THE WAR
ILLUSTRATED

GENERAL SIR ARCHIBALD WAVELL, K.C.B.

Frontis.

THE WAR
Illustrated

Complete Record of the Conflict
by Land and Sea and in the Air

Edited by

SIR JOHN HAMMERTON

Volume Three

The THIRD VOLUME OF THE WAR ILLUSTRATED contains the weekly issues from No. 45 to No. 70. Within these pages the most world-shaking events in all history are faithfully and succinctly described, accompanied with an unrivalled wealth of photographic illustration. In the note to Volume 2, the Editor remarked that " no comparable mirror of these exciting and historic times exists," a statement which he can confidently re-affirm in respect to the present volume. He also said that what the following volumes would have to present he could not dare to guess.

Look over the contents of this Third Volume and you will see how well advised was the restraint upon the imagination, although the greatest disasters of the war had already befallen us—Norway, Holland, Belgium, and the iniquitous defection of our allies, the French. The Battle for Britain is the main concern of the period covered by the present volume ; a battle that has by no means ended. But a battle of which none of us fears the eventual issue. It is heartening that within the pages of this Third Volume the glorious achievements of our Army of the Nile and of our worthy allies the Greeks in Albania are pictured and described so that it ends on a note of high hope and confidence in the outcome of the struggle, no matter what trials still await us.

The General Index has been carefully compiled to facilitate ready reference to any of the literary or pictorial contents of the volume, and a glance at it will suffice to indicate the wide scope and thoroughness of our contemporary chronicle of the conflict

Published 2000
Cover Design © 2000
TRIDENT PRESS INTERNATIONAL
ISBN 1-58279-102-3 Single Edition
ISBN 1-58279-020-5 Special Combined Edition*
*Contains Volume 3 & 4 Unabridged
Printed in Croatia

A NEW GROUP OF WAR LEADERS

KING GEORGE II OF THE HELLENES

Son of King Constantine, he was King of Greece for the first time from 1922 to 1923, and after 12 years of exile was restored in 1935.

GENERAL ALEXANDER PAPAGOS

After serving in the Turkish wars, he reorganized the Greek Army and on the outbreak of war against Italy became C.-in-C.

GENERAL JOHN METAXAS

In his early days a soldier—he was Chief of the Greek General Staff in 1913—he entered the political arena and in 1936 became Prime Minister. Since 1938 he has been virtual Dictator.

AIR VICE-MARSHAL J. H. D'ALBIAC, D.S.O.

Now in command of the British Forces in Greece, he has the distinction of having served in the Army and the Royal Naval Air Service before he joined the R.A.F.

Photos, Hay Wrightson, Planet News, Wide World, and British Official: Crown Copyright

VICE-ADMIRAL SIR J. F. SOMERVILLE
After serving in the Royal Navy from 1898 to 1939, he was recalled to active service on the outbreak of war, and his name will henceforth be associated with Dunkirk, Oran, and Taranto.

ADMIRAL SIR A. B. CUNNINGHAM
Commander-in-Chief of the Royal Navy in the Mediterranean since 1939, he has done his utmost to get the Italians to attempt to justify their boast that the Mediterranean is *their* sea.

ADMIRAL J. C. TOVEY
From 1938 to 1940 he commanded the destroyer flotillas of the Mediterranean Fleet; then he was appointed Commander-in-Chief of the Home Fleet—the post Beatty held in the Great War.

CAPTAIN E. S. FOGARTY FEGEN, V.C.
Captain of the Auxiliary Cruiser "Jervis Bay," he engaged a Nazi raider in the Atlantic on November 5, 1940, and so saved 33 out of his convoy of 38 ships. He was awarded a posthumous V.C.

Photos, Topical Press, Universal Press, and British Official: Crown Copyright

AIR MARSHAL SIR CHARLES PORTAL

A colonel in the Army at the age of 25, after the Great War he joined the R.A.F. In this war he was C. in C. of the Bomber Command before being appointed Chief of the Air Staff.

AIR MARSHAL W. SHOLTO DOUGLAS

From the Artillery he transferred to the R.F.C. in 1915 and commanded fighter squadrons in France. His present appointment is that of Air Officer Commander-in-Chief, Fighter Command.

AIR MARSHAL SIR A. BARRATT

Now in charge of the Army Cooperation Command of the R.A.F., he went to France in 1914 with the R.F.C., later seeing many years of distinguished service with the Air Arm in India.

AIR MARSHAL SIR R. PEIRSE

Deputy Chief of the Air Staff at the Air Ministry since 1937, he was appointed Chief of the Bomber Command in November, 1940. He served in France throughout the Great War.

Photos, Elliott & Fry; British Official: Crown Copyright; Planet News, and Sport & General

General Index to Volume Three

*T*HIS *Index is designed to give ready reference to the whole of the literary and pictorial contents of* THE WAR ILLUSTRATED. *Individual subjects and persons of importance are indexed under their own headings, while references are included to general subjects such as Greece, War in; France; Italy, etc. Page Numbers in italics indicate illustrations.*

List of Maps and Plans

Errata and Addenda

Page 83. Caption to top photograph. For "wing gun of a Browning Gladiator aircraft." *read* "wing Browning gun of a Gladiator aircraft."

" 120. Centre column, 4th line from bottom. For "2.1 per cent" *read* "21 per cent."

" 150. Bottom photograph, 2nd line of caption For "the airport in Jersey" *read* "the acrodrome at Le Bourg, Guernsey."

" 167. Bottom row, last portrait, 2nd line of caption. For "D.S.M." *read* "O.B.E."

Page 192. Bottom photograph, caption. This photograph shows the Naval Training Ship "Caledonia," formerly the White Star liner "Majestic." *Not* the "Scotstoun."

" 197. Caption, 3rd line. For "a Nazi fighter" *read* "a Junkers Ju. 87B dive-bomber."

" 203. Caption, 2nd line. For "Fiat motor works" *read* "Itala motor works."

" 209. Centre photograph, caption, 3rd line. For "one of the wings" *read* "the rudder."

Page 211. Caption, lines 9 and 10. For "Dornier bomber" *read* "Messerschmitt fighter"; line 15, for "Messerschmitts" *read* "Dornier bombers."

" 237. Centre photograph, caption. 2nd line. For "Dornier bomber" *read* "Heinkel He.111K."

" 346. Table of German and British Aircraft Losses, item Sept. 13. For "26" (German losses) *read* "2."

" 451. Bottom photograph is upside down.

Page 508. Column 1, line 6 from bottom. For "third largest" *read* "fifth largest."

" 559. Fourth portrait in fourth row, caption. For "Wing-Commander F. V. Beamish" *read* "Commander Charles St. J. Beamish."

" 567. Column 1, line 10 from top. For "P. & O liner" *read* "New Zealand Shipping Company liner."

" 618. Bottom caption should *read* "left to right, Major-General Gambier-Parry, General Metaxas, and a Greek General."

July 12th, 1940 *The War Illustrated*

Vol. 3   A Permanent Picture Record of the Second Great War   **No. 45**

It was a bitter moment for France when German troops marched past the Arc de Triomphe and the Unknown Soldier's grave.   Hitler, pondering on the scene above, might well remember that the Arch was begun by Napoleon to commemorate those victories of 1805-1806 which made him as much master of Europe as the German dictator is today, with only Britain standing out ; yet before the Arch was finished Napoleon was a prisoner at St. Helena and his vast Empire had crumbled into ruin.   This photograph was wirelessed to New York and flown to England in a Clipper 'plane.

Photo, Keystone

On France Descends the Silence of Defeat

While the extent and nature of the German victory had hardly penetrated to the masses of the French people, the rigorous censorship enforced by the Nazis and the Bordeaux Government alike could not hide the signs of defeat and subjection described here.

ON France, once so gay and gallant, has descended the sombre silence of defeat and despair.

The " 75's " have ceased to roar, the chatter of the machine-guns has died away. But not only has been stilled the voice of war. A heavy blanket of depression weighs down the spirits of a people naturally animated ; a Press renowned for its strident notes has been muted at the behest of Dr. Goebbels ; from the broadcasting stations come the programmes permitted by the conqueror, and from Radio Paris speaks the " traitor of Stuttgart," Paul Ferdonnet ; at half-past nine on these July evenings, when on the café terraces the loungers sipping their cafés and apéritifs have still light enough to read their papers, a firm curfew order is enforced, and only those holding a pass issued by the German Kommandantur are allowed in the streets.

anticipation of the evil things that tomorrow may bring.

The French soldiers, too, are there—hundreds of thousands of men who did all that brave men could do, but who have been defeated by things beyond their control and outside their leaders' reckoning. Now in sullen groups they plod along the roads in dejected fashion to the depots where they will hand over their arms to the conquerors and then be permitted to proceed to their homes—if homes, indeed, they still have. As for the 900,000 of their comrades who surrendered during the battle, it has been decreed that they shall remain in the enemy's prison-camps until the German triumph shall be secure.

In the occupied territory—and all the France that matters is now occupied by the Germans—a people whose ancestors first listened to and broadcast

den to make any personal contact with French prisoners of war without the consent of the German authorities, distribute unauthorized pamphlets and organize unauthorized public meetings or demonstrations, down tools or dismiss employees so as to injure German interests, publish

Before Hitler and Mussolini divided the carcass of their prey they met on June 18 in Munich of unhappy memory to consult on the terms to be offered to France. Here the Dictators are seen standing in their car to allow the crowds to get a better view of them.

Scattered over the war-pocked countryside are millions of unhappy folk who left their homes weeks ago and, maybe, hundreds of miles away, when they sensed and heard and felt the invaders' furious approach. Now that the war is over great masses of refugees, French, Belgian, and Dutch, are being herded almost like cattle into temporary camps which have been established at many places in order that the roads may be kept clear for the passage of the German troops. There the homeless pass their days and nights in a state of hungry squalor, their minds filled with the memory of the horrors of yesterday and with the

the intoxicating gospel of the " Rights of Man " is now governed by the decrees of a military dictatorship. Thus, on June 30th the Nazis decreed that any acts of violence against the German authorities or German citizens should be punished by death. At the same time it was sternly forbid-

Top, Otto Dietrich (left) Nazi Press Chief, and Karl Boehmer, head of the Nazi Foreign Press Dept., are seen at the tomb of Franço's Unknown Soldier. Lower photo shows a German heavy motorized unit passing the Obelisk in the Place de la Concorde, Paris.

Photos, Keystone and Associated Press

Nothing Is Wanting to Her Cup of Humiliation

anything harmful to the Reich, listen-in to non-German wireless broadcasts, and disseminate anti-German news. All arms were required to be delivered up within 24 hours, and also all wireless sets which had not been specially exempted.

Everywhere were the all-too-apparent signs of conquest, but perhaps in Paris was the humiliation of defeat most felt. Such reports as leaked out from the former French capital spoke of a city largely deserted by its populace, with many of its houses and shops still shuttered and closed. The cafés were open and the food supplies seemed to be adequate. Fond couples roamed the walks of the Bois de Boulogne, children sailed their boats on the pond or watched with fascinated eyes the grim antics of

In his diatribe of January 30, 1940, Hitler declared that M. Daladier, then French Premier, would "soon make the acquaintance of German and Austrian divisions." His words were recalled by the photograph below of Austrian troops in the Place de la Concorde. Another unwelcome visitor to the square was the Nazi aeroplane seen above which landed in the very narrow space available.

Punch and Judy amidst the pleasant greenery of the Luxembourg Gardens. But many of the factories were still out of action, and unemployment and short time were rife. Through the once-crowded streets passed no buses or taxis or private cars, although the trains of the "Metro" still rumbled through the smelly gloom. Plenty of German soldiers were to be seen, but for the most part they were sightseers being shown round by those of their officers who had visited or lived in Paris before the war. But the sights and sounds which the word "Paris" had meant to those peasant youths were denied them, for the gay creatures that once had given Paris its reputation of the "City of Light" had no place in a town where the strokes of nine sounded the curfew that none dare disobey.

After the entry of the German Army into Paris the people had to suffer in silence the spectacle of their conquerors viewing the sights of the city. In particular, the Arc de Triomphe, from which the swastika flag was flying, was visited by many German officers shown round by gendarmes.

Photos, Associated Press and Keystone

Why the German Army Won in France

Many reasons have been advanced for France's collapse, so complete and so sudden; but most of her critics are agreed that her army was outclassed, outmanoeuvred, and outfought by the German war machine. Some analysis of military effort of the two belligerents in the Battle of France is attempted here.

In the great battle of the West, which opened on May 10 and ended forty-seven days later on June 25, when the last of the French divisions laid down their arms, it has been estimated that the French Army lost 60,000 soldiers killed in action, and perhaps 300,000 wounded—this out of a total mobilized in France of about 2,780,000.

The figures are impressive enough, particularly when we look at them not in the mass as the military statistician sees them but as individuals, as men, young, middle-aged, and even old—when we remind ourselves that for every one of the 60,000 dead some woman weeps for son, husband, or lover, some child mourns a father, some *poilu* a comrade who in the danger and terror of the battle had stuck to him closer than a brother. The 300,000 wounded, too, will tax the country's hospitals for weeks and months; for all the years that remain to them tens of thousands of brave men will bear on their bodies and in their minds the scars of wounds, the marks of mutilation.

But compared with some of the battles of the Great War—battles which in their

result were far less decisive—the casualties suffered by France in this battle which decided her fate for the present, and perhaps for all time, can hardly be regarded as out of the way. On July 1, 1916, the opening day of the great offensive of the Somme, the British Army lost 56,000 men killed, wounded, and missing, and at Verdun in 1916 the French losses were approximately 350,000. Between August 21 and September 12, 1914, in three weeks of war, the French suffered losses amounting to some 600,000 men. Moreover, in the great battle of 1940, the French dead and wounded were far outnumbered by the prisoners taken by the Germans. In the first phase of the battle, when the armies were engaged in Belgium and north-eastern

France, the Germans were able to claim 350,000 French prisoners; and as the battle swept across France, another 600,000 poilus were herded into the German prison-camps. So great was the haul of prisoners, indeed, that it is obvious that something infinitely serious had happened to France's military machine.

In his speech to the Senate M. Reynaud spoke of "incredible mistakes" which had permitted the Germans to cross the Meuse; but the supreme blunderer was not General Corap, commander of that ill-fated Ninth Army, but General Gamelin and those (including General Weygand) who for years past had maintained that in this war France should assume a defensive attitude, calmly secure behind the fortress wall of the Maginot Line. In vain did men of the newer school—General de Gaulle, for instance—urge that the war should be one of movement, in which the supreme part would be played by mechanized units. The gentlemen of the staff were thinking in the terms of the Great War. Even the campaign in Poland, in which the Germans demonstrated their new tactics for all the world to see, seemed to leave them unmoved; as it had no effect on their practice it is reasonable to assume that its lessons never penetrated to their thought. They dreamed of a static war, and Hitler and Keitel willed that it should be a dynamic war.

For this type of warfare Hitler's army was well prepared. It was strong in tanks, large, small and medium; its artillery was numerous and first-class; its men were highly trained and were imbued with an almost mystical lust for battle such as had not been seen in Europe since the Moslem Arabs ceased to follow the trail of conquest. Moreover, the German air force, overwhelmingly superior to the French in number and possessed of more up-to-date 'planes, had been trained to act in the closest cooperation with the army —of which, indeed, it was a vital part. It was by the most skilful combination, the most daring use, of tank and gun and dive-bomber, that the Germans were able to pierce, thrust aside, or outflank one after another of the French defences.

Not only in the actual fighting did the Germans evince an extraordinary efficiency far surpassing that of their opponents, but this was also manifest in such things as the maintenance of their tanks and the arrangements made for refuelling, in the astonishing skill of their sappers, and the tremendous skill and energy displayed in getting stores and supplies to the front through country which had been ravaged and burnt out by their own war machine. True, their successes in this direction were furthered by their complete ruthlessness, evidenced by the way in which they machine-gunned or simply drove through or over the flocks of refugees who cluttered up the roads. But ruthlessness could never have won the battle; it was planning of the very highest and most detailed order, the keenest efficiency and the most whole-hearted zeal, that did that.

Top is the desolate scene in the main street of Avesnes-le-Aubert when the French Army was falling back before the mighty German onrush. Disabled French tanks almost blocked the road. Above, amidst the ruins wrought by their own guns in a Belgian village, a Nazi 37 mm. anti-tank-gun has been placed in position. The bicycle belongs to the leader of the gun crew.
Photos, E.N.A. and Keystone

On Vimy's Hill Sacred to Canada Hitler Triumphs

On July 26, 1936, King Edward VIII, accompanied by President Lebrun, unveiled the Canadian National War Memorial on Vimy Ridge (below ; air photo of ceremony, above). Four years later, after the Nazi triumph in the Battle of France, the Memorial was visited by Hitler accompanied by General Keitel (left).

ONE of the most glorious achievements of the Canadian Army in April 1917 was the storming of Vimy Ridge, and on the Ridge was erected a glorious monument on soil, as King Edward described it, "that is as surely Canada's as any acre within her nine provinces." The Memorial commemorates the sacrifice of 60,000 of the 600,000 soldiers of Canada's Expeditionary Force—as great a number, incidentally, as were killed of the 2,000,000 and more Frenchmen engaged in the Battle of France which ended in the surrender of June 1940.

Photos, Topical, Wide World, Keystone

How the Nazis Broke France's Fortress Line

From time immemorial Man has sheltered in fortresses designed to withstand a long
siege and to resist the strongest weapons of the age. Though every great war in Europe
for generations past has shown up the futility of the fortress against heavy artillery,
skilfully handled, military engineers continued to construct such systems. Here is the
story from German sources of the taking of Maubeuge.

ONE of the major surprises of the
German advance through France
and Flanders was the com-
parative ease with which the enemy
subdued or isolated some of the huge
fortresses constructed by the French and
Belgians especially to halt—if not to
hold up—the Nazi advance. Profiting,
presumably, from the lessons of the First
Great War, the military engineers took
steps to render these strongholds " impregnable." The latest resources of the
civil engineer were employed—immensely
strong steel and concrete construction ;
deep underground chambers for the personnel, ventilated and air-conditioned
so that men might live safely in them for
weeks ; all the most advanced mechanical
equipment for working the armament and
feeding the guns. The fortress systems
were planned so that by cross-fire one
fort could aid its neighbour, and in fact
all that science could do was done to
strengthen these works.

The fortress idea was extended to the
entire frontier between France and
Germany. France constructed her
Maginot Line, and Germany in emulation
built the Westwall. Along the Franco-
Belgian frontier extended a lighter zone
of defences that has been called the
" semi-Maginot Line." Here, then, were
the fortifications that should have rendered France safe against the Nazis.

Along the Maginot Line were individual
fortresses that had existed for many
years, and had been specially modernized. One of these was Maubeuge, which
in the First Great War had been invested
on August 25, 1914, and had capitulated
on September 7 ; during this period it
had immobilized the German VII Reserve
Corps, but after its surrender only two
battalions had been needed to act as
garrison, and the rest of the corps was
freed for the attack on the French army.
It might well have been expected that
the modernized Maubeuge would put
up a better show.

The Onslaught on Maubeuge

After the Nazis secured passage over
the Maastricht bridges, across the Meuse
and the Albert Canal (May 11), they
pushed on and isolated Liége (May 13),
subduing a number of the forts and continuing their advance southward. (Photos
in page 689 show how the Nazis dealt
with Eben Eymael, one of the Liége
forts.) Namur was reached and isolated
by May 15, and the enemy was able to
cross the Upper Meuse in several places.
A salient was forced in the Allied line
near Sedan (May 16) and quickly widened
out until it extended as far as Maubeuge
(by May 18), its loop running near Rethel,
Laon, St. Quentin, Le Cateau and
Landrecies. The enemy then turned
westward, after breaking through, and
there ensued the " Battle of the Bulge."

Maubeuge, then, played a vital part
in these events. Had the fortress been able
to offer a prolonged resistance the course
of history might have been different. What
actually happened is suggested by the
photos from German sources in the opposite page. The town of Maubeuge was
taken by storm troops on May 21. German
aeroplanes destroyed numbers of tanks
with which the French had hoped to stay
the enemy onrush.

A terrific artillery bombardment was
directed at the forts, and aeroplanes
dropped large-calibre bombs. Under
cover of the artillery support the German
storm troops crept nearer. Taking
advantage of natural cover afforded by
trees and the undulating nature of the
ground the artillery, both heavy and
light, was able to get within less than a
mile of the perimeter of the defensive
system, and eventually the main forts
were silenced. Most of the barbed wire
had been broken down by the bombardment ; and the infantry, with "pioneers" or
field engineers, thus approached the forts.

A terrible scene of destruction met their
gaze. The massive concrete walls had
cracked like nutshells, and the steel
reinforcing bars protruded. The cupola
of the fort—formed of 11-inch armour
plate—was gouged out as if it had been a
piece of cheese, and was twisted and
torn under the impact of the giant shells.

Forts or posts that continued to resist
were attacked by the infantry. Unless
the defenders promptly surrendered they
were next dealt with by the field engineers,
who piled sandbags to block up the
entrance; laid a heavy charge of explosive,
and fired it. If this did not suffice, holes
were bored in the walls and dynamite
exploded to shatter the structure. Systematically all the outlying posts were
reduced, and by May 24 this giant fortress
of the Maginot system had capitulated.

In effect, two days earlier, Maubeuge
had ceased to impede the German onrush.
So fell this modern wonder of ferro-con-
crete, on whose staying power and that of
others so much hope had been based.

It seems that the French people had
been afflicted with what has been called
" Maginot folly," and were lulled into
a false security. Borrowing from the
terminology of A.R.P., we might almost
say that " deep-shelter mentality " was
responsible for bringing about the collapse
of the French defence.

This photograph from a German source shows some of the defenders of Maubeuge being marched
off as prisoners of war after the capture of the town. The Germans admitted that not only the
fortress but the whole town was fiercely defended.

'Cracked like Nutshells' by the German Fire

This photograph, like others in this page depicting scenes in the capture of Maubeuge, is from a German source. It shows the post known as Des Sarts, one of the outlying forts that continued to offer a determined resistance after the fall of the main fortress at Maubeuge. At last, however, its heroic garrison had to surrender (photo, bottom right).

Left is seen the devastating effect of artillery fire and of the explosion of demolition charges laid by the field engineers who accompanied the storm troops in the assault on Maubeuge. When isolated machine-gun posts refused to surrender they were destroyed by explosives which "cracked the concrete structures as if they were nutshells."

Below is seen the cupola of one of the forts at Maubeuge, after the building had been destroyed by German artillery fire. According to the German account it was crippled by two direct hits, while other shots tore huge pieces from the 11-inch-thick metal. This massive steel dome could be rotated so as to bring the guns to bear, and it also had a rise-and-fall movement.

Beaten down by overwhelming force, the brave defenders of Des Sarts hoist the white flag of surrender (below). With most of its turrets put out of action and its guns silenced by the terrific hail of shell fire, the garrison had then to meet the frenzied onrush of the storm troops, and the field engineers were making ready to blow up the structure when at last the fort gave in.

(From " Die Wehrmacht ")

There Was Little Left in St. Malo for the Nazis

HEROISM of a remarkable kind was displayed in the evacuation of St. Malo, the famous port and tourist centre on the Brittany coast, just as the German troops drew near. The scene was described by Mr. Le Marquand, owner of an auxiliary yacht, when he returned to a British port. " I saw the total destruction of the harbour after all the British troops had been safely evacuated on June 18. The Germans were then reported to· be fast approaching, but the British naval officer in charge of the demolition party was amazingly cool. He would not allow his men to take any risks—he stood alone in the open to watch the destruction. Once, when four charges were ignited, it was doubtful whether all had exploded. The men were definite that three had, but some of them wanted to venture into the danger zone to see what had happened to the fourth. The officer refused to allow them to leave cover. A few seconds later a deafening explosion from the fourth charge hurled portions of dock gates into the air. Amid all this, the officer still took no cover, but stood alone while all the debris was flying about and dropping all around him. He seemed to have a charmed life."

Above is a view of St. Malo from the last British ship that left ; a petrol dump fired by the British is going up in flames. Left is some of the equipment of lorries saved from the port and brought over on the deck of a steamer.
Photos, " Daily Mirror " and Keystone

A GLOWING tribute was paid to the work of the British demolition party at St. Malo by the Countess de Pret. She had escaped from Belgium and was doing Red Cross work in France at the time of the German invasion. She eventually got from St. Malo to Brest in a small English yacht. The Countess said : " After all the scenes of panic in France it was wonderful to see the calmness with which the British officers and soldiers carried out their duties at St. Malo. Although the Germans were within a few miles, the British made a thorough job of the demolition of St. Malo harbour. They blew up everything, and the harbour will be out of use for at least two years. We also learned that the British had made Cherbourg useless as a port and had destroyed the harbour works there. . . . In France there was complete lack of organization. It was an inspiring contrast to land in England and to find everyone so calm and well disciplined."

Poles Stand Unyielding By Britain's Side

General Sikorski, who, after his arrival in London from France with the reconstituted Polish Army, specially posed for the photograph above. Right, the King greeting M. Raczkiewicz, the Polish President, on the latter's arrival in London from the South of France on June 21, 1940.

IN a broadcast to the Polish people from London on June 24, 1940, General Sikorski said : " At a time when the great body of our armies, safely back from France, is landing on the shores of Great Britain I would like to declare solemnly, in the name of the Polish Republic, that, animated by an indomitable will, we shall continue to fight shoulder to shoulder with the powerful British Empire for a free and independent Poland. A new phase of our armed effort is opened before the Polish Army, closely linked by its brotherhood of arms with the British Army. Together with our great British Ally we shall carry on in this effort. Our place today is in the line of battle. We are fulfilling our alliance with Great Britain. The Polish nation will persevere in the struggle against Germany to the end. The Polish units who took part in the battle for France fought with the utmost gallantry, earning the admiration of friends and the respect of the foe. Poland was the first country to fall victim to the enemy. Today, in spite of tremendous losses and enormous hardships, she remains the loyal ally of Great Britain. We have unshakable confidence in victory. The iron will of Great Britain to continue the struggle is subject to no doubt. Standing unyieldingly at her side, we shall win, bringing to you—and to Europe—deliverance.''

The Polish troops in France were eventually evacuated in two transports, which carried also a number of civilian refugees. Above, one of the ships is alongside the quay at a port in the West of England and the men are streaming down the gangway. They were in high spirits despite the latest misfortune that had befallen them ; and the Poles being a music-loving people, one of the first incidents after the arrival was an impromptu sing-song accompanied by two accordions, left.

Photos. E.N.A., Keystone, "News Chronicle," and G.P.U.

WHAT OF THE FRENCH COLONIAL EMPIRE?
The Possibilities of its Salvage for France

June 30, 1940

By The Editor

AT the moment of writing—God knows what the next news bulletin will tell us—the only hope of a France resurgent would seem to lie in Africa. It is worth remembering that Europe once narrowly escaped conquest from North Africa when the Moors brought to Spain, and even to some parts of Mediterranean France, a civilization in many ways superior to and assuredly more benign than that of Germany today, and far more vigorous than that which, for seven centuries, it displaced in the Iberian peninsula. And, now, if only Scipio's historic " Carry the war into Africa " could be reversed to " Carry on from Africa " and the French colonies there rally to the eventual salvation of France ! . . . If only !

The flag of France has been hauled down in all her European lands and even in Syria. Much of "the pleasant land of France" is now, and is likely to remain in the lifetime of most of us, both old and young, under the shadow of the Swastika. Such " honourable " freedom as she may exercise will be limited by the behests of her bosses in Berlin.

Let us make no mistake about that !

The octogenarian defeatist Marshal Pétain and his group of corrupt politicians who sold France into German serfdom on June 22 are the uttermost enemies of their own country that have ever appeared in its long and tempestuous history. Sorrow must mingle with indignation for the dreadful fate that has brought the name of one who once stood high in military skill and valour into everlasting reproach and abomination as his too-long life closes. A true soldier would have chosen a less inglorious ending.

THESE men around Pétain, at the moment of their country's greatest trial, were offered indissoluble friendship with their British allies—a magnificent gesture worthy of our great leader's vision and decision—Franco-British citizenship for all Frenchmen, equal status with all free men of Britain who are prepared to die rather than to bow beneath the Nazi yoke—they, *les misérables*, refused : some, like Pétain, from sheer senility ; others, like Laval, because their known traitorous leanings to Fascism and the idea of a Latin block (France, Italy, Spain) meant the saving of their skins and pe-haps their money-bags.

At the most critical moment in modern history these self-imposed leaders of unhappy, heroic France were content to acknowledge that something less than 300,000 Nazis in armed vehicles, on motor bicycles, in aeroplanes, had overcome what for years we have been told was " the finest army in Europe "—the mobilized Five Million of France. It is hard for a mind still sane to give credence to such a débâcle : but the facts are inexorable.

Will French Leadership Revive ?

FRENCH leadership is dead—in France. It must revive elsewhere—in Britain or in some foreign soil where the tricolor has not been hauled down. If not . . . then, indeed, a final farewell to the great France of history. Let that be understood. Nor is that a new thing : it is an old, old story. Historians are familiar with it through the ages.

When the spirit of old Rome was dying in the capital, the great province of Africa, where man had to be self-reliant and softness did not pay, was still vigorous and offering fight to the barbarian ; even the noble art of the serious theatre was flourishing in Timgad when it had degenerated into buffoonery at Rome. When Babylon was declining, more than a thousand years before, its one-time colony of Nineveh was rising in grandeur as the head of the powerful

(though historically sterile) Assyrian Empire —soon to overwhelm the motherland. Why should not a French Colonial Empire—if need be, independent of a Nazi-ruled France —arise today in power and potentiality far exceeding anything that will ever come out of France herself when she finally accepts the Peace terms—terms that will be vastly less " honourable " than the infamous Armistice conditions ? Why not ? We can at least hope that the spirit of France is not utterly extinguished.

THOUGH Mittelhauser in Syria has laid down his arms at the behest of the Bordeaux defeatists, Nogués, the successor of the great Lyautey in North Africa—despite the news of the alleged disarming of the Algerian forces—may yet prove of sterner stuff, and Britain can in due time look after any Fifth Column Syria which might prove a menace to the British Empire in the Near East.

Before I have finished the writing of this article the wireless may tell me that these hopes are vain . . . that the French débâcle is worse than I had dared to think. In such

Pétain : He Saved Paris—and Lost France
Photo, Sport and General

case nothing would remain for Britain but to regain for France, with the aid of such legions as General de Gaulle can rally, those Mediterranean lands which must be occupied and administered by a power friendly to Great Britain, as the British Empire begins to crumble on the day that the Mediterranean becomes for us a forbidden sea. And a catastrophe which Malcolm MacDonald, to my unforgotten horror, once envisaged — the not distant disintegration of our Empire— would have definitely begun.

Let Australia, New Zealand, Canada, South Africa, India—yes, even Egypt and Eire—recall his words and resolve that such a sundering of the Commonwealth shall not be if their individual effort can help to prevent it. " United we stand," divided . . .

THERE are no doubt many, like myself, at a time of life when ease and comfort should have been earned, who could still acquire both by sneaking off to America— California calls !—but are well content to see both disappear and to spurn those chances of escape from financial ruin and personal hardship still open to us, in order to see the Battle of Britain through, if so be we survive the ordeal. For, again make no mistake, that battle is about to be engaged.

From the window where I write these words I can see a long line of Martello towers—those sturdy little strong points erected in 1804 when Napoleon was preparing his fleet in Boulogne to invade England. These picturesque remnants

of Britain's preparedness to meet the invaders who did not come 136 years ago may even now prove of greater value to England than the much-vaunted Maginot Line to France— mainly because nobody is dreaming of sheltering behind them !

The Maginot Line, on which incredible millions that might have benefited the common people of France were squandered by muddle-headed militarists, passes into history with the less tangible, but no less valuable, South Sea Bubble. The Great Wall of China proved far more useful in its day, not to say Hadrian's, the remains of which we can still visit in Northumberland. But happily the French in Africa—North, West, and Equatorial—finely organized, as all of us who have travelled these countries can testify, have no Maginot Line to mesmerize them into false security. They have officers and men and native levies of real fighting power, all splendidly organized, fit to meet the best that Italy can pit against them. There lies some hope of resurgence. If it fails, France indeed has reached the end of the road, and is properly personified in the piteous figure of Pétain.

" France Is Lost Without Britain "

IT was once my fortune to take a long journey with the French general commanding the forces in Algeria. I have never forgotten the earnest manner in which he said " Britain and France must stand together, or France is lost." Note that he did not say " Britain was lost." He knew that Germany then—when Hitler was merely an obscure political agitator in Munich—was already planning day and night to be revenged on France. And his own people and the British were comfortably ignoring most that was going on. Especially he told me that the French people, unlike the British, despised their colonial kin.

" A Frenchman goes to one of our colonies solely to make money. Rarely to stay. Not even in the lovely environment of Mustapha at Algiers, or at Carthage, the suburb of Tunis, or at Rabat in Morocco or in the charming new French suburb at Fez—oh, no, Paris, Marseilles, or whichever his home town may be, is where his heart is and where he means one day to return."

" And why so," I asked, " for I should be happy to live in almost any of these North African places ? "

" Because in France to remain a ' colonial ' is to be an inferior Frenchman. A Lyonnais who has to go to Fez to make his fortune must justify himself by returning one day with his fortune to Lyons."

FRESH from all the loveliness of the Mustapha villas, and already well acquainted with the beauties of Morocco and certain French homes at Marrakesh, this came with something of a shock. It accounted for the anxious look in the eye of this earnest, able and highly intelligent French general when he said that without Britain France was " done." And that was sixteen years ago !

Not even now is France without Britain ; but it would be sheer idiocy to say that she has not betrayed Britain. Not the France *au cœur*, not the France of her fine, intrepid colonial commanders and hard-bitten warriors, but her rotten politicians—the very class that sneered at her own " colonials." It may be that the day of the colonial is at hand and that the motherland will be succoured in her hour of trial by the despised and rejected. That she can ever regain her position as one of the puissant powers of the world is open to doubt ; that her colonial empire may save her from sinking to the status of a minor power if it acts in full accord with the British Empire is (at the moment of writing) still a possibility.

The British Navy Moved—and Hitler Lost a Fleet

BRITAIN SEIZES THE FRENCH FLEET

Ministry of Information Statement, July 4, 1940

It will be recalled that the French Government, relying upon the promises of Germany and Italy not to use her Fleet against France's former Ally, undertook by the terms of the armistice to allow their Fleet to pass into the hands of the enemy.

His Majesty's Government, having lost all faith in promises made by the Governments of Germany and Italy, felt that they were compelled, not only in their own interests, but also in the hope of restoring the independence of France and the integrity of the French Empire, to take steps to ensure that the French Fleet should not be used against them by the common enemy.

With this object in view steps were taken in the early morning of July 3 to place all French men-of-war in British ports under British control.

At the same time French vessels in ports of North Africa were offered certain conditions designed solely for the purpose of keeping them out of German hands.

It was explained to the officer in command that if none of these conditions were accepted Great Britain was prepared to take every step in order to ensure that none of these vessels should be used against her.

His Majesty's Government deeply regret that the French admiral in command at Oran refused to accept any of the conditions proposed, with the inevitable result that action had to be taken.

From The Premier's Statement :

The Premier stated that, having taken over nearly 220 French warships in British ports, it was "with sincere sorrow" he had to announce the drastic measures taken in North African waters. At Oran a British battle squadron fired on the "Dunkerque," "Strasbourg" and other warships. The desired result was achieved and no British ship was affected. Ships at Alexandria were forbidden to leave harbour.

The battleship "Dunkerque" was the first of two new ships of the same class to be launched. She has a displacement of 26,500 tons, a speed of 29·5 knots, and carries a normal complement of 1,381. Her main armament is eight 13-in. guns. She was completed in October 1935, and at the outbreak of war her sister ship, the ["Strasbourg,"] was also with the French fleet. The "Dunkerque" was so heavily damaged in the fighting at Oran on July 3 that she was put out of action for many months. One vessel of the "Strasbourg" class ran ashore and was damaged ; another slipped out of harbour and was hit by an aerial torpedo. Left, seen from the stern of another ship is the French aircraft-carrier "Bearn." She is a ship of 22,146 tons, carrying 40 'planes ; originally built as a battleship but converted to her present purpose in 1923-1927.

At the beginning of the war France was strong in submarines, having 78 against the British Navy's 57. Above is the "Henri Poincare," one of 30 of the Redoubtable class. She has a surface displacement of 1,384 tons and carries eleven 21·7-in. torpedo tubes. Her complement is 67. So successful did this type prove that 30 of them were built. It was stated on July 4 that some French submarines, including one large one, were taken under control in British harbours.

Photos, I.N.A., Associated Press, Wide World

The "Georges Leygues," left, is one of France's smaller cruisers and she has five sister ships. She is of 7,600 tons and her main armament consists of nine 6-in. guns, while she carries eight 3·5-in. and eight 13-mm. A.A. guns. She has an aircraft catapult and carries four 'planes. Her speed is 31 knots and her complement is 540. Right are two French destroyers, the "Chacal" and the "Leopard," both of 2,126 tons, photographed during a pre-war visit to Portsmouth. By chance the White Ensign is flying close to them. For a complete statement of the French Navy see Vol. 2, page 710.

From 'Down Under' to the Defence of the Homeland

Towards the end of June thousands of Anzacs—to give to the Australians and New
Zealanders of today the name immortalized by the gallantry of their fathers at Gallipoli
and on the Somme—came ashore in Britain to help in the defence of the country which
to them is the Motherland.

"WHERE's this war?" demanded a strapping Australian as he marched down the gangway from the troopship and stepped for the first time on English soil. "Is there a war on here?" shouted the New Zealanders as they, too, drew near the quay. Then they poured ashore in their thousands, felt-hatted giants from the cattle ranges and the sheep runs, from the splendid cities and the little country towns of "Down Under." Superb in physique, splendidly armed and equipped, filled to overflowing with the high spirits traditionally associated with the men of the Dominions—right indeed was Mr. Geoffrey Shakespeare, Under-Secretary for the Dominions, when he said in his welcoming speech that "there will be a thrill in every heart when they learn that this magnificent body of men has arrived." Then in significant phrase he went on, "I pity your enemies, and I congratulate those fortunate enough to fight by your side."

Weeks had elapsed since, to the cheers and fervent good-byes of a vast concourse of people, they had left the ports on the other side of the world; and under the "sure shield" of ships of the Royal Navy and of the navies of Australia, New Zealand and Canada, they had made what proved to be an altogether uneventful passage. As one of their officers put it, "All the way across we have had no trouble, no incidents. We owe the Navy a tremendous debt. Our convoy was a fine target all the way over, but no enemy dared to attack us. There is no doubt who rules the seas."

They had called at Cape Town and Freetown on the West African coast, and now after voyaging eleven or twelve thousand miles they had arrived in Britain at one of the greatest hours in the Empire's history. As soon as the ships arrived a message of greeting was read to them from the King:

A few months ago I sent some words of welcome to the first contingents of the Second Australian Imperial Force and the New Zealand Expeditionary Force when they disembarked in the Middle East. It has fallen to your lot to come to the United Kingdom itself, and as you take your place beside us you find us in the forefront of the battle. To all I give a warm welcome, knowing the stern purpose that brings you from your distant homes. I send you my best wishes and I look forward to visiting you soon.

After his Majesty's message had been read, the General Officer commanding the disembarkation area read a message from Mr. Anthony Eden, Minister of War:

You come at a timely hour. The cause of the free nations needs every measure of support that can be given. With Australia and New Zealand represented in two theatres of war, with Canada and South Africa taking their full part, we can now present to our

enemy a truly imperial front—a front which, as he has learned from experience in the past, has never been, and never will be, broken by him.

The messages were received with cheers—and the messengers, let it be added, were given a reception, particularly by the Australians, which was described as boisterous! The spirit of the newcomers was well shown in the words of the New Zealand commander as he acknowledged the greetings. "We have entered the fight," said Brigadier Hargest, "boots and all!"

Then the legions of the Anzacs—including a detachment of Maoris who as they landed sang their battalion song, written on the voyage by Corporal Amohau—came ashore, entered the waiting trains and were sent on their way to their camps in the country. Both the commanders, it may be noted—Major-General H. G. Wynter, of the Australians, and Brigadier J. Hargest, M.P., Commander of the New Zealanders—served with the Anzacs in the Great War, and here and there amongst the officers and rankers of both contingents were to be found veterans who had met the Germans in the last war and were anxious to meet them in this. One of the men as he came up the gangway was carrying a German helmet which he had captured twenty years before: "I have come back to look for its owner," he told those who inquired about his trophy.

As it was in 1900, as it was again in 1914-1918, so it is yet again in 1940. Australia and New Zealand will both "be there."

Victor Blanco, centre, who is with the Australian Contingent in Great Britain, may be said to have come from the depths of the ocean to fight,
for "in private life" he is a pearl diver. He is here doing a war dance. One of the first desires of the Anzacs on landing was for newspapers,
and, left, Australians are devouring the news after disembarkation. Right, a New Zealander has found a willing guide in a London messenger boy.
Photos, Wide World, Central Press and Associated Press

Smiles, Cheers, Thumbs Up from the Dominions

Among the New Zealand troops that arrived in Britain at the end of June there was a large contingent of Maoris. Some sturdy warriors of that fine race are here seen leaning over the rail of the transport that brought them to this country.

At the battle of the Plate the "Ajax," two-thirds of the crew of whom were New Zealanders, gave a fine account of herself. Centre, are men of the New Zealand R.N.V.R., who were welcomed on June 25 at a British port by the High Commissioner for the Dominion, Mr. W. J. Jordan.

The Australian troops that reached our shores at the end of June were in high spirits. Here Australians are giving cheers for the King; in the foreground are the nurses who came with them.
Photos, Photographic News Agency and Fox

Nov. 11, 1918
June 21, 1940

How Great Was France

How Low Is She Fallen Now!

Twenty-two years after Foch's victory, the France of Pétain places herself beneath the heel of Hitler

IN the heart of the Forest of Compiègne there is a gla which will ever be associated with the most triumpha and most tragic moments in the history of modern Franc

When it first catches the historian's eye the trees whi surround it are bare and gaunt in their winter nakedne The wan sun has not yet risen, but there is enough light distinguish the dark shape of a railway coach. Up t steps of this coach, still before dawn, proceed the plenip tentiaries of triumphant France and her ally, Britain, a soon they are followed by the emissaries of that German which, after four years of terrific battle, has now been beat to the ground. Soon they are grouped within about t table, and under the stern eyes of Foch and Wemyss t German delegates put their signatures to their country and their army's complete surrender. This done, t victors leave the coach, and pose for a moment by the ste (left), Marshal Foch standing with Admiral Wemyss his right and General Weygand (in képi).

Twenty-two years pass away, and again history made in that same forest, that same clearing, that sam coach. But the circumstances are now different, far. is now France that is defeated, Germany that is the vict

Close on the heels of a German officer, General Huntzig leader of the French delegation, enters the coach (righ and then, seated at the table—the same table—beside h fellow delegate, Admiral Leluc, he listens while Gener Keitel, with von Brauchitsch and Hess on his left, and Hitle Goering, Raeder and Ribbentrop on his right, reads t preamble to the bitter terms now demanded of Fran as the price of peace.

Based upon photographs sent by radio to New York and flown England by Clipper 'plane. Photos, Associated Press, Wide W

Our Munitions are 'Vital to the Nation & the World'

On June 27 Mr. Herbert Morrison reported to the House of Commons on the first seven weeks of his tenure of the Ministry of Supply, " a task," as he said, " of very vital importance to the nation and indeed to the world." His speech told of an encouraging spurt in production, and some of his main points are given here.

IN recounting progress and production, said Mr. Morrison, he could not and ought not to give figures as to specific items but he was able to reveal something of the energetic measures taken to speed up all branches of supply.

Standardized Tank Production

WITH regard to the problem of tanks, we must remember that the strategy of the war was based in the spring of 1939 on a small army overseas, and the tank for a Continental army was a different tank from what would be required somewhere else.

There was no clarification of what we wanted. The list of tanks we were making was a very wide list.

Therefore the Tank Board made a recommendation which the Secretary for War and I thought was right—namely, that military opinion of what was broadly wanted must come, so far as possible, through one focal point. The question of design will be for the Board to decide ; then they must go ahead and produce it.

Tanks, in any case, cannot be produced at once. While a tank is not a warship, it is more like a warship than it is like a wheelbarrow. Production is bound to take time.

Therefore it was decided to concentrate in the meantime upon the greatest possible output of those tanks which had proved satisfactory

I have insisted that there must be no over-elaboration of design. Frills and fancy pieces are not vital. Some standardization was essential to quick production.

A New Weapon by the Million

On June 19, only a week ago, I gave orders for very large quantities—millions—of a certain weapon.

Already the output has reached nearly a quarter of a million a week—between four and five times the previous production, and that output will grow.

I think these facts are encouraging.

I am not going to say things are satisfactory. They could not be satisfactory in the circumstances of the case. I can only say they

INCREASES IN PRODUCTION

Monthly rate, June over April

Cruiser and infantry tanks ...	115 per cent
Guns (two items)	50 per cent
Guns (one item)	228 per cent
Small Arms	40 per cent to 186 per cent
Ammunition	35 per cent to 420 per cent

are coming nearer and nearer to satisfaction as the days pass along.

Big Orders for Materials

THE main element in supply is raw material, and this is a very extensive function of the Ministry.

Broadly speaking, the position can be described as satisfactory. **We recently placed very big orders in America and elsewhere for raw materials, and I have given instructions that it is better to be on the safe side and have too much rather than too little.**

We have to face the consequence of a possible siege.

As for machine tools, the sources of supply are manufacturers here, second-hand machines in dealers' hands, and American and foreign producers of new and second-hand machines.

Our importation of machine tools from abroad is reaching a very great figure. It is at the rate of over £1,500,000 per month.

A census of the use of machine tools has

been taken to make the best use of idle plant. A return of the results of that census is at present under classification.

Production the First Consideration

AT the beginning of the life of the present Government, Parliament gave us wide and sweeping powers over persons and property. I am not going to use these powers in pursuit of any particular pet theory of the Right or Left.

What I want is production. That is the real consideration.

Orders to Empire and U.S.A.

IN our imports of munitions from the Empire and the United States, we have to get the maximum possible abroad, and we have a comprehensive programme for purchases from abroad.

Orders totalling £5,000,000 have been placed in Canada in the last few weeks.

Australia is sending immediately small arms ammunition, bombs, shells and fuses, and all the available capacity of India is being taken up.

We have concentrated quite properly on immediate things and immediate production for the next few months.

But we are not going to forget the longer view, for we all hope that this period of the last few weeks will change, and we must have a long-term policy and we must think of an offensive as well as a defensive policy.

Mr. Herbert Morrison's clarion call to the nation has resulted in enormous increases in munitions ; the production of various types of tanks, e.g., has been more than doubled. One of the tanks is seen above undergoing tests. Top, Mr. Morrison.   *Photos, Fox and Topical Press*

'Go To It!' is the Munition Workers' Slogan

The truckload of 3·7-in. anti-aircraft shell - cases in the photograph, above, is being taken to a filling room. Later the cordite cartridge, primer and fuse will be added, these operations being known as the "complete round." Top right, a typical munition worker ; formerly she made ladies' hats, but now she stamps shell-cases.

The most careful precautions must be taken at factories where high explosives are handled to guard against anything being brought in that might cause an explosion. Below, left, is the barrier to the danger zone, marked "Clean" and "Dirty," at which special shoes without nails must be donned. The Military Assistant to the Superintendent is seen being fitted with them. Below, right, the pockets of a worker are being felt by a searcher to discover if there is any metal object in them. In his hand the man holds his packet of sandwiches.

Photos, Topical

Some of the famous Spitfire fighters are being assembled in the workshop. The photograph is from the official film "Behind the Guns," showing Britain's war effort.

AFTER Mr. Herbert Morrison had given the House of Commons figures of the increased output of munitions, quoted in page 16, he added : "I think the House will agree that, so far as these figures go, they show an encouraging spurt in production during these critical weeks. I do not claim that the credit for this entirely belongs to me. It belongs to the organization of the Ministry, and particularly it belongs to the fine response which the working people of the country have given to the appeals of Ministers and their response to the actions of Hitler and the most serious situation in France."

'If the Invader Comes'—How He Will Be Repulsed

Specially drawn for THE WAR ILLUSTRATED by Haworth

Britain's defence against invasion falls into three main parts :

(A) Timely warning by our air forces of impending enemy action ; preparation at points likely to be threatened first or mainly ; air and sea action against the invaders on the sea and in the air.

(B) Defence of our coastline by fixed and mobile artillery and by aircraft ; naval operations against transports and enemy escorts by our naval forces based on ports, to prevent or limit enemy landings; shore defence by our land forces, mobile bodies of whom would be rushed to threatened points to reinforce the troops normally massed there ; defence against aerial landings : L.D.V. patrols by night (perhaps later by day), backed up by patrolling units of the regular forces.

(C) Action against any troops landed by the Nazis. Roads would be blocked and defended ; threatened areas would be evacuated of most civilians and brought under military control. Zonal rather than linear defences are probable, and any forces securing a foothold would be isolated and dealt with piecemeal after they had penetrated a little way into the country.

OFFENCE

Stage 1.
Parachute troops would be dropped followed by parachute containers with machine-gun, sub-machine-guns, dynamite and ammunition, etc. These troops would be intended to take and hold a given piece of country until reinforcements arrived.

Stage 3.
Large troop-carrying 'planes full of heavily armed shock troops would then arrive. Some of the 'planes would carry light field artillery and heavier types of machine-guns. The Nazis are supposed to have dropped small tanks from the air in Holland. If this is so they would probably be introduced at this stage.

Stage 5.
Assuming that the Germans were able to hold off our defenders, and if they were able to take possession of a harbour or landing ground, they would bring in troop-ships and supply ships. To do this, of course, would mean facing our Navy, including submarine and torpedo boats, not to mention our heavy bombers. If successful they would then try to land medium and super-heavy tanks and various types of artillery. One of the first would be anti-aircraft guns to keep our bombers away whilst they rushed mechanized transport along the roads.

DEFENCE

Stage 2.
Local Defence Volunteers, having spotted the Germans, would give the alarm, and regular troops, armed with service rifles, tommy-guns and Lewis guns, could be rushed to the spot in fast trucks.

Stage 4.
Bren gun carriers mounting anti-tank rifles and Bren guns should be quickly concentrated. These, together with the very mobile gun-howitzer and trench mortar crews, would be able to give adequate support.

Stage 6.
By this time the intentions of the invaders would be clear, all roads would be blocked, and anti-tank devices brought into operation. Heavy mobile artillery rushed into position farther back could pound away at masses of vehicles and tanks thus held up. The Germans would undoubtedly use dive-bombers in an attempt to dislodge strong defence posts. During the evacuation from Dunkirk our fighter 'planes were able to deal very effectively with these dive-bombers. All this time more and more troops, guns and tanks could be brought up and concentrated where needed, and the same process could be repeated wherever and however often the Nazis attempted to invade.

Day by Day Britain's Home Defences Grow

Members and clerks of the London Stock Exchange are learning to defend the famous building in Throgmorton Street and, if need be, their own homes. Here an instructor of the Guards is demonstrating the working of a Bren Gun. On his left is Major Karo, O.C. Stock Exchange Cadets. Right, an air-raid shelter being built round the Henry Irving statue near Charing Cross.

IN his broadcast on Sunday, June 30, Mr. Chamberlain said that the enemy might try to invade us at any moment. "If he does try," he added, "we will fight him in the air and on the sea ; we will fight him on the beaches with every weapon we have. He may manage here and there to make a break through. If he does we will fight him on every road, in every village, and in every house, until he or we are utterly destroyed. If he is driven to evacuate as we had to evacuate from France, there will be no friendly fleet waiting for him ; there will be nothing waiting for him off the beaches of England but death and disaster."

The girls, left, working at high pressure at a factory in the Midlands, have yet found time to become efficient fire-fighters. Above is a poster written by a Glasgow newspaper-seller who treats raids as if they were football matches!

The men, left, are volunteers who joined a famous regiment now in the Eastern Command in April, 1940, and are learning with the aid of trestles and planks to clear obstacles during their training. The Lord of the Manor of Colyton, Devon, has the right to form an army of his servants and tenants in times of peril. It had not been exercised since 1646, during the Civil War, until the present Lord of the Manor, Mr. T. Newman, once again made use of the privilege. Right, he is seen in the grounds of his house drilling his men as L.D.V.s.   *Photos, Central Press, Marcel Lavelli, Keystone, Fox and G.P.U.*

Nazi Terror Reaches the Channel Islands

St. Helier, the capital of Jersey, was almost completely evacuated. Below are Channel Islanders who were brought to England in a great fleet of ships. Left, a mother and her two young children who endured a 20-hour voyage in a small boat.

ON July 1, 1940, German troops landed in the Channel Islands by air. Three days before the Home Office had announced that the Islands had been demilitarized, but, notwithstanding, Jersey and Guernsey were both bombed and defenceless civilians were machine-gunned, the death roll on the one island being 29 and 10 on the other. The casualties would have been far heavier had the greater part of the population not been already evacuated. Evacuation became inevitable when the Germans occupied the coast of France. As can be seen in the map, centre right, none of the islands is more than 40 miles distant from the French coast. A great fleet of ships, including paddle-steamers, cargo-boats and many small craft, carried men, women and children to western ports of England, though some of the islanders chose to remain behind.

Photos, Topical Press and Planet News

OUR SEARCHLIGHT ON THE WAR NEWS

Every week there are innumerable items of interest which, through pressure on our space, we are unable to describe in full, but which should nevertheless have their corner in our pages. Here, then, is the first of a series of selected war news paragraphs.

Norway and Her King

APART from Balkan royalties there are few crowned heads in Europe today, and of these, three, Queen Wilhelmina of Holland and the Kings of Norway and Albania, have sought refuge in Britain.

King Haakon arrived at a northern port from Bergen on June 10, with the Crown Prince and members of the Norwegian Government. In a proclamation to the Norwegian people it was explained that this move had been made by advice of the High Command and " to prevent further destruction of the yet intact parts of the country." It was added that the President of the Storting of Holland and the Army and Navy supported the King and Government.

The puppet Government set up in April by Germany was later superseded by the appointment of Reichkommissar Terboven. Inspired by his master in Berlin, this official has now suggested to the Storting that it should meet and formally request King Haakon to abdicate his throne.

Italians on the Run

PANIC has been created on the Eritrean side of the Sudan frontier by the sudden harassing raids of British light mechanized units. These armoured fighting patrols are wont to attack native enemy forces with machine-gun fire, inflicting casualties without loss to themselves. One such raid took place on June 29, when a troop of cavalry, 1,200 strong, was encountered in the neighbourhood of Kassala by two British light armoured vehicles. When our patrols opened fire the enemy scattered in disorder and made for the hills, leaving 50 casualties behind them. A week earlier in the same district a battalion of native infantry was routed with severe loss.

How Did Balbo Die ?

MYSTERY surrounds the death of Marshal Balbo, Italy's Governor-General in Libya. According to the official Italian communiqué, " on Friday, June 28, while flying over Tobruk during an action with the enemy, the 'plane piloted by Italo Balbo ... fell in flames." Also in the 'plane were Balbo's nephew, Signor Ferrara, his brother-in-law, Lt.-Pilot Florio Gino, and the Italian Consul-General in Libya. All were killed. Two days later, however, the British Foreign Office issued a categorical denial of this story. " No British aircraft were concerned in the crash of Marshal Balbo's machine, and there is no truth in the statement that he fell in battle," it read, though the British squadron which was operating over Tobruk stated that they saw a machine burning on the ground.

From the facts available it would seem that Marshal Balbo, chief rival of Mussolini in the affections of the Italian public, may have died as Von Fritsch died in Poland in September 1939. In Balbo's stead was appointed Marshal Graziani of Abyssinian fame—or ill-fame.

Hong Kong is Evacuating Too

FOLLOWING the virtual encirclement of Hong Kong, Britain's commercial and military outpost in China, it was decided to evacuate from the colony all the British women and children. The first batch, totalling 1,960, left Hong Kong in a crack liner of the Canadian Pacific on July 1. Several scores also made the passage in one of the big trans-Pacific clipper aeroplanes. Their destination was Manila, in the U.S.A. islands of the Philippines though later they may proceed to Brisbane and Sydney.

Roosevelt's New Rival

PRESIDENT ROOSEVELT has not yet decided whether or not he will run for a third term of the Presidency, but he is more likely to do so now that his opponents, the Republicans, have chosen as their candidate a man of strong personality and popular appeal—Mr. Wendell Willkie. Although he has never held any political office and had not the backing of the Republican Party machine, Mr. Wendell Willkie secured the nomination at the Party conference at Philadelphia on June 28 in the sixth ballot. The Presidential elections are due to be held next November.

Sending the Children Overseas

FIRST of Britain's children to be evacuated to the New World were 60 youngsters who landed at New York on July 1. These were sent over privately, but the Government has in course of preparation a scheme whereby some tens of thousands of children are to be evacuated to Canada ; later perhaps the scheme may be extended to the U.S.A. and to Australia and New Zealand. In large measure the expenses of the evacuation will be borne by the Government.

Britain on the Offensive

TANTALIZINGLY brief was the communiqué issued on June 26 by the Ministry of Information which told of the first raid on enemy territory. It read : " In cooperation with the Royal Air Force, naval and military raiders yesterday carried out successful reconnaissance of the enemy coastline. Landings were effected at a number of points and contact made with German troops. Casualties were inflicted and some enemy dead fell into our hands. Much useful information was obtained. Our forces suffered no casualties." The Nazis, of course, waxed scornful in their account of operations " limited to landing attempts on a very small scale by a few British ships at two points of the French Channel coast." These were " completely unsuccessful," and the German casualties were only two wounded...

Evacuation of thousands of selected children, not to the British countryside but across the Atlantic, was a scheme that seized the public imagination. Here are some children pleased with the idea of an American adventure.
Photo, Wide World

Syria Quits the War

WHAT will France's Empire do ? In Syria, at least, the position is now clear. On June 23 great enthusiasm was aroused in the territory by a stirring proclamation broadcast by M. Puaux, French High Commissioner, that General Mittelhauser had decided " to carry on the mission of France in Syria and to defend with indomitable energy the honour of France and of her flag."

There followed four days of anticlimax, of uncertainty, of dwindling enthusiasm, misgiving and perplexity, until, on June 27, it was announced that General Mittelhauser had reconsidered his position and had decided to fall in with the instructions of the Pétain Government ; to put it plainly, he had ordered the cessation of hostilities.

What was the reason for this change of front ? It may well be inferred that it was due to the personal intervention of General Weygand, who, immediately after the Syrian defiance, was reported to have flown to Beirut to remonstrate with the man who had succeeded him as head of the Allied forces in the Near East. Thus Italy, with one eye on the oil pipe-line reaching the Mediterranean at Tripoli, starts putting the screw on.

'Scharnhorst' in the Wars Again

HIT by shells from the battle-cruiser " Renown " off Narvik on April 9, bombed by a naval 'plane on June 13, torpedoed by H.M. submarine " Clyde " and hit by three aerial bombs a week later—the " Scharnhorst," Germany's 26,000-ton battleship, was attacked again on July 1. When lying in a floating-dock at Keil, undergoing repairs, she was heavily bombed and set on fire by aircraft of the Coastal Command.

They Torpedoed Their Friends !

LOADED with 1,500 Germans and Italians who were being sent from Britain to internment camps in Canada, the Leyland liner " Arandora Star " was torpedoed by a U-boat off the west coast of Ireland. News of the disaster was given in a German communiqué on July 3, but this did not add that the torpedo had caused the deaths of 500 or more of their friends !

Reports varying, inconclusive and in parts contradictory, came from Rome as to the manner of Marshal Balbo's death. The non-Axis world drew its own more definite conclusions. *Photo, L.N.A.*

Scared by Stalin, Carol Turns to Hitler

For many years King Carol of Rumania proved himself to be a most skilful walker of Europe's political tight-rope; for years he managed to maintain his own and his country's balance while surrounded by a horde of greedy neighbours. At last, however (as is told below), he was pushed, or fell, or jumped, from his precarious position.

WHEN Molotov, Stalin's Foreign Commissar, on June 26 sent an ultimatum to Rumania demanding the return of Bessarabia, "stolen from the Soviet Union in 1918," King Carol bowed at once to superior force. He knew only too well that of the two countries that had guaranteed his frontiers, France was now *hors de combat*, and Britain was involved in her own defence. So, in a sense of accommodating realism, he swallowed his oft-repeated words that Bessarabia had been, was, and ever would be, Rumanian. His Government offered to negotiate, but Molotov was in dictatorial mood, so on June 28 the Russian troops crossed the Dniester and occupied Kishinev, the Bessarabian capital, and other towns near the frontier, and by July 1 the occupation of the entire province was complete.

Perhaps there were some grounds for Russia's claim, inasmuch as Bessarabia was part of the Tsar's empire from 1812, when it was ceded by the Turks, until 1917, when a not altogether representative "Council of the Land" proclaimed local autonomy, followed early in the next year by a declaration of Bessarabia's union with Rumania. The Soviet Union never formally acquiesced in the loss of the province, and it was well understood that at the first favourable opportunity Russia would do her best to recover it. That moment, so Stalin judged with his usual flair, had now come.

Lying between the rivers Dniester and Pruth, Bessarabia is most fertile in the north, where it forms part of the famous Black Earth region; the central area, though well watered by tributaries of the two great rivers, tends to be marshy, while parts are thickly forested with beech, oak and birch; in the south, adjoining the delta of the Danube, there are stretches of sand, salt marshes and lagoons. Practically all the population of some 3,000,000 are engaged on the land, raising crops of grain, fruit and tobacco, tending their vineyards, rearing numbers of sheep, cattle, horses, and pigs.

In the towns, particularly in Chisinau (Kishinev), there is a large Jewish element, but the province as a whole may well be described as one of Europe's "crazy quilt" areas. The Rumanians account for between 50 and 60 per cent, while the Russians and Ukrainians amount to rather less than 25 per cent. The balance is made up of Bulgarians, Turks, Germans, Magyars and Jews. On racial grounds, then, Russia could make small claim for the restitution of the province.

At the same time, however, it must be admitted that the Rumanians, whose numerical strength lies in the country rather than in the towns, have treated the minorities in a not altogether enlightened fashion. In the Russia of the Tsars Bessarabia was the most backward province, and it has been the most backward province of Greater Rumania. In 1897 only 19·4 per cent of the inhabitants over six years of age could read, and by 1930 the percentage had risen to only 38·1.

If Russia had some claim to Bessarabia on historical grounds, it had none to those northern regions of Bukovina which were coupled with Bessarabia in Stalin's ultimatum. Frankly enough, Molotov described its handing over as "a compensation, if only an unimportant one, for the immense loss which the Soviet Union and the population of Bessarabia have suffered through the twenty-two years' rule of Rumania in Bessarabia." Before 1918 the Bukovina was not Russian but Austrian, and of its population of about a million, 40 per cent speak Rumanian and 33 per cent Ukrainian. In the northern districts of Cernauti (the capital) and Storojinet the Ukrainians are in the majority, and this fact may have weighed with Stalin, who only a few months earlier incorporated so many million Polish Ukrainians within the bounds of the Soviet State.

Having restored Bessarabia at Stalin's behest, King Carol apparently feared similar demands from Hungary and Bulgaria. He turned, therefore, to the only Power which might be able to restrain their revisionist aspirations—Germany, and on July 1 it was announced that Rumania's foreign policy would be reorientated "as determined by the new European order in course of establishment," and that therefore Rumania had renounced the Anglo-French guarantee of April 13, 1939. An envoy was sent to Berlin to appeal (so it was said) for military assistance, and though this was refused Rumania continued to take all possible precautions against invasion.

The Russian occupation of Bessarabia and Northern Bukovina was begun on June 28 and completed on July 1. The map above shows the portions ceded by Rumania to Russia. The River Dniester, below, forms a natural boundary between the U.S.S.R. and Bessarabia. The buildings in the foreground are fishing huts.
Photos, Fox, Dorien Leigh

I Was in Charge of 450 French Wounded

The heroic work of British Red Cross nurses on the beach at Dunkirk
is described in page 646, Vol. 2. Here is the story of another nurse's
heroism at Dunkirk—that of Mme. Casimir-Périer, a French army
nurse, who swam out to a British destroyer to fetch help for the
wounded in her charge.

Mme. Casimir-Périer, whose part in the retreat to Dunkirk is told in this page, photographed at an English resort where she was
resting after her ordeal.
Photo, Associated Press

DURING the battle of Flanders the ambulance unit to which Mme. Casimir-Périer was attached took up quarters in an abandoned hotel near Dunkirk, and prepared to receive 100 wounded.

On the first day 400 wounded came in. The second day there were 700 more. The doctors and other officers from the unit were lent to a field hospital two miles away, and the worst cases were transferred there.

Soon the road between the two hospitals became almost impassable, owing to heavy shell fire and aerial bombardment. Mme. Casimir-Périer and other assistants were left to carry on. The local reservoir had been bombed, and water had to be rationed. Each wounded man had one tumblerful a day. There was none for washing.

The order was given to evacuate. Nearly 450 wounded were put in forty-three ambulances to go to Dunkirk jetty. Eleven of the ambulances never got there. They were bombed and left flaming on the road.

When Dunkirk beach was reached the ambulance attendants went back to continue their work, and Mme. Casimir-Périer was left with about 300 wounded men in her charge.

She said : "Some I left shielded from the sun under the lighthouse on the jetty. The others hid under a pier on the hot sand. Poor fellows—but what brave fellows.

"Some of them needed a surgeon all to themselves, but they were grand and cheerful. They shouted jokes to each other, and referred to me as ' the little green monkey,' because I was darting about from one to the other. I gave them what comfort I could, and then said I must leave them for an hour or two to go and search for the officers, as there was no one to give orders.

"I left a French rifleman in charge—a great big fellow, with a wound in the face. Don't let a single one leave here until I return,' I said. They waved to me as I went.

"I returned to the hospital, and found no one there. I went on to the other hospital and found it had been terribly bombed. Still I could not find the officers. Someone said they had gone to a fort some five miles away.

"I set out on foot. The bombing, the shelling, and the machine-gunning all this time were frightful. An incendiary bomb fell right at my feet. It scorched my legs and face.

"Still I could not find the officers. I realized they must be either dead or helping wounded somewhere else, and I must rely on myself.

"I returned to the beach. I had been away for six hours. The boys seemed pleased to see me. I waited with them as the day lengthened. Then an English trawler, the King George,' came in. I helped get the poor fellows aboard, and waved to them as they steamed away.

"After that I went back to have another look at the road to the other hospital, where 150 of the most seriously wounded were lying. I had promised I would bring them help, but I could see that it would be almost impossible to travel that road and live.

"Then I looked seaward, and saw a British destroyer a long way out. I dropped my clothes on the beach and started swimming out to it in brassière and shorts.

"I think I swam for three-quarters of an hour. I was nearly drowning when the sailors hauled me aboard. They took me in front of an officer. I told him I needed help, and he said, ' Madame, you shall have it.'

"I was so filthy and covered with oil, and ashamed of myself, that I went back in the water again, and started swimming for the shore. One of the destroyer's motor-boats overtook me, and they lifted me in.

"The sailors got all the wounded in the destroyer in wonderfully quick time, using four motor-boats."—" *Daily Express.*"

How We Bombed the Maastricht Bridges

In earlier pages of "The War Illustrated" (Vol. 2, p.p. 574, 581, 631, and 654) reference has been made to the magnificent feat of an R.A.F. Bomber Squadron which blew up the bridges at Maastricht —a feat which evoked the message " Messieurs, je vous remercie " (Thank you, gentlemen) from General Georges. Now we record the story broadcast by a sergeant observer who was one of the two survivors of the action.

THE two bridges at Maastricht should have been blown up on the night of May 11, but for some unknown reason they were left standing. It was absolutely necessary that the bridges should be destroyed, for they were the only route open to the enemy.

One Squadron Leader asked for volunteers, and there is no need for me to say that not a single one of us hesitated. I wasn't present at the actual time, but when I arrived my pilot told me he had put my name down, and I'm glad he did.

Maastricht was about 100 miles away from our aerodrome, but from the preparations we made for the journey you might have thought we were off for a journey across miles of uncharted land. We are thorough about all our routes, of course, but the vital importance of this raid made us even more careful. It was absolutely essential that we should not waste any time in finding the bridges, and it was absolutely essential that they should be destroyed.

Five aircraft set out on the task. One flight of three were detailed to destroy the larger bridge, and the other two aircraft— in one of which I was the observer—had the smaller bridge to deal with. We were given a fighter escort of three aircraft, which

Here is a scene in a street of Dunkirk during the terrible bombardments from the air which Mme. Casimir-Périer describes. An ambulance is once more the victim of the bomber Robert Montgomery, the American film star, who served with an ambulance in France, declared that a vehicle without the Red Cross was safer than one with it. *Photo, British Official: Crown Copyright*

Two important bridges over the River Maas and the Albert Canal were heavily bombed by the R.A.F. in the middle of May.   The Germans put up a terrific barrage when the British 'planes appeared, but the R.A.F. pilots delivered their attack at 6,000 feet, diving to 2,000 feet as they dropped their bombs.   This German photograph of Maastricht, taken during the raid, gives a vivid impression of the intensity of the attack. (See photograph in Vol. 2, page 581.)

Photo, Associated Press

cheered us up quite a lot, but unfortunately we were not to have their company for long. When we were about 20 miles from the target 30 Messerschmitts tried to intercept us, but we continued on our course while the three fighters went into the attack.   The odds were ten to one, but even so several of those Messerschmitts were brought down.

So we arrived near Maastricht.   All the company we had was more enemy fighters and heavier anti-aircraft fire.   The Messerschmitts attacked us from the rear.   The first I knew about it was when our rear gunner shouted to me, " Enemy fighters on our tail—look out, Taffy ! "   Our pilot turned and took evasive action, while the gunner shot one of them down.   That seemed to frighten the others, for they soon sheered off.   The barrage was terrific—the worst I have ever struck—and as we neared our target we saw the flight of three bombers, now returning home, caught in the thick of the enemy's fire.   All three were lost.

The big bridge looked badly knocked about and was sagging in the middle.   It had been hit by the bombs dropped by the three bombers ahead of us.   When we delivered our attack we were about 6,000 feet up.   We dived down to 2,000—one aircraft close behind the other, and dropped our load. Looking down, we saw that our bridge now matched the other.   It sagged in the middle, and its iron girders were sticking out all over the place.   Immediately after we had dropped our bombs we turned for home, but the barrage was there waiting for us.   It was even worse than before, and it was not long before our aircraft began to show signs of damage.   Soon the rear gunner shouted, " They have got our tanks ! " and as it looked as if the machine was going up in fire, the pilot gave orders to abandon aircraft.

I Was Taken for a Boche !

The rear gunner jumped first.   We saw nothing of him after that, though we hope he is all right.   Then I jumped.   The pilot remained with his machine and managed to bring it down safely.

When I jumped we were near Liége, and on the way down I saw I was going straight for the River Meuse, so I pulled my rigging cord on one side and altered direction to make sure of falling somewhere in the town. But as I came near the ground I saw a reception committee waiting for me.   Hundreds of people were dashing about from one street to another and all were pointing at me.   As I got nearer I realized that the mob was angry ;   they were shouting and waving their fists.   I then began to wonder whether

the river wouldn't be safer after all, but by that time it was too late to change my mind.

I landed in a small cottage back garden, and before I had had time to disentangle myself from my gear the crowd rushed into the next-door garden and dragged me over the fence, shouting " Sale Boche "—that means " Dirty German "—and other insulting remarks.   I shouted back " Je suis anglais," but either they didn't believe me or didn't understand my French.

Soon they had dragged me into the street where there were hundreds of people waiting. Men and women held my arms and an angry old man got ready to shoot me.   Again I

shouted " Anglais !   Anglais ! " and I am glad to say somebody must have thought it just possible that I was telling the truth, for the old man was prevailed upon to hand me over to the police.   On the way to the police-station, burly women tried to hit me ; and then suddenly, out of the blue, I was spoken to in English by a Belgian woman who offered to act as my interpreter.   I was grateful to her.   She persuaded the police to send me to the Commandant of Liége Fortress.   He believed my story, offered me hospitality, gave me a bicycle and a map, and put me on the road to Namur.   So, after an adventurous journey, I arrived in England.

I Served as a Woman in the French Army

Sharing the dangers of the French Army, of which it was officially recognized as a unit, the Anglo-French Ambulance Corps had a hazardous journey from the front to Bordeaux.   The story of the women ambulance drivers' endurance and heroism is told exclusively to " The War Illustrated " by Miss Dorothy M. Clarke.

OUR contract was for six months as soldiers of France, and the French Government had passed a special decree to enable us—46 British women, members of the Anglo-French Ambulance Corps—to serve as " petticoat " poilus.

We left England at the beginning of April in a troopship seen off by numerous cameras, for the novelty of our mission had stirred the imagination of the Press.   Our ten days' stay in Paris rivalled that of any film star ; we were fêted and photographed wherever we went.   Then on April 13 at an impressive ceremony in the Place des Invalides we and our 22 ambulances were handed over officially to the French Army.   We were attached to the Dépôt de Guerre du Train No. 19 and posted to Compiegne.

At first our duties consisted of transporting sick and accident cases, and we grumbled because we had so little to do.   But when on the morning of May 10 we were awakened by the sound of bursting bombs we knew that war on the Western Front had started in earnest and there was no further time to slack or grouse.   From then onwards, working in twenty-four hour shifts, we drove our ambulances day and night as a never-ending stream of wounded poured into the five local hospitals.

Compiègne itself was subjected to a heavy bombardment.   For days the raids went on continuously from dawn to dusk.   Then our passengers were not confined to members of the Forces and we carried wounded civilians as well.   Some of the patients we

brought in were children and tiny babies. The rain of incendiary bombs set whole streets on fire and soon the place was a burning shambles.   The senior officer in the town gave permission for the troops to save what goods they could, and so amidst crackling flames and falling masonry we ran with the soldiers from street to street and building to building, filling kit-bags and haversacks with packets of food, bottles of wine, silk stockings, cameras, shoes, gloves, dress material, etc.   It was one of the most exciting days of our lives ;   but after the excitement came the depression.

Water, gas, electricity, telephone, telegraph were all cut off.   The railway line was severed.   Any shops which remained intact were closed ;   and nearly all the inhabitants of the place fled south.   But the fighting services, and the personnel of the largest hospital—Royallieu—remained.

We had never expected to go to the Front, and we did not go, but the Front came to us. A couple of weeks passed, and then at 2 o'clock one morning we were roused suddenly from our beds, told to pack and be ready to leave in a quarter of an hour.   This marked the beginning of that great and rapid retreat before the German advance, which spread in ever-growing momentum from the north to the south of France.

Always on the run, we had seldom time to stay for more than a few hours in any one place ;   we were driving day and night, carrying the unfortunate wounded with us. Sometimes our patients were lying on

These Women Played a Manful Part in the Great Retreat

Miss D. M. Clarke, of the Anglo-French Ambulance, who tells of her adventures in this and the previous page. Right is one of the ambulances ditched during the retreat.

stretchers in the ambulances for as long as 22 hours at a time.

During the retreat from Fontainebleau we lost our field kitchen, three male cooks, and all our food. After this major disaster, for the next ten days we were officially without food, money, or billets. We lived on carrots and lettuces out of the ground ; an occasional hen's egg, and a few biscuits and sardines which we managed to acquire. At night we slept in our ambulances in the fields and forests. If we washed at all we did so in wayside streams, or beneath a village pump ; but hot water was an unknown luxury. And all this time we were subjected continually to aerial bombardment, so that our tin hats never left our sides.

The Germans advanced so rapidly that at one time the enemy was only three and a half miles behind us. In the general hurry and disorganization we lost all touch with military headquarters, and for some days were without official orders and petrol.

We were posted as missing, but by sheer good luck managed to reach Bordeaux and get on board a Polish troopship—one of the last boats to leave—on the day on which the armistice was signed. With deep regret we left our ambulances behind us on the quay-side. As we embarked in the harbour we were bombed, and at sea we were chased by a submarine, so that when in a few days we reached a north of England port never had the shores of home appear more welcome.

The Royallieu Hospital, Compiègne, at which the Anglo-French Ambulance Corps was first stationed. When the German Army approached the buildings were abandoned, and the unit began the long retreat which ended only at Bordeaux.

Here are women of the Anglo-French Ambulance Corps taking a hurried meal by the roadside during their long retreat. Before the Royallieu Hospital was evacuated, Compiègne had been heavily bombed by the Germans. Right, destruction wrought in one street while the Corps was still gallantly carrying on its work of mercy.

Photos, D. M. Clarke, exclusive to THE WAR ILLUSTRATED

What Twelve Days of Air War Cost Germany

Air Raids on Britain and Germany: Debits and Credits, June 18—July 1

ON BRITAIN	Casualties	Enemy Losses	ON GERMANY, &c.	British Losses	ON BRITAIN	Casualties	Enemy Losses	ON GERMANY, &c.	British Losses
June 18–19 Essex, Cambridgeshire, Lincolnshire, Norfolk, Suffolk, Northamptonshire	12 k. 90 i.	7	**June 18–19** Bremen—O.f. Hamburg—O.f. Kastrop—O.f. Misburg—O.: P. Sterkrade—O.: P. Gladbach, Wesel, Arsbrech—R. Schwerte—M. Düsseldorf—R.: A.W. Soest—M. Cologne (nr.)—T. Schilau—P. Cologne—A.W.f.	3 m.	**June 25–26** S.E. Scotland ; Wales : Midlands ; N.E., S., S.E. and S.W. England	4 k. 13 i.	5	**June 25–26** Arnhem and Borkum—A. Linhen—R. Hamm—R. Dorsten—R. Osterfeld—M. Monheim—O. Bremen—A.W. Cologne—F. (c.). Heligoland—D. (a.). (fighter shot down.). Bomoen—A.	Nil
June 19–20 East and South Coasts	8 k. 60 i.	3 2*	**June 19–20** Lünen, Hamm, Bielefeld, Münster, Düren, Schwerte, Euskirchen, München-Gladbach, Hamborn, Emmerich, Hamburg, Brunsbüttel, Norderney—O.; A.W.; B.; M.; A.; T. Rouen—A.	1 m.	**June 26–27** N.E. Scotland ; N.E., E. and S.E. England	slight	3	**June 26–27** Gelsenkirchen—O. Soest—R. Texel, Helder, Schipol, Waalhaven, De Kooy—A. Dortmund, Bonn, Handorf, Langenhagen—A. Cologne—O. Ludwigshaven—F.(c.). Osnabruck, Rheydt, Hamm, Soest —M.; R. Willemsoord, Genemuiden—L.; D.K	2 m.
June 20–21 N.E., E. & S.E. England	0	?	**June 20–21** Schipol—A. Rouen—A. Haamstede—A. Paderborn—A. Münster—A. Hitzacker—A.W. Ludwigshaven—M. Osterfeld—M.; S.; Essen—M, Calais—G.E.	} 2 m. 1 l.	**June 27–28** S.E. England	very slight	1	**June 27–28** Misburg—O.f. Bremen—O. Salzbergen—F. Helder and Texel—N. (b.: one Heinkel dest.) Denmark and N. Germany—m.o. bombed. Nyborg, W. of Copenhagen—O.f.	Nil
June 21–22 E., N.E., S. & S.E. England	3 k. 3 i.	?	**June 21–22** Bremen—A.W. Kassel—A.W.; A. Rothenburg—A. Göttingen—S. Huntlosen—A. Hamburg (N. of)—A. Rheine (nr)—T. Osnabruck and Bremen, rly. between—T. Lingen—T. Essen—A.W. (Krupps). Hanover (nr.)—O. Willemsoord—O.	2 m. 1 l.	**June 28–29** S. Wales ; E. England	5 i.	?	**June 28–29** N.W. Germany—F. (c.): M.: R.: C.: A. Dormagen, S. of Düsseldorf—F. f. Hochst—F. (c.) f. Monheim (nr.)—F. Cologne (E. of)—blast fur. b. Osnabruck, Soest, Hamm —M.	Nil
June 22–23 Nil			**June 22–23** Merville, W. of Lille—A.	1 l.	**June 29–30** S. and E. Coasts ; Midlands ; town in Scotland	2 k. 8 i.	? ?	**June 29–30** Abbeville—A. Hochst—F. (c.) f. Dortmund—Ems Canal—b. Soest, Schwerte, Hamm and Gremburg — M. Baden. Cologne—m.o. b. Bois de Chimay—m.o. b. Norderney, Borkum, Schipol—A. Barga, Münster—A. Merville—A.	3 m.
June 23–24 Nil			**June 23–24** Germany and Holland—A.; R. (daylight) Mecklenburg, Ruhr, Rhineland —A.W.; M.; R. Hamburg—?	3 m. Several m.	**June 30—July 1** E. England, Wales, W. England ; E. Scotland	1 i.	1†	**June 30—July 1** Merville—A. Hamburg—O. f. Darmstadt area—b. f. Bremen—O. Haltern, 10 m. W. of—D. (a.). Hanover — M. Osnabruck, Dülmen—M.; R. Norderney —A. Huntlosen—A. Dortmund—A.	3 m. Nil
June 24–25 E. Counties, Midlands, town in S.W. England	5 k. 20 i.	?	**June 24–25** Eindhoven, Schipol, Waalhaven, De Kooy—A. Mülheim, Kassel—A.; A.W.f. Helder—N.f. Dortmund—O.: M. Deichshausen—A.W. Emmerich (nr.)—R.	Nil					

* By balloon barrage.   **KEY TO THE TABLE**   *† Float 'plane.*

A. aerodrome : **a.** ammunition : **AW.** aircraft works.   **GE.** gun emplacement ; **i.** injured ; **k.** killed ; **L.**   **N.** naval base : **O.** oil depot, stores or refinery.
B. bridge : **b.** bombed : **C.** canal ; **c.** chemical.   locks ; **l.** lost ; **M.** marshalling yard ; **m.** missing ;   **P.** power station ; **p.** petrol ; **R.** railway.
D. dump ; **DK.** docks ; **F.** factory ; **f.** set on fire.   **m.o.** military objectives.   **S.** stores or warehouses ; **T.** trains.

German 'Planes Down

German Airmen Killed or Captured

Civilian Killed

In the diagram above the Nazi losses in machines and crews are compared with British civilian deaths. Taking 4 airmen to each of 22 bombers brought down about 90 were killed or captured as against 46 civilians killed—not more than one-tenth of British road casualties during May 1940. The map shows the very wide range of the regular air battlefield over Germany.   *Courtesy of "Evening Standard"*

THE tables printed here attempt a comparison between the results of the Nazi raids upon Britain and those carried out upon military objectives in Germany or enemy-occupied territory. Air raids have to be accepted as a hard necessity of war. The results must be judged by military standards and endured, as they are, without undue concern.

Map legend:
Airfields X
Air Factories, Stores, Munition Works & Power Stas. . . . . ▲
Oil Dumps . . . . . ■
Bridges, Junctions & Marshalling Yards . . . . . ●
Other Objectives . . . . . O

0   100 MILES

Night and Day the R.A.F. Hits the Nazis Hard

Here is the scene when aircraft of the Fleet Air Arm had bombed and completely wrecked a new Nazi big gun emplacement on the cliffs near Calais on June 20. The second of two bombs has made a direct hit. The aircraft were led by a young Canadian airman who had twice photographed the position under heavy fire. On the right a salvo of ten bombs can be seen falling on the oil storage tanks at Monheim, seven miles north of Cologne.

The photograph left explains the reference to bombing marshalling yards, appearing so frequently in Air Ministry bulletins. A "stick" of three bombs is dropping on the marshalling yards at Hamm, the junction of the main lines from Munster and Hamburg to Dortmund.

Photos, British Official: Crown Copyright

OUR DIARY OF THE WAR

Wednesday, June 26, 1940

Announced that General de Gaulle was forming **French volunteer legion** in Great Britain, and also setting up French centre for armament and scientific research.

M. Corbin, French Ambassador in London, **resigned.**

Air Ministry announced that Coastal Command aircraft wrecked German aerodrome at **Bomoen,** near Bergen.

R.A.F. made daylight raids into Germany, oil plants and other objectives were bombed. During night aircraft attacked seaplane bases at **Texel** and **Helder,** and many aerodromes in Holland and Germany.

R.A.F. scored successes in Africa, raids being carried out on aerodromes at **Gura** and **Macaaca,** and on **Assab.**

German aircraft appeared over Britain during night of June 26-27. Bombs were dropped in North-East England, North-East Scotland and in other areas. **Three raiders shot down.**

Five raids made on **Malta.**

Thursday, June 27

Russia presented 24-hour **ultimatum to Rumania** requiring cession of Bessarabia and Northern Bukovina, and satisfaction of other demands.

New seat of Pétain Government reported to be Clermont-Ferrand.

General Mittelhauser, French C.-in-C. in Near East, announced that **hostilities** had **ceased in Syria.**

French Government dismissed Governors-General of **Indo-China** and of **Madagascar.**

R.A.F. bombers made daylight raids into Germany. Oil refineries near **Hanover** and at **Bremen** hit.

Other formations attacked military objectives in Denmark and North Germany. Oil tanks at **Nyborg,** west of Copenhagen, set on fire.

Enemy aircraft crossed British coast during night. Anti-aircraft defences and R.A.F. fighters went into action.

Friday, June 28

British Government gave formal recognition to General de Gaulle.

After unsuccessful attempt to negotiate, **Rumania ceded Bessarabia and Northern**

German battleship "Scharnhorst" which during the period June 13—July 2 had suffered persistent and successful attack by British aircraft and submarines.

Bukovina to Russia. Soviet aircraft and motorized columns began taking possession. General mobilization proclaimed in Rumania.

Channel Islands, which had been demilitarized and partly evacuated, **bombed and machine-gunned** by enemy 'planes. Thirty-nine persons killed.

Coastal Command aircraft blew up ammunition store at **Willemsoord,** Holland.

THE POETS & THE WAR
XXVIII
1904—1940
BY SIR ROBERT VANSITTART

Was I not faithful to you from the first?
    When have I ever failed you since my youth?
I loved without illusion, knew the worst,
    But felt the best was nearer to the truth.

You were indulgent too and open-eyed
    To the shortcomings I was frank to own.
So we were mingled, destined side by side
    To face a world we could not face alone.

Did you keep faith with me? When all was well
    Yes; but I clave to you when all was not.
And, when temptation touched your citadel,
    Your weakness won again, and you forgot——

Forgot your Self, and freedom and your friends,
    Even interest; and now our vaunted glow
Becomes a blush, as the long story ends
    In sorry separation at Bordeaux.

You hate me now; you will not hate me less
    If I go on unshaken by your fall,
If *for your sake,* devoid of bitterness,
    I face the world without you after all.
                                    —*The Times*

R.A.F. successfully raided petrol and bomb dumps at **Macaaca,** Eritrea. Effective raid carried out on desert aerodrome at **El Gubbi.**

Nazi raiders crossed East Coast during night of June 28-29. Anti-aircraft defences were in action. Few bombs dropped in South Wales and near East Coast.

Italians raided **Mersa Matruh,** but without doing serious damage.

Admiralty announced that H.M. submarine "Tetrarch" had sunk German transport off south coast of Norway.

Announced that Canadian destroyer "Fraser" had been lost off Bordeaux.

H.M. trawler "Myrtle" reported mined.

Saturday, June 29

Russian troops continued process of occupying Bessarabia and Northern Bukovina.

Rome announced that **Marshal Balbo,** Governor-General of Libya, had been **killed** in air battle over **Tobruk** on June 28. British Foreign Office denied that any aircraft of R.A.F. was concerned in the crash.

Admiralty announced that an **Italian destroyer** had been **sunk** in the Mediterranean, and **two Italian U-boats destroyed** in the East Indies.

R.A.F. again attacked harbour at **Willemsoord.** Chemical factory at Hochst, near **Frankfurt,** was bombed and set on fire. Dortmund-Ems canal attacked.

Two British light tanks routed 1,200 Italian cavalry across Eritrean frontier.

Raiders crossed British coasts during

night. Bombs dropped at number of points, including Bristol Channel area. **Heinkel raider shot down** off coast of Scotland.

Sunday, June 30

Bucharest reported serious **clashes between Russian troops** advancing into Bessarabia **and retiring Rumanian forces.**

French, Italian, and German delegations to Armistice Commission assembled at Wiesbaden and proceedings opened.

R.A.F. bombers again attacked **Merville** aerodrome and also railway objectives at **Vignacourt,** north of Abbeville.

Non-stop attacks on Germany continued. Oil storage tanks at **Hamburg** hit and set burning. Further raids made on enemy aerodromes, including **Norderney.**

Five Messerschmitts shot down and seven others probably destroyed by formations of Hurricane fighters over France.

Enemy aircraft again crossed British coasts during night. R.A.F. fighters **shot down float 'plane** off North-East coast.

Admiralty announced that H.M. submarine "Grampus" was overdue and must be considered lost.

Malta had 50th air-raid.

Monday, July 1

Rumania renounced Anglo-French guarantee of her integrity.

Russians completed occupation of ceded territories in Rumania.

British Foreign Office issued statement that Government cannot allow Syria or the Lebanon to be occupied by a hostile Power.

German bombers raided Britain during evening and night. Incendiary bombs dropped on North-East Coast. **Two raiders shot down** by R.A.F. fighters.

High explosive bomb dropped on town on North-East coast of Scotland. Twelve persons killed and 18 injured.

Enemy landings on Jersey and Guernsey officially announced.

Oil refinery at **Augusta,** Sicily, set on fire by R.A.F. Aerodrome at **Gondar,** Abyssinia, severely damaged, and other successful raids made in **Kenya area.**

Marshal Graziani arrived in Libya as C.-in-C. of Italian Forces in North Africa in succession to Marshal Balbo.

British cargo steamers "Empire Toucan," "Guido" and "Zarian" reported torpedoed.

Evacuation from **Hong Kong** began.

Tuesday, July 2

Four more Italian submarines reported sunk in Mediterranean.

R.A.F. raided Kiel in early morning and heavily **bombed battleship "Scharnhorst."** Docks were set on fire.

Other R.A.F. aircraft attacked aerodromes in Germany, and ammunition barges on canals at **Rotterdam.**

Macaaca, Eritrea, bombed again, and three more Italian aircraft destroyed.

Nazi raiders bombed North-East Coast towns during evening. Twelve persons killed and 123 injured. Enemy aircraft also dropped bombs in open country in South-West England and over Wales.

British liner **"Arandora Star,"** carrying 1,500 German and Italian internees to Canada, **sunk by U-boat** off west of Ireland.

British tanker "Athellaird" reported torpedoed in mid-Atlantic.

Berlin issued casualty figures purporting to show total losses (156,492) in France and Flanders.

Wednesday, July 3

British Fleet seized all French warships in British harbours. Those in North African ports which refused conditions offered were fired upon, and many damaged. Ships at Alexandria were refused permission to leave. Many ships and sailors accepted British control.

SHE WILL NOT FIRE HER GUNS FOR HITLER

These British sailors, waving to men ashore, are in possession of one of the French warships taken over by the Royal Navy on July 3, 1940, at Plymouth, Portsmouth and Sheerness. They were boarded by superior forces, and, except in the case of the submarine "Surcouf," there was no untoward incident. For the time being, at least, the French ships were allowed still to fly the tricolour.

Photo, G.P.U.

How France's Warships Were Saved From Hitler

Following Marshal Pétain's appeal to the Nazis for an armistice, the fate of the French Fleet became a matter of the gravest interest to Britain, now left as the only bulwark of Western civilization. To prevent its falling into enemy hands was imperative, but it was only, alas, by a display of the most resolute British force that this was achieved.

FACING Keitel and his semicircle of grim-faced Nazis in the railway coach at Compiègne, Admiral Leluc signed away the French Navy to Germany. True, Article 8 of the Franco-German armistice contained the words "demobilization" and "disarmament," and also Germany's "solemn declaration" that she would not use the French Fleet during the war or claim it on the conclusion of peace. But few outside Pétain's Government—and perhaps few inside it, save the senile pessimist who was its head—can have put any trust in the written word. Hitler's vows are made to be broken, and we may be sure that the French ships would not have been allowed to rot and rust in the French harbours, but in the Fuehrer's good time would have been added to Mussolini's fleet and what was left of his own. By such a concentration of naval might Britain's sea power might well have been challenged with some possibility, even probability, of success.

But Mr. Churchill and his Government and the Admiralty chiefs decided otherwise. Britain's own salvation demanded the strongest action, and after deliberating a question which Mr. Churchill described as being more grim and sombre than any in his experience, they unitedly took the decision "with aching hearts but with clear vision."

Oran on the North African coast, the great French naval base, is an artificial harbour, and some of the land on which the shore buildings stand has been reclaimed from the sea.

The 10,000 - ton French aircraft carrier "Commandant Teste" was reported among the ships destroyed by the British Fleet at Oran on July 3.

"Early yesterday morning," Mr. Churchill told the House of Commons on July 4, "after all preparations had been made, we took the greater part of the French Fleet under our control or else called upon them with adequate force to comply with our requirements."

First, those ships were secured which had come into harbour at Portsmouth, Plymouth and Sheerness—two battleships, two light cruisers, some submarines, eight destroyers and some 200 smaller, but none the less extremely useful, mine-sweeping and anti-submarine craft. The operation was carried out without resistance or bloodshed, with the exception of a scuffle on the monster submarine "Surcouf," in which one British officer and an A.B. and one French officer were killed.

Captain C. S. Holland, R.N., who presented Admiral Somerville's ultimatum to Admiral Gensoul, was at one time British Naval Attaché in Paris.
Photos, G.P.U. and Associated Press

Most of France's naval strength was concentrated in the Mediterranean at Alexandria and Oran. At the former a French fleet, consisting of a battleship, four cruisers, and a number of smaller ships, was lying beside a strong British battle fleet. After negotiations the French admiral, Admiral Godfroy, complied with the British demands.

"Thanks to the friendship formed between the French and British crews," ran an official report issued in Cairo on July 7, "demobilization of the French fleet at Alexandria has been carried out without difficulty in a spirit of complete understanding."

There remained the fleet at Oran and its adjacent military port of Mers-el-Kebir on the western side of Algeria. Here were assembled two of the finest of France's vessels, the "Dunkerque" and "Strasbourg"; two other battleships, the "Bretagne" and "Provence"; several light cruisers, and a number of destroyers, submarines, and other vessels. On the morning of July 3, Captain Holland, who had arrived in a destroyer, requested an interview with the French commander, Admiral Gensoul, and on being refused presented a document whose vital fourth paragraph began:

It is impossible for us, your comrades up to now, to allow your fine ships to fall into the power of the German or Italian enemy. We are determined to fight on to the end, and if we win, as we think we shall, we shall never forget that France was our Ally, that our interests are the same as hers, and that our common enemy is Germany. Should we conquer we solemnly declare that we shall restore the greatness and territory of France.

Then it proceeded to demand that the French should either :

(a) Sail with us and continue the fight.

(b) Sail with reduced crews under our control to a British port. . . .

(c) Alternatively, if you feel bound to stipulate that your ships shall not be used against Germany or Italy, then sail with us with reduced crews to some French port in the West Indies—Martinique, for instance—where they can be demilitarized to our satisfaction or perhaps entrusted to the United States to remain over until the end of the war, the crews being liberated.

If you refuse these fair offers I must with profound regret require you to sink your ships within six hours.

Failing the above, I have the orders of His Majesty's Government to use whatever force may be necessary to prevent your ships falling into German or Italian hands.

Unfortunately, none of these alternatives proved acceptable. After parleys which continued nearly all day, Admiral Gensoul, acting, no doubt, in accordance with orders dictated from Wiesbaden, where the Franco-German Armistice Commission was in session, announced his intention of fighting.

Some hours earlier a British battle squadron, with cruisers and destroyers,

And by Force or Persuasion Secured by Britain

British sailors boarded most of the French ships that had sought shelter in British ports soon after their surrender to the Royal Navy had been demanded.

had arrived off Oran under the command of Vice-Admiral Sir James Somerville. Admiral Somerville now received instructions from London to complete his mission before night fell, and at 5.58 he opened fire on the powerful French fleet, which was protected by shore batteries. At 6 p.m., to quote Mr. Churchill, he reported that he was heavily engaged.

"The action lasted some 10 minutes, and was followed by heavy attacks from our naval aircraft carried in the ' Ark Royal.' At 7.20 Admiral Somerville forwarded a further report which stated that a battle cruiser of the Strasbourg class (later identified as the ' Dunkerque ') was damaged and ashore, that

These are some of the first photographs to be taken of the French warships now in British waters. In one are some of the smaller craft, which include destroyers, submarine chasers, torpedo boats and patrol vessels. Another shows a French battleship of the Bretagne class in a British port.

Photos, P.N.A., Keystone and G.P.U.

In British Ports & at Alexandria Peace Prevailed—

Perhaps the most interesting of the French vessels taken over on July 3 was the monster submarine " Surcouf," readily identifiable by the unique seaplane hangar amidships.

Lieut.-Commander Dennis Sprague, R.N., was shot in a scuffle aboard the "Surcouf" while leading the boarding-party on July 3. Three days later his body was borne to the grave with full naval honours on July 6.

Photos, Vandyk and G.P.U.

The " Richelieu " was lying at Dakar in French West Africa, and a British naval force was dispatched to Dakar with orders to present to the French admiral there proposals similar to those offered to his colleague at Oran. As no satisfactory reply was received within the time limit specified, a twofold attack was delivered upon the " Richelieu " in the early hours of July 8. First a ship's boat, under the command

a battleship of the ' Bretagne ' class had been sunk, and another of the same class had been heavily damaged, that two French destroyers and a seaplane carrier, the ' Commandant Teste ' were also sunk or burned.''

While what Mr. Churchill well described as " this melancholy action " was being fought, the " Strasbourg " and some other vessels (later reported to be five cruisers, some torpedo boats, and several smaller vessels) managed to slip out of harbour, and eventually reached Toulon, although the " Strasbourg " was hit by at least one torpedo from a 'plane of the Fleet Air Arm. " None of the British ships engaged in the action was in any way affected in gun-power or mobility by the heavy fire directed on

them," said Mr. Churchill, and it was later announced that the casualties were remarkably small—two wounded and two missing.

The French, however, had a very different tale to tell. Quoting what it claimed was a French Admiralty communiqué, the German News Agency said that only two survivors were rescued from the " Bretagne," and of the complements of the " Dunkerque," " Provence," and " Mogador," 200 were dead or missing and 150 were wounded. Other French official reports said that more than 1,000 French sailors were killed, wounded, or missing as a result of the battle.

The next day the battle was renewed, and on July 6 units of the Fleet Air Arm raided Oran again and secured six hits on the " Dunkerque," already crippled and driven ashore. So ended the battle of Oran, the first large-scale action since Trafalgar in which British ships had been arrayed against French. Throughout the action the Italian Navy, for whose reception, as Mr. Churchill said, " we had also made arrangements," and which was considerably stronger than the fleet we used at Oran, kept prudently out of reach.

By now all France's capital ships were accounted for with the exception of the two largest, the " Richelieu," only just completed, and the " Jean Bart " still under construction.

THE ACTION AGAINST FRANCE'S NAVY
July 4—10

Name	Tonnage	
Battleships		
Richelieu	35,000	Completed, but not in commission; put out of action by British Navy at Dakar on July 8.
Jean Bart	35,000	Afloat, but not completed.
Strasbourg... ...	26,500	Torpedoed after gaining open sea at Oran. Reached Toulon.
Dunkerque ...	26,500	Badly damaged at Oran and ashore ; bombed later.
Bretagne		One sunk, one heavily
Provence		damaged at Oran. Two
Courbet	22,189	in British ports, one
Paris		at Alexandria.
Lorraine		
Aircraft Carrier		
Béarn	22,146	Reported (July 8) at Martinique.
Aircraft Transport		
Commandant Teste	10,000	Reported sunk or burned at Oran.
Cruisers		
Algérie		
Four of the Suffren		
class	10,000	Three at Alexandria.
Two of the Duquesne class ...		
Ten light cruisers of varying tonnage		Two in British ports ; one at Alexandria ; five reached Toulon.
Destroyers & Torpedo Boats, etc.		
Over 70 vessels	2,800 downward	Eight in British ports ; Mogador and another sunk or burned at Oran.
Submarines		
Surcouf	3,000	In British port.
Forty-five first-class craft		
Over forty second-class craft... ...		Some in British hands.
Small craft ...		Over 200 in British ports and more at Alexandria and Oran.

Note.—Under construction (some may have been put into service): 2 battleships 3 cruisers and many destroyers and smaller craft.

The ships at Alexandria were demilitarized by agreement on July 7.

—But at Oran and Dakar They Fought it Out

of Lt.-Commander R. H. Bristowe, was sent into the harbour and dropped depth charges close under the stern of the warship as she lay at anchor in the shallow water, so as to damage her propellers and steering gear. Then the main attack was developed by aircraft of the Fleet Air Arm which secured at least five hits with their torpedoes on the battleship's mighty frame. Air reconnaissances revealed that the " Richelieu " had a list to port and was down by the stern, while a large quantity of oil fuel covered the water around the ship. As for the " Jean Bart," Mr. Alexander, Britain's First Lord of the Admiralty, told the House of Commons on July 9 that he preferred not to say where she was.

With howls of rage the Germans received the news of these Nelson-like strokes. Mr. Churchill was assailed with the foulest vituperation, and in French Government circles, too, there was the most bitter denunciation, talk of a stab in the back, " all the more hateful as it was made by our Allies of yesterday." But in Britain and overseas, and in America in particular there was nothing but praise for the resolute way in which a most tragic dilemma had been resolved.

Nevertheless, there was no triumphing in Britain over the issue of the " melancholy action " of Oran. Rather there was the profoundest regret that the stroke should have been made necessary by the treachery of Pétain's government.

The opinion of Frenchmen in England was well expressed by General de Gaulle when he asked the British people to

" spare us and spare themselves from any interpretation of this tragedy as a direct naval success." That, he said in a broadcast, would be unfair. " The French ships at Oran were in fact incapable of fighting. They were at their moorings unable to manoeuvre or scatter, with officers and crews who had been corroded for a fortnight by the worst moral sufferings. They gave to the British ships the advantage of the first salvos, which, as everyone knows, are decisive at sea at such a short range. Their destruction is not the result of a fight. Nevertheless," he concluded, " I would rather know that the ' Dunkerque '—our beautiful, our beloved, our powerful ' Dunkerque '—is aground at Oran than see her one day manned by Germans shelling English ports or Algiers, Casablanca, or Dakar."

Mr. Churchill himself had no need of apology. " I leave the judgement of our action with confidence to Parliament," he declared in the course of his magnificent oration in the House of Commons on July 4. " I leave it to the nation. I leave it to the United States. I leave it to the world and history."

Lieut.-Commander R. H. Bristowe, hero of the brilliant exploit by which depth charges were exploded against the stern of the " Richelieu."

Broadcasting on July 4 Mr. A. V. Alexander, while deploring the bitter road which led " from the glorious cooperation of two navies at Dunkirk to the melancholy action at Oran," paid a high tribute to " the spirit which burned in Admiral Somerville and his men."
Photos, " Daily Mirror " and Associated Press

The " Richelieu," France's greatest battleship, laid down in 1935 was only completed recently, and no photographs of her ready for sea are available. A naval artist's reconstruction of her from technical data, however, shows her truly formidable appearance. This great 35,000-ton ship carried eight 15-in. and fifteen 6-in. guns, besides 18 anti-aircraft guns. Remarkable features are the towering superstructure and strangely shaped funnel.
Specially drawn for The War Illustrated by Laurence Dunne

Where and Why the Battle of France Was Lost

First Full Account of the Military Failure
Which Led to the French Capitulation

Perhaps it was only natural that the Bordeaux Government should endeavour to explain
its desertion of the Allied cause by putting the blame for France's collapse on the B.E.F.
So that the reader may judge for himself, we give below M. Baudouin's charges and an
account of the Battle of the Gap largely based on a statement by a senior staff officer.

AFTER the defeat, the inquest. In a statement issued from Vichy on July 5, M. Baudouin, Marshal Pétain's Foreign Minister, gave a description of the military events, as decisive as they were disastrous, of the past few weeks—a description which was obviously dictated by the desire to curry favour with his Nazi masters by belittling the contribution made by the B.E.F. to the Allied cause.

The first serious strategic error (said M. Baudouin) was on May 10, when the French left their trenches at England's demand and rushed to the Low Countries. General Weygand, in an attempt to close the Artois gap, asked the British to strike south while the French pushed north. General Sir Edmund Ironside agreed ; but the British delayed for two days, and then suddenly abandoned Arras and raced north towards the ports, while the German divisions poured in. It was General Weygand's opinion that if the British had obeyed orders the gap could have been closed.

General Weygand asked for British troops and aircraft on the Somme-Aisne front, but only five of the 40 air squadrons engaged were British, and no British troops ever arrived.

Two days later a senior staff officer of the B.E.F. replied in London to M. Baudouin, giving the first really detailed and authoritative account of the battle by one who was actually there and in a position to know. While refraining from recrimination or criticizing in any way the French High Command, he urged that the allegation that the B.E.F. had failed to comply with the Weygand Plan " ought to be knocked on the head " forthwith. Then he proceeded with his description, opening with the events of May 19—the day on which General Weygand succeeded General Gamelin in the supreme command.

Slowing Up the Germans

On that day the B.E.F. had fallen back from its position east of Brussels and Louvain to the line of the Escaut Canal, where it had seven divisions in the line and two in reserve. It had been obvious to the British Command that the British right rear was likely to be placed in a dangerous position, and so steps had been extemporized by improvised forces at Lens, Béthune, Douai and Arras to protect the right rear, not only of the B.E.F. but also of the First French Army. These improvised forces were recruited from partly trained Territorial divisions, three of which had been sent out to France some weeks before for work on aerodromes and roads. They had had a certain amount of training, but they were

not fighting formations, for while they were armed with rifles, a certain proportion of machine-guns, and a few anti-tank weapons, they had no artillery. Nevertheless, they were thrown into the battle and they fought very gallantly indeed. By their defence of Arras and

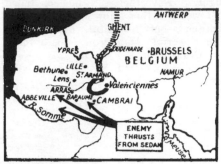

May 19. The position in Flanders when General Weygand succeeded Gamelin. The shaded line represents the Belgian Army ; white dotted line, the B.E.F. ; black, the First French Army.

May 22. With the view of closing the gap at Cambrai, General Weygand planned that the B.E.F. and the First French Army should attempt to join up with the French forces attacking from the Somme.
By courtesy of the " Daily Mail "

certain vital river and canal crossings they considerably slowed down the German drive to the coast.

On May 19 on the left of the B.E.F. was the Belgian Army from Oudenarde to Ghent and the sea, while on the right was the First French Army of between eight and ten divisions, extending in a curved line from St. Amand to Valenciennes. These French divisions were in a considerable state of disorganization, for they had fought their way back from the line at Namur and had been subjected to an attack which was probably heavier than any that had so far been launched against the B.E.F. They had been pushed back, and at each stage had lost more and more of their equipment until by now they were undoubtedly in a bad way. Several days were fully occupied in reorganizing and trying to regain some cohesion.

South of the First French Army was the gap of some thirty miles to the

Somme, and by May 19 this gap had been in existence for about a week, and all the French efforts to plug the hole had been unsuccessful. During that week something like eight German armoured divisions, followed by perhaps eight motorized divisions, had been pouring through the gap and creating untold havoc and disruption beyond. The situation was still very obscure, and so conflicting were the reports that no one could be sure whether the French or the Germans held the bridgeheads. This, then, was the position which confronted General Weygand when he took over the supreme command.

Planning to Close the Gap

On May 20, General Ironside, Chief of the Imperial General Staff, went to G.H.Q. to discuss the position with Generals Billotte and Blanchard. By this time it was quite clear that an effort had to be made to push forces from the B.E.F. and the First French Army in a southward direction to try to regain contact with the French on the Somme ; it was also clear that to do that an attack was necessary. There could be no question of an unhindered march through the area of the gap, because the Germans were in occupation of it. In any case, a considerable amount of preparation had to be done.

The B.E.F. had only two divisions in reserve on May 20, and it was decided that these two divisions, the 5th and 50th, would carry out an attack from Arras, which was still held by their comrades to the south, and across the Scarpe River. The attack was to be supported on the right or western flank by elements of the First French Cavalry (Mechanized) Corps. General Billotte agreed to this plan, and said that part of the First French Army would be available to continue the British left flank and cooperate with it in the southerly direction.

That attack was timed for 2 o'clock on May 21, but on the morning of that day the British were informed that the French division on their left were not ready to attack and would not be ready before May 22. Nevertheless, it was obvious that the sooner the attack was launched the greater its chance of success. Time was pressing. The longer the gap was left open, the more Germans were able to pour through it. In these circumstances Lord Gort made his own decision, resolving that, even though the French were not in a position to support

Where the B.E.F. Fought Hard to Close the Gap

It was at Ypres (seen right, after suffering damage from the German onrush) that on May 22 General Billotte explained to Lord Gort and the King of the Belgians the French plan for a combined counter-attack intended to close the Somme gap.

Two British divisions made a counter-attack on the morning of May 21, maintaining their positions until almost surrounded by the Germans and then being withdrawn. The photo below shows a typical scene during the operations—British Army lorries of a convoy forging along under heavy bombardment.

On May 22 the King of the Belgians, Lord Gort and General Billotte met at Ypres. General Billotte (seen in the photo below) commanded the first group of French armies, but he also had "power of co-ordination" of the French, British, and Belgian Armies. At this meeting he explained General Weygand's plan to close the Somme gap. That night, on his way back to headquarters after the Ypres meeting, General Billotte was killed in a car accident.

Photos, British Official: Crown Copyright; Fox, E.N.A., Topical Press

In order to hamper and delay the German advance the B.E.F. were compelled to destroy or seriously damage roads and railways in the threatened zones—a fact which made more difficult any counter-attacks against the enemy. Here (left) is a railway station on a main line to the French coast, after British Royal Engineers had rendered it useless to the Nazis.

Weygand's Plan Came Too Late to Save the Day

the B.E.F.'s left, the attack should be delivered.

Delivered it was, and the British divisions reached their first objective south of Arras and inflicted heavy casualties on the Germans. Many prisoners were taken, but the very heavy opposition which was encountered showed that it was now not merely a question of dealing with a few raiding columns of German armoured divisions, but of meeting strong bodies of infantry which were consolidating the position.

For the next two days the two divisions fought very hard, especially in front of Arras. All that time the Germans were working round their western flank, and on May 23 they had almost surrounded the British. On the evening of that day Lord Gort decided he could not keep his men there any longer or they would be surrounded and captured. So they were withdrawn, just in time, eastwards to Douai.

Gort in Conference at Ypres

Meanwhile, there had been a meeting at Ypres on May 22, attended by the King of the Belgians, Lord Gort, and General Billotte, commanding the First French Army, who had also been given "power of co-ordination" between the French, British, and Belgian armies. Earlier in the day General Weygand had paid a flying visit from Paris to explain his intentions, but unfortunately Lord Gort did not receive the message announcing the visit until the next day and so did not see General Weygand.

At the meeting at Ypres on May 22, General Billotte explained the plan which General Weygand had devised for closing the gap which extended from Douai to the Somme. In brief, it was intended that an attack should be made by the French from the south from the direction of Roye northwards to join an attack to be made from the north by the First French Army and the B.E.F., then in the neighbourhood of Douai and Valenciennes. Instructions were telegraphed from London on May 23 that the plan should be carried out, and so Lord Gort proceeded to General Blanchard—for in the meantime, by one of those unlucky chances which so often upset the best laid plans, General Billotte had been killed in a car accident while returning to his headquarters after the Ypres meeting—with the proposal that an attack should be made in a southerly direction in accordance with what General Weygand had in mind. This attack was to be made by two British divisions and three French divisions with the objective of the railway at Havrincourt and Marcoing, and it was hoped that the French would be able to join up in the attack from the south. The date suggested by Lord Gort for the attack was

May 26, although the French would have preferred that it should have been launched a day earlier. It was pointed out, however, that the two British divisions involved were those which had been engaged at Arras and the Scarpe—without French support—and had only just been withdrawn from the line, whereas the French had had six days to reorganize.

Another question which had to be considered was the munitions situation, which was by no means "rosy." The munitions available in France at that time were just a "gun issue"—160 rounds

May 26. Why the Weygand Plan failed. If the attack as contemplated had been delivered, the two British divisions would have found themselves in a trap—the shaded area—with the Germans thrusting through the collapsed Belgian defences on the north and rapidly approaching the Channel ports on the south.
By courtesy of the "Daily Mail"

per gun—and the B.E.F. were short of small arms munitions. Attempts to land munitions by parachute had not been too successful because the Germans learned of it and started to attack the aeroplanes bringing the munitions over.

In the way of food supplies there were in the country supplies for only two and a half days, and the forces were put on half rations. Some months before, as a matter of precaution, seven days' supplies of munitions had been brought north of the Somme in case of interruptions of supplies from the air. It was not air attack, but the German armoured forces which cut them off from their supplies. Nevertheless, they had sufficient munitions for what they had to do.

Another preoccupation presented itself on May 25, when the Belgians were attacked and were driven northwards in disorder. It had been hoped that if the Belgian forces were obliged to withdraw they would be able to revolve and establish themselves on the Ypres Canal, and so continue to form part of a line on the left of the B.E.F., but what actually happened was that the Germans rushed up from Courtrai, pushed the Belgians northwards towards Bruges, and opened up a new danger of the possible encirclement of the left flank of the B.E.F.

Lord Gort had one brigade in reserve, and that was pushed up to the left flank near Ypres. That was not enough. The Belgians were giving, it was all too obvious. At 6 p.m. Lord Gort saw that the situation on his left flank, far from

being likely to improve, was likely to get much worse. Therefore, he decided that first the 50th Division, to be followed later by the 5th Division, instead of attacking to their south, had to go to the Belgian front at once. Had he decided otherwise it would have meant another arm of the pincers going towards Dunkirk and cutting off the British forces.

When he made his decision to take these two divisions away from the attack which was to be staged, the Commander-in-Chief realized that the French would probably take it as an excuse or as a reason for not attacking themselves. The British did not think there was the least likelihood of the French carrying out an attack unless they were very strongly supported by British troops. But that risk had to be accepted. General Blanchard was informed that these two divisions were no longer available for an attack in a southern direction.

When General Blanchard was visited by British staff officers on the morning of May 26 they found him obviously disturbed by the situation; indeed, he and his staff were working out plans for withdrawal as fast as possible—the only thing he could do, in fact.

In truth, General Weygand's plan was admirable—on paper; in fact, as a plan it was the only one available. The trouble was, however, that it came too late because, first, there were too many Germans in the area, and, second, before it could be brought into operation the British left flank composed of King Leopold's army had disappeared, and there were not sufficient reserves to deal with both flanks at the same time.

When Leopold Surrendered

It should be realized that at about this time the B.E.F. was extended along a line of 75 miles, which obviously did not allow of any reserves for charging. The British, unsupported by the French except for their First Cavalry Corps, had put everything they had in reserve into the attack developed two days before the Weygand Plan was evolved. So far as their left flank was concerned, the position became hopeless when at eleven o'clock on the night of May 27 it was learned that the King of the Belgians was asking for an armistice at midnight.

As for the other part of the Weygand Plan—that the French should attack northwards—this never matured at all; in fact, it may be stated that the French gained no ground whatsoever.

In the words of the senior staff officer, "We kept on waiting for news of the attack from the south, but nothing happened. We regarded ourselves as something like a beleaguered garrison which could make a sortie, but the relief of the garrison must come from the outside."

France's Fair Face Befouled by the Nazis

HOW terrible was the devastation wrought in the fair land of France by the Nazi "Blitzkrieg" will be in evidence from these photographs. Wherever the Nazi monster trod there was left a trail of destruction, as by the most brutal methods Hitler sought to destroy the morale of the civilian population and to drive out the inhabitants in terror to crowd the roads and embarrass the defending forces. Then, too, more damage was caused by the blowing up of bridges by the defenders and by other measures intended to hold up the Nazi advance. Though France was at war with Germany for 9 months and 19 days, only 39 days elapsed from the beginning of the western offensive (by the invasion of the Low Countries) to the day when Marshal Pétain announced that France must give up the fight. That such a panic-stricken surrender was untimely is indicated by the fact that isolated bands fought on in ignorance of the shameful armistice : e.g., the 22,000 heroes of the Maginot defences who held out until June 22, when they were ordered to yield.

The Nazi army passed this way in the great drive to the south of France. Above is the once picturesque little town of St. Père, a hundred miles south of Paris, now but a shattered shell.

Bridge after bridge was blown up by the French in their last desperate attempt to stem the German tide. Right is one of the broken bridges across the Seine, alongside of which the Nazis built a pontoon bridge for their troops to cross.

As they retreated the French destroyed most of the munition factories in France. Below is one of them smashed beyond repair and useless for any purpose except providing scrap metal.

Photos, Associated Press

This scene will recall sad memories of the last war, for it is Fort Mare, near Verdun, the scene of bitter fighting in the long, heroic and successful defence of the fortress in 1916-1917. These shellholes were not made then but in June, 1940, when the fort quickly fell to the Nazis.

More Signs That Britain Is Really Awake

Bomb "snuffers," which may greatly lessen the danger from incendiary bombs, are now being made. At the end of a long handle is a dome-shaped wire frame coated inside and outside with asbestos fibre. There is no need to wear fireproof clothing to handle such extinguishers.

Here, in a peaceful meadow on an English farm, disused carts and wagons have been so disposed as to make an enemy landing from the air a very risky proceeding.

The evacuation of livestock from certain areas of Southern and Eastern England was one of the defence measures taken in view of the possibility of invasion. A large proportion of the four-footed "evacuees" were sheep and here some of them are arriving at a goods yard on the start of their journey.   *Photo, Keystone*

Mr. Winston Churchill, who is Minister of Defence as well as Prime Minister, visited the South Coast on July 2 and inspected defence measures. He is seen above leaving a Brighton hotel near which some 5,000 people assembled to cheer him. It was a strangely changed Brighton that greeted the Prime Minister, for the seaward side of the promenade is now forbidden ground to civilians and has no other promenaders than soldiers and police. *Photos, "News Chronicle" and Fox*

Anderson Shelters Stand Up To The Test

This shelter in a south-west town of England kept a family of four safe from a bomb that fell a few yards away and almost buried it in debris. Even the gramophone (below) which they had taken with them to pass away the time was retrieved intact.

Though a German bomb fell close beside this Anderson shelter in the east of England, making the crater seen here, the two occupants were not injured.

NO better tribute to the efficacy of the Anderson shelter could be desired than that given by these photographs of the erections after German aerial bombs had fallen close beside them. Three are on the very brink of bomb craters, and in no case did the enemy missile fall more than a few yards away. It will be noted that the corrugated steel walls and roof have been well covered and backed up with earth, in accordance with the official directions ; the thickness should be 15 inches at top and 30 inches at the sides. Another important point is to ensure that the entrance is shielded by a neighbouring brick wall, or by a baffle made of bags or boxes of earth or sand piled up high enough to protect the opening from blast or splinters. Only by attention to these points can the full security of the Anderson shelter be obtained.

Despite the destruction wrought on near-by houses by a Nazi bomb, this shelter was left intact, and none of its occupants was harmed.

Photos, Fox and " Daily Mirror "

Over the Channel Islands Flies the German Flag!

With sorrow the British people heard the news that, following demilitarization and partial evacuation, the Channel Islands had been bombed by Nazi 'planes and then occupied by enemy detachments. Some account of the invasion is given below, and in page 51 is an eye-witness account by a citizen of Jersey.

SINCE 1066 the Channel Islands—then part of the dominions of William the Conqueror, Duke of Normandy —have been attached to the British Crown. For nearly 900 years the islanders, despite their French speech and their many peculiar ways and ancient privileges, have been among the most loyal of English subjects. Once or twice the islands have been taken by the French, but today it is the soldiers of Hitler who lord it over Jersey and Guernsey, Alderney, Sark, and their girdle of rocky islets.

There was much blowing of trumpets by the Germans over their first capture of British territory. The announcement was made in the shape of a special communiqué of the German High Command, broadcast after the rendering of the Nazi battle song " We are off to fight against England," and it read as follows : " On June 30 the British island of Guernsey was captured in a daring *coup de main* by detachments of the German Air Force. In an air fight a German reconnaissance aeroplane shot down two Bristol Blenheim bombers. On July 1 the island of Jersey was occupied by surprise in the same manner."

There was nothing daring about the capture, however, nor was there anything in the nature of a surprise. None of the islands is farther than thirty miles from the French coast, and as soon as northern France was overrun by the Nazis it

became obvious that the Channel Islands might be invaded at any moment. Considerations of prestige and of sentiment might have demanded that the islands should have been defended against hostile attack, but to do so would have meant the detachment of forces—military, naval and air—which might well be better employed elsewhere. None the less, it must have been with a heavy heart that the authorities took the decision to abandon to the enemy territory which was as English as any in England.

In the last week of June it was decided to demilitarize the islands and to evacuate a considerable part of the population.

As soon as the Channel Islands were evacuated, a Channel Islands Relief Committee was formed in London. Inquiries are here being answered at the Committee's offices.

The Royal Guernsey Militia and the Jersey Militia were disbanded, and so, too, were the recently formed detachments of Local Defence Volunteers. The people were told that if they wished to leave for England they had only a few hours in which to pack, as boats were already waiting at the ports to take them across the Channel.

During the next few days the customary placidity of the islands was rudely shattered. Houses which had been homes for generations were left in a shuttered abandonment. Potato and tomato fields were ploughed up, and though many of the great herds of Jersey and Guernsey cattle were shipped across the water, many, too, had to be destroyed. Motorcars driven to the ports were offered for sale at £1 apiece, but not a purchaser was forthcoming. Many a shopkeeper about to leave for England gave away his goods, and in the public-houses drinks were to be had for the asking. As there was no room on the boats for pets, the dogs and cats were shot, and so great was the run on the vet's services that the owners had to line up while their dumb friends were dispatched.

Of the total population of rather more than 90,000, some 25,000 sought safety in England. For the most part the refugees were young men of military age, women and children. They were evacuated by a motley collection of vessels, which included trawlers, potato boats, and even a coal boat, and had to face a passage which even to Weymouth took twenty-four hours, and many of the vessels had only ship's-biscuits and water on board.

For the majority of the islanders, however, the ties of home were too strong to be severed with such suddenness, and in their resolve to stay on they were supported by the example of many of the leading members of their little communities. Thus, the Jersey States of Parliament announced that " we are remaining at our posts to carry on our duties, and we are all of us keeping with us in these islands our wives and families." In Guernsey, the King's Procureur told his people that he would inform the Nazis when they came that the Islanders had no arms and would offer no resistance, and would ask that their enforced submission should not be abused ; and Mrs. Hathaway, Dame of Sark, similarly intimated that she was remaining in her diminutive domain.

By June 28 the evacuation was practically completed and the islands had been demilitarized, but this latter fact did not prevent the Nazis from delivering a murder-raid. So for a space the Channel Islands became German.

On the day after the Germans occupied the Channel Islands, the local newspapers appeared as usual. They were free only in the sense that they were given away. The front page of this newspaper shows the use to which they were put by the Germans. They told the people that if they did not submit to their new rulers they would feel the whole force of Nazi ruthlessness.

Photos, " Daily Mirror" and Central News

The Fleet Air Arm is Quick Off the Mark

THE Fleet Air Arm is the off-spring of the Royal Navy, and it has already proved itself worthy of the glorious record of its sire. In the long operations in Norway the F.A.A. showed the finest qualities of fighting airmen. Then in the bombing of the French battleship, "Dunkerque" after she had been damaged and had run ashore in Oran Harbour, the Naval airmen finally put "paid" to her account. During the same week-end, the F.A.A. made very effective attacks at Bergen, Catania and Tobruk. Finally, it was the bombs dropped on the "Richelieu" by the F.A.A., after Lieut.-Commander Bristowe had dropped depth charges under her stern, that put her out of action for a very long time to come.

One of the most recent types of biplane to be introduced into any of the British fighting services is the Fairey Albacore. Aircraft of this type are now used by the Fleet Air Arm as torpedo-bombers.

Another type of aircraft largely used by the Fleet Air Arm as fighters and dive-bombers is the Blackburn Skua. These machines carry a crew of two and are armed with five machine-guns as well as their load of bombs. Above left, before starting on a raid the wing machine-guns are being loaded up by men of the F.A.A. A formation flight of these 'planes, as finely illustrated in the lower photograph, is an imposing spectacle and the pilots "keep station" with all the accuracy of their brother officers in the ships of the Royal Navy.

Photos, Charles E. Brown and Central Press

The Pity of It! That Dunkirk Should Be

During the attack on the French Fleet at Oran on July 3 the 25,000-ton battleship "Dunkerque" was damaged and driven ashore. In order to put her completely out of action she was attacked on July 6 by aircraft of the Fleet Air Arm and hit by six torpedoes. Inset, Admiral Gensoul, in command of the French vessels at Oran.

The "Strasbourg," which, though torpedoed by the Fleet Air Arm, escaped to Toulon, is a sister ship of the "Dunkerque." Right, the destroyer "Mogador," 2,884 tons—one of two sunk or burned at Oran—photographed in a British harbour.
Photos, Keystone, P. A. Vicary and Associated Press

wed by the 'Melancholy Action' at Oran

oval we see the harbour of Mers-el-Kebir at Oran, where ice-Admiral Somerville's dramatic seizure of the French eet took place. In the background the fort, which was in tion against the British Fleet, can be seen through the mist.

H.M.S. " Hood," which was stated in a French communiqué to have been in Vice-Admiral Somerville's squadron at Oran, is the largest battleship in the Royal Navy—indeed, afloat.

op right is Vice-Admiral Sir James Somerville, on whom rested the terrible duty of ordering the British Fleet fire on the French ships at Oran. Immediately above is the French battleship "Provence," completed n 1915. She belongs to the " Bretagne " class, two of which were accounted for by the Royal Navy at Oran.

Photos, Chas. E. Brown, Sport & General, Pierre Boucher and " The Times "

CRUEL indeed was the dilemma in which the British Government were placed by Marshal Pétain's decision—" with full knowledge," as Mr. Churchill phrased it, " of the consequences and of our dangers, and after rejecting all our appeals at the moment when they were abandoning the alliance and breaking the engagements which fortified us "—to place the French Fleet in the power of that enemy which up to so recently had been the enemy of France as well as of Britain. But, in the circumstances, Britain could do no other than she did. So was fought on July 3, 1940, the " melancholy action " at Oran.

Britain on the Offensive Against Italy

Although it was the Italians who declared war against Britain, they displayed little eagerness to start the fray. Rather, from the very first day of the struggle, it was Britain who assumed the offensive, whether it be on the land or on the sea or in the air. Some account of the initial operations has been given in Page 692, Vol. II and here we continue the story into July.

AFTER a month of war, British troops operating from their bases in Egypt dominated some 3,500 square miles of Italian Libya. By day and by night they pushed out patrols along the frontier from the Mediterranean coast to below Jarabub, nearly 150 miles to the south.

In all the discomfort of the desert—and the desert, what with the torrid sun and the high wind loaded with sand and dust, can be exceedingly uncomfortable—the British troops raided and skirmished

This sketch map of the Eastern Mediterranean region illustrates the operations against Italy. Important places in Libya and Egypt and on the frontier are indicated.

in the most vigorous fashion. On the other hand, the Libyan levies of the Italians seemed to have little heart for the struggle; even the officers, though Italians for the most part, seemed to be little more enthusiastic, particularly those of them who knew how flimsy were the lines of communication which linked them with the homeland and how easily these might be cut.

Nor did the enemy morale show to better advantage in the far south, where Italian East Africa borders on the Sudan. Here towards the end of June there was a clash between a strong force of Italian native cavalry totalling 1,200 sabres, and two British light armoured vehicles out on patrol. When the British advanced and opened fire with their machine-guns, the enemy scattered in panic in all directions, leaving 50 of their number behind them. In the same district a few days earlier another small British patrol routed a battalion of Eritrean infantry, inflicting on them severe losses.

It was in this neighbourhood that the Italians claimed what they described as "an important success"—the capture of Kassala and Gallabat, but their success, which actually was unimportant, was dearly bought, for in the attack they lost 300 men, eight light tanks, and two aircraft. On the farther side of the Italian

dominion in Abyssinia, patrols drawn from the Somaliland Camel Corps raided one Italian frontier post after the other, and here, too, the victors commented adversely on the morale of the enemy, noting in particular a disinclination to come to close quarters.

In the air Italy showed a more enterprising spirit, and her 'planes were frequently in action against the British base at Malta—which on June 23 experienced its thirty-ninth raid, carried out by some 60 'planes; the naval base at Alexandria, where some of the bombs fell on King Farouk's private estate; Sollum, Port Sudan, and Mersa Matruh; and—only a day or two before France quitted the war—the French naval base at Bizerta. But this display of vigour had to be paid for, and already by July 3 the total number of Italian machines definitely destroyed by the R.A.F., quite apart from those shot down by the anti-aircraft defences, amounted to 74, with about 30 so severely damaged as to be probably out of commission.

One of the R.A.F.'s best days was July 4, when six British fighters engaged nine enemy fighters over Sidi Barrani, on Egypt's Mediterranean coast, and shot down seven. Another successful British operation was carried out on July 6 by aircraft of the Fleet Air Arm and the R.A.F. against Italian warships sheltering

in the harbour of Tobruk, Libya; and on the same day aircraft of the Fleet Air Arm attacked the aerodrome of Catania, in Sicily, leaving it in flames.

Nor did the Italians put up a better show on the sea. While Vice-Admiral Somerville's squadron was heavily engaged with the French ships at Oran, the Italian Navy was careful to keep at a distance, although, as Mr. Churchill phrased it, we had made arrangements for its reception.

On July 9 a large Italian force was engaged by the British Fleet, but although one of their battleships and a cruiser were hit they disappointed the Royal Navy by escaping to the shelter of the coastal minefield. The Italian submarines were busy—with disastrous consequences to themselves. At the beginning of July it was announced that 14 Italian submarines had been destroyed in 20 days.

Many of these were destroyed by flying boats attached to the Middle East Command, but one was captured by a naval trawler. Read the communiqué issued by the Admiralty on June 23:

"H.M. Trawler 'Moonstone' was on patrol in the Gulf of Aden when the periscope of a submerged submarine was sighted. The trawler at once attacked with depth charges. These brought the submarine to the surface. The submarine engaged the trawler with her entire armament, consisting of torpedoes, two 3-in. guns and smaller guns. The trawler replied with her 4-in. gun and a Lewis gun, and scored hits on the submarine with 4-in. shells. The submarine subsequently surrendered, and was brought into Aden as a prize."

The captain and several officers of the submarine were killed, but three officers and 37 ratings were taken prisoner. There were great rejoicings in Aden when the submarine was brought in flying the White Ensign above the Italian flag.

H.M. Trawler "Moonstone" furnished one of the epics of anti-submarine warfare. On patrol in the Gulf of Aden she captured and successfully took into port an Italian submarine taking prisoner three officers and 37 ratings.

Photo, Wright & Logan

Bombers in Action in Sun-baked East Africa

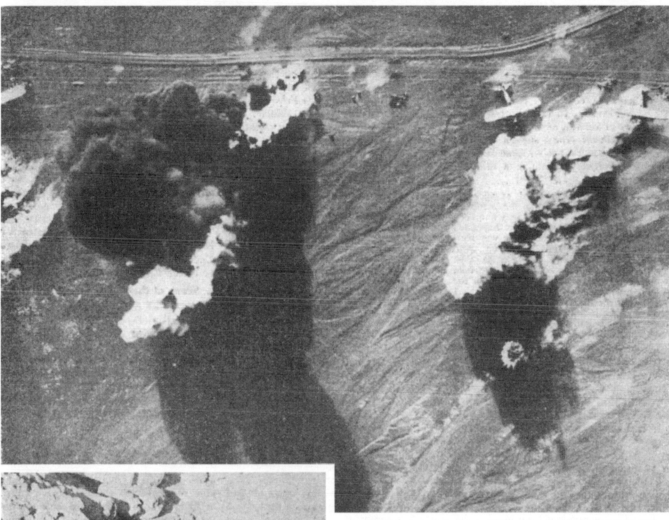

Aerodromes, forts and other military objectives in Italian East Africa
have received constant attention from bombers of the R.A.F., with such
successful results as are recorded in this photograph. In an Italian
aerodrome three tri-motor Caproni bombers have been set on fire.
British Official photo: Crown Copyright

The success of Italian bombers in East Africa has not been considerable. Here we see British troops taking cover during an Italian air raid
on the Libya-Egypt frontier, while on the right a bomb is bursting in a
British camp while raiders were overhead. *Photos, British Movietone News*

Mussolini's 'Hard and Bloody' War Against France

If Mussolini and his tame propagandists may be believed Italy's 13-day war with France reflected the greatest glory on the triumphant Italian arms. Here we give the Duce's published account of the battle and also the story of the " Battle of Mentone"—incorporating material gleaned from an informative article in " The New Statesman and Nation."

ACCORDING to the Italians there was a big battle in the French Alps in the course of Italy's 13-day war with France. In this short struggle —we have it on the authority of Signor Mussolini himself—the " superb " Italian troops " crushed France's Alpine Maginot Line in a four-day battle in a blinding snowstorm."

The French troops resisted savagely to the end—that is to say, till the armistice and even a few hours after, for they had been kept in ignorance of what had happened in the rest of France. The battle was hard and bloody. Thousands of men who became casualties bear evidence to this. The names of those who fell on the field of honour will be made known. As for the wounded whom I visited in the hospitals I declare that it is difficult to find in the whole world another race which through the most cruel physical sufferings could show as much calm and stoicism as the Italian race.

These are the words of Mussolini, written on the morrow of the " battle " to the Prince of Piedmont, Italian Crown Prince and Commander of the Italian Forces in the West, and published after the Duce's visit to the front on July 1.

It is a matter of history that though Mussolini declared war on France on June 10 and hostilities were announced to begin at midnight, the Italians did not deliver their first attack on the Alpine front until June 21, the day on which the French delegates in the forest glade at Compiègne had been handed the

German armistice terms. But they made no real advance until June 24, which was the very day on which the French signed the armistice with Italy at Rome. An Italian communiqué of that day stated :

On the Alpine front from Mont Blanc to the sea our troops started a general attack on June 21. The formidable enemy defences built into the rock on the high mountains, the strong reactions on the part of the enemy, who was firmly resolved to oppose our advance, and the bad atmospheric conditions, did not check the advance of our troops, who scored notable successes everywhere. An Italian contingent managed to gain possession of certain fortifications, such as the fort of Chanaillet, near Briançon, and the fort of Razet, in the lower Roya valley. Entire Italian units reached the valley of the Isère, Arc, Guil, Ubaye, Tinée, and Vésubie, penetrating the enemy's fortified lines and threatening the whole enemy front. The advance of our troops proceeds along the entire front.

By the time the " Cease fire " had sounded the Italians had advanced over the frontier a distance of some two miles. . . .

Mussolini's visit to the front on July 1 was described in ecstatic terms by a commentator on the Rome wireless, and his account was supplemented by details of the attack on the " Alpine Maginot " couched in almost lyrical terms. The spokesman described the French positions as having been " made impregnable by Nature and military art," and so prepared his hearers for an account of " a magnificent out-

flanking attack undertaken by a direct assault on the fortified town of Mentone."

All who have visited the Riviera will know that to describe Mentone as a fortified town is, to put it mildly, an exaggeration. The memories most visitors bring away from Mentone are of a pleasant seaside town, shuttered and somnolent during most of the day, where large numbers of retired British preachers and missionaries and military gentlemen of the " Colonel Blimp " variety read " The Times " and " The Spectator " in English reading-rooms, drink regularly English tea and Scotch whisky, and go to the English church on Sunday.

Scene of the ' Magnificent Attack '

Like most of the other towns on the French Riviera Mentone is built on a narrow strip of coast, behind which rise in rapid succession the ramparts of the Alps ; and a few hundred yards beyond the English church the road crosses a little gorge into Italy.

With this picture in our minds, talk of " magnificent outflanking attack, "direct assault," and " fortified town " is simply fantastic. But if we are to believe the Rome commentator, " after several days of tireless fighting against enormous odds, our gallant troops entered Mentone," and " our troops were supported by an artillery train which came through the tunnel under La Mortola, and shelled the strongly held town in which the enemy was maintaining an obstinate resistance." Though " obstinately resisting " the defenders do not seem to have blown up the narrow bridge mentioned above ; nor was the railway along the coast very much damaged by " the pounding of the great guns from the southernmost forts of the Alpine Maginot."

" A desolate sight presented itself to the eyes of the Duce," went on the commentator, " in that once charming resort. The streets were littered with trees blown down by the power of our shells. The shutters of many shops in the main street had been blown in. The villas and great hotels stood gaunt and deserted with all the glass of their windows gone. Everything bore witness to the heroism of our conquering army on that bitterly contested battlefield."

Later reports confirmed that Mentone was, indeed, in ruins, its streets filled with shellholes and its only inhabitants hungry cats ; but the havoc had been wrought by French guns after the Italian occupation on June 23.

Such is the story of " the Battle of Mentone," which, as a writer in " The New Statesman " has put it, " may well go down to the future impartial chronicler as one of the biggest military frauds of history."

In this much-camouflaged car Benito Mussolini (seen standing) visited the " battlefields " of the Alpine Front. He was escorted by Marshal Badoglio, Chief of the General Staff, and Signor Soddu, Under-Secretary of the Italian War Ministry. Later a party of foreign journalists was conducted over the " zones of operations " where Italy fought her " safety-first " war with France.

Photo, Associated Press

Shipping Our Enemies to Safety !

Ssome of the first German prisoners of war to arrive in Canada, where they will be interned " for the duration," are watched by an armed guard.

WHEN the Nazi High Command joyfully announced the sinking of the British liner " Arandora Star " off the west coast of Ireland, they did not add that she carried about 1,500 Germans and Italians on their way to Canada for internment. Of these, 470 Italians and 143 Germans lost their lives, largely owing to the fact that the subjects of the Axis Powers fought fiercely to be the first in the lifeboats. The U-boat was commanded by Captain Prien, who in October 1939 torpedoed the " Royal Oak " in Scapa Flow.

The 15,000-ton British liner " Arandora Star " was sunk by a U-boat off the west coast of Ireland on July 2. German prisoners are going on board a British transport to be taken overseas for internment.
Photos. Associated Press and Keystone

Hitler Intensifies the Air War Against Britain

In twenty days the Germans lost at least twenty bombers in fruitless raids on Britain— despite the adoption of daylight raids from July 1. Only two British fighters were lost during this period. On July 10 a resounding victory was achieved.

IN his war commentary broadcast on July 4 Air Marshal Sir Philip Joubert explained the Air Ministry's reasons for not disclosing the precise whereabouts of places raided by the Germans, and also for official reticence about the amount of material damage done. If we did not publish these particulars the enemy was obliged to send over aircraft to reconnoitre and take photographs, which gave our pilots another chance to have a go at the Nazis. The Air Marshal also made it clear that British figures for air losses were correct, whereas the Nazi claims were exaggerated and mendacious.

During the seven days ending July 7 the Royal Air Force maintained its destructive raids on German aerodromes, seaplane bases, aircraft works and other such objectives. Oil refineries and storage depots were raided again and again without intermission, and in all these operations our losses were remarkably low. The enemy's raids upon Britain were no more successful than those he had made the week before, although on the evening of July 1 he began to send his pilots over in daylight. Perhaps the Nazi pilots were feeling their way, but these raids gave very useful experience to our defence organizations—both in the air and on the ground—and some remarkable successes were gained.

Heinkel Extinguished in the Sea

On the night of June 26–27 a squadron leader piloting one of our Hurricanes was directed to his quarry by "a tremendous concentration of searchlights" on his starboard beam, striking the base of a cloud and reflected upwards. In his own words :

I turned right and immediately saw three aircraft flying towards my nose at 7,000 feet just above light cloud. I came close up underneath the last bomber, ∴ . a Heinkel 111. I fastened on his tail beneath and behind. . . . The bomber went into a slight dive quite slowly at 160 miles per hour. I found myself coming up right behind him, so I got into a comfortable position and opened fire at about 4,000 feet. . . . The Heinkel continued the same shallow dive. I gave it four bursts and then saw a glow inside the machine. It steepened its dive slightly, and as I thought we must be getting near the sea I pumped in all the rest of my rounds. The glow increased and the inside of the machine was obviously on fire.

Breaking away to the right at 500 feet, I watched him continue down but could not see him strike the water. After climbing to 1,000 feet and dropping a parachute flare I could see the bomber lying on the water with a cloud of black smoke blowing from its rear section.

Another of the bombers—a Junkers 88 —was attacked by a Spitfire pilot over the East Coast. His bullets struck a bomb rack and the enemy aircraft exploded in mid-air. The third raider was a Heinkel : it was tackled off the south coast by one of our Blenheim aircraft, and turned away. The Blenheim pilot considered that the Heinkel had been damaged and the rear gunner killed by "four heavy short bursts" delivered from dead astern. The pilot was enthusiastic about the work of the searchlight men. "The lights were very effective," he said. "They never left the target and never illuminated our aircraft."

Here are some episodes from the daylight raids on Britain during July 3. The raids were of the "hit-and-run" type and in most cases the Nazi bombers approached the coasts singly.

In the morning three Spitfire pilots, after attacking a Dornier "Flying Pencil" bomber, watched it turn on its back and crash into the sea off the East Coast. The Spitfires then attacked and badly damaged another Dornier, which made off. Later in the morning a fighter pilot fired three bursts at a third Dornier 17, 12,000 feet up off the N.E. Coast, but aided by the clouds, the raider escaped destruction. Some little while after, a bomber, believed to be a Heinkel 111, fell into the sea off Aberdeenshire, following a stiff combat with our Spitfires.

In the early afternoon two Spitfires shot down another "Flying Pencil," this time off the S.E. Coast. A Junkers 88 was brought down off the Scottish coast, and a Hurricane patrol attacked and damaged a Dornier 215 while on patrol off the East Coast. Other Hurricanes badly punished a Heinkel 111 they had intercepted over the English Channel. To cap this day's work, Spitfires raced out to sea shortly after 7 p.m. to intercept yet another Nazi bomber; six minutes after taking off, they had shot it down in flames.

In the destruction of military objectives the Germans accomplished next to nothing. The other side of the account is shown in the table printed in this page. Moreover, by July 8 (in twenty days), at least fifty Nazi raiders had been lost and 118 aircraft destroyed in German raids since the war began. Out of the 4,000 aircraft computed to have been lost by the enemy in all by early July, 2,500 were accounted for by the Royal Air Force. Then the Nazis came over in greater strength—and lost more. In the greatest air victory since June 18, 150 raiders attacked over the South and East Coasts on July 10: 14 Nazi bombers and fighters were shot down, and 23 others seriously damaged. Two only of our fighters were lost, and of these one pilot was rescued.

Air Raids on Britain and Germany: Debits and Credits
July 1—8 (*Continued from page 26*)

ON BRITAIN	Casualties	Enemy Losses	ON GERMANY	British Losses
July 1–2			**July 1–2**	
N.E. Coast of Scotland	12 k. 18 i.	2	Kiel—N.b. ; D.K. b.* ; Homburg—O. ; Hamm—B. ; Duisburg (nr.)—m.o.;Meiderich—blst. fur. ; Deichshausen — A.W. ; Wesel, Cologne, Venlo, Texel—A. ; Rotterdam—C.	4 m.
Bristol Channel area	4 i.			
N.E. England Wales	7 i.			
July 2–3			**July 2–3**	
N.E. Coast ; S. & S.W. England Wales	13 k. 123 i.	1	Denmark and Belgium—A. ; Ruhr ; Westphalia—L.C. b.; Hamburg ; Dortmund—m.o. ; Zeebrugge—D.K. Texel, Ymuiden — A. (one Me 109 shot down)	Nil 1 m.
July 3–4			**July 3–4**	
N.E. England ; Scotland ; E. & S.W. England	2 k. 22 i.	7 (and 6 dmgd.)	Evere, nr. Brussels ; Ypenburg, nr. Hague—A.	Nil
E. Counties	Nil		Wyverne, St. Omer ; Aachen—A. ; De Kooy, Merville—A.	1 m.
			Neumunster, Osnabruck, Lunen, Hamburg—R.	Nil
			Rotterdam—C.	Nil
July 4–5			**July 4–5**	
Channel Coast (Portland)	few i.	1 bmr. 1 fightr.	Hanover, Emmerich—O.f. ; Hamm, Soest — m. o. b. ;	
S.W. Counties	none	1	Amsterdam ; Brussels—A.	1. m.
N.E., S.E. & S.W.	none		Dutch Coast (off)—Patrol vessels damaged.	2 m.
			Wilhelmshaven, Emden, Kiel —N.; Dortmund-Ems Canal —C ; Hamburg, Osnabruck, Hamm, Schwerte, Cologne —L.C. ; Varel, Harburg, Aachen, Bremen, Wenzendorf—A.W.	1 m.
July 5–6			**July 5–6**	
S.W. England ; E. Riding, Yorks ; on Kent Coast	few i.	?	Deichshausen—A.W. ; Waalhaven & Flushing—A.	2 m.
N.E. England	none		Kiel & Wilhelmshaven—N. ; D.K. Cuxhaven, Hamburg—	
S.E. Coast, bombs on town	7 k. some i.	1	D.K.; Cologne—R. ; Schipol & Texel—A.	1 m.
July 6–7			**July 6–7**	
N.E. Coast		1	Knocke—A. ; Evreux, Ypenburg—A. ; Zwolle & Katwijk—C.	
S. Coast	few cas.	1		1 m.
N.E. Coast	few k.		Bremen & Kiel—S.Y. ; Emden —A.R. ; Brunsbüttel—C.	2 m.
S. Devon	some k.		Norderney & Hornum—S.B.	
S. Coast	few k.			
July 7–8			**July 7–8**	
S. Coast	1 k.	7	Eschwege—A. (1 a/c. dest.)	nil
Channel Coast	others i.		N. France—m.o. (1 fighter sht. dwn.)	
W. Country	some k.			
S.W. England	1 k. 1 i.		Ludwigshaven & Frankfurt— m.o.; Osnabruck, Soest, Hamm, Ruhrort - Hafen, Gremberg—R. ; Wilhelmshaven — N.; Duisburg-Ruhrort—C.; Heide, Westerland, Hornum, Wesel —A.; Rotterdam, Brussels —A.	2 m.
N.E. Coast (3 fighters m.)	few i.			
			Boulogne (supply ship b.)	2 m.
			* "Scharnhorst" bombed.	

KEY TO TABLE
A. aerodrome ; **a.** ammunition ; **A.W.** aircraft works ; **A.R.** armament works ; **B.** bridge ; **b.** bombed ; **blst. fur.** blast furnaces ; **C.** canal, barges, etc.; **c.** chemical ; **D.** dump ; **D.K.** docks ; **F.** factory ; **f.** set on fire ; **G.E.** gun emplacement ; **L.** locks ; **L.C.** lines of communication ; **M.** marshalling yard ; **m.o.** military objectives ; **N.** naval base ; **O.** oil depot, stores or refinery ; **P.** power station ; **p.** petrol ; **R.** railway ; **S.** stores or warehouses ; **S.B.** seaplane base ; **S.Y.** shipbuilding yard.

In the Front Line With Our Searchlight-Men

TRAVELLING along the South Coast we approached at dusk searchlight stations whence one can sometimes see the German beams across the Channel. Here between 20 and 30 miles from the enemy the armed darkness seemed to wait and listen, and the half-seen familiar English countryside and seaside became strangely exciting.

" You should have been here the day before yesterday," said the corporal in charge who was once a stockbroker's clerk. " We had a bit of fun." Their fun was front-line stuff—a private battle of their own. These, perched on their bare headland, with a Dornier, flying round and round, trying to mop them up with machine-gun fire. " The first day we had new potatoes in our ration," said the acting cook sadly, " and I never had time to cook them."

They fought the Dornier as he circled. Then they were bombed. " There are five craters flanking this site, and they didn't half make a mess of my pots and pans," added the cook.

Suddenly to the south-west of us bright bayonets of light began to probe the night. " That's him," muttered the N.C.O. with satisfaction. The men on the sound detector stretched their huge mechanical ears towards the searching beams. " Hostile aircraft approaching," they confirmed.

" Target south-west engage ! " The two men in the shadows round the lamp stood ready. The sizzle of violet smoke, and our light was erect, throwing a pallor of violet moonshine over the site. The sound of 'planes was near now. Neighbouring beams searched with us with canny cooperation. Everyone was tense, sighting with all the power of the huge swinging lamp, and ready for bombs or for the sudden dive attack down the beam itself.

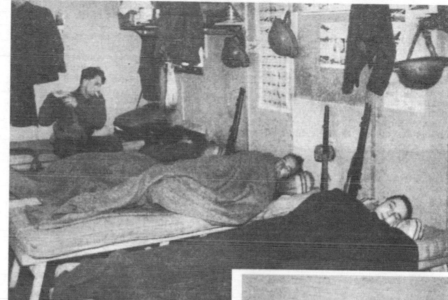

All through the night the searchlight men are on the qui vive, but with the dawn they take their well-earned rest—with uniforms and equipment handy.

At last the pleasant English command " douse ! " broke the beam off and the watchers were left to blink in utter darkness and discuss their luck.—*Story by John Pudney of the " News Chronicle," and photos exclusive to* THE WAR ILLUSTRATED.

Taken by Barnet Saidman, " News Chronicle " staff photographer, these photographs show a searchlight crew actually in action when bombs were dropped near by. In the morning five craters were open to inspection.

OUR SEARCHLIGHT ON THE WAR NEWS

Among the many items of war interest which cannot, for obvious reasons, be given in
full in our pages, we select week by week a number which are recorded in brief.
This is the second of the series.

"HOLD Calais to the end" was the order given to the officer commanding that heroic British brigade which, by drawing off two German heavy armoured divisions destined to cut off the B.E.F., allowed time for the evacuation from Dunkirk.

The officer in question was Brigadier Claude Nicholson, 42 years of age, former Commander of the 16th/5th Lancers, and,

Brigadier Claude Nicholson, the man who said "No Surrender" to the Germans at Calais. He joined the 16th Lancers, and when war broke out was in command of the Imperial Defence College.
Photo, Universal Pictorial Press

according to Sir Hubert Gough, "the most brilliant officer of his standing in the British Army . . . the most able and clear-headed soldier of his age." The units taking part in this epic resistance were the Rifle Brigade, a battalion of the 60th Rifles, a battalion of the Queen Victoria's Rifles, a battalion of the Royal Tank Regiment, gunners of a Royal Artillery searchlight regiment, and a number of French troops—in all about 4,000 men.

Seriously handicapped by lack of equipment, including vehicles and ammunition lost in landing, fighting without sleep or rest and with very little food or water, the heroic troops were gradually forced from the outer limits of the city to the centre, and finally to the Old Citadel, their commander being always in the thick of the fight. As a German newspaper described it : "House by house had to be conquered. The Englishmen had made every house a fortress."

After four days (May 23-26) of merciless attack, the Germans demanded immediate surrender. Brigadier Nicholson's answer was an uncompromising "No !" So the enemy brought up dive bombers, and more German troops pressed into the town, followed by tanks. Still the garrison fought on, until by the evening of May 26 their ammunition as well as their food had run out, and there was silence. Vice-Admiral Ramsay, who organized the amazing Armada that brought the men from Dunkirk, said : "We could not send in supplies or bring off the wounded. It was horrible to be so close and yet to be powerless to help them."

The fact that this gallant force was unaware of the immense strategic importance of their stubborn defence further enhances its valour, and to their intrepid, imperturbable commander, now a prisoner of war in Germany, is primarily due the credit for a story of heroism that, as Mr. Churchill put it, "added another page to the glories of the light divisions."

'Skulking, Swaggering Louts!'

SUCH was the description given by the ship's crew of most of the first batch of German prisoners of war and civilian internees who reached Canada early in July. Their guard, about 250 British officers and men, heaved a sigh of relief on reaching Quebec, for they had had only about two nights' sleep out of seven.

The younger Germans, especially the airmen, had shown themselves particularly true to the Nazi ideal, having behaved throughout the voyage in a truculent, arrogant manner, insulting their guards, whose tolerance and courtesy were strained to the uttermost. On landing, most of them tore their gas masks into shreds, to prevent them being returned to England.

But there were few complaints of the behaviour of the older officers, and none at all of that of the merchant seamen who, embarrassed and shamed by the manners of their compatriots, thanked the British officers and crew on behalf of the German marine for the kindness and consideration received.

Further Exploits of the 'Snapper'

H.M. SUBMARINE "Snapper" is a little ship of 670 tons, carrying an armament of six torpedo tubes and one 3-in. gun, and a crew of 40, commanded by Lt. W. D. A. King. But her achievements are in no proportion to her size. During the Norwegian campaign she sank four transport and supply ships, and her commander was awarded the D.S.O.

On July 7 the Admiralty proudly announced that she had torpedoed five more enemy vessels. "Our submarines continue to harass and inflict serious losses upon German sea communications with Norway. H.M. submarine 'Snapper' sighted a convoy of supply ships escorted by an armed trawler and aircraft. The 'Snapper' attacked and hit two ships with torpedoes. The remnants of the convoy scattered and made in disorder for the shelter of a fjord. Later the 'Snapper' sighted a large convoy escorted by armed trawlers and aircraft. A successful attack was carried out and three ships were hit with torpedoes."

Still They Fought On!

CUT off from the world in the fortifications which they had been ordered to defend to the end, 22,000 troops in the Maginot Line were still fighting five days after the signing of the armistice. The French Command could not contact them, and so they remained unaware of the "Cease Fire" order, until a method of approach was devised by the perplexed delegates of the Franco-German Armistice Commission, sitting at Wiesbaden.

King George to the Islanders

ADMINISTRATION of the Channel Islands, which were demilitarized and partly evacuated at the end of June, lay largely in the hands of two officials, the Bailiffs of Jersey and of Guernsey, and to them King George has recently addressed a personal message of sympathy and hope.

"For strategic reasons," said His Majesty, "it has been found necessary to withdraw the armed forces from the Channel Islands. I deeply regret the necessity, and I wish to assure my people in the Islands that in taking this decision my Government have not been unmindful of their position. It is in their interest that this step should be taken in the present circumstances. The long association of the Islands with the Crown, and the loyal service the people of the Islands have rendered to my ancestors and myself, are guarantees that the link between us will remain unbroken. I know that my people in the Islands will look forward with the same confidence as I do to the day when the resolute fortitude with which we face our present difficulties will reap the reward of victory."

French Embassy to Withdraw

DIPLOMATIC relations with France virtually ceased with the withdrawal of the British ambassador, Sir Ronald Campbell, from Bordeaux, but it was not until July 8 that the Foreign Office was informed by the Marquis de Castellane, French Chargé d'Affaires, that he had received instructions from the Pétain Government to withdraw the French Embassy staff from London.

M. Corbin, the Ambassador, had already resigned on June 26, after seven years' service, during which he had gained the trust and friendship of the British Government. He left the charge of the Embassy with M. Roger Cambon, till then occupying the post of Counsellor. On July 5, following a formal protest to the Foreign Office against the action of the British Fleet in the Mediterranean, he in turn tendered his resignation to the Pétain Government. To the Marquis de Castellane thus fell the melancholy duty of putting up the shutters of the house in Albert Gate, once the brilliant centre and haunt of diplomacy, culture, wit and beauty.

H.M. submarine "Snapper," commanded by Lt. W. D. A. King, whose latest achievements are described in this page, is here seen returning from one of her previous voyages.
Photo; "Daily Mirror"

Eye Witness Stories of Episodes
and Adventures in the
Second Great War

I Heard the Horst Wessel Song in Jersey

A refugee from Jersey, while waiting for nightfall to escape from the island, saw Nazi troops pass within a few yards of him. Reaching England safely, he told his story to Laurence Wilkinson of the " Daily Express "—the full, dramatic account of the German occupation of the Channel Islands.

MY wife and daughter left Jersey immediately the Lieutenant-Governor announced that the island was to be demilitarized.

The last of the troops and guns were leaving the harbour as the first of the stream of civilians boarded the ships awaiting them. There were thousands—men, women and children—carrying every ounce they could.

Things were quiet for a day or two after they had gone, but everywhere I met people who had tried to get away from the island, only to find there was no more ship accommodation. The mail boats were crammed.

Then on Friday (June 28) the German 'planes came over, bombing and machine-gunning, killing and wounding civilians indiscriminately. We didn't have a chance. There wasn't a gun, not even a revolver, left in the island. I was in a car on the coast road when two bombers came roaring low at us from the direction of the harbour. I flung myself down by the sea wall. The bullets spattered all around me.

On Saturday morning they came over again, but did no damage. On Sunday they came skimming over the housetops—huge Heinkels—singly, at intervals of half an hour.

At 5 a.m. I was awakened by the roar of a dive bomber. He swooped very low and dropped something on to a roof.

Someone climbed up and found it was a German flag. Attached to it was an ultimatum from the general commanding the Nazi air force in Normandy.

It was taken to the Bailiff, Mr. Alex Coutanche, who ordered it to be printed and posted up all over the island. By the evening there were white flags showing from houses all over the island. The Germans were already in the streets. They had arrived at 5 p.m.

By that time I had made my plans for escape, though I had little hope of their succeeding.

I tried to buy a passage to England in a motor-boat. The owner wanted £50, then backed out at the last moment, after I had made all preparations to leave.

Then I met the captain of a Dutch cargo vessel which had come to collect potatoes. In the air raid of Friday his cook had been injured, and the skipper had taken him to hospital. In his absence the crew had gone off with the ship, leaving the captain stranded.

Another man pointed out a motor-boat left by an Englishman who had gone in the general evacuation. We decided to take it to England and hand it over to its owner.

We got two loaves, a large jar of water, and a chart of the Channel. Then we hid inside the boat, and waited for darkness and high water. A man on the quay begged a passage. I knew it lessened our chances, but we agreed to take him. I told him to come back later, and not to breathe a word to a soul.

This is the text of the ultimatum given to the Governor of the Island of Jersey on July 1 by the Commander of the German Air Forces in Normandy. It will be noted that " every hostile action" was threatened with bombardment by the Nazis

A woman of about fifty drove up in a car and begged a passage. I said she could come. She turned to a man lounging on the quay and said, " Do you want my car ? You can have it."

The man said, " What's the use of a car ? I can't even drive." But he said he would have it, as it was free.

The woman told me she had just seen the Germans in the town. She said they were lined up, heavily armed, with motor-cycles, with which they had landed from 'planes.

I gave orders, " No smoking, no talking, no moving about. If you don't obey these instructions it's the finish for all of us."

Twilight was coming on when I heard voices. I crept to the hatch and peeped out. I saw between fifty and eighty German soldiers swinging along shouting the Horst Wessel song.

They marched past within ten or fifteen yards of us and went up to the fort. After that I saw motor-cyclists patrolling. Otherwise there was not a soul to be seen.

The boat started to float. We put up the sails, but there was not a breath of wind. We got hold of a rope tied farther along the quay-side, and tried to haul ourselves out.

It took us almost an hour to travel fifty feet. We thought we should be caught in the middle of the harbour. We dared not start the engines.

We had just got through the harbour mouth when we started the engines. We took a circuitous, amateurish route. North-west of Guernsey the engines seized-up for lack of oil. We heard scores of 'planes and expected them to spot us at any moment. We heard the sound of many explosions from the island.

We thanked heaven for a mist which came up at that moment. But we had to have oil. I searched among our provisions and found 3 lbs. of butter. We melted it on the exhaust pipe and poured it into the sump. The engine ran the whole day until eight o'clock that night on Jersey butter.

We were within twelve miles of the English coast when darkness fell. There was a big swell and our engines failed. Then an air raid started. The German bombers dropped flares. Searchlights swept the sky, then coastal guns blazed into action.

At daybreak a cutter spotted us and towed us in more dead than alive. Someone made us coffee. Everybody shook hands, thanked everybody else, and then drifted away—perhaps never to meet again.

Marooned For Six Days on a Breton Island

Volunteer demolition squads from the Royal Engineers helped in the destruction of French harbour works. One of these parties working at Brest had the added excitement of being marooned off the Breton coast. Their story was told exclusively to "The War Illustrated."

WE reached Brest about 9 o'clock in the morning of June 18, said the corporal, and spent most of the afternoon preparing the gear for our job of demolition.

The town of Brest did not seem to have suffered much, although there had been several air raids on the docks. People were still in the town, but the French naval staff moved out while we were there. We saw them going out—all kinds of ships, from merchant ships to the big submarine "Surcouf."

Working in cooperation with the Navy, we actually finished our demolition work (which included the blowing-up of heavy cranes) about 9.30, and left the place blazing merrily. We boarded a motor-boat which had been detailed us with one leading seaman to get across the harbour. There was a strong wind blowing which brought down thick clouds of black smoke from the oil dumps we had fired. This probably saved us from the German 'planes, but it caused us to miss our way and lose the ship we should have boarded.

We hung about outside the harbour until getting on for midnight, and then, as we had plenty of fuel on board, our captain decided to make a dash for England. The boat was a 35-ft. motor launch, and there were fifteen of us on board—Royal Engineers and one sailor. We were all seasick, and she was pitching and tossing dreadfully, and at 6 o'clock in the morning the engine broke down and we drifted for about 36 hours back on to the coast of Brittany. We failed to attract the attention of any ships and had just about given up hope of being picked up when a couple of Frenchmen came out in a

small fishing smack and towed us into the shore.

Here there was a crowd of villagers who told us that the Germans were about eight kilometres away. They suggested we should change our clothing so that we could mingle with them and get away as civilians, and they made arrangements to take us to another place which they did not think the Bosche had reached. Our uniforms and equipment were taken away and burnt ; all we kept were just our boots and socks and they gave us all their clothes—we looked a proper ragged lot when we'd finished! This was Thursday morning, and we had had no food to speak of since Monday (there's no time for food on demolition duty!). While we were waiting for a lorry to take us to this other port they had news that the Bosche had got through and we were encircled.

It was then decided to send us to a small island where it was thought we would be safe until arrangements could be made for us to be taken to England. We were only just in time, and soon after the Bosche came through the town. We lay low until it was dark, and then we went into a cottage. Here we had to stay for six days with no food other than the potatoes and carrots we dug up, and a little milk which one of us got from the cow. The only available water was very dirty, but fortunately we had one rainy day, and that just saved us. We were also very short of cigarettes. Every day, regularly at about 11 o'clock and 4 o'clock, a German patrol 'plane came over the island, during which time we lay low.

On the following Wednesay evening we saw a small fishing boat coming out to us, and, thinking it might contain Germans, we scattered. We were very glad to see some Frenchmen land, and they told us they had heard from the villagers that we wanted to get back to England and they were willing to take us if we were willing to take the risk. So we climbed aboard and set off for England, where we arrived after 20 hours.

We 'Clouted' the German and Escaped

After wandering for days through German-occupied France, disguised as Belgian refugees, four young B.E.F. men escaped in a commandeered boat and reached England. They were Pte. Halls of Deal, Fus. Davies of Rochdale, Lce.-Bomb. Croft of Stoke-on-Trent, and Corp. Patrick Hanley of Deal, who tells their story in his own words.

DESCRIBING his experiences, Corporal Hanley said : I went across to Boulogne after ten days' leave, and the first thing I heard was that the Germans were advancing on the town. I was sent out with a party on to the Boulogne-St. Omer road, where we put up a barrier against German tanks, known to be approaching.

Eventually we were confronted by a 10-mile-long enemy armoured convoy, and the order was given " Every man for himself." With Private A. Halls, of Deal, and Lance-

Bombardier J. Croft, of Stoke-on-Trent, we got to a wood, where we hid for the night. In the morning we found we were surrounded by the mechanized German column, and we were taken prisoner and kept for eight days in a locked church.

The German sentry came round about every hour to see that we were all right. On the eighth day I said to my companions : " We've had enough of this. If he comes round to-night I'm going to clout him." Well, he came round once too often. We got away into another wood, where we hid for four days, without food or water, except for a little milk we were able to get from some cows. The water was filthy and made us ill.

We managed to stagger into a barn, where we were found by a farmer, who gave us food. Then we met some Belgian refugees, who gave us some civilian clothes, and we disguised ourselves as refugees and set out to find the British or French armies.

We met a British subject in a French town who told us where he thought the French Army was. When we got there we found the Germans in possession. We decided to try to cross the Somme, but the way was choked with refugees. We then tried to rejoin the French at Lille, but, on arrival, found the Germans there, too.

We picked up a bicycle and one of us who had blistered feet went ahead on it as a sort of advance guard. We got back to Boulogne, having completed a circle—a vicious circle.

In one of the villages we passed through we were challenged by German soldiers, who were looking for spies, and since we couldn't produce our "Belgian refugee" papers we were taken to the Commandant. We were marched through the streets at the point of a revolver. I cannot speak Belgian, but fortunately neither could the Commandant, and he gave us the benefit of the doubt.

We got to the coast in time to see three British bombers destroy the German headquarters and do other damage. Our problem was to find a boat, and we reconnoitred the beach disguised as beachcombers, with our trousers rolled up and a piece of seaweed over our shoulders. Eventually two French girls told us of a garage where there was a boat

This photograph was taken during the withdrawal of the Allied Forces from Brest, the great French naval base in Brittany. It shows the smoke rising from a great conflagration when powder and petrol stores were blown up to prevent them falling into Nazi hands. Every effort was made to render the French ports through which the British forces passed useless to the Nazis, and the work was done by demolition parties with skill and daring.

Photo Fox

Here are the our young men whose great adventure is described in these pages. They are, left to right, Lance-Bombardier H. Croft, Fusilier S. Davies, Private A. Halls, and Corporal P. Hanley. The photograph was taken just after they had arrived safely home looking little the worse for their long ordeal.   *Photo, Topical*

abandoned by a doctor. The boat was white ; we stole some paint and painted it black.

Just as we were about to launch it we heard a shout and saw someone dashing towards us. We thought we had been spotted, but it turned out to be a French soldier. We took him aboard, and he brought a lieutenant with him.

One man sat in the stern with a compass as we rowed. The French girls had given us food, but we didn't need it—we were all sick except Halls. They even gave us a Union Jack —to wave in case we should see British 'planes —and a bag full of corks to plug the boat in case we should be machine-gunned.

We rowed like mad and managed to get clear before daylight. Still rowing until there were blisters on our hands, we saw a boat on the following morning and were picked up and landed at an English seaside town.

We Saw Cherbourg Wrecked By Explosion

Passengers two miles out at sea on the last ship to leave Cherbourg on June 19 saw the whole quayside fall in ruins as British Marines blew up the docks. This story of the end of the great French port was told by a French naval officer when he arrived in England.

ON June 18 we were told to expect a British tank division, which had fought a gallant rearguard action on the Somme, where the front was cracking and then later on the Seine.

They came rumbling into Cherbourg in the evening. Half the population had already left. Those who had resolved to stay were putting up their shutters and barricading themselves in their houses. The Germans were only a few miles away.

We started embarking about nine o'clock in the morning. Outside on all the roads leading into the town French infantry were guarding the approaches from behind barricades.

All along the quays there were British Marines drilling holes to lay dynamite. The big quay where passengers used to land from America was a weird sight. Hundreds of army vehicles stood wheel to wheel. Under this quayside were hundreds of sticks of dynamite.

The first to be got aboard were the British tanks. An officer volunteered to take two small tanks out of the town to clear the roads of any Germans.

When he got to the last barricade guarding the town, the French infantry holding it told him they were awaiting orders to evacuate and move south.

The British tank officer said to them : " Well, have a good look at these tanks, and don't fire when we come back, if you are still here."

The two tanks sailed through, and after patrolling a mile of two they turned back. Immediately they got to the barricade the officer opened the turret of the tank and waved his British tin helmet. Then he had to duck back as a machine-gun opened fire on him from the barricade.

There was nothing for it but to fight, and, after about fifteen minutes the tanks demolished the barricade and overcame the defenders. Anxious to find out why they had been attacked, the officer got down and examined the arms of the dead. They were all German, though the barricade defenders wore French uniforms. They were parachutists dropped overnight.

When the two tanks arrived at the quayside the embarkation was almost complete. They had only just time to go on board themselves. Power had been cut off, and the cranes could not be used to lift the tanks on board. So they were sent crashing down the rocks to the sea. At twelve o'clock the last ship put out. I was on board. The only craft in the harbour was a small motor-boat manned by British marines, lying in the shelter of the breakwater, and waiting to touch a switch which would send the docks of Cherbourg, and all those lorries lined on the quayside sky high.

From two miles out at sea we saw the great port's end. The long lines of quays lifted slowly into the air, then suddenly broke into segments, while hundreds of minor explosions broke out. Then a great column of smoke rose up over the port and hung there like a black cloud in the sky as we headed for England.—(" *Evening Standard.*")

During the final retreat of the B.E.F. from France, it was possible to save far more equipment than was the case when the men from Dunkirk were taken off, under heavy fire, from the sands. Men and material after the retreat from Paris southward were embarked from ports that were well equipped for handling heavy cargoes. Here is the scene at Cherbourg when an almost endless stream of British Army lorries rumbled on to the quays and were safely embarked for Britain.   *Photo, British Official : Crown Copyright*

Miss England Is Busier Than Ever

Photo, Fox

Thatchers are still busy in many parts of Britain, and the younger men who have joined the Army are being replaced by women. Here one of the latter is learning the ancient craft.

Above, some of the Forestry Section of the Women's Land Army are at work with a cross-cut saw in one of the many British forests under the Forestry Commission. Bill-posting is not an easy task for women, especially when big sheets have to be handled from ladders. The London woman below is, however, making a good job of putting up a huge " Go To It " poster.

Photos, L.N.A. and Planet News

These girls are tending lathes in one of the shops of a great Sheffield steel works which is turning out war material of various kinds. Since the war many girls have been employed there to work machine tools. *Photo, Central Press*

Above, in a British small-arms factory, a woman is piling up completed magazines for Bren guns. The war has caused some cities to employ policewomen for the first time. Right, a Manchester police recruit on her first day of duty is making notes. *Photos, Wide World and Keystone*

'Waste Not, Want Not' is the Motto for Wartime

During a great salvage campaign that followed an appeal by the Lord Mayor of Newcastle, householders contributed many thousands of bottles. Here workmen are sorting a great dump of them. They were distributed for Army use.

The two towers of the Crystal Palace, above, are being demolished for old iron. Left, a load of waste paper salved at East Ham is being taken to the mills to be repulped.

The Borough of Holborn, in whose area are many hotels and restaurants, makes every day a valuable collection of waste food to be used for feeding pigs.

IN the House of Commons on June 27 Mr. Herbert Morrison stated that the voluntary effort for salvage had not been altogether successful. In consequence a new Ministry of Supply order made the collection of salvage compulsory for all local authorities with a population exceeding 10,000. In this page are scenes at some of the salvage dumps. Expert sorters are at work all day separating and grading the great mass of material received. They deal with 92 grades of bottles, 13 grades of non-ferrous metals, various grades of paper, rag and other forms of refuse. It is the duty of householders to put all waste paper and cardboard, scrap metal and bones in separate bundles to be called for by collectors, who may be the Council dustmen, rag and bone merchants, or voluntary organizations.

Photos, Central Press, Planet News and Keystone

Above, a great consignment of iron and steel scrap, collected under the Iron and Steel Control's salvage scheme, is being loaded by a magnetic crane for transport to the smelting furnaces.

OUR DIARY OF THE WAR

WEDNESDAY, JULY 3, 1940

Sea Affair. French ships in British ports were placed under control. Following refusal of Admiral at Oran to accept conditions offered, British battle squadron opened fire, sank one battleship and damaged other units. French ships at Alexandria were forbidden by Britain to leave port.

French liner " Champlain " reported sunk by mine off La Pallice, Bay of Biscay.

Air War. R.A.F. bombers carried out daylight raids in Belgium and Holland. Dive attacks made on aerodromes at Ypenburg, The Hague, and at Evere, Brussels.

Night raids made on aerodromes at Aachen, De Kooy and Merville.

Coastal Command aircraft bombed enemy bases at Texel and Ymuiden.

Campaign against Italy. Number of Italian aircraft destroyed in Middle East since beginning of hostilities reached 60.

Home Front. Daylight raids over England and Scotland. Seven German bombers shot down. Six civilians killed and 78 injured. Train on South Coast bombed ; driver killed.

General. Germany refused Rumania's request for a treaty of alliance or military assistance.

THURSDAY, JULY 4

Sea Affair. Premier made statement in House of Commons on British seizure of French warships and action off Oran.

Pétain Government announced that French warships at Alexandria had been ordered to leave. If escape was impossible, Hitler ordered that they must be scuttled.

French Admiralty ordered warships at present on high seas to intercept British merchant vessels.

Air War. R.A.F. made daylight raids on oil refineries at Hanover and Emmerich. Aerodromes at Amsterdam and Brussels attacked.

During night R.A.F. carried out attacks on naval bases at Wilhelmshaven, Emden and Kiel ; on Dortmund-Ems Canal ; on lines of communication at Hamburg, Cologne and elsewhere ; on aerodromes at Varel, Hamburg, Aachen and Brussels.

Campaign against Italy. Nine enemy fighters shot down by R.A.F. near Sidi Barrani, Western Desert.

Small British garrisons at Kassala and Gallabat, Sudan frontier, withdrew after heavy mechanized enemy attack in which enemy lost 8 tanks, two aircraft and 300 men.

Home Front. Enemy aircraft approached Channel coast. At Portland naval auxiliary vessel was set on fire, and a tug and lighter sunk. Eleven civilians killed. Bombs dropped on South-Western counties, but no military objectives hit. One bomber and one fighter shot down.

General. Rumanian Government resigned. M. Gigurtu succeeded M. Tatarescu as Premier and formed a new Cabinet.

FRIDAY, JULY 5

Sea Affair. Germany announced that Article 8 of Armistice terms, providing for demobilization and disarming of French Fleet, would be suspended.

R.A.F. sank large German supply ship off Dutch coast and damaged another. Nazi A.A. gunship turned turtle after bombing by Hudson 'plane.

Air War. R.A.F. bombers made daylight raids on aircraft factory at Deichshausen and on aerodromes at Waalhaven and Flushing.

During night bombers again raided naval bases at Kiel and Wilhelmshaven. Docks at Cuxhaven and Hamburg attacked. Cologne railway junction bombed. Aerodromes at Schiphol and Texel attacked.

Gibraltar experienced first air raid when French naval air squadrons attacked shipping. No damage or casualties reported.

Campaign against Italy. In Libya, Blenheim bombers attacked large troop and motor transport concentrations near Bardia. Another formation bombed El Gubbi.

Home Front. Scattered raids over England during night. Slight damage and few casualties.

General. Pétain Government declared it was severing all diplomatic relations with Great Britain.

Announced that supply of oil from Iraq to Tripoli in Syria had been cut off.

Count Ciano left Rome for Berlin.

SATURDAY, JULY 6

Sea Affair. Fleet Air Arm machines secured six hits on French battleship " Dunkerque," grounded at Oran.

Demobilization of French Fleet at Alexandria proceeded, after acceptance by Admiral Godfroy of British proposals for preventing the ships being used by the enemy.

Air War. R.A.F. bombed aerodromes at Knocke, Evreux and Ypenburg.

During night shipbuilding yards at Bremen and Kiel, and armament depot at Emden, were attacked. Seaplane bases at Norderney and Hornum bombed.

Enemy made three raids on Malta. One, probably two, of raiders brought down.

Campaign against Italy. Fleet Air Arm and R.A.F. attacked Italian warships sheltering in harbour of Tobruk, Libya, eight direct hits being obtained. Other units attacked aerodrome at Catania, Sicily.

Home Front. Nazi 'planes flew over town in South Devon. High explosive bomb caused few casualties. Raiders driven off by fighters and A.A. guns. Bombs also dropped over South Coast area.

Enemy bomber shot down into sea off Aberdeenshire after 100-mile chase.

Heinkel shot down by Spitfire off South-East Coast.

SUNDAY, JULY 7

Sea Affair. Admiralty announced that H.M. submarine " Snapper " had torpedoed five German supply ships under convoy.

Air War. R.A.F. bombers made daylight raids into Germany, penetrating more than 300 miles. Aerodrome at Eschwege extensively damaged. In Northern France, a British bomber had running fight with five Messerschmitts and shot one down.

Bergen oil tanks set on fire by Fleet Air Arm. During night bombers attacked military targets at Ludwigshaven and Frankfurt, and rail communications at many places in North Germany. Hits registered on naval barracks at Wilhelmshaven and on canal basin at Duisberg-Ruhrort. Aerodromes in North Friesian Islands were bombed, as were airports of Rotterdam and Brussels.

Home Front. Bombs were dropped in coastal districts in West Country ; some houses destroyed and five persons killed. Dornier " pencil " damaged by A.A. fire and believed to have come down.

Slight enemy activity over British coasts during night. Three Dorniers shot down by Hurricane fighters.

Three enemy fighters shot down by R.A.F. Spitfires off South-East Coast.

MONDAY, JULY 8

Sea Affair. Admiralty announced that H.M. destroyer " Whirlwind " had been sunk by U-boat.

French battleship " Richelieu," lying at Dakar, French West Africa, put out of action by depth charges and aerial torpedoes, after her commander had refused four

alternative methods of peaceably putting her beyond reach of enemy control.

French warships at Casablanca reported to have put to sea.

Air War. R.A.F. attacked Ostend : large enemy supply ship hit, canal lock gates and naval storehouses damaged. Bombs dropped on enemy barges on canals at Zwolle, Haten, Weest, Elberg, and Delft.

Other aircraft bombed Danish harbour of Aalborg and patrol vessels off the coast. Aerodromes in enemy occupation at Soissons and Douai were damaged.

During night Kiel and Wilhelmshaven were again bombed. Damage done to oil refineries at Homburg, and to aerodromes at Waalhaven, Amsterdam and Brussels.

Three air raids on Malta, in addition to seven during week-end. Three, probably five, raiders destroyed.

Campaign against Italy. Mersa Matruh, Western Desert, bombed by enemy ; no damage, no casualties.

Home Front. Daylight raids made over Britain, from extreme South-West to North-East coast. Little damage caused and few casualties. Eight enemy aircraft known to to shot down, and others disabled.

Minister of Food announced immediate rationing of tea to 2 oz. per head per week.

General. Stated that nine B.E.F. divisions rescued from Dunkirk had been fully reorganized.

French Embassy in London to be withdrawn.

Reported that British Government had lodged protest with Swedish Government against latter's decision to allow transport of German troops and materials of war across Swedish territory.

Announced that King Haakon had refused German request, through Norwegian Storting, to abdicate.

TUESDAY, JULY 9

Sea Affair. Commander-in-Chief, Mediterranean, reported that he had made contact east of Malta with Italian forces, including two battleships and number of cruisers. Enemy immediately retired behind smoke screen, but a hit was obtained on one battleship. Cruiser hit by torpedo from Fleet Air Arm machine. Enemy was being pursued.

In another part of Mediterranean H.M. submarine " Parthian " sank Italian U-boat.

Another British naval force based on Gibraltar carried out sweep towards Central Mediterranean ; four enemy aircraft were destroyed and three heavily damaged.

Coastal Command aircraft attacked enemy shipping off Danish coast, including two minesweepers, one of which was damaged, and two supply ships, both of which suffered.

Air War. Coastal Command bombers attacked Bergen. Another formation bombed aircraft on Sola aerodrome at Stavanger.

R.A.F. made night raids on naval dockyards at Wilhelmshaven, Bremen, goods yards in the Ruhr, oil refineries at Manheim, and aerodromes at Borkum, Texel, Schiphol and Waalhaven.

Campaign against Italy. R.A.F. raids were reported on Diredawa, Zula and Massawa, Italian East Africa, considerable damage being done.

Enemy columns endeavouring to raise siege of Fort Capuzzo, Western Desert, successfully engaged.

Home Front. Eight enemy aircraft brought down, one of which was towed in, and several others severely damaged during raids on various parts of Britain. Some damage done to premises at Bristol Channel port. Six persons killed in Welsh area.

General. House of Commons approved further Vote of Credit of £1,000,000,000 for war expenditure.

Hitler-Ciano talks in Berlin continued.

French Chamber and Senate at Vichy voted full powers to Marshal Pétain to promulgate by decree a new Constitution.

A FEW THOUSAND TONS OF OIL GOERING WON'T GET

This remarkable and unique photograph shows a 'plane of the Royal Air Force actually in action in maintaining the blockade.   Our bomber, far above the sea, has successfully attacked an enemy tanker carrying much needed supplies of oil to the enemy.   Ablaze from stem to stern the tanker is sinking in the Channel off the French coast.   The photograph was taken from another bomber of the same formation.   *Photo, P.N.A.*

Italy Goes Over the Top in East Africa

After several weeks during which Italian offensive operations in Africa were confined to
air raids, Mussolini carried the war into enemy country by launching attacks across the
frontier into the Sudan and Kenya. Some description of the opening actions is given below.

MOYALE has come into history with a rush. For years it has sweltered in a modest obscurity, just one of the many posts which line the frontier between Britain's colony of Kenya and Italian Abyssinia. In the centre of the compound stands tiny Fort Harrington surrounded by a few thatched buildings and mud huts within a fortified wall. No main road, no railway, passes through it, nor is it on any great caravan route ; its sole importance arises from the wells of fresh water which lie outside the walls but within the encircling wire.

Beyond Moyale, just across the bare

there was a further attack in force accompanied by a fierce bombardment, in the course of which a thousand shells fell on the fort in the space of a few hours. Finally, the garrison was withdrawn on the night of Sunday, July 14, and joined the relief force according to plan.

In Italy the capture of Moyale was hailed as a momentous victory, but perhaps with more reason the Italians could congratulate themselves on the seizure on July 3 of the Sudanese town of Kassala on the Eritrean frontier, and Gallabat, a hundred miles or so to the south. Kassala ranks as one of the principal towns of the Anglo-Egyptian

Sudan, as it has a population of some 6,000 and is a station on the railway which links Khartoum with Port Sudan on the Red Sea. Four days later Kurmuk, 200 miles to the south-west of Gallabat beyond the Blue Nile, also fell to the Italian arms. While none of these posts was of any strategic value, their capture was the work of considerable forces.

However unimportant in themselves, these operations may be taken as indicative of Mussolini's resolve to take the offensive in East Africa, whether it be because he feels that something of the kind is necessary to restore Italian prestige after the inglorious happenings which marked

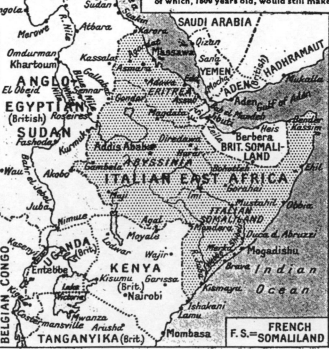

Italy's entry into the war set Rome feverishly to work on A.R.P. Here workmen are sandbagging arches of the Colosseum, the massive masonry of which, 1800 years old, would still make a good air-raid shelter. *Photo, A.P.*

valley through which runs the frontier, stands the Italian fort of Agal, built high up on a steep hill. From June 1936, when the Abyssinians were driven out of Agal by Mussolini's legions, Italians and British have faced each other across the valley ; and following Italy's entry into the war on the side of Germany against Britain the Italian authorities in East Africa concentrated a considerable body of troops at Agal with the obvious intention of attacking British Moyale.

On June 28 the attack opened with a heavy bombardment by field guns and an assault by Italian regulars. This was driven off, but the Italians attacked again on July 1 and on the following day, when there was a successful counter-attack by the little garrison of King's African Rifles. On July 5 intermittent shelling began, and on July 9

the opening weeks of the war, or because he is really determined to venture on a campaign of imperial conquest.

For such a campaign Abyssinia might be regarded as well situated, for it is surrounded by British territory containing a number of objectives within easy reach of Italian warplanes operating from bases in Abyssinia. Nor is a land offensive out of the question, westwards against the Sudan, or to the south against Uganda and Kenya, and perhaps farther south still across the Equator into Tanganyika and even Rhodesia — which is next door, as it were, to the Union of South Africa. It is true that in such operations vast distances would have to be covered,

This map shows those parts of N. and E. Africa where the British and Italian forces are engaged in land operations from Libya to Kenya. See Vol. II, p. 664, for N. Africa as a whole and p. 613 for Egypt and Suez. Note how all Italian East Africa is cut off from Italy, while the British hold the Red Sea and the Indian Ocean

In N. Africa Our Prison Camps Begin to Fill

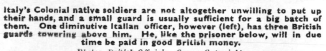

Italy's Colonial native soldiers are not altogether unwilling to put up their hands, and a small guard is usually sufficient for a big batch of them. One diminutive Italian officer, however (left), has three British guards towering above him. He, like the prisoner below, will in due time be paid in good British money.

Photos, British Official: Crown Copyright

Outpost Fighting in the Sudan and Kenya

This aerial photograph taken over Malta during a raid by Italian bombers gives some idea of the warmth of their reception by A.A. guns. In the split second of the exposure, 17 shells can be seen bursting in the air.
Photo, Associated Press

first line, behind which the defence forces of the South African Union and the Rhodesias would be enabled to muster, while inexhaustible reinforcements might be brought across the ocean from India.

Moreover, the Italian position in Abyssinia is none too happy. Mussolini has boasted long and often of the Italian conquest, but in truth considerable areas of the huge country have never been conquered. Of the 5,000,000 tribesfolk, many are actively hostile and the rest are filled with a hate which requires but a spark to become inflamed into furious activity. If any considerable portion of the Italian garrison were withdrawn, then Abyssinia as a whole might revolt.

Again, the Italians in Abyssinia are in effect beleaguered. The shells which were fired with such lavish profusion into Moyale, the bombs which have been dropped on our Red Sea ports, the petrol used up in the raids into the Sudan, can never be replaced until Italy can break the British blockade. Finally, Abyssinia is not a self-supporting country so far as the white man is concerned; and it might well be that long before the Italian motorized columns had reached the Equator, the central stronghold of Italy's new empire in East Africa would have been compelled to capitulate by that most efficient of war's handmaidens—famine.

but in the light of the experience of the last few months it would be unwise to assume that armoured cars cannot penetrate any country, however difficult, however vast. Moreover, much of the African terrain—the flat bush country and the veldt in particular—makes easy going for mechanical transport. Motorized columns can carry their own water as easily as their own petrol; and distances which only a few years ago required weeks to be covered by the long trains of natives walking in single file can now be traversed in a few days.

But the invader who endeavoured to press on for any considerable distance down the " All Red route " which leads from Egypt to the Cape would be exposed to many dangers. His ever-lengthening lines of communication might be threatened at a thousand points, and in view of Britain's command of the seas he could hardly expect to receive reinforcements or supplies from the coast. Opposed to him would be considerable and constantly-growing military forces, which, though they might be inferior in mechanized equipment, would be his superior in all else. The King's African Rifles, whose battalions are distributed in Nyasaland, Tanganyika, Kenya, and Uganda, would constitute a formidable

Among the doughty native warriors that the Italians are meeting in Africa, none are better fighters or more loyal to the British Empire than the King's African Rifles, men of which famous regiment are here seen at bayonet practice. The K.A.R., whose headquarters are at Nairobi, Kenya Colony, did excellent service in the fighting at Moyale in July.
Photo, P.N.A

War in France as the Nazi Cameramen Saw It

Here a German cameraman has registered a success for the R.A.F., some of whose bombers have just passed overhead, leaving damaged 'planes and an oil dump on fire.

This gunner of a French tank is holding up his hands in surrender to German soldiers only because he has no alternative. The rest of the crew are dead. He can shoot, but alone he cannot handle the tank, which is disabled, so the bitter moment comes.

The destruction of this bridge across a railway made it necessary for the advancing German infantry to clamber across the rails, but their transport could not pass that way. Inset is a Nazi light anti-tank gun in action with infantry, mopping up in a French village. Most German units include soldier photographers who obtain these action pictures. *Photos, Central Press and Keystone*

'Back to the Bourbons' Won't Save France

Pathetic indeed is the spectacle of France, so long the torch-bearer of light and liberty, but now the scene of a tyranny which has its inspiration in the autocracy of the Bourbon kings, fortified by the harsh brutality, the comprehensive efficiency of the Fascist state. Here is a sketch, by E. Royston Pike, of Pétain's France on Bastille Day.

JULY 14, " le quatorze juillet," is the day on which France has been accustomed to remember the storming of the Bastille by the Paris mob in 1789—the episode which is taken as marking the opening of the great French Revolution. But in the celebrations of 1940 the prevailing note was one not of jubilation but of " meditation "—and meditation not on the military triumphs, the striking achievements, which flowed from that day of turbulent action, but on the events of the last few weeks which have destroyed France as a great Power.

The France of Pétain shrinks in senile aversion from the boisterous rejoicings with which Bastille Day has been for so long celebrated. There is little in the aged Marshal of the spirit of Danton ; and under his guidance, dragooned by his police, intimidated by his soldiery, the French people may soon hang their heads when they read the inscription " Liberté, Egalité, Fraternité,"

"THAT'S NOT FRANCE!"

Cartoon by Low, by permission of the " Evening Standard "

which inspired their fathers to such tremendous deeds and created such a dust and clatter in the worm-eaten fabric of 18th-century Europe.

There is little of the " Rights of Man " in the new Constitution which was voted by the National Assembly in the Grand Casino at Vichy on the afternoon of July 10. There were a few protesting voices, a few votes cast in opposition, but the proposals submitted by the Pétain-Laval Government for the suppression of France's parliamentary democracy in favour of a Totalitarian regime were passed by overwhelming majorities. In the Senate only one vote was cast against, and in the Chamber only three ; but it is significant that at the meeting of the National Assembly, composed of Senate and Chamber sitting together, where the vote was secret, the hostile votes rose to 80 out of 649. The next day the constitution of the Third Republic, so high-sounding on paper but operated with such cunning disregard for the public weal, was abrogated in large measure ; and by three " Constitutional Acts "

supreme power passed into the hands of the old Marshal.

" We, Philippe Pétain, Marshal of France," read the first, " declare on the basis of the Constitutional Law of July 10, 1940, that we assume the functions of Chief of the French State." Those functions, sweeping enough in all conscience, are set out in the first Article of Constitutional Act, No. 2.

"The Chief of the French State has full Governmental powers. He appoints and removes Ministers and Secretaries of State, who are responsible to him alone.

The head of the State holds legislative power with the Ministerial Council, firstly until new Assemblies are formed, and secondly by his own decision and in the same form after the formation of these Assemblies in the case of great external tension or internal crisis. Under the same circumstances he can decree measures of taxation.

He proclaims the laws and is responsible for carrying them into effect.

He appoints all holders of civil and military offices for whose appointment the law does not provide other methods.

He commands the armed forces.

He holds the right of pardon and amnesty.

Ministers and ambassadors of foreign Powers shall be accredited to him. He conducts negotiations and ratifies.

He can declare a state of siege in one or more parts of the country.

He can declare war only by previous agreement with [the Legislative Assemblies."

All provisions of the Constitution of 1875 incompatible with the foregoing were repealed, and " We, Philippe Pétain, Marshal of France," ordered in conclusion that the French Senate and Chamber of Deputies should remain in existence until the Assemblies contemplated were formed, although they would not meet unless summoned by the Chief of State. " Done at Vichy, July 11, 1940. Signed, Pétain."

Before the promulgation of these decrees the Marshal called on President Lebrun to inform him that he intended to assume the functions of the President of the Council (Prime Minister) and of the President of the French Republic, in order that responsibility for the direction of affairs in the present exceptional circumstances should rest on his shoulders alone. M. Lebrun, we are told, acquiesced and " put his powers at the disposal of Marshal Pétain."

That night the new Chief of the French State addressed his people over the wireless. The new State, he said, would be Totalitarian, with himself at the head ; under him and

directly responsible to him would be twelve Ministers and twelve Under-Secretaries of State. Administration should be simplified and decentralized, and henceforth the administrative unit would be the thirty or so provinces that existed before 1789. In each of these a governor would be appointed, who, to a large extent, would take the place of the Prefects of the present 90 departments. It was intended that the seat of the Government should be Versailles, which the German Government had been asked to " liberate."

International capitalism and international socialism, which, so he declared, had gone hand in hand in order to exploit France, were a thing of the past, and it was now necessary to fight against all internationalism. " The basis of our State," went on the man whom the German wireless was quick to call France's Fuehrer, " must be Work, Family, and Fatherland."

So, slain by a gang of semi-Fascist politicians and Clerical generals, the Third Republic followed into the grave the Second, murdered in 1852 by Napoleon the Little (as Victor Hugo called him), and the First, which Napoleon Bonaparte made the stepping-stone of empire. In its place the world saw an attempted revival—in some measure, at least—of that country of peasants governed by an all-powerful monarch which is what the history books tell us was the France of the Bourbons. True, at Versailles there is to rule no Louis XIV but a Chief of State—but, none the less, he will be possessed of powers just as autocratic as those enjoyed by the " Sun King " of 250 years ago.

The names of the old provinces—Dauphiné, Gascony, Anjou, Berry, Languedoc, and the rest—hardly met with outside works of fiction, are to find their places once again on the map. Perhaps ere long the royalist dream kept alive by Charles Maurras and Léon Daudet in the columns of " Action Française " may be realized, and there will sit on the throne of his ancestors His Majesty, King Henry V.

Uneasy Jostling of the Ages

This strange mixture of political ideals and machinery, in which the age of Louis XIV jostles that which, by German historians at least, will be described as Hitler's, led to no modification of the Nazi attitude towards conquered France. There were sneers in Germany at the " superficial imitation of German social and political reconstruction," while Alfred Rosenberg, Nazism's ideologue-in-chief, wrote gloatingly that " the French Revolution of 1789 has been buried at Vichy by the French themselves."

While France was " meditating," while Germany was sneering, in London Bastille Day of 1940 was described by General de Gaulle, leader of "Les Français Libres," as " a day of dawning hope," if one of mourning for their country. These remembered that the column in the Place de la Bastille is not only dedicated to the heroes of July 14, 1789, but also commemorates those who in July 1830 drove from Paris the last of the reactionary Bourbons.

In London Hope Yet Flamed for France on July 14

The great French national festival of Quatorze Juillet did not pass unnoticed by French soldiers in Britain who are still determined to carry on the fight, but the occasion was one of solemn resolve rather than martial pageantry. The chief incident of the day was the laying of a wreath on the Cenotaph in White-hall. The guard of honour seen here, which General de Gaulle inspected, was typical of the best of the French fighting forces.

JULY 14 has for 150 years been France's great festival of freedom, for on that day in 1789 the Bastille, great fortress-prison of Paris, symbol of the despotic power that had reduced the French people to virtual slavery, was stormed and its prisoners released. The site is now marked by a bronze column surmounted by a figure of Liberty. Formerly the anniversary was celebrated by a great military parade on the Champs-Elysées. This year it was only the Frenchmen in Britain who could commemorate the day as free people.

General de Gaulle, as he laid the wreath on the Cenotaph in London, was watched with sorrow but also with hope by many French spectators. He placed a wreath also on the plinth of the statue of Marshal Foch at Victoria (left).

In former years the supreme moment of the great military parade that commemorated July 14 in Paris was at the Arc de Triomphe, where the salute was taken. This year only Nazi transport rumbled past the spot. Right, is a French soldier with Bren gun at the Cenotaph ceremony in London.
Photos, Topical, Planet News, G.P.U. and Keystone

'We're Sailing Against England' Sing the Nazis

SAID Mr. Churchill on June 19, 1940, "The enemy is crafty, cunning and full of novel treacheries and strategies." Parachutists—once airily discounted as an offensive arm—have already proved their deadly efficiency. But little has yet been heard of another ingenious Nazi air weapon —the troop-carrying glider train, reported to have been tried out in secret during the invasion of the Low Countries. How this stealthy and speedily reinforced method of attack would work is shown in page 604, Volume II, an essential to its use on a large scale being hundreds of trained glider pilots. Germany, ever methodical, has provided them by sponsoring gliding as a sport in pre-war years, and in the exclusive photographs in these two pages, taken as late as August 1939 we see how the potential invaders were trained (see further in page 66).

The German pupil-pilot is ready for a first flight. Crash-helmeted, he has his shoulder-straps tightened and the catapult is hooked on.

" Take it easy and the machine will do the rest ! "—the instructor's words ring in the pupil's ears as he clings to the padded spar in front and awaits zero hour (centre). Then (lower photo) up and away! The men who hold the glider's tail have let go ; the taut elastic rope whips the machine into the air, leaving the crew still running down a hillside "somewhere in Germany." It looks a long way down to the valley, but, as British glider pilots quickly learned, it is only necessary to be calm and to relax that "death-grip" on the joystick.

Photos exclusive to THE WAR ILLUSTRATED

Is This How They Hope to Invade Britain?

Crashes are not infrequent, and here a German class has taken an hour's rest from flying to fix up a broken machine. Favourable wind conditions being essential for the more advanced stages of gliding, the "wind-clock" and "wind-sock" (right) are eagerly watched for a "soaring wind."

Nearing proficiency at last, the pilot-to-be sets out to pass his final tests with a more elaborate and manoeuvrable machine. The wind blows strongly and he turns to the right along the slope which deflects the air current upwards, lifting him like a piece of thistledown (centre). To qualify he must keep aloft for five minutes and land without damage. Thenceforward (above) he may soar to great heights, swooping and climbing above the rolling landscape for hours on end. The application of gliding to wartime purposes is discussed in page 66.   *Photos exclusive to* THE WAR ILLUSTRATED

In a Stilly Night They May Come In Gliders

In the much-threatened invasion of Britain Hitler may be expected to use every means—
fair or foul, orthodox and altogether novel—which may seem to serve his purpose.
Among them may well be the employment of troop-carrying gliders such as are
described in the article given below.

IF and when Hitler's men come to Britain they will do so by sea—in surface vessels, submarines, or amphibious craft—and/or by air, when the means employed will include troop-carrying 'planes and perhaps gliders. The use of the latter opens out interesting possibilities.

It is suggested that gliders, or even trains of gliders, consisting of two or more linked together, will be drawn in

their total weight 37 per cent might represent that of the structure, and 63 per cent that of the men carried. It is suggested that a glider would be able to carry as many as ten fully-armed soldiers, each weighing about 160 pounds carrying equipment amounting to another 90, or 250 pounds in all.

Even if only four or five men were carried by each glider, they would constitute a military unit as compared with the

can make use of quite small fields or open spaces dotted here and there with trees, ditches, and obstacles of one kind or another. It does not matter in the least if the glider is wrecked, provided its passengers are not hurt or too badly shaken.

Yet another advantage of this method of troop transport may be mentioned. The glider is not only silent, and so its approach is very difficult to detect— particularly at night when, we may assume, it would be most generally if not always used—but its pilot can pick up sounds from the ground which in the case of an aeroplane would be completely drowned by the roar of the engine. Gliding noiselessly above the darkened earth, he can hear the sound of marching feet, the rumble of tanks, the clanking of guns, even the shouted orders of direction. With the information thus gained he can come to earth in a spot most vitally dangerous to the defence.

'Dead Meat' for the Fighters

On the other hand, the glider has certain disadvantages. In the first place the cruising speed of the towing aeroplane is reduced from say 140 m.p.h. to 120 m.p.h. This perhaps is not a very serious matter, but the glider itself, when it is cast off by the towing machine somewhere over the coast, is reduced to a speed which may be almost no speed at all, although, if its pilot knows how to take advantage of every favourable current of air, it may succeed in keeping up until it has covered a distance of some 15 or 20 miles. But while in the air it is, of course, the easiest of targets, being both unarmed and unarmoured. It might be shot down by anti-aircraft fire, or if its control cables remained intact and its tail were not shot off, it might at length glide to the ground, when (it is more than likely) it would disclose to the rapidly assembled L.D.V.s a little collection of bullet-riddled corpses.

Such trifling catastrophes would, however, count little with the Nazi air chiefs; what are young Germans for but to be slaughtered for the Fatherland? If the glider method of transporting troops gives promise of being effective, even in only a small way, then it may well be that it will be tried.

It is not without interest to the defenders of Britain, then, that (if report speaks true) the Germans for some weeks past have been assembling a fleet of gliders at Vaernes, the aerodrome near Trondheim on the Norwegian coast, and maybe they are busy on this project at other points much more reasonably situated on the opposite coast to ours.

Aerial "trains," which it has been suggested might be used for invasion, were successfully experimented with in the United States for peaceful purposes some years ago. Here, gliders are being towed over New York City by one powered 'plane. On returning to the aerodrome they were slipped one by one and glided safely to ground.   *Photo, Wide World*

the wake of high-powered troop-carrying aeroplanes. "The outstanding advantage of transporting troops by towed glider (as well as in the troop-carrier itself)," says a writer in a recent issue of "Flight," "is that the number is increased merely by a small reduction of speed. With twenty in the troop-carrier and ten in the glider, the increase in number is 50 per cent, a worthwhile figure."

The gliders would be of light construction, wood and canvas chiefly; and of

individual parachutist who has to wait for his fellows to join him before he can make an attack in force. Moreover, as the gliders are capable of being guided, several might be made to land in the same field or open space, whereas parachutists are dropped in extended order.

One great advantage the glider has over the troop-carrying aeroplane is that, whereas the latter requires a large open space free from all obstacles, the glider, landing at as low a speed as 30 m.p.h.,

Nazi Parachutists in Action—the First Photographs

This photograph was taken when the Nazis were terrifying the people of Belgium by parachute troops. It shows parachutists descending from 'planes over a Belgian town. The two larger photographs in this page are among the first of this method of air invasion to reach this country.

A flight of parachutist reinforcements is descending on the snowclad countryside of Norway. The photograph reached London on July 11, 1940. Like others of the German Army in action, it was radioed to America and brought by Clipper mail to Great Britain. Inset, Nazi parachute troops who have just landed are watching some of their dive-bombers at the fiendish work of spreading terror among helpless civilians, work in which they will soon take part themselves.

Photos, Keystone and Associated Press

300 British Rifles Held 12 Miles of Front

Based on official and eye-witness accounts, the story we give below tells of just one
small force of British soldiers involved in the maelstrom of the great battle of the
Somme fought in the early summer of 1940.   It is a story of a most gallant fight crowned
by a triumphant escape from beneath the very wheels of Hitler's war machine.

VICKFORCE was the name given to five scratch battalions of the B.E.F., hastily organized on May 19—the day on which Weygand was put into Gamelin's shoes in the hope that he would be able to frame a plan to check the German advance, already thrusting deep towards the Channel coast of northern France. Dieppe, Le Havre and Rouen had not yet fallen, and if they were to be saved a stand had to be made between the Somme and the Seine. The position chosen was along the Béthune, a little river which enters the Channel at Dieppe, and a wooded ridge

on its south-western bank ; on this line Vickforce dug itself in.

For ten days the men mined bridges, erected wire obstacles, built road blocks, concealed anti-tank rifles and Bren guns in strong emplacements ; and in a brave attempt to bluff the enemy into the belief that they were stronger far than they were, set up in dummy emplacements spoof soldiers made of sandbags, wearing steel helmets and armed with tent poles. So day and night they laboured, and as they laboured there poured over and through them without intermission columns of refugees and troops and military transport escaping from the Germans who had smashed the French line at Abbeville and Amiens. After ten days the little force was reorganized as the Beauman Division, under Major-General A. B. Beauman, and it then had three battalions of about 700 men each. One of the three was known as " Newcomb's Rifles " and commanded by Lieut.-Colonel L. E. C. Perowne, of the Royal Engineers.

From May 19 until June 8 this gallant collection of British oddments stood somewhat aloof from the confused battle on the Somme, although they were subjected to air bombing every day. Time and again German armoured vehicles and motorized infantry approached, but

always they withdrew without an attack. At length, however, the battle drew very near, and it became apparent that the Béthune line, in one section of which 300 rifles were now strung out along 12 miles of front—about 1 man to 70 yards—could not be held much longer unless it were strongly reinforced.

By June 7 the situation could hardly be graver, and a scheme of withdrawal in small parties moving independently through the broken wooded country to the ferries over the Seine west of Rouen was worked out in careful detail.   The scheme was given the code name " Robin

By way of pictorial accompaniment to the intensely interesting story of Newcomb's Rifles, we give here photographs of its commander, Lt.-Col. L. E. C. Perowne, R.E. (right), and Major-Gen. A. B. Beauman, C.B.E., D.S.O. (left), who commanded the scratch division of which it was part ; while below is Caudebec, very much as it appeared on June 10, 1940. At Caudebec the Seine is wide and swift-flowing, and it was no mean feat to swim across and bring back the ferry-boat—one such as is shown in our picture—which the obstinate ferryman had tied up on the opposite shore.

Photo, Bassano, E.N.A. & Lafayette

How 'Newcomb's Rifles' Crossed the Seine

When the French Army in Northern France began to break, retreat was forced upon the British Army. The full story cannot yet be told and may never be known, but it is certain that many units, separated like Newcomb's Rifles from the main body of the army, showed the utmost heroism in making their way to the coast and putting up at intervals a resistance to enemy forces that seemed overwhelming. Here is one such unit making a stand in a ditch beside a road, determined to die rather than surrender.

Photo, British Official : Crown Copyright

Hood," and late in the afternoon of the next day the order went out to the companies : " Robin Hood ; blow all bridges and craters before leaving. Take particular care against air observation. No especial hurry." So the 2,000-odd British soldiers began to thread their disciplined way through forest paths and a countryside cluttered with the debris of armies in retreat and a populace in flight.

In what follows we tell only of Newcomb's Rifles, but the other two battalions had the same task and performed it not less competently. Towards the evening of June 9 detachments of the Newcomb's were nearing the Seine. The Germans were in Rouen and were sending out to the north mobile columns of tanks and truck-borne infantry to cut off the retreat ; the small river towns of Caudebec and Duclair were choked with wreckage, human and material ; Duclair, moreover, had been bombed and was in flames, and dense smoke from burning oil tanks drifted low across the woods. In the dusk the battalion's commander set out in his car to " C " Company, who were nearest Rouen, and carried their headquarters staff in several journeys to Fontaine. On his last journey he ran into a concertina wire in the dark—wire put up around a number of German tanks parked for the night ! At once he drew

heavy fire and the car was wrecked, though fortunately there were no casualties. Colonel Perowne and his Intelligence Officer, covering the escape of their party, were pursued with bursts of rifle fire, but managed to slip away through the trees. At Fontaine they found the French ferry boats tied up on the south bank, and as their crews remained deaf to every call the Headquarters Staff spent the night in a lair amongst the rocks.

Meanwhile, battalion rear headquarters, who had taken refuge for the night in a barn, were surprised by four enemy tanks which drove along the road from Rouen at dawn, spraying woods and hedges at random with machine-gun fire. Watching through cracks in the barn door, the little party of British soldiers saw the first tank turn in at the farm gate. Without losing a moment one man crawled out of the barn unnoticed and opened a second gate. Then at his signal the rest flung open the barn door and dashed out in their small car and on two motor-cycles. Picking up their comrade, they got clear away, despite the wild volleys of the enemy.

At the same time the headquarters company was threading its way by compass through the forest of Trait, avoiding all the roads and paths which by this time were held by the enemy. For more than six hours the company commander fol-

lowed an accurate course in the thick of the smoke-filled forest, and emerged through the trees within a few hundred yards of the ferry which was his objective.

Early on June 10 the ferries resumed operation, although the approaches to them were jammed with refugees and military transport. At 6 o'clock Caudebec was bombed and fires were started, and air attacks were continuous all day. In the midst of the work of crossing the ferry captain refused to return from the far bank, and as he ignored the furious ringing of the bell, volunteers swam the river and placed him under armed guard. At long last the crossing was completed, the refugees and French troops being sent across first, and then, when the approaches to the ferry had been cleared, the British troops and their transport brought up the rear. In this way four-fifths of Newcomb's Rifles crossed the Seine with all their arms and baggage.

Still their troubles were by no means at an end, and they had more than a week of adventure interspersed with some hard fighting before on June 19 they arrived with their transport on the Quai Normandie at Cherbourg and embarked for England—22 officers and 310 other ranks, with 29 anti-tank guns and 15 Bren guns. It was a fine ending to a fine episode.

'Should the Invader Come to Britain We Sh:

Britain is now a beleaguered island, and on every hand there are signs of a calmly-taken and resolutely-held determination to defend it to the last. Among the precautions are anti-tank obstacles manned by soldiers who call upon every passing motorist to show his credentials (above).

In all the ancient towns and villages men of the Home Guard, as Mr. Churchill prefers to call them, are learning or re-learning the use of the rifle; here, for instance, the local L.D.V.s are on parade in the colonnaded market-place of Chipping Campden in the Cotswolds. The other photographs in these pages show

Photos, Associated Press, G.P.

fend Every Village, Every Town, Every City'

The Prime Minister to Britain and the World
July 14, 1940

EVER before, in the last War or in this, have we had in this ...d an army comparable in quality, ...ment, or numbers to that which ...ds here on guard tonight. We ... a million and a half men in the ...sh Army under arms tonight. ... every week of June and July has ... their organization, their defences, ... their striking power advance by ... and bounds.

...hind these, as a means of ...ruction for parachutists, air-borne ...ders, and any traitors that may ...und in our midst—and I do not ...ve there are many, and they will ... short shrift—we have more than ... million of the Local Defence

Volunteers, or, as they are much better called, The Home Guard. . . .

SHOULD the invader come, there will be no placid lying down of the people in submission before him as we have seen—alas !—in other countries. We shall defend every village, every town, and every city. The vast mass of London itself, fought street by street, could easily devour an entire hostile army, and we would rather see London laid in ruins and ashes than that it should be tamely and abjectly enslaved. I am bound to state these facts, because it is necessary to inform our people of our intentions and thus to reassure them.

His Majesty inspecting a barricade on the South Coast on July 11 ; a member of an A.A. gun crew handling a 3·7-in. shell ; and a concrete obstacle placed on an open space to prevent enemy 'planes landing.

" and Topical

In Dover's Straits the Nazis Swooped

Towards the close of a beautiful day (July 14)—one so clear that from Kent's shore the white cliffs of France could be clearly seen—a convoy of Allied merchantmen was steaming steadily up Channel. Suddenly forty dive - bombing Junkers, escorted by Messerschmitt fighters, plunged out of the sky.

Some impression of the dramatic scene is conveyed in this photograph taken when the battle was at its height. On the right, two bombs have fallen just astern of an escorting destroyer; note the huge column of water from one burst. The small white splashes mark the impact of bomb fragments, while white puffs proceed from the destroyer's belching A.A. guns.

Nine of the Nazi war-planes were shot down into the sea, but no damage was caused to our ships. The convoy continued on its way.

Photo, British Newsreels Assn. Film

DEFENCE AND THE OFFENSIVE
The War Spirit of the British Peoples
By the Editor

I AM astonished that one of my readers accuses me of being too pessimistic. In all the many words I have written about the War pessimism is the one thing I have sought to avoid. Nor will I allow the charge to pass. To look with open eyes at the known facts and to record them as "things seen," however depressing or terrifying the facts, is not to be a pessimist.

In the last war there was a Colonel Maude, whose lectures were very popular. I attended several. He showed us—with many large-scale maps—how we were winning all along the line! In the Shaftesbury Theatre late in 1915 I remember one evening when I sat next to Sir Frederick and Lady Pollock, who wildly applauded Colonel Maude when he "proved" to us that in a few more weeks we would have beaten the Germans and sent them helter-skelter for Berlin. All very pathetic to recall, but true. I am glad that we have no Colonel Maude today to lull us into happy somnolence in cushioned stalls.

A pessimist has been defined as one who has lived much with optimists. So far as I am concerned the reverse holds true. In some measure I believe in our eventual victory just because I have passed much of my time recently in the company of pessimists.

Mr. Priestley (he is no pessimist), in one of his masterly broadcasts, asked us to regard Britain as a "fortress." At the moment I agreed; but I am not too sure that fortress is the best word. Britain is far, far more than any fortress, symbolic or actual. She is the refuge, the homeland, the exhaustless reservoir of all that makes for freedom and sanity in this lunatic world today. A fortress suggests something that can be not only besieged, but reduced; whose holders are surrounded, beleaguered, awaiting succour from without. No picture of Britain today could less truly represent our position, perilous though the hour may be. Britain cannot be besieged or blockaded so long as the mightiest Navy in the world holds the seas, and that Navy signifies so many bits of Britain afloat!

The Mighty Inspiration of Freedom

IN this little island of ours, whose people have built up the benignest empire the world has ever seen, the forces of defence and offence are mighty, yet their might is as nothing to the inspiration which informs every man and woman with the desire, the determination, the decision to stand for that freedom in which they were born and for which they are prepared to die. These are greater things than guns—or butter.

Among the epic stories of the Spanish Civil War that will inspire hundreds of volumes for years to come, the heroic resistance of the Nationalists (the Franco rebels) in the Alcazar at Toledo and the self-sacrifice of the Republicans who, with a loss of two thousand men, captured the Cuartel, at Madrid, from the rebel garrison will be retold a thousand times. In both instances the things of the spirit triumphed over all material things. So will it be with the so-called "fortress" of Britain. Fortress indeed; what of the Maginot Line, what of Belgium's Liége forts and Albert Canal, what of Holland's flooded defence areas, what of Rumania's "Carol's Ditch"?—nothing! Fortresses. Playthings. Chimeras. Stuff for bombing or ignoring.

"All wars are fought in the spirit," says the poet. And all history supports him. It is in the spirit that we shall meet and defeat the German menace to Great Britain.

It has been my fortune in the last week or two to see "close-ups" of what we are doing to throw back any German attack upon our homeland. Tank traps, strong points, barricades, miles of wiring can be seen in five minutes' walk from where I write. The appointment of General Ironside as Chief of Home Defence was a wise decision. It came when we knew that France was about to betray us by capitulation. Let us thank our Leader for the wisdom of that decision. The result has been to transform Britain and the British into a country defended in every corner and a nation eager to maintain its freedom against the assaults of barbarism, while still holding the high seas and preparing the blows which in her good time will make her enemies reel in regions far from these shores.

Britain Ready as Never Before

BRITAIN today is ready as at no time in her history to meet the invader. And the one thing which we can be sure of in our study of Hitler and Nazism is that the chances of attack bear an inverse ratio to the chances of successful defence.

From what I have personally witnessed, and still more from what I have been authoritatively informed of, the chances of a successful invasion of Great Britain—excepting, and only for the moment, Eire—are small. That there may be some, indeed many, attempts which we shall have to repel—and doubtless some surprises—I do not doubt. These will take toll of life and property in our island, but all such attacks I am convinced will be thwarted or repulsed. Parts of Britain may feel the invader's heel, but they will have no more than transient trouble to endure—trouble for which we are prepared and hourly improving our preparedness. "The Battle of Britain"—to which these daily coastal battles in the air and sporadic bombings are as preliminary skirmishes—can have but one issue: the discomfiture of the enemy, if he ever attempts a decisive invasion. An event of which one may still entertain some doubt.

But to what purpose all this? you may ask. The answer is that if Nazi Germany fails, or funks, in the Big Thing she has met her first defeat—and her first defeat may well prove final.

Meanwhile there is Italy to be mentioned. I am indeed misguided if Fascist Italy can ever have more than a "nuisance value" in this War. In Britain's good time the Mediterranean and its lands will be cleared of the Italian forces that at present exist there, and he who believes that these jackals will ever strike a paralysing blow at Britain is, in the fullest sense of the term, defeatist. From the cowards of Caporetto we have little more to expect than material for slaughter. History records many a strange alliance in times of war but none more grotesque than that between the vigorous and militant Nazis and the clamorous Fascisti, whose inferiority complex inspires the grandiloquent nonsense of their Duce in his public utterances on "the bloody battle of Mentone" and the high-speed flight of their fleet on July 9.

One of many pronouncements which time has falsified was Earl Baldwin's that "the frontier of Britain is the Rhine." When first spoken it sounded true enough, but today the Rhine is not even the frontier of France, though we may hope that it will be so again. Today, however, the frontier of freedom is Great Britain, behind whose arms and valiance the many millions in the United States are sheltering, and in which downtrodden millions in Europe are still trusting.

Look at a map of the British Empire and you will find no spot on it of military or naval importance where the Union Jack has been hauled down—save only in the Channel Islands, which with the German occupation of Western France, to which these islands are more closely related geographically than to Britain, became too difficult to defend against aerial attack. Our Empire stands unscathed and will assuredly emerge stronger and more closely knit than ever from the final stages of the conflict. With the solitary exception of Eire, every self-governing Dominion in the British Commonwealth is as completely at war with the Nazi-Fascist aggressors as Britain herself. Large forces of Anzacs and Canadians stand in Great Britain ready to join in any effort that may yet be needed to engage and destroy the mightest armada that Germany can muster.

We Shall Win Through to Victory

WE have been brought to our present position of defence by a series of unpredictable disasters on the Continent, but, above all, by the collapse of France, whose ineffective resistance to the German impact, compared with the heroic stand of Poland has actually lowered her militarily to an inferior category and will remain for all time the crowning disillusionment of the Second Great War.

From the terrible situation in which the iniquitous defection of France has placed Britain, her sworn ally, and all the other countries that had looked to France and her great empire for cooperation when their crucial hours arrived—Poland, Norway, Holland, Belgium—Britain and the British Empire, in cooperation with such Polish forces as have been re-formed, with the Dutch Empire, still loyal to its motherland, with the French legions now reshaping in Great Britain, and possibly with far greater collaboration from certain French colonies than the traitor government of France is striving to prevent, we shall emerge victorious—if not next year, then, as Mr. Churchill has promised us, in 1942, restoring France to a regime more worthy of her people and the other temporary victims of Nazi fury to a new era of peace, preserving the British Empire intact and confining a baffled Germany to an ample "living room," though less extensive than her cheap victories have given her for the moment.

... And Still the Dutch Don't Love the Nazis!

In the first few weeks of their occupation of the Low Countries the Nazis professed
much sympathy for the poor Dutch who had been so misled by their Queen and her
advisers, but ere long they discovered that smooth words could not blot out their manifold and all-too-horrible transgressions against a once-free people.

**Dr. Seyss Inquart,
the Nazi governor of
Holland.**
*Photo, International
Graphic Press*

WHEN, after four days of the most bitterly contested struggle, the Dutch still maintained their resistance against the German invaders, the Nazi war lords determined to teach them a terrible lesson. That lesson was delivered on May 14, when two squadrons of German bombers flew over Rotterdam and ploughed a "veritable furrow of destruction" across the heart of the city.

When they had passed, nearly two square miles of closely-packed streets and houses had been laid waste, so that only four or five buildings were left standing ; the rest of the area was one vast heap of rubbish and mangled bodies. Three weeks later corpses were still being recovered from the ruins at the rate of 300 a day ; and in all 30,000 men, women, and children were computed to have perished, slain by the bombs or burnt to death in the tremendous fires which ensued, or drowned in the underground shelters when these were flooded by burst water mains.

With characteristic effrontery the German authorities claimed that only three hundred people had been killed by their bombardment, whereupon a clergyman of the city, when holding a service in commemoration of the dead in his parish a few days afterwards, said : " I commemorate the three hundred dead in our city, of whom eight hundred fell in my parish alone."

Only a German—perhaps only a Nazi German—could see anything strange in the fact that after this demonstration of military frightfulness the Dutch were still in refractory mood, still displaying a reluctance to cooperate with the new administrators. So widespread was the spirit of opposition that within a few weeks the Germans were compelled to take notice of it and to threaten still further terrors.

Early in July General Christiansen, the German Commander-in-Chief in Dutch occupied territory, issued a proclamation directed against " specific manifestations of Dutch hostility," of which he mentioned in particular " the repeated failure of the Dutch land and sea forces to salute the German soldiers in the prescribed manner," " demonstrations in favour of the former Dutch Government or

members thereof," " insults to the justified pride of the German soldiers," " actions which damage German prestige and afford evidence of lack of respect for Germany," and, finally, " brawls with German soldiers." These manifestations of " a foolish spirit " must stop immediately, it was declared ; otherwise the most stern penalties, including death, would be imposed.

" Those who sympathize in word or deed with England and those who do not communicate the names of such sympathizers to the German authorities " were also threatened with the death penalty ; and it was made clear that the Germans have grounds for believing that in their bombing activities in Holland the R.A.F. have been provided with valuable information by sympathizers in the country. As the Dutch News Agency pointed out, a clearer admission of the

That part of the great Dutch port of Rotterdam which was bombed to utter destruction on
May 14, as shown in the R.A.F. photograph in the opposite page, is here seen from the air as it
was in the days of peace. Nazi terrorism was directed at the very heart of the city.
Photo, " The Times "

effectiveness and accuracy of the R.A.F. attacks and of the falsehood of the German accusations of " senseless and wanton attacks of the R.A.F. on non-military objects " can hardly be imagined.

But the Germans have not contented themselves with threats : indeed, in every way possible they are endeavouring to break the spirit of Dutch independence. Newspapers have been suspended for days or weeks because of their alleged " unfriendly attitude " towards the invaders and " their one-sided propaganda"; there can be little doubt that before long some of the Dutch editors will be joining their German colleagues in the concentration camps. Tens of thousands of Dutch

subjects are being conscripted under the orders of Seyss Inquart, the Nazi governor of Holland, to do heavy manual labour in Germany ; and a number are reported to have already arrived in the Ruhr and the Rhineland.

It has been reported, too, that high officials of the Netherlands State have been dismissed from office because they have refused to bow the knee in the courts of Hitler. Among these are the Burgomaster of The Hague, Jonkheer de Monchy, and General Winkelman, the Dutch Commander-in-Chief, who, after leading the forces in the brief but by no means inglorious campaign against the invader, was commissioned by Queen Wilhelmina to negotiate with the conquerors after she and her Government had been compelled to leave the country. It was announced in Amsterdam on July 3 that General Winkelman had been

arrested and sent to Germany as a prisoner of war, because he and his subordinates had not observed the conditions laid down for the demobilization of the Dutch Army and that disturbances had resulted in consequence. " It is in the supreme interest of the people," read the last sentence of the communiqué, " to see to it that no further disturbances of the demobilization shall occur." In effect, General Winkelman was carried away as a hostage for his people's good behaviour. All these evidences of repression indicate that Holland is not yet crushed, and give reason for hope that, in spite of all the Nazis can do, she never will be crushed.

Nazi Horror in Rotterdam—Here 30,000 Perished

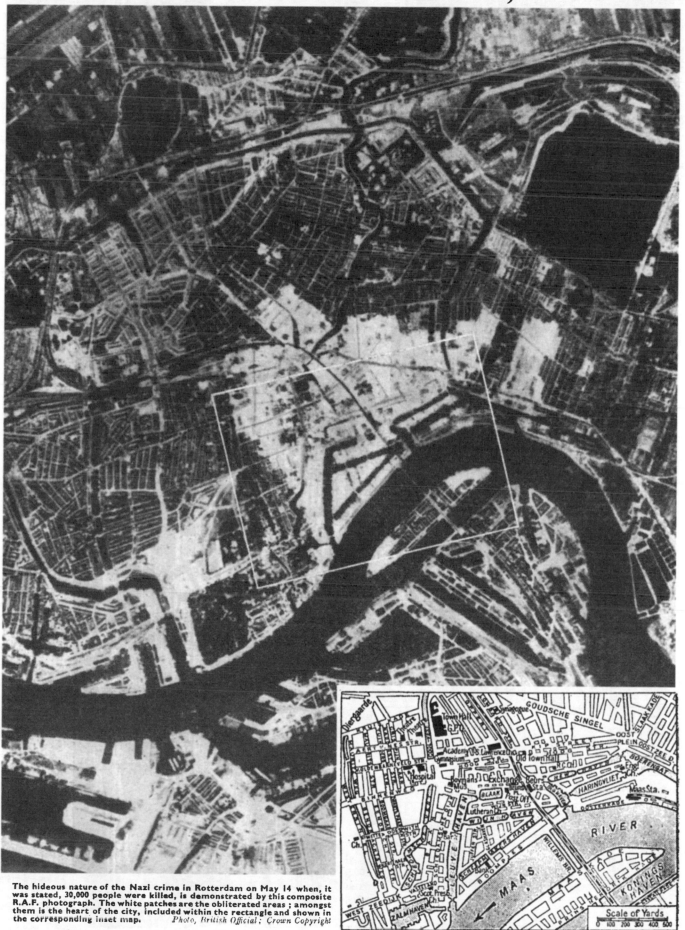

The hideous nature of the Nazi crime in Rotterdam on May 14 when, it was stated, 30,000 people were killed, is demonstrated by this composite R.A.F. photograph. The white patches are the obliterated areas; amongst them is the heart of the city, included within the rectangle and shown in the corresponding inset map.   *Photo, British Official; Crown Copyright*

Oil, Basis of Modern War

Picture-Diagram of its Production from the Rock to the Tanker

Specially prepared by Haworth for
THE WAR ILLUSTRATED

In this diagram, based upon the latest and most authoritative technical data now available, the elaborate story of oil, the fluid upon which the whole of modern warfare depends, is clarified.

SECTION OF AN OILFIELD

A — Water Well — Oil Well — Gas Well — Oil Well — Oil Well

Oil Bearing Limestone

B — Drill Rig — Donkey Engine — Drill Pipe — Spare Sections of Drill Pipe stacked until wanted — Drill Head constantly changed to keep sharp

C — DETAIL OF DRILL HEAD — Cutters

D — Well Head Machinery & Brick Surround — Remote Flow Control

E — Gas Absorption Plant Separator — Gas — Liquid — Storage Depot — Relay Pumps

These Saucer shaped "Bunds" prevent Oil being lost in leakage

Escape Vents for Oil Gases

Flexible Armoured Connecting Pipe

Tanker Pipe System — Oil Tanks Here

Oil Field — Pipe Line — Hills 3000 Feet High — Pipe Line

ALL THESE RE-FUELLED FROM ONE LARGE TANKER
1 Battleship
3 Cruisers
5 Destroyers

OIL WELLS. Oil is found in limestone rock at about 2,000 ft. depth, in the form of dark-coloured froth in fissures in the rock. This froth is composed of 60 volumes of gas to one of liquid. **Diagram A.** A section through an oilfield, showing how the seam of oil-bearing rock is sandwiched between others containing water. Gas and water shafts are sunk to enable the pressure to be controlled. **Diagram B.** A drill rig, a tower to facilitate the handling of the long lengths of drill pipe.

DRILLING.

Diagram C. The drill head shown in detail. The small eccentrically-mounted wheels cut out the earth and the cutters in the body of the drill head grind smooth the sides of the bore. The drill is rotated by a small donkey engine. As drilling proceeds a kind of mud is pumped into the hollow drill pipe, and is returned upwards between the pipe and the bore. Before the last few feet are pierced the bore is lined with steel or concrete, and well head machinery is placed in position. When the oil-bearing rock is pierced gas pressure forces the oil upwards

Diagram D. The well-head machinery with the brick or concrete surround. The flow of oil from the well is controlled by a large wheel on the lay shaft.

Diagram E. The oil is then separated into liquid and gas. These gases, which were formerly wasted, contain many valuable hydrocarbons which are absorbed in special plant and finally added to the liquid oil. The stored oil is pumped to the oil-tanker many miles away. In some cases the oil pipe-line has to pass over mountains 3,000 ft. high, and along 150 miles of pipe-line.

THE OIL TANKER. The tanker is moored close to the oil storage-tanks. Shore pumps force the oil into the ship's huge tanks through armoured flexible pipes. A 10,000-ton tanker can be filled in a day, and as many as 6 different grades or types of oil can be taken on together. The loading must be carefully done, due allowance being made for change from hot to cool climate. After each voyage the ship's tanks must be cleaned and made gas-free. The term oil includes petrol, lubricating oils, heavy furnace oils, as well as other types, and various grades of each type.

Oil is Still a Pressing Problem For the Nazis

As is pointed out in this article, Germany's oil position may have been somewhat improved as the result of her series of conquests. Yet while Hitler has won great victories on the Continent it is for Britain and not for Germany that oil gushes out in the U.S.A. and Irak, in Mexico and Venezuela, in Dutch East Indies and in Iran.

IT must be admitted that up to now oil has served Hitler well, and his stocks have been sufficient to win for him the most startling victories. In some respects, indeed, Germany's oil position may have been improved as one result of her series of conquests. In Denmark, for instance, she is said to have secured some 200,000 tons, and in Norway, too, a year's supply of petrol was included in the booty. Then there can be little doubt that in Holland the invaders have been able to lay their hands on considerable stocks of oil, though our demolition squads and raiding airmen have done their best to destroy the great oil tanks at Rotterdam and elsewhere. Even in France, although a number of oil tanks—in particular at Rouen and Le Havre—have been bombed to destruction, it is considered that the Germans have acquired at least a million tons, which it is estimated would keep their war machine in active operation for a month.

What has Germany got from Rumania ?

These gains, however, cannot be regarded as other than temporary, and against them must be set the enormous expenditure of oil in the over-running of western Europe. More substantial are the gains which must be expected to accrue to Germany as a result of Rumania's adhesion to the Axis. Since the war began Rumania has been the principal source of Germany's oil imports, and the Nazis may now expect to receive not a mere proportion of her oil production but the whole, amounting to six or seven million tons per annum—and this despite the fact that 80 per cent of the oil concessions are in the hands of French and British companies. Following Carol's approach to Hitler at the beginning of July the engineers of these companies were ordered to quit Rumania, and the Rumanian Government also demanded the return of some 3,000 railway tank wagons leased to British interests and seized more than half of the fleet of French tank barges on the Danube.

Quite apart from politics, indeed, economic considerations must lead to the diversion of Rumania's oil to Germany. Where else, indeed, can she send it with the route via the Black Sea to the Mediterranean closed following the collapse of France and the entry of Italy into the war ? More than ever before of Rumania's oil may be expected to go up the Danube to Germany.

There is yet a third route—the railway which connects the oil-fields at Ploesti, north of Bucharest, and Bacau on the eastern flank of the Carpathians, through Cernauti (Czernowitz), across the frontier into Poland, through the Galician oil-field to Lwow, and thence westward via Cracow into German Silesia. But this railway, so important strategically as well as economically, is under the control of Russia, for not only did the Soviet win the race for the Galician oil-fields in September 1939, but on June 28, 1940 Stalin's Red Army occupied the northern districts of the Bukovina, of which Cernauti is the capital. At Cernauti railways from Poland, Russia, and Bucharest meet, and Stalin's seizure of the place is an indication of his resolve to control so far as possible the flow of Rumanian oil to the state which, though today, ranking as an ally, may be tomorrow an enemy.

This may well have been a motive for the occupation of Bessarabia only a hundred miles from the Rumanian oil-fields, and the domination of the Black Sea ports from which in normal times the product is exported.

Through those ports Germany receives large quantities of oil shipped across the Black Sea from Batum, the export centre of the enormously productive Russian oil-fields in the Caucasus. With any improvement of Anglo-Russian relations, it might be hoped that the supply of Soviet oil to Germany would be diminished, or at least not increased. But already Germany and Italy are being denied any share of the petroleum produced in the Irakian oil-fields in Mosul and Kirkuk and carried across Syria by pipe-line to Tripolis on the eastern Mediterranean coast, as it was announced on July 6 that an agreement between the British Government, the Government of Irak and the Irak Petroleum Company had provided for the cutting of this northern pipe-line and the diversion of the entire flow through the southern pipe-line which runs across Palestine, reaching the sea at Haifa. From Irak Italy received considerable supplies of oil before her entry into the war against the Allies, and in the past much of that oil, we have good reason to believe, has been diverted to Germany's use. But now the process must be reversed as Mussolini's oil stocks are used up by his 'planes and warships and tanks, operating over vast distances in the war against Britain.

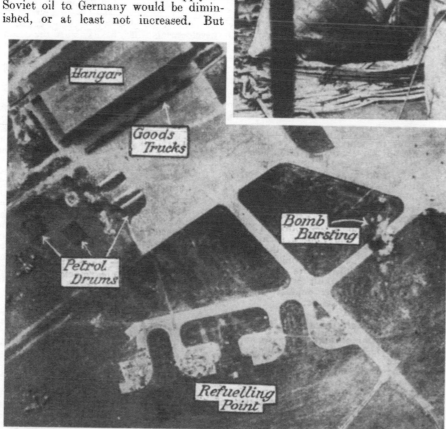

In view of the vital importance of oil to Hitler's war-machine, the R.A.F. has made a point of raiding the petrol dumps scattered along the enemy's front. Among them was that at the aerodrome at Eschwege, in Germany, 20 miles east of Cassel. Top, petroleum tanks in Amsterdam harbour after bombing by the R.A.F. *Photos, British Official, Crown Copyright; and Associated Press*

OUR SEARCHLIGHT ON THE WAR NEWS

Among the many items of war interest which cannot, for obvious reasons, be given in
full in our pages, we select week by week a number which are recorded in brief.
This is the third of the series.

ON May 14 the War Office announced that a new home-front force was being formed, to be known as the Local Defence Volunteers, whose duty it would be to deal with possible landings of enemy parachute troops in Britain.

Within two hours harassed officials all over the country were trying to cope with the thousands of men and youths who rushed to enrol, thankful that at last there was a form of national defence which they could undertake from which neither their age nor their occupation need exclude them.

L.C.C. park keepers, many of whom are ex-Service men, are training as Local Defence Volunteers. Here are three at aiming practice, with a sergeant-instructor showing a member of the squad how to check up on rifle sights.
Photo, Planet News

Eight weeks later, on July 8, it was stated that the L.D.V.s, or, in Mr. Churchill's happy phrase, the "Home Guard," numbered 1,060,000.

Germany Put in Her Place

THE fearless way in which Turkey, through her Prime Minister, has reacted to Nazi propaganda, has created satisfaction in London and profound annoyance in Berlin. Germany's whispering campaign, deliberately designed by Von Papen, the German ambassador, to undermine the confidence of the nation, her circulation of false reports, her systematic attempts to embroil Turkey with Russia, at length provoked Dr. Saydam to plain speaking at Ankara on July 12.

"Those who make accusations against Turkey and seek to influence her overlook one important point: the Turkey of today is not the dead and rotten Ottoman Empire. At the time of the Empire such intrigue benefited its authors. But the present Turkish rulers . . . have only one programme: the interests of Turkey, the security of the Turkish Republic. Such are the considerations omitted when this propaganda was conceived."

Abyssinia Britain's Ally

AFTER a prolonged and arduous campaign in 1935-36, conducted with every circumstance of ruthlessness and cruelty, Italy annexed Abyssinia, or such portions of it as she was able to control. But the country never really came to terms with its conquerors, and bitter hostility, coupled with outbursts of guerilla warfare, have darkened the four years of occupation. When Italy entered the European war, Abyssinia's hopes of freedom revived. Since that day she has been officially acknowledged by Britain as an ally, and on July 15 it was announced that Abyssinian troops were fighting side by side with Sudanese troops against Italians.

Swedish 'Neutrality'

GREAT BRITAIN, faced with a legitimate grievance, has protested to the Swedish Government against the latter's decision to allow German troops and war materials to be transported across her territory. Bearing in mind Sweden's refusal to allow Allied forces passage to Finland, the inconsistency seems particularly glaring.

On April 12, following the invasion of Norway, Herr Hansson, Prime Minister, stated his country's foreign policy: "Sweden is determined to observe her principle of strict neutrality. This means that she reserves the rights of independent judgement. It is not in accordance with strict neutrality to allow any scope for foreign enterprise." But early in July these brave words were ignored, and, trying to justify the concession to Hitler, Herr Hansson explained: "While hostilities were going on in Norway transit was subject to restrictions, and requests for the delivery of arms and munitions to either party were rejected. The situation is now different . . . It is evident that we cannot disregard developments which have entailed the occupation, entirely or partly, of seven countries, and the signing of an armistice in France."

In Sweden's eyes, might evidently makes all things right.

Czechs to Fight for Britain

THE dramatic evacuation of the Czechoslovak Army from France has been successfully completed by the arrival in England of the final contingent, led by the Commander-in-Chief, General S. Ingr.

When the French Government requested an armistice, two regiments of the Czech Army were in action on the Loire front, serving with two French divisions. Abandoned by the French units, the heroic Czechs rejected the order to cease fighting, and established contact with the British Government. Obeying Admiralty and War Office instructions, all Czech troops in France started to converge upon a certain French port. Here, after innumerable complications, two transports of the British Navy departed with the first contingent. But the units from the front were still far from the coast when the French forbade further embarkation. Baffled but resolute, General Ingr started negotiating with the French High Command while he and his staff awaited the arrival of the weary men from the fighting line. By the time they arrived permission had been granted, and evacuation proceeded.

Even more adventurous was the escape of the Czech Air Force. This consisted of about 200 first-line pilots, then engaged in severe fighting, about 300 pilots under training, and 200 air mechanics. When France capitulated the British Air Ministry announced that it would bring all the airmen to England, and instructions were broadcast by the B.B.C. Two days later they began to arrive. Some were flown in British bombers. Others eluded French control and landed in their own 'planes. Still others flew to North Africa. The rest assembled at Atlantic ports.

There are now two Czechoslovak camps in Britain. As Dr. Benes, head of the Czech National Committee (soon to receive recognition as the Czech Government), declared on June 19: "We are remaining here and shall remain here to fight for our future together with Great Britain, this great nation, however matters may turn out."

Mr. Churchill Again Responsible

THE Nazis have fastened with avidity on the Premier's assertion that London will be "fought street by street," for here, ready to hand, is their excuse for not regarding the capital as an open city. His reference to the defence of "every village, every town, every city" is interpreted by a German News Agency as a direct incitement to francs-tireurs, and for the fate of these misguided defenders, against whom terrible reprisals will be launched, Mr. Churchill will be solely responsible. But the Home Guard remains unmoved.

Pans Into 'Planes

"GIVE us your aluminium," cried Lord Beaverbrook, Minister for Aircraft Production, to the women of Britain, "and we will turn your pots and pans into Spitfires and Hurricanes, Blenheims and Wellingtons." And as one woman the housewives of Britain

Lord Beaverbrook's appeal to housewives for aluminium goods brought an immediate and overwhelming response. Lady Lucas Tooth, in charge of the W.V.S. at Chelsea, is here seen receiving contributions at the Town Hall.
Photo, Fox

rushed to the 1,600 dumps hastily organized by the Women's Voluntary Services, not only with their pots, pans and kettles, but with aluminium hot water bottles, mincers and dredgers, shoe-trees and hair curlers, cigarette cases, finger plates and door handles, motorcar registration plates and bicycle mudguards. One contribution to a Westminster dump was an artificial leg, and to Chelsea was brought a racing car with an aluminium body. Hundreds of tons of this light-weight metal have been collected within a few days.

I WAS THERE!

Eye Witness Stories of Episodes
and Adventures in the
Second Great War

I Captured a Nazi Airman on the Farm

Here, in her own words, is the story of a woman who, when told that one of the crew of a 'plane shot down by British fighters had landed by parachute near her home, rose valiantly to the occasion, captured and disarmed him, and later handed him over to the police.

THE heroine of this stirring episode is Mrs. Nora Cardwell, wife of an officer in the Local Defence Volunteers of a district on the North-East Coast. Her pluck and presence of mind were honoured within 24 hours by the award of the Medal of the Order of the British Empire, Civil Division. When told of the award Mrs. Cardwell remarked : I am beginning to think I was very foolish and that if I had had time to think I should have retreated. I thought that if the man had got into the house he might pull himself together and show fight. My one idea was, now or never.

Here is Mrs. Cardwell's account of her experience :

One of my farm men came to the door and said some German parachutists were coming down. I went to the telephone but found it was out of order. I told a boy to go on his bicycle for the police. But in the meantime I had to do something. We had been told that we had to deal with these parachutists very quickly before they had a chance to do any damage.

I went out into the garden and saw the airman limping across the paddock towards the house. There were two or three people about, but they did not do anything, so I walked up to the man and told him to put his hands up. He did not understand until I made signs and he then raised his hands in the air. I pointed to the automatic pistol in his belt and he handed it to me.

He was about 6 ft. 3 in. tall and about 25 years of age. I walked with him in front of me to the road. We waited for about half an hour before the police and soldiers arrived and took him away.

The tail of the shattered Nazi bomber shot down on July 9 during a daylight raid ; the Swastika was pierced by bullets.

The Front of Our Ship Was Blown Away

Among the survivors of H.M. Destroyer "Whirlwind," whose loss was announced by the Admiralty on July 8, was Leading Stoker C. A. Cairns. His story of the torpedoing of his ship and of his escape was told exclusively to "The War Illustrated."

RECOUNTING his experiences with the discretion which is officially required, Leading Stoker Cairns said :

I had just come off duty and was resting in the canteen flat reading a book when there was a terrific explosion.

I was flung through the air and fell into an oil tank. The inrush of water floated me clear and I managed to grab one of the twisted girders and succeeded in scrambling out of the tank. We crawled towards the stern to await and hope for rescue. We were unable to launch the boats as they had been damaged.

Here is Mrs. Cardwell, who captured a German airman after he had landed by parachute on the East Coast on July 9. British fighters had sent his machine crashing down.
Photos, "News Chronicle"

H.M. Destroyer "Whirlwind" sank on July 8 after being hit by a torpedo. She belonged to the Admiralty "W" class of which nine ships were built during the last war. They have a displacement of 1,100 tons with a speed of 31 knots and carry six 21-in. torpedo tubes. Their normal complement is 134. A stoker's story is told in this page.
Photo, Wright & Logan

Eventually a British aeroplane appeared and after circling round twice went away, apparently for assistance.

While we were waiting, the officers amongst us served out tots of whiskey. The spirits of the men were excellent and the discipline good. Later another warship hove in sight and after a while we were taken aboard her. We saw the "Whirlwind" go down as we were steaming away.

I did not sustain any serious injury, but I was soaked through and covered with oil from the tank into which I had fallen, so that the baths and change of clothes we were provided with on the rescue ship were very much appreciated.

We Dodged the Germans for 21 Days

More than three weeks after their capture at St. Valery during the British retreat from the Somme, two twenty-year-old privates in the Queen's Own Cameron Highlanders reached London, weary, ragged and half starved, but irrepressibly elated at the success of so daring an escape. Here is the story of their resource and fortitude as it was told to Basil Cardew, "Daily Express" Staff Reporter.

WE could have held out, but the French let us down. When the French surrendered we were 6,000 strong. We had to lay down our arms, too, not because we could not fight on—we all wanted to—but because we had no more food or ammunition.

So the Germans just walked in and herded us into a field—the whole 6,000—just like cattle. That day we were formed up and made to march, as we thought, towards Belgium. As we marched the Germans guarded the road with armoured cars and infantry armed with Tommy-guns.

After we had trudged for eight miles we had a whispered talk and decided to make a break for it. On an agreed sign we broke from the main column, and in the general mix-up we managed to slip into a French peasant's house which was empty.

After the troops had passed we managed to crawl out of the back of the house into some woods. We were so tired we just lay down and slept. When it got dark we crept out. No one was about. We knew it was no use trying to work our way back by the way we came. The roads were thick with anti-aircraft guns, machine-gun posts and armoured cars.

So we started on a cross-country detour, skipping the roads as much as we could. When we started we had no food, guns, or any idea of where we were going. We knew the gamble we were taking. But it was worth it.

It took us twenty-one days to get back to the coast. We had no food for the first four days. That made six days altogether, because we had had none for two days before we were captured. On the fourth day of our escape we found a bottle of French rum in an abandoned lorry. Then we came to a potato field, and dug up a few potatoes with our jack knives—the only equipment we had. That meal of rum and raw potatoes was like a banquet. But we kept most of the rum, for we knew it would have to last us a long time.

Next night we came to a big house. It was dark then, and before we had a chance to get cover we walked right into a German sentry. He was sound asleep, with his rifle at his side. He did not waken.

About 200 yards past the headquarters we took shelter in a house that we thought was unoccupied. Luckily we didn't stay downstairs. After a search of the house in the darkness we slept in the attic on a double bed. In the morning voices woke us up. They were German. We crawled under our bed and waited for the worst. But the Huns had beds downstairs and they tucked in. We waited all day, not daring to move or cough. In the evening they went out—we watched them from a window.

As we crept downstairs we saw a loaf left by the Nazis. Heavens, how we wanted it. But discretion won and we left it and crawled into some woods. Then discretion lost. We were so hungry that we decided to go back. We scrounged that loaf and it tasted to us better than a slap-up dinner.

Our next stop was at a big mansion. It was derelict, but in the kitchen we found tinned meat left by some French officers, scraps of bread, butter, sugar and rice. At night we heard cows mooing and we crept out with jugs. The cows were tethered and feeding in a field. We milked them each night. We had ten pints in one night, and made rice pudding on the anthracite cooker. Every night for four nights we milked those cows.

These smiling lads are the two Cameron Highlanders whose thrilling story, told in this page, shows that they worthily upheld the traditions of their great regiment.
Photo, "Daily Express"

Then, fit again, we made for the coast. We were only two miles from port. We spent many nights looking for a boat to cross the Channel. At last we found one, a 20-foot French fishing smack lying in a river.

Four more days were spent getting stores from the mansion aboard the boat, and then we had to wait another four for a suitable tide. Luckily we both knew how to sail a boat and fix a course by the stars and the sun.

It was a stormy, dark night when we started on our final dash. We were challenged at the mouth of the harbour. Machine-gun bursts followed us, but we kept at our oars until we were too exhausted to carry on. Somehow we got the mast up and put our boat under sail.

We took turns at the wheel while the other slept on deck. We were shipping too much water to sleep below. By six o'clock that evening we sighted England.

Three British vessels were moving along the coast. The last of these sighted us and came across at full speed. We couldn't speak. We just looked at each other and grabbed hands.

Typical of the British spirit is Mr. Percy H. Tibble, landlord of a Hampshire inn. He is here showing an airman the toy pistol with which he "held up" three Nazi airmen when they came down near his house, and compelled them to surrender.
Photo, Central Press

Why the Nazis Lost 140 Aircraft in Eight Days

Our Hurricane and Spitfire fighters, with a rate of fire of 9,600 rounds per minute from their eight machine-guns, are superior to the German fighters, which in fact they almost disregard in attacking the escorted bombers. Moreover, our fighters are more manoeuvrable than those of the enemy.

DURING the week ending July 13 the Nazis inaugurated massed attacks by daylight on our shipping convoys, in an attempt at blockading our coast. They came over with very large fighter escorts. Thus on July 10 our Spitfires over the South-east coast met a Dornier bomber with an escort of 30 Me 109s, flying in three layers between 8,000 and 12,000 feet. Two enemy fighters were shot down and two more damaged. Later, Spitfires met several Dorniers heavily protected by fighters. " It was like a cylinder of circling enemy aircraft," said one of our pilots. He climbed to the top of the " cylinder," did a spiral dive down the inside, attacked a Me 109 and a Dornier bomber, and put them both out. On this day the enemy lost for certain 15 aircraft, and others were badly damaged. We lost two British fighters, one pilot escaping. The conclusion to be drawn from these heavy fighter escorts is plain : so strong are the British defences that only thus closely guarded dare the Nazis send across their bombing aircraft.

There are two main reasons for the fighter superiority so disliked by the enemy. In initiative and daring, in readiness to take on bigger odds, our pilots and crews are far better than their opposite numbers in the Luftwaffe. Then again, our Hurricanes and Spitfires are better fighting machines, armed with eight Browning machine-guns firing forward. A converging fire at a rate of 1,200 rounds each gun per minute can be delivered, brought to bear at a point 250 yards in front of the aircraft. Against this terrific fire-power the German bomber can bring to bear only one at a time of its three movable machine-guns.

The German fighters are armed with one cannon (or shell gun) and four machine-guns, or with two cannon and two machine guns. From actual experience our Royal Air Force has found its own armament of all machine-guns to be superior. The German fighters, moreover, are said to be less manoeuvrable than our own.

The dauntless spirit of our airmen is exemplified by the story of a fighter pilot who recently shot down a Dornier 17. He had lost both legs in a pre-war crash. Invalided out of the R.A.F., he eventually became so skilful in the use of his metal legs that he resumed his cricket, and could also play tennis and squash. On the outbreak of war he "argued his way" into an R.A.F. Volunteer Reserve Medical Board and insisted he was fit for flying. The President of the Board persuaded the doctor to send him to a central flying school for a test. He passed with flying colours and went to a fighter squadron. In a " mild crash " a few months ago both his metal legs were bent, but an artificer put them straight, and within half an hour he was up in the air again. Now he is leading a squadron of Canadians.

Our ground defences have come remarkably well out of the first large-scale raids,

Flying Officer D. R. S. Bader, the legless R.A.F. pilot whose exploit in shooting down a Dornier 17 is related in this page, is now leading a fighter squadron of Canadians.

Photo, Sport & General

which began on June 18. The A.A. gunners have done very accurate work, and besides putting up fierce protective barrages have shot down a dozen or more enemy aircraft during the week under review. As to the convoys, the enemy raids have had negligible effect, and it is doubtful if even the Germans themselves believe that a decisive result can be gained by these attacks.

Now let us take a glance at the figures for the raids. In eight days the enemy lost 90 aircraft and fifty more were so badly punished that it is doubtful if more than a few could have reached home. This was accomplished with the loss of only thirteen of our fighters. During the period from June 18 to July 7 the Nazis lost 37 aircraft. Thus in the last four weeks twice as many German aircraft have been destroyed as during the 9½ months from the outbreak of war to June 17, when the enemy lost 63 machines in raids on Britain.

While our Royal Air Force has thus put up such a good show in the defence of Britain, its bomber squadrons have ceaselessly carried the war into the enemy's country. On the night of July 13-14, for example, fourteen enemy aerodromes in Holland and Germany were bombed ; other objectives included :

" Docks at Hamburg. Wilhelmshaven and Emden ; aircraft factories at Bremen and Deichshausen ; oil refineries at Monheim and Hamburg ; supply factories at Grevenbroich, Gelsenkirchen and Hamburg ; and goods yards at Hamm, Osnabruck and Soest."

All our aircraft returned safely ; one bomber on his homeward way even shot down an enemy fighter ! On the following night eight other enemy aerodromes and seaplane bases were attacked. No wonder that, faced with this kind of activity night after night, thousands of Germans from the raided regions are said to be fleeing to Czechoslovakia, Poland and other places of safety. All these targets are chosen in relation to the enemy's probable plans for the invasion of Britain : day by day our forces endeavour to nip in the bud any major operations at marshalling men, material or transport.

Highly significant, too, is the statement by our Air Ministry that the success of the R.A.F. attacks is " contributing effectively to a reduction in striking power of the German Air Force."

This Messerschmitt fighter 'plane was shot down during a recent raid on South-east England. The muzzles of the wing guns can be seen protruding. Air Ministry officials are examining the wreckage of the machine while a sentry mounts guard.   *Photo, Graphic Photo Union*

British Sea Power Still the Ruling War Factor

British merchant shipping inevitably suffered a higher rate of loss in June owing to the French collapse, the addition of 130 Italian submarines to the attacking forces, and renewed German activity in the Atlantic. But the rise in the average rate of sinkings was slight, total enemy losses were at least equal to the Allied, and enemy ships had been cleared off the oceans.

THE capitulation of France caused a rise in the amount of Allied shipping casualties during the month of June. The German occupation of the French Atlantic coastline caused inevitable losses among the British and Allied ships which were diverted from their normal peaceful occupations to assist in the evacuation of Allied personnel and material from the French ports. During June 40,946 tons gross of British

merchant ships were sunk by submarine and bombing attacks, in addition to 129,625 tons of Allied shipping. This compares with the 30,000 tons odd which were lost during the evacuation of Dunkirk in the previous month.

As far as concerns the sinking of merchant ships which were engaged on their normal voyages, the slight rise in the average rate of sinkings was due to the renewed activities of German submarines in the Atlantic from Gibraltar to Eire. They were dispatched there at the beginning of the month (as the renewed sinking of neutral vessels testified) to cooperate with the Italians when they were ready to declare war. The entry of Italy into the war also added some 130 submarines to the enemy fleet, and a few sinkings were made in a hitherto safe area, the Mediterranean. The British total of losses in this way, however, amounted only to 184,654 tons gross, a weekly average of only about 46,000 tons ; while neutral flags, mainly Greek, Finnish, and

Swedish, lost 73,864 tons gross (according to the Admiralty figures).

Three armed merchant cruisers were lost during June. They were the Cunard White Star liners "Andania" and "Carinthia," and the former Anchor liner "Caledonia," which had been renamed "Scotstoun." Another passenger liner in use as an auxiliary, the Orient liner "Orama," was sunk by superior enemy forces in a small naval encounter during the evacuation of Narvik. These four losses totalled 71,113 tons gross,

The world shipping situation by the end of June was completely changed. German and Italian shipping had been cleared from the seas. Norwegian, Danish, Dutch, and Belgian shipping were added to the strength of the Allies. The French surrender left the fate of many French ships in doubt, but some were retained in the service of Great Britain and the remaining Allies, while the others will not be permitted to sail at large. The only neutral European maritime nations left in operation by the middle of June were Greece and Sweden, and possibly Finland. These ships are mostly employed in worldwide tramp trades, and are therefore available for charter by Great Britain.

Hitler's success on the Continent had the counter-advantage of simplifying the economic blockade, and the control stations at the Orkneys, the Downs and Gibraltar were dispensed with. But contraband control did not therefore come to an end. During the month of June, 53,048 tons of contraband was intercepted, including 42,000 tons of petrol.

Although the anti-submarine fleet was depleted by naval operations off French ports, losses of ships in convoy were maintained at a low level. In the first ten months of the war, 27,247 merchant ships, British, Allied, and neutral, had been convoyed with the loss of only 40, a proportion of only 1 in 681.

Of individual losses it is difficult to speak, because of the reticence of the Admiralty in announcing casualties. Information that is too detailed would be of assistance to the enemy. It is known, however, that the Blue Star liner

"Wellington Star " was torpedoed in the Atlantic by a German submarine. She was a brand-new refrigerated cargo liner of 12,382 tons gross. Another large loss was the French liner "Champlain," which was reported to have struck an enemy mine off the French coast. A coincidence was the torpedoing of the Ellerman Wilson cargo liner "Guido" (3,921 tons) exactly 25 years after her predecessor of the same name met a similar fate.

'Around All the Power of the Navy'
From the Prime Minister's Broadcast, July 14 1940

AROUND all lies the power of the Royal Navy, with over 1,000 armed ships under the White Ensign, patrolling the seas, capable of transferring its force very readily to the protection of any part of the British Empire which may be threatened —capable also of keeping open our communication with the New World, from whom, as the struggle deepens, increasing aid will come. Is it not remarkable that after 10 months of unlimited U-boat and air attack upon our commerce, our food reserves are higher than they have ever been, and we have a substantially larger tonnage under our own flag, apart from great numbers of foreign ships in our control, than we had at the beginning of the war?

To offset the total Allied losses up to the end of June (1,430,523 tons gross) are the ships captured from the enemy. The seizure of about 75,000 tons of Italian shipping in June brought this total up to about 335,000 tons gross. Thus Allied and enemy losses were about equal, just over a million tons, after ten months of war. But Allied ships still had command of the sea, while enemy shipping had been driven off the oceans altogether. The enemy has little means available of replacing his losses, except by new building.

Over a million tons of ships are building in British yards alone, while Britain has also strengthened her fleet by purchase from overseas. Meanwhile, the fleets of her other Allies are wholly at the service of the Allied cause, and she is able to charter neutral ships, which the enemy cannot do. British sea power is, in fact, still the ruling factor in a Continental war.

This diagram puts into picture form the comparative losses for June and the whole war period of the enemy, British and neutrals.

Merchant Shipping Losses in Ten Months of War			
	Sept. 3-June 2 *Tons gross*	June 3-30 *Tons gross*	Totals Sept. 3-July 1 *Tons gross*
BRITISH :			
Liners, cargo vessels, etc. ...	764,945	184,654	949,599
Lost in naval operations ...	33,983	40,946	74,929
Naval auxiliaries ...	24,667	71,113	95,780
Naval trawlers ...	12,804	131	12,935
Totals	836,399	296,844	1,133,243
ALLIED	167,655	129,625	297,280
Totals	1,004,054	426,469	1,430,523
NEUTRAL	598,905	73,864	672,769
Totals	1,602,959	500,333	2,103,292
Enemy Losses to July 1			
	Sunk	Captured	Total
GERMAN	617,000	260,000	877,000
ITALIAN	169,000	75,000	244,000
	786,000	335,000	1,121,000

Eire Has an Air Force, Small but Good

Important work is being done by the ground staff in the control room. These two recruits are undergoing instruction at Baldonnel.

Ammunition is being loaded into a wing gun of a Browning Gladiator aircraft before starting on a flight. Such 'planes are among those used for the training of the personnel of the Eire Air Corps.

COMPARED with the air forces of other countries, Eire's Air Corps is insignificant in the number both of its men and machines. Yet the men are highly trained and may be expected, if put to the test, to show all the daring and fighting spirit of their race. Some of the most famous types of British aeroplanes are numbered among their machines, including Avro Ansons, Gloster Gladiators, Lysanders, and Supermarine Walruses. The headquarters of the Eire Air Corps is at Baldonnel Aerodrome, Clondalkin, Co. Dublin, where the service units are stationed. There is also a Flying Training School where pilots are trained. The technical ground staff is maintained by a scheme by which boys of from $16\frac{1}{2}$ to $17\frac{1}{2}$ years of age are admitted to an apprentice school and, after a period of three years' training, become qualified as skilled mechanics.

A Lewis gunner is in the cockpit of a Lysander aircraft (circle) ready to take off during his training at Baldonnel. The actual training of the gunners is done with camera guns which look something like Lewis guns, but carry nothing more deadly than films. Above, a Walrus Amphibian at Baldonnel Flying School.

These pilots under training at Baldonnel are lined up before their machines, fully equipped. There is no lack of cadets, and as soon as they have qualified they are passed out for service with the fighter squadrons, reconnaissance squadrons, and coastal patrol squadrons.
Photos, Keystone and G.P.U.

OUR DIARY OF THE WAR

WEDNESDAY, JULY 10, 1940

Sea Affair. Aircraft of Fleet Air Arm sank Italian destroyer and hulk used for storeship in harbour north of Augusta, Sicily.

Dutch tanker " Lucrecia " reported sunk by U-boat on July 7.

Latvian steamer sunk by German 'planes.

Air War. R.A.F. bombers delivered daylight attack on aerodromes at St. Omer and Amiens.

Malta raided ; no damage, few casualties.

Campaign against Italy. Blenheim bombers set fire to petrol dump near Tobruk, Libya. Several raids carried out on Macaaca aerodrome. Italians still persistently attacking British Moyale, on Kenya-Abyssinia frontier.

Sudanese police post at Kurmuk reported captured by enemy on July 7.

Home Front. Large-scale fighting took place all day off South and East coasts of England. Fourteen enemy aircraft shot down, and 23 severely damaged.

Bombs dropped in South Wales, damaging some buildings, and minor damage reported from districts in South of England. Damage done to residential district on South Coast ; four persons killed. Fleeing civilians machine-gunned.

General. British Union of Fascists banned as illegal.

French National Assembly accorded full powers to Pétain Government by 569 votes to 80.

THURSDAY, JULY 11

Sea Affair. H.M. patrol yacht " Warr.or II " sunk by enemy bomber.

Iranian cargo-boat " Beme " sunk by Italian submarine.

Reported that Italian troopship "Paganini" caught fire and sank on June 28 off Durazzo, with loss of 220 Italian and Albanian officers and men.

Air War. Dawn raid made on Boulogne aerodrome ; five enemy aircraft believed destroyed and others severely damaged.

R.A.F. bombers attacked military objectives in France and Low Countries. Aerodromes, barges and other targets bombed.

During night R.A.F. bombers extensively damaged enemy aerodromes in Holland. Munition works at Ludwigshaven and near Cologne bombed, blast furnaces at Siegburg attacked, dock buildings at Bremen damaged.

Home Front. Twenty-three enemy aircraft shot down and many more damaged when enemy bombers made daylight raids on shipping and other objectives round British coasts. Some damage and casualties reported.

Lord Craigavon stated that Mr. de Valera

had rejected offer concerning joint defence of Northern Ireland and Eire.

General. Marshal Pétain announced formation of new Government composed of 12 Ministers, with himself as Chief of the French State, and also appointment of 12 Governors of French Provinces.

FRIDAY, JULY 12

Air War. R.A.F. bombers made night raids on Emden and Kiel.

Campaign against Italy. Two enemy columns approaching Fort Capuzzo were effectively engaged.

From Mr. Churchill's Broadcast
July 14, 1940

I CAN easily understand how sympathetic on-lookers across the Atlantic or anxious friends in the yet unravaged countries of Europe, who cannot measure our resources or our resolve, may have feared for our survival when they saw so many States and kingdoms torn to pieces in a few weeks, or even days, by the monstrous force of the Nazi war machine. But Hitler has not yet been withstood by a great nation with a will-power the equal of his own. Many of these countries have been poisoned by intrigue before they were struck down by violence. They have been rotted from within before they were smitten from without. How else can you explain what has happened to France, to the French Army, to the French people, to the leaders of the French people ?

But here in our island we are in good health and in good heart. We have seen how Hitler prepared in scientific detail the plans for destroying the neighbour countries of Germany. He had his plans for Poland, and his plans for Norway. He had his plans for Denmark. He had his plans all worked out for the doom of the peaceful, trustful Dutch. And, of course, for the Belgians. We have seen how the French were undermined and overthrown. We may therefore be sure that there is a plan, perhaps built up over years, for destroying Great Britain, which, after all, has the honour to be his main and foremost enemy. . . .

ALL depends now upon the whole life-strength of the British race in every part of the world, and of all our associated peoples and of all our well-wishers in every land doing their utmost night and day, giving all, daring all, enduring all, to the utmost, to the end. This is no war of chieftains or of princes, of dynasties or national ambitions. It is a war of peoples and of causes. There are vast numbers, not only in this Island but in every land, who will render faithful service in this way, but whose names will never be known, whose deeds will never be recorded. This is the war of the Unknown Warriors. But let all strive without failing in faith or in duty, and the dark curse of Hitler will be lifted from our age.

Stated that Italian air losses in operations against Britain are now well over 100 mark.

Home Front. Eleven enemy bombers destroyed during raids round Britain. Raiders reported in South-west of England and in Wales, and over Scotland.

SATURDAY, JULY 13

Air War. R.A.F. Bomber Command made further night attacks on various objectives in Germany, including docks at Hamburg, Bremen, Wilhelmshaven, and Emden, factories, oil refineries and goods yards. Fourteen enemy aerodromes in Holland and Germany also attacked.

Coastal Command aircraft bombed munition dumps at Harlingen, on Dutch coast, and barges near Bruges.

Italian aircraft raided Aden and Malta.

Campaign against Italy. Small British garrison at Moyale still holding out.

R.A.F. made raids on El Aden, El Gubbi, and Bardia, and on shipping at Tobruk.

Home Front. Six bombers and six fighters shot down during enemy raids on shipping, and on land areas in England, Scotland, and Wales. Damage slight and casualties few, since many bombs fell in open country.

SUNDAY, JULY 14.

Sea Affair. Admiralty announced that H.M. destroyer " Escort " had been lost in the Western Mediterranean.

Air War. R.A.F. bombers attacked by night 'plane factory at Bremen, oil refineries at Bremen and Hamburg, goods yards at Hamm and Soest, and other military objectives.

Other aircraft bombed aerodromes in Holland and Germany.

Coastal Command aircraft attacked oil storage depot at Ghent.

Gibraltar raided three times. Bombers driven off by A.A. guns.

Campaign against Italy. British aircraft raided Italian posts in Libya and Eritrea. Shipping in Tobruk harbour again attacked.

Garrison in British Moyale, Kenya frontier, withdrew after holding out for five days.

Home Front. Air battle over Straits of Dover, when about 40 Junkers dive bombers and escorting Messerschmitts attacked a convoy. Five bombers and two fighters destroyed by R.A.F. fighters and A.A. guns.

General. Frenchmen in London, led by General de Gaulle, celebrated " Le Quatorze Juillet."

MONDAY, JULY 15

Sea Affair. Admiralty announced that H.M. submarine " Shark " was overdue and must be considered lost.

Air War. R.A.F. bombers attacked aerodromes at Lisieux and Evreux in Normandy. During night they again attacked those of Norderney and De Kooy.

Others bombed oil refineries at Hanover and targets at Paderborn, Hamm, and Osnabruck.

Coastal Command aircraft caused large fires in warehouses at Willemsoord harbour.

Palestine suffered first air raid when hostile aeroplanes dropped bombs over Haifa area.

Home Front. Enemy raiders bombed South Coast town, killing four people. Bombs were also dropped in other areas in England, and in South Wales.

TUESDAY, JULY 16

Sea Affair. C.-in-C., Mediterranean Fleet, disclosed that 20 Italian aircraft had been brought down during action between British and Italian fleets off Calabria on July 9.

Thirteen British merchant ships lost through enemy action during week ended July 7.

Air War. R.A.F. bombers attacked aerodromes in Northern France and barge concentrations near Armentières.

Enemy 'plane brought down in flames during raid on Malta. R.A.F. fighter shot down, first British casualty in five weeks' fighting.

Campaign against Italy. R.A.F. reconnaissances reported into Libya as far as Tocra, 30 miles north of Benghazi, and bombing raids on Tobruk, Bardia, and El Gazala.

Home Front. Three bombers brought down in sea off coast of Britain by fighters.

H.M. submarine " Shark," stated on July 15 to be overdue and considered lost, was of 760 tons displacement, with an armament of six torpedo tubes and one 3-in. gun. She was completed in 1934, and was a sister ship of the " Spearfish," " Salmon " and " Snapper." Inset is Lt.-Commander P. N. Buckley, lost with the rest of his crew.

Photos, Wright & Logan, G.P.U.

HERE'S A SMILE FOR HIS MAJESTY FROM THE NIGHT SHIFT

This group of workmen in a shell-producing factory in Southern England are idle only for a moment because they are watching the King talking to some of their mates while his Majesty was visiting the workers during the night shift.   The factory's motto is " Work like hell and it's hell for Hitler."   So well has it been lived up to that the daily production is double that of the last war.

Photo, P.N.A.

When the Highland Brigades Had To Surrender

In the war of 1914-1918 the 51st (Highland) Division of Territorials covered itself with glory, and already in this war it has seen some of the hardest fighting. Below we give the story of its stand on the Somme and the eventual surrender of two of its brigades, as described by Mr. Douglas Williams in the " Daily Telegraph," from material supplied him by the only officer of the two brigades to escape to England (see also page 108).

ON May 20, ten days after the Germans invaded Holland and Belgium, the 51st (Highland) Division was holding a portion of the French line in front of the Maginot forts in the Metz area. Three weeks later, in the storm of the German Blitzkrieg, two of its brigades found themselves prisoners of war ; the third, the 154th (Black Watch and Argylls), was on its way home to England, having been evacuated from Havre on June 11.

The French High Command had decided to send this division north to the Somme. After delay and much confusion owing to repeated change of orders, in the course of which the division's artillery and transport became temporarily lost, it finally arrived, on May 27, on the line of the River Bresle, from which it was sent forward to the Abbeville area to defend the Somme bridgeheads, in conjunction with units of the French Ninth Corps. Very heavy fighting developed from June 1 onwards, and combined attacks by the French, assisted by the 152nd and 153rd Brigades, at dawn on June 4 failed to secure the bridgehead, and the division suffered heavy casualties, especially the 152nd Brigade (Seaforths and Camerons).

A particularly brilliant incident of this day's fighting was the highly successful attack by the Gordons against enemy forces strongly entrenched in the Grand Bois ; the position was carried after the most gallant fighting, and the whole wood was cleared of the enemy.

Heavy enemy pressure, however, finally made a withdrawal inevitable, and the division fell back again to the line of the Bresle, where at one time it occupied a front more than 18 miles long. These positions were held for only three days ; then on the night of June 8 a further withdrawal was carried out to the line of the Bethune. Next morning (June 9) the 154th Brigade was detached and ordered to defend the Havre area, to take up a line running due south from Fécamp, in the hope that it could hold it until the other two brigades could join them.

Finally, on the evening of June 10, the remaining two brigades moved back along

the coast-line via Dieppe, to take up their final positions round St. Valery-en-Caux. A bridgehead was formed around St. Valery, the southern portion being held by units of the French Ninth Corps, the eastern face by the 153rd Brigade, and the western area by the 152nd Brigade. The following day the enemy appeared in force and launched heavy attacks with large numbers of tanks, assisted by very accurate mortar fire and the co-operation of masses of aircraft, against which, apart from ground fire, we had little protection.

Heavy casualties were suffered by the 153rd Brigade (Gordon Highlanders and Black

At the height of the German offensive the 51st (Highland) Division, which had been holding a part of the Maginot Line defences, became involved in the Allied retreat. The opening of June found it on the Somme, and on June 12 two of its brigades—the 152nd and 153rd—were compelled to surrender at St. Valery (lower photo). Its third brigade, the 154th, was more fortunate, for it was evacuated to England from the great base port of Le Havre (upper photo) on June 11.

Photos, E.N.A. and Wide World

At St. Valery All Was Lost Save Honour

Taken in France while it was still "all quiet on the Western Front," this photograph shows Gordon Highlanders being inspected by a French general at British G.H.Q.

One of the two brigades forced to surrender at St. Valery, the 152nd was composed of Seaforth and Cameron Highlanders. In this photograph a guard mounted by the Camerons is seen being inspected by the C.O., while inset is a smiling sergeant of the Seaforths.

Photos, Photographic News Agency and British Official : Crown Copyright

Watch). The men, however, held on gallantly throughout the day and the enemy failed to break through at any point on the eastern wing. Increasing fire, however, especially from heavy mortars, guided by accurate direction from the air, made the line ever more difficult to hold. At night the order was received to withdraw to the beaches and for the troops to embark at St. Valery, where vessels were to be sent to receive them. A rendezvous was given at St. Valery railway-station, and embarkation was to begin at 2 a.m. on June 12.

Gen. Fortune's final order to his division, dated St. Valery June 11, was to the effect that the Navy would probably make an effort to take the division off by boat, perhaps that night, or in two nights. All ranks must realize that the operation could be achieved only by the full co-operation of everyone, and that the utmost discipline must prevail. Men would board boats with equipment and arms ; vehicles would be rendered useless. Finally, if the enemy should attack before the whole force was evacuated, all ranks must realize that it would be up to them to defeat them. The enemy might attack with tanks, but we had anti-tank guns. If the infantry could stop the enemy's infantry, that was all that was required, while our anti-tank guns and rifles could inflict casualties on the enemy's armoured fighting vehicles.

The withdrawal was successfully made, and the men arrived near their rendezvous, where news was received that the embarkation could not be proceeded with. It appeared that the previous day, while our two brigades had successfully held their positions, the French Ninth Corps had been forced back, permitting the enemy to get round behind the British positions and occupy the port. Harbour and beaches were already occupied by the enemy, with tanks, mortars and machine-guns commanding every point of embarkation.

At 8 a.m. the French capitulated and handed over the town to the Germans. There was therefore no further hope of escape, and the remnant of the division, totalling about 150 to 200 officers and between 4,000 and 5,000 men, was taken prisoner by the enemy, together with the French Ninth Corps.

One of the unhappiest aspects of this tragic event was the fact that at Veules les Roses, a little port a few miles eastward of St. Valery, a large number of other British troops were at that moment being embarked. Had the 51st Division but known of this undoubtedly a great many of the men could have marched there without difficulty and got away.

When captured the British troops, while exhausted, short of food, and worn out by continuous marching and fighting in hot weather, were in high spirits and full of fight. They were not inconsiderately treated by their captors, though it was clear that the Germans had never expected such a large bag.

"Over 26,000 prisoners were taken," announced the German High Command, "including five French generals and one British."

Rations at first were scanty, a loaf of rye bread being divided among six, and water was short. The first day they were marched 12 miles to a camp near by, but after that conditions improved, and their subsequent movements were by motor-lorry.

Major-Gen. V. M. Fortune, G.O.C. of the division, was treated with special attention, and was permitted to keep his motor-car, his A.D.C. and his servant. Similar courtesies were shown to the two brigadiers with him.

How the Stage Was Set for the French Armistice

Hitler exploited to the full the dramatic possibilities of the fact that he was able to impose the humiliating terms on France by clever stage management. He dictated them on June 21 in the railway coach in the Forest of Compiègne in which British and French delegates imposed the armistice terms of November, 1918, on Germany. A preliminary ceremony was a parade of German troops round the coach (right).

First the coach was drawn out of the pavilion in which it was housed (see photograph in page 708, Vol. 2) into the position above the memorial slab on which it stood in November, 1918. Below is the coach with some of the German soldiers who helped to put it in position.

Two of the French delegates are here arriving in the Forest of Compiègne to sign the armistice terms. Between the two German officers are M. Noel and General Huntziger. In the photograph on the left is Hitler in his supreme hour when, after the French delegation had received the terms, he left the coach. In the first row, left to right, are General von Brauchitsch, C.-in-C. of the Army; Admiral Raeder, C.-in-C. of the Navy, Hitler and Goering. In the second row are Hess and von Ribbentrop. (These photographs like those in pages 14-15 come, of course, from German sources.)

Photos, Associated Press

Where the Nazis Came: French Towns Then and Now

The town of Vitry-le-Francois, which was Joffre's headquarters in the early weeks of the last war, had this very ornate gate. In the early days of June 1940 the town was bombarded by the Germans during the fighting on the Marne, and, right, it is seen in flames.

Nine years ago the beautiful old city of Orleans (left), shrine of Joan of Arc, was en fête for the celebration of the fifth centenary of France's great deliverance. This year it fell before the Germans and was badly damaged by gunfire. Above is one of its devastated streets.

These two photographs show Rethel, the small town on the Aisne which endured four years of German occupation in the last war. In one is seen the Church of St. Nicolas in the days of peace, while in the other débris is being cleared away after the German entry in June 1940.

Photos, E.N.A., Associated Press, and Wide World

Will Hitler Come With a Fleet of Barges?

Just as Napoleon at Boulogne threatened an invasion of England 136 years ago, so today Hitler stands on that same shore, threatening, blustering—and preparing. Amongst his preparations are said to be an armada of small craft, of which (as is told below) he has a number of varied kinds and uses at his disposal.

NIGHT after night for weeks past—and sometimes during the day, too—amongst the objectives of Britain's bombers in the raids on Germany and German-occupied Europe have been concentrations of barges in the waterways of Holland and Belgium and Northern France. The reason is obvious; those barges which have been splintered and burnt or left high and dry on the banks of canals whose lock-gates have been blown up, may well have been chosen for inclusion in that armada which Hitler is reported to be assembling for his oft-threatened invasion of England.

Certainly the Fuehrer has plenty of vessels to choose from, vessels of many different shapes and sizes, vessels designed for many a varied use. There are the great barges, some so big that they can carry the contents of three hundred 10-ton coal wagons which in peace time make the passage up and down the Rhine and Maas. There are the Diesel-engined river craft which have appeared in increasing numbers of recent years on the waterways of the Low Countries and of Eastern France as far as the Swiss border; many of these make coastal trips from Rotterdam to Antwerp, and there is little doubt that given reasonably fine weather they could make the passage of the North Sea

sufficient size and of sufficiently strong construction to carry tanks, field artillery, anti-aircraft guns, and heavy equipment.

We may presume that they would be assembled at a number of enemy ports on the coast of Western Europe—in particular, Rotterdam, the Hook of Holland, Flushing, Antwerp and the Scheldt estuary, Zeebrugge, Dunkirk, Calais, and Boulogne; Brest and Cherbourg might be used if it were decided to attempt a landing in the south-west of England or on the shores of Ireland. Numerous as these possible assembly points are, we have good reason to believe that several of them have been so damaged by British demolition squads and aircraft that for a time, at least, they must be quite unusable. Moreover, the communiqués of the R.A.F. abundantly testify that Boulogne, Calais, and the rest are closely watched, and any suspicious concentrations are immediately bombed.

Of the bases mentioned, probably Flushing and Antwerp are the nearest to England of those which are reasonably intact. To make the crossing from the Scheldt to the Lincolnshire coast the armada would have to travel some 240 miles, but to the Kent coast the distance would be only some 135 miles. The slow-moving barges would require from 24 to

unable to stop the embarkation of the B.E.F. and French from Dunkirk—in the broad daylight of early summer.

As we have been told by Mr. Churchill, even five divisions (say, 100,000 men), very lightly equipped,

" would require 200 to 250 ships, and with modern air reconnaissance and photography it would not be easy to collect such an armada, marshal it, and conduct it across the sea, without any powerful naval forces to escort it and with the very great possibility that it would be intercepted long before it reached the coast and the men all drowned in the sea, or at the worst blown to pieces with their equipment while they were trying to land."

Then, in addition, there is a great system of minefields, recently strongly reinforced.

If the weather were fine and the sea fairly calm, if the British Navy were temporarily or permanently out of the picture, if the Germans had superiority in the air, if they had a reasonable share of Hitler's customary luck—then the passage across the narrow seas might be made by these lumbering, slow-moving flotillas of strangely-assorted craft. But there are altogether too many " ifs."

When Napoleon prepared a similar invasion he was in some ways much better situated than is Hitler. He was able to assemble his great army of 100,000 men at Boulogne without any fear of bombing attacks or prying reconnaissance 'planes; he had practically the whole Continent under his complete control, political and economic; he had collected a great fleet of flat-bottomed ships which had to fear no lurking submarines, no raiding 'planes, no speeding warships, but simply men-of-war which were dependent on the wind for their movement.

Yet for two years Napoleon waited, and then in a fit of disgust shook his fist at the unassailable white cliffs of England, and marched away to Ulm and Austerlitz. Will Hitler have to, or could he, wait so long?

Hitler's invading army might cross the North Sea in bluff-bowed motor craft like the "Rapid," 190 tons, seen above. Many of these vessels were engaged in trade with British ports, carrying merchandise from Holland. Some are a good deal larger, and all are built especially to stand rough seas.

under their own power. Then there are the big cargo lighters used extensively in the docks of Amsterdam; the powerful ferry boats, driven by steam or Diesel engines, which are used for crossing the Scheldt between Antwerp and Flushing; there are the tugs attached to the Dutch and Belgian ports, and the big flat-bottomed paddle tugs which paddle their way up and down the Rhine. Again, there are the Dutch motor coasters, 500 to 600 tons apiece, engined with Diesels, which are good sea boats and are often used to cross the North Sea.

Altogether there must be some hundreds of small craft which might be used to carry considerable numbers of German troops across the narrow strip of water which separates the Continent from our own shores: and quite a number of these boats are of a

48 hours to make the crossing, and it need hardly be said that it should be quite impossible for them to move any distance, even in thick fog, without their presence being discovered by the British Navy and the R.A.F. Even air action alone might be expected to have a devastating effect on the flotilla, although it should be remembered that the German air force was

All Hitler's army would have to be carried in shallow-draught ships and barges or lighters. Suitable craft are Dutch coastal motor barges such as this. They are good sea-boats and are familiar to many Londoners, for they are of sufficiently shallow draught to enable them to be navigated as far up the Thames as Kingston.

Photos. Nautical Photo Agency

Waterways of the Reich Bombed by the R.A.F.

Careful photographic reconnaissance carried out with astounding daring by the R.A.F. made possible the successful bombing of the aqueduct of the Dortmund-Ems Canal, announced on July 17. The top photograph, one of those taken by the reconnaissance 'planes, shows barge traffic on the canal which was used largely to transport munitions. The photograph immediately above proves incontestably how successful the raid was. Large craters can be seen in the canal bed, some of them 30 feet across, and all the water has drained away. Further details are given in page 110.

Duisburg, an important town lying between the Rhine and the Ruhr, with which rivers it is connected by a canal, was also bombed by the R.A.F. The Parallel Harbour is here seen photographed from the air, showing a wharf which was damaged by the raiders. Owing to the heavy damage caused to roads and railways by R.A.F. raids, the Nazis had been obliged to divert much traffic to their inland waterways.

Photos, British Official: Crown Copyright, and G.P.U.

The Admiral Was Disappointed With the Italians

For the first few weeks of the Anglo-Italian war there was little to record in the way of naval operations, but in July there were several brushes between the two fleets which are described in the article that follows. As will be seen, they were inconclusive actions because the Italians refused to venture their main fleet in a prolonged combat with Britain's battle squadrons.

IF we may believe Mussolini's propagandists, the Mediterranean has been swept clean of Britain's warships and the sea is now what imperial-minded Italians have so long claimed it ought to be, an Italian lake. How, then, shall we explain the presence in both the western and eastern basins of the Mediterranean of powerful squadrons of the Royal Navy—squadrons so powerful that they were able to engage Italy's battle fleet and after the engagement maintain their patrol?

There for a certainty they were on Tuesday, July 9—one force based on Gibraltar. including H.M.S. " Hood " and H.M.S.

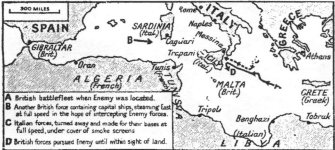

A British battlefleet when Enemy was located.
B Another British force containing capital ships, steaming East at full speed in the hope of intercepting Enemy forces.
C Italian forces, turned away and made for their bases at full speed, under cover of smoke screens
D British forces pursued Enemy until within sight of land.

This map of a portion of the Mediterranean shows the movements of British and Italian ships during the action of July 9, 1940, when the Italian fleet turned away and fled to harbour.

" Ark Royal," carrying out a sweep towards the Central Mediterranean, and carrying it out successfully despite heavy air attacks by Italian bombers and without encountering any of the enemy's surface ships ; while simultaneously another force was conducting a similar reconnaissance in the Ionian Sea to the west of Crete.

This second fleet was under the command of Admiral Sir Andrew Cunningham, British C.-in-C. in the Mediterranean, and consisted of a squadron of light cruisers supported by several battleships. During the morning they sighted an enemy force consisting of two battleships, a large number of cruisers, among which were some 8-in. gun cruisers, and approximately 25 destroyers. Early in the afternoon contact was made by the two cruiser forces, but after a brief period of intense fire the Italian cruisers retired as soon as they came within

the extreme range of the British battleships. A few salvos were exchanged between the battleships on either side, and one of the Italian vessels sustained a hit with a 15-in. shell. Then an intense smoke screen was laid down by the Italian destroyers, and behind this their ships, big and small, retired at full speed. The action then developed into a chase, the enemy being pursued until the coast of Italy came within sight. There, lying off shore, our forces remained to offer battle until the evening, despite a succession of bombing attacks by waves of Italian aircraft.

It would, indeed, have been suicide on the part of the Italian squadron to attempt a prolonged action, for, according to a Rome account, the British squadron included three of the Barham class battleships, each of which mounts eight 15-in. guns, against which the Italians had ranged two battleships of the Cavour class, reconstructed vessels carrying ten 12·6-in. guns apiece. In terms of fire-power the British battleships could fire 95,000 lb. of shell per minute as compared with 36,000 lb. from the Italian ships.

In the light of this superiority of fire-power we may see what little value there is in the claim made in the Italian communiqué that " at the close of the night the British squadron proceeded in a southerly direction pursued by Italian naval forces." The truth of the matter would seem to be that the British squadron approached as near as possible to the Italian coast, which, if it were Taranto, as has been suggested, would be a matter of some 15 miles. Then, when it became evident that the enemy had no intention of renewing the battle, the British squadron continued its operations, which included the convoying of a number of ships through the eastern Mediterranean.

In the course of the battle one of the Italian battleships was hit and the Italians

admitted the loss of 29 men killed and 69 wounded ; they also announced that they had lost a submarine and the destroyer " Zeffiro." On the other hand, no hits were made by the enemy by bomb or gunfire on the British ships, and a number of enemy aircraft—twenty in all—were shot down.

Of course, Mussolini claimed the action as a triumph. In an Order of the Day to the Italian Navy he told them : " You have obtained our first naval victory—you have taught the enemy by direct hits, by gunfire, that one cannot challengingly approach the Italian coast." The Italian communiqués further claimed that many of the British ships had been hit by bombs, shells, or torpedoes, that an aircraft-carrier had been " rendered motionless " by a bomb, and that " one ship, probably a battleship, was sunk "—claims which our Admiralty hardly took the trouble to deny.

Ten days later came the news of a further British success against the Italian fleet in the Mediterranean. About 7.30 on the morning of July 19 H.M.A.S. " Sydney," accompanied by a small destroyer force, engaged two Italian cruisers to the north-westward of Crete. The enemy ships altered their course south-westwards and endeavoured to escape, but the British ships made a determined attack, and the " Sydney's " fire was so accurate that one of the Italian ships, the 6-in.-gun cruiser " Bartolomeo Colleoni," was hit in a vital spot and forced to reduce speed, when the British destroyers completed her destruction. The second cruiser, of the same class, was chased and hit several times, but her superior speed saved her from a similar fate.

As the " Bartolomeo Colleoni " went down, 545 of her crew were rescued by boats lowered from the British ships ; and it is unpleasant to have to record that while they were engaged in this work they were bombed time and again by Italian 'planes.

In his report on the running fight of July 9 Admiral Cunningham described it as " a disappointing action," but, however disappointing to the British, it must have been still more so to those Italians who have been deluded into believing that Britain's sea power is a thing of yesterday.

It is not often that the camera can give the lie direct to Nazi and Fascist distortions of the truth, but this photograph is one of the exceptions. It shows an Italian battleship of the " Conti di Cavour " class fleeing before the British Fleet. A salvo from a British battleship is falling ahead of her, and the guns from her after-turret (trained aft) have just fired, thus proving incontestably that it was the British ships that pursued the Italian ships, and not vice versa as the Italians claimed.

Photo, Associated Press

H.M.A.S. "Sydney" and Her Victim

Named after the light cruiser that sank the "Emden" in November, 1914, the new "Sydney" (top photo, 6,830 tons, completed 1935) of the Royal Australian Navy sank in a running fight N.W. of Crete, on July 19, the Italian cruiser "Bartolomeo Colleoni" (5,069 tons, lower photo), claimed to be the fastest in the world. Both carried eight 6-in. guns, but the Italian's speed was at least 37 knots against the 32·5 knots of H.M.A.S. "Sydney." Inset, Capt. J. A. Collins, R.A.N., of the "Sydney," who was awarded the C.B.   *Photos, Charles E. Brown, Wide World and Associated Press*

They Are in Britain's Battle-Line in Africa

IN the ranks of Britain's armies in Africa are to be found soldiers of many different races—white, black, and brown, inheritors of vastly different traditions, dwellers in many a widely-contrasted stage of culture. Out of a wealth of types and personalities we illustrate in this page a selection which, however inadequate, may make some claim to be reasonably typical. Natives of the Kenya highlands, the deserts of Somaliland, and the tropical zone of West Africa here take their place beside soldiers of the white races drawn from the vast open spaces of Rhodesia and the towns and villages of the Union of South Africa.

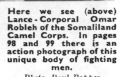

Here is a sergeant-major of the King's African Rifles, that fine body whose battle honours include " Ashanti 1900," " Somaliland 1901-1904," and " East Africa 1914-1918."

Photo, William Davis

Here we see (above) Lance - Corporal Omar Robleh of the Somaliland Camel Corps. In pages 98 and 99 there is an action photograph of this unique body of fighting men.

Photo, Paul Popper

In large measure the defence of the British Commonwealth in Africa falls upon the defence forces of the Union of South Africa, which enjoy a high reputation for spirit and efficiency. Below, some soldiers of the Union are at practice with a Bren gun.

Photo, Fox

The Royal West African frontier force consists of the Nigeria Regiment, the Gold Coast Regiment, the Sierra Leone Battalion, and the Gambia Company. Some men of the last-named are shown below during training. In the Great War the Company fought in the Cameroons and East Africa.

Photo, P.N.A.

The riflemen seen in our centre photograph are part of the defence forces of the great colony of Southern Rhodesia. They are engaged in mortar practice at the camp at Bulawayo.

Photo, Courtesy of S. Rhodesia Government

The Empire's Part in the Battle of Britain

As the weeks pass the British Empire—that " great empire " which Hitler prophesied on
July 19 " will be destroyed "—grows more and more united in its determination to defeat
the Totalitarian might. Realizing the urgent need of air power reinforcement, the Colonies,
as related here, are making magnificent contributions to the new Colonial Air Armada.

THROUGHOUT history no Empire has shown greater cohesion in war than the British Empire in 1940. There is an enthusiasm and enterprise in defence which holds the attention of all free peoples now that the heart of the Empire remains the last stronghold of freedom in Europe.

From possessions distributed throughout the Seven Seas every form of assistance for the Battle of Britain is pouring in to build up the armed forces and the financial strength of the Motherland. At the moment the most outstanding help in Empire defence develops from the air-mindedness of Britons overseas. From India to the Gold Coast, from Malaya to the Falkland Islands, they appreciate that their safety depends upon mobile forces to protect key points, forces possibly thousands of miles away, which the international situation has made vital strongholds for the preservation of the unity of the Empire. Thus it is not difficult to see how British-Australasian sea trade and Gibraltar are definitely interlocked.

Funds have been started by newspapers, individuals, organizations throughout the Colonies, the Dependencies and in India to buy aircraft for a special force within the Royal Air Force. This has become known as the Colonial Air Armada—a significant striking force of 40 heavy bombers and 160 Spitfires, capable of smothering the enemy with 100 tons of explosives daily.

Sections of this Air Armada are to be named after the donors, and machines will be named within the sections according to portions of the donors' territories. We can expect soon to hear of the Natal Squadron, the Malaya Squadron and the like ; Zanzibar's two Spitfires, for which £20,000 has been sent, are to be known as " Zanzibar " and " Pemba." But, let it be noted, they will not be so marked. The name will not; of course, be written on the fuselage, and squadron names will not be inscribed on aircraft either. So, like troops in modern battle, the only identification of Air Armada machines will be in R.A.F. records—but after the " show " the Press, and thus the donors, will learn what their gifts have been doing. The manning of this Special Force, as far as circumstances permit, will

be by men from overseas. The ideal set up will be for men from Hong Kong to operate Hong Kong gift machines.

The Dominions have not so far contributed to the Air Gift Fund because they have their own air forces, which naturally receive first attention. As they are self-governing communities, their war effort is associated

How deeply affected by the war are the people of South Africa is shown by the fact that in every city in the Union there is a daily two minutes' pause at noon for silent prayer. This is the scene in the famous Adderley Street, Cape Town, during the silence.

Not only the great Dominions but the smallest islands within the Empire are standing to arms, and here are two scenes, thousands of miles apart, but both typical. In one, on the small island of Bermuda, soldiers of the Volunteer Rifle Corps are on guard at a wireless station, a link in Imperial communications. Right, the veteran Empire statesman and soldier, General Smuts, is inspecting South African infantry at Johannesburg.

Photos, courtesy South African Government, and P.N.A.

Empire Men & Women Serve in the Homeland

Newfoundland, the oldest of British Colonies, has sent many of her stalwart sons to fight for the Mother Country. Among a contingent that recently arrived in Britain were a number of artillerymen. They were well trained and soon took up their part in home defence. Some of them are here seen at practice with a 9·2-in. howitzer.

Photo, Central Press

On July 16, 1940, Mr. R. B. Bennett, a former Prime Minister of Canada, presented to the High Commissioner of Canada, Mr. Vincent Massey, on behalf of the Canadian Red Cross Society, a hospital with 600 beds, built on a site in the Home Counties given by Lord and Lady Astor. The ceremony took place in front of the building, and right are some of the Canadian nurses who, with a contingent of troops, were present at the ceremony.

Photo, L.N.A.

'Colonial Air Armada' For Defence of Empire

with all sorts of domestic considerations which do not affect the Colonies. If war develops beyond Europe they are more likely, being larger, to suffer individual attack. Self-sufficiency in defence is their major consideration. Thus India has covered all potentially vulnerable areas with an observer and air-raid warning system, modelled upon the British one with sirens, wardens and the like. Canada has built an aluminium refining factory near Ottawa which can turn out as much aluminium as the whole of Germany could at the start of this war.

Some Gifts for the Colonial Air Armada

Ceylon—State Council	... ...	£375,000	
" "Times of Ceylon " Fund		15,000	
Private donations ...	...	5,000	£395,000
Malaya—" Straits Times " }			
" Straits Echo " }		227,000	
" Malay Mail "	...	45,000	£272,000
Gold Coast—Government Gift	...	100,000	
Government Loan		500,000	
" Gold Coast Spitfire Fund "	... ...	15,000	£615,000
Trinidad business men	... ...		42,000
Falkland Islands ...	... ...		50,000
Hong Kong—" South China Morning Post " }			
" Hong Kong Telegraph " }			40,662
Bengal Residents ...	... ...		40,000
British Guiana—Residents...	...	30,000	
" Georgetown Fund "		10,000	40,000
Zanzibar Executive Council	...		20,000
Natal—" Speed the 'Planes Fund "			201,000
Jamaica—" Jamaica Gleaner " ...			20,000
Windward Islands—St. Vincent Arrowroot Assn.			5,000
Bahamas-Nassau—Private donations			5,000
			£1,745,662

Australia has put its all in under the same motto as in 1914 : " To the last man, to the last shilling." Munition and aircraft workers exceed 17,000, and besides Maribyrnong and Lithgow, four very large new munitions plants are going up.

From the granaries of the Empire food is pouring into this country also. Canada has 431,500,000 bushels exportable surplus waiting for ships. Her bacon is coming quickly to supplement the depleted supplies since Denmark fell beneath the Swastika. Australian wool is filling ships' holds after an excellent clip. New Zealand butter, mutton

This artist's impression of bombers and fighters of the Colonial Air Armada (40 bombers, 160 fighters in all) symbolizes the magnificent war contribution of the Colonies.
Photo, British Official : Crown Copyright

and the like have never reached so high a rate of production. And the navies, armies and air forces of the Dominions are expanding with that speed which typifies the New World.

Australia, out of a population of less than 7,000,000 has 150,000 men serving in these forces. Canada, with 11,000,000 people, when recently authorized units have been filled will have 200,000 men under arms. New Zealand, with 1,500,000 people, has rallied about 75,000 men to the colours. India is creating a new army of 100,000 men in addition to her Navy and Air Force, services which are quite distinct from the British Forces in India. South Africa, out of the 2,000,000 Europeans available for service, has 80,000 under arms.

India, too, has made generous aircraft contributions. Here Sir Alexander Murray, a well-known Indian business man, is handing over to Captain Balfour, Under Secretary of State for Air, a flight of 'planes presented by the East India Fund. *Photo, P.N.A.*

Across the Arid Plains of East Africa Races a

One of the finest and at the same time most picturesque regiments among the British forces in Africa is the Somaliland Camel Corps, a troop of which is seen here on the great plain of Tugwijaleh, which is covered with grass burnt so yellow that it reflects the heat of the sun more fiercely than sand. The men of the Camel Corps are used to such conditions, and their white officers quickly become inured to them. In peacetime the Camel Corps number just over 400 officers and men.

# of Britain's Famed Somaliland Camel Corps

In the fighting against the Italians in East Africa, the Somaliland Camel Corps have greatly distinguished themselves. They have made frequent daring raids across the frontiers, a typical one being that in the middle of July, when they raided the Abyssinian frontier post of Daberabo and destroyed 20,000 rounds of ammunition—a most important piece of work, for the Italians have many hundred miles of frontier to guard with no hope of replenishing their ammunition.

Come Hitler's Men Where'er They May

A month's experience of air raids showed that the danger of flying window glass was serious. Precautions include the fixing of strips of gummed paper, lace fabric and wire netting. In the instance shown above, where a bomb fell only 25 yards away, gummed paper strips saved the windows of one house while its neighbour lost every pane. In other cases paper strips proved inferior to gummed lace at greater distances.

With the immense speed-up of home defence preparations the King became much occupied with inspections of new works and counter-invasion training. Here he watches an incoming patrol of the Scots Guards held up at a post. Note the position of the patrol's rifle.

The women of a Lancashire mill have made their own rifle range, learned to shoot, and now take turns of duty with the night watchman. The oldest and youngest of them are a "grannie" of 51 and a girl of 19, seen here.

"Should the invader come," said the Prime Minister, "there will be no placid lying down of the people." These photographs represent but a few of uncounted aspects of home defence. Left, padlocked chains immobilize an unattended lorry. Above, in the West Country tree trunks with wheels attached are quickly swung across the road.

Photos, Fox, "Daily Mirror," P.N.A., Planet and Topical Press

The Men of Britain Have Their Reception Ready

The Prime Minister was given a rousing welcome by the troops when he visited the Southern Command in the middle of July. Mr. Churchill is seen in circle with Lieut.-General Sir Alan Brooke, who on July 19 was appointed C.-in-C., Home Forces.

Mr. Churchill closely examined the defence works during his tour of inspection, and is seen, left, emerging from a blockhouse. The photo above shows troops jumping out of a lorry to take part in defence exercises watched by the Premier.

British Official Photographs: Crown Copyright

September 1939 : the Polish War in Retrospect

To earlier pages of " The War Illustrated " E. Royston Pike has contributed many an
article on Poland's struggle against the invader, but none has given him more pleasure
in the writing as this further tribute to a little country's magnificent defence, reviewed in
the light of that latest and most disastrous of the War's phases, the Battle of France.

FOR seventeen days, from September 1 to September 17, Poland resisted the whole weight, the fullest force, of Germany's military might, and even after that fateful Sunday when Stalin delivered his all-too-effective stab in the back, Polish resistance was continued until early in October (or for 35 days in all) by isolated remnants of the army and by beleaguered towns and cities. Nine months later Hitler turned against France, and in 35 days, reckoning from May 14, when his troops smashed the French Ninth Army at Sedan,

Moreover, the Germans possessed a great superiority in armament and fire power ; for example, one German infantry division = 84 guns, 136 machine-guns, 54 trench mortars, and 54 anti-tank guns ; while one Polish infantry division = 48 guns, 60 machine-guns, 18 trench mortars, and 27 anti-tank guns.

Not only were the Poles far weaker in men, guns and 'planes than the enemy, but they were given an impossible problem in strategy. Poland had no Maginot Line, and possesses practically nothing in the

11 already amounted to 91,000 killed and 146,000 wounded, a total of nearly 240,000, with 413 aeroplanes shot down and 461 tanks destroyed or put out of action. Only the Nazi archivists can say how wide, one way or the other, are these figures of the mark ; but the most conservative estimate puts the German losses at 130,000. The Polish losses were on a corresponding scale ; probably in proportion to the numbers engaged they were even greater, for against Germany's immensely superior mechanized armament the Poles had nothing to oppose but their bodies. One estimate puts them at 150,000— of whom 35,000 were killed.

In addition to this prodigal outpouring of blood on the battlefields, Poland was sorely wounded in every city, town and village as the warplanes of the enemy killed and destroyed everyone and everything that had the misfortune to be shadowed by their ominous wings. The war in Poland was a total war, and women and children and old men were slaughtered as a matter of policy, in the hope of spreading panic and disruption behind the lines.

Strikingly revealing and filled with human appeal are the photographs taken by Julien Bryan, the American cameraman, in Warsaw in the days during and immediately following the terrible siege of September, 1939. Above is one of them—one showing Warsaw's citizens constructing with feverish haste shelters which they hoped would shield them and theirs from the death-dealing bombs rained down by an unending succession of Nazi warplanes.

to June 17, when the French applied for an armistice, he brought to the ground the country which for centuries had been accounted one of the greatest military powers on the Continent.

When the Germans invaded Poland on September 1, 1939, they were possessed of every military advantage. Poland was taken by surprise, but even if her mobilization had been complete she would still have been heavily outnumbered, for at the most she could have mustered about 4,000,000 men ; in fact, only a million were mobilized in time to take part in the September campaign.

Germany had already concentrated along the Polish frontier some 1,300,000 men— between 60 and 70 divisions of infantry, 15 armoured and motorized divisions, and at least 2,000 warplanes, including 1,100 bombers. Against these Poland could range, even on paper, only 22 divisions of infantry, one mechanized brigade and, worse still, only 300 first-line warplanes. In the event, however, six infantry divisions went into action incomplete, and two could not be mobilized at all. Thus the German effectives were three times superior in infantry and twenty times superior in armoured and motorized divisions, and six or seven times stronger in the air.

shape of natural obstacles. The attack was developed along an open front of about 1,600 miles, unfortified and unfortifiable ; and from her territory in East Prussia Germany was able not only to cut off the Poles in the Corridor and Posen, but to deliver a powerful attack from the north flank, while the main attack was directed from the west.

From the first the hopelessness of many of the Polish positions must have been obvious to attacker and defender alike, yet to the eternal glory of the Polish arms let it be remembered, to take just one example, that the little outpost of Hela, attacked though it was from land, sea and air, held out until October 1. Even the end of the campaign did not see the end of resistance, for during the weeks that followed reports trickled through to the outside world of guerilla bands continuing the struggle from fastnesses in the Carpathians and the eastern marshes.

At length the war was over and Poland was a conquered country. But the Germans had had to pay dearly for their victory. True, in his speech to the Reichstag on October 6 Hitler said that the German losses were 10,572 killed, 30,322 wounded and 3,400 missing—a total of 44,294. German documents which fell into Polish hands go to show that the Nazi losses up to September

For Weeks They Held the Pass

While the battle was in progress, while the Polish divisions were fighting first on the frontier, then on the line of the rivers Narew— Vistula—San, then in the south-east on the Dniester and Stryj, while Warsaw maintained itself as a flaming stronghold of Polish independence—the great armies of France were enabled to mobilize and take up their positions undisturbed in the Maginot Line and Britain was given a breathing-space in which to fill some of the gaps in her defences which ought to have been closed years before.

In vain Poland looked to her Allies for assistance in the mortal struggle in which she was engaged. Whatever the reason for their failure to help, it is a fact that not a French or British 'plane flew to join the hard-pressed Poles, not a French or British warship went to the succour of the Polish sailors and soldiers fighting for their lives and their country's honour at Gdynia. Then and for months afterwards, the Germans had no need to worry overmuch about black-out or A.R.P., for we were careful to let it be known that the 'planes they heard at night were loaded with leaflets and not bombs.

By the middle of that sunburned September there seemed to be good reason to believe that the Polish front would shortly be stabilized ; the main German onslaught had been slowed up and in several places there had been smashing counter-attacks, notably General Sosnowski's near Lwow. But at the exactly-timed moment Russia intervened and struck the blow which brought Poland to her knees. Even so, it was not until September 22 that Lwow surrendered to the Russians ; Warsaw fought on, a burning shambles, until September 27 ; and the Hela Peninsula held out for two days more.

Great in battle, Poland did not lose her greatness in defeat. Many a German within her bounds contributed to her downfall by spying and sabotage in the cause of the enemy, but amongst the Poles themselves there were none to glory in the role of Fifth

The Poles Fought Even Better Than We Thought

Hundreds of thousands of Poles were carried away by the Nazis as prisoners of war to serve as serfs on the farms and in the camps and factories of the Reich. Here are some of them at dinner-time.   *Photo, E.N.A.*

execution yards echo with the shouts of defiance, the bold calls of liberty. A brigade of Polish Carpathian Chasseurs fought heroically side by side with the British and French in Norway, while Polish legions in France, after helping to garrison the Maginot Line, fought when the French themselves had given up the fight ; one division managed to carry out its orders to break through the German ring and reach this country, where today it forms part of the garrison of the British fortress.

" Our place today," said General Sikorski in a broadcast to the Polish nation on June 24, just after the French capitulation, " is in the line of battle. We are fulfilling our alliance with Great Britain. The Polish nation will persevere in the struggle against Germany to the end."

Columnist, none who sought to anticipate the notoriety of Quisling. In vain did the Nazi Governor-General invite Poles of eminence to form a Cabinet under his direction ; one and all of those approached refused the dubious honour, and Frank's rule was denied even the rottenest rags of legality.

On the morrow of defeat in Poland there were few recriminations and no gibings, no snarling attacks, on the allies of yesterday. The Polish fleet was not employed as a bargaining counter to curry favour with the victor, but such of the ships as survived sailed away through innumerable hazards to honourable service with the Navy of Britain. Poland's politicians and generals were not made of very heroic stuff, perhaps, but Moscicki and Beck preferred to leave their country rather than stay to make terms with the enemy. There were no histrionics in Warsaw about defending every street, every square, every house ; when Lord Mayor Starzynski said, " We shall fight to the last man if we have to go down fighting," he meant what he said, and the men and women of Warsaw meant it, too. They *did* fight, in a spirit of hopeless passion, in a mood of sublime unreasonableness, so that the name of Warsaw will ring down the ages as a symbol of the most desperate valour.

' Poland Always Faithful '

Turning the pages, the blood-stained pages, of Poland's history, one is caught up time and again by some instance, pathetic if it were not so noble, of the faithfulness of Poles to their country, to their religion, to their culture and ideals, to the men they have trusted and loved. Not for nothing is Poland's motto *Polonia semper fidelis.*

Through the horrors of the Russian campaign Napoleon's Polish legion followed him with unswerving fidelity — followed him (though they did not travel so fast) in the retreat from Moscow that marked the wane of his star, to the field of Waterloo, where in the grave of his hopes many of his gallant Polish lancers, too, found their grave.

Nearly a year has passed since the campaign ended, but the Nazis, despite all their terrorism, have to walk warily in conquered Poland, with their pistols at the ready. Hate glares at them from every doorway, spits at them in the dark ; and the very gibbets and

Here is another of the striking photographs taken by Julien Bryan in the siege of Warsaw. In the open, surrounded by such of their household goods as they have been able to salvage from the ruins of their burnt or blasted homes, a little group of unhappy folk are striving to maintain as far as may be the decencies of human existence.

Spain is Not at All Eager to Go to War Again

In the last war Spain was a neutral ; in this she is a non-belligerent. But her position
is by no means certain, for, as is made clear below, while the great mass of the people
are sick of war, a constant pull is exercised by the Axis Powers.

SPAIN is not at war—in her attitude of
"non-belligerency" she has copied
Mussolini's Italy, in this as in so
many other things—but little more than a
year has passed since she was in the throes
of a struggle even more deadly, more
ferocious, than that which during the last
nine months has devastated the smiling plains
of Poland and of France. Between July 18,
1936, when General Franco raised the
standard of revolt in Spanish Morocco,
until March 28, 1939, when Madrid surrendered to his triumphant columns, nearly
half a million Spaniards were killed on the
battlefields of the Spanish Civil War.
Hundreds of thousands more were wounded ;
and yet a further vast unaccountable host of
civilians, men, women and children, old and
young, people of every class, every party,
every sect, met a bloody end.

"The wounds of civil war are deeply
felt," wrote Lucan, born in the Spain
of 1,900 years ago, but the mighty duel of
Pompey and Julius Caesar which he described, terrible and deadly as it was, did not
leave such a train of slaughter, such a legacy
of hate, as that which is Spain's most recent
memory. Eighteen months have passed
since the noise of battle died away, but still
(so it is said) there are a million prisoners in
Franco's gaols, and every week numbers of
unhappy men are taken from their cells to
face the firing squads. In every town and
village, in every street, there are men whose
maimed and mutilated bodies are the mute
witnesses of the fierce fights in which they
have been engaged. On every hand there
are soldiers and armed policemen, for the
peace which reigns in Spain today is the
peace of the conqueror. On every hand,
too, there are crowds of sad-looking folk,
for there is not a home in Spain which does
not mourn a father or a brother, a husband
or a son, who rests for ever beneath the
shattered walls of Bilbao or Toledo, on the
stricken fields of Brunete and Teruel, or in
the blackened ruins of Guernica and Madrid.
Everywhere, too, there are signs of poverty
and distress in which all classes are involved.
There are queues outside the "Auxilio
Social"—soup kitchens perhaps we should
call them ; there are shops filled with goods,
but the prices are high, and beyond the
reach of most ; rationing is widespread—
even cigarettes are rationed to the extent of
three packets a week—and in every seven
there are three meatless days.

Impoverished, laid waste, the flower of her
young manhood slain or maimed—small
wonder that Spain shivers with apprehension

at even the thought of becoming
involved in the war. With most
of the Spanish Press pro-
German, with 60,000 Germans
still in the country—one of the
legacies of the Civil War period
when Hitler helped Mussolini
in "non-intervention"—the
propagandists of the Axis
Powers make a great show
of activity. They do their best
to stir up anti-British feeling,
and in particular endeavour to
stimulate a demand for the
return of Gibraltar. It seemed
the other day that they had
succeeded to some extent when
on July 17 General Franco, in
a speech to Army, Navy and
Air Force officers in Madrid,
declared that it was Spain's
duty and mission to obtain a
mandate over Gibraltar. "We
have 2,000,000 soldiers," he
said, "prepared to stand up
for Spain's rights," and there
have been demonstrations in
Madrid by University students
and other irresponsibles demanding not only Gibraltar
and the cession of Oran, but
the return to Spanish ownership of the rich mines of Rio
Tinto and Peñarroya.

Spain's strategic importance can readily be seen in this general map which includes Spanish Morocco.
Exhausted by her Civil War, Spain, in her role as non-belligerent in the present conflict, is beset with difficulties
since both Hitler and Mussolini cast greedy eyes upon the mineral wealth of the country.

'Non-Belligerency' is Franco's Choice—As Yet

After France's capitulation, a steady stream of refugees passed into Spain. They came on foot and in cars, with as many of their belongings as it was possible to take from their homes. Rows of French cars are here seen lined up at the Franco-Spanish frontier.

That Germany is fully aware of the immense economic importance of Spain is evidenced by the care with which the Nazis have cut a corridor across France and along the western seaboard to the frontier in the Pyrenees. From Irun through Bordeaux to Tours and Paris runs a vital railway which is now a highway from Spain to Germany, along which will be transported vast quantities of iron ore from the Bilbao mines only 80 miles from Irun, and from the rich deposits of Oviedo and Santander ; copper ore from Sevilla, Cordoba and Huelva ; zinc from Santander, Murcia, and Vizcaya and other places in Northern Spain. Thus it will be seen that there was more than a mere martial flourish in the parade of German mechanized forces on the frontier facing the Spanish guards.

Spanish Aid for Germany

With such vast and rich economic resources waiting to be tapped, Hitler may perhaps agree to Franco's Spain remaining non-belligerent, just as for months he acquiesced in a similar attitude on the part of Mussolini's Italy. Indeed, it may well be to his great advantage to do so, for Spain may take the place of Italy as his back-door through which will be poured vast quantities of goods of one kind and another which will help to keep Germany's war machine, not to mention her home front, in healthy functioning. Already there are reports from New York of shipments of oil and oil products to Spain greatly in excess of last year's exports, which suggests that Germany and Italy may both be getting vital oil supplies through the blockade by this route. There is also a story that British military equipment left behind in France by the B.E.F. is being sent to Spain by the Germans with the intention that the Spaniards shall sell it back to Britain for American dollars, with which Spain may buy oil from South America, which in turn will be sent to Germany in payment for the British military equipment ! But even if at a later date the situation should change and it would suit Hitler that Spain should enter the war as a partner of the Axis Powers, it is not at all certain that Franco would answer the Fuehrer's whistle. Spain has a long seaboard, and her outlying islands — Minorca, Majorca, the Canaries, and the rest — would be an easy

Sir Samuel Hoare, Ambassador Extraordinary in Spain, is here seen leaving the Royal Palace at Madrid where he presented his credentials to General Franco on June 8.

prey to the British fleet. Moreover, Spain shares the Iberian Peninsula with Portugal, which for 500 years has been Britain's ally. To Portugal in 1808 went the British Expeditionary Force, which after years of fighting brought the vast edifice of Napoleonic power crashing to the ground. Franco, we may be sure, has read his history. Yet another factor making for peace is the influence of the Vatican, still great in a Spain which, nominally at least, is predominantly Catholic.

On June 14, Spanish forces marched into Tangier, the international zone of Morocco. The first to enter the town were Spanish marines, seen here, landed from the minelayer, "Vulcane."

OUR SEARCHLIGHT ON THE WAR NEWS

Among the many items of war interest which cannot, for obvious reasons, be given in
full in our pages, we select week by week a number which are recorded in brief.
This is the fourth of the series.

'Britain An Impregnable Fortress'

So said General Smuts on July 21, broadcasting to Britain and the United States. " Nothing that has happened so far in the war justifies the inference that the fate of Britain will follow that of the other countries that have been overrun. The correct inference is just the opposite. How different, indeed, how unique, the case of Britain is, is forcibly illustrated by the most astounding incident of the whole war. I refer to the escape of the British Expeditionary Force at Dunkirk. If ever a force was trapped and doomed, it was the B.E.F. at Dunkirk. The German Government announced that it was trapped, and their High Command concentrated the bulk of their vast bombing force in an effort to achieve this crowning victory. . . If the German Army and Air Force together could not succeed in their attack at a single point like Dunkirk, how can they fairly hope to succeed in an attack on such a huge area as Britain, where, moreover, every physical and moral factor would be vastly in favour of the defence ? . . . If Dunkirk has any message for us it is the heartening one that Britain will prove an impregnable fortress against which Germany's might will be launched in vain. If that attack fails, Hitler is lost and all Europe, aye, the whole world, is saved.''

Town of Missing Men

The " very gallant band of brothers " depicted in Vol. 2, page 657, were partly recruited from Kendal in Westmorland. Into a " Pals " company of the 4th battalion of the Border Regiment went 90 men from this little town, and most of them have been officially reported as missing, after being cut off in a wood near the Somme. One family or more in every street has received this notification concerning a young husband or son, but the courageous women keep on hoping, for more than once the intimation has been followed by another, announcing that the missing man is now a prisoner of war. So Kendal's lost men may still return.

Shot Down Three Before Sinking

H.M. destroyer " Brazen," commanded by Lieut.-Commander Sir Michael Culme-Seymour, has been lost by enemy action. She sank while being towed into port, having been badly damaged in an encounter with enemy aircraft. But the Nazi bombers did not have it all their own way, for the destroyer shot down three during the engagement. One crashed alongside, the

second was given a direct hit in the nose with a 3-in. shell, while the third received a direct hit abaft the port engine. There was no loss of life on the destroyer.

Falmouth To Cardiff via Belfast

Steps were taken by the Royal Navy early in July to guard against any attempted German invasion of Ireland or the west coast of England from Scandinavian ports by the laying of a minefield, 1,000 miles in length, between the Orkneys and Iceland, and Iceland and Greenland.

The Admiralty has now announced that mines are also barring the way into the Irish Sea from the south, so that ships wishing to reach the Bristol Channel will have to pass round the north of Ireland. The minefield extends to about 50 miles at its widest point. This latest exploit of H.M. minelayers renders still more hazardous any scheme of Nazi invasion by sea.

Seeing Nineveh from a Dining Car

The Baghdad Railway is completed. Deprived, owing to the war, of the ceremonies befitting the end of so vast and romantic an undertaking, the first passenger train to leave Baghdad for Istanbul started quietly on its journey in the evening of July 17.

First planned by Germany 50 years ago to link Europe with the East, the great Berlin-Byzantium-Baghdad-Basra scheme had a chequered history. By 1914 the Germans had completed the section between Baghdad and Samarra. British engineers then extended the line as far as Baiji. The final section from Baiji to Telkuchuk, a matter of 200 miles, took four years to build and cost 3¼ million pounds.

In normal times the traveller from London will take seven days to reach Baghdad, changing twice only—at the English Channel and at the Bosporus. Approaching Mosul

in his luxurious compartment, he will be able to glance at the little Arab town built on the site of the great Assyrian city of Nineveh. Should he extend his journey to Basra—changing at Baghdad because the railway gauge is different—he can descry across the desolate plain the sandy mounds and the still impressive Ziggurat which are all that is left of Ur of the Chaldees, the city built about 2400 B.C., the city of Abraham.

By courtesy of the " News Chronicle "

The minefield laid towards the end of July in the southern approaches to the Bristol Channel and the Irish Sea extends from the north-west Cornish coast, between Hartland Point and Trevose Head, to the limit of the Eire territorial waters, as shown.

Hitler's Latest ' Peace ' Appeal

On July 19 Hitler delivered himself of another of the fantastic " peace " harangues to which the world has become accustomed. Three days later Mr. Mackenzie King, in the Canadian House of Commons, voiced the feelings both of Britain and her Dominions in a few caustic comments.

The speech, he said, abounded in those historical falsehoods which had characterized all Hitler's utterances since the outbreak of war ; his words had been a succession of promises made and broken, and his works had been cruelty, rapine, bloodshed, and violence. " Hitler's claim that the speech is an appeal to reason deceives nobody. It is almost entirely a threat of dire calamity to millions of innocent beings, and exhibits an even greater reliance on violence than previous utterances. Such a speech calls for no reply. It answers itself, and the only appropriate comment is that, so far as the future of the war is concerned, deception has run its course.''

Even more disdainful was the comment of the American announcer at a radio network of 31 Pacific Coast stations before he faded out the Fuehrer's speech : " We feel sure our American listeners will concur with our opinion that Mr. Hitler should not be permitted to use our American facilities to justify his crimes against civilization itself.''

On July 22 the Admiralty announced the loss of H.M.S. " Brazen." The destroyer received damage during an attack by enemy aircraft and subsequently sank while being towed into port. During the engagement she shot down three German 'planes. Built in 1928, the " Brazen " had a displacement of 1,360 tons, with a speed of 35 knots and a complement of 138.

Photo, Planet News

I WAS THERE!

Eye Witness Stories of Episodes
and Adventures in the
Second Great War

We Drifted for Six Days on a Raft

Thirteen seamen who, after their ship had been sunk by a U-boat,
withstood six days of privation on a raft have added another page
of dogged courage and endurance to Britain's sea history. The
story of their ordeal, as narrated below, was told by a survivor when
he landed in England.

AFTER their ship was torpedoed on
the morning of a Friday she sank,
and the survivors were left in one
lifeboat and on a raft. The position was a
very long way from land, but the U-boat
did not come to the surface or make any
attempt to save life. Describing their subsequent experiences, one of the survivors
said :

The raft was taken in tow by the lifeboat
and we paddled throughout Friday and that
night. During Saturday forenoon the
weather deteriorated, and finally the tow
parted. Before anything could be done
to pass a new tow, the raft and the lifeboat
had been driven far apart, and soon lost
sight of one another. There was nothing
we on the raft could do in the squally weather
except put out a sea anchor. This was done,
and, from a very small compass which one

man had in the top of his fountain pen, we
were able to glean some idea of the direction
in which we were drifting.

On the raft were three rifles and some
ammunition. During the night of Saturday
we fired the tracer ammunition into the air
in the hope of attracting attention. It was
unavailing. On Sunday morning a liner was
sighted, but those on board failed to see the
raft in the rough sea and she went on her
way. We were out of luck. By that time
we had started to ration our water supply,
allowing one milk tin full per day to each
of the thirteen men on the raft, half the
ration being issued about ten a.m. and the
other half about ten p.m.

Late on Sunday evening heavy swell was
encountered, and the raft capsized, throwing
us into the water. Two of the three rifles
were lost, as was some of the scanty store of

food, but fortunately all the men succeeded
in regaining the raft, and the water store
was not lost.

On two occasions on Monday ships were
sighted, but again we failed to attract attention. We had no means of making or lighting
flares, and nothing which could be used as a
mast on which clothing could be hoisted
as a distress signal. From Monday to
Thursday nothing at all was sighted. Nevertheless, all the men remained in good spirits.

Early on the morning of Thursday a
German U-boat appeared. It approached
the raft to within twenty yards. We saw
that on the bridge of the U-boat there was a
machine-gun which was kept trained on
us. We therefore ostentatiously threw overboard the one remaining rifle. The U-boat
circled slowly close round the raft. Then
the U-boat commander waved and went
away.

The thirteen of us had been clinging to the
raft for nearly six days, and were suffering
from privations, exposure, and salt-water
sores. Yet we were relieved at not being
taken prisoner, and celebrated by having
a double ration of water.

Later that day British destroyers appeared
and rescued us from the raft.

Here are seen the survivors of the torpedoed ship being rescued by a British destroyer, after they had spent six days on a raft in stormy seas. Suffering
acutely from privation, they narrowly escaped being made prisoners by a U-boat which circled close to their raft. Later the same day British destroyers
appeared and rescued the exhausted men.

Photo, "Daily Mirror"—Exclusive to THE WAR ILLUSTRATED

The Germans Even Gave Us Cigarettes

Among the members of the B.E.F. who succeeded in escaping to England after being captured by the Germans was an army officer of the 51st Division (see page 86). He was accompanied on his journey through France and across the Channel by a naval captain, in whose words the following account of their adventures is given.

TELLING the story of his adventures, the naval officer said he was captured at Havre, where he had gone, under heavy machine-gun fire from the cliffs, to the end of the pier in order to destroy his papers. He went on :

I took shelter behind a heap of stones, into which the Germans fired continuously and kept calling on me to surrender.

Ultimately, as they kept reducing the size of the heap of stones, there was little cover, so I had to surrender to a German general. I found myself on the top of the cliff with other prisoners, some of whom were severely wounded. There were no doctors.

The next day we were marched to a transit camp. The Germans, confronted with a number of prisoners, had very little food and all we had that day was a little rye bread. We were told that anyone attempting to escape would be shot.

The next day we were taken farther east by bus to the next camp, and it then became clear to me that if I was to escape it would have to be from here. I met an Army officer who was also determined to escape and together we made a careful examination of the sentry posts and position of the machine-guns, and decided to make an escape the next day.

Towards evening we took advantage of all the sentries' attention being directed to some movement in another part of the camp. We climbed through the barbed wire and hid ourselves in a bed of nettles, waiting there for four hours until dark.

We had agreed that we would pose as refugees, he Belgian, as he spoke French fluently, and I Flemish. As a disguise I had secured a pair of French sailors' " bags," which I wore over my uniform trousers, and to hide my uniform coat I put on top of it a blue golfing jacket that I had been wearing underneath for warmth. Later I picked up a peasant's cap and a voluminous overcoat.

We tramped back towards the coast by night, walking across the fields and through woods, avoiding roads and villages as much as possible, though once we crossed a main road along which German motorized units were passing. Sometimes at a house we got a drop of milk and a crust. Once we had the luxury of a bowl of soup. But that was the nearest we got to a meal for the five days it took us to find a port in which we could pick up a boat.

The picking-up, I am afraid, had to be quite unauthorized. It would have been fatal for any fisherman to help us. The Germans were absolutely ruthless and shot anyone suspected of helping men to escape from France. We saw what looked like a hopeful craft at anchor half a mile out from the shore at one small port, and as there were dinghies drawn up on the beach we saw a hope of getting off to it after dark.

We were on the pier in our refugees' disguise when two German soldiers started to chat to us and ask what there was to do or to see in the place. We spun our refugee yarn to them, chatted for a bit, and then at the end one of them offered us each a cigarette. It was the only smoke I had for eleven days.

At ten o'clock that night it was dark and raining hard, and we put off in a dinghy. When we got to the boat we found that the mast was housed and we had no idea how to get it up, and the engine refused to start. It was an awful moment, for the boat was pitching about badly at her anchor and we were both so weak that we were seasick.

After a considerable struggle we brought the engine to life, and it lasted just long enough to get us through the sandbanks into the open water. Then it died, and in the dark we made some sort of a job of stepping the mast and getting the mainsail and foresail up. By dawn we were some distance off the shore, and we hoped we were not visible.

We sailed all that day, tacking to and fro, except for one ghastly period of three hours when we had a flat calm. The engine had come to life once or twice during the day, but just then, when we wanted it, it died again. A carrier pigeon dropped on board and we fixed a message to it, but the poor thing was even more exhausted than we were. When we launched the bird it flew dazed into the sea and was drowned.

With dusk the wind rose again, and during the night we made good progress. In the morning, ten days after I had landed in France, I caught sight of the English coast.

We were in too weak a state by this time to alter our course, so we sailed straight on until we came to harbour, where the local coast watchers, policemen and fishermen gave us food and made us comfortable.—(*Press Association*.)

Jerry Machine-Gunned Our Little Boat

While engaged in whelk-fishing a few miles from their home port, three fishermen—Cyril Grimes, Roland Grimes and Joseph Barnes— were machine-gunned by a German 'plane which swooped upon their small craft. The story of their escape is told exclusively to " The War Illustrated " by the skipper, Mr. Cyril Grimes.

THE crew of the 25-foot whelker were among those who responded to the appeal for boats for the evacuation of Dunkirk. They had returned, quiet heroes of that historic adventure, to their occupation of whelk-fishing when the German 'plane swooped upon them. Describing its murderous attack, Mr. Cyril Grimes, the skipper of the boat, said :

We were about ten miles out, and we were gathering in the whelks when we were machine-gunned. Earlier in the day we had seen the 'plane going westward at a great height, and at the time I said that it was a rum-looking 'plane. Then it came back. I think it may have been bombing somewhere, and as it was heading for home the Germans saw us. It was in a direct line for us, and it seemed that we were in its path.

I looked up and saw the iron crosses painted underneath the 'plane, which was at a height of four to six hundred feet. I was going to say that there was a Jerry coming towards us, but there was not time. The Jerry was travelling at about 200 miles per hour, and he began machine-gunning us. He flew directly over the boat, and we at once turned our engine off and threw ourselves to the bottom of the boat. The bullets flew all round the boat, but none of us was hit, nor was the boat. Some of the bullets were only a few inches away from me, and if anyone had been leaning over the starboard side he must have been hit.

The machine-gunning went on for a short time ; it must have been for a few seconds, but it seemed like hours. The 'plane then flew away to the east at a great speed. I raised myself in the boat and looked over the side, and as I saw that the 'plane was banking I thought that it was coming back for us, but it turned and went off.

I have never had anything like that happen to me before, and I don't want it to happen again—it was too close to be comfortable. There was another boat about a mile away, the crew of which thought that it was one of our own 'planes practising ! We were gathering in our whelks at the time we were attacked, and the Jerry must have been able to see what we were doing. It just shows you that the Germans will do anything.

Undaunted after being machine-gunned the previous day by a Nazi 'plane, the crew of this East Anglian whelker are seen preparing to cast off for another fishing. They saved themselves during the German attack by lying flat in their boat.
Photo, Claud Fisher

They Have Won Honour in Freedom's Cause

Lt. B. M. H. Shand, M.C., 12th Lancers. He covered the withdrawal of a column in face of fire from four tanks.

Lt.-Col. H. Lumsden, D.S.O., 12th Lancers. In the retreat he was responsible for the fine work of the regiment.

2nd Lt. J. W. P. Rhodes, M.C., Gordons. On three occasions he led fighting patrols among the enemy.

2nd Lt. E. C. Mann, D.S.O., 12th Lancers. At the Yser Canal his leadership held up superior forces for seven hours.

2nd Lt. E. P. G. Miller Mundy, M.C., 12th Lancers. For skilful handling of his cars often under heavy fire.

Flt. Sgt. G. A. Powell, D.F.M. Despite his wounds after air attack at Stavanger, he flew home 370 miles.

Sgt. H. Cartwright, D.F.M., proved a most efficient fighter against enemy aircraft, having himself shot down four.

A/Sq. Ldr. J. R. Kayll, D.S.O., D.F.C. For inspiring leadership of his squadron which destroyed 32 enemy 'planes.

Actg. Flt. Lieut. J. A. Leathart, D.S.O. Led his squadron in a number of offensive patrols against odds.

Pilot Officer D. H. Grice, D.F.C. Displayed great courage in attacking enemy aircraft and destroyed six.

Cdr. J. H. Allison, D.S.O. Took a gallant part in bringing off the British Expeditionary Force from Dunkirk.

Dr. A. G. Rewcastle. The first woman doctor to be given the rank of Surgeon Lieutenant, R.N.V.R.

Skipper J. Mugridge, D.S.C. For minesweeping services, most dangerous but least dramatic of war work afloat.

Cpl. Joan Pearson, Medal, O.B.E. For protecting injured pilot from bomb splinters with her body.

Lt. Cdr. R. E. Courage, D.S.O. Took part in the first battle of Narvik and greatly distinguished himself.

Pilot Officer A. C. Deere, D.F.C. Displayed great courage in many combats against superior numbers.

Sgt. G. A. Craig, D.F.M. Pressed home attacks over Oslo aerodrome, despite heavy opposition.

Flt. Lieut. R. H. A. Lee, D.S.O. Given in addition to his D.F.C. for his "intense desire to engage the enemy."

Flying Officer K. H. Blair, D.F.C. On one occasion, after being badly shaken by bomb, he took part in a patrol.

Squad. Ldr. L. E. Jarman, D.F.C. Decorated for gallantry in aerial combat. He is one of many New Zealand pilots.

Squad. Ldr. P. J. H. Halahan, D.F.C. For leadership of his squadron which brought down 70 enemy 'planes.

Ldg. Aircraftsman, J. K. S. Fisher, D.F.M. Wireless operator in a bomber, wounded, but continued his duties.

Flt. Lieut. J. S. Soden, D.S.O. For shooting down five enemy 'planes. Once outnumbered 50 to 1.

Actg. Flt. Lt. S. F. Coutts-Wood, D.F.C. He was decorated for gallantry in attacks on objectives on the Continent.

Flying Officer P. R. Walker, D.F.C. In two engagements at heavy odds, he accounted for ten enemy aircraft.

Raids Cannot Shake Our 'Indomitable Resolution'

Damage to military objectives was negligible, and the attacks on convoys were ineffective.
For every 6½ civilian casualties Hitler lost one aircraft ; for every two casualties he lost
one airman.   The R.A.F. and the A.A. forces shot down 5·8 enemy aircraft for every
British fighter lost.

IN a month's Nazi raids on Britain, beginning on June 18, 336 civilians were killed and 476 seriously injured. This information was given in the first of the Air Ministry's monthly reports on air raid casualties, which added that the largest number killed in any locality on any occasion was 32. In order to withhold valuable information from the enemy about the precise result of any particular raids, Mr. Churchill told Parliament on July 18 that all casualties would be notified locally, but in

twin-engined two-seater Messerschmitt 110 fighters for bombing our convoys. Three of our Hurricanes on patrol off the South Coast encountered sixteen of the converted Messerschmitts flying line-astern to bomb a convoy. Upon attack by our machines the enemy formation turned away, but not before one of them had been sent down into the sea and another set on fire.

Many observers have borne testimony to the fine spirit and high morale of residents in the coastal zones which have been the object of Nazi raids. Material damage has been slight, and as regards military objectives also these raids have been a failure. Taking the month's totals of casualties, it is seen that the number killed is less than that of victims of fatal road accidents over a similar period. British civilians can be relied on to present a brave front to any of Hitler's frightfulness, however much it may be intensified in the future.

Looking at the other side of the aerial war, there is an increasing sign that the R.A.F. raids are having a big effect morally as well

Miraculous escapes by German airmen, when their machines were shot down by British fighters over the Channel on July 19, are seen in these vivid photographs. Those on the left show a pilot descending by parachute above the clouds, and then nearing one of the ships he had been trying to attack. Above, two survivors are waiting in their rubber boat for help. *Photos, British Official: Crown Copyright; and "Daily Mirror."*
Exclusive to THE WAR ILLUSTRATED

aqueduct this canal is carried over the River Ems, and the R.A.F. determined to strike here. Models of the aqueduct were constructed and picked R.A.F. crews were given special instructions on the methods to be used. Results are seen in the photographs in page 91. Afterwards one captain said : " If we had not seen the models and the photographs beforehand we could easily have made a mistake, for there were several places which more or less resembled our target."

Debits and Credits in One Month's Raids June 18—July 18, 1940	
Nazi aircraft destroyed ... ... 140 (90 bombers ; 50 fighters)	British civilian casualties ... ... 902 (336 killed ; 476 seriously injured)
Germany lost 1 aircraft for every 6½ persons killed or injured	
,, ,, 1 airman ,, 2 ,, ,,	
,, ,, 5·8 aircraft ,, 1 fighter machine lost by Britain	

Pages could be filled with accounts of the nightly bombing raids on enemy objectives— accounts in which the same strategic points figure again and again. No respite is allowed. Hitler, in his speech to the Reichstag on July 19, repeated the lie that our airmen aim at the civil population ; no one who scans the British Air Ministry reports of the daily and nightly raids on Germany can have the slightest doubt that our men are concerned with military objectives only, and that they get on to their mark.

Dutch reports testify to the accuracy of our work and to the havoc caused. It is said that many trains for Germany laden with Dutch farm produce and vegetables have had to return to Holland because railway tracks had been wrecked by our airmen. Road traffic also had been similarly disorganized. Many similar reports

future reproduction of this figure in the Press, either individually or in aggregate, would be forbidden. A monthly statement would be given in Parliament and in the Press.

In approximately one month's raids on Britain the Germans have lost about 140 aircraft, of which fifty were fighters. With them have been killed or captured nearly 430 airmen—offsetting the 400 airmen prisoners returned to Germany by the Pétain government. Only 24 British fighter aircraft were lost over the period mentioned, with the pilots and crews—20 men in all. To the figures for German losses must be added another hundred aircraft so badly damaged as to be unlikely to get back. On July 21 the Germans began to employ their

as materially. On July 16 adverse weather conditions prevented our airmen paying their usual visits on the other side of the enemy line, and so, for the first time in thirty successive nights, our bombers did not operate.

More news was released about the fine exploit of bombing the Dortmund-Ems Canal. It seems that our pilots had so damaged German trains and railways that the enemy turned to his canal system more and more for the transport of iron ore and other essentials to the Ruhr factories. Barges big enough to take two train-loads of munitions were brought into use, and the Dortmund-Ems Canal was a vital waterway for the purpose in question. At a double

come from other quarters. According to a German engineer from Hamburg the damage done to locks and factories was terrific, and the population was in a state of nervous tension. Whenever an aeroplane engine was heard, everyone made for the shelters and stayed there for hours. A German woman said that the air raids in Western Germany had made life there unendurable.

Up to the present Hitler's raids on Britain have failed. Though, in the words of Lord Halifax on July 23, " he is preparing to direct the whole of German might against this country," he cannot succeed. For " in every part of Britain, in great towns and remote villages alike, there is only one spirit, a spirit of indomitable resolution."

They Hold Our First Line of Shore Defence

The veteran sailors who are Britain's first line of shore defence are seen in these photographs at their vigil. (1) A coastguard is taking the compass bearing of a ship close in shore. (2) A passing ship has just been sighted from a coastguard station. (3) The flashlamp signalling apparatus used by the coastguard at night is being got into position.

SINCE the outbreak of war the Coastguard Service has had new and onerous duties thrown upon it. In peacetime it was concerned chiefly in keeping a watch for ships in distress, in warning them against danger, in helping in the saving of life, and in watching for any attempts to land smuggled goods from small motor boats— a traffic which then was causing considerable trouble. Now, besides their ordinary duties, the coastguards must watch for enemy 'planes, surface ships and submarines approaching the coast.

The Service is manned by naval pensioners and men with a knowledge of local conditions. It grew out of the Preventive Service and was controlled by the Admiralty from 1858 to 1923, when it was transferred to the Board of Trade; when the Ministry of Shipping was set up in October 1939 it took over the Coastguard Service. On May 28, 1940, the control of the force was again assumed by the Admiralty.

For coastguard purposes the United Kingdom is divided into twelve divisions, each in the charge of a Captain or Commander of the Royal Navy.

One of the chief life-saving duties of the Coastguard Service is rescue work by the rocket apparatus. (4) Here men of the Coastguard are examining the breeches buoy. (5) Coastguards flag-signalling to a ship close in shore.

Photos, L.N.A.

OUR DIARY OF THE WAR

WEDNESDAY, JULY 17   *319th Day*
At Sea—Admiralty reported sinking of ocean-going U-boat in Atlantic after being twice bombed by Australian flying-boat.

H.M. merchant cruiser " Vandyck " reported sunk by air attack on June 10.

In the Air—Air Ministry disclosed that as result of recent planned action of R.A.F., double aqueduct of Dortmund-Ems canal had been put out of action.

R.A.F. made further attacks on barge concentrations in Holland and Belgium.

Coastal Command aircraft shot down enemy bomber in Channel.

During night British bombers attacked aerodromes at Merville and Hertogenbosch. Oil depots in the Ruhr and Ghent set on fire.

War Against Italy—Further raids on Tobruk harbour during night of July 16-17. Other objectives attacked at El Gubbi, Libya, and at Assab and Agordat, Eritrea.

Home Front—Single raider dropped 11 bombs in South-East England. Woman and child killed and others injured.

THURSDAY, JULY 18   *320th Day*
On the Sea—Admiralty announced loss of H.M. destroyer " Imogen " as result of collision in dense fog.

H.M. trawler " Rinovia " attacked off South Coast by enemy aircraft, one of which she shot down.

In the Air—R.A.F. bombers made daylight raids on barge concentrations near Rotterdam, on Boulogne harbour, warehouses at Le Havre and aerodrome at St. Omer.

During night Coastal Command aircraft bombed naval base at Emden, harbours of Harlingen and Willemsoord, and supply depot at Ghent.

R.A.F. made night raids on aircraft factories, and oil depots at Bremen, Krupp's works at Essen, supply trains, and other military objectives in Germany.

War Against Italy — R.A.F. bombers made successful raids on Italian bases in Libya, Eritrea and Abyssinia, including Tobruk, Neghelli and Agordat.

Italians raided Mersa Matruh. Enemy bomber crashed and caught fire.

Home Front — Enemy bomber shot down off South Coast. Single raider dropped high explosive bombs on town in S.E. Scotland during night ; large tenement badly damaged and some fatal casualties.

Raider over N.E. Scotland chased out to sea after 30-minute fight.

Another Nazi 'plane flew over town in S.E. England. Fighters went up, battle took place over centre of town, and enemy was reported shot down.

Announced that Germans lost their 200th aircraft in raids on Britain since war began.

Shipping — Ministry of Shipping announced that French merchant ships in U.K. ports were being requisitioned to serve common war effort, and would fly both flags.

Japan — Premier announced that Agreement had been made with Japan to stop for three months transit of war supplies to China through Burma and Hongkong.

THE POETS & THE WAR
XXIX
BRIEF HOUR
By Ben Davies

' Do not men die fast enough without being destroyed by each other ? Can any man be insensible of the brevity of life ? and can he who knows it, think life too long !'—
Fénelon

We who with careless hands have tossed this gem
Now see it dim and fade before our eyes,
And with a sense awakening and wise,
Seek no release nor pity, but condemn
Our easy valuation, and the hours,
Fleet and flying, that with subtle speed
Filched opportunities that may have freed
Us from this servience to ugly powers.
And seeing now this transient bubble fade,
With a grim humour we are yet content
To see the remnant in some ideal spent ;
And, till before Time's altar we are laid,
To make of every hour a day to hold
The dreams that live though we do not grow old.

FRIDAY, JULY 19   *321st Day*
On the Sea — Italy's fastest cruiser, " Bartolomeo Colleoni," was sunk, and another put to flight off Crete, by Australian cruiser " Sydney " and small destroyer force.

Admiralty announced that two British merchant ships, " King John " and " Davisian," had been sunk in region of West Indies by enemy raider, believed to be converted merchant vessel.

In the Air — R.A.F. made night raids on enemy aerodromes and seaplane bases along coast of N.W. Germany and northern Holland. Aircraft factories, oil plants and railway communications also bombed.

Coastal Command aircraft attacked naval base at Emden and Dutch port of Harlingen.

Home Front — Twelve enemy aircraft shot down round Britain's coasts, ten being destroyed while attacking shipping in Channel.

Sir Alan Brooke succeeded Sir Edmund Ironside as C.-in-C. Home Forces. Lord Gort was appointed Inspector-General to Forces in Training.

General — President Roosevelt announced his acceptance of nomination for third term.

Hitler made " final appeal for peace " in speech to Reichstag.

SATURDAY, JULY 20   *322nd Day*
In the Air — R.A.F. made night raid on naval base at Wilhelmshaven. Oil refineries at Hamburg and Bremen and shipping in Emden harbour also bombed. Coastal Command bombers fired oil tanks near Rotterdam.

Fleet Air Arm attacked Tobruk and secured hits on oiler and transports.

Home Front — Twenty-one German aircraft brought down in raids on Britain, 18 by fighters and three by A.A. guns.

Thirty-five raiders attacked convoy in English Channel. Shipping in harbour in south of England was also attacked.

Ministry of Home Security stated that during month beginning June 18, total of 336 civilians had been killed in enemy air raids, and 476 seriously injured.

SUNDAY, JULY 21   *323rd Day*
On the Sea — Admiralty announced that H.M. submarine " Salmon " was considerably overdue and must be presumed lost.

H.M. trawler " Crestflower " reported sunk by enemy aircraft.

In the Air — R.A.F. and French bombers attacked oil depots at Rotterdam, and Bremen ; aircraft factories at Wismar, Bremen, Rotenburg, Kassel, and Gottingen ; goods yards at Hamm and Soest ; and aerodromes in France, Holland and Belgium.

Coastal Command aircraft bombed 14,000-ton enemy supply ship. Other aircraft set fire to oil tanks at Ghent.

Home Front — Enemy raids reported over various areas of Britain. In English Channel six Hurricanes encountered 80 Dorniers and Messerschmitts. Four raiders shot down.

Empire — General Smuts broadcast to United Kingdom and U.S.A. on a free Europe.

Czechoslovak Govt. — British recognition granted to Provisional Czechoslovak Government, with Dr. Benes as Premier.

MONDAY, JULY 22   *324th Day*
On the Sea — Admiralty announced that H.M. destroyer " Brazen " had been lost through attack by enemy aircraft.

In the Air — R.A.F. bombers made night attacks on aircraft factories and oil plants in Germany, and on aerodromes in France, Holland and Germany.

Coastal Command aircraft attacked docks and petrol stores at Amsterdam, barge concentrations at Helder, and shipping at Dunkirk. Fleet Air Arm raided Bergen.

War against Italy — Cairo reported heavy raids during week-end by R.A.F. bombers on Tobruk, El Gubbi and Bardia in Libya, and Asmara and Assab in Eritrea.

Home Front — Enemy aircraft reported late at night over England and Scotland, greatest activity being in N.E. and S.E. Scotland. Bombs dropped at many coastal points, including Thames Estuary.

Dornier shot down by Hurricane fighters off South Coast. Two, possibly three, German aircraft believed brought down by A.A. guns during raid over S.W. England.

Lord Halifax made broadcast speech in reply to Hitler.

TUESDAY, JULY 23   *325th Day*
On the Sea — Admiralty announced that H.M. trawler " Campina " had been sunk by enemy mine.

In the Air — R.A.F. made widespread raids on aircraft factories, oil depots, twelve aerodromes, and other targets in Holland and Germany.

Coastal Command aircraft attacked patrol boats in Dunkirk harbour, oil tanks at Flushing and docks at Amsterdam.

War Against Italy — R.A.F. secured direct hits on submarine jetty in Tobruk harbour. El Gubbi and El Adem also attacked.

S. African Air Force made four raids on Diredawa aerodrome, Abyssinia.

Home Front — Dornier 17 shot down by R.A.F. fighters near N.E. coast of Scotland. Coastal Command aircraft shot down enemy flying boat in same area.

Third War Budget, presented by Sir Kingsley Wood. Income tax raised to 8/6. Higher duties on tobacco, wines, beer and entertainments.

France — Pétain Government announced that M. Daladier and three members of his Cabinet are to be tried on charge of war responsibility.

Lt-Gen. Sir Alan Brooke, K.C.B., D.S.O., who commanded the Second Corps of the B.E.F. in France, has been appointed Commander-in-Chief of the Home Forces in succession to Sir Edmund Ironside.
Photo, Planet News

THE HEIGHT OF AERIAL BATTLE IN THE VICTORY OF DOVER

What may be described without exaggeration as being the world's most dramatic air-raid picture is this of Dover Harbour at the height of the German bombing attack delivered on Monday, July 29. The sky is peppered with anti-aircraft shells, through which dodge five of the Nazi dive-bombers— Junkers 87. Two bombs are exploding near shipping lying at anchor, not one of which was damaged, as may be seen from the photograph in page 120 taken from the same point after the raiders had passed. Altogether 80 German 'planes took part, and of these 17 were accounted for.

Photo Associated Press; Exclusive to The War Illustrated

This Is the Europe Fuehrer Adolf Wants to Build

Intoxicated by his successes on the Continent, Adolf Hitler is now reported to be busily engaged in preparing plans for the remaking of Europe according to his heart's desire. What lines his proposals may be expected to take are described here by E. Royston Pike.

HITLER has dreamed a dream, and is fast giving it shape and size and form. It is the dream of a United Europe which through so many centuries of the Middle Ages entangled Popes and Emperors in a web of rivalry and war ; the dream which came to Napoleon in the watches of the night, disturbed by the gnawing cancer in his stomach or the blood-spattered wraiths of the men who died at Marengo or on the road from Moscow ; the dream which might have been realized at Versailles if Clemenceau had not been so old, Lloyd George so opportunist, if Wilson had not been so filled with the stuffiness of the professor's study. Once and once only has that dream come down to earth, when eighteen hundred years ago "absolute power under the guidance of virtue and wisdom "—the phrase is Gibbon's —ruled the Roman Empire from the wall of Antonine between the Forth and Clyde to the deserts of Persia, 3,000 miles and more away. Now it has fallen to Adolf, son of Schuecklgruber, customs-collector at Braunau, to attempt afresh what Charlemagne and Innocent and Napoleon failed to do. And shall Hitler succeed where they failed ?

Not only is Hitler possessed of the sublimest self-confidence, not only does he display a ruthlessness which Machiavelli might have regarded with wondering admiration, but he has at his disposal a military force, a martial equipment, such as (fortunately, perhaps) has never been granted to any of his predecessors on the road of empire. With these aids and advantages he has effected a clearance in Europe which surpasses even that effected by the men who 150 years ago set out to conquer Europe to the tune of the Marseillaise and with the intoxicating words "Liberté, Egalité, Fraternité " emblazoned on their banners. In a few short weeks he has driven kings and queens from their thrones, presidents and cabinets into exile ; countries have been overrun, peoples enslaved, constitutions swept away, the political framework of great states dissolved and the whole structure of Western society undermined and sent crashing into ruin.

So complete a victory, so vast a triumph, could never have been won on the field of battle alone. Hitler's generals have achieved great victories in the field, but they could not have triumphed

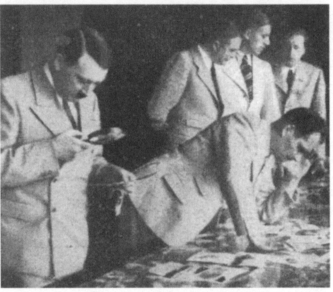

The man who might be Emperor Adolf I is here seen inspecting with the closest interest documents and photographs which fell into his hands when the Nazis captured what had been only recently French General Headquarters.

From the " Berliner Illustrierte Zeitung "

without the work of his spies, his saboteurs, his agents of one kind and another in all the countries he has ruined. Not fighting but treachery has been the lever which has brought down Holland and Belgium, N o r w a y and France.

In all the assailed countries he has had no difficulty in finding tools who were willing to play his game, to serve his purpose — politicians on the make who would rather be lackeys of the powerful foe than nobodies in opposition, newspaper proprietors willing to accept favours and even hard cash, rich men whose money-bags outweighed their patriotism, capitalists who still deluded themselves into believing that Hitler is a bulwark against the Bolshevik flood, young men who have received education but no jobs, public officials whose eyes have been dazzled by the glittering prizes thrown open to obscure men in a Europe where the old order has been swept away.

This is the really tremendous fact about Hitler's victory. Better far had it been if his victory had been won on the battlefield only, for nations defeated in war have often recovered in the years of peace, as Prussia recovered after Jena, as France recovered after Waterloo and Sedan. But in this war the rot has gone deep ; the disasters in the field have been combined with assaults on the social and economic structure delivered not from without, but from within, by such men as Quisling, Mussert, Henlein, and Laval, to choose just four out of the portrait-gallery of defeatists.

Because his victory has been won not only by the Nazi generals and the Nazi soldiers who stormed the forts of Verdun, who swamped the guns on the Somme in such an abandon of ideological intoxication, but by men within the gates of his victims, Hitler can now indulge in an orgy of planning and reconstruction such as even Napoleon can hardly have dreamed of. He plays with nations, he juggles with boundaries. He calls this people " home to the Reich," and dispatches that to a prison camp. For him Europe is a chequer-board about whose squares men and women by the thousand, by the tens of thousand, are moved as the veriest pawns.

Now at length we are in a position to see something of those things to come which have long been stirring in Hitler's fecund brain. The Europe nurtured in the ideals of democratic liberalism, the Europe which

In the new Europe which Hitler is planning to build Alsace-Lorraine will almost certainly be among the territories " restored " to the Reich. Perhaps this explains the eagerness with which all traces of the war are being removed from the region. This photograph shows a German labour unit cleaning up the wreckage caused by the bombardment of an Alsatian town.   *Photo, Keystone*

Only He Would Be Free in an Empire of Slaves!

enshrines the traditions born of 2,000 years and more of civilized existence, is to be swept away, and in its place we are to find a continent from which such liberties as we have known are to be banished for evermore. Europe is to be imprisoned in a system of rigid caste, such as for thousands of years has held the Indian spirit in an unyielding, inelastic grasp. It is to be like a pyramid at whose summit will flaunt in riches and such elegancies as have survived the chieftains of the Nazi state. Closely associated with them is a vast army of bureaucrats in every country of the Nazi Reich. Below these is the great mass of the German people, men and women supposedly of the purest Nordic race, with never a grandparent in whose veins runs a single drop of Jewish blood; these are to have the satisfaction, such as it is, of knowing that they belong to the dominant race and that, hard-worked and deprived of individual liberty as they are, there are other peoples within the bounds of their empire who are worked harder still and have even fewer rights and privileges. These constitute the next layer of the pyramid—the Czechs and the Poles, the Scandinavians and the Dutch, the Belgians and the French, whose function it will be to serve as hewers of wood and drawers of water for the privileged race above them. But theirs is not the last layer: there are still the lesser breeds without the law, the Jews and the "niggers" who are doomed to an existence which even coolies would not envy.

Just as individual men and women will be predestined to belong to one or other of the social grades, so each country in the Europe of the Nazi Reich is to have its settled place. Never again is Europe to be a patchwork of sovereign independent states each with its government and its army, its host of customs officials, collected within and behind a high tariff wall. So far, it may be said, so good; for of all the disastrous mistakes committed by the treaty-makers at Versailles, surely the worst was the creation of this jigsaw puzzle in which countries which economics decreed should be interdependent were given the right to strive to maintain an independent self-sufficiency.

Everything For the Germans

But closer acquaintance with the Nazi plan leads to disillusion. Hitler is no disciple of Cobden, but in his planning is solely concerned with what he considers to be the welfare of the German people. Germany itself is to be the manufactory of the Empire, and its workers engaged at the skilled and most profitable tasks will naturally receive the highest wages and enjoy the best advantages of labour. But the other lands are in their economics as in their political structure to be made completely subordinate. Denmark is to be a farm supplying butter and eggs and bacon for the breakfast-tables of Germany, Poland and Rumania are to be granaries, Holland is to be a nation of carriers, while France is to revert to the land of peasants, such as it was in the days of the Louis, but henceforth producing wine and corn for the refreshment of the Nazis.

There is to be a similar "division of labour" even amongst the cities; Munich seems to be destined to be the capital of

So far as is possible the industries of France will be transferred to Germany, but even if not transferred, it is highly unlikely that the Nazis would allow the famous Creusot works (which Nazi soldiers are regarding above) to continue to function. These were established by the Schneider brothers in 1836 and for years have been the most important of France's ordnance factories.

Greater Germany. Nuremberg, perhaps, will recover its imperial standing, and its quaint old houses may look down on Emperor Adolf I riding through its streets with his characteristic forelock peeping incongruously from beneath the crown of the Holy Roman Empire.

Then there is Paris. Paris is scheduled to be the "fun city" of the Reich—the place to which the Nazi chiefs will repair when they have tired of their stolid fraus and their pudding-faced fräuleins. Its factories may be permitted to continue their output of ladies' handbags and powder-puffs, but it will be pre-eminently the city of the nude and naughty, of lovelies and lingerie, whose boulevards will be the perpetual parade-ground of the international of the demi-monde.

This is the Europe that Hitler would build, Adolf Hitler, the son of Schueck'-gruber; Adolf Hitler, the "conquering Fuehrer," who but for the mistakes, the faults, the sins and crimes of little men in high places might still be peddling his picture-postcards to the tourists in Vienna.

Following the military breakdown of France the Nazis laid greedy hands on all the war material that had not been exhausted by the weeks of battle. Perhaps the most valuable item in their booty was the petrol supplies. As seen here, they hastened to fill their depleted tanks from France's oil reserves.

Photos, Associated Press

The Nazis Glory Over Their Fallen Foe

The fullest possible use of the camera is made by the Nazis for home propaganda by displaying the completeness of the German triumph over France. Left, an obviously staged photograph of steel helmets said to have been thrown down on the field by defeated French soldiers. They will go to the scrap-heap, as does all the metal booty. Below, men of a German Salvage Corps collecting French helmets and damaged rifles and machine-guns, also to be melted down to make other munitions.

The Germans have stripped Paris of every commodity of which they were short. Here a wholesale tobacconist's warehouse has been turned into a depot for Nazi troops.

In those parts of France which the Germans think they will never hand back, Nazi " Artisan Work Companies " are removing all the scars of war. In the photograph above, trenches are being filled in and barbed wire taken away from former French front-line positions in Alsace. Meanwhile the ordinary folk of France are a sorrowful people, as is witnessed by the sad faces of these citizens of Bordeaux leaving the 1914-18 war memorial after the signing of the Armistice that betrayed them.

Photos, "New York Times,"
E.N.A. and Keystone

These Were the Last Defenders of Arras

Here we give another chapter in the story of the British Expeditionary Force's great fight against the Nazi hordes in the early summer of 1940. It is told in the words of Mr. Douglas Williams, War Correspondent of the "Daily Telegraph," through whose courtesy we are enabled to reprint it here.

OF all the towns in the B.E.F. area of Northern France, none except Dunkirk is better known to British soldiers or to the British public than Arras, a comfortable little market-town of 20,000 people, whose ancient cobble-stones through the centuries have echoed to the marching feet of armies of all nations.

From October, 1939, to May, 1940, Arras was the nerve-centre of the British Expeditionary Force. There Lord Gort had his headquarters, and through its glass-domed station in packed trains, or down its main streets in rattling lorries, passed at one time or other most of the units that made up the B.E.F.

It may, therefore, be of special interest to describe its siege, and its defence by a heroic but inadequate garrison until, reduced to a shambles of shattered brick, with its streets ankle-deep in broken glass, the burning city was finally abandoned to the advancing Panzer divisions of the German Army.

The story begins on May 18, when rear G.H.Q.—Lord Gort's advanced headquarters at that time being in Belgium—decided, under the threat of enemy tanks reported as near as St. Quentin, to retire. The defence of the city and the surrounding area was handed over to Gen. Petre, summoned from his 12th Division Headquarters at Abbeville, who later came under the orders of General

as construction companies, supply details, and the like, and a somewhat battered French armoured division. Except for the Welsh Guards, the British troops, whose duties up to that time had been largely

Major-General R. L. Petre, to whom Lord Gort handed over the command at Arras, fought in the last war in Gallipoli and Mesopotamia.
Photo, Lafayette

civilian, were necessarily ill-trained and ill-equipped to meet the formidable enemy. There was little or no artillery available, although later a battery of 25-pounders was lent by the 5th Division and a two-pounder anti-tank battery came from the 50th Division.

General Petre established his headquarters in the ancient pile of the Palais St. Vaast, whose underground cellars furnished perfect protection against air raids. Two officers were lent to him as Staff officers, but he had no clerks and no communications but a few gallant dispatch riders (plus a wireless set which worked intermittently) and one cipher officer. He was almost completely cut off from G.H.Q., except for the rare arrival of a liaison officer after a perilous trip over heavily shelled roads ; he fully realized that the enemy was determined, at all costs, to capture Arras—a key city in the communications of Northern France.

Ammunition was plentiful, and there were stocks of food, including one of the N.A.A.F.I. depots, the luxurious stores of which, distributed gratis, were much enjoyed.

By this time the population of the city had dwindled to a mere 3,000, all of whom had sought refuge in civil A.R.P. shelters or in the famous caves, formed by the excavation through centuries of local building stone, in which during previous sieges the

Arras was almost destroyed during the last war, but was completely restored, as this photograph of the Grande Place shows. Now the town has undergone a second martyrdom.
Photo, A. J. Insull, Copyright A.P. Ltd.

Franklyn as G.O.C. of the area, with headquarters at Vimy.

Available troops, necessarily scanty, were disposed to the best advantage to meet the Germans. The 36th Infantry Brigade (commanded by Brigadier Roupell, V.C.), which was subsequently overrun by the Germans, was posted round Doullens, to guard the back areas, with one battalion (Royal West Kents) detached to guard the Somme crossings at Péronne. Two brigades of the 23rd Division, Territorials, were strung along the Canal du Nord, to face the enemy coming through the 20-mile gap they had made in that area.

For the defence of the city itself were available one battalion of Welsh Guards, some mixed units of G.H.Q. troops, such

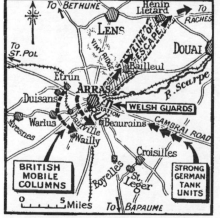

In this map is seen the final line of retreat of the British forces from Arras after it was evident that overwhelmingly superior German forces made it impossible to hold out.
Courtesy of the " Daily Telegraph "

Here is the Palais St. Vaast, formerly the Abbey of St. Vaast, which General Petre defended so gallantly. It was rebuilt as a palace by Cardinal Rohan in 1754.
Photo, E.N.A.

people of Arras had taken shelter from the enemy. The streets were deserted, houses and shops shuttered.

The defending troops were posted along the southern and eastern perimeter of the city in hastily constructed strong points and machine-gun posts. From May 20 heavy fighting developed, with frequent raids by dive bombers, which caused some casualties and made communications difficult. Welcome reinforcements arrived in the shape of the Green Howards and the Royal Northumberland Fusiliers, but enemy pressure was such that General Petre decided that he could not continue to hold the outskirts of the town on the south, and a withdrawal was ordered to the line of the railway station.

The bridge over the cutting was blown up,

Another Chapter in the Undying Story of the B.E.F.

Amongst the regiments which defended the Palais St. Vaast at Arras was a detachment of Welsh Guards, than whom, said a British soldier eye-witness, " I never hope to meet a braver crowd of men." These Welsh Guardsmen are training in patrol work early in 1940 in a French village that was wrecked by shell-fire in 1914-1918.

and the cutting itself, six or seven railway lines broad at that point, was converted into an impenetrable tank obstacle by piling railway trains together four or five deep. Engines with open throttles were allowed to smash into each other until the whole area was a solid mass of jumbled carriages and smashed rolling-stock, behind which, and from the windows of houses on the main square facing the station, the British garrison took up its new defensive position.

Heavy incendiary bombing was carried out by the enemy that afternoon. It started many fires, which, owing to lack of wind, continued to smoulder, covering the whole city with a pall of black smoke. By May 22 the pressure round the town had become intense, and Lord Gort, through General Franklyn, decided that some kind of offensive was essential.

The purpose of the attack was twofold. First, G.H.Q. was very anxious to make some co-operative attempt southwards to join hands with the French, who were under-

stood to be on the eve of launching their eagerly awaited counter-attack northwards. Secondly, it was hoped to relieve the Arras garrison.

The task was entrusted to General Martell, of the 50th Division, who was given for the purpose one of his own brigades, consisting of Durham Light Infantry and a tank brigade.

General Martell was instructed to clear an area about 10 miles deep and four miles wide, west and south of Arras, by forming his forces into two small mobile columns which would advance along parallel lines a few miles apart. His troops had had little rest for several days, and, moreover, it was their first encounter with the Germans. Therefore the test was a high one for Territorials, and high praise is due to them for their gallantry.

Each column consisted of the following : one infantry battalion, one anti-tank battery, one battery 18-pounders, one company machine-guns, one tank battalion.

The operation went well in its initial

stages. The left column did fine work, put many enemy tanks out of action, captured 400 prisoners, and killed many Germans. The right column made some progress, but was held up by unexpectedly heavy enemy forces, and was also upset by the erratic behaviour of the French armoured division, which, while co-operating with our forces, mistook our troops for Germans and opened fire on them. Unfortunately also about this time both commanding officers of the tank battalion were killed, while the commander of one of the infantry battalions was also killed when the tank in which he was riding suffered a direct hit from a German field-gun.

By 6 p.m. it became evident that further progress was impossible ; from observation points reinforcements of enemy tanks, with infantry in buses, could be seen moving down the road from Cambrai. Some were destroyed by direct fire, but the pressure became greater and greater, and heavy counter-attacks were launched on the anti-tank localities which the two columns had established at Beaurains and Warlus.

The enemy also began a series of desperate attempts to cross the River Scarpe. A bridging train was destroyed by our artillery, but the German infantry continued to press forward in waves to launch their assault boats. Our Bren guns could not fire fast enough to cope with the packed masses of Germans, who dashed forward frantically. suffering tremendous losses.

At Last the Order to Withdraw

In view of the enemy's obvious superiority in strength, both columns began to withdraw north of the city, where General Petre's force had already realized that they could not hold out much longer. With much of the city burning, the streets harassed hourly by dive-bombing and with continual alarms at points all round the perimeter, defence was becoming more and more difficult. German forces, some of them appearing in various disguises, had already reached the area of the citadel, and preparations were discussed for a last stand at the Palais.

Finally, at 1.30 on the morning of May 24, a dishevelled and exhausted liaison officer arrived at General Petre's headquarters, after a five-hour motor trip, with orders from Lord Gort for a general withdrawal. Only two hours remained before daybreak, but the evacuation took place in perfect order.

It was started down the Douai road, but just outside Arras it was found that the bridge over the Scarpe had been prematurely blown up. It was at first considered a misfortune, but later turned out to be a blessing in disguise, for a scouting party of some twenty which had crossed the broken span were captured by a large party of Germans a short way down the road. The remaining columns were then switched to the Henin-Lietard road, which at that time was the only free exit from the beleaguered city, the Germans having occupied at least 330 deg. of the perimeter.

All that morning General Petre's force, together with remnants of the 5th and 50th Divisions, moved in a packed mass, nose to tail, down the narrow road ; but, by some dispensation of Providence, not a single German 'plane was in the air, and the whole force reached comparative safety north of Douai without interference or casualties.

Another of the regiments whose names will ever be associated with the gallant defence of Arras is the Northumberland Fusiliers, who formed welcome reinforcements at the height of the enemy pressure. Here is a motor-cycle battalion of the famous regiment passing through a French village soon after the arrival of the B.E.F. in France in the autumn of 1939.

Photos, British Official : Crown Copyright

Air Blockade Is a Game That Two Can Play

Of late weeks there have been some new developments in the technique of the blockade, whether applied by Germany or by Britain. Here we review one fresh aspect—the air war against the vital centres of communication.

SINCE the day war began the Nazis have been doing their very utmost to blockade Britain. First they tried submarines, and then, when the U-boat menace proved not so successful as they had hoped, they developed the magnetic mine dropped by 'planes in the traffic channels close to our coast. But it was not long before the secret of the magnetic mine was out and the minelaying 'planes were chased away. So the Nazis had to think again.

Grand-Admiral Raeder had had his turn; now it was Field-Marshal Goering's. Plans were laid for an air blockade of the British Isles, and ere long they were in operation. Day after day the Nazi raiders crossed the North Sea or the English Channel and dropped their bombs as near as possible to the targets which had been selected. Unfortunately for them, most of the targets were thoroughly well defended, and so a number of bombs were unloaded on fields and

of the British workers that it was recently decided that only if raiders were actually overhead would production of vital munitions be stopped, and already arrangements are being made for production to be carried on during the long hours of dark of wintertime.

Meanwhile, Britain is not content with a defensive war, but by means of the bombing 'planes of the R.A.F. is developing day and night an offensive of the greatest intensity. There is not a city or town in western and north western Germany which has not learnt to dread the ominous note of our bombers, and neutral observers have told of the damage that has been caused to material and to morale. Dr. Goebbels may persist in telling the German people that the British air raiders are quite harmless, but the people of Hamburg, the Ruhr, and the Rhineland know better. Not for nothing is the German radio now urging the public to pay attention to the

Attack on English Channel Convoy
July 25, 1940

21 Coastal Vessels attacked by waves of 30 aircraft.

Sunk	 5	Total tons ..	.. 5,104
Damaged	.. 5	,, ,, ...	.. 5,133

2 Destroyers damaged by dive-bombers after attack by 9 Nazi M.T.B.s.

Nazi aircraft shot down   29

neglected subject of A.R.P., while many towns hitherto regarded as being quite safe are being evacuated. So great damage has been caused to certain German factories in the western part of the country that night shifts have had to be suspended for a week at a time, and detailed scales of allowances to be made to workpeople who lose work as a result of the air raids have been published in the German press.

Again, how disconcerting must have been the discovery that not only Nazi warplanes can lay mines! For some time past British bombers have been sowing mines in German waters, along the coast and in the river estuaries, and so the British sea blockade of Germany has been extended far beyond where the surface minelayers can penetrate, to (for example) the farthest limits of Germany's Baltic coast.

Thus more and more it becomes apparent that Hitler cannot win the war until the R.A.F. has been crushed—and what chance is there of that when the youth of the Empire is a vast reservoir of potential pilots and gunners, and to the product of Britain's aircraft factories now speeding ahead under the vigorous direction of Lord Beaverbrook is added the output of those many factories in America which, so he tells us, are being planned for the production of a total output of 3,000 'planes a month?

This, one of the first photographs taken of Germany's attempted blockade of Britain from the air, shows a convoy off the south-east coast being attacked by Nazi dive-bombers.
Photo, Planet News

commons or in the open sea without damage.

Blockade by air is not on all fours with blockade by sea. The aim of the submarine and of the surface-raider is to prevent ships arriving at their destinations in our ports, but the air blockader, though he may attempt to sink ships in convoy, finds his principal targets in the ports to which the ships must come; the lines of communication—railways, roads, goods yards, warehouses, and so on—along which the cargoes must pass to their destinations; and those destinations, whether they be munition works, where steel is converted into big guns or aluminium into aeroplanes, or the petroleum dumps where the petrol and oil from America and Iran are stored in bulk, or the food depots where are assembled the vast quantities of food supplies brought from every corner of the globe.

Certainly in a country so thickly populated and so highly industrialized as Britain, targets of this description are exceedingly numerous, and the really surprising thing is not that the Nazis come over so frequently, but that up to now, at least, the damage and disruption caused have been trifling. Such is the spirit

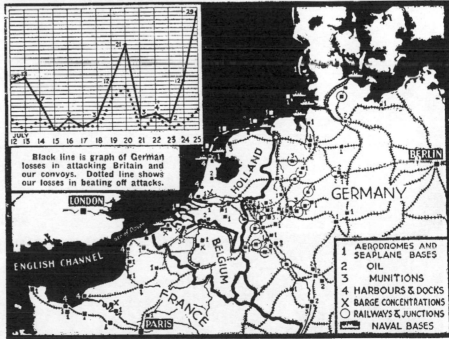

Black line is graph of German losses in attacking Britain and our convoys. Dotted line shows our losses in beating off attacks.

This map and the curve above tell part of the story of blockade and counter-blockade by air. While, of course, the losses in convoy by air attack cannot be revealed, the Admiralty stated that up to July 8 only 47 ships had been lost in convoy since the war began. The graph covers the period July 12 to 25 and the map 1,000 raids by the R.A.F. on Germany and German-occupied territory.

Courtesy of " The Daily Mail "

This Battle of Dover Was Won in the Sky

What was described as the R.A.F.'s finest triumph was won over Dover Harbour on July 29, when an attack by wave after wave of Junkers and Messerschmitts was blown to pieces without being able to cause damage of the slightest importance to ship or harbour. Here is an impression of the principal incidents in that day of glorious battle.

DOVER on a sunny morning in late July. White cliffs crowned by the old castle's massive keep, crescent of houses with a long arm of buildings reaching out into the harbour, quays and breakwaters, and the basins of placid water disturbed by the tireless scurry of many ships, great and small.

First above the town a solitary Nazi 'plane appeared on a reconnaissance flight. Then shortly afterwards there dived from out of the sun a horde of German warplanes—30 or more Junkers 87 dive-bombers, protected by some 50 Messerschmitt fighters. In wave after wave the bombers swooped down on the harbour and the flotilla of varied craft, while above them the German fighters endeavoured to form a series of protective layers in the sky.

They Saw the Bombs Fall

But the defences were alert, and in a moment they blazed into action. A terrific anti-aircraft barrage was flung aloft, and two of the leading bombers received direct hits. The others came on, however, in their almost vertical dives. Those who watched on shore could see the bombs being released from the racks, could watch them as they fell; spouts of water rose high into the air and the boats in the harbour bobbed up and down like corks. On shore the houses shook with the reverberations of the bursting bombs and the crash of gunfire.

The Germans, we are given to understand, believed that there must be a time-lag between the moment of the bombers' assault and the arrival of the defending squadrons of fighters, but even before the dive-bombers

had time to pull out of their dives, their escort was being attacked on every side by British Hurricanes and Spitfires. The sky became one vast battlefield in which the 'planes of friend and foe dived and twisted and somersaulted in the frenzy of battle. Eye-witnesses said the German machines seemed to fall like autumn leaves. One squadron of Spitfires sent four Messerschmitts and a bomber crashing into the sea, and a squadron of Hurricanes made a score of four Junkers and a fighter. One Spitfire pilot attacked three Junkers in succession; the first fell into the water after his opening burst of fire, the second went down in flames, and the third flew away crippled. In another battle two German machines followed each other in flames into the sea, while the British fighter responsible for their destruction flew along the sea-front just above the roofs on its way back to its base; its fuselage was riddled by bullets, but those who glimpsed it from below said they saw someone waving as if in triumph from the cockpit.

"For a time," said an onlooker, "there was a violent scrap up there. Machines were diving, machine-guns blazing away, and engines roaring as dogfights went on in different parts of the sky." Then after half-an-hour of this fierce fighting the Nazis, despite a pronounced numerical superiority at the outset, had had enough. In those 30 minutes eight of the dive-bombing Junkers had been destroyed and nine of the escorting Messerschmitts—17 out of a possible total of 80 enemy 'planes engaged, a 2·1 per cent loss. Their formations shattered, the survivors flew away across the Channel, closely pursued by the Hurricanes and Spitfires.

Shortly afterwards several more of the Nazi 'planes which had taken part in the battle came to a sudden end. One raider was shot down over the Channel just as he had dropped three whistling bombs near some small fishing boats. "We were trawling," said the skipper of one of the boats when he arrived safe back in harbour, "when suddenly a big black 'plane came out of the clouds not more than 500 feet above and dropped three bombs. The bombs exploded some distance away and almost lifted our small boats out of the sea." The boats made for the shore, but as they turned they heard machine-gun firing, and looking up they saw three British fighters tackling the German machine. *That* Junkers did not get back to Germany.

So closed the fiercest air battle to date that the war has seen. A massed onslaught on one of Britain's most important naval strongholds had been delivered and had been beaten off with heavy loss to the enemy, while not a single bomb fell on shore and the defenders' losses amounted to but one 'plane down and two damaged.

The Sky Was Cleared in An Hour

It all happened in less than an hour. Then the sky was clear again save for the British fighters cavorting in triumph above the coast they had so well defended. And Dover Castle, which from the days the Romans came has lived through so many turbulent centuries, weathered so many storms of war, withstood so many threats of invasion, looked out to sea as the enduring symbol of England's indomitable might.

In page 113 we reproduce a photograph of the determined Nazi dive-bombing raid on Dover, showing the attack in full swing. Junkers 87s have swooped on their targets, loosed salvos of bombs and zoomed away, while great fountains of spray leap into the air and the calm waters of the harbour heave and pitch so that the sheltering ships bob about like corks. Here is the same scene a moment or two later. Every boat is unharmed, exactly in the position it occupied in the earlier photograph—all the Nazis' audacity and high explosive have been wasted once again.
Photo, Exclusive to THE WAR ILLUSTRATED·

After the Greatest of All Battles in the Blue

From the greatest aerial battle ever fought, that during the Dover raid on July 29, 1940, the British 'planes engaged returned to their base keeping excellent formation.   Here are some on the way home after their ever-memorable victory when, in the space of 30 minutes, 17 Nazi aircraft were shot down.   That day the raiders lost 14 bombers and 7 fighters.

This photograph and that in the centre show the smiling imperturbability of the pilots who had been up to fight the Nazi air armada. In one a pilot officer is showing a comrade, as evidence of his narrow escape, a bullet hole in his flying helmet (marked by arrow), as if it were all in a day's work. In the other a group of pilots are basking in the sun on their aerodrome and comparing notes on their battle experiences.

Photos. Fox

Italy's Navy Is Not Spoiling for a Fight

Above is the Italian cruiser "Gorizia," one of a class of four of 10,000-ton warships carrying eight 8-in. guns. She is seen at a pre-war review with a flight of seaplanes flying over her. Left, the "Conte di Cavour," one of four reconstructed Italian battleships of 23,622 tons, carrying ten 12.6-in. guns; in the foreground is an auxiliary craft.

Photos, L.E.A.; International Graphic Press

THE Royal Italian Navy has not so far given a very good account of itself. On July 9, in the Mediterranean, two Italian battleships and a number of cruisers made off under cover of a smoke screen after one shell from a British capital ship had hit an Italian battleship (see page 92), while the sinking of the " Bartolomeo Colleoni " by H.M.A.S. " Sydney " on July 19 was admitted by one of the captured officers of the Italian ship to be due to the " cheek " of the Australian cruiser in attacking a ship that was technically her superior. In many of the units of the Italian Navy armament has been restricted to get lightness and speed, while in some cases more and heavier guns than the tonnage seems to warrant are carried. Thus, in the matter of design many Italian warships are faulty, according to British ideas. Another disadvantage of the Italian Navy is that about 60 per cent of the personnel are conscripts, thus leaving what is little more than a skeleton crew of fully-trained and experienced seamen. At the outbreak of war the Italian Fleet stood fifth in strength among the navies of the world, but the dispersal of the French Navy now puts it fourth. In " mosquito " craft, that is, torpedo-boats and motor torpedo-boats, it is exceptionally strong.

The Army at Home Has New 'Mosquito' Cars

Below is a close-up view of an " Ironside " with one of its crew. These little cars are not only very fast, but can negotiate the roughest country.

The German rush through the Low Countries and France proved the great value of small but extremely mobile mechanized units, and the British Army has profited by the lesson. The result is the new small armoured cars, nicknamed " Ironsides," with which a famous cavalry regiment has been equipped. In the photographs at the top of the page and at the foot, cars of this type are seen in action during exercises.

Above, men are leaping from their cars with their guns ; while below, with the " Ironside " under cover of trees, they advance at the double. Right is a squadron of " Ironsides " with the crews lined up to receive instructions from their officer.

British Official Photographs ; Crown Copyright

Britain's Gallant Defenders Are 'On Their Toes'

The men defending Britain's coast are "on their toes," and day by day practice is making them perfect in all the work that will be required of them in the event of invasion. Right are just a handful of the men that Nazis would find waiting for them at the top of the English cliffs.

Invaders would also get a hot welcome from such a strong point as that below. It is a pill-box carefully camouflaged, on the top of which a Bren gun is mounted to counter any attempt by dive-bombers to destroy the position.

The Secretary of State for War, Mr. Anthony Eden, visited various points in the British land defences in the week ending July 20. He is here seen inspecting a naval gun on a land mounting placed in a disused gateway. In front is the tackle by which the gun is drawn out from its camouflage among the trees.

There has been a marked increase in the number of enemy bombers brought down by British A.A. guns, and even when direct hits are not scored the terrific barrage put up is often more than the hostile aircraft can face. The photograph, left, shows an anti-aircraft gun with an imposing array of shells all ready for action.

Photos, British Official: Crown Copyright, and G.P.U.

One of the 80 Raiders Destroyed in One Week

Survivors of the crew of the Dornier whose blazing end is illustrated in this page. The one above is a stretcher case, but the other (right) is probably suffering from nothing worse than shock. He seems surprised at being so well treated.

July's last weeks were black for Nazi bombers; in one day, July 25, no fewer than 28 'planes were brought down—up to then the record number for one day's bag—and four days later 25 were reported down, most of them in the battle above Dover harbour. In the period July 23-29 over 80 were destroyed. One of the victims was this Dornier 17M, whose crew of three were lucky to escape alive when the machine was shot down in flames. Below the 'plane is seen burning a minute or two after it hit the ground, while on the left is a close-up view of the front fuselage and one of the wings when the flames had burnt out, but smoke was still rising from the shattered frame and engine.

Photos, L.N.A.

When the 'Lancastria' Went Down T

LYING at anchor in the harbour of St. Nazaire, the giant Cunarder "Lancastria" was sunk on Monday, June 17, by a salvo of bombs dropped by Nazi warplanes. Before the war the "Lancastria" was one of the most famous of cruising liners, but for some time past she had been a troopship, and when she met her end she had just completed the embarkation of a large number of personnel of the B.E.F. and the R.A.F. in France. Altogether there were some 5,000 people on board, including some French refugees. Of these 2,477 are known to have been saved. The large photograph shows some of the survivors at the West Country port to which they were taken by the rescuing vessels. In circle above is Lt. R. Haynes, 50th Company, A.M.P.C., who with his company of 250 men got on the "Lancastria," but only 40 survived. The other photo shows injured survivors helping one another.

Photos exclusive to THE WAR ILLUSTRATED

en of the B.E.F. Escaped to Wear Uniform Again

en of the B.E.F. Escaped to Wear Uniform Again

Abyssinia May Soon Be Aflame With Revolt

For some time we have heard little of what is happening in Abyssinia, but now the country which four or five years ago filled the headlines is once more coming into the news. All the signs go to suggest that revolt against the Italian rule is imminent.

UNTIL it was dark the flying boat rocked at its moorings among the warships anchored in the great harbour of Alexandria. Then a boat put off and a slight figure, closely muffled in a cloak, was smuggled ashore, while an artificially-provoked commotion distracted the attention of inquisitive bystanders assembled on the quayside.

Through the dark streets the little party hurried to the Italian Yacht Club—taken over by the British authorities since the outbreak of Anglo-Italian hostilities—and there the man of mystery was taken into a washroom, where at three hours' notice officers of the R.A.F. had made hasty arrangements for his arrival. The muffling robes were thrown aside and there stood revealed in civilian dress His Imperial Majesty, Haile Selassie, Emperor of Abyssinia, who, after four years of exile, was now returning to his own country from England.

'I Will Be Wearing the Crown'

The Emperor made the first stage of his trip by flying straight across Nazi-occupied France in a 'plane provided by the British Government; he slept peacefully much of the time, curled up in his seat and wrapped in rugs. From Malta he flew on to Alexandria, and now for a few hours he laughed and joked with his British hosts—'' I claim to be the only man who has entertained an Emperor in a washroom,'' said one of the senior officers afterwards—who toasted success to the Abyssinian campaign that was shortly to begin, in Italian Chianti brought up from the club's cellars. The Emperor invited his hosts to visit him at any time that they were passing through Addis Ababa, and to the pilot who brought him from England he gave a

gold watch engraved with a crown. '' When next you see me,'' he said, '' I will be wearing the crown.'' He then changed into a brand-new, smartly cut uniform of an Ethiopian generalissimo, on which blazed all his many medals and decorations. After cordial farewells he muffled himself in his cloak again and followed a guide to the waiting 'plane. Soon he was on his way, and towards the end of July he was reported to have arrived in Khartoum, where a house was placed at his disposal by the Government of the Sudan. From there he proceeded to make contact with the chiefs in Abyssinia who had either stood out against the Italian invader or were only waiting a favourable opportunity to throw off the Italian yoke.

Since May, 1936, when Haile Selassie was driven from Addis Ababa, Abyssinia has been accounted part of the Italian Empire of East Africa. But the country has never been wholly subdued, although in the war itself the Italians employed an army of 500,000 men equipped with all the most modern war material and employing to the full poison gas and intensive bombing, and the army of occupation amounted at one time to as many as a quarter of a million men—and may still do so.

But Abyssinia is a vast country of 350,000 square miles—about six times the size of England and Wales—largely mountainous, some of it hardly explored, and most of it in a very backward stage of development, particularly in the matter of communications. Of its 7,000,000 people—Abyssinians proper or Amharas (about 2,000,000), Gallas, Somalis, Danakil, and negroes—many have never been brought under effective Italian rule; particularly in the western regions bordering on the Sudan the tribesfolk have maintained a state of isolated independence. The people as a whole have shown little inclination to adopt that Fascist culture which has been thrust upon them at the point of the bayonet, and that guerrilla warfare which has never completely died down will certainly be intensified now that Haile Selassie is once again within hail.

They Raid the Enemy for Arms

According to report Britain is providing arms and ammunition for the tribesmen who are revolting against Italian rule, and many thousands of Abyssinians have already armed themselves at the expense of the Italians. '' It began in a small way,'' we are told by Miss Sylvia Pankhurst, who has done so much to keep alive the cause of Abyssinian independence. '' The Italians had a small isolated post. One night a party of chiefs stole up, surprised the sentries, took their weapons, held up the rest of the garrison, and captured the twenty rifles in the fort and

In 1936 the Emperor Haile Selassie, centre, was driven from Abyssinia, where he had reigned for six years. Now, with British support, he is somewhere in the Sudan endeavouring to rally his old chiefs to revolt against Italian domination. News travels apace in Africa, yet some time must elapse before a feasible plan of revolt is worked out. In the lower photographs, taken before the Italian seizure of Abyssinia, are two warrior chiefs who may perhaps soon be in the firing-line again.   *Photos, Hay Wrightson and Keystone*

Italy's New-Won Empire Trembling in the Balance

all the ammunition. After that Italian convoys began mysteriously to disappear. They set out but never reached their destinations. The number of armed Abyssinians grew. It is still growing. Today the Italian rulers are afraid to go outside their fortified posts unless with heavily-guarded convoys, and even then they are ambushed and wiped out.''

For some time past Ras Abeba Arragai, the chief who after Haile Selassie's departure carried on the struggle for national independence, has been making continuous headway, until today the whole of the northwest corner of the country, save for four or five towns, is under Abyssinian rule ; there are also areas of resistance in the eastern and central regions, even within a hundred miles of Addis Ababa, where the Viceroy, the Duke of Aosta, who succeeded Graziani in 1937, has his headquarters.

Italians on the Defensive

True, the Abyssinians in revolt are faced by an enormous army of Italians vastly superior in equipment and training, but it must be remembered that the Italians in Abyssinia are in the position of a beleaguered force. No supplies can reach them from outside, and it is estimated that unless they are relieved, across the desert from Libya or from the Red Sea, they will be facing exhaustion by the end of the year. As things are, life has been rendered a constant nightmare for the Italians by the guerrilla attacks which have been of late increasing in number and intensity.

Four years ago the Abyssinians were the first victim of the Totalitarian States on the prowl ; they were thrown to the Italian wolf because France and Britain believed that the dictators' appetite could be appeased by the sacrifice of other countries, other peoples, than their own. History may have to tell that it was the first victim which was the first to be restored.

Italy's full energies were put into the building of roads as soon as she had overrun Abyssinia. Over 20,000 navvies were employed on the work, and here some of them, veiled against the all-pervading dust, are off to work. Right, the Italian viceroy harangues a crowd of natives.

Photos, Mondiale

The map shows the boundaries of Abyssinia old and new. The frontiers before the Italian conquest are given and also the readjustments made later when Mussolini believed that his triumph was complete.

'Off the Map' but the Village Has Gone to War

SINCE September 1939 the peaceful English countryside has undergone a dramatic transformation. Every village is now vigorously playing its part in Britain's war effort. Hamlets that once formed quiet, secluded communities have new populations and new interests —the tide of war has been felt in the remotest parts of Britain's countryside. Mansions and large houses, farms and cottages, have been filled with townspeople; new faces have appeared in the village schoolroom and the "pub." War which produces strange, unexpected conditions and problems has brought fresh interests to thousands of countryfolk. The spirit of comradeship has been remarkable; a very real sense of unity has developed as a result of altered conditions and changing lives.

The three stalwarts of the village (top right) have enjoyed for years the shade of the elm tree. Now the tree has been cut down in connexion with defence measures, and here we see them contemplating the sawn-up trunk.

The air-raid warden has delivered 300 new filter pieces for the village gas-masks; he is seen in circle fitting one of them. Across the village street this ancient lorry (above), laden with stones and concrete, forms a ready barricade.

The district postmaster, a veteran of the Boer War, is in the Home Guard. His companion, in the Home Guard also, is a groom. Here they are on their way to duty, passing the village green with its memorial and salvage heap.

Story and photos, "News Chronicle": exclusive to THE WAR ILLUSTRATED

Waitresses and Maids Make Big Bombers Now

In the finishing shop two girl workers, left, are painting and cellophaning the wooden strips in the inside of a fuselage that is nearing completion. Above, a panel of a 'plane is being riveted by two of the hands with pneumatic riveters.

HELPING to make the Wellington bomber—that lovely pattern of deadly efficiency which cruises the sky at 250 m.p.h., ranging 3,000 miles at a flight—is part of women's work in wartime. The Wellington is built on the geodetic principle (something like a curved metal skeleton) mostly of duralumin, and it is in the building-up of the component sections that the women are employed, and in later stages on the covering of wings and fuselage with canvas. These bomber-building women have a business-like uniform of their own. It is compulsory for the rank and file to wear dungarees—in the machine-shops blue, in the dope shops khaki, and so on. Inspectors wear green, supervisors white. Two sets of dungarees, two caps, and gloves are issued to them every year.

From story by John and Crystal Pudney in " News Chronicle "

A drilling machine, above, calls for careful work, and the young girl shown earns about £2 a week working 11½ hours a day. Right, a squad of needlewomen sewing the fabric on a wing. A special stitch similar to a lock-stitch is used, and this sewing is carried out entirely by women workers, whose numbers have vastly increased of late.

Photos, exclusive to THE WAR ILLUSTRATED

Hope Is a Luxury in the Nazi Prison Camps

For obvious reasons the Germans do their best to keep their prisoners of war hidden
behind a thick veil of secrecy, but from time to time information leaks out which enables
us to form some picture, however inadequate, of their sad plight.

OF all Europe's unhappy millions—and who in Hitler-ridden Europe can be really happy ?—perhaps the most miserable are those whose life is the living hell of the German concentration camps. Hardly less miserable, however, can be the lot of the great host of soldiers who, after the excitements of war, are now compelled to languish behind the barbed wire of the prison camps.

There are hundreds of thousands of them, wearing the uniforms—ragged and dirty now—of all the defeated nations of the Continent. Poles and Norwegians, Dutch and Belgians and Frenchmen—they are all represented in the prison camps. In some, too, there are British soldiers, men who were wounded in the great retreat and had to be left behind or were surrounded like the gallant 51st Division when the line in France was overwhelmed by the German hordes.

Most numerous are the French soldiers who surrendered in crowds as soon as the news of the armistice negotiations reached the front. Before the close of the Battle of France the Germans claimed to have taken nearly a million prisoners, and that number may well have been exceeded.

Concentrated in prisoner-of-war camps in occupied France and in Germany, these unhappy *poilus* are living under conditions of extreme squalor, suffering the pangs of hunger, threatened by pestilence, tormented by half-healed wounds, and clothed in verminous rags. The filth of the camps was unbelievable, said Mr. J. L. Luhan of the American Hospital Ambulance Service, on his return from a visit to some of them a few weeks after the armistice. At a camp of 5,000 prisoners at St. Cloud, where Mr. Luhan distributed food, clothing, oranges, cigarettes, and drinks, the most pressing demand was for beef cubes, chocolate, and fresh bread. It seems that the prisoners were being given mouldy German bread

instead of the fresh French bread to which they had been accustomed. The responsibility for maintaining the prisoners was laid on the French Government by a clause in the armistice, but the lack of transport and difficulties put in the way by the German authorities often prevented food from arriving at the camps. So poor were the supplies that Marshal Pétain was compelled to protest to the German authorities.

At the camp at St. Cloud a number of French negro troops were imprisoned, and the Germans, in accordance with their boasted sense of racial superiority, discriminated against them in every way. When the American visitors called the attention of a German doctor to an unattended case of strangulated hernia in a black colonial, they were told : " We must distinguish between black and white ; the French must learn that."

No Release for French Prisoners

The Franco-German armistice brought release to those German soldiers who had been captured by the French, but not to the French taken prisoner by the Germans, who it was decreed should remain in German hands until the conclusion of peace. A week or two later a suggestion in a French paper that French prisoners should be released now that hostilities were over was denounced in a German semi-official statement as " a piece of unparalleled effrontery." Evidently, the statement continued, the French people had misunderstood German leniency, and had forgotten that after the last war it was years, and not weeks, before it was found convenient to begin the release of German prisoners.

Worse, even, than the plight of the French prisoners of war is that of the Poles, 700,000 of whom were transported to Germany in the weeks following the close of the Polish campaign in September 1939. The fate

of these men is indeed tragic, particularly those who are interned in concentration camps in the Reich. Typical camps are those of Lansdorf, near Vienna, and Luckenwalde, near Berlin, where during the whole of the bitter winter the huts in which the Polish prisoners were detained—250 men to each hut—were unheated, no blankets were supplied, and the men spent their nights wrapped in overcoats and sleeping on straw which was changed only once every two months. The only food supplied to them was sugarless coffee and 6 ozs. of bread per head, but soldiers who were put to work sawing wood or digging potatoes received a supplementary ration of a few potatoes in the morning, one loaf of bread for three men at midday, and potatoes with a small quantity of coffee in the evening. No meat or fat was given to the prisoners, and their families in Poland were distressed by the constant demands for bread and fats which were received. So meagre were the rations that the half-starved unfortunates were reduced to gathering rotting cabbages, bones, garbage—anything, indeed, that was more or less edible.

After some months of this sort of treatment great numbers of the prisoners collapsed in health, when they were sent back to Poland. Often, we are told, they looked more like ghosts than human beings when they staggered out of the train ; many of them were suffering from frostbite and were crippled for life. Their moral state was as bad as their physical, which is not surprising when one remembers the terrible conditions of their confinement, the inadequacy of their nourishment, the lack of warm clothing, the absence of the most elementary sanitary arrangements, of medical care and medicines, and many humiliations and the corporal and other punishments of every kind to which they were subjected just as the whims of their hard-faced warders dictated.

The terms of the Franco-German armistice provided for the release of all German prisoners of war. The French, however, were not treated with the same consideration, and here a long column of captive *poilus* are seen marching through a town on the road from Lille to Tournai.

Britain Still Has Brave and Faithful Allies

General Sikorski, C.-in-C. of the Polish forces, is receiving a gift of a German sub-machine-gun from some of his officers who took it from a Nazi parachute soldier near Narvik. Centre, the Duke of Kent with Polish officers while inspecting an R.A.F. training school in Scotland.

The morale and spirits of the Polish Army are high, and sing-songs of national music sustain their ardour. Here one of the songs is being recorded for broadcasting.

AMONG the Polish and Czech soldiers now in Britain are veterans of two campaigns, for many of the Poles fought in Norway and afterwards in France. The Czech Legion were with the French 7th Army and took part in the great retreat to the south. They embarked on French merchant ships, but after the Armistice had been signed at Compiègne they were ordered ashore. Eventually many of them were brought off by British warships, while others were taken on board an Egyptian merchant ship and eventually reached a British port. The Czech Government in Britain has now been officially recognized.

Typical of the fine Czech soldiers who are continuing the fight for freedom is this contingent entering a camp in Britain. Throughout their campaigns in Norway and France their padres have accompanied them, and shared all their dangers and hardships.　　*Photos, Keystone, Fox, Topical and Planet News*

OUR SEARCHLIGHT ON THE WAR NEWS

Czech Government Gets To Work

IN a Mayfair house, 114, Park Street, W.1, Dr. Benes is setting up the machinery of the Provisional Czechoslovak Government, formally recognized by Britain on July 23. Within a day several members of the new Cabinet were sworn in, including M. Jan Masaryk, former Minister in London, who is to be Minister of Foreign Affairs. The main effort of the new Government will be the organization of Czech forces on land and in the air, so as to take their share in the defence of Britain and the defeat of Nazism. On July 26 Dr. Benes inspected and addressed the remnant of the Czech Legion, now withdrawn from France and collected in a camp in North-West England.

'Free French' Services in England

IT is thought that one effect of the " Meknes " outrage will be to gain new recruits for the French armies now being reorganized in this country. In the South of England there is not only the great camp of the " Free French " soldiers, but another consisting of thousands of men of 42 nationalities under the command of French officers —the famous Foreign Legion.

In addition, the Admiralty has announced that a number of French warships which arrived in our ports before the signing of the Franco-German armistice are now being manned and prepared for sea by officers and men of the " Free French " naval forces, of which Admiral Muselier is the head. One such ship has already taken active part in recent successful operations.

The story of how French airmen reached this country after the capitulation has already been told. They are still arriving, and pilots of the French Armée de l'Air were stated to have participated with the R.A.F. in raids over Germany on July 21 and July 29.

Why Aerial Supremacy Will Come

IN quality our airmen easily excel the Nazis, and there is good reason to believe that our machines are far better than any that Germany has yet put into the air. Only in numbers has Britain lagged behind hitherto, and here the tide will soon turn. Our home production is now double that of a year ago ; aircraft production in Canada, too, has been doubled, and, as Lord Beaverbrook disclosed on July 25, the output of aircraft for Britain in the United States is to be increased by an additional 3,000 per month. Eleven thousand aeroplanes have been ordered in the U.S.A. by the British Purchasing Commission, and of these 2,800 have so far been delivered. Even allowing for the set-back due to the French débâcle,

we are probably now making or receiving every month more aircraft than are being turned out in Germany. Moreover, our own production curve is rising steeply, whereas that for the German output must be falling. Our airmen are harassing enemy aircraft works by daily raids, and Britain's home defences take a steady and increasing toll of raiding aeroplanes. All these factors are making for that preponderance in the air which will allow Britain eventually to take up the offensive again.

'With Love From H. to M.'

WHO can deny that when Dictators decide to give a present it is conceived on a big scale ? Did not Hitler give Stalin half of Poland ? He has now sent to Mussolini an anti-aircraft train equipped with sixteen guns. Formal presentation of the train was made at a station on the coast near Rome by the German General Ritter von Pohl, in the presence of many distinguished German and Italian representatives. The Duce remarked that the gift was " another proof of the indissoluble fraternity of arms binding the great German people to the Italian people in war and peace," and carefully tested all sixteen guns before returning to Rome.

It is to be hoped that his gunners will not repeat the mistake made both at Venice and Rome when agitated A.A. batteries fired at what proved to be their own bombers. . . . . . Or is it ?

America's 'Keep Out!' to the Nazis

AT Havana, capital of the Republic of Cuba, the foreign ministers of the 21 American republics have just met as the Pan-American Conference. Economic problems were prominent on the agenda, but more important was what Mr. Cordell Hull described as " the threat to our security arising from activities directed from outside our hemisphere ; an attempt to acquire domination of the Americas by foreign governments." Everyone knew that the U.S.A.'s Secretary of State was referring to the Nazis, and unanimous approval was given to the Act of Havana, one of whose clauses stated that no transfers of sovereignty of colonies of non-American countries in the Western hemisphere would be recognized or accepted. Moreover, steps might be taken by Pan-American countries to occupy such colonies as a temporary defence measure.

Heavy Losses of the Nazi Raiders

ON July 25 our defences accounted for 28 German raiders, with the loss of only five of our fighters, and this was no isolated achievement : on July 11 we brought

down 23 ; the next best was 21 shot down on July 20. On July 29 the enemy made a fierce attack on Dover, losing seventeen 'planes in the short space of half an hour. Since the first mass raids on Britain (June 18) 249 Nazi aircraft had been destroyed up to July 29, an average of nearly six a day.

Rumania's Unfriendly Attitude

FOLLOWING the detention of three Rumanian vessels by the British authorities at Port Said, H.M. Government on July 29 lodged a formal protest in Bucharest against a series of measures taken recently by the Rumanian

Vice-Admiral Muselier has been appointed by General de Gaulle to the command of the French Naval and Air Forces that are still fighting side by side with Britain.
Photo, Central Press

Government, all of which were designed to injure British interests. Restrictions were placed on the movements of British shipping in the Danube, British engineers and officials of the oil industry were expelled, and the British and Dutch-owned Astra Romana Oil Corporation virtually expropriated. All these acts, together with the summoning of the Rumanian Premier and the Foreign Minister to Berchtesgaden, mark an intensification of the Nazi drive to gain control of Rumania's oil industry. It was stated that the July shipments of oil to Germany would total about 180,000 tons, and that this purchase alone would suffice to keep 6,000 aeroplanes completely fuelled for more than a month.

Strange 'Planes Over Britain

ONE of the twelve enemy aircraft brought down while raiding this country on July 24 was an American dive bomber, a Chance Voight 156, which had evidently been captured from the French. Such 'planes may soon be flown by British pilots in their raids over Germany. A few days earlier one of our Hurricanes shot down in the English Channel a Messerschmitt 110, which was probably the first Nazi fighter to be used against Britain as a bomber. It was designed as a twin-engined fighter, and by converting it into a bomber both its range and striking power must have been sacrificed, since the long-range tanks and probably the rear guns also would have been removed.

Deadly 'Speed Boats'

MOTOR torpedo craft, known as "E" boats, are being used by the Nazis to attack British convoys in the Channel. These small but deadly craft are, in a way, a development of the racing " speed boat." Revolutionary principles of design have made possible present-day types, which can attain a speed of more than 40 knots. But the M.T.B. is a fair-weather craft, and even then failed at Dunkirk.

On July 23 the British Government recognized the Czech National Committee as a Provisional Czechoslovak Government, which will have its headquarters in London. Here Dr. Benes on the right watches a member of his Cabinet take the oath of office. *Photo, Planet News*

I WAS THERE!

I Was One of the Lucky Ones of the 51st

"Seeing that only a few hundreds out of 6,000 of the 51st Division got away from St. Valery," writes A. Borman, formerly a member of the staff of our publication "World War : 1914-18," and now a sergeant in the Royal Artillery, "I consider myself one of the most lucky." Here is his adventurous story, told exclusively to "The War Illustrated." For the full story of the Division see pages 86-87.

As a pre-war Territorial, I felt highly honoured when my battery was put in the 51st Division, which in the last war had so high a reputation for fighting spirit. After we went out to France we were on garrison duty in the Maginot Line, and even after the great offensive had begun we enjoyed ourselves for some weeks in the fight against the enemy. Then, quite suddenly, we were ordered to travel across France to try and break through the big bulge which had developed in the Allied line.

Much to our disgust, we were never able to do so, but our division lined up beside the French army on the Somme and defended Abbeville until the order came to retreat. Then we dropped back, all the time under heavy fire, until we got to that very charming little place, St. Valery-en-Caux (see photo in page 86).

The Germans held the town and, converted for the time being into infantry, my battery marched down the road and fought in St.

Valery until we had captured it. We had rather an exciting time in the place as the Germans were giving us all they had with machine-guns, trench-mortars and field-guns; indeed, after a time, a little group of us, seventeen in all, lost touch with our unit altogether, and it felt then as if we were the only British soldiers in the town. Eventually we regained our unit, and news came through to us about midnight on June 11 that boats were on the way to take us off; so, under the command of Major Mullens, we marched down to the harbour, where we were halted and told to about turn.

There we found that the boats we had expected would not be coming.

Then, to our amazement, Major Mullens marched us away from the harbour up a hill into a wood, where we waited from three o'clock in the morning until six. Then the major called us together and told us that he had very grave news indeed ; in fact, that most of the division had had to surrender. He himself, however, was determined not to surrender if he could help it, and any man who wished to follow him could do so at his own risk. With that he said, "I'm off !" and started running through the wood. Needless to say, we all followed him as closely as we could.

He led us for six miles under continuous machine-gun and trench-mortar fire, until eventually we arrived at a small village called Veules-les-Roses, where to our joy we discovered many British and French small craft. Even then we were still under very heavy fire from batteries mounted along the

Sir Michael Culme-Seymour, in command of the "Brazen," was promoted to the rank of Lieut.-Commander in 1939. The "Brazen" was his first command. A photograph of the destroyer appears in page 106.
Photo, Universal Pictorial Press

shore, and every man of us felt gratified indeed when one of H.M. destroyers arrived and answered them back very effectively.

Before long we were taken on board one or other of the waiting boats. Here I was not so lucky, for I got taken on board a French boat which went back to Cherbourg, where we remained for several more days engaged in the defence of the port. Eventually I got taken back to England in a coal boat to a South Coast port. The day after we arrived in England we were simply horrified to hear that France had capitulated.

Sergeant A. Borman, whose stirring story is told in this page, was serving in the R.H.A. attached to the 51st Division.

We Made Sure the Captain Jumped, Too

Before she sank under terrific bombing, the destroyer "Brazen" (see page 106) shot down three German aircraft. The story of the ship's gallant fighting finish is here told by Leading Stoker Phillips who, with all his shipmates, was saved from the sinking ship.

Leading Stoker Phillips spoke with admiration of the heroism of the crew of the "Brazen," who continued to fight on with the ship going down under them.

They took on about 50 German 'planes, brought down three, damaged another two so badly that they probably would not get home, and successfully drew the 'planes away from the convoy.

Despite merciless machine-gunning of the deck, every man on board was saved and only five were wounded.

Describing the end of the ship, Stoker Phillips said :

The ship began to sink amidships. The Germans dived on us continually with bombs and raked the decks with machine-guns.

Paddling about in water, the gunners kept up a continuous fire to such effect that two more German 'planes were unlikely to get home.

Another destroyer came up and, still under

heavy fire, we began to get off our wounded. Some of them were terribly burned.

The rest of the crew went forward to try and balance the ship in the water. The other destroyer got a wire out and began to tow us, but our ship broke and many of the men found themselves in the water.

The captain was still on the bridge, and called for volunteers to try and save the ship. I was helping a wounded man off, so I stayed with some others who were still on board.

The captain had to get off the bridge, as it went under water, and then, as the rest of the ship went down, he gave the order to jump. We made sure that he jumped as well.

After swimming about in the water for some time the men were picked up and landed back in port.

On the jetty the captain told us he wanted us all to serve with him again, and I hope we all go, because it's a fine crew. We took the rap, but we certainly saved the convoy. When we had finished with Jerry they had no bombs left.—(London "Evening News.")

136   *The War Illustrated*   *August 9th,* 1940

IIIIIIIIIIIIIIIIIIIIIIIIIIIIIIIIIIIIIIIIIIIIIIIIIIIIIIIIIIIIIIIIIIIIIIIIIIIIIIIIIIIIIIIIIIIIIIIIII I WAS THERE! IIIIIIIIIIIIIIIIIIIIIIIIIIIIIIIIIIIIIIIIIIIII

We Swam in Oil When 'Lancastria' Sank

None of the sea disasters of the war is likely to surpass in human suffering the wreck of the troopship "Lancastria," which was bombed and sunk in St. Nazaire harbour on June 17.   Here are some survivors' stories of the tragic and pitiable scenes they witnessed, and of coolness and heroism in the face of catastrophe.

Sister Chamley, of the Church Army, photographed after her arrival in London, was one of two sisters who risked their lives to give a chance to the soldiers.
Photo, Topical

THIS is the story an Army officer told. I was on deck saying goodbye to two friends when the aeroplanes first came over.   The 'planes were only 200 feet up.   I thought they were British.   Then the "Lancastria" was hit.   As she went down I waited until her deck was awash, then stepped into the sea.   I still had on my tin hat.   It was just as well, because when we were all in the water the 'planes still went on dropping bombs.   As they hit the sea their force lifted us right out of it.

The most dreadful thing was the cries of those who couldn't swim and there weren't enough lifebelts to go round.   You heard, " Help me !   I can't swim "—and you couldn't do anything.

But the courage shown was magnificent. Those who could swim sang as they swam.

I managed to get into a lifeboat, but it was soon so overcrowded that it turned turtle and we were all back in the sea.   I clambered on the keel, holding a paddle I had somehow collected.   With it I pulled more men up with me.   But they all crowded to one end, and suddenly the keel up-ended and we were in the sea for the third time.

After that I started swimming and was picked up by a tug.

A member of the "Lancastria's" crew who tried to launch one of the lifeboats described the scenes on deck.   He said :

As soon as we were struck I pushed my way through the mass of soldiers towards one of the lifeboats.   Already it was full right up with men, and when I moved them the others all surged towards the boat hoping they would get a place aboard.

Just then the " Lancastria " gave a terrific lurch to port and all the men were thrown from one side of her to the other.   I slid on my back down the deck, which was an enormous slant.   I was flung into the sea, which can only be described as being one almost solid mass of men clinging together like flies and covered with thick black oil. Some of them were horribly burnt by the explosion, others were hanging on to debris, others were swimming until they finally sank ; it was every man for himself.

All this time the three aeroplanes were still above us and they continually swooped and bombed the oily waters and their machine-gunners fired on the men struggling for their lives in the water.

Miss Fernande Tips, whose father is managing director of the Belgian branch of the Fairey Aviation Company, said :

I was with my mother, two brothers and a maid in the dining-room when the ship was bombed.   We all wore lifebelts as we ate.

As each bomb fell all we could see was a sort of shadow, followed by thousands of splinters.   Something hit me very hard in the eye and there was a terrific bang.

We tried to stick together.   We went up slanting stairs to the deck.   After that I lost trace of my mother and brothers.   My mother swam about for three hours before she was picked up.

Captain R. Sharp, the " Lancastria's " commander, said :

I was in my cabin when the bombs hit us, all four in one salvo.   I was on the bridge when the ship sank, and I was thrown into the water.   I was supported for four hours by my lifebelt ; then I saw one of my own ship's lifeboats in charge of Murphy, an Irish quartermaster, and McLeod, a Scottish quartermaster.

Murphy called to McLeod : " Holy smoke, there's the captain." There were a number of Frenchmen in the boat, and with their help they hauled me aboard.

I am a heavy man, and I was as slippery as an eel because of the oil on my clothes and the lifebelt.

Two Church Army workers, Sisters Troot and Chamley, said : Through an open porthole we saw a black cloud in the sky moving very fast.   It turned out to be five or six aeroplanes which, as soon as they were over the ship, released bombs.   We rushed on deck and, hearing the order " Women and children first," got into a lifeboat while men were sliding into the sea by ropes and others leapt overboard.

The German 'planes swept down and we saw the spurts as their bullets struck the water where men swam for their lives.

As our boat moved away from the side of the ship, soldiers watching through a porthole saw that we were wearing our lifebelts. They shouted, " Give us a chance," and we took off the belts and flung them into the sea.   The soldiers jumped in after them.   We saw R.A.F. 'planes arrive and drop lifebelts.

When the first warship arrived there was a great cheer and cries of " The Navy's here." (" *Daily Express* " and *Press Association*.)

From the deck of a trawler, about 900 men of the survivors of the " Lancastria " were taken on board a transport.   Here the trawler, so crowded as to render her unseaworthy, is alongside the transport.

Men of the 'Lancastria' Gritted Their Teeth and Smiled at Death

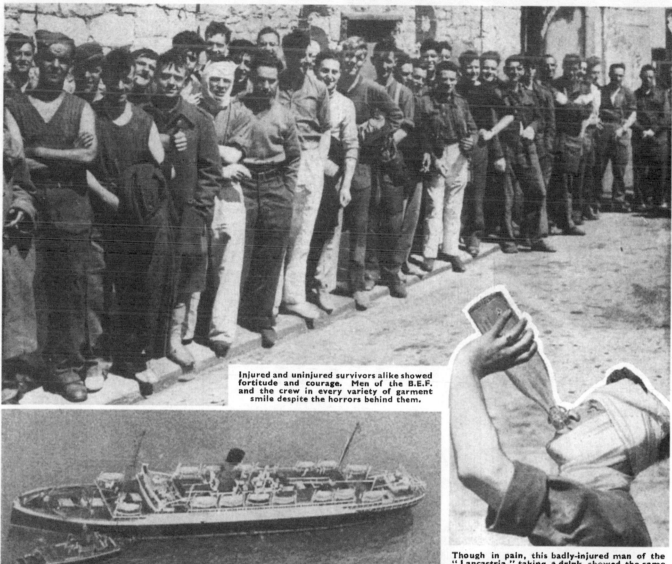

Injured and uninjured survivors alike showed fortitude and courage. Men of the B.E.F. and the crew in every variety of garment smile despite the horrors behind them.

Though in pain, this badly-injured man of the "Lancastria," taking a drink, showed the same unbreakable spirit as his shipmates.

When the news arrived that a ship carrying survivors of the troopship "Lancastria" was approaching a West of England port, doctors, nurses, stretcher-bearers and ambulances were hurried to the docks. Left, is the scene when stretcher cases were being carried to the ambulances. Right, a group of the survivors, among whom is Mme. Tips (seated third from the front, right), whose daughter Fernande tells her story in page 136, and her two sons. Left centre is the "Lancastria," 16,432 tons, as she was before the war—a popular Cunard White Star liner.

Top and bottom photographs exclusive to THE WAR ILLUSTRATED

British Personalities of the War

Wing-Commander Sir Louis Greig, appointed Personal Air Secretary to the Air Minister, Sir Archibald Sinclair, on July 28. A prisoner of war in 1914, he managed to get an exchange in time to watch the battle of Jutland from Jellicoe's flagship.

Mr. W. L. Stephenson, appointed Director-General of Equipment in the Ministry of Aircraft Production on July 23, is a Chairman of Woolworth & Co., Ltd. He will be concerned with additional fittings for aircraft, such as radio panels and other accessories.

Earl of Athlone, K.G., installed Governor-General of Canada on June 21, is a brother of Queen Mary. He married Princess Alice in 1904. Lord Athlone served in the Boer War, and during the last war he was mentioned twice in despatches. From 1923 to 1931 he was Governor-General of South Africa.

Adm. Sir Andrew Cunningham, K.C.B., appointed Commander-in-Chief in the Mediterranean in 1939. He was Deputy Chief of Naval Staff and Lord Commissioner of the Admiralty, 1938-39. He commanded the Battle Cruiser Squadron and was second-in-command in the Mediterranean, 1937-38. Admiral Cunningham served in the first Great War from 1915 to 1918, and earned the D.S.O., with two bars.

General H. R. Pownall, appointed Inspector-General of the Home Guard on June 20, a new post necessitated by the growing importance of the volunteers. General Pownall was Chief of the General Staff under Viscount Gort in the B.E.F. He will now act under Lieut.-General Sir Alan Brooke, Commander-in-Chief of the Home Forces. General Pownall won the D.S.O. and M.C. during the last war.

Brigadier G. R. Pearkes, V.C., was appointed General Officer Commanding, First Canadian Division, on July 16. He went to Canada as a young man, and in 1909 joined the Royal North-West Mounted Police. Enlisting in the Canadian Expeditionary Force in 1914, he won the V.C. in 1918, and also holds the D.S.O. and M.C.

Sir (Percy) James Grigg, K.C.B., Permanent Under Secretary of State for War since 1939, is Chairman of the Standing Committee appointed on July 29 to consider the working of the War Office with a view to simplification for wartime conditions. He was Finance Member of the Government of India from 1934 to 1939.

Lieut.-General Sir Clive Liddell, K.C.B., was appointed Governor and Commander-in-Chief at Gibraltar in 1939. He entered the Army in 1902, and in the last war won the D.S.O. Sir Clive commanded the 8th Infantry Brigade, 1931-34; the 4th Division, 1935-37; and was Adjutant-General to the Forces, 1937-39,

Photos, Hay Wrightson, Vandyk, L.N.A., Evening Standard, Topical, Elliott & Fry, Howard Coster

The Army Wins Its First Victoria Crosses

It is a tragic fact that of the five Victoria Crosses as yet won during this war all but one were posthumously awarded. Of them one went to the Royal Navy and two to the Royal Air Force (see Vol. II, pages 631 and 654). Now two are allotted to soldiers who greatly distinguished themselves in actions before Dunkirk and on the Scheldt as told below.

OF all the great conflicts in history, this war is surely most noted for falsifying all reasonable predictions as to the course of events and for producing the "unexpected." It would have been a rash man to prophesy that nine long months of this vital struggle would elapse before the British Army won its first Victoria Cross. But so it was. It needed Dunkirk to produce the occasion and the men.

On July 30, 1940, the War Office announced that the highest British decoration for valour had been awarded for conduct in

Capt. Ervine-Andrews, V.C. who, during the retirement on Dunkirk at the end of May personally accounted for seventeen Nazis with his rifle alone.   *Photo, " Daily Mirror "*

the field outstanding even at a time when brave deeds and heroic sacrifices were of hourly occurrence. The two soldiers singled out for such signal honour were :

> Lieutenant (now Captain) Harold Marcus Ervine-Andrews, of the East Lancashire Regiment, and
>
> The late Lance-Corporal Harry Nicholls, of the Grenadier Guards.

The dignified pages of the " London Gazette " glow with unwonted life and colour as they set forth the stirring story of these great deeds.

Capt. Ervine-Andrews won his V.C. " for most conspicuous gallantry on active service on the night of May 31–June 1, 1940." The official announcement continues :

Capt. Ervine-Andrews took over about 1,000 yards of the defences in front of Dunkirk.

His line extended along the Canal de Bergues, and the enemy attacked at dawn. For over 10 hours, notwithstanding intense artillery, mortar and machine-gun fire, and in the face of vastly superior enemy forces, Capt. Ervine-Andrews and his company held their position.

The enemy, however, succeeded in crossing the canal on both flanks, and, owing to

superior enemy forces, a company of Capt. Ervine-Andrews' own battalion, which was dispatched to protect his flanks, was unable to gain contact with him.

There being danger of one of his platoons being driven in, he called for volunteers to fill the gap. Then, going forward, he climbed on to the top of a straw-roofed barn, from which he engaged the enemy with rifle and light automatic fire, though, at the time, the enemy were sending mortar-bombs and armour-piercing bullets through the roof.

Capt. Ervine-Andrews personally accounted for 17 of the enemy with his rifle and for many more with a Bren gun.

Later, when the house which he held had been shattered by enemy fire and set alight, and all his ammunition had been expended, he sent back his wounded in the remaining carrier.

He then collected the remaining eight men of his company from this forward position, and, when almost completely surrounded, led them back to the cover afforded by the company in the rear, swimming or wading up to the chin in water for over a mile.

Having brought all that remained of his company safely back, he once again took up position.

Throughout this action Capt. Ervine-Andrews displayed courage, tenacity, and devotion to duty worthy of the highest traditions of the British Army, and his magnificent example imbued his own troops with the dauntless fighting spirit which he himself displayed.

Born on July 29, 1911, Capt. Ervine-Andrews joined the East Lancashire Regiment and saw service during the North-West Frontier campaign in 1936-37. Here, too, he gained distinction being mentioned in dispatches. Safely evacuated from Dunkirk, he has now been appointed liaison officer at Cambridge airport.

His companion in honour, Lance-Corporal Nicholls, was twenty-five years old and a native of Nottingham. He was particularly keen on boxing and fought for his battalion in Army championships. Since the thrilling deeds which earned him his decoration, he has most regrettably been reported as having been killed in action.

The official account of Lance-Cpl. Nicholls' bravery says ;

On May 21 Lance-Cpl. Nicholls was commanding a section in the right-forward platoon when the company was ordered to counter-attack.

At the very start of the advance he was wounded in the arm by shrapnel, but continued to lead his section forward.

As the company came over a small ridge the enemy opened heavy machine-gun fire at close range. Lance-Cpl. Nicholls, realizing the danger to the company, immediately seized a Bren gun and dashed forward towards the machine-guns, firing from the hip.

He succeeded in silencing first one machine-gun and then two other machine-guns, in spite of being again severely wounded.

Lance-Cpl. Nicholls then went on up to a higher piece of ground and engaged the German infantry massed behind, causing many casualties and continuing to fire until he had no more ammunition left. He was wounded at least four times in all, but absolutely refused to give in.

There is no doubt that his gallant action was instrumental in enabling his company to reach its objective and in causing the enemy to fall back across the River Scheldt.

This delightfully human photograph of the late Lance-Corporal Harry Nicholls, one of the Army's first two V.C.'s, was taken shortly before his death. He is seen with his wife and baby daughter at his home in Nottingham. Lance-Corporal Nicholls was wounded at least four times, but absolutely refused to give in.
Photo, " Daily Mirror "

OUR DIARY OF THE WAR

WEDNESDAY, JULY 24   *326th day*

On the Sea—German warship torpedoed in North Sea by Swordship aircraft of Fleet Air Arm.

British motor torpedo-boat sighted six enemy M.T.B.'s and engaged them. Enemy made off, but at least one was hit.

News was released of sinking on June 17 of liner " Lancastria " which was bombed by enemy aircraft off St. Nazaire during final evacuation of B.E.F. Death roll of about 2,500, mostly British soldiers.

In the Air—R.A.F. made night raids on docks at Emden, Wilhelmshaven and Hamburg, aircraft factories at Wismar and Wenzendorf, and seaplane bases at Borkum and Texel.

Haifa bombed by hostile aircraft causing an oil fire ; 46 people killed and 88 injured.

War Against Italy—R.A.F. bombers successfully attacked ammunition dump south of Bardia, Libya. Patrolling Gladiators shot down four enemy fighters and disabled a fifth. Hangars at Macaaca damaged.

Home Front.—Twelve enemy aircraft, including an American dive-bomber captured from the French, destroyed in and around Britain. Biggest air battle was fought off S.E. coast.

Rumania—Rumanian Government took over control of Astra Romana Oil Company, owned by British and Dutch interests.

THURSDAY, JULY 25   *327th day*

On the Sea—French merchant ship " Meknes," repatriating 1,300 French naval officers and men, sunk off Portland during night of July 24-25 by enemy motor torpedo-boat. Over 300 missing.

Admiralty announced that H.M. trawlers " Kingston Galena " and " Rodino " have been lost through enemy action.

Italy admitted loss of another submarine, the 16th.

Portuguese steamer " Alfa " reported sunk by German 'planes on July 15.

In the Air—R.A.F. made night raids on oil supplies, aircraft factories and aerodromes in North-West Germany and Holland. Hamburg docks and the Dortmund-Ems canal were also attacked.

Announced that in last three months R.A.F. had made more than 1,000 large-scale raids into Germany and German-occupied territory.

War Against Italy—Eritrean ports of Massawa and Assab were attacked by R.A.F. bombers. Four raids made on Macaaca.

Home Front—During air attacks on Channel convoy five small vessels were sunk and five others damaged. Nine enemy torpedo-boats then attacked but were engaged and chased away by two British destroyers and two M.T.B.'s. These were in turn attacked by German dive-bombers and both destroyers received some damage.

Twenty-eight enemy aircraft destroyed during widespread attacks on shipping in Channel and round other parts of the coast.

Rumania—Obeying Hitler's summons, Rumanian Premier, M. Gigurtu, and Foreign Minister arrived at Berchtesgaden.

General—Red Cross Sale at Christie's closed after realizing £84,023.

FRIDAY, JULY 26   *328th day*

On the Sea—Admiralty announced that H.M. trawler " Fleming " had been lost in action between two trawlers and four German dive-bombers.

In the Air—R.A.F. made daylight raids on Dortmund power station and Dutch aerodromes of Schiphol and Waalhaven. Owing to adverse weather conditions, night raids were confined to attacks on oil depots at Cherbourg, St. Nazaire, and Nantes.

Gibraltar suffered bombing attacks, but only slight damage was done. No casualties.

War Against Italy—Raid by R.A.F. bombers on Derna aerodrome, Libya, resulted in damage to six enemy aircraft. Successful attacks were carried out on Assab, Eritrea.

Italian aircraft bombed Mersa Matruh six times. Four casualties and slight damage.

Home Front—During the night German bombers were reported over S.E. England. Other districts raided were S.W. England and Wales. Air fight took place off Northern Ireland when convoy was attacked. At least four raiders shot down by home air defences.

Balkans—Rumanian Premier and Foreign Minister had " talks " with Hitler and Ribbentrop. They left the same evening for Rome. Stated that Rumanian merchant ship and two tankers have been detained by British authorities at Port Said.

Bulgarian Premier and Foreign Minister arrived at Salzburg.

General—M. Avenol resigned office of Secretary-General of League of Nations.

SATURDAY, JULY 27   *329th day*

On the Sea—Coastal Command aircraft successfully bombed enemy supply ship off Norwegian coast. Another left in sinking condition off Dutch coast.

In the Air—R.A.F. bombed Nordsee Canal, N. Holland, barges at Stavoren, in Friesland,

Sunk without warning by a German motor torpedo-boat on July 25 the French liner " Meknes " was taking repatriated French sailors back to France with all lights on and the French flag illuminated. Nine officers and 374 men were reported missing out of 1,277 on board.
Photo, " News Chronicle "

oil depots at Hamburg and Amsterdam, docks at Wilhelmshaven and Bremen, and eight enemy aerodromes in Holland and Germany.

Enemy bombers made three raids on Malta, but damage was slight.

Home Front—During night of July 26-27 a bomber was brought down off S.E. coast. Four daylight raiders, including a seaplane, shot down. Night raids were on a small scale, chiefly in areas of Wales and S.W. England.

Empire—Sydney radio announced that a total of 125,000 men had volunteered for the Royal Australian Air Force.

Balkans—Hitler received Bulgarian Premier and Foreign Minister at Berchtesgaden.

Rumanian Premier and Foreign Minister had conversations with Mussolini and Ciano at Rome.

Japan—Eleven prominent British subjects detained by Japanese gendarmerie.

SUNDAY, JULY 28   *330th day*

In the Air—Four enemy aeroplanes were brought down off Malta by R.A.F.

Three raids in preceding 30 hours were reported from Alexandria. Aden was raided, but damage done was superficial.

During the night of July 28-29 the R.A.F. bombed German oil tanks at Cherbourg and seventeen aerodromes in Germany, Holland, Belgium, and Northern France

War Against Italy—Air operations over Libya, East Africa, and the Mediterranean resulted in the destruction of nine Italian 'planes.

French pilots and crews with the R.A.F. carried out reconnaissance over Diredawa, Abyssinia.

Home Front—Nine German aircraft destroyed in fights over and around our coasts. At least 70 aircraft took part in aerial engagements over countryside of S.E. England at a great height ; in this combat five enemy fighters were shot down.

Enemy bomber shot down off S.W. coast, and a second one in S.E. England.

Empire—Reported that first Royal Canadian Air Force fighter squadron, fully equipped, had reached England.

France—Nazis stopped at 5 a.m. all traffic between occupied and unoccupied areas, trains being held up at Moulins.

General—Hitler received Dr. Tiso, President of Slovak Republic, and the Slovak Premier at Berchtesgaden.

Earl of Perth resigned his post as chief adviser on foreign publicity to Ministry of Information.

MONDAY, JULY 29   *331st day*

On the Sea—H.M.S. "Guillemot," a patrol vessel, shot down a German dive-bomber.

Admiralty announced that H.M. destroyer "Wren" had been lost in action with enemy aircraft, during which H.M.S. "Montrose" shot down two enemy bombers.

In the Air—R.A.F. bombers made daylight raids over Germany and the Low Countries. Barges were hit at Emden and Hamburg, and aerodromes in Germany and Holland were attacked.

During the night of July 29-30 R.A.F. bombers, accompanied by French airmen, attacked oil refineries, shipping, and road and rail communications in North West Germany, the Ruhr and the Low Countries.

Following announcement that German seaplanes marked with Red Cross had been used for reconnaissance work, the British Government warned the German Government that ambulance aircraft which do not comply with the requirements of the Red Cross Convention do so at their peril.

Italian aircraft raided Aden, causing negligible damage and nineteen casualties.

Home Front—In a big air attack on Dover Harbour, seventeen of the eighty German 'planes engaged were brought down in half an hour ; four more German 'planes destroyed off our coasts during the day.

Secretary of State for War announced that standing committee of business men had been set up to consider reorganization of War Office procedure.

Empire—Announced that a strong contingent of troops from South Africa had arrived in Kenya.

Japan—Japanese Foreign Office issued statement accusing arrested British subjects of espionage.

Rumania—British Note delivered in Bucharest protesting against Rumanian interference with British oil interests.

TUESDAY, JULY 30   *332nd day*

First Army V.C.'s—Announced that Victoria Crosses have been awarded to Lt. (now Capt.) H. M. Ervine-Andrews, East Lancashire Regiment and (posthumously) to Lance-Cpl. H. Nicholls, Grenadier Guards.

TANKS ARE PART OF THE ENGLISH COUNTRYSIDE IN SUMMER NOW

People in many parts of Britain have grown accustomed to the sight and sound of tanks and other armoured fighting vehicles speeding through the village streets or lumbering along over open country during exercises. Today, however, these vehicles take on a new significance : Britain is in the battle zone, and the tanks are on active service ; light tanks like these, seen emerging from a narrow and tortuous country lane, will be in the forefront to repel the Nazi invader, should he effect a landing on our soil.

Photo, British Official : Crown Copyright

Japan Wants All the Far East to Herself

During the Great War of 1914–1918 Britain and Japan were firm allies, but in this struggle British diplomacy has to meet a Japanese Government which seems more ready to seek the favour of the Axis Powers. Here we give an account of Japan's rise to greatness and of her imperial aims, which may be read in conjunction with the arrests of Englishmen in Japan early in August and similar manifestations of hostility.

JAPAN is so much of a Great Power nowadays that it is difficult to realize that only a little over seventy years ago she was a medieval empire, a feudal State which foreigners were forbidden to enter and natives forbidden to leave. There are many men still living who learned their geography from school-books in which Japan was hardly mentioned, for about it so little was known. Only in 1867 did she burst the eggshell in which for so many centuries she

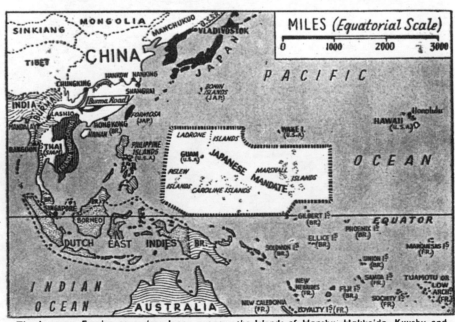

Prince Fumimaro Konoye, who formed a new Japanese Cabinet on July 21, 1940, was born in 1891 and is a member of one of the five most noble families of the Japanese Empire.

had been confined, and under the leadership of the younger members of the Samurai, as the feudal nobles were called, stepped out on the road which, in the course of a few decades, should place her on a level with the Great Powers of the Western World.

With unparalleled rapidity Japan was modernized on the best Western models. A democratic constitution was set up with an elected parliament and a responsible cabinet, although the Emperor, whom only foreigners call the Mikado, retained the title of "Imperial Son of Heaven of Great Japan," and with the title his divine honours and privileges. A great navy came into being, patterned on that of Britain; a great army, too, of which Germany, so recently triumphant over the French at Sedan, was the inspiration. From a self-supporting agricultural community Japan became a great industrialist nation and, again after the Western models, she began to look overseas for markets and for raw materials. Japanese Imperialism had been born.

Japan's first war was with China in 1894; the bone of contention was Korea, which passed as a result to Japan. In 1902 came the Anglo-Japanese Alliance—which endured until 1922—and, so fortified, Japan felt strong enough to challenge the power of the Russians who were her rivals in the penetration of the great territory of Manchuria. To the surprise of the world—though not, we may presume, of the British Government—she annihilated the Russian fleet in the great battle of Tsushima and captured Port Arthur after a tremendous battle. With her hold on Manchuria confirmed she went into the Great War as Britain's ally, and again emerged with substantial fruits of victory. She was now not only a Far Eastern power but a world power, and her statesmen now began to talk of a "new order in Asia" in which Japan should play the dominant part. In pursuance of these vast imperial designs her armies in 1931 converted Manchuria into the puppet state of Manchukuo, and six years later invaded the mainland of China. That war still goes on—one of the greatest which history records if regard be had to its extent and the number of men engaged.

After three years of fighting the Japanese have occupied most of the northern and coastal regions of China, although in the interior provinces the government of General Chiang Kai-shek, operating now from Chungking, still maintains a vigorous and not unsuccessful resistance. Since a state of formal war has never been declared—the Japanese refer to the conflict as the "Chinese affair"—Chiang Kai-shek has been able to

secure from abroad quantities of raw material —from Britain by way of Hong Kong and the Burma Road (see map), from French Indo-China and from Russia, whose Mongolian frontier marches for hundreds of miles with China's in the west. Those doors the Japanese are making desperate efforts to close, and not without success. Thus on July 19, 1940, Mr. Churchill announced that the export of arms and ammunition to China from Hong Kong had been prohibited for the past eighteen months and that now the government of Burma had instituted a similar embargo for a period of three months. Indo-China faded from the picture following France's military collapse, and so only Russia is now left to the Chungking govern-

Mr. Yosuke Matsuoka was appointed Foreign Minister in Prince Konoye's new pro-Fascist Government. He was born in 1880.
Photos, Associated Press

The Japanese Empire comprises Japan proper—the Islands of Honshu, Hokkaido, Kyushu and Shikoku; southern Sakhalin to the north; Korea (Chosen), across the Sea of Japan on the Asiatic mainland; and Formosa (Taiwan). The total area is 260,000 square miles, with a population of nearly a hundred millions. In addition there are the mandated territories—the Marshall, Caroline, Ladrone and Pelew Islands.

But Chiang Kai-shek's China Still Bars the Way

The Japanese have frequently bombed Chungking, to which city the seat of the Chinese Government was transferred from Nanking in 1937. Here a squadron of 24 Japanese bombers is on its way to attack the capital.

ment as a source of war material. But the " only " is a big one ; and besides, Chiang Kai-shek has been rapidly developing munition production in his own territory.

But even if Chinese resistance should be crushed, Japan's imperial aims would still remain unsatisfied. Following Germany's defeat of Holland and of France, Mr. Arita, the then Japanese Foreign Minister, proclaimed a sort of Monroe Doctrine over Eastern Asia, in particular the Netherlands Indies and French Indo-China. Arita's successor, Mr. Yosuke Matsuoka, went still farther when at the beginning of August he declared that Japan was intent on establishing a new order in greater Eastern Asia, which had as its foundation the solidarity of Japan and Manchukuo and China.

If this be the foundation, we have some grounds for speculation concerning the vast edifice which is to be erected upon it. The Japanese have a word for it—" Nanyo "— which may be translated as " South Seas," but is capable of being applied to any or all of the territories which lie between Tahiti and Java. Thus, Nanyo may include the Philippines, Indo-China, Thailand (Siam), British Malaya and the Straits Settlements, with Singapore, North Borneo and Sarawak, the Dutch East Indies, Portuguese Timor, and all the islands of the South Seas, including New Guinea and the Solomons. Some Japanese expansionists of an even more exuberant fancy would stretch Nanyo so that it would take in India, Australia, and even Africa.

For the execution of these far from modest schemes, Japan can rely on the third most powerful navy in the world—it ranks next after Britain's and that of the United States—and an army of some 3,000,000 men and an Air Force of some 3,000 and more 'planes. Her generals are efficient, her soldiers brave and tenacious, and her military equipment of good quality. Yet three years of the most bitter fighting have not sufficed for the reduction of the Chinese national resistance, whether of the armies of Chiang Kai-shek (amounting to between two and three million men) or of the guerilla forces with which China's vast area is liberally besprinkled. Two-thirds of the Japanese land forces are fully occupied in China, together with most of her mechanized units and front line warplanes. Already the Japanese casualties are said to amount to between one million and one and a half million.

Japan's approach to the Axis Powers was signalized by the presence of the 10,000-ton Japanese cruiser "Asigara" at Kiel on August 24, 1937, for a German Naval review. The white ship beyond her is the " Grille," used by Hitler for reviews.

Under the strain of long-continued war Japan is rapidly becoming a Totalitarian State after the Fascist model. The two parties which for years have shared the government the Minseito and the Seiyukai, which may be very loosely described as Liberal and Conservative respectively—are in dissolution and are merging with the Social Mass Party—up to recently socialistic in its trend—in a single party such as is to be found in all the Totalitarian States.

A few years ago it would have been confidently argued that Japan would have been incapable of sustaining so great an effort for more than a year or two. But a state efficiently organized for war can set at naught the dicta of the economists and the financial experts. And Japan is efficient. Nevertheless, there are many signs of war weariness in Japan, of widespread impoverishment. The budgets are astronomical ; forty per cent of the national income is absorbed for war purposes. There is a shortage of coal and iron and of practically all the other materials that are also war materials. The cost of living is rocketing ; prices are rising and wages lag far behind. True, Japan has conquered vast territories capable of returning enormous dividends ; but when will she have the time to exploit them, and where will she obtain the capital necessary for that exploitation ?

These men are Japanese marines such as have landed at the Chinese ports. They are armed with sub-machine-guns. Not only in its organization but in its methods of training and uniforms the Japanese Navy is closely imitative of the navies of the Western Powers

Photos, Wide World, Associated Press

Berliners Must Heil the 'Conquering Fuehrer' Or—!

After the capitulation of France Hitler returned, in the middle of June 1940, in triumph to Berlin, where cheering crowds acclaimed their Fuehrer in the flag-bedecked streets. In the top photograph Hitler is seen flanked by Nazi military and naval leaders as he reviews a guard of honour. Left to right, General von Brauchitsch, Admiral Raeder, General Keitel, the Fuehrer, Marshal Goering, and an officer who is obviously proud of the company he is in. In the lower picture Hitler is seen standing up in characteristic pose in his car as he passes the Berlin Chancellery.

Photos, Keystone and Associated Press

Another Ten Millions for the Hammer and Sickle

Continuing his career of more or less peaceful conquest, Stalin has just incorporated
the Baltic States and Bessarabia in the Soviet realm, thus bringing ten million fresh
subjects beneath the Red banner on which is emblazoned the Hammer and Sickle. These
developments are the subject of what follows.

STALIN, we may well believe, has every
reason to be pleased with the way the
war is going. While the other Great
Powers of the world are exhausting their
national resources and their armaments in
war or in preparations for war, Russia is
accumulating hers in peace. As the war
proceeds the peoples of Western Europe sink
deeper and deeper in the mire of poverty and
ruin ; the economic structure is strained to
the verge of collapse, society is face to face
with imminent dissolution—all things that
must bring joy to the heart of a missionary-
minded Bolshevik.

But there are still more concrete gains to be
recorded. In the autumn of 1939 Stalin re-
incorporated in the Soviet realm large
territories in Poland which were once reigned
over by the last of the Tsars but were lost in

After the Soviet invasion of Bessarabia
numbers of the inhabitants fled into other
districts of Rumania. Above are some of a
large party resting after reaching Bucharest.
Photo, Keystone

the revolutionary wars, and even attached to
them the region about Cracow and the
Galician oilfields which were part of the
empire of the old Francis Joseph. A few weeks
later he converted the three Baltic republics
of Estonia, Latvia and Lithuania into satellite
states, and then, after a brief but bloody war,
compelled Finland to cede territories which,
though small in area, were of considerable
strategic importance. For a few months he
paused in his career of aggression, but by
midsummer of 1940 he was once again on
the warpath.

In the middle of June the three Baltic
states were presented with ultimatums from
the Soviet government demanding free
passage for Soviet troops and the formation
of governments which would " enjoy the
confidence of the Soviet Union." The
ultimatums were accepted, and in a few hours
Soviet troops had occupied the chief towns
and Soviet warships steamed into the ports.
In Lithuania, Estonia, and Latvia the governments resigned and fresh ministers, known
for their pro-Soviet sympathies, reigned in
their stead. Then the people were asked to
say Yes or No to the establishment of a Soviet
regime and the incorporation of their little
countries in the Soviet Union. The results of
the elections were a foregone conclusion ; by

overwhelming majorities the answer in all
alike was Yes.

Still another of Stalin's peaceful conquests
is to be recorded. On June 27 King Carol of
Rumania was the recipient of a Soviet ultimatum demanding the restitution of Bessarabia and the cession of Northern Bukovina.
Bessarabia had once been Russian, but no
such claim could be made for Bukovina,
which before 1918 had been Austrian. Carol
was in no position to quibble, however, and
within 24 hours Russian troops had crossed
the frontier and were busily engaged in
occupying the territory demanded. Thus
within one short month Russia's frontiers were
extended to the Danube in the south and
along 800 miles of the Baltic coastline in the
north. Taking the year's gains as a whole,
a frontier of 2,000 miles, entirely land and

The strategic barrier of newly-acquired territory (see key), stretching from the Baltic to
the Black Sea, which Stalin has built up
between the U.S.S.R. and its neighbours.

so destitute of natural obstacles as to be
almost indefensible, has been exchanged for
one 200 miles shorter, and far easier to defend,
based as it is on the Baltic coast, the River
Bug, the Carpathian Mountains, the River
Pruth and the northern arm of the Danube
delta. Stalin, it is clear, thinks that trouble
may come from Germany's side of the
frontier—and is getting ready for it.

Moreover, as M. Molotov, the Soviet
Prime Minister and Minister of Foreign
Affairs, told the Supreme Council of the
Soviet Union assembled in Moscow on
August 1, the Union's population would be
increased by 2,880,000 inhabitants of Lithuania, 1,950,000 of Latvia, and 1,120,000 of
Estonia. To these should be added the
Bessarabian population and that of Northern
Bukovina—making 10,000,000 in all. If
to these be added the more than 13,000,000
inhabitants of Western Ukraine and
Western White Russia, the increase in the
population of the Soviet Union in the past
year is in excess of 23,000,000. (" It is worth
mentioning," he said in an aside, " that
nineteen-twentieths of that population
formerly formed part of the U.S.S.R., but
had been forcibly taken from it by the
Western Imperialist Powers when the U.S.S.R.
was weak.") Thus the Soviet Union, he
proudly claimed, will now speak in the name
of at least 193,000,000 people, not counting
the natural increase in 1939-1940.

Baltic States' Short Life

Of the most recent additions to the
U.S.S.R. power, Bessarabia can hardly be
worse off under Russian rule than she was
under Rumanian. Such regrets as there are
may be spared for the three little Baltic
republics which, after only 22 years of
independence, are now re-united to Russia.

But perhaps they attempted too much in
1918, when they broke loose from a Russia
in the throes of civil war. In the first flush of
their enthusiasm for independence they
could hardly be expected to weigh the cost of
maintaining armies, navies, parliaments,
diplomatic representatives and so on, when
their populations were so poor and few, and
their territories so small. It will be noted
that even today the people of Lithuania,
Estonia and Latvia added together amount
to 2,000,000 fewer than the Londoners who
live in the Metropolitan Police District.

But in these 20 years they have had at least
the experience of self-government, and it is
to be hoped that as federated republics in the
U.S.S.R. they will continue to enjoy some
measure of cultural autonomy. Certainly in
some directions—in education, in peasant
agriculture and cooperative marketing—
Estonia and Latvia have much to teach
that Russia might do well to learn.

If there is to be any lesson deduced from
their fate it is surely that in the modern world
there is no place for political pocket-hand-
kerchiefs—little States which have neither the
men nor the means to maintain an independent existence. Surrounded on every side by
monster States, they must inevitably gravitate
to one or the other. Who shall say that the
Baltic States have not made the wiser choice ?

The Indomitable Men of the Cliffs of St. Valery

Though not to be compared in magnitude with the magnificent withdrawal from Dunkirk,
the evacuation of British forces from the Dieppe coast was marked by heroism every
whit as great. The story of how our troops were got away from St. Valery-en-Caux, as
told to Mr. Douglas Williams of the "Daily Telegraph," is given here in summarized form.

ON the Normandy coast, between Dieppe and Fécamp, is the little town of St. Valery-en-Caux, clustered on either side of its harbour in a hollow of the cliffs, which here rise up steeply some 150 feet above the beaches. A little way along the coast towards Dieppe is the village of Veules-les-Roses, set in a picturesque valley and having its own tiny beach between two cliffs. Here, on the night of June 12, 1940, were gathered several hundred British soldiers who had managed to evade the Germans when two brigades of the 51st Highland Division were compelled to surrender to the enemy [see Mr. Williams' account in pages 86-87]. Some belonged to an R.A.S.C. Petrol Company, and after days of hard driving under heavy shell-fire had reached La Chapelle, 7-8 miles E. of St. Valery, on June 10. Orders were given to destroy all vehicles not needed for transport of their own personnel, and to move on to the village of Neville, ten miles S. of St. Valery. As the column drove out at midnight, an enemy barrage was creeping up to within 100 yards of the parking place.

After three hours of snail-like progress over bad roads in pitch darkness they reached Neville early on June 11 and began to organize the village to resist the enemy. But in the afternoon the car park was located by enemy aircraft, shelled, and set on fire ; eleven vehicles were destroyed. All the men escaped injury, however, and the unit was ordered to make its way to the beach at St. Valery—there to await the C.O., who, on a push-cycle, had gone to report at divisional headquarters. H.Q. had moved, and so the officer returned to Neville, destroyed all petrol supplies there, and made for St. Valery.

At the outskirts of the town he was stopped by heavy shelling, and so turned eastwards in the direction of Veules, hoping that he would come across his men later. On the way he had collected a number of stragglers. At Veules they found themselves on the cliff top, 150 feet or more above the beaches, with no apparent means of descending in safety.

An attempt was made to get through a wood that ran down to the beach, but the enemy was there in force, and a dozen of our men were picked off as they tried in single file to cross a gap. There was nothing for it but to retrace their way to the cliff top, where the party was joined by part of the missing Petrol Company.

It was now well after midnight, and something had to be done quickly if they were not all to be taken like rats in a trap at the coming of daylight. A signaller N.C.O. flashed a message in Morse to ships waiting in the Channel off St. Valery, warning the boats to stand by, while others of the party sought frantically for ropes or other means of descending the steep cliffs.

Pulling up a wire fence, men unwound it and lowered this makeshift "rope" over the cliff edge. They tried to climb down on it, but it broke and several men fell headlong.

Down a Rope of Rifle Slings

There was a windlass standing on the edge of the cliff, and the men found a wire hawser, which they attached. Some tried to descend this way, but the hawser was greasy and their hands slipped, so that more fell to the bottom. Then someone thought of their rifle slings. These were made of very stout webbing, and if they could be joined securely might furnish a lifeline by which the men could reach the beach below. By reef knots and the use of the stout brass clips at the ends the slings were fashioned into a "rope" and it was tested. It held, and for seven long hours it stood the strain while all the party at the cliff top slid down gingerly.

GERMANS SHELL & MACHINE-GUN FROM WOODS

FROM DIEPPE

Veules-les-Roses

CAILLEVILLE

TOWN CUT OFF AND FIRED

St. Valery en Caux

ALL SORTS OF BOATS CAME TO THE RESCUE

SMALL CAVES IN WHICH SOLDIERS HID

TROOPS CRAWLED ALONG BEACH

ENGLISH CHANNEL

This short stretch of coast shows the little ports of St. Valery-en-Caux and Veules-les-Roses, linked by the line of caves which provided hiding-places for men of the B.E.F. during the epic evacuation of our forces from the French shores.
By courtesy of the "Daily Telegraph"

The day was well advanced before the Commanding Officer—last of them to descend —made his way down to the beach, but mercifully there was a projecting piece of cliff that seems to have hidden the entire scene from the Germans near by. Not a shot was fired during the slow and perilous adventure. Below the men found boats that took them off to the waiting transports—from the jaws of death.

Cave Refuges of St. Valery

Meanwhile, at St. Valery itself, stirring events were happening. Up to noon on June 11 things had been pretty quiet. There were many Allied troops there, including cavalry and infantry regiments and numerous smaller parties who had lost touch with their own formations. A few minutes after midday a deafening crash was the prelude to a close and heavy bombardment by the enemy, who had come round the town along the edge of the cliff and were shelling the troops in the valley below.

The account of what followed is compiled from the personal narrative of a gunner in the B.E.F. who was present. There was a scramble for what little cover could be got ; from pier and promenade men fled down to the beaches. Some made their way up to the

town to fight the incoming enemy ; a few found boats and rowed out seawards, while others stripped and tried to swim out. Discarding greatcoats, many men made their way over the shingle to places where the towering cliffs gave some shelter ; the tide was coming in, but luckily it turned before reaching the refugees high on the shore.

In the town there was much shelling and machine-gun fire. The enemy sent out two boats filled with soldiers, who rowed along parallel with the shore and machine-gunned those sheltering there. Until dusk, seven hours later, it would not be safe to stir far away, but on hands and knees they made their way over the shingle towards Veules-les-Roses, a mile and a half away. Here and there the men found caves in the chalk cliffs and so gained shelter. Fifty or so—mostly Seaforth Highlanders—were cooped up in a cave seven feet wide and twenty feet long

They had little food and no water, and suffered intensely as the time went on. All the while there was a furious bombardment going on, and lumps of chalk and rock fell from the roof of the cave. At dusk they were joined by a number of French stragglers, and men stood along the foot of the cliffs two and three deep in places.

Tired out with the strain of waiting for ships that did not come, the men dropped off to sleep. There were many false reports, but about 2 a.m. there really were vessels off shore. At 2.30 a.m. a ship's lifeboat came to take off the soldiers to a cargo vessel some 300 yards out The trip took 25 minutes out and back, and only twenty-five to thirty men could be carried at a time.

A second boat was brought into service, and things went more quickly ; later others came to the beach—now running the gauntlet of enemy shell-fire, as the Germans searched for the ships with their artillery. About 5 a.m. aircraft began dive-bombing over the beach, and also machine-gunned the rescuers and waiting troops. But visibility was poor, and the troops fired back with rifles and machine-guns and brought down at least one Nazi.

Dawn disclosed a beach still filled with soldiers, formed up in queues and waiting their turn for the boats. Many more men had filtered in from Veules during the night. Now the enemy started to shell the beaches from woods on the left of Veules. Soon the trees were ablaze, and shells fells around the lifeboats. But under the supervision of the Royal Marines, who laughed and sang and jocularly called out "Cheer up ! " "To hell with the Germans ! " the task went on methodically until at last all were got away. The gunner of the B.E.F. from whose story this account is compiled tells how, as the last transport steamed away, one of the Marines turned to him and said reflectively : "Dunkirk ?—that was a picnic ! "

What the Nazi Cameramen 'Snapped' in France

The rapidity of the German advance through France is suggested by this photograph showing some mounted police following up the tanks and infantry through a village, still in flames, in which there had been heavy fighting. This and the other photographs in this page are German, and reached London through a neutral source.

Photo, Keystone

These big French guns, similar to that seen in page 263, Vol. 2, of "The War Illustrated" are now in German hands, and are being drawn away from their original positions, possibly for use against France's former Allies.

The photograph below was taken on the road from Amiens to Abbeville. A private car has struck a land mine, and the force of the explosion has blown it to pieces, part of the chassis lodging high up in a tall tree.

Here, piled high, are French rifles and machine-guns that fell into German hands, a very few among the hundreds of thousands captured. According to the German description the photograph was taken in the Moselle area soon after the French Army in that district had laid down its arms. *Photos, Keystone & E.N.A.*

Everybody Has A Good Word For A.R.P. Now

Much has been published of late concerning the activities of the A.R.P. organization
in particular localities which have received the attention of Hitler's bombers. This article
is in the nature of a valuation of the work being done by Civil Defence as a whole.

FOR months and months the great army of A.R.P. had a very dull time of it. They had answered the call for volunteers in the spirit of most willing service, and if they did not look forward to any pleasurable experience—after all, it's no fun being bombed !—they fully expected to be called upon very shortly to do their bit when Hitler's raiders were overhead. But the bombers were slow in coming, and it would not have been surprising if some of the first flush of enthusiasm had passed away, and the men and women who wore the badges of A.R.P. and A.F.S., the Red Cross and St. John, had got more than a little tired of waiting.

But even during the long dark days of winter—a winter, moreover, which was more bitter than almost any within the memory of living men—they never relaxed their vigilance. The A.R.P. wardens went on their patrols ; the stretcher and rescue parties, the demolition and decontamination squads, practised to make perfect ; the first-aiders manned their posts and dressing-stations, and the men of the Auxiliary Fire Service on many an occasion proved their value as the reserve arm of the " regulars."

In the War's Front Line

But at last Hitler's bombers did come, and the A.R.P. army showed at once that the months of waiting had not been wasted. They went into action in the most efficient fashion, and from every part of the country where bombs have fallen there come tributes to their courage and their devotion to duty. More than one has been killed while performing his task, and others have been wounded more or less seriously.

Today the personnel of Civil Defence—A.R.P., A.F.S., First Aid, Rescue and Decontamination Parties, and so on—now total one and a half million, and it should not be forgotten that, with the exception of some 200,000, every man and woman in this great host is a volunteer, receiving no payment for the services they render in their hours, often very scanty, of leisure. In many parts of the country, including some

large towns, the whole of the personnel consists of unpaid volunteers. In the larger cities it is impossible for various reasons to rely entirely on voluntary service, and here the paid staff constitute the essential nucleus of Civil Defence ; they form the stand-by parties who go on duty when actual raids occur and in the course of every week they put in 72 hours of regular work. There is no difference in spirit, however, between the full-time and the part-time personnel, and in case after case over ninety per cent of the part-time volunteers have turned out on receipt of an air-raid alarm — and they have done this not just once in a while but night after night.

In general, the organization built up during the months of waiting has worked exceedingly well when put to the grim test of actual bombing. It has almost become the rule that hardly have the bombs finished dropping when the " first attendance " has arrived on the spot. Indeed, there have been many cases when the personnel have gone about their work——helping the injured, rescuing those buried beneath debris, fighting fires, and so on—while bombs have been crashing round about them. Many a life has been saved by their promptitude ; many a fire which might have become a big blaze has been put out by A.R.P. wardens armed with stirrup pumps before it has had time to spread from the attic or room in which the incendiary bomb came to rest.

It is only natural that actual experience should have dictated certain changes in the

When a stirrup pump is used to extinguish a fire the man holding the nozzle of the hose should keep his face as near the ground as possible and have an axe handy to deal with obstacles.
From a set of A.R.P. lantern slides made by Photocrafts, Ltd.

organization and should have revealed the necessity for alteration in minor details of equipment ; but on the whole the experience of actual raids has not revealed the need for any essential modification in the organization of A.R.P. throughout the country, and from every hand there accumulates a mass of evidence of the confidence which people who live in the towns and districts actually raided have come to repose in the local Civil Defence.

There has never been anything very wrong about the morale of the British public, and their traditional sang-froid has been amply demonstrated. But all the same, the people in some of our " frontier towns "—the women who follow their children's example and go early to bed, fully expecting that the middle hours of the night will be spent in their shelter ; the workers who after a full day's toil in the munition factory go to bed with some of their clothes on, so as to be ready for the nocturnal dash—these derive considerable help and encouragement from the example of the warden coolly patrolling the streets as he blows his whistle, the A.F.S. men getting to work with their trailer pumps, and the women in overalls and nurses' garb ready to deal with the injured whether it be just a cut or a crushed limb.

Less than a year ago Sir Edward Evans, one of the two Commissioners for the London Defence, referred to "Cinderella, the new baby of National Defence," and pleaded that Cinderella has got to be given her chance in life, and she still has a great deal to learn. Now, after the experience of a few weeks' air raids, we may say that already the A.R.P. " Cinderella " has not only been given her chance but has shown beyond any question that she knows how to seize it.

Anti-gas respirators are a most important part of the A.R.P. workers' equipment. They must be carried at the "ready," so that they can be quickly adjusted over the head. To ensure that this is done, training is given in donning the respirators in any position, and here an A.R.P. squad in Esher are putting on their masks while lying on the ground.
Photo, Pictorial Illustrations

Ready For Any Bombs That Find a Mark

The A.R.P. service does tactical exercises, learning how to bring the necessary appliances to a raided area in the shortest possible time. A large-scale map and models are here being used for instruction at an A.R.P. headquarters in the South-East.

This photograph and that in the centre show the right and the wrong way to deal with an incendiary bomb. The hose or stirrup pump should be pointed upwards from some distance away, so that only a fine spray falls upon its flames. Too strong a jet of water, directed on to the bomb, will spread the flames.

These A.R.P workers fully equipped in anti-gas clothing are miners at a Lancashire colliery undergoing one of their frequent spells of practice, so as to be ready for any emergency.

Right, an A.R.P. demolition squad is actually at work on the ruins of a bombed house in North England.

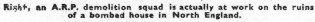
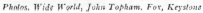

Photos, Wide World, John Topham, Fox, Keystone

Winston Sees That All Is Ready for Adolf

Mr. Churchill investigated every point of interest during his visit to the north-east coast on July 31. Top right he is inspecting the emplacement of a big gun ; above, he has climbed a sandbagged strongpoint to speak to the men ; right, he tries a Tommy gun.

TO the shipyard workers whom he met on his tour of inspection in the North-East on July 31 Mr. Churchill said that the country urgently needed the craft they were building, and that theirs was, therefore, most essential work. He thanked them for the great effort they were making to speed up output, and added that, though he did not know if Hitler had "missed the bus," whatever happened Adolf would not have such a comfortable journey as he might have had a few months ago. When he got back to Downing Street the Premier issued the warning that "Our sense of growing strength and preparedness must not lead to the slightest relaxation of vigilance or moral alertness."

When making his speech to the shipyard workers, during their dinner hour, Mr. Churchill stood on the running-board of his car so that those at the back of the crowd could both hear and see him.

Photos, British Official : Crown Copyright

Watchmen & Watchdogs Are Britain's Home Guard

Any parachutists attempting to land in London's parks would find men of the Home Guard waiting for them. Here park-keepers in their familiar brown uniforms are being trained.

In a typical English country scene, Home Guards, protected by sandbags, are "sighting" a low-flying aeroplane by way of practice.

The railways have their own Home Guard, a force of 200,000 men who guard both main lines and branches. Here one of them is seen on patrol at a junction.

Where there are wide open spaces to be patrolled, dogs have been enlisted to help the Home Guards. Alsatians and mastiffs are the breeds most favoured, and centre is "Nell," an Alsatian, who is on the alert beside her master on moorlands in north-west England. Members of the Mid-Devon Hunt, enrolled in the Home Guard, patrol Dartmoor on horseback. They work in pickets of three, and above, on the beautiful Middle Tor, a picket is waiting at the end of a turn of duty for the approaching relief.

Photos, British Official : Crown Copyright; Fox, Keystone and "The Times"

The Swastika's Shadow Over 21 Republics

No corner of the world is safe from the nefarious activities of Hitler's missionaries, but outside Europe the lands of Central and South America are perhaps the most exposed to his attentions. Here some of the plottings of recent months are reported.

THERE are twenty-one Republics in Latin America, and there is not one of the twenty-one which is safe from Nazi intrigue—not one but may be the stage of a Nazi putsch.

Hitler has long had his eyes on the republics of Central and South America. They are so rich in minerals, their soil is so fertile, their area so vast, their people so few. And of those people hundreds of thousands are of German descent, speak the German tongue and retain in large measure their German sympathies and outlook. Whether by force of arms or by insidious economic penetration Hitler hopes to bring within the orbit of German rule a considerable area of America south of the United States.

Mr. Cordell Hull, U.S.A. Secretary of State, arriving at the Pan-American Conference held at Havana at the end of July 1940. He is seen between Mrs. Cordell Hull and Mr. George Messersmith, U.S. Ambassador to Cuba.
Photo, Associated Press

Indeed, it is believed that plans are already in existence for the creation of what the Nazi conquistadores are pleased to call the " New Germany," which would comprise a great slice of territory including the northern half of Chile and the Argentine, the whole of Uruguay, Paraguay, and Bolivia and the southern districts of Brazil. In all these countries German agents have been busy in spreading the Nazi gospel.

The headquarters of the Nazi movement in South America is reported to be at Montevideo, Uruguay's capital on the River Plate. Uruguay has a population of only a little more than 2,000,000, and its army is insignificant, so that a handful of armed Fifth Columnists might well expect to seize the country in the space of a few hours or days. Only recently, indeed, details have been revealed of a Nazi plot for the military seizure of the country by shock troops.

A fully-documented exposure of the plot was published in the Montevideo newspapers of June 21. A series of *stutzpunkts* (supporting points) had been arranged at such strategic centres as railway junctions, aerodromes, and the principal towns on the

frontier where they faced a parallel set of *stutzpunkts* in the Argentine and Brazil, whence help from Nazi sympathizers was expected to be forthcoming. The existence of a Nazi political organization with cells in all parts of the country was proved, and such features of the Nazi state as the Hitler Youth Movement, the Labour Front, and the Gestapo had all been in full activity. It was suggested that the German Minister, Dr. Langman, who was much in the public eye during the " Graf Spee " incident of December, 1939, had abused his diplomatic privilege by importing into the country, by way of the Legation bags, propaganda material, cinema apparatus and wireless equipment. Furthermore, Nazi supporters had wormed themselves into key posts in the republic's administration. Stocks of arms had been accumulated at various points, and the plotters were waiting for nothing more than the word from Berlin. Fortunately the Uruguayan government were warned in time, and following a secret session the Minister of the Interior was empowered to ban societies which spread anti-democratic ideas, used foreign symbols, uniforms or salutes. At the same time Nazi agents were rounded up throughout the country.

Germans on the Pacific Coast

After Uruguay, Chile is perhaps the country most likely to receive the attention of the Nazi plotters. A considerable proportion of its population of some 4,000,000 is of German origin, and there are some parts of the country, particularly in the neighbourhood of Valdivia, which might be mistaken for the Reich itself, so preponderant is the German element, so evident the signs of German " kultur," so general the " Heil Hitlers ! " and the swastika buttons in the young men's coats. At the beginning of July a Santiago newspaper reported that the Chilean government had obtained knowledge of a Nazi putsch which was being organized in the country by 50,000 Germans in key places who had made plans to seize the most important mines and power plants.

Argentina, too, has a considerable German element. There is a local Nazi party which indulges in Jew baiting and takes an all too keen interest in what is taught in the 200 German schools. On July 27 the Argentine newspapers published photographs of arms, ammunition and military equipment, the swastika flag and portraits of Hitler, which had been seized by the gendarmes when they

raided the houses of some known Nazi sympathizers in the Misiones territory in the extreme north-east of the country. There was also found a manifesto urging the Germans of Argentina to overthrow the government. It may be supposed, however, that the radicalism which is so powerful an influence in the Argentine is too well grounded to be seriously disturbed by intrigues of this kind.

They Prefer Garibaldi to ' Musso '

In Brazil the danger might be expected to come from the Italian element rather than from the German. There are large Italian colonies in the country, but, as a general rule, while the Italians of the upper and middle classes are of Fascist inclination the workers have been nurtured in the Socialist, Trade Union, and radical traditions. Indeed, as the Buenos Aires correspondent of " The Times " has put it, " the Italy of Latin America is not that of Mussolini but is the Italy of Garibaldi and of Mateotti." But even in Brazil there are said to be a quarter of a million Germans—and where there are Germans there we may expect to find trouble-makers in the cause of international Nazism.

In all the other countries of South America the Nazis have been busy—in Paraguay and Peru, in Bolivia—whose army was once instructed by Ernst Roehm, who returned to Germany in 1932 and two years later was murdered in Hitler's blood bath of June 30—in the republics of the north, in Mexico and the West Indies, even in little Panama, where at the beginning of August the American authorities in the Canal zone arrested 81 aliens. So busy have the Nazis been, indeed, that Col. Frank Knox, President Roosevelt's Secretary of the Navy, has warned his country of the deadly peril in which it may find itself if a foreign Power gains a foothold in the Americas.

Before the Pan-American Conference the Nazis intensified their propaganda in the South American republics. One of the efforts was the sending of large batches of books for free distribution by their agents. Here some of the books are being packed for dispatch to the Argentine.
Photo, Associated Press

Destroyers Are Always on the Mark!

The crew of a destroyer are doing useful work in their off time, above, by practising shooting with miniature rifles. The man, right, has draped over his shoulders bands of ammunition for A.A. machine-guns.

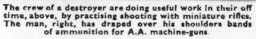

Though all modern ships carry mechanical sounding apparatus, the lead is still swung. Left, one of a destroyer's crew is taking soundings in this way.

Boarding an enemy ship, which is in reality storming it, is still a part of naval warfare, as the case of the " Altmark " showed. Above, men of a destroyer are at boarding practice. They are lying down as the impact of the two ships meeting might throw them off their feet.

Right, an anti-aircraft unit on board a destroyer is in action, often its most frequent form of fighting, as many air encounters show.

Photos, L.N.A.

Once They Fought in Powder and Pigtai

Sailors on land and soldiers on sea, the Corps of the Royal Marines is surely fully entitled to its motto of " Per mare, per terram " (by sea, by land).
They first came into being in " King Charles's Golden Days "—in 1664, to be more precise—and as long ago as 1827 King George IV granted the Corps
the globe and laurel as " its most proper and most distinctive badge," for no colours or crest could possibly contain the names of all the fights in which
it has taken part by sea and land.

ow the 'Jollies' Go To War in Goggles!

In their nearly 300 years of glorious life the Royal Marines have fought with almost every weapon—except bows and arrows !—and under almost every conceivable circumstance of land and sea warfare, but today they have to be ready for conditions such as never faced them when they helped to capture Gibraltar in 1704, or fought the French in Napoleon's time. As this photograph, taken of Royal Marines marching out of a camp on England's west coast for anti-gas exercises, shows their modern panoply includes anti-gas equipment.

The New Balance of the Navies After Oran

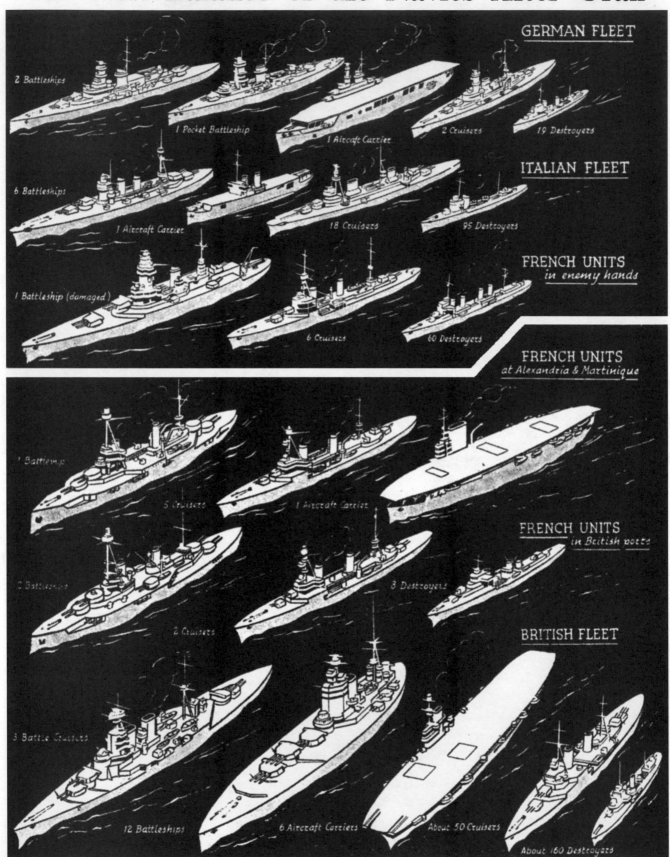

GERMAN FLEET

2 Battleships
1 Pocket Battleship
1 Aircraft Carrier
2 Cruisers
19 Destroyers

ITALIAN FLEET

6 Battleships
1 Aircraft Carrier
18 Cruisers
95 Destroyers

FRENCH UNITS
in enemy hands

1 Battleship (damaged)
6 Cruisers
60 Destroyers

FRENCH UNITS
at Alexandria & Martinique

1 Battleship
5 Cruisers
1 Aircraft Carrier

FRENCH UNITS
in British ports

2 Battleships
2 Cruisers
3 Destroyers

BRITISH FLEET

3 Battle Cruisers
12 Battleships
6 Aircraft Carriers
About 50 Cruisers
About 160 Destroyers

THE AXIS' FLEET—The total strength of the enemy at sea must now be reckoned to include the German and Italian Navies and the ships of the French Navy that were treacherously handed over to the Nazis. The total number of the various classes of ships on this basis is **9 battleships, 1 pocket battleship, 26 cruisers, 174 destroyers, 2 aircraft carriers.**

BRITISH & 'FREE FRENCH' FLEET—Balanced against the now very small Nazi fleet, the substantial, though untried, Italian fleet of 120 ships and the seized French ships must be set the British Navy and the ships of the French Navy now in British hands. The totals are **14 battleships, 3 battle cruisers, about 52 cruisers, about 168 destroyers and 6 aircraft carriers.**

These figures must be taken as approximate to the extent that they do not include the ships that have been added to the British Navy since the outbreak of war. This diagram represents in accurate picture form the main types of war vessels in the navies concerned. In the opposite page the naval forces are so presented that a clear idea of their relative strengths is given.

Diagram specially drawn for THE WAR ILLUSTRATED *by Lawrence Dunn*

Striking Forces of Axis and Allied Fleets Compared

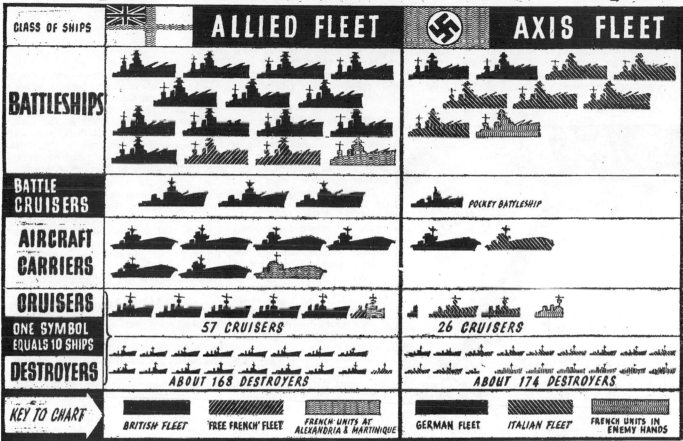

CLASS OF SHIPS	ALLIED FLEET	AXIS FLEET
BATTLESHIPS		
BATTLE CRUISERS		POCKET BATTLESHIP
AIRCRAFT CARRIERS		
CRUISERS (ONE SYMBOL EQUALS 10 SHIPS)	57 CRUISERS	26 CRUISERS
DESTROYERS	ABOUT 168 DESTROYERS	ABOUT 174 DESTROYERS

KEY TO CHART: BRITISH FLEET — 'FREE FRENCH' FLEET — FRENCH UNITS AT ALEXANDRIA & MARTINIQUE — GERMAN FLEET — ITALIAN FLEET — FRENCH UNITS IN ENEMY HANDS

This chart presents in comparative form the numerical strength of the Allied Fleet and of those opposing Britain shown in technically accurate detail opposite. The diagram at right indicates graphically, in the same order as that above, the magnitude of the two groups. Notable and significant is the Axis weakness in capital ships.

GERMANY's navy suffered what M. Paul Reynaud called "irreparable mutilation" during one short week of the Norwegian campaign. Of her pocket battleships she lost the "Admiral Scheer" (another—"Admiral Graf Spee"—was scuttled by the crew after the Battle of the River Plate). Of her two 26,000-ton battleships she lost the "Gneisenau," while the other ("Scharnhorst") was damaged by H.M.S. "Renown." In cruisers she lost the "Blücher" (10,000 tons), "Karlsruhe" (6,000 tons), "Emden" (5,400 tons) and another, unidentified. This left her with a single heavy cruiser and one—or perhaps two—of lighter displacement. Her destroyer strength was almost halved, and today she herself has only nineteen of these vitally important craft, so far as is known.

Under the Treaty of Versailles, Germany was limited to a displacement of 10,000 tons for her biggest warships, and to guns of not larger calibre than 11 inches. Therefore she turned out the much vaunted pocket battleships intended to out-gun any cruisers and to be faster than existing battleships. The remaining big battleship, "Scharnhorst," has a nominal speed of 27 knots.

Nazis Robbed of Naval Spoils in France

By his victory over France Hitler no doubt hoped to redress his naval losses and attain something like parity with Britain, but although the French fleet was ordered by the Pétain Government to be surrendered to Germany, Britain's prompt action robbed the Nazis of the spoils. In a melancholy but necessary action at Oran on July 3 the battleship "Dunkerque" was put out of action and later bombed by the R.A.F.; one battleship of the "Bretagne" class was sunk and another badly damaged; the aircraft transport "Commandant

Teste" was destroyed, and two destroyers were put out of action. Though another battleship, the "Strasbourg," was torpedoed, she managed to escape capture and made her way to a French port.

On July 8 the 35,000-ton battleship "Richelieu," completed but not yet commissioned, was put out of action as she lay in harbour at Dakar. Her sister ship, "Jean Bart," uncompleted, is believed to be under British surveillance. By arrangement with the French admiral in command at Alexandria, certain French warships there (including a battleship of the "Bretagne" class and five cruisers) were demobilized. About the future destiny of the aircraft carrier "Béarn," at Martinique with a number of small naval units, some uncertainty remains.

What Britain is Known to Hold

On July 3 French warships in British ports were taken under control by the Royal Navy, and thus Hitler was deprived of the use of two battleships, two cruisers and eight destroyers. It is in destroyer strength that the enemy, on paper, has something like parity. As our diagram shows, Germany can now control 174 destroyers, including those of the Italian navy and some 60 French ones that were surrendered under the armistice. Against these the Royal Navy can pit its own force of about 160, plus eight taken over from the French.

In capital ships Britain has an imposing and overwhelming preponderance—three battle cruisers and twelve battleships of her own, and two former French battleships. Italy has two new battleships of the "Littorio" class (35,000 tons), completed recently, and two more on the stocks. Besides these there are the four of the "Conte di Cavour" class, built in 1911-1913 and very drastically reconstructed in 1933-1937.

COMPARATIVE STRENGTH OF FLEETS— ALLIED | AXIS

Italy's Columns Invade British Somaliland

The launching of an attack by Italian forces on British Somaliland from the adjoining districts of Abyssinia was announced in Cairo on August 6. Here we tell of the country and the people thus brought into the zone of war.

IN all the many lands that go to make up the British Empire, British Somaliland, which the Italians invaded on August 4, is perhaps the least valuable. Nature has bestowed on it few of her gifts, and man has found it difficult to live in a country of

This map shows the direction of the Italian attack on British Somaliland which opened on August 4. The black arrows, right, indicate the direction of the Italian thrust while the arrow top left shows the threatened advance along the Egyptian coast.

By courtesy of the " Daily Telegraph "

such burning heat and so parched and barren a ground. Yet it is under British protection, and Mussolini would dearly love to be able to tell his people that his soldiers had conquered territory which had flown the British flag.

When the Italian columns crossed the frontier on that first Sunday in August the rainy season was not over—it usually lasts from April until October—but, even so, the invaders would find little water to slake their thirst and to refill their boiling radiators. There are no rivers save in the coastal belt, and even there they cannot be relied upon : in the vast interior of the country there are nothing but seasonal streams and wells few and far between. These wells, we may be sure, will be put out of action long before the Italians reach them.

For the most part, Somaliland is a vast plateau or series of plateaux which, when they near the coast, end in precipices 1,500 to 2,000 feet high, down whose descent wander goat and camel tracks to the coastal plain. Even this plain is almost waterless, and its nature may be guessed from its name, Guban, which in the Somali tongue means " burning." The Italian columns made their way towards Odweina, Hargeisa and Gara Gara, three places in the south which may perhaps be described as towns ;

Hargeisa, indeed, has a population of some 15,000. Odweina and Hargeisa were soon passed by the Italian motorized columns —the central column consisted of two colonial brigades, say 6,000 to 7,000 men, with guns and tanks—but between these places and Berbera and the coast of the Gulf of Aden, the invaders' prime objective, lie a hundred miles or so of rocky desert, crossed from east to west by two mountain ranges.

The first they will encounter, the Golis, has peaks rising to a height of 9,500 feet — peaks which are crowned in some places with forests of mountain cedar ; but for the rest the country they will traverse is covered with tall, coarse grass or with thick thornbush or jungle. Vast stretches of it are sandy desert ; in the mountainous heart of the country they will have to negotiate gorges, jagged and deep.

On their way through this inhospitable land they will meet few people, for of the 350,000 native folk the great majority are nomad tribesmen, who will certainly not stay to make a close acquaintance with the roaring columns of tanks and mechanized transport.

From the point of view of physique the Somalis constitute a splendid type. The men, hunters for the most part, are slim and wiry, and the women when in the flower of life are barbaric beauties. But men and women soon grow old, for the life they live is a hard one—one of constant wandering in search of food, which all too often is not easy to come by. Some of

them breed camels, sheep and cattle, living on their milk and meat and moving with them across the plains in search of fresh grass and water ; some are wandering hunters, men who are outcasts from their tribes and live a life as lonely as it is dangerous ; yet others are more or less settled, living in the villages near the coast or in Berbera and Zeila (occupied without resistance by the Italians on Aug. 5), whose whitewashed houses look out on the waters of the Gulf of Aden.

As a race the Somalis are fighters, and seldom is one encountered without his spear, shield and sword—and perhaps a gun. Under white officers they make excellent soldiers, and the Somaliland Camel Corps —one of the crack native regiments of the British Empire, and now partially mechanized —may be relied upon to put up a stern resistance against the Italian invaders.

' Mad Mullah ' on the Warpath

Not so many years ago some of the Somali tribes under the leadership of one Mohammed bin Abdullah, who called himself the Mahdi and whom we called the " Mad Mullah," carried on a little war against the British forces in occupation of the country. There was severe fighting in 1900 and again in 1903, when an expedition was undertaken against the Mullah by a mixed force of Indian and African tribes supported by British and Boer mounted infantry. After considerable fighting and some reverses, the Mullah was defeated in 1904, but he maintained his position in the country and ten years later overran a large part of the Protectorate. Not until 1920, when 'planes of the Royal Air Force were brought into operation against him, were his activities brought to an end. The Mullah himself died in Abyssinia in 1921. Since then the country has enjoyed the blessings of peace, and there is much that is good to show for the years of British occupation.

The Italian forces invading the Somaliland Protectorate on August 4, 1940, found ground forces as well as the R.A.F. cooperating in the defence. Among the former was the Somaliland Camel Corps, King's African Rifles, men of which are here seen showing the flag on the Somaliland-Abyssinian frontier. The tree is in Abyssinia.

Photo, Paul Popper

May the Nazis' Stay in Jersey Be Brief!

GOOD reasons enough have been advanced for the abandonment of the Channel Islands to the enemy ; but those reasons do not appeal to everyone. " It was honestly meant," said Lord Portsea in the House of Lords on August 1, " but in my view there was a smell of cowardice about it." Lord Portsea belongs to an old Jersey family— his father was one of the judges of the Royal Court of Jersey—and the bitterness of his words will be understood. The Channel Islands had not been conquered for over a thousand years, he went on ; the argument that the inhabitants had at least been spared the horrors of modern warfare and bombardment was, in his opinion, a Pétain argument, and he had no sympathy with it. " I am a very old man," he added, " but do not imagine that because the sands of life are running out those sands are less hallowed. They are hoarded with miserly care. I say to this House in all honesty that if I could go to submit to that bombardment with any chance whatever of recovering those islands I would go today." In conclusion, he appealed to the Government to " do something for my fellow-countrymen "—an appeal which was at once answered in the most sympathetic spirit by the Duke of Devonshire.

Among those who were evacuated from the Channel Islands were a number of the Jersey Militia, who are now undergoing military training in Britain. One of them is seen on the right taking cover when on outpost duty.

It was only to be expected that the Nazis should make the utmost possible use of their occupation of the Channel Islands. Here we have one of the photographs which were used for propaganda purposes in the Reich ; it shows the swastika flag flying above the airport in Jersey. The Germans used the phrase " captured," but actually there was no military action save for a particularly disgraceful exhibition of bombing and machine-gunning of defenceless civilians carried out when the Islands had been demilitarized. Fortunately, many of the inhabitants had been evacuated, or the loss of life would have been even greater than it was.

Photos, British Official : Crown Copyright ; Associated Press

British and Nazi Ways with Red Cross Aeroplanes

Photos, " News Chronicle " and Topical

This is one of the Airspeed " Oxford " ambulances in flight. Adjoining the usual distinguishing mark of British 'planes, the Red Cross is painted on the side of the fuselage.

The ambulance 'planes might almost be called flying hospitals, for among other equipment they carry oxygen cylinders. In the circle, oxygen is being administered. Above, a stretcher case is being put on board. As can be seen in the photograph, top right, the undercarriages of the ambulance 'planes are exceptionally low, so that access to the interior is easy.

ON July 27 the Princess Royal handed over two Airspeed " Oxford " aeroplanes to the R.A.F. They had been subscribed for by the Girl Guides of the Empire, and were the first air ambulances specially constructed for the R.A.F. in this war, converted troop-carrying aircraft having been previously used for ambulance work. They are elaborately equipped. Inside the ambulance there is accommodation for two stretcher cases and two sitting patients. Besides oxygen apparatus, the 'planes carry emergency surgical equipment and have lavatory accommodation. They also carry wireless operators. The presentation was made in the presence of a number of Girl Guides and Brownies. The two 'planes, which cost £7,500 each, were paid for out of a fund of £48,475 raised by the Guides in less than three months.

This is a Nazi Red Cross seaplane which was brought down in the English Channel at the end of July. It had been known for some time that the German claim that these 'planes were engaged in rescue work was utterly false, and in an Air Ministry statement it was now revealed that one of several 'planes bearing the Red Cross that had been brought down near England had been used as a communication aircraft by General-Major Tittel and also to make war films for the German propaganda service.

Birthday Guns With Love from Fuehrer to Duce

German and Italian soldiers are seen above mounting guard over the armoured train presented by Hitler to Mussolini. Right, Mussolini is leaving the train after inspecting it.

ON July 22, a few days before Mussolini's last birthday he received from Hitler a gift of an anti-aircraft train. It consisted of two armoured coaches with 16 anti-aircraft guns mounted on the roofs. It is possible that under certain circumstances it may be a useful refuge for the Duce, but meanwhile he has declared that it is another proof of the indissoluble fraternity of arms binding the great German people to the Italian people in war and peace. The presentation was made by General Ritter von Pohl at a railway station near Rome, and Mussolini personally tested all the guns.

Prince Umberto, Crown Prince of Italy, who commanded the Italian Army that gained a " victory " over France when she had already been betrayed, is inspecting troops and anti-aircraft guns on July 12. *Photos, Associated Press*

OUR SEARCHLIGHT ON THE WAR NEWS

'Alcantara II' Finds a Raider

ON July 28 the armed merchant cruiser "Alcantara" tackled and damaged an enemy commerce raider in the South Atlantic. The British vessel, formerly of the Royal Mail Line, was commanded by Captain J. G. P. Ingham, D.S.O., R.N.

That the Nazis should have thought it worth while to drop leaflets over England giving extracts from Hitler's speech causes great amusement to this A.R.P. man, who could, had he wished, have read the tirade a fort-night earlier in his morning paper.

Photo, Associated Press

The raider was the "Narvik," a fast converted merchant ship, mounting four guns on each broadside. On being hit by the "Alcantara" she turned away, making use of her smoke floats to evade pursuit. But for the chance that one of her shots holed the engine room and reduced the "Alcantara's" speed, the raider would no doubt have been brought to book. As it was she "sustained damage affecting her fighting efficiency." An earlier R.M.S. "Alcantara" figured in a stirring encounter of a similar nature 24 years ago, when she challenged and engaged the disguised raider "Greif." She herself was sunk, but not before so damaging the raider that the latter was easily finished off by two other ships of the patrol.

Nazis Lose 240 Aircraft in July Raids

DURING the month of July in raids on Britain and on convoys near our coasts at least 240 German aircraft have been shot down by the R.A.F. and our ground defences. Personnel numbering at least six hundred were killed or taken prisoner during this period. These facts are given in an Air Ministry communiqué of July 31. They are strictly accurate figures for losses actually reported by our airmen; many more enemy aircraft have been put out of action in the air, though not shot down, and others destroyed on the ground.

Rome Fires On Her Own Aircraft

BEFORE Italy entered the war she declared that Rome was an open city and not subject to bombing under international law. She has since shown some nervousness about the matter, and not long ago the A.A. defences of Venice opened fire at what they thought were raiding aeroplanes—and brought down two of their own bombers ! On the night of July 22 the guns of the Rome defences fired at aircraft flying over the city. The aircraft in question were Italian ones. The official Italian communiqué announced

that two people were injured by A.A. splinters ; the official German news agency said that two civilians were killed and four others injured—but did not mention that these casualties were due to Italian guns.

Perhaps this legendary aerial attack on Rome will go down in Axis history alongside the alleged raid by the R.A.F. on civilians at Freiburg-im-Breisgau, to which Hitler referred in his speech of July 19.

Foreign Legion to Fight With Britain

A REGIMENT of the famous Foreign Legion is included in General de Gaulle's Army of Free Frenchmen. This unit was the first to enter Narvik when the port and town were captured by the Allies last May. After the withdrawal from Norway the legionaries went into line on the French front before Rennes, but had to fall back with the Allied armies after three days. Today they are in Britain, armed, equipped and ready for anything that turns up. The gallantry of the Legion in Norway—where the regiment fought alongside the Chasseurs Alpins—won them many decorations.

British Transatlantic Wartime Flight

HITLER's desperate boast that his air and naval forces are successfully blockading Britain is disproved daily with ever-increasing emphasis. Our food ships reach harbour unscathed ; troops from our far-flung Empire land unmolested at British ports ; our bombers take off for a night's work over North-West Germany and return to breakfast at their base ; and on Sunday, August 4, a civilian flying-boat reached New York after an uneventful 16-hour crossing of the 2,370 miles of sea that lie between the United Kingdom and Newfoundland. She is the British Overseas Airways Corporation flying-boat "Clare," a vessel of 23 tons, piloted by Capt. J. C. Kelly Rogers with a crew of three, and she carried passengers and 112 lb. of mail, including copies of Saturday's London newspapers, which were thus available for New York readers the day after publication. This successful flight marked the resumption of the British Transatlantic Air Service. The "Clare's" sister ship the "Clyde" will also take part in the programme.

Leader of Free Frenchmen

GENERAL DE GAULLE has issued a message to the Army of Free Frenchmen in England, of which a translation is here given.

TO ALL FRENCHMEN

France has lost a battle! But France has not lost the war!

A makeshift Government may have capitulated, giving way to panic, forgetting honour, delivering their country into slavery. Yet nothing is lost !

Nothing is lost, because this war is a world war. In the free universe, immense forces have not yet been brought into play. Some day these forces will crush the enemy. On that day France must be present at the victory. She will then regain her liberty and her greatness. That is my goal, my only goal !

That is why I ask all Frenchmen, wherever they may be, to unite with me in action, in sacrifice and in hope.

Our country is in danger of Death. Let us fight to save it. LONG LIVE FRANCE !

The General has been untiring in his efforts to weld together the new force of Frenchmen eager to fight alongside Britain. On August 3, broadcasting to France and the French Colonial Empire, he questioned whether the French colonies would "consent to be surrendered, starved, put to fire and sword to pander to the terrors which the roaring of Hitler and the barking of Mussolini strike into the hearts of the old men of Vichy." It will be remembered that on July 6 a Court at Toulouse sentenced General de Gaulle

in his absence to four years' imprisonment "for refusing to obey orders and for inciting soldiers to disobey." At the same time the Pétain Government announced that French persons serving with the British forces would be liable to penalties ranging from hard labour to death. But with the "Meknes" affair in mind it is not likely that many Frenchmen will be prevented from joining General de Gaulle by such threats, or by the fact that on August 2 he himself was condemned to death by the Military Court of the Thirteenth Region of France.

Hitler's Leaflet Reprisal

IT is difficult to believe that Goebbels' organization is so maladroit as to think that the leaflets which German airmen dropped over Britain at the beginning of August would have any influence on public opinion. Unlike the leaflets which British airmen dropped over Germany at the beginning of the war, Goebbels' productions did not tell anything new, or even anything interesting, for the contents—Hitler's speech to the Reichstag on July 19—had appeared in full or in fair summary in British newspapers the morning after its delivery. Moreover, a large part of the leaflet was taken up with lists of German army officers promoted, a matter of no conceivable interest to Britons. But if there is any doubt about the motives behind this clumsy propaganda there is none about the reactions of its recipients. In at least one village the lucky finders of the leaflets sold them as souvenirs for a few pence apiece and thus raised a fund for Red Cross needs.

South African 'Bitter-Enders'

ALMOST every town in the Union of South Africa is represented in the advance guard of volunteer troops who were welcomed on July 31 by the Governor of Kenya, Sir Henry Moore. The Force includes all auxiliaries such as engineers, signallers, motor transport and medical services, and among the troops are barristers, "Springboks" and business men. "You are volunteers of your

Two French sailors outside General de Gaulle's London headquarters, on the anniversary of the outbreak of the war of 1914–1918, reading his stirring call to all Frenchmen to rally to the cause of freedom and France.

Photo, Associated Press

own choice," General Smuts had told them in his farewell address. "Your children will be proud of you. We South Africans reserve our respect and pride for bitter-enders, for those who go all out; who take their life in their own hands for their country and their people."

I WAS THERE!

A Heinkel Fell On Our Deck

When the Scottish steamer "Highlander" steamed into port on Friday, August 2, the wreckage of a Heinkel was draped over her stern. Here is the story of how her crew shot down this and another German bomber with their Lewis gun as they told it to W. A. Nicholson, of the "Daily Mail."

A T midnight on Thursday, August 1, the "Highlander" was steaming along off the north-east coast of Scotland when the drone of a 'plane was heard. Captain W. Gifford and the rest of the crew peered into the darkness trying to guess whether it was friend or foe. They did not have to wait long. As the 'plane roared overhead machine-gun bullets spattered on the decks around them, and jets of spray spurted up from the sea where aerial torpedoes had fallen.

Standing by the "Highlander's" Lewis gun were George Anderson, of Leith, and Laurie Halcrow, a young Shetlander. They were joined by Bert Whyman, a seaman from Southampton, and William Birnie, another Shetlander. The raider swooped twice across the ship, coming lower and lower, but Anderson held his fire. Describing what happened, he said :

The 'plane was flying low over us and for a time I could not see it because of the super-structure of the boat. So I aimed at where I thought the 'plane would be. . . .

I let go everything I had. What luck ! As I pressed the trigger the black shape of the machine came right into the sight, and I kept pumping lead into it as fast as I could.

It lurched in the sky over the ship about 30 ft. away, and then crashed. We dodged to escape it as it fell.

One wing caught the side of the bridge, tearing away some of the railings and smashing the lifeboat. The other wing fell over the deck on which we were standing, and smashed the railings and the wheel of one of the derricks.

There was a terrific din, but above it we could hear the cries of the German crew.

The body of the machine then broke away from the wings, and, bursting into flames, crashed into the sea. The crew had no chance to escape.

Then a second Heinkel appeared and dived to the attack.

Laurie Halcrow, who lost his brother through enemy action at sea six weeks ago, clutched Anderson's arm and shouted :

Give me a go, George. I'll give them what they gave my brother !

Like Anderson, young Halcrow waited his chance as the raider swooped to drop an aerial torpedo and machine-gun the decks. As he said :

He came closer and closer and as he got really near I let him have it. I must have scored a direct hit for the raider crashed straight into the sea.

Captain Gifford summed up by saying :

It was a grand night's work. Two or three of the men were slightly wounded, but Anderson was luckiest of all.

One bullet struck his steel helmet and another flew so close to his nose that it scratched his upper lip!—(" Daily Mail.")

George Anderson, of the "Highlander," who, with his shipmate A. Whyman, was awarded the medal of the O.B.E. for shooting down two German bombers. Others of the crew were commended.   *Photo, Planet News*

We Were Besieged For Six Days in Arras

From May 18 to May 24 a small and gallant B.E.F. garrison held the Palais St. Vaast during the historic siege of Arras. The story of their ordeal, as told here by Douglas Williams, "Daily Telegraph" war correspondent, was based on the diary of a soldier in the garrison.

T HE diary begins on May 18, when a detachment of Welsh Guards and a number of odd details separated from their units moved into the Palais St. Vaast at Arras. Here General Petre, commanding the garrison, had set up his headquarters. The story goes on :

We took up positions of defence and, as far as we were able, fortified the building by stripping the library shelves and piling the musty old volumes into the window recesses. Every man had a rifle with plenty of ammunition and, in addition, there were some Tommy-guns, hand grenades and a few Bren guns.

In the road outside was an anti-tank gun and a few light tanks. At the start food was fairly good and plentiful, and we were able to have regular meals. The food was prepared a mile or so away and brought to the Palais in vacuum containers, but, as the air raids became more intense, delivery became more difficult, until one day the Germans landed two direct hits on the kitchen, killing 13 men and destroying all the equipment. After that we had to depend on beef and biscuit from surplus rations, until we luckily discovered the existence of the N.A.A.F.I. canteen near the station, about half a mile from the Palais.

The padre of the Welsh Guards, a gallant and fearless man, used to drive to this canteen every day in his little car, indifferent to the bombs that were dropping, and would return loaded with such delicacies as chicken in glass jars, tinned tongue, galantine, sweet biscuits, and all the cigarettes we could smoke.

We were much bothered by refugees, of whom several hundred had taken shelter in the cellars of the Palais. Among them were spies, some of whom were captured and summarily "dealt with." Sniping from buildings near by was incessant, and houses were frequently raided to catch these traitors.

We spent most of our time, because of incessant air raids, in the cellars, varied by long spells of sentry duty at the windows on the floors above, watching some suspicious corner until our trigger fingers ached.

Our greatest problem was water. The big water tower had been destroyed by a bomb, and what was left had been so heavily treated with chlorine by the Medical Officer lest it should prove to have been poisoned that it was almost undrinkable. Water for

Having brought down two German raiders in twenty minutes, the 1,216-ton "Highlander" sailed proudly home with the wreckage of one Heinkel perched on her poop. Here the debris is being removed. The ship's master, Capt. W. Gifford, was given the O.B.E.   *Photo, Planet News*

The Petite Place of Arras, twice devastated in 25 years, is here seen in times of peace with the Hôtel de Ville in the background and the market in progress, in the foreground.
Photo, E.N.A.

washing was scanty, and after a bomb had fallen in the ornamental fishpond in the garden none of us could shave or wash.

All communication with the outside had been cut. A wireless van containing a transmitting set, which had been brought to us by some Green Howards, sent as reinforcements, was hit by a mortar shell the day it arrived and, with its personnel, was blown sky high.

As the week wore on things became worse. The Germans were closing in all around the perimeter of the city, air raids were so frequent that there was little or no sleep for the garrison, casualties increased, and there was nothing to drink except bottled beer and minerals taken from damaged grocery shops.

One amusing incident enlivened this bad period. A football being used for exercise by men off duty was kicked so hard that it went out of sight. Next day reports were received that an unexploded bomb had been located in the Palais schoolroom and the area was roped off, with sentries posted to keep people away until an expert arrived — to find, of course, that the bomb was only our muddy football.

Finally, shortly after midnight of May 24 we received orders for immediate evacuation. By some miracle 20 of our vehicles parked in the square had survived, and as many as possible of the garrison, with as much kit as could be carried, piled into them, the others following on foot.

Officers of the Welsh Guards refused to ride and marched with their men. We were told to make for Douai by the one narrow strip of country that was still believed to be free from enemy tanks, and as I left the Palais, for the first time since the siege, I was horrified to see the state to which bombing had reduced the city.

Bodies of refugees killed by air raids or shells, dead horses, cats and dogs lay about. Not a single building appeared to have escaped damage. Some had disappeared,

others were reduced to heaps of rubble. Every street was thick with broken brick, smashed glass, and splintered furniture. Although it was in the middle of the night, the glow from blazing buildings made the streets as light as day. Both the Grande Place and the Petite Place were a shambles.

When our convoy reached the outskirts of Douai, there, marching in perfect order along the road, were the Welsh Guards, still led by their officers afoot, every man with complete equipment, some even carrying Bren gun parts. It was a grand and stimulating sight to see such an example of discipline and training triumph over disorder and confusion.

I never hope to meet a braver crowd of men than those Welsh Guards. Every time there was a call for volunteers for some specially dangerous job they would crowd around their officer, each man trying to catch his eye. They did wonderful work amid scenes of horror when the big French hospital of St. Jean was bombed by German low-flying airmen. The attack was deliberately made at less than 100 ft., although the building was marked by a huge red cross, painted in the forecourt, and clearly visible from 10,000 ft. or higher.

Our convoy finally reached the coast at Dunkirk and we all embarked safely for England.

Going Home to France the Nazi Sank Us

While transporting French naval officers and men from England to France the " Meknes " was sunk by a German motor torpedo-boat on July 24, though her name and nationality were plainly marked. The survivors were filled with indignation at this action by the Germans, as seen in the following stories of English-speaking French sailors, based on a broadcast interview with Charles Gardner.

ONE of the French sailors who survived the sinking of the " Meknes " said :
I had just finished playing cards with some friends in my cabin when I heard the machine-guns. I went up on deck, but I couldn't see anything because it was too dark. The next moment, however, I saw tracer bullets above the ship, so I crossed over to the port side, but I still couldn't see anything.

The ship was brightly lit—all the lights were on as if it was pre-war—the name of the ship was clearly shown on both sides, and the French flag was lighted with a searchlight, so it had not entered our heads to think of an enemy. I thought it must be a battle boat, and I put on my lifebelt.

Then the machine-gunning started again. Things became very serious because he machine-gunned all the port side of the ship, making holes in all the lifeboats. The starboard lifeboats were all right ; there were

about five or six, I think, and they all got down except one, which threw all its men down into the sea.

I managed to get into a lifeboat all right, and we were some way from the " Meknes " when she sank. We did not see anything of the attacking boat, but we thought it must be a kind of speedboat. That's all we could imagine. We took to the lifeboat at 11 o'clock at night and were picked up at 7.30 in the morning.

Another survivor said :

When we were taken on board the British destroyers we were given hot drinks and food, and we dried our clothes. We were very grateful to the British sailors for their hospitality. I must point out that the French flag on the " Meknes " was well illuminated by the searchlight, and the enemy must have seen it, but this did not restrain them from sinking the ship.

The " Meknes " was a 6,127-ton liner of the Compagnie Générale Transatlantique. When she sailed on her fatal voyage she carried a complement of nine officers and 90 seamen, while her passengers numbered 99 naval officers and 1,080 ratings, 2 women and 1 child, all French. Of these nine officers and 374 men were not accounted for.
Photo, Central Press

I Saw a Convoy Bombed in the Channel

German bombing attacks on English ports and coastal shipping increased in violence during July, and many fierce fights were waged by the Navy and Air Force. A dramatic impression of one of these battles in the Channel is given in the following story by Ronald Walker of the " News Chronicle."

WAR happened suddenly over the Channel on July 25. So suddenly that I was rather startled. It was the first real war I had seen since I got back from being war correspondent with the R.A.F.

It was a pleasant sunny morning. Soldiers whistled as they polished their anti-aircraft guns. Two sailors sucked ices and wondered

whether " Jerry would have a go today." Despite the fortified state of the front, the soldiers and the sailors, it seemed improbable that Calais, across the Channel, was full of nasty Germans with evil intentions. . . .

Softly at first as to be just a murmur came the vibrating sound of aero engines. The German machines were so high that it was not possible to see them at first. Against the blue of the sky they betrayed themselves by leaving the trails of white smoke or cloud from the engine exhausts. Then we picked out a flight or two, so high that they were no bigger than moths. The sound of engines swelled as the Spitfire fighters came roaring up from their near-by bases. They climbed into the blue heights and in no time the sky was criss-crossed with streaks of white as the British pilots went into the rough and tumble.

From their battlefield the faint staccato rattle of machine-guns came drifting down, oddly distinct from the rising and falling note of the engines as they dived and climbed. The battling machines came lower and the noise increased. A new whistling note was added as Nazi bombers dropped very large "eggs" on the harbour.

As the enemy aircraft came nearer the shore guns opened up. The windows of the boarding-houses sounded like a crazy tap drummer. At the gun post on the front the crew grinned with a sort of cat-like satisfaction as they crammed the clips of shells into the breech.

The Germans, having dropped their bombs, turned for home. The dog-fight dwindled. Our fighters went off home after making a final search of the sky for intruders. All was quiet again . . . .

This story continues about two and a half hours later. Round the headland came, steaming slowly, the ships in line, 21 small cargo boats convoyed by two armed trawlers.

The attack was without warning. Through the cloud layer overhead swooped the German dive bombers. The air was filled with the sound of their fury, and the cliffs echoed with the roar of the bombs which rocked the little ships.

Two disappeared in a welter of smoke and water. When it cleared they were both sinking rapidly. Companion ships slowed down and waited to help. From the port fast motor-boats raced out to rescue the crews. Twice the enemy dived. Another ship was sinking. Others were hit.

The remaining ships formed again into line and continued. It was a splendid demonstration of the splendid courage of the British merchant seaman. High above them British fighters raced about.

Half an hour later the Germans crept through the clouds again and came hurtling down on the ships. Two more were badly hit. Quickly they listed and in a few minutes were gone. Again the survivors reformed and went off down the Channel.

One of the smaller ships came limping towards the shore. It was slowly settling down by the stern. Just in time her skipper beached his ship. It was loaded with cement. A German bomb had struck the hold fair and square, sending showers of cement over the skipper and his men. On the beach helpers found the skipper a fearsome spectacle. Blood from his wounds in the head, shoulder and arm, formed the cement into a bloody concrete. He refused assistance and said, " Look after the men."

Then he let himself loose. He raged up and down the beach. " Look at my —— ship," he roared. " Look what those —— have done. Let me get near the —— They won't drive me off the sea, the ——"

That is why the convoy always goes on.

We Were Looking for Trouble & Found It!

Here, in his own words, is the dramatic account of an aerial dog-fight from the point of view of a fighter pilot. Told by an R.A.F. Squadron Leader who has since won the D.S.O., it appeared in the American magazine " Life."

WE got a " Stand by " early in the morning of the first day of the Dunkirk evacuation, and at 9 a.m. we got our orders. There were 12 of us and, climbing to 20,000 feet, we headed across the North Sea.

We kept well together, but, of course, kept radio silence. We knew every inch of the coastline to which we were heading, but even without that knowledge there was no mistaking Dunkirk. Only a few minutes after leaving Britain and at our height we could see the pillars of smoke rising from the burning town and the villages all the way up from Calais.

At 4,000 ft. we were beetling along still looking for trouble when I saw a Hun formation of about 60 machines— 20 bombers and 40 fighters—at about 15,000 ft. and cursed the height we had lost.

The fighters, mostly Messerschmitts, heeled over and came screaming down at us and the next second we were in the thick of it. That attack developed like most dog-fights into individual scraps. It was at about 10,000 ft. that I found myself on the tail of my first Hun, a Messerschmitt 110.

Most of my instruments I remember had gone crazy in the course of the violent manœuvring. I remember particularly that my gyro was spinning wildly and the artificial horizon had vanished somewhere into the interior of the instrument panel, calmly turning up its bottom and showing me the maker's stamp and the words Air Ministry Mark IV, or something like that.

Down went the Messerschmitt again with me close on his tail. With the great speed of the dive my controls were freezing solid, and I was fighting the stick hard to bring the Hun up into the centre of my sights. When you get them there they stick, in fact, it's hard to get them out. Once there you can hold them for ever.

I thumbed the trigger button just once, twice. I smelt the cordite fumes blowing back from my Brownings as the 1,200 squirts a minute from each of them went into him. I saw the little spurts of flame as the tracers struck. For a fraction of a second I saw the back outline of the pilot's head half slewed round to see what was after him before, presumably, he ceased to know.

I looked around for the rest, but they were gone. My own scrap had brought me about 50 miles inland, so I turned and headed back, noticing with a shock that my petrol reserve was just enough to get me home, provided that I ran into no more trouble.

Out over the North Sea and on the way back to the station I clicked on the radio and called up the pilots of my squadron one by one : " How are you ? Did you get any ? " The first one came back jubilantly— he had got one. Then the rest—all of them had got one or two. Two didn't answer . . . .

The next day I saw some Junkers guarded by Messerschmitts bombing a torpedo-boat and some small rescue craft packed with troops far below. Chancing the anti-aircraft fire from the torpedo-boat, we plunged in. The Huns never saw us coming. Every one of us got one in that first dive.

Stick back and screaming up again, we re-formed and then down once more. This time the Huns had scattered, and it wasn't so easy. I got on to one Messerschmitt who was scramming for home and got a squirt in. There was the usual burst of smoke from his engine as he went down. I followed and I'm glad I did. Biding my time I let him have it.

I didn't know then how the rest of my squadron had got on with the Messerschmitt swarm they had got into above Dunkirk, but on the way back the first to answer my radio call said that he had got four. Then he suddenly said, " Oh, hell, my engine's packed up." Then, " I'm on fire."

There was silence for a second or two and he said, " Yippee ! There's a destroyer downstairs. I'm baling out." A second later I heard him mutter, " But how ? "

It is, as a matter of fact, not easy to bale out of a Spitfire. The best way is to turn her over on her back and drop out through the hood—if you can. That, we found out later, was exactly what he had done.

Here is one of the Supermarine Spitfires which have so often met Nazi Messerschmitts in " dog-fights " and worsted them. These 'planes carry eight machine-guns and are single-seater fighters. The Squadron Leader whose story is told in this page encountered his first Messerschmitt at 10,000 feet.
Photo, Charles E. Brown

Mr. Briton'll See It Through

These women are among those who have responded to the call for workers to make hurdles for trench revetments.

Now that the overrunning of Norway has cut off a large part of Britain's supply of wood pulp for paper, substitutes are being used. Here reeds that grow prolifically on the Norfolk Broads are being cut for papermaking.

One of the latest efforts of London to help the men in khaki or blue from overseas and from distant parts of the British Isles is the establishment of an Information Bureau (seen above) in Trafalgar Square. For soldiers it is an "inquire within for everything," and this Canadian leaving it certainly looks satisfied. One of the places many of the troops want to visit is the Zoo, and there they may see such an unusual sight as that right—one of the Zoo's A.R.P. fire-fighters practising with his hose from the back of a Bactrian camel.

The removal of the official ban on military bands reminds us of a very old industry—the making of drumheads. Here are scenes in the workshop, at New Eltham, Kent, of Mr. Horace Loosley, whose family have been engaged for 200 years in this craft, still entirely carried out by hand. Left, Mr. Loosley is sorting side-drum heads, while, right, one man is about to stretch a skin over a frame for drying, and another is shaving a skin to the correct thickness and smoothness.

Photos, " Daily Mirror," L.N.A., Topical, Fox and John Topham

Men Who Have Won Honour in Freedom's Cause

Aircraftman A. Meadows, D.F.M., for conspicuous bravery in the air. He bombed enemy troops at Bardia, Libya.

Flying Officer D. F. B. Skeen, D.F.C., for courage in the air against superior enemy forces.

Wing-Cdr. J. W. Gillan, D.F.C., for displaying courage and devotion to duty during air operations.

Wing-Cdr. G. W. T. Tuttle, O.B.E., for his outstanding work as staff officer.

Flying Officer W. H. Rhodes-Moorhouse, D.F.C., for destroying five enemy aircraft and for great courage.

Capt. A. Head, Life Guards, M.C., for displaying disregard of danger during evacuation of B.E.F. at Boulogne.

2nd Lieut. Irwin, M.C., for showing courage and resource during the evacuation of the B.E.F. at Dunkirk.

Wing-Cdr. the Earl of Bandon, D.S.O., for gallantry and devotion to duty in air operations.

Brigadier Dennis Furlong, D.S.O., for remarkable leadership during the withdrawal of the B.E.F. from Belgium.

Lieut. R. D. McLeod, R.E., M.C., for his services during the Norwegian campaign.

Surgeon-Lieut. K. W. Donald, D.S.C., for gallantry in H.M.S. "Hotspur" during first Battle of Narvik.

Cdr. H. St. L. Nicholson R.N., a bar to his D.S.O. Senior officer of destroyer force with H.M.A.S. "Sydney."

Cdr. J. T. Lean, R N., D.S.O., for skill and devotion to duty in the second Battle of Narvik, April 13.

Cdr. H. Lawman, D.S.O., of H.M.S. "Hotspur," for gallantry during the first Battle of Narvik, April 10.

Paymaster-Lieut. Stanning, D.S.O., of H.M.S. "Hardy," for conspicuous bravery at Narvik.

Bat. S.-Maj. H. O. Jarvis, D.C.M., for conspicuous bravery, rescuing a wounded officer under shell fire at Arras.

Maj. H. C. Stockwell, Royal Welch Fusiliers, D.S.O., for "soldierly qualities" during Norwegian campaign.

Lance-Corporal H. A. Sims, Royal Inniskilling Dragoons, M.M., for gallantry at Dunkirk.

Lieut.-Col. H. B. Hibbert, D.S.O., for his splendid leadership during the Norwegian campaign.

Pte. H. J. Williams, M.M., for carrying on at Wytschaete after one of his arms had been blown off.

Rev. T. L. Laying, a bar to his M.C., for showing great courage and helping wounded at Dunkirk.

C. P. Officer T. Fork, D.S.M., for gallantry in rendering mines washed ashore safe.

Commissioned Gunner A. Gantry, D.S.C., for the same dangerous work as C.P.O. Fork.

Leading Seaman W. Wills, D.S.M., for gallantry in rendering mines washed ashore safe.

A. R. Warden D. L. Jones, D.S.M., for meritorious service during an air raid. First warden to be thus decorated.

OUR DIARY OF THE WAR

TUESDAY, JULY 30, 1940   *332nd Day*
On the Sea—Greek tanker " Hermione," under charter to Italian Government, reported sunk by British forces on July 28.

H.M. patrol yacht " Gulzar " reported sunk on July 29 by air attack.

Minister of Economic Warfare announced extension of British blockade to cover whole of Europe and North Africa.

In the Air—R.A.F. made day and night attacks on aerodromes, barges, oil storage plants, and other targets in Northern France and Low Countries.

Coastal Command aircraft attacked gun emplacements on Norwegian coast. Other aircraft attacked naval base at Emden.

War against Italy—R.A.F. made eight raids on Italian positions near Kassala.

Home Front—Sporadic enemy raids on Britain. One fighter and two bombers brought down.

Japan—Lord Halifax made vigorous protest to Japanese Ambassador against arrest of British subjects in Japan.

General—Award of Army's two first V.C.s. Germans closed German-Swiss frontier.

WEDNESDAY, JULY 31   *333rd Day*
On the Sea—Announced that disguised German raider had been damaged in battle with H.M.S. " Alcantara," armed merchant cruiser, off Brazilian coast.

H.M. destroyer " Delight " reported sunk following air attack.

In the Air—R.A.F. made daylight raids on aerodromes in Germany and on shipping. During operations one enemy fighter and a seaplane were brought down.

War against Italy—Two more raids by R.A.F. on Kassala when severe damage was done on machine-gun and A.A. posts. Direct hits registered on hangars at Macaaca.

Nairobi reported sharp engagement at Dobel, on Kenya-Abyssinia border.

Enemy fighter shot down off Malta. One British machine brought down.

Home Front—High-flying German raiders appeared over S.E. England. One shot down.

Air Ministry announced that at least 240 raiders were destroyed during July.

Japan—Four of arrested Britons in Japan were released.

THURSDAY, AUGUST 1   *334th Day*
On the Sea—Announced that R.A.F. sank two U-boats in Mediterranean in July.

During night of August 1-2 British steamer " Highlander " fought battle with enemy aircraft in North Sea and destroyed two.

Enemy 'plane attacking convoy in North Sea was shot down by escorting vessel H.M.S. " Weston."

Irish steamer " Kerry Head " attacked by German bomber off Co. Cork.

In the Air—R.A.F. bombed aerodromes at Dortmund, Leeuwarden and Haamstede, Krupp's works at Essen, oil refineries and other targets in N.W. Germany.

Coastal Command aircraft dropped bombs on enemy aerodrome at Cherbourg.

Fleet Air Arm bombed enemy radio station and supply ship off Norwegian coast.

War against Italy—R.A.F. bombed ammunition dump at Bardia, Libya, oil refinery near Massawa and hangars at Asmara.

Home Front—Two enemy aircraft shot down in Channel.

Single raider dropped bombs on Norwich, causing five civilian deaths and some damage.

During preceding night bombs were dropped in neighbourhood of Thames Estuary and Bristol Channel.

Japan—Stated that Japan had released seven of thirteen arrested Britons.

Russia—M. Molotov reaffirmed Russia's neutrality.

FRIDAY, AUGUST 2   *335th Day*
On the Sea—H.M. trawler " Cape Finisterre " sank after engaging four enemy aircraft, one of which she shot down.

In the Air—R.A.F. made daylight raids on aerodromes in France, Belgium and Holland. Night attacks made on oil depots at Emden, Hamburg, Salzbergen and other centres.

War against Italy—R.A.F. raided bulk fuel installations at Zula, Eritrea. Oil depot at Accico and aerodrome at Asmara attacked. S.A. Air Force raided Iavello aerodrome.

Fleet Air Arm successfully attacked Italian aerodrome at Cagliari, Sardinia.

Home Front—Lord Beaverbrook joined War Cabinet.

German night raiders over S.E. coast driven off by machine-gun posts and ships' batteries. Enemy 'planes also reported over N.W. England and a Welsh town.

German aircraft dropped leaflets in Southern England containing translation of Hitler's Reichstag speech of July 19.

SATURDAY, AUGUST 3   *336th Day*
In the Air—R.A.F. bombers continued to harass enemy aerodromes, including Schiphol, Haamstede and Abbeville. Night attacks were made on oil tanks at Rotterdam and oil plants in the Ruhr and Rhineland. Naval base at Kiel also raided.

War against Italy—Three enemy bombers attacking ship in Berbera harbour were intercepted and damaged by British fighters.

R.A.F. made three successful raids on Derna (Libya) harbour and aerodrome.

Home Front—Enemy aircraft dropped bombs on waste land in S.E. England.

SUNDAY, AUGUST 4   *337th Day*
On the Sea—Two British trawlers reported having shot down a Dornier which had attacked them in the English Channel.

Italy admitted loss of seventeenth submarine.

In the Air—R.A.F. made night raids on oil plant at Sterkrade, in the Ruhr, leaving it in flames. Successful attack also made on Krefeld aerodrome.

Three Blenheims of Coastal Command routed four Messerschmitts off French coast; severely damaging two.

War against Italy—Italians invaded British Somaliland, advancing at three points, and were resisted by British land and air forces.

Italian base at Bir el Gobi, Libya, bombed by R.A.F. On their way there five British machines engaged 50 enemy fighters and destroyed three.

Enemy aircraft raided Sidi Barrani and Mersa Matruh.

Home Front—German raiders did minor damage in S.W. England.

During night of August 3-4 enemy aircraft dropped bombs on areas of Thames Estuary, East Coast of Scotland and Wales. No damage or casualties reported.

Japan—Release of three more arrested Britons was announced.

Japanese nationals arrested in London, in Singapore and other British possessions.

General—Germans closed part of frontier between France and Switzerland.

MONDAY, AUGUST 5   *338th Day*
On the Sea—H.M.S. " Alcantara " left Rio de Janeiro to resume search for raider.

Admiralty announced that H.M. minesweeping trawler " Marsona " had been sunk by enemy mine.

In the Air—R.A.F. made night raids on targets at Wismar, Kiel, Hamburg and Hamm, and aerodromes at Schiphol and Borkum.

War against Italy—Reported that King's African Rifles had occupied Todenyang in Abyssinia, near Kenya-Sudan border.

Italian column occupied Zeila (British Somaliland) without opposition. Hargeisa captured by strong enemy force.

Home Front—Four enemy fighters shot down near S.E. coast by Spitfires. Raiders were reported over S.E. England, Wales, and over a N.E. coastal town.

Empire—Reported that two drafts of reinforcements for Second Australian Imperial Force had arrived in England.

U.S.A.—President Roosevelt and American Attorney-General addressed Governors of 42 States on legislation for suppression of fifth column activities.

General—Military agreement signed in London by British and Polish Governments.

British flying-boat " Clare " reached New York, completing first of series of trans-Atlantic flights.

TUESDAY, AUGUST 6   *339th Day*
On the Sea—Admiralty announced that H.M. trawlers " Drummer " and " Oswaldian " had been sunk by mines.

Greek steamer " Loula " reported sunk by Italian submarine.

In the Air—Hampered by cloud, R.A.F. abandoned many targets. Le Bourget airport and aerodromes in Holland and N. Germany were bombed.

War against Italy—Middle East H.Q. stated that during first phase of operations in Western Desert, now ending, a small British mobile force had completely dominated Eastern Libya.

Oadweina (British Somaliland) occupied by enemy.

Enemy aircraft raided Haifa, but only slight damage and few casualties resulted.

Home Front—German bomber shot down off East Coast.

Empire—First contingent of airmen from S. Rhodesia for service with R.A.F. arrived at British port.

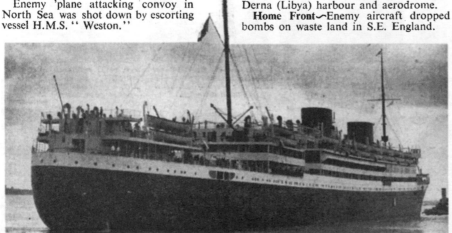

The armed merchant cruiser H.M.S. " Alcantara," which waged a gallant fight against a German raider in the South Atlantic, is a former Royal Mail Line ship of 22,181 tons. The story of the engagement is told in page 162. The Brazilian Government granted permission for the "Alcantara" to remain at Rio de Janeiro until the slight damage she had sustained had been repaired. She left Rio to resume her search for the raider on August 5.
Photo, L.N.A.

Photo, Planet News

A MESSERSCHMITT ACHIEVES A BLOODLESS VICTORY

This remarkable photograph was taken off the south-east coast of England on August 14, when a German fighter 'plane had succeeded in bringing down one of the barrage balloons on which the Nazi 'planes had been making concerted attacks during the week. The " victorious " Messerschmitt is scurrying away, while the balloon comes down, a mass of smoke and flame. From the head of the balloon are hanging the cables and guy ropes that menace the dive bomber. The destroyed balloon is quickly replaced by a new one.

Now May Begin the Battle for Our Empire

When Mussolini's columns invaded British Somaliland they started a new war—one
which may well develop into a struggle for the British Empire and its associated States.
Perhaps this essay by E. Royston Pike in the interpretation of the Dictators' designs
may serve as a guide-post through the confusing events of the day.

THERE was little to choose between one side of the frontier and the other; as far as sun-tortured eyes could see the waste of glittering sand lay spread out in a vast shimmering expanse, broken here and there by tufts of coarse grass, patches of prickly scrub, an occasional cluster of palms within whose grateful shade lay pools of life-giving water. As the Italian columns chugged and snorted and rattled their way across where their maps told them the frontier should be, they disturbed a grunting camel or two, antelopes flashed past, vultures rose in croaking protest from piles of whitening bones.

So on August 4 Italian columns from Abyssinia began the invasion of British Somaliland. But we may be sure that something more than that torrid triangle of African earth was needed to set Mussolini's

at the chosen moment he dispatched his soldiers, his tanks and 'planes on the road to the south-east where lay the lands of wheat and oil. But, to his disgust, the way to the Ukraine came to be barred by the rival dictator of the Kremlin. Hitler had to abandon half Poland to the Russians; and when, months later, he aimed at the Black

Sea through Rumania, the Russians again stepped in, seizing Bessarabia, commanding the Danube mouth, and throwing the mantle of their protection over that most Slav of all the Balkan States, Bulgaria. As for the way across the Balkans, it is barred for the moment by Rumania, while Turkey glowers from her fastnesses in Asia Minor.

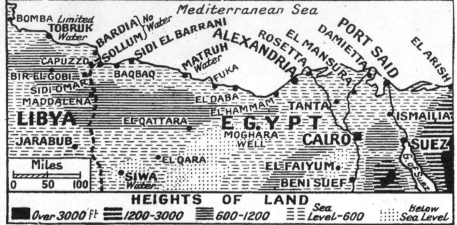

HEIGHTS OF LAND

■ Over 3000 Ft ▦ 1200-3000 ▤ 600-1200 ≡ Sea Level-600 ⋮ Below Sea Level

In the event of an Italian invasion of Egypt, their troops would have to cross many hundred miles of desert. This map shows the route they must follow — largely waterless.

So now it is Mussolini's turn. While the left arm of the pincers is halted in the Balkans —those pincers which it may be presumed are intended to include within their grasp the whole of the Near East—the right arm is now being extended in a vast, sweeping movement through Libya to Somaliland and Aden at the Red Sea's gate.

Fortune has been kind to Mussolini of late, for while France was still fighting at Britain's side the Italian arm of the pincers could move hardly at all. With a large French army in Tunis the Italians in Libya

Here is a scene on the great strategic road which runs the whole length of the coast of Libya. Mussolini opened it personally in 1937 with great ceremony.

war machine in operation and so expose his newly-won empire to all the changes and chances that war brings in its train. Somaliland was not the word that the Dictators spoke—or shouted rather—along the telephone wires that connect the Chancellery in Berlin with the cabinet in the Palazzo Venezia. Hitler and Mussolini are after a much bigger prize than that; not Berbera merely, but Baghdad and Basra—to mention but the names that alliteration brings to mind. Theirs is a vision of empire, of a vast imperial realm incorporating some of the fairest and richest of the provinces which—so they do their best to make themselves believe—a decadent Britain is about to let slip.

That part of the scheme which Hitler has devised is but a revival of the Pan-German project which in the Kaiser's day was crystallized in the phrase, "Berlin to Baghdad." The disasters of 1918 deflated for the time being the balloon of German pride, but it was soon blown up again by the frantic mouthing of Hitler's oratory; and

These Egyptian soldiers on manoeuvres in the desert belong to an army which is placed high amongst the fighting forces of the Near East. Of late it has been modernized in every way.

Photos, Sport & General and Keystone

In the Near East Britain's Soldiers Await It

These men of the South Staffordshire Regiment in Egypt are doing a spell of training with the Bren guns to greet low-flying aircraft. Below, men of the York and Lancaster Regiment are taking the most welcome of all drinks in the desert—cold water.

Air defences in Palestine have reached a high state of preparedness, and the anti-aircraft units are always on the alert. Above, one of the gun crews is in action during practice, but though the men are stripped to the waist they wear their steel helmets—by no means a comfortable form of headgear compared with the pith helmet that is generally worn in the East. In the desert adequate protection and camouflage for the guns is not always possible, but the Bren gun post, left, held by men of the King's Own Yorkshire Regiment, is well concealed.

Photos, British Official: Crown Copyright

Vast Indeed are the Two Dictators' Designs

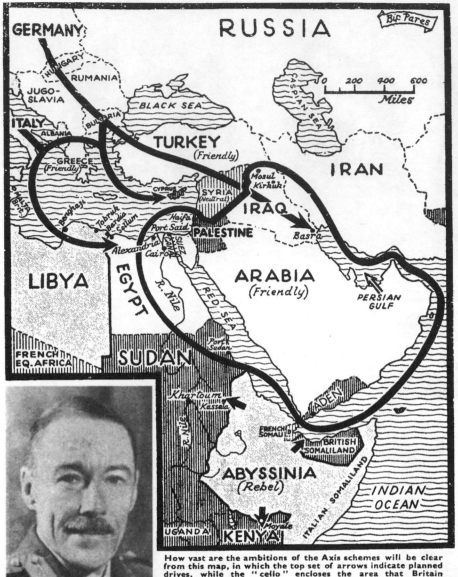

How vast are the ambitions of the Axis schemes will be clear from this map, in which the top set of arrows indicate planned drives, while the "cello" encloses the area that Britain must surely hold. Left, Lt.-Gen. Sir Philip Neame, V.C., who took over the command of the British Forces in Palestine and Transjordan early in August, 1940.
Photo, "Daily Mirror"

But between the dream and its accomplishment lies—what? First the Navy of Britain and the British Commonwealth, which is far superior to the navies of Germany and Italy combined. Moreover, it is the Navy which, since the Dutch wars of the seventeenth century, has never lost a battle. For two hundred years and more Britain's warships have controlled the Mediterranean—not to mention the Seven Seas; and still today, despite all Mussolini's boasts about "Mare Nostrum," the British flag braves the breeze within sight of Italy's heavily-defended shores.

On land the forces which may be ranged to meet the legions of the Dictators are far smaller than those which would have taken the field prior to France's collapse. But Britain's army in the Near East, outnumbered though it may be by the Italians, is far superior in fighting spirit. The Anzacs are in Egypt—and the men who smashed the Kaiser's finest regiments on the Western Front 25 years ago are little likely to fear the worst that the Italians can do. They have British regulars at their side, men trained to war through the arduous years of peace; Indian troops, too, warriors of races which for centuries made war their pastime, their very life. Before Mussolini's soldiers can reach the banks of the Canal they must cross some five or six hundred miles, much of it desert, entirely waterless; and they must march along one narrow road within sight of the sea, within range the whole way of the guns of Britain's ships.

Then there are Britain's allies and the possible allies of tomorrow. There is Turkey, which never forgets that the Italian programme of expansion includes the whole of her Mediterranean coasts; there is Greece, which is also fearful of Mussolini's designs; there are Irak and Iran, neither likely to sacrifice their independence without a blow; there are Egypt and the Sudan, and ranged on the southern frontier of Italian East Africa are the 'planes and battalions which South Africa has sent to the war. Then, finally, there is Russia—that vast enigma which hovers on Hitler's flank.

had to envisage a war on two fronts, and having envisaged it they shrank from it in alarm. Now, however, that Tunis, like Metropolitan France, is out of the war, Mussolini's 250,000 men in Libya are set free from that hampering fear of an attack in the rear and may now perhaps march on Egypt—that prize which has fascinated the gaze of conquerors through all the ages—and from the Nile to the Canal is but a step.

This seized, Britain's communications between the Mediterranean and India, the Cape and Australia, would be cut in their most vital spot and from Suez the Italian legions might expect to continue their career of conquest through Palestine and on to Irak and even Iran. Here, too, France may be said to have played into Mussolini's hands, for until recently a great French army stood to arms in Syria ready and eager to help Britain in the defence of the Near East.

But not only the Near East would be brought into the new war zone. While the German 'planes continued to dash themselves in a frenzy of onslaught on the defences of the British fortress, Spain's war-weary soldiers would be gingered and goaded into an attack on Britain's stronghold of Gibraltar, so that with both Gibraltar and Suez lost the British fleet might be caught in the Mediterranean trap. Italian columns might dash across the desert to the upper waters of the Nile in the Sudan. Khartoum would be threatened from Abyssinia; Port Said and Aden, Berbera and Sokotra, the islands of the Persian Gulf and the great oil refineries at Abadan, Basra where the great rivers of Mesopotamia meet—all would hear the guns. Still the imperial looters would not be satisfied. Alexander refreshed his tattered legions in the waters of the Indus; through all his most vigorous years India was to Napoleon a tantalizing dream. Where Alexander succeeded and Napoleon dreamed, might not Hitler dream and succeed?

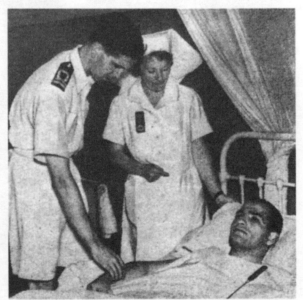

A British R.N.R. surgeon in a hospital in the Near East is examining an Italian pilot-officer, one of the many brought down by the R.A.F.   *Photo, British Official: Crown Copyright*

The Air Battle of Britain: First Phase Opens

In the six days August 8-13 the German air attack on our south and south-eastern coasts, airfields and certain harbours, including Dover and Portsmouth, developed with such fury that British and American observers declared that the Battle of Britain had opened. In four days of massed attacks the Nazis are known to have lost 265 machines against 70 R.A.F. casualties. Here are some high-lights in this epic of defence.

From the outbreak of war it has been expected that Germany, sooner or later, would launch massed aerial attacks upon Britain, by hundreds of aircraft; these assaults would precede—some said they would supersede—attacks by land and sea forces. Thus when, on August 8, there opened a large-scale bombing raid on British shipping in the Channel it was suspected that Hitler might have a more important objective, and that now, in fact, the Battle of Britain was about to begin.

It was preceded by an attack before daylight by enemy motor torpedo-boats; three coasting vessels in the convoy were hit by torpedoes, but one E-boat was sunk and another damaged. Between 9 and 9.30 a.m. came the first air attack, by Junkers 87 dive-bombers escorted by fighters. Six bombers and three escorts were destroyed by one Hurricane squadron, which, before the day was out, was to account in all for 21 enemy aircraft.

The squadron leader said:

"We climbed to 16,000 ft. and, looking down, saw a large formation of Junkers 87s approaching from the sun, with Messerschmitt 109s stepped up behind to 20,000 ft. We approached unobserved out of the sun and went in to attack the rear Junkers 87s before the enemy fighters could interfere.

"I gave a five seconds' burst to one bomber and broke off to engage two Messerschmitt 109s. There was a dogfight. The enemy fighters were half rolling and diving and zooming in climbing turns. They were painted silver.

"I fired two five seconds' bursts at one and saw it dive into the sea. Then I followed another up in a zoom and caught him as he stalled."

At 11.30 a.m., in still larger formation, the enemy renewed his attack. Three Hurricanes of the squadron already mentioned encountered ten Me 110s and shot down three, together with an Me 109. The latter was a decoy, and when it had drawn off the Hurricanes the Me 110s were intended to take the R.A.F. machines by surprise. But in the words of one of our pilots, "the Messerschmitt overacted the part."

At 4 p.m. the enemy made his final attempt, this time throwing in nearly 150 bombers and

GERMAN & BRITISH AIRCRAFT LOSSES		
German to April 30, 1940		
Total announced West Front, North Sea, Britain, Scandinavia		195
Unofficial estimate of additional 'planes damaged in Norway		200
	German	British
May	1,990	258
June	276	177
July	245	115
Aug 1-13...	280	109
Grand Totals, May to Aug.	2,791	659
Daily Results, August 1-13		
Aug. 1-7	10	15
8	62	18
9	1	1
10	1	4
11	66	29
12	62	17
13	78	25
Totals ...	280	109

Notes.—Figures for **May** cover Dunkirk operations and include aircraft destroyed by French. Probable number of enemy aircraft brought down by British during that month is 1,500 out of the total 1,990.

June-July figures include results of mass raids on Britain beginning June 18.

August figures include the four large-scale attacks on convoys and southern ports.

British losses include operations over German and occupied territory.

None of the figures include aircraft bombed on the ground or so damaged in combat as to be unlikely to reach home.

fighters. He was no more successful, and by 5 o'clock, when he relinquished the battle, had lost 60 aircraft—24 being dive-bombers. Some 400 enemy machines were sighted by our pilots, but it is probable that the number in use that day was considerably less, since the Nazis could so readily fly back to their base in France to refuel, and renew the attack.

British losses were 16 fighters, and the pilots of three were saved. During the second

This leader of a Hurricane Fighter Squadron was shot down over the North Sea, but luckily rescued by a minesweeper. By six o'clock next morning he was in the air again.

Another of our fighter pilots just after action; he wears the ribbon of the D.F.C., awarded for bringing down five Nazi aircraft in a single day.

After the engine of an R.A.F. 'plane has been carefully overhauled, as shown in the photograph in page 175, it is run on the ground at full throttle. Here a Spitfire is being put to this final test, with men leaning on the tail planes to steady the machine. The engines of Spitfires are Rolls-Royce Merlins II or III.

Photos, Associated Press and Wide World

This sergeant-pilot of a Hurricane was photographed as he landed after a successful encounter with Messerschmitts. With his colleagues above, he is typical of our defenders.

Tremendous Is the Barrage Nazis Must Meet

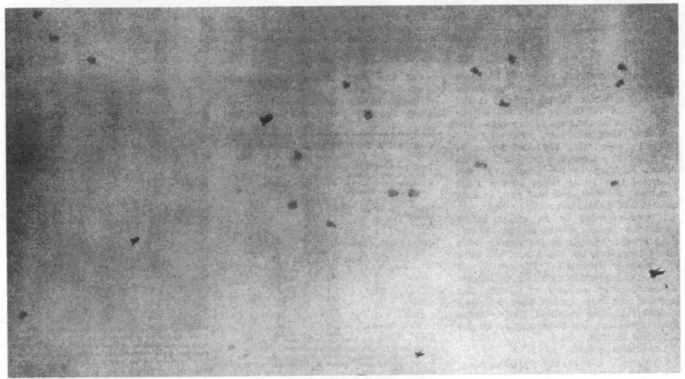

The top photo shows an aerial attack (on August 10) on barrage balloons on the Channel coast. Shells from anti-aircraft guns, seen bursting, forced the Nazis to fly high. In the lower photograph (taken on August 11) two barrage balloons are falling in flames, but before the enemy bombers, waiting high above, could dive on to their quarry they were routed by R.A.F. fighters.

Photos, Associated Press and Planet News

phase of the battle a Spitfire squadron off the French coast had chased seven Me 109s over the sea and destroyed six of them.

Thus the Nazis lost at least fifteen per cent of their aircraft engaged in the struggle. Now let us see how little they gained. By the light of flares dropped by aircraft, while it was still dark, their E-boats had been able to torpedo and sink three vessels of the convoy—which consisted of twenty small ships totalling about 18,000 tons—the combined tonnage of those lost was about 2,500. To these must be added two ships sunk by bombers (2,450 tons), making in all just under 5,000 tons of shipping destroyed. Smarting, doubtless, under their defeat, the Nazis claimed to have sunk by E-boat three vessels totalling 17,000 tons, and to have

bombed to destruction a further twelve, totalling 55,000 tons ! Later claims were still more grotesque.

On Sunday, August 11, 400 Nazi aircraft made a series of attacks on Channel ports—and lost another 65 machines. From 7.30 a.m. until nearly eleven o'clock Dover was the objective, and out of some sixty enemy machines engaged our Spitfires destroyed ten and the gunners shot down three. Meanwhile, at 10 o'clock, a force of 200 bombers and fighters made a fierce attempt to get over Portland, and about 150 actually reached the coast. Spitfire and Hurricane squadrons broke up the enemy formations and picked them off in a long series of dog-fights that lasted until well after midday. Forty of the raiders crashed

into the sea or on the land, two being brought down by A.A. gunners.

An R.A.F. auxiliary squadron destroyed ten Messerschmitts ; the Hurricane squadron which had got so fine a bag on the previous Thursday shot down five. Minor damage was done to two Naval vessels by splinters, while bombs that fell on shore damaged a hospital and other Naval buildings.

Next the Nazis attacked E. of Dover, towards the North Foreland. Going into battle now for the fourth time, the squadron of Spitfires which had begun the day's fighting encountered thirty Me 109s at 4,000 feet up, dodging in and out of the clouds. Four Spitfires gave chase and shot down two of the enemy. The same squadron an hour before, when ordered to patrol over a convoy off the East Anglian coast, came up against 40 Me 110 Jaguar bombers about to dive down on to the ships. The enemy was taken by surprise and was too late to form a protective circle ; ten of them were shot down into the sea. With the attack on the Foreland the enemy's assault petered out, though in the evening there was a mild flare-up, which ended in his losing a Dornier 17 and a Junkers 88. Thus in this day's operations he had lost 65 aircraft, and had gained nothing of consequence. Our own losses were 26 fighters, two pilots being saved.

Monday morning (August 12) saw the beginning of a further assault on our Channel ports. The attacks began over the Kent coast, on a bigger scale even than before, hundreds of aircraft being engaged. Later they extended to the Isle of Wight and to Portsmouth. Two hundred machines are said to have set out for the Dockyard town, but only about 50 got through the barrage. They dive-bombed on to the dockyard, but met with little success. Two small harbour service craft were sunk, a jetty was damaged, and a store was set on fire. In the town itself a railway station was hit and other buildings set on fire.

Dive-bombers Don't Like Balloons Above the Sea!

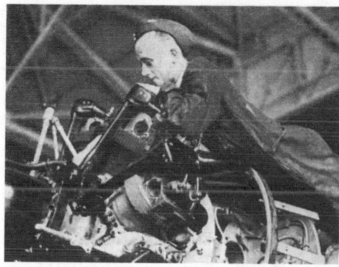

In the evening about seventy bombers and fighters attacked a town on the S.E. coast, dropping bombs in pairs. Little damage was done, and casualties were few. In this day's battles the Germans lost 61 aircraft, while 13 of our own fighters failed to return.

Early on Tuesday, August 13, the air battle was renewed. From the Thames Estuary to the Sussex coast waves of bombers and fighters came over. In the afternoon the attack concentrated on the Southampton region and the coast of Kent. At the rate of one a minute, enemy machines were sent crashing down by our fighters. Some bombs were dropped on a district of Hampshire. In the evening several R.A.F. aerodromes in S.E. England were attacked; bombs were also dropped in the Isle of Wight and in country districts of Berkshire and Wiltshire. This day's operations cost the Luftwaffe 78 aircraft; only 13 of our own machines were destroyed, and only three of our pilots killed.

In four forays the Nazis lost at least 265 aircraft, while the R.A.F. casualties were 70 fighter machines. The R.A.F. were remarkably successful in intercepting the raiders. With incomparable courage and magnificent élan our fighter pilots tackled the enemy—as always, at great odds—and upset his plans. As far as the blockade is concerned, our

The ground staffs (known to themselves by the mysterious name "Irks"), which ensure that our bombers and fighters take the air in perfect trim are a vital factor in the success of British 'planes. Above, a mechanic checks the engine of a medium bomber; and, right, an armourer loads up magazines for eight-gun fighters.

convoys still sail up the Channel to home ports, undeterred by E-boat attacks or aerial savagery. A novel feature was the towing of their own barrage of balloons by ships of the convoy, as a defence against dive-bombing. How effective in this respect is the balloon barrage was indicated by the fact that raiders have sought to shoot down the balloons. Observers in a southern region witnessed what looked like a dress rehearsal of smoke-screening by an enemy formation flying high up over the coast.

Whether the Nazi air assaults in mass were part merely of an intensified war on our shipping, whether they were a test of our air strength, or whether they might turn out to be the prelude to the Battle of Britain, were questions raised in many minds. Morale—of citizen and armed forces alike—could not have been higher.

This dramatic photograph shows a scene during the great aerial battle over the English Channel on August 8, 1940. Towards the close of the long combat, when a convoy, protected by its own barrage balloons (two of which can be seen on the right), was passing, 150 Nazi 'planes swooped upon it. On the left of the photograph an Anson reconnaissance 'plane is taking its part in the defence of the convoy.

Photos, G.P.U., Fox and Planet News

Canada Is in the Front Line Now—And Knows It

Great as was Canada's effort in the last war, expressed in men and money and materials,
already she can say with pride that it is being rivalled during the present struggle: indeed,
in some directions, it is already surpassed. Some details of her contributions to the
Commonwealth's might are given below.

BEFORE the war there were some who declared that Canada would never again be involved in a European struggle. They pointed out that of the men who rushed to join Canada's Expeditionary Force in 1914 at least half had been born in Britain, and they further noted that since 1914 Canada has received very few immigrants from the United Kingdom. On this basis of fact they proceeded to argue that the call of Britain at bay would not meet with anything like the response of 1914. They even suggested that if Canada did go to war she would do so not as a united nation but as one facing the prospect of disruption.

Yet, as so often has happened in the history of the British Commonwealth, the prophets of gloom have been confounded. Within a week of Britain's declaration of

The Earl of Athlone, who succeeded Lord Tweedsmuir as Governor-General of Canada, is here seen inspecting the Guard of Honour when he arrived at Ottawa on June 19.

shortly it will number 10,000. This rapid expansion has enabled some of the seven Canadian destroyers (" Assiniboine," " Fraser," " Ottawa," " Restigouche," " St. Laurent," " Saguenay " and " Skeena ") to be transferred across the Atlantic to serve with their comrades of the Royal Navy.

Then there is the Royal Canadian Air Force, whose strength last June was 15,594, and since then it has been largely extended. Indeed, men are being enlisted in the R.C.A.F. at the rate of 1,000 a week, under the direction of the air ace of the last war, Air Marshal W. A. Bishop, who shot down 72 enemy 'planes and on whose chest are the ribbons of the V.C., D.S.O. and bar, D.F.C., and the Croix de Guerre.

The first contingent of the R.C.A.F., complete with its own 'planes and full equipment, was reported to be in England on June 22, and a few weeks later Mr. Vincent Massey, the Canadian High Commissioner in London, inspected the first all-Canadian Fighter Squadron to cooperate in the defence of Britain. This squadron's personnel is composed partly of men drawn from the original No. 1 Fighter Squadron of the R.C.A.F. and partly from auxiliary airmen who, only a few months earlier, were sitting at their desks in Montreal or working on the farms of every province in the Dominion. From the outbreak of war they have been on patrol

A strict examination is made of every vessel approaching the ports on Canada's eastern coast, and the orders of the captain of this smart little ship engaged in the work must be strictly obeyed.

war against Germany, Canada, too, declared war—and not a divided Canada, but one in which there was a union such as had never been seen before. Indeed, it may be said that for the first time in her history Canada spoke with one voice as a united nation; and so far from there being any slackening in her resolve, the months that have passed since September 1939 have seen a bounding intensification of the Dominion's war effort in every field.

Canada's first division landed in Britain a week before Christmas, and the stream of men across the Atlantic still continues. Canadian troops are performing garrison duties in the British West Indies, so freeing the British regulars for duty elsewhere; a Canadian contingent landed in Iceland last June, thus ensuring that Hitler's conquest of Denmark should not be extended to the North Atlantic; there are Canadian troops also in Newfoundland. Altogether, Canada had at the end of June 113,593 men under arms, and of these, be it noted, not ten per cent are British born, though all were volunteers. They were born in Canada; to them

Canada, like Britain, leaves nothing to chance. At her Bren gun factory at Toronto armed guards watch round its high fences and stand at the entrances night and day. Circle, one of the guards examines the pass of a man seeking admittance. Above is a big gun at a fort near Halifax, Nova Scotia, ready to give a warm welcome to any marauder.

Photos, Fox, Canadian Official, P.N.A. and Planet News

Canada and not Britain is the Mother Country, the homeland. Yet in their tens of thousands they have enlisted and have crossed the Atlantic just as their fathers did before them.

Since the outbreak of war the personnel of the Royal Canadian Navy has been increased from 1,700 to over 7,000 men, and very

in their Hurricanes—Canadian-built—over the Atlantic, off the shores of Newfoundland and Nova Scotia, and gaining experience in escorting convoys reaching Canadian waters from England.

This Air Force expansion is in addition to Canada's magnificent work in conjunction with the Empire Air Training Scheme, which,

War's Perils Have Nerved a United Nation

it will be remembered, is principally centred in Canada. Shortly after its inception it was stated that when the organization reached its peak of efficiency the Canadian Aviation Schools would be turning out 25,000 to 30,000 pilots, observers, air gunners and wireless operators in a single year. Canada's share in the scheme was estimated to be about 350,000 dollars out of a total cost of 600,000,000 dollars (say £150,000,000).

'Planes, Tanks and Guns

This brings us to the mobilization of Canada's industry for the purposes of the war. Towards the end of July the Canadian Ministry of Munitions and Supply announced that every Canadian resource for the manufacture of aircraft would be kept fully employed for the next eighteen months and any Canadian aircraft factories not at present employed in the production of training and service aeroplanes would receive orders to produce fighter aircraft of various types up to capacity. In the last week of July the Canadian factories turned out 25 completed 'planes, and by early in 1941 it is estimated that 360 completed 'planes will be produced each month.

Very impressive was the survey of progress given to the House of Commons in Ottawa by Mr. C. D. Howe, Minister of Munitions and Supply, on July 30. " Perhaps no country in the world," he said, " is producing automotive equipment in the volume that now obtains in Canada. At present about 600 mechanized units per day are being produced, and in another month or two this figure will be substantially increased." Plans have been completed for producing tanks at the rate of one a day, and in the matter of shipbuilding five modern minesweepers and 28 anti-submarine craft would be completed by the end of the year. As for munitions, Canada was producing vast quantities of Lee-Enfield rifles, Bren guns, Colt-Browning machine-guns for

Here is a view of the Treasury Benches when Canada's Finance Minister, Col. Hon. J. L. Ralston, presented the Dominion's billion dollar war budget to the House of Commons in Ottawa on June 24. Left to right in front row are Rt. Hon. E. Lapointe, Minister of Justice ; the Prime Minister, Rt. Hon. W. L. Mackenzie King; Col. Ralston; Hon. T. A. Crerar, Minister of Mines and Resources; Hon. P. J. A. Cardin, K.C., Minister of PublicWorks; and Hon. J. E. Michaud, Minister of Fisheries. Just behind Col. Ralston are Hon. Ian Mackenzie, Minister of Pensions and National Health (left), and Hon. C. G. Power, Postmaster-General and Minister of National Defence for Air. To their right are Hon. Norman McLarty, Minister of Labour, and Hon. J. A. McKinnon, Minister of Trade and Commerce.   *Photo, Planet News*

aeroplanes, sub-machine-guns, 2-lb. anti-aircraft guns, 25-lb. quickfiring guns, 40 mm. anti-tank guns, 20 mm. Hispano-Suiza aircraft cannon, as well as shells and ammunition of many kinds. Uniforms ? Why, said Mr. Howe, " we have bought enough cloth to stretch from Ottawa to Berlin and back."

But perhaps the most impressive indication of Canada's will to win was the introduction of conscription of Canada's man-power from

the ages of 18 to 45 for home defence, combined with a National Register and the setting-up of a Department of National War Service to direct the mobilization of individuals and groups for the better prosecution of the struggle. In the light of these measures it is plain that Canada realizes that, as her Prime Minister, Mr. Mackenzie King, has stated, " She is on the front line for the first time."

The Royal Canadian Air Force is training pilots by the thousand to help the R.A.F., and the base at Ontario is the largest of the schools in the Empire Air Training Scheme. Here is a parade of flyers who are undergoing the final stages of their instruction.   *Photo. Fox*

After Three Years China Is Still Unsubdued

In a recent page (see page 142) we have given some account of Japan's imperial designs
in Eastern Asia, but space forbade more than a passing mention of that great adventure
in which she is engaged, the subjugation of China. Now we proceed to give more details
of the struggle which is perhaps most deserving of the title of the world's greatest war.

ONE evening at the beginning of July in 1937 some Chinese sentries on guard at the Marco Polo bridge outside Peking exchanged shots with a body of Japanese troops who were engaged on manoeuvres in the neighbourhood. Some said the Chinese were the first to fire, others put the blame on the Japanese ; but whoever fired them, those shots started a war which is still going on—a war which has caused a loss of life beyond computation, which has laid waste provinces, which has destroyed the homes of millions and, powerfully supported by its handmaidens of famine, flood and pestilence, has contributed one of the most terrible chapters to the story of man's inhumanity to man.

For years before the Sino-Japanese war began China had been passing through one of the most troubled periods of her age-long history. Those troubles may be said to have begun in the opening years of this century, when the crust of Chinese culture was broken by the impact of Western ideas. In 1912 the government by emperors which had existed for more than two thousand years was abolished in favour of a democratic republic, and the last of the Manchus—Pu-Yi, who was only three when he succeeded his uncle three years before as Emperor Hsuan T'ung—went into retirement. In his place China had a President in the person of Marshal Yuan Shi-Kai, but Young China found its leader in Dr. Sun Yat-sen (1866-1925), who for many years had been the chief organizer and leader of the Chinese Nationalist Revolutionary Party, the Kuomintang, and had given it the Three Principles—

Hongkong, Britain's outpost in South China, is now cut off from the interior by a wedge of Japanese-occupied territory. Here is one of the big coastal guns on the island's rocky coast. Top right is China's generalissimo, Marshal Chiang Kai-shek.
Photos, Topical

Nationalism, Democracy and what may be not too adequately described as Social Justice or Livelihood of the People—which are still the basis of the programme of the party of reform.

Sun Yat-sen succeeded in establishing a republican government at Canton, capital of South China, and for years there was a struggle between this democratic government of the south and the war lords who ruled in—perhaps it would be better to say, fought over—the northern provinces following the death of Yuan Shi-Kai in 1916. The situation became still more confused in 1923, when the influence of Russian Communism extended to Central China and the Kuomintang was reorganized under the guidance of Michael Borodin, Stalin's agent,

on the model of the Russian Communist party. Thereby was introduced a cleavage in the ranks of the reformers which became still more marked on the death of Sun Yat-sen from cancer in 1925.

Thenceforward for several years China was distracted by the bloody rivalry of a number of war lords, who fought each other, the Communists, and the Republicans of the South with equal zest. Ultimately one of the warring generals—Marshal Chiang Kai-shek—defeated the rest and in 1928 became president of a national Chinese government set up in Nanking. Even yet, however, China was not at peace for the Communists and the left-wing government at Canton persisted in their opposition to the Marshal.

A year or two passed, and there was some possibility of better things in store for China ; but in 1931 the Japanese invaded Manchuria and converted it into the puppet state of Manchukuo with, for its Emperor, Henry Pu Yi, who had been driven from the Chinese imperial throne nineteen years before.

During the next few years Chiang Kai-shek found his principal occupation in fighting his rivals in the south, and it was not until those shots were fired at the bridge outside Peking on July 7, 1937, that the feud of conservatives and radicals in China showed signs of being subordinated to a united resistance against the common foe.

After a year of bitter fighting about one-third of China had come under Japanese

After three years of war the position in China is as shown on this map, which also includes the Japanese Empire (criss-crossed). The arrows indicate the direction of Japan's aspirations.

War in the Far East Rivals That of the West

control. Their troops were in occupation of the principal towns and means of communication from Manchukuo to the frontier posts at Shanghai. They held the great cities of Peking, Tiéntsin and Nanking, the provinces of Chahar, Chihli, Shantung, Kiangsu and Anhwei; their troops were on both sides of the Yangtse and to the north were approaching the Hwang Ho or Yellow River.

Following the capture of Nanking, Chiang Kai-shek retreated on Hankow; but in October 1938 this, too, was occupied by the Japanese, and in the same month Canton was captured from the sea. The Chinese National Government now transferred its capital to Chungking, some 500 miles to the west, in the remote province of Szechwan. For some months the Japanese endeavoured to consolidate their conquests; then in the spring of 1939 they extended their hold on the Chinese coast by seizing Swatow and the island of Hainan, thus making it still more difficult for Chiang Kai-shek to

Here is a picture from the front somewhere in China: Japanese troops are advancing cautiously up a gully in pursuit of men of Chiang Kai-shek's army, which, oft-defeated, is still unbeaten.
Photo, Domei News Photo Service

Now another year has passed, and in that year Japan's soldiers have still further enlarged the sphere of Japanese occupation, so that now the maps show that practically the whole of the coast and most of the eastern and central provinces are under Japanese control. But the true position can hardly be gauged from any map, for the situation changes almost from week to week.

In those areas which the Japanese have occupied in force they are doing their best to exploit the economic resources of the country, and they are also intent on exploiting any differences which may come to light in the ranks of the Chinese themselves. Thus in March 1940 a " Central Government of China " was set up at Nanking by

the Japanese with Dr. Wang Ching-wei, who was formerly an associate of Sun Yat-sen and a member of the central committee of the Kuomintang, as its president. But Chiang Kai-shek's government at Chungking still maintains its resistance to the invader, and there is no reason to doubt that it continues to enjoy the allegiance and support of the majority of the Chinese people.

After three years of war, then, the liquidation of the " Chinese incident," as the Japanese style it, seems as far off as ever. The Japanese are fighting to fulfil what they regard as their natural destiny as the leaders of civilization in the Far East. The Chinese, for their part, are defending their soil against the invader; they are fighting for their independence as a people.

No one can say with certainty how many Chinese and Japanese have already perished in the course of this colossal struggle, but every estimate is made in millions, and to the losses suffered by the troops must be added the huge casualties of the civilian populace.

Mr. Churchill announced on July 18 that the Burma Road had been closed for three months to war traffic. The road, which is 726 miles long, was completed in 1938; here is the steel cable suspension bridge that carries it over the Mekong river.

import war material from overseas. But to some extent this disability was remedied by the opening of the " back doors " in Kansu, leading to Asiatic Russia, and the " Burma Road," running from Yunnan in the southwest to Lashio in Burma, where it connects with the railway to Mandalay and Rangoon.

Meanwhile, the Chinese national forces were not inactive. There were vigorous counter-attacks at many places on all fronts; the guerilla warfare developed on a large scale behind the Japanese lines in the provinces which, though they had occupied, they had never subdued; the Communist 8th Route Army established itself at Yenanfu in Shensi, which soon became the principal centre of the Chinese progressive forces; and, in accordance with the " scorched-earth policy " the country was systematically laid waste before the Japanese, so that their progress into the interior was hindered and their victory made barren indeed.

One of the most terrible air raids the world has seen was made by 24 Japanese bombers on Chungking on May 4, 1940. Terrible fires started amidst the flimsy houses and burned for 48 hours; one-fifth of the city was destroyed, and the casualties numbered about 10,000.
Photo, Eigner

The Nazis Say that London's Port Is Empty!

Dr. Goebbels' propaganda machine boasts repeatedly that the Nazi air blockade of the Channel and the English coast is so successful that the Port of London is empty of shipping. But the truth—as shown by the photographs in pages 180-183, taken on August 6—is that the Port is absolutely crowded with vessels bringing food and other supplies to Britain from the seven seas. This exclusive story, by John Pudney, is printed by arrangement with the "News Chronicle."

"I'VE just walked across the dock from one side to the other, stepping from one loaded or unloaded lighter to another," said the lighterman.

"And I've come down here to the docks because the Germans say the Port of London is empty," I said.

"I'd like to know how Jerry can claim that," said the lighterman. "We've not seen any Jerries down here. How can he have seen us ? As for the port being closed—just look across there, the way I have come."

Around the huge, busy dock are strung head to tail the defensively armed ocean-going food ships. In the basin are clusters of lighters and barges like black water-lilies against the steep ships' sides. The London docks are no place for casual conversation these days. I cannot print some of the answers given in reply to my snooping ; they are neither polite nor do they give anything away. A grim and determined discretion covers the great muscular activity of London's dockers.

When I had identified and explained myself to the men lumping flour from Canada into the hold of a barge—who I was and why I was there—they volunteered a great deal of opinion about the Nazis, never ceasing to shift the flour bags, as they were on piecework.

Briefly, Messrs. Ted Bussey, Bob Norton and Ted Furze said : " Tell your readers and, whatever you do, tell Hitler, there is plenty of grub down here. We've not been as busy as this for weeks, and farther up the quay you'll find more bags of flour being unloaded from Australia." They roar with

laughter. " And wouldn't old Hitler have a shock to get covered with flour, same as you are ! "

It is the custom of lightermen to stand by and gossip with some dignity while their small vessels are being loaded by the dockers.

The crew—one gaunt and knowledgeable waterman—of the lighter " Assistance " told me that he had been waiting about for a couple of days, as his lighter was being loaded with match blocks and timber from Canada destined for match-making.

The timber comes from the big ship in fits and starts, because of the method with which it is packed. " There's not been as many of us as this to be seen in this basin together for many a long day," he said.

Like a white flower among the black water-lilies is a Thames sailing barge, the " Lady Maud," loading a cargo of meal. Dick Amner, her Suffolk-born skipper, is a little ashamed of the use to which his sailing craft has been put, for she is not using her sails at all at the moment, but is acting as a " dumb " barge, being towed up the river with her cargo.

For one who can yarn about as many sailing-barge races as he can, this is a melancholy existence, but it goes to show that there is actually so much business in the port at present that there are not enough barges and lighters to go round. Sailing barges, such as the " Lady Maud," have had to be used to transport food through London.

Going down the quay in search of the meat ships, I passed a vessel from the Cape landing a cargo of fruit, tobacco and copper.

You get the feeling of actual food being landed most dramatically when you see cranes lifting 95 carcasses of New Zealand meat at a time. These are arranged with great artistry in a canvas " net " before they are slung ashore, and the hatchwayman in charge of the unloading tells me that the dockers, great amateur gardeners, call the flower-like arrangement of stacked carcasses a " Zinnia."

A great economy has been effected in Australasian shipping space by a new method of " telescoping " each individual carcass before it is frozen on the other side. The hind legs are neatly doubled up inside the carcass, which then takes up only two-thirds of the space it would normally take.

Discretion forbids all details of the food-stuffs passing through London's waterways. The hatchwayman himself says : " Sometimes of an evening they say to me, ' Where are you working, Charlie ? ' and I say, ' Mind your own business,' even though it is one of my best friends, looking for a job. It's the only thing you can do, isn't it ? "

The fantastic Nazi statements for home consumption that the Channel is now controlled by Germany and the Port of London effectually blockaded are utterly disproved by these photographs and those in pages 181-183. The top photograph is of an electric truck at the London Docks laden with flour from Australia. Below is the scene in one of London's great docks only two days before the massive convoy raids when 61 Nazi raiders were shot down. Ships from every quarter of the globe crowd the quays and basins, while lighters stand by to take the cargoes farther up the river.

Photos, " News Chronicle," exclusive to THE WAR ILLUSTRATED

From the Empire's Limits Argosies Come

Skipper Dick Amner of the sailing barge "Lady Maud" is here seen at the wheel. Owing to the great mass of cargoes that has to be taken from the docks his craft is now a "dumb" barge and is towed instead of sailing.

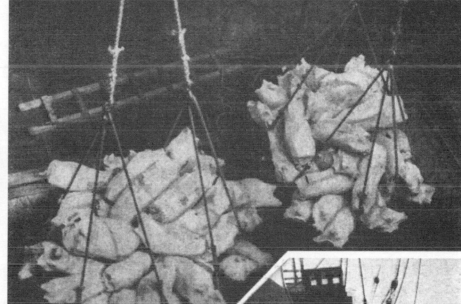

A cargo of meat from New Zealand is being unloaded, above. So well have supplies come in, despite massed air attacks on convoys, that imports from Australia and New Zealand are able to be curtailed. Meat intended for the French army has also arrived in this country and most of the cold storage depots are full. The logs, for pulping, being loaded into a lighter, left, are part of the invaluable contribution of Canada's forests to the Empire's war effort.

Photos, "News Chronicle," exclusive to THE WAR ILLUSTRATED

When the Scandinavian countries were cut off from Britain one of the most serious losses was the wood pulp formerly imported from them for the manufacture of paper. Canada has partly made up the deficiency, and, above, paper from the Dominion is being unloaded in the London Docks. Manufactured paper takes up less cargo space than the raw material. Britain has purchased the whole of the Australian wool clip, and at the left some of the bales of wool are seen at the docks.

Goebbels' Biggest Lie Is Answered

Germany Claims that Her Air Force Destroys British Convoys and Blockades the Channel and the Thames — But the Port of London Has Never Been Busier

Germany's great ports are dead for the duration of the war. Most of what is left of her merchant shipping lies idle at the quays, the furnaces drawn, and only shipkeepers on board, while only a few small coasting vessels enter or leave. The warehouses which once held Germany's imports from all quarters of the globe are empty, while others are still filled with goods for export which there is no possibility of carrying overseas. The Nazis would have their subject peoples believe that London, too, has lost its trade and that Britain's greatest port has been closed by the German blockade. They actually claimed on August 10 that "almost a million tons of British merchant shipping had been sunk in the last three weeks ! "

This photograph and those in pages 180-81 were taken on August 6 in London's docks. Ships loading and unloading lie alongside the quays ; hundreds of lighters are assembled to take on board their shares of the cargoes, and such scenes as this are of everyday occurrence. The Nazi leaders cannot explain them away, and so they resort to their favourite weapon in the war of propaganda— lies, more lies, and yet more lies.

Photo from the "News Chronicle," exclusive to THE WAR ILLUSTRATED

Why the Bomber Often Misses the Convoy

WIDTH OF SHIP e.g. 30 yds. TRAVERSED BY PLANE in ¼ sec.

SIZE of SHIP e.g. 250 yds. x 30 yds. TRAVERSED in 1½ secs.

Attacking *across* a ship's course (left, above), the bomber has only a quarter-second in which to release his missile. If he attacks *along* the vessel's course (right), which is seldom possible, he has 1½ seconds' grace. The ship, of course, is also moving, which adds other complications to the bomb-aimer's difficult task.

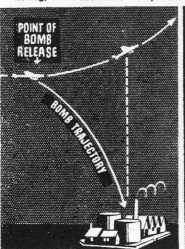

POINT OF BOMB RELEASE

BOMB TRAJECTORY

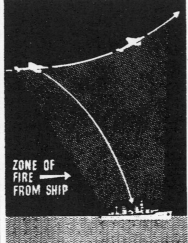

ZONE OF FIRE FROM SHIP

When attacking a land target (left), the bomb-aimer may release his bombs a mile or more before his aircraft comes over it. Against a fast-moving objective (right) the bomber must actually enter the zone of fire (tinted) for any accuracy.

Haworth's diagram shows the bomb-aimer and, behind, his pilot. Together they steady the 'plane and get it on the right course. Then the aimer sets his sights : A, height scale ; B, back-sight ; C, speed adjustment ; D, wind-speed adjustment ; E, compass ; F, fore-sight ; G, point (between arrows) where target must appear for correct bomb release.

"*Daily Mail*"

IN the diagram below, the aircraft is assumed to be flying at 250 miles per hour (approx. 366 feet per second). At 12,000 feet the bomb must be released some 10,000 feet before the aircraft comes over the target. Having ascertained the height and speed of the aircraft the bomb-aimer sets A and C (see Haworth's diagram above) ; next he adjusts the wind-speed screw D, and the fore-sight F is brought to the correct position. Tail-drift is compensated by adjusting a control just below F. All the while the bomb-aimer guides the pilot by observing the compass E. A check-up is made over back-sight and fore-sight, and when at last the target appears between the two arrows G, the bomb-release switch in the aimer's right hand is pressed.

THE six diagrams above and below illustrate difficulties of accurate bombing of moving targets as in recent large-scale attacks on convoys (pages 173-175). The faster (and more modern) the aircraft, the greater the chance of inaccuracy. It is a matter of split seconds to gauge the exact moment of bomb release when attacking, for example, a fast-moving warship. In dive-bombing, to avoid some of these uncertainties, the pilot comes down steeply. He attains greater accuracy, but runs a far bigger risk of destruction.

ZONE OF ANTI-AIRCRAFT FIRE

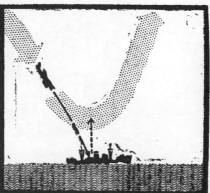

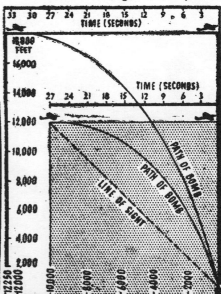

TIME (SECONDS)
33 30 27 24 21 18 15 12 9 6 3

18,000 FEET

TIME (SECONDS)
27 24 21 18 15 12 9 6 3

16,000

14,000

12,000

10,000

8,000

6,000

4,000

2,000

PATH OF BOMB

PATH OF BOMB

LINE OF SIGHT

12,250 12,000   10,000   8,000   6,000   4,000   2,000

Flying low to improve his chance of hitting the target (left), the bomber enters the fire zone at an angle difficult for the gunner ; but before he can turn away, after releasing bombs, he must come towards the target and thereby present a better mark for the gunner. Right, diagram of dive-bombing : the tinted portion shows how the bomber zooms up and away after dropping his delayed action bomb.
Based upon diagrams from the "Evening Standard."

The bomb must be released a calculated distance before the aircraft comes over the target. This diagram shows the path of a missile released at a height of 12,000 and 18,000 feet respectively.

Historic Regiments on the Home Front

The Royal Norfolk Regiment, formerly the 9th Foot, was raised in 1685 to assist in crushing Monmouth's rebellion. In the last war its strength rose to 20 battalions. The Yorkshire Regiment (Princess Alexandra of Wales's Own), formerly the 19th Foot, was long popularly known as the "Green Howards," and in 1920 this was made its official name. It derives from Sir Charles Howard, who was its colonel from 1738 to 1748, and the green facing of the uniforms. In the last war it had 24 battalions.

The Green Howards

Royal Norfolk Regt.

The Green Howards, who have already fought in France, are here seen manning Bren guns in one of the thousands of blockhouses on the Home Front, prepared to receive the Nazi invaders. In the circle other men of the regiment, also armed with Bren guns, are jumping into an anti-aircraft post.

Men of the Norfolk Regiment are seen left moving up a communication trench, now a not unusual feature of the landscape in some parts of Britain, to attack an "enemy" pill box. Above, they have arrived in the forward trench and are preparing to make their last dash forward towards their objective.

Photos, British Official : Crown Copyright

A Dutchman Sees Life In Hitler's Navy

This first-hand account of conditions in the German Navy has been written by a young
Dutchman who served some time on the " Scharnhorst " and " was given hell " on the
" Deutschland."   We have his name—but in view of his concluding remarks it may be
as well not to mention it !

I GOT into Hitler's Navy by accident, and I got out of it by sheer good luck. What happened between those events is a story that will remain seared in my memory till my dying day.

The sea is in my blood, for I'm a Netherlander, born in Rotterdam ; and that is how I first met tough old Captain Scharf, of the German Merchant Service. He gave me my first job at sea, and two years later, when he became Commander of the S.S. " Europa," I was given my first full-time job on the famous Nazi liner.

I wanted action ; the life aboard the " Europa " was dull. Capt. Scharf's Oberliet-zur-See suggested that I should apply to be transferred to Naval duties at Kiel. They were short of men (this was in 1937, at the height of the Nazi naval re-building boom), and my Dutch nationality was not thought likely to be a bar.

It was not. Within ten days I was enrolled as one of the " Gefolgschaft " (worker-followers) at the Deutsche Werke, largest of the State naval shipbuilding yards at Kiel. They paid me 62 pfennigs an hour, and six marks a week had to go in compulsory contributions —Nazi Party, Winter Relief, Sick Fund, and so on. Each Saturday I drew the equivalent of £1 8s. for a week of 50 hours !

They put me on assembling gun-turrets and electrical gun controls for 14-inch guns— heavy work that brought some fifty of us to a take-it-easy strike stage. There was a row. An appeal was made to Admiral Heusinger von Waldegg, the Krupps expert who tries to combine the extreme jobs of being " workers' trustee " on the shipyard Union list, and of being Chairman of the Deutsche Werke board !

Admiral von Waldegg solved our troubles in a way typical of this crafty old sea-dog. He agreed with us that conditions were tough at Deutsche Werke, as there was such a big rearmament drive, but suggested that we should go along to the Germania shipyards, also in Kiel, as there were better jobs going.

We went—only to discover that Admiral von Waldegg is also boss of the Germania Yards—and that as " temporarily unclassified " workers we should be de-graded to a rate of only 50 pf. an hour !

Some of my mates took jobs at this sweatshop rate, but as I knew the most popular young " Leutnant-zur-See " aboard the " Scharnhorst," I spent a night in the docks and then set off on a hike for Stettin (a walk about as far as from Manchester to London), and waited for my " Leutnant-zur-See " pal to come ashore.

My last few marks were spent in a cheering kümmel with him at the Hotel Bismarck, and so my first Navy job was sealed ! While the " Scharnhorst " was at the Stettin naval

base I was to study at the Kiel " Marineschule," and by the time the " Scharnhorst " set off on manoeuvres I would be a fully-fledged member of the "Reichskriegsmarine" (Navy, to you !).

I sat down and studied with 80 other lads— some tough U-boat chaps up for a refresher course, a few young " Vollmatrose " (" A.B.s ") from the " Graf Spee " . . . my particular pal being a certain Hans Munschmeyer, whose father fought in the Great War alongside von Spee himself, and was killed in the battle of the Falkland Isles. We little dreamed then that the " Graf Spee " would meet a similar fate. In less than two months I did a " crammer " course on Nazi Navy material.

Pay was nil ; pocket-money and beer-allowance equal to about 1s. 8d. a week. We

These young German sailors are in the big classroom at the Kiel Marine-schule (Naval School), where new recruits receive part of their training and men already trained take advanced courses.   *Photo, Keystone*

got up at 6.0 each morning, learned every jerk in the " Exerzierreglement " (drill book), worked all day on naval technical stuff, seamanship and gunnery, and then sang ourselves to sleep at nights with Nazi marching-songs and their rather bawdy Naval versions !

During my first trip in the " Scharnhorst " we were on manoeuvres for nearly two months off southern Norway and the North Sea. They soon nicknamed me a " Meckerer "—" grouser " (literally one who bleats like a goat), but I wasn't by any means the only grumbler aboard the " Scharnhorst."

We worked 10-hour shifts except when there was gunnery practice, when it was nothing to be on duty for nearly 14 hours at a stretch. We slept eight in a tiny cabin aft, and at over 15 knots it was almost impossible to sleep owing to the thump in the screw-shaftings.   Food was plentiful, but spoiled by bad cooking ; we did, however, get more fresh meat than I have ever seen before or since in naval or civilian centres of Germany, and as the refrigerators of the " Scharnhorst " are fairly small we didn't carry a lot of old stock.

There were Gestapo men aboard the " Scharnhorst." Some were junior officers, some were just ordinary " Vollmatrose " like myself. If there was any critical talk of the Nazi Party in the wardroom, or if any of the A.B.s like myself happened to criticize the news we got over the radio, somebody was sure to sneak on us as not being a good " Volksgenosse," that is, a " Comrade of the Nation." Sudden disappearances of men, or transference of officers, were often due to Gestapo spying. I learned to keep my mouth shut.

I helped to scrub and polish the decks and fittings, and when duty took me up on the control top, the tripod foremast or under the barbettes, I took no interest in the officers' business. The only pals I had were aboard the " Emden," at present the only medium-class cruiser of the Nazi Navy left afloat. The others, the " Nurnberg," " L e i p z i g," " K ö l n," " Königsberg " and " Karlsruhe," all now at the bottom, all carried chaps who had studied and worked at Kiel with me. We were all young. Average age aboard the " Scharnhorst " was 22.

After a brief period on the aircraft-carrier " Graf Zeppelin," where I learned to fly a twin-engined Messerschmitt, I was suddenly, for purposes of discipline, transferred to the " Deutschland " (since renamed " Lützow "). There was an impression that the Naval authorities wanted to tighten up on discipline. As I see it now, plans were already then being made for composite action of Navy and Luftwaffe in readiness for the Norwegian campaign.

We were given hell on the " Deutschland." Each Oberliet-zur-See had been given special instructions to see that we were worked to breakdown pitch. Our quarters were worse than on the " Scharnhorst," and for a whole week I had to sleep on deck by the " Katapultflugzeug " (catapult-plane), despite the bitter cold.

Then came the River Plate battle. In the Reichskriegsmarine we heard the news first, and it caused a tremendous tightening up of discipline. The " higher-ups " must also have known about the coming Norway action, for training was intensified.

Those freezing nights on deck, combined with the fact that I was getting too much starchy food and little red meat, gave me a bad cold, and then pneumonia. I came back in a Swedish tramp-steamer, and at Kiel was given a 10-day travel pass with " Auf Krankenurlaub " (on sick-leave) printed across it in red. That pass gave me free travel to the Dutch border, and within five hours I was back safe in Rotterdam. I've over-stayed my " Krankenurlaub " by months, but as I'm not going to be fool enough to go back into Hitler's Navy, I'll let Admiral Raeder worry about my desertion !

E-Boats Will Do No Better Than U-Boats

At sea several of the crew of a Nazi motor torpedo-boat are look-out men, watching for some suitable prey not too well guarded. The men at left have just sighted a promising target. Speed and shallow draught are the greatest assets of these small craft, and their object is to dash in towards the quarry, fire their torpedoes and retreat as fast as possible. "Full speed ahead" is the order, and below one of these German motor torpedo-boats is seen going "all out" at about forty knots, making a wake that rises above the stern.

AT the outbreak of war Germany had a comparatively small number of motor torpedo-boats, but, as they can be built far more cheaply and more quickly than submarines, she speeded up construction of an improved design known as E-boats or "Night Hawks." These craft were active in the Channel from July 1940 onwards, but there is good reason to believe the Royal Navy has got the mastery of this latest menace. The E-boats carry a crew of 19 officers and men. Besides torpedoes they are armed with 1½-in. automatic shell guns, and they have a range of about 600 miles. They are very low in the water and therefore difficult to spot from a distance, but can sight even a small coasting steamer long before they themselves can be observed. E-boats are driven by Diesel engines, which, when they are going at full speed, make a roar that can be heard far off, but at low speeds are almost inaudible.

While a motor torpedo-boat approaches its quarry a man stands by each torpedo tube ready to fire when the signal is given ; in the circle is one of them with his hand poised above the lever that operates the torpedo. Above some of the Nazi E-boats are seen at their moorings in a German harbour.

Photos, Fox and International Graphic Press

African Soldiers Are Proud to Fight for

(1) **A typical N.C.O. of the Gold Coast Regiment.** Promotion fills native soldiers with intense pride.

(2) **An officer carries the Colour of a battalion of the Gold Coast Regiment** at the opening of the 1940 session of the Legislative Council.

(3) **This drum-major of the Sierra Leone Battalion** is proud of his gorgeous uniform.

(4) **Men of the same battalion marching through Freetown.** Despite their smart appearance all the men are barefoot, for the native African soldier does not take kindly to boots.

Photos, Lubinski

THERE are two separate forces of native troops in the British African Colonies—the Royal West African Frontier Force, men of which are seen in this page, and the King's African Rifles, seen opposite. The Royal West African Frontier Force consists of the Nigeria Regiment, the Gold Coast Regiment, the Sierra Leone Battalion and the Gambia Company. The Force was originally constituted in 1899, and is controlled by the Colonial Office and the War Office, the officers being chosen from the British Army. At the outbreak of war the Nigeria Regiment numbered five battalions of infantry, two batteries of artillery, a company of engineers and a signal section, while the Gold Coast Regiment consisted of three battalions of infantry, a battery of artillery and a signal section. Both regiments fought with gallantry in the African campaigns of the last war, and have now crossed Africa to fight again on the eastern side.

King and Country, for Empire and Freedom

THE King's African Rifles dates back to 1896, and was the first recognized military force in equatorial Africa. It was then known as the British Central Africa Rifles, but in 1901 received its present title. Within a short time there were six battalions, and at first their chief task was combating slave raiders; but during the First Great War the regiment was on active service from August 1914 until November 1918, and quickly rose to 22 battalions, with a strength of 1,423 British officers, 2,046 British N.C.O's and 31,955 rank and file. The figures show how important a part the regiment played in the defeat of Colonial Germany, and all their other service, fine as it was, was dwarfed by their campaigns in the First Great War.

Men of the King's African Rifles pride themselves on their smartness and discipline, and these two photographs show men of the Nyasaland battalion. Top, a class for non-commissioned officers is at drill, while in the lower photograph men in fatigue uniform are drawn up for a kit inspection. A high authority has said of the African troops that " the fighting qualities are uniformly good whatever the regiment."

Photos, Topical

OUR SEARCHLIGHT ON THE WAR NEWS

New York Backs R.A.F.

ON August 9 and 12, the days following the great aerial battles in the Channel, all the New York papers gave pride of place to reports from London, acclaiming on their front pages Britain's mastery in the air, rushing out new editions as more details became available, and making use of every word of the rather scrappy information which was all that their London correspondents could send them at the time. The German versions of the same engagements, with their fantastic lists of successes, were, significantly enough, relegated to inside pages.

His Life to Save Others

HAD he baled out when his stricken machine caught fire during the great air battle of August 8, Flying-Officer D. N. Grice might have saved his own life. But in that case the burning 'plane would have crashed over houses in the centre of the town. Instead, this heroic pilot stuck to his controls, skimmed over the roof-tops, losing height all the time, turned the machine with consummate skill to avoid a building on the cliff

Flying-Officer D. N. Grice, who so gallantly sacrificed his life, had been married only nine months. His home is at Ealing, and the Mayor of the Borough has opened a fund to provide a memorial. *Photo, Associated Press*

edge, and finally crashed in the sea 50 yards from the water's edge. When, a few minutes later, motor launches reached the spot, they found only burnt-out wreckage.

In the President's Bad Books

AFTER being publicly reprimanded by Mr. Sumner Welles, U.S. Acting Secretary of State, for an indiscreet interview given in London to the Press Association on August 6, Mr. John W. Cudahy, American Ambassador to Belgium, was summoned home by President Roosevelt and left England on August 10.

Mr. Cudahy had defended King Leopold's decision to surrender, saying that it would be applauded when the truth was known. He stated that the Belgians' supply of wheat would last until the middle of September or early October, and that Britain should lift the blockade to prevent famine. But what caused particular resentment in the States was a comparison he made between German and American soldiers which was unfavourable to the latter. Mr. Welles declared that Mr. Cudahy had given the interview " in

violation of standing instructions of the State Department," and that his views " must not be construed as representing the views of the Government."

'The Pilots We Cannot Replace'

SO said Mr. Garfield Weston, M.P. for Macclesfield, on August 9, as he handed to the Minister for Aircraft Production a cheque for £100,000 to cover the cost of replacing sixteen Hurricanes and Spitfires lost in the previous day's great air battle over the Channel. The pilots, indeed, cannot be replaced, but their successors can avenge them if the 'planes are forthcoming, and this point is being increasingly appreciated by the British people. Mr. Weston's splendid gift is one of many devoted to the same end. On July 28 Lord Beaverbrook announced that he had received over £2,000,000 from the public for the purchase of aircraft, and every day gifts both large and small pour in to him. The city of Worcester recently subscribed £10,000 for two fighter aircraft. Richmond, Surrey, has opened a Spitfire fund ; Hendon, Middlesex, intends to raise £20,000 to buy four Hurricanes ; Portsmouth has collected £11,000 for two fighters. The aim of the Newsagents' Spitfire Fund is to defray the cost of at least one squadron. The Gaumont-British Picture Corporation has launched a scheme to provide a flight of three Spitfires. From the Empire and the Colonies come great money gifts earmarked for the purchase of aircraft with which to protect the Mother Country and, through her, their own existence.

G-Men Hunt the Saboteurs

THE Norwegian cargo steamer " Lista " left New York en route for Liverpool on August 7. During the night an explosion, followed by a fire, occurred in her hold, and a tug, urgently summoned, beached her in flames near the entrance to the Ambrose Channel in New York harbour. The Federal Bureau of Investigation, popularly known as the G-men, started investigations into the cause of the fire, which, it is suspected, was the result of an incendiary bomb planted by Nazi agents.

This treacherous attack on a small merchant vessel gives point to the disclosures made two days earlier to President Roosevelt by Mr. Edgar Hoover, chief of the G-men, on acts of sabotage against the U.S. defence programme. These included the putting of emery dust in aeroplane engines and scrap metal in naval vessel engines. It was reported that the bureau had handled 16,885 cases of sabotage since the European war broke out, and a strong warning was given to every American city to examine its utility undertakings and to ensure their protection against subversive agents whose plans, it had been discovered, included many terrible means of creating destruction.

Lord Milne and A.M.P.C.

THE Auxiliary Military Pioneer Corps, whose G.O.C. is, appropriately enough, Major-General L. W. Amps, was formed in November 1939 to carry out manual work not done by civilians. It is composed largely of old soldiers of the 1914-1918 war, and younger men with slight physical defects which make them unfit for front-line service. Since its inception it has developed into a combatant corps, being armed with rifles and bayonets as well as with mattocks, picks and spades. We have already called attention to the magnificent work and courage of this valuable auxiliary (*see* Vol. 1, p. 501, and Vol. 2, pp. 233, 467, 596, 656), of which Field-Marshal Lord Milne was appointed Colonel Commandant on July 2. On August 5 he inspected a group of Amps

which became famous in the battles of Flanders. It was the last to leave Boulogne on May 24, after defending the harbour for days, under gruelling enemy fire, with any and every weapon they could " scrounge." Five hundred out of 1,100 men were killed or reported missing. One of this group recently received the Military Medal for a

Field-Marshal Lord Milne, Colonel Commandant of the Auxiliary Military Pioneer Corps, is here seen talking to one of the men engaged in heavy work. Lord Milne is 73 years of age.
Photo, Planet News

typical act of great bravery. Major-General Amps, who accompanied Lord Milne on his visit to the camp, was a colonel of the Buffs in the last war, when he was awarded the V.C.

Haw Haw's Understudy

AN American journalist, Mr. Warren Irvin, recently returned from Berlin, has made some interesting revelations about Berlin's English radio announcers. It seems that in the waiting-room of the broadcasting station were caricatures of various speakers, including one of the British Fascist, William Joyce, better known here as Lord Haw Haw. After the latter's identity had been exposed another announcer, whose mother is English and father German, was told " You had better be Lord Haw Haw tonight." At least two other Britons are employed at the Nazi station, but their names were carefully concealed, and in front of neutrals they always struggled along in faulty German.

Australian Flying Calamity

TRAGEDY smote Australia on August 13, when an aeroplane which was carrying three members of the Commonwealth Cabinet and the Chief of the Army General Staff crashed on the point of landing at Canberra. The ten occupants of the aircraft, all of whom were killed, were Brigadier G. A. Street, Minister of the Army ; Mr. J. V. Fairbairn, Air Minister ; Sir Henry Gullett, Vice-President of the Executive Council ; General Sir Cyril Brudenell White, Chief of the Australian General Staff ; Lieut.-Colonel Francis Thornthwaite, a Staff officer ; Mr. R. E. Elford, secretary to Mr. Fairbairn ; and an R.A.A.F. crew of four.

The 'plane was a Lockheed-Hudson bomber, used because the party, which had flown from Melbourne for a Cabinet meeting, was larger than could be contained in the machine ordinarily used. This disaster is a grievous blow to Mr. Menzies' Government.

I WAS THERE!

Eye Witness Stories of Episodes and Adventures in the Second Great War

My Squadron Shot 21 Nazis in One Day

A dramatic account of one of the three big air battles in the Channel on August 8, August 11 and August 12 was given by a flight commander whose squadron had shot down no fewer than 32 enemy aircraft during these engagements. He was himself shot down on the morning of August 12, the day on which he broadcast his adventures. Here is the fighter pilot's story in his own words.

THE other flight of my squadron took off at half-past eight the other morning to patrol the convoys sailing down the Channel south of the Isle of Wight. My flight took off shortly after that. We were lucky to find that the first two formations of dive bombers, Junkers 87, were left to us. We went straight at them; some of them turned back at once, but others went on to the convoy and attacked. We shot up a few of the bombers, and then got mixed up with their escorting Messerschmitt 109s. I remember seeing two of them, about a quarter of a mile away, coming straight at me at sixteen thousand feet. Suddenly, for no reason at all, one of them did a half-roll and went straight down. I followed, but although I had not fired at him, and so far as I could see no one else did either, he went straight into the sea. It just looked as though he committed suicide. I was so astonished that I could not believe my eyes.

While I was watching for others, there was a crash behind my head; a bullet came through my hood, passed through the back of my helmet, tore through the back of my goggles, and—before I knew where I was— the hood had flown back and my goggles had disappeared. After that, all we could see were enemy bombers and fighters going like mad for home.

The squadron got six bombers and three fighters, for certain, and six others were damaged at that time. I, myself, got one fighter. The balloons which the convoy carried (see illustration page 175) had certainly put the dive bombers off their stroke.

Later, the whole squadron was sent up to investigate a raid off Beachy Head. We went up to more than twenty thousand feet and saw at between thirty thousand and thirty-five thousand feet no fewer than thirty-six Messerschmitt 110s. They swung round and returned towards France when

they saw us, and as we were unable to reach them, we turned, and were then told over the radio telephone that a battle was going on south of the Isle of Wight. We had fifty miles to go to the convoy. I myself led the three machines in my section to a point well south of the island. There we saw two separate squadrons of Messerschmitt 110s.

Something went wrong with my radio set; I could hear the squadron leader calling: "Where are they?" knowing that I had spotted some, but he could not receive my message. So there were the three of us, circling high above the Messerschmitts, which were now flying in an uncompleted circle at about four thousand feet. We were at sixteen thousand feet. I was curious to know why they were circling round like that, and we decided to have a crack. We went down on them; the Messerschmitt which was at the end of the circling line of fighters was shot into the sea immediately. Well, we broke up that happy little circle quite effec-

tively; all three of us got at least one. I think we must have taken them by surprise.

We started climbing again, but after a minute I thought I would like to go back and find out what was happening. I flew over another circle of enemy fighters for about five minutes, until they had all cleared off. Then I went down, and saw one of their pilots in the water. He was easy to see, for all around him was a big patch of green vapour, a special method used by the Germans when they get into the water. It shows their friends where they are—you can see the green vapour five miles away.

While I was investigating this I was attacked by a Messerschmitt 110 which I suppose I had overlooked. I skidded round and climbed for him, but he broke away to my left. I was still turning, and at about a thousand feet I stalled. He was right in my gun-sight. I just gave him a quick burst— he heeled over and went straight into the sea, and broke up. He was really a sitting bird. Then we went home.

Our day's bag by then was fourteen enemy aircraft, and in the third action of that day we made it up to twenty-one. Our squadron's score must now be well over seventy. We shot down our first enemy on May 22nd— until then we hadn't had any luck, but by the end of the Dunkirk show our score was about thirty.

Coming Back From Kiel Our Bomber Sank

The announcement by the Air Ministry that "one of our aircraft failed to return" does not always mean that the crew are lost. It frequently happens that, as related in the following story by a sergeant-pilot, the airmen are picked up by Naval units and reach their bases safely.

THE sergeant-pilot of a bomber said: We had been attacking Kiel, and had spent some 90 minutes over our target, flying most of the time through a very hot barrage. The shells, which were bursting right above us, showered above the aircraft rather like golden rain.

After hitting our objective with our bombs, we started for home, but unfortunately we ran into thick fog, so we climbed above the clouds. Just after dawn broke we came

below the clouds again to find that we were still over the sea. The petrol was almost exhausted, and first one and then the other engine petered out, and there was nothing for it but to alight on the water.

We glided down from 3,500 feet, but with visibility patchy and extending sometimes to only about 50 yards, we realized that we were likely to spend an unpleasantly long time in the dinghy.

When we were about 100 feet up I saw a

Hitler hopes that the intensive bombardment of Britain will shake the morale of the people, but this photograph does not suggest that anyone is "nervy." It was taken at Berwick, between Eastbourne and Lewes, on the morning after an aerial battle during which a Messerschmitt had been brought down in a cornfield. The young people, who must have heard the aerial combat and perhaps the sound of bombs, have evidently no feeling but curiosity about this 'plane that should have terrorized them.
Photo, Associated Press

naval trawler, and we came down about a mile from her. As we passed her we tried to indicate by pointing seawards that we were coming down and wanted her help. At first the crew thought that we were giving a low-flying exhibition and they were taken aback when we hit the water. Coming down was rather like hitting a concrete pavement, and the impact knocked both engines off the machine.

The aircraft went under water, but came up again within a second or two, with the cockpits half full. The crew had been standing by and in a few moments they had launched a dinghy and got aboard it. I jumped into the sea, and then, pushing the dinghy away from the aircraft, which threatened to sink at any moment, I swam behind it for a short distance after which the other fellows hauled me in.

In a few minutes the trawler's lifeboat was heading towards us and soon we were on board the ship. The crew lent us an assortment of clothes while ours were drying against the funnel, and I got the skipper's socks.

Later we steamed right over an enemy magnetic minefield. A naval patrol vessel hailed our skipper and asked him if he realized that he was right on top of it.

" Of course I do, but it doesn't bother us," reported the skipper nonchalantly through his megaphone. We arrived back at our base still wearing our motley collection of borrowed garments, part R.A.F., part Naval and part civilian.

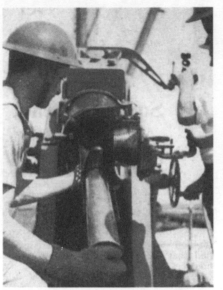

The highest courage and first-rate marksmanship have been shown by the men who man the guns of merchant ships. Here some of them are loading a 12-pounder gun.
Photo, Fred. G. Shaw

Our Gunners Fought Waist-Deep in Water

The 17,000-ton " Scotstoun " (once the Anchor Line " Caledonia ") was on the North Atlantic patrol when she was torpedoed and sunk on June 13. The story of her last hour, reprinted from " Life," is told here by a member of the crew, Signalman Ronald Gold, who pays special tribute to the gallantry of his gunner shipmates.

THE first torpedo which struck the " Scotstoun " shattered the steering gear and screws, rendering the ship helpless. It also ripped open the after-hold, and wrecked the wireless aerial.

Signalman Ronald Gold said he was immediately ordered to run up as many ensigns as he could. He went on :

Getting up an ensign on each available mast is always a first step when a warship goes into action. The ensign goes up and stays up till the ship goes down. We get as many up as we can in case some get shot away. I got three ensigns hoisted on the foremast, mainmast and on the gaff aft. It wasn't easy, because the radio aerial was in a tangle on the decks and the aftermast was leaning over all skew-whiff.

Then I reported back to the bridge. From the bridge and in between my jobs I had a good view of the action spot, and from the other signalman I learned a lot about the beginning of it.

Nobody seemed to have spotted the source of the attack before the first torpedo struck. Then two ocean-going U-boats were discovered far out on the starboard quarter, their periscopes barely feathering the sea's spume that overlaid the heavy swell.

The alarm sounded immediately on the klaxons, and a few minutes later our 6-inch and stern high-angle guns began their uproar. The ship lay wallowing in the trough of the swells—a wide-open target— and torpedo after torpedo came at her from the hidden submarines, which, however, were kept at a distance by our gun barrage.

The gun crews could see the torpedoes coming at them so, throughout the action, one of the stern high-angle guns, depressed to its lowest point, was actually firing at the torpedoes and diverted several from their course. I myself observed at least six bounce out of the water and go speeding harmlessly past the ship.

I saw the marvellous high-angle gun on the stern hard at it pumping shot in front of the torpedo wakes which were coming at us now and again.

And I saw something else. Just as I got to the bridge I saw a radio operator coming down from the broken aftermast. Somehow he had managed to climb up that mast and re-rig the aerial, and now he was racing towards the radio cabin. I learned afterwards that within three minutes of reaching the radio room he had managed to get a code message over. Those three minutes helped to save us, because a minute later the last two torpedoes hit us, wrecking the radio apparatus and the aerial—for good this time.

The next minutes are a bit of a blank, with the ship going over further the whole time. But I remember watching the water creep up round one of the gun crews hard at work on a 6-inch.

First knee deep, then waist deep in water, they held the shells high above their heads as they fed their gun. Then, as the increasing angle of the sinking ship put the gun out of action, they went and helped at another.

It's not my job to dish out praise, but I thought those men were great. All of them had seen the wrecked radio aerial and knew that they had little hope of assistance or rescue. They didn't know that a message had got through.

They were hundreds of miles away from the steamship lanes, and over a week's boat journey away from the nearest land. British warships were unlikely to visit the area and the relief vessel on this beat was not due for a long time. But they kept on.

Then, as gun after gun was submerged, the order came : " Abandon ship."

I saw the captain come out of the control tower and stalk down the starboard wing of the bridge and stare along the side. He was hatless, his white hair blowing about in the wind. We waited, but we weren't surprised when he half turned around and said over his shoulder : " Take to the boats." The message was passed on, and one after another the gun crews went to their boat stations or slid over the side on to rafts.

But the stern high-angle gun kept on to the end with the corpses of two of its crew who had been killed during the first explosion washing about in the waves at its base. At length that stopped, and survivors climbed up the steeply sloping deck and joined the captain, the doctor, the chief gunnery instructor and the rest of us on the bridge.

The " killick " (Navy slang for petty-officer, so-called from the anchor, or killick, he wears on his sleeve badge) came out with the confidential code books and handed some to me. It was his responsibility to see that these books went to the bottom. Before I left the bridge I heard the captain say to the other officers : " Well, I don't think we have done so badly, gentlemen. We've still got three ensigns up and the guns going to the last."

From my boat I saw the captain holding grimly on to the bridge rail, and heard him order the other officers over the side. But at a nod from the first lieutenant the little group seized him by the arms and plunged with him down the sloping bridge and into the water, where a boat picked them up.

Some of the men were singing as we pulled away to watch the " Scotstoun " go down. The lieutenant in my boat stood up and called for three cheers for her. Those who could stand up cheered, and I could hear those in the other boats and rafts do the same. Then she was gone.

Just after midday a Coastal Command 'plane appeared, circled over us twice, and then flashed with an Aldis lamp : " Cheer up, there's a destroyer coming."

It arrived, and I have never seen anything so neat and quick as the way it got us aboard. Rope ends came down and the sailors simply yanked us on deck like fish.

The " Scotstoun " is here seen in harbour when as the Anchor liner, " Caledonia," she sailed as a merchant ship. Ships of the Anchor Line in peacetime plied on the North Atlantic and to the East.
Photo, Wide World

My Day Over The Mediterranean

The thrills and dangers of a British air patrol in the Mediterranean—a typical day's work for the men who keep the sea clear for the convoys—are vividly depicted in the following story by Alexander Clifford, " Daily Mail " special correspondent, who accompanied the crew of an R.A.F. flying-boat on patrol.

WE made an early take-off. The sun was rising as we began to scour miles of the motionless Mediterranean for enemy submarines and shipping. As we approached Sicily, with Etna looming in the background, we spotted something.

The pilot swung the machine towards it, and the something took shape as an escorted water-carrying vessel of the sort Mussolini uses for supplying his troops in Libya.

Our crew were at action stations. I was holding my breath. The flying-boat went into a steep dive. Three bombs went screaming down. The sea swirled up in foam as they dropped immediately behind the vessel's stern. The smaller escorting ships went scurrying away.

It was only a few minutes after this that we were first attacked. I knew nothing until a noise like violent typewriters suddenly broke out all over the fuselage of our 'plane. Tumblers leaped from their rack and burst about my ears. Something ripped through the seat of my shorts. Whether it was a bullet or a splinter of glass I did not look to see.

Bullets pinged around me. I tore open the communicating door and looked aft. The Italian fighter which had attacked us was hurtling towards the blue sea in flames. But the rear gunner who had shot it down was slumped across his gun. Both our midships gunners had blood trickling down their legs.

Smoke was pouring up from where incendiary bullets had struck. I felt a spray of petrol in my face. For a minute it seemed that we were hopelessly afire.

" Get ready in case we have to bale out," said the navigator to me as we passed each other carrying extinguishers and tins of water.

We stamped and we doused and we managed to control the main outbursts. For some time after this we kept our eyes skinned for smoking rags and cushions.

We moved the wounded forward and bound up their injuries. Fortunately they had only flesh wounds in the legs.

There was urgent work to be done everywhere. And we were still flying along the coast of Sicily, where Mussolini's fighter squadrons are based.

The fitter, who had now manned the rear gun turret, waved to me. Our rudder mechanism was damaged. I clambered up to tell the pilot, but he already knew. He was using his engines to steer.

Then I took down a message for transmission to headquarters. But we could not send it. Our radio was soused with petrol, and we dared not risk a short-circuit. There were holes everywhere, but the machine kept flying on as though nothing had happened. The crew moved about their emergency duties completely calm.

Then came the next attack. I watched our gunners pumping bullets at Breda monoplanes as they swooped above us, soaring dizzily into the deep blue sky and diving down along our length with guns blazing.

I was too busy to count the number of attacks on our 'planes, but one enemy machine dived out of sight, apparently out of control. The gunner who shot him believes that he must have crashed.

When Malta came in sight the Italians were still attacking. But with all guns firing we made them keep their distance. No further damage was done. A bullet struck one of our gunners' goggles, but the glass did not break.

As the enemy 'planes finally sheered off back towards their bases, we set to work stopping holes in the hold preparatory to alighting on the sea.

We knew that our petrol and oil could not last much longer. With our hearts in our mouths we flew low over Malta's minefields and alighted safely.

The coolness of our pilot, the magnificent teamwork of our crew had saved our lives for all of us, and a costly flying boat for Britain.

Lance-Corporal John Lee Warner, whose story of his adventurous escape from France is told on this page, is here seen walking in London.
Photo, Planet News

I Trekked Across France to Spain

On August 2, Lance-Corporal John Lee Warner, of the Queen's Royal Regiment, reached London from Lisbon in time to celebrate his 21st birthday. While with the B.E.F. he was captured by the Germans, and after escaping from them wandered for six weeks across France into Spain. Here is his story.

WE were stationed just north of Abbeville, and on Sunday, May 19, dug trenches all day. I was in charge of the forward section of the forward company for the battalion.

Next day the Germans bombed us regularly every hour. At 5.30 in the evening we got the " stand-by for immediate action," and half an hour later the German tanks arrived. From that minute hell was let loose. It is a curious sensation to have these tanks firing at you. You hear a crack and then the shrapnel flies.

In my section of 11 men only two were wounded, but after two hours of this I decided to send a man back to see what we should do. He returned to say there was no platoon headquarters and no company headquarters. They had gone without being able to get word up to us.

I decided to withdraw, and we crept away, harassed all the time by snipers.

That night we hid in a barn, and when things had got a little quiet I went out to have a look round. In the village I found an abandoned lorry. We cranked it up and set off in the direction of Abbeville.

Suddenly ahead a red light flashed. I thought it was our rearguard and pulled up.

A man jumped on the running-board and held a Tommy-gun at my head. I switched on the lights. He was a Jerry, and ahead, stretched out as far as we could see, were two columns of German tanks.

I decided to surrender. I felt I was the biggest fool in the Army, until next morning we were joined by 10,000 French and 1,200 British prisoners.

We marched off in columns of three with six men and two lorries mounted with machine-guns to act as guards. All the way along the road men were making their escape by jumping into the hedges as we turned a corner, but I felt too sick to try anything.

Eventually we got to Beaucourt-sur-Ancre and by this time I was fed up and damned hungry, for we got little, if anything, to eat. It was decided to park us there for the night and move on next morning.

Prisoners were still being brought in and one of these was wearing civilian clothes. I made a bargain with him and we swopped.

We were all in a wheat granary with plenty of haystacks about. I climbed to the top of one of these, made a hole six feet deep, and hid there. Next morning the troops moved off, and I had started on my escape with the advantage of civilian clothes.

This was May 27, and I made my was northwards towards Dunkirk, because we heard stories about what was going on there. Eventually I came across a small house beside the railway line near Arras, broke in and rested up there, eating all the food I could lay hands on.

On the sixth day there I heard a knock on the door and saw a Jerry. He asked me where my wife was. I said she had gone into Arras because she was afraid of the bombs. He could speak less French than I could, so I got away with it, but he ordered me to go to Arras and get her.

Next day I stuck a notice on the door saying I had gone to Arras and would be back in two days.

I made my way to Etaples and there a man gave me a bike which proved a godsend. I was trying for the coast and a boat, but failed to get a boat at either Boulogne or Calais. Then someone stole my bike, so I hiked back to Etaples and went across to Le Touquet.

When sleeping in an empty house there, some Germans entered and arrested me. I was threatened by the military commandant to be shot as a spy, because I was still in the clothes of a French workman.

The commandant got so mad with me that he kicked me down half a dozen steps, but that was the only time a German touched me. They put me in the backyard of a house with 18 other British and 80 French prisoners, but I escaped that night through a window which the guards had overlooked.

Then I made my way towards Spain and eventually got to the frontier. But I had no exit visa and was arrested by a gendarme. I told the chief of police my story, and he pointed out a way I could get across over the hills.

After that it was plain sailing. I got assistance from British Consuls, and reached London in time to celebrate my 21st birthday. (" Evening News.")

Let the Trumpets Sound, the Spirit-stirring Drum !

After months of "cold storage," military bands were allowed in July to make cheerful music again. At one of the R.A.F. stations members of several famous dance bands, some of whom are seen left, are to be found, and while they are being trained as service bandsmen they have formed a dance band, the "Squadronairs," for the station. Meanwhile, at Aldershot they are training other Army bandsmen, some of whom are seen "in action" below.

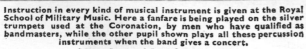

Instruction in every kind of musical instrument is given at the Royal School of Military Music. Here a fanfare is being played on the silver trumpets used at the Coronation, by men who have qualified as bandmasters, while the other pupil shown plays all these percussion instruments when the band gives a concert.

Photos, Sport and General, L.N.A., Fox

British Personalities of the War

Rt. Hon. Clement R. Attlee, P.C., M.P., who for some years has been the leader of the Labour Party in the House of Commons, is now achieving fresh distinction as Mr. Churchill's deputy. He is a member of the inner War Cabinet and holds the office of Lord Privy Seal. Born in 1883, he became secretary of Toynbee Hall and a lecturer at the London School of Economics. In the Great War he served in the South Lancashires and the Tank Corps in Gallipoli, Mesopotamia and France, and held the rank of major. He has represented Limehouse since 1922, and in Ramsay MacDonald's ministries was Under-Secretary of State for War, Chancellor of the Duchy of Lancaster and Postmaster General.

Rt. Hon. Albert V. Alexander, P.C., M.P., is one of the Cooperative M.P.s, representing the Hillsborough division of Sheffield, and has often crossed swords with Lord Beaverbrook when the latter's newspapers have championed the small trader against the " Co-op." Now, however, they are on the best of terms, for Mr. Alexander, as First Lord of the Admiralty, wants 'planes for the Fleet Air Arm—and Lord Beaverbrook knows how to get them ! He was born in 1885, and, unlike most cabinet ministers, has the distinction of being educated at an elementary school. He was First Lord of the Admiralty from 1929 to 1931, and Mr. Churchill put him back there in May 1940.

Mr. Frank Pick, who in August was appointed Director-General of the Ministry of Information, was until recently Vice-Chairman of the London Passenger Transport Board. Almost his whole working life, indeed, has been spent in the service of London Transport, for he joined the Underground Group in 1906 and for many years was Lord Ashfield's right-hand man. He, too, it was who put the travelling millions by 'bus and tube in his debt by making the posters things of beauty with their scenes of London's country.

Mr. W. G. Weston, M.P., on August 9 handed a cheque for £100,000 to Lord Beaverbrook, Minister for Aircraft Production, with the request that he should buy with it sixteen Hurricane or Spitfire fighters to replace those lost in the great battle above the Channel the day before. Born in Canada 42 years ago, he served in the Great War and then, returning to Canada, built up one of the biggest bakery firms in the Empire. In November 1939 he was returned unopposed as M.P. for Macclesfield.

Rt. Hon. Arthur Greenwood, P.C., M.P., as Minister without Portfolio is the member of the inner War Cabinet charged with the supervision of economic affairs—he presides over the Economic Policy Committee—and in this capacity he told the House of Commons on August 7 of the present position of the blockade. One of Labour's most trusted leaders, he was first elected to the House of Commons in 1922 ; in 1924 he was Parliamentary Secretary to the Ministry of Health, and from 1929 to 1931 was Minister of Health. Since 1932 he has represented Wakefield. In his earlier days he was lecturer in economics in the University of Leeds, and towards the end of the last War was Assistant Secretary of the Ministry of Reconstruction. He has written much on economic and social conditions.

Rt. Hon. Herbert S. Morrison, P.C., M.P., as Minister of Supply occupies one of the key posts in Mr. Churchill's win-the-war Government. He is a Londoner and was born in 1888, and from the elementary school he passed in rapid succession from errand boy to shop assistant, from telephone operator to newspaper circulation manager ; then he entered London politics and as Secretary of the London Labour Party was organizer of the Labour triumph of 1934, which ended a long period of control by the Municipal Reformers. From 1934 until 1940 he was Leader of the Labour Party in the L.C.C. In the House of Commons he was elected for South Hackney in 1923, in 1929, and again in 1935. In Ramsay MacDonald's second Government he was Minister of Transport.

Photos, Central Press, Fox, Lafayette

OUR DIARY OF THE WAR

WEDNESDAY, AUGUST 7, 1940 *340th Day*

On the Sea⁓Announced that British liner "Accra" was sunk off west coast of Eire when two U-boats attacked convoy on July 26. Nineteen persons missing. Both U-boats were destroyed.

Admiralty announced that H.M. minesweeping trawler "River Clyde" had been sunk by enemy mine.

In the Air⁓R.A.F. bombers made daylight raids on aerodromes at Cherbourg and Hamstede. At night bombers attacked Homburg oil plant, Kiel dockyard, store depots at Hamm, and aerodromes in N.W. Germany.

Skuas of Fleet Air Arm successfully bombed oil depot near Bergen.

War against Italy⁓No further enemy advance into British Somaliland.

R.A.F. bombed shipping and store buildings at Bardia, and submarine bases at Massawa.

Home Front⁓Raiders appeared during night over widespread areas in Britain, but damage from bombs dropped was slight.

Director-General of Ministry of Information, Sir Kenneth Lee, resigned. Mr. Frank Pick appointed to the post.

General⁓Agreement concluded between British Government and Gen. de Gaulle concerning organization, employment and conditions of service of French Volunteer Force in Britain.

THURSDAY, AUGUST 8 *341st Day*

On the Sea⁓Admiralty announced that H.M. submarine "Oswald" was overdue and must be presumed lost.

British liner "Kemmerdine" overdue and presumed lost.

In the Air⁓R.A.F. bombed aerodromes of Schiphol and Valkenburg. Coastal Command aircraft shot down a Messerschmitt off Le Havre.

Night raids made on Hamburg docks, supply depots at Hamm, Soest and Cologne. Mine-laying in enemy harbours and estuaries continued.

War against Italy⁓Enemy columns from Hargeisa and Oadwina, Somaliland, reported to be advancing northwards.

Big air battle over Sidi-Amar, Libya, when Gladiators engaged much larger force of Italian fighters. Fifteen of latter were destroyed. Two British aircraft missing.

Walrus aircraft of Fleet Air Arm, operating from H.M. Australian cruiser "Hobart," made dive-bombing attacks on Italian H.Q. at Zeila, causing damage and casualties.

Italian aircraft made unsuccessful bombing attacks on British warships in Gulf of Aden.

Home Front⁓Sixty-one raiders shot down in Channel during big air fight. Waves of German dive bombers attacked British convoy, considerably damaging several. Eighteen British aircraft down, but three of their pilots safe.

Air battle followed attacks by motor torpedo boats (E-boats), which sank three coastal vessels in a convoy. One E-boat sunk and another damaged.

Enemy aircraft dropped bombs over wide area of Britain. Little damage reported except from N.E. England, where a sanatorium and shop property suffered. There were a number of casualties.

FRIDAY, AUGUST 9 *342nd Day*

On the Sea⁓Norwegian steamer "Toran" reported sunk.

In the Air⁓R.A.F. attacked aerodrome at Guernsey, setting it on fire.

British bombers raided seaplane base at Poulmic, near Brest. Other aircraft fired Nazi oil tanks at Flushing and damaged works at Ludwigshaven and Cologne.

War against Italy⁓In Somaliland, enemy positions on Hargeisa-Jugargan road were attacked. Italian fighters raided Berbera.

R.A.F. attacked shipping in Tobruk harbour. Massawa was successfully bombed.

S. African Air Force bombed Neghelli aerodrome, Abyssinia, destroying two aircraft and damaging others.

Home Front⁓Single raider dropped bombs on N.E. coastal town, causing damage and casualties before being shot down.

Balloon barrage defences and S.E. coastal town attacked by German fighters with machine-guns.

During night raiders dropped bombs over many areas in England. In north-west they destroyed several houses and caused fatal casualties.

Rumania⁓Government agreed to cede part of the Dobruja to Bulgaria. Exchange of populations to involve transfer of 100,000 Rumanians.

General⁓War Office announced that British troops stationed in Shanghai and North China are being withdrawn for service elsewhere.

SATURDAY, AUGUST 10 *343rd Day*

On the Sea⁓H. M. submarine "Odin" considerably overdue and presumed lost.

In the Air⁓R.A.F. made daylight attacks on enemy aerodromes in Holland and France, including Schiphol, Querqueville, Flushing, Caen, Dinard and Guernsey.

Night objectives included Hamburg docks, Wilhelmshaven, oil tanks at Frankfurt and Homburg, and supplies at Hamm and Soest.

War against Italy⁓Italian advance in Somaliland continued. French airmen reported to be taking part in R.A.F.'s operations in Africa. Italian aircraft raided Aden.

Home Front⁓Sporadic German raids reported in England and Wales. Twelve high explosive bombs dropped near town in S.E.

General⁓Syria closed frontier to British and other combatant subjects of military age.

SUNDAY, AUGUST 11 *344th Day*

On the Sea⁓Admiralty announced that Egyptian liner "Mahomed Ali El-Kebir" had been sunk by U-boat in Atlantic while carrying troops. Survivors 740 out of 860.

In the Air⁓R.A.F. bombed aerodromes at Dinard, Caen and Guernsey, and seaplane slipway at Brest. Coastal Command aircraft shot down enemy fighter off French coast.

Night raids made on oil plants at Dortmund, Gelsenkirche, Wanne Eickel and Cherbourg. Military targets bombed at Dusseldorf, Hamm and Soest.

War against Italy⁓Enemy made general attack on British positions covering Jugargan Pass, but was repulsed.

Home Front⁓About 400 German 'planes launched attacks on balloon barrage in Straits of Dover, on Weymouth and Portland, and on shipping off East Coast. Sixty-five enemy aircraft destroyed. Twenty-six British fighters missing ; two pilots safe.

Some damage done to houses, churches, naval buildings, including a hospital, and communications. Two warships sustained minor damage from splinters.

Albania⁓Revolt which started in Miriditi district said to be spreading and to have resulted so far in 400 Italian casualties.

General⁓Nazi leader in S. America, Arnulf Fuhrmann, arrested in Argentina.

MONDAY, AUGUST 12 *345th Day*

In the Air⁓R.A.F. bombed Gotha airframe factory and other targets in N.W. Germany, Holland and France.

Raids made on 17 aerodromes and seaplane base at Borkum. Harbour at Helder bombed by R.A.F. and Fleet Air Arm.

Home Front⁓Sixty-two enemy machines destroyed in course of large-scale raids on South Coast. Attacks began over Kent coast and extended later to Isle of Wight and Portsmouth. Thirteen British fighters missing.

Minor damage done to outskirts of H.M. dockyard. Number of buildings, including railway station, hit in Portsmouth. Church and houses damaged in Isle of Wight.

Extensive night raids by enemy bombers over England and Wales.

TUESDAY, AUGUST 13 *346th Day*

On the Sea⁓Running fights took place between British motor torpedo boats and German light naval forces, in which one Nazi ship was rammed.

Admiralty announced that H.M. minesweeping trawlers "Tamarisk" and "Pyrope" sank following air attack.

In the Air⁓R.A.F. carried out daylight operations over area extending from Jutland to Bay of Biscay ; targets included aerodromes at Waalhaven, Hingene, Caen, Cherbourg, Morlaix, and seaplane base at Brest. Twelve aircraft did not return.

During night large force of R.A.F. bombers seriously damaged Caproni aircraft works at Milan and Fiat plant at Turin.

Other bombers attacked Junkers factories at Dessau, 60 miles S.W. of Berlin, and at Bernburg, munition works at Luenen and Grevenbroich, military targets in the Ruhr, and 14 aerodromes in Germany, Holland, Belgium and France.

War against Italy⁓Enemy attacks on Jugargan positions, Somaliland, renewed but with scant success. Column advancing along coast road from Zeila engaged by British aircraft and gunfire from H.M. ships.

Engagements in Gallabat area, Sudan, resulted in withdrawal of enemy with losses.

Home Front⁓All-day air battle along South Coast. Seventy-eight German aircraft shot down. Thirteen British fighters lost, but pilots of ten reported to be safe.

Mass attacks made on Southampton. Bombs dropped in Isle of Wight and country districts of Berks, Hants and Wilts. R.A.F. aerodromes in S.E. England attacked.

Empire⁓Three Australian ministers, army chief of staff, and other prominent officials killed in air crash at Canberra.

France⁓French "war guilt" trials opened in secret session at Riom.

THE R.A.F. 'CLAWED THEM DOWN' BY THE HUNDRED

In his broadcast on August 17 the Minister of Information, Mr. Duff Cooper, reassured those who were half inclined to think that the figures for the Nazi machines brought down were too good to be true. People in the raided areas have no doubts, however, for they have actually witnessed many such scenes as this, which was photographed on August 18. In the top photograph a Nazi fighter is seen behind a house coming to earth. It immediately burst into flames, and the large photograph shows what happened to it a second or two later.

Photos, G.P.U.

When It's Action the Black Watch Are Snappy!

The Black Watch is now with the Army in the south of England. Top left, men of the regiment are advancing through a farm during exercises. For quick movement the regiment now has bicycles, as seen above.

The Black Watch had experience of parachute troops while they were with the B.E.F. in Flanders, and the knowledge they gained in countering this invasion from the air is being put to good use in their exercises. Above, during exercises an alarm of parachutists has been raised and the men move off at top speed. In the circle a very realistic incident during training is seen when men are taking flying leaps across a crowded trench.

Photos, British Official : Crown Copyright

It Was a Very Tight Corner at Wytschaete

In the retreat to Dunkirk in May 1940, a great part was played by the artillery who covered the withdrawal with their fire. Here is the story, based on official records, of one of the many brilliant rearguard actions—one in which the gunners and the Royal Scots Fusiliers shared the honours.

ON Sunday, May 26, a regiment of the Royal Artillery received orders to proceed to Wytschaete—" White Sheet " to soldiers of 1914-1918—in Belgium. The regiment had hardly returned to its billets at La Marquette and a portion of the gun troops had not yet returned from Pont-à-Marc. It was decided, however, to send all the regimental headquarter groups to a rendezvous in the woods on the other side of the village.

The second-in-command went on ahead to reconnoitre suitable " hides " and the best route in for the guns. Although the column was continually held up by refugees the regiment was safely hidden and the reconnaissance carried out. Throughout the deployment enemy bombers were active. The second-in-command's rendezvous and regimental headquarters " hide " were bombed but suffered no casualties.

The infantry at this time were holding a line along the Ypres-Commines Canal, thence along the railway line north of the canal to a point where the railway crossed the canal, and so on to Ypres itself. The patrols for their part were well forward, the idea being to withdraw to the canal line as soon as contact had been made with the enemy. This was carried out according to plan.

After one quiet day things began to liven up. The enemy attacked in force, and the artillery regiment fired continually on troop concentrations and trench-mortars. Attempts were also made to locate a battery which had proved most troublesome to our infantry.

The situation gradually deteriorated. Observation-post lines were cut and wireless communications jammed. At one time it seemed that the lines on both flanks had gone, but the infantry brigadier went round all his battalions and the line was again stabilized. Many of the infantry who had fallen back on the gun positions re-formed and went forward. Odd rifles abandoned by dead and wounded men were collected at the gun positions for future use.

The problem of communication remained. It was decided to send one officer from each battery forward into the line to establish contact with the forward company headquarters and direct fire. One officer went forward in the regiment's sole remaining armoured observation vehicle, the other on foot. At one time the latter officer was actually several hundred yards in front of

the infantry. The reports received from him were invaluable in clarifying the situation.

The officer in the armoured vehicle succeeded in going about a mile before a shell burst overhead and wounded his assistant. He proceeded on foot a mile and a half, finally reaching a drive leading up to a château. Here he found a company of Royal Scots Fusiliers practically surrounded, and so, under heavy fire from three sides, he made his way back with the intention of calling for battery fire. But it seemed certain that the company of Royal Scots Fusiliers could not escape being surrounded, and in fact very few of these men did get back. Nevertheless, all possible support was given to them, but the difficulty of maintaining communication made observed fire almost impossible, and it remained for regimental headquarters, battery command posts, and troop command posts to use their own initiative in deciding suitable targets.

Firing Over Open Sights

Enemy shelling which had been continuous all the day increased after nightfall, and it became obvious that a further attack was pending. The situation as regards our own infantry remained obscure. The commanding officer gave orders to troop commanders to order individual gun control at their own discretion.

A troop near Saint Eloi supporting the left flank was able, through telephonic communication with the Northamptons and a Manchesters' machine-gun company, to prevent a break-through on the left of the line. An officer of this troop, having spent a day at the observation post, knew the area well, and under his direction a line was laid out to the Northamptons and Manchesters, who were then able to call for fire

whenever it was needed. On more than one occasion battery fire was put down.

In the small hours the guns were firing over open sights, and all spare personnel were armed with rifles and Bren guns to give every possible help to the infantry. The enemy advanced again and again to within a few hundred yards of our positions, but each time he was driven back by the artillery's guns at point-blank range and by small-arms fire. At three in the morning things had quietened down, though there was intermittent machine-gun and shell fire, and an hour later orders were received to withdraw and occupy positions near Kemmel.

The Germans attacked again at 4.30 a.m. All troops except the most advanced were safely withdrawn. The most advanced troop, however, owing to the boggy state of the ground were compelled to winch their guns out, one by one—a two-hour task. Two guns had been removed and were on the road, and the other two were being winched out, when suddenly the enemy appeared over the ridge. The troop commander ordered that the two remaining guns should be rendered useless, and the first two guns were immediately sent off to the rear under heavy fire. The sergeant detailed to remove the firing-pins of the guns was severely wounded, but was rescued after a counter-attack by the infantry.

The counter-attack began at midday, when reinforcements arrived in the form of an infantry brigade. They deployed in front of the gun positions where the line had for a time been stabilized. They counter-attacked, and the line was restored.

Many times during the anxious hours of the action at Wytschaete the line looked like going. The infantry was heavily out-numbered and continually subjected to machine-gun fire, trench-mortar fire and dive-bombing. All ranks had been many days and nights without sleep, yet when the order to withdraw was given, many a man was at a loss to understand the reason for it.

The little Belgian town of Wytschaete, on the Messines Ridge 4 miles south of Ypres, around which the incidents related in this page occurred, is seen, top left, as it was rebuilt after its destruction in the last war. Above, a gun of the R.A. drawn by a tractor is crossing into Belgian territory for the last stand at the end of May, 1940.
Photos, British Official : Crown Copyright ; and A. J. Insall, Copyright A.P.

Libya Provides Targets for Britain's Navy

This striking picture of a British cruiser bombarding a fort on the coast of Italian Libya from close in shore was taken a few days after hostilities began. There was another bombardment by British naval guns on August 17 when Fort Capuzzo and Bardia were the targets. Left, a British officer is observing the effect of the salvos.

One of the guns of a cruiser that bombarded the coast of Libya is here seen in action, while the smoke from its last shot drifts away. The decks are cleared for action and not a man is visible, but the gun crews are keeping up the hail of shells with automatic regularity.

The Italian airman above is manning one of the machine-guns of a bomber that attacked British ships in the Mediterranean. Machine-gunning and bombing brought no success, and the photograph, right, shows why. British seamanship was too good, and skilful handling made it possible to dodge the bombs, which are seen dropping harmlessly into the sea.

Photos, Movietone-Gaumont Newsreels and Associated Press

Prestige Was the Chief Casualty in Somaliland

After a fortnight of war the campaign in Somaliland came to an end on August 19 when the British forces were successfully evacuated. As pointed out below, the withdrawal, though it may temporarily have a depressing influence on British prestige in Africa, was thoroughly justified on strategical grounds.

For a few days after their occupation of Oadweina and Hargeisa on August 5 the Italians halted their advance while they made preparations for the attack on the main British positions in the mountains which lay between them and Berbera, the port, some fifty miles distant, which was their objective.

By August 9 the two columns which had occupied Hargeisa and Oadweina had joined hands and an attack by light and medium tanks was delivered against the British forward positions at Kodayira. After some sharp fighting the British forces, under the command of Brigadier A. R. Chater, withdrew to the main defence lines at Tugargan, situated at the foot of the plateau. On Sunday, August 11, the Italians opened their main onslaught, subjecting the troops occupying the Tugargan lines and the reserve positions to the rear to heavy bombing and machine-gunning. Then at noon the Italian infantry, Blackshirts for the most part, assaulted the trenches and the battle continued all day, even far into the hours of dark. Though heavily outnumbered, the defenders maintained their positions, but in one place the line was broken for a short time and two guns were put out of action.

By now the Italians had brought into action the greater part of two divisions—say, nine to ten thousand men—complete with artillery, 25 tanks, and other armoured vehicles, and after four days' hard fighting the little British force of five infantry battalions and the Camel Corps was forced to abandon its positions on Mill Hill and Observation Hill in the Tugargan Pass. Outside Berbera there was a fierce battle at Barkasan, in which the Italians were severely handled by a Scottish battalion, and an attack from Zeila along the coast was also repelled.

The situation of the British forces in Somaliland was now officially admitted to be critical. In the last communiqué issued by the British Near East Command in Cairo on the night of August 18 it was stated that : " In Somaliland yesterday (Saturday) the enemy again renewed their determined attacks with picked Italian troops supported by artillery, tanks and aircraft. The British force continues to fight with the utmost gallantry, inflicting important losses on the enemy and contesting every yard in its withdrawal towards Berbera."

Then on the next day it was announced in London that the campaign in Somaliland was at an end, for the whole of the British force, including the wounded and many loyal natives, had been safely evacuated on August 17 and 18 by ships of the Royal Navy and carried away to Aden. All the guns except the two whose loss is mentioned above were embarked ; and of the material, stores, and equipment, a great part had been evacuated and the remainder destroyed.

" British, Rhodesian, Indian, African, and Somali troops," stated the War Office communiqué, " working in the closest co-operation with the Royal Navy and the R.A.F., have carried out the role assigned to them with conspicuous skill and bravery against greatly superior strength. Enemy losses, particularly among Blackshirt units,

Berbera, from which the British troops in Somaliland were evacuated on August 17 and 18, is the most important port of British Somaliland and the capital of the Protectorate established in 1884. The town now numbers 20,000 inhabitants, and above is one of its chief streets.
Photo, Keystone

have been heavy, and out of all proportion to our own."

Then the statement went on to review the position that had presented itself to the British Command. The original Allied dispositions in Somaliland were based on a scheme of close Franco-British cooperation, under which the French at Jibuti were to hold

This great column of smoke rose into the air when Fort Maddalena, the Italian stronghold on the coast of Libya, was bombarded by the British on June 17. Other photographs of this successful operation appear in page 202.
Photo, British Official : Movietone-Gaumont-Newsreel

the right flank, the pivot of the whole position. When France suddenly withdrew from the war, so that more than half of the available Allied force was neutralized, a new and grave situation was at once created.

Three alternatives were open. The most obvious would have been to reinforce British Somaliland in sufficient strength to ensure its safety, but this could not be done without employing important reserves and thereby weakening the reserves in other theatres of war more immediately important than Somaliland. The second alternative was the immediate and unresisting evacuation ; but this, too, was turned down, as it would have meant giving up British territory without fighting and thereby losing the opportunity of inflicting losses on the enemy in men and material, which would be difficult to replace.

The third course—the one chosen—was to remain with our small force, using it to inflict the maximum losses on the enemy until withdrawal became inevitable.

The news of the withdrawal was received with very mixed feelings. While, on the one hand, it was generally admitted that the Italians had conquered a territory which was economically unprofitable and of small value strategically—for the Italians in Eritrea were just as well, or as little, able to close the Red Sea and blockade Aden, as they are now from Berbera—on the other hand, it must be confessed that British prestige in Africa has received a severe blow. Native tribesmen are unable to appreciate the finer points of strategy, and the one thing that would be plain to them was that the British had been driven out of a territory which they had occupied for some sixty years, and had held against a long succession of native revolts—driven out, moreover, by the Italians whom hitherto it had been the fashion to despise.

But prestige can be paid for too dearly, and if it were a question of choosing between hanging on to Somaliland and adding a much needed reinforcement to the garrison of Egypt, then there could be no hesitation. After all, the ultimate fate of British Somaliland will not be decided by those days of fighting in its own bleak and barren passes, but on other fields of battle much nearer the heart of Britain's empire

They Hoisted the White Flag on Fort Maddalena

These photographs of British raids into Libya are the first showing this campaign to reach London. One of the early successes was the capture of the Italian fort of Maddalena (see map in page 170) on June 14. Left, from the watch-tower of the fort an Italian displays a white flag; while above, British armoured cars are moving forward to take possession of it.

Very considerable damage was inflicted on Italian motorized units during the advance; in centre, left, are the burned-out remains of a car on the desert. One of the first things investigated by the British troops when they took possession of the post was the well, centre right. The water was found to be undrinkable.

A substantial amount of material fell into the hands of the British. Left, Italian light anti-tank guns are being examined by British officers. The surprising discovery was made that most of them had been fired but a few times, which suggests that the gun crews had been taken by surprise.

Photos : British Paramount, Movietone and Gaumont News-reels

SMOKING STRICTLY PROHIBITED منع شرب الدخان قطعيا

Britain's Bombers Hit Back With A Vengeance

As if to prove that Britain has energy enough and to spare even at the height of the Nazi air onslaught on her shores, bombers of the R.A.F. delivered smashing attacks on military objectives in Germany and also in Italy. Thrice in one week Italy's most vital aircraft works at Milan and Turin were attacked, and in the same week great industrial plants in Germany were subjected to tremendous bombardment.

MILAN and Turin were first attacked by British aircraft when the war was but a few hours old. That attack took the Italian defences by surprise and much damage was done, but that damage was as nothing compared with that wreaked on the night of August 13. As the raiders made for home across the Alps in the early hours of the following morning they left behind them smashed factories, many of them on fire, and even when high above the mountains the dull glare from the blazing Caproni works could still be seen reflected in the southern sky.

Flying some 1,600 miles from their bases in England, the raiders had to climb up to three miles high to surmount the snow-capped peaks. "From south-eastern France," said one of the pilots on his return, "we could, from our great height, see Switzerland in the distance like a fairyland of bright neutrality in a pool of ink." But they had little time to admire the glorious spectacle of the Jungfrau and Mont Blanc, whose snowy flanks glittered superbly in the moonlight. Shortly before midnight they appeared above Italy's industrial north, and soon their bombs were raining down on the Fiat aviation works at Turin. Here several direct hits were scored, and through the holes in the roof incendiary bombs were dropped, which at once engendered a fierce blaze, followed by several explosions. The pilots who took up the attack at 1 o'clock had no need to be told that they were over their targets. From 10,000 feet they dropped fresh salvos of high explosive and more incendiary bombs, which spread still further the blazing area.

Railway sidings some distance to the west of the aircraft works were also hit, and a road and railway junction to the south of Turin was attacked. Simultaneously, the Caproni works at Milan, which turn out Italy's bombing aircraft, were badly damaged. All the British raiders reported seeing bursts on the target. One salvo of incendiary bombs fell in a line down the length of the buildings, and as heavy bombs

followed them there came a series of large explosions. A stick of high explosive was dropped across the hangars on the adjoining aerodrome, and others played havoc with the seaplane station at the south end of a large reservoir. By 1 o'clock several fires were raging in the target area, but many more direct hits were scored before the raiders made for home. The Italian defences were apparently taken completely by surprise, and the anti-aircraft fire was scanty and ineffective. As dawn was breaking all the aircraft engaged on the flight flew back across the Alps and the slowly awakening French countryside and arrived back safely, with the exception of one machine which came down in the sea near our coast. But even here the crew were picked up and landed in safety. All the crews were, as one observer put it, "begrimed but hale, hearty and full of good cheer. They all had had a good go at the targets, and know that their bombs found their mark."

Havoc in the Junkers Factory

On the same night the vast Junkers factory at Dessau, one of Germany's main centres of aircraft production, was bombed time and again by 'planes of the R.A.F. Bomber Command. The raiders attacked in relays for over an hour, and although high clouds obscured the moon parachute flares effectively illuminated the target. The crew of one aircraft reported that one of their bombs had hit and destroyed the main power house. Other bombs had severely damaged the airframe assembly sheds and a large sheet-metal shop. In the course of another attack, delivered from only 1,000 feet up, one of the experimental shops was directly hit and blew up. Coincidently with this attack, other British raiders were bombing a subsidiary Junkers factory at Bernburg where the airframes for Junkers dive-bombers and troop transports are produced. Munition factories at Lünen, north-west of Dortmund, and in the neighbourhood of Düsseldorf were also attacked, and in every case fires were started by incendiary bombs. Among other targets found in Western Germany

were a blast furnace near Cologne, and a large oil refinery at Hanover.

On August 15 the R.A.F. struck at the industrial region of the Ruhr; amongst their victims was the great Krupps' armament factory at Essen. The same night R.A.F. bombers again crossed the Alps to attack the Caproni factory in Milan and the Fiat works at Turin, and blast furnaces at Genoa also received their attention. One of the crew remarked: "the blast furnace was much more blasted when we left."

The next night the great I.G. synthetic oil plant at Leuna, north-east of Leipzig—the works where in normal times 400,000 tons of oil are produced each year—was attacked in force by R.A.F. bombers for the first time. An intense barrage from heavy and light anti-aircraft guns, pom-poms and machine-guns, all working in close co-operation with batteries of searchlights, met the attackers, but failed to prevent them from making a series of devastating assaults. Oil storage tanks were left ablaze. One of the high smoke-stacks of the factory collapsed and the hundreds of bombs dropped left a chain of fires from which columns of dense smoke poured. Other new targets attacked on that night were the benzine oil plant at Bohlen, the Carl Zeiss plant at Jena, and a Messerschmitt factory at Augsburg. In every case they came in for severe punishment. On the 19th the famous yards at Hamm were bombed for the 52nd time.

The raiders were back again in force over Italy on the night of Sunday, August 18, when for the third time in a week the workers in the Caproni and Fiat concerns scurried to shelter as 'planes were reported overhead. Yet the next morning, no doubt, they and the German workers at the great aluminium works at Rheinfelden on the German-Swiss frontier—which in the course of the same night was struck by salvo after salvo of heavy bombs so that the fires from its blazing sheds could be seen 20 miles away—read that Britain was staggering under the hammer blows of Goering's air force, and was certainly in no position to hit back!

This was a principal target of the R.A.F. attacks between August 13 and August 18. The famous Fiat Motor Works at Turin, now turned to aircraft production, were bombed three times by the R.A.F. and badly damaged.

Photo, E.N.A.

Dutch and Norwegians Are Still With Us

Prince Bernhard visited on August 14 the men of the Dutch Air Force now in Britain. Right, with Dutch and British officers, he is inspecting a flying-boat. Above, the Dutch pilot and crew of a seaplane are examining its gun.
Photos, P.N.A. and " Daily Mirror "

During a visit to the north-east coast in August, the Duke of Kent inspected coastal defences and naval establishments. At one post a Dutch minelayer now co-operating in the work of the British Navy was lying, and His Royal Highness is seen left, making an inspection of the ship.
Photo, British Official: Crown Copyright

The officers whose countries have been overrun by the Nazis, but who have come to Britain to continue the fight, are kept in close touch with the latest equipment and methods of the British Army. On August 10 a party of Army leaders and officers visited the head-quarters of a British division. Among them were Poles, Czechs, Norwegians, Dutch and Belgians. Below, General Fleischer, Norwegian Commander - in - Chief, is handling a Bren gun.
Photo, G.P.U.

The " Sleipner " (below), a Norwegian patrol ship, received a letter of commendation from the British Admiralty for her help during the British landings in Norway. She shot down six enemy aircraft and damaged six more.

British Official: Crown Copyright

TWELVE MONTHS AFTER
Some Second Thoughts on Failure and Success in the War

By the Editor

" I TOLD you so ! " There are no more hateful words of tongue or pen. None more futile. None so apt to be uttered by those who would pass for knowledgeable folk. So easy to be wise after the event, perhaps having made a 'good guess before it.

Not in that frame of mind is this article written. The intention is to assess certain fairly obvious errors that have led to the present stage of the War, as a help to understanding the strange, eventful history of its first year, now so near to completion.

All wars are won by reason of mistakes as much as by reason of careful calculation. In the War of 1914-18, mistakes on both sides counted for not less than the brilliance of strategy, the bravery of men, the luck of weather. The initial mistake of Von Kluck in his rush for the Channel ports provided the opportunity for the Battle of the Marne, one of the most decisive of the War.

The mistake of the Huns in sending each newly-made Zeppelin to terrorize London, in their eagerly impatient effort to break our spirit by sheer frightfulness, only taught us how to develop a defence which, in time, destroyed every Zeppelin that could be sent, even when they could muster as many as thirteen for one raid. Had the first use of that arm been withheld until at least a score of these Leviathans could have showered their bombs upon an unready London the history of the Zeppelin would have been very different—and a more painful memory for Londoners.

How We Wasted Our Tanks in 1916

THE British were not less ill-advised in prematurely launching the greatest mechanical device of the War : the tank. This British invention has proved in German hands the chief weapon of the mechanized Nazi armies that have swept over half of Europe in 1940. Forty-seven of them went into action at the Battle of the Somme on September 15, 1916. Another six months of preparation and ten times that number, better able to withstand armour-piercing bullets and handled by carefully trained crews, would have given an entirely new turn to the War in 1917.

A catalogue of mistakes that were made by both sides—fortunately in greater measure by the Germans—in those fateful four years would be as surprising in length as pointless in purpose at this moment when war conditions differ more from those of 1914 than these differed from the Crimean War. Let us consider only one or two aspects of the present conflict where the avoidance of certain mistakes, political and military, would have brought us earlier within sight of that final victory in which we have greater reason today to believe than at any time since September 3, 1939.

" I have made only one mistake about the War," said a friend to me the other day ; " I said it would never happen." A week before Hitler screeched to the world that he was going into Poland " to stop this lunacy," a well-known writer on international affairs assured me ; " It'll only be another Munich." Myself, I had for months asserted my belief in the coming of the War—yet took no steps to safeguard my own financial position,

which may be regarded as evidence that I only half believed in what I maintained as a probability. The sub-conscious effect, perhaps, of that hope which springs eternal in the human breast ! Today I sadly wish I had had the courage of my convictions. Yet that side of it is a minuscular matter, mentioned merely to indicate how hard it is to make a personal decision even when your examination of a complex problem appeals to you as correct.

Cardinal Mistake of September 1939

So far as the general public is concerned it may be said with reason that even in the week preceding the fateful September 3, 1939, the great mass of peace-loving people in the Western democracies clung desperately to the hope of Peace, and when the Beast of Berlin screamed his final challenge to Civilization his demoniacal voice was heard by ears that only half-reacted on minds incredulous.

With the dread outbreak of War the cardinal mistake was made. So far as can be judged the British Government and the people of the British Empire were entirely confident that in the political and military leaders of the French Republic they had strong and faithful allies. To an eminent French publicist I said a week or two before the fateful day : " My one fear is the rotten state of your political parties, your ever-changing governments of Left, Centre, and Right." To which he replied by drawing on the white cloth of our dining-table an ingenious and amusing diagram of French political parties (everyone of them admittedly corrupt) and saying : " But in the moment of national danger all coalesce as one."

Events have proved him mistaken, despite his forty-five years of activity in Anglo-French literature and politics. In reality these innumerable dissident parties, each with its own dirty axe to grind, never " got together." It was no united France that stood side by side with a united British Empire to withstand the onslaught of the Nazi-Hun. The France that mobilized was a nation trudging unwillingly to war, with no heart for the impending struggle, lulled into a state of unheroic apathy by its effete military leaders who, having built some two hundred miles of concrete bombproof shelters for its soldiers between Switzerland and Luxembourg, felt they could " sit pretty " and take whatever blows the enemy might direct upon these cosy retreats, which are now being shown to their conquerors by French officers as mighty curiosities of self-deception.

The Maginot Line, on which for years a whole library of books and journalism had been written by authors of every nation, was the great illusion on which France relied. And not France only, but her allies and her friends. History will record that no vainer memorial of human effort exists anywhere on the surface of the globe.

We British (knowing no better) were beguiled by it no less. We might with good reason accuse our own military leaders of failing to discern its futility. But had not British military experts gone to Poland in the months preceding the Nazi avalanche and

pronounced the picturesque Polish cavalry and infantry and handful of airmen able to withstand the mechanized might of Germany for two or three months ? No braver allies than the Poles proved themselves could have been desired, but . . .

Mistakes ! Had not the same British experts eight months in which to discover the pitiful weakness of the thin defences strung along the Belgian frontier between Luxembourg and the sea? And what did they do to strengthen and deepen them ? Ask ye the stalwart Scottish soldiers who now languish in Nazi prison camps.

There were reasons. Yes. The unworthy son of King Albert had long been under Nazi influence. His pronounced personal objection to the extension of the Maginot Line in its full defensive strength, his significant rejection of friendship with the Allies in 1936 and formal declaration of a neutrality his country was unable to maintain, might have prepared both France and Britain for his final act of betrayal. And that, be it known, did not come until he had only too much reason for believing that France was about to crumble, headlong surrender being a desperate effort to save his own land from complete destruction in the impending débâcle.

When Loyalty Was Ill-Advised

WAS the British Government at that terrible moment of time unaware of the vast catastrophe in store for Europe ? Why was the finest army that ever left British shores exposed to the dire disaster that overtook it ? The only answer must be : Britain's deep and abiding sense of loyalty to her allies ; a loyalty that outstepped all considerations of self-interest and even went beyond the bounds of common caution. A loyalty that was truly heroic but not less truly ill-advised, for though the people of Britain had no suspicion of that " something rotten in the state of " France, the Intelligence Department of the British Government must have known more and our military leaders might have risked less.

One of the prime causes of the tremendous débâcle—what a subject for a new Zola is here !—lay in the fact that the French Government held the citizens of the Republic in shackles of ignorance which rivalled those of the Nazi censorship. From September of 1939 until the Hunnish hordes had overrun the coasts of France and were closing even upon Paris, a censorship worthy of Hitler himself held the French people in total ignorance of the true state of affairs and would seem to have kept the stark truth even from our own leaders until it was too late. A people in ignorance of the events that are happening to its fighting forces is a people prepared for the panic and confusion that are ever the rewards of the ignorant. In these dark months France had been betrayed by its squabbling politicians and by its supine army leaders, and with France her allies and her friends throughout the world.

Your mistakes and my mistakes in our view of the changing fortunes of the War can be largely traced to this censorship which muzzled the Press of France and produced a smoke-screen of rumour and doubt behind which the Fifth Column of Defeatism

They Show Maginot Secrets to Their Conquerors

Here is one of the most tragic of all documentary proofs of France's humiliation, for it shows the last phase of the taking of the vaunted Maginot Line. The French Army and the French nation believed blindly in its impregnability, but before ten months of war had passed it was in German hands. Yet, as this photograph suggests, those who manned it were not greatly downcast, for the French officers displaying the underground workings to German officers almost seem to exhibit pleasure in explaining to them the mechanical perfection of the greatest military illusion of all time.

contrived its diabolical work. The sinister figures of Laval, Bonnet, Prouvost and the senile Pétain were all busy behind this smoke-screen, with the appalling results we are witnessing today.

But the French collapse really began long before the outbreak of war. The Popular Front must share with the subversive Fascists the blame for disintegrating the strength of France at a time when a truly united Republic was her one hope of survival. The general slackness of the people, the limp condition of all parties in the State, save only those who wrought underground for the destruction of popular government, could produce nothing but defeat. And no spectacle is more distressing than to witness today Admiral Abrial, who did so brilliantly at Dunkirk, acting as the tool of Nazi conquerors in controlling Algeria for Pétain and the controlled government of Vichy instead of holding the torch of a Free France where it could have burned to splendid purpose.

French North Africa, had there been a spark of genuine fire of freedom in the hearts of France's leaders, might well have rallied to the rehabilitation of the motherland. The craven response of the pro-consuls who held power in Morocco, Algeria and Tunisia—to which we must add those of Syria, Indo-China. Madagascar and Equatorial Africa—and the fleet commanders at Oran and elsewhere, put that great possibility of an early renascence out of sight and laid a grievous burden upon the British naval and military forces in and around the Mediterranean which would never otherwise have had to be envisaged.

The obedience of these French colonial chiefs to the behests of Vichy, which is no more than bending the knee to the Nazis, has increased the difficulties of Britain's task a hundredfold and played into the hands of the despicable Mussolini. France will surely live to lament her betrayal of the Allied cause at the great hour of crisis, and her only hope of surviving and regaining some measure of her former greatness lies in the spirited co-operation of those Free Frenchmen who rally to the leadership of General de Gaulle. The liars who said that Britain would fight to the last Frenchman may now enjoy the spectacle of France fighting to the last Britisher !

The Tragic Mistake of Scapa Flow

WHAT shall one say about the first big mistake on the British side—the failure between the crisis of 1938 and the outbreak of war to make Scapa Flow secure against submarine attack ? Something will be said about that one day, though meanwhile those responsible for the neglect which led to the loss of the " Royal Oak," and the utterly useless sacrifice of over 800 of our highly trained naval officers and men, walk about unbranded. Some day—not today. But this earliest mistake of those entrusted with the Defence of the Realm must not be forgotten in any assessment of error. What, too, about the mistake in our failure to pile up supplies ? Those critical months that were wasted by a department whose chief (his name is never mentioned now) took such obvious pleasure in stating how much he was spending—with how little to show for it !

Meanwhile some of these mistakes can be written off against the all-important vindication of the R.A.F. in the Battle of Britain. It is clear " beyond a peradventure," as President Wilson phrased it, that not only man for man, but machine for machine, the R.A.F. is master of the German Luftwaffe, and the lag of British production which gave a quantitative ascendancy to the Hun has given a qualitative ascendancy to the British.

All motorists know how quickly " last year's models " diminish in value. The same quick decline applies to warplanes, and the fact that the British machines are mainly " this year's models," by very reason of the need to recover that lag, is one of the secrets of our superiority in the air.

One only, for the men are more than the machines, and the magnificent youth of Britain and the Empire that flies our machines has proved itself worthy of immortal fame. All knighthood pales to insignificance before their achievement.

The supreme mistake will ever remain our simple faith in French integrity and the defensive value of the Maginot Line. It is pitiful to consider the deluded millions throughout the world who witnessed the film propaganda of that vast work which gave weakness an illusion of strength and fear the quality of force. Sergeant Maginot's name was to live as the Saviour of France. It will live more likely to signify the snare that caught his country for the invading Hun, and forced Britain to stand alone as the last bulwark of Democracy, the ultimate defender of Civilization, in which most splendid effort in the history of mankind she will surely prevail.

Not All Vichy's Waters Can Wash Out Their Guilt

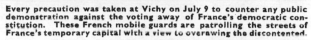

Every precaution was taken at Vichy on July 9 to counter any public demonstration against the voting away of France's democratic constitution. These French mobile guards are patrolling the streets of France's temporary capital with a view to overawing the discontented.

NATIONAL ASSEMBLY was the name given to the body responsible for the opening stages of the French Revolution, but in more recent years it has been applied to joint sittings of the Chamber of Deputies and the Senate. On July 9 the National Assembly met at Vichy, having been called together to give Marshal Pétain's Government full powers to draft a new constitution. Out of 649 representatives of the people" who were present, only 80 dared to vote against surrendering all that France had gained in the long fight for freedom. Nearly 300 Senators and Deputies were absent.

After the collapse of France, when Vichy became the capital, the hotels which had been hospitals were quickly turned into Government offices. Here is one of them, with official cars parked outside.

The National Assembly met on July 9 in the theatre of the Casino de Vichy, not altogether an inappropriate setting for the meeting of a body quite unrepresentative of the people in whose name they professed to act. Above, this strange assembly is seen in session under the presidency of M. Jeanneney, while the Speaker's desk is occupied by M. Laval. Left centre, M. Laval, to whom France's betrayal was largely due, is seen arriving at the Assembly.

Photos, Wide World

Occupied or Unoccupied, All France is Miserable

This picture of life in the two zones of France in defeat is depressing enough, but no words could do justice to an appallingly depressing theme. So great is the disaster that has overcome them that the mass of the French people are still too stunned to grasp it in all the fullness of its enormity.

THERE are two executioners in France today—two, because there are two Frances, one in the occupation of the Nazis and the other the France of Pétain and his fellow old men of Vichy. But the people who live on either side of the " Chinese wall " which the Germans have erected across France are equally miserable. Of the past they do not care to think, of the future they do not dare to think ; their concern is only with the present, and grim enough that present is.

In the occupied zone the Germans are everywhere. Particularly in Paris are they seen goose-stepping through the streets, gazing in the shop windows, doing the " sights," sipping their drinks on the café terraces. Their bands play martial music in the parks, the swastika flies from the roofs of the leading hotels and principal buildings ; the shops are thronged by officers and men in field grey, buying silk stockings and dainty lingerie and other feminine knick-knacks to be sent to their wives and sweethearts in the Reich. Thanks to the money-changing racket worked by the Nazi authorities, the things in the shops are cheap to the Germans although shockingly dear when they have to

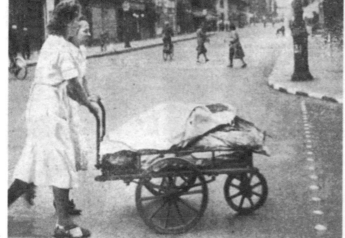

be bought with hard-earned French francs ; so all the little shops which deal in works of art, jewelry, and the vast variety of luxury goods made in the Paris factories are being rapidly cleared of their stocks.

Still after many weeks of German occupation there are no taxis in the Paris streets, and no buses ; only the underground is operating ; thousands of Parisians of both sexes are now depending on the bicycle as never before. There is a curfew at nine o'clock, and on its sounding the city which for generations has enjoyed a world-wide reputation as the " City of Light and Laughter " is sunk in nocturnal silence. The penalty for being out without a pass issued by the German authorities is a night in jail. Many hundreds of thousands of the Parisians are still scattered through the

length and breadth of France, and those who have remained in the city go about their day's work in a state of sullen resignation. They have little to complain of concerning the conduct of the conquerors, who, indeed, exert themselves to win the good graces of the conquered.

One of the most frequently seen of the propaganda posters pasted up by the Nazis in town and village is one showing a fatherly-looking German soldier carrying a French baby in his arms with the slogan underneath, " The Nazis are the children's friends." Some 5,000,000 French people are now being fed, clothed, and sheltered by the invaders. " Yes, they are kind," one French girl is reported to have said, " but it is difficult to be grateful."

Between the occupied and the unoccupied zones there is little communication, with the result that the economic condition of the

In a region of occupied France men of the Gestapo are removing the French direction sign in a shell-wrecked town and substituting a German one. Left, two women are wheeling a hand-cart across a Paris street, usually crowded with traffic, but now, owing to the petrol shortage, almost deserted.

Photos, Planet News and Keystone

country is becoming more deplorable every day. Pétain's France, i.e., the unoccupied zone, comprises less than a third of France's total area and produces only one-eighth of the country's agricultural produce and one-tenth of its revenue ; yet it is now being called on to feed more than half the country's normal population. Within its bounds are 10,000,000 refugees and over 1,000,000 demobilized French soldiers, while the government at Vichy is also responsible for the maintenance of the million and more French prisoners taken by the Germans. In Brittany and Normandy the enormous quantities of foodstuffs which in normal times would have been exported to Britain are now piled up and perishing ; but in the Pétain zone a famine is almost within measurable distance, for southern France

produces very little wheat and few livestock with the exception of pigs and poultry, although it has a superabundance of grapes, fruit and vegetables. North France and South France are mutually dependent, but the Nazis, content with having seized the rich northern half of the country, are little concerned with the conditions which prevail in that part they have left to Pétain.

What they *are* concerned with is the fostering of any latent germ of hostility between the unoccupied and occupied zones. They have nothing but contempt for the Vichy government, although it suits them, for the moment, to connive at its existence, and

to the Parisian proletariat Hitler's propagandists address themselves with glowing accounts of the " Socialist " organizations established in the Nazi Reich. Then in talks and newspapers addressed to every class of Frenchman, the Nazis do their utmost to stimulate that anti-British feeling which, despite the comradeship of the last war, cemented on so many a blood-soaked field, lies not very deep in the French national conscience.

Neither in Paris nor in Vichy are there any signs of French national resurgence ; for that we must look to London and de Gaulle. Pétain and the men of Vichy, indeed, seem to be wallowing in a bath of humility which other people would call humiliation ; those of them who are religious seem to believe that a new and purified France will be born out of the present sacrifices. For their part they are endeavouring to create a France which will be as muffled in its life as in its politics and ideas.

It may seem a small point that Pétain's government has forbidden sunbathing and the wearing of two-piece bathing costumes at the seaside resorts of the Riviera and the Atlantic coasts ; but this reversion to the prudery of yesterday is significant of the whole outlook of the men whom defeat has called to the helm of France

Australia's 'Porcupines' Have Plenty of Prickles!

Some idea of the great size of the Short-Sunderland flying-boats can be gathered from this photograph of a mechanic climbing to the top of one of the wings to examine the aerial.

The photographs in this page show routine incidents with the Short-Sunderland flying-boats manned by the Royal Australian Air Force. Above is a wing of one of the 'planes forming part of a convoy escort that has come down low to inspect three of the ships.

THE Royal Australian Flying-Boat Squadron has been operating with the Coastal Command since April, 1940. Besides its ordinary routine work, some of the flying-boats have performed the duties of air-liners, having carried important personages to and from different parts of Europe during the crisis in mid-June caused by the surrender of France. One of the Short-Sunderlands —they are called "Flying Porcupines" by the Germans—which are the machines used by the squadron, took Mr. A. V. Alexander to Bordeaux when, as stated by Mr. Churchill in the House of Commons on June 16, he went to confer with the French Government about the future of the French Fleet. Another was on its way home from Malta when it was instructed to call at Gibraltar and pick up and bring home Vice-Admiral Muselier, who is now in command of the Free French Navy and Air Force in Great Britain. Another Sunderland of the squadron carried Lord Lloyd, the Colonial Secretary, to France, to discuss the position of the French colonies ; while a 'plane of the squadron carried Lord Gort and Mr. Duff Cooper to Rabat on their fruitless effort to clear up the Moroccan situation. Finally, one of its 'planes carried the Emperor Haile Selassie to Egypt. The Short-Sunderland flying-boats are the largest flying-boats used by the R.A.F. and carry a crew of seven. They are armed with seven machine-guns. During four months of its operations the squadron had a record of 2,500 flying hours, and many of the pilots have recently averaged 900 miles flying a day.

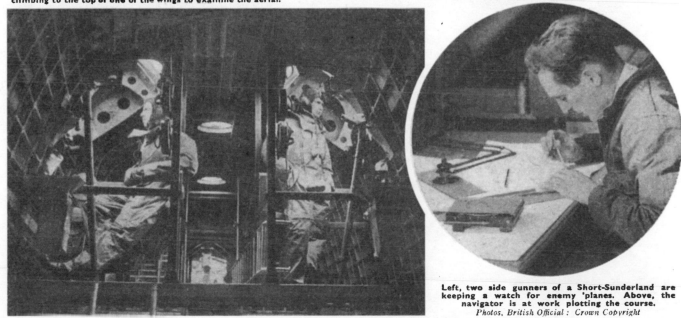

Left, two side gunners of a Short-Sunderland are keeping a watch for enemy 'planes. Above, the navigator is at work plotting the course.

Photos, British Official : Crown Copyright

'I Asked for an Air Force & Marshal Goering Has

IN a grandiloquent passage Hitler has declared that he told Goering to give him the finest air force in the world, and he gave it him. Certainly of late months the German air force, built up with such surreptitious efficiency through the years of Germany's rearmament before the war, has achieved some striking triumphs. With utter ruthlessness the air terror has been loosed not only on the soldiers but on the civilian populations of Poland and Norway, of Belgium and France. Defences have been razed, towns laid waste, peoples bludgeoned into submission. Now in the Battle of Britain the air army which has devastated the Continent is turned against these islands ; and now for the first time the Luftwaffe is meeting its match.

Photos, G.P.U., Keystone, Cent.

e the Finest in the World'—Samples Now in Britain

THESE photographs, taken within a few hours of each other in mid-August, show a mere handful of the hundreds of German 'planes battered to destruction against the British bastion. (1) a Dornier bomber shot down over the Kent coast taken away in triumph ; (2) a German machine completely burned out ; (3) one of many Messerschmitts shot down on August 13 ; (4) two little English girls, seated on the broken fuselage of a Nazi bomber, examining souvenirs ; (5) a Dornier "flying pencil" bomber with engines on fire diving to destruction ; (6) on guard beside the crumpled wreckage of a Croydon raider ; (7) examining a parachute and gun taken from a Heinkel ; (8) the Navy on guard beside a wreck in Scotland ; (9) this Messerschmitt crashed in flames.

Daily Mirror," Associated Press

Britain's Defenders Beat Back the Nazi Raiders

Carrying out its much-boasted programme, the Nazi air force went a stage further with the assault on Britain. After the coastal shipping it was the turn of ports, naval bases and aerodromes to be attacked. Then the raiders ventured further, and came against the full strength of our defences. Events no longer went according to plan, and they met with the crushing defeats here told.

IT is now clear that it was indeed the Battle of Britain that opened on August 8 with mass air attacks on Britain's shipping. Raids on harbours, naval bases and dockyards and on aerodromes near the coast followed, but no vital damage was done anywhere to our protective and defensive organization. Then the Nazi bombers flew farther inland and tried to wreck airfields, destroy power stations, and damage roads and railways. Last, there followed abortive attacks on London itself.

On August 14 it seemed that the tempo had moderated. Only scattered attacks were made, apart from one on Kent about midday, when large formations of bombers and fighter escorts tried to put our aerodromes out of action. A light A.A. battery brought two down; a heavy battery shot down one and damaged another, which was finished off by Lewis gunners.

Over the Channel off Dover and Folkestone other raiders were repulsed by Spitfire squadrons. In less than an hour the skies were again clear of the enemy. Later in the day six Dorniers attacked a lightship. A single Hurricane raced out to sea to the rescue, and got in two bursts on the tail of the last Dornier, sending it down into the sea. Boats which went out to pick up the crew of the lightship, now slowly sinking, were machine-gunned by another German aircraft. Bombs were dropped on Southampton in the

Tyne, the battles raged. Twenty-two raiders were destroyed by anti-aircraft fire. The 4·5 A.A. guns brought down Junkers and Dorniers almost invisible at great heights; the quick-firing Bofors guns caught dive-bombers on their downward swoop and made them end it in flames; Lewis guns of the searchlight posts claimed others.

During the Eastbourne raid several men took refuge under a Corporation lorry, but the protection was insufficient and they were killed; the lorry, as can be seen, was not completely destroyed.
Photos, Wide World and "News Chronicle"

Coming in over the S.E. coast in waves of 54 bombers, the Nazis unsuccessfully attacked R.A.F. aerodromes. Thirty raiders flew in very high over one South-coast town. But our fighters were ready, and six Dornier bombers were shot down into the sea. In an afternoon attack a church received a direct hit. Later that day eighty bombers raided a coastal town in the same area; all the bombs fell near the sea front, demolishing several houses and wrecking a hall and a chapel. One raider machine-gunned men working on a hillside and wounded seven.

Crossing the N.E. coast on Thursday afternoon, in the biggest raid on that area so far, bombers attacked a residential district of Sunderland and also the Tyneside, doing little material damage. Two children were killed while playing in a field; three raiders were brought down.

Thursday evening saw still more intensive efforts by the Nazis, who came in over the S.E. and S.W. coasts in waves. Except in isolated instances, they failed. Thirty of our fighters repulsed 200 of the enemy, destroying

at least twenty. Our barrage balloons were the object of especial attack, but any shot down were speedily replaced.

Between twenty and thirty dive-bombers attacked Croydon in the late afternoon. Beginning their dive when three miles away, they swooped down to a few hundred feet and loosed their missiles. No serious damage

A Heinkel bomber was shot down when Nazi bombers flew over Eastbourne on August 16. One Nazi airman's parachute failed to open, and above, his body is being lowered from the roof of a school on which it fell.

was done to the airport, but nearby buildings were wrecked and a number of people were killed and injured. In the battle with our fighters that followed, **not one of the enemy** escaped.

When this thumb presses the switch a Nazi bomber may soon crash. It controls the fire of all the eight guns of a Spitfire fighter, and when they go into action a spray of 9,690 bullets a minute meets the enemy
Photo, Associated Press

afternoon. Thirty-one raiders were brought down this day, against seven British fighters lost.

On Thursday, August 15, the Luftwaffe (the 'Air Arm') brought more than a thousand bombers and fighters against England, and lost the remarkable **total of 180 aircraft**. Our own losses were 34 fighters. Along a front of 500 miles, from Plymouth to the

King Congratulates Fighter Squadrons

The Secretary of State for Air received on August 16 the following message from His Majesty the King:

Please convey my warmest congratulations to the Fighter Squadrons who, in recent days, have been so heavily engaged in the defence of our country.

I, like all their compatriots, have read with ever-increasing admiration the story of their daily victories. I wish them continued success and the best of luck.

GEORGE, R.I.

When the Air Battle First Raged Round London

After the raid on a London suburb on August 16, everyone carried on. Here, in a damaged shoe shop, the proprietress next day sold shoes as usual.

Women took an active part in rescue work and in tending the injured. Above, nuns are going about their work of mercy in a station in a south-western suburb of London which had been damaged by a bomb.

The men of the Home Guard, left, shot down a German bomber with 180 rounds of rifle fire during the raid on Southern England on August 18, while they were being machine-gunned. They were photographed at their post on the following day.

The driver of this milk van caught in Fleet Street during an air-raid warning has done the right thing—tethered his horse to the back of the van and taken refuge in a shelter. Right is a church in a south-western suburb of London that suffered damage during the raid of August 16.

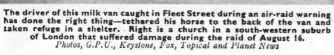

Photos, G.P.U., Keystone, Fox, Topical and Planet News

Gunners on the Ground Share the Glory

Another of Thursday's raiders met its doom from a new device to frustrate enemy aircraft. The announcement was made in the following form : " A German bomber was caught by one of the aeroplane traps erected by the Ministry of Transport for the military authorities and was completely wrecked, all the occupants being killed." These traps are said to be overhead constructions made of wire and designed to protect important points on the highways.

The German High Command, following its policy of mendacity in these matters, admitted the loss of only 32 aircraft in Thursday's battles ; to this our Air Ministry's rejoinder was that, although most of the fighting took place over the sea—a striking commentary on the success of our defence—the wreckage of 49 enemy aircraft was strewn over the English countryside !

Hitler's first attempt on London took place on Friday, August 16, when the sirens sounded soon after midday and again at a little after 5 p.m. A large force of bombers and fighters approached the S.E. coast at midday. Those that turned inland were frustrated by our fighters. Others, entering the Thames Estuary, dropped bombs on either side. Despite the intense barrage some raiders passed round the S.E. side of the Metropolis but dropped no bombs.

In the afternoon an airfield on the South coast was attacked. Later the enemy tried again to get past the defences of the capital. Making their way up the Thames Estuary, some of the Nazis reached a south-western suburb, where bombs were dropped on a station. A school was bombed and gunned, but all the children but one had gone home, and the remaining youngster was unhurt. A train had just come in at the station, and people who had alighted were mostly on the stairway when a bomb struck the booking office. Another bomb wrecked six houses in one block. Delay-action bombs also were dropped by the raiders, and some did not explode until Sunday night.

R.A.F. aerodromes were singled out by the Nazis in this day's raids. Patrolling near one airfield, a squadron of Spitfires caught eleven dive-bombers swooping down to attack. All the enemy were destroyed. In the evening the German onslaught was renewed at a number of points. Though attacks were made over a wide area, little damage was done. In all, **75 Nazi aircraft were destroyed** ; we lost 22 fighters.

On Saturday the enemy displayed little activity. One Nazi bomber was destroyed by the R.A.F.

The lure of London brought about on Sunday, August 18, an even heavier defeat of the Nazi aerial legions. Six hundred German raiders crossed the S. and S.E. coasts about 1 p.m. and made mainly for aerodromes and harbours. Formations of about eighty bombers flew line abreast in sections of three, making a huge rectangle. Circling in front and above went their fighter escorts.

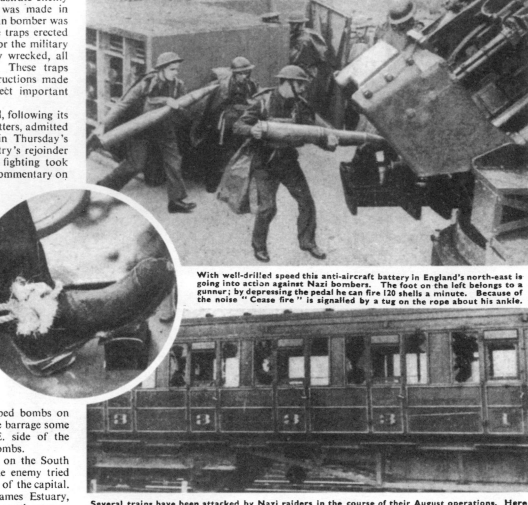

With well-drilled speed this anti-aircraft battery in England's north-east is going into action against Nazi bombers. The foot on the left belongs to a gunner; by depressing the pedal he can fire 120 shells a minute. Because of the noise " Cease fire " is signalled by a tug on the rope about his ankle.

Several trains have been attacked by Nazi raiders in the course of their August operations. Here is one of them which, when it had been brought to a standstill because the bombers were overhead, was struck by bomb splinters.   *Photos, G.P.U. and Associated Press.*

Entire enemy squadrons were wiped out by our Hurricanes and Spitfires.

Bombs were dropped on the outer fringe of South London, and for the first time the London A.A. guns were in action. Nearly a hundred raiders tried to get through the defences of Croydon. Fifteen were shot down by our fighters, while the A.A. gunners accounted for a number more.

In the evening large formations crossed the coast near Dover and the North Foreland and made their way along the Thames Estuary. They were met by a terrific barrage, and their formations were broken up by our fighters. With heavy loss the raiders were driven back over the Channel and the North Sea. So ended the second attempt to raid London ; out of six hundred aircraft engaged in the operations **152 were destroyed**—21 by A.A. gunners and 2 by Lewis gun crews. Twenty-two British fighters were lost.

Tuesday, August 20, was a day of scattered activity over a wide area by small numbers of raiders. Incidents at South-Western towns included the machine-gunning of bathers on a beach, and of Home Guards on duty at the top of a cliff. Bombs demolished houses. During the night steelworks in the Black Country had been the object of attack, and other places in the Midlands and North-East were bombed. Seven raiders were shot down.

GERMAN & BRITISH AIRCRAFT LOSSES
German to April 30, 1941

Total announced West Front, North Sea, Britain, Scandinavia		195
Unofficial estimate of additional 'planes damaged in Norway		200

	German	British
May	1,990	258
June	276	177
July	245	115
Aug. 1-20	731	212
Grand Totals, May to Aug. ...	**3,242**	**762**

Daily Results, August 1-20

Aug.	German Losses	British Losses	British Pilots Saved	Aug.	German Losses	British Losses	British Pilots Saved
				Bt.fwd.	280	109	16
1-7	10	15	—	14	31	11	2
8	62	18	3	15	180	37	17
9	1	1	0	16	75	25	14
10	1	4	0	17	1	0	—
11	66	29	2	18	152	22	12
12	62	17	1	19	5	6	2
13	78	25	10	20	7	2	1
	280	**109**	**16**		**731**	**212**	**64**

Notes.—Figures for **May** cover Dunkirk operations and include aircraft destroyed by French. Probable number brought down by British during that month is 1,500 out of the total 1,990.

The main attack on Britain began on Aug. 8—up to the 20th there were 8 mass attacks.

None of the figures include aircraft bombed on the ground or so damaged as to be unlikely to reach home.

On Aug. 20 the Air Minister stated that Germany had lost **701 aircraft** since Aug. 8, in attacks on Britain, with more than **1,500 personnel**. Our own losses were **192 aircraft** and **90 personnel**. Our A.A. guns had shot down 57 German raiders in the period.

WE STAND ERECT ON THE ROAD TO VICTORY

Mr. Churchill's most inspiring survey of our position after a year of war, given to Parliament on August 20, impressed the whole non-Axis world. Here, selected from the speech, are a series of passages, notable for their splendid phrasing and for their clear presentation of Britain's invincible will to victory.

ALTHOUGH this war is in fact only a continuation of the last, very great differences in its character are apparent. In the last war millions of men fought by hurling enormous masses of steel at one another. In this war nothing of this kind has yet appeared. It is a conflict of strategy, of organization, of technical apparatus, science, mechanics, and moral . . . . There is another far more obvious difference from 1914. The whole of the warring nations are engaged ; not only the soldiers, but the entire population, men, women and children. The fronts are everywhere. The trenches are dug in the towns and streets. Every village is fortified. Every road is barred. The front line runs through the factories. The workmen are soldiers, with different weapons but the same courage.

There seems to be every reason to believe that this new kind of war is well suited to the genius and the resources of the British nation and British Empire and that once we get properly equipped and properly started a war of this kind will be more favourable to us than the sombre mass slaughters of the Somme and Passchendaele. If it is a case of the whole nation fighting and suffering together, that ought to suit us too, because **we are the most united of all the nations, because we entered the war with the national will and with our eyes open, because we have been nurtured in freedom and individual responsibility, and are the products not of totalitarian uniformity but of tolerance and variety.**

Hitler is now sprawled over Europe. Our offensive springs are being slowly compressed, and we must resolutely and methodically prepare ourselves for the campaigns of 1941 and 1942. Two or three years are not a long time even in our short precarious lives ; they are nothing in the history of a nation, and when we are doing the finest thing in the world and have the honour to be the sole champion of freedom of all Europe we must not grudge these years or weary as we toil and struggle through them. . . . **The road to victory may not be so long as we expect, but we have no right to count on this. Be it long or short, rough or smooth, we mean to reach our journey's end.**

'We Stand . . . Masters of Our Fate'

RATHER more than a quarter of a year has passed since the new Government came into power in this country. What a cataract of disaster has poured out upon us since then ! The trustful Dutch overwhelmed ; their beloved and respected Sovereign driven into exile ; the peaceful city of Rotterdam the scene of a massacre as hideous and brutal as anything in the Thirty Years' War. Belgium invaded and beaten down ; our own fine Expeditionary Force, which King Leopold called to his rescue, cut off and almost captured, escaping as it seemed only by a miracle and with the loss of all its equipment.

Our ally France out. Italy is against us. All France in the power of the enemy, all its arsenals and vast masses of military material converted or convertible to the enemy's use. A puppet Government set up at Vichy which may at any moment be forced to become our foe. The whole Western seaboard of Europe from the North Cape to the Spanish frontier in German hands. All the ports, all the air fields on this immense front employed against us as potential springboards of invasion.

Moreover, the German air power numerically so far outstripping ours has been brought so close to our island that what we used to dread greatly has come to pass and the hostile bombers not only reach our shores in a few minutes and from many directions, but can be escorted by their fighting aircraft. If we had been confronted at the beginning of May with such a prospect it would have seemed incredible that at the end of a period of horror and disaster, or at this point in a period of horror and disaster, **we should stand erect, sure of ourselves, masters of our fate, and with the conviction of final victory burning unquenchable in our hearts.**

'No One Flinched or Wavered'

Let us see what has happened on the other side of the scales. The British nation and the British Empire, finding themselves alone, stood undismayed against disaster. No one flinched or wavered ; nay, some who formerly thought of peace now think only of war. Our people are united and resolved as they have never been before. Death and ruin have become small things compared with the shame of defeat or failure of duty. We cannot tell what lies ahead. It may be that even greater ordeals lie before us. We shall face whatever is coming to us. We are sure of ourselves and of our cause, and here is the supreme fact which has emerged in these months of trial.

Meanwhile, we have not only fortified our hearts but our island. We have rearmed and rebuilt our Armies in a degree which would have been deemed impossible a few months ago. We have ferried across the Atlantic, thanks to our friends over there, an immense mass of munitions of all kinds, cannon, rifles, machine-guns, cartridges, and shells, all safely landed without the loss of a gun or a round. The output of our own factories working as they have never worked before has poured forth to the troops. The whole British Army is at home. More than 2,000,000 determined men have rifles and bayonets in their hands to-night and three-quarters of them are in regular military formation. **We have never had Armies like this in our island in time of war. The whole island bristles against invaders from the sea or from the air. . .**

Our Navy is far stronger than it was at the beginning of the war. The great flow of new construction set on foot at the outbreak is now beginning to come in.

We hope our friends across the ocean will send us timely reinforcements to bridge the gap between the peace flotillas of 1939 and the war flotillas of 1941. There is no difficulty in sending such aid. The seas and oceans are open.

The U-boats are contained. The magnetic mine in many areas is, up to the present time, effectively mastered. **The merchant tonnage under the British flag after a year of unlimited U-boat war, after eight months of intensive mining attack, is larger than when we began.**

Why do I say all this ? Not assuredly to boast ; not to give the slightest countenance to complacency . . . I say it because the fact that the British Empire stands invincible, and that Nazidom can still be resisted, will kindle again the spark of hope in the breasts of hundreds of millions of downtrodden or despairing men and women throughout Europe, and far beyond its bounds, and that from these sparks there will presently come a cleansing and devouring flame.

The great air battle which has been in progress over this island for the last few weeks has recently attained a high intensity. It is too soon to attempt to assign limits either to its scale or to its duration. We must certainly expect that greater efforts will be made by the enemy than any he has so far put forth. Hostile air fields are still being developed in France and the Low Countries, and the movement of squadrons and material for attacking us is still proceeding. . . .

On the other hand, the conditions and course of the fighting have so far been favourable to us. . . . Whereas in France our fighter aircraft were wont to inflict a loss of two or three to one upon the Germans, whereas in the fighting at Dunkirk, which was a kind of no-man's-land, a loss of about three or four to one, we expected that in an attack on this island we should achieve a larger ratio. This has certainly come true. . . .

The enemy is, of course, far more numerous than we are. But our new production already, I am advised, largely exceeds his, and the American production is only just beginning to flow in. It is a fact, as I can see from our daily returns, that **our fighter and bomber strengths are now, after all this fighting, larger than they have ever been. . . .**

The gratitude of every home in our island, in our Empire, and, indeed, throughout the world, except in the abodes of the guilty, goes out to the British airmen who, undaunted by odds, unwearied by their constant challenge and mortal danger, are turning the tide of world war by their prowess and by their devotion. **Never in the field of human conflict was so much owed by so many to so few.**

All hearts go out to the fighter pilots, whose brilliant actions we see with our own eyes day after day, but we must never forget that all the time, night after night, month after month, our bomber squadrons travel far into Germany, find their targets in the darkness by the highest navigational skill, aim their attacks, often under the heaviest fire, often at serious loss, with deliberate, careful precision, and inflict shattering blows upon the whole of the technical and warmaking structure of the Nazi power. . . . I have no hesitation in saying that this process of bombing the military industries and communications of Germany, and the air bases and storage depots from which we are attacked, which will continue upon an ever increasing scale until the end of the war, and may in another year attain dimensions hitherto undreamed of, assures **one of the surest, if not the shortest of all roads to victory. . . .**

*　　　*　　　*　　　*

Guiding the Course of History

Before we can undertake the task of rebuilding we have not only to be convinced ourselves, but we have to convince all other countries that the Nazi tyranny is going to be finally broken. **The right to guide the course of world history is the noblest prize of victory.** We are still toiling up the hill, we have not yet reached the crest-line, we cannot survey the landscape or even imagine what its condition will be when that longed-for morning comes. The task which lies before us immediately is at once more practical, more simple, and more stern. I hope—indeed I pray—that we shall not be found unworthy of our victory if after toil and tribulation it is granted to us. **For the rest we have to gain the victory. That is our task.**

Greece Has Good Reason to Fear Italy

After the invasion of Albania by Italy in 1939 a guarantee against aggression was given to Greece by Britain and France. On the outbreak of the European War, Greece took up a position of strict neutrality, but in August 1940, following the collapse of France, one of Greece's two guarantors, Italy adopted an attitude of distinct truculence against her little neighbour across the Ionian Sea.

No country in the Balkans watches Italy with closer attention than Greece. The average Greek does not trust Italy. He resents the Italian occupation since 1922 of the Dodecanese, islands which have been inhabited by Greeks for centuries. Not only has Italy strongly fortified the Dodecanese and equipped them with aerodromes and naval bases, which are a direct threat to Greece, but she has regimented the Greek inhabitants. They are even forbidden to wear blue shirts, and the Greek considers blue to be his national colour.

The Italian occupation of Albania gave Italy a common land frontier with Greece. Greece eyes suspiciously the construction of a railway from Durazzo in Albania, ostensibly for the purpose of transporting ore from the mining district of Labinoti to the Greek frontier, but which might also very well serve strategic needs.

The Greeks have a horror of war. Their last war, they are fond of pointing out, lasted from 1912 (the beginning of the Balkan Wars) to 1922, when the Greek armies which had invaded Asia Minor were defeated by the New Turkey.

Greece was a signatory of the Balkan Pact of 1934, and has a treaty of friendship and neutrality with her neighbour Turkey, whereby she undertakes to prevent the transport of troops, munitions, or armaments through her territory to any State attacking Turkey, and to consult with Turkey immediately war breaks out involving Turkey or Greece.

Greece is only too well aware of her extremely vulnerable position vis-à-vis Italy. Her exposed coastline, while it has many valuable harbours (notably Piraeus and Salonika), is longer than the Spanish and Portuguese coastline combined. Corfu, although a Greek island, has obvious attractions as a naval harbour to an ambitious Power. Athens is only 46 minutes' flying time from Lero in the Dodecanese, while there is hardly an important Greek town which could not be reached in under an hour from Italy or from Italian-controlled Albania.

Greece's 200 aircraft, British, German, and French, are varied in military value,

General John Metaxas has been the Greek Premier, Minister of Foreign Affairs and Acting Minister of War since 1936, and in 1938 he assumed virtual dictatorship.

and the largest naval unit is the 9,450-ton cruiser "Averoff," mounting four 9.2-inch and eight 7.5-inch guns.

If Greece could bar the approaches to Salonika, by the aid of her numerous small naval craft and by the mining of the channels between the Aegean Islands, she would be very well satisfied with her naval effort. She has, of course, fortified her islands, bays and narrows.

The Greek army has been trained largely by French officers and is a very different force from that which retreated from Asia Minor in 1922. There are some 700,000 well-trained men ready for an emergency, although the normal strength of the army is only 65,000. The chief danger to be envisaged is from Albania, and one of Greece's five army corps has been stationed at Yannina to cover the approaches to Greece from the Albanian frontier. The others are garrisoned in Athens, Salonika, Larisa, and Drama.

The Drama army corps is an additional safeguard for Salonika and the Aegean coast, and in the event of war it might be reinforced by the Turkish Thracian army, stationed on the other side of the River Maritsa, since the Turks have just as much interest as the Greeks in safeguarding Salonika, the fall of which would seriously hamper aid to Yugoslavia, Greece, and possibly Rumania.

Greece, unhappily, is a poor country. In recent years she has spent one-third of her total revenue on defence, but her total expenditure amounted to only £8,242,000. The deficiency of the Greek army in tanks, the lack of aircraft, and the absence of capital ships in her fleet make her reluctant to go to war, except in the most extreme circumstances.

That war might be forced upon her, however, was made apparent in August 1940, when Italy, never too friendly, displayed many signs of increasing hostility. The Duce is nothing if not predatory, and with France out

This sketch map displays both Greece's dangerous position in relation to Italy and Italian Albania and her extremely long coastline. Points of military interest are the mine-net between Samos and Athens, and the Metaxas defence line facing Albania.

Once More the Balkans Are a Storm Centre

of the way he no doubt thought that Britain, with her heavy commitments at home and in Egypt, would be unable to render Greece any very effective assistance. It was not difficult to foment a quarrel, and what might well have been a casus belli was found in one Daout Hoggia, a bandit who was murdered in Albania towards the end of July by two fellow Albanians who fled to Greece, where they were arrested. The murdered Hoggia was suddenly given the status of an Albanian patriot, and as Albania and Italy were now one, Italy demanded that the two assassins should be handed over. Before this could be done, however, the Italian propaganda machine was launched against the Greeks, who were accused of anti-Italian activities on the Greco-Albanian frontier.

Relations were further strained by the torpedoing of one of Greece's only two

Seen beneath the 9·2-inch guns of the cruiser " Averoff " (top right) are two of the fastest destroyers of the Greek Navy; above, one of the " Averoff's " A.A. guns.
Photos, Keystone

cruisers—the 2,115-ton " Helle "—off the Aegean island of Tinos on August 15. An Italian submarine was suspected, and the Italians admitted · that they might have mistaken the " Helle " for an English cruiser. A day or two later two Greek destroyers were attacked by Italian bombers, and again a similar excuse was proffered. The Duce's government now asked that, if the Greek fleet saw fit to leave their harbours, they should give notice to the Italians beforehand.

As likely as not, these attacks were intended to persuade the Greeks that they would do well to abandon the British guarantee and substitute for it an understanding with Italy. But General Metaxas, the Greek Dictator, who as recently as August 3—the fourth anniversary of his accession to power—had renewed the declaration of Greek neutrality, found the Italian acts as unconvincing as their arguments.

The training of the Greek Air Force is modelled on that of the R.A.F. These cadets, who have almost completed their training, parade for a National Fête. King George II of Greece (circle), who is essentially a soldier king, is here seen giving advice to infantry during manoeuvres.
Photos, Keystone and Planet News

The Merchant Navy Defies Hitler's Blockade

The fantastic claims made by Nazi propaganda of the mastery by air power over British shipping (see pages 180-183) are easily disposed of. Although the July total was 27,000 tons higher than for June (see page 82), Goebbels' million tons is here shown to be a fivefold magnification. Convoys continue with full confidence to sail the British seas.

THE first stage of the Battle of Britain was a strong assault against the sea power of Germany's greatest enemy. Submarines which had been withdrawn from service before the Battle of France were sent out to sea again in June in a concentrated attack against merchant shipping. From newly-acquired air bases in France and Belgium wave upon wave of dive-bombers launched attacks against convoys in the English Channel and ports and dockyards on the south and south-eastern coasts of Britain.

The submarines, through sheer numbers, were bound to score a number of successes. British merchant shipping losses were undoubtedly heavy, compared with the previous months of the war, for 211,974 tons gross were sunk during the four weeks July 1 to 28. But this figure is insignificant compared with the claims made by the Nazis.

Fantastic stories were circulated by the Goebbels " lie factories " that more than a million tons of British shipping had been sunk in three weeks of air battles over the Channel. This was merely an attempt to compensate for the heavy losses suffered by the German Air Force in their struggle to force their will over British sea power and close the Channel to shipping and thus rob the country of the services of its major port—London.

The month of July proved that Goering's theory that air power could master sea power was incapable of realization. In the first concentrated air attack on a convoy in the Channel the Nazis sent about 250 dive-bombers and fighters against a small escort of coastal vessels. More than 50 Nazi aircraft were quickly shot down by Hurricanes and Spitfires and by anti-aircraft fire from the escorting ships, and only five small vessels of about 5,000 tons were sunk. Five more of the same tonnage were damaged and had to go to port for repairs, but the attack was a conspicuous failure. In the enemy raid on the harbour of Dover seventeen machines were shot down within the space of half an hour. Only one small vessel was sunk and no other damage was done (see full accounts in pages 114 and 120).

The merchant ships proved themselves perfectly capable of defending themselves from air attack. The 1,000-ton passenger vessel " Highlander," operating in the North Sea, was attacked by three Heinkels. The gunner on board the little ship held his fire until one of the 'planes came well within range, preparatory to bombing. He fired his gun and scored a hit. The aeroplane fell apart, the body of it falling across the poop of the ship (see page 163). The two other 'planes then started to attack, but another burst from the ship's gun brought the second raider down into the sea.

Merchant Shipping War Losses

	Sept. 3 to July 28 Tons gross	July 1 to 28 Tons gross
BRITISH :		
Cargo vessels	1,164,953	211,974
Lost in naval operations	74,929	—
Naval auxiliaries	109,021	—
Naval trawlers	15,235	2,300
Totals ...	1,364,139	214,274
ALLIED	334,625	26,148
Totals ...	1,698,763	240,422
NEUTRAL	737,932	59,595
Totals ...	2,436,695	300,017

Enemy Losses to August 4

	Sunk	Captured	Total
GERMAN ...	658,000	260,000	918,000
ITALIAN ...	105,000	150,000	255,000
Totals ...	763,000	410,000	1,173,000

In addition, 26,000 tons of neutral tonnage under enemy control have been sunk.

The third, seeing what had happened to his comrades, sheered off.

After more than a month of this sort of attack, despite all the Nazi boasts about the command of the Channel, convoys of merchant ships sometimes extending five miles in length calmly plough up and down the Channel, well escorted and confident. Many of the convoys have now been supplied with their own barrage balloons, to counteract the efforts of the dive bombers coming low over their difficult targets.

The major part of the British shipping losses were attributed to the submarine assault. Stationed in the Atlantic from Eire to Gibraltar, large forces of enemy submarines would bide their time for an attack against a carefully-selected target, be it an Allied or a neutral ship. Neutrals suffered

heavily, but according to the official Admiralty figures lost only 59,595 tons gross during July. It can safely be stated that this estimate is a very conservative one. During the previous month, for instance, Admiralty sources stated that the enemy had sunk about 75,000 tons of neutral shipping. Yet a report from Athens later said that no fewer than 14 Greek ships alone, of more than 61,000 tons, had been sunk during the month, with a loss of 21 lives.

Submarine warfare comes in waves. When the enemy's strength is sent out from its bases in a massed attack on shipping, it has a definite effect on the number of sinkings. But those submarines must go back to their bases to refuel—those of them that have escaped destruction at the hands of the Navy and the Air Force Coastal Command. Then the wave of losses subsides until the next combined attack is launched.

One notable achievement of the submarines was the sinking of the " Arandora Star," an unescorted liner which was conveying Italian and Nazi internees and prisoners of war to Canada. The submarine was responsible for the loss of many enemy lives. At the end of the month the Elder Dempster liner " Accra," on her way to West Africa with passengers and mails, was sunk by torpedoes fired from two submarines. Within a few minutes those submarines met their timely end.

Meanwhile, July heralded the appearance of another Nazi armed raider. Disguised as a merchantman, and flying the Swedish flag, this vessel succeeded in sinking the cargo liners " Davisian " and " King John " in West Indian waters. It was not long before that raider had an unsuccessful encounter with the armed merchant cruiser "Alcantara," in the South Atlantic.

The month of July was a real trial of strength between the Nazi forces and British sea power. Armed raiders, submarines, aeroplanes and " E-boats " were employed with intensity, but they failed to make any appreciable difference to the continuous flow of British imports and exports. Minelaying aeroplanes attempted to close harbours to shipping, but if the minelayers were not brought down, the mines were as quickly swept as they were laid. The E-boats, enemy torpedo boats · which occasionally issued from French ports to make sporadic torpedo attacks against convoys, received harsh treatment from escorting vessels. Despite all the weapons and the favourable bases in their possession the Germans were unable to impose their will upon the Merchant Navy. Hitler's widely proclaimed " blockade " of Britain was his first major defeat ; yet the British blockade is still a reality—in July 45,300 tons of contraband goods were seized, 34,600 tons being from neutral ships bound mainly to Italian ports.

MERCHANT SHIPPING LOSSES in 11 months of WAR

★*Each Symbol :-* ⬛ *represents* 100,000 *tons.*

BRITISH	JULY 1 – JULY 28 1940 1940	SEPT 3 – JULY 28 1939 1940
Liners, Cargo Vessels Etc.	211,974 TONS	1,164,953 TONS
Lost in Naval Operations	2,300 "	199,185 "
TOTAL	214,274 "	1,364,138 "
ALLIED	26,148 "	334,625 "
TOTAL	240,422 "	1,698,763 "
NEUTRAL	59,595 "	737,932 "

TOTAL BRITISH, ALLIED AND NEUTRAL LOSSES

300,017 TONS	2,436,695 TONS

ENEMY LOSSES TO AUGUST 4th 1940

	Sunk	Captured	Total
GERMAN	658,000 TONS	260,000 TONS	918,000 TONS
ITALIAN	105,000 "	150,000 "	255,000 "
TOTAL	763,000 TONS	410,000 TONS	1,173,000 TONS

26,000 TONS OF NEUTRAL TONNAGE UNDER ENEMY CONTROL HAVE BEEN SUNK

This picture diagram continues from page 82 the story of the successful resistance of the British Merchant Navy to the enemy's fiercest air and submarine attacks. The Italian figures have been corrected by later information.

I WAS THERE!

Eye Witness Stories of Episodes
and Adventures in the
Second Great War

We Saw The Bombers Fall Like Leaves

Sunday, August 18, is a day that will ever be remembered by hundreds of thousands of Londoners, who were involuntary eye witnesses of a great air battle above their heads. Here, exclusively told to "The War Illustrated," is the story of what Mr. H. G. Earle, of The Amalgamated Press staff, saw when picnicking in Surrey.

I WAS spending the day with my family at a famous beauty spot on a ridge of hills overlooking the weald of Surrey and Kent. The position may be easily compared to that of a spectator on the cliffs of Dover overlooking the Channel. The whole panorama of the beautiful Surrey countryside is before one, and it was here that we were about to partake of our lunch. But very shortly the enemy bombers were heard high up above in close packed formation.

Anti-aircraft batteries opened fire immediately, and the sky seemed full of fighter aircraft going up in pursuit. My family and I seated ourselves with our backs to a large beech tree, as I thought this afforded the best protection under the circumstances. In a few seconds a large German bomber hurtled out of the sky like a falling leaf. The pilot managed to regain some control when near the earth and it seemed as if a safe landing might have been possible, but he made a sudden dive, hitting the ground, and the machine immediately burst into an inferno of flame and smoke. It was a terrible scene, taking place just down below us in the valley in broad sunlight. This, by the way, was the only time when my younger daughter—she is only 5—showed even the smallest signs of any distress. Our fighters were zooming in all directions and we could hear the rattle of machine-gun fire above us.

A big black German bomber planed right across our vision about 300 feet from the earth, and with engines off, obviously trying to land, when to our amazement there was a burst of machine-gun fire as he scraped over the roof of a farmhouse very near to a golf course. It was astonishing to us that the occupants of the machine in such a perilous position could still machine-gun a farmhouse as they passed over the roof and pancaked into a field half a mile further along apparently undamaged. We were told by someone who was near the field that the machine was a Dornier. While this was going on anti-aircraft batteries were sending up shells at a terrific rate. Shells were bursting in the wood behind us, and we felt that any moment some splinters might descend upon us. After a very short interval we saw a formation of Spitfires bring down two more bombers on the distant hills.

It was then that my wife pointed out to me one of our fighters that was obviously in difficulties. He was spiralling towards earth and his destruction seemed imminent when, much to our relief and amazement, he zoomed into a vertical climb. He must have realized that he was going to hit the ground. At the top of the vertical climb the parachute opened and the pilot fell out of the machine and landed safely. As he dropped, his machine fell to the ground like a stone.

Then a group of German bombers, hotly pursued by our fighters, were seen making the best of their way to the coast.

I looked at my watch; the action had lasted thirty-five minutes. Our tense nerves relaxed. It was then we began to realise the perilous position we had been in. The Battle of Britain had been a reality to us. We had seen with admiration the wonderful fighting quality of our fighter pilots. The Surrey countryside was peaceful once again, and the only evidence of the battle was the smoking ruins of the German bombers in the fields below us.

After that we continued our lunch. Just after six o'clock we arrived home, to find that a bomb had dropped six doors away from our house, shattering many windows and sending tiles flying in all directions !

On Sunday, August 18, as told in this page, the peace of the Surrey countryside was suddenly shattered by the roar of anti-aircraft fire as German bombers rapidly approached in close formation. This photograph of a Nazi Junkers 87, which was taken the same week-end on the S.E. coast, shows the Nazis actually machine-gunning an A.A. gun emplacement in which a cameraman was stationed. As such it is probably the closest picture so far taken in England of raiders in action.

Photo; Associated Press

I Watched Them Bomb A Lightship

On August 14, 1940, six German dive-bombers bombed and machine-gunned a lightship off the south-east coast, killing two of the crew of nine and injuring the rest.　Hilde Marchant's dramatic eye-witness story of this outrage is published here by arrangement with the " Daily Express."

LYING in a ditch on the top of a cliff, I was watching a terrific battle between 200 'planes.

While our fighters were engaged, six German bombers rested quietly in the clouds over the sea.　As the battle spread inland they felt safe enough to swoop down on the undefended lightship.

I saw them pierce the shadowy sky, and in my innocence believed they were going to join the battle over land.　Instead, they straightened out in one long black line and began to make for the ship.

It rocked from side to side as the bombs crashed in the water around—bad shots even with a sitting target.　Men from two lorries that had stopped by the roadside shrieked curses at them and shook with anger.

How close it was !　We could see the swastikas and watch the bombs fly, and how helpless we all felt !　Men were being bombed and not one of us could do a thing except curse.

The little ship had been anchored in that bay for many years, and through fogs and gales had diverted the shipping of all nations from a nest of treacherous sand and rock.　Yes, all ships—even German merchantmen—had been sent in peace and out of danger by the little red ship which now lurched from side to side.

Through the din of the engines we heard a harsh, quick rattle.　The crew were being machine-gunned.　The wreck of the ship was not enough ; the pilots sought slaughter . .

Down came those screeching black 'planes, right over my head, pausing only to turn their machine-guns on the men who fumbled at the side of their ship to get a dinghy out. It is dirty, cruel fighting, and we must harden ourselves and know the terms of Hitler's total war.

The 'planes swung up and turned for a second dive.　The first was right above me and turning for a second chance, when a fresh sound came into the sky.

Three Spitfires streaked low over the cliffs. I cheered and cheered, and the men on the roadside yelled, " Go after the black swine ! "

They did.　The Germans flattened out and began to scramble for the clouds again. But our fighters, embittered by the pathetic wreckage below, tore into the six bombers. At least three of them were brought down, and one was so badly damaged it is unlikely it got back home.

I saw one German 'plane rock out of its path and begin to drop.　Black smoke and flame blistered the sky.　The machine skidded for a mile low over the water ; then it sank with a great splash—and with a loud cheer from me.

A second German 'plane seemed to stumble about the sky, then disappeared into the clouds again.　They got away to report their magnificent morning's work— how they found an unprotected lightship and machine-gunned the crew, and how they managed to fly into the clouds when they were challenged to fight.

They did not pause to see the rest of the story I watched from the cliff head. The overladen dinghy got away from the sinking ship, and a motor-boat from the harbour ploughed out to them.

A Spitfire hovered around, protecting the rescue work.　As the boat picked up the men the lightship sank stern first.

A second motor-yacht came out and searched the water for some miles around. At first I thought they were looking for survivors from the lightship, but soon I realized they were looking for the crew of the German bomber that had crashed.

The Spitfire guided them to the wreckage.　In the first moments of unreasoned anger at the savage display I had seen so closely I felt that those men should drown. Yet later I knew we need not behave like Germans in our fighting.

I met James Easton, the master of the lightship, on his way to the station.　His face was still twitching, and he limped from a bullet wound in the leg.

" We were having our dinner when the 'planes came over," he said.　" The deck was open, and there was no cover, so we crouched down against the ship's side.

" She rocked like mad.　We were thrown all over the deck.　Then we heard machine-gun bullets hammering the deck.

" A couple of lads were killed with the first shot.　I got one in the leg, and all of us got peppered.　We dragged ourselves over to the dinghy and got it loose before the last lot were on top of us.

" We got away just as the Spitfires came after them, and though we were exhausted and bleeding it was a grand sight."

He was in a hurry when I saw him, still shaking, and with his face bleeding.　He had a train to catch.　What for ?　" To send in a report and see about a new lighter."

We Puzzled the Germans With Our Gaelic

Three Scottish soldiers who escaped after capture by the Germans wandered across France to a Spanish port, puzzling German interrogators and evading recapture by replying to all questions in Gaelic.　The story of their odyssey was broadcast by one of the three and is reprinted here by arrangement with " The Listener."

IT took us one month and three days to get from France back to Ballachulish. At the beginning of May thirty-five of us, fighting two thousand Germans, were defending a small house.　We were completely surrounded, and on the last day the shells were coming over " two-a-penny." We were captured about 2.30 in the afternoon and they began to march us north towards Belgium.　One day we were passing through a big town and I saw that we could have broken away, but we weren't together and I wasn't going without my pals.

Two days after that we came into a village. That night we slept in a Sports Stadium. We made a little shack for ourselves ; Sandy Blood (that's what we call Macdonald), big Willie Kemp and myself.　We made our plans that night.　The French people were putting pails of water at the roadside for the prisoners as they were marching along. Of course there was always a rush for the water, and during one rush we three kept on past the pails and round the end of a house into the garden.　There was a French boy in the garden and he pointed to a bush. We went and hid there and the boy brought us civilian clothes and a map, and later his mother came out with food.　We waited there until the column had passed and then set off over the country.

We were trying to get back behind the Maginot Line because we had no idea what was taking place.　Well, one night we came over a ridge, and, looking down, saw the Vimy War Memorial.　Sitting up there we had a conference and decided to walk by night.　I took a chimney stack for a landmark and we marched till we passed it. Then we lost our direction and had to sleep under a haystack.　When we awoke up in the morning and looked across the road we saw a bivouac in front of us and supply lorries and horses.　They were only fifty

The ruthless bombing of the lightship by Junkers is vividly shown here.　A bomb has fallen close to the ship, and the next bomb scored a direct hit.　Contrary to all rules of maritime warfare the Nazis did not hesitate to attack a defenceless craft—a ship whose purpose was to serve sailors of every nation.　　　*Photo, " Daily Mirror "*

August 30th, 1940　　　　　The War Illustrated　　　　　221

IIIIIIIIIIIIIIIIIIIIIIIIIIIIIIIIIIIIIIIIIIIIIIIIIIIIIIIIIIIIIIIIIIIIII I WAS THERE! IIIIIIIIIIIIIIIIIIIIIIIIIIIIIIIIIIIIIIIIIIIIIIIIIIIIIIIIIIIIIIIIIIIIIII

As related in this page, a party of Scottish soldiers only succeeded in crossing the frontier into Spain by repeated and determined efforts. Here are seen the pomp and ceremony when the Nazis took over the international post at Irun.
Photo, Keystone

yards away, and there was a German cavalry regiment there, too. We were in a field of sugar-beet, so we walked along the rows pretending that we were picking weeds, and got out of sight.

We were constantly running up against the Germans, but we always pretended to be refugees and got away with it. Several French people recognized us as British soldiers and gave us food and *vin rouge*. One night I fell ill, so we lay down in a pigsty where there was plenty of clean straw. Two Jerries came in, just looking to see what they could find. My pals pointed at me and said : " Camarade, malade," and the Jerries said : " Slomber," meaning " Sleep on." I was better in the morning, and as we were walking along the road a German lorry stopped and gave us a lift for about eight kilometres. They thought we were Belgian refugees.

Later we came into a place that was all smashed to blazes and found a bicycle shop. It was smashed as well, but we managed to rig up three bicycles and did about forty kilometres the first morning we had them. Then one day as we were looking at the sign-post at a cross-road, a German came up and asked us for our papers. When we said we had none, he set us to work emptying French ammunition and equipment that they had captured. We denied that we were English and spoke Gaelic the whole time, which the Germans couldn't understand. They tried eight interpreters on us, but it was no good. Then they produced a map and asked us to point out where we came from. Big Willie put his finger as far north as he could reach, in Russia, and, when they saw that, they let us go.

With a bit of luck and our Gaelic, we went on south until we came to the Pyrenees. Up in the mountains there we met a muleteer —a young fellow—and he led us straight into a Spanish Military Camp. They were quite decent to us there, but put us back over the frontier into France. We walked down the road about a kilometre and then turned back to get into Spain again. Altogether we tried three times, and at last succeeded by swimming the river with the Spanish soldiers only a hundred yards away from us. We slept in our wet clothes on a hillside. In the morning we did some nudist bathing while our clothes dried, and then when we got up to the top of the hill we saw the port we were looking for. It was a strange, foreign-looking port ; but when I saw it I was sure that it wouldn't be long before I saw Ballachulish again.

How We Got to Egypt with Our 'Planes

In addition to the French airmen who escaped to England after the armistice to continue the fight under General de Gaulle, others flew their 'planes from Syria to Egypt and joined up with the R.A.F. The escapade of one such party of " deserters " is described here by their leader.

A NUMBER of French airmen joined the British forces as soon as possible after the armistice, and many more would have done so had their machines not been put out of action on orders by the Pétain Government. Usually this was done by cutting the rudder wires or removing engine parts. In spite of this, many Frenchmen managed to escape and are continuing the fight.

The leader of a party of airmen who reached Egypt from Syria said :

All the boys of the section under my command volunteered to fight on with the British, but the undertaking was not without its risks. I was still thinking what to do when, in the course of a chat with a superior officer, he said, "If I were you, having good 'planes at my disposal, I wouldn't be here." He added, "Besides, I won't be in camp tomorrow."

"Thanks, monsieur, I get it," I replied, and immediately prepared my plans with my comrades. We knew the magnetos of the engines were disconnected, but we could manage to fix that, so we decided that zero hour should be three o'clock in the morning. Before departing I left a letter to my colonel saying that we were convinced we were no more bound to obey a Government under the control of the enemy.

In one way and another the news of our intention became known. We had to turn down, with regret, at least fifty chaps willing to join us. Another obstacle had to be overcome, as it was announced that a platoon, with two machine-guns, had been placed near the hangars and ordered to shoot any approaching silhouette.

Some of us wavered, but I decided that as leader I should be the first silhouette. I came up to the sergeant, whom I knew, and explained to him that my section had received orders to fly to a neighbouring base immediately. He replied, "Come on, you can't fool me. I know you are crossing to the British. But look—I am going with you." I could not but agree, although we were overloaded with stolen equipment, including several machine-guns and boxes of ammunition.

We taxied as silently as possible away from the barracks, and when in the middle of the ground we opened the throttle fully and went off. So overloaded were the 'planes that they left the ground only after a run of about 800 yards instead of the usual run of 400 yards. We steered a course for Egypt, where we were greeted in the most friendly fashion. Here we are now ready for the fight.

Although we are technically war-time deserters, sentenced to death, I have a hunch that I and all who acted as I did will have the opportunity to parade once again at the Arc de Triomphe in a free France.—*British United Press.*

Mechanics of the French Air Force tuning up a fighter before the capitulation. Many such 'planes were later successfully transferred to British units.
Photo, Service Cinématographique de l'Air

OUR SEARCHLIGHT ON THE WAR

Splinters Mystery Solved

HEAVY fragments of grooved steel, some of them still red-hot, were picked up in two areas on the South-East Coast following two heavy explosions on August 13. The explosions, which were not preceded by the characteristic noise of falling bombs, wrecked some houses, killed two A.R.P. workers, and injured many others. The splinters were later examined by experts who pronounced them to be pieces of shell fired from long-range German guns.

'Britain Delivers the Goods'

A TEXTILE firm in Bradford had the happy idea of stencilling on its export packing cases the cheerful slogan "Britain Delivers the Goods," surmounted by a Union Jack. So excellent did this seem to the Export Council of the Board of Trade that similar stencils were sent to thousands of exporting firms. Some have adopted a variant of the wording: "Shipped in a British ship under the protection of the British Navy." Both slogans will serve to impress the consignees with our confidence of outwitting Hitler's vaunted blockade.

The Last Boat Floated Off

TROOPS on board the Egyptian transport liner "Mahomed Ali El-Kebir" were just about to turn in when she was torpedoed at dusk on August 11. At their officers' orders they fell in on the canting deck, each detachment waiting in perfect discipline for its turn to take to the boats. The ship's officers stated that the loss of life (120 out of 860) would have been much greater had it not been for the skilled help of the naval ratings aboard the transport, and that the cheerfulness and "wisecracking" of the naval ratings were a powerful moral factor. The last boat was not lowered, but floated off the deck of the sinking ship. When all boats and rafts were clear there were still about thirty officers and men left, for one boat had been destroyed in the explosion. Diving into the sea—"Come on, mates. There'll always be an England. Let's swim to it," cried one of them—they were later picked up by a British warship.

New Tanks for Old

IN the Midlands is a factory—one of many taken over for this purpose—where expert and responsible workers are engaged in reconditioning tanks and other armoured vehicles. Some of these casualties arrive so severely damaged as almost to appear total wrecks, but after being entirely dismantled, rebuilt and repaired, every small detail being carefully overhauled and rigorously tested, they leave the factory to all intents and purposes as good as new. Such an achievement is a tribute to our engineering craftsmen, as well as a contribution of great economic importance to our war effort.

German 'Paraspooks'

WITH his usual happy knack, "Peterborough" of the "Daily Telegraph" has applied the term "paraspooks" to the German parachutists who, according to a Nazi broadcaster came down in the Midlands and the North in the early hours of August 14. Between 70 and 80 parachutes were dropped, each capable of bearing a weight of 400 lb., all with Nazi markings, and sometimes accompanied by bags containing instructions purporting to be operation orders. But in many instances the harness had not been undone, and in some cases Home Guards were on the spot to collect them when they landed. Hundreds of troops and police scoured the countryside, but no trace of German soldiers or arms was discovered, and on August 15 it was officially announced that the scheme had evidently been faked by the Germans in the hope of creating panic.

American Armed Ships Off Greenland

AS far back as April President Roosevelt issued a veiled warning that any German attempt to occupy Greenland would be an infringement of the Monroe Doctrine. But it seems—and who can blame him?—that he does not trust Hitler, and two specially armed U.S.A. cutters, the "George W. Campbell" and the "Northland," have now been sent to Greenland waters as a precautionary measure against annexation for the establishment of German air bases.

V.C. OF NAMSOS
Lt. R. B. Stannard, H.M. Trawler 'Arab'

IT was announced on August 16 that the second naval V.C. of the war had been conferred on Lieut. R. B. Stannard, R.N.R., for "outstanding valour and devotion to duty" at Namsos. The first British naval detachment landed at Namsos on April 14, and between then and May 1, when the British troops were withdrawn, Lieut. Stannard made his gallant stand. The official announcement of the award stated that when enemy bombing attacks had set on fire many tons of hand grenades on Namsos wharf, with no shore water supply available, Lieut. Stannard ran the "Arab's" bows against the wharf and held her there. Sending all but two of his crew aft, he then endeavoured for two hours to extinguish the fire with hoses from the forecastle. He persisted in this work till the attempt had to be given up as hopeless. After helping other ships against air attacks, he placed his own damaged vessel under shelter of a cliff, and landed his crew and those of two other trawlers and established an armed camp. Here those off duty could rest while he attacked enemy aircraft which approached by day and kept anti-submarine watch during the night. When another trawler near by was hit and set on fire by a bomb, he, with two others, boarded "Arab" and moved her 100 yards before the other vessel blew up. Finally, when leaving the fjord, he was attacked by a German bomber, which ordered him to steer east or be sunk. He held on his course, reserved his fire till the enemy was within 800 yards and then brought the aircraft down. Throughout a period of five days the "Arab" was subjected to 31 bombing attacks, and the camp and Lewis gun positions ashore were repeatedly machine-gunned and bombed; yet the defensive position was so well planned that only one man was wounded. Lieut. Stannard ultimately brought his damaged ship back to an English port.

DORTMUND-EMS CANAL V.C.
Flight Lieut. R. A. Learoyd

THE first bombing of the Dortmund-Ems Canal, one of Germany's great inland waterways, was announced on July 17 (see page 91, Vol. 3), and Flight Lieutenant Learoyd was engaged in these operations. The feat for which he was awarded the V.C. was thus officially described:

This officer, as first pilot of a Hampden aircraft, has repeatedly shown the highest conception of his duty and complete indifference to personal danger in making attacks at the lowest altitudes regardless of opposition. On the night of August 12 he was detailed to attack a special objective on the Dortmund-Ems Canal. He had attacked this objective on a previous occasion, and was well aware of the risks entailed. To achieve success it was necessary to approach from a direction well-known to the enemy, through a lane of specially disposed anti-aircraft defences and in the face of the most intense point-blank fire from guns of all calibres. The reception of the preceding aircraft might well have deterred the stoutest heart, all being hit and two lost. Flight Lieutenant Learoyd, nevertheless, made his attack at 150 ft., his aircraft being repeatedly hit and large pieces of the main planes torn away. He was almost blinded by the glare of searchlights at close range, but pressed home his attack with the greatest resolution and skill. He subsequently brought his wrecked aircraft home and, as the landing flaps were inoperative and the undercarriage indicators out of action, waited for dawn in the vicinity of his aerodrome before landing, which he accomplished without causing injury to his crew or further damage to the aircraft. The high courage and skill which this officer has invariably displayed on many occasions in the face of the enemy set an example which is unsurpassed.

Lieut. R. B. Stannard, who is 37, entered the Merchant Service in the Port Line and was afterwards an Orient Line officer.

Flight Lieut. Learoyd, born at Folkestone in 1913, joined the R.A.F. as a short service commissioned officer in 1936.

They Have Won Honour in Freedom's Cause

Pilot Officer A. W. Dunn, D.F.C. for gallantry. After bombing the Ruhr he flew home on one engine.

Pilot Officer L. W. J. Watt, D.F.C. for displaying bravery in the air. He shot down a Messerschmitt.

Sergt. J. M. Dawson, D.F.M. for gallantry. Though he was wounded, he finished his job.

Sergt. B. L. Savill, D.F.M. for bravery. He continued over his charts with the reserve pilot.

Pilot Officer L. J. Drogo-Montagu, D.F.C. for bravery. He was reserve pilot and bandaged the wounded.

These five officers were engaged in the same raid.

Capt. P. Rowell, Lincolnshire Regt., M.C. for displaying courage during B.E.F. evacuation at Dunkirk.

Warrant Officer H. E. Atkins, M.B.E. for displaying gallantry during the evacuation of B.E.F. at Dunkirk.

Q.M. Sergt. Burridge, of Portsmouth, M.B.E. for displaying bravery and devotion to duty.

Lieut. Wallace Anderson, M.C. for conspicuous bravery and devotion to duty in the face of great danger.

Col. (temp. Brigadier) C. G. Phillips, bar to his D.S.O. for zeal and ability displayed during Norwegian campaign.

Miss A. Ralph, Royal Red Cross 1st Class, highest honour in nursing. Matron-in-chief of Q.A.R.N.N. service.

Miss H. McFeat, Royal Red Cross for displaying untiring devotion to duty in nursing the wounded.

Miss Catherine M. Roy, C.B.E. for displaying great devotion to duty in carrying out her work.

Miss A. Murrie, Royal Red Cross for services to nursing, and displaying devotion to duty.

Matron L. Phillips, Royal Red Cross for services to nursing and displaying devotion to duty.

Capt. G. F. Stevens-Guille, R.N., of H.M.S. "Codrington," bar to his D.S.O. for conspicuous bravery.

Lieut. William King, R.N., of H.M. Submarine "Snapper," bar to his D.S.O. for bravery off Norway.

The Rev. A. T. A. Naylor, D.S.O. for his splendid work in France. Assistant Chaplain to the Forces.

Capt. George Creasy, R.N., D.S.O. for conspicuous bravery shown while on active service.

Lieut.-Cmdr. Viscount Mandeville, O.B.E. for displaying outstanding courage in rescuing wounded men.

Squadron-Leader John Ellis, D.F.C. for displaying great initiative and leadership during Dunkirk evacuation.

Squadron-Leader C. W. Pearce, D.F.C. for his daring action in the sinking of an enemy submarine.

Flight-Sergt. F. G. Berry, D.F.M. for displaying exceptional qualities as a leader during Dunkirk evacuation.

Flight-Lieut. John Simpson, D.F.C. for conspicuous courage in the air against the enemy while wounded.

Flying Officer Eustace Holden, D.F.C. for destroying 4 enemy aircraft and helping to destroy others.

OUR DIARY OF THE WAR

NESDAY, AUGUST 14, 1940
347th Day

ie Sea—H.M. destroyers "Malcolm" "Verity" made contact with six Nazi trawlers and three E-boats. Three vessels seen to be hit.

.dmiralty announced that H.M. cruiser Transylvania" had been sunk by U-boat.

H.M. minesweeping trawler "Elizabeth Angela" reported sunk by air attack.

Swedish steamer "Mongolia" sank in Kiel Bay after explosion.

In the Air—R.A.F. made night attacks on oil refineries and refining plants near Bordeaux. Other bomber formations attacked railway sidings and power station at Cologne.

Both day and night attacks were made on aerodromes in Northern France.

War against Italy — Italians launched violent attacks against British positions in Somaliland, and, after serious losses, compelled our forces to fall back.

Home Front—Thirty-one enemy aircraft destroyed in renewed attacks on British coasts. Seven British fighters down but two pilots safe. Raids made on barrage balloons at Dover, and lightship bombed. Scattered attacks in various areas, including Southampton and Hastings.

THURSDAY, AUGUST 15   *348th Day*

In the Air—R.A.F. again bombed Fiat factory at Turin and Caproni aircraft works at Milan. Blast furnace at Genoa hit.

Other bombers attacked oil plants at Gelsenkirchen and Reisholz, munition factories at Luenen, Essen, Gladbach and Dusseldorf, wharves at Emmerich, supply depots at Hamm and Soest, and several aerodromes in France, Holland and Germany. Dock basin at Helder attacked by Coastal Command aircraft.

War against Italy—In Somaliland British forces continued to hold reserve positions against renewed enemy pressure.

R.A.F. raided Bomba (Libya), damaging float 'planes and flying-boats in harbour. Successful raids made on Macaaca (Eritrea), Jigjiga and Dessie (Abyssinia).

Malta raided by enemy bombers and fighters. Alexandria raided.

Home Front—One thousand enemy aircraft took part in onslaught from Tyne to Plymouth, of which 180 were destroyed by R.A.F. and A.A. defences. Thirty-four British fighters lost, but 17 pilots safe.

Train and houses hit at Seaham Harbour; bombs dropped at Sunderland; industrial premises at Rochester damaged; aerodromes in S.E. attacked; Hastings bombed; unsuccessful attack on Portland. In evening Croydon airport was raided.

Greece—Greek light cruiser "Helle" torpedoed by unidentified submarine while anchored off island of Tinos.

FRIDAY, AUGUST 16   *349th Day*

On the Sea—Reported that five unarmed trawlers fishing off west coat of Scotland had been bombed and machine-gunned by German 'plane.

In the Air—Night raids by R.A.F. bombers over Central Germany. Synthetic oil works at Leuna, near Leipzig, fired. Other objectives were benzine oil plant at Bohlen, Zeiss plant at Jena, Messerschmitt factory at Augsberg, aircraft stores at Kolleda, Junkers works at Bernburg.

Coastal Command aircraft damaged Nazi A.A. ship in Stavanger Fjord.

War against Italy—In Somaliland British bombers attacked Zeila and Adadleh. Italian bombers attempted to raid Berbera, but were intercepted by French aircraft which shot down two and drove off the others.

Tobruk harbour again raided by R.A.F. and considerable damage done.

Home Front—Intense air attacks again made on S.E. areas. Two raids made on London area, when a number of persons were killed. Damage done at Tilbury and Northfleet and in south-western suburbs.

Bombs dropped in Isle of Wight and in country districts in Herts, Essex, Surrey, Hants and Oxfordshire. Deliberate attack made on Eastbourne. Damage and casualties at R.A.F. aerodrome.

Seventy-five enemy aircraft destroyed. Twenty-two British fighters reported lost, but 14 pilots safe.

U.S.A.—President Roosevelt announced that U.S. Government were holding talks with British Government with regard to acquisition of naval and air bases for defence of Western Hemisphere.

Greece—Two Greek destroyers reported to have been bombed by Italian aircraft while en route for Tinos Island. Two Greek cargo boats torpedoed and sunk, and a third bombed.

SATURDAY, AUGUST 17   *350th Day*

On the Sea—Admiralty announced that H.M. submarine "Orpheus" was overdue and presumed lost.

Disclosed that French destroyer "Maille Breze" sank in April near a British port after series of explosions.

In the Air—R.A.F. dropped 3 tons of high explosive bombs and showers of incendiaries on Boulogne, inflicting severe damage. Twenty-six enemy aerodromes raided.

War against Italy—Italian forces withdrew from Fort Capuzzo, following bombardment of the fort and of Bardia by battleships and cruisers of British Mediterranean Fleet. British fighters escorting the Fleet shot down nine enemy 'planes.

In Somaliland enemy renewed determined attacks with picked Italian troops, artillery, tanks and aircraft. British Force withdrew towards Berbera, contesting every yard.

Home Front—No German raid reported between dawn and midnight.

U.S.A.—President Roosevelt and Canadian Premier stated that Canada and U.S.A. were setting up joint Defence Board.

SUNDAY, AUGUST 18   *351st Day*

In the Air—R.A.F. again bombed Italian aircraft factories at Milan and Turin. Other aircraft attacked aluminium works at Bad Rheinfelden, and chemical works at Waldshut. Aerodromes at Freiburg and Habsheim heavily damaged.

Coastal Command aircraft made another successful attack on Boulogne harbour.

War against Italy—R.A.F. made first raid on Addis Ababa, securing hits on hangars.

Home Front—Six hundred bombers and fighters made mass raids on Britain, attempting to reach London. Dog-fights over outer fringe of South London area, where at least one bomber was shot down.

Air fighting extended over Thames estuary, Kent, Surrey, Sussex, Hants and the Channel. Attempts made to bomb train, bus and Green Line coach in S.E. area.

Enemy lost 152 aircraft. Twenty-two British fighters missing, but 12 pilots safe.

MONDAY, AUGUST 19   *352nd Day*

On the Sea—Skua aircraft of Fleet Air Arm attacked two enemy transports at Haugesund, Norway, one being hit.

In the Air—R.A.F. carried out daylight reconnaissances over Holland and North Sea. A.A. position near Amsterdam and aerodrome at Flushing bombed. During night 30 enemy aerodromes were attacked.

Other aircraft bombed naval base at Kiel, oil refinery at Hanover, power station at Zschornewitz, north of Leipzig, Dortmund-Ems Canal and other lines of communication. Oil tanks near Bordeaux attacked.

War against Italy—War Office announced that British forces in Somaliland had been successfully evacuated.

During night R.A.F. bombers attacked Derna harbour, petrol dump at Bir el Gobi, and aerodrome at El Gubbi.

Home Front—Enemy raids on Britain were on minor scale. Five aircraft brought down. Three British fighters lost but pilots of two safe. Dock in South Wales and several aerodromes were attacked.

TUESDAY, AUGUST 20   *353rd Day*

On the Sea—Survivors of British freighter torpedoed without warning in Atlantic landed in Northern Ireland.

Mail steamer "St. Patrick" attacked by three German bombers off south Wexford coast.

In the Air—R.A.F. made daylight raids on enemy aerodromes. Coastal Command aircraft attacked two German destroyers in North Sea, damaging one.

War against Italy—Middle Fast G.H.Q. reported that whole of British force evacuated from Berbera had reached Aden with bulk of equipment.

R.A.F. bombed hangars and railway station at Diredawa, aerodrome at Dessie, and railway buildings at Kassala.

Ineffective raids on Malta and Gibraltar.

Home Front—Waves of German bombers, accompanied by fighters, crossed S.E. coast and were met with fierce A.A. fire and later engaged by R.A.F. fighters. Enemy lost nine aircraft, Britain two.

During preceding night enemy operated singly over widespread areas of England, South Wales and a few districts of Scotland. German aeroplane crashed in Co. Kerry.

H.M. submarine "Orpheus" (Lieut.-Commander J. A. S. Wise, R.N.) was reported on August 17 to be considerably overdue and presumed lost. Sister ship to the "Odin" and "Oswald," she was completed in 1930 and had a displacement of 1,475 tons. Her armament consisted of eight torpedo tubes and one 4-in. gun, and her complement was 53 officers and men.

Photo, Wright and Logan

The War Illustrated

RUNNING THE GAUNTLET OF GERMANY'S CROSS-CHANNEL GUNFIRE

This small British merchant ship was among those in the convoy shelled in the Straits of Dover for the first time by long-range German guns from the French coast on August 22, 1940. Astern of her is a destroyer. It was estimated by observers that from 80 to 100 shells were fired, but the convoy kept on and not a single ship was hit. Later German 'planes flew over the convoy and dropped bombs, but these too missed their mark. *Photo, Keystone*

The First Year of the War Seen in Retrospect:
by Maj.-Gen. Sir Charles Gwynn, K.C.B., D.S.O.

Now that the war has lasted for a year it may be well to review the strategical situations
and developments which have marked its course. Here, then, is such a review, as
authoritative as it is comprehensive, written by Major-General Sir Charles Gwynn,
Military Critic of the " Daily Telegraph and Morning Post " and Joint Editor of " The
Second Great War."

THIS war is one between a nation whose aggressive policy has committed it to offensive action and peace-loving nations who have relied on their power of defence and their superior economic position to wear down the resources of her aggressor.

At the outset, Germany's hopes lay in achieving rapid and decisive success. The Allies, for their part, were prepared to fight a long war, relying mainly on the stranglehold of the blockade and a steadily increasing development of their resources to secure a position which would enable them to dictate their terms.

Germany's advantage lay in that the initiative rested with her, that she could take action at her selected time, and that her opponents were so scattered that she could fall on the weaker while standing on the defensive against the stronger when and where it suited her purpose. Moreover, she had no scruples about attacking neutral countries if invasion of their territories would place her in a favourable position. The action of the Allies, on the other hand, was restricted by respect for the rights of neutrals and by scruples in the use of the air arm, which was the only weapon with which they could carry war into the enemy country. Germany was, therefore, well placed to employ both offensive and defensive action to further her designs.

A glance at the map of Europe shows how favourably Germany was placed to exploit her advantages. It will be seen, although there was no fighting till September 1939, that the war really began when Germany entered Austria in March 1938. That move turned the flank of Czechoslovakia's carefully-prepared defences. At Munich, in September 1938, she was induced to surrender her defences, and in March 1939 Germany occupied the whole country. Employing

lies, Fifth Column activities and threats of ruthless air warfare, Hitler had achieved two strategic victories without striking a blow. Poland, which had been induced to take some part in the elimination of Czechoslovakia instead of coming to her assistance, was now exposed to attack. Hitler had thrown off the mask and his ambitions were revealed. Poland was to be his next victim. France and Britain decided that, even at the risk of a world war, they must call a halt to Nazi aggression.

But it was impossible to save Poland. Outmatched numerically and in armaments, she could also be attacked from three sides. Moreover, her industries on which her armament supplies depended lay in the most exposed part of the country. Her armies were stationed to defend them, right between the jaws of the German pincers. But the Poles relied on mobility and manoeuvre and no great fortified position had been constructed.

Without a declaration of war, Hitler launched his attack. In the first surprise the small Polish air force was wiped out by German bombers before it could leave the ground. Then German armoured divisions cut through the Polish armies or through the gaps between them. Infantry and artillery masses followed. The jaws of the pincers began to close, and retreat to escape them

was inevitable. But orderly, well coordinated retreat was impossible. The German armoured divisions, closely supported by aircraft, had already penetrated deep into the country, disrupting the organization of control on which skilful manoeuvre in retreat depends. Confusion reigned in rear of the Polish armies, intensified by the action of parachutists who blew up bridges, cut telephone wires and damaged railways, aided by the large German element of the Polish population. The country was riddled

General Hans von Seeckt, who commanded the small German Army permitted by the Treaty of Versailles and laid plans for its subsequent development on a grand scale ; he died in 1936, before his machine could be launched. Top, Polish soldiers in action, in September, 1939.
Photos, Wide World and Planet News

with Fifth Columnists. Gallantly as the Poles fought—and their resistance at Warsaw was a memorable feat of arms—the end was inevitable. The Russian stab in the back eliminated the last hope that a remnant of Poland's armies might continue the struggle with their back to Rumania, through whom the Allies might have sent supplies.

Could France and Britain have saved Poland ? The answer must be, No. Their armies, still unprepared, were confronted by the strongly fortified Siegfried Line, attacks on which would almost certainly have failed. Their air forces, though they

Illustrating the Polish campaign of September 1-17, 1939, this map shows the direction taken by the principal German drives. As in France nine months later armoured and motorized columns, preceded by waves of bombing 'planes, blasted the road to victory.

A Study in the Strategy of the Land Campaigns

might have reached Poland, could not have operated there for lack of equipped bases. To have attacked Western Germany would have involved initiating a form of warfare against which the Allies had set their faces, since it involved dangers to non-combatants. Moreover, German reprisals would have interfered with the development of French resources.

With the end of the Polish campaign a long lull set in during which only sea power remained active.

Hitler was not yet fully prepared for a life and death struggle with Britain and France. It is probable that he expected that the Allies would accept the *fait accompli* and give him a respite in which to prepare for his next move. The peace offensive which he launched to that end failed, however. He could, therefore, neither force the issue nor could he avoid it. Germany was feeling the effects of the blockade, and her own counter-blockade of Britain by submarines and mines was having no success. It was a situation which must have tested Hitler's nerve, but Dictators cannot draw back.

Hitler Makes His Choice

What were the alternatives open to him ?

(1) He could stand on the defensive, hoping with the help of counter-blockade measures to wear down the determination of the Allies. That, however, meant sacrificing the initiative and exposing his people to long periods of hardships with no successes to buoy up their spirits.

(2) He might attempt to crush the morale of the British and French people by launching an unrestricted air attack on them. His air force, numerically, was still greatly superior to that of the Allies. There were, however, strong arguments against such a course. The German people would have suffered from reprisals. Damage, irreplaceable owing to the blockade, might be inflicted on German munition and other industrial establishments.

Moreover, air attack on Britain presented difficulties. She could be reached by bombers, but she was out of range of fighting aircraft, which experience had shown were necessary as escorts to bombers. Experience had shown,

Most of the European countries engaged in the war of 1914-1918 were also involved in that which broke out in 1939, but (as this map makes clear) the alinement of the belligerents varied considerably. Only Sweden, Switzerland and Spain escaped the one war and (as yet) the other.

too, that the moral effect of bombing was often to irritate rather than to cow.

(3) Counting on the inability of the Allies to attack, he could wait to expand his army and air force, make good the wastage of the Polish campaign, and then, at his chosen moment, use his army and his air force combined in one desperate attempt to secure decisive victory.

When he decided on the last course we do not know, but preparations for it must have been put in hand with the greatest vigour from the beginning of the lull. The Allies could also, of course, use the lull to develop their strength ; but, as we now know, they did not take full advantage of the opportunity. Worse still, the French lost some of their ardour during the months of idleness and, according to neutral observers, became obsessed with the idea that all that would be required of them would be the comparatively easy task of defending the Maginot Line. During the lull the invasion of Finland served to distract attention from the main arena, and the gallant fight made by the little

Hitler owed much of his rapid success in Norway, as elsewhere, to the Fifth Column, and all too seldom were the nefarious activities of the traitors nipped in the bud. Here French soldiers, forming part of the Allied Expeditionary Force, are marching off a batch to a concentration camp.
Photo, Service Cinématographique de la Marine

On Land the Rush of Mechanized Armament

Here is one of the German mechanized columns which, as described in this chapter, formed the spearhead of the German attack against the Allied flank on May 14. The heavily armoured German cars find that their progress is impeded by concrete barriers that narrow the track down until it is only a few feet wide.
Photo, Keystone

Finnish army against desperate odds tended to encourage Allied confidence in the powers of defence.

Then came the invasion of Norway and Denmark. This may have been intended by Hitler to cause dispersion of the Allied forces ; or it may be that he had not finally decided to risk a great offensive, and desired to have Norway as a base for counter-blockade measures in case he finally decided on a defensive policy.

In the event he acquired a useful asset, but probably at a higher price than he expected. The petrol and food supplies he looted were of immediate value to him, and he eliminated the possibility of Norway, under Allied pressure, becoming a less complaisant neutral. Although the venture had cost him dear, it certainly helped to strengthen Hitler's prestige as an invincible and ruthless conqueror.

Fortunately, the Allies decided not to throw good money after bad, but cut down their commitments in Norway when it was seen that it was hopeless to save her. If they had not done so they might have become involved in a side show that would have placed a heavy strain on their navies and shipping resources.

We now come to Hitler's Blitzkrieg, his great effort to achieve a rapid decision. Let us look at the weapon his General Staff had sharpened for him. It was specially designed for offensive action, though it could equally be used to parry.

General Von Seeckt, who organized the small army allowed to Germany by the Treaty of Versailles, made the original sketch of the weapon to be forged if and when the rearmament of the Reich became possible. He visualized an army in two parts. First, a highly mobile, strongly armed spearhead, mainly composed of armoured vehicles, which by a rapid surprise blow might hope

to penetrate the enemy's defences ; it could then spread confusion in the enemy's rear, disrupting his system of command and seizing strategical points. Behind the spearhead would come the rest of the army, composed of slower-moving but powerful formations of infantry and artillery, which would enter and enlarge the gap and take advantage of the confusion.

Von Seeckt's successors accepted his basic conception and, when Germany rearmed, perfected it. To give power to the army, which all Germans had been brought up to look on as their main weapon, it was decided to use the air arm in close cooperation with it. Armoured vehicles are partially blind ; aircraft could give them eyes. Armoured fast-moving vehicles could not bring with them sufficient guns and ammunition to crush well-entrenched positions ; bombing aircraft could supplement deficiencies of artillery. Moreover, attack from the air, which troops on the ground find themselves unable to answer, produces moral effect much greater than that caused by the actual casualties it inflicts.

Rôle of Germany's Air Force

There was, however, of course, nothing to prevent the German air arm being used independently and ruthlessly if occasion made such use effective. But the German air force, with little time available for training during the process of rapid rearmament, specialized in army cooperation—not on air combat and navigation to the same extent as, for instance, did the R.A.F.

As a further aid to increasing the confusion caused by the rapid action of the mechanized spearhead, the idea of using parachute troops was borrowed from the Russians. It was used with effect in Poland and Norway ; and, in the latter campaign, the situation necessitated the employment of troop-carrying air-

craft. Those campaigns too showed that the idea of rotting the fibre of his opponents by propaganda and corruption, expounded in Hitler's "Mein Kampf," could play an immense part in strategy and increase the effectiveness of parachute troops.

That was the weapon, depending for its power less on new and powerful weapons than on the nice adjustment of its constituents for cooperation. How could it be used ? The Maginot Line closed the French frontier, and evidently the German General Staff refused to risk blunting or breaking their weapon in a direct attack on it.

More neutral countries must be added to the list of Hitler's victims in furtherance of his plans if they refused to surrender their rights. And the Low Countries obviously stood in his way. Once again Flanders was to be the cockpit of Europe.

War in Europe's Cockpit

While the lull continued, the Low Countries had been useful to Germany as a source of supplies and as providing loopholes in the blockade. But if the war was to be won by a Blitzkrieg their value in that respect became of less importance. Instead, they were required to provide access to France and to furnish bases for air and submarine attack on Britain. There were, too, other considerations. If Holland and Belgium were invaded Hitler knew that a large portion of the Allied armies would move to their assistance, leaving the positions prepared with much labour on the Franco-Belgian frontier. It was true that Holland and Belgium had strengthened their own defences, but, in the hopes of maintaining their neutrality, they had refused to make any plans with the Allies as to the nature of the assistance they would require. Under these circumstances it was probable that the comparatively small and poorly-equipped Dutch and Belgian armies would suffer severely before help reached them ; and that the Allies' contingent, drawn out of its defences, would be encountered under conditions of more or less open warfare—conditions for which the German army was specially trained and had had experience in Poland.

Invasion of the Low Countries and a frontal encounter with the Allied armies, while still on the move, formed the primary element in the German plan. But such an encounter might lead only to the orderly retirement of the Allies, reinforced by Belgian and Dutch troops, to prepared positions on which static warfare conditions would develop. A Blitzkrieg required a more decisive success. A successful withdrawal had, therefore, to be prevented and an attack in flank would obviously make withdrawal difficult. The Allies' flanks were, however, protected by the sea on one hand and by the formidable obstacle of the Meuse river on the other. East of the Meuse, too, Luxembourg and the Belgian Ardennes, hilly country with poor railway communications and few roads, presented obstacles to a mass flanking attack. A surprise attack by swift-moving and powerful mechanized formations might, however, find a weak spot. If such an attack succeeded, far-reaching results would be attained. If it failed, the main attack in the north could still go on and at the worst the German army could stand on the defensive, having at least secured bases in Holland and

In the Air Hordes of Terror-inspiring 'Planes

Belgium favourable for air attack on Britain. Such were the main features of the German plan to avoid desperate attacks on the Maginot Line.

On May 10 Holland and Belgium were invaded. The Dutch and Belgian troops fought gallantly, but mechanized divisions and air bombardment succeeded in making gaps in their lines. The Dutch fell back behind their main inundation defences and there they offered stout resistance, till air-borne troops, assisted by Fifth Columnists, created an ulcer at Rotterdam in their rear. It was, however, the threat of reducing their towns to ruins by bombing attacks that caused them to lay down their arms. To show what they were prepared to do, the Germans had deliberately destroyed a large part of Rotterdam.

The Belgians also fought well, but the capture of a bridge over the Albert Canal, which formed their main line of defence in the north, compelled a gradual retirement to a second line running from Antwerp to Namur along the line of the Dyle. Perhaps the Germans, deliberately, did not press the pursuit with too great energy. Certainly they did not use their air force to any great extent to hamper the advance northwards of the Allies, who had at once responded to Belgium's call for help. By the fifth day of the invasion, therefore, the Allied armies, fully committed, were taking up their positions on the Dyle line. The junction of the defending forces had been accomplished, and there seemed fair prospects of stemming the German invasion.

Then, on May 14, the German flank attack was delivered ; and for this the spearhead was used. Mechanized columns, which had been driving back the weak Belgian detachments in the Ardennes, appeared on the Meuse. At Sedan and Dinant vital bridges were captured undamaged ; at Sedan especially there was an onrush of heavy tanks. The defence, surprised and demoralized by bombing attacks, collapsed. The spearhead had broken through.

The causes of the disaster are not yet fully known and need not be dwelt on. It is evident, however, that it was not solely due to the invulnerability of the new heavy tanks the Germans brought into action, for their vulnerability was subsequently established. Whatever the causes, demoralization spread ; and the gap was widened and remained open. Armoured divisions poured through and, supported by infantry carried in lorries, swung rapidly westwards, cutting the communications of the armies in Belgium. In the confusion caused, the extent of the danger may not have been at once appreciated

and there appears to have been some delay in ordering the retreat, obviously necessary. It may have been thought that the German thrust would spend itself and become immobilized owing to supply difficulties. Counter-attacks would then restore the situation. By living on the country, drawing petrol from roadside pumps, and by capture of depots, the spearhead, however, maintained its mobility and, encountering little opposition, reached the coast. The lorry-borne infantry, acting defensively, secured the corridor through which it had passed against weak counter-attacks. Where, we may ask, were the French reserves, especially mobile armoured formations which might have delivered a powerful counter-blow ?

Pressed from the north by the main German army, hampered by hordes of refugees, it was impossible for the armies in Belgium to cut a way through to the south. The story of the retreat to Dunkirk needs no repetition. Gallant fighting by all services saved the personnel of the B.E.F. But German strategy had won the day, though, man for man and weapon for weapon, the German army had no superiority.

France Swept to Destruction

The success of the great coup, which probably exceeded German expectations, left the heart of France exposed to attack. She had lost a large part of her army, and almost all the assistance Britain could give her on land. Her prepared defensive positions had been overrun ; the Maginot Line had not only lost its value but had become a subject for derision and recrimination. Italy was in her rear. Worst of all, her army and her leaders, political and military, had become demoralized. Germany gave them no time to recover. With amazing speed her army, in spite of its great exertions in Belgium, advanced south, sweeping away Weygand's attempts to organize resistance. France surrendered ; and Britain, greatly

weakened, was left standing alone. German strategy, German belief in offensive action supported by diabolic ingenuity and ruthlessness, German readiness to take risks, had triumphed.

Hitler might well have expected Britain to give up an unequal struggle, but Britain stood firm in her determination, not merely to defend herself, but, in the end, to destroy Nazidom. Her Island Fortress was manned and strengthened before Hitler could reorganize his forces. Her Navy tightened its stranglehold and included Italy in its grasp. Her Air Force performed prodigies in defending her shores and in carrying war into the heart of Germany.

Hitler, after a year of victories, is faced by a new strategic problem, more difficult and involving greater risks than those which confronted him when he could use the whole strength of his army for the destruction of France. His army is halted by the sea. To send even part of it across involves tremendous difficulties and dangers. He must depend almost entirely on his air force to achieve the quick victory he needs. But his air force has met a formidable antagonist, one superior in combat and one that can carry warfare into the heart of Germany.

Can Hitler's General Staff find a solution to his problem before the stranglehold of Britain's Navy and the offensive attacks of her Air Force paralyse Nazi power ?

Opening on May 10, the Battle of the West swiftly extended over the Low Countries and Northern France. The principal drives are indicated above, culminating in the thrust to the coast at Calais which led to the retreat from Dunkirk.

In the lightning invasions of neutral countries which the Germans achieved in the first year of war, the Luftwaffe played an important part in acting as the eyes of the mechanized columns, as well as in spreading terror among the civilians. Above, German bombers are going into action in conjunction with the mechanized army. Preparation for this was the chief part of German airmen's training, to the neglect of air combat and navigation.

Undertones of War on the Western Front

For the first eight months of the Second Great War it was almost true to say that it was "All quiet on the Western Front"—certainly far truer than at any time between 1914 and 1918. There were artillery bombardments—our upper photograph shows a big German gun in action against the French lines—and on the one side and the other a state of constant alertness was preserved. The men on the right are poilus in the forward defences of the Maginot Line with their rifles trained on the opposite loopholes in the West Wall.

Photos, British Official, Central News, E. N. A., and Planet News

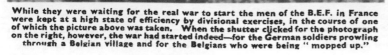

While they were waiting for the real war to start the men of the B.E.F. in France were kept at a high state of efficiency by divisional exercises, in the course of one of which the picture above was taken. When the shutter clicked for the photograph on the right, however, the war had started indeed—for the German soldiers prowling through a Belgian village and for the Belgians who were being "mopped up."

One Tremendous Year of History

by E. Royston Pike

An impressionistic survey by the Literary Editor of "The War Illustrated," who week by week throughout the year, has described the course of the war and painted the background—historical and geographic, social and economic—against which the immense drama has pursued its earth-shaking course.

BEFORE their wireless sets, in castle drawing-rooms and cottage parlours, in club lounges and the bars of village inns, they grouped themselves the men and women who remembered the last war. These were they to whom the joyous clatter of the maroons on November 11, 1918 had sounded deliverance; they had believed in their hearts that henceforth of a certainty there should be no more war. Since then twenty-one years had passed, and as they stood there they looked around on the children that the years had brought—looked at them for the first time with eyes of pity, half ashamed of the begetting and conceiving that had given them entrance into such a world.

Into a silence that was almost too deep to be borne cut the sombre tones of Mr. Chamberlain's voice. He was sitting at his desk in Downing Street. "This morning the British Ambassador in Berlin . . . a final Note . . . unless we heard from them by 11 o'clock . . . war would exist between us. I have to tell you now that no such undertaking has been received, and that consequently this country is at war with Germany." Slowly the words so heavily charged with fate broke the stillness. "It is the evil things that we shall be fighting against—brute force, bad faith, injustice, oppression, and persecution. . . ."

The tension was broken, and with voices a little strained, perhaps, the flow of chatter was resumed. There was a clatter of knives and forks as they laid the tables for dinner. Behind the bars they were busy filling up the tankards of the men whose memories were of Gallipoli and the Somme.

Then the note of drama was sounded again. Above the medley of homely sounds and familiar voices wailed the shriek of the air-raid sirens. For a second or two they thought that it could not be true, but all doubts were dispelled by the blasts of the wardens' whistles. Swiftly they reacted according to their mood and circumstance. Some went out into the garden and scanned the skies. Some shepherded their little ones beneath the kitchen table. The streets were cleared for the most part by the bustling wardens and police, who looked more than a little self-conscious in their steel helmets. There was a steady troop of people into the air-raid shelters; and beside the buses parked along the kerbs the drivers and conductors exchanged their reminiscences of war.

After a few minutes another siren sounded, and the flow of life went on. The blinking crowds emerged from their subterranean refuges; the sky-gazers became conscious of their empty glasses; the suburban housewives rushed to see what the passing minutes had done to the Sunday joint. Life went on, but not as before. The war had begun, and that very night the waning moon splashed its cold light over the stricken "Athenia," first of the U-boats' victims.

For Poland's thirty-three millions the war had begun three days before, when at 4.30 on the morning of September 1 Hitler had launched his legions across her frontier. Already the Poles had experienced in large measure the pains and passions of war.

Germany's prison ship, the "Altmark," had almost reached home when on February 16, 1940, the prisoners heard the thrilling words, "The Navy is here!" This photograph was taken after the "Cossack's" daring attack.

putting up a most gallant resistance, but against the armed might of the invader the Poles were like a naked and weaponless man fighting a deadly duel with one completely armoured and armed to the teeth.

Yet nothing could daunt the natural valour of the Polish soldiers. They fought as the Poles throughout the centuries have always fought when defending their native soil against the invader. To the German tanks and armoured cars, to the roaring hordes of bombers, the Poles replied with the rattle of musketry; with fantastic bravery their horsemen charged the steel cavalry of the enemy. Thousands turned a deaf ear to the order to retreat, and died on the line they had resolved to defend to the uttermost; their comrades withdrew ever nearer to their country's heart, turning now and again to rend the foe with fury when he presumed too much on his superiority of arms and men.

For seventeen days the campaign in Poland continued, and then on September 17 Poland was stabbed in the back by Russia. Yet, even so, the Poles abandoned nothing but hope of victory. Warsaw, though completely surrounded, kept the Germans at bay for another ten days; and for weeks and months news trickled through to the outside world of bands of Polish soldiers and irregulars who had refused to lay down their arms.

And, though defeated, Poland never made peace. A year has passed since Hitler proudly boasted that the German Army had won a victory unprecedented in history, but a Polish Government is in London, and a Polish Army, having covered itself with glory in Norway and in France, forms part of the garrison of the British fortress. Polish airmen fly beside their British comrades; and in Poland itself the millions of Poles are living and working for the day of revenge.

While through those days of blazing September sunshine German and Pole were locked in combat, in the west France's great army was mobilized and took up its position in the Maginot Line—that monument of misplaced confidence, as a few

One of the most striking of the many amazing victories won by the Finns over the Russians was that of Suomussalmi, where in the opening days of the New Year the Finns annihilated the 44th Division of the Red Army. Among the booty were 43 tanks.

Already their country was bleeding from a multitude of wounds. Within a few hours their air force had been driven from the skies or flamed to heaven in blazing ruin. On a front of some 1,600 miles her armies were

From September 8-28, 1939, Warsaw, under the leadership of her stout-hearted Mayor, M. Starzynski, maintained a heroic resistance against the besieging Germans. Not until a large part of the city had been converted into a smoking shambles did Poland's capital surrender.

Photos, Julien Bryan and Planet News

Broken by the Brutal Hands of Barbarians

months later it was proved to be—while Britain, all too slowly at first, set about the mustering of her mighty forces and resources. As in all the wars for centuries past the Royal Navy patrolled the ~~~s and kept them open despite all that U-b. .., surface raider, and mine could do. With the single exception of Eire all the family of nations who comprise the British Commonwealth rushed to stand side by side with Britain in the hour of her mortal danger. " We stand with Britain," said Australia's Prime Minister, and the same day, September 3, New Zealand joined her in declaring war against Germany. Three days later South Africa came into the war, with General Smuts once again at her helm ; and on September 10 Canada, united as never before, ranged herself beside her sister nations. From the princes and peoples of India, from the islands of the Indies and of the southern seas, from the colonies and protectorates and mandated territories of Africa—from every corner of the Empire, from every people in the Commonwealth, sounded the answering note of passionate loyalty to the ideals which Britain, not for the first time in her history, had drawn the sword to defend.

While the war was still only a few hours old, men were rushing to enlist in the Empire's armies, and on September 12 it was officially announced that the vanguard of a new British Expeditionary Force had landed in France. Very different in many ways was the new B.E.F. from the old—how the

" P.B.I." of 1914-1918 would have appreciated the motorized transport of 1939 !— but the spirit of the men was as high and the reception given to them by the French people was as whole-hearted. Soon the men of khaki had taken their places at the front ; and on them, in their billets and defence lines, descended the long months of winter—a winter marked by no event more exciting than a trench raid, a winter of rain and wind, of ice and snow and frost, more bitter than any within the memory of living men.

Glorious Battle of the Plate

It was indeed a miserable winter, one which exhausted the bodies and depressed the spirits of the millions on either side whom war had torn from their homes and settled occupations and flung into situations novel and dangerous. Only one ray of light illumined the December weeks, and that was composed of the funeral flames of one of Germany's much-vaunted pocket battleships. All the world outside Nazidom was thrilled by the story of the " Graf Spee," chased into the neutral harbour of Montevideo by Harwood's three British cruisers ; all the world, including Nazidom, listened-in to Montevideo on the night of December 17 when the " Graf Spee," her wounds hastily patched, sailed out into the River Plate to meet her end. Some thought she would fight, some that she would surrender ; few there were who had anticipated that inglorious end on a mud bank in the river, where the pride of Hitler's navy blazed and smoked into a tangled mass of scrap metal.

Only for a few days were men's eyes turned towards the sunny waters of the South Atlantic ; for the most part during the weeks that closed the old year and opened the new their attention was riveted by the extraordinary struggle in the snows of Finland, where a little people defended themselves against the Russian colossus. In October, following his seizure of half

Poland, Stalin had stretched out his hands to the three little Baltic republics, Estonia, Latvia, and Lithuania, and without any difficulty had converted them into puppet States. He tried the same thing with Finland, and, perhaps to his surprise and certainly to the world's, the Finns dared to resist him.

Outnumbered by twenty or thirty to one, with few 'planes and little mechanized equipment, the Finns maintained a resistance hardly equalled for heroism in the whole history of war. In " General Winter " they found a most puissant ally, and tens of thousands of Russians were wrapped by the snows of Finland in the sleep of death. Hundreds of 'planes were brought down by the Finnish marksmen ; hundreds of tanks sank to disaster in the snowdrifts ; villages with strange-sounding names sprang into fame as the battlefields where a few thousand of Finnish soldiers had defeated, nay crushed, the choicest regiments of the Red Army. On the Mannerheim Line in the Karelian Isthmus the Finns made a superb stand, and when at last it was outflanked rather than overrun, the military critics spoke somewhat pityingly of its planning and construction. The Maginot Line was so very much better . . .

At last Russia's uncountable hosts crashed their way through to victory. Finland submitted to Stalin's will. But never, so long as men continue to delight in deeds of bravery, will Finland's fight be forgotten.

Finland's surrender was dated March 12, but still Scandinavia remained in the very forefront of the news. There was much diplomatic parleying—sometimes in not very diplomatic language—between the Allies and Norway concerning the use of Norwegian territorial waters by ships conveying Swedish iron-ore from the Atlantic port of Narvik to the German harbours. Once, on February 16, Britain's destroyers invaded Norway's waters and intercepted the " Altmark," Germany's prison-ship of infamous repute, which was conveying a number of British merchant-seamen as prisoners-of-war to Germany. The daring adventure was cheered to the echo at home and abroad, while Germany shrieked with unavailing rage.

Early in the next month—on April 8—the Allies mined Norwegian waters so as to bar the passage of Germany's ore ships, and the next day Germany retaliated with a move which had obviously been prepared long before, for the ships which disgorged their cargoes of armed men on to the quays of Narvik, Bergen, and Trondheim had already arrived in good time for zero hour.

So began the German invasion of Norway —one of the strangest incidents in a year full of strangenesses. A few hundred German soldiers marched unopposed into Oslo, and, while a military band kept the people quiet with martial music, occupied all the strategic points until

On April 9 and again on April 13, 1940, the British Navy struck at the German warships at Narvik. Here is one of the German destroyers that was set on fire.

After little more than a fortnight in Norway the Allied forces were withdrawn ; this photograph shows British troops embarking at Namsos. Left, German soldiers hoisting the swastika flag over the palace of King Leopold of the Belgians at Laeken, near Brussels.
Photos, British Official : Crown Copyright ; Central Press, and Planet News

Europe Will Be Saved by Britain's Example

they could be strongly reinforced by sea and air. Too late the Osloans awoke to the fact that they had been bluffed into surrender; too late Norway as a whole realized her folly in not linking her fortunes with those of the Allies, relying instead on an out-of-date conception of neutrality.

Off the coast of Norway Britain's fleet, supported by Norwegian guns, took heavy toll of Hitler's navy, but the evil had been done. Thousands of German soldiers had entered the country, thousands more arrived day by day, and when the Allied Expeditionary Force landed at Namsos and Aandalsnes, they were not only opposed by an enemy immensely superior in arms and numbers, but from beginning to end they were subjected to an aerial bombardment as demoralizing as it was devastating. Landing in the middle of April, the British troops were withdrawn in the first days of May. It was an ill-conceived adventure. Not for the first time—and not, alas, for the last—Germany's opponents had taken action too late.

In Britain the news of the evacuation of the British troops from Norway was received with anger and disgust. Until but a day or two before the withdrawal the people had been buoyed up by hopes of victory based on the most extravagant reports received from neutral sources, which the British authorities, while not confirming, had done little to "debunk." When the truth became known the re-action was all the more violent. There were bitter speeches in the House of Commons, and Mr. Chamberlain's Government, already undermined by months of criticism because of its failure to grasp the realities of a great and grim situation, tottered to its fall. On May 10 it crashed, and other and greater things crashed with it, for on that day the Nazis invaded Holland and Belgium.

Churchill, Man of the Hour

While on this side of the North Sea Britain girded up her loins under the inspiring leadership of Winston Churchill, Hitler's war machine crashed its way across the dykes and fields, through and over the towns, of the Low Countries. Holland's resistance lasted a mere five days, but in those five days the Dutch did all that brave men could do. Only when the heart of Rotterdam had been made a shambles by squadrons of Hitler's bombers, only when the whole of the Netherlands had been converted into a battlefield in which the invaders were all too ably assisted by Fifth Columnists and parachute troops dropped from the skies, only when a quarter of her little army had fallen on the field of battle—only then did Holland sue for peace.

In Belgium the struggle was more prolonged, for King Leopold appealed for help to Britain and France, who immediately denuded their fronts in France by rushing divisions to his aid. On the very first day of invasion the British Expeditionary Force crossed into Belgium, and a few days later was in action beyond Louvain. But in the

In five days—May 10-14, 1940—the German invaders overran Holland. This German motorized unit is crossing the Maas by barge, the hatch-covers making a runway.

French sector there were "incredible mistakes," and when the German armoured divisions poured in an uninterrupted flood across the Meuse the Allies in Belgium were forced to retreat. For days there was a veritable welter of battle, a confusion of warring columns, one vast morass of tragedy. Along roads packed with a populace fleeing in terror from the German bombers, British and Belgians and French strove to maintain a fighting front.

But the Germans hit hard and even harder. On May 28 Leopold of the Belgians ordered his men to lay down their arms, and with the French armies on their right verging on collapse, the British retreated to the coast in a desperate bid for survival. From Dunkirk from May 30 to June 4 a motley armada snatched the khaki army from the very jaws of the German pincers. The B.E.F. lived to fight another day, but with the loss of all its equipment. It was indeed, as Mr. Churchill said, both a miracle of deliverance and a colossal military disaster.

Still all was not lost in France—at least, so it seemed. On May 19 Weygand supplanted Gamelin, and with pathetic faith the French trusted him to work that miracle which alone could save their country. On the Somme and Aisne the old general endeavoured to form a line of resistance, but the new type of war in which the armies were engaged demanded too much of brains which had learnt little since 1918. The tide of German victories was unstemmed. On June 14 the Germans goose-stepped through Paris, and on June 21 France's plenipotentiaries sat in the railway coach at Compiegne where 22 years before Foch had dictated terms to a defeated Germany.

Now it was France's turn to taste the bitterness of defeat, and Hitler saw to it that France's cup of misery and humiliation was filled to overflowing. Just before the final capitulation of France as a military power, Mussolini deemed the moment opportune for

On June 21, 1940, France's delegates arrived at Compiègne to negotiate their country's surrender (circle). Just before France's capitulation Italy declared war; in the lower photograph an Italian warship is in action against the British squadron on July 9. *Photos, Keystone and Associated Press*

intervention, and in the streets of Mentone his troops won what he, at least, described as a great and glorious victory.

In nine months Poland had been conquered, Norway overrun, Denmark seized, Holland subjugated, Belgium crushed. Now France was flung on the altar of sacrifice. Under Pétain and the men of Vichy she bowed to every German demand. At the old Marshal's behest no opposition was forthcoming from the French colonies, and even France's Navy would have passed into Germany's possession if it had not been put out of action or seized by the navy of the country which until so recently had been her firm ally. The battle of Oran on July 3 was perhaps the year's saddest day.

On the continent of Europe Hitler now strutted as the greatest conqueror of all time. Only Britain stood out against him. So, as the first year of war drew to its close, against Britain the Fuehrer discharged his fleets of bombers and fighters, while along the 2,000-mile coast from the North Cape to the Pyrenees he plotted and prepared for that invasion which he confidently predicted would bring Britain to her knees. Alone she stood against a continent in arms. And yet not alone, for beside and behind her were grouped the mighty nations of the English-speaking world. There was never a false note in her trumpet-blast of defiance. "We stand on the road to victory," said Mr. Churchill in his magnificent oration in the House of Commons on August 20, and "we mean to reach our journey's end."

'Mid Falling Bombs London's Firefighters Go To It

Photo L.N.A.

The City of London experienced its first air raid of the war on the night of Saturday-Sunday, August 24-25, 1940. A number of high explosive and incendiary bombs were dropped, and a big fire was started in a warehouse block which received a direct hit. The fire was prevented from spreading by the London Fire Brigade and the A.F.S. This spectacular photograph was taken when the raid was still in progress. This was the first real test under war conditions of the A.F.S., and they behaved as seasoned firemen. A particularly high tribute was paid to the A.F.S. women and girls, who " stuck to their posts like heroines."

Photo L.N.A.

London is Bombed by Stealthy Night Raiders

Owing no doubt to the heavy losses it had sustained in mass attacks on Britain, the Luftwaffe first reverted to sporadic raids and then cautiously combined these with operations by larger formations. Still the losses of Nazi pilots were enormous, so the Nazi airmen came in at night by stealth, and on August 24 the first bombs fell on Central London.

I N the third week of August the Luftwaffe again changed its tactics and resumed mass attacks by day, though sporadic " hit-and-run " raids were not abandoned. In what proved to be the first of a series of night raids on London the Nazis, during the night of Thursday, August 22, dropped bombs on several outer suburbs. The next night, for the first time, bombs fell on Central London.

Another notable change was that the enemy no longer made any pretence of confining his raids to objects or places of military importance. By night there might be some little excuse for him, owing to the efficient blacking out of our towns ; but even by day, when he could quite clearly distinguish his targets, he dropped bombs on churches, cinemas, blocks of flats, working-class houses and similar objectives, the destruction of which could not possibly aid him directly in waging the war.

On Wednesday, August 21, the Nazis made mainly for our aerodromes, where only slight damage was caused. Two dive-bombers attacked a town in the South-east. The first dropped screaming bombs that did little harm ; the second launched a torpedo, and eight houses out of a row were demolished. In a raid on a Midland city several bombs dropped in close succession and killed and injured a number of people, including children. When a Dornier bomber was shot down two of the crew surrendered to farm workers ; the third was captured by the wife of a Home Guard, who ran to the scene with her boy of 14 (he snatched up his father's rifle as he went). In the evening the raiders again attacked R.A.F. aerodromes, but few ventured far over the coast.

Soon after midday on Thursday, German coastal guns bombarded a British convoy in the Channel, but no ship of the convoy or escort was hit. Later the convoy suffered aerial attack, but our fighters engaged the raiders and drove them off, shooting down one machine. Elsewhere few enemy aircraft crossed our coasts and no bombs fell on land.

In the early morning of Friday bombs were dropped by single raiders on London

suburbs. In one locality, where ten bombs fell, a cinema was wrecked. Fires were caused in houses where other bombs fell, but the A.R.P. services soon got everything well in hand. Delay-action bombs were used by the enemy. Strangely enough, in another raided suburb some miles away another cinema was destroyed. In this district five bombs had fallen close together, yet comparatively little damage had been done and not one fatal casualty was reported.

The Sergeant-Pilot of a " Spitfire," who had to bale out after shooting down a bomber and came down in the Channel, is here being brought ashore in a rowing boat.

Here a motor boat is going all out to attempt to rescue the crew of a German bomber brought down into the sea in flames. Left, an injured German airman is being helped on his arrival in London.

During Friday various parts of Britain were raided by solitary bombers in what seemed to be pointless operations. Murderous machine-gun fire was opened on people on beaches and others in the streets. Late at night a few bombs were dropped on the outskirts of London but caused no casualties.

Saturday was an eventful day that ushered in a week-end packed with incident. After shelling Dover from the French coast in the

This photograph shows Folkestone as it appeared when seen from the east on August 26, 1940. About noon on that day enemy aircraft dropped many bombs on the town, destroying houses on the sea front.

Photos, Planet News, Keystone and Fox

While Nazi Raiders Over Britain are a Nuisance

The seats of this cinema in a London suburb were smashed to fragments when a bomb wrecked the building during a night raid on August 22.

This house was demolished in the raid on London on August 25, only one wall being left standing. Two fireplaces are all that now remain of an Englishman's home.
Photos, Keystone & Fox

London's six-hour raid on August 27 was the first of the Nazis' "nuisance" raids. Here is a baker's premises which were damaged. Employees hurriedly left and the loaves were spoiled.

morning the enemy made an aerial attack on the town, doing little damage. Then Ramsgate was very heavily bombed, entire rows of houses being demolished. The local gasworks was set on fire, and after firemen had got to work on the conflagration the raiders came back again to machine-gun them. Ramsgate, like a neighbouring resort, has contrived spacious shelters in tunnels through the chalk beneath the town. Here some 60,000 persons can take refuge quickly and in security. At Manston aerodrome, near Ramsgate, considerable damage was done to buildings by raiders. Another R.A.F. aerodrome also was attacked and persons killed.

At Portsmouth, several working-class and residential districts were very severely bombed and hundreds of people rendered homeless. The attack was made by forty aircraft which were so harassed by our defences that they dropped their bombs indiscriminately over a wide area. In the main shopping district of Southsea, near by, scores of windows were blown out. People in a Portsmouth cinema had a narrow escape when a direct hit wrecked the building; the roof and gallery fell in, but most of the audience had left when the sirens sounded and only eight persons of the few left were killed. In raids on a south-eastern area "Molotov's bread-baskets" filled with incendiary bombs were dropped.

At 8.30 a.m. and again at 3.30 p.m. the sirens sounded in the London area, but the raiders got only as far as the outskirts. Half an hour before midnight there came another warning, after two bomb explosions had

GERMAN & BRITISH AIRCRAFT LOSSES
German to April 30, 1940

							German	British
Total announced West Front, North Sea, Britain, Scandinavia	...	...	...	...	...			195
Unofficial estimate of additional 'planes damaged in Norway...	...	...	...	...	...			200
May	...	...	...	...	...		1,990	258
June	...	...	...	...	...		276	177
July	...	...	...	...	...		245	115
Aug. 1-27	...	...	...	...	...		1,022	282
Totals, May to Aug.	...	...	...				**3,533**	**832**

DAILY RESULTS, August 1-27

	German Losses	British Losses	British Pilots Saved		German Losses	British Losses	British Pilots Saved
Aug.				Bt.fwd.	675	191	52
1-7	10	15	—	Aug			
8	62	18	3	18	152	22	12
9	1	1	0	19	5	6	2
10	1	4	0	20	7	2	1
11	66	29	2	21	13	1	1
12	62	17	1	22	10	4	2
13	78	15	10	23	4	0	—
14	31	11	2	24	50	21	12
15	183	34	17	25	55	17	3
16	180	37	17	26	47	17	11
17	1	0	—	27	4	1	—
	675	191	52	**Totals**	**1,022**	**282**	**96**

Notes.—The main attack on Britain began on Aug. 8— up to the 27th there were 13 mass attacks.

None of the figures include aircraft bombed on the ground or so damaged as to be unlikely to reach home.

On Aug. 20 the Air Minister stated that Germany had lost **701 aircraft** since Aug. 8, in attacks on Britain, with more than **1,500 personnel**. By Aug. 27 German losses had increased to **1,012 machines** in 20 days. Our A.A. guns had shot down many more German raiders than had been expected. British losses in the period Aug. 8-27 were **267 aircraft** and **186 pilots**.

been heard near the central area. A screaming bomb fell on a large commercial building in the City. Flames rose 150 feet high from the fire that resulted, and soon the intense heat had set other buildings ablaze near by. The glow could be seen for miles, and it was an hour before the outbreak could be got under control by a large force of regular and A.F.S. personnel.

From adjoining buildings jets were directed on to the main blaze through broken windows, and the steady work of the fire-fighters began to take effect. The City church of St. Giles, Cripplegate, was struck by a bomb which blew in part of the wall and damaged the windows. A statue of Milton outside was overturned. Another bomb fell in the quadrangle of an L.C.C. block of flats and did no harm. In a suburb another large fire was caused when a factory was hit by incendiaries. A group of houses across the road became involved, but the occupants were taken to shelters and no one was hurt. Smaller fires broke out after hits by incendiary bombs, but prompt action soon got them under control.

The behaviour of the people called forth the highest admiration.

On the following Monday everyone went about his business with coolness and a determination that Hitler's terror-tactics should fail. But, stung by this indiscriminate bombing of centres of population, people began to ask when Berlin's turn would come.

More massed attacks by day were made on Sunday, August 25. A force of eighty bombers and fighters tried to come in over the Dorset coast, but were driven off with heavy losses. At least 24 enemy machines were shot down.

Britain's Bombers Carry the War to Berlin

After the air raid on London on August 24 the cat (left) returned to a wrecked warehouse next day. The rabbit was a survivor of August 22, when its owners' home was destroyed.

Another formation bombed the Scilly Isles, one person being killed.

Twelve Spitfires, in a battle over Portland, during which 43 raiders in all were shot down, accounted for a dozen of the enemy—three Do 17s, six Me 110s and three Me 109s. Ten pilots returned to their base ; of the remaining two, one baled out safely and the other was picked up by a steamer. Magnificent work was done also by a Hurricane squadron —six Messerschmitts shot down and three others shattered. Another Spitfire squadron shot down six Messerschmitt Jaguar fighter-bombers, part of a force that came over in waves, three and a half miles up in the air.

Night attacks were made over a wide region in the South and also in the Midlands —where for several hours waves of bombers came over. Hundreds of incendiary bombs were dropped, but little damage was done except to house property. Bombers reached the outskirts of London, and a few bombs were dropped ; little damage was done. In all fifty-five enemy aircraft were shot down on Sunday.

The R.A.F. bombed military objectives in the Berlin area during Sunday night, but the Air Ministry was careful to make it clear that this—the first bombing raid on the enemy capital—was in no sense a reprisal for the bombing of London. The next night (August 26-27) selected military objectives again were

attacked, though poor weather conditions hampered our pilots. A.A. batteries and searchlight concentrations on the outskirts of the German capital were bombed also.

While the R.A.F. bombers were thus carrying the war into Germany the enemy on Monday made his biggest and longest night raid on Britain. Sounding at 9.30 p.m., the London sirens sent people into shelters, and not till nearly four o'clock on Tuesday morning was the " Raiders Passed " signal heard. For six hours bomber after bomber, flying very high, tried to get through to the capital. Bombs were dropped on the outskirts of Central London, and in outlying districts. Three raiders were shot down, and little damage was done. The night attacks were widespread, raiders coming in along a 500-mile stretch of coast.

Earlier in the day London had had another warning, when raiders tried to approach by the Thames Estuary, but were engaged and scattered by our fighters. On Monday afternoon three waves of enemy aircraft had attacked along the S.E. coast. Some tried to destroy the balloon barrage at Dover, while others swooped down over Folkestone and

dive-bombed at a low level. Essex and Sussex were attacked by raiders coming over the Thames Estuary. Another wave, late in the afternoon, concentrated on Portsmouth. In all areas the enemy was repulsed with heavy losses by our fighters. Forty-six raiders were brought down, with the loss to the R.A.F. of 15 machines (11 pilots saved).

Though small formations of enemy aircraft came over the Channel coast on Tuesday, August 27, few ventured far inland ; three were shot down. At night London had two warnings—at about 9.30 and again a little after midnight. The raiders were checked at the outer defences and mostly jettisoned their bombs. A few incendiary bombs fell in the London area and did little damage ; there were no casualties reported. On every hand it was clear that the raids had merely stiffened the Londoners' morale. In most places of amusement artistes and audience helped each other to while away the hours until the " Raiders Passed " sounded. Railway and road transport held back their services so that belated passengers might get home in time, after a brief respite, to take up anew the day's war effort.

These anti-aircraft gunners of a battery in England are examining with justifiable pride evidence of their success. The mass of tangled wreckage is the remains of a Dornier bomber which they brought down with their first shot when it was about to drop its " eggs " over England.

Above is one of the houses at Ramsgate that was practically destroyed on August 24, when about 250 bombs were dropped on the town. But Ramsgate has one of the finest air raid shelters in the country. Three and a half miles of tunnels excavated in the chalk on which it is built, provided refuge for 11,000 people, but there was room for well over 40,000 more. Right is an undamaged shelter behind a house at Portsmouth ; the house was destroyed by a bomb on August 24. The raiders bombs have not affected the famous dockyard. *Photos, Fox, Topical, Central Press, Planet News and G.P.U.*

For Centuries to Come These Episodes Will R

MILESTONES of the FIRST TW

1.—*SEPTEMBER 1, 1939.* At dawn the
Army marched into Poland, and, de
broken bridges, made rapid progress

2.—*SEPTEMBER, 1939.* The first troop
new B.E.F. landed in France.

3.—*NOVEMBER 4, 1939.* President
signed the " cash and carry " Neut
in Washington.

4.—*DECEMBER, 1939.* Russian aeroplane
Finnish towns and civilians with i
bombs.

5.—*DECEMBER 17, 1939.* The " Adm
Spee," badly damaged by the c
" Exeter," " Achilles " and " Aj
scuttled outside Montevideo harbo

6.—*FEBRUARY 12, 1940.* The first troo
2nd Australian Imperial Force a
N.Z.E.F. disembarked at Suez.

he Opening Year of the World's Greatest War

of the SECOND GREAT WAR

H 18, 1940.   Hitler and Mussolini met
ennero on the Brenner Pass to discuss
plans.

14-19, 1940.   First British troops landed
orway, to be warmly greeted by the
ace.

0, 1940.   At dawn, without any warning,
an troops marched into Belgium and
nd.

26 - JUNE 4, 1940.   By the amazing
try of the Army and Navy, four-fifths of
E.F. was evacuated from Dunkirk.

14, 1940.   The tragic day on which
an troops for the second time in 70
marched into Paris.

JST, 1940.   In the midst of the aerial
zkrieg " the Nazis made repeated
ks on the British balloon barrage.

Across the Channel Whined the German Shells

For the first time in her history England was shelled from across the sea when in the course of the battle of August 1940 German guns, mounted on the French coast not far from Calais, bombarded not only a convoy of merchantmen passing through the Straits but the land in the region of Dover.

THE first shells to arrive on British soil from across the Channel killed two A.R.P. workers and wrecked some houses in the Dover area on the morning of August 13. At first it was thought that bombs had been dropped—a reasonable supposition enough in view of the hundreds of bombs which had been unloaded on the South-east coast for days and weeks before—but as no aeroplane had been seen nor had the noise of falling bombs been heard, it was concluded that not bombs but shells were responsible. This view was supported by the metal splinters picked up, as these resembled shell fragments rather than bomb splinters.

A few days later all doubts were removed when German heavy guns established in emplacements on the French coast not only shelled a convoy of eighteen merchantmen steaming up the Straits of Dover, past "Hell's Corner," scene of some of the greatest of German air raids, but later in the same day bombarded the Dover area.

"Shortly before noon today," read an Admiralty and Air Ministry communiqué issued on August 22, "one of our convoys in the vicinity of the Straits of Dover came under fire from heavy guns mounted on the French coast. The warships escorting the convoy at once laid smoke screens to conceal the convoy from the enemy. Although some shells fell fairly close to ships, no ship of the convoy or escort was hit or received damage."

Firing from a distance of some 20 to 23 miles, the German guns bombarded the ships as they passed through the narrowest part of the Channel from near Folkestone to opposite Dover harbour. Groups of people assembled on the white cliffs of Kent saw the flashes of the guns coming from the French coast, and a few seconds later watched huge fountains of water spurting around the ships, followed by the sound of terrific explosions, which shook the very ground. As mentioned in the communiqué, the escort ships shielded their charges with a dense smoke screen, and the eighty or a hundred shells fired in the course of an hour or so failed to reach their target. In any case, as naval experts pointed out, it is exceedingly difficult to hit a target moving on the sea at such a distance.

About 9 o'clock that evening the German guns opened fire on the English coast. The bombardment lasted for nearly three-quarters of an hour, and was opened by a salvo of three shells, which screamed their way across the narrow Channel and crashed into some buildings behind the sea-front of Dover, throwing up a column of sparks and debris. Other shells followed in quick succession.

But hardly had the shelling begun when R.A.F. bombers took the air and in a few minutes were subjecting the German batteries to a tremendous aerial bombardment. Those who were watching from the Kent coast saw numerous flares coming down the sky, streams of orange shells or "flaming onions," and white flashes as of bombs bursting. Hardly a sound could be heard across the 20 miles of intervening water, but the flashes and bursts, and the German searchlights excitedly probing the night sky, proved beyond a doubt that the gunners across the sea were not having at all a nice time.

The first of the British bombers was over its objective—somewhere in the neighbourhood of Cape Gris Nez between Calais and Boulogne—soon after 9.30, and others took up the attack at intervals until 3.35 a.m. High-explosive bombs and incendiaries were dropped at Cape Gris Nez and at battery positions located near Audembert and St. Inglevert in the same area—and this despite intense anti-aircraft fire from the German guns as the British 'planes approached the French coast. On the next night the R.A.F. were up above Cape Gris Nez again with a force of medium bombers, and they repeatedly bombed the gun positions from heights ranging from 10,000 to 4,000 feet ; and their visit was repeated on the night of Sunday, August 25. The Germans, for their part, also continued their spasmodic shelling of the Dover region, with resulting damage to property and some loss of life.

Some military experts expressed the opinion that the Germans were using guns of about 12-inch calibre, firing them from emplacements set a few miles from the coast ; possibly the guns themselves are on railway mountings, so that after firing they can be moved back into camouflaged security. Others went further and suggested that they were 15-in. or 14-in. French guns from the Maginot Line—guns which had been primarily designed for shelling German towns in the Saar and Rhineland at a distance of 20 to 30 miles, although so far as is known, and for whatever reason, they were never actually fired. In any case they are not "freak" guns, such as was "Big Bertha," the gun which, throwing a shell of 9·1-in. calibre of stream-line shape, shelled Paris towards the end of the last war at a range of nearly 75 miles.

Nor are the Germans alone in being able to fire across the Channel, for it was revealed that on the same day as the convoy ran the gauntlet of German shell-fire in the Straits of Dover, British gunners fired a few rounds at the German positions near Calais.

Such long-range bombardment has a nuisance value, but its military effects are hardly likely to be important. It would have to be a very heavy bombardment indeed, and one very long sustained, to drive, say, British troops from their positions on the Kent coast ; and if Hitler is depending on his big guns at Calais to secure the Channel for his army of invasion he is likely to be disappointed.

The Straits of Dover, showing regions within the range of guns at Calais, Cape Gris Nez, and Boulogne.
Courtesy of the "Daily Telegraph"

Above is the upper part of a church at Dover wrecked by a German shell fired on August 22. In the remarkable photograph below, taken from the British coast during the bombardment, flashes from the German guns (right) can be seen, and (on the left) a parachute flare dropped by one of the British 'planes that showered bombs on the German gun emplacements. *Photos, Associated Press*

Hitler's Coast Guns Did Not Stop the Convoy

These unique photographs were taken on August 22 on board one of the escorting warships of the convoy which was the first to be shelled by the big guns on the French coast. The convoy is seen ploughing bravely on while a salvo of shells falls amidst it.

Alec McMallen (above), ship's carpenter of one of the vessels in the convoy, was contentedly smoking his pipe when he got to port. Right, the commander of an escort ship watches Nazi bombers overhead.

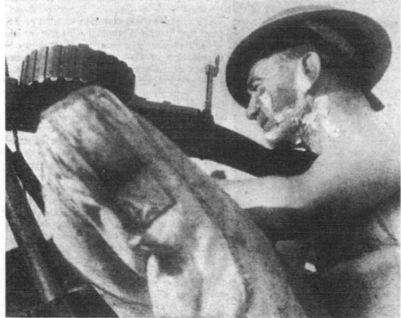

Directly an attack is imminent every man on the escorting warships is instantly at his action station. The gunner above was shaving when the call came, and did not even wait to wash the lather from his face. Right is Signalman K. Stene, who was busy all through the bombardment.   *Photos. Central Press and Sport and General*

John Bull and Uncle Sam Keep Rolling Along!

The war is coming very near to America—so near that, with a speed and unanimity
which would have been altogether out of the question only a few months ago, the U.S.A.
is not only adding to her own defences but is abandoning her long-cherished and
carefully-preserved isolation.

SITTING at his desk at the White House, President Roosevelt greeted the newspapermen on August 16 with his customary affability. Indeed, he made it clear that he was particularly glad to see them, because he had three announcements to make of very great importance, present and future.

When the pressmen were all attention the President announced in slow, carefully-chosen words that the United States Government had entered into conversations with the British Government with regard to the acquisition of naval and air bases for the defence of the Western Hemisphere, and especially of the Panama Canal.

This was indeed headline news, but the President had not finished. Mr. Roosevelt went on to say that, in addition to conferring with the British Government, his Government was carrying on conversations with the Canadian Government concerning the defence of America. Finally, he announced that, at the invitation of Mr. Churchill, military and naval officers of the U.S.A. were already in Britain as observers of the great battle now raging.

It was understood that a day or two before Mr. Roosevelt and Mr. Churchill had been in communication—presumably by way of the Transatlantic telephone—and had discussed the possibility of the U.S.A. leasing naval and air bases from Great Britain. The situation of the bases was not made public, but it was generally believed that the negotiations concerned Newfoundland, Bermuda, and that great chain of British islands composed of the Bahamas, Jamaica, Leeward and Windward Islands and Trinidad, and British Guiana on the mainland of South America. Bases established in any of these territories would supplement the present

American naval and air bases in Cuba, Puerto Rico, and the Panama Canal zone, and would obviously constitute an immense reinforcement to the defences of the Panama Canal, perhaps the most vital of America's lines of communication.

In effect, the Caribbean Sea would be closed against unwelcome intruders—and on the subject of intruders Mr. Churchill and President Roosevelt may be relied upon to think alike. Only one non-American Power threatens the safety of the Canal and the integrity of some or all of the Latin-American republics, and that power is Nazi Germany.

So much for the southern defences of the U.S.A. Turning now to the north, we see that vast undefended frontier—the longest undefended frontier in the world—which for nearly 3,000 miles separates the U.S.A. and Canada. America has no fear of Canadian aggression, just as Canada has no fear of American designs on her territory. But such is the range of modern aircraft that it is not outside the bounds of possibility that Hitler

On this map America's principal naval and air bases guarding the entrance to the Panama Canal are shown by crosses. The white circles indicate British possessions where the United States hopes to lease other bases.
Courtesy of the " Daily Mail "

should attempt to establish air bases on the frozen shores of America's far north, as well as in Greenland and Iceland. It was with intense interest and considerable relief that Americans learnt that Canadian and British troops were holding Iceland against Hitler; and they greeted with a chorus of approval President Roosevelt's announcement that an arrangement was being negotiated with Canada whereby the U.S.A. would move troops to Canada whenever it might be necessary to repel a threat to the security of the one country or the other.

On August 17 President Roosevelt met Mr. Mackenzie King, the Canadian Prime Minister, at Ogdensburg on the American side of the St. Lawrence, and the meeting resulted in an agreement that a Permanent Joint Board on Defence should be set up to commence immediately studies relating to sea, land, and air problems. In a broad sense, the authorized statement declared, it would consider the defence of the northern half of the Western Hemisphere.

Two years before, when making his famous goodwill visit to Canada, President Roosevelt had made the declaration that " I give to you the assurance that the people of the United States will not stand idly by if domination of Canadian soil is threatened by any other empire "; and two days later Premier Mackenzie King had said that " We, too, have our obligations as a good friendly neighbour, and one of them is to see that at our own instance our country is made as immune from attack or possible invasion as we can reasonably be expected to make it ; and that, should the occasion ever arise, enemy forces should not be able to pursue their way by land, sea, or air to the United States across Canadian territory." Now the understanding and the resolve were carried a big step further. The U.S.A. made it as plain as could be that an attack on Canada would be an attack on the U.S.A., and would be resisted at once by the great republic with all her armed might.

Closely linked in the popular mind with the question of bases and the defence conversations with Canada—though the connexion was carefully disowned by President Roosevelt—was the suggestion that the U.S.A. should sell a number of out-of-date destroyers to Great Britain. In the matter of destroyers the U.S.A. Navy is the strongest

The assurance given by Lord Lloyd, Britain's Colonial Secretary, to the Bermuda House of Assembly in August 1940, that "there is no question of Bermuda, or any part of it, being separated from the British Empire," followed close upon a visit of the Duke of Windsor to the island on his way to the Bahamas. His Royal Highness is here seen inspecting a naval guard of honour on his arrival in Bermuda on August 8.   *Photo, Planet News*

The Destroyers Are Ready—Will Britain Get Them?

Here, in this remarkable photograph of Philadelphia Dockyard, are some 130 of the American warships which were laid up after the last war. Nearly all are destroyers, of which it is hoped that at least 50 will be transferred to the British Navy. Most of these are of the same type, of about 1,100 tons, with a speed on trials of 35 knots.
Photo, Central Press

in the world, with its 237 destroyers actually built and 60 more on the stocks ; but of the former, 167 are "obsolete," in the sense that they are more than 16 years old ; in fact, they were built towards the end of the last war. For some time before the present war most of them had been lying in the American naval yards, but when war broke out in Europe President Roosevelt ordered that they should be reconditioned so that they could be employed on the neutrality patrol in the North Atlantic—" to watch what is going on," as the President put it.

On August 4, in a broadcast to the American nation, General Pershing, who was Commander-in-Chief of the American Expeditionary Force in 1917, urged that the United States should make available to Britain at least 50 of these over-age destroyers as part of its help in defending democracy and assisting the security of the U.S.A. If the destroyers so sent helped to save the British Fleet, then America herself might be saved from another war. " We shall be failing in our duty to America," he added, " if we do not do it."

The suggestion was taken up in many quarters, and it was generally believed that President Roosevelt himself strongly favoured it. As for his opponents of the Republican

Party, Mr. Wendell Willkie, in the speech accepting his nomination as Republican candidate for the Presidency, at least gave his tacit approval when he said that "We must honestly face our relationship with Great Britain. We must admit that the loss of the British Fleet would greatly weaken our defence. This is because the British Fleet has for years controlled the Atlantic, leaving us free to concentrate on the Pacific. If the British Fleet were lost or captured, the Atlantic might be dominated by Germany, a power hostile to our way of life, controlling in that event most of the ships and shipbuilding facilities in Europe. This would be a calamity for us. We might be exposed to attack on the Atlantic. Our defence would be weakened until we could build a navy and air force strong enough to defend both coasts."

Before the destroyers could be sold to Britain, however, it might be necessary to repeal a law passed in 1917 forbidding the sale of vessels constructed for the U.S.A. Navy, and perhaps special legislation would be involved. It was suggested that the destroyers might be transferred to Canada

instead of to Britain direct, or that they might be disposed of to private firms as "scrap" on the understanding that they should be resold to Britain. Whatever the method adopted, the American public welcomed the idea that the destroyers should be made available for Britain, more particularly in view of Mr. Churchill's declaration to the Commons on August 20 that His Majesty's Government had informed the United States Government, "spontaneously, and without being asked or offered any inducement," that they were ready to place defence facilities at their disposal by leasing sites in our Transatlantic possessions.

They welcomed it, in a word, as but one illustration of that working together which, to quote Mr. Churchill again, would cause America and Britain to become "somewhat mixed up together in some of their affairs for mutual and general advantage." With gladness in their hearts they heard him applaud the process of Anglo-American mingling. "Like the Mississippi, it just keeps rolling along. Let it roll. Let it roll on full flood, inexorable, irresistible, benignant, to broader lands and better days."

Twenty Acres of Scrap Torn Down from the Sky

FROM August 8 to August 27 the total " bag " of enemy aircraft credited to the R.A.F. was over 1,000. Many of these fell on British soil, and as a result the Royal Air Force, as a side-line of its heroic exploits, made a generous contribution to the Minister of Supply's call for scrap metal. The photograph at the top of the page was taken at one of the big dumps covering no fewer than 20 acres. The great mass of twisted and broken metal is a veritable graveyard of the remains of Nazi fighters and bombers. They are worth thousands of pounds as scrap. First examined by technicians, who search for any new features of construction, workmen, who obviously enjoy their task, then break up the fuselage and engine for melting down. About 160 men are employed merely in piling up the lorry-loads of wrecks.

Photos, Associated Press and Topical

R.E.s Dig Up Time Bombs Like Potatoes!

The Nazi air raids on Britain have the double purpose of attacking military objectives and spreading terror among the civilian population. For the latter the enemy has two new weapons—the "screaming" bomb and the delayed-action bomb. Many of the bombs fall deep into the earth and do not explode until hours or even days later. Some that fell in a London suburb on Friday, August 16, did not explode until the following Sunday morning. Therefore, in bombed districts everyone should avoid small holes in the ground and recently disturbed earth, for there may be a delayed-action bomb beneath.

Time Bomb Diagrams :

A is the fuse in the tail; as soon as the bomb strikes the ground a trigger is released which allows acid to reach the metal plate, B. The acid gradually eats through the plate and eventually reaches the fuse, so firing the explosive, C. The bomb is fitted with an armour-piercing nose-cap, D. Right, a delayed-action bomb has got home. The deeper it penetrates into the earth, the greater the damage it does.

Diagrams courtesy of the "Daily Mail"

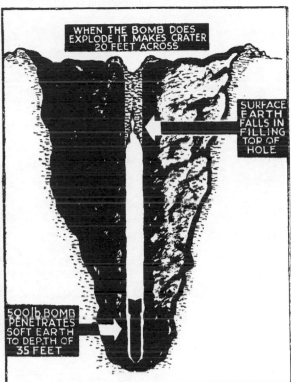

WHEN THE BOMB DOES EXPLODE IT MAKES CRATER 20 FEET ACROSS

SURFACE EARTH FALLS IN FILLING TOP OF HOLE

500 lb. BOMB PENETRATES SOFT EARTH TO DEPTH OF 35 FEET

Here men of the Royal Engineers are digging on a spot where a delayed-action bomb is known to have fallen. They are now only just below the surface, but they will have to go much deeper and, as seen below, towards the end of the excavation the earth has to be taken out carefully and hoisted to the surface.

THE dangerous work of dealing with delayed-action bombs falls to the lot of the Royal Engineers, and in this page they are seen carrying out their life-saving work. There are two methods of rendering the bombs harmless, depending on the place in which they fall. If on open ground, well away from anything to which they might cause damage, they are exploded where they lie. When this is done they form craters as much as 20 feet in diameter. If, however, bombs fall close to buildings another method must obviously be used, so the bombs are dug out and carted away, to be exploded where they can do no harm. The work is carried out by the officer in command, after consulting with the local authorities, and the men have become so used to their dangerous task, and have learned so thoroughly the best method of dealing with each individual case, that they go about their work as calmly as if they were digging potatoes.

Above is a squad of the R.E. specially qualified to tackle delayed-action bombs ; they have just dealt faithfully with another one, the latest of many. At times they may have to dig down as much as twenty feet before they find their quarry.

Photos, L.N.A.

More Chevrons for the Minesweepers' Funnels

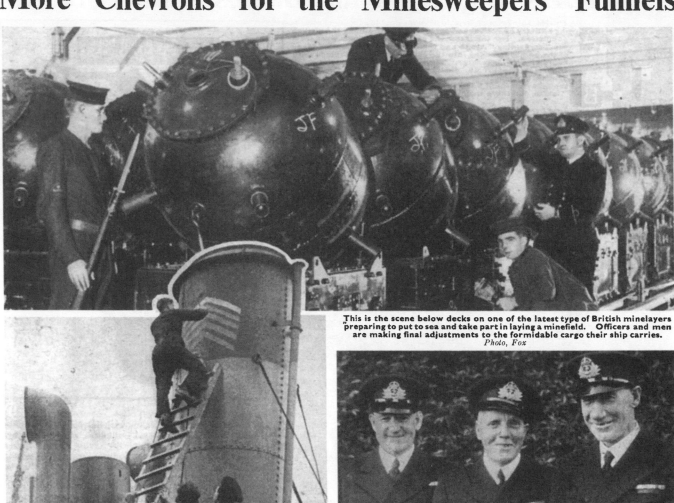

This is the scene below decks on one of the latest type of British minelayers preparing to put to sea and take part in laying a minefield. Officers and men are making final adjustments to the formidable cargo their ship carries.
Photo, Fox

These three skippers of minesweepers—which before the war were trawlers—were decorated by the King with the Distinguished Service Cross on June 10 for "unfailing courage and devotion to duty." They are, left to right, George Abernethy, Isaac Parkinson and Thomas Fraser.

These men of the mine-sweeping trawler "Cordella" are among the crews who paint chevrons on their ships' funnels to record the number of mines they have destroyed. Above, the ship's artist is at work on the fifth chevron. Right, a minesweeper has just earned another chevron, for the mine it has caught explodes harmlessly astern.

Photos, "Daily Mirror" and Associated Press

Eye Witness Stories of Episodes and Adventures in the Second Great War

Sixty Shells Dropped Round My Ship

A new form of attack on shipping was begun on August 22, when German batteries on the French coast between Boulogne and Calais unsuccessfully shelled a convoy passing up the Channel. The following eye-witness stories of the attack were told by captains of ships in the convoy to Laurence Wilkinson, of the "Daily Express."

STEAMING up the Channel on August 22, Captain George Hunter had just commented to his chief engineer on their luck in having sailed round the coast for nearly a year of war without a scratch. Then suddenly there was a crash on the seaward side of the ship, and three great spouts of water shot in the air.

Describing the scene afterwards, Captain Hunt said :

We both looked, but nothing was said. I thought, " Have I spoken too soon ? "

I looked out of the window on the bridge, but I could not see any aircraft. That seemed funny. What else could it have been but bombs?

It was all quiet for a bit. We were puzzled, but the convoy went on as though nothing had happened. Then, suddenly, " Wham ! Swoosh ! " And there were three more mountains of water shooting up—uncomfortably near.

After that it got a bit monotonous. The salvos of shells came over at almost regular intervals of five minutes.

I sent the chief engineer down below. I had a feeling that we were going to get a packet of trouble, and I thought it was no good both of us being killed.

He had not been down below more than a few minutes when the next salvo shook the ship. The bridge was awash with about a foot of water from the spouts. I got my ankles wet. There must have been a 'plane high up in the sky spotting for the Germans.

The naval vessels escorting us did a first-class job. They shepherded us through, telling us where and how to steam, and at what speed. To give us cover, they raced about us throwing out a smokescreen.

The shelling seemed to be coming from all the way along the coast between Boulogne and Calais. We could see the flashes of the guns, and in the seconds that followed we wondered if any one was going to get a packet.

Then we heard the whistle and the thud and saw the waterspouts.

In between salvos I rummaged around to collect any shell splinters I could find. I put

Captain George Hunter who was in command of one of the ships in the convoy that was bombed in the Channel on August 22, is here seen on the bridge after his ship reached port.

some aside in a handkerchief. I thought the Admiralty might like to have a look at them and, anyway, they'll do as souvenirs.

The stuff they were throwing over was heavy, wicked stuff. I guessed they must have been from heavy guns.

I thought, " I seem to be getting some-

This photograph gives some idea of the ordeal through which the convoy, of which Captain Hunter's ship formed part, passed. As the ships steamed up Channel on a perfect day through sunlit waters, the batteries on the French coast opened fire. The convoy turned as close in shore as possible, yet beneath the white cliffs of England shells still hailed upon them. That they should have escaped without loss was a heartening proof both of bad German marksmanship and good British seamanship.
Photos, Associated Press

The escape of the convoy that was shelled from the French coast was in some measure due to the speed and great efficiency with which the escorting destroyers laid smoke screens and dropped smoke floats. Here, during the attack described by Captains Hunter and Storm in these pages, a destroyer is sending out a smoke screen which in a few minutes will make the whole convoy invisible both from the air and the sea.
Photo, Fox

body else's share," because time and again the salvos seemed to be coming near to me, and I nearly always got a throwback in the way of shrapnel. Other ships in the convoy seemed to be missing a good bit of the fun.

Quite sixty shells dropped around my ship. It was a nasty experience. Bombing from an aeroplane is not so bad, as I found out later in the day when bombers attacked us.

Before they had half done their job, our Spitfires came roaring down on to them, scattering them like dust. You never saw flying like it. Our fellows were marvellous. The Germans just took one look at them, and then seemed to vanish out of the sky.

A somewhat different view was held by the master of another ship in the convoy, Captain Archibald Storm, who said:

We were in the rear of the convoy and saw the first shells drop. A couple of them dropped into the sea between my ship and the shore, and then another couple came.

Some of the other ships probably never saw those four shells. I think they were just trial shots, so that the spotting 'plane could put the gunners on their target.

Nothing happened after that for about half an hour. We were still wondering what it was all about when the shelling started in earnest.

If it was intended for us it was well off the mark, though other skippers in the convoy may have had worse luck than me.

I took my ship through the first big convoy attack in the Channel—the attack which started at night with German E-boats firing torpedoes and raking us with machine-guns in the darkness, and ended up with a terrific bombing attack.

Compared with that, today's experience was not very frightening. It struck me as more of a try-out than a serious attack.

waiting on the wall when we got back, and the odd thing was that only one of them, the police-sergeant, moved to help me get the canoe out of the water. And nobody in that crowd had sufficient presence of mind to offer me a coat, although all I had on was my pyjamas, and they were soaking wet!

Miss Peggy Prince is here seen standing beside the small clinker-built canoe with which she effected the rescue described in this page
Photo, " Daily Mirror "

I Rescued An Airman In My Canoe

A gallant rescue was performed on August 14, 1940, by Miss Peggy Prince, who paddled a canoe some two miles out into the Channel and picked up one of the crew of an R.A.F. bomber. The next day, Miss Prince broadcast the story of her adventures, and it is given below in her own words.

AT twenty to six on the morning of August 14 there was a terrific hammering on the door of the house, and we found a couple of soldiers, who had come to tell us that there was an aircraft down in the sea about two and a half miles out.

They came to our house because I have a ten-foot Canadian type canoe, about the only boat left in the neighbourhood. They asked if they could borrow the canoe to go out to rescue any of the survivors from the 'plane. They thought it was a German bomber. I didn't know these men or whether they could manage a canoe; my canoe is only three feet wide and not so easy for a novice. So I asked them if they knew anything about canoes, and they didn't, so I said I'd go along.

We carried the canoe over three rolls of barbed wire, over a concrete wall and down a ladder to the beach. One of the soldiers said he was going to come with me, and I fitted him carefully into the canoe. He insisted on bringing his gun, in case there was any " funny " business, and so we set off.

By this time the aeroplane had sunk. She had sunk even before we got the canoe launched, and we'd been in such a hurry to get her down that I hadn't any time to take any bearings from the land. I tried to steer for a buoy which seemed to be near the spot.

When we got out near the buoy I stood up, but I couldn't see anything at all, and the canoe was leaking, so I turned back.

When we got back to land there were quite a lot of people, and they told me that there were three people in the sea, swimming a little bit farther than the point we had reached. So I set out again, but this time I left the soldier behind. It was about a couple of miles I had to go, and this time one of our Hurricanes flew over me and led me to the place, where I picked up a sergeant of the R.A.F. A motor fishing boat had come out and was picking up the other two.

I have no idea how the sergeant got into the canoe without overturning it. He had swum to the buoy for which I had been making, and I tried to hold the canoe steady while he climbed in; but he was very exhausted. I wrapped my coat around him and paddled back. On the second journey out it was a bit of a race between me and the fishing-boat, but I was determined to get one of the men after having been out once already. The sergeant told me afterwards that, when he saw the canoe coming, he made up his mind that he would be rescued by the canoe, so he submerged to keep out of the way of the fishing-boat.

There were well over a score of people

We Ran Into a German Balloon Barrage

Some fighter pilots' experiences have already been told in this series (see pages 165 and 191). The contrasting dangers and difficulties of the R.A.F. bomber squadrons are vividly described in the following account of some exciting incidents during night raids over Germany during the month of August.

A TWENTY-THREE-YEAR-OLD pilot in a heavy bomber squadron, broadcasting an account of some of his experiences on August 14, said :

We had a bit of excitement a few nights back when we ran slap into the middle of a German balloon barrage. Our luck was in. Not only did we get away with it, but we brought one of the balloons down.

Our target that night was a synthetic oil plant at a place called Gelsenkirchen, which is in the middle of the Ruhr. It was a dark night—very dark—and we had come down to about six thousand feet to find the target. We dropped our flares and located and bombed the works, then we climbed and went back to see what results we'd had. My second pilot was flying the 'plane. I'd been down in the bomb-aimer's position, which is in the nose of the aircraft, doing the bombing.

Suddenly I saw a long dark shape silhouetted against the clouds, then, as the searchlights played across them, I saw three more, about a hundred yards away. By now I'd gone up from the bomb-aimer's position and was standing beside the second pilot. I gave instructions to the gunners to open fire at the balloons, and we started to turn away to starboard to get away from them. Immediately afterwards the second pilot threw the aircraft into a very steep right-hand turn, for he'd seen another balloon coming straight up in front of him. It had loomed up out of the darkness dead ahead and our wing tip just caught the fabric. If the pilot hadn't yanked the aircraft over quickly we should have flown right into it, the envelope would have wrapped itself round the 'plane, and that would have been the end of the trip. But all that happened was that the aircraft bucked a bit ; then there was a terrific explosion which we could hear even above the roar of the engines and I imagine the Germans were minus one balloon, though we couldn't see what happened.

When we climbed up higher we found we'd been flying along a row of balloons, right in the thick of them. It was pretty amazing that we hadn't hit a few more, for when we'd been bombing we must have been all among the cables.

Another raid which I shan't forget in a hurry happened just before this balloon incident. On this occasion we were bombing the railway marshalling yards at Hamm. There's an important railway traffic centre here, and it seems to be selected as a target most nights in the week. When we took off the weather was pretty poor, and at seven thousand feet it was freezing. Over the North Sea we struck heavy banks of cloud. I climbed to fourteen thousand feet, but even at that height we couldn't get out of it—so we just carried on flying through cloud. When we were about fifteen minutes away from our target, the port engine began to splutter and the engine revolutions dropped. I realized that we'd probably got ice in the carburettor. Then the starboard engine spluttered, and soon both engines ceased to give any power at all. Our air-speed indicator packed up, so did the altimeter. We didn't know whether we had flying speed or how high we were.

The second pilot and I were flying the machine between us while he was fixing the warm air control which had become disengaged. This is an arrangement by which the air, instead of being sucked straight in, is warmed up by the heat of the engine before being passed through to the carburettor. He'd got both his hands on the warm air lever, forcing it down as far as it would go, and he'd got his feet on the rudders, while I grabbed the stick, keeping the aircraft on an even keel, I could tell by the feel of it that we were going down very quickly. The wings had a thick layer of ice on them, and one couldn't see through the windscreen because that too was covered in ice. It didn't matter very much about that, because it was so dark and we were still in cloud. I decided that if the engines didn't come on within another four or five seconds, I'd give the order to abandon the aircraft. I'd got the words on the tip of my tongue, when the port engine spluttered a couple of times and began to pick up again.

It would still have been impossible to maintain height with the amount of ice we had on the aircraft, but I decided to hang on a little longer before giving the order to bale out. The starboard engine picked up, and after a bit more spluttering, both engines started working normally again.

The Germans place great confidence in their balloon barrage. Here is one of them ready to take the air. The crew waits for the order to send it up.
Photo, Wide World

Members of a Nazi barrage crew maintain a vigilant watch as a balloon ascends above oil refineries "somewhere in Germany."
Photo, Wide World

We flew on for another half-minute or so, and then the altimeter started registering. I looked at the height and found it was approximately four thousand feet, which meant we'd come down in a dive about eleven thousand feet.

We were just recovering from this when we ran into an electrical storm. The effect was so weird that I began to wonder whether we hadn't arrived in another world. Everything seemed outlined in a blue haze. The propellors made shining spinning circles. The two guns in the front turret were pointing up in the air and there was the same blue haze round them, too. The front gunner reported that there were sparks jumping from one gun to another ; the rear gunner afterwards said that for a minute he thought his guns were actually firing and he couldn't understand it. As I looked at the second pilot's face, I saw that it was ringed with blue. The tips of his fingers had the same blue haze round them. It covered the instrument panel and ran along the leading edges of the wings. That lasted about two minutes, and was one of the weirdest experiences I have ever had.

We flew on and arrived over our target area. The cloud was still so heavy that it was impossible to locate the marshalling yards, so we turned and came back, and on the way we bombed the alternative military target which had been allotted to us. Three fighters picked us up near Rotterdam. First of all the rear gunner reported one enemy aircraft apparently trailing us, then he was joined by a couple of his pals. The gunner got all ready for a bit of a scrap, but they didn't attack and we arrived back at the base without further incident.

OUR SEARCHLIGHT ON THE WAR

French Ships to be Demobilized

AFTER France surrendered there arose problems concerning the future of three French naval vessels—the aircraft carrier " Béarn," the cruiser " Emile Bertin," and the training cruiser " Jeanne D'Arc "—which were in Western Hemisphere waters at Martinique and Guadeloupe. Discussions took place between the U.S. Administration, the French Embassy in Washington, the Consulate at Martinique, and the French Commander of the " Emile Bertin," who felt that he must obey orders and return to France, even at the cost of fighting. Agreement was reached, and the three French ships are to be decommissioned. There remains the problem of the 100 American 'planes aboard the " Béarn." Britain claims them because she assumed liability for all orders of the Anglo-French Purchasing Commission. At any rate, they are out of Hitler's reach.

Bigger and Better Bombers

TWICE as powerful as those at present in use and carrying far greater bomb loads, bristling with gun positions, very fast, gigantic in size yet easy to handle and manoeuvre—such is the verdict of pilots who have tested the new secret British bombers shortly coming into service against the enemy. In addition to this impressive new model, the Wellington has been provided with a new type of engine, similar to that fitted to fighter machines, which enables the former speed of 260 miles per hour to be considerably exceeded.

Twisting the Rope

ACCORDING to the " New York Times " Marshal Pétain admits that Hitler is putting pressure on the Vichy Government. " The Germans hold the rope and twist it whenever they consider that the accord is not being carried out." Every day brings new evidence of the arch-bully's policy. On August 21 a decree was issued by General Weygand dismissing 180 French Army commanders who had taken part in operations against the Germans. The following day, General de Gaulle, announced that " 800 aeroplanes, supremely essential for the defence of France in Africa, are leaving Morocco, Algeria and Tunisia for Istres, there to be placed at the disposition of the enemy." Squads of the Gestapo now at Marseilles give orders conflicting with those issued from Vichy. Some 50,000 Germans from the Ruhr and Rhineland have arrived in the French capital in order to be out of reach of R.A.F. bombing raids. So proceeds the " honourable peace as between soldiers " foretold by Marshal Pétain.

Commander Ben Bryant of the " Sealion," leaving his submarine with his First Lieut., John Bromage, on their return to harbour after desperate adventures in Norwegian waters.

Canadian Destroyer to the Rescue

WHEN the " Arandora Star," en route to Canada with many hundreds of German and Italian internees, was torpedoed by a U-boat on July 2, 1940, the Canadian destroyer " St. Laurent " (Commander H. G. de Wolf, R.C.N.) was 84 sea miles away. She covered the distance in under three hours, and, guided by a Sunderland flying-boat to where the survivors were crowded in lifeboats or clinging to wreckage, engaged in the work of rescue until the flying-boat reported that no more survivors were in sight. Then with more than 850 survivors on board the " St. Laurent " set course for a Scottish port, where she arrived 17 hours later—at 6.30 a.m. on July 3. The 850 survivors were crammed in somehow, and on their way to safety were given a breakfast of porridge and one egg each. Cocoa and soup were also provided, and those people who looked as if they needed it were given a tot of rum.

' Sealion ' Survives Depth Charges

WHEN the British submarine " Sealion " (*see* Vol. II, pp. 462 and 504) returned to her base in August 1940, Commander B. Bryant had a thrilling story to tell. When off the Norwegian coast the " Sealion " was about to torpedo a 9,000-ton German merchantman. Suddenly the convoy of which she was a part changed course and one ship came straight for the submarine. There was a grinding, crashing shock as " Sealion's " periscope and hull were struck a glancing blow. Then came an hour of depth charging, but the little vessel survived it all. After a time she was surfaced and her crew found the heavy metal masts and the periscope shafts swinging wildly. All through the night they worked to make fast the wreckage, but perhaps the most hazardous job fell to Chief Petty Officer R. Clark, who fitted up an emergency wireless aerial.

' Criminals Trained for Murder '

THE arming of the Home Guard with rifles provoked violent attacks in the Nazi press and on the Berlin radio. "The British Government is releasing criminals from prison and training them for murder," said the announcer bitterly. "Every Englishman who agrees to act as a franc-tireur is digging his own grave. Churchill is leading the British civil population on a fatal path." How much more will be resented the decision to equip certain units of the Home Guard with light machine-guns purchased in America, with millions of rounds of ammunition.

V.C. OF A BROKEN BRIDGE
2nd. Lieut. R. W. Annand

THE Victoria Cross has been awarded to 2nd Lieut. R. W. Annand, Durham Light Infantry, for most conspicuous gallantry on May 13-16, 1940, when the platoon under his command was on the south side of the River Dyle, astride a blown bridge. During the night a strong attack was beaten off, but about 11 a.m. the enemy again launched a violent attack and pushed forward a bridging party into the sunken bottom of the river; 2nd Lieut. Annand attacked this party, but when ammunition ran out he went forward himself over open ground, with total disregard for enemy mortar and machine-gun fire. Reaching the top of the bridge, he drove out the party below, inflicting over 20 casualties with hand grenades. Having been wounded, he rejoined his platoon, had his wound dressed, and then carried on in command. During the evening another attack was launched, and again 2nd Lieut. Annand went forward with hand grenades and inflicted heavy casualties on the enemy. When the order to withdraw was received he withdrew his platoon, but learning on the way back that his batman was wounded and had been left behind, he returned at once to the former position and brought him back in a wheelbarrow before losing consciousness as the result of wounds.

2nd Lieut. R. W. Annand was on the Supplementary Reserve of the Durham Light Infantry at the outbreak of war. Before joining the Army in 1937 he was a Sub.-Lieut. in the R.N.V.R.

C.S.M. Gristock was 34. He entered the Army at the age of 14 as a band boy in the Queen's Bays. Later he transferred to the Norfolks. His V.C. was the first won for that regiment.

Photos, British Official : Crown Copyright ; and " Daily Mirror "

V.C. WON IN BELGIUM,
Coy. Sergeant-Major G. Gristock

C.S.M. GRISTOCK, of the Norfolk Regiment, was awarded the V.C. for most conspicuous gallantry on May 21, 1940, when his company was holding a position on the line of the River Escaut, south of Tournai. After a prolonged attack, the enemy succeeded in breaking through beyond the company's right flank, which was consequently threatened. Coy. Sergeant-Major Gristock, having organized a party of eight riflemen from company headquarters, went forward to cover the right flank. Realizing that an enemy machine-gun had moved forward to a position from which it was inflicting heavy casualties on his company, C.S.M. Gristock went on, with one man as connecting file, to try to put it out of action. While advancing, he came under heavy machine-gun fire from the opposite bank, and was severely wounded in both legs, his right knee being badly smashed. He nevertheless gained his fire-position, some 20 yards from the enemy machine-gun post, undetected, and by well-aimed rapid fire killed the machine-gun crew of four and put their gun out of action. He then dragged himself back to the right flank position, from which he refused to be evacuated until contact with the battalion on the right had been established and the line once more made good. He has since died from his wounds.

More Drops of Bitterness in France's Cup

One more humiliation was suffered by France when the Chamber of Deputies, once her stronghold of freedom, was hung with swastika banners and filled with officials of the Nazi-governed city assembled to hear Hitler's "Appeal to reason" speech, relayed from the Reichstag on July 19. In the circle below a Nazi soldier wanders among the trenches at Vimy Ridge, which, with the sand-bags filled with concrete, were preserved as a lasting memorial of the heroism shown there in the last war.

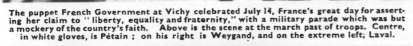

The puppet French Government at Vichy celebrated July 14, France's great day for assert-ing her claim to "liberty, equality and fraternity," with a military parade which was but a mockery of the country's faith. Above is the scene at the march past of troops. Centre, in white gloves, is Pétain ; on his right is Weygand, and on the extreme left; Laval.

Many of the people of Brussels can remember the German occupation of their city in the last war, and they are not greatly upset by the company of German soldiers, who are often seen reading the Nazi war publication "West Front" outside the cafés.

Left, German soldiers are walking in front of hangars at Le Bourget, the great airport of Paris — one of many fine French aerodromes which have come into the hands of the Nazis but are receiving constant attention from the R.A.F.

Photos, Wide World and Keystone

OUR DIARY OF THE WAR

WEDNESDAY, AUGUST 21, 1940
354th day

In the Air—R.A.F. Coastal Command aircraft, after attacking two enemy ships in North Sea, engaged seven escort Messerschmitts and shot one down. British machine damaged but landed safely.

Daylight attacks made on enemy aerodromes. Night raids on oil refineries at Magdeburg and Hanover; on aerodromes at Caen, Abbeville and Quakenbrueck, near Hanover; on island of Texel; and key railway centres in the Ruhr and Rhineland.

War against Italy—R.A.F. raided Sidi el Tmimi, seriously damaging three Italian aircraft and seaplane jetty at Bomba.

Reported that South African Air Force had made bombing expedition from Mega, Western Abyssinia, to Indian Ocean, raiding all enemy aerodromes, Mega wireless station, and other targets.

Home Front—Enemy made short raids by single aircraft on British coasts. Damage to one aerodrome, a Yorks town and a residential district on South Coast. Aerial torpedo wrecked eight cottages in S.E. town. Thirteen raiders destroyed; one British fighter lost, but pilot safe.

Balkans—Rumanian Government agreed to cede Southern Dobruja to Bulgaria.

THURSDAY, AUGUST 22
355th day

On the Sea—German guns mounted near Calais and Boulogne bombarded convoy in Straits of Dover, but without result. Convoy was also attacked from air, but no ship hit. One raider destroyed, the 1,000th brought down round British coasts since June 16.

Air attack made on British convoy off N.E. Coast. Bombers driven off by escorting vessels and Spitfires.

In the Air—R.A.F. made heavy sustained attacks on German gun positions along French coast.

Bomber squadrons made night raids on many targets in Germany, including aircraft factory at Frankfurt and power station near Cologne. Attacks also made on 22 aerodromes in Germany and occupied territory.

War against Italy—Reported that R.A.F. had bombed many targets in Libya on August 20, including Tobruk harbour, and landing-grounds at Tobruk and El Adem.

R.A.F. raided Bomba roadsteads in Libya, sinking two submarines, a destroyer and a submarine depot ship. Successful attack made on landing-ground at Derna.

Alexandria raided, but damage slight.

Home Front—During evening German long-range guns shelled Dover area. Some damage to buildings and a number of casualties. British land guns shelled France.

Single raiders reported over wide area of England and Wales. Ten shot down. Four British fighters lost, but two pilots safe.

Greece—Announced in Athens that British Navy and Air Force would aid Greece in event of an attack.

FRIDAY, AUGUST 23
356th day

On the Sea—Enemy raider reported at large in Tasman Sea, having attacked British steamer "Turakina" on August 20.

Canadian cargo steamer "Geraldine Mary" reported sunk by enemy action off Irish coast.

British ship "Havildar" torpedoed off north coast of Ireland.

In the Air—R.A.F. made further heavy attacks on German gun emplacements near Gris Nez.

During night British bombers raided twenty aerodromes and seaplane bases in France and Holland, railway sidings at Mannheim and objectives in the Ruhr.

War against Italy—Italians reported to have reoccupied site of Fort Capuzzo.

Home Front—Enemy aircraft over London in early hours of morning. Many bombs dropped, but damage done comparatively slight. Two cinemas and a church hit. During day and evening raiders operated singly in widely separated areas, including London. Machine-gun attacks in Midlands. Residential areas in S.E. bombed, and damage done to N.E. coastal town. Enemy lost four machines, Britain none.

SATURDAY, AUGUST 24
357th day

On the Sea—H.M. trawler "Arctic Trapper" shot down two Nazi 'planes which had attacked her.

H.M. minesweeping trawler "Resparko" reported sunk as result of air attack.

In the Air—R.A.F. made hour-long bombing raid on Daimler Benz plant at Stuttgart, and also attacked nitrogen plant at Ludwigshafen, synthetic oil plant at Frankfurt and power station near Cologne.

German long-range gun positions again bombed. Further attacks also made on 20 aerodromes in occupied territory.

War against Italy—R.A.F. bombers attacked industrial targets in N.W. Italy.

During the night of August 23-24 British naval forces penetrated into the harbour of Bardia, Libya, and engaged targets at point-blank range; the seaplane base at Bomba was also bombarded.

Home Front—Resumption of mass bombing raids on England. In afternoon came two waves, one of 300, the other of 500 bombers with escorting fighters,

Two attempts to reach London beaten back, but in a third, at 11.30 p.m., some bombs were dropped. Portsmouth raided; Ramsgate gas works hit and Manston aerodrome damaged. Dover again shelled from French coast and later bombed from air, but suffered only slightly. Fierce air battles fought above the Straits.

Fifty-two raiders shot down. Nineteen British fighters lost, but 12 pilots safe.

Balkans—Rumano-Hungarian negotiations on Transylvanian question broke down.

SUNDAY, AUGUST 25
358th day

On the Sea—Reported that H.M. submarine "Sealion" had returned to her base after voyage in which she sank an enemy supply ship, chased a U-boat, and was rammed while attacking a convoy.

In the Air—R.A.F. attacked big armament works and other targets in Berlin area. Enemy aerodromes in Holland, Belgium and Northern France also raided.

Coastal Command flying-boat attacked enemy flying-boats in Tromso area of Norway, sinking two and damaging others.

Home Front—Fifty-five German 'planes brought down during mass attacks on Britain, 43 being destroyed in fierce battle off Portland. Thirteen R.A.F. machines missing, but pilots of four safe. Two bombs dropped on Scilly Isles. London again raided during night. St Giles, Cripplegate, and other buildings in City area damaged.

MONDAY, AUGUST 26
359th day

On the Sea—Admiralty announced that H.M. Destroyer "Hostile" had been sunk by enemy mine.

In the Air—R.A.F. bombers made daylight and night attacks on twenty-seven aerodromes in Germany, Holland, Belgium and occupied France. During the night strong attacks were made on the synthetic oil plant at Leuna and the oil depot at Frankfurt. Aircraft factory at Frankfurt, explosives factory at Griesheim, and various objectives at Hoechst, Cologne, Leipzig, Hamm and Schwerte heavily bombed.

War against Italy—During night of August 26-27 R.A.F. bombers attacked Fiat works at Turin and other factories near Milan.

Announced from Cairo that R.A.F. had raided military objectives in Mogadishu, Italian Somaliland, and the airfield of Dessie in Abyssinia; Galabat, Metema, Bardia and El Adem also attacked.

Home Front—Three main mass attacks made on Britain, ending with 6-hour raid alarm in London during night. 'Planes approached the capital one or two at a time, but few bombs were dropped; one enemy bomber shot down by anti-aircraft fire. Great battle over Thames estuary.

Folkestone raided about noon by strong force of bombers and fighters. Large number of bombs dropped and damage done to private property. This raid followed by fierce engagement over Dover and Straits.

Two towns in Midlands attacked during the night, fires being caused and damage done to industrial property.

Scilly Isles again raided. First German raid on Eire. Four villages in Co. Wexford bombed.

Forty-seven raiders destroyed. Fifteen British fighters lost but pilots of 11 safe.

General—Governor of the Territory of the Chad, French Equatorial Africa, announced that it refused to accept capitulation and would continue to fight on side of Britain.

TUESDAY, AUGUST 27
360th day

On the Sea—Admiralty announced that H.M. Submarine "Spearfish," considerably overdue, must be presumed lost.

In the Air—R.A.F. bombed docks at Kiel and Wilhelmshafen, Messerschmitt factory at Augsburg, oil tanks and supply depots at Mannheim, and several aerodromes. Oil tanks near Bordeaux, near Brest and at Cherbourg also attacked.

War against Italy—R.A.F. bombed Fiat works at Turin and Marelli magneto factory at Sesto Saiovannni.

R.A.F. raided Harar and Dessie, Abyssinia.

Enemy attacked Haifa, but damage was negligible and casualties few.

Home Front—Enemy air activity slight during the day; three enemy aircraft shot down. During the night widely dispersed attacks over Britain, including London.

Balkans—Axis Powers reported to be intervening in Transylvanian dispute.

H.M.S. "Hostile" was sunk by an enemy mine on August 26. With four sister ships she took part in the gallant attack on German destroyers in Narvik Bay on April 10 and was damaged as a result of the action. H.M.S. "Hostile" belonged to the "Hero" class; her displacement was 1,340 tons with a speed of 36 knots. She carried a complement of 145.

EVER A FIGHTER, THE PREMIER IS ALONGSIDE THE FIGHT

Determined as always to see for himself, the Prime Minister has visited many of Britain's coast defences. On August 28 he was at Dover when Nazi 'planes renewed their attack on the town and there was a fierce aerial fight overhead. Mr. Churchill, wearing a steel helmet, mounted to a vantage point and watched the progress of the battle with keen appreciation of the skill and daring of the British fighters.

Photo, British Official: Crown Copyright

The Grenadiers Lived Up To Their Reputation

Continuing our series of chapters describing the fighting of the B.E.F. in France in the early summer of 1940, we now give the story of the Grenadier Guards, who did magnificent work in covering the retreat to Dunkirk. It is based on information received from official sources, and makes a little epic of amazing gallantry and fortitude.

IT was into no unknown country that three battalions of the Grenadier Guards advanced on May 11, 1940, when the B.E.F. was rushed into Belgium in answer to Leopold's appeal. The Grenadiers fought their first action at Dunkirk in 1658—that Dunkirk to which nearly 300 years later they were to make a fighting retreat. On their colours are " Namur 1695 " and the names

and established a machine-gun post. This was engaged and destroyed by the battalion's mortars.

Nothing of moment occurred on the next day, although both "X" and "Y" battalions were subjected to heavy shelling. But the German thrust through the French armies farther to the south had turned the line of the Dyle, and the British were ordered to withdraw to positions farther back on the River Dendre near Ninove. This was accomplished in orderly fashion despite bombing and machine-gun attacks by enemy aircraft and the crowding of the roads by refugees and straggling Belgian soldiers.

On the Dendre, on May 18, the three battalions found themselves side by side. Presently, a German patrol of motor-cycles headed by a motor-car appeared on the opposite bank of the river, just as the commander of one company of " Y " battalion was making a reconnaissance. He himself opened fire with an anti-tank rifle and knocked out the car. A burst from a Bren gun then swept the motor-cyclists, who took refuge in

"X" and "Y" battalions held the Escaut position for four days, before withdrawing to a prepared position on the Gort Line east of Roubaix, which they held for another three or four days. On the Gort Line a patrol of "Y" battalion had an interesting experience. It was reconnoitring a farm when the farmer offered the men coffee and then disappeared. Within 20 minutes the patrol was surrounded by the enemy. It put up a spirited resistance, killing many Germans, and suffered no casualties.

When the decision was taken to evacuate the B.E.F., the battalions were soon on the move again in the direction of Dunkirk. "Z" battalion had just crossed the River Lys after a long and tiring march when it was learnt that the enemy had broken through on the right, between Commines and Ypres, and that the battalion was to restore the situation. It made a counter-attack and, after a hazardous advance across open country, the battalion reached its objective and held it in spite of repeated and determined enemy efforts. Eventually it was ordered to withdraw to Messines and then it made its way to Moeres, where it was ordered to be ready to support a brigade which was being hard-pressed south of Furnes. The ground was reconnoitred but the battalion's services were not called upon.

Fierce Fighting at Furnes

Meanwhile, "X" and "Y" battalions marched on Furnes, where again there was a danger of the enemy breaking through. A reconnaissance party consisting of the Commanding Officer of "Y" and two company commanders came under fire and were all hit. A young officer found them lying in an exposed position in the main street of the town which was raked by machine-gun fire. Displaying complete disregard of his own safety, under heavy machine-gun and rifle fire, he carried the Commanding Officer who was dead and the two company commanders who were wounded into the doorway of a house. But the enemy's fire was so heavy that no stretcher-bearers could approach, and an entry had to be forced from the back. "X" and "Y" battalions took up positions and were subjected to an intense and accurate bombardment which was obviously directed by enemy agents on the spot, and a telephone was actually found in the church tower. A reserve ammunition truck was hit and set on fire, but the mortar bombs were unloaded before they could explode and were put to good use in blowing up two German mortar positions. Many houses in the town were burning furiously, and the situation was made still more uncomfortable by the fact that little artillery support was available and no counter-battery fire could be given. Meanwhile, the enemy launched repeated and determined attacks and attempted to cross the canal on rubber boats. All these attempts were frustrated; a section of "Y" battalion under a lance-corporal drove out and killed 20 Germans while itself suffering only one casualty.

Farther to the north two line battalions were hard pressed and a gap was opened between them. Soon after midday news reached "Y" battalion headquarters that the enemy was crossing the canal unopposed. The same young officer who had dragged the dead C.O. and the two wounded company commanders into cover was sent to learn the exact situation. He had with him the Bren carrier platoon. By resolute leadership he

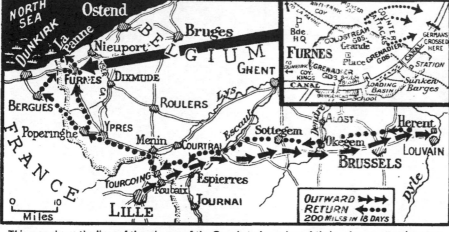

This map shows the lines of the advance of the Guards to Louvain and their subsequent retirement. The map inset, showing the counter-attack at Furnes, is from a sketch map by Brigadier J. A. C. Whitaker, who was himself at Furnes. Top, one of the Grenadier Guards lights his pipe.
Photo, British Official : Crown Copyright ; map courtesy of " The Daily Telegraph "

of Marlborough's four great victories—Blenheim, Ramillies, Oudenarde, and Malplaquet—and Waterloo. Then during the Great War the Grenadiers were continuously in action in Flanders : Mons, Ypres, Passchendaele and Lys are but a few of their battle-honours earned in the four years' campaign. Now they were in Flanders again.

Battalions which we may call "X" and "Y" advanced rapidly from the French frontier to take over part of the line of the River Dyle at Louvain. "Y" battalion was in support of "X"; "Z" battalion, belonging to a different corps, was in reserve behind the Dyle farther to the south. Actual fighting began on May 14, when strong enemy fighting patrols engaged "X" battalion in Louvain and along the railway to the north. At the same time there was considerable enemy air activity and shelling. Sniping by Fifth Columnists and parachutists added to the difficulties.

On the following day some enemy troops succeeded in infiltrating between "X" battalion and that on its right. An immediate counter-attack by a company with some Bren gun carriers drove the Germans out and restored the situation. Next, there was trouble on the left where the Germans crossed a canal

a house, and mortar fire destroyed the house. No more trouble was experienced from the enemy patrol, but in the fighting which now ensued the sniping activities of Fifth Columnists continued to be very troublesome.

By this time the German break-through to the south necessitated a new withdrawal to the line of the River Escaut (Scheldt). The Grenadier battalions took up positions on the western bank of the river, with their left on Helchin. On May 21 the enemy opened violent artillery, mortar and machine-gun fire and launched numerous determined attacks. These were repulsed, but in one place a crossing was forced and some companies of "Z" battalion had to fall back. The position was under direct enemy observation, there was no cover, and every movement drew destructive fire. The crew of a Bren gun carrier did splendid work driving across country and spotting the positions of the enemy machine-guns. A counter-attack was immediately ordered, and it was then that Lance-Corporal H. Nicholls picked up a Bren gun and, firing from the hip as he ran, silenced three machine-guns and inflicted heavy casualties on massed enemy infantry who were forced back across the Escaut. For this action Lance-Corporal Nicholls was awarded the V.C. (*see* page 139).

They Held Up the Foe on the Road to Dunkirk

These are some of the Grenadier Guardsmen whose gallant conduct is described in this article. They are Bren gunners in a forward position before the retreat.

rallied the troops on the spot and led them back to the canal in a counter-attack. His action averted an enemy break-through between the brigade area and the sea.

During this time the transport column and other details of "Z" battalion had been ordered to the neighbourhood of Dunkirk, there to destroy all their trucks except those carrying arms, food and ammunition. All the vehicles were present and in good order, and the melancholy task of destruction was duly performed. The personnel then made their way to the sea at La Panne, where there was indescribable confusion. Trucks, wagons and cars abandoned under orders by British units were being plundered and driven away by civilians and other nondescript people. The men of the transport column armed themselves with all the Bren guns and anti-tank rifles they could collect and established a post across the road, enforcing order and putting a stop to the pilfering. Next, they contributed to the defence of the position at Furnes by holding a front of half a mile along the canal east of the town. The situation at Furnes was saved and the final withdrawal to the sea made possible.

This was not the first time that the Grenadiers had covered the withdrawal of a British army. In 1809, Sir John Moore was watching the troops coming into Corunna when he said : " Look at that body of men in the distance ; they are the Guards by the way they are marching." In 1940 a divisional staff officer, checking up the units as they were withdrawing, was heard to say as a battalion of Grenadiers marched through : " These must be the Guards."

The sea front of La Panne (once a popular Belgian seaside resort), where " Z " battalion of the Grenadiers reached the sea, is here seen as the troops found it, lined with deserted houses, and cluttered with derelict anti-aircraft guns and all the rack and ruin of war. In peacetime its sands were crowded with holiday-makers.   *Photos, British Official : Crown Copyright; and E.N.A.*

We Have More Than Held Our Own in the Air
by Major F. A. de V. Robertson, V.D.

Here the work of the various Air Force Commands is analysed during the three successive phases of the war in the first year of hostilities—the maritime, military and purely aerial stages. Lessons taught by the year's experience are made clear by Major Robertson, of the Editorial staff of "Flight."

To judge the lessons taught by the first year of air warfare one should start by getting the background clear in one's mind. The Royal Air Force is a separate Service, and so is the Regia Aeronautica of Italy; but the Luftwaffe is, as the German word indicates, the air arm of the German Army. It has proved itself formidable when working in conjunction with German ground troops, but when sent to work independently, as in its efforts against Britain and British sea power, it has not been impressive.

We have the Royal Air Force and the Fleet Air Arm. The latter is a branch of the Navy, though on occasions it has worked with the R.A.F. The Royal Air Force is

of all. It is prepared to co-operate with the Navy or the Army, and also to undertake independent action on its own. It has had to perform all three functions in this first year of the war.

The British Army does not possess an air arm of its own, but a certain number of special squadrons are allotted to it by the R.A.F. These army co-operation squadrons are trained and equipped for tactical reconnaissance and to spot for the artillery. When we send an expeditionary force to the Continent it is necessary for the R.A.F. to provide fighter squadrons to protect the A.C. squadrons, and also bomber squadrons to reconnoitre far behind the enemy's lines and to bomb his back areas. These are known

all stages of the war, but at first it was the whole war, so far as Britain was concerned.

All through this stage the Coastal Command was the most active branch of the R.A.F., and its activities have never been abated. Its flying-boats (the Sunderland being the foremost type) and its Anson and Hudson landplanes ceaselessly scoured the seas in search of U-boats and enemy surface craft, and kept the Navy well informed of nearly all movements. Its aircraft bombed and sank a number of German submarines, but such successes gave no measure of the utility of its work. If an aircraft sighted a periscope it informed the Navy at once, and that patch of sea was soon made unhealthy for under-water work. Often the Coastal machines met Heinkel 111 bombers or Dornier 18 flying-boats, and, though our machines were not intended for air fighting, the crews never hesitated to attack. The excellent marksmanship of our highly-trained air gunners resulted in many victories.

The Bomber Fails Against the Navy

During this period the Fighter Command remained in a state of " exasperated anticipation," as someone described the feelings of the pilots. They did sentry-go up and down our coasts, and pounced with avidity on any Heinkel 111 which they encountered. The obsolescent types of German bombers employed could not stand up to a Hurricane or Spitfire, and could escape only by taking refuge in a cloud. Our fighters easily defeated the German attempts to bomb the Fleet in the Forth and at Scapa Flow, and one must marvel at the weakness of the bomber formations which the enemy sent against such important objectives. It was an instance of the ineptitude of the Luftwaffe in independent action.

The Bomber Command also joined in the task of helping the Navy. It made several spirited attacks on German naval bases, and when enemy seaplanes began to deposit magnetic mines off our coasts, the Bomber Command started a series of "security patrols" over the seaplane bases in the Frisian Islands which very much curtailed the activities of the minelayers.

When German naval forces emerged into the North Sea our bombers attacked them, as German bombers likewise assailed British naval forces. From these encounters two tactical lessons emerged. It is very difficult to bomb a moving warship from a great height; but if a bomber came low it ran into the furious anti-aircraft fire from the ships. The multiple pom-poms on our warships proved extremely effective, and it soon became evident that bombers were unable to prevent a Navy from carrying on its work. This was a surprise to many foreign observers, and told heavily in favour of the British cause.

The other tactical lesson from these operations was the tremendous advantage conferred on British bombers by the adoption of the power-operated gun turret. This turret, which may have up to four machine-guns, is elevated, depressed, or traversed by the power of the engines without any muscular exertion by the gunner. The German

Germany made full use of her immense air force when she overran Norway in April, 1940. Here a German 'plane is flying over the forests near Oslo, dropping bombs not only on troops but on the defenceless civilians who fled from the capital when the Germans landed.   *Photo, Keystone*

organized in three active Commands in this country, and there are Overseas Commands, of which the Middle East, with headquarters at Cairo, is the most important. In Great Britain there are the Bomber, the Fighter, and the Coastal Commands.

The Coastal Command works mainly with the Navy. Its chief duty is reconnaissance over the seas round the British Isles, which is carried out by squadrons of flying-boats and squadrons of landplanes.

The Fighter Command exists primarily for the air defence of Britain. In addition to its squadrons of fighter aircraft, it has under its control the squadrons of the Balloon Barrage and the Observer Corps. It also has operational control over the anti-aircraft guns and the searchlight battalions provided by the War Office.

The Bomber Command is the most flexible

as the Air Component of the Expeditionary Force. While the B.E.F. was stationary in France the Bomber Command sent over to that country a number of its squadrons, which would thus have a shorter distance to fly to reach Germany. They were known as the Advanced Air Striking Force, and were not under Army command.

So far as Britain is concerned, the war has consisted of three phases : the first maritime, the second military (using that word to mean operations by the Army), and the third aerial.

In the first stage the Royal Navy established a blockade of Germany, swept German commerce off the seas, and practically confined the small German navy to its harbours until it was able to destroy most of it during the Norway campaign. Of course, this naval blockade has continued through

Britain's Air Commands are Nearing Supremacy

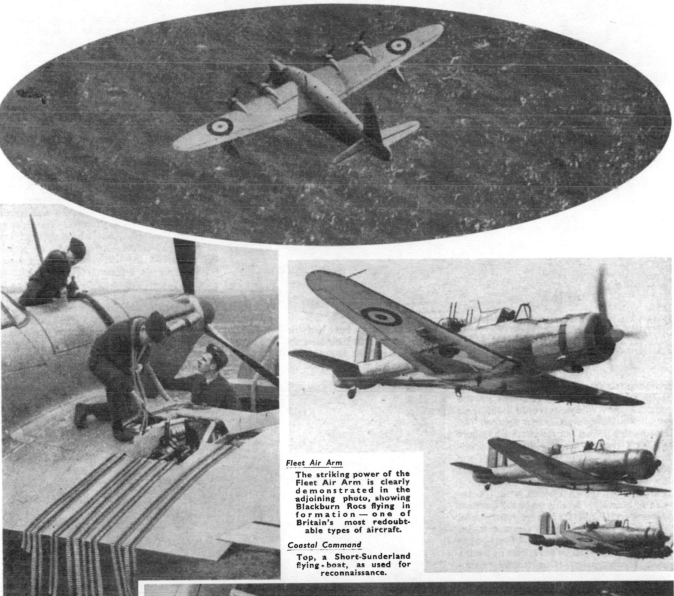

Fleet Air Arm

The striking power of the Fleet Air Arm is clearly demonstrated in the adjoining photo, showing Blackburn Rocs flying in formation — one of Britain's most redoubtable types of aircraft.

Coastal Command

Top, a Short-Sunderland flying-boat, as used for reconnaissance.

Fighter Command

In this page the work of the Three Commands of the R.A.F. and the Fleet Air Arm is symbolized. An aspect in the servicing of Fighter Command machines is shown above, where armourers at an aerodrome in England are immediately recharging the guns of a Hurricane just back from a combat with Nazi aircraft over the coast.

Bomber Command

The work of the ground staff with the Bomber Command is a vital contribution to the defence of Britain. Right, armourers are fitting bombs to a machine preparatory to a flight over enemy territory. The work requires the utmost care and precision to ensure that there is instant release when the button that frees the bomb is pressed.

Photos, L.N.A., Charles E. Brown, Central Press, and Topical

Germany's 'Luftwaffe' Meets Its Match at Last

These pilots of Italian aircraft are receiving instructions from an officer at an aerodrome in Italy before starting out to attack one of the few objectives in the Mediterranean they can reach. Against the chief of them, Malta, they have had little success.
Photo, Wide World

German Armies, but had not sufficient numbers to prevent their advance. The chief lesson of this phase is that an army is badly handicapped if it is short of aircraft. The

same applies also to shortage of tanks or any other weapon.

The third stage began with the collapse of France. The glorious incident of Dunkirk taught another lesson. The situation of the British troops gave an apparently ideal opportunity to the German bombers to annihilate our force. But the Fighter Command was thrown into the fray. Our Spitfires, Hurricanes, and Defiants shot down the German bombers in fantastic numbers, and the B.E.F. was substantially saved. What had been thought impossible was actually accomplished. The German bomber force was badly defeated.

Then followed the purely aerial phase of the war. The Bomber Command began an independent campaign against German munition works, particularly oil plants and stores, as well as other military targets. The damage done was immense, but we cannot yet say to what extent the German war effort has been injured. At the same time the Luftwaffe began an independent bombing campaign against this country, possibly as a preparation for an attempt at invasion. Being able to use French aerodromes, the Germans sent short-range fighters (which are more efficient than long-range fighters) to escort their bombers. Our Hurricanes and Spitfires could and did master the escorts, but fighting them took time, and gave the enemy bombers

doctrine was that a bomber's best defence was speed, not armament, and that proved wrong. Our Wellingtons could hold their own when attacked by German fighters.

During this period our long-range bombers flew over Germany nearly every night dropping leaflets. The propaganda value of the leaflets was doubtful, but the training of our pilots and navigators was most useful.

The land campaign opened with the invasion of Norway. In this stage the German dive-bombers (Junkers 87) were most useful in preparing the way for the German tanks. Effective use was also made of air-borne troops, either dropped by parachute or landed from a troop-carrier. Our Bomber Command furiously attacked the rear of the

Above, on the seashore in South-east England, are the remains of a German bomber after meeting British fighters. Left is a Heinkel brought down by a British A.A. battery during the fighting in Belgium in May 1940.
Photos, British Official : Crown Copyright ; L.N.A.

a chance to do their work. Even so, the German bombing results were poor. The resounding successes of our fighters, at small cost to themselves, are known to all ; but had they been able to concentrate on shooting down only bombers, their victory would have been even more complete.

Of the war against Italy it is too early to say much. The Regia Aeronautica has not been able to drive the Royal Navy out of the Mediterranean, and its rather antiquated types of aircraft have been easily beaten by our Gladiator biplanes. Our Blenheims and other bombers have done considerable damage to Italian naval bases, aerodromes, and other objectives. The R.A.F. Command of the Middle East has every reason to be proud of itself.

Air Battle for London Raged Yet More Fiercely

In the week following the first bombing of London in the night of August 23-24 furious attacks were made repeatedly, but every day attack was beaten off and the raiders never penetrated the barrage defences of the centre. Changing tactics and varied formations, attacks on aerodromes and the Thames Estuary were alike unsuccessful.

DISTURBED by their enormous losses the Nazis showed during a short period, August 24 to September 3, what appeared as indecision both in strategy and tactics. Bomber losses proved so costly that they took to the use of improvised fighter-bombers which should in theory combine the swiftness and ease of manoeuvre of the fighter with the death-dealing power of the bomber. But our Fighter Command soon countered this move, and dozens of Messerschmitt single and two-engined bombers were brought down. At the other extreme the Luftwaffe threw into the struggle their new four-engined bombing craft—an enormous machine with all a giant's vulnerability, but with great striking power once it could safely be brought over its target.

The enemy tried every imaginable shift and dodge to elude our defences, using decoy formations that screened other units ready to dash through and search out our airfields. After forgoing mass raids for a time in favour of smaller and scattered attacks they came over again in large formations, which split up in small sections when across the Channel and so endeavoured to disperse our defenders. Ever larger fighter escorts were provided for the raiding bombers, and for a few days the ratio of our losses increased, but soon dropped again to the " one-British-to-four-German " ratio which the courage and skill of our fighter pilots had established.

GERMAN & BRITISH AIRCRAFT LOSSES
FIRST YEAR OF THE WAR

German to April 30, 1940

Total announced West Front, North Sea, Britain, Scandinavia ... 195

					German	British
May	...	...	...	...	1,990	258
June	...	...	...	...	276	177
July	...	...	...	...	245	115
Aug	...	...	...	...	1,210	373
Sept. 1-2	...	...	...	...	80	34
Totals, May to Sept. 2			...		3,801	957

Daily Results, August 1 to Sept. 2

	German Losses	British Losses	British Pilots Saved		German Losses	British Losses	British Pilots Saved
				Bt.fwd.	852	222	63
Aug.				**Aug.**			
1-7	10	15	—	22	10	4	2
8	62	18	3	23	4	0	—
9	1	1	0	24	50	21	12
10	1	4	0	25	55	17	3
11	66	29	2	26	47	17	11
12	62	17	1	27	5	1	0
13	78	25	10	28	29	14	7
14	31	11	2	29	11	12	7
15	183	34	17	30	62	27	15
16	180	37	17	31	85	39	25
17	1	0	—				
18	152	22	12		1,213	374	159
19	5	6	2	**Sept.**			
20	7	2	1	1	25	16	9
21	13	1	1	2	55	18	8
	852	222	68	Totals	1,293	408	167

Notes.—Figures for **May** cover Dunkirk operations and include aircraft destroyed by French. Probable number brought down by British during that month is 1,500 out of the total 1,990.

The main attack on Britain began on Aug. 8—up to Sept. 2nd there were 18 mass attacks.

None of the figures include aircraft bombed on the ground or so damaged as to be unlikely to reach home.

During the first year of war, announced an Air Ministry communiqué of September 2, our Fighter Command pilots shot down **1,730** German raiders—destroying **964** enemy bombers and fighters during August alone. Our anti-aircraft gunners during the year shot down **192** raiders. The Aeronautical Correspondent of " The Times " estimated that the all-in loss to the German air force in all campaigns during the year would be about 7,000 aircraft, and the corresponding British loss about 1,500.

Another tactic was the extension of the night bombing raids: enemy aircraft quartered the country and individual bombers dropped missiles with little heed for targets of military value. It was suggested, in fact, that the enemy's object was to keep our sirens sounding and to hold up industrial production.

London's third night raid in the week came on Wednesday, August 28. The sirens sounded at 9 o'clock, and for seven hours thereafter single enemy raiders were over the area. Many people were thus prevented from making their way home, but as soon as the shelters disgorged the waiting crowds the transport services got the wayfarers to their destinations. Many incendiary bombs were dropped, but prompt action by the A.R.P. workers localized the trouble and prevented serious fires. Anderson shelters saved several lives when explosive bombs fell near, but in one case a shelter suffered a direct hit and was blown out of the ground, four people being killed.

Aerodromes in the Home Counties were the object of massed attacks by large formations on Friday, August 30. The raiders came over in three successive waves at short intervals. A great battle developed and they were scattered and driven back. Some enemy aircraft approached London, where the warning sounded soon after midday, but were foiled by our fighters and anti-aircraft

A hugh bomb crater made in the outskirts of London on the night of August 29/30 is seen above. Right, the tail of a British Hurricane damaged in a fight, yet the pilot brought it home.

Ramsgate people in their tunnel (see p. 237) during a raid. An American report stated that though over 1,200 houses were destroyed, total casualties were but 28 killed and 45 injured, due to this excellent shelter.

The South-East Bears the Brunt of the Nazi Attack

The men who man the balloon barrage are not only on the defensive, but on occasion they can take the offensive very successfully. Left, some of them are in action at the end of August during a raid on the barrage. A Messerschmitt attacked a balloon affectionately known as " Matilda." It succeeded and, right, are the tangled remains. But "Matilda" was avenged, for her crew poured 100 rounds of rifle fire into the Messerschmitt and it dropped into the sea in flames.

Photos, Planet News

gunners. Later in the afternoon London had its twentieth air raid warning since war began, but the " Raiders Passed " came fifteen minutes later. Yet another alarm came about an hour after, keeping people under cover for some ninety minutes. Fierce battles raged above the outer suburbs and a round dozen of raiders met their doom in such encounters.

Night raiders made their appearance at a little after 9 p.m., and soon our fighters were heard overhead giving chase. Over the London area both high explosive and incendiary bombs were dropped, apparently at random, and considerable damage was done to houses in various districts. Next morning, with but a brief interval, the enemy resumed his attacks by day, and during Saturday the sirens sounded at 8.27 and 10.40 a.m., 1.5 and 5.49 p.m., and again in the evening at 9.49 and 11.30. The most desperate attempts were made by raiders to reach our aerodromes, to which no serious damage was done, however.

In the course of the day dive-bombers attacked a suburban town thronged with shoppers, and in another suburb a low-flying Nazi 'plane turned its guns on to people in the streets. In all these encounters the

raiders lost heavily, as the figures printed in the table in page 259 demonstrate.

In the fourth attack during Saturday some three hundred raiders were engaged ; typical of the formations was one in which 20 Junkers bombers were escorted by three times that number of Me 109's. Our Spitfires chased the bombers back to France and shot down one over the Kent coast ; they also destroyed one of the Messerschmitts.

On Sunday, September 1, more attempts were made on our aerodromes in Kent, Surrey and Essex. Enemy fighters in advance laid a mark consisting of a ring of smoke, and the bombers then attempted to drop their missiles on the area outlined. But as this marking was an advertisement to our waiting Spitfires and Hurricanes the enemy device necessarily had little value. Enemy formations of 100 to 150 were employed in the day's largest raid, between 1 and 2 p.m., with considerably smaller forces later, at 3 p.m. The battle surged to and fro and at one time exciting air fights were waged over the outer ring of London suburbs.

Coming up the Thames Estuary on Tuesday afternoon, September 3, a force of Nazi aircraft made strenuous attempts to get past our barrage, which in the past had always

baffled them. Three of one bomber formation, for example, were shot down by our A.A. gunners within two minutes, and another shortly afterwards. Mass attacks were made again and again, but all failed before the barrage of fire put up by our ground defences. As soon as the formations had been scattered our fighters went in and completed the rout.

Again on Tuesday waves of enemy raiders tried to force a way up the Estuary but without success. London was warned and took to its shelters, but its guns never came into action. In the morning 250 'planes attacked the defences of S.E. England, and later in the day a wave of 150 aircraft was employed; but these great armies of the air withered away before the barrage and the keen offensive of our fighters. Once again the Luftwaffe had failed. The first year's War in the Air, then completed, gave the enemy no success in his major aim —the subjugation of Britain's air defences and the terrorization of her people.

On August 3 a force of 100 Nazi bombers made a savage raid on a town in the Thames Estuary. The worst feature of the raid was dive bombing by four 'planes that sprayed buildings with bullets. One, a Dornier 17, was shot down by Lewis gun fire and, left, are Gunners Harris and Howland who did it. Above, the Dornier is burning on the beach. Right, a member of its crew under guard.

Photos, Fox

The Lights of London Town—1940 Pattern

This remarkable photograph was taken from the roof of a high building in Fleet Street during one of the night raids over London towards the end of August. The exposure lasted 90 minutes. The searchlight has just caught a Nazi bomber, while the diagonal streak is the light from a parachute flare. In the upper part of the photograph anti-aircraft shells are bursting. The streaks of light across the photograph are caused by the movements of the stars during the long exposure.

Photo, Associated Press

What the R.A.F. Did to Germany in August

During the month of August the Royal Air Force made about two hundred raids on Germany or enemy-occupied regions, and the table printed in page 263 records operations at 284 points. A brief analysis of these raids is given. So numerous were the aerodromes attacked that eventually the Air Ministry ceased to specify them individually and gave instead the bulk results.

GERMANY was somewhat slow to take up night bombing to any large extent. It was thought that, concentrating on fighter production and the building of day-bomber types, she had been perforce obliged to put up with a smaller output of the heavier class of bomber. Then, too, until the collapse of France, night bombing raids on Britain involved some difficulties. Comparatively few of the Nazi pilots had been trained or were experienced in night operations, and few could have had knowledge of our terrain. Perhaps, added to all these factors and surpassing them in importance, was the circumstance that Hitler had infused into his army and air force—high command and operating personnel alike—the notion of a blitzkrieg in which victory should be won by a short series of dashing actions against much inferior opponents.

Whatever the causes that led to Hitler's postponement of his major land effort until the early summer of 1940, this respite enabled Britain to build up a far greater Air Force and instil into its gallant members that spirit which today finds its expression in the heroic successes achieved against the four-to-one superiority in numbers of the invading Luftwaffe.

Then, right from the outbreak of hostilities, the R.A.F. carried the war into the enemy country and, when Britain's policy at last permitted, undertook the persistent raiding of military objectives on land. During one month alone, according to an official statement issued early in August, the R.A.F. had dropped 33,431 bombs on Germany or German-occupied territory, while the Nazis had been able in the same period to drop on Britain only 6,987 bombs.

Aerodromes and aircraft factories, of course, are among the most important objectives. Air Chief Marshal Sir Robert Brooke-Popham, speaking recently about factors of air superiority, stressed the great danger of pressing for local defence, and said that probably the best defence for Derby (for instance) would be a bomber squadron in Norfolk which attacked aircraft factories in Dessau. Now at Dessau, 69 miles S.W. of Berlin, are the gigantic works of the Junkers organization, where bombers and troop-carriers are built. There is another Junkers factory at Bernburg, not far from Magdeburg.

Both these places were bombed by the R.A.F. on August 13. Three nights later Bernburg was revisited, the factory and its test airfield being severely damaged. On August 28 another raid, on an even larger scale, was made by the R.A.F. on Dessau. Fires broke out which could be seen for 60 miles; clouds of smoke rose to 300 feet. In the words of one of our pilots, " it seemed as though the whole place were ablaze. I am sure that it won't turn out any more Junkers for a while." On August 16 the Messerschmitt works at Augsburg was bombed severely; it was raided again on the 27th. Other aircraft factories were bombed during the month by the R.A.F., who turned in a new direction to harry Germany's 'plane production. Previously they had punished the aircraft works at Gotha, Cassel and Bremen, and also the Dornier seaplane establishment at Wismar.

Aerodromes without number have been systematically raided night after night. During one part of August the Air Ministry's communiqués specified eleven in Germany, twelve in Holland (one bombed twice, four bombed three times and one raided six times) and a score in German-occupied France. In fact, later in the month the communiqués ceased to particularize, and just lumped them together in one total,

This heavy bomber is being prepared for one of the nightly raids over Germany. A train of low trucks takes the bombs to the 'plane, but some of them may come back, for, as Mr. Churchill said in his message to the Bomber Command (see page 264), pilots have brought their bombs home rather than loose them when it was difficult to hit the precise military objectives prescribed. The map shows the towns and industrial areas that have been bombed by the R.A.F. Since May 10 the R.A.F. have raided Germany itself nearly 600 times. *Photo, L.N.A. Map, courtesy of the "Daily Express"*

Over 280 Raids on Enemy Territory in 31 Days

Many of the raids over Germany have been carried out by Wellington bombers and in this photograph one of them, taking off for a flight over enemy territory, is soaring above another of the same type. These 'planes are armed with six machine-guns, besides bombs, and carry a crew of five.
Photo, Wide World

saying : " Many aerodromes were attacked."

Oil products are the life-blood of aircraft engines, so let us see what the R.A.F. did during the month to destroy Germany's stocks, demolish her refineries and hydrogenation plants and hamper the transport of oil and petrol. Seventeen oil stores, refineries or synthetic production works were raided : Homburg on August 6, 7 and 10 ; Frankfurt on August 10, 16, 22 and 24 ; the huge works at Sterkrade on August 4 and 23, and the Gelsenkirchen oil plant on August 1, 3, 11 and 15.

During the Sterkrade raid of the 22nd " lines of H.E. bombs were seen to straddle the target ; a direct hit is believed to have been scored on the pumping station, and fires were started with incendiary bombs." The huge hydrogenation plant at Leuna, near Leipzig, has a production of about half a million tons of coal-oil per annum : on August 16 the R.A.F. bombed it for the first time. Despite a fierce barrage our machines dropped hundreds of bombs. The main plant extends for almost 1½ miles, and along the entire range of buildings there was a chain of fires. On the 26th Leuna was again heavily attacked by the R.A.F. On the same night other R.A.F. machines bombed the benzine refinery at Bohlen, said to turn out 180,000 tons yearly.

On the 15th two installations at Gelsenkirchen (five miles N. of Essen) were selected for punishment, when two separate raiding forces bombed them systematically for two hours. One crew, which had scored eight direct hits, counted at least twenty-five fires raging. Another large oil refinery near-by was attacked also. The restriction of oil imports has made Germany's plants for producing oil from coal and lignite more valuable, and it was these works which the R.A.F. so successfully bombed at the end of the month.

In quite another direction, after a flight of some 600 miles, our bomber squadrons attacked the aluminium works at Rheinefelden, on the Rhine, ten miles E. of Basle. For one and a half hours bombs were rained on the extensive plant, our pilots coming down as low as 1,500 feet at times. Enormous damage was done over a wide area : many fires were started until, to our bomber crews, the entire expanse of buildings seemed ablaze.

Among chemical factories, munition works and metal works bombed were those at Lunen, Grevenbroich, Ludwigshafen, Griesheim and, last but not least, the Krupp works at Essen. The Daimler-Benz motor works at Stuttgart was bombed on the 24th. Here armament and armoured-cars are manufactured. The resulting conflagration could be seen from a distance of 60 miles.

For transport, Germany relies a great deal on her inland waterways, especially as her over-worked railway system has been repeatedly disorganized by our bombers. Two important canals are the Dortmund-Ems, linking up the Ruhr with Emden, and the Weser-Elbe canal, connecting the two rivers. The former has become historic through the exploits of our pilots : it was bombed again on the 19th, when also a low-level attack was made on the Weser-Elbe canal. The same night a strong R.A.F. force attacked Kiel dockyard, and rail communications over a wide area were dislocated by successful attacks on Bremen, Wunstorf and Geseke.

The marshalling yard at Hamm was bombed for the fifty-second time on this same 19th of August, and on the 22nd, together with the goods siding at Soest, was bombed " as usual." Much other damage was done to road and rail communications in vital zones. Then, too, the electric power stations received attention ; those at Herdecke and Hattingen were bombed on August 11 ; that at Zschornewitz on the 19th ; Knapsack was raided on the 22nd and 24th, and the station at Kelsterbach, near Frankfurt, on August 27. In the light of these facts no one can doubt that the aircraft production and maintenance of the enemy is being seriously hindered by this offensive defence of our shores against the aerial terror.

One Month's R.A.F. Raids on Germany and Enemy-Occupied Territory

(Compiled from Official Air Ministry Communiqués)

Numbers following place-names denote the days in August on which raids were made

Aerodromes	Aerodromes	Chemical Works, Munition Works, Metal Works, etc.	Oil Refineries, Hydrogenation Works, Oil Stores and Depots
Abbeville, 3	Merville, 23		Berlin, 30,
Arnhem, 31	Morlaix, 14	**Berlin, 28**	Bottrop, 3, 22, 29
Berlin, 30, 31	Montebourg, 19	Cologne, 9, 10	Bohlen, 16
Borkum, 5	Munster, 9	Essen, 1, 15, 29	Castrop-Rauxel, 11
Boulogne, 14, 20	Nivelles, 26	Griesheim, 22, 26	Cherbourg, 30
Breat, 11, 19, 27	Orleans, 19, 23	Grevenbroich, 13	Coblenz, 22
Bricy, 19	Ostend, 19	Hoechst, 26	Cologne, 29, 31
Brussels, 19	Plouescar, 24, 26	Jena, 16	Dortmund, 11, 28
Caen, 10, 11, 20, 23	Rennes, 19, 23	Leverkusen, 26, 31	Flushing, 9
Chartres, 15	Saarguemines, 24	Ludwigshafen, 9, 24, 25	Frankfurt, 10, 16, 22, 24, 26
Cherbourg, 1, 7, 10, 11	St. Brieuc, 23	Lunen, 13, 15	Gelsenkirchen, 1, 3, 11, 15, 29, 30
Crefeld, 4, 6, 10	St. Inglevert, 19	Mors, 6	Gironde Estuary, 14, 19, 27
Darmstadt, 24	St. Omer, 19, 22, 23, 26	Rheinefelden, 18	Hanover, 19
Deauville, 22	Schihpol, 3, 5, 6, 8, 9, 10	Ruhrort-Hafen, 9, 22	Homburg, 6, 7, 10
De Kooy, 26	Soesterberg, 6, 19	Waldshut, 18	Kamen, 1
De Mors, 22	Texel, 6, 26		Leuna, 16, 26
Dietholz, 19	Trier, 9	**Power Stations**	Magdeburg, 30, 31
Dinard, 11, 22, 23, 24	Vannes, 23	Cologne, 8, 10	Mannheim, 27
Dortmund, 1	Valkenburg, 8	Duisburg, 29	Monheim, 3
Eindhoven, 6, 9, 23	Venlo, 6, 9	Hattingen, 11	Ostermoor, 19
Flushing, 10, 19, 24	Vierzon, 24	Herdecke, 11	Rotterdam, 3, 31
Freiburg, 18	Villacoublay, 19, 23	Kelsterbach, 27	Reisholz, 1, 6, 15, 28
Gilze Rijen, 6, 9	Waalhaven, 10	Knapsack, 22, 24	St. Nazaire, 29
Gladbach-Rheydt, 6	Werl, 9	Zschornewitz, 19	Salzbergen, 19
Glicy, 23	Wizernes, 14		Sterkrade, 4, 23
Guernsey, 9, 10, 11	Ypenburg, 6	**Railway Junctions, Marshalling Yards, Supply Depots**	
Guipavas, 19, 23		Bremen, 19, 30	**Naval Bases, Docks, Harbours, etc.**
Haamstede, 1, 3, 7	**Aircraft Factories, Aircraft Stores, etc.**	Coblenz, 22	Borkum, 15
Haarlem, 24		Crefeld, 1	Boulogne, 14, 17, 18, 30, 31
Habsheim, 18	Augsburg, 16, 17	Duisburg, 10, 13, 22, 26	Dieppe, 23
Holtenau, 7	Berlin, 30	Geseke, 19	Duisburg, 22
Husum, 7	Bernburg, 13, 16	Hamm, 1, 5, 6, 7, 8, 9, 10, 11, 15, 19, 22, 26, 29, 30, 31	Emden, 30, 31
Jagel, 19	Frankfurt, 13, 22, 26	Hanover, 31	Hamburg, 5, 8, 10, 30
Lanveoc, 19, 22, 23	Dessau, 13, 27, 28	Mannheim, 1, 22, 23, 27	Helder, 15
Lastrup, 31	Kochem, 13	Neheim, 19, 24	Kiel, 3, 5, 7, 19, 20, 27
Le Bourget, 6	Kolleda, 16	Osnabruck, 31	Wilhelmshaven, 10, 27
Le Crotoy, 19	**Leipzig, 28**	Roermonde, 13	
Leeuwarden, 1, 5, 15, 19	Munchen-Gladbach, 13	Schwerte, 6	**Canals**
Le Poulmic, 9, 23	Stuttgart, 24	Soest, 8, 9, 11, 15, 22, 29, 30, 31	Dortmund-Ems, 19
Lingen, 23	Wismar, 5	Wunstorf, 19	Weser-Elbe, 19
Lisieux, 19, 22, 23			

Total No. of Raids, Aug. 1-31 ... 283

R.A.F. Shatters the Myth of Berlin's Immunity

Berlin and its environs were raided four times by the Royal Air Force during a week beginning on August 25 and selected military objectives were heavily damaged. In no sense a reprisal for the enemy raids on London, the R.A.F. operations were an extension of the strategy that for months past had dealt hammer blows at key points in enemy territory.

ON August 8 the Nazis began their massed aerial attacks on Britain, and eight days later there were two raids on London itself. Whatever may have been the motives that caused Hitler so long to delay the attack on our capital city we may be sure that expediency governed his action. For long months our Air Force had been striking at hundreds of aerodromes, factories, transport lines and other key points night after night—with great success and surprisingly few losses. The Nazis might well have suspected that any intensification of their own raids would provoke even greater activity on the part of the R.A.F., and they

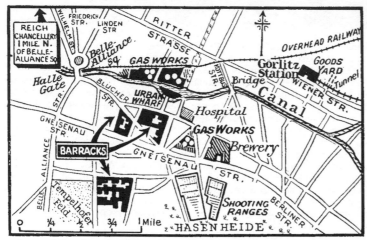

Some of the places in Berlin which suffered damage by our raids during the period August 25-31 are here indicated.
Courtesy of the " Daily Telegraph "

might also have feared raids on their own capital, which they had often boasted was impregnable to air attack. Yet, driven by the imperative need to strike at Britain's vitals and to bolster up the morale of his own people, Hitler was compelled to send his airmen against London.

On the night of August 25 bombers of the Royal Air Force attacked armament factories in the Berlin area, thus opening a new phase in the air war. It must be emphasized that though this was the first time that bombs were dropped in the region of Berlin, the German capital had in fact been at the mercy of our bombers for months past, since many of our pilots had made the journey in every sort of weather since last autumn. During March, for instance, Berlin was visited five times in six nights by the R.A.F. The Air Ministry pointed out that the raid of Sunday night was not a reprisal for the Nazi attacks on London. It was, of course, merely a quite legitimate extension of our bombing attacks on military objectives, an analysis of which for the month of August is printed in page 263.

Berlin's raid warning lasted just over an hour and a quarter; ten heavy explosions were heard within a few minutes of the sirens sounding. Later there were other detonations and much gunfire. The German A.A. guns were in action for nearly three hours. Leaflets as well as bombs were dropped by our machines. An American

correspondent said that next day three streets in the German capital had been roped off; according to a Stockholm report certain streets were strewn with shell splinters and leaflets.

On the night of Wednesday, August 28, "important targets in the Berlin area were heavily bombed," said an Air Ministry announcement. Both high explosive and incendiary bombs were employed, and the objectives included works vital to war production. Aircraft drawn' from two squadrons made a special attack on one objective only four miles from the centre of the city. A neutral report stated that at a point in the Kottbusserstrasse a time bomb embedded in the roadway was a menace to Berlin's underground railway.

Next day the German broadcasting stations warned people to go to shelters directly they heard A.A. gunfire. Newspapers described the British bombing as "wilful murder" and as "Churchill's deliberate manoeuvre to terrorize the German population." It was stated that ten persons were killed and 28 injured.

Fifteen tons of bombs were dropped in the Berlin area on Friday night (August 30-31) by the Royal Air Force. Objectives included a factory making war material, a petroleum

store, and aerodromes. The raid lasted between two and three hours, and intense opposition was encountered from the ground defences.

On Saturday night, Aug. 31–Sept. 1, for the fourth time during the week, Berlin was raided. This time our bombers singled out lighting installations, an aero-engine factory, and an aerodrome in the German city and its environs. Visibility was poor, and to the west of Berlin the entire region for a distance of 70 miles was covered with a bank of low cloud. Now and then a break in the clouds enabled our pilots to catch a glimpse of one of the many lakes in the district and thus to get their bearings.

Thus was the myth of Berlin's invulnerability destroyed. Its people had been told that the city was so well protected by A.A. batteries that no raider would be able to get through. This was a foolish exaggeration, and bound to bring about its own disproof. By contrast, Britons were told long ago by the Government that it was practically impossible to prevent some raiders penetrating their defences by night (and, with less probability, by day) given a sufficiently determined attack. Instead of being buoyed up by false and delusive hopes of immunity they rely on a quiet courage to face the perils and a determination to play a citizen's part in the Battle of Britain.

On the night of August 28, during a three-hour raid on Berlin, our bombers penetrated the enemy barrage and attacked selected targets. This radio photograph shows damage done by two bombs which fell in Kottbusserstrasse, about half a mile from the Görlitzer railway station (see plan above).
Photo, Associated Press

How the Raiders May Be Spotted

Diagrams for the Non-technical Man.

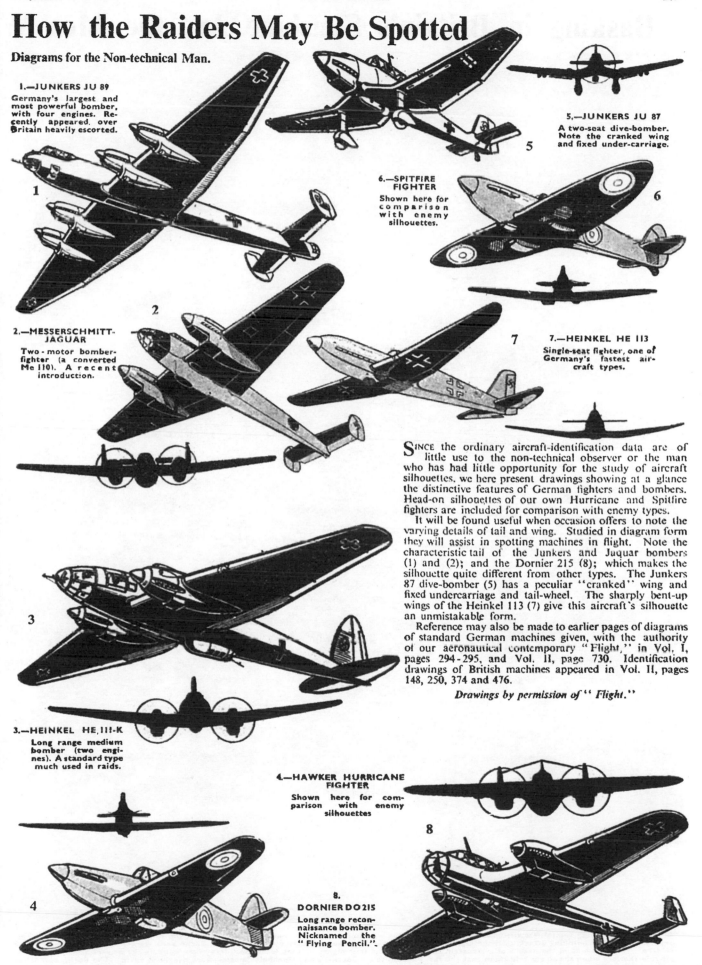

1.—JUNKERS JU 89
Germany's largest and most powerful bomber, with four engines. Recently appeared over Britain heavily escorted.

2.—MESSERSCHMITT-JAGUAR
Two - motor bomber-fighter (a converted Me 110). A recent introduction.

3.—HEINKEL HE, 111-K
Long range medium bomber (two engines). A standard type much used in raids.

4.—HAWKER HURRICANE FIGHTER
Shown here for comparison with enemy silhouettes

5.—JUNKERS JU 87
A two-seat dive-bomber. Note the cranked wing and fixed under-carriage.

6.—SPITFIRE FIGHTER
Shown here for comparison with enemy silhouettes.

7.—HEINKEL HE 113
Single-seat fighter, one of Germany's fastest aircraft types.

8. DORNIER DO 215
Long range reconnaissance bomber. Nicknamed the "Flying Pencil."

SINCE the ordinary aircraft-identification data are of little use to the non-technical observer or the man who has had little opportunity for the study of aircraft silhouettes, we here present drawings showing at a glance the distinctive features of German fighters and bombers. Head-on silhouettes of our own Hurricane and Spitfire fighters are included for comparison with enemy types.

It will be found useful when occasion offers to note the varying details of tail and wing. Studied in diagram form they will assist in spotting machines in flight. Note the characteristic tail of the Junkers and Jaguar bombers (1) and (2); and the Dornier 215 (8); which makes the silhouette quite different from other types. The Junkers 87 dive-bomber (5) has a peculiar "cranked" wing and fixed undercarriage and tail-wheel. The sharply bent-up wings of the Heinkel 113 (7) give this aircraft's silhouette an unmistakable form.

Reference may also be made to earlier pages of diagrams of standard German machines given, with the authority of our aeronautical contemporary "Flight," in Vol. I, pages 294-295, and Vol. II, page 730. Identification drawings of British machines appeared in Vol. II, pages 148, 250, 374 and 476.

Drawings by permission of "Flight."

Basking in Britain's Sunshine Are the Men Wh

Although the German capital was visited in the early days of the war on more than one occasion by 'planes of the R.A.F. dropping leaflets, it did not experience its first bombing attack until the night of Sunday, August 25, when military objectives in the Berlin area were heavily bombed by R.A.F. raiders. This raid was in the nature of a "curtain raiser," and on four nights of that week Berliners were kept awake or sent scurrying to their air-raid shelters when the sirens told them that the R.A.F.—despite all Goering's and Goebbels' boasts—were overhead again. The Berlin authorities maintained that small damage was done, but they took the precaution of roping off those districts which had been most affected : and their denials

v Hours Before Were Keeping Berliners Awake

were hardly borne out by the newspapers, which were lavish in such headlines as " Murder," " Shameful, cowardly act " " Systematic Churchill manoeuvre to place German population under murderous terror." And Hitler himself in his tirade of September 4 screamed against the British " pirates " who perpetrated the " nuisance of nightly and planless bomb-throwing." Both in Britain and in Germany there were suggestions that the raids on Berlin were in the nature of reprisals for the German raids on London, but this was denied by British air authorities. As always, the R.A.F. continues to concentrate on strictly military objectives, of which there are plenty in the Berlin area.

Two Nazis Fell to the 'Arctic Trapper's' Guns

"WE thought it was 'Good-night, nurse'," said the skipper of the "Arctic Trapper" with the usual gift of understatement practised by those at sea. He was describing the moment at which his gun crew had already brought down one Nazi and the other Nazis—five of them—turned and made a determined attack on him to avenge their comrades. The "Arctic Trapper" is a Grimsby trawler built for the North Sea fishing and familiar with the run out of Grimsby to Spitsbergen or Iceland.

"She looks shabby, mind you," admitted the engineer who accompanied us in the launch which put out to take aboard the "Arctic Trapper's" mail. "But she's a right ship. You should see her moving." The sirens had just gone on land when we came aboard, and Skipper William Hilldrith mentioned casually enough : "You'll see all the boys manning their action stations just as they were the other day." That "other day" was the day the "Arctic Trapper" brought down two German 'planes with her one gun, a score which brought congratulations from the First Lord of the Admiralty.

"The wife's got that telegram," said the skipper. "Otherwise you could see it." But I did see the young ex-railway porter from Grantham, who is the gunner, and his gun crew, all Grimsby fishermen, who shot down the second Nazi 'plane while machine-

Skipper William Hilldrith, of the Grimsby trawler "Arctic Trapper," all ready to put to sea again, despite the Nazi bombers, just after his ship's gallant exploit.

gun fire from a German formation was swishing about them. On the wrists of these men are home-made identity disks. These are painfully shaped by hand and are punched out with the seamen's names. They are made of parts of German 'planes which have been brought down.

"That's what made us steam towards them so fast," said the crew. And the recipe for shooting down Nazi 'planes ?

"You want to get the first shot in," said the young gunner. "They must be in range, of course."

George Kirby photographed them as they waited at their gun stations, while the sirens screeched across the water from the land : heavy-eyed but eager, they waited for them, unshaven but alert at their precious gun. The raiders passed and the "Arctic Trapper" was ordered off to a new position as we left.

"She don't look up to much, but she moves lovely," ruminated the engineer. And the little boat that smacked down two of the ineffectual eagles sent to terrify the South Coast of England sailed by across our stern, solid and small in the sunset.

Story by John Pudney and photographs by F.G.Kirby, "News Chronicle" staff photographer. Exclusive to THE WAR ILLUSTRATED

Members of the trawler's crew have a little fun with a trophy they picked up off Margate. It is a rubber boat carried by a German raider. Below, the gun crew are manning the 12-pdr. with which they brought down the Nazi bomber at the end of August.

In the circle is the shabby, but gallant, little "Arctic Trapper" at sea off Ramsgate. In addition to the 12-pdr. the "Arctic Trapper" carries a Lewis gun to deal with low-flying 'planes. Below, the crew are ready for action.

Alsace Is Already German Once Again

When the Germans defeated France in 1870 they demanded, and received in due course,
Alsace-Lorraine as part of the price of victory. In 1940 they have not yet formally
demanded it, but there is no doubt that they will do so, and in the meantime they are
acting as if the cession had been already made. Here by way of background we tell
something of Alsace-Lorraine's troubled history.

In Alsace-Lorraine there are no " Avenue Maréchal Foch " nowadays ; they have all been changed into " Adolf Hitler Strasse." In the towns and villages they are taking down the French place names and putting up signboards in German. French advertising signs are rapidly disappearing, and placards advertising German newspapers have been pasted over the French posters calling for subscriptions to the National Defence loans. The hotel names are being Germanized also, and the names above the shops. But perhaps the most prominent of all evidences of the Germanizing process are the outlines of names over

created German Empire the whole of Alsace and a large part of Lorraine, including the great town of Metz.

From 1871 until 1918 Alsace-Lorraine, as the ceded territories were now officially styled, was under German rule. For the first twenty years it was governed from Berlin by dictatorial decrees, but following the fall of Bismarck in 1890 the young Kaiser, Wilhelm II—the " recluse of Doorn," as we have come to know him—embarked on a more liberal policy which reconciled many of the populace to German rule, although they still maintained their love for French culture, their devotion to the ideals of old France.

In 1911 the Kaiser granted Alsace-Lorraine a constitution, and the process of Germanization was greatly helped by developments in France herself, where the markedly hostile attitude adopted by the Government towards the Catholic Church deeply offended the Alsatians, who were and are devoted Catholics. At this time the Alsatian Clerical Party, strongest in numbers of all their political groups, became affiliated to the German Centre Party. Yet just before the Great War relations between the Alsatians and the Germans were worse than they had been

Demobilized after their country's defeat, these French soldiers are entraining for their homes—if homes the war has still left them. Some of them, maybe, are Alsatians, and on arrival they will find that their beautiful province is being rapidly Germanized.   *Photo, Wide World*

shop-fronts whose former owners were Jews ; here the names have been torn away or scrawled over, and almost without exception the windows beneath have been smashed and the interior of the shop ransacked and wrecked. In the streets little children sometimes wave the swastika flag, and more and more it is becoming the custom to give the Hitler salute beneath the shadow of the great cathedral in Strasbourg which Goethe knew and loved.

Out of its 2,000 years of history Alsace-Lorraine—more properly Alsace and Lorraine, for until 1871 they were two distinct provinces—has spent many centuries under German rule. For nearly 800 years following the break-up of Charlemagne's empire Lorraine was a more or less independent dukedom loosely attached to the Germanic Holy Roman Empire. Alsace was still more German in speech and culture—its people still speak a German dialect—and for many centuries its principal cities were virtually independent. In 1648, however, it was annexed to France following the Thirty Years' War, and in 1766 Lorraine, too, was united to the French crown. Both provinces remained French until 1871 when, following the disastrous Franco-German war, Bismarck compelled France to surrender to the newly-

for years, following several incidents in which German soldiers had adopted a most truculent attitude against Alsatian civilians. During the four years of the Great War the inhabitants of Alsace-Lorraine were in a most difficult, even terrible, position, and it was with unbounded joy that they welcomed the French troops as liberators in October, 1918.

Hard on the heels of the retreating Germans the French reoccupied their lost provinces ; in 1919 Alsace-Lorraine was formally restored to France by the Treaty of Versailles, and the mourning robes which for nearly 50 years had muffled the statue of Strasbourg in the Place de la Concorde were removed. The re-annexation of Alsace-Lorraine advanced France to the position of one of the most important European steel producers, for Lorraine has vast iron deposits and considerable coal resources which had been organized by Germany on a basis of large-scale capitalism. But it also brought with it problems which the highly centralized and altogether secular French Republic found it difficult to solve The Alsatians had possessed under the Kaiser a considerable measure of local government, and had learned to look to Strasbourg as their centre ; now they were required to turn to Paris for inspiration and direction. Still more important was the

fact that in Alsace-Lorraine the Concordat with the Papacy had been maintained so that the Catholic priests were paid by the State and the children were taught the Catholic faith in State-aided schools. While just after the war the provincial assemblies which the Germans had permitted were swept away, the " Cartel des Gauches " of 1924 under Herriot and Briand proposed that religious teaching in the national schools should be suppressed. But in face of a boycott of the schools, Herriot was obliged to compromise.

But the religious and provincial susceptibilities of the Alsace-Lorrainers had been roused, and in 1926 an autonomist organization was founded—the " Elsass-Lothringer Heimatbund " (Home League of Alsace-Lorraine)—under the leadership of Eugen Ricklin, who had been a member of the German Reichstag and of the Alsace-Lorraine Landtag. Its programme included the recognition of Alsace-Lorrainers as a national minority, political autonomy with an Alsace-Lorraine local parliament, and the placing of the German language on an equality with French. Poincaré, who was himself a Lorrainer, endeavoured to suppress the movement with a high hand, banning the autonomist newspapers and arresting the chief leaders. Ricklin and his lieutenant, Rossé, were tried at Colmar in 1928 on a charge of plotting against the State, but their condemnation and sentence to a term of imprisonment made them popular martyrs and they were soon amnestied.

Supported by Catholic and Democratic elements the autonomists won increasing influence, and of the thirty deputies returned by Alsace-Lorraine to the last Chamber in Paris, six were declared autonomists. The autonomists always denied that they sought for reunion with Germany, but of late years there has been a pronounced National Socialist movement in the provinces, actively supported from within the Reich. Even after the war began they were active, and one of their number, C. P. Roos, was shot in October, 1939, as a German spy.

But now the Alsatian Nazis are having their way. Politically, the anschluss has already been effected with the installation of Herr Wagner as Chief of Civilian Administration ; it is rumoured that Alsace will form part of a new province, Gau Ober-Rhein, with Karlsruhe as its capital. " Henceforth," declared Herr Wagner soon after his appointment, " there will be no Alsace problem ; the clean-up neglected in 1871 will be made ; all the foreign elements in the country will be expelled because they have striven to maintain a perpetual state of dissension." The economic anschluss is also in progress, for already the customs barrier between Alsace and the Reich has been swept away and instead a new barrier has been erected between the province and France ; the Alsatians have been given ration cards for bread, flour, meat, and sugar, such as their German neighbours have possessed for years, and in the restaurants they serve ersatz coffee and tea.

Paris Is Not Allowed to Forget

These German soldiers are rummaging among the books on the famous stalls beside the Seine, perhaps in the hope of finding a German novel wherewith to while away the hours of boredom.   Below is a demobilized French soldier who with heavy heart has returned to his workbench.

Every day the people of Paris suffer the humili-ation of seeing Nazi soldiers sightseeing in their beautiful city.   Right, a wounded captain of the French Army wheeled out by his wife.

The German troops seen above enjoy the triumph of sounding the tattoo by torchlight in the quadrangle at Versailles beside the statue of Louis XIV.   Right, a Nazi military band is playing in the Place de l'Etoile, near the Arc de Triomphe in Paris.
                                    Photos, Wide World and E.N.A.

The King Greets Frenchmen Who Are Still Free

On August 24, 1940, the King made his first inspection of General de Gaulle's Free French forces, at a camp in the South of England. Above, the King is seen with General de Gaulle on his arrival. His Majesty is acknowledging the Royal salute of the guard of honour.

Since it has been re-armed and re-equipped, General de Gaulle's Army has undergone an intensive course of training, both infantry and mechanized units constantly taking part in exercises. Left, French soldiers are in "action" with rifles and a trench mortar.

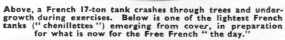

Above, a French 17-ton tank crashes through trees and undergrowth during exercises. Below is one of the lightest French tanks ("chenillettes") emerging from cover, in preparation for what is now for the Free French "the day."

The crews of French warships that came to Britain have been in action against enemy aircraft and have accounted for at least one raider. Above, the gunners of one of the famous French 75-mm. A.A. guns "at the alert" during a raid.

Photos, P.N.A., Planet News and L.N.A.

Transylvania : Latest Victim of Power Politics

Rumania, so largely the creation of the Versailles settlement, was at once threatened when the " Diktat " came to be repudiated. She restored Bessarabia to Russia and the Southern Dobrudja to Bulgaria, but jibbed at Hungary's Transylvanian demands. Here we tell of the contested province and of the Vienna Award of August 30, 1940.

THOSE who remember their Latin will know that Transylvania means "beyond the woods " (i.e. in this case, from Hungary), and both in Hungarian and Rumanian its names signify " forest land." It is a country well deserving of its beautiful name—a country of hill and mountain, of rich pastures on which graze cattle and horses and sheep, of great fields of corn, of orchards and vineyards. It has its industrial side, too, for there is many an ancient town with factories and mines.

Sheltered within the embrace of the Carpathian mountains, it has escaped many of the great wars which have devastated Europe to east and west, but its very isolation, combined with its natural riches, has made it a land to which the feet of the wandering peoples have gladly turned. Thus it is that today it is the despair of those tidy souls who would have every country inhabited by one people and one people alone, for in Transylvania there are many peoples of many different races, speaking many different tongues, worshipping according to many different rites. And, moreover, they are exceedingly intermingled.

Once a part of the Roman province of Dacia, Transylvania was overrun by wave after wave of barbarian tribes, the chief and last of whom were the Magyars, or Hungarians. In the middle ages the population consisted of the great mass of Romano-Dacians—from whom the present-day Rumanians are descended—and the three dominating " nations," the Magyars, the Szekelers (also of the Magyar race), and the Saxons. The last were German colonists who had arrived in the country in the 12th century and established themselves in the Siebenbürgen (the " seven strong towns "), of which Sibiu (Hermannstadt) and Brasov (Kronstadt) were the most important. For many centuries the Magyars constituted the ruling race ; the Rumanians—Wallachians or Vlachs they were styled—although they numbered more than half of the total popula-

tion, were looked down upon and were subjected to religious persecution inasmuch as their religion was that of the Orthodox Church, while the Hungarians were Catholics.

From 1003, when Transylvania was conquered by King Stephen of Hungary, until 1526, Transylvania was part of the Hungarian kingdom, and it was so again from 1691 to 1848 and from 1868 until October 1918, when, following the collapse of the Austro-Hungarian Empire, the Rumanians of Transylvania and of the adjoining Hungarian districts on the west proclaimed their independence of Hungary, and a few weeks later voted for union with the kingdom of Rumania.

Now it was the Rumanians who were the dominant race, and the Hungarians deeply resented their new-found subjection. Under the " Red " dictatorship of Bela Kun the Hungarians invaded Transylvania in 1919, but were driven out by the Rumanians, who in turn occupied (and looted) Budapest. Hungarian protests were disregarded by the victorious Allies, and by the Treaty of Trianon of 1920 the whole of Transylvania was granted to Rumania, together with large stretches of territory on the west.

Carol in Hitler's Trap

Hungary was never reconciled to the situation created by the Treaty of Trianon, and never ceased to demand the return of at least the western fringe of Rumania and a large part of Transylvania. When Carol bowed to Stalin's demands and restored Bessarabia to Russia, when a few weeks later Bulgaria demanded the return of her lost territory in Southern Dobrudja and after a short negotiation was promised it—Hungary became increasingly clamorous in her demands for the restoration of the territory lost in 1920. King Carol threw over the British guarantee in the hope of ingratiating himself with the Axis Powers, but he soon found himself in a pretty dilemma, for Hitler, desirous of strengthening Germany's protégée, Hungary, worked out a plan whereby Rumania would

cede to Hungary both territory and population. According to report, this provided that the frontier districts of Crisana and Maramures, in which the Magyars are in the majority, were to be restored to Hungary, together with sufficient adjoining territory to provide a home for the half-million Szekelers, who were to be removed from the region in the Carpathians where they and their ancestors had lived for 800 or 900 years, while the farms and towns they vacated were to be taken over by Rumanians " brought home " from Hungary. But the plan failed to satisfy Hungary, who was now demanding the whole of Transylvania up to the line of the River Maros.

Then another solution was suggested—that Transylvania should be constituted an independent State, divided into cantons, on the lines of Switzerland.

But finally Hitler decreed otherwise. At a meeting in Vienna on August 30, attended by Von Ribbentrop, Count Ciano, Count Csaky, and M. Manoilescu, Foreign Ministers of Germany, Italy, Hungary and Rumania respectively, it was decided that about two-thirds of Transylvania should be restored to Hungary. The line of division was drawn in the most arbitrary fashion from the Hungaro-Rumanian frontier south of Oradea across the middle of the country to the Carpathians north-east of Brasov. Hungary received some 20,000 square miles of Transylvanian territory, including Cluj the capital, territory inhabited by about 2,500,000 people, of whom more than a million are Rumanians, not to mention some hundreds of thousands of people of German descent. The award, indeed, was altogether contrary to the principle of racial distribution, for many hundreds of thousands of Hungarians were left in the Rumanian portion.

Bitterly must King Carol and his advisers have regretted their denunciation of the British guarantee. They chose to put their trust in Hitler, and now in the space of a few weeks were called upon to pay the price. The Government communiqué issued on the day of the Vienna award stated that "the arbitration of the Axis Powers concerning the Hungarian-Rumanian dispute has been accepted as a result of the ultimative demands formulated by Germany and Italy." Report had it that if the award were not accepted forthwith, then Germany would not only aid her Hungarian vassal in seizing the territory awarded, but might herself go farther and occupy the whole of Rumania.

In Transylvania the news of the partition was received with anguish, and in particular Dr. Maniu, Leader of the National Peasant Party, protested. In Cluj and other Transyl-

Cluj—the Germans call it Klausenburg and the Hungarians Kolozsvar —is situated in hilly country on the banks of the Szamos, a tributary of the Theiss. Its most prominent feature is the fine Gothic church of St. Michael. Its population of 100,000 is made up of Magyars (about half), Rumanians, Jews and Germans.   *Photo, E.N.A.*

Now Hungary Takes a Slice of Rumania

vanian towns crowds paraded the streets singing patriotic songs and shouting that they preferred war to surrender, while others knelt in prayer in the public squares. But these demonstrations were soon banned by the Rumanian Government, fearful that it might jeopardize what the Vienna arbitrators had left. By September 13, it was announced, the whole of the awarded territory should pass into the hands of Hungary.

But there were few even in Hungary who believed that the Transylvanian problem had been settled, and none in Transylvania itself. For Transylvania is a word charged with emotional importance for Rumanians and Hungarians alike. The Magyars can never forget that the country was ruled by St. Stephen nine centuries ago, while the Rumanians for their part recall that all through the centuries of Transylvania's history the backbone of its people have been the men of Rumanian race, that it was the birthplace of the Rumanian language and the seed-plot of the national revival which, a century ago, gave rise to the Rumania of today.

| RUMANIA TOTAL POPULATION 19,500,000 | RUMANIANS 14,250,000 | UKRAINIANS 800,000 | RUSSIANS 500,000 | HUNGARIANS 1,400,000 |
| | GERMANS 750,000 | BULGARIANS 450,000 | TURKS 250,000 | OTHERS 1,100,000 |

Adapted from the "New York Times," this map well shows the tangle of races which have produced Rumania's minority problems. Figures are approximate, from Russian and Rumanian sources.

Following the Great War Rumania was more than doubled in territorty, but in 1940 she has been compelled to restore much of the territory she gained in 1917-1920. First, Bessarabia and Northern Bukovina to Russia; then the Southern Dobrudja to Bulgaria; and, finally, about two-thirds of Transylvania to Hungary.

This mountain scene is typical of the countryside of Southern Transylvania, a land of uplands stretching towards the Carpathians and its southern extension, the Transylvanian Alps. Most of the latter, including Les Monts Fagarash, where this photograph was taken, were left to Rumania by the Vienna award of 1940.

Scattered in little pockets throughout the wide expanse of Transylvania are groups of the Magyar race—people who cherish the memory of the days when they were the dominant nation and who, since the Treaty of Trianon of 1920 gave them to Rumania, have never ceased to hope for the coming of the day that would restore them to Hungary.

Photos, Dorien Leigh and Mondiale

Black France Declares for Liberty

First of the French colonial Governors to join De Gaulle was M. Eboué (left), Governor of the Chad ; he is a negro—the first to hold so high a rank in France's Empire—and was born in Cayenne, French Guiana, 56 years ago. Above is a typical riverside scene in Chad.

Once a German colony, French Cameroons was mandated to France by the League of Nations in 1920 ; left is a view in Duala, the chief port. Above is a chieftain from one of its northern districts.

METROPOLITAN France is enslaved, but to an ever-increasing extent the French Empire overseas is refusing to obey the defeatists of Vichy and, instead, is pledging its support to General de Gaulle. In a broadcast to the French people on August 27 the leader of all Free Frenchmen announced that on August 26 the Governor of the Territory of the Chad in French Equatorial Africa had declared that the Territory refused to accept capitulation and would continue to fight on the side of Great Britain. Response to the Chad's example was soon forthcoming, for on August 29 it was announced that the Free French flag was flying over the whole of French Equatorial Africa and French Cameroons, thus completing a solid block of anti-Axis territory right across Africa ; and later the Society Islands (including Tahiti) and the Marquesas joined General de Gaulle, while Martinique and Guadeloupe were reported to be on the brink of doing so.

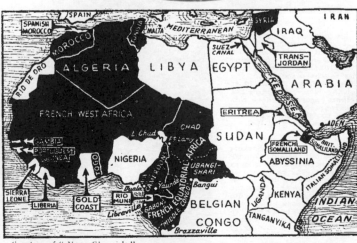

Courtesy of " News Chronicle "

Capital of French Equatorial Africa is Brazzaville (circle). Left is Libreville, capital of Gabun, one of the four divisions of the Colony. The strategical importance of France's colonies in West Africa will be obvious from the map.

Photos. E.N.A., Wide World, and Dorien Leigh

I WAS THERE!

Eye Witness Stories of Episodes and Adventures in the Second Great War

We Were the First to Bomb Berlin

The week of August 25-31, 1940, saw the first bombing attacks by the R.A.F. on military objectives in the Berlin area. In spite of formidable concentrations of searchlights and anti-aircraft guns, the attacks were pressed home successfully, and here we give some eye-witness stories by airmen who took part in these night raids.

ALTHOUGH August 25 was the first occasion since the outbreak of war on which the R.A.F. made bombing attacks in the Berlin area, many of our bomber pilots are familiar with this journey, having made it in every kind of weather during past months.

One pilot, describing the first raid on Berlin, which was his twenty-fifth of the war, said :

When at the " briefing " before we started the intelligence officer mentioned Berlin, everybody was pleased. After the " briefing " we went to the crew room and worked out our course and how we intended to go in. Then we had a bit of dinner. The weather was bad right from the start ; as soon as we gained any height at all we ran into heavy cloud, and during the journey we caught sight of only three small gaps in the cloud.

For at least two-thirds of the way there was very heavy anti-aircraft fire, much more than usual. One might almost have thought that the Germans were expecting us. Twice I had to take violent evasive action to escape the shells.

When we arrived over Berlin there was a formidable concentration of guns and search-lights. We cruised around for half an hour before we located the target, and all the time the guns were popping off at us quite accurately. Then suddenly we saw a small gap beginning to open in the clouds three or four miles away, and we made for it.

First of all we thought we could see a main-road junction. Then the hole in the clouds widened still more and we saw that we were right. Next we caught sight of the reflection of the moon on a lake, and these two points gave us our position. Working down the lake we got on to our target. More " Flak " (A.A. fire) and searchlights than ever started, and we could not keep a steady enough course to bomb the first time. So we did a preliminary canter. Then we went away, and two or three minutes later we came back. We didn't dare to go very far away because, having had that bit of luck in finding the place, we were afraid of losing it once more in the clouds. We went just far enough to shake off the guns and search-lights, and then came back over the target.

By this time the friendly gap had opened up just a bit more. Having dropped our bombs we turned away, dodging violently because the guns were getting warm again. We could see a large red fire burning, and then the clouds finally closed over the scene.

In another raid on Berlin, aircraft drawn from two squadrons made a special attack on one objective only four miles from the centre of the city. Every pilot in the two squadrons wanted to be in on the raid. " You could not have bought a seat in any of the aircraft for any amount of money," said a senior Intelligence Officer.

A young pilot officer broadcast a description of this raid. He said :

We reached the Dutch coast, then we flew on across Germany towards the Dümmer See. That was where we met the first serious opposition, and I decided to climb higher because of the " Flak " (A.A. fire). From this point onwards we were under continuous fire all the way to Berlin—a good 200 miles. There was hardly a break between any of the guns and searchlight concentrations. Several times the aircraft was shaken, and I could see bursts of fire immediately under-neath us, and also about 50 yards off the port wing, dead on our height.

As we approached Berlin there seemed to be a semi-circle of heavy guns to the west of the city firing outwards. Once we had passed those there was very little opposition. . . . As we approached we had seen for some time a large fire burning on the south-east outskirts of Berlin, so we went to have a look at it. We knew that somebody else from the squadron—loaded with incendiary bombs—had gone in earlier to try to set our target on fire to help the rest who were following to find it.

We flew right across the centre of Berlin. If we had been bombing indiscriminately we could have put our bombs down there, but our instructions were to bomb the target and the target only. We were warned about that in no uncertain way. As we got nearer to this fire I could make out the girders of a huge gutted building, which was blazing fiercely.

We circled round above it, then when we had satisfied ourselves that this was the target I decided to go in and attack. We flew away a bit to the east, turned round and made a dive attack. Running up on to the target we met with no anti-aircraft fire at all, so that we were able to carry out a careful attack. It was just like a bit of practice bombing—" left, left ; right, right ; left "—and so on.

They opened up on us when we dropped our bombs, so we got out as quickly as we could, but as soon as we got a little distance away we turned to have a look to see if we could observe any results. There were four fires burning beside the big red one which we had seen earlier. They were intensely white and they formed a long line across the target. Going back it was much the same as it was on the inward journey, except that if anything the " Flak " and searchlights were even more intense, and they certainly continued for a greater distance—right back as far as the Zuider Zee.

Some of the personnel who took part in a big raid on Berlin are seen talking to the Intelligence Officer at their station. These men helped to shatter the legend created by the Nazis that their capital was so well protected by A.A. batteries that no enemy raider could get within bomb-dropping distance. So one more Nazi boast was disproved !

Photo, Fox

I Saw the Nazi Pilot's Frenzied Face

Alarming, indeed, was the experience of some dwellers in a South London suburb during a daylight air raid, when it appeared as if a Heinkel must crash straight into their house. So close did the 'plane come that, as described below, they looked right into the terrified face of the Nazi pilot.

THE Heinkel was heading straight for the house where I had taken cover. The householder, his wife, three children, and I stood helpless, fatally fascinated, as the Nazi bomber loomed larger and larger, until its shape filled the view from the French windows behind which we stood.

It was at this moment we caught sight of the pilot's face.

The glimpse was a momentary one, but none of us in that room will forget the horror of the Nazi's expression.

Helmeted and goggled as he was, there could be no mistaking the frenzied fear which lurked behind the wide open eyes and tensed cheek-bones.

It was the face of a man harassed and hunted to the extremity of human endurance, the face of a man beyond hope of escape, and resigned to the impending crash and total destruction.

Then, as if by a miracle, the 'plane lifted at the last moment, and we glimpsed its pursuer, a British Spitfire, pumping bullets at an incredible rate from all of its eight guns.

The Heinkel crashed a mile away—one almost regrets that its pilot will not be able to report his experience to his messmates in Germany.—(*Reynolds News*.)

I Enjoyed My First Parachute Descent

An R.A.F. officer, who broadcast his story on August 28, told how he brought down two Messerschmitts during a fight off the South Coast before having to bale out. This was his first parachute descent, and he seems to have found it on the whole an enjoyable experience.

IT was a lovely evening and the wind was warm about us as we passed through the slip-stream of our aircraft to our cockpits. We were to patrol the coast at 10,000 feet.

We were flying east when three enemy aircraft were seen flying west in the clouds overhead. I told our leader that I would climb with my flight above the clouds and investigate. As I did this, twelve Messerschmitt 109 fighters emerged from the clouds. Still climbing, I made for the sun and turned and gave the order for my flight to break up and attack. In a moment our battle began— our six Hurricanes against the enemy's twelve.

The eighteen aircraft chased round and round, in and out of the cloud. I chose my first opponent. He seemed to be dreaming, and I quickly got on to his tail and gave him a short burst which damaged him. I flew in closer and gave him a second dose. It was enough. He dived out of control; and I followed him down to 6,000 feet. There I circled for a minute or two and watched him dive vertically into the calm sea.

I opened my hood for a breath of fresh air and looked about the sky. There was no sign of either the enemy or my own flight. I was alone, so I climbed back into the cloud, which was thin and misty.

Then three Messerschmitts, flying in line astern, crossed in front of me—so close that I could see the black crosses on their wings and fuselage. I opened fire on number three in the formation, and we went round and round in decreasing circles. I was lucky again. I had the pleasure of seeing my bullets hit him. Pieces of his wings flew off. Black smoke came from just behind his cockpit. He dived and I fired one more burst at him, directly from astern.

We were doing a phenomenal speed, and then my ammunition gave out—just as the other two Messerschmitts attacked me. I twisted and turned, but they were too accurate. I could hear the deafening thud of their bullets. Pieces of my aircraft seemed to be flying off in all directions; my engine was damaged and I could not climb back to the cloud where I might have lost my pursuers. Then came a cold, stinging pain in my left foot. One of the Jerry bullets had found its mark, but it really did not hurt.

I was about to dive to the sea and make my escape, low down, when the control column became useless in my hand. Black smoke poured into the cockpit and I could not see. I knew that the time had come for me to depart.

I was at about 10,000 feet, but some miles out to sea. I lifted my seat, undid my strap and opened the hood. The wind became my ally. A hand—actually, the slip-stream catching under my helmet—seemed to lift me out of the cockpit. It was a pleasant sensation. I was in mid-air, floating down peacefully in the cool breeze. I had to remind myself to pull my ripcord and open my parachute.

When the first jerk was over I swung like a pendulum. This was not so pleasant, but I soon settled down, and I was able to enjoy a full view of the world below—the beach, some miles away, with soldiers—and the long line of villas in a coastal town. There was no sensation of speed. But the ripples on the water became bigger—the soldiers on the beach became nearer.

I had one minute of anxiety. As I floated down, one of the Messerschmitts appeared. The pilot circled round me and I was just a little alarmed. Would he shoot ? Well, he didn't. He behaved quite well. He opened his hood, waved to me and then dived towards the sea and made off towards France.

The wind was still friendly. It was carrying me in towards the beach. I took out my cigarettes and lit one with my lighter without any difficulty. Ages seemed to pass. As I came nearer and nearer to the coast, I could hear the all-clear sirens, and, passing over the houses on the sea-front, I could see the people coming out of their shelters and looking up at me. I had descended to about 1,000 feet. I began to sway a little, and I could hear my parachute flapping, like the sound of a sail in a small boat. The soldiers' faces were quite clear, but I must have looked English, even at one thousand feet—which was comforting.

For the first time since the enemy pilot circled around me, I became anxious. Was I to end my escapade by being banged against a seaside villa ? It did not seem possible that I could reach the fields beyond. The journey ended in a cucumber frame, after I had pushed myself free of a house with my foot.

And now I come to a pleasant recollection —in spite of my foot and my painful landing. The people in that seaside town were wonderful. A woman appeared with a cup of tea in one second. Then a policeman with a whisky-and-soda. I drank the whisky-and-soda first, then the tea. A blanket appeared, then the ambulance. I remember one amusing incident as I was lifted into the ambulance.

A little boy of seven came over to me with cigarettes, and he said : " Good luck, sir. When I grow up I'm going to be an airman, too."

In the last war, to be shot down meant almost certain death for the airman. Nowadays, however, he has an excellent chance of survival, thanks to his parachute, which, as seen here, is carefully tested in the wind to safeguard against the possibility of tears or flaws.   *Photo, Topical*

Destroyers for Bases—and Everyone Is Pleased!

Widely hailed as one of the most important events in the history of the British Commonwealth and of the United States of America, the Anglo-American Naval Agreement was concluded in Washington on September 3, 1940. An anticipation of its terms has been given in page 242 ; now we give it in detail, together with the text of the official Notes.

"**A**N epochal and far-reaching act in preparation for continental defence in the face of grave danger." These were the words used by President Roosevelt in his special message to Congress on September 3 to describe the Anglo-American Naval Agreement which had just been signed in Washington, whereby Britain leased to the U.S.A. a number of naval and air bases in the Atlantic, and America transferred to Britain 50 destroyers.

Four of the bases—on the Avalon Peninsula and the south coast of Newfoundland, and on the east coast and the Great Bay of Bermuda—were, stated Mr. Roosevelt, " gifts generously given and gladly received " ; or as the British Note from Lord Lothian to Mr. Cordell Hull, dated September 2, put it, they were granted freely and without consideration, " in view of the basis of friendship and sympathetic interest of His Majesty's Government in the United Kingdom in the national security of the United States, and their desire to strengthen the ability of the United States to cooperate effectively with other nations of the Americas in defence of the Western Hemisphere." A glance at the map will show that Canada equally with the U.S.A. may be defended from Newfoundland and Bermuda.

The remaining bases—on the eastern side of the Bahamas, the southern coast of Jamaica, the western coast of St. Lucia, the west coast of Trinidad, in the Gulf of Paria, in the island of Antigua and in British Guiana within 50 miles of Georgetown—were stated to be leased " in exchange for

naval and military equipment and material which the United States will transfer to His Majesty's Government " ; and there was no secret of the fact that this equipment and material would take the shape of fifty of America's surplus destroyers—vessels which were " obsolete " in the sense that they were over sixteen years old, but which were perfectly serviceable and would constitute a most timely strengthening of Britain's naval forces in an arm of the service which has suffered comparatively heavy losses.

All of the bases referred to in the Agreement, together with the " facilities for entrance thereto and protection thereof," will be leased to the United States for a period of 99 years, free of rent and charges other than compensation to the owners of private property for any losses or damage they may sustain arising out of the bases' establishment ; it was stressed that there was no question of any surrender of British sovereignty in the territories affected.

" The Agreement," continued President Roosevelt in his message to Congress, " is not inconsistent in any sense with our status at peace ; still less is it a threat against any nation. It is an epochal and far-reaching act in preparation for continental defence in the face of grave danger. . . .

" Preparation for defence is an inalienable prerogative of a sovereign State, and under present circumstances this exercise of a sovereign right is essential for the maintenance of our peace and safety. This is the most important action in reinforcement of our national defence that has been taken since the Louisiana purchase. Then, as now, con-

Here is a U.S.A. destroyer of the type of those being exchanged for bases in the Atlantic. The ships were to be sailed to Canadian ports and handed over to the Royal Navy.

siderations of safety against attack from overseas was fundamental. The value to the Western Hemisphere of these outposts of security is beyond calculation. The need for them has long been recognized by those primarily charged with the duty of charting and organizing our own nation's naval and military defence. They are essential to the protection of the Panama Canal, Central America, and the northern portion of South America, the Antilles, Canada, Mexico, and our own eastern and Gulf of Mexico seaboards. Their consequent importance in hemispheric defence is obvious, and for these reasons I have taken advantage of the present opportunity to acquire them."

The Louisiana purchase referred to by the President was effected in 1803, when Napoleon sold to the infant U.S.A. the whole of the vast territory of Louisiana, approximately a million square miles, for some 27,000,000 dollars. For the Virgin Islands purchased from Denmark in 1917 the U.S.A. paid 25,000,000 dollars. The destroyers which are to be received in return for the bases are valued at approximately 84,000,000 dollars—say £21,250,000.

Of the fifty destroyers, eight were stated to be immediately available and would be sailed to Canadian ports and handed over in the course of the next day or two ; the remainder were all in Atlantic ports and would shortly be handed over. All the vessels are of 1,060 to 1,190 tons, speed 35 knots, and equipped with either 5-inch or 4-inch guns and twelve 21-inch torpedo tubes, i.e. the same as in the Royal Navy, but they will need to be fitted with the British degaussing belt and the " Asdic " anti-submarine gear. Soon the whole fifty will be playing their part in maintaining the blockade of German Europe and in shepherding Britain's convoys through the seven seas.

How immensely valuable to the U.S.A. are the British concessions of naval and air bases in the Atlantic and Caribbean Sea will be clear from this map. Combined with the bases in Cuba and Puerto Rico they form a chain guarding the Panama Canal from the east. The Newfoundland and Bermuda bases will assist in Canada's defence—hence their free grant. *Courtesy " News Chronicle "*

OUR SEARCHLIGHT ON THE WAR

Business Men Versus U-Boats

An auxiliary squadron of the R.A.F. Coastal Command, whose job is to escort shipping convoys, is achieving great success in spotting submarines that lie in wait. It has attacked nine within the last two months, two of which were almost certainly destroyed and three others damaged. These results are all the more remarkable in that the squadron consists almost entirely of professional and business men, tradesmen, factory hands and clerks from a Scottish city near the air station. Among the flight commanders are a chartered accountant and a P.T. instructor, while the commanding officer was head of a firm of building contractors.

American Refugee Ship in Port

After a rough voyage the U.S. refugee ship "American Legion," which left Petsamo, in Finland, on August 16, arrived safely in New York harbour on August 28. Among her 900 passengers she carried the Crown Princess of Norway and her three children, and a number of American diplomatists, including Mrs. Borden Harriman, U.S. Minister to Norway. Germany had done her best to make propaganda out of this rescue mission, denouncing the voyage as " wanton " and as " criminal folly," and predicting certain destruction of the ship. While in the danger zone life-belts were worn the whole time except during eating and sleeping, the number of look-outs was doubled, and constant lifeboat drills were held. On the last 500 miles two American destroyers provided an escort in honour of Princess Martha, and to indicate that the exiled Royal family are still recognized as the rulers of Norway.

' Not Flying—But Miracles '

The skill and resource of our pilots are demonstrated not only in the daily toll they take of enemy aircraft, but in the remarkable way in which they nurse their own wounded machines and land them safely. Two inspiring accounts of such achievements were reported on August 31. The first told of a Coastal Command aircraft, an American-built Hudson. It had been badly damaged by a high-explosive A.A. shell, which took its nose right off during a dive-bombing attack on two enemy destroyers near Denmark. Both pilot and navigator, who had been acting as bomb-aimer, were injured, but together they managed to stop the dive, got the 'plane on to an even keel, and, amazed that she could fly at all with such severe damage to the fuselage, piloted her home through a raging storm and made an excellent landing. " When we went in to report," remarked the navigator, " I found a bit of shrapnel in my leg. I was so cold that I pulled it out quite cleanly myself without feeling it."

The other damaged machine was a Hurricane fighter, which, when landed, was found to have a big hole in the starboard wing and through the starboard side of the fuselage. Moreover, it was stated that " one

of the ailerons of the main port wing had suffered enough damage to bring down many a machine. In addition, the fuel tank had been pierced, and the rudder half shot away." Notwithstanding all this, the intrepid pilot, wounded in one eye and one shoulder, but with justifiable faith in the toughness and quality of what was left of his British-built aircraft, succeeded in making a safe landing in a small field near Folkestone after a 20-mile glide. " It's not flying," pronounced one technical expert, after examining the riddled 'plane, " it's a miracle."

Vichy 'Axes' the Diplomats

M. Baudouin, Foreign Secretary in the Vichy Government, has imposed " compulsory retirement " on 83 officials of the French diplomatic service, including 15 Ministers, 3 Counsellors of Embassy, and 19 consuls-general. It is evident that Germany's intention has been to remove diplomatists who hold a pro-British and democratic outlook, for the Marquis de Castellane, former chargé d'affaires in London, has already been appointed to fill one of the vacancies, as " the French Government wishes to recognize the tact which he showed in a particularly delicate situation."

British Workers Defy Hitler

It has been found that after a raid work in British factories has either consciously or unconsciously speeded up. In one Midland factory the output was only a fraction below normal during the week when it suffered from a bombing raid, while the following week the output increased by 33 per cent. Moreover, workers everywhere are anxious to have the shelter regulations so modified that they need not abandon their tasks unless bombing attacks appear imminent.

Torpedoing the Children

A British ship which was carrying 320 children and other passengers to Canada was torpedoed in the Atlantic during the night of August 30. Every child has returned safe and sound and none is any the worse for the two nights at sea after the

These smiling children are some of the 320 bound for Canada who were rescued when their ship was torpedoed in the Atlantic. The photograph was taken when they arrived at a northern port on September 1.
Photo, " Daily Mirror "

torpedoing. Mr. Geoffrey Shakespeare, M.P., Chairman of the Children's Oversea Reception Board, which arranged the evacuation, reported that the sailors and passengers were emphatic in praise of the pluck, cheerfulness and orderly behaviour of the children.

They assembled at their correct boat stations inside 3½ minutes and, as one enthusiast put it, they bore themselves "like Guardsmen on parade."

Heroes of the Home Front

Two railwaymen, sub-ganger George Frederick Keen and lengthman George Henry Leach, have, by their gallantry, saved a burning ammunition train from destruction. The train, which consisted of about 50 wagons, was standing on a single-line railway when it was bombed during the

Sub-ganger George Keen, who at midnight on August 22 saved an S.R. ammunition train around which incendiary bombs were falling, shows how he detached the ignited wagons from the train.
Photo, G.P.U.

night of August 22, the third truck being hit. Mr. Keen first helped people in neighbouring cottages to shelter and ten minutes later was joined by Mr. Leach, who, hearing the bombing, had rushed by bicycle from his home two miles away. Keen then called for military volunteers from a near-by salvage depot, and was also joined by five auxiliary firemen. By this time the wagon was burning fiercely and explosions were taking place in other trucks. Keen tried to separate the first two wagons, but the heat was too great, and he therefore led his working party to the other end of the train, where each wagon in turn was uncoupled and laboriously shifted by hand 300 yards to safety. The official report stated that but for the action of Keen and Leach in starting to move the wagons, the train might have been destroyed.

Red Cross ' Cover ' Again Invoked

The remarkable mixture of cunning and naïveté in the Nazi character has once more been in evidence. Through the Swiss Government Britain has received from Germany a proposal that 64 Nazi vessels, to be distinguished by Red Cross markings, should be allowed to range unmolested in the Channel and North Sea—ostensibly, to rescue German airmen who had been shot down ; actually, it may well be surmised, to reconnoitre our defence arrangements. The British Government has naturally rejected the proposal, at the same time reminding Germany of many deliberate attacks upon British hospital ships and carriers, including the actual sinking of the hospital ships " Maid of Kent," " Brighton " and " Paris." It is noteworthy that the day this announcement was made (August 31) the Air Ministry reported that an R.A.F. pilot who had baled out at 15,000 feet was dead when he reached the ground, his body riddled with bullets from three Messerschmitts which had savagely attacked him during his descent.

A.F.S. Girls Ready to Fight the Incendiaries

Throughout nearly a year of inaction the Auxiliary Fire Service kept alert, and recent raids have shown that during the long wait it had become a highly efficient force. Wolverhampton A.F.S. girls have learned all a fireman's duties, and in the photographs in this page they are seen at practice. Above, the tin hat is donned with little concern for the exact angle, while, right, the gumboots go on. Left, two members of the force are directing the hose at a practice fire.

Quickness in getting into action when a fire has started is acquired by such constant practice that every movement becomes almost automatic. Here girls of the Wolverhampton A.F.S. are running out the hose from pumps while at drill.

Photos, "News Chronicle" staff photographer, R. Girling

OUR DIARY OF THE WAR

WEDNESDAY, AUGUST 28, 1940
361st day

On the Sea—Shelling of steamer " British Commander " by unknown vessel in Indian Ocean was reported by a New York wireless station. Finnish steamer " Elle " sunk by U-boat off west coast of Ireland.

In the Air—During night R.A.F. heavily bombed targets in Berlin. Other squadrons attacked air-frame factory at Leipzig; Junkers works at Dessau; oil-plants at Reisholz, Dortmund and Nordenham; and several aerodromes.

Skua aircraft of Fleet Air Arm successfully attacked oil depot, motor patrol vessel and supply ship along Norwegian coast.

Home Front—Heavy air attacks over Kent coast and Thames estuary. R.A.F. fighters and A.A. batteries split up raiding formations and series of fights took place at high altitudes. Few bombs dropped.

Night raid on London. Parachute flares and incendiary bombs dropped. Some damage done and casualties caused. Many towns in South-east, Midlands, S.W. coast and N.W. coast also raided.

Twenty-nine enemy aircraft shot down. Fourteen British machines lost, but pilots of seven safe.

Balkans—Announced that Hitler had summoned Foreign Ministers of Hungary and Rumania to conference in Vienna on Transylvanian dispute.

THURSDAY, AUGUST 29
362nd day

In the Air—R.A.F. carried out daylight raids on aerodromes in Holland and on convoys and shipping along Dutch coast. During night bombers attacked Krupp's works at Essen; oil refineries and plants at Gelsenkirchen, Bottrop and St. Nazaire; power stations at Duisburg and Reisholz; military targets in the Ruhr; goods yards at Hamm and Soest; aerodromes in Germany, Holland, Belgium and France.

War against Italy—South African Air Force raided Mogadishu, Italian Somaliland, and destroyed hundreds of motor transport vehicles. R.A.F. attacked Massawa.

Home Front—Big enemy bomber formations attacked Kent-Sussex coast in two main raids, but were dispersed.

Bombs dropped and civilians machine-gunned in Scilly Isles. South-west town also machine-gunned, and few bombs dropped in South of England.

During night two bombs were dropped in London area. Raiders also reported over Midlands, S.E. inland area and towns in S.W., N.W. and N.E. areas.

Eleven enemy aircraft destroyed. Twelve British fighters lost, but pilots of seven safe.

Balkans—Ribbentrop and Ciano conferred in Vienna with Hungarian Premier and Foreign Minister. Later Rumanian Foreign Minister joined discussions.

U.S.A.—Bill providing for compulsory military service passed the Senate.

Africa—French Congo and Cameroons repudiated Pétain Govt. and joined Allies.

FRIDAY, AUGUST 30
363rd day

On the Sea—Evacuee ship taking 320 British children to Canada torpedoed during night in Atlantic. One casualty, ship's purser.

In the Air—During night R.A.F. again raided Berlin. Direct hits secured on military targets including petrol installations, aircraft factories and aerodromes. Electrical works and railway junction badly damaged.

Other aircraft bombed quays and railway sidings at Boulogne. Still others attacked oil depots at Gelsenkirchen, Magdeburg and Cherbourg; dock warehouses at Hamburg; goods yards at Bremen, Hamm and Soest; shipping at Emden; gun emplacements at Cap Gris Nez; and aerodromes in Germany and Holland.

Home Front—Great air battles fought over London area all day and night. High explosive and incendiary bombs dropped.

Bombs dropped indiscriminately in Kent and Surrey. Slight damage reported. Attempts made to attack R.A.F. aerodromes in Home Counties. At one town industrial premises damaged and number of casualties.

Late at night enemy 'planes were reported over 11 towns besides London area.

Sixty-two enemy aircraft destroyed. Twenty-seven British fighters lost, but pilots of fifteen safe.

Balkans—Rumania yielded to Axis terms and agreed to cede to Hungary whole of Northern Transylvania and three Szekla provinces.

SATURDAY, AUGUST 31
364th day

On the Sea—Admiralty announced that H.M. armed merchant cruiser " Dunwegan Castle " had been sunk by U-boat.

THE POETS & THE WAR
XXXI
ENGLAND AT BAY
BY D. S. MacColl

Outnumbered, trapped, " invaded," unbefriended,
   She conquered in the air
Yet one more post of empire, and transcended
   The seas, her ancient share;
By sons from near and far redeemed anew,
   By hundreds against myriads defended,
" So many by so few."

              —*The Times*

In the Air—During night R.A.F. bombed lighting installations, aero-engine factory and aerodrome at Berlin; oil plants at Cologne and Magdeburg; goods yards at Hamm, Soest, Osnabruck and Hanover; shipping at Emden; various industrial targets and aerodromes.

Fleet Air Arm and Coastal Command attacked oil tanks at Rotterdam.

War against Italy—R.A.F. successfully bombed Italian air bases in Libya. Raid also made on Agordat, Eritrea.

Home Front—Enemy attacks against aerodromes in S.E. area renewed. Raids also made on aerodromes in Thames estuary, and on one in East Anglia.

Fierce battle fought over London area during afternoon and evening.

Waves of bombers appeared over a N.E. town during night, and over a N.W. coastal district. Considerable damage done and a number of casualties.

Eighty-eight German aircraft destroyed. Thirty-nine British machines lost, but pilots of 25 safe.

SUNDAY, SEPTEMBER 1
365th day

In the Air—R.A.F. made daylight raids on aerodromes of Ypenburg and Schiphol. Coastal Command aircraft bombed submarine and E-boat base at Lorient on west coast of France.

During night R.A.F. raided Munich for first time, attacking aero-engine works. Other targets included Emden docks; oil plants at Nordenham, Hanover and Ludwigshafen; munition works at Bitterfeld and Leipzig; engine works at Stuttgart; railway sidings at Soest and Mannheim; power station at Kassel.

War against Italy—R.A.F. again crossed Alps and bombed Fiat works at Turin and at Lingotto. Other targets were railway bridge over R. Po, and Marrelli works near Milan.

Assab, Italian port on Red Sea, heavily bombed by R.A.F.

Home Front—Further raids by large enemy formations on S.E. coast. Some bombers reached Croydon, but most were turned back by fighters and A.A. defences. Bombs dropped in Kent and Surrey, causing some damage and casualties.

Twenty-five Nazi aircraft destroyed. Sixteen British fighters lost, but pilots of nine safe.

Balkans—Demonstrations and riots occurred in Rumania as protest against cession of Transylvanian territory.

Africa—Announced that another French colony, Gabun, had joined Allies.

MONDAY, SEPTEMBER 2
366th day

On the Sea—Admiralty announced that H.M. sloop " Penzance " had been sunk by U-boat.

In the Air—R.A.F. bombers made night attacks on dynamite works at Schlebusch and Bayer explosive works near Cologne; oil installations at Ludwigshafen and Frankfurt; Bosch factory at Stuttgart; Dortmund-Ems canal; French port of Lorient; gun emplacements at Cap Gris Nez.

Coastal Command aircraft bombed supply ships off Dutch coast, oil tanks at Flushing, and Ostend harbour.

War against Italy—R.A.F. bombed important railway junction and electric power station at Genoa.

R.A.F. renewed attacks on Assab, Eritrea.

Home Front—Repeated attempts by big enemy formations to bomb Kent and Thames estuary aerodromes, and to reach London, were beaten off by fighters and A.A. gunners. Series of dramatic air battles took place, one being over a S.E. coast town.

During night enemy activity was widespread but on smaller scale. Attacks mainly directed against Bristol Channel and South Wales area.

Fifty-five Germans raiders destroyed. Eighteen British fighters lost, but pilots of eight safe.

TUESDAY, SEPTEMBER 3
367th day

On the Sea—Admiralty announced that Norwegian motor torpedo-boat, co-operating with British naval forces, had shot down a German bomber.

Swedish steamer " Alida Gorthon " reported torpedoed off west coast of Ireland.

In the Air—R.A.F. bombers made night attacks on military targets in the Black Forest, in forests in Hartz Mts. and in Grunewald forests north of Berlin. Many fires started, causing explosions.

Bombs dropped on power stations, gasworks and armament factory in Berlin; oil tanks at Magdeburg; goods yards at Hamm and Schwerte; blast furnace at Merzig; several Dutch and German aerodromes.

Other aircraft attacked barge concentrations in Beveland Canal and Scheldt estuary, and Ostend docks.

From 9 p.m. until 1 a.m. attacks made on advanced striking bases of German Air Force in Pas-de-Calais area.

Home Front—Two waves of German bombers and fighters attempted to reach aerodromes in London area, but were repulsed by R.A.F. in Thames estuary.

Twenty-five enemy machines shot down. Fifteen British fighters down, but pilots of eight safe.

Balkans—Demonstrations in Transylvania continued and clashes took place between Hungarian and Rumanian troops.

Iron Guard in Bucharest attempted a coup d'état to depose King Carol, but failed.

General—U.S.A. agreed to transfer immediately to Royal Navy 50 over-age destroyers in exchange for bases in British possessions along Atlantic sea-board.

French possession of Tahiti joined General de Gaulle.

NAZI 'SKY-WRITERS' LEAVE THEIR TRAIL ABOVE ST. PAUL'S

Fascinated by what looked like " sky-writing " by enemy aeroplanes overhead, thousands of Londoners forgot to search for shelter and kept their eyes glued on the sky.   This photograph was taken from a building in Fleet Street on September 6, 1940, between 8.49 and 9.59 a.m., when enemy aeroplanes were circling over the City of London drawing strange patterns against the sky.   Actually their production is involuntary, being due to the action of cold air on the exhaust at a great height.

Photo, Planet News

When Tank Fought Tank Near Arras

When the Battle of the West opened there were two Army Tank battalions with the B.E.F. and both were heavily engaged in the operations that preceded the evacuation from Dunkirk. Here we tell of the exploits of one of the battalions as described in the "Daily Telegraph" by Mr. Douglas Williams.

ON May 12, two days after the Germans marched into the Low Countries, a battalion of British tanks which had been engaged in training exercises over open country west of Arras, received rush orders to move into Belgium to join the main body of the B.E.F., which had already crossed the frontier. The tanks were sent by rail and the men followed in their vehicles.

After a few days in Belgium the battalion was ordered back to Orchies, in the old Gort Line, and from there was again withdrawn to Vimy and placed under the orders of the 50th Division to assist in the counter-attack which Gen. Martell was organizing to relieve the Arras garrison.

It arrived in the Bois de la Folie, near Vimy, shortly after dawn on May 21, and while the men, who had been on the move all night, snatched a bite of breakfast and a brief rest, the officers hurried to a house in Petit Vimy to receive the operation orders.

The counter-attack was to take place that same afternoon, and the battalion was given a start line along a railway track south-west of Arras. Despite the fact that the battalion had moved 300 miles in less than 10 days, with practically no opportunity for the maintenance and repair of vehicles, 38 Mark I. tanks (weighing about 10 tons each, with a crew of two and armed with Vickers machine-guns) were available, plus seven Mark II. tanks (weighing 25 tons, carrying a crew of four, and armed with the two-pounder anti-tank gun) borrowed from another unit.

Sharp at 11 a.m. all moved off in proper order towards the start line, while the commanding officer and the adjutant went forward in light tanks to make contact with the battalion of Durham Light Infantry which they were instructed to support. On arrival, however, at Anzin St. Aubin, where the rendezvous had been given, they found that the infantry had not arrived, and they did not, in fact, put in an appearance until an hour later, having been delayed en route.

The attack, however, began promptly at 2 p.m., and as the tanks rolled forward they came into immediate contact with the enemy in strong force. The crossing of the railway was made difficult by the fact that it was here running through a cutting and could be crossed only at a few places, and, in the hope of clearing out enemy forces which were holding them up, the seven large tanks were ordered forward to deal with them. They were not seen again and were presumably either captured or immobilized.

Shortly afterwards the remainder of the tank force came under heavy fire from anti-tank guns, but they had no trouble in silencing the enemy as soon as the latter's positions were given away by the flash of the first discharge. The German crews packed up and moved off in a hurry at the first burst of our machine-gun fire.

The enemy infantry showed no great courage. On many occasions parties of them came running towards the British tanks, undoing their ammunition and revolver belts as they did so, and handing these in through the flaps to the British crews inside.

In other cases, so terrified were the Germans that in their eagerness to surrender they even climbed on top of the tanks and perched there with their hands in the air. Others lay down, shamming dead, and one tank, investigating a gravel pit, found no fewer than 50 Germans lying huddled together, hoping they would be passed over as dead, though in this they were disillusioned.

By this time the battle had spread out over a large area and had developed into individual fighting by individual tanks. A number of our tanks had had to be discarded owing to mechanical breakdowns, and the wireless communication sets on those still engaged were out of action or could not be used, as there had been no time to tune in all the sets on the same frequency.

We were inflicting heavy losses, and matters were progressing very favourably until the commanding officer, still directing the battle from his light tank, was killed by a direct hit from a German field battery at point-blank range as he stood up in the control tower.

There were still about a dozen tanks in this area. These were collected together by the senior officer present, and he led them to contact the Durham Light Infantry, who were now observed advancing across country in "open order" with their rifles at the "ready" and with Germans emerging from the crops around them with their hands up surrendering.

Further on, the British tanks suddenly came upon a collection of German vehicles, including two enormous six-wheeled petrol containers. They opened immediate fire and destroyed the lot, including the petrol tanks, holding thousands of gallons, which burnt fiercely.

By this time contact with the infantry had again been lost, and it later appeared that the D.L.I. had suffered heavy losses from a German dive-bombing attack which had forced the men to disperse into cover.

All the afternoon fighting continued until, towards the evening, the tanks rallied behind the infantry which were found again holding a position at Beaurains. Operations were confused, and neither side had any clear information where the other was.

At about nine o'clock, when the Tank Adjutant was holding a conference at a cross-road with the Acting Commanding Officer of the D.L.I. (the C.O. having become a

On this map can be traced the movements of the tanks during the action described in this chapter.
Courtesy of the "Daily Telegraph"

German and British Tanks in the Battle of France

This German light tank is passing through a ruined French village during the thrust to the coast of Northern France. It was the skilful use of these light armoured units that made the Nazi success possible.

Photo, Keystone

and five big German ones. For ten minutes, violent fighting continued at this point-blank range, with tanks on each side shooting at gun flashes from the other side. Finally, the British tanks dropped a smoke candle, which caused a lull for a couple of minutes, and then fighting was resumed with greater intensity.

Luckily for us, because by this time ammunition was running low, the Germans decided that they had had enough, and lumbered away into the darkness.

By this time it was 10 o'clock, and in the absence of definite orders the tank commanders were instructed to withdraw, and started their way back to Vimy. They returned cross-country, passing a wood full of burning German vehicles, and after crossing the River Scarpe at Anzin they reached their encampment in the Bois de la Folie just as dawn was breaking.

casualty), they heard a rumble of tanks approaching. It was dark by this time, with a heavy pall of smoke from burning vehicles covering the countryside. The Durham officer insisted that the tanks were German; the adjutant was equally positive that they were British.

Finally, the adjutant decided to walk forward and find out for himself, and as he met the leading tank he tapped on the visor with a couple of maps he held in his hand. The tank stopped, and to his horror a couple of German heads popped out of the flaps! He turned and ran like a hare 300 yards down the road, with the Germans shooting at him with all they had.

The burst of fire had warned the British tanks of the enemy's proximity, and a heavy pitched battle ensued at less than 300 yards' range between the ten small British tanks

The tank may be regarded as the most important arm of the modern army, and, among other functions, it has entirely superseded the cavalry. The centre and lower photos in this page were taken with the tanks of the B.E.F. in France early in 1940. Centre, two of the crew of a tank are at the alert during night exercises. Above, a British tank is moving forward somewhere in France.

Photos, British Official : Crown Copyright

Three Arms of German Might in Occupied France

The Nazi propaganda which issued this photograph stated this U-boat was returning from one of the long trips made possible by the occupation of French ports.

At a Nazi aerodrome in France, raiders from England are describing their exploits to Gen. Milch, Inspector-Gen. of the Luftwaffe, second from left, and Marshal Goering.

Every unit of the German army is provided with expert photographers (see page 329, Vol. 2), for propaganda purposes. Those above are operating a large telephoto camera.

This photograph is a poor effort in propaganda, for the Nazi soldiers, lined up for roll call in a French village near Dunkirk, are distinctly shabby. On a roof behind are two men with an A.A. gun. Signposts bearing German names have been put up beside the French ones. Centre, supplies of petrol are being issued. Strict economy in petrol is enforced in the German army, spilling even drops being punishable.

Photos, E.N.A. and Associated Press

What We Have Learned in a Year's A.R.P.

BY SIR ALEXANDER ROUSE, C.I.E.

Here, appropriate to the experiences of the citizens of this country stoically enduring daily air attacks, is a review of the lessons officially drawn from the experiences of the first twelve months' work in A.R.P. Sir Alexander Rouse writes with the authority of his position of Chief Engineer to the Ministry of Home Security.

AFTER a year of war it is possible to review the results of bombing and compare them with the effects which were anticipated and on which the shelter policy of the Government was based. That policy was designed to give protection from the splinters and blast of a heavy high explosive bomb bursting within 50 ft. of a structure or shelter, and it may be said with confidence that the effects experienced have been less devastating than anticipated.

Dwelling-houses are completely destroyed only by a direct hit somewhere near the centre. Hits near the side, or near-misses, only remove part of the house, and unless the occupants happen to be in this part they have usually escaped without serious injury, and even when the house had been completely destroyed, survivors have often been rescued from the debris. I have seen a case where a heavy bomb exploded so close to two semi-detached houses that the walls were within the crater, which was 40 ft. wide and about 10 ft. deep ; the houses were laid completely flat.

A woman with her baby who were in the upper storey were, however, taken from the wreckage suffering only from bruises, having been protected by a couch which turned upside down on top of them. That was luck. In another case a girl took shelter under the kitchen table and in spite of the whole house coming down she was rescued unhurt but naturally a little shaken, and affirmed that Hitler was not going to frighten her ! In the former case the woman and the baby were lucky, but in the latter the girl took a sensible precaution. In all houses there are places which are safer than others, and if there is no time to get into the shelter it is always worth while getting into the safest place possible, having thought out beforehand where such places are.

The shelters which have been provided or recommended by the Government have all come up to expectations in providing protection and have even proved more efficacious. The Anderson steel shelter has stood up to bombs at a distance of only 10 ft. away, provided that it has been covered with the correct amount of earth, that is, 15 inches on top and 30 inches at the sides and back. It is deplorable, however, that so many people have not taken the trouble to give the correct amount of earth, and disaster has followed in many cases of which examples are given in the photographs.

In the official instructions for the erection of these shelters it was stated that if the entrance was within 15 ft. of the house or substantial wall, no baffle wall in front was necessary as it was considered that anything falling closer than this would be pretty sure to wreck the shelter. Experience, however, has proved that even if the shelter is only 6 feet or 8 feet from the house or wall a very large additional amount of protection is given by erecting a baffle wall, since a bomb falling between house and baffle wall will very possibly not hurt the occupants of the shelter.

So much has been said by the Press about the protection afforded by the Anderson steel shelters that the popular fancy, which was once inclined to scorn them, is now clamouring for them and is inclined to reject the more substantial surface brick shelter with $13\frac{1}{2}$ in. brick walls.

This is quite erroneous, as these brick shelters have equally proved their worth. No case has been recorded of splinters from a bomb penetrating a $13\frac{1}{2}$-inch wall except when the explosion has been so close as practically

The photograph above shows the necessity of the covering of earth over an Anderson shelter. It was riddled with splinters from a bomb bursting 20 feet away. Left, is a shelter with no earth over the back, a bomb burst 15 feet away and splinters killed two of the occupants.
Photos, Ministry of Home Security

to destroy the wall. In fact, few splinters, except from very heavy bombs exploding near by, have penetrated even 9-inch walls.

As regards trenches, few cases have been reported of near-misses, but in all cases reported they have more than come up to expectations.

Basements, too, have served their purpose well. In fact, under smaller buildings such as domestic residences of 2 or even 3 storeys, they have, even when unstrutted, sufficiently withstood the weight of debris which has been produced by the demolition of the house above to prevent fatal injury to the occupants.

The value of the home as an air-raid shelter has been proved over and over again.

Strange Indeed are the Ways of Blast

Many tributes have been paid to the steel Anderson shelters, which have proved so effective in saving lives threatened by bombs. Very effective, too are the surface shelters, built of brick and concrete. A row of such shelters was put up to afford protection to people living in a street of small houses in a northern town. A bomb fell only 25 ft. away from the shelter to the left of the photograph, but, as can be seen the shelter, like others in the row, was undamaged.

The effect of a heavy bomb on a row of houses in a colliery district is seen in the photograph, right. A heavy bomb fell only 20 feet from the back wall, but the casualties were three children in the back lane who were killed. Despite the severe damage, the people in the houses escaped injury.

The photograph left shows the front of the same houses. They exemplify the unexpected results that sometimes follow from a high explosive bomb. Though the bomb fell at the back of the houses, the damage was greater on the street side for the front walls collapsed while those at the back withstood the shock. This was probably due to the way in which the shock of the explosion from the bottom of the crater travelled through the ground.

Courtesy of the Ministry of Home Security

They Used Their Homes as Shelters—and Lived

A narrow room on the ground floor with stout walls affords excellent protection. In the demolished house above three people escaped with slight injuries by sheltering in the front hall. Next door (see photo of both halls at right) people in the hall were quite uninjured.

Photos, courtesy of Ministry of Home Security

Casualties in houses from bomb splinters have been negligible and these have been due to people carelessly standing near windows or doors. The casualties in dwelling-houses have been mainly due either to direct hits, when the occupants were damaged by the debris and blast, or else to flying glass from bombs exploding near by. In a survey of 650 cases in urban areas, about a quarter of the casualties have been due to flying glass striking people either in their own houses or in the streets. The importance of protecting windows by pasting netting or other fabric or even stout paper over the glass has been emphasized by innumerable examples.

Where occupants of houses have taken the trouble to study the pamphlet " Your Home as an Air Raid Shelter " and to select the best part of the house for a refuge room, they have been safe, even where the house was partially demolished by a direct hit. A narrow room or passage with the maximum amount of solid brickwork around it, such as the hall or the space under the stairs, has survived in a very large number of cases.

One thing that has emerged from the tactics adopted by the enemy is that, unless the whole country is to be constantly prevented from working by day or sleeping by night owing to incessant air-raid warnings, there must be a risk of bombs being dropped without any warning, and this is a risk which all of us, I am sure, are prepared to take. This risk, however, emphasizes the extreme importance of taking cover whether in a building or in the streets, particularly in the latter. In the pamphlet entitled " Air Raids " (published by the Stationery Office in June last) there is a diagram which indicates the degree of risk incurred when taking cover or lying down as compared with standing in the open. This diagram is reproduced here. Subsequent statistics of casualties incurred confirm its correctness— particularly in respect of the danger of standing in the open.

An enormous number of incendiary bombs have been dropped in this country, but comparatively few have caused serious fires. Many of these fall harmlessly in open spaces and many are " duds." In the daily reports which I receive I read this sort of thing :

" A number of incendiary bombs were dropped in Blanktown—damage was slight and all were dealt with by the occupants of houses or air-raid wardens with sand and stirrup pumps."

In fact, there is no great danger that incendiary bombs will produce devastating fire in residential areas if every citizen is prepared to deal promptly with them.

I would call the attention of readers finally to the importance of taking the best cover available or even lying down on hearing anti-aircraft fire or bombs dropping in the vicinity.

The danger from bomb splinters to anyone standing in the streets is clearly shown in the photograph below and the diagram in the left-hand column.

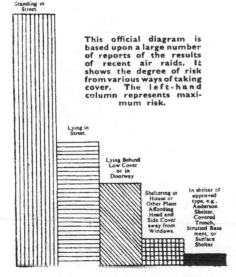

This official diagram is based upon a large number of reports of the results of recent air raids. It shows the degree of risk from various ways of taking cover. The left-hand column represents maximum risk.

Standing in Street.

Lying in Street.

Lying Behind Low Cover or in Doorway

Sheltering in House or Other Place Affording Head and Side Cover away from Windows.

In shelter of approved type, e.g., Anderson Shelter, Covered Trench, Strutted Basement, or Surface Shelter

The main stream of splinters from an exploding bomb flies upwards and a person lying down would probably have escaped all of them. Anyone standing (see outlined figure) runs an infinitely greater hazard.

Italy's Water Supplies Are The Things To Hit

Already Italy has been raided time and again by the bombers of the R.A.F., and with the coming of longer and darker nights this long-distance offensive will no doubt be intensified. Certainly, there are plenty of targets for the R.A.F.'s attention, and amongst the most important is—water !

IF Mussolini liked he could boast that his fleet comprises ships such as are to be found in no other of the big navies of the world. But he does not like, for mention of the *Nave Distillatrice* (distilling ship) and the *Navi Cisterna per Acqua* (water carriers) is an all too grim reminder that the overseas possessions of the Italian Empire are almost entirely dependent for their water on supplies brought from home.

Thousands of Italians in Libya—Marshal Graziani and his staff, the officials and the soldiers, black and white ; the settlers in groves and plantations—all are dependent for their lives on the regular arrival of the water-ships ; every house has a cistern, but the rains are inadequate to keep them filled. On the sun-baked rocks of Pantellaria, the little island between Tunis and Sicily which Mussolini has converted into a miniature Gibraltar, not a drop of rain falls throughout the year ; Rhodes, principal of the

each with carrying capacity of 950 tons. Next rank five of rather more than 1,000 tons apiece, the " Flegetonte," " Scrivia," " Tirso," " Garigliano," and " Sesia " ; all five are driven by Diesel engines, and the last four have been fitted for mine-laying as well as for water-carrying. The remaining eleven,. " Metauro," " Sile," " Sebeto," " Arno," " Brenta," " Bormida," " Mincio," " Adige," and " Frigido "—range from 780 tons in the case of the " Adige," to the little Japanese-built " Frigido," which has a tonnage of 398.

Small and ungainly in appearance, lightly armoured (if at all) and armed with nothing heavier than 4·7-inch guns—many have machine-guns only—these ships are nevertheless among the most important of those which fly the Italian flag. Indeed, it may be said that Mussolini could spare some of his biggest fighting ships rather than suffer the loss of his fleet of water tankers.

group in the Colle Isarco," Miss Elisabeth Mackenzie, former Rome correspondent of the " News Chronicle " has written in that newspaper, " would disrupt Milan's great electrically operated industrial network and paralyse the electric railways running through the Brenner Pass, thus jeopardizing Italian coal supplies from Germany. In the same way the destruction of the Direttissima, one of the stations of the Tonale Group and situated near Prato, would bring to a stand-still fast railway services between Sicily and Bolzano."

" The destruction of the Fiat works at Lingotto," says Miss Mackenzie, " does not cripple or even halt arms ouptut in that sector, as the underground factory situated at near-by Moncalieri can take up and continue production. But, if the power stations in the Val d'Aosta system were hit, the factory of Moncalieri as well as countless others would be at a standstill."

Italy's electrical power plants are built on the edges of the rivers from which they derive their water, and they constitute landmarks which cannot be camouflaged. Here is one of them which has been already bombed by the R.A.F.—the great hydro-electric station at Valdo in North Italy. Above right is the Italian water-distilling ship " Citta di Siracusa."
Photos, E.N.A. and Jane's " Fighting Ships "

Dodecanese group and Italy's most important naval base in the eastern Mediterranean, has a few winter torrents, but their supply is quite inadequate for the needs of the garrison. As for Abyssinia, there is a rainy season in the summer, but from October to March the rainfall dribbles into nothingness.

The water distilling ship is the " Citta di Siracusa," 3,593 tons, built in 1910 ; she is fitted with Ansaldo distilling plant and can produce 190 tons of fresh water daily. More important are the water-tankers, of which there are 22 named in the current Italian naval list.

At their head are three ships built in 1936-1937 : " Isonzo," " Po," and " Volturno." They are of 3,336 tons, oil-fired, and have a capacity of 2,000 tons. Next rank the " Dalmazia " and " Istria," built at Fiume in 1922-1923 ; with a tonnage of 2,900 they can carry 1,800 tons of water. Not much smaller is the " Ticino," and then come " Pagano " and " Verde," 1,432 tons,

For without water men cannot fight—or live. These ships, then, may well be regarded as the ripest of targets for Britain's submarines.

Italian water supplies can also provide our bombers with a target. To a very large extent Italian industry and everyday life are dependent on electricity, and of Italy's 1,198 power plants, 809 are situated in the northern regions, well within bombing range of 'planes operating from England— a fact which has been more than demonstrated by the nightly raids on the great armament and munition works at Milan and Turin.

" A direct hit on one of the plants of the Cardano

ITALY'S VITAL TARGETS

On this map are marked the positions of the principal Italian hydro-electric stations and the rivers from which they derive their power. More so than any other big Power, Italy is dependent on her electrical network for her very life.

Courtesy of "News Chronicle"

1. BARDONECCHIA
2. ROSONE
3. VENINA
4. S. FRANCESCO
5. SONICO
6. CARDANO
7. RIVA
8. FADALTO
9. GALLETO
10. ACQUARIA NUOVA
11. COGHINAS
12. AMPOLINA
13. RONCO
14. PONT
15. BORGO TECINU
16. SUSA
17. PAESANA
18. SAMPEYRE
19. DRONERO
20. TENDA
21. DOLCEACQUA
22. DIRETTISSIMA
23. MINCIO

Italian Fighters and Bombers

Six of Italy's Modern but Slow Machines

SO far the much-vaunted Italian Air Force (Regia Aeronautica) has failed to gather many laurels. The British Air Force has already established an ascendancy over it at least as great as that over the German Air Force. Italy's precise strength in 'planes is known only approximately. Shortage of raw material has retarded new construction, but according to a German estimate before the war Italy possessed about 4,000 fighting warplanes, though there is reason to believe that this was a characteristically bombastic Nazi assumption, and that the actual number of first-line machines is much less. There are upwards of thirty types, but a large proportion are outclassed.

1.—SAVOIA-MARCHETTI S 79
Used for bombing and reconnaissance. Has a range of 1,100 miles, with a maximum speed of 270 m.p.h. Three Alfa Romeo engines (126 RC 34) with a total of 2,250 h.p. Wing span, 69 ft. 6 in. Armed with three 12·7-m.m. machine-guns.

2.—CAPRONI CA 311
Another type of bombing and reconnaissance machine, armed with three 7·7-m.m. machine-guns. The top speed is about 253 m.p.h. Two Piaggio PXVII engines (1,260 h.p.) Wing span, 53 ft. 1½ in.

3.—SAVOIA-MARCHETTI S 81
A three-engined bomber with a speed of 210 m.p.h. and a range of 1,100 miles. Three Piaggio Stella X RC engines (2,100 h.p.). Wing span, 78 ft. 8½ in. Armed with six 7·7-m.m. machine-guns.

Drawings taken by permission from "Chart of Italian Aircraft" issued by "Flight" Publishing Co. Ltd., Dorset House, Stamford Street, London, S.E.

4.—MACCHI C 200
A modern single-seater fighter with a top speed of 313 m.p.h. and a ceiling of 33,000 ft. The engine is a Fiat A 74 RC 38 (radial), developing 840 h.p. Armed with two 12·7-m.m. machine-guns, firing forward. Wing span, 34 ft. 8 in.

5.—FIAT CR 42
A biplane fighter (above and below) somewhat resembling the Gloster Gladiator. Armed with two 12·7-m.m. guns. Has a Fiat A 39 RA engine of 550 h.p., the top speed being 240 m.p.h. Wing span, 31 ft. 2 in. Range 520 miles.

Fighters

AMONG Mussolini's more modern fighters are the Macchi C 200 (shown here) and the Fiat G 50. Single-seat monoplanes, with a radial engine, they are said to be robust and capable of easy manoeuvre, but their speed as judged by R.A.F. standards is low. Two 12·7-m.m. machine-guns are fitted, which fire forward. Somewhat of an anachronism among these fighter craft is the Fiat CR 42 (shown at left), a biplane machine resembling types that Britain is steadily replacing by others of more modern design.

Bombers

Italy's three-engined bombers include the Savoia-Marchetti S 79 and S 81 (top). The engines resemble our Bristol Pegasus type. As representative of the twin-engined bombing craft we illustrate the Savoia-Marchetti S 85 (below), designed for dive-bombing and ground attack. Another two-motor bomber, the Fiat BR 20, is armed with four machine-guns.

Seaplanes

The Regia Aeronautica comprises also about 340 seaplanes and flying-boats, many of them fast becoming obsolete. The provision of this comparatively large number indicates apparently that Italy intends to take the utmost advantage of her island bases. Among the fastest seaplanes are the three-motor Cant Z.506B.

6.—SAVOIA-MARCHETTI S 85
One of the newer twin-engine types developed for dive-bombing and "ground strafing." The head-on view (above and right) shows the diving brakes lowered. Two Piaggio PXVII engines, giving 1,260 h.p.

War's Curtain-Raiser in the Western Desert

One of the prisoners taken by the British during the operations early in June in Libya was Major-General Romolo La Strucci, who is seen above with a British officer.

This British officer and sergeant are examining an Italian light tank which was badly smashed and put out of action by a British armoured car unit during operations in the forward area of the Libyan frontier.

The photograph, centre, shows a British soldier examining a captured Italian field gun that has sustained very unusual damage as the result of a direct hit from a British gun, a hole having been pierced clean through the barrel. Early in September the largest convoy of British troops ever to reach Egypt arrived at Egyptian ports. Men and war material came from Britain, Rhodesia, India and Australia. Thousands of technicians, infantrymen, and R.A.F pilots with quantities of munitions were transported and the voyage was made without sighting a single Italian submarine or warship.

Photos, British Official : Crown Copyright

When a Bomb Fell at Buckingham Palace

At 1.30 on the morning of Tuesday, September 10, a time bomb exploded on the terrace of Buckingham Palace just outside the King's sitting-room. It had been dropped a few hours before by one of the Nazi raiders, and when it went off it wrecked the swimming pool and a corner of the terrace, and also broke scores of windows. Their Majesties were not in the Palace at the time, but shortly after it had exploded they went to inspect the damage (upper photo) In our second photograph the King talks with Mr. Churchill while the Queen chats with the demolition squad.   *Photos, Wide World*

London's Blackout Pierced by Leaping Fires

The blackout of London was completely countered by one of the great fires started by the Nazi raid on London on the afternoon of Saturday, September 7. Above is the scene looking down the Thames with the Tower Bridge silhouetted against the glare.

Each night the fires they started helped the Nazi raiders to find quite other than military objectives. Symbolic of the spirit of the people is the scene in the circle. In the garden of a small London house a Union Jack fluttered from a flagstaff. The next morning, the house was in ruins about it, but the flag still fluttered above them. Above is one of the streets bombed on September 8, photographed the next day.

Photos, Wide World, Daily Mirror, Planet News

Fire Fighters Did a Man's Job in the Battle of London

On Saturday, September 7, fires were started in dockland by the first large-scale daylight raid on London. By the following afternoon, however, the efforts of the London Fire Brigade and the A.F.S. had brought them under control. Here a fireman deals with the smouldering debris of a large dock building. *Planet News*

While firemen were at work at the docks, they were bombed and machine-gunned. Circle, an A.F.S. man points to a bullet hole in his pump. Right, seeing that all is in order. *Photos, G.P.U.*

The destruction caused by falling bombs can be gauged from this photograph of a Woolworth store in South London, destroyed on the night of August 29, 1940. *Wide World*

Goering Sends His Bombers to London, but th

London, September 8, a housewife (left) carries on with the Sunday dinner. Above, an air warden who acted as midwife during a raid seen with mother and child.

In the circle, centre, the King is seen with people in East London whose homes had been bombed, when he visited a devastated area on September 9. Sisters of Mercy, left, were among those who helped to comfort the people. One of the first thoughts of the carmen, above, in a bombed area, was for the safety of their horses.

Photos, " Daily Mirror," Fox and Wide World

e of the Empire's Capital City Are Undaunted

Where bombs cut off the supply, drawing water from a horse trough caused smiles. Nurses of a London hospital, right, cheerfully rescued some possessions.

Air-raid shelters saved many thousands of lives during the intensive bombing of London and here some schoolboys find themselves safe in the congenial company of soldiers. On September 8-9 London was bombed for nearly ten hours, the raid beginning at dusk. Next day, firemen, right, were still at work on the smouldering ruins of buildings.

Photos, Keystone and Fox

London Feels the Full Blast of Nazi Fury

With the mass raids that began on September 7—mass-murder raids they might well be styled—London became the chief objective of the Nazis' aerial onslaught. Some details of the days' and nights' horror, shot by many a gleam of human heroism, are given below.

GERMAN air activities during Wednesday and Thursday September 4 and 5 gave little hint of the murderous raids that were to shock the world during the days to come. On the night of Tuesday, September 3, bombs were dropped in the Bristol Channel area and the north-west of Britain. Though buildings were wrecked there were few casualties. Next morning there began the usual raids on aerodromes in Kent and Essex. In London itself, during Wednesday, the sirens sounded at 9.19 a.m., at 1.27 p.m., and finally at 9.5 p.m. The last raid continued practically all night. Though many fires were started they were soon put out and the damage was inconsiderable. In the London area damage and casualties were very slight. A.A. gunners shot down their 200th raider during this day.

When large numbers of enemy aircraft crossed the coast on Thursday morning some managed to get through to the outskirts of London, where, in the south, they damaged communications to some little extent.

In the afternoon a large force crossed the Kent coast and then split up into two groups, being joined by others which had followed. Ranging along both sides of the Thames Estuary, they tried to bomb aerodromes but were frustrated by our fighters. They dropped bombs on an industrial undertaking. In the first attempt, made at 9 a.m., about 250 bombers and fighters had been employed, coming over in waves of 20 to 30. At half-past two came another mass attack, which lasted two hours. London's third alarm of the day was at 9.18 p.m.,

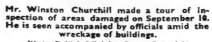

Mr. Winston Churchill made a tour of inspection of areas damaged on September 10. He is seen accompanied by officials amid the wreckage of buildings.
Photo, British Official : Crown Copyright

ushering in a raid which continued until Friday morning. Although a large public shelter in a London square was hit by a bomb, only two out of the thousand persons within were hurt.

With hardly a respite the enemy raids began again at 8.30 a.m. on Friday. In an hour our fighters shot down between thirty and forty enemy aircraft. Most of the fighting took place over Kent and Sussex, and fine work was done by a Polish squadron. In three raids some 650 German aircraft were engaged—300 in the morning, 200 about midday when the Kent coast was again the objective, and 100, followed later by another 50, in the late afternoon.

A few minutes before 9 p.m. two bombs were dropped in the London area by a single aeroplane. Baffled by the fierce barrage, other raiders sheered off and attempted to get through from another direction, again without success. Flares were used by the enemy to light up his targets, and both fire-bombs and demolition bombs were dropped in many districts. The sixth raid of the day lasted from 11.34 p.m. to 1.4 a.m. on Saturday.

In seven days the A.A. gunners had shot down 61 raiders, a remarkable achievement of an arm whose main purpose had been

marked out as the putting up of a defensive barrage to keep the raiders flying high. Our fighters and ground defences together destroyed some 154 enemy aircraft in the four days September 3-6, with a loss to the R.A.F. of 71 machines and 30 pilots.

On Saturday, September 7, Hitler launched what was doubtless intended to be a crucial attack on London and the south-east, from which the Nazis probably expected results like those achieved in the mass onslaught on Rotterdam in May. Five hundred raiders took part, and nearly a quarter of them fell victim to our fighters and gunners. The first attack lasted 1½ hours, and as the enemy machines flew up the Thames Estuary they were met by a curtain of fire more terrible and destructive than any previously encountered. But by sheer numerical superiority they managed to force some of the bombers past our outer defences, and to drop bombs on aerodromes in Kent, Surrey and Sussex. Making for the London

During an intensive night raid of nine-and-a-half hours over London, civilian buildings were, as often, the chief victims. A hospital was hit, and one of the nurses is seen viewing the damage to her home.
Photo, Planet News

The curious effect of a bomb blast. This 'bus, apparently climbing a house in a North London square, was fortunately empty at the time of the explosion. Driver, conductor and passengers had already taken shelter.
Photo, " Daily Mirror"

Mark of the Nazis on Humble East End Homes

" The enemy has now thrown off all pretence of confining himself to military targets," said an official communiqué on the raids over London issued on September 10. There could be no better proof of the truth of these words than this photograph, taken on September 6, of a row of small houses in the East End of London after a raid. At the best, only a few belongings such as these women carry were saved undamaged.

Photo, British Official ; Crown Copyright

But 'We Can Stick It' Say the Cockneys

Few military objectives were hit during the Nazis' night raids on London. On September 8 the alarm lasted about eight hours and bombs fell heavily on a wide area. The interior of a church is seen which suffered considerable damage, though the walls are still intact.   *Photo, Planet News*

opposition—all pretence of discrimination must have been abandoned and the raids became a fury of wanton destruction and mass murder. By a thousand-to-one chance a bomb falling on a very strong underground shelter, where a thousand people were taking refuge, went down through a narrow ventilating shaft. About 14 were killed and 40 injured, but there was no panic.

Three London hospitals (one each in the Central, South-west and Eastern districts) were bombed on Sunday night in a ten-hour orgy of blind savagery, as one London newspaper termed it, which began at dusk. The raiders closed in on the Metropolis about 8 p.m. and again sought out the East End. But this time Central London also suffered severely. Two muséums were damaged. In one London hospital heavy bombs fell on the sleeping quarters of the night staff, and four masseuses and two nurses were trapped.

When an aerial torpedo demolished a block of flats in the East End more than fifty

Docks, the main force flew up the river, with ferocious dog-fights developing all the way along from the coast. They reached the eastern districts of London and attacked industrial plants on both sides of the Thames. Many incendiary bombs were dropped, and fires were started which later served as beacons to guide the night raiders.

In the late afternoon other large formations (numbering 250 in all) came over the coast and headed up the Estuary : for eight and a quarter hours—until dawn, in fact—the Nazis' desperate attempts went on to subjugate London. They failed, in the face of the incomparable skill and daring of our fighter pilots and the splendidly organized

and manned ground defences. A.A. gunners during Saturday shot down 28 raiders, and 75 were destroyed by our pilots. The casualties were 306 killed and 1,337 injured. Of material damage there was plenty as the result of this indiscriminate attack on non-military targets. The densely populated East End of London appeared to have been deliberately selected for punishment.

In South London another crowded area around the Elephant and Castle was bombed after flares had shown the Nazi pilots the nature of their target.

At first the raiders kept mainly to military objectives, but later in the day—stung to desperation, perhaps by the strength of our

GERMAN & BRITISH AIRCRAFT LOSSES
German to April 30, 1940

Total announced West Front, North Sea, Britain, Scandinavia				...	...	195
					German	British
May ...	...	...	...	...	1,990	258
June ...	...	...	...	...	276	177
July ...	...	...	...	...	245	115
Aug.*	...	...	...	...	1,110	310
Sept. 1-11	...	...	...	...	502	198
Totals, May to Sept. 11			...		**4,123**	**1,058**

Daily Results.			German Losses	British Losses	Br. Pilots Saved
Sept. 1	...	...	25	15	9
„ 2	...	...	55	50	10
„ 3	...	...	25	15	8
„ 4	...	...	54	17	12
„ 5	...	...	39	20	·9
„ 6	...	·..	46	19	12
„ 7	...	...	103	22	9
„ 8	...	...	11	3	1
„ 9	...	...	52	13	6
„ 10	...	...	2	0	—
„ 11	...	...	90	24	7
			502	198	83

None of the figures include aircraft bombed on the ground or so damaged as to be unlikely to reach home.

*Corrected Total. Owing to a misprint, incorrect figures were given in previous list (page 259).

Air Raid Casualties During August : 1,075 killed, 1,261 seriously injured.
During Mass Raids on London. Sept. 7 : 306 killed ; 1,337 injured. Sept. 8 : 286 killed ; about 1,400 injured. Sept. 9 : about 400 killed 1,400 injured.

people were killed ; twelve families had taken refuge in a buttressed ground floor of the building. London railways were disorganized by damage done near one terminus, but other services were improvised on Monday, September 9. The death roll was 286 ; about 1,400 were seriously injured.

After a quiet day London heard the sirens at 5.10 p.m., but the enemy was soon forced to flee. Some damage was done by individual raiders. At 8.49 p.m. the night attacks began. "Bombs were scattered at random over London without any distinction of objectives," said an Air Ministry communiqué of Tuesday, September 10. "They have fallen in the City and caused fires in the immediate vicinity of St. Paul's Cathedral and the Guildhall. They have fallen on a large maternity hospital which was twice attacked, a number of casualties being caused." Other targets were a poor-law institution for the aged, an L.C.C. housing estate, and large numbers of workmen's cottages in the East End.

Warehouses near St. Paul's were set on fire and so damaged as to be past saving, though the blaze was localized.

A well-known cinema in the Central London district received a direct hit during a fierce night raid. Nazi fury has been chiefly confined to residential quarters, churches and places of entertainment. Some extent of the damage can readily be seen from this photograph.
Photo, Bertram Park

In A Crescendo of Fury the Air War Goes On

Although in September the bombing of London suggested that the Nazis had abandoned all pretence of seeking only military objectives, we may trace some method in their madness of destructive rage. The various stages in the aerial offensive are outlined below.

"THE air battle continues," said Mr. Churchill in the House of Commons on September 5. " In July there was a great deal of air activity, August has been a real fighting month . . . we must be prepared for heavier fighting in this month of September."

Within less than 48 hours events more than justified the Premier's words of warning. In the afternoon of Saturday, September 7, a cloud of German raiders appeared above London—the first of many mass raids on the Empire's capital. Within a few hours hundreds of Londoners—humble, altogether defenceless folk for the most part—were killed, and thousands were injured more or less seriously ; hundreds of little homes were shattered, hospitals were laid in ruins, many

London. I personally assumed command of these victorious German airmen, who for the first time have been attacking London in broad daylight, accompanied by their brave fighter comrades."

But important as the propaganda value of the raids on London must be in Germany, it is far more reasonable to suppose that the bombing is part of a deliberate plan—a plan which has for its object the actual conquest of these islands by an army of invasion. Following the collapse of France in June the Germans at once began moving their air force nearer to the coast, occupying in particular all the principal aerodromes in northern France. From there they delivered their large-scale attacks on the convoys of merchantmen in the Channel ; after a time these

been manifested beyond a doubt to all the world, and to none more so than to the Nazis themselves and their Italian allies. For weeks before the mass attacks on London began the population of the Ruhr and the Rhineland had known what it is like to spend the hours of night in uncomfortable shelters while without are the roar of gunfire and the ominous thudding of bombs.

After a time the range of the raiders was extended to the lines of communication and the aircraft factories, doubtless in the hope of dislocating the one and so hampering the work of the other that it would be impossible for Britain to achieve not merely equality with Germany in the air, but that superiority which is her aim. In these objectives, too, Germany has signally failed, for the transport

---

BRITAIN'S MOST CRITICAL HOUR : THE PREMIER'S HISTORIC WORDS

INVASION—TO BE OR NOT TO BE?

THE effort by Germany to secure daylight mastery of the air over England is the crux of the whole war. So far it has failed conspicuously . . . Nevertheless, all Hitler's preparations for invasion on a great scale are steadily going forward.

Several hundreds of self-propelled barges are moving down the coast of Europe from the German and Dutch harbours to the ports of Northern France from Dunkirk to Brest, and beyond Brest to the French harbours in the Bay of Biscay.

Besides this, convoys of merchant ships in tens and dozens are being moved through the Straits of Dover into the Channel and along from port to port under the protection of the new batteries which the Germans have built on the French shores. There are now considerable gatherings of shipping in the German, Dutch, Belgian and French harbours, all the way from Hamburg to Brest. Finally, there are some preparations made of ships to carry an invading force from the Norwegian harbours.

Behind these clusters of ships are barges and very large numbers of German troops awaiting the order to go on board and set out on their very dangerous and uncertain voyage across the seas. We cannot tell when they will try to come. We cannot be sure that, in fact, they will try at all, but no one should blind himself to the fact that heavy full-scale invasion of these islands is being prepared with all the German thoroughness of method, and may be launched at any time on England, Scotland, or Ireland, or upon all three. If this invasion is going to be tried at all, it does not seem it can be long delayed. The weather may break at any time.

Therefore we must regard the next week or so as a very important week in our history. It ranks with the days when the Spanish Armada was approaching the Channel and Drake was finishing his game of bowls, or when Nelson stood between us and Napoleon's Grand Army at Boulogne.

We have read about all this in the history books, but what is happening now is on a far greater scale and of far more consequence to the life and future of the world and its civilization than those brave old days of the past.

Every man and woman will therefore prepare himself to do his duty, whatever it may be, with special pride and care. It is with devout but sure confidence that I say : " Let God defend the right."

AERIAL WAR OVER LONDON

THE cruel, wanton, indiscriminate bombings of London are part of Hitler's invasion plan. He hopes, by killing large numbers of civilians and women and children, that he will terrorise and cow the people of this mighty Imperial city and make them a burden and anxiety to the Government, and thus distract our attention unduly from the ferocious onslaught he is preparing.

Little does he know the spirit of the British nation or the tough fibre of the Londoners, whose forbears played a leading part in the establishment of Parliamentary institutions, and who have been bred to value freedom far above their lives.

This wicked man, the repository and embodiment of many forms of soul-destroying hatred ; this monstrous product of former wrongs and shames, has now resolved to try to break our famous island spirit by a process of indiscriminate slaughter and destruction.

What he has done is to kindle a fire in British hearts here and all over the world which will glow long after all traces of the conflagrations he has caused in London have been removed. He has lighted a fire which will burn with a steady and consuming flame until the last vestiges of Nazi tyranny have been burnt out of Europe, and until the old world and the new can join hands to rebuild the temples of man's freedom and man's honour upon foundations which will not soon or easily be overthrown.

This is the time for everyone to stand together and hold firm, as they are doing. I express my admiration for the exemplary manner in which all the A.R.P. services of London are being discharged. Especially the fire brigades, whose work has been so heavy and also dangerous.

All the world that is still free marvels at the composure and fortitude with which the citizens of London are facing and surmounting the great ordeal to which they are subjected, the end of which or the severity of which cannot yet be foreseen.

It is a message of good cheer to our fighting forces, on the seas, in the air and in our waiting armies, in all their posts and stations, that we send them from the capital city. They know that they have behind them a people who will not flinch or weary of the struggle, hard and protracted though it will be, but that we shall rather draw from the heart of suffering itself the means of inspiration and survival, and of a victory won, not only for ourselves but for all—a victory won not only for our own time, but for the long and better days that are to come.

Extracted from Mr. Winston Churchill's Broadcast of September 11, 1940.

---

public buildings hit, and the means of communication temporarily dislocated.

Why was it that only now after a full year of war London became the target of Nazi bombs ? Hitler would have us believe that he had spared the great city out of magnanimity ; he simply hated to think of the thousands of innocent people who would become involved in the holocaust. . . . In his surprise speech at Berlin on September 4 he shouted that if the British did not cease their attack on the German cities, then " we will simply raze theirs. We will call a halt to these night pirates. If the British throw two or three thousands of bombs we will unload 150, 180, yes, 200 thousand. . . ."

The creator and captain of the Luftwaffe made a similar boast. In a broadcast from his headquarters in Northern France on September 8, Field Marshal Goering said : " Now is the historic hour when for the first time the German Air Force has struck at the heart of the enemy. After all the British provocative attacks on Berlin the Fuehrer decided to order reprisal blows against

ceased, perhaps because they had proved in almost every case too costly.

Then came the turn of the ports—Dover, Folkestone, Portsmouth, Southampton, Weymouth, and the rest—and the aerodromes in the coastal districts. No doubt it was intended that after a short time the ports should be incapable of receiving and handling shipping, and the aerodromes would be put out of action so that Britain's fighters would have to operate at an ever greater distance from the coast. But not only have the ports, both naval and commercial, continued to remain open, but the R.A.F. have not had to evacuate a single aerodrome in the southern and south-eastern areas.

Nor have the Germans succeeded in wearing down the defence ; the reserves of fighter aircraft and of the men to fly them are not only large but are constantly replenished, and it has not been found necessary for additional fighters to be drafted to the coast from other regions. That the offensive power of the R.A.F. has not been diminished by the fierce struggle in which they are engaged has

system has continued to function and the aircraft factories week by week beat their own records of completed machines.

There remains the question of morale. The Germans are firm believers in the doctrine of frightfulness, and from what they were able to accomplish in Poland and Holland, in Belgium and France, they may well believe that in course of time the British public must crack under the strain of heavy and sustained air bombardment, just as the peoples of the Continent have done. But, as Mr. Churchill phrased it, " we have no doubt that the whole nation, taking its example from our airmen, will stand up to it, grim and gay " ; and the American correspondents in London have not been able to find words strong enough to express their admiration of the way in which the people of Britain are standing up to their ordeal. As for London, the official communiqué issued on September 9 rendered them no more than their due when it said that " its citizens have met the blind savagery of these latest night attacks with admirable courage and resource."

From the Signal 'Raider Over' to the 'All Clear'

Many enemy raiders attacking the West of England cross the Dorsetshire coast. Above, watchers have sighted a Nazi 'plane. One points to it while the other beats an iron bar to call the gunners to their posts.

When the enemy is in sight, one of the men manning the station hoists a warning flag, left. Above, the crew of the anti-aircraft gun run at top speed to their action stations.

Here the men are at their gun waiting for the observers to give them the signal that the raider is within range, when they can pepper it. Beside the gun-pit is a store of ammunition, right, from which it is handed out to the gun crew.

Photos, "News Chronicle" staff photographer, I. Saidman, exclusive to THE WAR ILLUSTRATED

The raider was driven off, but before going lightened his 'plane by dropping some of his bombs. Left, the smoke is rising from the crater made by one of them. Above, after the raid the gun crew have a sing-song, but the spotter is still watching.

Rumania Finds a Scapegoat in King Carol

After ten years of uneasy tenure of Rumania's throne, reputedly the most dangerous
of the few still left in this modern world, Carol abdicated on September 6 and sought
refuge in Switzerland. Something of his colourful career is told below.

BEFORE it was light on the morning of Saturday, September 7, King Carol of Rumania left his country, an exile for the second time. He left behind him a capital whose streets were filled with demonstrators, where police and Iron Guards had been battling near the royal palace and troops had been called out to use arms and tear gas against the rioters.

A few hours before King Carol had abdicated in the great marble throne-room of the palace in Bucharest. " I have decided to abdicate," he declared in the proclamation he made to his people, " in face of the misfortunes which have come to this country. I hope by this sacrifice to save my country, and I hope it will not be in vain." So King Carol abdicated, and for the second time in his nineteen years of life his son heard the blare of trumpets and the people shouting " God save King Michael ! "

What a lifetime of romance and danger could the royal fugitive look back upon as the train bore him across the Balkans to Switzerland and retirement ! Not yet 47 years old, he was the son of King Ferdinand I who succeeded his uncle, Carol I, in 1914 ; and

Proclaimed King in 1940 for the second time, King Michael of Rumania was born in 1921 and succeeded his grandfather, Ferdinand in 1927, but three years later was supplanted by his father Carol II.

Dr. Julius Maniu (left) is leader of the Rumanian National Peasant Party, and has twice been Prime Minister. Right, is General Ion Antonescu who was released from the monastery in which he had been imprisoned following his denunciation of the Bessarabian cession, to become Dictator of Rumania on September 4.
Photos, Wide World and Associated Press

his mother, Queen Marie, was a daughter of the Duke of Edinburgh. From the days of his youth Carol was a thorn in the flesh to his father, although he shared to a large extent his mother's love for England and things English. Towards the end of the Great War he fell in love with one Mlle. Zizi Lambrino, daughter of a Rumanian artillery officer, and to the surprise of the world and the disgust of his family, married her. A year or two later, however, he consented to the annulment of the marriage ; and in 1921 he married Princess Helena, daughter of King Constantine of Greece. A son was born to the young couple in October of the same year—Prince Mihai, the King Michael of today, but in a very short time Carol tired of his wife, and found a new love in the person of Magda Lupescu, who divorced her husband, an army officer, when the prince became enamoured of her.

For the second time Carol was compelled to choose between the woman he loved and his right to the throne, and for the second time he chose the woman. " A woman of great intelligence and commanding personality, with flaming red hair," writes John Gunther, " her charms were such that Carol gave up a throne for her." He quarrelled violently with Ferdinand and Marie, deserted his princess, and for some time wandered with Lupescu about Europe. When King Ferdinand died in 1927 Carol was still an exile, and his son Prince Michael, then a boy of six years old, was proclaimed King as Michael I with a Council of Regency. For three years Carol and Lupescu continued in their Surrey home or passed from hotel to hotel on the Continent.

Then in June 1930 he made a dramatic come-back. He arrived in Bucharest by aeroplane, and in a few days his restoration was complete. King Michael became Prince of Alba Julia and was packed off to school again. Shortly afterwards Mme. Lupescu also came back to Bucharest, and there she lived until the other day in a house not far from the Palace.

For ten years Carol ruled the country, at first through a facade of allegedly non-party governments, and then latterly as a dictator, in fact if not in name. His part was a difficult one to play, for Rumania was honeycombed with minorities whose claims were more or less actively supported by the countries surrounding her, three of whom had

been despoiled in 1919 to make Rumania great.

Though himself half a Hohenzollern and possessed, so it has been said, with a surreptitious admiration for Hitler, he found his chief opponents in the Fascist organization which sprang into being in Rumania—in particular, the Iron Guard, which, suppressed more than once and its leaders executed or " shot while trying to escape," still managed to maintain a subterranean existence.

In 1940 his difficulties came to a head, for following the radical transformation in the heart of Europe, all the countries with claims against Rumania were encouraged to make them. Faced already by so many foes, King Carol endeavoured to make a patched-up peace within. On June 21 he issued a decree creating a new National Party under his supreme leadership and including members of the Iron Guard and of the Peasant Party, headed by Dr. Maniu.

But the national unity was short-lived, and following the cession of Bessarabia and Bukovina to Russia, a number of Rumanian statesmen, including Dr. Maniu, and the leaders of the Liberal Party, Professor Jorga and M. Bratianu, issued a manifesto opposing further cession of Rumanian territory. But before August was out half Transylvania had been abandoned to Hungary by the Vienna Award (*see* page 272), Greater Rumania was in a state of collapse, and in the search for a scapegoat it was but natural that the Iron Guard in particular, should find him in the King.

On Sept. 4 M. Gigurtu, the pro-German premier who had accepted the ultimatum from the Axis Powers demanding the return of the greater part of Transylvania, was compelled to resign, and in his place King Carol appointed General Ion Antonescu, who the next day was granted Dictator's powers. Another day passed, and Antonescu presented a demand for the King's abdication. So once more Carol became an exile : and as his train crossed the frontier into Jugoslavia its windows were riddled with bullets. The Iron Guard had the last word.

King Carol II of Rumania was born in 1893 and supplanted his son, Michael, on the throne in 1930. Ten years later he was again an exile following the collapse of Greater Rumania.
Photo, Associated Press

OUR SEARCHLIGHT ON THE WAR

British Biscuits for the World

URGED on by Mr. F. D'Arcy Cooper, chairman of the Executive Committee of the Export Council, who told them they could have all the sugar and flour they wanted, biscuit manufacturers in Great Britain are cooperating to develop still further the already large export trade in cakes and biscuits. It is worth today half-a-million pounds a year, for the 400 different varieties are eaten in all the free countries of the world, each country having its own preference. Continental markets have, of course, closed, but new profitable markets have been opened with the U.S.A., South America, India, Malaya, Dutch East Indies, and various parts of the British Empire. The development of all export trade is now a matter of urgency, to provide additional foreign exchange for war supplies from overseas.

H.M.S. ' Truant ' to the Rescue

HERO—or should one, speaking of a ship, say heroine ?—of several remarkable exploits, including the sinking of the German cruiser " Karlsruhe," H.M. submarine " Truant " has added to her gallant history by rescuing a captive British crew. Here is the story. On patrol off Cape Finisterre, " Truant " surfaced to investigate the identity and business of a strange ship. The latter turned out to be the Norwegian merchantman " Tropic Sea," captured by an enemy raider and bound for Germany in charge of a prize crew. Also aboard were the captain and crew of the British steamer " Haxby," previously sunk by the raider. Unnerved by the advent of the submarine, the Germans scuttled the " Tropic Sea," and, with their British and Norwegian prisoners, took to the boats. H.M.S. " Truant," after a little competent sorting, took on board the 24 British seamen and the Norwegian captain and his wife. Having no room for more survivors, she left the remainder in their boats in the middle of a calm sea. She then got into touch with the R.A.F., whose flying-boats proceeded to their rescue, and have since brought one boat-load of Norwegians to England.

Negro Governor Shows the Way

MOST of the French possessions in Africa have now repudiated the Vichy Government and joined General de Gaulle. The lead was given by Chad Territory, whose Governor is a remarkable personality. He is M. Adolphe Félix Sylvestre Eboué, a negro born in 1884 in Cayenne, French Guiana, of African parentage. Holding a Government scholarship, he studied law and colonial administration at the Sorbonne, became Lieut.-Governor of the French Sudan and later on of Guadeloupe, West Indies. But the reforms he introduced into the sugar plantations in order to improve conditions for the native workers so alarmed the planters that they contrived to get him recalled " for consultation " with the French Colonial Office. The result was his transference to Chad, which he governs with marked success.

Dental Ambulance from U.S.A.

AMERICAN dentistry has always been renowned, and never more so than when it is combined with plastic surgery in the merciful rebuilding of an injured face or jaw. The American dental profession, with signal generosity and understanding, has presented to the British Ministry of Health a dental ambulance " as a symbol of the willingness of all American citizens to hold out a helping hand to the British people." It will be manned by a dental surgeon, a plastic surgeon, a dental mechanic and an anaesthetist, and is equipped as an emergency operating room which can be transported to treat on the spot any disfigured soldier or civilian who cannot be moved.

Ghost Ship Attacks German Navigation

BETWEEN August 18 and 26 six Nazi merchantmen, including a 10,000-ton tanker, were destroyed outside Oslo. In addition, hundreds of bodies in German uniforms have been washed up at various parts of the coast between Trondheim and Tromso. The authorities believe that they are from troopships which were bound for the Narvik sector. The Norwegians would like to assign responsibility for these sinkings to the torpedo-boat " Sleipner," whose exploits, real or mythical, a few months ago fired popular imagination. Another theory is that British submarines are active in this area. One thing is certain, that, in spite of every precaution, Germany is finding navigation very precarious all along the Scandinavian coast.

Syria Under Axis Control

WITH a lack of ostentation strangely at variance with the character of Dictator States, an Italian armistice commission arrived at Beirut on August 28 and set to work at once, in spite of a strong undercurrent of hostility on the part of the inhabitants. It is stated than an inventory of military material is being made, and that the removal or destruction of war equipment such as 'planes, armoured cars and guns is

THIRD V.C. FOR THE NAVY

ON September 3rd it was announced that the posthumous award of a V.C., the tenth of the present war, had been made to Leading Seaman Jack Foreman Mantle, of H.M.S. Foylebank, a 5,600-ton motor ship of the Bank Line, which was attacked by enemy aircraft on July 4. Mantle, who was in charge of a pom-pom, had his left leg shattered by a bomb early in the action, but he nevertheless remained at his gun. The ship's electric power failed, whereupon he continued firing with hand gear only.

He was wounded again in many places, and the official report stated : " Between the bursts of fire he had time to reflect on the grievous injuries of which he was soon to die ; but his great courage bore him up till the end of the fight, when he fell by the gun he had so valiantly served." ·

one of the objectives of the commission. Four thousand demobilized men of the garrison have already been returned to France, and Italians, formerly interned, have been released. The French High Commissioner, M. Puaux, has urged upon the population the need for discipline, hard work and an avoidance of profiteering. Rationing of meat has begun, and there is a shortage of sugar, rice, and especially of petrol, due to the stoppage of supplies by sea.

Saved from the ' Orzel '

THE Polish submarine " Orzel " was, on June 13, presumed to be lost with all hands as her return from patrol was so long overdue. Word has now been received, via Stockholm, that part of her crew were rescued by the Germans and sent to hospital at Gdynia. This is good news indeed, for the " Orzel " was famous for many daring exploits. When Hitler invaded Poland at the beginning of September 1939, she was trapped in port at Gdynia, but escaped to sea in spite of an attack from the Nazi fleet. On September 15, when she put into Tallinn to land her sick captain, the Estonian authorities made an attempt to intern her, and confiscated her charts, breech-blocks and most of her torpedoes. The crew of the submarine, however, did not see eye to eye with them, and they overpowered the guards, cut through the mooring ropes and made their way to sea once more. This story has been told in Page 511, Volume I. A month later, after incredible experiences, the " Orzel " was proudly escorted into harbour by a British destroyer, and thereafter threw in her lot with the Royal Navy. Later she distinguished herself by sinking a German transport carrying troops to Norway.

' Leaves of Fire '

HITLER'S much advertised " new weapons " seem to have fizzled out or missed their mark. Quietly, without preliminary warning, the R.A.F. have introduced a new weapon which is creating havoc among the enemy's war supplies. It is an incendiary weapon, described as a self-igniting leaf, and is designed to set fire to military stores standing in the open, to arsenals, ammunition dumps, concentrations of trucks or lorries, and also, under suitable conditions, to woods in which an ammunition plant or a military depot lies concealed. The " leaf," or celluloid card, is 2 inches square, and 250,000 can be carried in one 'plane. The indignant Germans have already stated that they cause poisoning, but this is, of course, false. They are not poisonous, but, like any other incendiary bomb, they cause burns. More than a million have been scattered over a wide area in Germany lately during the daring night raids carried out by the R.A.F., particularly over the Black Forest and the dense woods of the Harz Mountains.

V.C., Reported Dead, Now Safe

ON August 6, King George presented privately to Mrs. Harry Nicholls, wife of Lance-Corporal Harry Nicholls, of the Grenadier Guards, the Victoria Cross won by her husband on May 21 for an act of great gallantry against the enemy on the banks of the Scheldt (see page 139). At the very start of the action he had been severely wounded in the arm, but continued to engage the German infantry, causing many casualties and making them fall back. He himself received three further wounds, and was believed to have died. But early in September Mrs. Nicholls received a telegram to say that her husband was safe and was reported to be a prisoner of war.

I WAS THERE!

Eye Witness Stories of Episodes
and Adventures in the
Second Great War

Our Shelter Shook—and So Did We

Saturday, September 7, 1940, saw the first of the mass raids on
London made with such savage ferocity by the Nazi bombers. The
area chiefly affected was the East End. The following story was
told us by a member of "The War Illustrated" staff—a sixteen-
year-old girl whose home is in the heart of Dockland

BEFORE the siren went at a quarter to five
in the afternoon we heard gun-fire and
'planes which we knew must be
"Jerries," so we all went into our Anderson
shelter—my father and mother, my brother
aged 13, and my little sister of 7. The
'planes came over in three lots—we could
hear them very plainly—and the guns sent
up a terrific barrage. We could hear bombs
whistling down all round us as we cowered
in the back of the shelter, expecting to be hit
every moment. Bombs were dropping in a
field behind us, and we thought that if they
didn't hit us they would surely hit our
house, where we had had to leave our poor
little dog. We could hear her barking
furiously at every explosion. Our shelter
shook, and so did we, but my small sister
went to sleep and never heard a thing. The
rest of us ate sweets and tried to pretend we
didn't mind. All the time fire-engines were
rushing past clanging their bells.

When the All Clear sounded and we
started to come out of the shelter, my brother
said, "Hasn't it got dark?" Father said
it was because we had been in the shelter—
but it wasn't. It was a great smoke cloud
all over the sky—awful thick, black smoke,
which made our faces dirty. We thought
for a moment that our house was on fire, but
it was the reflection from the burning buildings

farther down. We could see at least half-a-
dozen fires blazing and great flames shooting
up into the sky.

That same night when the "Jerries" came
back, my old school was hit by an incendiary
bomb. I saw one window bright with
flames, and when I looked again the whole
school was blazing. Only the four walls
were left standing. We had to go back into
our shelter before nine o'clock, and all spent
the rest of the night there. We lay on our
beds, but could not sleep because the noise
was so awful. But it didn't seem to worry
my brother and sister, and they slept peacefully.

We Dived to 800 Feet to Bomb Kiel

The naval dockyard at Kiel—a favourite objective of the R.A.F.—
was subjected to a swift attack by heavy bombers on August 27.
In the face of a fierce barrage of anti-aircraft fire, blinded at times
by the searchlights, one pilot came down to 800 feet over the docks
to drop his bombs. Here is his own dramatic story of the scene.

DESCRIBING the raid from start to finish,
the bomber pilot said :

Going out the weather was fairly
good and we came out about fifteen miles
North of the target, managed to get a good
" pinpoint " and then turned and flew south.
There was no enemy activity of any descrip-

tion while we were going down to the target,
no " Flak " and no searchlights. We flew
along at about thirteen thousand feet and
then came round slightly east of the target.

One searchlight picked us up and then
suddenly we seemed to be in the centre of
the biggest collection of anti-aircraft bursts
and searchlights I have ever seen. They all
came on at once—just as though somebody
had pushed over a switch. We flew on,
taking ordinary evasive action. We dropped
a flare, but with all this " Flak " coming up
we didn't have time to wait and see what
happened.

We had worked it all out before we took
off, and I was manoeuvring to try to get the
target in between us and the moon, though
unfortunately the moon was only just coming
up and wasn't very bright. From my height
I could definitely make out the shape of the
Mole. There was no mistaking it. I
decided to take the odd chance and we went
down in a dive to 800 feet.

I was trying to keep the target just underneath the nose of the aircraft all the time.
We got up a dickens of a speed. I estimate
we were doing about 350 m.p.h. on the clock.
When we got down to about 8,000 they had
about 15 searchlights on us. The heavy
" Flak " had been coming up all the time,
and now the light " Flak " started. It just
came straight up at us ; I have never seen so
much before.

I thought, we couldn't go back, having got
so far, so we just carried on. The lower we
went the more intense the " Flak " became.
Now and then I was able to catch a glimpse
of the Mole in front of us. It was impossible
to say for certain whether there was a ship
there or not ; I saw a long dark shape to the
west of it which certainly looked like a ship.

We just carried on diving. I gave the
order to release the bombs at 800 feet. Then
straight away we shot down to one hundred
feet over the Mole and just above the water.
There seemed to be more searchlights than
ever. At times I was blinded. It was
impossible to see the results of the bombing.

Suddenly, in front of me I saw a lot of
trees coming up straight ahead. One of the
searchlights, flattening out to try to catch us,

Following the mass air raid on the afternoon of September 7 great fires broke out in London's
dockland. This photograph, taken a few hours later, shows London's familiar outline silhouetted
against a flame-lit sky. On the left is St. Paul's, and on the right the Tower Bridge (marked
by an arrow). In the centre (arrow), is the summit of the Monument which was erected in
1677 to commemorate the Great Fire of London of 1666. *Photo, " News Chronicle "*

304   *The War Illustrated*   September 20th, 1940

||||||||||||||||||||||||||||||||||||||||||||||||||||||||||||||||||| I WAS THERE ! ||||||||||||||||||||||||||||||||||||||||||||||||||||||||||||||||||||

had illuminated them, just in time for me to see them. I pulled the aircraft up, and we went over the top. The trouble was we didn't dare go up too high because as soon as we did every gun in the place started opening up. I tried going up to 300 feet. But all the guns seemed to be banging away at us. It was incredible. We went down low again and flew over the town at about 100 feet.

The front and rear gunners were blazing away at the points of fire on the ground. They used up about 3,000 rounds between them. We must have stayed over the town for about ten minutes, just charging backwards and forwards trying to get away. Practically all the time we were at about 100 feet. I was trying to head west, but as soon as I did that they put up a terrific barrage in front of us.

I just hoped to get out of it, but I must say I never really expected that we would. We went south, zig-zagging all the time. We got about 15 miles away and then, although we were being shot at, we were able to gain height. As we went up we had to take violent evasive action all the time, but finally we got away.

While the Luftwaffe raided London the R.A.F. never ceased for a moment their bombardment of German territory. Here is a German A.A. gun in action during an alarm.

' All In the Day's Work' Says an A.F.S.

Inspecting raid damage in London on September 10, Mr. Churchill sympathized with auxiliary firemen who had been on duty for many hours. "Never mind, sir," said one of them. "It's all in the day's work." That this is typical of the A.F.S. is exemplified by this story by Mr. L. Bastin, an auxiliary from Shoreditch.

DURING the week-end raids of September 7-8, London's firemen and the Auxiliary Fire Service carried on their dangerous work while bombs dropped round them, and many were killed or injured.

Mr. L. F. Bastin, of the A.F.S., had worked continuously at a blaze from 5 o'clock on Saturday, September 7, until after midnight. Even an injured ankle did not stop him working. He refused to stop until a rescue squad made him.

Later, in hospital, he said :

I saw hundreds of firemen working with bombs dropping all round. I counted 12 bombs as the rescue squad carried me to a car a quarter of an hour away.

On the dockside itself, right among the heart of those fires, civilians were standing round helping. Young girls and old men formed human chains passing buckets of water to the firemen when we could not get water from the hydrant. The spirit of the people was marvellous. I never saw anything like it.

I saw great lorries burning up like matches. The fire-boats came up and helped.

When Mr. Bastin reached a first-aid post there were five more injured firemen. "One man," he said, "had taken cover in a doorway when he heard a bomb whistling. His face was covered with splinters from the wood blocks in the road. He never murmured."

Nurses and doctors at the post also carried on their work despite the bombs. The first aid men driving to pick up casualties always got through somehow when a bomb dropped ahead of them.

Throughout the worst of the bomb dropping police were still at work roping off streets and directing the services. Although they could see the stupendous size of the fire, firemen going to the blaze were singing "Roll Out the Barrel." *Daily Telegraph.*

When the German bombs were rained down on London the Fire Brigade—"regulars" and A.F.S.—went into action immediately. Here we see members of the London Fire Brigade tackling the situation created when a bomb fell in the street and set fire to gas escaping from a main.

I Flew With the R.A.F. Over Kassala

After the frontier fortress of Kassala in the Sudan was occupied by the Italians at the beginning of July, the garrison was subjected to continual attack by the R.A.F. A typical raid is described in the following dispatch by Alan Moorehead, of the "Daily Express."

I FLEW in a British bomber on a three-and-a-half hours' raid over Italian East Africa and the enemy border garrison at Kassala, during which wave after wave of British machines swept down in one of the biggest concentrated bombing attacks of the mid-Eastern war.

I went with the three pilots in my formation to get final instructions for the attack. Here on map and aerial photographs was the spot where the Italians had gate-crashed three thousand strong into Kassala ; here was the spot where troops were garrisoned, and here probably were machine-gun nests and A.A. batteries.

The commander said : " Bomb them, and strafe them with machine-gun fire, then reconnoitre along roads back into Eritrea."

A moment later I was scrambling into the cockpit of a bomber gingerly keeping my hands off the controls that led down to racks filled with bombs.

We shot up in a stream of dust over this country, which is half as big as Europe, where a man can die of thirst in a day and even Bedouins can scarcely scrape a living from the dead, brown rock and sand.

Across in the other machines, the rear gunners kept spinning their glasses in the turrets in search of enemy fighters.

Gratefully I took a couple of lumps of chewing gum from the young Canadian pilot and watched the minutes tick by. Even to veterans I imagine that this is a moment with the greatest strain — when you don't know what's in front or how you're going to succeed.

In the electric rush of action over the target you have only time for the thrill of absolute confidence and the attitude of " if it's coming to me, I can take it "—that is just fine. But these lads who have grown into seasoned fighters in the past months, showed no feeling either way . . . .

The leading pilot with a nod took us into the attack. From a considerable height we dived, turning and banking to avoid ground fire until we felt we could reach out and touch the target with our hands.

Noiseless above the scream of the motors, the tracer bullets skidded past the glass of the cockpit. Two bursts ripped through the leading bomber's starboard wing.

Our racks opened up and our first salvo was shot downwards on the huts. I heard nothing above the engines except the rat-tat-tat of our forward gun raking the compound from a few hundred feet. Even our bomb explosions did not break through the barrage of noise.

It seemed so easy then—not a sign of a living soul on the ground. All those ten thousand men had been driven to cover and the target was lying out there in a neat inviting pattern on the ground.

Yet we were under fire and there was that gash in the other machine's wing.

Then back from a long detour we were roaring down over Kassala again from an opposite direction.

This time our last load of bombs went down and strafing began in earnest. Three times we were on them with the same lurching side step and a last straight roaring dive.

As we turned to dive again the lads in my 'plane held on to the attack with set, intent faces. Clearly they had forgotten everything else in the world except this whirling little arena of battle.

I had got a splitting headache and felt mildly sick. But soon we were mounting again into the clear, steady air above, and turned for the long journey homeward.

Kassala, Sudanese frontier post, dominates a fertile area beyond which the River Gash loses itself in the desert. These brown basalt crags belong to the unscaled mountains—Jebel Kassala and Jebel Moktam.
Photo, E.N.A.

As we left the target three more dark shapes moved across the sky. The next Brtish formation was flying into the attack . . .

We Thought We had Rammed an E-boat

A British motor torpedo-boat put into port on August 15 with bedding stuffed into a big hole in her bows—the result of ramming an enemy ship much larger than herself. The "scrap" in the North Sea during which this incident occurred is described here by the commanders of the three M.T.B.s involved.

THE M.T.B.s are the Navy's smallest fighting ships, but they boast great speed and strength.

Three of them went out on patrol in the North Sea, captained by Lieut. Mannoch, Lieut. F. A. Hamilton-Hill, R.N.R., and Lieut. Stewart Gould.

Here is the story told on their return to port by Lieutenant Mannoch :

We were suddenly shelled by a vessel which must have seen our bow-waves from a long way off, for the phosphorescence shone brightly in the dense darkness

Next I saw two dark grey shapes ahead, moving slowly. I took them for E-boats, opened fire, and decided to ram one. When I got closer I found it was not an E-boat, but something larger.

I put the wheel over to avoid her, but we hit her six feet from the stern. Our ship climbed right on her upper deck and slewed to starboard before she slipped back in the water. By this time the other two M.T.B.s were on my starboard side, and the three of us gave the German some fierce fire. We were within 500 yards of her, firing at almost point-blank range.

I found our damage was causing trouble —a 10-foot hole in the bottom and a 6-foot hole on the port side. We stuffed all the bedding we could find into the holes, but the water came 3 feet above the mess-deck.

One of the other M.T.B.s took us in tow and we went ahead very slowly. We discovered an enemy vessel of the trawler type astern and we opened fire at 200 yards.

My crew told me they heard screams coming from her, and soon she turned away and broke off the action.

At dawn, on our way back to harbour, we met a Dornier flying-boat. Between the two of us we pumped about 1,000 rounds into her. The last we saw of her was dark smoke pouring from her exhaust as she made for home.

Lieut. Gould added his story:

We beat off an E-boat and then found what looked like another. She fired machine-guns, explosive shells, and grenades at us all at once. The grenades came from a kind of pneumatic gun.

We fired effectively at her gun flashes and had a running fight at 30 knots for about eight minutes. We beat her off, but ran into her again while looking for the damaged M.T.B., and had another five minutes' running fight.—(*Daily Mail.*)

Lieut. Mannoch, captain of the motor torpedo-boat which rammed an enemy warship, is seen right, with members of his ship's company, inspecting the damaged bow after the torpedo-boat had been taken from the water at her base.
Photo, Planet News

There Will Be No Nazi Aggression in Iceland

ON May 16, 1940, a little over a month after German troops had marched into Denmark, the British Foreign Office announced that British troops had landed in Iceland to secure the country against German invasion. Since then they have been reinforced by a detachment of Canadian soldiers—yet another example of the working of the spirit of Imperial fellowship. The photographs in this page show something of the life of the troops in Iceland and incidents in their preparation to defend the island against invasion. Left, men of the West Yorkshire Regiment are at anti-tank practice. Below, a Canadian officer is chatting with two Iceland women who are wearing their native costumes.

Battle dress is worn not only by the troops in Iceland, but by the men of the Royal Navy who are there on the work of maintaining communications with Britain and landing supplies. In the two photographs, centre, are soldiers and sailors who are making themselves at home in their strange surroundings. The equipment of the troops is excellent, and above are men of the Canadian " Royals " manning Bren gun carriers.

Photos, British Official: Crown Copyright

They Have Won Honour in Freedom's Cause

Capt. A. G. B. Wainwright, R.A., M.C., for displaying great courage. No task proved too difficult for him to undertake.

Major J. Murray Prain, Fife and Forfar Yeomanry, **D.S.O.,** for distinguished services in the field.

Maj. R. Graham, O.B.E., for displaying conspicuous bravery and devotion to duty in the course of military operations.

Maj. A. E. S. Adair, M.C., Grenadier Guards, **D.S.O.,** for displaying gallantry as well as splendid devotion to duty.

Lieut.-Col. Norman Coxwell-Rogers, Royal Engineers, **D.S.O.** for conspicuous bravery and courage during military operations.

Col. H. F. Grant-Suttie, D.S.O., M.C., C.B.E., for distinguished services rendered in the field against the enemy.

Capt. R. Pilkington, M.P., M.C., for great courage. As Parliamentary Secretary to Mr. O. Stanley, he resigned his job to join up.

Lieut. D. L. Rome, M.C., for displaying great courage and conspicuous gallantry during operations against the enemy.

Lance-Sergt. P. Brown, R.A., M.M., for displaying bravery in the field in the course of operations in Belgium.

Lieut.-Col. (Acting Brigdr.) A. L. Kent Lemon, York and Lancaster Regt., **C.B.E.,** for distinguished services in the field.

Lieut.-Com. J. E. H. McBeath, R.N., of H.M.S. "Venomous," **D.S.O.,** for gallant services during coastal operations.

Pilot-Officer R. M. Taylor, D.F.C., for displaying particularly good work as a fighter pilot extending over a long period.

Able-Seaman D. Wilson, of H.M.S. "Watchful," **D.S.M.,** for enterprise and courage displayed in stripping enemy mines.

Wing-Com. Lord Willoughby de Broke, R.A.F., A.F.C., for displaying untiring and devoted service in performing his duties.

Capt. W. Gifford, of s.s. "Highlander," **O.B.E.,** for splendid services. He and his crew shot down two enemy aircraft.

Squadron-Leader Selway, D.F.C., for displaying great gallantry as well as devotion to duty in air operations.

Squadron-Leader W. M. Churchill, D.S.O., and **D.F.C.,** for displaying courage and devotion to duty during operations in the air.

Pilot-Officer D. G. Gribble, D.F.C., for gallantry in the air. He destroyed 3 Messerschmitts and in addition damaged many others.

Pilot-Officer J. A. M. Reid, D.F.M., for skilful navigation during a reconnaissance. Promoted from Sergeant since award was announced.

Acting Flight-Lieut. P. W. Lynch-Blosse, D.F.C., for carrying out successful work in locating and bombing enemy targets.

Pilot-Officer J. A. A. Gibson, D.F.C., for destroying 8 enemy aircraft and for engaging and smashing a Junkers 87.

Sergt. Gamble, D.F.M., for great courage during air operations. Though he was badly wounded, he continued his job.

Pilot-Officer J. K. U. Blake McGrath, D.F.C., for displaying courage and determination. He destroyed at least 12 enemy aircraft.

Pilot-Officer P. C. F. Stevenson, D.F.C., for great courage during intensive air operations in the Channel and Thames Estuary.

Flying-Officer T. B. Fitzgerald, D.F.C. for courage in the air. Though he was wounded, he saved the lives of his crew.

OUR DIARY OF THE WAR

WEDNESDAY, SEPTEMBER 4, 1940
368th day

On the Sea—British naval units reported to have torpedoed German transport off Skagen on September 3.

Stockholm reported that between August 18 and 26, six German merchant ships were sunk off Norway.

Admiralty announced that H.M. mine-sweeping trawler " Royalo " had been sunk.

Reported that British liner " Avoceta " had fought battle with U-boat off Portuguese coast.

In the Air—R.A.F. bombed Calais and Boulogne. During night they penetrated enemy territory as far as Stettin, where synthetic oil plant was bombed. Other forces started fires amongst military stores in Harz Mts., Thuringian Forest, and Black Forest.

Attacks also made on power station and aircraft factory at Berlin ; oil stocks at Magdeburg ; goods yards at Nienburg ; aerodromes in France and Belgium.

Aircraft of Coastal Command attacked oil tanks at Cherbourg and docks at Terneuzen.

War against Italy—R.A.F. carried out sustained and successful raids on all principal aerodromes in Eastern Libya. Bombers of S. African Air Force raided Javello.

Home Front—In morning two forces of enemy aircraft attempted to bomb aerodromes in Kent and Essex, but were driven off. Later other formations crossed S.E. coast, some of which penetrated our defences. Bombs were dropped on a Medway town and in scattered areas in South-East.

During night raid on London A.A. defences put up heavy barrage. Scattered raids over the country. Most casualties occurred in two towns in North-East and one in South-West.

Fifty-four enemy aircraft destroyed. Seventeen British fighters down, but pilots of twelve safe.

Guns fired across the Channel from Dover.

Rumania—Premier, M. Gigurtu, and his Cabinet resigned. King Carol requested Gen. Antonescu, former Minister of National Defence and Chief of Staff, to form new Government.

THURSDAY, SEPTEMBER 5
369th day

On the Sea—Admiralty announced that there had been naval operations by British forces in Eastern and Western Mediterranean, extending over five days. Italian fleet turned tail ; Italian base in Dodecanese was bombarded, and Fleet Air Arm attacked aerodromes in Sardinia and the Dodecanese.

Reported that 37 survivors of torpedoed British ships " Penzance " and " Blairmore " had arrived at Baltimore.

Admiralty announced that H.M. destroyers " Ivanhoe " and " Esk " had been sunk.

In the Air—R.A.F. again bombed military objectives concealed in German forests. Other targets were synthetic oil plant at Stettin ; tanks at Kiel ; refineries at Hamburg and Regensburg ; Emden Docks ; goods yards at Hamm and Soest ; and many Dutch and German aerodromes.

Other forces heavily bombed port of Boulogne, gun positions at Gris Nez, and harbour at Calais.

War against Italy—R.A.F. attacked great Fiat works at Turin during night, causing heavy damage.

Enemy bombed Matruh, Egypt, causing slight damage but no casualties. Few bombs dropped at Suez.

Home Front—Enemy renewed attacks on Britain. Large formations attempted to attack aerodromes on both sides of Thames Estuary, but were driven back. Bombs dropped on industrial plants on Thames-side.

Several districts in Kent attacked ; part of a hospital demolished. Fierce air fighting reported over several parts of S.W. England,

but damage caused by bombs was slight.

London was again attacked, bombs being dropped during day on outskirts. During night high explosive and incendiaries did some damage. District in Wales also bombed.

Thirty-nine enemy aircraft destroyed. Twenty British fighters missing but pilots of nine safe.

Rumania—Royal decree dissolved Parliament. New Premier, Gen. Antonescu, given dictator's powers.

FRIDAY, SEPTEMBER 6
370th day

In the Air—R.A.F. raided Berlin during night for three hours. Targets which were hit included West power station, B.M.W. aero-engine works and Salzhof oil reservoir.

Attacks continued on military objectives concealed in Black Forest, and large fires and explosions ensued. Railway sidings at Krefeld, Hamm, Soest, Mannheim and Ehrang bombed with success.

Other formations bombed gun emplacements and aerodromes on French coast.

War against Italy—Enemy aircraft raided Haifa but were driven off.

Home Front—Big enemy air attacks repulsed over S.E. England, objectives being

THE POETS & THE WAR
XXXII
SONG OF A HOME GUARD
By Lord Dunsany

If with parachute and gun
The Nazis come and I get one,
Richer for his blood will blow
Kentish flowers which we know
On some sunny slope whereby
We encounter, he and I ;
Or stronger some dog-daisy grow
Underneath a summer sky.
Or, when the hills of chalk are dry
And golden are the stalks of grass,
Some patch of thyme with deeper glow
May cheer whoever chance to pass,
Or tempt and feed the wandering bee
With that blood from oversea ;
Or brighter shall a borage shine
Or sweeter smell some eglantine.
And just the same if he gets me.
—*Evening Standard*

R.A.F. aerodromes. In morning battle 34 raiders shot down in one hour. Bombs caused slight damage to one factory in Thames Valley. During afternoon enemy crossed Kent coast but were driven back. Later, five formations crossed North Kent coast. Fire was caused to industrial plant on north bank of Thames.

During night enemy penetrated into London area and high explosive and incendiary bombs were dropped. Elephant and Castle district suffered severely.

Damage done in North-West. Attack on cathedral town in West Country.

Forty-six raiders destroyed. Britain lost 19 fighters, but pilots of twelve safe.

Rumania—King Carol abdicated in favour of his son Prince Michael.

SATURDAY, SEPTEMBER 7
371st day

In the Air—R.A.F. made determined attacks on enemy shipping in Channel ports. Other bomber squadrons attacked Krupps' works and other targets in the Ruhr.

Further attacks made on war materials stored in Black Forest. Aerodromes bombed included those at Colmar, Gilze-Rijen, Wesel, Krefeld, Brussels, Querqueville, Soesterburg and Eindhoven.

War Against Italy—Enemy aircraft raided Port Sudan, causing little damage.

Home Front—Severe and widespread damage caused in heaviest German air attacks yet made on London. They began in afternoon and continued until dawn.

Raiders came in two waves and spread out, some making for aerodromes in Surrey, Kent and Essex, others for docks, others for London. Fiercest fighting raged from East London down to Thames estuary. Fires started and damage done to lighting and other public services. Two schools badly damaged. Casualties 306 killed, 1,397 seriously injured.

Enemy lost 103 machines. Britain lost twenty-two, but pilots of nine safe.

SUNDAY, SEPTEMBER 8
372nd day

On the Sea—Admiralty reported that aircraft of Fleet Air Arm had bombed two enemy supply ships off Norway, sinking one and severely damaging the other.

In the Air—During night strong bomber forces attacked French and Belgian Channel ports and convoys in North Sea. Raids on Hamburg, Bremen and Emden.

War Against Italy—British patrol from Kenya penetrated 16 miles into Abyssinia and inflicted casualties on garrison at Gorai.

Home Front—Towards midday large force of enemy aircraft approached coast north of Dover. They were hotly engaged and only small formations penetrated inland. Bombs fell mostly in rural areas.

From 8 p.m. raiders carried out prolonged attacks on London and were met by intense A.A. bombardment. Bombing became indiscriminate. Damaged premises included three hospitals, a church and two museums. Aerial torpedo partially demolished block of flats in E. London. Docks on both sides of Thames heavily bombarded. Casualties numbered 286 killed, approx. 1,400 badly injured.

Eleven Nazi 'planes shot down. Britain lost three, but one pilot safe.

MONDAY, SEPTEMBER 9
373rd day

On the Sea—Admiralty announced that in Mediterranean H.M. submarine " Osiris " had sunk one Italian supply ship, and H.M. submarine " Rorqual " two.

Aircraft of Fleet Air Arm reported to have attacked enemy supply ship in Haugesund, a tanker south of Bergen, and a German military hutment camp in Bergen area.

H.M. submarine " Phoenix " considerably overdue and presumed lost.

In the Air—R.A.F. raided Berlin and blew up Neukoln gasworks. Bombs dropped on naval dockyard at Hamburg ; shipyards and docks at Bremen, Kiel, Wilhelmshaven and Wismar ; goods yards at Krefeld and Brussels ; and several aerodromes.

Fresh and sustained attacks made on shipping and concentrations of invasion barges at Ostend, Calais, Boulogne, and Flushing, and on gun emplacements at Cap Gris Nez.

War against Italy—Fifty civilians killed when Italian 'planes bombed Tel-Aviv for first time.

R.A.F. bombers successfully attacked number of aerodromes in Libya.

Home Front—Day and night raids made on London. During evening bombs dropped in South London, town in Kent attacked, houses wrecked and people killed. Dog fight took place over Houses of Parliament when enemy were chased up river from London Bridge.

During night bombs were dropped at random. Some fell in City causing fires in immediate vicinity of St. Paul's Cathedral and Guildhall. Others hit large maternity hospital, children's hospital, Poor Law institution for the aged, Nurses' Home attached to a hospital, hall of a City Livery Company, workmen's dwellings in East End, and many other residential districts in West and North London.

Fifty-two raiders down. Thirteen R.A.F. fighters missing, but six pilots safe.

Dover area shelled from France during evening ; enemy's gunfire was returned.

THIS WAS THE END OF THE BOMBER THAT ATTACKED BUCKINGHAM PALACE

These spectacular photographs record the destruction of the Dornier bomber that, having raided Buckingham Palace, was destroyed by a British fighter in mid air and fell in bits and pieces over Victoria (see pages 322 and 332). Hit by the bullets of the fighter seen in lower part of the left-hand photograph the Nazi machine exploded and its tail and wing tips can be seen detached. In the right-hand photograph its twin tail is hurtling down. The fighter pilot's own story is given in page 332.

Photos, Exclusive to THE WAR ILLUSTRATED

Grenadiers Would Like to Meet Nazis Again!

THE Grenadier Guards more than maintained their great reputation for gallantry and steadiness during the retreat to Dunkirk and during the memorable scenes on the Dunes. Back in England their one desire was to have another meeting with the Nazi army. Now, in the North East of England, they are going through an intensive course of training in those tactics which their experience in France and Flanders taught them were most effective. To the Tommy.gun, the newest of all weapons, Guardsmen have taken kindly. They can do deadly execution with them by firing from the hip when advancing across open country and can make extremely effective use of them while going full speed on motor-cycles.

1. The Grenadier Guards making a charge while they utter fearsome cries to strike terror into the enemy. 2. A Guardsman armed with a Tommy gun uses it effectively from behind a tree. 3. With the Bren gun is Guardsman J. Nicholls, brother of Corpl. H. Nicholls, the Dunkirk V.C. of the Grenadiers. 4. Here, advancing through a smoke screen, are some of the Guards' Bren gun carriers.

Photos, Fox

The Empire Will Fight Till Victory Be Won

Now that we are well into the second year of the war we may discover no weakening of effort, no slackening of resolve, but, on the contrary, a tremendous intensification of the activities and preparations that make for victory. Here is a review of some of the outstanding achievements of the Commonwealth at war.

IN South Africa's Parliament at Cape Town they were debating the course of the war. General Hertzog, Leader of the Nationalists and former Prime Minister, had been arguing that the war was already lost and that Great Britain had no chance without allies against both Germany and Italy. Then General Smuts rose to reply.

"We are not going to be deflected from our course by Hitler's victories or glorification of Germany," he said. "We do not run away, we are not hands-uppers." He would not take the road of Pétain. "Nobody desires peace more than I. But I want to know what kind of peace I can expect." The opposition was prepared to conclude peace at any price, but he believed in only one kind of peace, peace through victory. "I would rather a thousand times be with England than with Germany. We want nothing to do with Nazidom and ' Heil Hitler! ' " South Africa's main line of defence, went on the General, was Kenya and the other African colonies, and South African troops were already there playing their part. Germany was beaten in 1918 despite her long series of victories ; she was a colossus with feet of clay, and it collapsed. In this war, so long as Britain maintained control of the sea and brought her air force to the first rank, there could be no question of victory for Germany, but on the other hand, every prospect of victory for those who opposed her. " General Hertzog," concluded the Premier amidst tremendous cheers, " asks how long South Africa will prosecute the war. I tell him now that we shall go on till we have achieved victory."

Not long before, General Smuts, who in addition to being Prime Minister of the Union of South Africa is C.-in-C. of the South African Forces, made a moving farewell to the troops about to set off for Kenya.

" As an old soldier," he said, " I know what your service as soldiers in the far north may mean to most of you. I express to you the gratitude of the people of South Africa for the choice you have made and the service you are prepared to offer your people and your country. More no man can do than offer his life for his friend. That offer, the highest and most solemn offer a man can make, you are making. We are proud of you.

" A nation is never proud of its hands-uppers, its fence-sitters, its players-for-safety. We South Africans reserve our respect and pride for bitter-enders, for those who go all out and take their life in their own hands for their country and their people. You are going north to meet the enemy where he can be found, not where he comes to find you—in your own homes. That, too, has been the tradition of South Africa. We did it in the last war."

They did it, indeed, as many of those who listened to General Smuts knew well—those who were sons of the men who held Delville

These young Australian pilots in training at Narromine aerodrome, Australia, are marching out to their 'planes for an instructional flight. They will complete their training in Canada.
Photo, Wide World

Wood on the Somme against the terrific German attacks in the summer of 1916.

So the Springboks left South Africa for the front in Kenya, and as the trains drew out from the station there arose from the packed carriages the Springbok war-cry. " Jubilwayo ! " shouted the leader, and in reply came the great chorus, " Gheegamalay-oo ! Gee ! Gheegamalay-oo ! Gee ! Gheegamalay-oo ! W-A-A-H ! "

Arrived in Kenya they were received by the Governor, Sir Henry Moore, who conveyed to them the King's message of greeting.

" Your presence here," said the Governor, " fighting side by side with units raised in the Rhodesias and in both East and West Africa (these, it may be mentioned, are the Gold Coast Regiment and the King's African Rifles) is a striking proof of the determination of all members of the British Commonwealth in Africa to present a united front against the King's enemies."

The South African Field Force is under the command of General Dickinson, and is a self-contained separately organized unit ; even the nurses and scores of girl clerks and stenographers that accompany it are all drawn from the Union.

In Australia the same magnificent spirit is abundantly manifest. " Unable to promise easy things," said Mr. R. G. Menzies, the Prime Minister, in a recent speech, " the Government ranges itself behind the brave inspiring policy of Mr. Churchill." Then in an account of the " honourable achievements " of the past year he revealed that 130,000 men had been raised for the Australian Imperial Force for service overseas, that many thousands more had been recruited for the Navy and Air Force, as well as 100,000

Like all the British Government Offices, the London offices of the Dominion High Commissioners have armed guards. Above, Australian soldiers are parading in the entrance hall of Australia House before taking up their posts. In the centre photograph, Australian soldiers in London are lending a hand in clearing wreckage caused by a bomb.
Photos, Sport & General

From Every Quarter They Come to Britain

One of the greatest assets of the Empire's air striking forces is the series of Canadian air-training stations such as this at Trenton, Ontario. The foreground group includes Air Vice-Marshal L. D. D. McKean, Chief Liaison Officer with the Canadian Air Force.

On June 6 it was announced that seven Canadian destroyers had arrived in British waters. Here men from one of them are landing in Britain for the first time.

Among the troops of Transjordania is the Arab Legion, enlisted from Beduins. This man of the Legion on sentry-go at a desert camp has an alarm clock hung on the post.

Photos, British Official and Canadian Official

for home defence. Furthermore, the Commonwealth's aircraft, shipbuilding, and munition industries had all been expanded so that in every direction Australia was putting her every ounce into the fight.

A similar story is to be told of New Zealand. Thousands of New Zealanders are side by side with the Australians in Egypt and Palestine and the British Isles, and at home in the Dominion she has in reserve an infantry division, a cavalry brigade, and a territorial force, shortly to be given intensive training.

Canada's war effort, too, has gained a tremendous impetus. An official review of the situation issued from Ottawa at the end of August stated that Canada would shortly have a corps of two complete divisions and ancillary troops in the United Kingdom, and that the third and fourth divisions, now practically complete, were being trained and equipped in Canada. The strength of the Canadian Active Service Force is 133,000, while the Non-Permanent Active Militia has nearly 50,000 actually enrolled. From October 1, 30,000 men will be called up each month under the recently passed Mobilization Act ; the first men affected are likely to be those of 21 and 22 years of age, who will be required to undergo a thirty-day period of training. The Royal Canadian Air Force has a strength of nearly 20,000 officers and airmen ; and the Royal Canadian Navy has 113 vessels in operation, manned by nearly 9,000 officers and men. In the near future a hundred more vessels will be added to Canada's fleet. In her shipyards two new destroyers are being built for the Royal Navy, and three merchant vessels are being converted into armed cruisers. Twenty-two schools established under the British Commonwealth Air Training Plan are now in operation ; and all the aerodromes, hangars, and buildings scheduled to open in 1941 will be completed before the end of this year. Following the collapse of France Canada intensified her efforts, particularly in the field of aircraft production, and to an ever-increasing extent Canada's industry is being turned over to war purposes, and enormous quantities of arms and munitions are being produced each week.

Because of her size and the enormous multitude of her peoples, because of her age-old history and wonderful culture, India occupies a unique place in the British Commonwealth of Nations. The intervention of Italy has brought her very near to the war, and her effective frontier now runs through the Mediterranean and the Red Sea, the Middle East and Malaya. In Egypt, Aden, and Singapore Indian and British forces are occupying these vital strategic links. Some thousands of Indian troops are already overseas, but the army in India is much stronger than it was when war broke out. Regular units are being reinforced, territorials embodied, garrison companies raised, and units for general service have been inspected from some of the Indian States. The Royal Indian Navy has been more than doubled, and the naval establishments at Bombay and Karachi have been correspondingly enlarged. Steps have been taken to increase the number of Indian officers commissioned each year. Then India is rapidly becoming one vast arsenal, turning out war materials of all kinds not only for the Indian forces in India and abroad, but for the United Kingdom, the Dominions, and their Allies. It has been stated that of the 40,000 items needed to equip a modern army, more than 20,000 are already being produced in India, and in the first eight months of the war the peak of production of the ordnance factories reached a peak which was touched only towards the end of the last war. Ex-

Never Has the 'Old Country' Called in Vain

pansion of the Air Force is also in hand, and large numbers of Indian pilots are being trained. Finally, an Indian defence savings movement has been launched, and is receiving immense contributions from princes and people alike.

Much the same story could be told of all the other members of the British family of nations. From every quarter the Government in London has received offers of help given without asking and without stint. To take just a few examples, Malta has raised extra battalions for the King's Own Malta Regiment, some 3,000 "parashots," and has contributed a battery now on overseas service. Malaya has made considerable financial contributions for the prosecution of our war effort, and is the home of an officers' cadet training unit for the Far East. Newfoundland, one of the first to respond to the call, has sent a heavy artillery regiment to the United Kingdom. Men, materials, ammunition—all are being given freely to the cause of Britain and the British Commonwealth.

"Take a deep breath," says the Army doctor who is taking the measurements of a new batch of recruits at Delhi for the 11/14th (Gurgaon) Punjab Regiment—one of the regiments making up India's territorial force. Circle: Machine-gunners of the Malay Regiment on manœuvres in Singapore.
Photos, Keystone & L.N.A.

This eighteen-pounder gun is being worked by members of the New Zealand Expeditionary Force, now in England. Below are some of the South African troops paraded at Nairobi on their arrival in Kenya, when through the Governor, Sir Henry Moore, they received a message from the King.
Photos, L.N.A. and South African Official

In Africa Italy Loses Five to One in Air Fights

The result of two successive raids in August by the R.A.F. in the Middle East is seen in the photograph, left, taken from a height of 4,000 feet when British bombers were attacking Asmara aerodrome. The building in the centre has suffered a direct hit, while on the right are ruins of buildings destroyed in a previous raid. In the photograph below a mechanic with a bomber squadron at a desert aerodrome in Egypt is overhauling the propeller of a machine.

These British aircraft armourers, browned by the desert sun, are preparing the deadly load of a bomber about to start off on a flight against an enemy position. Ammunition for the machine-guns is being wound, and bombs have been unpacked. The R.A.F. has attained even greater supremacy over the Italians in the Middle East than over the Germans in Europe. Up to the beginning of September, Italy had lost 250 'planes in aerial fights in Africa and Britain about one-fifth of that number.

Photos, British Official : Crown Copyright

Yet Mussolini Still Says It is 'Our Sea'

Above, an italian submarine in the Mediterranean has been sent to its last account by depth-charges dropped from a Sunderland flying-boat of the R.A.F. Eastern Command. A huge patch of oil tells with certainty of its fate. The photograph was taken from another 'plane.

The sinking of the crack Italian cruiser "Bartolomeo Colleoni" on July 19, 1940, by H.M.S. "Sydney" and a few destroyers has already been recounted (see page 92). Photographs now available show, right, the Italian ship as she sank with a column of black smoke rising from her, and, below, some of the survivors. They are coming alongside a British destroyer.

Photos, British Official : Crown copyright

THE Italian determination to make the Mediterranean " our own sea " is still very far from fulfilment, and the record of the Italian Navy so far cannot have given Mussolini much ground for hope that his ships may yet cover themselves with glory.

After the sinking of the " Bartolomeo Colleoni," on July 19, the Italian Fleet lay low until August 31, when it was reported that the enemy's main fleet of battleships, cruisers and destroyers was at sea. An immediate effort was made by the British forces to make contact, but as soon as the enemy got news that the British were approaching they turned tail. In the first six days of September search was made for the enemy in the Dodecanese bases but no warships were there. The Fleet Air Arm, however, bombed the bases, both there and on the island of Rhodes, while British warships bombarded military objectives in the Dodecanese Islands. Thus, in six days the Royal Navy made a clean sweep of the Mediterranean and made it possible for convoys of British troops reinforcing the Army in the Middle East to pass unmolested.

London Was in the Front Line of Air Battle

The Nazi attempt to destroy the morale of Londoners by air attack had, as American correspondents told the world, no chance of any kind of success. Yet Goering's Luftwaffe continued in the period here reviewed, September 12 to 18, their murderous and destructive bombing of the capital.

TALES of heroism, fortitude and quiet endurance that have consistently and continually come from the Provinces have now been matched by stories of magnificent bravery in London during the fierce and wanton assaults by Nazi bombers which began on September 7. Thus a child of 14, given up as dead when her home in south-west London was bombed to the ground on Monday night, was rescued on Friday after eight hours' tunnelling through a mountain of debris. Her story is told in detail in page 331.

During another raid, after one particularly loud crash, a warden dashed out into the darkness and, skirting a large crater in the road, came to a pile of bricks which had recently been a house. Climbing over some of these he called, "Is anybody there?" From the depths a male voice replied "Yes, an old lady and myself." "Is she all righ?" called the warden. "No, she's a little bothered to know where she is going to spend the rest of the night."

Goering Attacks King and Queen

Twice in the week bombs fell on Buckingham Palace, and in Friday's assault the attack must have been deliberate. The Royal Chapel was destroyed, but Their Majesties were unhurt. The King and Queen, who had made several visits to the poorer London quarters that suffered most in earlier raids, replied to a Cabinet message: "Like so many other people we have now had a personal experience of German barbarity, which only strengthens the resolution of us all to fight through to final victory." An incendiary bomb fell on the House of Lords, but was quickly extinguished. Other fire-bombs fell in Downing Street but did no damage. In all, eight City churches have been bombed. Half a dozen bombs fell near St. Paul's Cathedral, including a 1-ton missile buried near the West door (see page 326) and heavy H.E. bombs.

Nazi bombers seem to have selected any conspicuous and prominent buildings for attack, and 118 London schools have thus been put out of action, mostly in night raids. Hospitals also were bombed, some twice.

The Law Courts were hit, and one Chancery Court demolished. It was clear that the raids were as ruthless as the Nazis could make them in order to sap civilian morale.

On the night of Sep. 11 the raiders were met by a terrific barrage of A.A. fire, the like of which had never before been encountered. Round London was a veritable ring of bursting shells and, strangest of all, no searchlights were seen until later on in the night. It was obvious that a method of ranging and "prediction" different from and greatly superior to the visual one previously employed had come into use.

In the ordinary predictor certain optical instruments are kept focused on the raider. The apparatus forecasts the probable future course of the raider, giving out settings for ranging and sighting the A.A. guns (see p. 702, Vol. 2). Location by sound is done by an arrangement of microphones which are turned in various directions until the sound

of the aeroplane is heard at its loudest by the operators. Thus the bearing for a searchlight, for instance, is obtained. It was inferred that the new prediction method which staggered the Germans was based on a combination of these two principles.

The Strand was bombed on the night of September 16-17, but a huge crater in the roadway was all the damage done. Beyond it is the famous Church of St. Mary-le-Strand.

The raiders seem to have come over in bomber formation on that Wednesday night, instead of in ones or twos, and immediately they approached London's outer defences they were baffled, scattered and harassed by a curtain of bursting shells flung miles up into the air by our 4·7 A.A. guns. Coming down lower to avoid these they encountered still other missiles from other guns, until finally, at the lowest zone, they were frustrated by machine-gun fire.

Only a few raiders continued on their death-dealing mission; the majority turned back and made off. Though few were actually shot down, the new barrage had succeeded in protecting the great area of outer and inner London, and only a few bombs were dropped in the central part. The barrage cut down the death-roll for that night to 40, and only 170 were injured.

London's Curtain of Flying Steel

On Thursday night the protective curtain of steel came again into operation, even fiercer than on Wednesday, though not so continuous. Reports from New York said that warships of the Royal Navy, stationed in the Thames, were helping to put up the barrage around London. Fewer raiders got through than on Wednesday, and the main thrust seemed to have been diverted to other parts of Britain. Dockland and Central London in particular were well protected, though no guns were diverted from the defence of other districts.

On Friday London had its longest day raid, and when the sirens sounded at 9.45 a.m. (second time that morning) people on their way to work were obliged to shelter until nearly 2 o'clock. Lone raiders flew recklessly over Central London and dived down through the low clouds to bomb prominent buildings. In the afternoon, before a warning came, there was another tip-and-run raid. At 9.2 p.m., the usual night attack began; there were many raiders, but owing to the barrage they had to adopt different tactics. All their lanes of approach to the Metropolis were hedged by continuous screens of gunfire, and only a few got through to drop bombs. Comparatively little damage was done during this raid.

On Saturday it was learned that our balloon barrage had been improved and that the ballons could now be flown at a far greater height than hitherto. Early on Friday the new barrage had claimed its first enemy machine. Two raids of short duration on Saturday morning were followed by a third and fourth in which the Nazis reverted to mass formations and flung in three hundred bombers, striving to reach London from the South-east; it was believed that they were testing the defences in this sector. Another warning came at 7.49 p.m., with the "All Clear" at 9.1; just over half an hour later the sirens sounded again, but after twelve minutes the raid was over and a quiet night followed.

The Luftwaffe on Sunday, September 15, suffered its greatest setback since the beginning of mass raids, losing 185 machines and about 400 pilots. A month earlier, on Thursday,

Suburbia Saves What It Can From the Wreck

It is not only in the East End, tragic as it is, that Nazi hate has wrecked the people's homes. The little houses of the suburbs have also suffered their fury. In houses, such as these in S.W. London, that have been only partially wrecked, it is possible to salvage much of the furniture. In houses that have suffered direct hits, practically all has gone. The Queen is among those who have sent furniture and bedding to help those in the bombed area.

Photo, Central News

Those on Whom the Brunt of Air War Falls

August 15, 181 Nazi machines had been destroyed. Seven of Sunday's bag were shot down by A.A. gunners; out of the total, **131 were bombers.** The R.A.F. lost 25 fighters, but the pilots of twelve were saved. Since the raiding force had consisted of between 350 and 400 aircraft, the Nazis therefore lost about half of their number.

Top, a warden after hours of strenuous work is refreshed by a Salvation Army canteen. Circle, a child from a bombed Dockland home.

The R.A.F. went out to meet the enemy, brought many down over the Channel, harried them and broke up their formations. Over the coast our pilots destroyed more, and of the few that got through to London still others were shot down, falling at Victoria, Kennington, Herne Hill and Streatham on the south-eastern side of the Metropolis; one was brought down in Woolwich Arsenal.

A third attack was made on Buckingham Palace, where two time bombs fell during the midday raid. One of the dive-bombers concerned was shot to pieces in the air just after its missiles had fallen (see pages 309, 322 and 332). The Royal apartments were damaged by one bomb, but the second fell on to the lawn. Both were removed before they exploded. Incendiary bombs also fell in the Palace grounds and started grass fires.

One raider was shot down by the British steamer "Port Auckland" from the Thames; shells burst below the bomber and brought it crashing down on the river bank in flames. The first Nazi bomber to be brought down in London was the Dornier aircraft that had bombed Buckingham Palace and fell in the forecourt of Victoria Station. The pilot of the Hurricane that shot down the Nazi had to bale out of his damaged machine and landed in a Chelsea garden (see page 332). It was his first fight.

Sunday, September 15, saw the conclusion of a magnificent piece of work by the bomb disposal personnel and officials of the Gas Company, who saved St. Paul's from almost certain destruction. The full story of this heroic deed is told in page 326.

In Sunday night's raid three London hospitals were bombed. Attacks by small groups of bombers were made over a wide area, and the raiders in their game of hide and seek were favoured by the cloudy skies. After the "All Clear" at 5.35 a.m. there was a quiet spell of 4 hours. Monday's raids came at 9.59 and 10.55 a.m., at 12.12 p.m. and at 2.12—this last continuing until six o'clock in the evening. At 8.10 p.m. the night raids began again. A non-stop succession of attacks was made and the A.A. fire hardly diminished all night. Bombs fell in central London and in the east, north-

GERMAN & BRITISH AIRCRAFT LOSSES

German to April 30, 1940

			German	British
Total announced and estimated—West Front, North Sea, Britain, Scandinavia				350
May			1,990	258
June			276	177
July			245	115
Aug.*			1,110	310
Sept. 1-18			774	215
Totals, May to Sept. 18			**4,395**	**1,075**

Daily Results, Sept. 1-18

Sept.	German Losses	British Losses	British Pilots Saved	Bt. fwd.	Sept.	German Losses	British Losses	British Pilots Saved
						410	144	75
1	25	15	9		10	2	0	—
2	55	20	9		11	89	24	7
3	25	15	8		12	3	0	—
4	54	17	12		13	2	0	—
5	39	20	9		14	18	9	6
6	46	19	12		15	185	25	14
7	103	22	9		16	7	1	—
8	11	3	1		17	12	3	2
9	52	13	6		18	46	9	5
	410	**144**	**75**		**Totals**	**774**	**215**	**109**

None of the figures include aircraft bombed on the ground or so damaged as to be unlikely to reach home.
Additional German Losses. Sept. 11—4 shot down over Continent. Sept. 15—2 by Fleet Air Arm. Figures for Sept. 18 incomplete.

Mass Raid Casualties in London. Sept. 7: 306 killed; 1,337 injured. Sept. 8: 286 killed; about 1,400 injured. Sept. 9: about 400 killed, 1,400 injured.

Mr. Churchill stated that during the first half of September civilian casualties amounted to about 2,000 killed and 8,000 wounded, about four-fifths being in London. In the fighting services casualties were only 250.

German Aircraft Destroyed in Britain. From September 3, 1939 to September 17, 1940 the German machines destroyed around and over Britain totalled **2,178.** In that time 553 British aircraft were lost, 259 pilots being saved.

east and southern suburbs. Most of the fighting took place above the clouds.

In the raids of Tuesday night (Sept. 17) several large stores in the West End were damaged, among the premises being those of Bourne & Hollingsworth, D. H. Evans and John Lewis. Employees and members of the public taking refuge in shelters beneath some of the buildings were unhurt. Attacks were also made on the Eastern and Southern residential districts, and many families rendered homeless by this Nazi barbarity. The Lambeth Walk was bombed in recent raids. Under the most severe test, in imminent danger most of the time, the Auxiliary Fire and other A.R.P. services did splendid work.

The Secretary for Air, Sir Archibald Sinclair, in a speech on Wednesday, Sept. 18, said that owing to raids by our R.A.F. the German armament production had fallen by 30 per cent. He also stated that the problem of intercepting the night bomber was being worked at, and he was "able to look forward to a time when the pleasure of night bombing over Britain . . . would cease to be attractive to Field-Marshal Goering."

Homeless people from East London (left), gained refuge in Tube stations of the Underground for the night, and though their quarters were none too comfortable, the knowledge of perfect safety many feet below the surface brought both sleep and smiles.

Scenes of Havoc in Streets of Inner London

Top, when a bomb fell in this London roadway, a tram was blown aside; the passengers had already taken shelter. Left centre, the church of Our Lady of Victories in Kensington was burnt out after an oil bomb had dropped through the roof. Bottom left, this letter-box was left standing amid the wreckage of houses in a south-east district; the postman is taking his morning collection. Bottom right, an extraordinary effect of a bomb explosion: a channel was driven through a block of single apartments to a height of six stories, yet the explosion left the roof undamaged.

Photos, Topical, L.N.A., Keystone and Fox

Berlin and the Barges are Bombed Again

While the Nazi raiders continued their " blitzkrieg " against London, the bombers of the R.A.F. carried the war into the enemy's territory by delivering yet more fierce attacks on Berlin and on the barges and other craft which, if reports speak true, were collected for the purpose of invading Britain.

THE authorities in Berlin were in a very bad temper on the morning of September 11, for the bombers of the R.A.F. had been over the German capital again—that R.A.F. which the Berliners had been told so often would never be allowed to darken their skies. And now they had been over again—and the Berliners were asking questions.

In the statement it issued for public consumption the German News Agency was more than usually communicative. "The British bombed non-military objectives in Berlin again," it said, " on Tuesday night. Aided by clear moonlight they dropped a great number of bombs on the centre of the city and the western residential area—in fact, they just missed the United States Embassy. Fires and explosions damaged offices, hotels, and public and private buildings. Roof fires were quickly extinguished, but a number of works of art and quantities of fine furniture were damaged. The walls of some buildings were seriously damaged. Blast caved in the sides of several houses, and as others were threatening to collapse whole blocks in the centre of the city had to be evacuated."

When the Berliners went to work in the morning they were stated to have seen some of the damage done in the night hours. One bomb had hit the great Brandenburg Gate, another had struck the Reichstag building, and the Victory Column in the centre of the Tiergarten—Berlin's Hyde Park—had also been hit. Bombs had struck the house of the Society of German Engineers and the Academy of Arts—despite the fact that, as the News Agency put it, representatives of all nations had enjoyed the hospitality of the one, while the other had held exhibitions of both German and international art.

"This new attack on Berlin," concluded the statement, " reveals a definite plan to terrorize the civil population. The assassin Churchill has given the order to the R.A.F. to avoid all targets of military importance and to destroy as many monuments as possible. There can be only one answer to these cowardly crimes—the answer of the German Air Force."

In spite of their plaints the Nazis—whose headquarters are at Munich—would probably have preferred that the R.A.F. should make their long-distance attacks on Berlin rather than continue to concentrate the main force of their onslaught on the German industrial areas and those bases where for weeks past they have been accumulating the fleets which, so they hope and intend, will enable their armies of invasion to land on Britain's shores. Since the threat of invasion became acute Britain's bombers have given the Nazis no rest. Night after night, and in daytime as well, they have dropped thousands of tons of bombs on the harbour installations, shipbuilding yards, and dock basins of Hamburg and Bremen; they have inflicted tremendous damage on the railways of the Rhineland and the Ruhr, the junctions and the marshalling yards.

As for the bases on the " invasion coast " which stretches from Norway to France, there is not a port which has not been blasted time and again by the R.A.F. Now they are over Bergen when a flotilla of ships has been reported there; now it is Flushing and Ostend; now it is Boulogne and Calais, now Dunkirk or Le Havre, now Cherbourg or Brest which shivers beneath the avalanche of steel descending from the sky.

On Monday and Tuesday, September 16 and 17, one of the largest forces of British bombers so far used in the war was flung against the invasion bases on the other side of the Channel and wherever a concentration of barges was spotted by the air observers it was made the object of a tremendous bombardment. Great fires were started on the quays, and if, as was believed in some quarters, thousands of German troops had already gone on board the boats, the losses must have been very heavy.

Reports received in London show that the German plans for the invasion of Britain have been thrown into a state of chaos by our constant bombing. Although the Germans have been making the most strenuous endeavours to repair the damage done to their invasion organization, they are finding it increasingly difficult to counter the attacks of the R.A.F., who in the course of a single day's operations may bomb Berlin—the capital was heavily attacked again on the night of Sunday, September 15—and a number of Germany's most vital spots, while at the same time they inflict the most terrific losses on the German 'planes which ventured to engage in the Battle of London. No wonder the Nazi chiefs are riled!

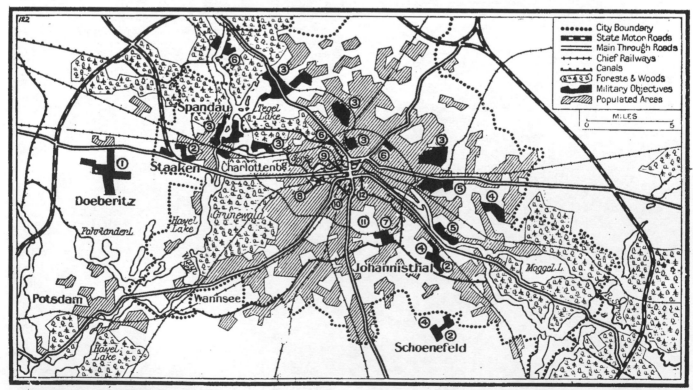

KEY TO MILITARY OBJECTIVES IN BERLIN

1.—Troop Centre.
2.—Air bases.
3.—Small arms and munition works.
4.—Aircraft Factories.
5.—Electrical Plants, etc.
6.—Gas Works.
7.—Telephone and wireless equipment works.
8.—Tiergarten.
9.—Reichstag.
10.—Hitler's Chancellery.
11.—Tempelhof (air port).
12.—Unter den Linden

When the R.A.F. bomb Berlin they do so not merely out of a determination to exact reprisals for the Nazi raids on London, but because in the German capital there are many objectives which are ranked most definitely as military. Some of the most outstanding of these are indicated on this map.

By courtesy of the " Evening Standard "

R.A.F. Strike at the Heart of Nazi Berlin

The Nazis have been reticent about the damage done in Berlin, but left is a photograph of one of the chief streets of the city after a visit from the R.A.F. Above is the Kroll Opera House, which is stated to have received a direct hit.

In circle is Potsdam station, close to the famous Palace, 16 miles from Berlin. It was struck by both incendiary and high explosive bombs on September 10. The great Brandenburger Tor (below), which stands at the top of Unter den Linden, Berlin's most famous street, was hit during a raid.

Photos, Keystone and E.N.A.

IN the early days of the war 'planes of the R.A.F. constantly flew over Berlin loosing pamphlets and gaining a useful knowledge of the lie of the city, which they have since put to good use in more deadly work. Bombs were dropped on the Nazi capital for the first time on August 25, and since then warnings have sent Berliners to their shelters for two or three hours almost every night, sometimes twice in a night.

Berlin's most famous park, the Tiergarten, lies just beyond the Brandenburg Gate in the heart of Berlin. There, too, bombs have fallen.

Photos, Dorien Leigh and Wide World

Palace and Hospital and Famous Shops—S•

Following the opening of the " blitzkrieg " against London
fashion against the famous buildings, the hospitals and other
on September 10, 13, 14 and 15 ; on the left workmen are cl
in Regent Street after a time-bomb had exploded in this

When on September, 13 Buckingham Palace was bombed for the second time
the Royal Chapel was damaged; as may be seen the altar collapsed, but the
priceless Gobelin tapestry above was unaffected by the blast. The raider responsible for the fourth attack was shot to pieces in the air (see page 332) and
right is the damage caused when his 'plane crashed on shops at Victoria Station.

the London Landmarks Hit by Nazi Bombs

's airmen seemed to aim their bombs in the most deliberate
...polis. Buckingham Palace was an early victim, being bombed
...fter a bomb had fallen in front on the 14th. Above is the scene
...hfare. Burlington Arcade (right) also sustained a direct hit.

In nearly all the raids made by the Germans on London, hospitals were hit—but
then hospitals have always been amongst the most frequent victims of Nazi
bombs. Above is the Westminster Bridge end of St. Thomas's Hospital which
was largely demolished by a huge bomb. Fortunately there were no wards in this
wing, otherwise the loss of life would certainly have been far greater than it was.

Ramsgate Has The World's Finest Shelters

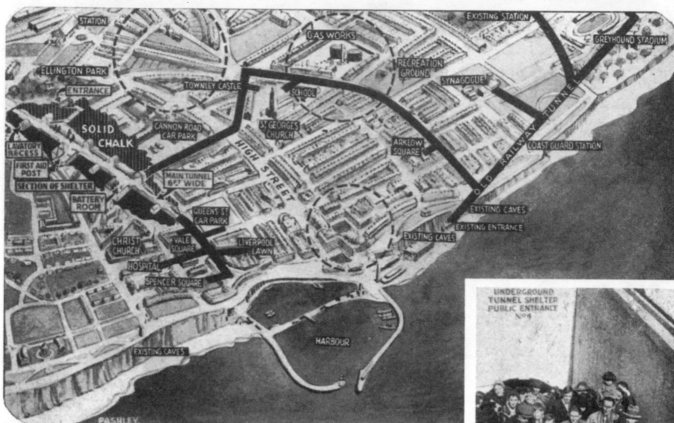

RAMSGATE, a pleasure resort and fishing port without any fortifications whatever, felt the full blast of the " blitzkrieg " while London was still untouched, and over 1,000 houses in the town have been destroyed (see page 237). Yet despite this, the loss of life has been comparatively small, thanks to the magnificent system of shelters designed by the borough engineer and surveyor, Mr. R. D. Brimmell. Ramsgate is built on chalk which is easily excavated and the tunnels cut through it need no lining. They lie about 60 feet below the surface and have a total length of four miles. A portion of this length consists of the disused tunnel through which the railway ran to the old Ramsgate Sands station until a new station was built at the back of the town. There are 22 entrances and from every part of the town one can be reached in five minutes. Owing to the formation of the land, no artificial ventilation is needed, for a natural current of air passes through the galleries. The scheme, once derided for its somewhat high cost, has been completely successful. In the picture map the run of the tunnels is seen. The large dotted circles indicate parts of the town most damaged.

Map-diagram by courtesy of the " News Chronicle" ; photos, Wide World and Associated Press

This is one of the many entrances to the tunnels with people leaving them after a raid.

Left, is one of the main streets of the town after a warning has sounded. Practically all the townsfolk are in the shelters and the traffic policeman has gone about other duties in his tin hat, leaving his helmet behind him. Centre is one of the galleries while it was under construction. Right is one of the entrances to the galleries in the higher part of the town (see also page 259).

London Hospitals Make Fine Objectives!

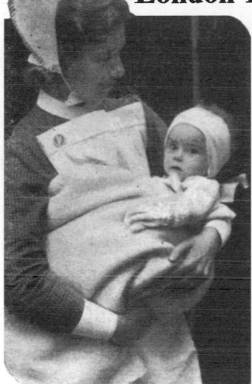

One of the three hospitals hit by German bombs on the night of September 9-10 was a children's hospital. Left, a small child is being moved to a place of safety. Above is a damaged ward of the hospital.

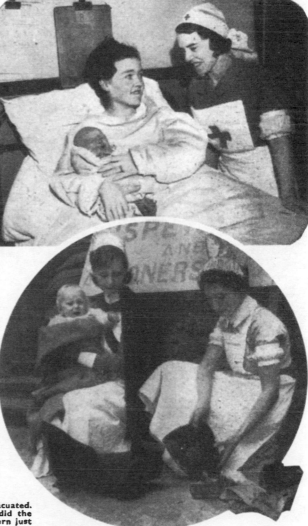

Above is a London hospital after the raid of September 10 ; it had already been evacuated. Right, a nurse of the children's hospital is shown fragments of the bomb that did the damage. Centre is one of the patients of a maternity hospital with her baby, born just before the hospital was bombed on September 9-10.

Photos, " Daily Mirror," Keystone, Graphic Photo Union, Planet News

Let Us Honour the Men Who Saved St. Paul's

Taken at speed to Hackney Marshes in a lorry driven by Lt. Davies, the bomb was there exploded. Here is the crater 100 ft. wide that it made there—and not on Ludgate Hill!

The bomb fell at an angle, and all the time that it was in the ground slipped through the clay ever nearer to the foundations of the Cathedral. The excavators of the Bomb Disposal Section had to dig down 27 ft. 6 ins. before they found it.

FOR four days St. Paul's Cathedral was in most terrible danger. In the course of the German air-raid on the night of September 11 a huge time-bomb—it proved to be a ton in weight and was about 8 ft. in length—was dropped in the roadway of Dean's Yard, close to the west end of the Cathedral. It was stated to be fitted with fuses that made it dangerous to touch. Members of the Bomb Disposal Section were soon on the scene and they worked without a break, faced first by fire from a broken gas main, and all the time by the most imminent danger of being blown to pieces, until the evening of September 15, when with the aid of two lorries joined in tandem they succeeded in dragging the bomb from its bed of clay.

Then the deadly missile was placed on a lorry and driven at top speed through streets, cleared by the police (owing to the great risk of its explosion) of all passers-by, to Hackney Marshes, where it was safely exploded, as seen in the photograph at the top of the page. At the next service held in the Cathedral there was a prayer of thanksgiving for "those men who performed a feat of outstanding heroism and skill yet regarded it as their job."

Here are the heroes who saved St. Paul's actually at work on the job. They are members of the Bomb Disposal Section, and looking down the hole they have dug is Lieut. R. Davies, their commander.

Photos, G.P.U.

Their Eyes Are Vital to R.A.F. and A.A. Guns Alike

Two men of the Observer Corps, left, are on duty. The spotter follows enemy 'planes with his binoculars, while the plotter sits beside him with an instrument that enables him to ascertain the height of the invader and the direction of his flight.

The chief observer is here seen at work. He has had long experience, and there is nothing about the recognition of enemy aircraft that he does not know. Among those who serve with him are farmers, gardeners, and a builder, while the chief is the postmaster of a neighbouring village. An officer of the R.A.F. said "their work is simply vital to us."

WHEN the sirens sound and the people go to their shelters, they little know that they owe this life-saving chance to the Observer Corps. These are the men who man the listening posts dotted throughout the countryside and no enemy raider can cross the coast without being detected by these invaluable volunteers. They are civilians of all ages and classes and their only uniform is blue dungarees and an armlet.

The shifts vary in length, and the least popular—especially in wintertime!—is that from 2 a.m. until 8 a.m. Full time observers are paid £3 a week, but all the part-time observers at this post and many others get 1s. 3d. an hour.

Here is a general view of the observation post in which the observer and plotter are at work. It stands in open country in the south-east of England and is manned by 18 men, none of whom has had less than four years' training, while a few have been in the Observer Corps since 1922.

Photos, " News Chronicle" staff photographer, F. G. Kirby; exclusive to THE WAR ILLUSTRATED

Hope For France Springs Anew in Africa

While Metropolitan France groans beneath the yoke of the conqueror, in the French Empire, particularly in Africa, there are signs of an increasing restiveness. This article discusses the attitude towards their colonies adopted by the French people in peacetime, and now in time of war.

WHEN France is defeated on the Continent she turns to Africa. So it was after the crash of Napoleon's empire; fifteen years after Waterloo a French army occupied Algiers and gradually brought the whole of the Bey's country under submission, and in the 1850s the French extended their hold on Senegal from the coast where their settlers had been established since early in the 17th century to far inland in the direction of the Niger, thus laying the foundations of the vast "Afrique Equatoriale Française" (A.E.F.) of today. At the same time "Afrique Occidentale Française" (A.O.F.) was also coming into being. The first French colonization in West Africa was on the Gabun river in 1841, and Libreville, the present capital, was founded in 1849.

and Ubangi-Shari. A.E.F. has an area of nearly a million square miles and is inhabited by some three million natives; A.O.F., with nearly two million square miles, has a population of 15 million natives.

Now in 1940 France is turning once again to Africa, but this time it is not a question of incorporating further territory in the French Empire, but of the French Empire showing the way to Metropolitan France. It was in French Equatorial Africa that the first signs of revolt against the defeatist policy of the Vichy Government were first made manifest, when on August 27 M. Eboué, Governor of the Chad, declared his allegiance to General de Gaulle, leader of the Free France movement in London. In a few days the whole of French Equatorial Africa had followed his lead.

and Tunis, or in war against the native tribes—the Riff in particular—in the case of Morocco. The name of France's most eminent and most successful colonial administrator, Marshal Lyautey, is associated with North Africa, and his period of office as Resident-General in Morocco, from 1917 to 1925, was particularly noteworthy. Algeria, indeed, has been developed to such an extent that it is not regarded as a colony but as almost an integral part of France; until the collapse last summer of the parliamentary regime it was represented by deputies and senators in Paris.

But the French are not a colonizing people like the Portuguese or the Spaniards, the Dutch or ourselves. They do not like emigrating, and if their financial careers or economic necessity required them to pass long years abroad, they are constantly buoyed up by the hope of spending their declining years in Paris or the province which gave them birth.

Taken as a whole, the French people tend

It was at Dakar, left, chief port of French West Africa, that France's finest battleship, the "Richelieu," took refuge after the case of the French surrender. On July 8 Lieut.-Commander R. H. Bristowe, R.N., with the most intrepid gallantry entered the harbour and completely disabled the great French ship with depth charges.
Photo, Fox

After the disaster of Sedan in 1870 a similar trend was manifest when successive French governments strove to build up a huge empire in the heart of Africa. They embarked on a race for territory with Britain and Germany, in particular striving to reach across the Congo to the headwaters of the Nile. In this they were unsuccessful, for when Major Marchand, crossing the Sahara from the Niger, reached Fashoda on the Upper Nile, in 1898, he was warned off by Lord Kitchener, who had just completed his conquest of the Sudan by defeating the Dervishes at Omdurman. Meanwhile, in North Africa, France's empire was growing apace; a protectorate was established over Tunis in 1881, and in 1912 over a very large part of Morocco.

After a century of imperial expansion France's empire in Africa extended right across the Sahara from the Mediterranean to the Gulf of Guinea. In the north are what used to be called the Barbary States—Morocco, Algeria, and Tunis; in the west, A.O.F. comprises Dahomey, French Guinea, French Sudan, the Ivory Coast, Mauretania, Niger, Senegal, and the mandate of Togoland; while in A.E.F. there are the territory of the Chad, Gabun, Middle Congo,

One of the strangest peoples in the French Empire is the Habbé tribe of negroes who dwell in the gorges of Bandiagara Falaise, 180 miles south of Timbuctoo, in French West Africa. Right are some villagers who dwell in thatched mud-houses, though many are still troglodytes living in caves cut in the cliffs.
Photo, Wide World

Perhaps it is a little strange that the first blow for liberty in France overseas should be struck in a region which has received but little attention from the French Colonial Office. For the most part French energies and French money have been expended in Algeria, Tunis, and Morocco, whether it be in public works, as in the case of Algeria

Central Africa Sounds Revolt Against Vichy

The Moroccan troops are among the finest in the French colonial army, and above is a typical private, proud of his uniform and his medals. He was photographed at a ceremonial parade.

In the history of France's colonial administration there have been innumerable scandals, and the treatment of the natives has often left much to be desired.

If the vast empire built up in Africa has been retained and maintained, it is because on the one hand France was jealous of the rival imperialisms of Britain and Germany, while on the other the spokesmen for the colonies could point to their vast economic resources and also to their usefulness as a reservoir for native soldiers.

Since the Great War, when France was " bled white," as the saying goes, at Verdun, she has come to rely more and more upon the black man in her ranks, and this in spite of the estimate that the fighting value of one French soldier is approximately that of ten Moroccan or Senegalese. This may be as may be, and it is only right to state that native troops, provided that they are well-officered and properly equipped, have proved their value time and again in many a hard-fought field in colonial wars.

But the importance of the revolt against the policy of Pétain in the French Empire has little to do with the value of the natives as fighting men. The accession of French Equatorial Africa and the adjoining mandated area of the Cameroons to General de Gaulle's Free France movement gives to Britain and her allies a broad belt of country stretching right across Africa from the Atlantic to Kenya, with cross communications (particularly by air) east by west, and so barring the road to an enemy advancing from the north. The gain, militarily speak-

to regard " their " colonies with hostility, or at least indifference ; they appear to be a nuisance which has arisen out of the misguided efforts of colonial administrators who had an urge for expansion, or who wanted to rival the territory-grabbing exploits of a predecessor or colleague in another part of the empire. The more Radical and Socialist they are in their opinions, the more the French dislike their colonial possessions and resent the fact that they have been foisted upon them—territories which have to be defended at the cost of blood and treasure, territories which constitute a constant temptation to shady financiers, company directors and exploiters of the natives and the natural resources.

These picturesque uniforms are those of another fine Moroccan regiment, one of whose duties is to guard the desert route. Moroccan soldiers fought with valour in France.

ing, is slight, because the French colonies were but lightly garrisoned. But strategically we cannot but profit immensely by the change in Central Africa from potential hostility to co-operation and alliance.

Still greater would be the gain if French North Africa follows the same road. Only because their western flank has been secured by France's defection have the Italians dared to make their thrust eastward against Egypt. If that flank is reconstituted, then Marshal Graziani will have to take measures to secure his rear against an attack by Franco-British forces operating from Tunis and supported, thanks to Britain's control of the Mediterranean, from the sea.

This being so, we can well understand the haste with which the Vichy government despatched General Weygand to " stop the rot " in North Africa. If Tunis and Algeria, Morocco and West Africa, follow the brave lead of Governor Eboué, then the defeatists whose plaint is that France is hopelessly beaten and so must obey every order issued by the Nazis, will be placed in an increasingly difficult, even finally impossible position.

Though small judged by the number of inhabitants, Koroko is one of the most important towns of the Ivory Coast which forms part of French West Africa. As the photograph above shows, its architectural style is primitive, yet the builders in mud have ambitious ideas, as the chief's house in the centre proves. All big buildings, such as mosques and markets, have much the same architectural features.
Photos, René Zuber, " Match," and Wide World

OUR SEARCHLIGHT ON THE WAR

Balloons and Kites Do Their Bit

THE enemy hates our balloon barrage, and with good reason. No dive-bombing attack can be made within an area protected by balloons. Moreover, although their function is primarily preventive, they have also brought down a number of enemy machines, such as the Heinkel which crashed in Wales on September 13, after colliding with a balloon stated to be of a new design which can be flown very high. The raiders are indignant at this impediment to their activities and have

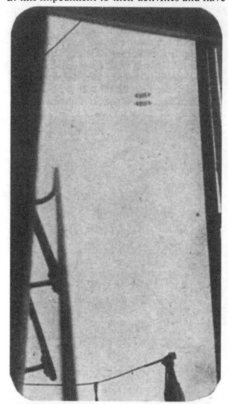

Box kites flying at great height are one of the devices used by convoys against low-flying Nazi bombers. Here one of them is seen from a Naval escort vessel in the Channel.
Photo, Sport & General

deliberately attacked them with machine-gun fire. Still less do they like the kites which, together with balloons, are now being used to protect convoys, and which played their part recently when an attacked convoy was got through the Straits of Dover without suffering loss. The box kite is small, and as the wire to which it is attached sways from one angle to another with every air current, the Nazi airman finds it impossible to estimate in which direction this cable will be stretching when he would like to swoop over the convoy.

Italian Leaflets Derided By Arabs

WHEN, on September 9, Italian raiders passed over Jaffa on their way to bomb Tel Aviv, leaflets were dropped over the town. It was evidently hoped that these would impress the Arabs with the invincibility of Italian arms, but they have merely caused amusement and derision. The translation reads : " Arabs of Palestine—The British have been driven from Somaliland by Italian forces, who are now advancing through Kenya to Egypt. Italians are masters of the skies over Malta and Gibraltar, and the rulers of the Mediterranean. Petrol stores at Haifa, stolen from you by the British, which you tried vainly to retrieve by destroying the pipeline, have now been destroyed by Italian bombs. If the British are defeated in Palestine you will recover the ownership and freedom of your land with the assistance of the Italians."

The irony of this appeal is not lost upon the Arabs, who know as well as anyone that the British Fleet still controls the Mediterranean, and that the Italian Navy is apt to consider discretion the better part of valour, and to make full speed for its home ports whenever the opportunity arises for an engagement with its opponents.

Veteran Skipper Defies Nazis

NAVAL officers are of the opinion—and who should judge better ?—that 'not enough is known of the bravery, devotion to duty and resource shown by the crews of the small coastal craft of the Merchant Service. Their only armament, as a rule, is a machine-gun, and with this they resist attack by bomber or U-boat. Here is a tale of how one of these heroic little boats defied an enemy raider. It was in the Thames Estuary on her way to London that this tiny collier was attacked by Nazi 'planes. One well-aimed bomb fell into a hold and penetrated right through the bottom of the vessel. But the 70-year-old skipper and his crew scorned to take to their single boat. Instead, they succeeded in beaching the craft just as she was on the point of sinking. There, between tides, temporary repairs were made. The little craft was then floated off and proceeded on her way, discharging her cargo in London port according to instructions. Further repairs were then effected, after which the skipper and his devoted crew immediately left for a northern port to continue this business of coal transport which they had carried on for nearly a year. It is good to know that this splendid veteran of the Merchant Service has been awarded the O.B.E., Civil Division.

King and Queen in A.R.P. Shelter

KING GEORGE and Queen Elizabeth, whose own home has suffered badly from German bombs, have made several tours to inspect the damage done in recent air raids in the East End and the outer suburbs, and to offer their sympathy to the people who had lost their relatives and homes. In the course of one of these, their Majesties, who were accompanied by Sir John Anderson, Minister of Home Security, took shelter beneath a police station when the sirens gave warning. Here were already gathered court officials, policemen, some A.R.P. workers, and the canteen staff. One of the latter prepared tea and the Royal visitors had a cup before continuing their tour after the sounding of the " All Clear."

Our Tough Railwaymen

WE have already recorded an act of courage and resource on the part of two railway workers (see page 278). Here is another story, again showing how they disregard their own safety when the good of the community is involved. The train service somewhere in the South of England was temporarily suspended because an unexploded bomb had fallen a short distance away from a main line signal box. Experts pronounced that the bomb could not be immediately disposed of, so it was decided to shunt thirty high-sided wagons loaded with coal on to the up line to serve as a screen for the down line, which could then be used for single-line traffic. This was done, and then, without a second thought, volunteers came forward and worked twenty-four important freight, newspaper, and fish trains past the danger spot before the bomb was removed by the Bomb Disposal Section.

Holland in London

PROFESSOR P. S. GERBRANDY, who has succeeded Jonkheer de Geer as Prime Minister of Holland, has stated that a Netherlands National Institute is to be established in London for " making known the intentions and the opinion of free Netherlanders, not only in Europe, but in the whole world, especially the Far East and the United States." It is understood that one of the first activities of the institute will be to organize an exhibition of modern Dutch art. The first Netherlands "Day of Freedom" was inaugurated on Sept. 17, when Queen Wilhelmina received a loyal address from her free subjects and expressed her unfaltering determination to lead the rest of her people back to freedom.

Nazis' Bill of Occupation

AS from June 25, France has to pay to Germany 20 million Reichsmarks a day for the upkeep of the army of occupation. The French Official Gazette, in making this statement on September 14, announced that a convention had been signed between the French Government and the Bank of France, by which the latter will advance to the State the sum of fifty thousand million francs for this purpose.

The Water-Bus At Last

ON September 13, with none of the ceremony that was surely its due, a river service on the Thames between Westminster Bridge and Woolwich was inaugurated by the Ministry of Transport, which hopes in this way to relieve congestion on the land routes to and from the City. The boats, which were well filled, hold round about 200 people. The complete journey, for which the fare is

River steamers which once plied up-stream from Westminster, have now been transferred to the London Passenger Transport Board, and, plying between Westminster and Woolwich, give Londoners an alternative route to work.
Photo, L.N.A.

9d. return, takes between one and two hours, with intermediate stops at the piers at the Tower, Cherry Gardens (Bermondsey), Tunnel (Wapping), West India Dock, Greenwich, and Brunswick, for East India Dock. London bus conductors collected their fares and then sat and surveyed the Capital from this novel viewpoint. Just as, almost unnoticed after the clamour of years, women were given the vote during the first Great War, so, during the second, Mr. A. P. Herbert sees one of the desires of his heart unexpectedly fulfilled.

I WAS THERE!

Eye Witness Stories of Episodes and Adventures in the Second Great War

We Dug for Eight Hours to Rescue a Girl

Among the A.R.P. services none does more heroic work than the demolition and rescue squads. One such party who tunnelled their way for eight hours into the debris of a London house found fourteen-year-old Mildred Castillo alive after four days. Their rescue of the girl is described by one of the party, Mr. George Woodward.

THE men who volunteered to tunnel their way into the debris of a house which had been bombed on Monday, September 9, were George Woodward, Wally Capon, and G. W. Pitman, and Mr. George Woodward afterwards said:

On Thursday, September 12, while removing the debris, I heard a voice say "Mama." I thought I was dreaming, because none of us ever anticipated finding anyone alive after being buried under such a great mass of wreckage for four days.

It gave me such a shock that I went for a little walk to steady my nerves. Then I went back to the other side and found a doorway full of debris. Again I heard the voice say "Mama," I was convinced, and I shouted. I got out some more debris and shouted again: "Who's there?" The voice replied: "Mildred." I called "All right, my dear, I'll soon be with you."

The three of us then began to make a tunnel with our hands, pulling at the debris. We had to remove it very gently because there was a danger that tons of it might slip. The whole of the ten men in Squad Two began working strenuously to get the wreckage out of our way.

Finally Capon, Pitman and I decided to take a chance, made a small hole, and one after another crawled into it, making it into a tunnel as we went. It was only big enough for us to lie flat on our tummies. We came to a wall and had to turn along it, and often as we pulled struts away earth fell in.

In time our tunnel was between 20 and 30 feet long and of a zig-zag formation, only big enough for us to squeeze through. After we had been at it 3½ hours we reached the girl's head, which, with one of her hands, was in a little cavity formed by a protecting beam. We passed her a rubber tube and poured glucose tea through it. Then Pitman gave her biscuits. She kept on asking for water, and eventually a doctor who was outside told us she could have some.

Then we started to clear her body up to the waist. We scraped away with our hands to free one leg at a time, continually passing the earth or pieces of debris between our legs to the one behind.

When we got the little girl free Capon lay on his face and told her to put her hands round his neck. Pitman clasped his hands over hers to keep them secure in their hold. Then all three of us wriggled backwards, pulling the girl and each other. After eight hours in the tunnel all four of us reached the open air.

Though the three of us worked in the tunnel we would not have succeeded but for the wonderful cooperation of all the Chelsea rescue squads.

The girl was marvellous. We sang to cheer her up and she tried to sing, too. We gave her a torch and she held it and moved it about to help us. She kissed us all when we finally reached her. She was conscious all the time we were working, and never cried. ("*News Chronicle.*")

Looking at this tangled ruin that was once a house in a district of south-west London it might well seem impossible that any human being could still be alive after the German bomb had sent it crashing down. Yet, as is told in this page, a girl, Mildred Castillo, did live beneath the load of broken timbers and smashed rubble—lived for four days, and was still alive and conscious when she was finally rescued. Her mother and brother were killed. This photograph shows the A.R.P. demolition squad who, spurred on by Mildred's faint cries, pushed through the debris.   *Photo, G.P.U.*

The German raiders who bombed Buckingham Palace and other London landmarks on Sunday, September 15, achieved some success—but only by paying a terrible price. Several of the Nazi bombers were shot to pieces in the air, and here we see the broken wing of a Dornier which crashed on a rooftop high above a street in the Victoria area. See also illustrations, pages 309 & 322.

What We Saw of the Victoria Bomber

After a week of intensive air raids, Londoners were cheered on Sunday, September 15, to see German bombers falling in the streets. The following eye-witness accounts of this thrilling morning were broadcast by Robin Duff and Edward Ward of the B.B.C., and we give, too, the story of the British pilot who brought the 'plane down.

A MEMBER of the B.B.C. staff, Robin Duff, said in his broadcast :

When I heard the drone of 'planes fighting that Sunday morning I rushed out of my flat in my pyjamas, and there in the sky I saw a Dornier 17 swooping down over St. George's Hospital, near Buckingham Palace. It was followed by a Spitfire. A few seconds later there was a great explosion in the air, and the German 'plane broke into pieces. As far as I could see only one of the crew baled out, and his parachute was already badly damaged by the explosion. The rest of the crew presumably had already been killed.

I have often seen German 'planes crashing to earth, but this was the first time that I had seen one smash up completely in the air. The engine and the bulk of the machine crashed into the forecourt of Victoria Station.

Some way farther down the road, on top of a house, came the tail of the machine. As for one wing, it fell just outside a public house, which must have been anything up to half a mile away. As I got near this pub —not in my pyjamas any longer—I heard an absolute babel of voices. I went in and found everybody talking at the tops of their voices, absolutely thrilled at what they had seen.

They had been through a good deal, these people, and the great anti-aircraft barrage that we had heard during the past few nights

had already put new heart into them, but that battered wing of a Dornier, lying in the street, encouraged them more than anything else in the world could do.

Another member of the B.B.C. staff, Edward Ward, said :

Just after mid-day on Sunday, September 15, one Hurricane brought down three German bombers over London. I was lucky enough to see part of the engagement.

Just after the alarm sounded I could hear the drone of several German bombers. Soon

bombs began to fall, some of them rather uncomfortably near. And then came a terrific rattle of machine-gun fire. I looked up in time to see one of our fighters weaving about among the bombers just under the clouds. Suddenly there was a terrific crash in the air as the Hurricane's guns found the bomb racks of one of the Germans. The German seemed just to disintegrate in the air. Two big pieces—the engines of the 'plane—hurtled down to earth, and bits and pieces floated down after them.

Soon after the German was hit there was a terrific screaming roar as a 'plane came hurtling down. At first I thought it was a dive bomber, but the crash told how the machine had hit the ground. It was the Hurricane, but the pilot, as it turned out, was safe. . . .

By the time I reached the spot where the Hurricane had crashed, there wasn't much to see ; just a heap of tangled aluminium on the pavement, and a hole in the road from which you could see the back part of the engine sticking out, but there was still less to be seen of the German bomber, a part of which had fallen about a quarter of a mile farther on.

The Pilot's Story

And here is the story told by the pilot who brought the 'plane down at Victoria Station. He is a Sergeant Pilot from West Kirby, in Cheshire, and it was his first fight. After he had shot down the enemy machine he had to jump by parachute. He said :

I was in the last section of my Squadron, and my Dornier victim took all that I had to give him. Bits flew off him and I broke away intending to turn and attack again. My windscreen was covered with black oil, and when I did attack again I think it must have been a different machine. Anyway, as soon as I fired a big flame shot up, and I must have got his petrol tanks.

I broke away again, and turned to make a head-on attack on another Dornier, firing a burst straight into its cockpit. At first I thought a piece of the Dornier had flown off, but then I saw it was a German baling out. I passed so near that I believe I touched the parachute.

As I made my final attack, my right wing struck something. I went into a terrific spin. There was no response from my controls.

I flung the hood back and struggled to get out. I must have been doing well over 400 m.p.h. when I finally got out of the cockpit. The wind was so strong it was like a piece of an airplane hitting me. People on the ground told me later that my parachute opened at only three hundred feet.

I spun across a house in Chelsea, got my feet down on a gutter, slid down the roof, and fell into the garden on my back. Then two girls came up to me, and I was so glad to see them that I kissed them both.

Like Soldiers My Children Stood on Deck

Hardly had a " mercy ship " carrying children to Canada left British shores in late August when a German submarine without shadow of excuse, torpedoed her. How magnificently the children met their adventure is told by a schoolmaster in charge.

THE children who were on the torpedoed ship were drawn from all parts of Great Britain and were being evacuated to Canada under the Government scheme. When they were brought ashore again on September 1 they seemed none the worse for their experience, and were all anxious to resume their journey.

Mr. C. H. Hindley, headmaster of Stoke School, Gosport, who had charge of the

contingent, told the story of what they regarded as an adventure with unashamed pride in " my children." He said :

The children were all in bed on the night of August 30 when the torpedo struck, shaking the ship from stem to stern.

Alarms were sounded immediately, and in a twinkling we were all at our appointed posts. Several boat drills carried out since we left harbour had them all well trained.

I WAS THERE!

Each group had been kept to one part of the ship, and they never took their lifebelts off except when they went to bed. Stewards and stewardesses were splendid. They never gave a thought for themselves or their property.

The children were in their life-jackets, coats hastily thrown over their pyjamas, and on the boat deck within 3½ minutes of the explosion. The older children helped the small ones on with their life-jackets. There was no panic, not a single cry.

They filed calmly to their stations like little soldiers, treating the whole thing as a great adventure.

Even as the lifeboats were slipping down to the water they started to sing " Roll out the Barrel." Their courage and cheerfulness inspired us all, racked as we were.

Three or four of the lifeboats had got away, but on examination it was thought that the ship could keep afloat and the captain attempted to recall the lifeboats.

Other ships were round us by this time. And the captain gave orders for all the remaining lifeboats—we had 24 in all—to be lowered. Within an hour and a half of the torpedo striking we were all safe on board other ships.

Many of the children were seasick in the boats. Those who were all right sang louder "to drown the sounds made by their sick companions," as they told me. It was wonderful to hear their voices rolling out over the waves of the dark and stormy Atlantic.

An eight-year-old youngster in my boat said : " Are we going on to Canada, sir ? " I replied, " I hope so." " That's good," said the boy. " We don't want Hitler to think he can beat us that easy."

There were willing hands on the rescue ships to help the children aboard, but the older boys and girls scorned offers of a lift. They climbed the swaying rope ladders as though seaborn.

The younger ones were hoisted aboard in slings. The boat lowered baskets and we simply dumped the kiddies in twos and threes and had them hoisted aboard. The kiddies thought it was great fun.

In the rescue ships the crews gave the children and their escorts everything : sweets, food, cigarettes and clothing. Some of the stewards sang and told stories to the children. (*Press Association.*)

We Were Sunk by a Nazi Q-Ship

Among the merchant ships waylaid and sunk by a disguised German raider operating off the West Indies was the 5,000-ton " King John " of Liverpool. The ship's carpenter, Mr. Burroughs, here tells how his ship was sunk and the crew's four days in an open boat.

ABOUT nine in the morning of July 13, 1940, the captain of the " King John " sighted another ship on the horizon. " Chips " Burroughs said :

We all had a look at it when it came nearer, because ninety per cent. of the ships on the seas these days seem to be British.

But this one was a foreigner. The cabin-boy next to me asked if she was carrying a gun, but all I could see was something square at the stern of the ship. It was one of four hidden six-inch guns.

The raider was flying the Swedish flag, and had Swedish colours painted on her sides. All of a sudden she opened fire. Four shells burst around us, sending red-hot jagged shrapnel flying everywhere. Then

there was another salvo of shells and another. With our one small gun we had no chance of fighting back. The raider had come up on us, innocently, had carefully fixed her gun sights and was firing at point-blank range.

A young Australian was at our gun, stripped to the waist, but he couldn't do anything. If he had fired back, he might have won fame for himself, but we should all have been blown to kingdom come. The captain gave the order to abandon ship.

I ran to my quarters, grabbed some tobacco, and put my best suit under my arm. Then I stopped to get a quick drink from the pump—because I guessed rightly that we might soon be suffering from thirst

in an open boat—and I dropped my best trousers, not once worn, and lost them.

They were still firing as we lowered the boat. There were nineteen in my boat and forty-one in the boat on the other side of the ship. When we were nearly two miles away a motor-launch from the German ship fired a machine-gun across our bows to make us stop. As they approached one of the officers shouted " Hands up."

They took our captain and chief engineer on board to be prisoners in the raider, and then they looked us over for souvenirs. One of the junior radio men had his savings of £25 in a cashbox on his lap. They took that. They took a sheath-knife from me.

Both our lifeboats were brought alongside the raider, and the Germans launched a third one, containing prisoners they had taken off the " Davisian," another British ship they had sunk just before us.

The " Davisian's " crew were amused about the way the Germans favoured the Scotsmen aboard. The Nazis seemed to have the idea that Scotland was only waiting the right moment to rebel against England, so they gave the Scotsmen a ration of cigarettes, and none to the Englishmen, so as to spread discontent !

We cast off in our lifeboat, hoisted the sails, and soon lost sight of the other boats. Luckily for us our captain had whispered to us the course we should follow just before the Germans came alongside.

His reckoning was dead right, though it took us four days and four nights to get to the island he had told us about. The sun beat down on us during those four long days. The skin peeled off our face and arms, and our lips were cracked.

We were rationed to a beakerful of water a day per man, and some of the men were getting desperate with thirst when the clouds broke and the rain came. We all opened our mouths to the sky, and sucked the water off our arms.

Then we saw land. It was a blessed sight. It was a tiny coral island, with no landing place except up an iron ladder up the cliffs. The only inhabitants were four lighthouse keepers. We were grateful for the food they gave us, and for the knowledge that we were safe. (" *Daily Express.*")

On her way from Britain to Canada a " mercy ship " loaded with 321 British children was torpedoed by a Nazi U-boat. Fortunately, as is told in this page, not one of the children was harmed and here we see some who were landed at a west coast port.   *Photo: Topical*

Yeomanry Regiments in Palestine

In this war, as in the last, Palestine is the temporary home of many of our most famous yeomanry regiments. Among those stationed there are the Cheshire and the Warwickshire Yeomanry, both of whom have "Gaza," "Jerusalem" and "Palestine 1917-1918" among their battle-honours.

Cheshire Yeomanry

Warwickshire Yeomanry

Arrived back in camp after a hard day's training, the good trooper's first consideration is for his mount (top left). Circles: the army farriers are on their job. Above, "spotting" for anything suspicious in sky or on land.

Such are the demands of mechanized warfare that most of the British cavalry regiments have now abandoned their horses and go into action in tanks. But there are exceptions, and one of the exceptions is this Yeomanry regiment which is making its way across the rocky terrain of the Holy Land. In the distance are some of those Palestinian hills which in the course of untold centuries have witnessed so many wars in this land of Armageddon.

Photos British Official: Crown Copyright

British Personalities of the War

Rt. Hon. Ernest Bevin, P.C., M.P., achieved fame as the "Dockers' K.C." in the years filled with labour troubles that succeeded the last war. He was born in 1884 in a Somersetshire village and went to work for a farmer at the age of eleven. Then he went to Bristol, where he organized the road transport workers—the first step in the career which was to give him the all-powerful position of General Secretary of the Transport and General Workers Union. For years he has been one of the chiefs of the Trade Union movement, and he was not even an M.P. when Mr. Churchill appointed him Minister of Labour in his "Win the War" Cabinet. Wandsworth Central, however, soon gave him the right to answer questions from the Treasury Bench.

Lord Woolton, Britain's Minister of Food was born 57 years ago. For years he has been one of the outstanding figures in the business world of the North of England—he is chairman of Lewis's and its chain of subsidiary drapery stores—and he was still Sir Frederick Marquis when, in 1939, he was made honorary adviser to the War Office and the Ministry of Supply on clothing for the army. Shortly afterwards he was appointed Director-General of Equipment and Stores on the Munitions Council, whence in April 1940 he was called by Mr. Chamberlain to take charge of the all-important new Ministry of Food—in which position he was confirmed by Mr. Churchill in the following month.

Rt. Hon. Ronald Hibbert Cross, P.C., M.P., was born in 1896 and is an old Etonian. After service in the Great War in the Duke of Lancaster's Own Yeomanry and the Royal Flying Corps from 1914 to 1918, he devoted himself to his profession of merchant banker. In 1931, however, he was one of the multitude of young Conservatives who were returned to the House of Commons in the "Slump" election of that year. He was returned again for the same seat, Rossendale, in Lancashire, in 1935. After serving as a Government Whip and as Vice-Chamberlain of the Royal Household, he became in 1938 Parliamentary Secretary of the Board of Trade and in the following year was made Minister of Economic Warfare. In Mr. Churchill's reshuffle he succeeded Mr. R. S. Hudson at the Ministry of Shipping.

Lord Beaverbrook, appointed by Mr. Churchill Minister for Aircraft Production on May 10 and a few weeks later given a seat in the War Cabinet as Minister without Portfolio, was born (William Maxwell Aitken) in Newcastle, New Brunswick, Canada, in 1879, the son of a Scottish minister. He made his first fortune in Canada, in cement, but came to England before the Great War, and in 1910 secured a seat in the House of Commons as Unionist M.P. for Ashton-under-Lyne. The next year he was knighted and in 1917 was raised to the peerage. In 1918 Mr. Lloyd George appointed him Minister of Information. By now he had secured control of the "Daily Express" and made it and the "Sunday Express" a power in the land. All through his public life he has been most keenly interested in the progress of flying and in the development of the economic resources of Britain and of the British Commonwealth, and still today these twin interests are his chief preoccupation.

Rt. Hon. Robert Spear Hudson, P.C., M.P., Minister of Agriculture, is wealthy because of the partiality shown by British housewives for the soap that bears his father's name. After Eton and Magdalen he entered the diplomatic service, and in 1924 first entered Parliament as M.P. for Whitehaven and in 1931 became member for Southport. Becoming Parliamentary Secretary to the Ministry of Labour, he was appointed Minister of Pensions in 1935, and two years later became head of the Department of Overseas Trade. About this time he came into prominence as leader of the band of younger Conservatives who wished for a more vigorous rearmament policy during the Chamberlain regime. Then in April 1940 he was made Minister of Shipping, and in the next month received the appointment of Minister of Agriculture in Mr. Churchill's administration.

Photos: Central Press, L.N.A., Topical Press, Planet News, and Vandyk

OUR DIARY OF THE WAR

TUESDAY, SEPTEMBER 10, 1940
374th day

On the Sea—Convoy off E. coast of Scotland attacked twice by bombers but reached its destination.

In the Air—During night R.A.F. secured repeated hits on Potsdam railway station, Berlin. Attacks also made on docks and airframe factory at Bremen, and naval barracks at Wilhelmshaven.

Other formations bombed barge concentrations, docks and harbours on French, Belgian and Dutch coasts, gun emplacements at Cap Gris Nez, railway targets at Duisberg and Brussels, and many aerodromes.

German reports stated that Reichstag and many other public buildings had been hit.

War against Italy—Aerodromes and harbours in E. Libya and Eritrea bombed by R.A.F. Enemy made ineffectual raids on Matruh and Khartum.

Home Front—Daytime reconnaissance raiders appeared over Central London. No bombs dropped, but some fell in Kent, Sussex and East Anglia. Enemy aircraft also reported over a Welsh town. Town on south bank of Thames Estuary attacked.

Delayed-action bomb seriously damaged north-west wing of Buckingham Palace.

Night raid on London began at 8.14 p.m. Incendiary bombs started many fires, but only one major one. Damage and casualties less than during preceding night. Large E. London maternity hospital hit, as well as hospital in Central district. Church in Central London burnt to the ground. Bond St. and Burlington Arcade hit.

Two enemy bombers shot down.

Long-range guns on both sides of Straits of Dover resumed shelling in early morning.

WEDNESDAY, SEPTEMBER 11 *375th day*

On the Sea—Admiralty announced that Navy was constantly in action against German shipping and ports.

In the Air—R.A.F. bombed railway stations, goods yards and an aerodrome at Berlin, docks and shipyards at Hamburg, Bremen and Wilhelmshaven, oil plant at Monheim, explosive factory at Frankfurt, goods yards at Hamm, Cologne, Coblentz, Mannheim and Ehrang, railway junction at Namur, and aerodromes in Germany and Holland.

Other forces bombed barge concentrations, docks and shipping at Channel Ports.

Coastal Command aircraft attacked enemy convoys off Dunkirk and Cap Gris Nez, sinking one supply ship and damaging two.

Home Front—Main enemy activity over Britain began about 3 p.m. when large number of aircraft approached London area. Polish squadron and another squadron of Hurricanes engaged them, broke up their formations and chased them out to sea. Bombs were jettisoned in Surrey and Sussex. Some fell on S. coast town, causing casualties.

Night raids were met by violent A.A. barrage with new heavy guns. Main force of offensive directed against S. London and suburbs. Two hospitals, many houses, and small factories hit. Regent St. damaged. Delayed-action bomb fell near St. Paul's.

Enemy lost 89 aircraft ; Britain lost 24 fighters, but pilots of seven safe. Casualties in London were 150 killed and about 430 severely wounded.

Dive-bombing attack made on Dover area, accompanied by violent shelling from Cap Gris Nez. British guns replied.

THURSDAY, SEPTEMBER 12 *376th day*

In the Air—Coastal Command aircraft bombed shipping off Le Havre.

During night R.A.F. bombers attacked oil stores, shipping and docks at Emden, and docks at Flushing, causing large fires.

Other forces bombed key distribution centres at Osnabruck, Hamm, Schwerte, Ehrang and Brussels. Norderney seaplane base and several aerodromes attacked.

War against Italy—Enemy's defences west of Egyptian frontier reported to be thickening.

Home Front—Day raids on Britain included attacks by single aircraft on several towns in S. England and on one in N.E.

At night terrific A.A. barrage again started in London area, but enemy attacks were sporadic. Incendiary bombs fell in N.W. district and caused some damage. Elsewhere widespread attacks caused relatively small damage and few casualties. Two towns in Midlands and one on S. coast attacked.

Enemy lost three machines ; Britain none.

FRIDAY, SEPTEMBER 13 *377th day*

On the Sea—Belgian steamer " Ville de Mons " reported sunk on September 1.

In the Air—British machines made daylight attack on convoy of tankers off mole of Zeebrugge ; one ship exploded.

During night R.A.F. heavily bombed invasion bases on enemy coasts.

War against Italy—Italians crossed Egyptian frontier and occupied Sollum and Customs post at Musaid.

Home Front—During long daytime raid bombs fell on Buckingham Palace wrecking Royal Chapel and injuring three employees. Incendiaries were dropped on Downing St., but no damage was done. Oil bomb damaged roof of House of Lords. Big hospital bombed for second time. Many incendiary bombs dropped.

Attacks made on several districts in S.E. England. Considerable damage to one Essex town, but no casualties. Later, bombs fell in one district of Central London, in Eastbourne and in Kent and Surrey. Incendiaries also fell in Northern Ireland.

During night raiders flew over London area in relays at 10-minute intervals. Incendiary bombs fell in a S.W. square. A post-office and a library were wrecked and many shops damaged. In South Wales bombs caused damage in one town.

Enemy lost two aircraft ; Britain none.

River service of water buses inaugurated between Westminster Bridge and Woolwich.

SATURDAY, SEPTEMBER 14 *378th day*

In the Air—During night R.A.F. made heavy sustained attacks on shipping, barge concentrations and military equipment and stores at Channel ports, including Antwerp.

They also bombed supply depots at Osnabruck, Mannheim, Aachen, Hamm, Krefeld and Brussels, and rail communications at Rheine, Ahaus, Sundern, Husten and West-Hofen.

Gun emplacements at Cap Gris Nez and several enemy aerodromes were bombed.

War against Italy—Italian aircraft raided Malta but were driven off after dog fights.

Home Front—During daylight attacks bombs were dropped in S.W. London. In a south-coast town the town hall and a hospital were hit. Damage and casualties at Brighton and Eastbourne. Church and houses demolished at Ipswich. High-explosive bombs damaged town in N.W. England.

Time bomb exploded in front of Buckingham Palace, doing only slight damage.

Night raids on London were sporadic. Bombs fell in suburbs and outlying districts ; in two of these blocks of houses were hit. Fire started in City. Bombs damaged houses in Midlands town.

Enemy lost 18 machines. Nine British fighters missing, but pilots of six safe.

U.S.A.—Congress finally approved Conscription Bill.

SUNDAY, SEPTEMBER 15 *379th day*

On the Sea—H.M. minesweeping trawlers " Libra " and " Conquistador " destroyed enemy aircraft by gunfire. British steamer " Port Auckland " shot down bomber.

In the Air—R.A.F. again bombed military objectives in Berlin. Heavy attacks made on war supplies, barges and shipping at dockyards and ports along North Sea and Channel coasts. Direct hit on warship off Terschelling. Le Havre quays wrecked.

Other forces attacked distribution centres at Hamm, Osnabruck, Soest and Krefeld, and railway junction at Rheine.

Coastal Command aircraft sank supply ship off Ijmuiden, and two supply ships in convoy off Dutch coast.

War against Italy—Reported from Cairo that Italian forces continued eastward advance along coast, reaching point about 20 miles from Sollum. Enemy harried by R.A.F. and artillery fire from mobile guns.

R.A.F. fighters shot down six enemy bombers in Libya and Western desert.

Home Front—Severe defeat inflicted on German Air Force, when 185 machines were destroyed. Britain lost 25 fighters, but 14 pilots were safe.

Attacks launched in two main waves over Dover area were met by our fighters. Intense air battles over Kent coast, Maidstone, Canterbury, above Medway and Thames Estuary. Two formations penetrated London area and bombs were dropped. Buckingham Palace hit, damaging Queen's apartments. Elsewhere houses demolished, fires started and damage done to water mains.

Time bomb which fell near St. Paul's on Wednesday safely removed to Hackney Marshes, where it was blown up.

Among other places, enemy machines crashed at Kennington Oval, Streatham and Victoria.

In afternoon two small attacks made on Portland and Southampton area.

Night raids on London began soon after 8 o'clock. Raiders met by heavy barrage, but some reached Central London. Three hospitals hit ; damage done to houses, commercial premises and other buildings.

Enemy aircraft reported during night over S.W. England, Midlands, and S.E. Scotland.

Rumania—General Antonescu announced formation of new Government under direction of Iron Guard, with himself as Leader of the State and Prime Minister.

MONDAY, SEPTEMBER 16 *380th day*

In the Air.—R.A.F. carried out daylight raids on Calais, Ostend, Dunkirk and Veere. Convoys of barges attacked off Zeebrugge and Ostend. Haamstede aerodrome also bombed.

Adverse weather prevented night raids, as accurate bombing would have been impossible.

War Against Italy.—Advance guard of Italian invaders of Egypt reached Sidi Barrani, 60 miles from Libyan frontier, although harassed by R.A.F.

Asmara aerodrome, Eritrea, successfully attacked.

Home Front—Long-range guns were in action in morning on both sides of Channel.

Large formations of enemy aircraft crossed S.E. coast about 8 a.m. and attempted to penetrate inland, but were driven off. Later small numbers crossed the coast and a few bombs fell at several points.

• Intense A.A. barrage put up at night when raiders approached London in successive relays of small groups. Bombs fell in many parts and surrounding suburbs. Many famous West-end streets and squares damaged. Another hospital hit. Fires were caused but were quickly held under control. In Home Counties most bombs fell in rural areas. Towns in Midlands and North-West suffered damage and casualties. Six bombers destroyed during night, four by A.A. guns.

Germany lost 7 aircraft, Britain one.

HE LEADS THOSE WHO ARE WAITING TO THROW THE NAZIS BACK INTO THE SEA

" I would actually welcome the invasion. . . . I would welcome the opportunity of throwing the Germans back into the sea.   They have done it twice to us, and it is about time we got some of our own back."   In making this declaration General Sir Alan Brooke, Commander-in-Chief Home Forces, speaks from the immense experience gained with the B.E.F. when he was in command of the Second Corps and as Commander of the new Expeditionary Force sent to France after Dunkirk.   In this photograph General Brooke (right) is standing beside Major-General Percival and Lieutenant-General Sir Ronald Adam.

Photo, British Official : Crown Copyright

Hats Off to the Men Who 'Kill' the Bombs!

Courage of a very high order is required in the men of the Bomb Disposal Sections of the
Royal Engineers whose job it is to dig up and destroy the time-bombs distributed by Nazi
raiders. Some of their deeds of heroism are described here, and tribute is paid also to
some civilian workers well worthy of inclusion in the heroes' ranks.

Not until the monster time-bomb was successfully removed from the hole which it had dug close to the foundations of St. Paul's Cathedral (see page 326) did the nation wake up to the existence in their midst of a body of men whose heroism is of that supreme kind—the cold-blooded. Yet those four days of dangerous toil at the top of Ludgate Hill was but one incident out of many such. Since the Nazi raiders started dropping time-bombs in their attacks on London and the provinces, the Bomb Disposal Sections of the Royal Engineers, whose principal job it is to dig out the bombs, take them away to some convenient open space and there explode them, have been kept exceedingly busy. By day and by night they have toiled so that that dislocation of our communications, that interruption of the nation's business, which are the Nazis' objectives, shall be as short as possible.

For the most part, their heroic labours go unrecorded in the Press, because, as the soldiers themselves put it, "it's all in the day's work." Only when instances of exceptional gallantry have received official recognition do we hear anything about them. Recently, on September 17, the "London Gazette" announced that the King had been pleased to approve awards of the Medal of the Military Division of the Most Excellent Order of the British Empire, for Gallantry (now the George Cross), to four members of the Bomb Disposal Sections of the Royal Engineers; and it went on to tell in the most matter-of-fact way of the heroic deeds that had been recognized by the grant of this Cross, which ranks next to the V.C.

The first was Lieutenant E. W. Reynolds, 101/102 Bomb Disposal Sections, who on August 17, 1940, was sent to investigate a 250-kilo bomb which had fallen in a garden among some council houses and had not exploded.

"Digging down 17 ft. he found that it had a new type of fuse, about which no instructions had at that time been received. Finding that traffic was suspended on the road and that the inhabitants had had to be cleared out of their houses, he removed the fuse and found that it had a clockwork delayed action. The risk that he took was great, and merit of his action was the greater for lack of exact knowledge of the type of fuse he was dealing with." A fortnight later, on September 3, he was summoned to deal with another unexploded bomb found amongst the debris of some wrecked business premises. He found on arrival that it had a clockwork fuse which was still ticking; and, suggesting that the sooner it was dealt with the better, stated that he was willing to do so forthwith. "In view of the damage to property that would have been caused by the explosion of such a large bomb in such a congested area and especially of the possible effect on the public morale, permission was given and Lieutenant Reynolds immediately extracted the fuse and rendered the bomb inoperative."

Next we have the story of Second Lieutenant E. E. Talbot, 103 Bomb Disposal Section, who on August 24-25, after having been present for the whole time, 12½ hours, taken to dig down to an unexploded bomb, diagnosed when it was brought to the surface that it was of the delay-action type, and ordered his men to a safe distance while he examined it.

"As the bomb appeared to be of a new type, Lieutenant Talbot decided to remove it to a place where it could do no damage if it exploded. Still keeping his men under cover, he carried the bomb on his shoulder for some 200 yards and placed it in a safe spot. From the start of the work there was a risk of the bomb going off, and Lieut. Talbot set a fine example of courage and devotion to duty."

Our third story concerns Second Lieutenant W. L. Andrews, who on August 26, while in charge of Nos. 22 and 23 Bomb Disposal Sections, experienced some difficulty in trying to extricate the fuse of a bomb.

"After withdrawing it about 1½ in. the fuse dropped back into position actuated by what appeared to be magnetism or a spring. Removal was attempted several times without success. 2nd Lieutenant Andrews then placed his section under cover, and after tying a piece of cord to the ring of the fuse discharger, pulled, with the result that the bomb exploded. He was blown a considerable distance, and two of the men received splinter wounds. Throughout, 2nd. Lieut. Andrews displayed great coolness and keeness in the interests of the Service."

When Five Sappers Were Killed.

Finally, we are told of Lance-Sergeant W. J. Button, No. 48 Bomb Disposal Section, who on August 18 was ordered with his section to continue the work of excavating an unexploded bomb.

"Although he knew well that, owing to the time already spent on excavation, the bomb was liable to explode at any moment, he continued the work of his section with great coolness. The bomb eventually exploded, killing five sappers of the section, and throwing Lance-Sergeant Button a considerable distance. Although considerably shaken, he behaved with great coolness, collected the rest of his section at a safe distance, ascertained that none of them was injured, notified the first-aid detachment, and reported to his section officer by telephone."

But not only soldiers are engaged in combating the menace of the time-bomb; there are civilians whose daily work takes them into the same deadly field. To take one instance, there were the employees of the Gas Light and Coke Company, who were called in to deal with the gas main which had been set on fire by the bomb at St. Paul's and who had to put out the fire before Lieutenant Davies and his men could get to work digging out the bomb. When they first arrived on the scene they found that two of the Royal Engineers were already badly gassed, and the foreman and his mate promptly applied artificial respiration. Then he and three of his gang cut off the gas supply and got the fire brigade to flood the main with water. Later, there was a second outbreak of fire, and again the flow of gas was cut off and the fire brought under control. In peacetime gangs of gas workers are always in a state of readiness to deal with any damage which may happen to the mains, particularly through fire; in wartime their responsibilities are immensely increased, and as for danger—well, who would be keen on tackling the flames which are licking the crater at the bottom of which is a huge bomb which may go off at any moment?

These men, seen at their depot, form part of the heroic contingent of the Bomb Disposal Section of the Royal Engineers which removed the one-ton time-bomb that buried itself close by St. Paul's Cathedral on September 11. On September 15 the bomb was taken to Hackney Marshes, where it made a 100-ft. crater when exploded (see page 326).   *Photo, L.N.A.*

Their Heroism Is of the Cool-Blooded Sort

Deeds calling for that supreme form of courage, that in cold-blood, are performed by the men of the Royal Engineers who deal with delayed-action bombs. A one-ton bomb similar to that which threatened St. Paul's Cathedral fell, by a strange irony, close to the German Hospital in London. It penetrated 20 feet into the ground. As this photograph shows, the earth dug away could be removed only a bucketful at a time. The bomb was got safely away and there were no casualties, as all patients had been evacuated.

Photo, Topical

De Gaulle: Standard-Bearer of 'Free Frenchmen'

Before the war few had heard the name of General de Gaulle. Today, however, he has achieved widespread recognition as the man who, when France at the direction of the men of Vichy abandoned the fight, raised the standard of Free France. In preparing this article we have been indebted to '' De Gaulle's France and the Key to the Coming Invasion of Germany,'' by James Marlow (Simpkin Marshall, Ltd.).

INSIDE France the prevailing mood is one of defeatism; and so far as the men of Vichy can ensure it the same spirit prevails in the overseas dominions of the French Republic. But in London a Free French movement has been born—a movement which day by day goes from strength to strength. Its founder, its leader, and its inspiration is General Charles de Gaulle;

General de Gaulle, founder of the Free France movement designed to counter the defeatist policy of the Pétain Government, arrived at Dakar on September 23 in an attempt to secure French West Africa. Disappointed in his reception, however, and unwilling to shed French blood, he withdrew.

and his right to speak and act for that part of the French people and the French armed forces which have refused to grovel before the Nazis at Pétain's behest was acknowledged by the British Government on June 28.

General de Gaulle was born at Lille in 1890. In 1910 he entered the famous military academy of St. Cyr, and in due course was granted a commission in the 33rd Infantry Regiment and fought with distinction as lieutenant and company commander in the World War. He had already been twice wounded when in the course of the terrific fighting at Douaumont, the fort at Verdun which cost the lives of so many thousands of fighters, he was struck by a shell splinter and

was carried away into captivity on a German stretcher. After the Armistice he served under General Weygand in Poland in 1920-1921, and then there followed years of varied military duty at home and abroad. In 1937 he was given the command of a brigade of tanks with the rank of colonel.

By now he had achieved widespread recognition as an expert on the subject of mechanized warfare. Between 1932 and 1939 he published a number of papers and three books on the subject, one of which—'' Vers l' Armée de Métier'' was not only highly extolled by M. Reynaud, later French Premier, but was read with the very greatest of interest by German workers in the same field. Indeed, the Germans seem to have profited by the book far more than the French, for the French generals, and the politicians who supported them, looked with extreme disfavour on the man who had the temerity to suggest that the Maginot Line could be overrun by an avalanche of tanks. To them de Gaulle appeared as a crank: today, but too late, they must recognize that he was all too sound a prophet.

At the beginning of 1940, when the war on the Western Front seemed to have arrived at a position of stalemate, de Gaulle submitted a memorandum to the military authorities in Paris entitled '' The Advent of Mechanized Force,'' in which he urged once again the adoption of an offensive technique based on the use of mechanized armoured forces. '' In the present conflict,'' he wrote, '' as in all those that have preceded it, to be inactive is to be beaten. In order that we should be in a position to act and not only to remain passive, we must create a new instrument. Mechanized power, whether terrestrial, aerial or naval, would enable us to preserve ourselves from future attacks from Germany, to seize her strongholds and bases, to expel her from the regions which she has already or shall have captured, to blockade her, bombard her; in fact, to drive our weapons into her vitals from every side.''

This memorandum, like its predecessors, was pigeon-holed, but M. Reynaud found in it fresh confirmation of the views which he had expressed even some years before. Shortly after M. Reynaud became Premier, Colonel de Gaulle was made a General and given command of the 4th Armoured Division. In the month of fierce struggle which followed de Gaulle was one of the few French generals who won any considerable successes: at Laon between May 16 and May 19 he launched several successful counter-attacks with his armoured divisions, and he repeated the performance at Abbeville a fortnight later. Concerning the latter General Weygand paid a high tribute to him in an Order of the Day:

One of the most powerful recruits to General de Gaulle's Free France movement is General Georges Catroux, who until his supersession by the Vichy Government was Governor-General of the great colony of French Indo-China. Born in Algeria 63 years ago, General Catroux was one of Marshal Lyautey's most able subordinates in Morocco, and during the present war commanded the Mulhouse Division and later an army corps in Algeria.
Photos, Howard Coster and L.N.A.

Tanks!   More Tanks!   Hundreds of Tanks!

So steady is the stream of volunteers for General de Gaulle's Army of Free Frenchmen that recruiting offices have been opened in London. Above, some volunteers are being interviewed.

follow General de Gaulle as a Free Frenchman serving Free France.   Before September was out, General de Gaulle himself had proceeded to Dakar in an attempt to rally the patriotic forces in West Africa.

Looking into the future, General de Gaulle sees the time not far off when Germany will be wearied and exhausted, while against her the forces of her enemies have accumulated tremendously.   Then, he declares, is the time when we must attack.   " Not with an expeditionary force of men in battle-dress with rifles at the slope.   Tanks and Guns. More Guns and more Tanks. Thousands, tens of thousands of Aeroplanes.''

" This admirable, audacious and energetic leader attacked on May 30th and 31st at the south of Abbeville towards the enemy bridgehead very strongly held, breaking through German resistance and advancing 15 kilometres (nearly 10 miles) inside the enemy lines and capturing many hundreds of prisoners and considerable material.''

Then, early in June, Reynaud called him to his side in Paris, giving him the appointment of Under-Secretary of State for National Defence and War.   In every way he supported his chief during that terrible week when the news from the front was uniformly bad ; he was sent to London to consult with Mr. Churchill, and was present at Tours when the British Premier came by 'plane to stimulate Reynaud's flagging spirit.   Later still he was in Bordeaux doing his best to persuade the French Government to carry on the fight from Africa.   Again he paid a flying visit to London, and heard from Mr. Churchill's lips the tremendous proposal for Anglo-French union.   But when he returned to Bordeaux, Reynaud had fallen and Pétain and Weygand reigned in his stead—the old men who wanted only to negotiate surrender with the enemy. So de Gaulle hurried back to England, and there devoted himself to the self-chosen task of organizing French resistance from the capital of the empire which would have remained France's firm and faithful ally.   In one of his early broadcasts to the French people he uttered a trumpet call to liberty-loving Frenchmen wherever they might be throughout the world.   " The war is not lost,'' he averred, " the country is not dead, hope is not extinct.   *Vive la France !* ''

His challenge did not go unheeded.   In France there were, no doubt, thousands who would have cheered and helped him if they could, but on them lay the heavy hand of the Nazis and their puppets of Vichy.   Abroad, however, in the vast territories of the French Colonial Empire some of those who listened were stirred into action, and the first step of what was shortly to become a formidable revolt against Pétain, and all that Pétain stands for, was taken in Chad in the heart of French Equatorial Africa, where Governor Éboué declared that henceforth he would

Although they are wearing British battle-dress uniform, the tricolour badge and the word " France '' worn on the shoulders of these soldiers show that they have become members of General de Gaulle's army of Free Frenchmen.   Other French articles in their equipment are their rifles and headgear—steel helmets or berets as the occasion may demand.

Photos, L.N.A. and Keystone

Dakar's Guns Make Answer to De Gaulle

When it was announced that General de Gaulle was heading an expedition of Free
Frenchmen to Dakar, it was confidently anticipated that very shortly French West Africa
would, like Chad and the other Equatorial colonies, rally to the cause of Free France.
But as told here, the expedition ended in most disappointing fashion.

ON the morning of Monday, September 23, General de Gaulle appeared off Dakar, and called on this key-town of France's empire in West Africa to rally to the flag of Free France.

For weeks past, ever since the humiliating armistice concluded in the railway coach at Compiègne. Dakar had been the scene of a number of manifestations suggesting that there were many in the colony who looked with sympathy on the resistance to the Vichy

Gaulle came to the decision to invade it himself at the head of a Free French force, military, naval, and air.

His preparations complete, he and his troops sailed from England in French ships under the French ensign and escorted by battleships of the Free French Navy. Accompanying the expedition were considerable British naval forces, but these were in the nature of supplementary protection.

As soon as he arrived off Dakar, General

which was lying in the harbour, did not cease, fire was returned ; and on both sides hits were secured and casualties incurred. Then three French submarines made attacks on the British vessels, with the result that two of the former were sunk, although the entire crew of one were picked up.

Reports of the fighting were both sparse and contradictory, and it was not clear whether there were engaged on the side of the defenders the six French vessels—the cruisers " Montcalm," " George Leygues," " Gloire," and three destroyers—which a few days earlier had passed through the Straits of Gibraltar on their way from Toulon to Dakar. No explanation had been vouchsafed for this naval move except the suggestion that the ships were intended to guard France's sea communications and food supplies coming from West Africa, but as likely as not it was dictated by the distinct danger that General de Gaulle's Free France movement showed signs of securing the upper hand at Dakar.

The arrival of the French warships was, indeed, so opportune as to suggest that somehow or other knowledge of the De Gaulle expedition had reached Vichy ; and this view is supported by the fact that all those Frenchmen who had expressed sympathy for the Free France movement had been imprisoned by order of M. Boisson shortly before the expedition came in sight. Some surprise was expressed in London that the " Montcalm " and the rest had been allowed to pass through the Straits of Gibraltar, but it may have been thought that there were elements in the vessels who might be expected to declare for Free France as soon as they escaped from the control of Vichy.

But even so, as the official statement issued in London on September 26 made it clear, " it is no part of the policy of the British Government to interfere with the movements of French men-of-war so long as they are not destined for any ports under German control." For this reason no hindrance was put in the way of the vessels in question passing through the Straits of Gibraltar, although when later, having reached Dakar without interference, they put to sea again steaming south they were headed back to Dakar by ships of the Royal Navy, as it was thought that they might be intending to interfere with the situation existing in French Equatorial Africa which had already declared for General de Gaulle.

The statement concluded with words which came as a deep disappointment not only to the supporters of Free France, but to Britain and Britain's friends. " When it became plain that only a major operation of war could secure the fall of Dakar it was decided to discontinue hostilities, as it had never been the intention of his Majesty's Government to enter into serious warlike operations against those Frenchmen who felt it their duty to obey the commands of the Vichy Government. General de Gaulle himself was most anxious that he should not be the cause of bloodshed to his fellow-countrymen. The forces concerned are therefore now being withdrawn from the region of Dakar."

One of the three French cruisers which were sent from Toulon to Dakar, the " Gloire," is seen here. She is a ship of 7,600 tons, launched in 1935, and carries nine 6-inch guns and sixteen anti-aircraft guns. With her went her sister ships, " Montcalm " and " Georges Leygues." Their guns would be no match for those of a British battleship.   *Photo, René Zubr*

Government which was being organized by General de Gaulle from London. These manifestations assumed such proportions that the order went forth from Vichy that Governor Cayla should be replaced by Governor Boisson, who was more likely to be amenable to their dictates. Then came reports that German and Italian officers were going by air to Dakar in increasing numbers, under the pretext of freeing certain of their nationals who had been imprisoned during the war, although it was obvious that their principal aim was the control of the air bases there.

Meanwhile the spirit of resistance in at least a considerable element of the population never ceased to grow, and it was fostered both by the economic paralysis and by the rallying to de Gaulle of French Equatorial Africa.

It was, then, with the three-fold aim of responding to the desire of the population for a repudiation of the German yoke, to free the economic life of French West Africa from the slavery imposed by the Armistice, and to prevent the colony from falling into the hands of the Germans, that General de

de Gaulle informed Admiral de Laborde, in command of the French naval base there, that in a desire to avoid all bloodshed he was about to send emissaries ashore under a flag of truce. The Admiral replied that he would refuse to see them, and when the emissaries, unarmed and in an unarmed launch, flying the French ensign and the white flag, drew near to the harbour their boat was fired on by the French authorities in the port, and two of the little party were seriously wounded. Shortly afterwards General de Gaulle himself attempted a peaceful landing of his troops, but when the Dakar forts fired on his sloops killing several members of the crews and wounding a large number, the General decided to remove his troops and his ships to a distance.

The batteries of the port also opened fire on the British warships which were standing by, and before returning the French fire the Admiral Commanding signalled ; " Will be compelled to return fire unless fire ceases." As the fire of the shore batteries, and also of the great French battleship " Richelieu,"

When the R.H.A. Stood at Bay at Hondeghem

Of all the close-range fighting between British and German troops in France during the last few days of May, 1940, there was no more gallantly contested engagement than that of the defence of Hondeghem village by " K " battery of the Royal Horse Artillery. This story of the action was assembled by Mr. Douglas Williams, of the " Daily Telegraph," from accounts by two officers and the battery sergeant-major.

ON May 26 enemy forces were in full flood along the main road from St. Omer to Mt. Cassel in their thrust to the Channel ports. Strategically sited and immediately in the direct line of their advance lay the village of Hondeghem. To delay the enemy it was vital to defend it, and the task was allotted to K Battery, R.H.A.

The battery commander selected a small headquarter staff and F troop of four guns for the purpose. No infantry were available, and the only additional garrison was a detachment of 80 men and one officer of a searchlight unit.

The village formed a virtual outpost in the widely dispersed British line, and its defence was far from easy. The defenders' armament was restricted to four 18-pounder guns, Bren and Lewis guns, and rifles.

By the evening of May 26 final arrangements had been made. Two guns were posted on the outskirts to command the roads by which the Germans would probably come, and the two others were placed at strategic points inside the village. Bren and Lewis guns were located in makeshift strong points, chiefly in the upper windows of houses.

The night passed quietly in an atmosphere of great tension, as scouts had reported the enemy in force concealed in woods only four miles away. At 7.30 a.m. word was received by a dispatch rider that the two outer guns (I and J sub-sections) had engaged the enemy and destroyed a number of vehicles and two or three tanks as they advanced down the main road. Those two sub-sections were quickly overwhelmed by an avalanche of tanks and were both out of action and the crews captured or disabled within 10 minutes of the opening of the battle.

Such a set-back so early in the day was a serious matter, and all considerations were now centred on the defence of the village itself. Armoured vehicles and supporting parties of German infantry began to penetrate its outer perimeter, and the two remaining guns were immediately in action, registering hit after hit at short range on the enemy as they tried to place machine-guns in house windows as they advanced.

A Shell through the Cookhouse

The enemy managed to get one machine-gun into position in the battery's cookhouse, but just as they were about to open fire L sub-section gun, gallantly handled, under intense fire, with the same precision as if the men were deploying during gun-laying practice, put a round straight through the cookhouse wall, effectively silencing the post.

The cookhouse was set on fire and all the day's food was destroyed, but the enemy gun was knocked out, and later the dead crew were discovered in the embers of the building. The remains of the German machine-gun are now a prized memento in the battery.

Another enemy gun was located by K sub-section gun behind a farmhouse which had served as a park for the battery vehicles. Although some of our men might have been there, it was essential to silence the gun, so the 18-pounder was trained on the farmhouse

and the first round brought the whole place down in a shower of plaster and dust. Another four rounds were pumped in to make sure, and the machine-gun was not heard again. One British driver who was in the farmhouse had a miraculous escape and rejoined his unit little the worse.

Both K and L guns were now hotly engaged, firing point-blank at 100 yards range, using Fuse 1. So close were the Germans that the gun crews were being attacked with hand grenades, but casualties, apart from the total loss of J and I sub-sections, remained small, only one man having been killed and two wounded. Both guns were in very exposed positions, but they maintained a fast rate of accurate fire; every round took effect.

About 1 p.m. large numbers of German light and medium tanks were seen from the top of Hondeghem church approaching Cassel and Hazebrouck. It was the last observation made from that position, for the enemy then shelled and demolished the church.

Attacked from All Sides

Machine-gun fire was now coming from all sides, and both 18-pounders had frequently to change position, their crews manhandling them up and down the village street and firing from all angles. Meantime, help came from an unexpected quarter. D troop of the battery, on the slope of Mt. Cassel, and controlled by wireless, opened up a defensive barrage. So accurate was their shooting that although at one time their shells were dropping within 50 yards of the two guns in the village street not a single round fell among their own people. Unfortunately, three of D's four guns were put out of action.

When ammunition ran low the gun could fire only once every five minutes; but the enemy's activity, too, seemed to die down a little, while battery drivers, with rifles, did some excellent work taking pot shots at the enemy from windows.

At 3.30 p.m. it became apparent that the small garrison could hold out no longer. Ammunition was almost gone; all food supplies had been destroyed; no reinforcements, except one small detachment of Fife and Forfar Yeomanry, had appeared; and they were in danger of being surrounded.

At 4.15 p.m. the withdrawal was ordered and the two guns and the two wounded men were sent off ahead, for a rendezvous at St. Sylvestre, some two miles away on the road to Cassel. The remainder followed later by a different route.

At St. Sylvestre, however, the main road running through the village was found to be held by German medium tanks, and positions were hastily found around the church where a group of some 20 R.A.S.C. men armed with rifles and Bren guns joined the action. The enemy were by now aware of the British troops' arrival, and a volley of hand grenades suddenly started from behind the tombstones.

Germans appeared on all sides and the Troop Commander decided that they could be dislodged only by a direct charge. Two parties with bayonets fixed advanced round

each side of the churchyard wall, each man shouting, as ordered, at the top of his voice. A terrible roar went up. The psychological effect was just what had been calculated. Three or four Germans were shot, and the rest, throwing away their rifles, broke in a panic and were routed.

Both guns were now again brought into action from the graveyard, and fired what little ammunition was left into the neighbouring houses. One gun was limbered up to its quad (four-wheel drive) for a change of position, but both gun and quad were blown to pieces by two direct hits from a German gun firing along the road.

Though the situation then began to look desperate the men were no whit disheartened, and were still full of fight. Charges were made by small parties against houses where Germans were hidden, and K's one remaining gun continued firing until its last round.

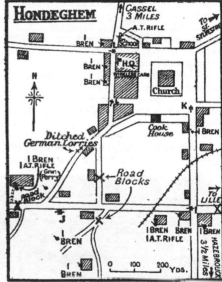

Where K Battery of the R.H.A. made its gallant fight on May 27th, 1940.
Courtesy, " Daily Telegraph "

As it was now late and enemy lights, presumably summoning reinforcements, had been observed, it was decided to make a dash to escape. The men piled into the remaining lorries, while the one gun left (L sub-section) was put out of action and abandoned.

Away went the British vehicles, under fire from German tanks in the fields. There was a sharp left turn and then a right turn in the road commanded by a German machine-gun. This S had to be taken at speed and the first vehicle was ditched at the second curve. The occupants, luckily, were able to scramble into the third vehicle, which got safely past. The second meanwhile had negotiated the first turn, but the driver missed the second and went straight through a hedge into a field. As the ground was dry he rejoined the road as it skirted the field.

Escaping at last from German machine-gun fire, the convoy went on in comparative safety and after a mile or so startled a party of the East Riding Yeomanry by arriving alive by the very road they had just mined !

London Still the Main Target of Nazi Bombs

The air battle for London in the week September 18 to 24 continued with hardly abated fury, mainly by night, rising to a fresh level of destruction in the central area on the night of September 24-25. Widely scattered attacks were also made in the provinces.

So far Hitler has failed utterly in the two main objects of his air attack on Britain. He has not attained aerial superiority in our skies, and his terror-raids have not provoked in our people a desire for peace negotiations ! To a Briton it is almost inconceivable that anyone could expect the second result, though the ordeal has been trying, especially to the workers of the eastern and southern districts of the Metropolis. Some unfortunates, bombed out of their homes, have been turned out a second time by attacks on West End districts in whose unoccupied flats they had been placed, but the spirit of the people has been magnificent.

The Luftwaffe continued its attacks on aerodromes, but was foiled again by our alert and well organized ground defences and by our ever-ready fighters. Striving to wear down our fighter strength and to cause the R.A.F. to use up its reserve, Hitler sent over his own fighters in hundreds, and brought into service even faster and later-built aircraft—the best that his designers had contrived—which were being saved up for a lateroccasion. But up to September 25, 876 enemy aircraft were destroyed for certain in raids on Britain, while the R.A.F. lost only 237 machines and 115 pilots.

Night bombers get through our defences— in small numbers and much harassed and hampered—but the war can certainly not be won by destroying small houses in the East End and big shops in West London. There are signs that our fighter aircraft are beginning to play a greater part in night interception, and we may be sure that our

gunners will put up even a fiercer barrage as time goes on. The Secretary for Air has hinted that other steps are being taken to curtail the activity of Goering's young men by night as well as by day.

The heroism and devotion to duty of bomb disposal units of the Royal Engineers was recognized officially by the award of the E.G.M. (Medal of the O.B.E. for Gallantry) to Lieut. E. W. Reynolds, 2nd Lieuts. E. E. Talbot and W. L. Andrews, and Lance-Sergt. W. J. Button, announced in the " Gazette " of Sept. 17.

On the night of Wednesday, Sept. 18, the London barrage was resumed when raiders (mostly single machines) came over. Bombs were dropped in the suburbs and damage was done in the West End also. During what was described as a day of continuous air engagements, mainly over the South-eastern area of England, the Nazis lost 46 aircraft to nine of ours destroyed (five of our pilots saved). Five separate waves of bombers and fighters came over, attacks beginning at 9.30 a.m. and not ceasing until 8 o'clock on Wednesday evening. The Nazis were very roughly handled by our fighters, and jettisoned their bombs in some cases on the mere approach of our Hurricanes or Spitfires.

On Wednesday, too, the Merseyside area experienced its fiercest raid. More than a hundred high-explosive bombs were dropped at night, besides many incendiaries. Fine work continued to be done by the A.A. gunners, who brought down 16 raiders in nine nights. An even more satisfactory

result was that when the Nazis encountered our barrage on the fringe of the Metropolitan area many of them turned tail after dropping their bombs there and then over open country. Thus it was that only a few got through to London. Time after time the challenge of the guns would be heard, following the sound of approaching aircraft ; after two or three rounds there would come the scream of bombs and then the shattering explosions as the missiles reached the ground. The raiders tried new routes, but batteries of mobile A.A. guns came into position and kept the Nazis on the run.

No large-scale raid was made during Thursday, the 19th, and of the few enemy aircraft that carried out hit-and-run attacks, five were shot down. Of two which dropped bombs on East London, one was brought down by our fighters. At night a number of raiders, flying singly, approached the capital from the north-west, using a new route and travelling at a low altitude. The barrage sounded fiercer than ever before, and many more searchlights were in operation.

On Friday morning, the 20th, some two hundred enemy aircraft flew inland over the Kent coast—to be met by a multitude of British fighters. Hurricanes and Spitfires closed in around the leading formations, and after a hot engagement sent them back over the Channel, where the fight continued. There was also a fierce fight over the Thames Estuary, but though a warning was given in London the danger had soon passed and no raider got nearer than the outskirts of the capital on the east

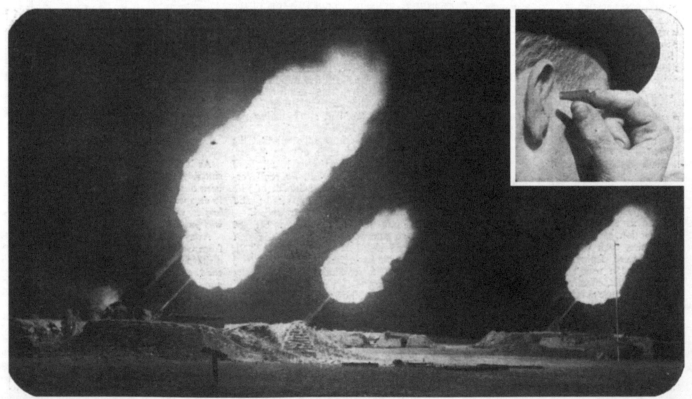

One of the first photographs to be taken of the fierce anti-aircraft batteries whose powerful barrage has proved the terror of enemy night-bombers. Guns and crews are here seen in action in the Central London's area during a night raid. London's nightly resistance to Nazi attackers has been aptly compared with that of Verdun in the last war.   Inset is seen one off the new ear-plugs which deaden the noise of guns and exploding bombs.

Photos, Central Press and Topical

Indiscriminate Bombing Brings Tragedy in Its Train

Here is the story of this Anderson shelter. Three people were taking refuge in it when a bomb destroyed their house. Blown into the air, the shelter landed in the next garden and the occupants staggered out unhurt. And unhurt, too, was the Sunday dinner they had with them (left).

Seventeen hours' continuous toil were necessary to rescue Thomas Reaves, a London taxi driver, from the ruins of a garage. He is seen above being lowered from the building on a stretcher. For 15 hours he had been fed by a doctor through a tube, right. Alas, all the efforts were unavailing, for he died later in hospital. His wife, to whom he had been married only two months, was with him and was killed.

Photos, " Daily Mirror "

The Capital Makes the Best of a Bad Job

Pegasus, the winged horse on the summit of the bombed Inner Temple Library, came safely to earth when the turret was pulled down. Top, he is carried away ; centre, in flight.

GERMAN & BRITISH AIRCRAFT LOSSES
German to April 30, 1940

Total announced and estimated—West Front, North Sea, Britain, Scandinavia... 350

	German	British
May	1,990	258
June	276	177
July	245	115
Aug.	1,110	310
Sept. 1-25	878	241
Totals, May to Sept. 25 ...	**4,499**	**1,101**

Daily Results.

Sept.	German Losses	British Losses	British Pilots Saved	Sept.	German Losses	British Losses	British Pilots Saved
				Bt. fwd. Sept.	506	168	82
1	25	15	9	14	18	9	6
2	55	20	9	15	232	25	14
3	25	15	8	16	7	1	—
4	54	17	12	17	12	3	2
5	39	20	9	18	46	9	5
6	46	19	12	19	5	0	—
7	103	22	9	20	4	7	3
8	11	3	1	21	2	0	—
9	52	13	6	22	1	0	—
10	2	0	—	23	11	11	8
11	89	24	7	24	8	4	2
12	3	0	—	25	26	4	3
13	26	0	—				
	506	**168**	**82**	**Totals**	**878**	**241**	**125**

None of the figures include aircraft bombed on the ground or so damaged as to be unlikely to reach home. **Additional German Losses.** Sept. 11: 4 shot down over Continent. Sept. 15: 2 by Fleet Air Arm. Revealed on Sept. 26 that 47 more shot down on Sept. 15 : total, 232. Figures for Sept. 25 incomplete. **Civilian Casualties.** Intensive air attacks on Britain began on Aug. 8. Casualties during August 1,075 killed, 1,261 seriously injured.

Mr. Churchill stated that during the first half of September civilian casualties amounted to about 2,000 killed and 8,000 wounded, about four-fifths being in London. In the fighting services casualties were only 250. **Mass Raid Casualties in London.** Sept. 7 : 306 killed ; 1,337 injured. Sept. 8 : 286 killed ; about 1,400 injured. Sept. 9 : about 400 killed, 1,400 injured. **German Aircraft Destroyed in Britain.** From September 3, 1939 to September 24, 1940 the German machines destroyed around and over Britain totalled 2,256. In that time 579 British aircraft were lost, 280 pilots being saved.

and south-east, where a few bombs were dropped. In the morning bombs at Brighton caused some fatal casualties.

There were two distinct raids on Friday night. In the earlier one several raiders got through to Central London, where a church hall and a manufacturing establishment adjoining it were set on fire. Underneath the hall was a refuge, but people sheltering there were unhurt. Many fires were started in South and South-east London, but were soon got under control. After a short interval there came a more intense raid on much the same localities.

A.A. gunners shot down a Junkers 88 bomber at Merton, Surrey, early in the morning. The pilot was killed and another of the crew came down in a parachute at Balham, three miles away. In its fall the bomber demolished a house, but only two people were injured. Occupants of the house were in their Anderson shelter and were unscathed. Next door an Anderson shelter was crushed flat, but the people had taken refuge beneath the stairs and thus escaped.

People going to work in the East End on Saturday morning, the 21st, were killed by bombs dropped by a lone raider. A factory and shops were hit, and several houses destroyed also. During the day the enemy made several attacks by single raiders or small formations, mainly over South-east England. About midday bombers tried to reach London but were stopped on the outskirts. A bomber was shot down in the afternoon.

In London's fifteenth night raid, over sixty hostile aircraft took part, flying up the

Lambeth has earned fresh fame. Here, after the raid of September 17, great-hearted people of the district are doing their famous walk.

Shops that have been bombed have carried on as best they could. Here at a desk on the pavement business is being carried on.

Lord Redesdale is one of those who have put their mansions in the West End at the disposal of the authorities to house refugees. Here is the scene in the ballroom of his town house.

Photos, G.P.U., Fox and Keystone

London's Face is Scarred But Her Heart is Sound

A Messerschmitt 110 that was being pursued and machine-gunned by a Spitfire plunged down to the sea, narrowly missing Folkestone harbour pier (above).

Photos, "Daily Mirror," exclusive to THE WAR ILLUSTRATED

THE NOISE BOMBS MAKE

RECENTLY a bomb fell just outside the gate of St. Dunstan's headquarters. It made a crater 36 ft. wide and 15 ft. deep. Some of the staff were in the air raid shelter, the door of which was 33 ft. from the crater. Its door was splintered to pieces and sucked out by the intense vacuum which follows an explosion.

The people inside experienced a few minutes of extreme anxiety because they did not know whether they were hurt or not, or whether the roof might come down. But luckily all was well.

The air raid shelter in which my wife and I were sleeping was about 90 ft. from the bomb crater. I was standing outside the shelter. Two or three bombs dropped, but I could hear by the noise they made coming down that they were some distance away. If the whistling noise remains more or less constant, you can be sure the bomb is at any rate 200 or 300 yards away, possibly more. If, on the other hand, the bomb is really dropping on to you, or very near to you, you are immediately aware that the whistling noise is getting rapidly louder. These were not screaming bombs but ordinary high-explosive bombs, which make a whistling like a shell approaching, and a little like the swish of a rocket.

I went into the shelter, sitting on the step. Then I heard this bomb coming down, and immediately recognized that it was coming near. The whistling, sizzling noise increased terrifically as the bomb drew nearer. I had time to wake my wife up, tell her to put her fingers in her mouth, which is a good way of ensuring that the mouth is open to protect the ears, and to shut the door of the shelter.

If you really hear the bomb as I did from the time it leaves the aeroplane it is surprising how long it takes to come down. I think a bomb falls at 150 m.p.h., whereas sound travels at about 720 m.p.h., so that the noise comes well in advance of the missile. One of the St. Dunstan's buildings was between us and the bomb, so that we did not receive the direct blast, but it was sufficient to shake the whole shelter and fill it with dust. A second or two after the explosion a large quantity of rubble and other debris came down on the shelter.

The interesting thing about this is that we, and all the others concerned, are less apprehensive now than we were before.—*Sir Ian Fraser writing in " St. Dunstan's Review.*

Large fighter formations, bent on the destruction of R.A.F. aircraft, took part in Monday's daylight raids. They were repulsed and sent back across the Channel, but losses were approximately equal on both sides. Later in the day there were attacks on our coastal towns, and at Eastbourne a single enemy aircraft dropped 28 bombs, demolishing houses in a working-class neighbourhood. Among the enemy machines that crossed the Kent coast was a gigantic four-engined bomber, with a very large escort. Together with these and the smaller bombers it turned tail in face of our fighters.

Two raiders were shot down on Monday night, and during the following day eight more Nazi machines were destroyed. Several attempts were made by the enemy to reach London during Tuesday, but his massed formations were broken up long before they got to the outskirts of the capital.

Thousands of incendiary bombs were dropped in the London area on Tuesday night. The warning sounded after an enemy reconnaissance machine had circled over the central areas. Many fires were caused, some by large oil-bombs, but the fire fighters in all cases soon got them under control. Five London hospitals were bombed, and one of Wren's City churches suffered a little damage. A college, two large stores, and a police-station were among the buildings that also suffered.

Air Marshal Sir A. Barratt disclosed on Sept. 25 that the figure of 185 German raiders down on Sep. 15 should be increased by 47 more that " almost certainly came down."

The German 'plane finally plunged into the sea (left), sending up a huge column of water; and when the spray died down, the tail was sticking out of the water (above). When it was all over, the pilot of the Spitfire could be seen by spectators on shore doing the " victory roll " (right).

Estuary early on Saturday evening. Two determined attacks were made, but, met and hotly engaged by Hurricanes and Spitfires, they were soon driven off. Four raiders were accounted for by A.A. gunners; one, trapped by the searchlights, was brought down by a direct hit; another, flying towards Central London, was blown to pieces in the air; a third was shot down near Bognor; the fourth was crippled by the guns and finished off by a fighter. More hospitals and churches were bombed.

Sunday, September 22, was marked by little enemy activity, though lone raiders came over East Anglia and the London area and dropped bombs. At night, however, a terrific clamour broke out as our guns came into action against a continual stream of Nazi bombers that approached the Metropolitan area from various directions. Fires started by an early raid were speedily put out by the A.F.S., so that the glow should not help later arrivals.

The Nazi air raids on London have done no serious damage to military objectives or to anything that could seriously interfere with the war machine. Therefore, photographs of many of London's bombed buildings have been published. This photograph, however, is typical of all that the Nazis dare publish of the work of the R.A.F. in Berlin—an unrecognizable military objective.

Shadow of the Big Bomber Over Humble Homes

Mr. and Mrs. Grimmond (left) are seen amidst the ruins of their home in south-east London, which was bombed on September 22. The hand of fate has been heavy upon them, for on September 17 five of their twelve children were drowned when the ship which was taking them to Canada was torpedoed. Right is a page from their little daughter's last letter.

Two Formidable Aircraft: German and an American They Will Soon Meet

WHEN many hundreds of her bombers have been shot down in flames over Britain's seas and countryside, Germany is now turning to the use of very much bigger machines than those she has hitherto used, no doubt in the hope that they will be able to stand up better against the all too deadly attacks of our Spitfires and Hurricanes. One four-engined giant bomber recently identified amongst its cloud of satellite Messerschmitts is the Focke-Wulf Condor (below right). This machine was originally designed as a passenger-carrying 'plane, and made its first flight from Berlin to Croydon on June 24, 1938; its four engines give a speed of 200 m.p.h., some 100 m.p.h. less than that of corresponding types in the R.A.F.

Our fighter pilots could ask for nothing better as a target, and it is hardly surprising that its appearances above our coast have been few and brief, and exceedingly well escorted. Its only advantage is that it has an exceptionally long range, for it has proved its capability of doing the journey from Berlin to New York non-stop. It is interesting to note that the German factory where the original Condors were produced is reported to have been practically wiped out in the course of recent R.A.F. bombing raids.

Another huge German bomber is the Junkers 88, several of which have been shot down recently in south-east England.

One of these was found to be of the newest make—not more than four months old—and on its fuselage was painted an emblematic red dragon.

Much more powerful and with an even greater range is the American "Flying Fortress" (above) bomber which R.A.F. pilots will shortly be employing in their raids over Germany. It is a monoplane with four engines and is armed with both cannons and machine-guns: and its maximum range of three thousand miles will make a mere nothing of a trip from British aerodromes to Berlin and back again.

The "Flying Fortress" is built by the Boeing Aircraft Co., and it is probable that the bombers supplied to Britain will be of the very latest type, the 30-ton B15 which has a wing span of 150 feet.

Mines or Bombs, They Make a Good Job of It

One of the duties of the Bomber Command is laying minefields in enemy waters, and for this duty special aircraft are employed. Above, a mine is being fixed in the slings of a Hampden bomber. More than 30 minefields have been laid in this way, from the Norwegian coast to the Bay of Biscay.
Photo, "The Times"

Germany's great industrial district, the Ruhr, has been persistently bombed by the R.A.F., and its position makes it an easier target than many of those to which the R.A.F. has made nightly visits. Here is one of the great railway marshalling yards between Hamm and Dortmund. This yard, together with the blast furnaces of the Union Iron and Steel works seen in the photograph, had been attacked over 60 times by September 21. The chief railway centre is Hamm, and the map, centre, suggests its importance.
Photo, E.N.A.

Though Hell Falls From Heaven, London M

Though time-bombs have put the butchers' shops out of action the housewives will not be deprived of their Sunday joint. In the market-place in a south-east suburb the steel-helmeted butcher is exchanging meat for coupons, and above his van floats in proud defiance the Union Jack.

To minimize the risk of injury from flying glass, some of London's buses were fitted with anti-blast netting (above). Right, a grocer who had been bombed out opens a mobile shop.

" Big
splinter
than th
time

T
The
Willia
New Y

Toda
very b
freedo
city w
Londo
attack
Londo
resista

Brit
tress.
from
of our
—the

The
It is t
brunt
and b
especia
key to

I as
go to
of the
only t
securi

The
La Gu

Bra
ened
admir
you.

as Ever the Things that Make For Life

So savage was the Nazi onslaught on the thickly-populated regions of the East End that hundreds of families were made homeless. Communal kitchens were thereupon established for those whose own had been destroyed.

Amongst the civilian heroes must be counted the men whose job it is to deal with damaged gas mains (left) and the emergency repair of hundreds of broken windows.

A Visit to Czech Airmen in Britain

Somewhere in Britain a Czechoslovak Air Force has come into being and two squadrons are now attached to the R.A.F. Below we have an account of a visit paid to one of their aerodromes by Mr. Henry Baerlein.

I is highly probable that if this article is translated for Herr Hitler he will lose his notorious patience, this time with the Czechs. A number of them, airmen and other fighters, unwilling to remain in their homeland, temporarily under his yoke, made their way, not without peril, across the closely guarded frontiers, and after serving in Poland and France a good many of them have joined the forces in this country. A visit I have just made to an aerodrome, part of which is allocated to them, has been a delightful and inspiring experience. The Czech airmen are the happiest of warriors, for now they know that they can concentrate on the fight with none of the complications which unfortunately overtook them in France and with 'planes whose excellence they fully realize. That they know how to handle them is proved by the fact that up to the day of my visit they had brought down nineteen Nazi 'planes and lost only a single pilot, with three or four others for a while in hospital.

What strikes one at first is the modesty with which these young men speak of their exploits. Most of them had a hard time in escaping from the German sentries and the Gestapo; while in France, where they destroyed over a hundred German machines, they were not always met with consideration. Thus when they were told to proceed from Central France to Perpignan, near the Spanish frontier, they were informed on arriving there that no petrol was available for them. Perhaps the French in their own agitation did not realize what would happen to the Czechs if they should fall into German hands. If one of them is missing from the Protectorate his mother receives a call from a Gestapo man, who asks if the son is in a foreign army. The mother replies that she does not know.

" Then I can tell you," says the man, " for he fell some days ago." If the woman faints or exhibits her emotion in some way the Gestapo man regards the evidence as complete.

The Escape from France

So it was most necessary for the Czechs to get away from France. By one means or another they flew to Algiers ; one to whom I spoke found a barrel of petrol and a small ladle with which it took him three hours to replenish his reservoir. In Algiers there was chaos, and in Morocco, where the Czechs spent ten days in anxious idleness, the commander of the garrison finally ordered that the magnetos should be removed from every 'plane and that black troops should prevent access to the hangars. A most capable Czech officer arranged for all his compatriot airmen to reach either Gibraltar or Lisbon, he himself being the last to leave, and if he had not been in mufti the Gestapo would have laid hands upon him.

" We do not wish to speak ill of the French," said the airmen, " now they are in such misfortune, but after all the Germans are neighbours of ours, we know them well, and it was a shock for us in France to find that, instead of German method and organization, there was such light-heartedness, coupled with scorn for the Germans, and at the same

time a yearning for peace. As for the French 'planes, too many had been hastily constructed, though a very good one was produced about a month before the collapse. But it is no exaggeration to say that the material in England is 100 per cent better. It is splendid to fly over here."

Naturally it does not suit the Germans that the country which they are " protecting " should have these representatives in Britain. One day the German wireless declared that the vessel containing the Czech airmen had been sunk ; a few days later the same wireless station urged all the Czechs to go home, adding that they would not be punished by the Protecting Power if they followed this advice. As a matter of fact no Czech airman lost his life on the voyage, and not all of them came to England by the routes I have mentioned. One of our bombers, for instance, brought more than thirty whom it had luckily picked up somewhere in France. They embarked at such brief notice that some were clad in pyjamas and some were barefoot.

On August 6, Dr. Benes, President of the Provisional Czechoslovak Government, visited two Czech squadrons attached to the R.A.F. in England. Above, Dr. Benes chats to one of the pilots just about to take off. Left, a typical Czech pilot.
Photos, P.N.A. and G.P.U.

" We are sometimes asked," said one of the airmen, " why we did not bring more of our own 'planes from Czechoslovakia. When Hitler marched into Prague in March, 1939, and most of us decided to leave, the weather was terrible and the drifts of snow made it very difficult for us to move our 'planes. Besides, we considered that if we were to land in a foreign country with these 'planes we might be extradited to the Germans, for no country was at war with them, and they would of course have accused us of theft, which is an extraditable offence."

When President Benes visited his airmen he referred to the British Government's recognition of his own Government as " the first hopeful turning point in the history of the Czechoslovak nation after Munich. Now we have started again to rise and I have a justified confidence that the Republic will be restored as a strong, free, democratic and happy State, even better than it was before." The President concluded : " You Czechoslovak airmen will, perhaps, be the first to enter the struggle here in Great Britain. Some of you will, perhaps, visit in the air our dear Motherland and will, perhaps, fly over our beautiful Prague. Then you will be the bearers of our most sacred ideals and messengers of our future victory."

The German radio in Prague replied to this by alluding to " the irresponsible activity of certain Czech emigrants," and stated that " the Czech nation believes in the Fuehrer's word and in the future of the Greater German Reich." That is wishful thinking on the part of Goebbels, for the whole Czech nation, looking forward with serene confidence to the hour of its liberation, hears with delight of the activity of certain emigrants in Britain, some on the ground and others in the air.

Czechs Help to Down the Nazis Over London

TWO Czechoslovak units are now stationed with the R.A.F.—
a bomber squadron and a fighter squadron. In both the flying personnel and ground maintenance staffs are all Czechoslovaks, many of whom have been in action above France and Britain since the beginning of the war. Hardly had the force been constituted when early in September the fighter squadron shot down six Messerschmitt 110s and one Dornier 215 bomber, approaching London by way of the Thames Estuary. The Czechs in their Hurricanes dived on the Nazis out of the sun, each choosing one of the enemy to attack, and probably the first the enemy knew of their approach was the hail of bullets which began to hit them. One of the Czech pilots had to bale out, but apart from that not a single one of the Hurricanes had a bullet-hole to show that they had been in action. As soon as he landed one of the Czechs asked, "When do we take off again?"

This Czech sergeant-pilot, now with the R.A.F., was one of a trio of world-famous aerobatic performers; his comrades were killed in France.

Circle: Seated on the ground before him, these Czech aircraftmen are listening with keen appreciation to the Czech officer who is explaining the details of a British Spitfire. They are members of one of the Czech squadrons now serving with the R.A.F. in England.

Dr. Eduard Benes, who was President of Czechoslovakia from 1935 to 1938 and is now President of the Provisional Czechoslovak Government in London, is here seen at an English flying field chatting to crews of the Czechoslovak Bomber Squadron, now attached to the R.A.F., and some of their English "guides."

Photos, E.N.A. & G.P.U.

Graziani Takes the Road Into Egypt

Egypt was invaded by the Italians on September 13, but the Egyptian Government failed
as yet to find in the stroke any reason for declaring war. Only a waste of desert was
involved, and (as we tell below) the British strategy was directed towards drawing the
enemy ever deeper into the inhospitable wilderness.

BENEATH a blazing sun and through an
all-enveloping haze of white dust
Marshal Graziani's army of invasion
crossed the frontier from Libya into Egypt
on September 13. Preceded by a screen of
4·7 anti-tank guns mounted on armoured
cars and tiny Fiat two-man tanks, the Italian
tanks, lorries, and infantry moved across the
stony desert in two long columns like a black
stream of ants. The first followed the line
of the coast, where they had the advantage
of a good road ; but the second, some miles
to the south, had nothing better than the
rough track which winds along the edge or
escarpment of the desert plateau.

Again the advance was resumed, and on
September 16 Graziani could claim the
capture of Sidi Barrani, 35 miles east of
Bugbug and 60 miles inside the Egyptian
frontier, or 75 miles by way of the coast.
Hardly had the Italians captured the village
when mines laid by the British before their
evacuation were detonated, and, as an eye-
witness put it, " the entire village full of
enemy troops appeared to be blown into
the air by the explosion."

At Sidi Barrani the Italians set foot on
the macadamized road which runs from Sidi
Barrani through Mersa Matruh to Alexandria. But Alexandria is 250 miles and

an easy and speedy victory. Behind him
stretched for 150 miles the thin line of his
communications. All his supplies—including every drop of water intended for the
parched throats of men or for boiling radiators
—have to be brought along the coastal road,
within full view of the ships of the Royal Navy
and without a vestige of shade to screen them
from the reconnaissance 'planes of the R.A.F.

Outnumbered Five to One

True, he had an enormous superiority of
men—at least ten infantry battalions each
consisting of about 1,000 men, supported by
numbers of light and medium tanks and
armoured cars, anti-aircraft and field artillery, and a considerable proportion of the
Italian Air Force, while behind him in
Libya were reserves numbering perhaps
200,000 or 250,000 men. The British, for
their part, were outnumbered by at least five
to one ; but, on the other hand, the Army
under the command of General Sir Henry
Wilson was generally admitted to be a
splendid force, one hardened by months of
training in this very desert. Admitted, the
Italians had made some progress into Egyptian territory, but, as a British spokesman
affirmed in Cairo, it had never been the
intention to defend " that long desert line
running southwards from Sollum, but certainly we~shall defend Egypt proper, the
Delta, and Nile valley." So at Mersa
Matruh the British force, composed of
British regulars, Australians, New Zealanders and Indians; awaited the Italian
approach. Though not even at Mersa
Matruh would the Battle of Egypt be fought.
Better far that the Italians should be drawn
ever deeper and deeper along the coast road,
exposed all the time to attacks from the air
and to bombardment from Britain's ships
along the Mediterranean shore, until somewhere west of Alexandria they should be

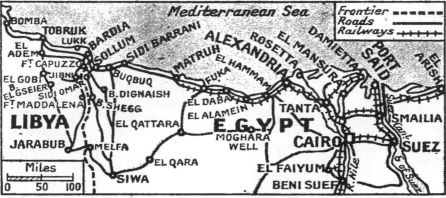

In invading Egypt the Italian columns are following for the most part the coast road which runs
from Libya along the Mediterranean shore to Alexandria, Britain's naval base in Egypt. From
Matruh the road is paralleled by a railway. By September 16 the Italians had reached Sidi
Barrani, 60 miles inside Egypt.

Having passed through the wire defences
that mark the frontier, the Italians occupied
Fort Musaid, a customs post now deserted
and crumbling into ruin. Then they came
down to the sea at Sollum through a pass
which proved a death-trap for many of
Graziani's men, for not only had one stretch
of it been mined by the British engineers, but
here and there in the rocks on the hillside
Bren gunners had established themselves and
took heavy toll of the marchers with next to
no loss to themselves. The Italians also
discovered to their cost that the coast road
from Tobruk had also been mined.

' Capture ' of Sollum

Mussolini's propaganda department
worked itself into a high state of excitement
over the capture of Sollum, and, indeed, in
its taking the Italians expended great quantities of shot and shell. But in fact for weeks
past the place had been held by a mere
handful of British troops, and even these
had been withdrawn under cover of darkness when the invasion began. For three
days the Italians shelled the village before,
they charged to the assault, and great must
have been their chagrin when, clambering
over what was left of the walls, now pounded
into their original dust, they discovered that
the place was an empty shell.

From Sollum Graziani's columns, keeping
close to the shore, arrived at Bugbug, some
25 miles inside Egypt. Here a big motor
transport convoy forming part of the vanguard was heavily attacked by a number of
British bombers, who swooped in from the
sea and left many of the vehicles in flames.

more beyond Sidi Barrani, and Graziani's
columns had still 95 miles to march before
they would come up against the main British
defences at Mersa Matruh. The Italians
had done well to cover 75 miles in four
days of hard fighting and marching, but
Marshal Graziani, hard-bitten old soldier
that he is, can have suffered no illusions of

The conditions that the Artillery has to face in the Middle East are very different from those
which prevail in the West. This gun in action against the Italians in North Africa has to do its
work in the open desert with no natural camouflage or protection of any sort. Owing to the
extreme heat, even steel helmets must be discarded.
Photo, British Official: Crown Copyright

Over the Desert the Italians Move Like Ants

The pair of caterpillar armoured cars (above) are being polished up after their day in the desert. Their equipment includes an anti-aircraft gun, which has inspired the crew of one of them to name their ship of the desert "Fly Flapper." Circle, the camera of a reconnaissance 'plane bringing back invaluable records is being carefully unloaded.

the town of Atbara, where it might not only cut the railway between Khartoum and Cairo, but move eastwards along the line to Port Sudan, Britain's halfway house on the Red Sea.

But (presuming on the possibility) the capture of Khartoum and the overrunning of the Sudan, however damaging to British prestige in Africa, would not be deadly; the battleground where the decision will be sought and made by force of arms is, we may be sure, somewhere within the "Fertile Crescent" which runs through western Egypt, across the Delta and the Suez Canal into Palestine. Somewhere in that semicircle of history-soaked land the Battle of the British Empire will almost certainly be fought.

brought to battle on a field that the defenders had chosen.

Such, we may suppose, is the strategy of Britain's Command in the Near East; but Sir Archibald Wavell, sitting in his office at Cairo, has to think not only of the Italian columns crawling along the Egyptian coast, but of other columns which may be moving across the desert towards the upper reaches of the Nile. It may well be that Mussolini has given the order to Graziani to launch several such columns from Libya or from Italian East Africa. One, we may suppose, might take the route from Libya south-east across 400 miles of desert, hopping from one oasis to another, to Wadi Halfa on the Nile, where Egypt meets the Anglo-Egyptian Sudan. Another might strike from the recently captured Kassala on the Sudan-Eritrea frontier due west across the desert to Khartoum, headquarters of the Sudanese administration; while a third, also operating from Kassala, might be directed down the Atbara to its confluence with the Nile at

The hardships of desert warfare are immensely increased by the burning sun beating down from a cloudless sky. There is no natural shade, but the resourceful British soldier often makes his own. These officers of an armoured car carry a big umbrella to protect them when they halt.

Photos, British Official: Crown Copyright

Our Merchant Navy is Stronger Than Ever

This article is, in part, a review of the position of Britain's mercantile marine after a year of Hitler's unrestricted sea warfare. On balance it was actually stronger at the end of 12 months by 100,000 tons. Events of the shipping war in August are also recounted.

WHEN Germany began the war in September 1939, having already sent her submarines and supply ships to strategic points on the important trade routes, it is reasonable to presume that she hoped to equal, or better, the record of sinkings during the height of the U-boat campaign in 1917. In the five months from March to July of that year, the enemy sank over 2,000,000 tons gross of British shipping, equivalent to an annual loss of 4,881,000 tons. By submarine, magnetic mine and bombing aeroplane, it was anticipated that at least this tonnage would be sunk during the first year of the Second Great War, particularly since the average size of our merchant ships had increased during the intervening 20 years. Plans for the blockade of Great Britain were therefore based on the assumption that over five million tons of British shipping would be sunk each year.

Indeed, in a flight of fancy, it was claimed by the Nazis that 5,078,038 tons gross had been sunk up to August 4.

As the tables in this page show, the results fell far short of claims and expectations, in spite of the assistance during the latter months of Italy, with her numerous submarines and motor torpedo boats. If armed merchant cruisers, transports and so on (converted passenger liners) are included, the British losses from September 3, 1939, to September 1, 1940, amounted to under 1¾ million tons.

That is one side of the picture. On the other are the tonnage gains. Owing to captures from the two enemies, purchases from neutrals, and new shipbuilding, the tonnage under the British flag was actually greater at the end of the first year than when war was declared. In addition, losses from marine hazards, more numerous owing to wartime navigation difficulties, had been more than

Merchant Shipping War Losses After a Year of War

	Sep. 3, 1939–July 28, 1940	July 28–Sept 1	Sep. 3, 1939–Sep. 1, 1940
BRITISH :	Tons gross	Tons gross	Tons gross
Liners, cargo vessels	1,215,114	258,850	1,473,964
Lost in naval operations ...	70,316	—	70,316
Naval auxiliaries ...	111,813	39,220	151,033
Naval trawlers ...	15,235	1,870	17,105
Totals ...	1,412,478	299,940	1,712,418
ALLIED	436,335	26,586	462,921
Totals ...	1,848,813	326,526	2,175,339
NEUTRAL	722,394	46,819	769,213
Totals ...	2,571,207	373,345	2,944,552

Enemy Losses to September 1, 1940

	Sunk	Captured	Total
GERMAN...	705,000	258,000	963,000
ITALIAN	123,000	150,000	273,000
Totals ...	828,000	408,000	1,236,000

In addition, about 33,000 tons of neutral shipping under enemy control have been sunk.

offset by the ships of Denmark and France which came under British control when these countries were occupied by Germany.

On balance the British mercantile marine alone, apart from Allied ships or vessels chartered from neutrals, was stronger at the end of the first year of war by a little over 100,000 tons gross.

The overrunning by Hitler's armies of most of the Continent of Europe completely altered the shipping situation. On the one hand it added about 6,250,000 tons to the Allied fleets (though some of this was already chartered by the British Ministry of Shipping); but, on the other, it meant that Britain had to draw her supplies of food and raw materials from farther afield. The nearest source, at one time the English Channel or the North Sea, was now, practically speaking, the North Atlantic. The new Allied tonnage could not, therefore, be regarded as a net addition, since more ships were required to transport a given tonnage of goods in a given period than before.

Another factor in the situation, however, was that British ships no longer had to main-

Merchant Shipping Balance Sheet for First Year of the War

British Tonnage, Sept. 1939		17,892,000
CREDITS		
Captures to Sept. 1, 1940		408,000
Danish and French ships (temporary possession)		800,000
*Purchase and building to Sept. 1, 1940 ...		800,000
Total		2,008,000
Add Allied Tonnage :		
Norwegian		3,750,000
Dutch...		2,000,000
Belgian and Polish		500,000
Total British and Allied		8,258,000
Neutral tonnage chartered		750,000
Total " Credits "		9,003,000
DEBITS		
British war losses, mercantile		1,544,000
" " Naval auxiliaries ...		168,000
†Allied war losses (May–Sept.)		263,000
*British marine losses		190,000
Total " Debits " ...		2,165,000
NET GAIN		6,843,000
British and Allied Tonnage, Sept. 1, 1940		**24,735,000**

* Approximate figures. † From date neutrals became Allies.

One of the new merchant ships that are being built at a rate that more than keeps pace with the losses through enemy submarine activity is here seen just about to glide down the slipway. All the old ceremony of christening the ship is dispensed with.

British Seamen Make Vain the Nazi Claims

This cheery party of sailors and soldiers are some of the 620 survivors of the transport, " Mohamed Ali El-Kebir," which was torpedoed and sunk in the Atlantic. They are here seen when they arrived at a London station on August 13, 1940. Most of them were wearing borrowed clothes. Every man was ready to go to sea again.
Photo, Central Press

tain in food, equipment and other supplies a large Expeditionary Force in France. At the same time, they were relieved of considerable demands from France herself, for our former Ally was by no means self-supporting in ships.

Taking every consideration into account, the shipping situation at the end of August was very much more favourable than when war was declared. It was still, and always will be, the most vital part of Britain's defensive armour.

All was not, however, plain sailing. The rate of sinkings had increased during June, July and August, and the losses in August were the highest of any month since the war began. This was due partly to intensified submarine activity—the vessels operating from new bases along the Belgian and French coasts, and aided by Italian vessels and trained crews—partly to more extensive bombing, also directed from new bases, and partly to the depletion of the Allied anti-submarine forces after the capitulation of France. In spite of the higher loss rate, however, a considerable reserve of tonnage remained in hand and there was no cause for alarm.

August also saw a new development in the campaign against British shipping. On the 22nd of this month batteries of heavy guns fired on a large convoy moving up the English Channel (see pages 225 and 247). The new menace was, of course, expected, and the escorting warships quickly laid a smoke screen. Although the range was short, as the ships were steaming about halfway between the two coasts, and although more than 100 shells were fired, none of the ships—which were later attacked from the air—was sunk nor seriously damaged.

Large-scale air attacks on coastal convoys began earlier in the month, but they were attended by such a high loss of aeroplanes and so little success that they were abandoned before the end of August. In the first of these attacks, on August 9, about 400 German aircraft took part in a series of raids. They succeeded in sinking only two small ships of 2,540 tons, though seven more—all coastal vessels—were damaged. Sixty German aircraft were shot down. Following this raid, coastal convoys were equipped with barrage balloons. The Germans also made more use of their motor torpedo boats, or E-boats, gaining another advantage from the possession of the Channel ports. On the same day that 400 aeroplanes sank only two

coasters, three other ships were sunk by two of these craft, which are larger and slower than their British counterparts.

There was further news of German commerce raiders during August. Early in the month the report was received that the disguised merchant ship " Narvik," mounting four guns on each broadside, had been engaged in the South Atlantic by the auxiliary cruiser H.M.S. " Alcantara," an ex-Royal Mail liner. The " Narvik " had sunk the cargo liners " King John " and " Davisian " a week or so earlier. The " Alcantara " scored a hit, but the " Narvik " escaped with the aid of smoke floats, after a lucky shot succeeded in reducing the speed of the British ship. Towards the end of the month the British liner " Turakina," of 9,691 tons, was shelled by an unknown raider in the Tasman Sea and a few days later the same fate befell the tanker " British Commander " in the Indian Ocean. Either of these losses may have been caused by the " Narvik."

Two more British armed merchant cruisers were sunk in August, both by torpedoes. They were the " Transylvania," of 16,923 tons gross, a former Anchor liner, and the " Dunvegan Castle " of 15,007 tons, a liner built for the Union-Castle intermediate passenger service to South Africa in 1936. They brought the losses of auxiliary cruisers

during the first year of the war to seven of 113,141 tons gross, all ex-passenger liners—one owned by the P. & O. Company, two by the Cunard White Star, two by the Anchor Line and one each by the Lamport & Holt and Union-Castle lines.

A transport, the " Mohamed Ali El-Kebir," 7,290 tons, formerly owned by the Pharaonic Mail S.S. Co., was also torpedoed in the Atlantic. The attack was made at dusk, and heavy seas were running. About 740 troops and crew were saved, but 120 were drowned, most of them soldiers who were in their bunks at the time of the explosion. It is a remarkable tribute to the Navy that during twelve months of war, when thousands of troops were convoyed, only three transports (including a small ship of 689 tons) were lost, apart from the evacuation of the B.E.F. from France, when all sorts and sizes of ships never intended for transport duties were employed.

At the end of a year of war, continually active at sea, the British Royal and Merchant Navies were stronger than at the start. The most vulnerable and most vital force of this island country, its shipping, was secure.

Despite Nazi claims, the Channel still remains an open road for British convoys, and the Port of London still carries on. Here, photographed from an escorting warship, is a convoy of small merchant ships proceeding up-Channel, unmolested either by U-boats or coast batteries.

OUR SEARCHLIGHT ON THE WAR

He Defied Hitler—and Died

ACCORDING to reports current in Batavia, Netherlands Indies, General Winkelman, former Commander-in-Chief of the Dutch Army, has died in Berlin. After four days of heroic resistance to the German invaders, with Rotterdam in ruins and many other cities helplessly awaiting a similar fate, it was General Winkelman who had the terrible duty to order the "Cease Fire" and to explain to the Dutch people why further resistance was unavailing. Later he defied the enemy in occupation by circularizing his troops with a statement exposing the German White Book on the invasion of the

General Winkelman, C.-in-C. of the Dutch Army, in a broadcast after the Army had laid down its arms, said : "The war was completely one-sided. To have gone on would have meant that still more innocent victims would have fallen."   *Photo, Planet News*

Low Countries. In July he was sent as a hostage to Berlin because he and his subordinates "had not observed the rules laid down for the demobilization of the Dutch forces." Now comes the report of his death from "heart failure."

Trinkets Dropped Over London

ITALIAN pilots who came over with the Nazi airmen on one of their raids made their presence known by showering trinkets over London—rings, medallions and other bits of imitation jewelery, all bearing inscriptions in Italian. One such ring, made of pewter, showed a head of Mussolini, chin thrust out, tin hat on head, and the words "Tireremo diritti," which can mean either "We shall forge ahead" or "We shall shoot straight." A medallion was inscribed with an exhortation addressed to Italians to preserve unity and follow their Leader. It is thought that this rather childish procedure is designed to encourage Italian fifth columnists in their activities, should the failure of the raiders weaken or undermine their resolution.

'Planes From Dutch East Indies

THE sum of five million guilders has recently been raised by the Netherlands Indies for the purchase of 40 Spitfires and 18 Lockheed Hudson bombers. Queen Wilhelmina offered them to King George "for the furtherance of our common cause, and as a tribute to the magnificent work of the R.A.F." The King, accepting the offer, said : "Such a noble tribute to the unremitting work of the R.A.F. both in attack

and defence will be a great encouragement to them." Following this gift came a cable to Lord Beaverbrook from the British Spitfire Fund at Batavia, remitting their first instalment of £5,000.

Fate of Tel Aviv Raiders

ON September 9 a number of Italian 'planes bombed Tel Aviv, the modern Jewish coastal town north of Jaffa. Bombs were dropped indiscriminately, far from any possible military objectives. Houses were destroyed, fires were started, and the resulting casualties were 111 killed and 151 severely wounded. But Nemesis overtook the raiders returning to their base, and four of them crashed mysteriously on or near the Turkish coast. One nose-dived into the sea and was seen no more. Two made good descents on the water and the wings of their aircraft kept them afloat for a few hours. Italian Red Cross 'planes picked up some members of their crews, but it was thought that six men were drowned. The pilot of the fourth raider had evidently been interrupted in his death-dealing task, for he jettisoned half his cargo of bombs into the sea before landing on the shore with one of his three engines burnt out.

Tate Gallery Bombed

ONE of London's buildings to suffer in the recent raids was the Tate Gallery, Millbank. A heavy bomb burst close by it, the blast shattering the entire glass roof and damaging the east wall. Mr. John Rothenstein and a staff of eight were in the building at the time, but none were hurt. Owing to the director's foresight not a single picture was exposed to injury, for during six days before and after the outbreak of war works of art to the number of 4,000 were distributed in safe places throughout the country, far from military objectives. The rest repose in the cellars of the Tate. Except for the east wall, no structural damage was done, and the new Duveen Gallery, apart from its glass roof, escaped unharmed.

The Civilians' V.C.

IN the course of his inspiring broadcast on September 23 H.M. the King announced the creation of "a new mark of honour for men and women in all walks of civilian life,"

to consist of the George Cross, ranking next to the Victoria Cross, and the George Medal for wider distribution. A statement issued later from Downing Street said that, although the immediate object of the institution of the George Cross is to reward acts of gallantry arising out of enemy action, it will also be awarded for other brave deeds. It will take the place of the Medal of the Order of the British Empire for Gallantry, the E.G.M., which will be absorbed. There will be a small Military Division of the Cross to permit of its award on occasion to members of the Fighting Services. The George Medal will rank with medals awarded for gallantry and distinguished conduct. Lord Chatfield is to act as chairman of the Committee on Gallantry Awards for Civil Defence.

Naming Our New Destroyers

THE naming of the fifty destroyers transferred from the U.S. Navy to our own, and now on their way to this country, has been under earnest consideration. One M.P. would have liked them to retain their original names ; another asked whether they might not be called after our Colonies. But the inspired suggestion of a woman—Miss Tania Long, American correspondent on the London staff of the New York "Herald Tribune"—has provided a happy solution to the problem. As Mr. Alexander, First Lord of the Admiralty, announced on September 17, they are to be the names of towns and villages common to both countries. The leading destroyer of the first flotilla is to be named Churchill, a place-name found in North Devon, in Somerset, in Worcestershire (twice), and in Oxfordshire, near Chipping Norton, as well as in Nevada and three other parts of the U.S.A., and in Canada. "By the happiest of coincidences," commented a "Manchester Guardian" leader writer, "there is also a living Churchill whose surname is not unassociated with the war effort of this country and therefore with the hopes of all those who care for liberty on the other side of the Atlantic." The other ships of this flotilla will be known as Caldwell, Cameron, Castleton, Chelsea, Chesterfield, Clare, Campbeltown. Names on a similar basis for the other flotillas will shortly be announced.

Two of the American destroyers which are being transferred by the United States to the British Navy are being given a final clean up before sailing for Canadian waters to be handed over to British crews. They still bear their original numbers, but their new names will be given at their final overhaul.   *Photo, Planet News*

I WAS THERE !

Eye Witness Stories of Episodes
and Adventures in the
Second Great War

We Were Roof-Watching in Oxford Street

When Oxford Street, London, was bombed during the night of September 17, three famous stores—John Lewis, D. H. Evans and Bourne & Hollingsworth—were severely damaged, but the employees and others in the shelters below the shops sustained no casualties. Members of the staffs here give their experiences.

A WATCHMAN in John Lewis's —the store which was most severely damaged—said:

I was on the seventh floor, on my way to relieve the other watch, when what I believed to be a torpedo-bomb came crashing into the side of the building near the roof.

There were two more bombs, high explosive, I think, and then came a shower of oil-bombs. By this time I was pretty stunned, having been knocked clean through a door.

It was a miracle that I was able to clamber to my feet. I don't know how I got down to the ground floor. I think I must have been blown by subsequent explosions.

Our first concern was for the people in the shelters below the building. By this time flames were spouting from the top storey.

There were more than a hundred people in one shelter and they got out fairly easily. There were several hundreds in the other shelters stretching right under the basement, and we got them away safely to a shelter in another store.

Our job was made very much easier by the splendid way the people behaved.

Sixteen-year-old Albert Bondfield, of Lewis's, was having his first spell as a roof-watcher on the night of the raid. He summed the situation up by saying: " We did have a night of it," and described his experiences as follows:

We drew lots for which watches we should do on the roof an hour at a spell, and when Mr. Dines and I drew the time we did I thought it was the perfect time, because the last bombs near us came down then.

While we were waiting for our relief, there was a scream. We threw ourselves against the sandbags, and then a bomb hit the building. Mr. Dines 'phoned down, and I climbed down the ladder on to the roof to make a more detailed report. I had just time to get against the sandbags when another bomb landed.

I 'phoned that down just as another whistled by. I put the 'phone down quick and clutched the sandbags. They came away in my hand from the blast.

Albert Bondfield, generally known as " Bonny," is here seen in his steel helmet cheerful and smiling after a " night of it," his first experience as a roof watcher.
Photo, Associated Press

Then we found the 'phone was dead. The fire was getting near, so we thought we might go. We climbed down the iron ladder and got into the building. The floor was all covered with broken bits. We went through a door that had been blown out and got to the basement.

A fireman had been hurt, so I went for the ambulance with Mr. Taylor and then fetched a doctor from Harley Street.

We gave the girls in the shelter a pick-a-back through the water from the automatic fire sprinkler. Some were more scared of being dropped in the wet than of the bombs.

Then we hunted round in the water and salvaged our things. . . . I wouldn't say I wasn't afraid. But we thought the first one was right on top of us. When it wasn't, we didn't worry any more.

Miss M. Holmes, an employee of D. H. Evans, said:

Some time ago the firm gave us the option of sleeping in our private shelter, and last night about sixty of us were in the shelter when the raid started.

We were all undressed and in our beds when we heard the first bomb dropping, but not one of us made a move.

Many of the girls started cracking jokes about what they would do to Hitler if their window displays were upset.

Later we were joined by girls from Lewis's. Then, at midnight, a warden came down and told us we would all have to go to another shelter because Lewis's had been hit.

We got out of bed and dressed. Then quite unhurriedly and calmly we made our way into Oxford Street. Not one of the girls showed the slightest sign of alarm, and we made our way to other shelters near by and settled down for the night.

An official of the firm said:

It was really wonderful to see how calm the girls were. They walked out although the raider was still overhead and the stores next door were on fire.—" *Evening News* " *and* " *Daily Express*."

The famous Oxford Street drapery stores of John Lewis are here seen after they had been struck by high-explosive and oil bombs on the night of September 17. A fierce fire raged for many hours and on the left of the photograph the jet of water from a fire engine can be seen still playing on the smouldering ruins the next day.
Photo, " News Chronicle "

During its long history Rhodes has been involved in many wars. Today it is an important Italian naval base, and on Sept. 5, as is
told below, it was bombed and shelled by the
British. Here is a view of the Old Town.
Photo, Fox

I Saw the Naval Attack on Rhodes

On September 5, 1940, a British battle squadron attacked the Italian
submarine base at Rhodes, while British sea bombers raided the air
bases on the island. The following dramatic impression of this
action came from the "Daily Express" reporter, Alan Moorehead,
who was aboard the flagship of the British squadron.

RHODES had never been raided before.
    It used to be a dreaming summer
island of roses and wine, of fisherfolk
and holiday-makers, peaceful monasteries
and pine forests.

Mussolini turned it into a secret hide-out
from which his submarines, bombers and
torpedo-boats have been waylaying neutral
and belligerent ships alike as they traded up
to Greece and the Dardanelles. On September 5 it was caught unawares.

We got what we had hoped for when,
the night before, sailors, airmen and gunners
received their final orders from the flagship.

An hour before sunrise the fleet was in
position lapped by a long easy swell. One
after another, over fifty miles of ocean,
silhouettes of the battleships and cruisers,
destroyers and aircraft carriers detached
themselves from the sea mist.

By a sickly yellow dawn light I could just
see our bombers sweeping off the deck from
the nearest aircraft carrier, each one heavily
laden with ochre-coloured bombs. The
leaders circled our flagship until the last
machines were clear. Then they wheeled
upward together in formation.

Away on the horizon the "Sydney" was
already in action. Spouting smoke columns
showed where her 6-inch shells were hitting.
Then Calato awoke to find its petrol dump
exploding and half a dozen aircraft blazing
on the ground and the barracks in flames.

At Maritza the green airfield of Tuat lies
under a monastery in a cup of hills. Five-
hundred-pound bombs thudded straight
through the two main hangars. Workshops
and barracks took fire and another petrol
tank went up with a roar.

As the 'planes left there was a cannonade
and minor explosions. Then a terrific blast
and a ribbon of black smoke reached far
across the sea within sight of the ships eighty
miles away.

Italian airmen, recovering from the first
shock, ran from the blazing hangars and
frantically took off. Before our bombers
could return three were brought down and
one more had to make a forced landing.
Our only other loss occurred when one of
our machines accidentally tipped off the
aircraft carrier. Its crew of three were
rescued by a destroyer.

While this was happening the rest of the
bombers came tearing back triumphantly
over the fleet and made their landings easily
despite a rising sea. One after another they
disappeared by hydraulic lifts into the
carrier.

By now it was daylight and the naval
gunners were ready for any Italian reply.
It came shortly after ten o'clock as we were
steaming away from the islands.

The first salvo of bombs seemed to come
clear out of the sun and it thrust up a green
wall of water away to the right of the flagship.

The fleet's guns opened with an aching,
shuddering crash. Shells seemed to be bursting everywhere right across to the horizon.

I was caught typing behind one of the
four-inch guns and the typewriter flew from
my hands among a pile of books that tumbled
on to the floor. I abandoned all hope of
getting back my favourite perch behind the
bridge.

Bits of shrapnel spattered the deck. I
ducked and ran for the 15-inch gun turrets.
From there I watched bomb bursts on the
waves and twice followed with my eye
enemy bombers skimming past at 7,000 feet.

Patiently, on the outskirts of the fight,
the British pursuit 'planes waited. Then
when the Italians passed beyond gun range
they leaped in.

They had two down in ten minutes and
three more as good as finished, casting bits
off as they fled. That makes fourteen
certainly destroyed and eight probably for
the day.

Even in the late afternoon we were getting
occasional warnings, but the fleet steamed
steadily into cover of the darkness.

We Were Survivors from the Children's Ship

"This deed will shock the world," said Mr. Geoffrey Shakespeare,
Under-Secretary for the Dominions, when news came of the torpedoing of the "City of Benares" with 90 child evacuees aboard, 83 of
whom were lost. Heroism and endurance could not prevent darkness,
storm and cold from taking their toll of child life.

THE German submarine's attack was
    launched without warning after
    dark, when the liner was 600 miles
from land. Most of the 90 evacuee children
were in their cots or bunks when the torpedo
struck the ship. Heavy seas swamped many
of the boats, greatly hampering rescue work.
The survivors, after nearly 24 hours adrift
in boats and on rafts in bitterly cold weather
and showers of hail, were picked up by a
warship.

A moving story of the disaster was told by
Mr. Arthur Wimperis, the playwright, who
was a passenger on the torpedoed liner. He
said: I was in my cabin reading at 10 o'clock
in the evening when there was a terrific
crash, and one realized instantly that the ship
had been torpedoed. I put on my raincoat,
took my pipe and tobacco and went to my
boat station.

Among other people there were 20 children
mustered or to be mustered there. They
came pouring up from their quarters on the
lower deck. One did one's best to comfort
them. We stood by until all the children
had been safely stowed in our lifeboat, and a
couple of sailors were in their positions.

Then we slid down a couple of ropes and
got in ourselves and the order was given to
lower away. We were up to our armpits in
water in the boat. One could see fitfully
by the light of flares dropped from the deck.
We were tethered to the liner by a wire
hawser. It was most difficult to loosen
them, but we got the boat free in time.

The liner was now listing right over us to
starboard and going down fast. We had
one oar, the only thing not pitched out of the
boat when she was lowered by the bows, and
a Canadian friend and I shoved away for
all we were worth against the side of the
ship.

Shortly after we had got the lifeboat
clear the ship went down. I thought it was
the finish, but actually I never felt the
suction at all.

There was a fair sea running and our
boat floated off. The other boats did the
same. This was at 10.30, when my watch
stopped. We were completely awash all through
the night and our great difficulty was to
try and hold the children above the water.
We looked like people sitting in the sea, and
it was the same with the other boats.

Night of Horror When 83 Children Died in Torpedoed Liner

Two women survivors at a **West Coast port** after being landed from the " City of Benares " which was torpedoed in the Atlantic in the evening of September 17.
Photos, Associated Press

People died of exposure at intervals all through the night. Among them was the padre in charge of the children. We wrapped the children in blankets, but the blankets got washed away. Everything was awash.

Mr. Wimperis continued : Morning came, and then we had our worst time, because as soon as it was light storms of hail and wind got up and the sea became tremendous. We were pretty hard put to it to keep the boat from being capsized, but we managed somehow. The boats had drifted apart. We were the last to be picked up, but one raft was picked up afterwards.

I am glad to say that as the warship came up we in our boat stood up singing " Rule, Britannia!" We managed to make quite a noise, and later the warship's crew asked which boat it was which arrived with the occupants singing. " Full marks," they said.

Of the ten grown-up escorts with the children only two were saved. One of these, Mrs. Towns, said :

I was awakened by the explosion and heard children screaming. I shouted out :

" It's all right." I managed to muster my 15 children and got them to the boat deck. Most of mine were girls, and we bundled them into a lifeboat.

We were many hours in that boat. It was a horrible nightmare which will live for ever in my memory. One by one 14 of my 15 children died.

In the lifeboat we had condensed milk and biscuits. The trouble was to get the milk into our mouths before it was ruined by salt water. Waves kept pounding over us.

A story of extraordinary good fortune was that told by Mrs. Bech, of London. She

rescue us. When we found the warship we all stood up and cheered and shouted for the good old British Navy.

Barbara Bech told her story too.

After I got into the lifeboat I collapsed, and when I came round I looked for Mother.

I was frantic when I couldn't find her. I sat in that lifeboat for hours, terrified that the rest of the family had been lost.

Then when the warship picked us up we all saw each other. My mother, my brother, and my sister were the first people taken aboard the warship.—(" *Daily Telegraph* " and " *Daily Mail* ")

Mr. Geoffrey Shakespeare (right), Undersecretary for the Dominions and Chairman of the Children's Overseas Reception Board, listens to the purser's story.
Photo, G.P.U.

was travelling to Montreal with her three children, Barbara, aged 14, Sonia, 11, and Derek, 9, and all were saved.

Mrs. Bech said :

I believe I was one of the last to leave the ship. I got two of my children, Sonia and Derek, on to a raft and Barbara into a lifeboat. Then I jumped overboard, and by some miracle landed on the raft which held Sonia and Derek.

Twice during the many hours we drifted in the terrible seas Sonia was washed off the raft. A man helped me pull her back to safety each time.

Hour after hour passed. I had almost given up all hope. I even said to my little girl, " Darling, I think we'll take off our lifebelts and go to sleep in the water."

But Sonia said, " Oh, no, mummy, don't do that yet. I'm sure we'll be picked up."

A few minutes later a warship came into sight and we were saved.

Sonia Bech said :

When we got on deck after the torpedo struck we were told to go up to the bow. From there we climbed down a ladder and we found a raft, and we all scrambled on it. For hours we were tossed about in the water. We were soaked to the skin. Seas were washing over us.

When we lay down our heads were in the water. When we tried to sit up we were blown down again by the wind. We were all very worried about Barbara.

Another vessel took us off the raft. Then we learned that a warship was coming to

These three children (centre) were among the few rescued from the ship. They are seen happily in port. Mrs. Lilian Towns, above, a Government escort, who was rescued.
Photo, Keystone

They Sought Sanctuary in the Tube

" ISN'T it wonderful," said the jolly-faced charwoman from Marylebone, " that for only three-ha'pence you get a whole night's sleep ? "

We were sitting, she and I, sixty feet below the ground in one of the passage-ways of the Edgware Road tube station. It was only seven o'clock in the evening, but already the place was full of people spreading rugs and cushions on the floor, unpacking thermos flasks and settling themselves down for the night. Since six o'clock they had been streaming down the stairs from street level. They were laden with bundles and baskets ; now they lined each side of the passages, stairs and platform—a regiment of men, women and children come to find safety from the fury of the blitzkreig which had wrecked many of their homes.

In this giant dormitory was an atmosphere of much cheerfulness. Of the hundreds who were there, most had been down on three or four consecutive nights, and were laughing, talking, and swapping stories and the day's news with all the friendliness and interest of life - long neighbours. Families were divided ; fathers, behind a cloud of tobacco smoke and a screen of upheld newspapers, lined one side of the passage, while mothers settled their children off to sleep along the other. More and more people came pouring down the stairway. Soon there were no gaps in the serried ranks of settlers parked on each side of the walls. Yet no one attempted to fill up the space in the centre.

I took a train and travelled down the line to Piccadilly Circus. The platforms at every station along the way were thick with recumbent bodies. Some were already asleep,

oblivious to the noise of trains and the chatter going on around them ; others were propped up against the walls, talking and reading and knitting, eating apples and sandwiches, careful to put the scraps carefully into baskets or paper bags.

I got in the train again and went on to the Elephant and Castle. The station was more crowded than any I had seen, for here were people who had suffered the full force of the Air Terror; yet the atmosphere was gay and more wide-awake than at any other station. For these were the lion-hearted Cockneys,

whose spirit can never be broken and who would rather stay awake and crack a joke than go to sleep and miss one.

A guard came down the platform telling them that the sirens had gone and the nightly " blitz " was on. A rousing cheer went up, and I wondered why, until the guard smilingly explained that no more trains would run from that platform, and so everyone was at liberty to " doss down " on the cushions of the train which stood alongside. It was a race between the men, for the women preferred to stay beside their sleeping children.

From the story by Miss Patricia Ward, reproduced here by courtesy of the " Evening Standard" ; the photographs, showing scenes above and below ground, when London's tubes are being used as air-raid shelters, are reproduced here by courtesy of the " News Chronicle."

Surface Shelters Have Saved Thousands of Lives

For one reason or another the Government has decided against constructing deep underground shelters, preferring surface shelters which, as the photographs in this page show, have stood up quite well against the bombs. Right is a street in South London which was heavily bombed; the occupants of the houses were in the shelters built in the middle of the street and so escaped unscathed.

Below is another proof that surface shelters stand against all but a direct hit. The scene is a South Coast town on which the pirates of the air have showered many bombs. The public shelter had 159 people in it; it was undamaged and the occupants were unharmed when a bomb fell near by and covered it with debris.

Photos, Keystone

Above is the damage caused by a huge bomb that fell in the east of London. In the background are people saved by their shelters. Left is a village shelter in the north-west area that stood intact amidst ruin.

Photos, L.N.A.

OUR DIARY OF THE WAR

TUESDAY, SEPTEMBER 17, 1940 *381st day*

On the Sea—British cargo steamer " Thornlea " reported sunk by U-boat in Atlantic. Irish steamer " Luimneach " reported sunk in Atlantic on September 4 by gunfire from U-boat. Survivors of British cargo boat " St. Agnes," torpedoed off Portuguese coast, landed at Lisbon.

During night enemy torpedoed "City of Benares " carrying 90 children to Canada ; of 306 persons lost, 83 were children.

In the Air—R.A.F. bombers made daylight raids on port of Ostend, shipping at Zeebrugge, convoy of barges off Dutch coast, and aerodrome of Ymuiden.

During night R.A.F. made heavy and sustained attacks on eight invasion ports, damaging shipping and military stores. Gun emplacements near Cap Gris Nez attacked. Other forces bombed important distribution centres in Rhineland.

Coastal Command aircraft attacked Cherbourg harbour, sinking two supply ships.

War against Italy—Enemy attempted to consolidate their position in and around Sidi Barrani, where R.A.F. heavily bombed them. Royal Navy bombarded coast road to Sollum.

South African Air Force raided Mogadishu aerodrome for sixth time and also Javello.

Home Front—During day enemy made small-scale raids. Bombs fell in South and S.E. England ; 15th cent. church wrecked. At Portsmouth church and several houses hit. Casualties in S.W. London. About 5.15 p.m. large waves of aircraft crossed Kent coast and were scattered by R.A.F. fighters.

During night raids on London incendiary bombs fell in S.E. district. High explosives fell in West End ; three large stores in Oxford Street hit.

Houses and buildings damaged in Merseyside town and number of casualties caused.

Twelve German aircraft destroyed. Three British fighters lost, but pilots of two safe.

WEDNESDAY, SEPTEMBER 18 *382nd day*

On the Sea—H.M. submarine " Narwhal " reported much overdue and presumed lost.

In the Air—Coastal Command aircraft attacked convoy off Borkum, registering direct hit on enemy destroyer. Others raided Cherbourg and aerodrome of De Kooy.

During night R.A.F. bombers launched fiercest attack yet made on invasion ports. Other forces attacked distribution centres of Osnabruck, Ehrang, Hamm, Mannheim, and Brussels.

War against Italy—R.A.F. launched highly successful attack on enemy bases in Dodecanese Islands. Continuous raids made against enemy from Western Desert.

Home Front—Enemy daylight activity mainly confined to S.E. area, few aircraft reaching London. Bombs fell chiefly near Thames estuary, causing damage to houses.

At night A.A. barrage in London was resumed. Raiders bombed at random suburbs all round London ; several heavy bombs fell in West End area. Casualties were heavy.

Severe raid on Merseyside. Bombs also fell on towns in Lancs, Midlands, North-East, South-West and Home Counties. Damage done, but casualties relatively few.

Enemy lost 48 aircraft. Twelve British fighters lost, but pilots of nine safe.

THURSDAY, SEPTEMBER 19 *383rd day*

In the Air—R.A.F. bombed communications in Germany, including Dortmund-Ems Canal. Fires and explosions were caused at Ostend and Flushing. Dunkirk docks attacked, and several aerodromes.

War against Italy—C.-in-C. Mediterranean reported that Benghazi was attacked by Fleet Air Arm on Sept. 16. One merchant ship set on fire, one destroyer probably sunk, and other ships damaged. Further attack made on 19th, three large ships being set on fire.

Home Front—Small-scale daylight raids took place on Britain. Bombs fell in E. London, on coastal towns in Essex and Sussex, and at one point in West of England.

Night raids were chiefly directed against London and suburbs. Factory set on fire in East End. Escape shaft on underground shelter in N. London hit.

Bombs fell in Lancs, Essex, Surrey, Berks, and Kent, in Midlands and South-West.

Germany lost five aircraft ; Britain none.

FRIDAY, SEPTEMBER 20 *384th day*

On the Sea—Admiralty announced that H.M. submarine " Sturgeon " had sunk 10,000-ton enemy transport off northern point of Denmark on September 2.

THE POETS & THE WAR
XXXIII
WHEN THE STORY IS TOLD . . .
By G. M. Chaplin

(Written in a Fire Station Watchroom during a raid)

When in the after years the tale is told
Of these strange days while Britain stands
    at bay,
Holding the pass—as, at Thermopylae,
Leonidas—then write the names in gold,
Along with Dunkirk, Narvik, and the rest
Of Bermondsey, Whitechapel, Shoreditch,
    Bow,
Wapping and Rotherhithe ; who stood
    the test
Of total war, nor flinched beneath the
    blow.

The people of the little streets stood firm—
And Britain stands. Remember this,
    Mayfair,
Whitehall and City, when at last the term
Is set to battle ; think then of the share
So bravely borne, our freedom to defend,
By front line folk of Borough and East
    End.

              —Daily Telegraph

In the Air—R.A.F. again made concentrated attacks on invasion ports along French, Belgian and Dutch coasts.

Dortmund-Ems Canal again bombed. Supply train travelling towards Munster attacked, and bombs dropped on yards at Hamm, Ehrang, Krefeld, Mannheim and Soest.

Coastal Command aircraft scored direct hits on two supply ships off Dutch coast

War against Italy—R.A.F. bombed aerodrome at Menastir, Western Desert, and damaged motor transport at Sidi Barrani. In East Africa Diredawa and Berbera successfully bombed, as was Gura aerodrome.

Home Front—Large force of raiders crossed S.E. coast in morning, but were driven back by our fighters before reaching London area. Bombs fell in Brighton, resulting in damage and casualties.

During night gliding raider dived and dropped two bombs in Central London. Incendiaries fell in S.E. London.

Four German aircraft shot down. Britain lost seven fighters, but pilots of three safe.

SATURDAY, SEPTEMBER 21 *385th day*

In the Air—R.A.F. continued attacks by both day and night on invasion bases in Channel ports.

Aircraft of Coastal Command bombed convoy of twelve merchant ships near Boulogne. Large supply ship south of Borkum and two smaller ships near Dutch island of Ameland were successfully attacked.

War against Italy—R.A.F. bombed aerodrome and troop positions at Sidi Barrani

and made reconnaissance flights over enemy territory in Western Desert. S. African Air Force attacked Birkas.

Enemy made ineffectual raid on Alexandria. Haifa was raided, resulting in damage and casualties.

Home Front—During day enemy activities were limited to isolated operations in S.E. England by aircraft flying singly or in small numbers. Industrial building hit in E. London, causing casualties. Bombs fell in Surrey, Sussex and Essex, but little damage and few casualties were reported.

In evening 60 to 70 German aircraft flew from Thames Estuary towards London, but were driven off after numerous combats with our fighters. During night incendiary bombs fell on N.W. and S.W. districts of London, causing many small fires. Another hospital in Central area hit. Church in S.E. London destroyed.

Town in N.W. England attacked, causing damage to houses. Damage and casualties resulted from bombs in 20 towns and villages in S.E. outside London area.

Enemy lost two aircraft, Britain none.

SUNDAY, SEPTEMBER 22 *386th day*

On the Sea—Admiralty announced that H.M. sloop " Dundee " had been sunk by U-boat.

In the Air—R.A.F. carried out widespread operations in Germany, Holland, Belgium and France. Aluminium works at Lauta, north-east of Dresden, bombed, as were railways in this area.

Strong forces of bombers attacked docks harbours and shipping at Channel ports.

War against Italy—British naval forces attacked enemy positions in Sidi Barrani area. These were also bombed by R.A.F., as was Menastir aerodrome. Enemy attacked Malta, damaging ten houses in a village.

Home Front—During day isolated aircraft crossed E. and S.E. coasts. Bombs fell in country districts in East Anglia, Hants, Kent, two towns in Sussex and in N.W. and S.E. districts of London.

During night relays of single aircraft dropped bombs over widely scattered areas in London, damaging houses and industrial premises and causing casualties.

Bombs also fell on towns in S.E. England. Germany lost one aircraft, Britain none.

MONDAY, SEPTEMBER 23 *387th day*

In the Air—Throughout night R.A.F. heavily bombarded military objectives in and around Berlin, including Rangsdorf railway station, West and Wilmersdorf power stations, and two gas works.

Other forces bombed aircraft works at Wismar, lock gates on Kiel Canal, shipyards and docks at Hamburg and elsewhere, goods yards, railway communications and several aerodromes. Channel invasion ports again vigorously attacked.

War Against Italy—R.A.F. again attacked Mena tir aerodrome. Two raids made on Tobruk harbour.

Home Front—H.M. the King announced creation of new honours for civilians—the George Cross and the George Medal.

During day British fighters engaged large formations of enemy aircraft over Kent and Essex. Deliberate attacks made on Sussex seaside towns, particularly Eastbourne.

Night bombing over London again took place. Raiders flew over N.W. suburb and also over S. London. Bombs fell on outlying suburbs to South and East and in one district of Central London.

Enemy aircraft also reported over S.W. S.E., N.W. England, and Wales.

Nazis lost 11 aircraft. Britain also lost 11, but pilots of seven safe.

Africa—General de Gaulle, with a Free French Force, and accompanied by a British Naval Squadron, arrived off Dakar. Governor rejected ultimatum, and opened fire which was returned by British warships.

LONDON'S GREAT HIGHWAY SCARRED BUT BUSY AS EVER

Oxford Street, one of London's greatest shopping centres, along the north side of which are half a dozen famous stores, was bombed on Sept. 17 and 18. Very considerable damage was done, but Oxford Street carried on, and so did those who shop there. Here is Oxford Circus a day or two later, with Peter Robinson's famous shop on the left. The "alert" may sound again at any moment, but no one worries about that.

Photo, Keystone

'All the Brigands Are in One Camp'

In these words a Canadian newspaper, " The Toronto Globe and Mail," summed up
the Berlin Pact of September 27, 1940, concluded between Germany, Italy, and Japan.
The " tie-up " of the gangsters was indeed the outstanding feature of the Pact which,
as Mr. Cordell Hull, U.S.A. Secretary of State, said does not substantially alter the
situation already existing.

I N Berlin on September 27 Germany, Italy,
and Japan concluded a military, political
and economic Pact. It was signed in
the Ambassadors' Hall at the Chancellery
by von Ribbentrop, Count Ciano, Foreign
Ministers of the Axis Powers, and M. Kurusu,
Japanese Ambassador in Berlin, and after
the signature Herr Hitler made a solemn
entry into the hall and formally greeted the
plenipotentiaries. Statements were then
read in which it was declared that the
Governments of Germany, Italy, and Japan,
" recognizing that as a condition precedent
to any lasting peace all nations of the world
should be given each his own proper place,"
had decided to stand by and cooperate with
one another in Eastern Asia and in Europe,
so as to establish and maintain " a new
order of things calculated to promote mutual
prosperity and the welfare of the peoples concerned." The Pact's terms were then revealed:

1. Japan recognizes and respects the leadership of Germany and Italy in the establishment of
a new order in Europe.
2. Germany and Italy recognize and respect
the leadership of Japan in the establishment of a
new order in East Asia.
3. Germany, Italy, and Japan agree to cooperate in their efforts on the aforesaid lines.
They further undertake to assist one another
w.th all political, economic and military means
when one of the three contracting parties is
attacked by a Power at present not involved in
the European war or in the Sino-Japanese conflict.
4. With a view to implementing the present
Pact, joint technical commissions, the members
of which are to be appointed by Germany, Italy,
and Japan, will meet without delay.
5. Germany, Italy, and Japan affirm that the
terms do not in any way affect the political status
which exists at present as between each of the
three contracting parties and Soviet Russia.
6. The present Pact shall come into effect
immediately upon signature, and shall remain in
force 10 years from the date of its coming into
force. In due time before the expiration of the

said term the high contracting parties shall, at
the request of any of them, enter into negotiations
for its renewal.

When the document had been signed von
Ribbentrop read a long statement on behalf
of the Government of the Reich. He began
as usual with a reference to the " injustices
of the Treaty of Versailles," and spoke of
the " extraordinary modesty " which characterized the demands put forward by
Germany, who " felt herself entitled to a

When the Berlin Pact between Germany, Italy, and Japan was signed on September 27, the Japanese
signatory was M. Kurusu, Japan's Ambassador in Berlin. Above we see him (second from the right)
with a number of German notabilities on the occasion of an exhibition in Berlin designed to
further Japanese-German friendship.   *Photo, E.N.A.*

share of the good things of this earth. . . ."
The National Socialist Government, he
went on, was resolved in all circumstances to
assure to the German people their rights of
existence within a suitable living space at a
time when other nat-
ions had seen fit to
claim whole continents
for themselves; and
this determination co-
incided with that of
other nations, which,
like Germany, had been
denied their rightful
place in the world.

" The tripartite Pact,"
he went on, " which I
have just signed on behalf
of the Fuehrer, together
with the plenipotentiaries
of Italy and Japan, con-
stitutes a solemn affirm-
ation of partnership be-
tween Germany, Italy,
and Japan in a changing
world. The purpose of the
Pact is to secure a new
order of things in those
parts of Europe at present
engaged in war and to
establish that new order
under the common
leadership of Germany
and Italy: it secures also a
new order in Greater Asia
under the leadership of
Japan. The pact is not
only based on friendship
but on a community of
interests of three nations
striving for the same
social ideals."

Later he said that the Pact which had just
been signed was a " military alliance between
three of the mightiest States of the world,"
and served the cause of a just order of things,
both in Europe and in Greater Asia. Other
States would be welcomed into the bloc if any
desired to make its own contribution to the
restoration of peace, but any State which
" endeavours to interfere in the final phase
of the solution of problems in Europe and
the Far East by attacking one of the three

Powers signatory to the pact will have to
meet the combined strengths of three nations,
numbering 250,000,000 inhabitants. . . ."

In the Axis countries and in Japan it
seems to have been thought that the new
Pact would appear to be as earthshaking as
the Nazi-Soviet Pact of August 1939. But
those who thought on these lines were disappointed. For long it had been recognized
that Japan was practically a Fascist State;
it was reasonable to suppose, then, that at a
convenient moment she would put on a firmer
footing the understanding which existed.

Already, indeed, she had shown signs of a
determination to exploit to the full the
situation which had arisen in Eastern Asia,
following the collapse of Northern Europe
and the onslaught on Britain. Before June
was out the Japanese were bringing pressure
to bear on the French administration in
Indo-China both with a view to stopping the
flow of war material to China through Indo-
Chinese ports, and also securing a permanent
footing in France's great Oriental colony.
Towards the end of September both these
ends had been achieved. By an agreement
concluded at Hanoi, the capital of French
Indo-China, on September 22 Japan was
granted the right to land 6,000 troops in
Indo-China, to establish three air bases in
Tongking, to station some troops in Hai-
phong, and also to send troops across Indo-
China to attack the Chinese in Yunnan. At
the same time, Japanese emissaries played
their part in stirring up Thailand, or Siam,
to make demands on Indo-China for the

Time Bomb or Dud?
From the cartoon by Illingworth in the " Daily Mail"

Germany Italy and Japan Make a Trio In Berlin

In April 1940 the Japanese Air Force celebrated the fortieth year of its existence, and in honour of the event a film was made glorifying its murderous exploits over China. Above, 120 Japanese 'planes are making a special flight for the benefit of the cameraman.

restitution of certain territories which, so it was claimed, were once part of the Siamese kingdom; while others were busy in the Dutch East Indies, fomenting unrest.

Indo-China, the Netherlands Indies, Malaya, the Philippines, Hong-Kong and Singapore, and the northern parts of Australia —all these are included in what the Japanese hot-heads have come to regard as their " living space." But it cannot be fully realized until Britain, too, has been driven from the Pacific—and behind Britain stands

the United States, for it is inconceivable that America would suffer the Pacific to become a Japanese lake. Here it is that the Berlin Pact comes into the picture, inasmuch as it was obviously designed to frighten America. As plainly as possible within the bounds of diplomatic language, " Uncle Sam " was told that if he chose to enter the war on the side of Britain, then America would be attacked by Germany, Italy, and Japan.

So far from being intimidated, the U.S.A. regarded the Pact as a challenge, and on every hand there were demands that stronger action should be taken against the aggressors. Nor was there the slightest suggestion—as the Axis plotters no doubt intended—that America's war effort should be diverted to her own needs in view of the threat against her Pacific seaboard ; rather, the belief was intensified that Britain was fighting America's war and that it was up to America to give her all the assistance in her power.

At first sight it would seem that if there is any gainer from the Pact it is Germany and Italy, rather than Japan, who in the event of a war in the Pacific could expect to receive little or no help from her allies, while she would be exposed to attack by the American and British fleets in the Near East. But it must be admitted that one of her potential enemies is likely to be immobilized.

Although Clause Five of the Pact carefully preserves the status quo as regards the signatories and Soviet Russia, there can be little doubt that Clause Three has its application not only to the U.S.A. but to Soviet Russia. Japan need not fear an attack by her Russian neighbour, for Russia is given to understand that if she attacks Japan, then Japan's allies in Europe will attack her on the west.

Like the Nazis, the Japanese have made liberal use of the camera as an instrument of propaganda, and in the two lower photographs in this page we have illustrations of it—not perhaps very effective ones. They were taken in the course of operations against the Chinese ; centre, Japanese troops " mopping up " a Chinese position in Hupeh Province, and, below, a Japanese warship cooperating with troops landing in front of the Chinese firing line.

Photos, Domei News Agency

Singapore—Britain's Strong Point in the East

With Japan's formal adhesion to the Axis Powers, Germany and Italy, Singapore, Britain's great naval base in the Far East, assumes the very greatest importance. Below we tell something of its setting in time and place.

LYING off the very tip of the finger-like mainland of Malaya is the little island—it is only 27 miles by 14— of Singapore. It is at the cross-roads of south-eastern Asia, and the sea traffic of half the world converges on its quays. As great cities go it is a youngster, for in 1819 when Sir Stamford Raffles obtained the grant of the island from the Sultan of Johore it was a tropical jungle inhabited only by a few miserable fisherfolk. For many years it has been one of the world's great ports, but since 1923 it has developed into something more : today it is Britain's stronghold at the gateway of

and 75 feet deep, and can lift a 50,000-ton battleship. The dock was built on the Tyne in the Wallsend yards of Messrs. Swan, Hunter and Wigham Richardson, Ltd., and was towed to Singapore in two sections in 1928, the voyage of 8,500 miles taking four months ; it was a tight squeeze going through the Suez Canal ! Authorized by the British Government in 1923, cancelled by the Labour Government in the following year, and again authorized in 1930, the Singapore Base has cost more than £9,000,000 ; and in its construction 6,000,000 cubic yards of earth were excavated in moving the hills which happened

infantry battalions. There is also the Straits Settlements Volunteer Force, consisting of a battery of artillery and four battalions of infantry, together with signal sections and engineers.

Close to Singapore city is the civil airport, one of the most important on the route from Britain to Australia ; and on the north side of the island, a few miles to the east of the naval base, is the headquarters of the R.A.F. Far East Command, which before the war consisted of two bomber and two reconnaissance squadrons, together with an anti-aircraft cooperation unit.

Some years ago it was stated that the total Service population of Singapore—the military garrison and the men of the naval base and air force—numbered with their dependants some 12,000 persons, but there is no doubt that of recent months this number has been greatly added to. So successful have been the sanitary and anti-malaria precautions that Singapore, if not exactly a health resort, is a garrison station with quite a good health record.

Singapore city has a front of handsome clubs and grand hotels behind which are stifling narrow streets and close-packed blocks of native dwellings, where hundreds of thousands of coloured folk pass their lives in huddled squalor.

Cosmopolis of the Orient

Compared with, say, Penang, Singapore is drab and colourless enough ; all its buildings are modern, and there is none of the charm of the immemorial East. Yet the human scene is one of endless fascination. Chinese merchants, sedate, bespectacled, leaning back in rich cars ; Chinese rickshaw boys in blue dungarees and with perspiring faces beneath their peaked straw hats ; bearded Sikh policemen directing the varied traffic, Indian coolies, lithe and unsmiling ; Malay artisans and Japanese shop-keepers, islanders from the Dutch Indies, Eurasians of indefinite breed—all these mingle and go their ways with that silent concentration, that secret intensity of purpose, which is so typical of the East. As for the Europeans, they, too, are largely of international stock, though, of course, the British greatly predominate— merchants and civil servants, soldiers, sailors, and airmen, mechanics and tourists. For them—the European community, for the British officials, the staffs and garrison—life may be pleasant enough, for the clubs are models of their kind, and somewhere in the neighbourhood are a golf course, a cricket ground, a racecourse, and a polo field.

But of late months Singapore has had little time or inclination for these distractions of a peacetime existence. Although prior to Japan's adhesion to the Axis the war seemed very far away, the defence works have been extended, local volunteer services have been embodied, and numerous exercises have been performed in order to familiarize them with their wartime duties of mine-sweeping, local patrols, and so on. Last summer the war seemed to come quite near when the Governor announced that further defence works were being put in hand which would necessitate the removal of some of the shark-proof bathing centres established on the south coast and their replacement by barbed-wire entanglements.

Now the foresight of those who proposed and planned the Singapore Base has been fully justified. Singapore stands out against the new menace in the Orient as the base for Britain's, and perhaps America's, fleets, and as the outlying fortress of India's defence.

Japanese aggression in the Far East and the strengthening of the Berlin-Rome-Tokyo Axis have made Singapore, Britain's great Naval base in the Pacific, more important than ever. It is the scene of great aerial activity, and here Indian troops from the Punjab are practising with A.A. guns at sleeve targets.

Photo, Keystone

the Orient, her great naval base in the Far East, an island fortress, one of the most strongly defended in the world.

Singapore city is on the south coast of the island, and with its population of over half a million—British and Dutch and Eurasian, Chinese and Indian, Malay and Japanese— is a veritable cosmopolis. The naval base is on the opposite side of the island, looking across the Straits to the mainland of Johore. It was officially inaugurated on February 14, 1938, by Sir Shenton Thomas, Governor of the Straits Settlements, when he opened the new graving dock. This is 1,000 feet long and 130 feet wide, surrounded by concrete walls and deep enough to take any ship afloat. Another remarkable feature of the Base is the floating dock, the third largest of its kind in the world ; it is 853 feet long, 172 feet wide,

to be in the way, and 8,000,000 cubic yards of earth were used to fill up the swamps which covered the rest of the site.

It need hardly be said that the base is most strongly defended by land, sea, and air. At Changi, at the eastern entrance of the Straits of Johore, powerful coast batteries have been mounted, and there are many other batteries elsewhere in the island. No details of the defences have been officially published, but it has been often stated that guns of 15-inch and even 18-inch calibre have been mounted in the forts. There is also a considerable garrison, which numbered before the war some 7,000 of all ranks, and comprised two regiments of heavy artillery and one of anti-aircraft artillery, four fortress companies of the Royal Engineers and one of Royal Signals, and three British, one Indian, and one Malay

This Is the War of the Unknown Warriors

For the first time in the history of Britain—at least since the days of the Civil War—war
is being fought on the very doorsteps or rather over the very roofs of the British people.
How magnificently they, "the 'Unknown Warriors' of this war," as Mr. Churchill
describes them, have met the challenge, stood the strain, is told here.

"THE front line runs through the factories." This was one of the diamond phrases in which the brilliant oratory of Mr. Churchill has crystallized the war since he acceded to the Premiership on May 10

and masses. Ten thousand civilian casualties against three or four hundred military since the "blitzkrieg" began is the evidence.

It is even possible to put a date to the day when it became a people's war. It was on

of the much discussed poster put out by the previous Government—"Your Courage, Your Cheerfulness, Your Resolution, will bring us victory"—became for the first time apparent. No longer was this a private fight run by the Gorts and Ironsides, Gamelins, Chamberlains and Daladiers; everyone could join in—and everyone did.

And rightly is this burden borne by the people. For while Lord Haw-Haw has nightly proclaimed for a year that the war was wished upon the peaceful British public by their bellicose "ruling circles," the exact contrary is the truth. It was not so much Chamberlain, the Conservative, who declared war, as Greenwood, the Socialist, whose magnificent words, when he "spoke for England" in the Commons on Sept. 2, 1939, rang with the authentic tones of the people. It was not the "appeasing" ruling circles but the exasperated working classes who decided that a time had come to call a halt to Hitler.

It is just, then, that the people, who called for the war, should have to wage it and to bear its brunt. No one can call "Coward" to Britons. The townsfolk of Dover, daily bombed and shelled, buy themselves tin hats and go out to the shops with a smile; the gradely lads of Hull, of Middlesbrough, of Newcastle and all the north-east, whose nightly terrors for months Londoners are now only beginning to appreciate, carry on with that famous "grim determination" which some orators have praised without knowing what it means. The slow-thinking men and women of Somerset and the braw folk of Aberdeen have alike come to regard nightly bombings, with the destruction of their homes, as part of their ordinary life.

Such are the heroes and heroines of *this* war—the nameless multitude for whom there

The children of the East End have stood up bravely to bombing and the next morning are at play as usual. Here are some of them lending a hand with clearing up. A great find is a piece of shrapnel, and such relics of an air raid are greatly prized—the bigger the better.
Photo, Planet News

last. He might have added that the front line also runs through the homes—through every suburban villa, every slum tenement, every country mansion, in Great Britain. For this is a People's War: no affair of clashing armies or remote conflicts by sea, but an all-in wrestling bout of the millions

that May 10, when the leadership of the British people was taken over by the one man great enough for the task, and big enough to jettison party interests and "bring Labour in." On that day the complacent murmur of the drones was exchanged for the angry buzz of the workers. On that day the truth

Many workers in the City of London have arrived within walking distance of their offices only to find that the usual ways of approach are blocked. Here, steel-helmeted policemen are directing them by a safe way, but even the walking is made difficult by a network of hosepipes.
Photo, Central Press

Courage and Cockney Humour Go Well Together

is no V.C. or D.F.C. Every air raid borne by them without giving way to fright or defeatism is a defeat for the enemy. For an "air war" is above all a war of nerves. The prime military objective is the civilian morale; whichever side cracks first is the vanquished, whichever holds out against the bombs the victor. However great its army, however potent its air force and navy, a nation is defeated if its people lose heart; there is every reason to hope that the German nation is already losing heart, but none to suppose that the British will fail first.

Goebbels likes to imagine Britons "cowering in their shelters" while the glorious Luftwaffe rains indiscriminate fire and explosive upon our island. His mental pictures must be inspired by what he sees in Germany, for certainly none of his spies could report having glimpsed any such thing here. We have read how the Berliners shake their fists and impotently curse the R.A.F. In London shelters community singing is the order of the day—or rather night. The Cockney, armoured with humour, bears the long hours with what almost approaches grim amusement, and the spirit of the Old Contemptibles lives on in every basement, cellar and "Anderson" in the old city. Toiling 12 hours or more by day on essential work, sleeping perhaps less than 4 or 5 hours by night—they are tough, these Britons; their pride will not be broken.

Praise, too, the womenfolk of this island. Young London typists fight traffic chaos for hours to reach offices that may have been demolished overnight. In their flats and houses suburban wives and mothers struggle with the problems of rationing, cooking without gas, managing the children when the sirens go, making the same housekeeping allowance cover a 25 per cent increase in the cost of living — fighting the bogey of worry with every mental weapon they can call to their aid. No one who witnessed it will ever forget the courage of the mothers of London's East End during those terrible days and nights of the second week of September. Their houses were not palaces, their belongings few, but they spelt home to them. Their worlds came crashing round their ears on those awful nights, but, with grim faces red with crying but alive with righteous anger, they marched on—soldiers all.

A young man named Michael Foot, one of a famous line of

workers and speakers for freedom, has become, in the last few months, the spokesman of the people, the articulate voice in which the murmurings of the multi-

Several blocks of "luxury" flats in the West End which stood wholly or partly empty have been taken over to house those from less fortunate districts who have been rendered homeless. Here we see old people being taken to their new quarters with a few of their belongings.

tude are heard. He is, oddly enough, the leader writer of a Conservative journal, the "Evening Standard"—a fact which demonstrates how the classes of Britain have become, like Britain and the U.S.A., in Mr. Churchill's phrase, "mixed up together." Thus Michael Foot wrote on Friday, September 13, a day of terror in London:

The story of the East End of London is a terrible, tremendous story: a story of anger, hate, love, defiance; a story of whole streets where you can see women's eyes red with tears, but women's hearts overflowing with kindness towards their neighbours . . . . .

A woman sits on a rickety chair in the middle of a shattered row of dolls' houses, her family about her. She waves her hand at the pile of ruin which was once her own home and her neighbours'. "We don't care about all this stuff," she says, "our only feeling is for the lives of our folk." "How do you like this sort of life?" says a passerby. "Well," she replies, "it's nice and airy." She ties up in a paper bundle the last remnant of her possessions in this world. She hoists her child into her arms. She is off in search of shelter for the night. She is the mother who in "The Grapes of Wrath" stood up at the end after suffering afflictions beyond those of Job and boasted, "You can't lick the people." . . .

That is why the defection of France can never be repeated here. French courage rested on the Maginot Line; when it was overturned, the rulers failed the masses. British courage rests on no system of defence, not even on the sea; it is rooted in the hearts of the people. Our rulers dare not fail us. Out of the colossal defeat of Flanders we plucked the glorious victory of Dunkirk. Today, out of the raging hell of the Dunkirk of Dockland, rises the prideful shout of the ordinary Briton: "You can't lick the people!"

"Bombs or no bombs" the work must be done is evidently the conviction of this stouthearted Englishwoman. The day after the raid of September 21 was washing-day, and despite the destruction around the usual routine went on.

Photos, L.N.A.

Allies of Britain in the War—Dutch Airmen

WHEN Holland was invaded by the Germans many units of the Royal Dutch Naval Air Service flew to this country and at once began cooperation with the British Coastal Command on patrol work. In the messes they share with the R.A.F. they are very popular and many of them speak excellent English, while in their work they are ideal allies and trusted friends. In addition to escorting convoys the Dutch airmen have attacked several U-boats in the Atlantic, and they have a fine record of air combats in which they have shown themselves superior to the Nazis. Many of the pilots are using the 'planes in which they flew to Britain. They are Fokker T 8 W float 'planes, fitted with Wright-Whirlwind engines. The Fokker aeroplanes designed by the famous Dutch engineer were used by Germans in the last war and had a great reputation.

The Royal Dutch Air Force, now in Britain, has taken a valuable part in convoy patrols. Above, Dutch 'planes are flying down the coast to meet a convoy. Right is one of the gunners who have already accounted for several Nazi aircraft.

The Commander of a Dutch squadron gives final instructions to his pilots before starting off. The uniforms are the same as those of the British Navy, with distinguishing badges.

Photos, British Official : Crown Copyright

Triumphs of Fighter & Gunner in a Week's Air War

The story of the air battles over London and air- and sea-ports for the period September 25 to 30 reveals a continuing success in the fight against murderous Nazi attacks on civil life. The land mine, utterly useless for military purposes, was repeatedly employed.

ONCE again, in the story of the air battle for London and our Southern air-ports, the salient features were (1) the outstanding success of our fighter pilots, and (2) the triumph of our A.A. barrage. When Nazi aircraft have managed to evade our defenders the civilian casualties have been grievous, both by day and by night ; but save for some not important interruption of our transport network the enemy achieved little of military value.

Four-engined bombers have been used in night raids and have been tried out by day, but during daylight operations these unwieldy monsters have needed such a big escort of fighters that there would seem to be little advantage in their use. Another try-out was to drop " mines " on land objectives ; here the aim seems to be the use of a very large body of explosive, enclosed in a case of aluminium alloy, designed to explode on light contact without penetration of the surface. It has been a long-standing scheme of the Nazis to develop aerial bombs for use against " personnel "—in other words, for the murder of civilians and the destruction of their dwellings. The " land mine " is useless for real military purposes. Its rate of fall is slowed down so that it makes a sort of gliding flight, and when it detonates it spreads destruction and death over an area far wider than that affected by even a heavy bomb of the ordinary sort.

The work of our fighter pilots has been consistently splendid : to give a few examples, on September 25 the score was 26 for 4 ; September 26, 31 for 8 ; September 27, 133 for 34. The wonderful achievement of Friday, September 27, brought from the Premier a well-deserved message of congratulation.

In raids on London on Wednesday, September 25, the Nazis returned to the use of large bomber formations—for the first time since the colossal defeat of ten days previously, when they lost in all at least 232 aircraft. Twenty-six of their machines were shot down—twenty between Bristol and the English Channel—and nearly two-thirds were bombers. The Luftwaffe adopted a tight formation of bombers in an attempt to baffle

Coastal towns from Hastings to Southampton were raided late in the afternoon on Thursday, September 26. Two bomber formations approached the Isle of Wight at 4 o'clock ; in thirty minutes they lost 31 aircraft. A German communiqué claimed that the Spitfire works at Southampton were bombed. In one of two London alarms a Nazi airman who had baled out came down over a S.W. suburb of the capital. In the usual nightly attack incendiaries and high explosive bombs fell in the East End and the West and in Northern suburbs.

The tale of Nazi losses was carried well over the thousand mark on Friday, when 133 were shot down. One of the series of

The countryside of Kent and Sussex has been littered with crashed Nazi aeroplanes during the past months. London was later in making their acquaintance, and many people saw tangible proof of the success of the R.A.F. for the first time in the last week in September, when the remains of a Messerschmitt were taken through Parliament Square on a lorry.

On September 25 nearly 150 people were sheltering in the crypt of a parish church in South-east London, when it was severely damaged by a bomb dropped by the night raiders. All the occupants were got out unhurt by A.R.P. workers.

Photos, Fox and Keystone

our Hurricanes and Spitfires, about forty Junkers 88 each in two wedges, and groups of Dornier and Heinkel bombers in similar formations. Our pilots picked off one bomber after another, despite their escort.

A dead set was made on Bristol, which had its heaviest raid since the beginning of the war. There were two attacks, and in the second at least fifty Nazis were engaged, in two formations. Over Bournemouth, too, there were fierce dog fights. A limping Dornier bomber flew low over a South-eastern coastal town and turned its machine-guns on the streets, in a last desperate attempt to do its worst before it fell into the sea, its crew doubtless presuming on the gentlemanly treatment they would receive from our people, despite the dastardly outrage.

In Wednesday night's raids on London some of the enemy machines endeavoured to get through our defences from the North, with scant success. Others attacked from the South-east, but there again were foiled by the barrage. Heavier guns and shells of a new kind appeared to be in use, and also some strange artillery of smaller calibre.

daylight battles in the London area was watched by the King and Queen while on a tour of bombed areas. Three waves of Nazi raiders made for London and S.E. England, while a fourth attacked Bristol. Only thirty out of 180 which crossed the Kent coast just before nine in the morning reached London, all the rest being frustrated by our fighters and A.A. gunners. Those that did get through were mostly fighter-bombers with a limited power of offensive. All round the outer fringe of the Metropolitan area they were shot down. South-western suburbs suffered most in the bombing which took place, and workers in a factory shelter were killed and injured ; what looked like a deliberate attack was made also on a residential area in the same quarter. Deaths were caused by bombs that fell in a South London district that had previously suffered. At East Grinstead a Nazi four-engined bomber was shot down by our fighters.

Before the sirens sounded in the London area on Friday evening, September 27, there had been bursts of A.A. gunfire, and when raiders approached the Central area a very

No Thanks to the Nazis that They Escaped Death

Unexpected disasters and miraculous escapes have occurred during the night bombing of London. Left are a London woman and her daughter who escaped by lying under the kitchen table on which a mass of debris fell, only the mother sustaining a slight injury to her head. Right, a man, who was pinned in the house for nearly twenty hours by a beam which held him by the ankle, is being removed by A.R.P. workers. The only injury he sustained was to his ankle.

Photos, " Daily Mirror," Associated Press and Fox

The young soldier, right, is Gunner W. Stafford, R.A., whose twenty-one year old wife and his nineteen months' old son were trapped in an Anderson shelter, one of five which, as the photograph above shows, were buried when a bomb fell near them. By heroic efforts he saved both.

Londoners Lose Homes But Not Their Hearts

Here is the usual scene at one of the shelters under big blocks of London offices that are now being opened at night as well as in the day. The one in question is 8 ft. below the surface. With prams parked, mothers and children wait until the office workers leave.

Photo, Fox

GERMAN & BRITISH AIRCRAFT LOSSES

German to April 30, 1940

Total announced and estimated—West Front, North Sea, Britain, Scandinavia ... 350

	German	British
May	1,990	258
June	276	177
July	245	115
Aug.	1,110	3 10
Sept. 1-30	1,114	311
Totals, May to Sept. 30	**4,735**	**1,201**

Daily Results

Sept.	German Losses	British Losses	British Pilots Saved	Sept.	German Losses	British Losses	British Pilots Saved
				Bt. fwd. Sept.	756	202	112
1	25	15	9	16	7	—	—
2	55	20	12	17	12	3	2
3	25	15	8	18	48	12	9
4	54	17	12	19	5	—	—
5	39	20	9	20	4	7	3
6	46	19	19	21	2	—	—
7	103	22	9	22	1	—	—
8	11	3	1	23	13	4	3
9	52	13	6	24	8	4	3
10	2	—	—	25	26	4	3
11	89	24	7	26	34	8	3
12	3	—	—	27	133	34	16
13	2	—	—	28	6	7	—
14	18	9	6	29	10	4	2
15	232	25	14	30	49	22	12
	756	**202**	**112**	**Totals**	**1,114**	**311**	**167**

None of the figures include aircraft bombed on the ground or so damaged as to be unlikely to reach home.

Additional German Losses. Sept. 11 : 4 shot down over Continent. Sept. 15 : 2 by Fleet Air Arm. Revealed on Sept. 26 that 47 more shot down on Sept. 15. Figures for Sept. 30 incomplete ; 2 shot down by Blenheims over North Sea.

Civilian Casualties. Intensive air attacks on Britain began on Aug. 8. Casualties during August 1,075 killed, 1,261 seriously injured.

Mr. Churchill stated that during the first half of September civilian casualties amounted to about 2,000 killed and 8,000 wounded, about four-fifths being in London. In the fighting services casualties were only 250.

Mass Raid Casualties in London. Sept. 7 : 306 killed ; 1,337 injured. Sept. 8 : 286 killed ; about 1,400 injured. Sept. 9 : about 400 killed, 1,400 injured.

German Aircraft Destroyed in Britain. From September 3, 1939 to September 30, 1940 the German machines destroyed around and over Britain totalled 2,525. In that time 667 British aircraft were lost, 324 pilots being saved.

intense barrage opened up. Caught in a searchlight beam, one enemy machine was almost at once blown to bits in the air. The stiff barrage caused most of the visitors to find targets in the suburbs so that London received many high explosive and fire bombs.

Combats between British and German fighter aircraft distinguished Saturday's daylight raids, September 28. Early in the day a few out of many attackers got to East London and dropped a small number of bombs, one falling on an L.C.C. block of flats. No raider penetrated to London in the second attack, made about midday, but bombs were dropped on a South coast town, the Dornier's crew machine-gunning shoppers. Portsmouth was the objective of the enemy's third raid, later in the afternoon. The enemy forces consisted very largely of fighter aircraft, and the combats were mainly between fighter and fighter ; as a result losses on both sides were practically the same.

On Saturday night there were raids on London, South-east England, Merseyside, and the East Midlands. West and South London, and suburbs in those quarters, were bombed. Between midnight and Sunday morning three bombers were destroyed ; one by fighters, one by A.A. gunners, and the third by fouling a balloon cable. Four more were shot down before Sunday was out.

During Sunday, September 29, lone raiders took advantage of cloudy skies to approach towns and villages in S.E. England. In the Midlands and at Edinburgh also there were raids. Three times the " Alert " sounded in the London area during daylight, and soon after the last warning there began the most terrific barrage yet put up. Many thousands of rounds were fired and the guns never ceased to roar at Nazi planes which, singly or in twos and threes, tried to reach the Metropolis. As a result many of the raiders dropped their bombs and " mines " on towns and villages in the South and South-west and the Home Counties. The South and West of outer London came off worst and moderate damage was widespread.

On Monday, September 30, the Luftwaffe wound up the month with six massed attacks in daylight. Over 500 raiders crossed the coast. Few, however, reached London, and all attacks were smashed by the R.A.F. between 9 a.m. and 5.30 p.m. Their losses amounted to 47 machines brought down by

our fighters and two bombers shot down over the North Sea by Blenheims. It was calculated that the enemy lost nearly 150 personnel compared with only 10 British. A particularly fine achievement was the chase by an R.A.F. Polish squadron of 30 Dornier 215's from Beachy Head to France. The Poles shot down three of the Messerschmitt escorts and one of the Dorniers over France itself. This squadron had then exceeded a score of 100 enemy 'planes destroyed.

Major Walter Elliot of the Western Command stated on September 30 that the R.A.F. figures during the months of August and September meant that one German aeroplane had been brought down every 42 minutes ; this was equivalent to their present output. It was also satisfactory to note that as the month went on the A.A. gunners registered increasing successes. Out of ten Nazi machines destroyed over South-east England on Sept. 29, six were due to gunners.

The unconquerable spirit of the Londoner is something beyond the comprehension of all Nazis, for it is based on a great sense of humour. That spirit is very apparent in this photograph. These people have saved from their wrecked homes an harmonium, and a laughing crowd gives voice to " There'll always be an England."

Photo, " Daily Mirror"

Berlin Workers in Gas Masks—A Propaganda Lie

Lying Nazi propaganda often cuts both ways and here is an example. The photograph purports to show German workmen in a shelter during a British air raid and their masks suggest that the British have used gas—a palpable lie. An interesting feature is the shelter in which the Germans squat ; if this is typical, then the German shelters compare very unfavourably with the soundly constructed British shelters. As will be seen, it consists only of a wooden framework against which sandbags are piled.

The Incessant Bombing of Germany in September

The Royal Air Force visited Germany, and German-occupied territory on more than 440 occasions in September, striking fierce blows at every variety of military objective, as shown in the analytical table in page 377. The story is continued from page 262.

THIS month's tabulated analysis of the Royal Air Force's raids on German military objectives (printed in page 377) tells a marvellous story of incessant blows struck at vital aircraft works and armament factories, at power stations and at all the enemy's complex transport and communications system. It also discloses the gigantic and paralysing operations against concentrations of vessels massed for the invasion of Britain. In some quarters a demand has been made for what are termed "reprisals" against Germany for her bombing of non-military objectives. The best answer to Nazi terror tactics is an unremitting assault on the enemy's war machine—such as is being delivered, in fact, by our bombers.

Every Briton who steadfastly holds to his task despite the daily and nightly Nazi air raids is contributing to the success of the air war on Germany. If we all bear the burden without complaint there will be no call for the diversion of our striking force, and our bombers—mainly by night at present, but soon also by day—will be able to continue and increase their attacks on the objectives

in Germany that really matter. The nature of these objectives is shown by the Table opposite. During the period September 1—30 more than seventy attacks were made by the R.A.F. on aerodromes, airfields and seaplane bases; more than one-hundred and fifty on harbours, ports and naval depots (including, of course, the "invasion" bases); more than a hundred on railway junctions, goods depots, distributing centres and marshalling yards (by September 12 Hamm had been bombed for the sixtieth time); and over twenty on oil refineries, oil storage depots and convoys of oil tankers. To bomb the oil tanks at Regensburg (Czechoslovak frontier) our pilots had to make a 675-mile trip each way!

On September 3 Berlin was raided for the fifth time in nine days; two power stations, a gas works and an armament factory were bombed; main line railway tracks and others near the capital also were attacked; wooded areas in which arms factories were likely to be concealed were set on fire. On the 6th "a power station, oil targets and railway yards were hit." The B.M.W. aero engine works at Spandau were set on fire;

the Salzhof oil reservoir on the banks of the Tegel lake was "apparently badly damaged." Four days later the Potsdam railway station in the heart of Berlin was repeatedly hit with heavy bombs and several hundred incendiaries. On September 11 it was the turn of the Anhalter station; at the same time a large railway yard south of the Potsdam station was bombed. An A.A. battery in the Tiergarten was attacked, while both incendiaries and H.E. bombs were let fall on the Tempelhof airport.

Men from the Dominions figured in the raid on Berlin carried out on the night of September 15. A New Zealand wing commander lost his temper when one of his engines froze up at about twenty minutes' flying distance from the German capital; he had to let his bombs drop on an alternative objective and make for home, at first on a

This incendiary leaf was an R.A.F. "secret weapon" dropped in thousands and designed to take fire on exposure to oxygen (in the air) or sunlight. It consists of a fire pill packed with cottonwool treated to become self-igniting. The Nazis complained loudly and used it as an excuse for distributing gas-masks.
Photo, Associated Press

single engine. Other pilots had similar trials, but bombs were nevertheless dropped on the Tempelhof airport again, and on a power station damaged in a previous raid. A raid "on a much larger scale than any yet carried out" was made on September 23. The West power station and others at Wilmersdorf, Charlottenburg, Klingenberg and Moabit each "came in for a steady hammering; many fires were seen to break out—one aircraft alone started five large fires, which were visible from eighty miles away. Another aircraft reported a power station alight at four different points." Among other hits were the B.M.W. aero engine works, the Siemens cable works, and a railway junction. The attack was kept up for several hours, the raiding force being much the strongest so far sent to the German capital.

For the second night in succession Berlin was raided on September 24. The first of the attackers appeared over the city shortly after 10.30 p.m., and, evading the intense barrage of the ground defences, they swiftly located and bombed the great Siemens and Halske factories, which produce a large proportion of the electrical equipment used by the German armed forces. Soon after midnight it was the turn of Berlin's electrical power transformer and switching station at Friedrichsfelde—the plant which supplies much of the German capital's industrial current. About the same time the blast

Sent to America as anti-British propaganda, this photograph of a bombed tenement building in a German town carefully omitted any view of a nearby military objective attacked by the R.A.F. Americans knew how to balance it against the many hundreds of photographs, freely released, of ruthless destruction in London.
Photo, Associated Press.

442 Raids on Enemy Military Objectives

furnace in the south-eastern suburbs was struck and two sticks of bombs were dropped across a canal bridge not far from the Tempelhof aerodrome. Berlin was raided yet again on the night of September 25-26, when four separate attacks within an hour were made on power stations, railway junctions and other military objectives.

Among the many other places in Germany which on that same night felt the heavy hand of the R.A.F. were the dockyards at Kiel, and the return visit on the following night was even more successful.

Towards the end of the month weather conditions generally over north Germany tended to become unfavourable, but again and again numbers of our aircraft reached their objectives. In Berlin electric power stations were bombed, together with important rail centres and aerodromes in north Germany, the naval base at Wilhelmshaven and the munition works at Hanau near Frankfurt. On the night of Saturday, September 28, Berlin had its first experience of two raid alarms in one night, and the next night the warning period lasted for over five hours—the longest to date. That same night saw the R.A.F. offensive continued against the enemy's oil refineries, aircraft and munition factories, railways and aerodromes.

One new feature of the R.A.F.'s raids on Germany during September must be mentioned—what may well be described as one of Britain's secret weapons—a self-igniting leaf or card (see pp. 302, 376). Hundreds of thousands of these "leaves" were dropped in the course of several of the raids, and the effect of the new weapon is evidenced by the howls of rage with which its use was greeted by the Germans.

One Month's R.A.F. Raids on Germany and Enemy-Occupied Territory

(Compiled from Official Air Ministry Communiqués)

Numbers following place-names denote the days in September on which raids were made

Aerodromes
Abbeville, 3, 6
Barge, 10
Bergen op Zoom, 19
Berlin, 11, 15, 25
Boblingem, 2
Borkum, 11, 18
Brussels, 7, 12
Calais, 4, 6
Celle, 2, 9
Colmar, 7
Cuxhaven, 9
Deiplolz, 9
De Kooy, 3, 12, 14, 18, 20
Delmenhorst, 23
Deurne, 14
Dunkirk, 6, 8
Eindhoven, 7
Foret de Guines, 4, 6
Gifhorn, 23
Gilze-Rijen, 7
Haamstede, 16, 20, 30
Hage, 24
Hanover, 24
Hoya, 9
Husum, 11
Karlsruhe, 5
Krefeld, 7
Lastrup, 8
Le Touquet, 3, 6
Metalin, 11
Midlum, 17
Munster, 19, 26
Norderney, 5, 11, 12
Querqueville, 7
Schipol, 1, 9, 20
Soesterburg, 7, 23
Stade, 11
St. Omer, 3, 6
Texel, 5, 20, 23
Trier, 20
Vechta, 3
Wangerooge, 11
Wesel, 2
Wesermunde, 10, 17
Wurzburg, 5
Ymuiden, 17
Ypenburg, 1

Aircraft Factories, etc.
Barnstorf, 9
Berlin, 3, 6
Bremen, 10, 11
Essen, 7, 9

Leipzig, 1
Munich, 1
Rothenburg, 30
Wismar, 23

Chemical Works, Munition Works, Metal Works, etc.
Berlin, 3, 23, 25
Bitterfeld, 1, 29
Cologne, 2
Dusseldorf, 27
Frankfurt, 11
Hanau, 28
Laura, N.E. of Dresden, 22
Leipzig, 2
Leverkusen, 2
Maastricht, 20
Magdeburg, 30
Mannheim, 1
Merzig, 3
Rendsburg, 25
Schlebusch, 2
Stuttgart, 1, 2, 29
Zweibrucken, 7

Power Stations
Berlin, 3, 9, 23, 24, 25, 28
Frankfurt, 24 [30
Kassel, 1

Railway Junctions, Marshalling Yards, Depots
Aachen, 14
Ahaus Jnct., 14
Barnstorf, 9
Berlin, 11, 23, 25
Bremen, 30
Brussels,* 9, 10, 14, 17, 18, 20, 24
Celle, 9
Coblenz, 11, 19, 29
Cologne, 11, 28, 29
Dresden, 22
Duisberg, 10
Ehrang,* 6, 7, 11, 12, 14, 17, 18, 19, 20, 25, 29, 30
Emmerich, 12
Essen, 12
Hamburg, 15, 28
Hamm,* 3, 5, 6, 7, 11, 12, 14, 15, 17, 18, 20, 24, 25, 27
Hanau, 28, 29

Hanover, 23, 25, 28
Husten, S.E. of Dortmund, 14
Jetta, 14
Julich, N.E. of Aachen, 14
Krefeld,* 6, 9, 14, 15, 17, 18, 20
Lunen, 25
Magdeburg, 24
Mannheim,* 1, 6, 7, 11, 14, 18, 19, 20, 25, 27, 28, 30
Munich, 1 [29, 30
Munster, 23, 28
Neckarau, sth of Mannheim, 19
Osnabruck,* 12, 14, 15, 17, 18, 20, 25, 29, 30
Rheine, 14, 15
Schweren, 2, 17
Soest,* 1, 5, 6, 15, 17, 20, 27
Stockum, nr. Cologne, 17
Sundern, 14
Torgau, 22
West-Hofen Jnct., 14
*Main distributing centres.

Oil Refineries & Depots, Hydrogenation Works
Brest, 25
Flushing, 2, 9
Frankfurt, 2, 28
Gelsenkirken, 7
Hamburg, 5, 9
Hanover, 1, 9, 29, 30
Kiel, 5, 9
Leuna, 30
Ludwigshafen, 1, 2
Magdeburg, 3, 29
Monheim, 11
Nordenham, 1
Politz, nr. Stettin, 5
Regensburg, 5
Salzhof, 6
Zeebrugge, 13

Naval Bases, Docks, Harbours, etc.
Antwerp,* 13, 14, 15, 17, 18, 20, 21, 22, 25, 28
Boulogne,* 5, 6, 7, 8, 9, 11, 13, 14, 15, 18, 20, 21, 22, 23, 24, 25, 26, 28, 29, 30

Bremen, 9, 10, 11, 23, 26, 28
Bremerhaven, 11, 23
Brest, 22
Calais,* 5, 7, 8, 9, 10, 11, 13, 14, 15, 16, 17, 10, 20, 21, 22, 23, 24, 25, 26, 28, [30
Cuxhaven, 23, 30
Cherbourg, 17, 18, 24
Delfzil,* 5, 12, 24
Dieppe,* 10, 18
Dunkirk,* 7, 11, 13, 14, 15, 16, 17, 18, 19, 20, 21, 22, 25, 28, 30
Emden, 1, 5, 7, 8, 12
Fécamp*, 28
Flushing,* 11, 12, 14, 15, 17, 18, 19, 20, 21, 22, 25
Harfleur, 22
Hamburg,* 8, 11, 15, 17, 24, 30
Ijmuiden, 14, 15, 17
Ijsselmond, 13
Le Havre,* 12, 15, 18, 22, 24, 26, 28, 30
Lorient, 1, 2, 27, 28 29
Ostend,* 2, 3, 7, 8, 9, 11, 13, 14, 15, 16, 17, 18, 19, 20, 21, 22, 24, 26, 29, 30
Rotterdam,* 21, 30 [30
St. Omer, 21
Terneuzen,* 3, 17, 21
Veere, 16, 19
Wilhelmshaven,* 9, 10, 11, 15, 28
Wismar, 9, 23
Zeebrugge,* 16, 17, 18, 20, 22
*Invasion bases

Canals
Beleland, 3
Bruges, 7, 14
Calais-St. Omer, 21
Dortmund-Ems, 2, 19, 20, 26
Halteren, 25
Kiel, 23, 25, 26, 27
Zutphen, 14

Gun Emplacements
Cap Gris Nez, 2, 5, 9, 10, 14, 15, 17, 18, 24, 26, 28, 29

Total No. of Raids Sep. 1-30 ... 442

The analytical table (above) of R.A.F. objectives in Germany successfully attacked in the month of September gives all possible proof of their military nature. It is a continuation of the impressive list for August given in page 263. Below, with radial distances from London, are shown the principal aerodromes in Germany and German-occupied territory known to be used by the enemy.

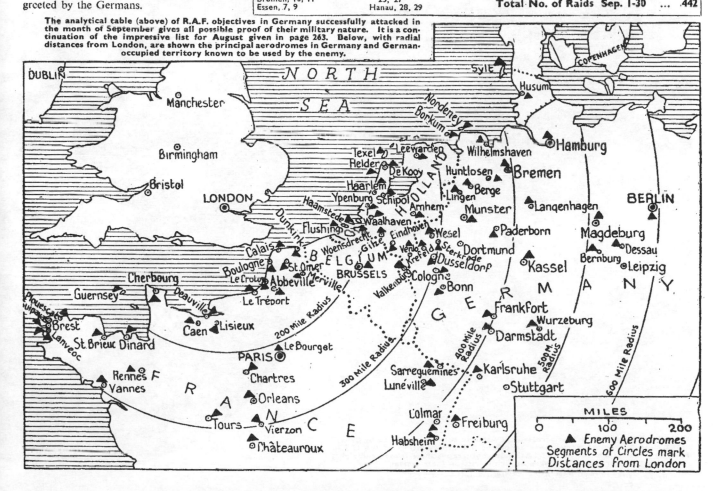

MILES
0   100   200

▲ Enemy Aerodromes
Segments of Circles mark
Distances from London

Once Under the Stars and Stripes They W

When the American destroyers crossed the Atlantic they were manned by British
crews although on each vessel were an officer and twenty ratings of the U.S.A.
Navy to " teach them the ropes."   As these photographs show (above and right)
the British sailors were in high spirits on their arrival.
Photos. Wide World, Central Press and Fox

elp to Win the War Under the Union Jack

we see the first of the 50 destroyers which Britain is receiving from America in exchange for the grant of sites for air and naval bases in North America ng British waters on September 28. " These are fine ships," said the captain of one of them, " delightful to handle, and I am certain that they will come up trumps when put to the test. Some of them were sinking U-boats in the last war, and they will sink more U-boats before this war is over."

Safely across the "Herring Pond," these members of the British crews of two of the destroyers—American once, but now British—shake hands on the conclusion of a fine trip; on the right some A.B.s are taking a look at an anti-aircraft gun.
Photos, Central Press and L.N.A.

They Make Strange Hauls Today

This skipper of a trawler is one of over ten thousand fishermen who have joined the Royal Naval Patrol Service, and are now engaged in the dangerous work of minesweeping.

The man in the engineroom of a trawler, above, watches the signals from the engineroom telegraph on the bridge. On the promptitude of his response to the skipper's orders the safety of ship and crew may depend. The crew have their moments of relaxation from their exacting duties, and enjoy a game of cards (left).

The "skipper," now a Lieut. Commander in the Royal Naval Reserve, is busy in his cabin with his charts (circle), for he is his own navigating officer.

The fishermen turned mine-sweepers have proved very handy men in changing to handling machine-guns. Right some of them are keen learners at a Lewis-gun course on the East Coast. *Photos, Fox*

'Food' for the Navy's Men and Guns

No praise can be too high for the fighting efficiency of the men of the Royal Navy, but it is not always remembered that without the work of the commissariat branches of the Admiralty the ships could not sail nor the guns be fired. Vast, indeed, are the responsibilities of the departments presided over by the Directors of Naval Ordnance, Naval Equipment, Naval Stores, Victualling and Contracts.

While the guns of one of Britain's monster battleships point menacingly to the sky, a fresh batch of 6-in. shells is unloaded from the ammunition ship and run across the deck to where the lift will lower them to the magazines. Circle, a 16-in. shell is being lowered on to the battleship's deck; it weighs a ton and will carry over ten miles.

Men as well as guns must be fed, and, right, beneath the shadow of the great bridge superstructure, Jack Tars are bringing aboard some of the food that will keep the ship's company of 1,500 men going for three months.

Photos, British Official: Crown Copyright

Here's To the Men Who Clear Up the Mess!

Amongst the brave men who are in the very front line of Civilian Britain in its fight
against the Nazi air raiders are the members of the Demolition Squads and the Rescue
Parties. Below we learn of what a district surveyor told a reporter on the " Evening
Standard " of the responsibilities of these men and of the really splendid way in which
they are shouldered.

WHEN bombs are dropped, unless they
fall in the middle of a vacant field
or in the sea, there is always an
aftermath of desolation and destruction to
be cleared away. If men and women have
been buried underneath the fallen buildings,
then they must be dug out and attended to
without delay ; if masses of debris block the
streets they must be cleared away ; if the
vital services are hit, which term includes not
only railways and tramways, but gas mains
and electric cables, water-pipes and sewers,
they, too, must be put right. All these
dangerous and difficult jobs are entrusted to
the demolition squads and rescue parties of
the Civil Defence organization.

Generally speaking, these are raised from
the outside staff of the various councils and
they are under the control of the district
surveyor. To take a typical instance, there
are seven squads operating from the headquarters of this south-west London district.

" They come on duty at eight o'clock in
the morning, and are supposed to be relieved
at eight o'clock at night—but recently there
have been so many demolished buildings to
cope with that they have not always been
able to relieve each other promptly," the
district surveyor in charge told me.

He said that the men were paid a little over
£3 a week, and that when they worked over-
time they did so without any extra wage.

" And, on their part, without any thought
of it," he added.

Crawling about wherever a bomb has torn
its path of terror and destruction, these
indomitable mercy men burrow and dig
through mountains of debris to free children
and women and men.

Most of the rescue brigade have been
recruited from the building trade.

They are the type of navvy whom before
the war you saw springing about the beams
and joists of half-erected buildings, eating
their lunchtime bread and cheese perched
in the most precarious positions, and
endlessly wisecracking with their mates.

They don't wisecrack any more. The
things they have seen since the bombardment
of London have stopped that.

Nor, when they're out on a job, do they
stop to eat—except if a Women's Voluntary
Service mobile canteen should come near
enough for them to grab a sandwich.

There are ten men in every squad : foreman, carpenter, plumber, bricklayer, and six
labourers, four of whom have been trained to
give first-aid.

" Sometimes," said the district surveyor,
" it is rather a long time before the debris
can be cleared enough to let the ambulance
men and stretcher parties through to where
people have been trapped.

" That is why our boys must know how
to be able to alleviate suffering right away."

When I called at headquarters there was
no one in the downstairs room where the
men sit waiting till they are called on duty ;
there was only a pile of their impedimenta—
picks and shovels and drills and the hooded
torches which, when the bombers are overhead, are the only light they have to work by.

All of the squads were out ; some still
working on the ruins caused in the night,
others at home on their 24 hours off duty.

Up against the walls of the little office
were propped such relics as the fin end of a
500 lb. bomb, dug out of the ruins of a
house ; a jagged piece of metal, eight inches
long, which had " come hurtling from a
wrecked upper floor and missed one of our
foremen by an inch."

" They are great men, these navvies,"
said the district surveyor quietly. " They
work through raids, with bombs crumping
round them and the continual danger of
houses collapsing on top of them, without
turning a hair.

" And they're not all young men either—
the best foreman we've got is a man of 70,
who's quicker on the job than any of them."

He told me that the men were standing
the terrific mental and physical strain of their
work with grand staunchness.

" Of course, it's no good pretending that
some of them don't suffer from shock—
they'd have to be robots not to, seeing the
things they do. And when that happens we
try to get them an extra hour or two's rest,
but that's not always easy to arrange these
days and nights of blitzkrieg."

I went with him to a row of houses two
blocks away, where a squad was working on
the havoc caused by two bombs which had
fallen, one on each side of the road.

The men were shoring up gaping walls,
knocking ragged ends of glass from windows,
digging a path through the mountainous pile
of bricks and rubble strewn over the road.

Two men, their faces white with dust,
looked out of a hole in a wall and shouted a
cheerful greeting.

" They're light-hearted about this particular job—by a miracle there were no casualties, for the people living in the houses most
badly hit had got out of London only a day
or two ago," said the district surveyor.

The demolition squads of London's A.R.P. have quickly become expert in dealing with the ruins
of houses that have been bombed. The photograph shows one of the men on a perilous perch
dealing with a cistern that hangs in mid air.
Photo : L N.A.

Every Hour Demolition Squads Risk Their Lives

A perilous job—disconnecting pipes from a heavy cistern in the roof of a bombed house. Circle, a car wrecked by a bomb in an area close to Oxford Street.

An A.R.P. squad is pulling down the dangerous wreckage of a block of flats. The photographs in this page were taken after the raid of Sept 22-23.

Photos, L.N.A., Wide World and Planet News

Out of the Frying-pan Into Spitfire

WHEN Lord Beaverbrook made an appeal for aluminium to build more Spitfires and Hurricanes, the housewives of Britain made a magnificent response and readily gave up favourite cooking utensils to go into the melting-pot. The photographs in this page show what became of them. (1) Another contribution from the housewife's kitchen is added to the pile. (2) When the contributions are received at the dump, those parts that are not pure aluminium are hammered off. (3) In the next process the pots and pans, after being cleansed, are put into the smelting furnace. (4) After being smelted, the aluminium is thrown from the furnace into ladles. (5) An asbestos-gloved workman pours the molten metal into standard-size moulds. (6) Before the ingots cooling in the moulds are quite cold, they are stamped with the words " pure aluminium." (7) Finally, the frying-pans and saucepans will form part of a Spitfire, such as this, or a Hurricane. The housewives who gave their pots and pans in response to the appeal have the satisfaction of knowing that they have made a very direct contribution to aircraft production and to the defence of their own homes.

Photos, Fox, Keystone, Central Press

New Flags for Old: Britain Takes Delivery

One of the 50 U.S.A. destroyers that have been taken over by the Royal Navy is here being brought out of dry dock at the Charlestown Navy Yard. She is "Aaron Ward," No. 132, but will receive in the British service a place-name common to Great Britain and the U.S.A.

When the destroyers were taken over by the Royal Navy at North American ports the American crews showed the British crews "the ropes" before they left. As the photograph proves, the two Navies were on the best of terms.

It was a memorable and historic moment when the Union Jack and the White Ensign were hoisted on the first batch of destroyers to be taken over. Here, the British flag is being broken simultaneously at the bows of the transferred destroyers.

The officers and crews that brought the American destroyers across the Atlantic were shipped from Britain to Canada as soon as the agreement was ratified. Ratings are here seen taking their kits on board their new ships. The accommodation for the crew differs considerably from that of British destroyers, but the standard of comfort is equally high.

Photos, International News Agency, Sport & General, and Keystone

OUR SEARCHLIGHT ON THE WAR

First Award to Home Guard

THE first member of the Home Guard to win a military decoration is Mr. Glyn Jones (see p. 391). His job was to defend a vital point. The post in question was bombed, one man being killed and another badly wounded. Young Mr. Jones, fortunately unhurt, first carried his wounded comrade to safety and then returned to his post and continued on guard, heedless of further bombs and much debris which fell around him. For his devotion to duty he has been awarded the Military Medal.

Londoners' Steadfast Confidence

AIR Marshal A. W. Bishop, V.C., Director of Recruiting for the Royal Canadian Air Force and a famous pilot of the last war, is full of admiration for the way the people of London are withstanding the Nazi air raids. "The British are a wonderful people," he said. "Everything is going on as usual. Such absolute steadfast confidence as Londoners display is incredible until seen." Such a tribute from "Billy" Bishop is worth having, for no man can possess greater courage and endurance. By the time he reached the age of 24 he had not only won the V.C., but the D.S.O., the M.C., the D.F.C. and a bar to the D.S.O. According to him the Empire air training scheme in Canada is "months and months ahead of schedule. The boys are magnificent, as good a type as any I have seen."

Wheeled Cavalry

ROUGH-RIDING of a new kind is being adopted as part of our defence against invaders. Members of this new and extremely mobile unit consist of crack motor cyclists, heroes of many a dirt track and hill-climbing trial. They will be stationed at strategic points, ready to tear off at top speed to deal with parachute or 'plane landings. If necessary they will cut straight across country. Tests which were recently made in the Western Command were of the most gruelling nature, but so experienced are these young riders in roaring up mountain-sides, leaping ditches and ponds, and emerging safely from spectacular skids, that this unit of cavalry on wheels will prove a formidable obstacle to enemy troops ill-advised enough to attempt a landing from the air.

Oldest Submarine's Latest Exploit

BRITAIN'S veteran submarine, H.M.S. H 49, was completed twenty-one years ago, and is thus nine years older than the official limit of supposed usefulness. Survivors of the H class are now used mainly for instructional purposes, but that H 49 is still taking part in active warfare is disclosed in an Admiralty communiqué of September 26. "British submarines continue to search out and take their toll of enemy shipping. Full information of their successes cannot be given without endangering their security, but it can now be stated that H.M. submarine H 49 (Lieut. M. A. Langley, R.N.) lately attacked a convoy of eight supply ships with torpedoes, two of which found their mark." In the same communiqué the Admiralty announced that the submarine "Tuna" reported the destruction of a large supply vessel screened by two enemy destroyers.

Captured Pilots Fear the Worst

HUNDREDS of Nazi pilots have been taken prisoner within the last few weeks, and the officers who examine them have all been struck by the invariable attitude of fear and suspicion with which any friendly advance is received. The average age is round about 20, and it is evident that these young pilots have been brought up to believe that the British are utterly ruthless and only too ready to wreak a cruel vengeance on any opponents who may fall into their hands. So the captives are apprehensive, silent and deeply suspicious of the slightest kindness shown. The skilled treatment given to those who are injured bewilders them, and they look for a "catch" somewhere. Food and drink may at first be refused on the grounds that these are probably poisoned, or constitute a bribe. Even after they are sufficiently reassured to accept the consideration offered them, they remain for the most part sullen and bad-mannered. Only a few, and these the youngest, break

Britain's Youngest V.C.

SERGT. JOHN HANNAH of the R.A.F., who is only eighteen years of age, has been awarded the V.C. in recognition of most conspicuous bravery. Here is the official account of the deed which has won for him the highest military honour; his own version is given in page 387.

On the night of September 15 Sergeant Hannah was the wireless operator air gunner in an aircraft engaged in a successful attack on enemy barge concentrations at Antwerp. The machine was subjected to intense anti-aircraft fire and received a direct hit from a projectile of an explosive and incendiary nature, which apparently burst inside the bomb compartment. A fire started and quickly enveloped the wireless operator's and rear gunner's cockpits. As both the port and starboard petrol tanks had been pierced, there was grave risk of the fire spreading.

Sergeant Hannah, on forcing his way through the fire to obtain two extinguishers, found that the rear gunner had had to leave the aircraft. He could have acted likewise, leaving through the bottom escape hatch or forward through the navigator's hatch, but he remained and fought the fire for 10 minutes, beating the flames with his log-book when the extinguishers were empty.

Meanwhile thousands of rounds of ammunition exploded in all directions. Hannah was almost blinded by the intense heat and fumes, but had the presence of mind to obtain relief by turning on his oxygen supply. Air admitted through the large holes caused by the projectile made the bomb compartment an inferno, and all the aluminium sheet metal on the floor of the cockpit was melted away, leaving only the cross bearers. Although receiving burns to his face and eyes, Sergeant Hannah succeeded in extinguishing the fire. He then crawled forward, ascertained that the navigator had left the aircraft, and passed the latter's log and maps to the pilot.

Sergeant Hannah, who is 18 years of age, displayed courage, coolness, and devotion to duty of the highest order, and by his action in remaining and successfully extinguishing the fire under conditions of the greatest danger and difficulty enabled the pilot to bring the aircraft safely to its base.

---

down under the strain of relief at their humane treatment. But all pay sincere, if grudging, tribute to the skill of the British fighter pilots who brought them down.

Homes for the Homeless

ON September 27 Mr. H. Willink, M.P., was appointed Special Commissioner for the Care and Rehousing of the Homeless of the London Region. He has many problems to face, one of the greatest being that so many people do not want to be moved out of their own district, even though good quarters may be found for them in another part of London. Another is the opposition, still felt by many parents, to being separated from their children, although the desirability of evacuating all school children to safe areas would seem obvious. Mr. Willink is considering, among other schemes, the provision of hostels for people who have to remain and work in London. Improvements in the organization for the immediate shelter of those who have been bombed out of their homes are rapidly taking effect, as well as arrangements for the transport of salvaged furniture belonging to those who have found homes elsewhere. Mr. Willink pays a high tribute to the pluck, patience and cheerfulness of the sufferers. "I have been deeply impressed," he said, "by the gratitude expressed to me by so many in the emergency rest shelters for the way they have been received there, and for the meals they are now able to get. Hundreds of officers are doing work to which they are quite unused and hundreds of volunteers are doing grand work. But very much remains to do, and London Region will go to it and do its utmost for those who have suffered in the front line."

British Airmen Saved After 84 Hours

AFTER a search lasting three and a half days, Hudson and Anson aircraft of the Coastal Command, working in close co-operation with British naval units, found the crew of a British bomber which had come down in the North Sea. During those 84 hours they had been adrift in a rubber dinghy on a rough sea. True to character, the Germans many times attempted to obstruct the efforts at rescue, sending Heinkels near one of the searching warships, so that Blenheim fighters were despatched as a protective patrol to drive them off. When the little dinghy was at last located, a container of food and tobacco was released from a 'plane and, after a little paddling, one man was seen to reach out and seize the waterproof bag. The rescue was eventually effected by a warship directed by flare floats to the spot, which was 70 miles nearer the coast than when the search started.

Will There Be a Holy War?

MUSSOLINI's attacks on their sacred places have so inflamed Moslems in Egypt, Palestine and India that their leaders are seeking to declare a holy war against Fascism. The movement started from the invasion of Egypt by Libya, and the bombing of Haifa and other places in Palestine. On September 23 the Mullah Sahib of Bhutan, in Peshawar, India, issued a call to action, and this has been taken up by Arab chiefs in Egypt. The Supreme Moslem Council in Palestine issued a manifesto expressing "detestation at the abominable attack on the mosque at Haifa and at the desecration of the cemetery there." Great resentment against Italy has been stirred up in Syria. In Egypt the Grand Senussi has also called for vengeance against the invader. As there are over 200,000,000 Moslems, the possibility of a religious war should certainly give Mussolini something to think about.

I WAS THERE!

Eye Witness Stories of Episodes
and Adventures in the
Second Great War

How We Saved Our Burning 'Plane

The official story of the heroic feat over Antwerp which won eighteen-year-old Sergeant Hannah of the R.A.F. his V.C. is given opposite. Here is his own account of the incident, making light both of his heroism and of his injuries which, unhappily, resulted in serious illness.

WRITING to his mother from hospital, Sergeant Hannah said :

Dear Mum,—At last I have managed to get a rest. As you see by my address, I am in " dock " (hospital). I suppose you will have had some official news that has got you all worried. Still I am O.K., and would have written sooner but only managed to get my eyes open this morning. Well, to tell you all about it, I am lucky to be alive.

We got caught in a terrific " ack-ack " barrage overby. Our 'plane went on fire. At the time it had singed my whiskers. I realized that we were liable to blow up any minute, so I made for my parachute, only to discover that it was on fire, too, so you can guess there was some panic.

By this time the navigator and gunner had baled out, and the 'plane was a blazing mass and a terrific target for the " ack-ack " and they were still letting away.

Still I did some quick thinking and started throwing all the flaming mass overboard. During this, ammunition on the kite was going off ten a penny with the heat.

Finally I got the fire out and the pilot and I limped home.

They rushed me to hospital right away, but I heard since then it caused a great sensation. They have " ack " chiefs, bomber command chiefs, and many more big noises having the kite photographed from all angles. I have had so many C.O.s and big shots visit me that I feel a big shot too !

I have had a telegram from an officer in command congratulating me on my conduct. Apparently it was the first time that a fire has been put out in the air.

My pilot is getting the D.F.C., so I expect that I will be getting something too. But, if you feel the way I do, you will be quite thankful that I am alive, without worrying what I am getting or am going to look like.

Well, if you could see me now I'm sure you would burst out laughing. They have my face all covered with a black plastic stuff, and my hair is still black from the smoke, so I look like a nigger. The nurses won't believe I have got fair hair. I am quite happy here. If what they tell me is true, my face should be practically clear when the stuff comes off. It is a new pattern stuff, and if it works I should be as good as new.

They were worrying about shock when I came in, but I seem to be O.K. The only snag I have is that I cannot eat. My skin is all frizzled up. You won't likely know me when you see me. I have gone thin already, and if they have changed my face I hope I don't get lost looking for my home !

The Air Officer Commanding the Hampden bomber group where Sergeant Hannah was stationed paid high tribute to his courage. He said :

Sergeant Hannah would have had every justification if he had left the burning aircraft. He could have escaped, but he remained in the rear cockpit, which must have rapidly become an inferno.

All the inflammable equipment inside the cockpit was alight and ammunition was exploding.

Sergeant Hannah very probably saved the life of his pilot. He certainly saved the aircraft when he must have known that his last chance of safety was apparently hopelessly jeopardized. No one who has seen the aircraft can be otherwise than amazed at his extraordinary presence of mind and extreme courage.

How We Found the 'Benares' Survivors

Forty-six survivors of the " City of Benares," including six evacuee children, were brought safely to port on September 26 after eight days' ordeal in an open lifeboat. Their miraculous rescue, here described, was primarily due to two Sunderland flying-boats.

THE commander of the warship which brought the survivors to port said :

The lifeboat was found eight days after the " City of Benares " was lost. All that time the crew had been moving, keeping their boat safely going through the storm, sometimes by sail and sometimes by a

" pedal screw "—by which a propeller can be turned by pedals in the boat.

The boys had been simply heroic. Not a complaint through the long days or the freezingly cold nights. Miss Cornish, the only woman in the boat, had been a perfect Florence Nightingale.

As darkness fell and the cold grew more intense, she set to work massaging the boys' legs to keep them from being frost-bitten.

The boys welcomed their turn at driving the lifeboat along with the pedals. It helped to keep them warm. So far out in the Atlantic the provisions and water had to be carefully rationed. Only enough was allowed to keep them alive.

A 'plane of the Fleet Air Arm that was escorting our boat spotted them. The boys told me that they saw the 'plane—just a speck thousands of feet above them—but they knew what it was, and they waved.

The pilot reported to us what he had seen, and we soon had them safe. It will take more than a Hun torpedo and days in an open boat to crush the spirit of lads like these.

It has been a happy task for us. Would that we could have brought more of them safely home.

It was cooperation by two Sunderland flying-boats, one belonging to the Royal Australian Air Force, which led to the rescue.

The captain of the second aircraft said :

The Sunderland we were relieving sent up a message just before going off patrol. The captain said he had sighted a boat.

We went straight to the place he indicated and found the boat at once. All the people in the boat were sitting or lying down except one man, who was at the tiller. Some amidships seemed to be in rather a bad way.

They had hoisted sail and were making what speed they could. When we got there we dropped a parachute bag filled with all the

This is the 'plane in which the very gallant deed which gained the Victoria Cross for Sergeant Hannah was enacted. Pilot Officer C. A. Connor, a young Canadian, who has himself received the D.F.C., is pointing out the details of the burnt-out cockpit to the Station Engineer Officer.
Photo, Central Press

388   The War Illustrated   October 11th, 1940

|||||||||||||||||||||||||||||||||||||||||||||||||||||||| **I WAS THERE!** ||||||||||||||||||||||||||||||||||||||||||||||||||||||||

These boys have just been rescued from the Atlantic after being eight days adrift in an open boat. They are five of the six children who with 40 adults were the last survivors from the " City of Benares " to be picked up. The number of children lost was thus 77 and not 83 as first announced (pages 360–61). Extreme left is Kenneth Sparks, hero of the rescue ; and circle, Miss Mary Cornish.

Photos, Keystone

food we had on board. We attached a life-jacket to keep it afloat.

We circled round and made them a signal that we were going to get help, but they had only a semaphore which we were travelling too fast to read. However, we made them understand that we were going to fetch a ship, which was about forty miles away.

Before leaving them I went down very low on the water and saw that it would be possible to land and take them on board if they could not be rescued otherwise.

Then we went to fetch a ship. We found a warship and signalled that there was a boatful of people and indicated their position. We flew back to the boat and then to the warship.

But she was not on the right course, so I signalled : " Follow me," and then flew directly over the ship towards the lifeboat. When I was getting near the lifeboat I dropped a smoke-flare which the warship saw and signalled " O.K."

We watched until we saw the warship actually stop alongside the lifeboat, and then, as we had received a signal telling us to return to base before dusk, we left.

Among those rescued, in addition to the six children, were British and Lascar seamen, Bohdan Nagorski, Polish director of a shipping company, Father O'Sullivan, a Roman Catholic priest, and Miss Cornish. The last two were acting as escorts.

Mr. Nagorski said :

We had made up our minds that there was no hope of our being rescued. We had been at sea in the open boat for eight days. We had no water and our food was practically gone. Suddenly we heard the roar of aeroplane engines. We looked up, and to our joy saw the flying-boat appear from the clouds. The pilot signalled to us and dropped food.

The flying-boat went up again and returned some time later simultaneously with the appearance of the British warship. We were taken aboard and revived by the crew.

Telling of his experiences after the ship had been torpedoed, Mr. Nagorski said :

We expected, to pick up one of the other ships but we never saw a sign of one. The six children on our boat behaved magnificently. After we had been two days on the sea we discovered a sail in the lifeboat, and between sailing and rowing we managed to make good headway. The officer in the boat decided to steer an easterly course, in the hope that he would ultimately reach the coast.

The next two days passed like a nightmare. Heavy seas burst over us time and again. It took us all our time to save the children from being carried overboard. Weather conditions improved but we had to weather other storms.

Without doubt the boys owe their lives to the heroism of Miss Mary Cornish, of London, one of the escorts and the only woman on board the lifeboat. Crouched in the pitifully confined space in the bows of the boat, she massaged the limbs of the boys and made up muscle exercises to counteract the terribly cramped position and bitter cold.

Thirteen-year-old Kenneth John Sparks, of Wembley, said :

The worst of it was rowing all day and night. We ate ship's biscuits, sardines and tinned salmon and had condensed milk and a little water to drink.

I was the first to see the flying-boat. I shouted and then we all prayed. We had to be lifted up the steps of the warship, as none of us could walk.

The last phase of the tragic story of the " City of Benares " is seen in this photograph. A destroyer has arrived on the scene to rescue the last survivors of the ill-fated ship in response to directions of the Sunderland flying-boat, to which 13-year-old Kenneth Sparks had " flag waved " the identity of the lifeboat with a handkerchief.

Photo, British Official : Crown Copyright

How We Torpedoed a Nazi Troopship

The sinking by H.M. submarine "Sturgeon" of a 10,000-ton German transport believed to be carrying between 3,000 and 4,000 troops took place on September 2 off the northern tip of Denmark. The exploit, which was carried out in spite of very difficult conditions and weather of a particularly heavy nature, was described as follows by an officer of the "Sturgeon."

We went up the Skagerrak and got into a position early on the morning of September 2. It was blowing quite hard and we saw nothing until an aeroplane came into sight just as it was getting dusk. About half an hour later the hydrophone operator reported that he heard very faintly the sound of a ship. The "Sturgeon" was brought right up and two or three minutes later two small German destroyers were sighted and just afterwards a very large transport.

Conditions were not very good. We were some distance from our quarry when we first saw her and were on her beam. She appeared to be steering a course for Oslo. Fortunately she was silhouetted against the light of the setting sun. We went to diving stations and brought the tubes to the ready and as soon as we could fired our torpedoes. The transport was going away from us.

As soon as we had fired a torpedo we submerged, but after a short time the commanding officer came up for a look. Everything was quiet, with the transport steaming on with her escorting destroyers. A moment or two later we heard a great explosion and the commanding officer, looking through the periscope, saw a gigantic column of smoke coming up from the transport. The smoke must have gone up some 2,000 feet. We went farther away from the transport and once an aeroplane came swooping around right over us, but we were not spotted.

After about ten minutes the transport burst into flames and became a blazing mass from stem to stern. It was a terrific sight. After an hour and a half she was settling down low into the water and quite obviously she was finished.

We went down to re-lay our torpedoes and when we came up to the surface again the transport had gone. There was nothing left but the two destroyers, with their searchlights on, picking up the survivors.

Lieut. G. D. A. Gregory, D.S.O., in command of the "Sturgeon," is here seen (extreme right) on the bridge when the submarine came home after her great exploit.
Photo, Topical Press

We had one bad moment, for as we came to the surface it was not realised that the searchlights were on and we came right into their beams. The destroyers were about three miles away and luckily they did not see us.

It was an extremely lucky shot at that range.

The ship, he said, was a single funnel, low-built Diesel vessel of about ten to twelve thousand tons. She was making north for a Norwegian port.

He added : Danish reports have stated that she had between three and four thousand troops on board. Whether these troops were intended for a possible invasion of Great Britain can only be a matter of speculation.

The ship's cook of the "Sturgeon" cooked 100 eggs for breakfast on the morning that the transport was torpedoed. Like that he is eating here, they were all hard-boiled.

The officer remarked that the day which ended so well started rather badly. He said :

We were not feeling too well because we had some extraordinarily hard-boiled eggs for breakfast. An A.B. does what cooking can be done, and when I asked how long he had boiled the eggs he replied : " Two and a half hours, sir." There were a hundred eggs to cook for three minutes each. He therefore multiplied one hundred by three, made a few other calculations, and boiled our eggs for two and a half hours !

Though the crews of submarines say it is a great life, it is certainly a cramped one, and one of their first desires when they come ashore is to stretch their legs. Bicycles give a good opportunity for this and also lessen the difficulties of transport, so when the "Sturgeon" arrived in port several bicycles went on board ready for ship's leave, but they will be landed before she puts to sea again.
Photos, "Daily Mirror"

Women in the Front Line of Britain's War

Above, nurses and students of the Great Ormonde Street Hospital help to build shelters for the roof-spotters. Oval, A.F.S. girls clearing the pavement in Oxford St.

Berwick Street Market, close to the shattered shops of Regent Street, still does business, but the girl in charge of the meat stall wears a steel helmet as a precaution while she serves.

The pavements of Bond Street, in which are many world-famous shops, are usually crowded in the busy hours with those who buy of the best. Today a novel fashion has appeared there—women who wear the A.R.P. uniform surmounted by a steel helmet; the new Civil Defence badge is embroidered on the sleeve of the uniform (centre). Below, nurses at the Children's Hospital are clearing up a damaged ward

Photos, Fox, G.P.U., Wide World, "Evening News" and Central Press

They Have Won Honour in Freedom's Cause

Capt. A. J. Biggs, who carried unexploded bombs a distance of several miles to a quarry, where they were destroyed.

Lieut. R. Davies, G.C. who, with members of Bomb Disposal Unit, saved St. Paul's Cathedral from the menace of a time-bomb.

Wing-Com. F. V. Beamish, A.F.C., D.S.O. for displaying courage in the air. He destroyed 2 Messerschmitts and a Dornier.

Squadron-Leader C. E. R. Tait, D.F.C. for conspicuous daring and courage during air operations against the enemy.

Squadron-Leader J. R. A. Peel, D.F.C. for displaying bravery and outstanding qualities as a leader during air operations.

Pilot Officer Whelan, R.A.F., D.F.C. for bravery and courage in the course of air operations against the enemy.

Squadron-Leader Charles Pearce, R.A.A.F., D.F.C. for bravery and devotion to duty in the course of air operations.

Pilot Sergt. H. J. L. Hallowes, bar to his D.F.M. for destroying 21 enemy aircraft and for his resolute daring.

Flight Lieut. J. F. Newman, D.F.C. for displaying great gallantry and devotion to duty in the course of air operations.

Act. Squadron-Leader M. N. Crossley, D.F.C., D.S.O. for bravery displayed in air operations. He destroyed 18 German aircraft.

Sub-Lieut. R. W. Timbrell, R.C.N., D.S.C. for displaying conspicuous bravery and devotion to duty while on active service.

Sub-Lieut. J. W. Golby, R.C.N.V.R., D.S.C. for displaying great gallantry and devotion to duty while on active service.

Volunteer Glyn Jones, M.M. for carrying a wounded man to safety. First Home Guard to receive a military decoration.

Comm. E. R. Conder, R.N., D.S.O. and D.F.C. for displaying bravery and conspicuous daring during naval operations.

Comm. H. Shove, R.N., D.S.C. for displaying conspicuous bravery and devotion to duty while on active service.

Squadron-Leader Strange, a bar to his D.F.C. for conspicuous bravery and devotion to duty in the air.

Flight Lieut. J. A. Cohen, R.A.A.F., D.F.C. for displaying courage and devotion to duty during air operations.

Flight Lieut. J. Sample, D.F.C. for displaying bravery in the air. He shot down 2 enemy aircraft.

Act. Flight-Lieut. E. C. Le Mesurier, D.F.C. for carrying out long reconnaissance flights over enemy territory.

Squadron Leader the Hon. M. Aitken, D.F.C. for gallantry and devotion to duty. He is Lord Beaverbrook's heir.

Col. Gordon Johnson, O.B.E. for displaying bravery and conspicuous devotion to duty while on active service.

Maj. F. Clarke, R.A.S.C., O.B.E. for displaying outstanding courage and devotion to duty while on active service.

Lieut.-Col. E. J. Medley, R.A., D.S.O. for displaying conspicuous gallantry and courage while on active service.

Temp. Lieut. (temp. Lieut.-Col.) R. O. Ward, O.B.E. (Military Div.) for displaying courage and gallantry in the field.

Maj. Henry Hopking, The Suffolk Regt., O.B.E. for displaying courage and gallantry while employed on active service.

OUR DIARY OF THE WAR

TUESDAY, SEPT. 24, 1940   *388th day*
On the Sea—Admiralty announced that H.M. submarine " Thames " was overdue and must be presumed lost.
In the Air—R.A.F. bombed enemy minesweepers in the Channel.
Coastal Command aircraft attacked Zeebrugge and naval station at Brest.
During the night R.A.F. heavy bombers successfully bombed military objectives in Berlin. Other forces attacked railways and goods yards, power station near Frankfurt-on-the-Oder, gun emplacements at Cap Gris Nez, many aerodromes and invasion ports.
Home Front—In morning two enemy formations of bombers and fighters attacked across Kent coast and area of Thames Estuary. Minor forces penetrated to London. Bombs fell in Thames-side towns and in East Kent. Southampton area was attacked. Damage and casualties also caused at Brighton.
Night raids were concentrated on Central London areas. Large numbers of incendiary bombs dropped. St. Clement Danes church damaged. Shops, private property, an hostel, a college and hospitals in W. and N. London damaged. Extensive raids made into Wales.
Enemy lost 8 aircraft. Four British fighters missing, but pilots of three safe.
General—Hundred bombs dropped on Gibraltar by aircraft of French types.

WEDNESDAY, SEPT. 25   *389th day*
On the Sea—Coastal Command flying-boat found in mid-Atlantic 46 survivors, including 6 children, of the evacuee ship, " City of Benares," torpedoed September 17.
In the Air—R.A.F. again bombed Berlin. Targets included railways, power stations, a munitions factory and Tempelhof aerodrome. Other forces attacked docks at Kiel, the " Scharnhorst " being hit ; goods yards at Osnabruck, Ehrang, Hamm, Mannheim and Hanover ; shipping, barges and stores at Antwerp, Flushing and four Channel ports.
Coastal Command aircraft bombed oil tanks at Brest.
War against Italy—British naval forces again shelled Sidi Barrani area. R.A.F. bombed Tobruk. Raids were carried out at Assab, Macacca and Berbera.
Enemy fighters flew over Malta. One shot down and two others damaged.
Home Front—Daylight attack made on Bristol. Minor enemy activity in S.E. England. Air battle took place over Bournemouth.
At night raiders flew low over London in spite of A.A. barrage. Parish church in S.E. damaged and another destroyed ; hospitals, schools, houses and business premises hit. In N.W. district heavy bombs seriously damaged a nursing-home, cinema, shops and about 200 houses. In W. district incendiaries preceded big explosive bombs ; and houses, shops and a hospital were hit.
Bombs were dropped in other parts of S.E. England and in the North West.
Twenty-six enemy aircraft destroyed. Four British fighters lost, but pilots of three safe.
General—Announced that Gen. de Gaulle had abandoned operations against Dakar.
French 'planes again raided Gibraltar, dropping about 300 bombs. Small ship in harbour sunk, and property damaged.

THURSDAY, SEPT. 26   *390th day*
On the Sea—Admiralty announced that H.M. submarines H 49 and " Tuna " had lately sunk three enemy supply vessels.
Italian torpedo-boat destroyer reported to have been sunk in Ionian Sea by British submarine.
In the Air—R.A.F. made further heavy attacks on Channel ports, particularly Le Havre. Kiel and other objectives in N.W. Germany were successfully bombed.
War against Italy—R.A.F. twice raided enemy concentrations at Sollum.

Home Front—In morning enemy aircraft flying singly approached E. and S. coasts, but few penetrated far. Bombs fell on N.E. coast. In afternoon attacks were made on coastal towns from Hastings to Southampton. Bombs fell in a Midlands town.
During night raids on London, flares, followed by high-explosive bombs, fell on North, West and Southern suburbs. Hospital, flats, shops, industrial premises and houses suffered. Incendiary bombs damaged premises in Central London. N.W. coastal town was heavily raided.
Enemy lost 34 aircraft. Eight British fighters lost, but pilots of three safe.
Dover was shelled for over an hour.

+-+-+-+-+-+-+-+-+-+-+-+-+-+-+-+-+-+-+

THE POETS & THE WAR
XXXIV
FOR THE TOWNS OF THE S.E. COAST
By EDWARD SHANKS

Since Britain rose above the seas,
    The seas have beaten on her shore,
An endless battery prolonged
    For half a million years or more.

The waves at shingle, sand and chalk
    Have clawed with endless enmity,
And still the island rests secure,
    Mistress, not vassal, of the sea.

We shall not fear this punier foe,
    Though he with poisoned talon strike,
We hold the coasts. The fate of all
    Who come against them is alike.

Remember, though, the fabled bells
    Of Dunwich, that, below the wave,
Ring for the victim of that war
    Out of her ancient, sea-drowned grave.

Remember, now, the little towns
    On which the raider throws his hate,
Which stand the brunt and keep our land,
    Impregnable, inviolate.

They shall not sink, like Dunwich, down
    Under a final conquering tide,
But when those sullen waves recede,
    Shall rise again, new-glorified.

When from our skies these storms are swept
    And earth and ocean both are free,
Margate and Ramsgate, Folkestone, Dover,
    Your bells shall sound above the sea.
                            —*Daily Sketch*

+-+-+-+-+-+-+-+-+-+-+-+-+-+-+-+-+-+-+

FRIDAY, SEPT. 27   *391st day*
On the Sea—Admiralty announced that H.M. trawler " Loch Inver " was overdue and must be presumed lost.
In the Air—R.A.F. carried out large-scale night attacks on enemy invasion bases, including French Atlantic port of Lorient.
Other forces operating over Germany bombed railway yards at Mannheim and Hamm, and munition factories at Dusseldorf.
War Against Italy—Enemy 'planes attempting to raid Haifa driven off.
Home Front—Mass attacks in S. England were intercepted and severe losses inflicted, especially near London. Three daylight attacks on London, when a few bombs caused damage to houses and an industrial building, and casualties resulted.
Enemy aircraft also reached outskirts of Bristol, where they were driven off by R.A.F. after lively engagements.
Germans lost 133 aircraft. Britain lost 34 fighters, but pilots of 16 safe.

British and German guns fought artillery duel across the Channel.
General—Germany, Italy and Japan signed 10-year military, political and economic Pact.

SATURDAY, SEPT. 28   *392nd day*
On the Sea—First flotilla of 50 transferred American destroyers arrived in British waters.
In the Air—R.A.F. again raided Berlin and electric power stations and A.A. guns positions were bombed. Elsewhere in N. Germany targets included railway centres and aerodromes. Fires and explosions caused at Wilhelmshaven. Munitions works at Hanau, near Frankfurt, severely damaged. Channel ports and enemy base at Lorient again attacked.
War Against Italy—S. African Air Force successfully raided Birikau, Italian Somaliland, for third time.
Home Front—During morning enemy aircraft, chiefly fighters, crossed S. E. coast and a few reached E. London. Bombs fell but damage was slight. Bombs also dropped on S. coast town. Enemy force approached Portsmouth area, but were driven off.
Night attacks were made on London, S.E. England, Merseyside and East Midlands. Both high explosive bombs and incendiaries were dropped. Shops in a S. London district extensively damaged. Wardens' post hit and nine perished. Isolation hospital and other buildings damaged in S.W. suburb.
Six German aircraft destroyed. Britain lost seven fighters.

SUNDAY, SEPT. 29   *393rd day*
On the Sea—Reported that survivors of British ships " Blair Angus " and " Elmwood," torpedoed on September 21, had landed at St. John's, Newfoundland.
In the Air—R.A.F. bombed oil refineries at Magdeburg and Hanover ; aluminium works at Bitterfeld ; gas works at Stuttgart ; goods yards at Osnabruck and Cologne ; and many enemy-occupied aerodromes.
Home Front—During daylight raids bombs were dropped at points on Thames Estuary, a S. coast village and one in Home Counties. Garage fired in Kent. Attacks also made in Midlands and in Edinburgh area.
Night raids were widespread. Many fires started in London, including serious one in City. In Home Counties attacks were heaviest south and west of London. Nurses' home and hospital in western suburb badly damaged. Large fires on Merseyside.
Ten enemy bombers destroyed. Four British fighters lost, but pilots of two safe.

MONDAY, SEPT. 30   *394th day*
In the Air—R.A.F. delivered big attack on German bases, particularly Calais and gun positions near Cap Gris Nez.
Military targets in Berlin bombed for four hours, including power stations, railways and factories. Other forces attacked oil refineries, munition factories, goods yards and railways in Germany, docks at Cuxhaven and Amsterdam, many enemy aerodromes and Channel ports.
Coastal Command and Fleet Air Arm attacked docks, shipping and petrol stores at Rotterdam, Ostend and elsewhere.
War Against Italy—R.A.F. attacked Libyan bases, main damage being done at Marawa.
Home Front—Six large daytime attacks launched against S.E. England and Bristol area. All were broken up after crossing coast, but one formation reached London. Bombs fell in western suburbs. Attacks made on several places in South-East, notably Bexhill and Hastings.
In night, incendiaries fell in Central London. Suburbs in N.W., N. and N.E. were bombed. Fires caused on Merseyside.
Enemy lost 49 aircraft. Britain lost 22 fighters, but 12 pilots safe.
Two artillery duels with long-range guns took place across Straits of Dover.

A PALPABLE HIT, BUT RICHARD'S SWORD UNBROKEN!

Marochetti's famous bronze statue of Richard Coeur de Lion in Old Palace Yard received very slight damage during a recent raid. A " palpable hit " by a Nazi bomb bends but does not break King Richard's sword. The bomb exploded in the courtyard of the House of Lords, and only slight damage was done to the windows. Glass was blown out and walls were chipped by flying debris, which also covered the golden thrones of the King and Queen. The bomb exploded between the building and the statue.

Photo. Planet News

France is Now Robbed of Food and Freedom

Now the mask is off in occupied France as in the unoccupied zones, and the peasant—
who is deprived of his pigs—and the bourgeois alike are forced to realize that, despite
the high-sounding promises of restoration and reconstruction from Vichy, their country
and themselves are helpless vassals of the Axis.　Here is a summary of recent news
through neutral and American sources.

WHATEVER the French leaders who gave in to Hitler expected from him, they have been disappointed. Both in occupied and in unoccupied France, according to accounts by neutral observers and escaped French and British nationals, conditions are appalling, with a slight bias for the better in the occupied region. With the example of the treatment of Poland before them, the renegades of the Pétain Government should have known better. Doubtless they expected special treatment, but, except that the full savagery of Hitler's soldiery has not yet fallen on the French, the fates of Poland and France do not differ greatly.

"What a city to loot," Blücher is reported to have said on gazing from St. Paul's upon the City of London. The same sentiment must have entered the mind of his twentieth-century imitator when the Fuehrer ascended the Eiffel Tower (now a national German monument, of which models stand on thousands of mantelshelves in the Fatherland) and gazed upon the wealth of Paris and northern France. Certainly plunder was the first thought of the German occupiers of the fair land of France. The German plan for that country is to reduce it to a nation of peasants—"peasants without pigs," as one observer laconically reports. With Germany as the industrial centre of Europe, the rest is to be a raw material and food producing reservoir, inhabited by serfs who will labour to the greater glory of the Herrenvolk. The plan is applied very simply. All movable industrial equipment of value and all skilled workers are being transferred to Germany from occupied France. To feed the Supermen of the Fatherland the country is being systematically robbed of crops, stocks, cattle, poultry and all farm produce. What the French have left to them—and it is very little—is doled out in miserable rations, amounting to about one-eighth of the amount consumed by the average Frenchman before the war. And to obtain these tiny quantities of food, long queues wait from dawn to dusk outside the shops, while well-fed Nazis roll by in luxurious cars, or great lorries, loaded with plundered provender, rumble eastwards.

Little Food, No Free Speech

The loss of his food is probably the hardest cross the Frenchman has to bear; next to it must come the loss of his political liberties and the rights of free speech. The word "Boche" is verboten and harsh punishment is meted out to anyone heard using it. In its place the word "doryphore" (potato bug) has emerged as the general term for German; doubtless this, too, will be a forbidden word when the Nazis realize its new application. The curfew means that the Parisian can visit his favourite café for only three short periods in the day—at breakfast, lunch and dinner times; entertainment is almost dead except for a few inferior Aryan cabarets brought over from Berlin; friendly visiting is forbidden (no parties of more than eight or so are allowed to forgather); private travel by car or train has ceased; bicycles, being the only mode of locomotion remaining except pedestrianism, are almost unobtainable. The shortage of soap may be endurable, but it is annoying. Less bearable is the shortage of fuel—coal, wood and oil—which, with autumn breezes blowing already and a hard winter in prospect, makes all France shiver in anticipation. There were great stocks of coal and coke in France, gathered together at the Government's request before the surrender; these have been confiscated and carried into Germany.

When the occupation began the French were pleasantly surprised to discover how friendly and urbane the billeted soldiery were, and to observe how generous the authorities seemed to be in the matter of censorship and individual liberties. They were soon disillusioned; within six weeks the velvet glove was removed and the grip of the iron hand was felt. The invaders' attitude entirely changed; whereas at first the French were smiled at and their children's heads patted for the benefit of photographers by Hitler's men, those same soldiers changed into their natural character of blond beast almost overnight. Herded along side streets because their favourite boulevards are reserved for the mighty ones, forbidden to walk in the Bois de Boulogne or along the Avenue Kléber and other famous thoroughfares, the Parisians were now received with hostile stares, curt, contemptuous phrases, and personal cruelty. The mask was off.

Germans Flock From the Ruhr

Into the Paris area have flocked the well-to-do families of the Ruhr and Rhineland, fleeing from the nightly visitations of the R.A.F. These, and the 2½ million soldiers in the occupied zone, together with 250,000 on furlough in Paris, also have to be fed luxuriously, while the semi-starved Parisian looks on. Letters to New York, printed in the American newspapers and reprinted in Britain, tell of the impotent anger of the ordinary Frenchman when he has to witness this degradation of his country. The soldiers he could bear—even admire; but these swine of civilians using Paris as a funkhole—pfui! Further, the cunning with which the Nazis have rigged the currency has rendered every German visitor wealthy and hopelessly impoverished even well-to-do French people. The French currency still exists, but with the franc at twenty to the mark a small fortune is required to purchase even minor luxuries.

These same letters—and reports brought into Spain and Portugal by neutral travellers and diplomats—all stress the same point. The first numb acceptance of the occupation has worn off. The Frenchman may be compelled to helpless silence, but he boils with suppressed rage.

Many of military age, required to enrol at the local kommandatur and firmly "invited" to volunteer for labour in Germany, have disappeared. Tyranny of this and other varieties are making the people realize at last the extent of the betrayal—both of France and of true democracy. They await the opportunity and the signal for revolt against their masters, of Berlin and of Vichy, knowing that their only hope lies in a British victory. They have lost all faith in Pétain

These residents of the famous French port of Le Havre are seen receiving an allowance of tinned ersatz soup from a depot run by the sisters of the N.S.V. or National Socialist Assistance. To judge from their expressions Nazi food does not appear delectable!
Photo, E.N.A.

In Conquered Paris the Velvet Glove is Off

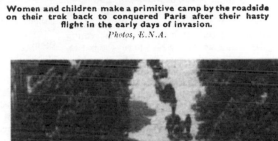

Women and children make a primitive camp by the roadside on their trek back to conquered Paris after their hasty flight in the early days of invasion.
Photos, E.N.A.

Refugees' street depôts, above, have become tragically frequent in occupied France. Notes pinned to the board ask for information concerning missing relatives and friends.

The famous Paris church of Sacre Coeur, which dominates the city from Montmartre, attracts Nazi soldiers as an object of special interest. They are seen on the steps. The Germans have been pouring their supplies into the French capital, and supply columns are seen, right, entering the deserted Paris streets.

What Has Fate In Store For Portugal?

Far from easy is the situation of Portugal, now the only remaining really neutral country in Western Europe. Here we have something to say of the past and present state of Britain's oldest ally and hint at the possibilities of tomorrow.

FOR more than five and a half centuries, since 1386 when our Edward III concluded the Treaty of Windsor with King John, England and Portugal have been allies, and it was in honour of this, the oldest alliance in history, that the Duke of Kent was the nation's guest at the celebrations in Lisbon last summer of the eighth centenary of Portugal's independence and the fourth centenary of her last liberation from Spanish rule. Her *last* liberation : ere long she may be once again brought under the dominion of Spain.

For Portugal is small and weak, and 1940 is proving a bad year for small and weak countries. " Portugal is such a little country," wrote Ralph Fox, the young English writer who gave his life on the battle-field, fighting for the Spanish Republic. " Its spare, swarthy peasants, in their black homespuns, with the black tasselled caps like woollen nightcaps, have to work so hard on the brown, burned-up earth, to pay so much for the little water to irrigate their parched fields, and the fields themselves are so tiny, hardly bigger than a middle-class Englishman's suburban garden. They work, with a little bread, a little fruit and wine, sometimes a little meat, to produce port wine and cork for exports. And the fishermen fight the Atlantic storms to get you sardines. That's all this little country gives the world—port, cork and sardines."

Long ago, when Europe was discovering the Indies and the Americas, Portugal was a Great Power and Lisbon, the capital, was perhaps the world's richest and most thriving port. But history showed that Portugal was too tiny and the Portuguese too few to discover new worlds, to colonize them, and to conduct their trade. Moreover, the great mass of the people were ever ignorant and miserable, the dupes of the Inquisition, the slaves of the Jesuits, the prey

of their royalties and rulers. The monarchy, restored in 1640 after a forced union with Spain which had endured for sixty years, lasted until 1910 when the young Manoel, who had succeeded his father, Carlos I, brutally murdered two years before, was sent into exile—to spend the years until his death at Twickenham in 1932 for the most part in England, in extremely comfortable and pleasant circumstances.

When Manoel left, Portugal became a republic, and in little over twenty years witnessed twenty-four revolutions and coups d'etat of one kind and another. The attempt to construct something that might be called a democracy was an utter failure. " Electors meet in vain where want makes them the slaves of the landlord or where superstition makes them the slaves of the priest," wrote Macaulay, and the great Whig would have found in modern Portugal abundant proof of the truth of his dictum. The last vestiges of a parliamentary regime were swept away in 1926 by a group of army officers, headed by Generals Carmona and da Costa, who at least showed some acumen in appointing to the post of Finance Minister

Dr. Salazar, the Premier and virtual dictator of Portugal, is here seen in the plain clothes he prefers to any uniform, making an inspection of an underground ammunition store.

While Europe has been in a state of turmoil the people of Portugal under a benevolent dictatorship have changed their mode of life very little. Here is the scene in the market-place of a small Portuguese town where the women make their purchases, sure at least that the other dictators will not rain death upon them from the skies.
Photos, Leicester Cotton and Planet News

With its long coast line Portugal has produced a hardy race of fishermen who besides fish for home consumption are responsible for one of their country's most important exports—sardines. The others are port and cork.

a professor at the University of Coimbra, one Dr. Antonio d'Oliveira Salazar. The don resigned after five days in office, but in 1928 Carmona, now ruling alone, appointed him again to the same post, and since 1932 Salazar has been premier and virtual dictator.

Salazar in himself is a very pleasant change from the common run of present-day dictators, and in his appointment and his subsequent career there has been displayed many a deviation from what has come to be accepted as the dictatorial norm. As a man he is intensely retiring though hardly

modest in his estimate of his own importance ; hardly a Portuguese would recognize him if he met him in the streets. He hardly ever appears in public and never wears a uniform ; he does not rant over the wireless or review goosestepping troops, or make spectacular appearances at great party demonstrations ; his photograph is seldom seen in the shop windows, although a press photograph, such as the one above, is occasionally permitted. If he has enemies, he knows how to get rid of them without employing such clumsy weapons as the bullet and the axe.

An Occupation Might Be Hitler's Achilles Heel

Lisbon's imposingly picturesque harbour and water-front along the River Tagus. At this dock the boats unload their cargoes of fish to the waiting fishwives some of whom are seen standing on the quayside. In contrast to the troubled Europe of today, this scene has a refreshingly peaceful appearance.

Portuguese troops are seen marching along a street of Oporto on their way to camp. Oporto, one of Europe's chief ports along the Western seaboard, preserves its commercial peacetime pursuits. The city is the centre of the port wine trade.

Photos, Branson de Cou, and Leicester Cotton

A new development in dictators, his dictatorship is not inspired by any revolutionary enthusiasm, any burning zeal to right the wrongs of the world by wiping out men and institutions and frontiers with ruthless gusto. The Nazi and the Fascist are like the Communist in believing that the success of their " movement " would liberate their peoples from the stranglehold of an outworn political system, from the chains of what they describe as " pluto-democracy " (or should it be " demo-plutocracy " ?). Salazar and the men who put and maintain him where he is have no sustaining belief in the virtue of revolution ; their blessed word is restoration, and they look not forward to a new order of society based on an all-powerful State, operating through a single party, but back to the " good old days " in which family and wealth and inherited influence are the things that " pull."

Salazar has no party of his own ; his movement strives to be genuinely national and his first success was in the complete suppression of the parties and factions which made Portuguese politics a foul disgrace. True, there is a Salazar militia for boys between eight and twelve, a Salazar youth movement ; true, Portugal is a police state, one in which spies are everywhere and the policemen are ever on the search for anything which to their not over-bright intelligence may appear subversive. But at least the uglier aspects of the dictatorships of Hitler and Mussolini are absent from that wielded by the one-time professor who is that well-nigh unique character, a dictator who shuns the limelight.

And some very solid achievements lie to his credit. He has balanced the budget and brought order into the national finances, although there are critics who whisper that the balancing has been achieved by omitting to include some inconvenient items, while the comparison between now and a few years ago is somewhat affected by taking the pseudo at different par of exchange. But Salazar has succeeded in doing what none of

his predecessors of the republican era managed to do ; he has remained in office for twelve years and may well remain there for many years to come.

But in that he will not have the determining word ; maybe that will be Franco's or Hitler's. Portugal today is the last independent neutral country in Western Europe, and how long she can continue such is problematic. Both Germany and Italy would like to have the line of her coast and the Azores for submarine and fleet bases whence they might threaten Britain's route to the Cape and South America and turn the flank of Gibraltar. Amongst the Falangists —the predominant party in Franco's Spain —there are many who are of the opinion that the whole of the Iberian peninsula should be under one flag, and that Spain's.

If the Axis Powers have not yet seized the whole of the Atlantic seaboard it is because Portugal is more valuable to them, at present, as a door through which may come supplies from America, than she would be as a base of attack against Britain. But some day, any day, they may decide otherwise, and then Portugal will follow so many other little countries of Europe in the Axis prison. As likely as not, there would be no military resistance, for Portugal's army has a peacetime strength of only 30,000 men.

And then ? Then history might well repeat itself. When Napoleon lorded it over Europe, it was to Portugal that Wellington's Expeditionary Force was dispatched. Portugal proved to be Napoleon's heel of Achilles ; it may prove to be Hitler's too.

Here Are Prisoners of War of Three Nations

This photograph of British officers who are prisoners in Germany was received through Lisbon. The camp is known as Oflag IX A. Two of the officers have been recognized. Bottom line, fourth from left : Lt. A. H. Bishop, R.A.O.C. Top, sixth from left : Capt. P. Scott-Martin, M.C., Royal West Kent Regt. Others will no doubt be recognized by friends and relations.

Left, German airmen taken prisoners in England at the end of September are entraining on their way to an internment camp. Nazi prisoners in Canada (above) do voluntary work for which they are paid 20 cents a day. The chance to earn is eagerly taken.
Photos, Br. Official : Crown Copyright ; Topical, Fox & Associated Press

A good haul of Italian prisoners has been made by the British during the operations in Libya. Above is the scene in a prisoners' camp. Naturally swarthy, the Italian soldiers baked by the desert sun have all the appearance of "men of colour."

British Fleet Sweeps the Mediterranean All Clear

During a patrol in the Mediterranean, a British destroyer attacked an Italian submarine with depth charges. Gunfire having destroyed the conning tower, the enemy ship surrendered. Top left, the submarine draws alongside the destroyer. Above is seen the captain's bridge on board a battleship while at sea.

On July 9 British naval forces in the Mediterranean made contact with Italian battleships, cruisers and destroyers. An enemy battleship was hit, but the enemy retired behind a smoke-screen and sought the safety of shore defences. Two shells are seen exploding (circle).

Photos, Associated Press; British Official Crown Copyright

These sailors have reached their home port. A sing-song accompanied by a piano accordion testifies to the high spirits of this battleship crew. White cap covers, white jumpers and shorts, instead of the heavy serge trousers of the ordinary uniform, are now warn in hot weather, adding greatly to the comfort of the ships' companies.

Photo, Central Press

Polish Airmen Are Fighting in Britain's War

Recently, Polish airmen fighting in the R.A.F. on R.A.F. machines, in British skies, against the common enemy, have achieved many successes. Here Mr. Henry Baerlein, who has visited, on behalf of "The War Illustrated," the headquarters of a Polish bomber squadron, tells something of their work and spirit.

WE have lately been told in official communiques that in mass attacks upon this country the Germans have encountered Polish fighter squadrons which have operated with marked success ; indeed, the magnificent dash and determination of this allied force has made people think that their psychology would be less adapted to bombers. That this is not so I have learned in the course of a recent visit to a bomber aerodrome, part of which is allocated to the Poles. Not only do they speak enthusiastically of the British machines they fly—

Poles began to participate in bombing expeditions, so that it was rather foolish of Goebbels to declare on the wireless that during the night of September 2-3 a Polish pilot accompanying a British raid to Berlin had flown on to Warsaw and given himself up. The Poles are anxious to reply to such a calumny when they receive the order to bomb Berlin.

The squadron-leader was likewise astonished and delighted that a young airman in this country has to pass through exactly the same curriculum now as in peacetime.

The gallant Polish airmen with the R.A.F., now in temporary exile, find the customs of their homeland particularly dear to them. Here some of them are rehearsing for an entertainment of Polish music and dancing in aid of their funds. They make costumes with white linen on which they paint characteristic designs. *Photo, Fox*

" we are," one of the pilots said to me, " terribly satisfied with them "—but the British authorities are just as appreciative of the work of these airmen.

Most of the Polish airmen who arrived in Britain were very experienced pilots, some in civilian and others in military flying, so that it was not long before they had accustomed themselves to our methods and machines. These, they say, are much easier to handle than the types which they flew in France. The fact also that our bombers are heavily armoured, so that they can reach their targets in spite of opposition, has greatly impressed them. Their one regret is that these machines cannot carry three times as many bombs. And, talking of bombs, a Polish squadron-leader told me of his astonishment when he saw how even in wartime our practice-bombs are so well made. " As beautifully formed," he said, " as jewels, and I realized how good must be the bombs we are given to drop."

It was in the middle of September that the

That this is not so in the German air force is obviously, he said, one of the reasons for their heavy losses. And how many of them have enough experience to attempt the feat of dive-bombing by night ?

Not all the members of this bomber squadron can speak English as well as that officer, but he told me that this matters surprisingly little, and especially is it so among the rank and file. For the first two weeks they talk to each other, somehow or other, about their 'planes, and then they feel quite capable of enlarging the conversation to include their girls. These Poles are perfectly at home in Britain, though in the winter they will think regretfully of the fortnight's skiing which was part of their ordinary service at home. They have not the smallest complaint to make of the food, and the squadron-leader became almost lyrical in alluding to the cook at another base who serves up a joint of beef partly well done, partly underdone, partly lean, partly fat, so that everyone is satisfied.

" As to our work," he said, " I believe that we are giving satisfaction." This, I afterwards ascertained, is an understatement, for the Poles have been doing splendidly. For instance, the squadron-leader had just received a letter from a young compatriot of his temporarily in hospital, whom he had known very well in Poland. There he shot down four Germans himself and, with another pilot, two more. Here, after a week's training, he went up, brought down one and was himself brought down and, as this happened at a height of less than 600 feet and he could discover no flat landing-place, his machine crashed, but the damage to himself was not serious. Going up on the next day, he shot down four Messerschmitts and a Heinkel, after which his machine caught fire and he was obliged to bale out, a proceeding rendered difficult—in fact, he said in his letter, it was the most difficult undertaking of his life—because his 'plane was in a diving position. This resulted in his being struck by the tail and he was pretty severely wounded in the leg. He is now hoping that this and the burns on his hands and face will not keep him in hospital.

While the squadron-leader had been talking three Polish officers (one of them a chaplain who, like his companions, was in the uniform of the R.A.F. with the word " Poland " as a shoulder badge) had come in from a neighbouring base. As it happened they had all been so busy in various ways that they had not had time to pick up much of our language, but the two air forces, said the squadron-leader, understood each other perfectly. He then translated for my benefit an incident which had occurred in the other squadron. A gunner was helping to take the flares out of a bomber on its return early one morning. The fourth one which he handled started to burn. He feared that it would explode and injure the two men still in the 'plane and the 'plane itself. So he grasped it in his arms, ran across a field and was gravely wounded when the explosion took place. The first question he put on recovering consciousness in hospital was with regard to the condition of the aircraft and his two comrades. The C.O. who told us of this affair remarked with a smile that " I would not have got it out of the man himself." The Polish airmen, like ours, he said, considered that the most harassing part of the day's work was the description of their exploits to the intelligence officers on their return. All they want to do then is to rest and go up again.

On October 1 the Polish Minister of Information, Prof. Stronski, contrasting the defences of Warsaw and London, declared the Polish fighting pilots were very happy to share in the Battle of London. The Polish Squadron 303 had shot down during September 1940 over 100 Nazi aircraft, and by their successes then were repaying the German Air Force for the tragic fate of Warsaw in September 1939. The squadron-leader of this No. 303 was wounded in a fierce battle over London and was decorated with the Virtuti Militari Cross on August 8 by General Sikorski.

They Are Ready in Thousands to Avenge Warsaw

The King shaking hands with a Polish airman when he visited one of the Fighter Command Stations to which a Polish squadron is attached.

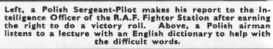

Left, a Polish Sergeant-Pilot makes his report to the Intelligence Officer of the R.A.F. Fighter Station after earning the right to do a victory roll. Above, a Polish airman listens to a lecture with an English dictionary to help with the difficult words.

Polish airmen have come to Britain in thousands eager to avenge the ruthless destruction the Nazis caused in Warsaw. They are now completing their training in the N.W. of England. Left, a Polish airman carries a bomb of which he hopes later to make good use. Right, another airman practises with the type of machine-gun with which his 'plane will be fitted.

Photos, Keystone, Central Press, Topical and Chas. E. Brown

London Carries On in the People's War

October opened with new variations of the air war on London and the country generally, but incidents were fewer and attacks on a smaller scale, though more prolonged. No large-scale victories could be recorded for the R.A.F., but in no way had Goering advanced towards his objective.

THE selection of Air-Marshal Sir Charles Portal to succeed Sir Cyril Newall as Air Chief Marshal (on the retirement of Sir Cyril to become Governor-General of New Zealand) may be taken as a significant portent of Britain's intention to intensify the air offensive against Germany. For since March last Sir Charles Portal as C.-in-C. of the Bomber Command had directed the work of our bombers in blocking the enemy's transport, slowing down his munition production and checking his plans for the invasion of Britain. The Bomber Command was taken over by Sir Richard Peirse, Vice-Chief of the Air Staff.

Bad weather—it was even bad enough to prevent the R.A.F. on two nights from making their customary raids on German objectives—may have accounted for the slackening of the enemy air attacks on Britain in the early days of October. But it is possible that the slowing down of Germany's assault may have been due to a realization that the blitzkrieg had failed, and to the withdrawal of aircraft for use in quite another theatre of war. Nor must there be left out of account

GERMAN & BRITISH AIRCRAFT LOSSES

German to April 30, 1940
Total announced and estimated—West Front, North Sea, Britain, Scandinavia 350

	German	British
May	1,990	258
June	276	177
July	245	115
Aug.	1,110	310
Sept. 1-30	1,114	311
Oct. 1-7	72	30
Totals, May to Oct. 7 ...	**4,807**	**1,701**

Daily Results

	German Losses	British Losses	British Pilots Saved		German Losses	British Losses	British Pilots Saved
Oct.							
1	5	3	—	4	3	1	—
2	10	1	—	5	23	9	7
3	2	—	—	6	2	—	
				7	27	16	10
Totals					**72**	**30**	**17**

None of the figures include aircraft bombed on the ground or so damaged as to be unlikely to reach home.

Civilian Casualties. Intensive air attacks on Britain began on Aug. 8. Casualties during August 1,075 killed, 1,261 seriously injured.

Mr. Churchill stated on Oct. 8 that up to Oct. 5 8,500 people had been killed and 13,000 seriously injured in air raids. Casualty figures had decreased steadily week by week since heavy raiding began on Sept. 7; from over 6,000 in the first week to just under 5,000 in the second, to about 4,000 in the third, and to under 3,000 in the last of the four weeks.

Mass Raid Casualties in London. Sept. 7: 306 killed; 1,337 injured. Sept. 8: 286 killed; about 1,400 injured. Sept. 9: about 400 killed, 1,400 injured.

German Aircraft Destroyed in Britain. From September 3, 1939 to Oct. 8, 1940, the German machines destroyed around and over Britain totalled 2,601. In that time 607 British aircraft were lost, 338 pilots being saved.

German Pilots Lost. Lord Croft, Under Secretary for War, stated recently that more German airmen alone had been slain or captured in the previous twelve weeks [i.e. July to September] than all the civilians they had murdered in Britain. Less British blood had been shed as the result of air attacks in 12 months than we frequently lost in a single hour in the Great War of 1914-18.

the heavy losses suffered by the Luftwaffe since the war began. Air Ministry figures to the end of September show that in combat between British and German air forces 3,644 German aircraft were destroyed against 1,417 British lost—316 of our pilots were saved. As to the total German aircraft losses in all theatres of war, the Air Correspondent of the "Daily Telegraph" worked out a figure of 6,500, more than half being bombers. This would mean that the Nazis had lost about 13,500 air personnel.

In daylight raids on the first day of October only a few enemy aircraft got through to London. Attacks in the South of England proved unsuccessful and the Nazi machines were repulsed near the coast. Five raiders were destroyed, three of our fighters being lost. Six "alerts" in all were given during the day and night. Soon after the first evening alarm was sounded the "Raiders Passed" was given, but after an hour's lull there was another warning. Generally the Nazis came over singly, making swift runs to the central area and then scurrying off as soon as bombs had been dropped. The North and North-western suburbs were attacked, and bombs fell also in East London. Many fire bombs fell, but were smothered and put out with little difficulty. Our A.A. gunners shot down one raider before it had time to drop its load; bomber and bombs exploded together.

There was a seven-hour daylight raid on Wednesday, October 2, and London had no fewer than six "alerts." In small lots of forty to eighty the Nazi machines crossed the Kent coast, but only odd machines got near London. Attacks were also made on South-western England, South Wales, and Essex. Swift retribution overtook a Dornier 17 which machine-gunned the streets of an Essex town—a trick which the Nazis have too often played of late. A few minutes afterwards it was shot down by a Hurricane.

At night the enemy aircraft came over in waves from two different directions, skirted the suburbs, and then turned in towards the Metropolis. As usual, they did some damage, but were prevented in their major object by our barrage. As Mr. Ernest Brown, Secretary for Scotland, well said in a speech made at this time, London was scarred by the nightly attacks but was undaunted. Hitler had failed to disrupt the life of the City.

Nine London districts were bombed by daylight on Thursday, but though there were many attacks few aircraft were engaged and it was generally lone raiders who flew over and dropped bombs at random. There were

All that remained of an A.R.P. lorry which was blown out of the street into this back garden when a bomb fell in a South-Western London street during a recent night raid. *Photo, "Daily Mirror"*

This clock on the mantelpiece of a London house which was bombed has been chiming regularly. A member of the A.R.P. is seen removing the time-piece from its lonely perch. *Photo, Fox*

They Go to Deep Shelters with High Hearts

On a short branch line of one of London's tubes trains have been stopped and the current cut off, and there between the rails many Londoners spend a safe night. The tunnel, about half a mile in length, is lit throughout by electric light.

Photo, Planet News

One of the first acts of Mr. Herbert Morrison after becoming Home Secretary and Minister of Home Defence was to visit air raid shelters and see the conditions for himself. Below, he is talking to mothers and children in a shelter in South-East London.

Photo, " News Chronicle "

The people of North-East England who suffered severely from air raids before London was touched have never quailed. The words in the photograph, left, were chalked in front of a house wrecked by a bomb.

Photo, Keystone

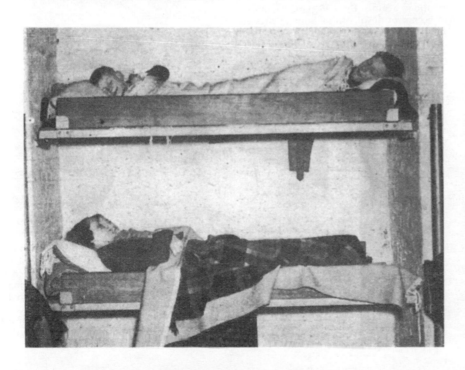

Part of the crypt of London's famous church, St. Martin-in-the-Fields, is reserved as an air raid shelter for women and children only, left. Above, a sand cave used as a deep shelter by people of a Kentish village.

Photos, Keystone and Planet News

Guns Roar Glorious Defiance to Nazi Bombers

A Messerschmitt 109 fighter, above, escorting a bomber was brought down near Maidstone. The pilot baled out watched by crowds of hop-pickers, who later had the satisfaction of seeing it as it is on right.   *Photos, Fox*

low clouds over London and people below could see nothing of what was happening in the air. Gunfire was heard, and the noise of aircraft engines, but life went on much as usual in the busy City and Central area. Two warnings were given during the night. Our fierce barrage prevented much mischief. Such raiders as got through did so by shutting off the engines and making a long and silent glide over their objective.

Low cloud on Friday enabled raiders to sneak in over London and drop bombs here and there during an " alert " lasting some hours. Apart from Central London, bombs fell also in Northern and Eastern districts and in suburbs on the South-west. A Hurricane pilot flew out of the clouds and found a Junkers 88 on mischief bent; the enemy was shot down. This sort of cloud hunting was common. A German communiqué gave the number of their losses as five machines, two more than claimed by the Air Ministry, who had not counted in two " probables."

All day Saturday fierce battles were fought in the air, and the enemy came over in big formations again. By 7.30 p.m. 23 raiders had been shot down. In an hour 18 Messerschmitt fighters were shot down over Kent and the Thames Estuary. Other raiders crossed the Dorset and Hampshire coasts but met with little success. Bombs fell in East and South-east London, dropped by isolated enemy machines flying very high. The barrage at night reached a new intensity and was continuous for long periods. Only at two points were bombs dropped in the London area, neither near the Central district.

A score of places in the Home Counties were bombed on Sunday, in hit-and-run raids made possible by cloudy conditions.

At night, after a brief " alert " early in the evening, probably when an enemy reconnaissance machine came over, there was an " all clear " until morning. Nevertheless

Mr. Churchill on the Bombing of London
Notes from his Speech of October 8

TO what extent has the full strength of the German Air Force been deployed ? Short-range dive bombers have been kept carefully out of the air fight since their very severe mauling on Aug. 15. It would seem, taking day and night together, nearly 400 of the German long-range heavy bombers have, on the average, visited our shores every 24 hours. We are doubtful whether this rate of sustained attack can be greatly exceeded. We believe that the German heavy bomber pilots are being worked at least as hard as, and it may be a great deal harder than, our own. The bulk of them do not seem capable of anything beyond blind bombing. On the whole, however, we may ... reach the provisional conclusion that the German average effort against this country absorbs a very considerable part of their forces and strength. We feel more confident now than we have ever been before ... It would take 10 years at the present rate for half the houses of London to be demolished ... On every side is the cry " We can take it."

the Nazis claimed that " London and numerous other targets in the South of England were again successfully attacked in spite of very difficult weather conditions. . . . In London a big gasworks exploded " ! A very clear proof how the Berlin communiqués are concocted.

At daylight on Monday there began big attacks on London and the South-east, the raiders coming up the Thames Estuary and over the coast of Kent as usual. Nearly 500 Nazi machines were involved, and there were five separate attempts on London. Only in

The guns of the London barrage whose roar the capital likes to hear when the 'planes are overhead badly need a cleaning next day. Left, hot water being poured through a barrel to open the pores of the metal and facilitate the removal of dirt and corrosion. Right, the man who pours in the hot water.

two cases did enemy aircraft penetrate the London defences, and even then very few bombs were dropped. A number of incendiary bombs fell in the Central area during the night, but the trouble was soon localized and the fires quickly extinguished. Attacks in the week were many and sometimes on a large scale, tactics were completely changed yet the military results were negligible.

London's Defences Are Beating The Night Bomber

Soon after the intensified murder raids on London began the increased fury of the A.A. gun barrage gave much satisfaction to the millions compelled to endure the indiscriminate Nazi bombings. Other defence methods were also operative, and here an acknowledged authority discusses the problems of night defence and forecasts increasing success in grappling with them.

ONE feature of the air war which showed a steadily increasing importance from the beginning until the time of the intensified aerial attacks on Great Britain of August and September was night bombing. And in countering it the greatest ingenuity was exercised.

Night bombing was begun by the Royal Air Force, which had carefully prepared for it and trained for it. The German air force, in so far as official statements from Berlin revealed its beliefs, held that military effect, which is the only kind of effect worth thinking about in war, could be secured only by day bombing.

Actually the Royal Air Force had evolved a method of night bombing which enabled it to hit at military targets by night with as great certainty as by day, the only difference being that the targets had to be chosen in relation to their position and also in relation to the weather.

Nights do occur occasionally when the illumination is so good that targets can be recognized almost as readily as by day. But on most nights the targets chosen must be of the " self-illuminated " variety if they are to be found without the use of parachute flares or the starting of fires at near-by points.

A good example of a self-illuminated target is a blast furnace. Another was the seaplane base at Sylt, which was one of the first land objectives attacked by the Royal Air Force during the war. Water can be distinguished from land on most nights, and when the shape of the shore or coastline is distinctive a target can be recognized by the conformations with as great accuracy as by day.

Any Target Was Permissible

The German air force had made many night raids before the main attacks on London began in August and September ; but they had been directed at military objectives, and as those objectives are extremely well camouflaged and as England is a country over which it is exceedingly difficult to find the way even by day, the German pilots in most cases missed their objectives altogether and dropped their bombs more often than not in open country. These small raids were the subject of many official communiqués and in all cases the damage was slight or even altogether non-existent.

But when the order was given to attack London both by night and by day the method selected was very different. It seems, from the results, that any big building which could be seen by the German night pilots was to be regarded as a permissible target, and that, supposing the buildings could not be distinguished at all owing to the darkness, any cluster of houses was to be regarded as a permissible target.

Thus the East End of London received a great many heavy attacks and vast numbers of dwelling houses there were destroyed. In addition, many big buildings in the West End were hit and much damage done to them. But there was no evidence that anything approaching a military target was selected by any pilot. Sometimes it did seem that power stations and railway stations were being selected, but then a large series of raids would intervene in which no bomb dropped near such objectives.

The fact that this random or semi-random method of bombing was adopted by the Germans made the problems of defence more difficult. For it is clear that an airman is bound to find some part of London if he sets out for it even on the darkest night. To try to prevent enemy aircraft getting to any part of London or other large cities, while at the same time maintaining adequate protection for the real military targets such as munitions works, was the essence of the defence problem.

London's Magnificent New Barrage

The solution, in so far as it had been arrived at by the beginning of October, was to obtain a high degree of coordination between the anti-aircraft guns, the balloon barrage and the night-flying fighters. The searchlights, which were used extensively at first, were used in a much reduced degree later for reasons which will appear.

The first point which had to be taken into account was that interception by night was a matter of extreme difficulty and could only be achieved on nights of good visibility and with a certain amount of luck. The night-flying fighter, in fact, had very severe limitations. It was imperative, therefore, to build up the defence by gun and balloon barrage for night work.

The guns made the first step. One night Londoners heard the night raiders met with a tremendous barrage of fire, more intense and more continuous than anything they had heard before. It was the outcome of the working of the first part of the new scheme.

Instead of waiting for " seen targets " only, the gunners had been instructed to fire on sound alone and also to use certain new instruments and new methods.

These included a new system of prediction. The ordinary predictor, used with the anti-aircraft guns, is a calculating machine which quickly produces results from certain figures which are fed into it by the gun crews, the resultant figures giving the gun position officer the information for sighting and fusing that he wants.

Now it is evident that the accuracy of the predictor's results is of two orders ; first, it makes the calculations correctly without exception and, therefore, in one part achieves 100 per cent accuracy ; second, the usefulness of its results in the actual firing depends upon the accuracy of the figures which are fed into it.

That is where the difficulty still lies. The height of the approaching aircraft must be correctly estimated, its speed and its course. Moreover, the predictor can only work on the assumption that that speed, course and height will remain the same or will be subject to alterations which are pure guesswork on the part of the gun crew. No gun crew and certainly no predictor can tell what an enemy pilot will do with his machine during the appreciable number of seconds a shell is in the air travelling towards its target.

When the new barrage system was instituted for the defence of London by night, the limitations of the predictor were taken into account and a wider system of prediction, based on certain probabilities, was adopted. In addition, the firing of the guns was grouped according to a specific pattern so as to increase still further the probabilities of a hit.

The entire system is one of probabilities. As such it was shown at once to be a great success. The searchlights were not used so extensively, so that the enemy night pilots no longer profited by their reflected light, but the sound locators came into more extensive play and enabled a barrage to be put up which did very effectively hamper the movements of enemy machines.

It did not bring them down in large numbers. Indeed, this was not expected. It is known that a fairly large number of anti-aircraft rounds must be fired—the number has been estimated at between 5,000 and 6,000—in order to shoot down a single enemy machine, but the barrage effectively held off the enemy.

Concurrently with the adoption of the new prediction system for the guns, there went an improvement in the effectiveness of the balloon barrage. This consisted in introducing new balloons and cables which could be flown higher, yet with the same lethal effect on any enemy machine which chanced to strike a cable.

Higher Balloons And Other Methods

Barrage balloon height is determined by cable weight. Cable weight is partly determined by lethal effect. It is of no use to fly a balloon very high if, in order to do so, the cable must be so light that it can easily be cut by a fast-flying aeroplane. Research into the properties of cables had been going on since the beginning of the war, and the result was the possibility of flying the balloons higher with the same protective effect.

An enemy machine was brought down by a high-flying balloon early in the series of night raids on London, and in general the balloon barrage may be said to have added its effect to that of the guns in limiting the area in which the enemy machines could work with any chance of getting away safely.

Guns and balloons were not the only methods being tried during the period of night raids in August, September and October in order to counter the night raiders. Enormous numbers of devices were constantly under review by scientific workers and technical experts. Some of these were confidently expected to show successful results when the preliminary work on them had been completed.

No more difficult type of attack to counter exists than the night-flying bomber which is seeking, not specific military targets, but any cluster of buildings it can find. But to every form of attack there is an appropriate defence, and it was recognized throughout the Royal Air Force that this form was no exception.

The Man and Woman in the Street Answer the

These unique photographs were taken within th
two minutes from the fall of a bomb, in a Lo
workers, themselves living in the district attack
more bombs may fall.   Above, they are dealing wit
is a rescued kitten.

Scenes of infinite pathos were enacted as the people were rescued from
their wrecked houses. The mother above being guided to a place of
refuge by an A.R.P. worker carries her unconscious child.   Right, A.R.P.
workers search a wrecked house in case there may be someone trapped in it.

n Their Own London Suburb as the Bombs Fall

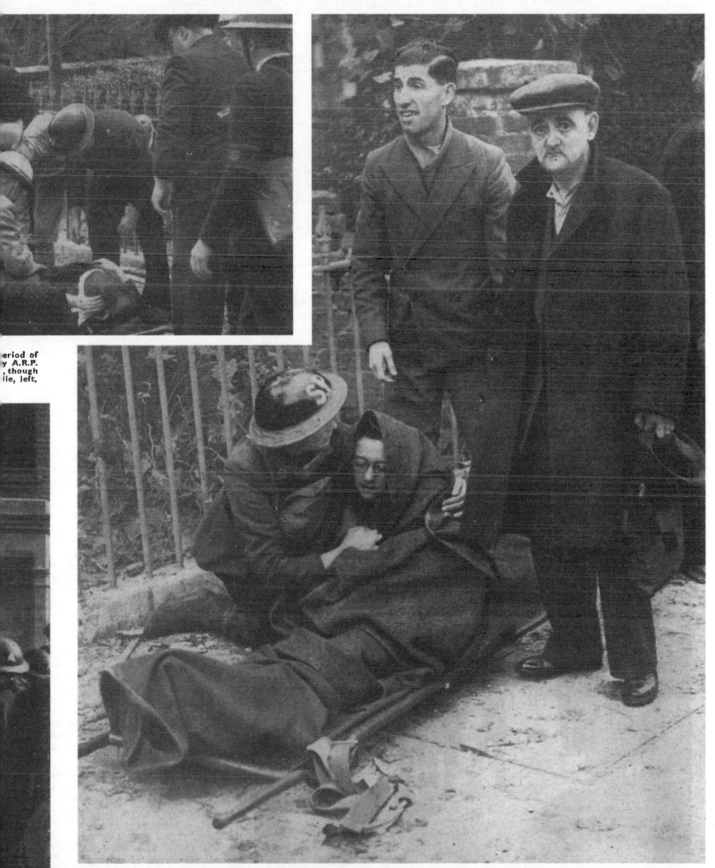

eriod of
y A.R.P.
, though
ile, left,

While the A.R.P. men risk their lives in rescuing the occupants of stricken homes the women of that fine body of front line workers show a no less gallant spirit in ministering to their suffering sisters. Above, one of them comforts a woman suffering from shock, and to her care her family can safely leave her.

Photos by Edward Dean, Exclusive to THE WAR ILLUSTRATED

Women On Active Service in the Battle of Britain

Since the War has come to the homeland, active service for women's organizations attached to the fighting forces has taken on an even more military aspect. Here Miss Peggy Scott describes the work, often under fire, of A.T.S., W.R.N.S., W.A.A.F. and W.F.P.

THE Battle of Britain has brought women for the first time into the front-line everywhere.

Even when several hundred of the Auxiliary Territorial Service—the A.T.S.—were in France in the spring of 1940, they were confined to areas on the lines of communication. The "Soldierettes," as the French people called them, took the places of men, except in the fighting line; there, the men had to cook and drive for themselves.

As a matter of fact, being in the front line has made less difference to the A.T.S. than to women in the civil services. They did everything for the men before, except fight. The only difference now is that when the men who usually work in the cook-house and orderly room at night go to their Action Stations, women take their places. At one unit in the South where women work in the cook-house during the day and men at night, some of the A.T.S. clerical staff take the places of the men in the cook-house when they go to their action stations. Certain commanding officers have had the A.T.S. trained to work the stirrup-pumps for fire-fighting.

The Battle of Britain has also perhaps speeded up the recruiting of the A.T.S. Over 30,000 women are already at work; practically wherever there are soldiers in the British Isles, there are A.T.S. helping them; but still more are wanted—about 10,000.

One of the best aids to recruiting occurred when the A.T.S. Unit returned from France. The Director A.T.S. inspected them after church parade. The remark of a man at the crossroads, obviously an old N.C.O., when Dame Helen Gwynne-Vaughan was Parliamentary Candidate for South London, came to mind as D.A.T.S. went carefully down the lines: "It's something to have a soldier, even if she is in petticoats!"

The woman who was Chief Controller of Queen Mary's Army Auxiliary Corps, British Armies in France, from its formation

The "Naafi," the girls who serve the beer, cigarettes, and extra foodstuffs to men of the Navy, Army, and Air Force, wear a khaki coat and skirt and soft felt hat, while on their shoulders are the distinctive colours of the Services—dark blue for the Navy, red for the Army, and light blue for the R.A.F. This photo shows some of the girls in their off-duty uniform.

in February 1917 until she was appointed in September 1918 to lead the Women's Royal Air Force, is in her element in the Army. She is a soldier's daughter.

Proudly she looked at the A.T.S. who had proved themselves. They seemed indeed old soldiers with B.E.F. on their tin hats and

recruits who were present were tremendously impressed by their smartness.

They had the experience of old soldiers, for they had been bombed and machine-gunned as the men had been in France. They were women picked for their efficiency before they went to France.

The success of the A.T.S. cooks has made the demand for them the greater. There have been complaints about the Army cooking since war began, but never of the cooking that the women do. It should be even better now that a woman Inspector of Catering to the Auxiliary Territorial Service has been appointed. Senior Commandant M. S. Froode will visit the cook-houses where women are working and see that the best use is being made of the rations. Until recently women were getting four-fifths of the men's rations, which were found to contain too much meat and too few eggs, milk, and vegetables for women's health.

Most of the caterers in the A.T.S. have domestic science certificates, but some ordinary cooks have done so well in the cook-house that after further training they have been promoted to officer rank. There is a Messing Officer, for instance, whose husband before the war was in charge of a block of flats where she did the catering.

It has been found that women cooks work better with their own section leader. There was a sergeant-cook who thought that the women should do the same shift as men, which was from 4 a.m. to 11 p.m., whereas the women worked in two shifts. There was also a sergeant-cook who did not like having women in his cook-house because he "couldn't swear at them!" Incidentally, the women liked working for this man.

Experts in other directions than cooking have been promoted to the charge of a platoon, including teleprinters and telephonists. Pay Experts have emerged, as women who are good at figures have learned the special system used in the Army. In the Records Office also women have proved themselves worthy of promotion. Many women in the A.T.S. were trained for this office before the war, so that they have been able to help with the extraordinary work which the evacuation from Dunkirk alone

Under orders for service in Kenya, these girls of the Women's Mechanized Transport Corps are learning to handle a situation—a ditched ambulance—which may well arise in East Africa. In charge of the unit is Mrs. Keith Newall (upper photo); note the springbok on her arm.

Photos, Fox and L.N.A.

In Navy, Army & Air Force They Do Men's Jobs

The signals branch of the Royal Air Force is of immense importance, and some 1,200 of the Women's Auxiliary Air Force are engaged as teleprinter and telephone operators. Two of the girls are seen above at work. Right is a woman dispatch rider of the W.R.N.S.
Photos, Wide World and Fox

involved. Special arrangements had to be made for dealing with the large number of men who could not be traced for a time.

The new A.T.S. Selection Board, which consists of the Director and the Assistant Directors in all the Military Commands, will consider in making promotions besides good service, special qualifications, for example in domestic science, languages, driving, and business experience. When the promotion concerns drivers or caterers, both the Inspector of M.T. Companies, and of Catering, will also be present.

The F.A.N.Y.s who became A.T.S. drivers have as their Inspector and Commandant of the Training School, Miss Baxter Ellis, late Chief Commandant of F.A.N.Y. These drivers still have the privilege of wearing the name F.A.N.Y. underneath " Women's Transport Service " on the sleeve.

Among the changes in the A.T.S. organization approved by the Army Council which have already taken effect are the following :—

(1) An Auxiliary Territorial Service Council has been formed under the supervision of the Adjutant-General, and consists of the following officers :—

(a) The Director of the Auxiliary Territorial Service, president. The Director is on the staff of the Adjutant-General and will be responsible under him for the administration of the Auxiliary Territorial Service.

(b) A senior A.T.S. officer attached to the staff of the Quartermaster-General, who will deal with the clothing, feeding, and accommodation of the Auxiliary Territorial Service.

(c) A senior A.T.S. officer attached to the staff of the Director of Military Training, who will be responsible for all branches of training in the Auxiliary Territorial Service.

(d) A woman doctor attached to the staff of the Director-General of Army Medical Services, who will be responsible for the health and general welfare of the Auxiliary Territorial Service.

The **Women's Royal Naval Service**— W.R.N.S.—although the Senior Women's Service, has only a strength of about one-fifth of the A.T.S. This Service, which is employed at the ports, has been on Active Service more or less since the war began. Wren cooks have fed the shipwrecked mariners all the time, and seen the ships gathering for convoy in the harbour. Always the Wrens are releasing men for service at

sea, and when the evacuation from Dunkirk came, that release was greatly valued.

Their friends sometimes think that they go to sea themselves, because they talk of " going aboard." Every fleet shore establishment is considered to be a ship, and the Wrens talk of the floor as the deck, and the kitchen as the galley. At first the Wrens were mostly girls whose homes were at the ports, so that nautical terms came easily to them, but recently a recruiting officer has been seeking the sea-loving girls inland, and they have more to learn. Because the W.R.N.S. is a small service, careful selection of personnel is possible, and some of them have called it the " snob-service." Discipline is stricter perhaps than in the other Services. When a W.R.N.S. Commandant saw a W.A.A.F. smoking as she walked along the front, she said : " I would not allow a Wren to do that outside, in uniform."

Active Service for the **Women's Auxiliary Air Service—the W.A.A.F.**—means much repairing of balloons by the fabric section,

which is composed largely of dressmakers and tailoresses, cooking for the men at Balloon Centres and Field Kitchens, and taking the places of the men in practically everything except flying. The W.A.A.F. substitute the men in the R.A.F. in small groups as the airmen are required for other work ; they do not move about in companies like the A.T.S. In each of the Services there is hush-hush work for women to do ; in the Air Force these girls are called " plotters." They are all well educated, some having University degrees.

The girls who cook at a field kitchen really know what Active Service conditions mean. The kitchen is probably a shack, the boilers are outside, and the mess-room is an open pavilion, boarded up.

There are about half as many W.A.A.F. as there are A.T.S. on Active Service, but recruiting is usually open.

Splendid work is being accomplished by the **Women Ferry Pilots.** R.A.F. pilots have other things to do than to fetch and deliver aeroplanes from factories to R.A.F. stations, and the Air Transport Auxiliary was formed when war began by British Airways. Men only were invited to join the A.T.A. at first, but very soon eight women were included, and Pauline Gower was appointed First Officer of the Women Ferry Pilots.

There are 25 Women Ferry Pilots flying every day with training machines for the R.A.F., and they hope soon to ferry also repaired aircraft from maintenance units to Squadron headquarters. Added to weather difficulties, the women pilots, who are unarmed, have to keep a sharp look-out for raiders : but that is Active Service.

The women who are also serving in the front line include the **Women's Land Army**, the **Mechanized Transport Corps**, the **Nurses** and the **V.A.D.s**, and all the **A.R.P. workers**, First Aid workers, the ambulance drivers, girls of the Auxiliary Fire Service, munitions workers, clothing and equipment makers, canteen workers, and those who escort children to the Dominions.

The A.T.S. now provides 50 per cent of its own motor drivers. A school has been established in Surrey where the future drivers undergo a course of instruction. Above, learners are having a lesson in dismantling and reassembling the gear-box and drive to be ready for any emergency.

London's War Ambulances are Always Under Fire

MANY a time last winter the men and women who had volunteered for the London Auxiliary Ambulance Service must have asked themselves, as they turned up at their stations day after day or night after night : " Isn't all this rather a waste of time ? "

I went out the other evening to one of those stations, in Greenwich, S.E., and spent the whole night there.

Phoney war ? Waste of time ? Indeed ! We were sitting, eight women and six men, in a sandbagged shelter erected in the playground of an L.C.C. school, Drawn up outside the shelter were seven ambulances, two Green Line coaches and six cars—the station's entire transport fleet.

Since the very first day of the blitz the town has sustained the savage blows of the Luftwaffe, and its A.R.P. workers have been tested as sternly as any in the land.

Before September 1940 many of them had never seen a bomb : twenty-five days and nights of intensive bombing have given them the confidence of veterans.

They have passed through the fire—literally so. I met two young men who one night drove an ambulance through a wall of flame to the scene of a bombing.

" Funny thing was," said one of them, " we never thought of the petrol. All I was worrying about was my trousers. I was afraid they would catch fire. But we got through unhurt.

" After that our only bad moment was when we picked up the casualty we'd been sent to fetch. The stretcher was so hot we could hardly hold it."

The strength of this ambulance unit is 68—43 women and 25 men. They work in 12-hour shifts, and they are paid the usual A.R.P. rates—£3 3s. 3d. for men and £2 3s. for women. The women include typists, factory workers, housewives and spinsters.

By day the unit occupies the infants' department of a school, the main school building being taken by the A.F.S. At night, as soon as the siren sounds, the men and women on duty take up their quarters in the shelter.

And there they sit and wait for the calls that come to them from the district A.R.P. control :

" *One ambulance and one car (for sitting cases) wanted immediately at ——* "

The drivers, men and women alike, go out in rotation, the car drivers alone, the ambulance drivers accompanied by an assistant—out under the splinters and the bombs, to pick up the casualties, take them to the nearest hospital and then return to the station.

If the telephone line that connects the district A.R.P. control with the ambulance shelter should break down, the messages are brought by dispatch rider.

All the ambulances and the cars already bear the scars of battle—dents and holes made by falling debris or falling splinters. I fancy the unit is secretly proud of them.

As a sideline to their ambulance work, two of the women members of the unit look after an " animals' detention post."

Every morning, after the " All Clear," they go round the bombed houses and pick

A woman driver examines the roof of an ambulance which is pitted with shell splinters after a journey to a bombed house.

up the pets that have been left homeless. The post itself—located in a garage—was bombed one night, and another garage

A driver (above) and a first-aid helper run to the ambulance from the shelter. Driver and members of first-aid party, left, are seen in their sandbagged shelter. After the " all-clear," below, animals are collected and are looked after until claimed.

had to be requisitioned. Now the flat above the second garage has been burned out by an incendiary.

No, it's anything but a phoney war out Greenwich way.

Story by William Forrest and photos by "News Chronicle" staff photographer, Ross-White. Exclusive to THE WAR ILLUSTRATED.

Through London's Battle the Railways Carry On

This railway van boy, wearing his tin hat, cheerfully swings himself behind the piled-up packages, apparently quite impervious to the menace of bombs.

The great London railway termini are prime military objectives—the nerve centres of the nation's transport—and in spite of air raid alarms and bombs the railways "just have to carry on." Here is a vivid description of the wartime working of " Metropolis " Station which William Forrest wrote for the " News Chronicle."

OF the thousands of bombs rained on London since the blitz began, some, no doubt, were aimed at " Metropolis " Station. None found its mark, and not for a single moment was the work of the station brought to a stop.

When the sirens sound Metropolis Station takes note, but carries on. Nor has it any " spotters " to give the warning of imminent danger and bring its work to a temporary halt. Night and day, raid or no raid, the trains steam in and out of Metropolis Station—more trains, and longer ones, than ever before.

As the stationmaster said to me, " The railway's just *got* to carry on."

He quoted impressive figures. In every weekday during the Battle of London 98 steam trains came in and out of Metropolis Station. Ten of these were run in duplicate, so that actually the number is 108. In addition, 110 suburban trains—known as " residentials "—came in and out daily.

In the first three weeks of September the booking office at Metropolis Station took as much money in passenger fares as in the whole of a normal September. And the parcels traffic one week was equal to that of pre-Christmas week.

Fifteen coaches used to be about the maximum for main-line trains. Now you can see the giant locomotives regularly pulling 17 coaches out of Metropolis, and sometimes even one or two more. And every compartment is loaded to the limit.

The stationmaster was loud in his praise of the child evacuees. " They're grand," he said. " The other day I watched them during an alarm. When the guns began to fire they all got terribly excited, but not with fear—no, they were arguing furiously about the sort of guns that were being fired ! "

" Not once," he added, " have I seen a case of panic at this station. I'm a Northerner myself, but I really must take off my hat to the Londoners."

The loud speaker broke in on our talk : " An air raid warning has just been sounded. Passengers can go to the shelters or proceed by their trains."

We walked out to the main departure platform. It was a daylight raid, but one of the more exciting ones, with the 'planes already over London and the guns firing briskly.

There were the booking offices still open—at first they used to close during raids, but now they carry on. There were the collectors punching the tickets at the barrier and forgetting that they ought to be wearing their steel helmets during a raid.

Here was the guard urging passengers to get aboard the train, where they would be safe from falling shrapnel. And at the far end of the platform I could see the tin-hatted heads of the driver and fireman protruding from the cab of the engine.

The driver had already arranged the special headlight code which tells the signalmen on the route that the train has already been informed of the raid.

In a few minutes—while the guns were still firing into the clouds—the whistle blew, the green flag waved, and the 4.10 for Somewhere in England steamed slowly out of Metropolis.

Until the train reached the limit of the air raid zone it would keep to a maximum of 15 m.p.h. Then, on entering the All Clear zone, it would be stopped at the first signal cabin and the driver informed of the All Clear. The normal headlight would at once be restored and the train proceed without speed restrictions. If it should later run into another air raid it would be stopped again, notified of the raid, change the headlight, and reduce the speed.

Inevitably the trains in and out of Metropolis run late. But they keep on running.

While the Alarm was still on I looked in at one of the signal cabins near the station. Like all the other railway personnel, the signalmen were still at their posts.

Besides their steel helmets they have been provided with steel boxes—one for each man and just big enough to hold him—in which they can take temporary cover if the bombs begin to fall perilously near. . . .

Darkness, and the night alarm. The buses stop, the taxis quit the streets. But passengers still make for Metropolis Station by Underground, and the trains are there to take them on their way.

A soldier is seen passing through the ticket barrier (circle), while, below, a porter hoists his heavily laden truck at the Parcels Office. Raid or no raid, the signalmen must carry on their job. They are seen, right, working the signals. They are given the extra protection of individual steel refuge boxes.

Photos, " News Chronicle ,"   Exclusive to THE WAR ILLUSTRATED

They Were The First To Win The George Cross

THE names of the first recipients of the newly-instituted George Cross and George Medal were announced on October 1, 1940. The following details are taken from the official accounts in the London Gazette of the deeds for which the awards were made.

Thomas Hopper Alderson, Part-time Worker (Detachment Leader), Rescue Parties, Bridlington, received the George Cross for sustained gallantry, enterprise, and devotion to duty during enemy air raids.

A PAIR of semi-detached houses at Bridlington was totally demolished in a recent air raid. One woman was trapped alive. Alderson tunnelled under unsafe wreckage and rescued her.

Some days later two five-storey buildings were totally demolished and debris penetrated into a cellar in which 11 persons were trapped. Six persons in one cellar, which had completely given way, were buried under debris. Alderson partly effected entrance to this cellar by tunnelling 13 ft. to 14 ft. under the main heap of wreckage and for three and a half hours he worked unceasingly. Although considerably bruised and in imminent danger from wreckage, coal gas leakage and enemy aircraft, he succeeded in releasing all the trapped persons.

On a third occasion some four-storey buildings were totally demolished. Five persons were trapped in a cellar. Alderson led the rescue work in excavating a tunnel from the pavement through the foundations to the cellar; he also personally tunnelled under the wreckage many feet into the cellar and rescued alive two persons (one of whom subsequently died) from under a massive refrigerator, which was in danger of further collapse.

A wall, three storeys high, which swayed in the gusty wind, was directly over the position where the rescue party were working.

Alderson worked almost continuously under the wreckage for five hours, during further air raid warnings and enemy aircraft overhead.

By his courage and devotion to duty without the slightest regard for his own safety, he set a fine example to the members of his rescue party, and their team work is worthy of the highest praise.

Temp. Lieut. Robert Davies, Royal Engineers, who was also awarded the George Cross, was the officer in charge of the party detailed to recover the bomb which fell in the vicinity of St. Paul's Cathedral.

SO conscious was this officer of the imminent danger to the Cathedral that regardless of personal risk he spared neither himself nor his men in their efforts to locate the bomb.

After unremitting effort, during which all ranks knew that an explosion might occur at any moment, the bomb was successfully extricated.

In order to shield his men from further danger, Lieutenant Davies himself drove the vehicle in which the bomb was removed and personally carried out its disposal.

Sapper George Cameron Wylie, Royal Engineers, the third recipient of the Cross, was a member of the Bomb Disposal Section engaged upon the recovery of the bomb which fell in the neighbourhood of St. Paul's Cathedral.

THE actual discovery and removal of the bomb fell to him. Sapper Wylie's untiring energy, courage, and disregard for danger were an outstanding example to his comrades.

The George Medal was awarded to the following fourteen men and women for individual or concerted acts of gallantry.

Ernest Herbert Harmer, Executive Chief Officer, and **Cyril William Arthur Brown,**

First civilian to win the George Cross, Mr. T. H. Alderson, of Bridlington, a detachment leader of the town's rescue parties.

Photo, " Daily Mirror "

Second Officer, Dover Fire Brigade, and **Alexander Edmund Campbell,** Section Officer, Dover A.F.S.

IN a recent large-scale attack by enemy bombers on Dover Harbour, fires were started in ships and oil stores. Air raids continued throughout the day. During the attacks all members of the Dover Fire Brigade and Auxiliary Fire Service engaged at the fires did excellent work in difficult and dangerous circumstances and the fires were eventually extinguished.

The individuals named above volunteered to return to a blazing ship containing explosives, in which they fought fires while enemy aircraft were still in the neighbourhood.

George Archibald Howe, manager, Shell-Mex and B.P. Ltd., **William Sigsworth,** manager, Anglo-American Oil Co., Ltd., **George Samuel Sewell,** engineer, Shell-Mex and B.P. Ltd., **Jack Owen,** fireman, Kingston-upon-Hull Fire Brigade, and **Clifford Turner,** leading fireman, Kingston-upon-Hull A.F.S.

DURING a recent air raid bombs were dropped on an oil depot, petrol tanks being pierced in several places, causing serious fires. Mr. Howe showed outstanding leadership and organization in fighting the fires and conspicuous bravery in entering the tank compound, which contained burning spirit, to open the valves so that the stock could be transferred. He was assisted by Mr. Sigsworth, who also entered the tank compound and who was untiring in his efforts to extinguish the flames.

Mr. Sewell led a party of men into the tank compound and was also continually on the tank roof while the gas inside was burning, endeavouring to extinguish the flames by playing foam over the tank top and placing sandbags over the roof curb. Fireman Owen volunteered to operate a hose on the top of an almost red-hot tank after wading through petrol and water to a depth of about four feet. His clothes were thus soaked with petrol and might have caught alight at any moment. Leading Fireman Turner volunteered to assist Mr. Howe in fixing hose on a tank-top surrounded

by flames from burning petrol. Their clothes were thus soaked with petrol and might have caught alight at any moment.

Miss Sonia Vera Carlyle Straw, Air Raid Warden, Carshalton.

DURING an air raid she volunteered to give assistance to the wounded. While the raid was in progress she attended a number of cases of badly injured women and children and treated several persons suffering from shock. She carried on entirely by herself without assistance for a considerable time until help came, and showed great courage and resource.

Two other women members of Civil Defence organizations, Mrs. **Dorothy Clarke,** Ambulance Driver, and Mrs. **Bessie Jane Hepburn,** Ambulance Attendant, both of Aldeburgh.

THEY showed courage of a high order and devotion to duty in rescuing a man badly injured in an explosion.

William Fisher, Dock Labourer, of Southampton, displayed great gallantry during an air raid.

HE rescued Gunner S. W. Jones, of the 21st Light A.A. Battery, from the Bofors gun-site on the roof of a building about 50 ft. above ground level. In the early part of the raid one man of the gun team was seriously wounded in the face and head.

Fire quickly broke out, and in addition to the ammunition which began to explode, ammonia gas fumes were released from a cold storage chamber below. The sergeant in charge of the gun realized the danger to his men and rightly ordered them to abandon the post. It was found impossible to get the wounded man over the parapet wall and down the ladder on to the crane platform.

Fisher then came up, and without hesitation made a rough seat of a sling rope and fastened it to the hook of the jib crane. After obtaining the assistance of the crane driver, he allowed himself to be hoisted on to the roof of the building. He then attached the sling under the arms of the wounded soldier and waited on the roof until he had been lowered on to the quay. The sling was then detached and returned once more to the roof for the rescuer himself to be lowered.

During such time as Fisher was on the roof he was in constant danger from the fire, the gas fumes, and the almost continuous explosions of shells. His conduct throughout was a fine example of initiative, bravery, and coolness.

Patrick King, Air Raid Warden, of Seaton Delaval.

DURING an air raid King was in his shelter when he heard a bomb explode. He ran towards the place where it had fallen and found that two semi-detached houses had almost collapsed. One of

Lance-Corporal G. C. Wylie, of the Bomb Disposal Squad (Royal Engineers), who helped to remove the one-ton unexploded bomb that menaced St. Paul's Cathedral.

Photo, Planet News

Lieut. Robert Davies, who commanded the Bomb Disposal Squad which dealt with the time-bomb outside St. Paul's. It was taken to Hackney Marshes and there exploded

Photo, Fox

Fourteen Men & Women Gained the First Medals

Second-Officer Cyril William Arthur Brown, of the Dover Fire Brigade, is on the extreme right of this group. The Dover firemen and A.F.S. fought fires in ships and oil stores.

Mrs. Bessie Jane Hepburn (right) and Mrs. Dorothy Clarke, ambulance workers, of Aldeburgh, Suffolk, who rescued a man injured in an explosion.

Miss Sonia Straw, Air Raid Warden, of Caterham, whose courage and resource during air-raids has been exceptional.

these was empty, but in the other was a blind lady who had sheltered under the stairs. King managed to get through the front door and ascertained by shouting that the blind woman, Miss Hannah Wilson, was alive but buried under the debris. He borrowed a fireman's axe from a fireman who was on the spot and pulled some of the debris out of the way with it. Some of the roof timbers were obstructing him so he sent for a saw with which he sawed off lengths and used them as supports to prevent further debris falling as he progressed. He had to struggle for a considerable time through the debris, meanwhile encouraging Miss Wilson and telling her what to do. He managed with considerable difficulty to reach her and to clear the debris off her body, and eventually to bring her out into the open. The house was in imminent danger of collapse and King showed great courage and presence of mind.

Frederick Ernest Rose, Maintenance Engineer.

He was in charge of the salvage party at the factory at which he is employed. Although a raid was in progress and bombs and debris were still falling, Rose led his two assistants into damaged buildings and, though hampered by flood water and darkness, personally extinguished fires which had been started among some magnesium.

He then led his men on to another affected area and assisted to check fires which had also broken out there. By his personal courage and coolness he was an outstanding example to others.

The New Honours for Civilians

Broadcasting to the nation from Buckingham Palace on September 23, at the height of the Battle of London, King George VI. announced the creation of a new honour for civilians in the following words :

Many and glorious are the deeds of gallantry done during these perilous but famous days. In order that they should be worthily and promptly recognized I have decided to create at once a new mark of honour for men and women in all walks of civilian life. I propose to give my name to this new distinction, which will consist of the George Cross, which will rank next to the Victoria Cross, and the George Medal for wider distribution.

Mr. Patrick King, Air Raid Warden, who rescued Miss Hannah Wilson—a blind woman—from a wrecked house. He is seen receiving Miss Wilson's congratulations.

Section-Officer A. E. Campbell, of Dover A.F.S., who is seen being cheered by his colleagues after the announcement of his award of the George Medal for bravery in returning to a blazing ship containing explosives.

Photos, " News Chronicle," " Daily Mirror," Topical Press

OUR SEARCHLIGHT ON THE WAR

British on the Turkana Front

WEST of Lake Rudolf, which lies mostly in Kenya but partly in Abyssinia, is the semi-arid Turkana country, remote from civilization and inhabited by a warrior tribe. It has now been revealed by a "Times" correspondent that for several weeks past South African troops, complete with all auxiliary services, have been holding the Turkana front, thus protecting the desert routes into Uganda and Kenya, guarding important water supplies and safeguarding the tribesmen from Italian raiding parties. The inhabitants are aware of the danger threatening from the Abyssinian frontier

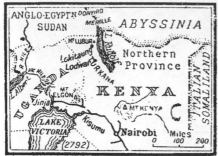

Showing the position of the Turkana frontier now being held by South African troops as a safeguard against raiders from Abyssinia.
Courtesy of "The Times"

and not only are they on the best of terms with the British troops, but they are themselves building defensive positions and helping to patrol the whole area.

Japanese Double Dealing

IT is said that Japan's treaty with Indo-China was made not solely in order to give her a back way into China, but also to enable her to have access to the great mineral and natural wealth of the French dependency. These include iron ore, of which Indo-China has exported about 90,000 tons to Japan in recent years ; coal, of which over two million metric tons are produced annually ; zinc, wolfram or tungsten, and tin. All of these would be of use to Japan in her manufacture of war supplies, and the maize which is one of the country's chief crops would provide a valuable source of edible fats.

They Can't Have It Both Ways

ON October 2 the announcer on the Bremen radio stated with satisfaction that German airmen raiding London had already caused 13,000 civilian casualties. The next evening, with still greater pride, he asserted that the aim of the bombers was so accurate that only military objectives were hit and no damage inflicted upon houses. "German airmen," said he, "take a great pride not only in hitting their targets but also in not allowing their aim to be interfered with by atmospheric or other conditions. After hitting their targets, warehouses and the like, the airmen return home with the gratifying knowledge that they have not destroyed or even damaged a single dwelling-house."

Dakar Under Martial Law

REPORTS from French West Africa show that in spite of the attitude of the Vichy-controlled authorities, the bulk of the population is favourable to General de Gaulle and his Free French Movement. The people of Dakar appear so determined that the Germans shall not annex the port that the local authorities have taken alarm, have declared a state of siege, and have placed machine-guns in position round the town in order to counteract any popular movement. The Dakar municipality has been dismissed

and a permanent court martial is dealing with a number of arrested persons. For fear of hostile demonstrations, the memorial services for the victims of the naval clash of September 23 were held on board the cruiser "Georges Leygues," instead of in the cathedral. All of which tends to prove that the inhabitants are more and more inclined to see in General de Gaulle the only possible defender of the interests of the French Empire.

Berlin's Voluntary Evacuation

THE scheme now in progress in Berlin for the evacuation of women and children to safe areas may be termed "voluntary" by the authorities, but actually it is one in which priority is being given to wives and children of members of the Nazi Party, and it is subsidized by party funds. This has all come to light since the issue of a denial by the Regional Governor of Berlin that a comprehensive official evacuation was taking place. The refuge zone is in the protectorate of Bohemia and Moravia. Private houses have been commandeered and public buildings requisitioned ; and in one district, that of Olomouc, 170,000 German civilians will be housed. In the Vyskov district the Czechs have been ordered to vacate 28 villages, and in the Brda district 22 villages must be placed entirely at the disposal of the Berlin population before the end of this year.

The Nazis Could Not Hold Him

LANCE-CORPORAL GILBERT DONALDSON, a young soldier of the Queen's Royal Regiment, has reached his home in Scotland after a series of exciting adventures in France. On May 20, when his section was hopelessly surrounded at Abbeville, Mr. Donaldson saw that it was time to withdraw, and, having discovered an abandoned lorry, he took with him two wounded comrades and started off. Very soon, however, he found himself in German hands, one of 14,000 prisoners with whom he marched from Beaumetz to Doullens, and thence to Beaucourt-sur-Ancre. Here he acquired a set of civilian clothes and, on May 27, having evaded his captors, he set off northwards and walked for some days. Then for six days he was hidden and fed in a railwayman's hut, but, hearing on the wireless that the Dunkirk evacuation was

Lance-Corporal Gilbert Donaldson at home in Scotland with his mother after his four-months' journey from Abbeville, during which he was twice taken prisoner by the Nazis.
Photo, Planet News

completed, he abandoned his plan and, helped by English civilians, one of whom lent him a bicycle, he made for Etaples. Here he was put in contact with two officers who were hiding in a deserted lighthouse. Their joint plan to sail for England in a small boat he had discovered miscarried, and after searching in vain for another boat in both Boulogne and Calais and losing his bicycle, the indomitable young soldier returned on foot to Etaples and crossed into Le Touquet. Here he was arrested and again imprisoned, but on June 23 he managed to escape and once more returned to Etaples. A French N.C.O. doing farm work gave him a new bicycle in exchange for a promissory note for 1,500 francs, payable after the war, and, much encouraged, Lance-Corporal Donaldson set out for Spain, via Paris. In this city he picked up a sergeant-major from the Gordon Highlanders and, with 500 francs given them by a retired British officer resident in Paris, the two men cycled to the frontier of the occupied territory and crossed it at Leches. Thence they reached Toulouse and Mr. Donaldson decided to make for Marseilles. After a fortnight in Marseilles endeavouring to obtain an exit permit and other necessary papers, he ultimately managed to find a route which brought him to safety.

No More Children Going Overseas

THE recent tragic sinking of the "City of Benares," when 77 children bound for Canada were among the 260 who perished, has caused the Government to suspend its Children's Evacuation Scheme during the present season. This decision has been reluctantly taken out of consideration of the best interests of the children themselves, for the dangers to which passenger vessels are exposed in the Atlantic, even when sailing in convoy, are enhanced by the gales and heavy seas prevailing during the winter months. Already 2,650 children have reached their temporary homes in other countries, but up to July applications in respect of some 200,000 children had been received by the Children's Overseas Reception Board, and the Government regrets the keen disappointment which will be felt by parents who hoped in this way to send their children to safety. It is, however, possible that operations may be renewed next spring if the conditions then obtaining make it desirable.

Captured 'Planes Tell Their Tale

WHEN a Nazi aircraft falls into the hands of the R.A.F. in comparatively good condition, technical experts make exhaustive examination of its equipment and test its performance. Much information has been obtained from such probings. It is noteworthy that more armour and armaments are now being used, presumably in an attempt to reduce the great toll taken by our fighters. For instance, a Junkers 88 dive bomber bearing the date August 7, 1940, was found to be equipped with six free machine-guns instead of the more usual three. On the other hand, one Messerschmitt shot down carried no armament of any kind—nothing but cameras. One fact that has come to light is that, although materials are good and workmanship sound, the performance of the German 'planes is inferior to that of their British counterparts. Thus Messerschmitts have less speed than Spitfires and Hurricanes and are less easily manoeuvred. When the superior skill of our British pilots is also taken into account, it will be seen that there is much here to encourage optimistic views on the outcome of the air war.

I WAS THERE!

Eye Witness Stories of Episodes and Adventures in the Second Great War.

I Saw London Firemen on the Job

A fine tribute to the men of the London fire services, who "think next to nothing of bombs" was dispatched to the "Chicago Daily News" by Helen Kirkpatrick, and here, by arrangement with the "Daily Telegraph," we publish her experience of a night with London's fire-fighters.

OUR first alarm of the evening had been caused by a handsome combination of a few high explosives and a "Molotov breadbasket," and it was a pretty good blaze even in the eyes of the A.F.S., who do not consider anything less than a five-alarm fire worthy of mention.

Strictly speaking, it was not the first alarm that had been sounded, but it was the first our fire-fighting friends in the gigantic control-room, feet underground, thought we should bother with. So we piled into a fire car and dashed off to a well-known Central London street.

About 30 pumps were working on it when we got there, after making our way along the glass-covered street.

A building opposite to the one afire had been razed by explosive, and we had to climb over heaps of bricks to get up to the front line where hoses were playing on the top of an office building.

"Watch it. Hose coming up," and we jumped aside as another powerful stream leapt into the air. The accumulation of hoses, firemen and police in the small area suggested that we had better make way, so we stood on the steps of an adjacent building. Just then came the now familiar whizz of an approaching bomb and someone yelled, "Down flat, everybody !"

Our fireman guide stuck out his foot to trip me up, but I was already flat by then inside a door. A thud and boom sounded down the street and everyone picked himself up. An instinctive dusting off of hands revealed a slight sticky warmth and a flashlight showed cuts from glass on the floor.

Everybody had them, and then someone thought of a bucket of water in a corner. It was passed around, and we all dipped in, wiped our hands and concentrated on the fire again.

It was well under control and only smoke with an occasional flicker poured from the top floors. It occurred to someone that an old-fashioned gas street light was going as merrily as in peacetime. "Anyone got a piece of soap ?" A policeman disappeared into the building and returned with a cake. As it smothered the gas out he called, "Hey, mate, don't forget to return it. I might want to wash me hands."

There wasn't much more to be seen there, so we moved off to the nearest fire station to find out if there were any more outbreaks requiring a visit. As we drove up to the station three distinct and successive whizzes sounded. We three back-seaters buried our heads in our hands, but not the firemen, who never turned a hair.

When the explosions sounded, hours later so it seemed to us, they were 50 yards away, and the car rocked like a ship in a storm. As we came out of our ostrich positions a sharp blow on the back of the car sent us to the exit with unparalleled speed. But it was only a bit of hot shrapnel, which dented the fender.

Behind us we saw a deep red glow, and without waiting further information we roared through the night towards it, not heeding the traffic lights and one-way streets. We made a pretty good guess at its location and arrived as a second group of pumps pulled up. It was another office building on the fringe of a residential area.

Our guide took charge of the hoses, and we ran them up through the building to the roof and clambered up after them—two firemen and myself. Twelve feet away the roof was a roaring inferno, and the hose was kicking like a mustang as the pressure increased. It was a narrow ledge, and I thought retreat downwards more interesting.

An elevator was still running to the top floor, with a woman warden bearing a tray of tea for the firemen. No sooner had my fire-officer guide established hoses in position and seen the fire was controlled than another broke out 500 yards down the street.

Off we went, and reached it before any pumps arrived. It was one of London's loveliest and oldest historic churches. Flames were eating the centuries-old beams like paper, and the beautiful stained-glass windows were cracking like chestnuts in a roaster. My firemen took charge, opening fireplugs for pumps which came up one every few seconds. I again retreated across the street.

A little Cockney emerged from a shelter and shook his fist at the sky. "What I'd like to do to that blankety-blank so-and-so. E can bomb our 'omes, but when 'e starts on that "—he pointed eloquently—" where's the blankety military hobjective round 'ere ? I arsks you."

There wasn't any answer to that one except an incendiary bomb, which bounced at our feet, sputtered away, and died out. The Cockney kicked it, then spat with more expression than any words.

A few more minor fires which only took minutes to put out, and the firemen dropped me at my hotel. They didn't refuse a drink, but apologized profusely for an "uneventful evening."

"Now, miss," said one of them, "I must be getting back to my fire," and off he went to search out more work in the black night, with bombs falling all round.

Today, when every other citizen of London is close to being a hero, the fire fighters stand out. There are no words to describe their fearlessness.

It is not only the damage that fires cause that helps the enemy but the fact that a big fire is a beacon light for the airmen who follow and often lights up whole districts. For this reason when a conflagration starts, the London fire services pour such a cataract of water from many hose pipes on the flames as is seen above.   *Photo, Fox*

We Found Ourselves in a French Prison

Two English girls—Miss Bessie Myers and Miss Mary Darby—who drove an ambulance in France, arrived in England in September 1940 after being prisoners of the Germans for three months. The story of their work under terrible conditions among French wounded and refugees, and of their imprisonment in Paris, is told here by Miss Myers.

IN June 1940 five women ambulance drivers who were attached to the French Army ran into a column of German tanks and were captured. When the Germans moved on after halting in a village square, however, three of the women drivers turned their wheels quickly and by accelerating in the opposite direction managed to escape. Miss Myers and Miss Darby were unlucky, for, telling her story, after her return home, Miss Myers said:

" Our ambulance was firing on only two cylinders, and it was hopeless to try to get away. At first the Germans treated us as a colossal joke—though actually I do not think they knew quite what to do with us. We were well treated and were passed on in charge of various officers.

" At Soissons the Commandant spoke of sending us to Germany, but we asked to be allowed to work among the wounded at the French hospital, and permission was given.

" I can't begin to describe the incredible filth and squalor that we found. Water supplies had been cut off by the retreating army, and a small bath three-quarters full of dirty water was our daily allowance to tend the whole of the French wounded.

" There was no organization at the hospital, and terribly wounded men had lain there three weeks with the grime of the battle still on them, and their blood-soaked clothes lying at the foot of the beds.

" We set to work to do what we could, but it seemed little enough. We were given a piece of cottonwool and a small bowl of water to wash three patients at a time. The food—soup and bread—came from the German kitchens, and there wasn't much of it.

" Then there were the refugees, in a huge camp near by. Some of the women were expecting babies, but there was no provision for them. We found one woman having her baby on a stretcher, without any attendance. We organized some sort of ward for the expectant mothers, and a midwife was found among the refugees. She stayed only two days, and when I saw the last of the ward the women were in the charge of one elderly Poilu.

" Suddenly we were arrested and ordered to move at half an hour's notice. I found out afterwards that one of the French doctors had denounced Mary Darby as a spy, and, of course, I was implicated.

" We were taken to Paris by car, and put in solitary confinement in the Cherche-Midi prison with other women political prisoners. Conditions were filthy, and we were eaten alive with vermin. We were not allowed to speak to other prisoners.

" For a month we were not allowed to see anyone but the warders—German soldiers convicted of minor ' crimes.' Then a civilian Gestapo agent came, and soon afterwards we were examined. Mary Darby answered questions for three and a half hours. She was very pale and exhausted, but insisted on standing by me while I was questioned for an hour.

" We were moved to the Fresnes prison, with others, and there we were able to talk. A Polish woman had been sentenced to 20 years' imprisonment for hiding Poles in Paris. Another woman had been given two years for saying ' Sale (foul) Boche ! ' in the hearing of a Gestapo agent. Another was serving six months for pulling down a poster depicting a German soldier nursing a French baby.

" After two days and nights we were released, and our belongings returned to us. We got in touch with Mr. Herman Huffer, whose ambulances we had been driving, and by his help got into Vichy, where we were presented to Marshal Petain. He thanked us in the name of France for what we had done."—*Daily Telegraph.*

Our Squadron Helped to Bring Down the 232

The air battle over London on Sunday, September 15, in which it was estimated that 232 German aircraft were shot down, has already been described by eye-witnesses on the ground (see page 332). Here we give an account of the fighting from the point of view of a Hurricane Squadron Leader, who broadcast his story on September 23.

AT lunch time on Sunday, September 15, my squadron was somewhere south of the Thames Estuary behind several other squadrons of Hurricanes and Spitfires.

The German bombers were three or four miles away when we first spotted them. We were at 17,000 feet and they were at about 19,000 feet. Their fighter escort was scattered around. The bombers were coming in towards London from the south-east, and at first we could not tell how many there were. We opened our throttles and started to climb up towards them, aiming for a point well ahead where we expected to contact them at their own height.

As we converged on them I saw there were about twenty of them, and it looked as though it were going to be a nice party, for the other squadrons of Hurricanes and Spitfires also turned to join in. By the time we reached a position near the bombers we were over London—central London, I should say. We had gained a little height on them, too, so when I gave the order to attack we were able to dive on them from their right.

Each of us selected his own target. Our first attack broke them up pretty nicely. The Dornier I attacked with a burst lasting several seconds began to turn to the left away from his friends. I gave him five seconds and he went away with white smoke streaming behind him.

As I broke away and started to make a steep climbing turn I looked over the side. I recognized the river immediately below me through a hole in the clouds. I saw the bends in the river, and the bridges, and idly wondered where I was. I didn't recognize it immediately, and then I saw Kennington Oval.

I noticed the covered stands round the Oval, and I thought to myself, " That is where they play cricket." It's queer how, in the middle of a battle, one can see something on the ground and think of something entirely different from the immediate job in hand. I remember I had a flashing thought—a sort of mental picture—of a big man with a beard, but at that moment I did not think of the name of W. G. Grace. It was just a swift, passing thought as I climbed back to the fight.

I found myself very soon below another Dornier which had white smoke coming from it. It was being attacked by two Hurricanes and a Spitfire, and it was still travelling north and turning slightly to the right. As I could not see anything else to attack at that moment, I went to join in. I climbed above him and did a diving attack on him.

Coming in to attack I noticed what appeared to be a red light shining in the rear gunner's cockpit, but when I got closer I realized I was looking right through the gunner's cockpit into the pilot and observer's cockpit beyond. The red light was fire.

I gave it a quick burst and as I passed him on the right I looked in through the big glass nose of the Dornier. It was like a furnace inside. He began to go down, and we watched. In a few seconds the tail came

Miss Bessie Myers, seen in her London flat, attends to her correspondence. One of two English girls who were for three months in the hands of the Nazis, Miss Myers drove an American ambulance attached to the 6th French Army.   *Photo, Sport and General*

Here are the remains of a German bomber recently brought down in South-West London. Part of a wing and fuselage can be seen lying on the roofs above the street, which appear to have suffered little damage.
Photo, Sport and General

off, and the bomber did a forward somersault and then went into a spin. After he had done two turns in his spin his wings broke off outboard of the engines, so that all that was left as the blazing aircraft fell was half a fuselage and the wing roots with the engines on the end of them. This dived straight down, just past the edge of a cloud, and then the cloud got in the way and I could see no more of him.

The battle was over by then. I couldn't see anything else to shoot at, so I flew home. Our squadron's score was five certainties—including one by the sergeant pilot who landed by parachute in a Chelsea garden (see page 332).

Our Hudson Tackled Seven Messerschmitts

The Coastal Command was specially commended by the War Cabinet in September 1940, both for its steady performance of " often unspectacular tasks " and for its more recent successes in offensive action. The following story, broadcast by the pilot of a Hudson, is typical of the work of this branch of the R.A.F.

A HUDSON reconnaissance aircraft of the Coastal Command of which I was the pilot attracted the unwelcome attention of seven Messerschmitt 109s over the North Sea. The fact that I lived to tell the tale is the best possible tribute to the skill of my crew and the fighting qualities of the American-built aircraft we were flying. We were patrolling near the Danish coast early in the afternoon, flying just below the clouds at about 2,000 feet, when we sighted two enemy supply ships ploughing along in heavy seas. We decided to attack.

Those of you who have seen Hudson aircraft, or their civil counterpart, the Lockheed 14, would hardly believe that these converted air-liners could do dive bombing attacks. It's rather like an omnibus in a T.T. race. But they *can* do it—and quite successfully. So I put the nose down, straight for one of the ships, and we dived 1,000 feet.

We released the bombs as we pulled out and they fell a few yards ahead of the target. I was busy climbing and turning for another attack, and the observer saw the bombs swamp the ship in foam. They exploded just under the bow and must have damaged it considerably. There was some A.A. fire at us, but it was weak and inaccurate.

We came round again for a repeat performance and started another dive. Just as we were whistling down nicely, I got a bit of a shock. Coming towards us from the east was a formation of seven enemy fighters—Messerschmitt 109s. They were in " V " formation and looked to me like a swarm of angry bees out for trouble. I decided that this was no place for a solitary reconnaissance aircraft, and increased my dive down to sea level.

The seven fighters closed on us and then the fun began. My crew immediately went to action stations. I opened up the engines as we switchbacked and skimmed over the waves. Each time we turned the wing-tips were almost in the water. The Messerschmitts came up, four on one side of us and three on the other. They were a good deal faster than us and kept flying in turn at our beams, delivering head-on attacks.

Our guns were blazing away and I remember looking behind me into the smoke-filled cabin to see how things were going. Our carrier-pigeon, slung from the roof in its basket, was looking down at all the racket with a very upstage expression. The pigeon seemed to be saying, " I suppose all this is necessary, but please finish it as soon as possible."

However, the fighters were still going strong and so were we! I kept track of their approaches by glancing over my shoulder. Each time a Messerschmitt approached I gave a slight movement to the controls which lifted us out of the line of fire. I could see the cannon shells and bullets zipping into the water, splashing and churning up foam. Not that we were unscathed! Four holes suddenly appeared in the window above my head, and shrapnel and bullets were coming into the cabin pretty steadily. I was flying in my shirt sleeves and had hung my tunic in the back of the cabin. When I took it down afterwards there were four nice clean bullet holes through the back, sleeves and side. I was glad I hadn't been in it!

From the continuous rattle of our guns I thought we had sustained no casualties, but after 20 minutes, when I looked back, I found that the wireless operator, a veteran of the last war, had a bullet wound in the arm. But he carried on until the enemy broke off the engagement.

Up till then I hadn't had much chance of using my front guns. But a change in tactics by the Nazi fighters gave me a chance of getting in some bursts. The seven Messerschmitts weren't getting much change from side attacks, so they began to come from ahead. That was just what I wanted. By turning my Hudson at them I got home several hundred rounds.

By this time we were climbing up towards the scattered clouds, where the fighters still continued their attacks and turned the battle into a grim sort of hide and seek. At last we shook them off and were able to take stock of our position. The fight had then lasted just over half an hour.

The wireless operator came to have his wound dressed by my navigator and the rear gunner asked permission to leave his turret. When he came forward we found he had been wounded in the leg and, like the wireless operator, had carried on without saying anything about it.

They had seen most of the fight and as their wounds were being bandaged I shouted above the noise of the engines, " Any luck ? " The gunner held up one finger and then pointed straight downwards and grinned. Then he held up another and pointed slantingly down. This meant that one Messerschmitt had gone down for certain and he had seen another gliding down to the sea apparently out of control. The wireless confirmed our successes.

We had a long slog back to England—about two hours in a damaged aircraft. In spite of the hard towsing I had given the engines they were behaving perfectly, but I knew we would have trouble with the undercarriage. Sure enough, when we tried to put it down to land, it would only go halfway. We signalled to the aerodrome staff that we were going to make an emergency landing. I sent all the crew to the back of the machine to ease the trim. Then we came in. The wheels supported us a little and we landed quite sweetly.

From East and South Come the Troops of Empire

In the British Army in the Middle East British, Dominion and Indian troops are serving. Recently reinforcements have been sent from India as well as from Britain. Above, Indian troops are lined up on the quayside after disembarking.

ONE possible result of the meeting of Hitler and Mussolini in the Brenner Pass is a great offensive in the Middle East. If it should come about the Axis Powers will find themselves faced by very formidable armies, for the sweep of the British Navy in the Eastern Mediterranean early in October enabled a large convoy of reinforcements to be landed, while more have come from Australia and India through the Red Sea.

Australian reinforcements, including a complete squadron of the Royal Australian Air Force, have also recently arrived at a Middle East port. Centre is the scene when the last stage of the R.A.A.F.'s journey had been completed by train. One of the men is taking his first lesson in the new currency from a small boy from whom he has made a purchase. Below is the scene after the arrival of a British troopship with troops disembarking by a pontoon bridge.

Photos, British Official: Crown Copyright

War Personalities—G.O.C.s of Home Commands

Maj.-Gen. D. G. Johnson, V.C. The new Commander-in-Chief of the Aldershot Command is fifty-six years of age and began his military career in the South Wales Borderers, attaining his present rank in 1938. In this war he commanded a division of the B.E.F. In the last war he served in France and Gallipoli and won the V.C. at the crossing of the Sambre Canal on November 4, 1918, in command of a battalion of the Royal Sussex. He got a bridge across the river and twice led the assault which turned defeat into victory.

Lt.-Gen. Sir R. F. Adam, D.S.O., G.O.C. Northern Command, began his military career in the Royal Artillery. He is 54 years of age. In the last war he served in France, Flanders and Italy, and was mentioned in despatches and awarded the D.S.O. and the O.B.E. During his career he has held many important appointments both at home and abroad; one of the last before he took over his present command in June 1940 was that of Deputy Chief of the Imperial General Staff.

Lt.-Gen. Sir G. C. Williams, C.M.G., D.S.O., has been G.O.C. in Chief of the Eastern Command since 1938. He entered the Army in 1900. In the last war he was mentioned in despatches seven times, promoted Brevet Major and Brevet Lieut.-Colonel, and was awarded the D.S.O. and C.M.G. He was promoted Brigadier-General in 1918, Major-General in 1934, and Lieut.-General in 1938. From 1920 to 1923 he served in India and in the latter year came home to take up the appointment of Deputy Military Secretary at the War Office. He was Army Instructor, Imperial Defence College, 1928-32, Chief Engineer and Commandant of the Aldershot Command 1932-4, Staff College, Quetta, 1934-7.

Gen. Sir R. Gordon-Finlayson, C.M.G., D.S.O., is G.O.C. of the Western Command. Fifty-nine years of age, he entered the Army in 1900. During the European war he was mentioned eight times in despatches and awarded the D.S.O. and C.M.G., and promoted Brevet-Colonel. In 1919 he served in North Russia. After the Great War he held several important staff appointments and subsequently commanded the Rawalpindi District, India, 1931-34, and from then until 1936 was Commander of the 3rd Division. From 1938 to 1939 he commanded the British troops in Egypt, and on his return to England assumed the appointment of Adjutant-General to the Forces up to June 1940.

Lt.-Gen. R. H. Carrington, D.S.O., has been G.O.C. in Chief, the Scottish Command, since February 1940. He is fifty-seven years of age and entered the Army in the Royal Field Artillery in 1901. He immediately saw active service in the South African war, 1901-2, and has five clasps to the Queen's medal. In the last war he was mentioned in despatches four times, awarded the D.S.O. and promoted Brevet Lieut.-Colonel. He was promoted Major-General in 1936 and Lieut.-General in 1940.

Maj.-Gen. C. J. E. Auchinleck, D.S.O., who took over the Southern Command when Sir Alan Brooke left it to command the Home Forces in July, 1940, has served during most of his career in the Indian Army, his last command before returning home being the Meerut District. In the last war he served in Egypt, Aden and Mesopotamia, was mentioned in despatches and awarded the D.S.O. and Croix de Guerre, and was promoted Brevet Lieut.-Colonel. His last appointment in India was that of Deputy Chief of General Staff, Army Headquarters.

Photos, "Daily Mirror," Bassano, Central Press, Russell, Elliott & Fry

OUR DIARY OF THE WAR

TUESDAY, OCT. 1, 1940   *395th day*

On the Sea—British liner " Highland Patriot " sunk by U-boat in Atlantic.

In the Air—R.A.F. bombers attacked munitions factory at Berlin ; power stations at Duisburg and Cologne ; oil plants, goods yards, railway junction, canal docks in N. Germany ; several enemy aerodromes and bases at Rotterdam, Flushing, and along the Channel coast, particularly Boulogne harbour and gun positions near Cap Gris Nez.

Coastal Command flying-boat fought 20-minute battle with three Messerschmitts off Ushant, damaged them and drove them off.

Home Front—Several abortive day attacks made on south of England. Small number of aircraft reached London and dropped bombs. Train and streets in S.E. district machine-gunned by Junkers bomber which was later brought down. Two Welsh coastal towns raided.

Night raiders flew over Central London in spite of intense A.A. barrage. Incendiaries and high-explosive bombs fell in N.W. and northern suburbs. Large hospital in E. London damaged. Heavy bomb struck houses in W. London and there were many casualties. Church burnt out in N. London.

Bombs fell on Merseyside town and several others in N.W. England. Houses and industrial buildings damaged and number of casualties. Midlands town heavily attacked. Bombs fell at numerous points in S.E. England, and also off Louth-Meath coast.

Enemy lost five 'planes, Britain three.

WEDNESDAY, OCTOBER 2   *396th day*

On the Sea—C.-in-C. Mediterranean reported that British naval forces carried out sweep in eastern and central Mediterranean from Sept. 29 to Oct. 2 and landed additional military forces at Malta. Fleet was attacked on several occasions from air, but only losses were on enemy's side. Naval and air base at Stampalia, Dodecanese Islands, was bombarded.

H.M. trawler " Recoil " reported overdue and must be presumed lost.

In the Air—R.A.F. bombed oil plants at Stettin, Hamburg, and Bottrop, Krupps' works at Essen, goods yards at Cologne, railway junction near Hamm, and several aerodromes. Other forces attacked docks at Hamburg and Wilhelmshaven, ports and shipping at Amsterdam, Rotterdam, Antwerp, Flushing, and Channel ports.

Home Front—Series of daylight attacks made on London, all being broken up by British fighters. Bombs fell on coastal towns in Kent and Sussex. Damage done to housing estate in S.E. London.

Night raids were widespread and included Scotland and N.W. England, as well as S.E. areas. Bombs were dropped indiscriminately in London area. Buildings damaged included famous public school in N.W. London, a Saxon church, a police station, many houses, flats and shops.

Ten enemy aircraft destroyed. Britain lost one fighter.

Dover was shelled from French coast.

THURSDAY, OCTOBER 3   *397th day*

On the Sea—Admiralty announced that H.M. yacht " Sappho " had been sunk, probably by enemy mine.

In the Air—R.A.F. bombers made daylight raids on coastal objectives, including Rotterdam harbour, shipping off Dunkirk, and oil depots near Cherbourg. Weather conditions prevented night-bombing operations.

Home Front—Single aircraft made daylight attacks. Bombs dropped at random in London, Thames Valley, Essex, Kent and Cornwall. Midlands city and small town were damaged. Train machine-gunned.

During small-scale night raids bombs fell in two S.E. districts of London and later in south and west districts. Bombs also fell on a Welsh town, town on S.W. coast and a village in S.E. England.

Enemy lost two aircraft, Britain none.

Mr. Chamberlain resigned. Sir John Anderson succeeded him as Lord President of the Council. Sir Kingsley Wood and Mr. Bevin joined War Cabinet, and other changes were made in the Government.

FRIDAY, OCTOBER 4   *398th day.*

On the Sea—Admiralty announced that within the last few weeks seven German and two Italian U-boats had been destroyed and others damaged.

Stated that H.M. submarine " Osiris " had sunk an Italian destroyer in Adriatic on Sept. 22.

Reported that aircraft of Fleet Air Arm had destroyed two supply ships off Norway.

In the Air—Weather conditions precluded any bombing operations by R.A.F.

War against Italy—R.A.F. made successful attacks on railway and rail junctions in Abyssinia and Eritrea. Extensive aerial reconnaissances over Libya and W. Desert.

Home Front—Number of single aircraft scattered bombs at random over S.E. England. One demolished three houses in Central London. S.W. suburb attacked. Houses in N. London destroyed. S.E. coastal town attacked ; historic castle hit and many houses destroyed.

During night raids bombs were dropped in Central London and in N.W. district, but attacks were on restricted scale.

Enemy lost three aircraft, Britain one.

General—Hitler and Mussolini and their Foreign Ministers met on the Brenner Pass for a 3-hour conference.

SATURDAY, OCTOBER 5   *399th day*

On the Sea—Air Ministry revealed that recently U-boat was destroyed by bombs dropped from Sunderland flying-boat.

In the Air—In spite of severe weather conditions R.A.F. carried out bombing raids on oil plant at Gelsenkirchen, Krupps' works at Essen and other targets.

Coastal Command aircraft attacked shipping and warehouses in Brest harbour and barge and motor transport concentrations at Gravelines.

War against Italy—R.A.F. raided Italian port and depot at Benghazi and fired warehouses and shipping. Raids also made on Tobruk and Bardia.

Air battle over Malta. One enemy fighter brought down and another disabled.

Home Front—Air battles took place over Kent and Sussex coasts. Hastings twice attacked, many houses being demolished.

Night attacks directed mainly against London and adjacent areas. Many fires caused but were quickly under control. Bombs were also dropped at number of places in eastern counties and in S.E. England.

Enemy lost 23 aircraft. Nine British fighters missing, but pilots of seven safe.

Sir Charles Portal became head of R.A.F. vice Sir Cyril Newall, appointed Governor-General of New Zealand.

SUNDAY, OCTOBER 6   *400th day*

In the Air—R.A.F. carried out daylight bombing raids on ports of Ostend, Calais and Boulogne, shipping and barge concentrations at Dutch bases, and Diepholz aerodrome.

Hudson aircraft of Coastal Command attacked two armed merchant vessels off Dutch coast. One Hudson was hit by ships' barrage, but pressed attack home, afterwards plunging in flames into the sea.

Home Front—Enemy aircraft flying singly attacked nearly 20 places in the Home Counties. One raider dropped bombs on a Midland town, and another in Central London. Houses were demolished at Folkestone and a Northants town.

Enemy lost two aircraft, Britain none.

Night was quietest since attacks began on Sept. 7. Few bombs fell near London.

MONDAY, OCTOBER 7   *401st day*

On the Sea—Admiralty announced that H.M. trawler " Comet " had been sunk by enemy mine.

Naval sources at Alexandria disclosed that two Italian submarines were sunk in Mediterranean recently, bringing number lost by Italy since she entered war up to 22.

In the Air—R.A.F. made day attacks on barge concentrations on Dutch coast and shipping at Le Havre. At night strong forces bombed military objectives in Berlin, including three main power stations.

Other forces bombed Fokker works at Amsterdam ; goods yards ; several aerodromes ; harbours and shipping at Lorient and Channel ports ; gun positions at Cap Gris Nez.

War against Italy—Reported that vital supply line had been cut by R.A.F. bombing of Aisha, station on railway line between Addis Ababa and Jibuti.

Home Front—Large numbers of enemy aircraft attacked Britain. Five attacks attempted on London, totalling about 450 'planes. Few bombs fell in S.E. London. Minor damage at Eastbourne, Dover and other towns. Two attacks in S.W. England.

During night high explosive and incendiary bombs fell in Central London. Damage reported from ten districts in London area. Elsewhere enemy aircraft were reported over N.W. and W. England, Midlands, Welsh coastal town, S.E. Scotland and Liverpool.

Nazis lost 27 aircraft. Sixteen British machines missing, but pilots of ten safe.

Balkans—German troops entered Rumania through Hungary and occupied oilfields.

New Ministers in the reconstructed Government include (left to right) Viscount Cranborne, Secretary for Dominion Affairs, who previously held office as Paymaster-General ; Capt. Oliver Lyttelton, who takes over the Board of Trade and is a newcomer to political life ; Lt.-Col. Moore-Brabazon, new Minister of Transport, who has been Parliamentary Secretary to this Ministry for two periods ; and Sir Andrew Duncan, who comes from the Board of Trade to be Minister of Supply.

Photos, Central Art Library ; L.N.A.

GAUNTLY ERECT IN A WILDERNESS OF RUIN

Amidst the devastation caused by high explosive bombs, there have been strange instances of what seemed the most fragile part of a building surviving. Here are the ruins of a big London block bombed on the night of September 11-12. Almost everything is levelled to the ground except a few concrete columns and the braced steel framework of the outside goods lift which stands undamaged with the control and motor cabin at the top; all the same, it has taken on a dangerous tilt.

Photo, Planet News

Eastward Ho! Stream the Banners of War

Perhaps it was to divert attention from the failure of the " Blitzkrieg " against Britain, perhaps it was in pursuance of some long-prepared plan; but certain it is that, following the Brenner meeting between Hitler and Mussolini on October 4, the Dictators acted as if they were about to embark on a campaign on the grand scale in the Near and Middle East.

WHEN Napoleon was balked in his long-cherished plan for the invasion of England, he turned away in a fit of furious disgust and flung himself and his armies across Europe to the southeast. Now Hitler has been balked in a very similar plan ; and, like Napoleon, he, too, takes the route to the south-east. " Boney " waited for a favourable wind and Villeneuve ; Hitler has been waiting for Goering to substantiate his boast that Germany has won supremacy in the air over the Channel and southern England. But the wind that Napoleon longed for never blew, and Villeneuve was caught by Nelson at Trafalgar ; Goering has flung wave after wave of his fighters and bombers against Britain's defences, all to no avail. And in 1940 as in 1805 Britain commands the narrow seas—that slender ditch which throughout the centuries has served so well " in the office of a wall or as a moat defensive . . . against the envy of less happier lands."

Now all eyes are turned from " England bound in with the triumphant sea," to the opposite corner of Europe. In the Continent dominated by Hitler as it was dominated by Napoleon before him, millions of men are in a state of instant readiness for war. Fleets of ships have been mustered, every "invasion" harbour is crammed with troops, armadas of warplanes are ticking over. Hitler and his arm of which shall reach out from Germany through the Balkans across the Dardanelles into Asia Minor, while the other, spreading from Italy along the northern shores of the Mediterranean, will meet its fellow somewhere in the middle of the Fertile Crescent — in Palestine, maybe. Both arms are already in operation. For weeks past Marshal Graziani and his Libyan levies have been concentrating and consolidating at Sidi Barrani, 60 miles inside the frontier of Egypt, while in the north German troops — they were called " tourists " to begin with and now they are " technicians " and " instructors "— are streaming through Hungary into Rumania, which in the course of a few weeks has been converted from an independent state into a truncated satellite of the German Reich. Encouraged by their easy success over Rumania, the Nazis hope that Greece, too, will suffer herself to be engorged. Yugoslavia ? The Yugoslavs—so the Axis spokesmen aver—will be only too pleased to save their skins at the expense of sacrificing some of their Dalmatian ports

Turkey is the great question mark in the Near East. Germany hopes to intimidate her ; the Turks speak of two million bayonets ready to defend their land. Above is a young Turkish bugler.
Photo, Keystone

to Italy. Bulgaria ? The Bulgars have just won back Southern Dobrudja with Germany's support ; they are asking now for the return by Greece of Dedeagatch, on the Aegean, which they held from 1913 to 1918, and Edirne—Adrianople as it used to be called—from Turkey. Only on Hitler's sufferance can these demands be satisfied ; Bulgaria, then, should surely open her gates to the German legions en route to the Black Sea. Turkey ? Ah, here is a distinct snag in the carefully prepared scheme.

Not for many years has Turkey been the " sick man of Europe " ; indeed, it is difficult to recognize in the Turkey of today the country which until a generation ago was a synonym for corruption, misgovernment, and crime in high places. There is all the difference in the world between the Turkey which Abdul the Damned ruled and the Turkey which Kemal Ataturk forged in the fires of disaster and defeat. Since 1453 the Turks have held Constantinople—Istanbul, to give it its present name—and with Constantinople those narrow straits, comprising the Bosporus, the Sea of Marmara, and the Dardanelles, which separate Europe from Asia. Xerxes crossed them in B.C. 480 when on his way to teach the rebellious Greeks a lesson ; the Crusaders went that way to fight the Saracens, and across the Straits the Turks entered Europe ; in 1915 thousands of British and Dominion troops died on Gallipoli in a vain attempt to open the Dardanelles to the Allies. The Turkey we fought in the Great War was the Turkey of the bad old days, yet the Turks on the Peninsula held at bay the crack troops of Britain and France, and forced them to take to their ships again.

No one who served in Gallipoli will be under any delusions as to the quality of " Johnny Turk " as a fighting man, and if it comes to fighting, then the Turkish army of today, numerous, well equipped, and well officered, may be relied upon to give an excellent account of itself. The Germans may be hoping that the Turks can be cajoled into maintaining their present state of neutrality, or perhaps they may be intimidated.

The two Dictators at their Brenner meeting on October 4 almost certainly studied a map of the area shown here. Hitler's finger probably traced the course of the upper arm of the " pincers "—through Rumania to Bulgaria and the Black Sea, across the Dardanelles into Turkey and on to Palestine. Mussolini's stumpy finger no doubt traced a path along the Mediterranean into Egypt. So the Dictators plan the fall of the British Empire.
Courtesy, " Daily Mail "

victory-flushed Nazis, Mussolini and his not-so-enthusiastic Fascists, are about to embark on a new venture. They have heard the call of the East : a call charged not with exotic beauty but with something far more tangible, far more real—booty. Already they dream of laying their greedy hands on the well-tilled fields of Egypt, the orange groves of Palestine, the pastures of Syria; already they finger the mineral wealth of Asiatic Turkey and dabble their hands in the oily slime that makes Mosul and Iran so desirable a prize. We know the outlines of their plan of campaign. It is to take the form of a vast pair of pincers, one

How the Axis 'Pincers' Are Intended to Operate

Marshal Graziani, Chief of Staff of the Royal Italian Army, is in command of the Italian troops invading Egypt. He was born in 1882 and holds the title of Marchese de Neghelli.
Photo, Associated Press

But judging from the latest reports from Ankara and Istanbul, there is never a suggestion of surrender in Turkey's present attitude. Indeed, on October 11, it was officially intimated by the Turkish wireless service that any Axis drive through Turkey would be met by 2,000,000 bayonets.

Turkey will fight, and not only in Asia. There is not the slightest indication that the present Turkish Government has any intention of ceding any territory in Europe or of being driven across the Straits. It must be with a certain grim amusement that the Turks—no longer Moslems and many of them atheists—listen to such schemes as the one recently attributed to the visionaries of the Axis : the one which would create a new Papal State in the south-eastern corner of Europe in which the Roman Church and the Greek would be reconciled ; Istanbul would become once again Constantinople, and St. Sophia would re-echo to the sounds of Christian worship. They remember how, after the last war, Italy claimed southern Anatolia for herself, and how the Greeks occupied a large part of Turkey in Asia— until they were driven out in hopeless rout and with terrific slaughter by Kemal in 1923. They still suspect Italy of having designs on their country ; and that Germany, too, has not forgotten the Kaiser's dream of German domination from Berlin to Baghdad.

Turkey, then, will fight, and in fighting she will probably be able to rely on the active support of her partners in the Saadabad Pact of 1937—Iran, Irak, and Afghanistan. Possibly Soviet Russia, too, would deem that the time had come to resist Axis penetration while it was still at the gates of Asia. Indeed,

immediately following what was in effect the occupation of Rumania by German troops, it was reported that negotiations had been opened between Turkey, the Soviet Union, Yugoslavia, Greece and Britain, on the question of the Nazi expansion eastwards. The report was denied in Moscow, but it was admitted that twenty Russian divisions had been concentrated on the Bessarabian border, while on the other side of the Pruth, German forces were also said to be in large numbers.

But if we allow for a whole collection of " ifs "—if the Germans can march through the Levant into Syria and Palestine, if Graziani can conquer Egypt and cross the Suez Canal, if Mussolini's navy can drive Britain's from the Eastern Mediterranean, if this and if the other—then perhaps the battle which will decide not only the fate of Britain and of her Empire but of the whole world, may be fought on that plain in northern Palestine where warred the kings of Canaan, where Saul was defeated by the Philistines, where King Josiah fled before Pharoah, and which to the ecstatic vision of the author of the Apocalypse appeared as the great battlefield on which shall be fought out the final struggle between the forces of good and of evil.

British armoured cars keep up a constant patrol on the stretch of desert in Irak which might be a happy hunting-ground for Fifth Columnists in German pay.
Photo, G.P.A.

Lying in the very centre of the Fertile Crescent, Palestine may well provide the battlefield where will be decided the fate not only of the British Empire but of the world. It is a mandate of the League of Nations to Britain, who is, of course, responsible for its defence. Above is an A.A. battery in Palestine during a practice shoot.
Photo, British Official : Crown Copyright

For War in the Pacific Bases Are All-Important

With Japan formally admitted to the Axis, it would seem that inevitably, sooner or later, the war must spread to the Pacific. In anticipation of such a conflict, the Great Powers—Britain, Japan and U.S.A.—have already established series of bases (detailed in this chapter) from which their battle fleets will operate.

FOR 2,000 years and more the Mediterranean was the centre of human history. Then in the 15th century with the discovery of America the North Atlantic became the ocean about which were grouped the rising powers of the world. Tomorrow the Atlantic may give place to the Pacific; indeed, it may be claimed that already the Pacific constitutes the stage on which the next great drama of Power-Politics will be played.

Until the development of the steamship the huge expanse of the Pacific—it covers a fourth of the globe's entire surface—proved a most formidable barrier to human intercourse. Its first appearance in world politics may be said to have been in 1894, when Japan defeated China and went on to secure a foothold on the Asiatic mainland in Korea. Ten years later the Russian fleets in the Far East were annihilated by the Japanese under Admiral Togo in the great battle of Tsushima

Pacific as well as the Atlantic, while Britain has immensely strengthened her position in the south-west corner of the ocean by the construction of the great naval base at Singapore.

Singapore is the keystone of British sea power in the Pacific, for a fleet operating therefrom is excellently placed for defending not only the Indian Empire and the British possessions in Malaya, but Australia and New Zealand as well. It is true that Hongkong on the south coast of China is far nearer to Japan, but Hongkong, though ranking as the world's third greatest port and remaining a great fortress and outpost of Britain's dominions, is unable to accommodate large modern ships, and it has lost much of its importance since the establishment of the base at Singapore; in the event of war it might even prove advisable to abandon Hongkong—at least, for the time being—in

for she has an inner line of naval bases extending from the Kurile Islands in the north to Formosa or even as far as the Chinese island of Hainan in the south, so that she could make the China Sea into as much a Japanese lake as the Sea of Japan is already. Moreover, the groups of islands in the middle of the Pacific provide the Japanese navy and naval arm with innumerable bases from which they might operate against Australasia as well as isolating the American bases at Guam and in the Philippines.

But if Japan's strategic positions in the Pacific may seem to menace those of the U.S.A. in the same area, the American positions constitute in their turn a direct threat to Japan. (Note that Japan's strategic line is north to south—roughly vertical—while the U.S.A.'s is longitudinal, east to west.) From Long Beach and Los Angeles in California, the U.S.A.'s principal Pacific base, right across to the Philippines there extends a long line of American bases, pointing like a spear at Japan's vitals. Nearest to America, but even so rather more than 2,000 miles from San Francisco, is Hawaii, where a great, strongly defended naval and air base has been constructed; the fortifications at Pearl Harbour are said to be even stronger than those of Singapore. From Hawaii the line of

Left to right: Admiral Harold R. Stark was appointed Chief of U.S. Naval Operations on January 1, 1938; Admiral T. C. Hart is in command of the U.S. Asiatic Fleet; Colonel Frank Knox, though a member of the Republican party and so nominally opposed to President Roosevelt in politics, accepted the post of Secretary for War in June, 1940; the Commander-in-Chief of the United States Navy, Admiral James Richardson.   *Photos, Topical Press, Wide World*

Straits, and Japan thus achieved unchallenged predominance in the Pacific; her only possible rival at that time was Britain, and in 1902 Britain and Japan had concluded an alliance. The Great War of 1914-18 made Japan's control of the Pacific still more absolute, for Russia, for the time being, at least, fell out of the running as a great power, and those possessions which Germany had managed to obtain in the Far East before the war passed to Japan as part of the fruits of victory. As for the U.S.A., she contented herself with maintaining a few warships at Manila in the Philippines.

By the Washington Treaty of 1922 Britain, Japan, and the U.S.A. agreed that the status quo at the time of the signing of the Treaty should be maintained with regard to fortifications and naval bases in the most important strategic positions in the Pacific—Hongkong, America's possessions in the Philippines, Guam, and the Aleutian Islands, and Formosa and the numerous groups of Japanese islands, being the chief concerned. But the Washington Treaty expired on December 31, 1936, and since then there has been no limit placed on the strengthening or extension of fortifications in the Pacific area. Today, Japan is still the most powerful of the Great Powers in the Pacific, but her predominance is not so great as it was, for the U.S.A. has fully awakened to the fact that she faces the

order to concentrate more effectively on Singapore, 1,700 miles to the south-west; only consideration of prestige, or what the Orientals call " face," would demand its prolonged defence.

To Britain the Pacific is one of several oceans which have to be patrolled and, if need be, defended; to Japan it is the only ocean that matters. From north to south along the whole of its western basin the territories of the Japanese Empire extend over nearly 4,000 miles, though, of course, they are widely separated by vast stretches of landless ocean. Towards the north are the islands of Japan proper with Korea on the mainland and the huge dependency of Manchukuo. Practically the whole of the Chinese coast, including the hinterland of Hongkong, is now in Japanese occupation, and by the agreement concluded at Hanoi on September 22 with the Government of French Indo-China, Japan has now a foothold in that enormously wealthy French colony.

Then there are the numerous Japanese islands—Formosa and the adjacent Pescadores, Bonin and Volcano Island between Japan and the groups in mid-Pacific—the Carolines, the Marshalls, the Marianas or Ladrones, and Pelew—groups which were formerly German, but of which Japan is the mandatory. In the event of war in the Pacific, then, Japan is well placed strategically,

outposts stretches across the ocean to Midway Island, Wake Island (where work on a new naval base has just been begun), Guam, in the middle of the Japanese area, to the Philippines, where there is another great American base at Manila. Then, in addition to this " strategic bridge " across the Pacific, the U.S.A. has a naval aircraft base at Sitka in Alaska, and a number of air stations and bases of one kind and another in the Aleutians, which constitute a sort of land bridge between America and Asia. Then there is also, of course, the Panama Canal, through which America's fleets in the Pacific can be speedily reinforced from the Atlantic.

But in the Pacific distances are measured in thousands of miles, and when considering the possibility of naval operations on a large scale it must be borne in mind that, though solitary cruisers may remain at sea for weeks, even for months, at a stretch, a properly equipped battle fleet can remain at sea under war conditions not longer than about four days—or, to put it in other words, cannot operate at a radius of much more than 2,000 miles without having to return to its base for refuelling. Indeed, to be within reach of attack by a battle fleet, the objective must be within two days voyaging at ordinary speed. It will be seen, then, that a fleet operating from Hawaii, which is 3,379 miles

Geography's Limits on the Battle Fleets

In September 1939 the United States Navy had 15 completed capital ships against Britain's 13. Here, steaming in line ahead, are five of America's great battleships. In the foreground is the "New Mexico," while astern of her are the "Maryland," "Tennessee," "Oklahoma" and "California." The "New Mexico," 33,400 tons, has twelve 14-in. guns; the "Maryland," 31,500 tons, has eight 16-in. guns; the "Tennessee," 32,300 tons, has twelve 14-in. guns; the "Oklahoma," 29,000 tons, has ten 14-in. guns, and the "California," 32,600 tons, has twelve 14-in. guns.
Photo, Wide World

from Tokyo, would find it difficult to come to grips with Japan; hence the importance to the U.S.A. of Guam, which is only some 1,700 miles from Tokyo, and of the Philippines, which are within easy reach of Formosa and Japanese positions in S.E. Asia.

But the Philippines are between 5,000 and 6,000 miles from Honolulu in Hawaii, and from Honolulu to California is another 2,500 miles. No wonder, then, that it is suggested that Britain should place at America's disposal her great base of Singapore, which is only 1,350 miles from Manila, and that Australia, too, should offer to lease her sites

for bases. Unless such accommodation is made available, it is difficult to see how America can play any great part in the defence of south-eastern Asia and Australasia against an aggressive Japan. But, given the bases, then the U.S.A. has a naval superiority over Japan which should prove decisive.

Scattered about the vast expanse of the Pacific Ocean are the bases of the three great Powers—Britain, Japan, and the U.S.A. Japan's bases run approximately north and south, from the islands of Japan proper through Bonin to the mandated groups, the Marianas, Marshalls, and Carolines; to the west lie the island of Formosa and the occupied territories in China and Indo-China. Britain's chief bases are at Singapore and Hongkong; while those of the U.S.A. lie across the ocean in a horizontal line, including Hawaii, Midway and Wake Islands, Guam, and the Philippines.

Courtesy "Evening Standard"

Heroes and Heroines All at London's Hospitals

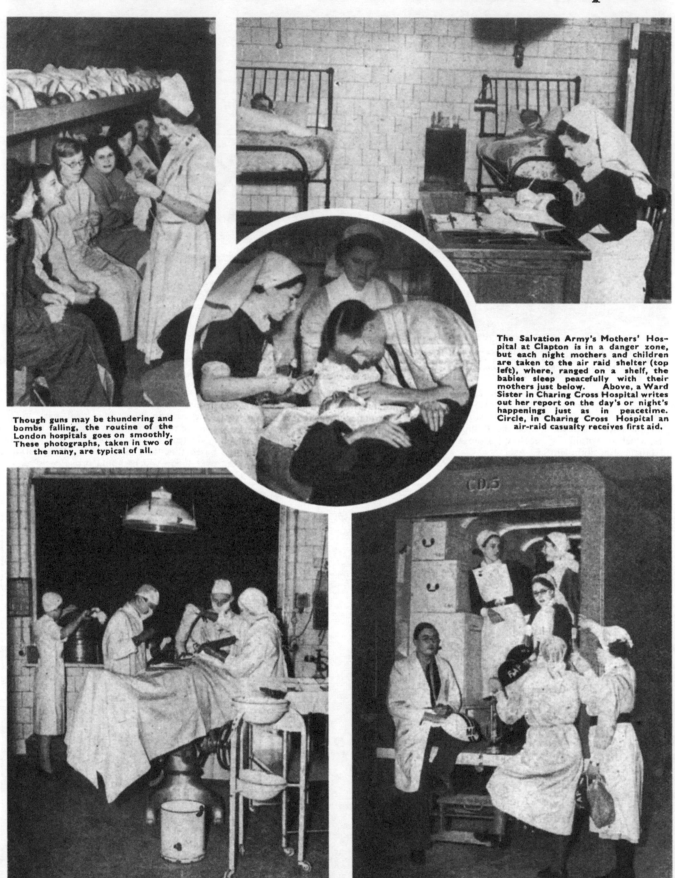

Though guns may be thundering and bombs falling, the routine of the London hospitals goes on smoothly. These photographs, taken in two of the many, are typical of all.

The Salvation Army's Mothers' Hospital at Clapton is in a danger zone, but each night mothers and children are taken to the air raid shelter (top left), where, ranged on a shelf, the babies sleep peacefully with their mothers just below. Above, a Ward Sister in Charing Cross Hospital writes out her report on the day's or night's happenings just as in peacetime. Circle, in Charing Cross Hospital an air-raid casualty receives first aid.

Left is the operating theatre of Charing Cross Hospital, where surgeons and nurses are carrying on. The hospital is in a centre that has suffered heavily, and near-by, under the famous Adelphi arches, mobile units (right), equipped with everything needed to give first aid to the injured, are always ready for an emergency. They carry all the instruments and dressings necessary for a large number of casualties.

Photos, " News Chronicle " and Fox

Britain Unshaken by Nazi Reprisal Attacks

Changing their tactics from lone night-flying bombers and heavily escorted day bombers, the Nazi air force made the greater part of their attacks during the period October 8 to 14 by fighter bombers. Considerable numbers were used by day and in smaller formations by night. Despite German boasts little evidence was to be seen of the culmination of ruin and terror that was claimed.

ACCORDING to a German communiqué of Oct. 8, the Luftwaffe on Monday night carried out an attack on London "which brought the succession of reprisal attacks which have shaken Britain to a culminating point." But next morning there were no signs of that culmination of savagery and destruction which Berlin claimed. Incendiary bombs were dropped, it is true, on a hospital whose location at the hub of the capital exposed it to daily and nightly risk, but the small fire arising was soon dealt with by the A.F.S. While engaged in this preventive work the firemen saw their own comrades from a near-by post being carried in on stretchers, maimed by the collapse of a fire station after a direct hit. There were piles of brick and masonry in some streets where other bombs had blasted away shops and office blocks, but nothing

to denote that overnight London had been visited by what Berlin described as "more bombers than ever." And nothing in the demeanour of the throngs on the way to work would have given any evidence of shaken morale.

A little later that same morning they showed amazing courage when bombers flew low over the capital and blew down buildings in several main thoroughfares,

Looking down on the roof at the east end of St Paul's Cathedral, through which a German bomb fell (circle). It made a rectangular hole 20 ft. by 10 ft. A further illustration is in page 431. Two chimney stacks (below) are freak remains after a fire which devastated London buildings after an air raid.
Photos, Central Press and L.N.A.

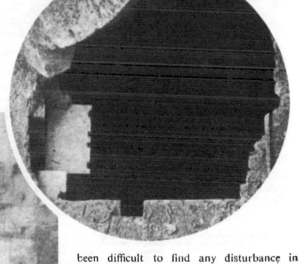

crowded with people. Some saw a bus destroyed and its driver and many passengers killed or wounded; others, when they heard the shriek of bombs, ran to shelter, and later went on their way to work undaunted. Tramcars were also damaged, and a train was struck by debris from a bomb explosion, but a couple of hours after it would have

been difficult to find any disturbance in Central London's complex transport system. The daily miracle of repair and restoration was performed.

The attack had been made by two formations of bombers and fighters which came in over the Kent coast. Only four or five out of fifty in the first lot got as far as Central London. A later wave was even less successful, for none got farther than the coast. Some of a third group got through and dropped a few bombs in the outer zone, but a fourth formation was repulsed.

At nightfall on Tuesday German heavy bombers resumed the attack, coming up the Estuary in a "procession." During the day's air battles five enemy aircraft were destroyed, and also two seaplanes, which were bagged by the Coastal Command. Mr. Charles Latham, leader of the London County Council, stated that in four weeks of night and day bombing only about one per cent of the Council's property had been damaged, and only about one in a hundred of the Council's tenants injured.

Small formations of fighter-bombers, flying high, attacked places in the south-east on Wednesday morning. One was blown to pieces in mid-air by A.A. fire over a south-eastern suburb of London, after being ringed around by bursting shells. A hospital was bombed, and it chanced that all the twenty-five patients were victims of previous raids. Happily they were got out without further injury.

Hardly had twilight fallen when the night raids began. Bright moonlight made it possible to follow the course of the raiders by the greyish trails of condensation from

On Hospitals & Animals the Random Bombs Fall

This was the scene of devastation at a large London hospital after the building had been hit by a heavy calibre bomb. A sixty-eight-year-old man was found to be alive underneath the mass of debris, and he was subsequently rescued.
Photo, " News Chronicle"

their exhausts. One of London's Wren churches was damaged by bombs that straddled the building. The top was torn off a bus near by, and its driver was injured in a shelter where he had taken cover. In another London street a Molotov " bread-basket " of incendiaries set fire to several buildings. Many flares were dropped by the bombers, but a number were put out by shots from A.A. guns. Two other ancient churches were damaged. By a direct hit on a shelter in the central area some thirty people were buried in debris, many casualties being caused.

During one of the raids in this period a bomb penetrated the roof of St. Paul's Cathedral and tons of stone fell upon the High Altar and Choir 90 feet below. Only the masterly execution of Wren's vaulting saved the building from worse destruction, for the bomb exploded either in the outer roof space or on the stone vaulting.

Twice during the morning of Thursday, October 10, enemy formations made for London, but were turned back over the Estuary. In a later attempt a single Nazi aircraft dropped one bomb in a London district, demolishing two houses and injuring four people. Widespread attacks were made at night, and bombs were dropped in some forty districts of London and the outskirts. Again many flares were seen, and our gunners had good practice in shooting out these beacons.

On Friday the enemy attacked mainly with converted Messerschmitts, coming over the coasts of Kent, Sussex and Dorset, and up the Thames Estuary. Some 350 aircraft took part. A Messerschmitt made a dive attack on Canterbury, and windows in the Cathedral were shattered. Happily most of the ancient stained glass had long ago been removed to a place of safety. Of a number of Dorniers which tried to bomb Liverpool, three were destroyed. Another Dornier

This pony, injured in an East End raid, is being housed and looked after at the People's Dispensary for Sick Animals farm at Ilford.
Photo, Fox

GERMAN & BRITISH AIRCRAFT LOSSES
German to April 30, 1940

Total announced and estimated—West Front, North Sea, Britain, Scandinavia **350**

	German	British
May	1,990	258
June	276	177
July	245	115
Aug.	1,110	310
Sept. 1-30	1,114	311
Oct. 1-14	110	59
Totals, May to Oct. ...	**4,815**	**1,230**

Daily Results

Oct.	German Losses	British Losses	British Pilots Saved	Oct.	German Losses	British Losses	British Pilots Saved
1	5	3	—	8	8	2	—
2	10	1	—	9	4	1	1
3	2	—	—	10	4	5	2
4	3	1	—	11	8	9	6
5	23	9	7	12	11	10	8
6	2	—	—	13	2	0	2
7	27	16	10	14	0	0	0
				Totals	**110**	**59**	**35**

None of the figures include aircraft bombed on the ground or so damaged as to be unlikely to reach home.

Civilian Casualties. Intensive air attacks on Britain began on Aug. 8. Casualties during August 1,075 killed, 1,261 seriously injured.

Mr. Churchill stated on Oct. 8 that up to Oct. 5 8,500 people had been killed and 13,000 seriously injured in air raids. Casualty figures had decreased steadily week by week since heavy raiding began on Sept. 7 ; from over 6,000 in the first week to just under 5,000 in the second, to about 4,000 in the third, and to under 3,000 in the last of the four weeks.

Mass Raid Casualties in London. Sept. 7 : 306 killed ; 1,337 injured. Sept. 8 : 286 killed ; about 1,400 injured. Sept. 9 : about 400 killed, 1,400 injured.

German Pilots Lost. Lord Croft, Under Secretary for War, stated recently that more German airmen alone had been slain or captured in the previous twelve weeks (i.e. July to September) than all the civilians they had murdered in Britain. Less British blood had been shed as the result of air attacks in 12 months than we frequently lost in a single hour in the Great War of 1914-18.

While Churches are Ruined They are Safe in Tubes

was shot down at Biggin Hill in Kent. Eighteen bombers making for London turned tail and abandoned their operation when a single Spitfire "worried" them.

In the evening our A.A. fire kept the raiders flying high. In London a block of flats was bombed for the third time. H.E. bombs in small number and also oil bombs were dropped in some other London districts. Enemy activity ceased rather earlier than usual. Owing to the enemy's changed tactics his losses were fewer, but his activities also were very much curtailed, and the change of plan in itself was a tribute to the effectiveness of our offensive defence.

The third of London's five daylight warnings on Saturday, October 12, was the two hundredth alert to be heard in the capital. Again the Nazis resorted to dive bombing, five houses in three roads on the outskirts of London being demolished and many others damaged. A bus was damaged and some passengers injured when a large block of buildings was bombed. Though the number of Nazi machines destroyed was comparatively small, the raiders were driven away without being able to do much harm.

Night raiders were heard as soon as it became dusk, but the "alert" was of short

These cheerful Londoners, secure for the night from the Nazi night raiders, are being entertained by a concert organized by E.N.S.A. in the Aldwych Tube shelter.
Photo, " News Chronicle "

duration. An underground railway station was hit and seven people killed. Elsewhere houses were demolished and flats wrecked.

Not till the afternoon did Sunday's air attacks begin, and the raiders were few in number. Some got to the outskirts of London, houses being damaged and fires started, but casualties were light. Very little activity was reported from other parts of Britain. The raiders flew high, and their vapour trails in the sky were everywhere to be seen over London as they twisted and doubled in order to try and elude our fighters. At night the "alert" was the signal for continuous activity for some time, as groups of bombers flew in and spread out on approaching London. Nearing the capital they came up against our barrage, and at least one Nazi was shot down by A.A. fire.

Single raiders dropped a few bombs at places in the Midlands and the South of England during daylight on Monday, October 14. Houses and shops were damaged in a Kent town, but elsewhere little harm was done and casualties were few. At night, however, London had what appeared to be its fiercest bombing up to date. Showers of fire bombs were dropped, a new type of missile being used which exploded on impact, Among buildings wrecked by H.E. bombs were a convent, a church, and a cinema, besides restaurants and office blocks. Brilliant moonlight seemed to render unnecessary the many flares which the Nazis dropped. In an institution for cripples four girl inmates were killed while in the maternity ward of a suburban hospital two nurses were injured, about fifty mothers with their infants being got out safely.

During the rush hour on Tuesday morning, and again a little later, small groups of Nazi raiders approached London. A hospital already damaged was hit again, fortunately without casualties. At least seventeen enemy machines were destroyed in these encounters.

One of Central London's most famous churches which has been bombed more than once. Though the beautiful interior was destroyed, the walls still stand, a melancholy skeleton.
Photo, Central Press

Nazi Ruthlessness Assails Our National Shrines

An incendiary bomb was dropped on St. Margaret's Church, Westminster, during one of the October raids on London, but, beyond the charred pews (right), and many windows blown out, little damage was done. The Speaker and M.P.s attend services in the church on special occasions, and the former has his own pew near the lectern. The church was erected in the reign of Edward I, but has undergone several restorations. There are many memorial plaques which were undamaged, and some fine stained glass windows.

A bomb which fell near Westminster Abbey about the same time damaged the exterior of Henry VII's Chapel, the most beautiful part of the Abbey, begun by Henry VII in 1503; in the main fabric the Chaucer memorial window above the tomb of the poet in Poets' Corner suffered damage to the glass, but the beautiful stone tracery was not injured.

Henry VII's Chapel is the Chapel of the Knights of the Bath, and some of their beautifully carved stalls were damaged by fire, above. A piece of masonry from the roof lies before them.

MANY celebrated London churches have been damaged as the result of the Nazi assaults upon the metropolis. As "military objectives" the damage they have sustained testifies to the wanton way in which the German pilots have let drop their bombs. Many historical buildings have suffered, though in the majority of cases the damage has mainly consisted of smashed stained glass windows, broken tiles and chipped stonework. Fires caused by incendiaries have been quickly extinguished, and, with one or two exceptions where the interiors of churches have been gutted, services are being resumed.

Photos, "News Chronicle" Staff Photographer:
Exclusive to THE WAR ILLUSTRATED

St. Paul's and the Abbey Are War Casualties

Wren's masterpiece, St. Paul's Cathedral, was hit by an enemy bomb during a recent raid on London.　The bomb penetrated the roof at the east end of the cathedral and demolished the High Altar, leaving the figure of Christ untouched.　No damage was done to the famous dome, which is separated from the altar by the choir, and the choir stalls with their exquisite Grinling Gibbons carvings were undamaged.　The High Altar dated from 1888, and the reredos, which suffered injury, was also erected at the close of the last century.

Photo, Planet News

When Enemy 'Planes Yield Their Secrets

The tail of this Messerschmitt 109 claims to record the destruction of thirteen R.A.F. 'planes, but the thirteenth proved unlucky, for the Nazi fighter was brought down by its intended "victim." R.A.F. sergeants, right, inspect the engine.

GERMAN bombers and fighters that have been brought down over Great Britain have given one or two "wrinkles" to our designers, as well as providing a knowledge of the weak spots of the enemy aircraft that has been put to good use by the R.A.F. Experts have been able to learn of every new advance made by the German designers and to consider its application to British aircraft. On the other hand, the suggestion that evidence of indifferent material and poor workmanship was found during the "post-mortems" on German aeroplanes has been proved untrue. Some of the material used does not reach British standards, but there is no evidence that the constructional defects are so great as to minimize the performance of the aircraft.

Examining the self-sealing petrol tank of a Junkers 88 bomber, the outside of which is made of vulcanized rubber. Below is seen a Heinkel 111 low-wing monoplane bomber.

A cannon gun from a Messerschmitt 110 which will not be used again. The menacing 4-gun mounting in the nose cowling of a Messerschmitt 110 is seen below.

Photos, Topical Press; Planet News; "News Chronicle"

R.A.F. Weave a Web of Destruction Over Germany

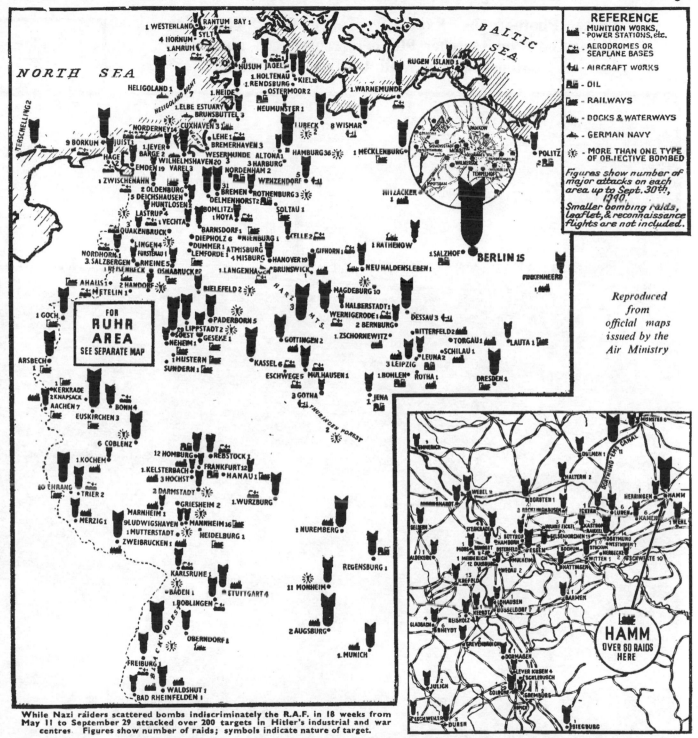

Reproduced from official maps issued by the Air Ministry

While Nazi raiders scattered bombs indiscriminately the R.A.F. in 18 weeks from May 11 to September 29 attacked over 200 targets in Hitler's industrial and war centres. Figures show number of raids; symbols indicate nature of target.

More than seven hundred times, on more than two hundred targets in Germany itself, the R.A.F. dropped bombs in less than five months. The maps printed above indicate the places, the type of objective attacked, and the number of raids made on these targets of prime military importance. Every raid formed part of a scientifically planned series designed to hit the enemy in his vitals—his armaments production, oil supplies, transport systems, docks, harbours, power stations, his aerodromes and seaplane bases.

In due course, when it came into the R.A.F. plan, the enemy's capital was visited and points of military importance were attacked. Three times in August (beginning on the night of the 26/27th) and twelve times in September our bombers were over Berlin and its suburbs, attacking power stations, factories, aerodromes, oil stores, railway stations and goods yards, gas works, blast furnaces, cable works and a host of other establishments. In the Ruhr area the Dortmund-Ems canal was repeatedly bombed, and thus the munitions it carried —already diverted from much-tried railways and roads—were prevented from reaching their destination. Similarly stocks of raw materials for the factories and works were stopped. The great marshalling yard at Hamm was bombed more than sixty times (see inset map). Here the Germans send an enormous quantity of goods wagons from all over the country: at the yard the trucks are made up into trains for their respective distributing points. It follows that if the

Hamm sidings be damaged and the work disorganized, goods of all sorts will pile up for days and the whole system will be put out of gear.

Another remarkable facet of the work of our bombers was the nightly attack on the ports, harbours, and river mouths where Hitler for months was assembling his invasion fleets. So terrible was the destruction wrought among his barges and other small craft that it was creditably reported that the enemy had withdrawn a great many barge convoys from the Straits to his North Sea ports, where they would be safer.

And it is indisputable that the R.A.F. attacks largely contributed to the delaying if not the total frustration of the German invasion plans.

After 31 Days and Nights of Ruthless Bombin

These Photographs Expressly Taken for "The War Illustrated" on October 9th, here reproduced absolutely untouched, may well become historic.

A City of Spires Untouched

Those who neither work nor live in London may well suppose from reading the reports in the newspapers of the damage caused by Nazi raiders that in large measure the Empire's capital has been laid waste. To show how mistaken is this impression we here reproduce two photographs exclusive to " The War Illustrated," taken on October 9, 1940, when the Battle of London had been in progress for rather more than a month. The photographs were taken from the roof of St. Paul's Cathedral looking down Ludgate Hill and the panorama is that seen looking west ; Note that the photographs overlap slightly, but are equally focussed on the same skyline.

From Law Courts to Ludgate Hill

All the landmarks which might be looked for in peacetime still stand erect. Looking from left to right we may pick out the tower and minaret of the Law Courts, and next the famous stepped spire of St. Bride's, Fleet Street. Farther back is the tower of the Masonic Temple in Queen Street, Holborn. The square tower with the four minarets is that of the Record Office in Chancery Lane, while in the foreground is Ludgate Hill with its railway bridge at the foot, and beyond it the offices of the " Daily Telegraph " and the " Daily Express." Half - way down Ludgate Hill on the right is the spire of St. Martin's Church.

High Holbor

Next on th
pany office
superstructu
the Memoria
we see St. M
just to the r
graph is the F
left of the se
Holborn, an
feature is the
Right of it is
                                                                              Ph

Old Massive Capital Stands Solid and Intact'

NIGHT after night and day after day since that Saturday afternoon of September 7, when the Nazis delivered the first of their mass attacks on London, Britain's capital has been the main objective of Hitler's sky-pirates. The destruction of property, as Mr. Churchill said on October 8, had been very considerable, but " we must not exaggerate the material damage that has been done. The papers are full of pictures of the demolished houses, but naturally they do not fill their restricted space with pictures of those which are left standing. If you go to the top of Primrose Hill or any of the other eminences of London, no one standing there and looking around would know that any harm had been done to our city. Statisticians may amuse themselves by calculating that after making allowances for the working of the law of diminishing returns—through some houses being struck twice or three times—it would take 10 years at the present rate for half the houses of London to be demolished "—and " a lot of things are going to happen to Herr Hitler and the Nazi regime before ten years are past ! "

To take these photographs our photographer mounted to one of those eminences of which the Prime Minister spoke—the outer gallery around the dome of St. Paul's Cathedral. He exposed his film on October 9, and from these photographs it is abundantly clear that, as Mr. Malcolm Macdonald, Minister of Health, told America in a broadcast on October 6, " though each night now adds to the sum of damage that is wrought, yet the old massive capital of this island, the city of its government and court of its kings for countless generations, stands solid and intact."

London Life in the Blitzkrieg: Getting Used to it!

In the mass of world-forces the death and destruction which we see around us today—
appalling and awesome as it may be to us who are existing in its midst—is no more
than a scratch upon the abounding life-energy of the world.   This little article, specially
contributed by a famous international journalist to "The War Illustrated," is a reminder
that even among the ruins "life goes on."

EVEN Hitler's total war in which gradually all the citizens of Britain have become directly involved cannot stop a thousand and one different entirely non-military pursuits. Life goes on, and we have to make the best of it.

Nature enables certain animals to adapt themselves—as a measure of self-protection—to their surroundings. They change their colour, their habits, their very shape in this process, which helps them to avoid a good many obvious risks to their life. The same is true of us. Khaki and camouflage are by no means the only outward signs of our astonishing adaptability.

Take, for instance, the question of earning one's living. While many established trades and professions have been badly hit, innumerable new ones have arisen almost overnight. Last year, when the introduction of the black-out created an immediate shortage of pocket torches and batteries, street traders within a few days had established a brisk trade in them ; or in gas-mask cases ; in black-out fittings ; gummed paper for the windows, and many other similar requisites. If you look at the street traders now you will find that they sell very different things—mostly in connexion with "Blitz" necessities—e.g., anti-splinter mixture for painting windows, or gadgets of all sorts that might come in handy in a shelter.

Chemists are doing a roaring trade in sedatives, sleeping draughts, ear-pads, mouth-pads, bandages and disinfectants. There is a big demand for identity disks, and some enterprising people sell and even engrave them in the street while you wait. Again, with over a dozen foreign newspapers now appearing in London there is a good opening not only for foreign type-setters and printers but also for newspaper vendors. In days gone by one could get a foreign paper only in one or two shops around Leicester Square or at the big Continental termini. Now they sell them all over London.

A successful business that appears to have been badly hit is "Paddy's Mobile Book Stall." Paddy, an enterprising Irishman and a tailor by trade, had developed an enormous business as a street bookseller. He had established a large stall outside Liberty's, and there he did a brisk trade not only in papers and magazines but also in books and Government publications. Hitler's bombs seem to have driven him from his accustomed pitch—no doubt only temporarily. By the way, the banning of "Guilty Men" provided him and many other street stalls with a best-seller.

Speaking of books, foreign dictionaries, London guides and English textbooks seem to be in great demand. On the other hand, authors and publishers complain that the normal book trade has been very badly hit indeed ; people have no money to buy books, so they say.

But furniture storage ; the manufacturing of all kinds of shelters, stirrup pumps, shovels, boarding-up material, bullet-proof waistcoats, life-saving jackets, siren suits and uniforms must be reckoned among the

flourishing trades at the moment. Then there are the junk shops where you can buy or sell anything from a grand piano to a tin hat.

Many of the established habits and traditions are being demolished, together with a few of London's buildings. Will there be a Lord Mayor's Show this year ? Indeed, is it desirable or technically possible ?

There is a slump in the demand for red-coated stentorian-voiced announcers at banquets. But, especially during the early months of the war, when bottle parties and clubs grew like mushrooms after the rain, there was a great demand for what Americans called "bouncers," i.e. chuckers-out.

The American "Jitney" system seems to have been transplanted to London ; people

Naturally enough the raids have slowed up postal collections and deliveries, but London's postmen, equipped with "tin hats," make their rounds in the bombed districts much as usual.   *Photo, Central Press*

not only share taxis, but there is quite an opening for private car hires at night when cabmen and some bus drivers go to shelter.

Incidentally, it is high time the bus drivers received a special word of thanks and commendation. Their job is a most trying one and they are doing it magnificently. To the difficulties of driving in the black-out have now been added the perils of bomb and shell splinter, while the constant changing of routes owing to traffic diversion is in itself an ordeal to any driver.

So many people have now become ambulant that one can say to one's lady friends : "And where did *you* spend last night ?" without risking a reprimand. It is interesting how, after many weeks of a rather silly snobbish attitude to sheltering (through the month of August "shelter crawling" was quite a popular pastime in

Mayfair), people have acquired the habit of going to shelter as soon as it gets dark.

Here again several new trades have arisen. Enterprising citizens have opened canteens in the shelters and are doing quite well selling tea or hot soup or sandwiches. Then there are some "tough guys" that hire themselves out to protect specific pitches for their clients. Shops selling folding beds and camp mattresses are doing well. Snorers in the shelters are a great problem ; to stop them from disturbing their fellow sleepers one or two places now employ "shelter shakers"—i.e. people who wake up the snorers as soon as they get too noisy.

This sudden necessity of communal sleeping raises many unexpected problems. Friendships are struck up and enmities established which will last a lifetime. They cut across all social barriers and they must act as an eye-opener to many a citizen. The ordeal brings out the sometimes hidden sterling qualities of some and the utter worthlessness of others. There is many a quarrelsome shelter pest who has to be dealt with next morning at the police court, and many a customer in shop or hotel who drives the staff crazy with pretentious demands for service and attention.

Most of the big hotels are benefiting from the "Blitz." Even people whose houses are as yet intact prefer living in larger and more solid buildings. Moreover, the gregarious instinct has unquestionably something to do with it : one hates being all by oneself in times like these, and the presence of others around becomes a necessity even for the most confirmed misanthrope.

While the hotels are doing well, the restaurants are hard hit. At night even those that occupy premises below street level are mostly deserted. But the first experiments in communal feeding are proving a great success.

Talleyrand observed that in times of great social upheavals people go in for the oddest of marriages. How true is that of today ? And where can even the luckiest ones go for a honeymoon ? Not only is it impossible to travel abroad, but half the British Isles must now be considered as protected areas. Again, with so many Londoners evacuated, there is hardly an hotel in the country where it is possible to obtain a bed, not to say a room.

When you suddenly have to evacuate your house what are the indispensable things you take with you ? Which of your belongings do you treasure most ? Thousands of people are faced with this problem every day, or rather every night. Then there is the question of domestic pets : we cannot take them to shelter, and we refuse to have them destroyed. But we are reluctant to leave them at home alone, so what is one to do ?

In this topsy-turvy world some people flourish, while many professions, including "the world's most ancient one," are practically ruined. But life goes on. Asked what he had been doing in the days of terror during the French Revolution, the Abbé Sieyès replied : "I have lived." If we can say as much a few years hence, we shall be lucky.

Despite Hitler's 'Blockade' We Deliver the Goods

The Union Jack and the slogan " Britain delivers the goods " stencilled on packing cases, left, is how a Manchester textile firm combines export trade and propaganda. Right, a small boy inside a packing case stows away for export British biscuits, the best in the world.

THE importance of sending goods abroad to pay for the British imports of war material and food was emphasized by Mr. F. D'Arcy Cooper, Chairman of the Export Council of the Board of Trade, in a speech on September 4, 1940. He said that since January 1 this year Britain's imports had averaged over £100,000,000 a month, and visible exports only £40,000,000, or a gap at the rate of £720,000,000 a year. Some of that gap was made up by invisible exports, interest on investments, shipping, banking, and insurance, but the remainder must be met by the sale of capital assets such as gold and securities. Food and the raw materials for the war must all be paid for, and the best way was by exports from this country. The exports trade had had a very difficult time since the beginning of the war. It was only natural that in the first few months the dislocation of business owing to war conditions severely upset our export trade. The Government appreciated the danger and in February appointed an Export Council, whose first task, among other things, was to coordinate industry according to the nature of the trades. From February to April the position of the export trade vastly improved ; in April our exports were greater than at any time since July 1930.

The excellence of the British products from the Staffordshire potteries has a world fame as widespread as that of Britain's textiles and biscuits, and there is still a great demand, not only from the Dominions, but from neutral countries, for British pottery. The girls in the photograph above are stacking up mugs destined for overseas markets as they come from the ovens.

Photos, Fox, Keystone and " Daily Mirror "

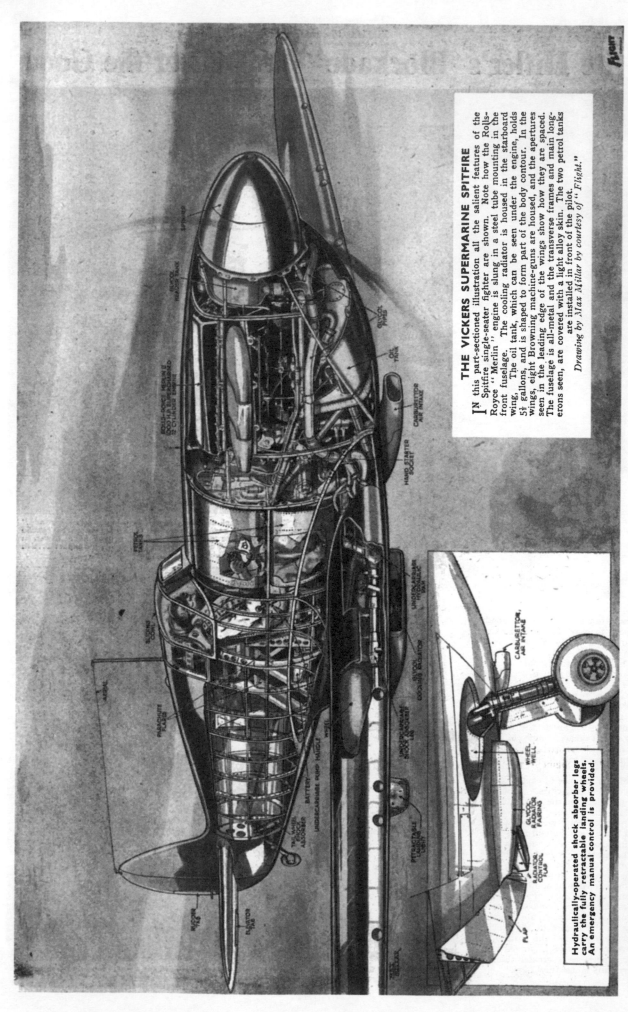

THE VICKERS SUPERMARINE SPITFIRE

IN this part-sectioned illustration all the salient features of the Rolls-Royce "Merlin" engine is slung in a steel tube mounting in the front fuselage. The cooling radiator is housed in the starboard wing. The oil tank, which can be seen under the engine, holds 5½ gallons, and is shaped to form part of the body contour. In the wings, eight Browning machine-guns are housed, and the apertures seen in the leading edge of the wings show how they are spaced. The fuselage is all-metal and the transverse frames and main longerons seen, are covered with a light alloy skin. The two petrol tanks are installed in front of the pilot.

Drawing by Max Millar by courtesy of "Flight."

Span 36 feet 10 inches.   Length 29 feet 11 inches.
Height 11 feet 5 inches.   Wing area 240 sq. feet.
Weight loaded 5,850 lb.   Engine power 1,030 h.p.
Initial rate of climb 2,300 feet a minute.

Hydraulically-operated shock absorber legs carry the fully retractable landing wheels. An emergency manual control is provided.

The Vickers Supermarine Spitfire was first produced in 1936, and after prolonged trials was supplied to the Royal Air Force in July, 1938. Originally it was designed as a four-gun fighter, but the specification was altered to include eight guns. An aeroplane with outstanding qualities as a fighting machine, it is rivalled only by the equally-famous Hawker Hurricane, which is powered with the same engine and is similarly armed. A special version of the Spitfire was built in 1938 in order to attack the world's speed record, and it attained a speed of 420 m.p.h. The present standard service version is now being built in huge numbers.

The Spitfire—The World's Finest Fighter

In all the annals of aerial warfare no finer fighter aeroplane ever existed than the Supermarine Spitfire. Time and time again as the conflict in Britain's skies continues our
Spitfire pilots, flying with unsurpassed skill and courage, roar up from their stations
to grapple with the Luftwaffe. Here Mr. Grenville Manton describes their capacities.

THE unremitting havoc the Spitfires and their pilots have poured into the enemy, the terrible toll they have taken of Messerschmitts, Heinkels and Dorniers in a few brief but breathless months, have aroused the admiration of the civilized world. And a fearful respect is held by Nazi airmen for that sleek, pugnacious monoplane.

Yet though no German fighter can compare with the Spitfire it is not a recently-evolved machine, but something of a veteran. Back in 1936 the prototype powered with a Rolls-Royce Merlin engine of 1,030 h.p. first appeared. Its designer was the late Mr. R. J. Mitchell, whose brilliance and genius resulted in those wonderful Schneider Trophy racing seaplanes, the S.5 and S.6. In a way the Spitfire is a descendant of those machines and its success is a legacy of the triumphs of its predecessors which were built specially for the Schneider contests thirteen years ago.

In its design and appearance the Spitfire is perfectly orthodox. There is nothing freakish or unusual about it. It looks what it is, a beautifully proportioned, clean-lined monoplane. It is of stressed-skin construction with a cantilever wing covered with alloy sheet. The tail unit, too, is cantilever, and with the exception of the rudder and elevators, which are covered with fabric, the covering is of aluminium alloy sheet.

The fuselage is built of metal, the framework being covered with an alloy "skin" which is attached with flush rivets to give a completely smooth surface. As on all modern fighting 'planes, the undercarriage is of the retractable type, the wheels and legs being tucked away into the underside of the wings when the machine is in flight. The retraction is controlled by an hydraulic system and there is also an emergency hand device.

Housed in the Spitfire's forbidding nose is its Rolls-Royce Merlin 12-cylinder Vee liquid-cooled engine of 1,250 h.p. The radiator is of special design and is housed in a duct beneath the starboard wing. The motor drives a Rotol three-blade controllable-pitch airscrew, the hub of which is fitted with a spinner. In front of the pilot are two petrol tanks, which together hold 85 gallons.

It Fires Over 20 Rounds a Second

The fuel is fed to the engine by pumps, and starting is effected by an electric starter and a manually-operated turning gear. The pilot sits in an enclosed cockpit, which is fitted with a sliding glass hatch and a hinged panel in the side of the fuselage. The wind shield fixed to the front of the cockpit is fitted with bullet-proof glass and there is a "fire-wall" arranged immediately behind the engine.

The armament of the Spitfire comprises eight machine-guns, all located in the wings, four on each side of the fuselage. These guns, which, with a rate of fire of 1,300 rounds per minute, are capable of producing a most shattering effect on enemy machines, are Brownings. They work on the barrel-recoil principle, and because they are mounted outside the propeller arc, they can be fired at maximum speed. This is not possible with guns which fire through the propeller, as they have to be synchronised in order to avoid

certain inevitable damage to the blades by bullets. In the equipment of the Spitfire a lot is squeezed into a little space. Besides having the full complement of normal flying and blind-flying instruments it carries a radio set, oxygen equipment for high altitude flying, a first-aid outfit, parachute flares and landing lights for night operations.

When, in July, 1938, the first batch of Spitfires was delivered to a fighter squadron, a new milestone was reached in the history of the Royal Air Force. It marked the extinction of the trusty and well-tried biplane fighter and opened up fresh developments in aerial warfare. When it was first introduced, though everyone was impressed by its tremendous speed, there were doubts expressed as to its suitability for service as a standard fighter. It was suggested that its

Under certain conditions of height and air temperature 'planes leave clear tracks in the sky from their exhausts. Here is such a record of an exciting chase over Kent by our fighters of five Nazi fighter bombers.
Photo, Wide World

Flights of Spitfires are a familiar sight in British - skies, and this fine and very characteristic formation plan shows how well the machines are handled.
By courtesy of "Flight"

immensely high speed would make it difficult to manoeuvre in combat, that it would be ineffective in "dog-fights" because it would be unable to twist and turn nimbly. Pilots, it was thought, would find it difficult and tricky to fly.

But months of war have proved all these contentions to be wrong. The Spitfire is easy and pleasant to fly, and it is used at night as well as by day. And, as has been proved again and again in the fighting over England, it has superlative qualities as a fighting machine. The Germans know this well, as many who have been shot down have revealed in explaining their defeat by such words as "Spitfire—too good."

As time has passed modifications have been made to the machine, each one adding to its speed and fighting power. At first, when it was fitted with a two-blade fixed-pitch wooden airscrew, its speed was 362 m.p.h. at 18,500 feet. Then by using a de Havilland controllable-pitch airscrew the speed was raised to 367 m.p.h. Changes were then made to the engine, a new fuel was employed, the Rotol airscrew was adopted, and the speed rose to 387 m.p.h.

Experts, ever striving for further improvements, have lately made it faster and more formidable than ever. And so the Spitfire remains, after four years, the swiftest and most deadly fighting aeroplane of the war against Hitler. Its companion, the Hurricane, is equally remarkable in its own field and it has received much less than its due from the public. This is partly because of the attention focussed on the somewhat faster Spitfire by the funds raised for it all over the country and Empire.

Little Foretastes of Tomorrow's 'Blitz' on Egypt

This Italian bomber was forced down on Egyptian territory, and has been on public exhibition at Alexandria. The people of the city may read in their own language (Arabic) the 'plane's story.
Photo, Wide World

Above, men of an infantry unit among the ruins of a Western desert fort captured by the British. Centre : a wireless operator at work in the desert. Right : Italian soldiers are seen entering Sidi Barrani. The buildings in the background have been shelled by the British Fleet.
Photos, British Official : Crown Copyright ; and Wide World

DUNKIRK TO DAKAR: CRISES OF THE SUMMER

It is opportune to present my readers with a brief but comprehensive review of the later political development of the War as many new and surprising changes are impending. I have therefore invited Mr. George Soloveytchik, one of the ablest and best informed commentators on international affairs, to contribute occasional articles in which he will give THE WAR ILLUSTRATED readers the advantage of his knowledge. A British subject, of Russian origin, Mr. Soloveytchik has long enjoyed access to the most authoritative sources of information.—ED.

LET us take stock of the situation. Its "debits" and "credits" are considerable.

The first few weeks of Hitler's "Blitz" had one rather striking political result. For the first time in many years Britain's international prestige began to rise again. Not only the neutrals, but even Germany's vassal countries were impressed by Britain's capacity "to take it." After two decades of smug complacency and escapism the British suddenly proceeded to give the world a display of their finest characteristics. Our prestige was still on the upgrade when a series of events once more threatened to cause us great damage in the eyes of the world. The abortive expedition to Dakar, the German-Italian-Japanese alliance, the sharp anti-British turn in Rumania, Italian progress on the Egyptian border, an ugly situation in Spain, and at home a shocking muddle over the shelter and evacuation questions each one of these setbacks (and only purblind fools can deny that they are setbacks!) would be unpleasant enough. But taken together they constitute a sum total of liability which must be liquidated as soon as possible.

Fortunately we have a Prime Minister who is not only fully alive to all these difficulties, but who has the courage to name them and to tell the nation the naked—if unpleasant—truth. No one in this country can sum up a situation in a phrase that is at once dramatic and succinct better than Mr. Churchill. In a recent speech he invited the British public to ponder " the cataract of disaster " that has poured over us during the last year. And at the time people were so overjoyed with the miracle of Dunkirk that they almost mistook it for victory it was Mr. Churchill who reminded them that this was really a colossal defeat and that " wars are not won by evacuations."

There is something at once tragic and noble in the fact that Mr. Churchill—the greatest of our many unheeded Cassandras—has to carry on his powerful shoulders responsibilities which would never have arisen if his warnings had been listened to in time. He became Prime Minister at the time of the Norwegian fiasco. The road from Narvik to Dakar was certainly not of his making, yet he has had to travel along it. He has managed to do so while keeping a cool head and a heart of oak a truly wonderful performance that is an inspiration to the whole nation.

His recent cabinet changes indicate determination to grapple with the vital domestic issues without delay. The shelter crisis and the evacuation problem are certain to receive both competent and energetic treatment from Mr. Herbert Morrison, while the latter's successor at the Ministry of Supply, Sir Andrew Duncan, is one of the few really outstanding newcomers to our administration since the war: Lord Woolton is another.

'Too Little and Too Late'

AND now for the international situation. With regard to the anti-British developments in Rumania, it has been obvious for a long time that the whole of south-eastern Europe is at Hitler's mercy. After the Austrian " Anschluss " and the sacrifice of Czecho-slovakia the Nazi grip over the whole Danubian area became so firmly established that only some super-imaginative stroke on our part might have affected the situation in our favour. The various Balkan governments made no secret of their fear of Hitler and of their desire to be bolstered up by us against his political and economic pressure

Certain opportunities, particularly in the economic field, were still open to us. What we did was " too little and too late." Had the special trading company, for which these countries and a few wise people in the city of London had been pleading in vain for years, been started in good time, Hitler's " Bloodless Invasion," together with its unavoidable political repercussions, might have been retarded or even nipped in the bud. Then, again, all the small nations of Europe were hoping for some British military and political success somewhere which would have proved a rallying point against the progress of Nazism ; alas, they looked in vain. So most of the Balkan governments threw in their hands in despair.

The Gangsters of Berlin and Moscow

TODAY the dominating influences in that part of the world are Nazi Germany and Soviet Russia, and nobody knows the exact nature of the understanding between the gangster of Berlin and the gangster of Moscow. It is unlikely that they would risk a conflict over Danubian, or indeed any other part of Europe. Their partnership may be an uneasy one, but they have far too many interests in common to allow their fundamental hatred of each other to lead them to an open clash.

Be this as it may, the fact remains that in Rumania at the moment we are powerless to protect our financial investments, our political interests, or even the lives of our citizens, and alas, much the same is true of the Far East. With the only difference, however, that in Rumania that situation is new, whereas in the case of Japan it has now lasted for an uncomfortably long time. The formal alliance between Japan, Italy and Germany does not greatly affect our position in this respect, and has been generally interpreted as a challenge to America and Soviet Russia rather than to us. But as an indication of the measure of importance attached by the Japanese Government to our good will it is pretty eloquent.

Then there is the Mediterranean situation. For years experts had been warning Mr. Chamberlain's Government that Mussolini and his " stooge " Franco constituted a challenge and even a danger to British interests there. Mr. Chamberlain did not share that view. Indeed, he was willing " to eat his hat " if the pact he made with Mussolini did not re-establish the proper balance of power in the Mediterranean. Mussolini, with unsurpassed cynicism, awaited the collapse of France to enter the war and to press forward at the time of our greatest embarrassment. So far his successes are more theoretical than real. Yet it is foolish for some of our official spokesmen to sneer at the Italians as they do, and then to be forced to abandon territory to them.

As to Spain, she seems now to be much in the same position as Italy was in the early months of the war : a non-belligerent but certainly not a neutral country, and one that is only awaiting an opportune moment to come out openly against us. Much responsibility for our difficulties in the Mediterranean belongs to the French. Not only did they refuse to utilize their own very considerable army stationed on the Italian border against Mussolini while there still was time, but it is an open secret that they prevented certain R.A.F. action contemplated by us which might have achieved some vital results from the very beginning.

Again, the disloyal behaviour of the French navy under Admiral Darlan's orders

and the resulting necessity of our action in Oran further contributed to our trials and tribulations, out of which, however, we extricated ourselves extremely well when everything is considered. The collapse of France would have been a sufficiently hard blow for us, in any case. But what makes things so much worse is the deliberate and sadistic way in which the malfeasant Vichy gang has sought to impede our actions since the French capitulation. Chief responsibility for that rests not with 84-year-old Pétain, but with Pierre Laval, a sinister personage and an avowed enemy of Britain.

It is incomprehensible that we should have allowed these men to thwart General de Gaulle's attempt to land at Dakar. To begin with, it may be asked : Why did we lend ourselves to this adventure which was obviously ill-timed and badly prepared ? And why did we let the " Vichy " ships through Gibraltar ? Again, having once become associated with this expedition, why did we not see it through ? It appears that General de Gaulle did not want to fire on his compatriots. How can any civil war be fought if that is to be the guiding principle ?

Further, it is quite clear that, at any rate, the spearhead of a German-Italian expeditionary corps is now at Dakar, so that it was no longer purely a question of fighting Frenchmen, but of the allied Franco-British forces fighting the Axis and its satellites. Had the Dakar expedition taken place a few weeks earlier, had it been better prepared and more carefully planned, this present fantastic situation would never have arisen. If General de Gaulle wants to save his movement from disgrace and disintegration, he must not merely avoid the repetition of such follies, but he must look for a spectacular success somewhere else. We, too, need a success, and we need it badly.

If the Italians Accept Battle . . . .

GREAT and decisive action is looming in the Mediterranean. Much in the future conduct of the war will depend on it. Our position there is fraught with considerable potentialities if only the Italians can be induced to accept open battle—which up to now they have been reluctant to do. Yet there is also another " if " ; if this time we avoid the mistakes that have led us from Narvik to Dakar. It is an old truism that the British are never ready for their trials, but always equal to them. Only we cannot " muddle through " this time, and no one knows it better than our present Prime Minister.

Through the follies of his predecessors, and owing to the collapse of France, we have found ourselves in a position of unprecedented gravity. Under his inspiring leadership we have stood up to our trials magnificently, but that is not enough. At home, we are enduring the bitterest of sieges night and day. Abroad we have nothing but difficulties in Europe and in the Far East.

True, we are not alone. The Empire is a pillar of moral and material strength to the Mother Country. Our Allies are each contributing their share to our effort. The great United States democracy is giving us much valuable help, and may give still more. Yet in this fight which we wage not only for our lives but for the future of mankind, the primary burden and the heaviest responsibility devolve on us. In facing our task we must make up our minds, once and for all, that we shall countenance no more Narviks, no more Dunkirks and no more Dakars.

OUR SEARCHLIGHT ON THE WAR

The Bullying of Norway

QUISLING has abolished the Norwegian flag and adopted a new one which shows a golden cross on a red ground. All portraits of King Haakon and other members of the Royal Family which may still be seen in public places, schools, official premises, etc., are to be removed and destroyed, although the ban does not yet extend to the thousands of portraits in private houses. The word " royal " is henceforth prohibited wherever it was used in commerce and industry. Royal names of streets and hotels must be altered ; incidentally, English names are also banned. Norwegian churches have been instructed to alter their set prayers, and particularly to remove from them all mention of the King and the Royal Family. Compulsory service for all Norwegian boys and girls is being introduced on the model of the German Arbeitsdienst. Jew-baiting has started, and in some districts a special notice has to be shown indicating that a shop is of Jewish ownership. Moreover, Jews are forbidden to practise as doctors or lawyers, or to enter or remain in any State service.

'Strangers' Guide to Flak'

FLAK is a contraction of a German phrase signifying anti-aircraft guns, and the British Air Ministry has thoughtfully issued a pamphlet full of information on the German air defences. There are, it seems, two kinds of Flak, light and heavy. The former are guns of from ¾ in. to 2 in. calibre, and fire shells weighing from ½ lb. to 3⅓ lb. The smallest will fire 160 rounds a minute with a range of 7,000 ft., while the largest fires 25 rounds a minute and has a range of more than three miles. Heavy Flak range from 3½ in. guns firing 15 rounds a minute and throwing shells to 20,000 feet, to the 4.7 in. firing ten 32 lb. shells a minute to a height of 30,000 ft. The heavy guns are directed by complicated instruments known as predictors, but the information obtained by this means can be rendered useless by pilots changing their course, height or speed the moment the gun is fired.

British Barrage Balloons in Sweden

A GALE in the Channel has once more driven a number of Britain's balloons towards Sweden, where they have caused a good deal of inconvenience and some damage to electric power cables. Stockholm's suburb, Sundyberg, was blacked out for a time, as well as some country parishes in southern Sweden. A Swedish air line has had to suspend its foreign services to Berlin, Helsinki and Moscow on account of the drifting balloons. Stormy weather may not be entirely responsible for the breaking away of these balloons. It is well known that our barrage is now being flown higher than previously, which involves a thinner cable of lighter weight. This is more lethal to raiding 'planes, but may well be less able to withstand a sou'wester.

Germany's New Five-Point Plan

SOME high officer of the Nazi Air Force, who describes the present operations against Great Britain as " merely an initial phase," has outlined a new plan for the air war as follows : (1) Absolute control of the Channel and English coastal areas ; (2) Progressive and complete annihilation of London, with all its military objectives and industrial production ; (3) A steady process of paralysis of Britain's technical, commercial, industrial and civil life ; (4) Demoralization of the civil population of London and the provinces ; (5) Progressive weakening of the British fighter force. This comprehensive plan looks well on paper and doubtless caused great satisfaction when submitted to the German High Command. Whether the pilots of the Luftwaffe regard it with the same optimism is open to question. For instance, upon point 5, the defeat of our fighter defence, hinges the success of the other four points of the plan, and fulfilment of this condition must appear, even to the German authorities, to be as far off as ever. To the British authorities, with their authentic records of 695 R.A.F. aircraft lost (of which 338 pilots were saved) against a total of 2,608 enemy machines destroyed over and around our coasts since war began, it is considerably more remote.

All-American R.A.F. Squadron

H.M. THE KING has approved the formation of a squadron in the R.A.F. to be composed entirely of pilots from the United States. It is to be known as the Eagle Squadron, and the badge consists of an American eagle with the letters " E.S." above it. The Commander is Colonel Charles Sweeny, who was one of the organizers of the group of American volunteers who came over in 1914 to join the French Army and later formed the " Escadrille Lafayette," which was responsible for the destruction of 199 German aircraft. The

Squadron-Leader W. E. G. Taylor of New York is in command of the first all-American R.A.F. Squadron to serve with the R.A.F. It is known as the Eagle Squadron, and members wear the Eagle badge on the sleeve.
Photo, British Official : Crown Copyright

fighting commanding officer is Squadron-Leader W. E. G. Taylor, who formerly served in the U.S. Naval Air Service. In August, 1939, this officer came to England and was granted a commission in the Fleet Air Arm. All the pilots, of whom 34 have already been enrolled, are volunteers with a great deal of flying experience. Three are stunt pilots and one a professional parachutist. Several were serving in France with the Allied Air Force, and after the Pétain surrender they set out for England by long and devious routes in order to continue their service in the fight for freedom.

British Pilot Sinks Submarines

THE recent award of the Distinguished Flying Cross to Acting Flight-Lieutenant William Weir Campbell, pilot of a flying-boat of the Middle East Command, was made in recognition of his daring and determined attacks on Italian submarines, by which two were destroyed with bombs and another with machine-gun fire. When the periscope of the first was sighted Flight-Lieutenant Campbell at once dived and released his bombs. There were two bursts abaft the conning-tower, and immediately the nose of the submarine rose sharply out of the water. Then the hull slid back vertically to the bottom. Air bubbles and oil at once began to appear on the sea and two hours later there was a large patch 300 by 500 yards across. Next day the same flying-boat sighted an Italian submarine on the surface, and again the flight-lieutenant dived to attack, scoring direct hits beside the conning-tower. Although in the open sea and in the face of an approaching storm, Flight-Lieutenant Campbell alighted, taxied the flying-boat among the wreckage and saved four of the submarine's crew. Because of the state of the sea, rescuing the survivors demanded the greatest skill and patience.

After they were safely aboard and a final search had been made, Flight-Lieutenant Campbell resumed his patrol, handing over the prisoners at the end of the day. On the return journey to the base this pilot sighted yet another submarine on the surface. This he machine-gunned, as he had no bombs left. After the second attack the submarine crash dived. It is reported that his special aptitude for dealing with submarines has earned for Flight-Lieutenant Campbell the nickname of " Dead-eye Dick " among his fellow pilots.

LIEUTENANT (ACTING CAPTAIN) ERIC C. T. WILSON, the East Surrey Regiment, attached Somaliland Camel Corps, was awarded the V.C. on Oct. 12, 1940, for conspicuous gallantry in Somaliland. The official account states that Captain Wilson was in command of machine-gun posts manned by Somali soldiers in the key position of Observation Hill, a defended post in the defensive organization of the Tug Argan Gap in British Somaliland.

The enemy attacked Observation Hill on August 11, 1940. Captain Wilson and Somali gunners under his command beat off the attack and opened fire on the enemy troops attacking Mill Hill, another post within his range. He inflicted such heavy casualties that the enemy, determined to put his guns out of action, brought up a pack battery to within 700 yards, and scored two direct hits through the loopholes of his defences, which, bursting within the post, wounded Captain Wilson severely in the right shoulder and in the left eye, several of his team being also wounded. His guns were blown off their stands, but he repaired and replaced them and, regardless of his wounds, carried on, while his Somali sergeant was killed beside him.

On August 12 and 14 the enemy again concentrated field artillery fire on Captain Wilson's guns, but he continued, with his wounds untended, to man them. On August 15, two of his machine-gun posts were blown to pieces, yet Captain Wilson, now suffering from malaria in addition to his wounds, still kept his own post in action. The enemy finally overran the post at 5 p.m. on August 15, when Captain Wilson was taken prisoner.

Sergeant Hannah Told Me the Fire Was Out

*Sergeant Hannah's story of the deed which won him his V.C.
has already been told (see page 387). Now we give the account of
the incident broadcast by Pilot-Officer Connor, who brought the
badly damaged aircraft and the injured sergeant safely home and
was himself awarded the D.F.C.*

IF anybody had told me that only half the
crew and three-quarters of the aeroplane
would return to England that night I
should have been inclined to laugh at them
—but that's what happened. . . .

As we came round for the second attack
we met a terrific barrage. We were hit in the
wing on the way down several times, and the
aircraft shook so much that it was not an easy
matter to keep control of it. However, we
released our bombs, and it was then that I
saw flames reflected in my windscreen, but I
was so busy taking violent evasive action
against the anti-aircraft guns that I didn't at
first give it any serious thought. While I
was avoiding the shells as best I could the
wireless operator (Sergeant Hannah) called
me on the inter-communication system and
announced, very quietly, in his marked Scots
accent : " The aircraft is on fire." I asked
him : " Is it very bad ? " He replied :
" Bad, but not too bad."

I gathered from this conversation and from
the fact that the reflection of the flames was
getting brighter and brighter, that the position
was fairly serious. I immediately warned the
crew to prepare to abandon the aircraft.

After three or four minutes of more shells
whizzing through us and past us I was
relieved to find that we were at last out
of range, and I think it must have been about
this time that my navigator and rear gunner
jumped for it. There is no doubt that the
navigator was convinced that there was

no chance of the aircraft surviving, while the
rear gunner apparently had no option. He
was literally burned out of his bottom cockpit.

The fact that the rear gunner did jump gave
Sergeant Hannah more freedom of movement. While he was fighting the flames with
his log book and with his hands I could feel
the heat getting nearer and nearer to the back
of my neck, but at the same time I noticed,
when I turned round, that the flames were
still some four or five feet away from me.
At first Hannah was wearing his oxygen
mask, but the fumes were evidently too strong
and he found himself beginning to suffocate.
So, without hesitation, he ripped the mask
off and dashed through the fire heedless
of the burns which he could not possibly
avoid.

After about 10 minutes, which seemed like
hours, I noticed the reflection in the windscreen had died down and that in place of the
heat at the back of my neck there was a
welcome and refreshingly cool breeze. I
asked the sergeant on the inter-communication system, which miraculously escaped
damage, how things were going. He said,
in his cheery manner : " The fire is out,
sir."

He scrambled into my cockpit and brought
me the navigator's maps so that I could steer
a course for home. In turning round to take
the maps from Sergeant Hannah I realized
what he had gone through. His face was
badly burnt, his flying suit was scorched all
over, and altogether he looked a sorry sight.
Through it all he was grinning, and I then
knew that although his injuries were severe
they were not as bad as they looked.

When I looked at the machine after landing, I found that the rear gunner's cockpit
and half the interior of the fuselage were
charred ruins (see picture in page 387).
There was a hole in the fuselage large enough
for a man to crawl through. There were
holes in the wings, but far more serious
were the holes in the petrol tanks, and how
the petrol did not catch alight and undo all
Sergeant Hannah's good work will remain
a mystery.

This photograph of Pilot Officer Connor,
whose exciting story of his flight with Sergeant
Hannah over Antwerp is recounted on this
page, was taken at his base.
Photo, Keystone

To make matters even worse, while he was
beating out the flames thousands of rounds
of ammunition were going off in all directions
and he had to fight his way through this fierce
internal barrage to save the aircraft. He did
not give his own safety a thought.

And Sergeant Hannah, modest as he is
courageous, said :

It seems to me that most of the credit
ought to go to Pilot-Officer Connor.

People don't fully realize that, while I
was doing my best with the fire, he was sitting
up aloft as cool as a cucumber, taking no
notice of the flames, which were only two
or three feet away from him, or the sounds
of bullets which were either whizzing close
to his head or hitting the armour plating
just above.

All the time I wondered whether we would
ever get out of the flaming aeroplane, but
when I realized how cool Pilot-Officer
Connor was I knew that, if things got too
bad, he would make an effort to land on the
water.

Thanks to him, we landed at our base.

The 'plane which accomplished this memorable flight was badly damaged. This photograph of part of the machine shows a large
hole made in the fuselage by a cannon shell.
Photo, British Official : Crown Copyright

I Watched the Navy Pound Cherbourg

*Early in the morning of Friday, October 11, a tremendous hammering
was given to the German-occupied port of Cherbourg by the guns of
the Royal Navy and the bombs of the Air Force. The following
eye-witness story of the naval bombardment was written by a press
correspondent with the fleet.*

WHEN the Navy, in its turn, struck at an
invasion port the Navy struck hard.

In the dark of the early morning
of October 11 our war vessels pounded the
basin and dock area of Cherbourg. The
bombardment was delivered by full broadsides from the ships and lasted for about
seventeen minutes. In that time, according to
an estimate made by a gunnery officer before
the official returns were rendered, some
thousands of shells were fired. These were

fired at an area perhaps a square mile in
extent in less than twenty minutes. And shells
are more destructive than bombs.

I went aboard one of the smaller ships as
the captain was telling his ship's company
the scheme for the night's operations. He
ended his cool and detailed narrative with,
" It's money for old rope." The men
grinned at that, and they grinned again in the
same way hours later. The enemy was not
only taken by surprise ; he was fooled.

The terrific bombardment of Cherbourg by British naval guns on the night of October 10-11,
considerably reduced the concentrations of enemy shipping in the German-occupied harbour.
During the operation no opposing force from the enemy was encountered. A blinding flash of
gunfire is seen directed at the invasion port.
Photo, British Official : Crown Copyright

"The Light Blues are doing nicely," our captain said as we sped stealthily across the Channel. From our position in the screen around the heavy ship we could see the flashes of A.A. fire from our target port. We could see the searchlights raking the sky. We turned 90 degrees to port and took up new positions.

Then hell was let loose. Every ship fired together. The night was shivered into half a hundred thunderclaps ; the ear-rattling yet hammer-like crack of the smaller guns, the bellowing of the bigger guns, deeper in tone than ours, yet as metallic and as cruel. Spiteful tongues of flame came from the ships, great rolling clouds of black smoke lit from within with red and orange light. Those on the bridge hid their eyes and covered their ears. I was dizzy and reeling for a moment, blinded by flash and silly with noise, in spite of my smoked glasses and plugged ears.

Once a searchlight came down to shine for a second across the sea. It was turned off and then up again, as though some know-all had said to its operator, "Don't be absurd." Yet the flashes of the guns were flaming signposts. Perhaps the defences were blinded by the fires ashore.

We turned sharply away for home without signals, for every manoeuvre since we had left our home port in the early dark had been done by the programme and the clock. Then and at last the shore batteries opened fire. We were rapidly lengthening the range—we must have been nearly a dozen miles away by now —but we heard the shells. But never a hit in the whole fleet. Star shells went up to spot us by and we thought we heard an aeroplane overhead. In the engine-room they were certain they heard the 'plane and felt the

thumps in the water and fancied for a time that we were being bombed. But we could see the flashes from the shore batteries. We put out a smoke-screen to fox the spotters. Soon we were out of range.

When I came up to the bridge an hour or so later in a glowing, misty, splendid dawn we were steaming into port. Our escort of two fighter squadrons was coming out in formation to meet us. We overtook a ship and exchanged no formal salutes as we slipped past. But its captain, the fleet senior officer,

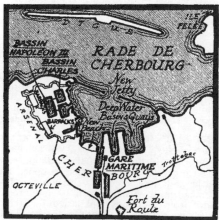

This map of Cherbourg Harbour shows the Bassin Napoléon where shells registered hits on dry docks, and the Gare Maritime where harbour works suffered badly.

waved his cap over his head from the bridge, and we all waved back. A signal from the commander of our ships winked its way by lamp along the line. "The flotilla carried out last night's operation very well."

A Royal Air Force pilot who was operating in the area at the same time broadcast an account of the bombardment. He said :

As we went over the English coast the glare and explosions appeared to be so close that I imagined at first we must be off our course, but it was Cherbourg all right—about 100 miles away. Clouds drifting across the scene were silhouetted against the white glow of flares which dropped incessantly over the target area from other aircraft, illuminating the place. As we neared it, the enemy ground defences completed the effect with searchlights," flaming onions," and anti-aircraft fire.

We were over the target area when suddenly the Navy let fly. It was like 500 thunderstorms rolled into one. One of my pilots said that even the tornadoes he had experienced in the Pacific Islands came nowhere near it. Every cloud flamed bright amber colour, and we could see the bursts of the first salvo plumb in the docks. Until then the ground defences had been blazing away at us, but this sudden blast from the sea "foxed" them absolutely. The searchlights went quite drunk, waving aimlessly about the sky ; the guns continued firing, but goodness knows what at. There was complete chaos down below. I said to my crew when we landed, "I have seen a few Fifths of November but what about October 11 ?"

When The Fleet Air Arm Goes Aloft

Carefully selected men are chosen for training at the Fleet Air Arm Schools, which, though on land, are named like ships, two of them being H.M.S. "Raven" and H.M.S. "Peregrine." An important part of the course deals with the recognition of British and enemy 'planes. Scale models are used for this purpose. A class is here being taken on H.M.S. "Peregrine" by a Sergeant Instructor of the R.A.F

When the Fleet Air Arm takes the air it is a quick change for those who go aloft in a new sense of the term. This rating slips on his flying kit over his uniform in double-quick time.

Air gunnery is an important part of the Fleet Air Arm training course. On board H.M.S. "Raven," a petty officer is giving instructions in the use of the Boulton Paul turret fitted with four Browning guns. Many successes against Nazi 'planes have been achieved, but figures have not been issued regularly.

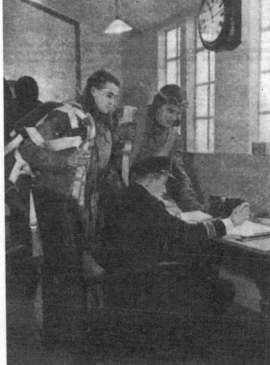

Map reading is an important part of the course for both pilots and observers. Here in the operations room of H.M.S. "Peregrine" charts are being studied before some of the learners set out on a practice flight. Right, last instructions are being given before taking off. *Photos, Topical*

Now We've Got the Tanks and the Men As Well

Above, left, tanks that were brought home damaged from France are being repaired and made ready for action again. Right, engines that have had a thorough overhaul are ready to be refitted. The works in which these photographs were taken specialize in quick tank repairs.

Two members of a tank crew preparing to set out are putting on their goggles and adjusting the earphones which enable them to communicate with one another above the noise of the tanks.

When the time comes for land fighting once more, there will be no lack of tanks or the men to man them, for day and night the British Army's strength in these and other mechanized units is being rapidly added to. There is an Officer Cadet Training Unit in the south of England where future commanders of land ships are trained. Above, cadets are waiting with their light tanks to start out for exercises. Right, the word to move off has been given, and amidst a cloud of dust one of the little tanks starts off at top speed.

Photos, Planet News

They Sleep in Safety Beneath London's Streets

This underground shelter in North London of the type standardized by the Government, with a four-tier chicken-coop bunk, makes comfortable accommodation for children. The little boy and his dog (oval) appear to enjoy their strange surroundings below ground.
Photos, Fox

This photograph was taken in the shelter of a block of flats in South-West London. The Warden, patrolling the district, checks the number of people in the shelter.
Photo, "News Chronicle"

Here is one family, and its dog, which has adapted itself comfortably to a shelter measuring only 7 ft. by 5 ft. in South-East London. There are electric light, radio, and home comforts generally.
Photo, John Topham

These people are settling down for a good night's rest in a Tube shelter. A mother prepares her little boy for sleep, while another child is seen already in bed, in a cot made from an orange box.
Photo, Keystone

OUR DIARY OF THE WAR

TUESDAY, OCT. 8, 1940   *402nd day*

In the Air—R.A.F. and Coastal Command aircraft made daylight attacks on ports of Boulogne and Lorient.

Night raids centred on naval bases of Bremen and Wilhelmshaven. Other forces attacked military objectives over wide area in Western Germany, Holland and enemy-occupied France. Night attacks on Channel ports continued.

War Against Italy—R.A.F. made bombing raids on Bardia and Sollum. Three attacks delivered on Assab. Enemy raided Aden, but caused no damage. Attempted raid on Malta was driven off with loss to enemy.

Home Front—In morning rush hour Nazi aircraft made low-diving attack on Central London. Buildings, shops, cafés and two buses wrecked. Number of fatal casualties. Bombs also fell indiscriminately on coastal towns in Kent and Sussex.

At night many incendiaries fell but failed to start fires. High explosive bombs shattered number of shops in one London district. Large London hospital hit; three wards wrecked. Raiders flying in pairs dropped large number of bombs over Thames estuary.

Eight German aircraft destroyed. Britain lost two fighters.

WEDNESDAY, OCT. 9   *403rd day*

In the Air—R.A.F. made daylight attacks on oil plant at Homburg, barges and bridges near Helder in Holland, Texel aerodrome, and shipping at Le Havre. During night our bombers carried out raids on widespread industrial and military objectives in Germany and enemy-occupied territory, including oil plant at Cologne, Krupps' works at Essen, and the Channel ports.

Aircraft of Coastal Command and Fleet Air Arm bombed shipping, naval quays and workshops at Brest. Hits were registered on destroyers.

War Against Italy—R.A.F. attacked shipping in Tobruk harbour, three ships being hit. Italians suffered heavy losses in skirmish with British patrol south of Buna, E. Africa.

Home Front—Britain attacked by small formations of high-flying fighter-bombers. Few penetrated beyond Kent and Sussex coasts, where minor damage was done. Some casualties and destruction in London.

London had 12-hour night raid. Bombs fell in 40 districts. Three churches severely damaged. Buses hit. Hotel cut in half; many houses damaged. Attacks were also made in several other parts of England.

Enemy lost four aircraft. One British fighter lost, but pilot safe.

THURSDAY, OCT. 10   *404th day*

On the Sea—During night heavy and light forces of Royal Navy bombarded Cherbourg where concentration of enemy shipping had been detected by R.A.F.

Admiralty announced that H.M. trawler " Kingston Sapphire " had been lost by U-boat action.

In the Air—R.A.F. bombers launched heavy attack on gun positions across Straits of Dover and on Calais. Raids by Coastal Command aircraft ranged from Den Helder on Dutch coast down Channel to Boulogne, Le Havre and Brest, where German destroyers were again bombed.

R.A.F. blew up oil storage tanks at Hamburg and started fires at Hanover, Cologne and several other places. Attacks were made on warships at Wilhelmshaven, Krupps' shipyards at Kiel, Fokker works at Amsterdam, and many other military targets.

War Against Italy—R.A.F. raided important military objectives at Benghazi, Libya. Fires were started and three ships in harbour received direct hits. Tobruk was also raided, as was Assab, Eritrea.

Home Front—Enemy aircraft made several attacks on coastal towns in Kent, Sussex and Thames estuary. Few bombs fell in one part of London. Hospital at Dover hit. Air battle over Maidstone. Bombers were twice over Liverpool and district.

During night bombs fell in 36 districts in London area and outskirts. Several houses demolished and others damaged in Thames estuary town. Bombs fell in Merseyside, Wales, W. England and Midlands.

Five enemy aircraft destroyed. Britain also lost five, but pilots of two safe.

German long-range guns shelled Dover area at dusk. British guns replied.

FRIDAY, OCT. 11   *405th day*

On the Sea—Admiralty announced that H.M. minesweeping trawler " Sea King " had been sunk by enemy mine.

In the Air—R.A.F. heavily bombed invasion bases on French coast during night. In spite of foggy weather some military

---

THE POETS & THE WAR
XXXV
LONDON
By A. A. MILNE.

(Si monumentum requiris, circumspice)

Old London's time-encrusted walls
  Are but the work of human hands.
What man has fashioned for us falls:
  What God has breathed into us stands.

What if the splendour of the past
  Is shattered into dust, we raise
A monument that shall outlast
  Even the Abbey's span of days.

On broken homes we set our feet
  And raise proud heads that all may see,
Immortal in each little street,
  The soul in its integrity.
             —*The Times*

---

objectives in Germany were attacked, as well as enemy-occupied Channel ports.

War Against Italy—R.A.F. carried out further raids over Benghazi and Tobruk. Asmara, Eritrea, was also bombed, as was Gura, Abyssinia.

Home Front—Formations of enemy aircraft, mostly bomb-carrying fighters, crossed coast on several occasions. Bombs fell in Kent, Sussex and Thames estuary. Damage to shops and houses. Windows of Canterbury Cathedral shattered. Three dive-bomb attacks on S.E. coast town.

During night raids more than 50 areas in London and Home Counties were attacked. Hospital for Incurables, R.C. convent, and London buses received direct hits. Merseyside and other towns in North-West again attacked.

Eight enemy aircraft destroyed. Nine British fighters lost, but pilots of six safe.

Violent artillery duel between British and German guns fought across Straits of Dover by moonlight.

SATURDAY, OCT. 12   *406th day*

On the Sea—Italy reported naval action off Malta during night of October 11-12, and admitted losses.

In the Air—During night R.A.F. bombers attacked military targets in Berlin, including power station, gas works and important goods yard. Raids also made on aluminium works at Heringen, Krupps' works at Essen, Fokker works at Amsterdam, oil plants at Cologne and Hanover, Dortmund-Ems

aqueduct, and other objectives. Channel ports and gun positions bombed.

War Against Italy—R.A.F. raided port of Bardia, Libya, and scored six direct hits. Fires and explosions were started at Tobruk. Javello aerodrome twice bombed by S. African Air Force.

Home Front—Daylight raiders dropped small number of bombs in London and suburban areas and in some places on south coast and in Kent and Surrey. At Hastings houses were demolished and a fire started.

During night raids a London underground railway station was hit and there were casualties. Another bomb fractured water and gas mains in a street. Many buildings demolished and damaged, including block of flats. Many hundreds of bombs fell in a Midland town and fires broke out. Three tenement houses wrecked and considerable other damage.

Enemy lost 11 aircraft. Ten British fighters missing, but pilots of eight safe.

Rumania—Four hundred uniformed officers and orderlies of German Army arrived in Bucharest.

SUNDAY, OCT. 13   *407th day*

In the Air—In spite of severe weather conditions R.A.F. attacked naval bases of Kiel and Wilhelmshaven; oil plants at Gelsenkirchen and Duisberg; Krupps' works at Essen, and other targets. Other formations bombed Domburg harbour and Mole at Zeebrugge.

War Against Italy—Nairobi announced that S. African Air Force had made fifth raid on Neghelli, S. Abyssinia, when considerable damage was done. British mechanized patrols inflicted heavy casualties on enemy S.E. of Kassala.

Home Front—Successive formations of enemy aircraft crossed Kent coast. Some reached London area and bombs fell. Many houses, a chapel and some shops damaged when bomb fell in allotments.

Night raids were heavy and 36 London districts suffered. Many casualties when large block of flats was hit. Hospital damaged by oil bomb. Church wrecked. Shelters hit and many people killed. Much damage to houses and shops.

Twenty provincial areas bombed. Six killed at home of mayor of East Anglian town. Liverpool tenement building hit, and two communal shelters in a N.E. town.

Two enemy aircraft destroyed. Britain lost two fighters, but both pilots safe.

MONDAY, OCT. 14   *408th day*

In the Air—R.A.F. bombed military objectives in Berlin; oil plants at Stettin and other centres; port of Le Havre; targets at Hamburg, Hanover and elsewhere, including several aerodromes.

War Against Italy—More raids carried out on Benghazi by R.A.F. bombers.

Home Front—Small-scale enemy activity during day. Bombs fell at scattered points in south of England and Midlands. Dive attack made on town in Home Counties; four houses and garage destroyed and some fatal casualties. Two raiders dived on East Anglian town causing damage and casualties in working-class area.

Night raids continuous and heavy. Fires started by strings of incendiaries. High explosives bombs fell in several residential areas. Famous church hit, shops wrecked. R.C. church and convent damaged. Music hall hit; cinema burnt out. Enemy planes also reported over Liverpool and another N.W. town, towns in S.W., East Anglia and Midlands.

Rumania—Uniformed Italian air officers arrived in Bucharest as part of Commission to supervise making of seaplane base at Rumanian port of Constanza. German troops continued to pour in.

Three Rumanian oil wells completely destroyed by fire near Baicoi.

'THAT'S THE WAY WE BUILD 'EM' IN BRITAIN'S SHIPYARDS

" You can take it from me that this ship is a good job of work," said a veteran of the shipyard, when one of Britain's new light cruisers slid down the
slipways at her launching.   Many other fine ships—not only cruisers, but battleships, destroyers, submarines, and the rest—have been added to the
Royal Navy of late months, so that more than ever it is now the most powerful fleet in the world.

Photo, P.N.A.

Britain Can Win—and Britain Will!

**A balance-sheet of victory—this in effect is what E. Royston Pike has written below.
Gloomy and threatening as was the prospect which opened upon us following France's
collapse, there are (as will be seen) the most solid grounds for confidence in the eventual
triumph of our Cause.**

Up to a few weeks ago perhaps the majority of thinking Americans, while they still hoped that Britain would win, yet in their heart of hearts thought her chances were pretty poor. While France was still erect and fighting the Allies had at least a fifty-fifty chance of winning; but when following the defeat of Poland, the seizure of Denmark, the collapse of the campaign in Norway, the overrunning of Holland and Belgium—when to this succession of hammer-blows there was added France's military downfall, then Britain's wellwishers in America thought that Britain's cause was as good as lost (there may have been some in Britain who thought so, too).

When the Battle of Britain opened they feared the worst. How could the little island in the mists of the North Sea maintain itself against a whole continent in arms? Every morning when they opened their newspapers they expected to read that Hitler's invasion fleets had sailed and that his Luftwaffe, operating now from aerodromes in France, was asserting its supremacy over the R.A.F. But day after day passed and Hitler's ships sailed no farther than the river mouths, while hundreds and thousands of his warplanes crashed in flaming ruin in the Channel—which the Royal Navy saw to it was still the English Channel—and in the green fields of southern England. August passed into September, September into October; and as week was added to week those thinking Americans—we need not concern ourselves with the unthinking ones—began to hope, where before they had only feared. Then came the Battle of London, and with never a dissenting voice all America rose up and cheered. Almost overnight opinion across the Atlantic underwent a complete change. Men no longer just hoped against hope that Britain would stand up against the enemy assault. They now firmly believed that she would continue to do so. Hitler himself may not know it, but America knows, as we know, that he has lost the Battle of London.

Britain will survive—that the Americans admit. But can she win? That, they say, is a different matter. Britain, they point out, has only 45 million souls, while Hitler has boasted in one of his more grandiloquent passages of the 200 millions he and Mussolini can draw upon. Hitler's figures are wrong as always, but it is a fact that in the Reich he controls some 70 million people, and as likely as not has under arms at this very moment four or five millions of trained soldiers. Against such a host how can Britain, gallant little Britain, prevail?

Here, perhaps, we may remind ourselves that modern wars are not won necessarily by the country with the biggest battalions; in the scales of battle, quantity is often outweighed by quality—the millions of cannon-fodder are no match for the hundreds of thousands who are equipped with all the latest instruments of death-dealing machinery.

Moreover, we must not forget—and Hitler and his Nazis we may be sure will never dare to let themselves forget—that in the continent they have overrun with such surprising ease there are millions of disgruntled folk—millions of unhappy people who, though their armies have been defeated in the field and they themselves bludgeoned into sub-

mission, are yet far from being reconciled with their state of virtual slavery. In all the countries which the Nazis have conquered there are millions, we may be sure, who are anxiously longing for the day of retribution; in Poland, in particular, there is a whole people—perhaps the best haters in Europe—who are sharpening the knives of revenge.

And in the Reich itself there are many—perhaps a third or a half of the whole—who in the days when they were permitted to express their preference never put a cross against the name of a Nazi candidate. For the time being, no doubt, they find it advisable to go with the stream, to "Heil Hitler" with the rest of them; being Germans, they no doubt take a pride in the striking victories achieved by German arms during the last year. But when the long-promised collapse of Britain does not come, when the war which should have finished last summer shows every sign of extending into next spring, when the R.A.F.'s visits to Berlin become more frequent and more prolonged, and when the Rhineland and the Ruhr become as devastated as Hamburg—then we may expect that the voices of criticism which at present are muffled by fear or stifled by success will make themselves heard in the Nazi Reich.

Then there is that mistake into which even many Britons so frequently fall—the mistake of identifying Britain with a couple of fair-sized islands, plus some 5,000 smaller ones, off the north-western coast of Europe. Britain is not just the British Isles; it is the British Isles and also the King's Dominions beyond the Seas. The British Empire—the Commonwealth is the better word—covers

Naturally enough, no details have been published of the new ships added to the Royal Navy since the war began, but this photograph shows one of the many launches. A fine cruiser has just taken the water in a British yard, after Mrs. Dorling, wife of Rear-Admiral J. W. S. Dorling, Assistant-Controller of the Navy, has in traditional fashion broken a bottle of champagne across her bows and given her a name which, though at present undisclosed, may one day be as famous as "Ajax" or "Achilles."

Photo, Keystone

These Facts and Figures Spell Victory

Canada's contribution to the armed forces of the Empire includes an ever-growing navy. Above we see some of the Royal Canadian Navy's more than 13,000 personnel marching along the quay of a port in Eastern Canada, where they took possession of some of the U.S.A. destroyers recently transferred to Britain.

a quarter of the land surface of the globe, and beneath the Union Jack one out of four of the world's teeming millions live out their lives. When Hitler boasts of his 200 millions, we of Britain may rejoin with our 500 millions.

Then in the matter of armed forces Germany has not any great preponderance—even now, when the Commonwealth is only just getting into the stride of war. In the British Isles today we know that there are more than 2,000,000 men standing to arms; Canada has raised over 200,000 men, Australia 230,000, New Zealand 150,000, and the Union of South Africa 100,000. Even before the war the Indian Army numbered nearly 350,000 men, and, though considerable contingents have been sent overseas, we know that the army in the Peninsula has not been diminished. So we might go on enumerating the warriors which the members of the imperial family of nations have put into the field or are now raising. But let us conclude our statistics with a mention of the Royal Navy, which today, as for 300 years past, is the supreme bulwark of our race and power. In 1939, with a personnel not far short of 150,000, it was the strongest in the world; it is far stronger today in men, and still more in ships. We must not forget, too, the mercantile marine of Britain and the British Dominions, which amounted to nearly 21,000,000 tons before hostilities began, and today, in spite of everything that the Nazis have been able to do, it is even larger. Germany's mercantile marine, on the other hand, is altogether immobilized, if not actually sunk or captured.

Coming now to natural resources, we hardly need the reminder that the British Empire is abundantly rich in all the raw materials which are also war materials. In some of them, indeed, she has almost a monopoly; the world's supply of nickel, for instance, is drawn almost entirely from Canada. Even in the matter of oil she is in

an excellent position, for she can draw her supplies from all the great oil-producing countries of the world, even though most of the oil wells are being operated under other flags.

Many another item could be included in this already encouraging balance-sheet: there is the contribution made to the common cause by our allies—for instance, by the Dutch East Indies, where there is a well-trained army of some 40,000 men, and the Belgian Congo, by the French colonies in Central Africa, and by the ships of Denmark and Norway (whose mercantile marine ranks as the third largest in the world), of Holland and Belgium. And there is also, of course,

the immense aid which is being rendered by the U.S.A., now aware at last that Britain is holding the first line of America's defences.

Strong in all the things that make for victory, then, is the British Commonwealth, and strongest of all in the belief that nerves its armies and inspires its workers—that the fight in which we are engaged is one not only for our survival and the Commonwealth's, but for the preservation and continued life of all those values which, evolved through all the centuries of recorded history, serve to distinguish us from the brutes that perish.

Once Germany's greatest port, Hamburg has been heavily bombed many times by the Royal Air Force, and this photograph must have been carefully chosen by the German Propaganda Department to show that the damage done is of no military importance. The fact is that docks, quays, and equipment are practically non-existent.

Photos, Associated Press

There is a Free Belgian Government in London Now

The sensational escape of Belgium's Prime Minister, M. Pierlot, and the Foreign Minister,
M. Spaak, from detention in Spain to London on October 22nd has greatly increased
the weight of Belgium's influence in the common struggle of the Allies to restore the
independence of the invaded countries.

O N the night of Tuesday, October 22nd,
the Belgian Prime Minister, M. Pierlot,
and his Foreign Minister, M. Spaak,
arrived in London after many weeks of trials
and tribulations.

Before attempting to assess what their
escape—first from France and then from
Spain—to this country means for the free
Belgian forces gallantly fighting by our side,
and also the importance to our own cause
of these ministers now being here, let us

merchant marine, and other assets outside
Germany's reach. But within a month
France, too, had collapsed.

On June 18th the Belgian Cabinet met at
Bordeaux to decide on a future course of
action, but no agreement could be reached
between the ministers.

Three of them wished to transfer the seat
of the government to London and to fight on
from Britain. These were M. Gutt, Minister
of Finance, M. de Vleeschauwer, Minister of

statesmen have for several months now been
operating the merchant marine, building up
an army, looking after refugees, and—chief
of all—administering the Belgian colonies
and mandated territories. But the position
remained somewhat anomalous as long as
the head of the government and the majority
of ministers were still in Vichy.

Finally, under German pressure, the
French withdrew recognition from the
various allied governments and broke off
diplomatic relations with them.

M M. Pierlot and Spaak tried to make their
way to Spain, but spent five days at
Perpignan before they were admitted to that
country. Permission to travel through Spain
was suddenly cancelled, and they had to stay
three nights in a meadow between the French
and the Spanish border. It was obvious that
the Germans were exerting their influence
over the Spanish authorities to prevent the
Belgian Premier and his Foreign Minister
from eventually travelling to Great Britain.
When the two Belgians at long last were
allowed to enter Spain, they were detained
for some weeks in a hotel and finally on
October 3rd they were arrested. Friendly
representations made on their behalf by
British and American diplomatic channels
proved of no avail. But eventually they
were, so to speak, snatched away under the
Germans' very noses and safely brought to
Britain by aeroplane.

This dramatic *dénouement* is important for
many reasons. In the first instance, it is a
good smack in the eye for the Germans and
it shows that after all the Gestapo is neither
omnipotent nor omnipresent in Spain.
Secondly, the arrival of these leading ministers
in London at long last clarifies the otherwise
somewhat involved Belgian position. It
strengthens our gallant allies immeasurably,
for now the forces of free and loyal Belgium
are represented by a small but vigorous
Cabinet that includes the four key men of the
national administration.

With such men in charge, the 25,000
Belgians now in Britain and the 13 million
whites and natives living in the Belgian
Congo or in the mandated territory of
Ruanda-Urundi, can look forward to competent and vigorous administration, while
we can rely on the maximum effort in both the
military and the economic sphere of a loyal
and courageous ally.

Belgium, so tiny on the map of Europe, has a large colonial Empire in Central Africa—the Congo
State of some 900,000 square miles with a population of nearly 11 millions. Above is the capital,
Leopoldville, which is situated on Stanley Pool, some 300 miles from the mouth of the Congo.
Photo, Dorien Leigh

recapitulate what happened to Belgium after
the surrender of King Leopold on May 27.

On that same day the Belgian Prime
Minister, M. Pierlot, announced that his
Cabinet had met in Paris and that, " having
examined the situation and envisaged all
possible developments, the Government were
unanimous in affirming their will to continue,
whatever happened, the struggle at the side
of the Allies until common victory was won."

During the month that followed Leopold's
surrender the Pierlot government continued
to function in France as the only legally
constituted Belgian government. First from
Paris, then from Tours, Bordeaux and finally
Vichy, it did what it could to carry on its
work. A new army was in process of
formation. There were the Colonies, the

Colonies, and M. Jaspar, Minister of Public
Health. The Premier, M. Pierlot, on the
other hand, supported by M. Spaak, the
Foreign Minister, and General Denis, the War
Minister, were in favour of remaining in
France and of following the French Cabinet
to Vichy, whereupon M. Jaspar left for
London on his own, while subsequently—by
official Cabinet decision—MM. Gutt and de
Vleeschauwer were sent to London, " thus
providing," as M. de Vleeschauwer put it,
" a tangible proof of the will of Belgium to
continue the common struggle and to ensure
the legal management of our country's vital
interests. We are therefore continuing the
struggle in the name of Belgium in a constitutional and legal manner."

From London these two able and energetic

Left to right : M. Hubert Pierlot, Belgian Prime Minister since 1939,
who arrived in London on October 22 ; M. Henri Jaspar, Minister of
Health ; M. Albert de Vleeschauwer, Minister for the Colonies ; Baron
Cartier de Marchienne, Belgian Ambassador to Britain ; M. Paul Henri
Spaak, Minister for Foreign Affairs.
Photos, " Daily Mirror," Planet News, G.P.U., Dorien Leigh.

'Too Right' Is 'Ajax's' Word For It!

While the Italian army of invasion was halted not far within the frontier of Egypt, Mussolini's navy, too, showed no signs of any great eagerness to give battle. Here we describe the action of October 12, when three Italian destoyers fell victims to H.M.S. "Ajax," of River Plate fame.

WHEN he stepped ashore at Alexandria on October 16, Admiral Sir Andrew Cunningham, Commander-in-Chief of the Royal Navy in the Mediterranean, had to tell of another most successful sweep of that sea which Mussolini would have his Italians believe is their private property. The British Fleet, the largest sent out into the Mediterranean since the war began, was seven days at sea, and its voyaging extended for some 3,000 miles in the eastern and central Mediterranean.

Unlike many of its predecessors, this sweep was marked by a brush with enemy forces. When about 80 miles south-east of Sicily at 2.30 on the morning of October 12, H.M.S. "Ajax"—one of the immortal trio of the Battle of the Plate—under the command of Captain E. D. B. McCarthy, R.N., made contact with three Italian destroyers. True to her reputation, "Ajax" at once engaged, and two of the Italian destroyers were sunk outright, while the third made off at top speed. This was hardly surprising, of course, for the "Ajax" is a cruiser of 6,985 tons, while the Italian destroyers were of the 679-ton "Airone" class.

Continuing her patrol "Ajax" sighted another enemy force, composed of one heavy cruiser and four destroyers. Again she engaged instantly, and succeeded in crippling one of the enemy destroyers, when the fall of darkness enabled the remainder of the enemy ships to escape.

Believing that "Ajax" was in touch with considerable enemy forces, H.M.S. "York" (Captain R. H. Portal, R.N.) came up in support, but no further contact was made with the enemy that night, although the pursuit went on. At dawn, however, with the assistance of aircraft of the Fleet Air Arm the damaged enemy destoyer was located in tow of another Italian destroyer which had gallantly come to her assistance. On "Ajax's" arrival the towing destroyer slipped the tow and made off at fast speed

towards Sicily, throwing out a smoke-screen as she sped. It was then ascertained that the damaged destoyer was the 620-ton "Artigliere," one of the latest class of large Italian destroyers. (She was completed in 1937, mounts four 4·7-inch guns, six smaller A.A. guns, and eight torpedo-tubes, and was designed for a speed of 39 knots.) Soon H.M.S. "York" was on the scene, and the "Artigliere's" crew at once began to abandon ship. "The crew were told to abandon ship immediately," said an eye-witness who was on the bridge of H.M.S. "Sydney" throughout the action, "and floats were thrown overboard for them. Then the 'York' fired a torpedo which hit the destroyer plumb in the magazine. The explosion was indescribable. A column of smoke shot 700 feet into the air, and the warship simply disappeared. One second it was lying on the surface, and the next it just was not there. Only a vast mushroom of smoke remained."

A wireless message was broadcast on the commercial wavelength of Italian stations giving the position of the survivors, and one of the British flying-boats was also successful in making wireless contact with an Italian hospital ship and led her to where the survivors from the destroyer were crowded in their boats and rafts, with the result that she was able to pick up a number of survivors. These messages were sent out in spite of the fact that the signals might give away the position of the British forces, and as Sicily was at no great distance an attack by Italian aircraft was to be expected at any moment. Indeed, "after breakfast," said the eye-witness we have already quoted, "we heard an Italian 'plane was shadowing us. Within a few minutes swift fighters had slipped off from an aircraft-carrier and almost immediately came the report 'Shadower shot down.' During lunchtime 12 enemy bombers came over in three formations at a great height. Every high-angle gun in the Fleet went into action, and peppered the

sky with white snowballs of smoke. The sea spouted up as the raiders unloaded their bombs. Other formations of bombers tried again later, but none pushed the attacks home. That evening we had great fun listening to the Italian radio, which claimed that we had lost a cruiser and 12 'planes and had an aircraft-carrier damaged. We sent a signal to the 'Ajax': 'Good work, Bonzer!' and Captain McCarthy, who has spent two years on the Australian station, flashed back: 'Too right!'"

In the action "Ajax" lost 13 killed and 22 wounded, and suffered only superficial damage which in no way impaired her fighting efficiency (though the Germans, with characteristic effrontery, announced that she had been sunk!); "York" suffered neither damage nor casualties.

The remainder of the sweep was quite uneventful save for an attack by torpedo-carrying aircraft on the 9,400-ton cruiser "Liverpool," which was slightly damaged.

Captain E. D. B. McCarthy, victor of the Mediterranean action of October 12, was appointed to command H.M.S. "Ajax," Sir Henry Harwood's flagship at the battle of the Plate, seen below, when she had been repaired and was recommissioned

Photos, Sport & General and G.P.U.

Keep Out of OUR Sea, Benito!
From the cartoon by Zec, courtesy of the "Daily Mirror"

The Burma Road is Open to Traffic Again

On July 18 Mr. Churchill announced that it had been decided to close the Burma Road to military traffic ; on October 8 he announced that it was to be reopened in ten days' time. How the road was built and why it is so important to China and to the world at large are told in the article that follows.

TRULY the Burma Road has a claim to be included amongst the wonders of the modern world—that Road which, running from Lashio in north-east Burma to Kunming, capital of the Chinese province of Yunnan, is now China's principal, indeed almost her only, outlet on to the wider world.

The Road was begun in October 1937 and was opened to traffic in December of the following year. For 726 miles it runs across some of the most difficult country in the world ; it is a miracle of engineering, and it may be doubted whether any other race but the Chinese could have built it, for its construction required enormous patience, dogged toil, and almost illimitable resources in manpower. Two hundred engineers were in charge of the job, and they had at their disposal 160,000 workers—Chinese coolies and their womenfolk, even their children. For fourteen months this great army of humble folk laboured where it was impossible to employ the machinery which Western engineers are accustomed to use. They were equipped for the most part with nothing more than those primitive hoes with which for thousands of years the Chinese have tilled their fields ; the rollers were of stone and drawn by oxen ; millions of tons of " dirt " were carted away in baskets borne on the backs of wiry women and slender girls. Here they cut into the side of a mountain or carted away a hill, basket-load by basket-load ; there they filled up a valley

The Burma Road begins at Lashio at the terminus of the railway from Rangoon and Mandalay ; from there it crosses the frontier into China, passes through Hsiakwan and thence on to Kunming. Here it connects with the main road leading to Chungking, capital of Free China.   *Courtesy of " The Times "*

in the same slow but relentless fashion. Great girders were lugged by human muscle for hundreds of miles until the swaying and flimsy rope bridges across the gorges were replaced by bridges of steel. In the road's length there are nearly 300 bridges, and not far short of 2,000 culverts had to be constructed to carry away the mountain waters. For fourteen months they toiled on the mountain roof of Asia in a country of gorge and precipice, through mighty forests where leopards and tigers roam.

At last their task was finished ; the Road, eight to twelve feet wide on the average, stretched its weary length across the mountains some 8,000 feet high, over two of Asia's greatest rivers, the Salween and Mekong, which, rising in the mountain plateau of Tibet, rush south with tempestuous force on their way, the one to the Bay of Bengal and the other to the South China Sea. The gradients are terrific ; the bends innumerable and hair-raising ; in many places there is a sheer drop of 2,000 feet from the road to the valley floor. The journey from Lashio to Kunming, where the Road joins the highway to Chungking, Free China's wartime capital, may be accomplished in six or seven days at the speed of 12 miles per hour which the lorries are able to average. Before the Road was closed to military traffic in July a hundred or so lorries a day passed along it, the principal loads on the up journey being petrol, cotton yarn, and other merchandise for Chiang Kai-shek's army, while on their return the lorries were laden with silk and tea, hides, tin, and tungsten.

When the Road was closed the traffic dwindled until only some ten or twenty lorries a day were passing along it. The closing must have been a heavy blow to Chiang Kai-shek, for the Road, since the occupation of the Chinese coast by the Japanese and more recently their establishment in Indo-China, is now China's life-line. The only alternative to it is the old Silk Road, immensely long and difficult, followed by the

The very spirit of ancient China breathes through this photograph taken in Hsiakwan, a town placed high up in the mountains of Yunnan. Through the archway passes the Burma Road on its way from Lashio in Burma to Kunming, capital of the Province of Yunnan. As soon as the Road was reopened on October 18 streams of lorries passed beneath the arch, conveying vital war stores to the hard-pressed army of Free China, whose headquarters are at Chungking.
Photo, Gerald Samson

Across the Mountains Runs China's Life-line

caravans from time. immemorial, leading from Sianfu into Sinkiang and Soviet Turkestan. It is true that the Road was closed during the rainy season, when the traffic in any case would have diminished; but the many critics of the closing maintain that it was unjust as well as impolitic to deprive Chiang.Kai-shek of any part of his petrol supplies while the Japanese aggressor was still permitted to receive unlimited supplies of petrol from America and the Dutch East Indies, scrap iron from America, and wool from Australia.

But in July, when it was decided to close the Road, France had just collapsed and Britain was expecting an invasion almost from hour to hour; in these circumstances it is understandable that the British Government should have decided upon making a friendly gesture to Japan in the hope that, as Mr. Churchill himself phrased it, the time so gained might lead to a solution just and equitable to both China and Japan.

The gesture failed, as so many other gestures of appeasement have failed in these last few years; and before the three months had elapsed the situation had radically changed for Britain. No longer did she fear invasion; even if it came she was ready for it. So when Japan made that gratuitous act of hostility, the Berlin Pact with Germany and Italy, Britain at once retaliated with a declaration that on Oct. 18 the Burma Road would be reopened to traffic of all kinds.

In anticipation of the reopening large numbers of lorries, fully laden with munitions and petrol, were gathered in Northern Burma, and as soon as October 18 dawned they were rushed across the frontier into China. At Lashio, where the railway from Rangoon and Mandalay ends and the Road begins, there was a tremendous congestion of munitions and other essential commodities destined for China; every warehouse was crammed to capacity, and great quantities of materials were stacked in fields around the town.

Before long, it was stated, some 20,000 tons of goods would be conveyed along the Road monthly.

In Tokyo it was professed that the opening of the Road would not make any appreciable difference to the course of the war in China, and there were many boasts that it would soon be put out of action by Japanese bombers operating from the aerodromes lately secured in Indo-China. Four days before the date fixed for the reopening Kunming, the Chinese terminus of the Road, was heavily bombed, and following the actual opening, raids were many and heavy. But the Chinese had taken every precaution possible and the Road "carried on."

In Free China the notice of the Road's reopening was received with intense relief, even joy. For years China has borne the brunt of aggression in the Far East, for years her fields have been trampled over by the invader, her people have been slaughtered in battle and exposed in their close-packed cities to the cruellest bombing—to which more often than not they have been unable to make reply. Now at long last they are given an indication that their struggle has not gone unnoticed—that those countries which are fighting Totalitarianism in the West are prepared to give some tangible assistance to the standard-bearers of liberty in the Orient.

Vast difficulties confronted the Chinese engineers in the construction of the Burma Road; all the more credit, then, to them for their massive achievement. At the top of the page we see gangs of Chinese labourers cutting an entrance to a tunnel; and the bottom photograph shows more of these indomitable toilers filling a gap in the mountains with "dirt" brought in hand-pushed barrows; in the middle picture a Chinese wayfarer, barefoot and carrying a heavy load, trudges along the Road.

Photos, Gerald Samson

Was September 16 Hitler's Invasion Day?

It may have been a rehearsal or it may have been the real thing ; whichever it was, Hitler's invasion fleet—if report speaks true—actually set out on September 16, only to be driven back in completest rout. Here we tell the story so far as it is at present made known

WHAT happened on September 16 ? Nothing less, it now seems probable, than an attempted invasion of England. In a bulletin issued by the Air Ministry on October 18, it was announced, quite parenthetically as it were, following an account of the continued hammer-blows of the R.A.F. on Germany's war machine, that " there is evidence, too, of the value of the R.A.F.'s determined attacks on the invasion ports. One report states that on September 16 many German troops were embarked, but were later taken off the ships. The invasion plans were not adopted because of the sustained offensive of the R.A.F."

That night the harvest moon, the brightest moon of the year, shone full. The sea was calm and the time of high tide propitious. Altogether it was an ideal night for an invasion. But the invasion plans failed because of the long sustained and devastating onslaught made by Sir Charles Portal's bombers on the shipping and barge concentrations assembled at the Channel ports.

Only the day before, it will be recalled, on Sunday, September 15, the R.A.F. had brought down 185 enemy aircraft in the course of the largest daylight mass attacks hitherto made by the Germans on this country. Those raids, there is little reason to doubt, were intended as the prelude to an invasion on a large scale—an invasion which should bring Britain to her knees and the war to a speedy conclusion.

At the time there were many stories in circulation concerning the supposed invasion attempt, and the English newspapers were full of accounts of smashing blows delivered at Hitler's barges assembled in the invasion bases ; on that same Sunday night the R.A.F. bombers left their mark on Hamburg and Wilhelmshaven, on Antwerp, Flushing and Ostend, on Dunkirk, Calais, Boulogne, and Le Havre.

A few days later some of the American papers were far more communicative. They did not hint at an invasion attempt ; rather they stated in the most definite terms that the armada of invasion had actually sailed. Thus the " New York Sun " stated that the barges—" very light, of wood and metal, and obviously intended solely for a one-way trip "—each contained 200 Germans with full equipment. " Evidently the Germans had counted on their airmen being able to silence the land batteries before these were able to annihilate the invaders, who were helpless because they did not carry artillery. . . . They sank under a withering fire as soon as they appeared. Meanwhile, detachments of the British Fleet appeared to the rear cutting off the barges from France."

The carnage was reported to have been terrific ; neutral observers stated that the number of killed, wounded, and drowned were to be counted in tens of thousands. All available hospital accommodation in and around the Channel ports had to be commandeered for the German wounded, and one report quoted a French doctor who said he had seen several thousand severely burned German soldiers in hospitals in occupied France ; they had been, said the doctor, on board transports and barges preparing for the invasion of England when they were caught by British oil bombs, and the flaming oil on the surface of the water burned the troops as they leapt into the sea.

Many stories were current, too, in the south of England concerning large numbers of dead Germans who, so it was said, had been washed ashore in several places. There were tales of closed lorries going to and from the beach at one point, of mysterious ambulances moving through the night ; nor was there any doubt that some dead Germans had actually been washed up, but it was officially stated that these were Nazi airmen whose 'planes had been shot down into the sea. Perhaps more to the point were the many stories published in American papers of large numbers of German dead being washed ashore in the neighbourhood of the invasion ports, particularly on the beaches near Le Havre, Calais, and Boulogne.

By way of explanation of these American reports and English rumours, responsible quarters in London expressed the opinion that a considerable proportion of the German divisions detailed for the invasion of England had actually embarked, when the fleet of flat-bottomed barges was caught by the bombers of the R.A.F., whose bombardment was so effective that the enemy fleet was obliged to put to sea, and lay a short distance from the French coast. Then rising winds compelled the vessels to return to their ports ; and the French people who had seen their departure and witnessed their return, concluded that the invasion had been attempted and had been driven back. Yet another explanation was that the R.A.F. bombers had caught the invasion fleet during a rehearsal.

But whatever happened on September 16, during that night and day in which the weather conditions, at least, were ideal for the implementing of Hitler's invasion boast, by nightfall the chance had been lost. A thick fog came down on the Straits of Dover blanketing the choppy sea and reducing visibility to a few hundred yards ; the full moon was obscured by dark rainclouds ; and a south-westerly gale howled through the night. It was a fitting end to the day which Hitler had chosen to be " Der Tag."

" Ready to invade Britain. Even minesweepers are useful as troop transports ; the joyful departure "—this is the caption supplied to this picture just received in London. How many of these men died on Sept. 16 ? *Photo, E.N.A.*

Once Again the Luftwaffe Changes Its Tactics

Continuing our review of Hitler's air offensive against this country, we have to note a change of tactics on the part of the Nazis, who found that the price demanded of their mass-bombers was too great. But no change could blunt the weapons of the R.A.F.

ABOUT the middle of October the German Air Force made further changes in its methods. No longer were its bombers squandered in vain attempts to wreak a terrible revenge on London and provincial cities ; instead, the Luftwaffe turned more and more to the use of the fast fighter-bombers which might have a better chance to elude our Hurricanes and Spitfires, but which could do far less damage when they did penetrate our defences here and there.

Another even more striking change was the virtual abandonment of precision bombing at comparatively low altitudes. The enemy bombers and fighter-bombers, in their daylight attacks, flew at 20,000 feet or even higher—a testimony to the accuracy of our A.A. gunfire and to the dauntless spirit of our fighter pilots. And by night also the raiders flew so high as to make anything like accurate aim impossible. These changes certainly diminished the German aircraft losses and at times brought the British and enemy losses to something like parity, but the essential fact is that the scale of the raids had to be reduced very considerably and mass attacks abandoned for the time. Thus those heavy bombing attacks—to which Hitler and Goering had pinned their faith as the instrument of Britain's demoralization and conquest—had indubitably failed, both in the assault on our aerodromes, aircraft factories and munition works, and in the destruction of our cities. And when Goering sent over hordes of fighters, in order to decimate our R.A.F., it was his own force that suffered.

It is now known that the raid on London on Tuesday morning (October 15) was on a rather large scale. Flying at 10,000 feet, three waves of German aircraft crossed the South-east coast about 9 o'clock and flew towards London. There was an interval of a few minutes between each wave, and the first was dispersed by our A.A. guns and driven back by fighters. Other enemy aircraft were turned back near Grays, in Essex, after flying up the Estuary. A few raiders got as far as London and dropped bombs as people were on their way to work. A hospital being repaired after a previous raid was again hit, some of the workers having hair-breadth escapes. Firemen who were dealing with an outbreak caused by Monday night's raids were gunned by Nazis. In all, 18 enemy aircraft were destroyed on Tuesday, 17 of them during daylight raids.

Something of a mass raid was made by the enemy on Tuesday night by groups of fighter-bombers and heavier machines. Oil bombs and H.E. were dropped in pairs in some places. In spite of the heavy nature of the attack on London and the suburbs the damage was less than on some earlier occasions. A hospital and a church suffered. A school in use as a shelter was hit by two bombs, and other public shelters were wrecked. Two enemy bombers were shot down, and in one case the machine (a Heinkel 111) blew up as it struck the ground. There was a heavy attack on the Midlands also. A German communiqué claimed that

over 1,000 aircraft had taken part in the night raid on London, and that they had dropped 1,000 tons of bombs. It also spoke of the bombers' "remarkable precision"!

There was very little enemy activity by day on Wednesday. Bombs were reported to have been dropped only at two places— a coast town in Scotland and one point in the West Country. At night the raiders dived down below the clouds to drop bombs and immediately regained shelter above. Four German bombers were shot down, one at Bishop's Stortford—the second in that locality during twenty-four hours ; others crashed at Denbigh, Frome, and near Harwich. At Liverpool a bomb fell on a surface shelter and killed a number of people. Dwelling-houses were demolished, but few industrial buildings were hit. There were some fires. Two hospitals in South-east England were damaged, and bombs fell in many other districts of Britain.

A few bombs were dropped on London by daylight raiders during Thursday, October 17. Generally the enemy aircraft flew very high. Attacks were made in the Kent area, and several bombs fell near Canterbury Cathedral, damaging the deanery. In the London area a three-storey building collapsed after being hit, falling against a shelter which, luckily, was empty. But in the wrecked building there were a number of casualties. The night raids were less extensive, and there were several lulls. The "raiders passed" was sounded much earlier than usual.

Friday (October 18) saw little activity by day, and only a small number of single aircraft came over. In the evening a museum in a London district was wrecked when four H.E. bombs fell ; a pedestrian was killed near by. Houses and a warden's post also were damaged, several wardens being injured and other persons killed. In another suburb a school, shops and houses were wrecked.

"Now, now, never mind. I won't let them hurt you!" From her wardens' post in a small Kentish village Mrs. Mary Couchman, just as bombs began to fall, saw some children playing in the street. They were frightened by the scream and the thud of the bombs, and she, gathering them in her arms, did her best to soothe them and shelter them with her own body.

Photo exclusive to THE WAR ILLUSTRATED

London Is Still the Nazis' Favourite Target

London's first "alert" on Saturday sounded in the afternoon, when an enemy bomber formation came inland towards the capital. No bombs were reported to have been dropped. Raids were made also on a town in the Midlands and on a coastal town in the South-east. Single enemy aircraft in each case were engaged, little damage being done and no casualties resulting. Big attacks were made at night on London, towns in the Midlands, and others in the North-east of England. Against London the air offensive continued until early morning. A hospital was hit and the medical school of another was set on fire. Shelters were demolished and a crowded café was wrecked. Many high-explosive and fire bombs fell in London suburbs.

There were four daytime "alerts" in London on Sunday, and pitched battles were going on high up in the sky during a great part of the day. The enemy concentrated his efforts on the South-east of England. Seven raiders were brought down, one crashing in a street at Woolwich. A few bombs were dropped in London, two falling at a place where many people were taking their morning "constitutional." A public-house was destroyed and the licensee buried under the wreckage. Outside a hall where service was about to be held—the ancient parish church had been damaged in a recent raid—fifteen bombs were dropped. But the hall was able to be used later for evensong.

Four bombers were brought down during Sunday night's raid on Britain : one crashed in Wiltshire, the crew of four descending by

Thousands of small panes of glass in Canterbury Cathedral were broken when a bomb was dropped nearby. An expert is at work removing pieces from a damaged window. The centuries-old stained glass had already been removed to safety. *Photo, Fox*

parachute and giving themselves up at various farmhouses. Of another, which fell between Harwich and Ipswich, the crew disappeared for a time. A piece of a Dornier gun-turret from a third raider was found

near Barnet on the outskirts of London. A fourth bomber is thought to have come down in the Channel off the Isle of Wight. London and the Midlands were the chief objectives of the enemy. In the Metropolis a hospital, an institution for the blind, and a church were bombed ; in another district a bomb fell at each end of one street. Surface shelters in various districts were hit ; a bomb struck a large public shelter with a glancing blow and blocked the entrance, but only three people were injured out of the 1,000 present, and those only slightly. The Midlands attacks lasted longer and were severe. Six bombs fell on a hospital.

Almost all day on Monday, October 21, there was evidence of raiding aircraft over London, but cloudy sky for most of the time hid them from sight. Intermittent gunfire was heard, and occasionally the sound of engines. Six bombs were dropped in one London district during the second " alert " ; four did little harm, but the rest fell on a row of small cottages and wrecked two. Two bombers flew low to make sure of this piece of terrorism. Three more bombs, dropped during the afternoon, smashed houses and damaged a water main.

Throughout Monday night, in spite of very misty conditions, there were persistent enemy attacks on London. The Merseyside area also came in for heavy bombing and Liverpool had its 200th raid of the war. Over London enemy aircraft flew continually, though the attack eased off after a while. A hospital and a maternity home were bombed, but there were no casualties, though a good deal of material damage was done. Elsewhere in the London area heavy H.E. bombs wrecked many houses. The Merseyside barrage kept the raiders flying high in that region and baffled their aim, but here again it was mainly houses that suffered. There were strong attacks on North-east coastal towns and on others in the Midlands.

The family above, bombed from their home, has salved a little furniture—the aspidistra and its pot being among the very few pieces undamaged. Circle is Mr. J. P. Hewett, of Hewell Street, Cardiff, known to his neighbours as "our man," and a typical self-sacrificing war worker. He served in the last war from 1914 to 1918 and now, at 50 years of age, works in a Government factory all day and is in a First Aid Post at night, while he also rouses the deaf people who cannot hear the sirens. *Photos, Planet News and Keystone*

In the 'Eagle' Squadron They Are Americans All

THE " Eagle " Squadron is the first R.A.F. squadron to be composed exclusively of American volunteer pilots. It has taken its place as an operational unit of the Fighter Command, and comprises thirty-four pilots. Colonel Charles Sweeny is the Squadron's Hon. Commanding Officer, and it was he who was primarily responsible for organizing this fine force. Squadron-Leader W. E. G. Taylor, its Commanding Officer, resigned from the U.S. Marine Corps Reserve at the outbreak of war so that he could obtain a commission in the Fleet Air Arm.

Here nine of the fastest Fighter Training machines, supplied to the Eagle Squadron for training purposes, are flying in splendid formation across the sky.

The Eagle Badge (circle) consists of a spread eagle surmounted by " E.S.," and is worn on the left arm. Col. Charles Sweeny (right), Hon. C.O.

Photos, P.N.A., British Official; Crown Copyright; " Daily Mirror "

Squadron-Leader W. E. G. Taylor (centre left) gives instructions to three Pilot Officers. Above, a group of American pilots en route to their machines, preparatory to a flight.

How Our Guns Drive Away the Raiders

Though the great barrage around London brought them into the limelight, our gunners had been doing sterling work for long months beforehand, putting into practice the maxims learnt during the days when most of them were " spare-time soldiers," for in the first instance our anti-aircraft batteries were manned by citizen soldiers of the Territorials.

THE terrific barrage that first met Nazi raiders over Britain on the night of Wednesday, September 11, was one of two main measures to defeat these stealthy terrorists ; others, to enable fighter aircraft to hunt down and destroy the enemy by night as by day, were the subject of active experiment and considerable achievement. Night bombing, to which the Germans were unwilling converts, is a confession of failure in the enemy's principal object—the subjugation of Britain—and was resorted to on a major scale only after mass raids by day had failed ignominiously. So far Britain's best defences have been the black-out and the barrage.

The name " box barrage " gives a very good impression of the curtain of fire with

40-mm. gun, which squirts out 2-pound shells at the rate of twenty-five a minute. Lower still it would be tackled by A.A. machine-guns and other arms.

One novel feature of the big barrage was the absence of searchlights, though these did come into operation later. The sky was fairly clear of cloud and the moon shone brilliantly, so prediction by sound apparatus was employed. The apparatus is secret and cannot be described, but a short account of the ordinary sound locator will be interesting. Mounted on a truck is an arrangement of four gigantic " ear-trumpets," three in a row vertically and another on a line at right angles, opposite the centre one of the vertical three. Two are " elevation " trumpets, while the

visual indication on a dial when the sound of the aeroplanes is received at its loudest.

In the next stage there come into operation a height-and-range-finder and the predictor. At the latter, two operators keep the target in view through telescopes, in manipulating which they set calculating machinery in motion within the predictor. A third operator " feeds in " the figures for the height of the aircraft—this information reaching him from the height-and-range-finder near by. The fourth and fifth operators are in charge of two dials, which they must " balance," on which appear the results of the other operators' manipulations.

Finally, all this is translated mechanically into movements of pointers over dials at the gun itself, by which the gunlayer aims his piece. As the approaching aircraft alters speed or direction the proper dial reading is communicated electrically to the gunlayer seated inside the steel shield of his 4·5. The important feature of the predictor is that it tells the gunlayer the probable *future* course of his quarry, and enables him to fire his shell to the point in the sky at which it should contact the raider.

' Shepherding ' the Raiders

Needless to say, these precise and powerful weapons must be properly organized and coordinated, in accordance with a carefully planned scheme. The various defence areas are quartered out, each having its defenders. In this three-dimensional warfare the very air above must be divided into different zones at suitable altitudes, and each region guarded by guns of appropriate range. Not only are the raiders shot at, hampered and harassed, they are also " shepherded," one might almost say—made to follow certain lanes in the air until they are brought up sharply against a barrier of exploding steel, in regions where the bombs they let fall can do the least harm. Because the night raiders may appear to pass overhead with impunity it must not be imagined that our defences are nodding ; there is probably a deep-laid scheme for their discomfiture selected by our gunners.

An enormously important factor in Britain's anti-aircraft defences are the searchlight units who work in conjunction with fighting aircraft and anti-aircraft guns. Here is seen a Lewis gun crew at a searchlight station in the London area. They are ever ready to repel low-flying attacks by the enemy.
Photo, Central Press

which the raiders are confronted and " boxed up," as it were. On the approach of an enemy aircraft the gunners are ready, and when the Nazi machine enters their area it is enclosed by a rectangle of bursting shells from our 3-in., 3·7-in. and (most deadly of all) 4·5-in. guns, to avoid which it must go higher or come down lower, or turn away from its path to the designed objective. In other words, only in flight can the raider find safety—and not always then. It is not surprising that many caught by the box barrage have jettisoned their bombs and scurried away. If the Nazi comes down lower it meets a concentrated fire from the Bofors

others are for obtaining the " bearing " of the aeroplane. The elevation listener manipulates his trumpets until he hears the sound with equal strength in both his earphones ; the bearing listener does the same, and so a sighting instrument on the sound locator is made to point in the direction of the aircraft. Linked up with the locator is a searchlight projector ; when the listening operators are satisfied that they have " got " the raider a signal is sent to the projector and the latter's beam is switched on ; it should then be right on to the target.

In order to lessen the fatigue of the listeners an electrical device can be used which gives a

Some British A.A. Guns Which Foil the Raiders

Type	Shell fired	Ceiling, ft.	Rate of fire (per min.)
40-mm. British version of the Swedish " Bofors " gun, used against low-flying aircraft. Shells loaded in " clips "	2 lb.	—	25
3-in. A.A. Type used in the war of 1914-18 and since improved. Mobile or fixed mounting	12 lb.	23,000	15
3·7-in. A.A. One of our principal weapons. Has a long barrel and is built as a fixed or a mobile gun	28 lb.	40,000	10
4·5-in. A.A. Our latest and best. With its steel armour shield enclosing the mechanism and protecting the gunners, it weighs 16 tons. Range like that of the 3·7-in. weapon, but fires a heavier shell which " gets there " more quickly	55 lb.	40,000	8

They Make the Noise at Night We Like to Hear!

The photographer who took these striking pictures spent a week at work with a section of London's anti-aircraft defences in order that he might photograph the guns of the barrage actually in action against the enemy.

This formidable gun forms part of an anti-aircraft battery in England. The battery has contributed very materially to the successes which A.A. guns have recently scored against Nazi raiders, for the knowledge of those who man it will be passed on to others, inasmuch as it is an officer-producing unit. Succes ful A.A. gunfire depends on the less spectacular work of the Gun Position Officer, seen at work (centre) with the predictor.

Photos, Central Press and Topical

'Never in the Field of Human Conflict

In his review of the progress of the war given to the House of Commons on August 20, the Prime Minister paid a tribute to the R.A.F. which will be recalled as long as our history and our fame endures. "The gratitude of every home in our island, in our Empire, and indeed, throughout the world," said Mr. Churchill, "except in the abodes of the guilty, goes out to the British airmen who, undaunted by odds, unwearied by their constant challenge and mortal danger, are turning the tide of world war by their prowess and by their devotion.   Never in the field of human conflict was so much owed

o Much Owed by So Many to So Few'

by so many to so few.'' When the Premier spoke, the Battle of Britain was in progress, but that of London had not yet been joined. If he had made his review a few weeks later he might have referred with still more force to those '' fighter pilots whose brilliant actions we see with our own eyes day after day.'' In this photograph are shown some of the chief defenders of the Metropolis—a Hurricane squadron, followed by Spitfires, speeding like silver arrows through the cloud-strewn sky on the way to intercept an enemy formation reported to be on the way to London.

Some of the Few to Whom We Many owe so Much

Behind the work of the fighter 'planes is a ground staff which directs all aerial activity. Left, the Adjutant and his assistants at a fighter squadron station are planning operations. Above, the order "Take the Air" has been given, and the pilots who have been driven to the aerodrome in lorries leap out to go to their machines.

Here a flight of Spitfires such as has driven off many daylight raiders is taking off for a flight over London after enemy aircraft have crossed the coast.

The work of defending Britain against enemy raiders is shared by the Spitfires with the Hurricanes, and for both types of 'planes Nazi airmen have a wholesome respect. These Hurricanes are flying in formation above the cloud layers after enemy aircraft have been reported near the London area in order to meet them before they begin their favourite manoeuvres of "cloud dodging" and unloading their bombs indiscriminately.

Photos, British Official: Crown Copyright; and Sport & General

Through the Night with London's Fire Fighters

Every night an armed guard is mounted at all the important fire stations to keep watch over the appliances and to keep unwelcome intruders away. The engines are always "ready on the run."

THE London Fire Brigade and the Auxiliary Fire Service have worked as one body since November 1939, and before long they will be combined as the London Fire Service. The A.F.S. men are now fully-trained firemen, for since the service was inaugurated they have undergone an intensive course of training ; even before London was systematically bombed they gained experience in fire fighting at some of the outbreaks of fire with which London firemen are always called upon to deal. There is also a women's section of the A.F.S. ; some of its members act as drivers of the cars of the chief officers, but their most important work lies in the control rooms. Several A.F.S. girls have died recently at the post of duty.

The indiscriminate bombing of London has struck at all quarters and all classes ; one district that has suffered heavily is the neighbourhood of Chancery Lane, home of the legal profession.

There is no time for stairs when an alarm is given, and the firemen slide down to the engines from their sleeping quarters on polished steel poles. They are often on the way to a fire within a minute.

Behind the work of the London Fire Brigade and the Auxiliary Fire Service is an elaborate control system which deals with the mobilization of the various units and controls their movements. Left, at work in a local control room; above, firemen are having a wash after returning from a fire.

Photos by "News Chronicle" Staff Photographer Ross-White, exclusive to THE WAR ILLUSTRATED; *and Planet News*

Learn the Anatomy of a Barrage Balloon!

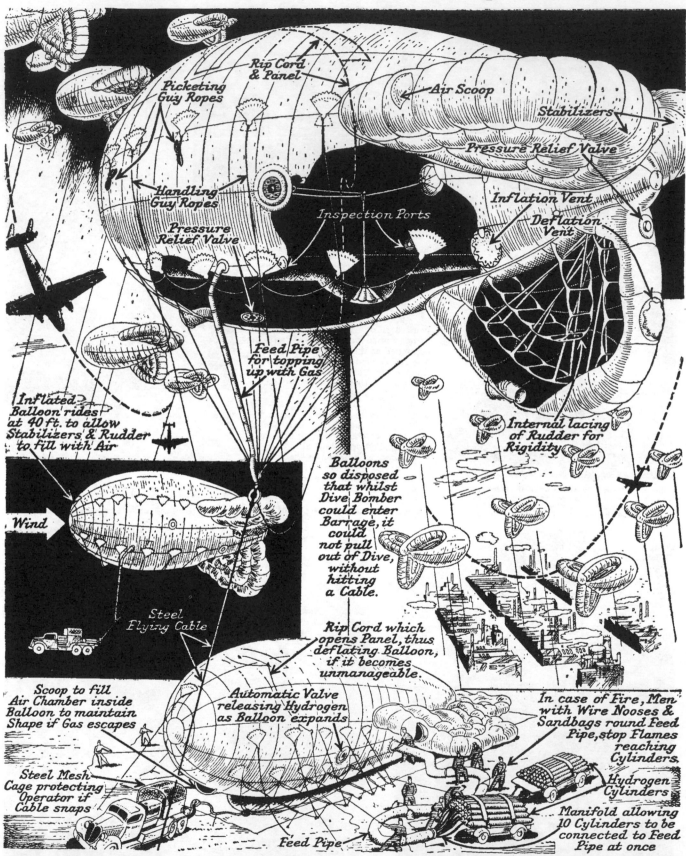

Rip Cord & Panel

Picketing Guy Ropes

Air Scoop

Stabilizers

Pressure Relief Valve

Handling Guy Ropes

Inspection Ports

Inflation Vent

Deflation Vent

Pressure Relief Valve

Feed Pipe for topping up with Gas

Internal lacing of Rudder for Rigidity

Inflated Balloon rides at 40 ft. to allow Stabilizers & Rudder to fill with Air

Wind

Steel Flying Cable

Balloons so disposed that whilst Dive Bomber could enter Barrage, it could not pull out of Dive, without hitting a Cable.

Rip Cord which opens Panel, thus deflating Balloon, if it becomes unmanageable.

Scoop to fill Air Chamber inside Balloon to maintain Shape if Gas escapes

Automatic Valve releasing Hydrogen as Balloon expands

In case of Fire, Men with Wire Nooses & Sandbags round Feed Pipe, stop Flames reaching Cylinders.

Steel Mesh Cage protecting Operator if Cable snaps

Hydrogen Cylinders

Manifold allowing 10 Cylinders to be connected to Feed Pipe at once

Feed Pipe

High up in the sky float the balloons that constitute the barrage which the Nazi dive-bombers most certainly do not like. Looked at from the ground some thousands of feet below, the balloons seem to be simple things enough ; closer inspection makes it clear that in fact theirs is quite a complicated anatomy. The principal details of their construction are revealed in this page of drawings, and it will be realized that to a balloon's making there goes a wealth of ingenuity and labour. Another point brought out by the diagram is that the way in which the balloons are disposed in the sky makes it impossible for a dive-bomber who has had the temerity to enter the barrage to pull out of his dive without hitting a cable and so crashing to earth. There have even been cases of a raider meeting his end by crashing into one of the balloons themselves. Many facts about our barrage balloons have been given in earlier pages, and opposite we tell of the way in which " wounded " balloons are made fit for return to duty ; here let us add that when filled with some 20,000 cubic feet of gas the balloons are 66 feet long and 30 feet high ; some 600 separate pieces of fabric, amounting in all to over 1,000 yards of 42-inch material go to the making of one balloon ; and the original cost of a balloon is about £500, while the gas alone costs £50.

'Wounded' Balloons Make Such Good Patients!

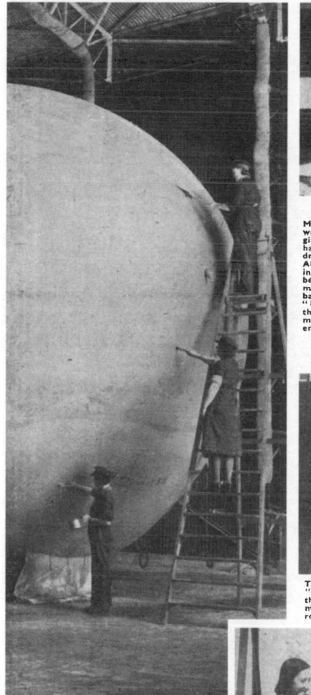

Much of the fabric repair work is done by W.A.A.F. girls ; they are experts in handling electrically-driven sewing machines. Above we see them repairing a huge length of rubberized fabric. An R.A.F. man, circle, is splicing balloon wires. At the "hospital" illustrated in this page, three hundred men and women are employed on balloon repair work.

Photos, Fox

These girls, left, are seen hard at work as they make the necessary repairs to an "injured" balloon. Complete spare balloons and parts are also housed in the "hospital." Packed in canvas covers, balloons are kept in store for replacement. Above, one is being put on a derrick for consignment to the store room.

Photos, Fox and Central Art Library

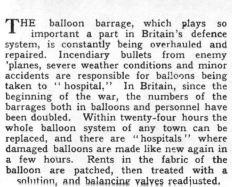

THE balloon barrage, which plays so important a part in Britain's defence system, is constantly being overhauled and repaired. Incendiary bullets from enemy 'planes, severe weather conditions and minor accidents are responsible for balloons being taken to "hospital," In Britain, since the beginning of the war, the numbers of the barrages both in balloons and personnel have been doubled. Within twenty-four hours the whole balloon system of any town can be replaced, and there are "hospitals" where damaged balloons are made like new again in a few hours. Rents in the fabric of the balloon are patched, then treated with a solution, and balancing valves readjusted.

These laughing members of the W.A.A.F. are pulling a trolley which is loaded with a repaired barrage balloon.   *Photo, Fox*

In a heavy sea a British battle-cruiser is putting out from port. The great weight of these ships and their high speed makes them inclined, like battleships, to cut through the waves rather than ride over them, while their comparatively low freeboard causes them to ship more water forward than would a merchant ship in similar weather. At the outbreak of war the British Navy had three battle-cruisers, "Hood," "Renown," and "Repulse," but no other navy had adopted this type of warship. The displacement of the "Renown" and "Repulse" is 32,000 tons, with a speed of 29 knots, but the "Hood," the largest warship afloat, has a displacement of 42,100 tons and a speed of 32 knots.

Photo, British Official: Crown Copyright

Tovey Now Holds the Post That Beatty Held

In the Great War they called it the Grand Fleet, and its commanders were in turn Jellicoe and Beatty ; in this war it is the Home Fleet, which until the other day was commanded by Admiral Sir Charles Forbes. Now, however, the C.-in-C. is Admiral Tovey, about whom, and another famous modern sea-dog, Rear-Admiral Sir Henry Harwood, we tell here.

BRITAIN'S Home Fleet—that great collection of battleships and cruisers, destroyers and smaller craft which keeps perpetual watch and ward over the North Atlantic, the North Sea, and the English Channel—has a new Commander-in-Chief. On October 17 it was announced by the Admiralty that Rear-Admiral J. C. Tovey, Commanding Destroyer Flotillas, Mediterranean, had been appointed Commander-in-Chief Home Fleet in succession to Admiral of the Fleet Sir Charles Forbes, with the acting rank of admiral.

Admiral Tovey is 54, and for the most part his 40 years in the Navy have been associated with the destroyer branch. In the last war he was in command of H.M. destroyer " Onslow " at the Battle of Jutland on May 31, 1916, and the gallant and skilful way in which he handled his ship came in for special mention after the action. First the " Onslow " and another destroyer, the " Moresby," tackled four of Admiral Hipper's light cruisers, until the two destroyers were met with so heavy and accurate a fire that they were forced to turn away. Foiled in this first attempt, the " Onslow " took station beside the " Lion," Admiral Beatty's flagship, and as the Admiral turned east, Tovey suddenly caught sight of the " Wiesbaden " in an excellent position for using his torpedoes, only 6,000 yards away. He dashed at her, firing as he went, until when within 2,000 yards he suddenly found himself too near to be comfortable to the enemy's battle cruisers. Though under the fire of the advancing ships, Tovey thought the opportunity of having a hit at so fine a target was one not to be missed, and at 8,000 yards he gave the order for all torpedoes to be fired. Unfortunately, at that very moment the " Onslow " was struck amidships by a heavy shell and so only one torpedo got off. But he had not finished yet,

Admiral J. C. Tovey takes command of the Royal Navy stationed in home waters, known as the Home Fleet. In the last war this force, first under Admiral Jellicoe and then under Admiral Beatty, was known as the Grand Fleet.
Photo, Universal Picture Press

and, passing close to the " Wiesbaden," he hit her fair and square under the conning tower.

Hardly had the noise of the explosion died away when another and far more important target suddenly presented itself. " Some five miles away," to quote the account of Sir Julian S. Corbett in " Naval Operations," " a whole line of German battleships loomed up in the mist advancing upon him at high speed. What was he to do ? He had two torpedoes in his tubes, but his engines were failing, his speed was down to ten knots, and to turn to attack meant almost certain destruction, and yet he turned. One destroyer more or less, so he reasoned, mattered little, while two torpedoes fired from an ideal position might materially affect the action, and in this admirable spirit of devotion he decided to attack again. Making for the advancing battleships, he waited till his sights were on, and at 8,000 yards fired his remaining torpedoes. Fair to cross the enemy's line they ran as he struggled away, but the Germans must have manoeuvred to avoid them, for there was no hit. So bold an attack with a crippled ship deserved a better result, but the sacrifice that he faced was not required of him, and two days later he got safely back to port." In fact, the " Onslow " was taken in tow by the " Defender," another crippled destroyer, and both ships succeeded in reaching Aberdeen on June 2.

From 1932 to 1934 he was in command of the battleship " Rodney," and from 1935—when he was promoted to Flag rank —to 1937 he was Commodore of the Royal

Rear-Admiral Sir Henry Harwood photographed at a public luncheon soon after his return to England from South America in mid-October. He had shortly before been knighted by the King.
Photo, Sport & General

Naval barracks at Chatham. In April, 1938, he was transferred to the Mediterranean to take command of the Destroyer Flotillas.

On the same day as Admiral Tovey's appointment to the Home Fleet was announced, Rear-Admiral Sir Henry Harwood, K.C.B., was appointed a Lord Commissioner of the Admiralty and an Assistant Chief of Naval Staff in succession to Vice-Admiral Sir Geoffrey Blake. Admiral Harwood's name will be for ever associated with the glorious battle of the River Plate of Dec. 13, 1939.

Every officer appointed to a staff job at the Admiralty is made a member of the crew of H.M.S. " President," the R.N.V.R. drill ship which lies off the Victoria Embankment, London, and the notice of Rear-Admiral Harwood's appointment declared that he had been " appointed to ' President ' for additional duty inside the Admiralty."

High proficiency in gunnery has distinguished the destroyer flotillas since the outbreak of war, and the men above, manning one of the small ships' A.A. guns, are typical of those who have made excellent practice against enemy aircraft. Admiral Tovey has been largely responsible for bringing the destroyer arm to its present state of efficiency.
Photo, Central Press

OUR SEARCHLIGHT ON THE WAR

German Lies Shown Up

THE Air Ministry, goaded beyond endurance by the lying communiqués of the German High Command, recently abandoned official reticence and gave chapter and verse in support of its statement that on a particular day eight Nazi aircraft had been destroyed. " The German High Command communiqué almost always contains an untrue statement of enemy air losses. Today's High Command communiqué, for example, only admits that three of their aircraft did not return from Tuesday's operations. In fact, as already announced, eight German aircraft were destroyed on Tuesday. Of these two were Heinkel float-'planes which were shot down in the sea without survivors.'' Details of the remaining six were then given, including the type of aircraft and any marks on it, the place where it came down, and the names of the crew. The Air Ministry added : " It will be appreciated that information of this nature may be of great value to the enemy and cannot be published as a general rule.''

America's New Air Base

JACKSONVILLE, Florida, is the site for the first of the U.S. Navy's great air bases which are to be built as part of the new defence programme. Its purpose will be twofold : it will serve primarily as the principal base of air operations from Newfoundland to the Panama Canal, and, secondly, as a training centre for pilots and aeroplane mechanics. As it is expected that three thousand mechanics will be under instruction at one time, thirty buildings, to be used as their training school, have already been erected, and enormous workshops are now under construction for the purpose of servicing naval aeroplanes from all over the U.S.A. The whole scheme is to cost 25 million dollars (£6,250,000) and will cover 3,360 acres.

Thumb-Screws on Syria

THE Axis Powers, through the agency of the Vichy Government, have succeeded in demoralizing both the army and civil service in Syria. Their ultimate aim is to secure the disarmament of the French forces and the surrender to Italy of vast quantities of war material and equipment. The army consisted of more than 100,000 men, of whom about half were native troops. Some 40,000 of the Europeans were reservists, and of these one-third have been, or are now being, repatriated to France. Moreover, the compulsory retirement, on the score of economy, of senior French officers and officials in the civil service, has resulted in the elimination of most of those who are pro-British or whose sympathies incline towards the Free French movement. Those that remain are forced to submit to the Vichy policy, for dismissal would deprive them of their pensions, and their families at home of their separation allowances. The Italian Armistice Commission, which arrived at Beirut soon after the collapse of France, has had to work very cautiously, owing to the ill-concealed dislike not only of the French, but of the Syrians and Lebanese too. Now, however, that the spirit of the army has deteriorated, the efforts to get Syria under the heel of the Dictators may meet with less resistance.

Free French Cause in Africa

WITH a view to encouraging the Free French movement in Africa, General de Gaulle arrived at Duala, Cameroons, on October 9. He telegraphed the following greeting to Mr. Churchill : " From French soil over which the enemy has no control I send to you and to the valiant peoples of the British Empire an expression of complete confidence and faithful friendship from 14,000,000 Frenchmen or French subjects already bound to me for the prosecution of the war by the side of the Allies until final victory.'' After conferences with Gen. de Larminat, whom he had appointed Governor-General of All Free French Colonies in Central Africa, Gen. de Gaulle is to continue his journey through the Cameroons to Lake Chad and thence to Cairo. In this city recruiting proceeds apace, and the Croix de Lorraine, the Free French emblem worn in the coat lapel, is very much in evidence among the French population. It is stated that Cairo is to be the centre of a network of world propaganda in the interests of Free France. In Tunis, which is Vichy-controlled territory, the underground Free French movement is steadily gaining adherents, and Gen. de Gaulle's presence in Africa is certain to spur on to further efforts all workers for the ultimate freedom of the great French Empire.

Starvation May Follow Nazi Looting

A REPORT has been issued in Washington in which the U.S. Commerce Department states that Germany will be to blame for any food shortage in Europe this coming winter. Germany already has larger food reserves than any other European country except Britain, and she is still adding to them, always at the expense of the plundered and occupied territories. In Norway the German Government has acquired and exported to its own storehouses the entire " crisis reserve " of potatoes, amounting to 300,000 tons, which the Norwegians, by increased cultivation last spring, had produced to meet the needs of their own people in the winter ahead. The Quislingist authorities have also concluded a new contract for supplying Germany with a further quantity of dried fish to the value of 4 million kronen. Foodstuffs such as eggs and meat are becoming scarce, for not only do the troops in occupation consume enormous quantities, but they also send parcels of food to their own homes. This is in addition to the regular official consignments.

In unoccupied France the food shortage is already becoming very serious, in spite of severe rationing. Such commodities as sugar, coffee, butter, chocolate, olive oil, soap and matches have disappeared. Little meat except mutton is available, and only by saving a week's ration can enough for a good meal be obtained. Sea fish is sometimes offered at coastal places, in spite of mines and submarines, but it does not reach inland towns. Because of transport difficulties the price of coal is prohibitive, so that wood is the only fuel available. Cold and semi-starvation will almost certainly be the lot of unhappy France for months to come.

Battered Libyan Ports

THE persistent bombing by the R.A.F. of Benghazi and Tobruk is causing grave concern to Italy. These two harbours have hitherto been largely used for importing supplies destined for troops on the Egyptian front, but as the result of British raids ships have been set on fire, quays damaged and dumps destroyed, and it is thought that Italian shipping will now have to proceed for unloading to Tripoli, very much farther west. One advantage of this arrangement will be that the crossing from Sicily is shorter, and is partly protected by minefields, but, on the other hand, the port is 500 miles from the Egyptian frontier, and to cover such a distance by road is both slow and costly.

PRINCESS ELIZABETH TO CHILDREN OF THE EMPIRE

On October 13, 1940, Princess Elizabeth made her first broadcast, an address to evacuee children at home and in the Empire. Her words were heard throughout this country, and by British children in Canada, the United States, South Africa, and elsewhere. The Princess said :

IN wishing you all " Good evening," I feel that I am speaking to friends and companions who have shared with my sister and myself many a happy Children's Hour.

Thousands of you in this country have had to leave your homes and be separated from your fathers and mothers. My sister, Margaret Rose, and I feel so much for you, as we know from experience what it means to be away from those we love most of all. To you, living in new surroundings, we send a message of true sympathy, and at the same time we would like to thank the kind people who have welcomed you to their homes in the country.

All of us children who are still at home think continually of our friends and relations who have gone overseas—who have travelled thousands of miles to find a wartime home and a kindly welcome in Canada, Australia, New Zealand, South Africa and the United States of America.

My sister and I feel we know quite a lot about these countries. Our father and mother have so often talked to us of their visits to different parts of the world. So it is not difficult for us to picture the sort of life you are all leading, and to think of all the new sights you must be seeing and the adventures you must be having.

But I am sure that you, too, are often thinking of the Old Country. I know you won't forget us ; it is just because we are not forgetting you that I want, on behalf of all the children at home, to send you our love and best wishes—to you and to your kind hosts as well.

Before I finish I can truthfully say to you all that we children at home are full of cheerfulness and courage. We are trying to do all we can to help our gallant sailors, soldiers and airmen, and we are trying, too, to bear our own share of the danger and sadness of war. We know, every one of us, that in the end all will be well ; for God will care for us and give us victory and peace. And when peace comes, remember it will be for us, the children of today, to make the world of tomorrow a better and happier place.

My sister is by my side, and we are both going to say good-night to you. Come on, Margaret.

Princess Margaret : Good-night.

Princess Elizabeth : Good-night and good luck to you all.

When Princess Elizabeth made her first broadcast on October 13, 1940, her sister, Princess Margaret, was sitting beside her, and the King and Queen were also in the room. Listeners were interested to note the resemblance of the Princess's voice to that of her mother.   *Photo, Planet News*

I WAS THERE!

Eye Witness Stories of Episodes
and Adventures in the
Second Great War

A Nazi Airman Landed In Our Meadow

During the summer and autumn of 1940 hundreds of Nazi airmen
from damaged 'planes came to earth in the English countryside.
Some of them landed uninjured and still aggressive in spirit, others
—like the central figure of the following episode described by Leslie
Thomas in the "Daily Express"—were broken in body and
apprehensive of ill treatment.

WHEN the ground under our running
feet shook as the German pilot's
body struck the spot where his torn
parachute dropped him, we were conscious
of only one thing. A man, perhaps terribly
smashed up, was lying there, groaning, in need
of help. We were only a pace or two from
him and he raised one hand in gesture of
surrender as he turned apprehensive eyes
towards us.

We had been gazing vainly up in search of
the high-flying attackers, the drone of whose
hundreds of engines made your head hum,
when we heard somewhere above us the noise
like the flack of a duster out of the window.

High up, just breaking through a white
cloud in which his machine had been sheltering, was a tiny black dot with a flapping white
thing following it down.

A man had baled out and his " brolly "
wasn't opening properly. He was dropping
and twisting and turning in the air in an
endeavour to get the crazy thing to function.
He was coming straight down in the teeth of
the wind, right into our meadow.

I remember shouting, " My God, his
parachute won't open," and dashing off at
top speed, just as you would if you saw a
chap coming a purler off a motor-bike in the
road.

Elsa was in the lead : she didn't stop even
to shout. She tore across the bit of meadow
and as she got up to the injured man she said
at once, " Gun ? " He only shook his head
and groaned.

Then we were kneeling beside him, Elsa
supporting him and saying reassuring things,
while I got his parachute adrift from the
harness, made it up into a pillow and started
to release the harness from him. She took
off his flying helmet and laid him back, his
face very white, lips swollen, and his mouth
and nose covered in blood. An ambulance
man, a member of the village first-aid squad,
arrived to examine him.

He was a little Nazi ; not at all the hector-
ing, medal-wearing, bully type. An educated
type of boy of about twenty-three or twenty-
four, with a few words of English which, with
my few fragments of German, helped us to
locate his injuries and reassure him that his
danger was over.

" Left foot broken," was his first remark.
The St. John man removed his boots, which,
we noticed, were ordinary walking boots, not
flying boots at all.

His eyes roved skywards, and I glanced up
and saw other parachutes, one of them
catching fire, gliding down from the sky, and
a black Dornier circling wildly with smoke
pouring from its tail. We learned afterwards
that one of his crew came down dead two
miles away on the end of his parachute.

Villagers, including the first-aid squad, now
began to arrive, and one good-humoured ass
came up and remarked, " You are a b——
fool, you know, to fight the English ! "

He was a lucky young Nazi that afternoon.
For all his terrible landing, which had made
me want to cover my eyes for fear of what I
was going to see, he appeared to have got off
with a pair of rather badly broken legs and a
bitten tongue. He didn't seem to have any

to him in brief sentences to help restore his
balance. " Goot, goot," he kept on saying.

Then, as a variation on an all-important
theme, " Would you be so very, very
kind . . . ? " At first she thought he was
going to make a request, but he was asking
for kind treatment. I suppose he had been
primed with stories of his fate if he fell into
British hands. . . . .

They took him away to hospital in an open
farm lorry, the village ambulance, and there
were cries of " Auf wiedersehen " from all
sides as he was lifted ever so carefully aboard
the stretcher.

This Nazi airman took to his parachute when his machine was shot down over the English countryside. The parachute failed to open properly and the German is seen wounded after landing. He
was afterwards taken to hospital in the village ambulance—an open lorry.   *Photo, " Daily Mirror "*

internal injury by his reactions, and his chief
concern was for his face.

" What here ? What here ? " he kept
asking, moving his hand vaguely in the
direction of his mouth. Elsa bathed his
mouth and nose and we both kept chatting

It had been his first flight over England
and he never reached London.

" I suppose I ought to hate him, when I
think he was on his way perhaps to bomb
mother," Elsa remarked, as we went indoors ;
" but I can't."

The 'Truant' Rescued Us After 134 Days

After being prisoners of the Nazis on the high seas for 134 days, the
crew of the British steamer " Haxby " were rescued by H.M. submarine " Truant " off Cape Finisterre. The following story of their
imprisonment and rescue was told by Captain Cornelius Arundell to
Laurence Wilkinson of the " Daily Express."

IT was about 6.30 in the morning of April
24, 1940, when the German raider,
flying Greek colours, suddenly opened
fire on the " Haxby " with four 6 in. guns.

We had no chance. The second salvo of
shells killed our gunner and smashed the gun
platform. They kept on firing after that for
about half an hour—with not a shot in return.

My ship was shattered and on fire, and
there were good men dead on the decks.
We had to swim for it, and after a long time

they picked us up from the planks and
wooden barrels to which we were clinging.

They put us into canvas suits and gave us
underwear and flannel shirts made out of
wood pulp. They sent us to our prison
quarters, three decks down.

They gave us a plate of black bread and
sausage. The bread was as hard as nails
and had half an inch of wet round the bottom.

When we went on deck for exercise for
one hour in the morning and one in the

afternoon we saw that we were in a fine ship, one of the Hamburg liners which before war was on the New York run. Furnishings and fittings were de luxe except where alterations had been made to give the ship powerful armament.

Our diet did not improve. There was no milk, no sugar, no tea. They gave us imitation coffee made from burnt corn and an imitation jam. Our staple diet was soup made from peas, beans or lentils.

We saw little of our captors. The captain, a grim-faced Prussian, never spoke until the day I left his ship to be transferred to the " Tropic Sea," a Norwegian ship which they had captured.

He then asked me if I had been treated well. I said I had no complaints, and added : " But I shall never forget that you killed sixteen of my men, firing at us while we were helpless."

He said : " Forget it, captain, there's a war on." I said : " I shall never forget and never forgive it." He shrugged his shoulders.

It was true that we hadn't been badly treated. The officers and men with whom we had dealings were like strangely deluded children. They believed that the war would be over in a matter of weeks, and they even had daily band practice on board so that the ship could be represented in " the victory march through Berlin," which they thought was soon to take place.

They believed that the British Navy had been swept from the seas, that South-east England was a desert of destruction, that the Port of London was shattered and useless, and that all England was starving and continuing the fight in desperation.

One morning Klaxon alarms sounded, and we were all locked in our quarters. There was a lot of scampering going on above our heads. Then the guns fired three times.

More than an hour later we saw through little peepholes in the wall of our prison room that some seamen were being brought on board. They were from the captured Norwegian ship " Tropic Sea."

Soon afterwards another ship came alongside. It was the German oiler " Winnetou," which had come out to refuel us. At this time we were kept in close confinement. We were twelve days locked in our quarters without exercise, and almost choked by oil fumes.

Then we were transferred to the " Tropic Sea " under armed guard.

They rigged up two machine-guns to cover any attempt to rush the lifeboats, and we were supervised by twenty guards, each armed with a revolver and a hand grenade.

The new captain, who was an officer from the first raider, called all the British and Norwegian prisoners on deck and told us : " There are six bombs hidden in this ship. If you try any tricks I will blow the whole thing sky high."

They kept on plugging at us with their propaganda. An officer had the special duty of converting us into good Nazis, and he seemed to think it was only a question of time before we saw the folly of our ways and realized that Hitler was a fine fellow and Churchill a low scoundrel. Among other startling statements, this propaganda officer said that only 3,000 British soldiers had escaped from Dunkirk and that every British port was closed by mines.

As we got nearer Europe we got a bit depressed. We thought there was no chance of rescue.

Then, at 5.30 on the morning of September 3, the alarm sounded through the ship again. We were told to get on deck with our lifebelts.

All the German officers seemed in a daze. When they first sighted the submarine they were convinced that it was a German which had come to escort them into port. They hadn't bargained for it being British.

The little submarine signalled : " Stop your ship, tell captain to put out boats, bring ship's papers."

I told the German captain, " He hasn't fired on you yet, and he won't if you behave.

Here is Capt. Cornelius Arundell, master of the freighter " Haxby," whose story of his captivity on a Nazi prison-ship for 134 days is recounted in this page. *Photo, Associated Press*

But if you try any monkey business I've a good idea what the consequences will be."

The Germans in my lifeboat refused to take us to the submarine, so I pushed the officer away from the tiller and told my men to row towards it for all they were worth. I knew that there were time bombs in the ship due to explode in a matter of minutes. We drew alongside the submarine and a young lieutenant pulled me aboard and said : " Welcome home." He had one of those Navy voices. It sounded like music in my ears.

Mine Was a Hot Night With 'Alf Bagwash'

Since the attack on London started we have come to recognize as heroes many men to whom and whose labour we hardly gave a thought in the days of peace. Among these are surely the men who take the newspapers from the printing-offices to the main-line stations on the first stage to our breakfast tables. This story by John Pudney is reprinted from the " News Chronicle."

PEOPLE are skipping from doorway to doorway—those who have to be out. On tall buildings there is a flush of false dawn from a distant fire.

Between the thunder of guns, like raindrops in a dark pool, sound London's clocks

striking the small hours, delicate and indifferent. On business of life and death fire appliances and A.R.P. vehicles streak through the streets.

In the shadows of Fleet Street rows of coloured news vans wait like teams of relay runners. " Awful " and " Bagwash," the news drivers, are discussing tonight's war with expert discrimination as they wait for the load of newspapers they are to take to the great main line termini.

" Chosen a hot night, you have, to watch the wheels go round," says " Alf Bagwash," whose passenger I am to be.

The Sky is Beginning to Whistle

We lumber off through the familiar, now rather frightening, streets. For six years, Alf tells me, he has driven newspapers to catch the train at " Eusterloo." Every night since " he started this —— game," he has driven on side-lights alone through these streets. . . .

" You don't half look funny when you shrink up like that in your corner," he says, interrupting himself.

I have sufficient reason to shrink. A couple of " diversions " have taken us well off the beaten course to " Eusterloo," and the sky is beginning to whistle.

We tumble out into an archway ; and your news pauses. . . .

" Alf Bagwash " tells me how he comes to bear this nickname ; and we proceed, our tires crunching on broken glass, the

Throughout the air " blitz " readers have received their newspapers with extraordinary regularity due not only to the indoor staff, but to the courage of such men as " Alf Bagwash," one of whose trips to " Eusterloo " through gunfire and bombs is described in this page. *Photo, " News Chronicle "*

windscreen momentarily dimmed by dust and smoke.

"You get a kind of first-hand knowledge of what's going on," says Alf, "and you get used to it."

More news is made even as we trundled through the shadows with the latest of everything. It is all that moves in London besides the vital services of the City fighting line.

We take what Alf calls "another little breather" for a matter of minutes in a shelter. "Shouldn't chance it, if I was you, mates," says a policeman when we decide to move on.

"I got a load in that van. Newspapers for the train," says Alf, conclusively clumping on his tin hat.

"Eusterloo" has taken us longer than we bargained for. But the train is there. And we bandy words with the other relay runners as they arrive.

Alf makes any journey possible, but I fancy I have spent far too much time "shrinking up" in my corner.

"Harry Awful" joins us. We calculate the time till dawn and, taking leave of the papers, retire to a long melancholy bar for tea.

I am most viciously scalded when all our cups jump out of our hands, and many frequenters of the bar flung themselves flat.

"Awful" and "Bagwash" captivate me by calling upon the depressed and recumbent company to sing.

Wallop again.

We are still alive then, and "Awful" says, "Thank Gawd the train's away, anyway."

How We Bombed Flushing Docks

During one of the R.A.F. raids on Flushing Docks one of our aircraft dived down to within a stone's throw of the ground and secured direct hits on buildings and an ammunition dump. The pilot, a young New Zealander, broadcast an account of this exploit, and here it is in his own words.

WE broke cloud just south of Flushing from along the coast. We waited for about 20 minutes to pin point it—just to make absolutely certain. Then we went up seaward and came in across the

The observer lies prone on the floor of the "bomb room" of his machine, his thumb on the bomb release, waiting for the precise second when he may drop his bombs.
Photo, Topical

docks. In the meantime they must have been getting all their guns ready. I thought we were going to glide in and catch them by surprise, but it didn't happen that way.

We were fairly low when they opened up. I have never seen anything like it—it didn't even seem worth trying to dodge the Flak, there was so much of it. I thought "Goodnight, nurse," put the nose down and hoped for the best. That wasn't being foolhardy. It was as good a way of getting out of it as any other.

The inside of the aircraft was reeking with cordite. Nobody said anything. Frankly, I thought we weren't going to get out of it, and I think the rest of them thought that too. I remember it flashing across my mind that if they did bring us down the aircraft would make a pretty good bomb load to land on them—I don't mean anything heroic, but

even if it was all up, we were going to hit the docks anyway.

The searchlights were holding us all the time. I just kept my eyes on the instruments and on the docks. If one had looked round one would have been blinded. As we went over, the bomb-aimer made certain all the bombs had gone. We dropped them and they landed right in the centre of the dock buildings.

Immediately we were thrown up to 600 feet. There were tremendous explosions. The second pilot was standing beside me. His knees buckled underneath him and he went down on the floor. I was just concentrating on trying to keep the aircraft in the air and to get away. More or less automatically I pushed the nose down, the throttles forward, and hoped for the best. There was a curtain of fire on all sides. We went through. I bet the Germans thought they had got one aircraft down all right, but we must have given them a terrific shaking.

The ships opened fire on us as well as all the guns on the shore. They seemed to have a ring of Flak ships round the harbour. The machine-gun tracer was making spirals in the air. They were using heavy arm quick-firing guns, too, and flaming onions by the dozen. The sky was absolutely full of it. We scooted along the edge of the sea. I could see the breakers quite clearly. By this time I was fighting with the stick. We sent out an S O S that we were likely to be coming down. I knew that we had been hit. I had felt the shells smack into the 'plane and I couldn't hold the aircraft properly.

I Never Thought We'd Make Home

We said we would have a crack at getting home. We told them that by wireless. I thought the rear gunner had been hit. He didn't answer when I spoke to him on the inter-communication set and I sent the second pilot along to his turret. We found that the gunner was all right, but that his inter-communication set had been put out of order. I told the second pilot to have a look at all control cables and keep his eye on the petrol gauges to see that the petrol tanks weren't leaking. The front gunner came out of his turret and stood by to operate the flotation gear in case we had to land on the water. At 15 to 20 miles out we could still see the flashes of explosions from the docks.

Frankly I never thought we'd make home. The aircraft was kicking like a bucking bronco. There were heavy clouds and I was flying on instruments all the way. It was raining most of the time. My arms were aching and seemed tied up in knots from the strain of holding the aircraft. Finally we got home, and I landed safely.

One of Hitler's chief invasion ports, Flushing, has been repeatedly bombed by the R.A.F., the concentrations of barges having suffered heavily. Here is seen part of Flushing's harbour, the Rotonde with the statue of Admiral de Ruyter at one end of the foremost quay. *Photo, E.N.A.*

In France Things Are Grim—Certainly Not Gay

To French printers in occupied France has fallen the unpleasant task of setting newspapers for the Nazis. Left is a scene in the office of " L'Echo de la Loire," the principal daily of Nantes ; the caption to the original German photograph reads, " A French printer unaccustomed to Gothic type (black letter) at work on the production of ' Der Stosstrupp ' " (The Storm Trooper). Right is one of the Nazi broadcasting cars which tell sad listeners the next instalment of regimentation which lies in store for them.

When war clouds first appeared on the horizon, precautions were taken by the French to destroy all the bridges across the Rhine on the frontier between France and Germany. Soon after the declaration of war the bridges were blown up, but after the Armistice one of the first works of restoration undertaken was the building of temporary structures to take their place. Above is one of them built by pioneers in 28 days ; beyond it are the remains of the old bridge.

Left is one of the long-range German guns mounted on the French coast which were intended to strike terror into the hearts of the people of Kent and to close the Straits of Dover to British convoys. In both purposes they signally failed. Right is Marshal Pétain receiving a party of American journalists at Vichy. He is said to have described the frontier between occupied and unoccupied France as " a noose round our necks," and to have declared that he yearned to meet " his old friend General Pershing."

Photos, E.N.A. and Keystone

They Have Won Honour in Freedom's Cause

Flight Lieut. Douglas Forsyth, D.F.C., for displaying great courage and gallantry during operations in the air.

Flying Officer Thomas Murray, D.F.C., for displaying bravery, conspicuous courage and devotion to duty during air operations.

Act. Flight Lieut. J. Jefferies, D.F.C., for destroying 4 enemy aircraft and severely damaging another two.

Flying Officer Peter Bennett, D.F.C., for displaying conspicuous courage and bravery against the enemy in the air.

Squadron - Leader Donald England, D.F.C., for displaying great courage and devotion to duty while engaged in air operations.

Capt. Quirk, of the Merchant Navy, O.B.E., for displaying courage and devotion to duty on active service.

Act. Flight Lieut. P. S Turner, D.F.C., for destroying 10 enemy aircraft during engagements over Dunkirk and Britain.

Flight Lieut. Peter Hanks, D.F.C., for displaying conspicuous bravery and devotion to duty during air operations.

Act. Flight Lieut. J. I. Kilmartin, D.F.C., for destroying 12 enemy aircraft. His determination made him a fine leader.

Capt. H. M. L. Waller, Royal Australian Navy, D.S.O., for displaying conspicuous bravery and daring while on active service.

Mr. G. A. Howe, Manager of Shell-Mex, Hull, G.M., for gallantry and leadership in fighting fire at oil depot.

Fireman J. Owen, G.M., for volunteering to operate a hose on top of an almost red-hot tank.

Mr. G. Sigsworth, G.M., for displaying courage and resource during oil depot fire at Hull. He assisted Mr. Howe.

Leading Fireman C. Turner, Hull Auxiliary Fire Services, G.M., for displaying outstanding courage in extinguishing fire.

Mr. G. S. Sewell, G.M., for working continuously on a tank roof while gas inside was burning.

Sergt. J. E. Mordin, D.C.M., for holding up 8 to 11 enemy tanks, and destroying several of them.

Mr. W. J. Jenkins, A.R.P. Cyclist, G.M., for delivering messages in a raid. He was twice blown off his machine.

Col. (Act. Maj.-Gen.) J. T. Crocker, C.B.E., for gallant and distinguished services against the enemy in the field.

Flight Lieut. W. Blackwood, D.F.C., for displaying outstanding courage and devotion to duty during operations in the air.

Sergt. E. R. Weston, R.A.M.C., M.M., for assisting wounded during evacuation of the B.E.F. from the French coast.

Pilot Officer W. Cunningham, D.F.C., for destroying 5 enemy aircraft, and displaying great personal gallantry in the air.

Flying Officer L. A. Haines, D.F.C., for shooting down 7 enemy aircraft and assisting in the destruction of another.

Act. Squadron-Leader Sir Archibald Hope, D.F.C., for destroying 4 enemy aircraft. He has completed 107 operational flights.

Cadet Arthur Mitchell, Cadet Corps Gallantry Medal, for driving a blazing lorry from a bombed building.

Act. Sergt. J. Blair, D.F.M., for having flown a 'plane 350 miles after the pilot had been killed

OUR DIARY OF THE WAR

TUESDAY, OCT. 15, 1940   *409th day*

On the Sea—C.-in-C. Mediterranean reported that H.M.S. "Ajax" sank three Italian destroyers in early hours of October 12. "Ajax" suffered superficial damage and some casualties. Following these contacts Fleet was attacked by enemy aircraft, at least four of which were shot down. H.M. cruiser "Liverpool" was damaged by aerial torpedo, but reached port safely.

Successes also reported by British submarines in Mediterranean; two armed merchant ships and two enemy supply ships sunk.

Dunkirk heavily bombarded during night by forces of Royal Navy.

In the Air—Main strength of R.A.F. bomber offensive concentrated on shipping and wharves at Kiel and Hamburg. Other forces attacked enemy oil plants, goods yards, railway junctions and industrial targets. Boulogne was heavily bombed.

Coastal Command Blenheims raided Flushing and Terneuzen. Other formations bombed Lorient and Brest.

War against Italy—Reported that on night of October 13 aircraft of Fleet Air Arm successfully bombed port of Lago, Dodecanese.

R.A.F. bombers carried out further attacks on Benghazi, Bardia, Capuzzo, Derna and Tobruk.

Home Front—Many daylight attacks by enemy aircraft, mostly fighters, and air battles took place over Kent coast, Thames estuary and elsewhere. Bombs fell in S. and E. London. Confectionery factory hit.

During night raiders came over in groups and dropped oil and high explosive bombs. London school used as shelter demolished, with heavy casualties. Many other buildings in various areas hit, including block of working-class flats, hospitals and shelters.

Eighteen enemy aircraft destroyed. Britain lost 15 fighters, but pilots of nine safe.

WEDNESDAY, OCTOBER 16   *410th day*

On the Sea—Admiralty stated that German convoy of three supply ships with two escort vessels had been destroyed.

In the Air—R.A.F. carried out successful bombing operations against naval bases and docks at Kiel, where extensive fires were started, Hamburg, Bremen and Cuxhaven. Other forces attacked oil plant at Leuna, munition factories and power station in Saxony.

War against Italy—Neghelli, Abyssinia, raided by S. African Air Force, damage being done to aerodrome. During night R.A.F. attacked shipping and military targets at Benghazi and Halfaya near Sollum.

Home Front—Enemy daylight raids were slight. Bombs fell in one Scottish coastal town and at one point in West country.

Indiscriminate night bombing in London area, but less heavy than of late. Communal shelter in Liverpool suffered direct hit. Ten high-explosive bombs dropped in S.E. town; hospitals hit. Other areas attacked were in S.W. England and Wales.

Enemy lost six aircraft, Britain none.

THURSDAY, OCTOBER 17   *411th day*

On the Sea—British naval forces engaged four enemy destroyers at extreme range 100 miles south-west of Land's End, but they escaped in gathering darkness. No damage sustained by British ships.

British long-range guns shelled German E-boat in Straits of Dover.

Admiralty announced loss by enemy action of H.M. trawlers "Resolvo," "Listrac" and "Warwick Deeping," and H.M. drifter "Summer Rose."

Vice-Admiral J. C. Tovey appointed C.-in-C. Home Fleet in succession to Admiral of the Fleet Sir Charles M. Forbes.

In the Air—Coastal Command aircraft made daylight attack on power station at Brest. Owing to unfavourable weather all R.A.F. night bomber operations were cancelled.

War against Italy—S. African Air Force bombed transport concentrations at Neghelli, Abyssinia.

Home Front—Series of attacks against S.E. England made by fighters flying at great height. Large forces of our fighters engaged them and split up formations, although some penetrated to London, where few bombs fell. Others fell in Kent and damage was done to deanery and precincts at Canterbury.

During longest night raid bombs were dropped in many areas in London. Fire station annexe hit. School destroyed. Block of council flats partly demolished.

Four enemy aircraft destroyed. Britain lost three fighters.

General—Burma Road was re-opened.

FRIDAY, OCTOBER 18   *412th day*

On the Sea—Enemy trawler sunk by British patrol vessel off French coast.

In the Air—Bad weather hampered R.A.F. bombers, but night raids were made on shipyards at Kiel and Hamburg, aluminium

works at Lunen, factory at Dortmund, wharves at Duisberg, goods yards at Schwerte, Osnabruck and Dortmund.

War against Italy—S. African Air Force, operating from Sudan, successfully raided Barentu aerodrome. R.A.F. bombers attacked Gura, Diredawa, Sollum, Benghazi and Dodecanese Islands. Rhodes was bombed, direct hits being obtained on aerodrome buildings.

Home Front—Small number of single aircraft dropped bombs in S.E. England and at one place in S.E. Scotland.

During night raids on London a local museum was wrecked and a school damaged. Britain lost one fighter.

Guns in action on both sides of Straits of Dover.

General—Japanese Air Force heavily bombed key bridges on Burma Road.

SATURDAY, OCTOBER 19   *413th day*

In the Air—Owing to adverse weather conditions night bombing of enemy targets was on reduced scale. Attacks made on railway yards at Osnabruck and on aerodrome in N. Holland.

War against Italy—R.A.F. carried out successful operations against enemy objectives at Benghazi and Berka (Libya), Halfaya (near Sollum), Maritza (Dodecanese Is.), and Diredawa (Abyssinia).

Italian aircraft bombed Arab state of Saudi Arabia. Oil centre of Bahrein Island, Persian Gulf, attacked.

Home Front—Little enemy activity during day. Bombs fell in Kent and in Midlands.

Three main attacks during night—against London, Midlands and towns in North-west. Heavy bombs and incendiaries fell in London and suburbs. Two public shelters hit. Four hospitals badly damaged; medical school set on fire. Crowded café wrecked. Social centre settlement damaged. Hotel struck.

Boys' college in S.E. England badly damaged. In Midlands block of tall houses shattered, church and two chapels damaged. Merseyside town attacked. Working-class property demolished in S.E. coastal town.

Two enemy aircraft shot down.

SUNDAY, OCTOBER 20   *414th day*

On the Sea—H.M. auxiliary patrol vessel "Girl Mary" reported lost.

In the Air—R.A.F. twice raided Berlin during night. Heavy explosive and incendiary bombs were dropped and many fires caused. Other targets were naval docks at Hamburg and Wilhelmshaven, industrial works, including Krupps' at Essen, and invasion ports.

Other forces heavily attacked industrial plants at Milan, Turin and Aosta.

Admiralty announced that German seaplane base at Tromsoe had been successfully attacked by naval aircraft.

War against Italy—R.A.F. carried out successful raid on Tobruk.

Cairo bombed for first time.

Home Front—Enemy day activity mainly over S.E. England. Bombs fell in London area and in Kent and Essex. Houses on L.C.C. estate demolished. Residential area of Thames estuary town attacked. Eleven bombs caused damage in S.E. coast town.

At night raiders flew over in groups, splitting up as they neared inner zone. In London area houses and other buildings were damaged and fires started. Small Midlands town and district heavily attacked.

Seven German aircraft destroyed. Three British fighters lost, but all pilots safe.

Heavy shelling from both sides across Straits of Dover.

MONDAY, OCTOBER 21   *415th day*

On the Sea—During night of Oct. 20-21 two Italian destroyers attacked British convoy in Red Sea. One, "Francesco Nullo," was chased and sunk by H.M.S. "Kimberley," which sustained slight damage. No other British vessel suffered.

R.A.F. bomber scored direct hit on enemy destroyer in Red Sea.

In the Air—R.A.F. made daylight raids on Boulogne and Gravelines. Other aircraft attacked enemy convoy off French coast, disabling one ship. Night attack on naval dockyard at Hamburg. Other targets included oil plant at Reisholz, various industrial works and Stade aerodrome.

War against Italy—R.A.F. raided working parties and motor transport between Sollum and Buq-Buq. Attacks made on Asmara and Gura (Eritrea) and Bahar Dar and Tessenei (Italian E. Africa).

Home Front—During day enemy reached London, Midlands and N.W. England. Flats and houses struck in London and outskirts; factory hit in Lancashire and damage done at points along Channel coast.

Night raiders on London mostly driven to outer areas by A.A. fire.

Heavy attack made on Merseyside. Midland town severely damaged. Other attacks made on N.E. town and urban and country districts in S.E. England.

Four enemy aircraft destroyed.

German long-range guns fired across Straits of Dover.

Purchase Tax came into operation.

Mr. Churchill broadcast to French nation.

AGAINST EVERY ATTACK BRITAIN'S BATTLESHIPS ARE ARMED

In the last war anti-aircraft guns formed only a slight part of the equipment of British warships. Today things are different, as this photograph, taken on the starboard side of a British battleship, shows. On the right are nine 16-in. guns ready to deal with surface ships, while above is the formidable array of those anti-aircraft guns which have given enemy aircraft attacking the fleet such a hot reception as to clear the Nazi mind of the delusion that the British Navy can be sunk from the skies.

Photo, British Official : Crown Copyright

Let Us Now Count Our Victories

Winter is coming, and with winter the dark nights, the fog, the wind and the rain. But the black-out will be lightened by expectation of victory, and in the article printed below E. Royston Pike, by bidding us remember the tremendous achievements of the past year, gives us hope and encouragement for the morrow.

WE ought to have rung our church bells on October 21 ; the towers and steeples ought to have rocked with joyous pealing. Some of those bells—those selfsame bells—rang out in jubilation when Howard sent his fireships among the towering galleons in Calais harbour, and the great Armada, its cables cut in panic, lumbered northwards to be shattered on the rocky shores of the Hebrides and Ireland. They rang out again when " Boney " struck his camp at Boulogne and marched away to easier victories on the Continent. After another hundred years they rang out again, when the boasts and menaces of the Kaiser faded away into thin air. They ought to have rung when an even greater threat, an even more imminent menace, was dispelled. They ought to have rung to celebrate the defeat of Hitler's invasion plan, for though his ships (or such of them as the R.A.F. have not burned or holed) are still in the invasion ports and half-a-million men are kicking their heels in idleness, ready to cross though all unwilling, every day that goes by brings us nearer to the fogs of autumn, the winter gales. Hitler may give the order, his men may embark. (Did they actually embark on September 16 ? We may never know. But the Germans over there in their billets and tents at Calais and Boulogne, in Le Havre and Dunkirk—*they* know ; they appreciate, we may be sure, the point of Mr. Churchill's grim allusion to the fishes, and they could cap the gruesome tales which we have been told with tales more gruesome, more fearful far.) But more likely Emperor Adolf has postponed his attempt until next year—and next year may very well be never.

We ought, then, to have rung our bells, we ought to have cheered and shouted ; the batteries should have thundered, the trumpets flourished ; we ought to have toasted England (forgive an Englishman's pride), England and Victory. And what better day could we have chosen for our rejoicings than the anniversary of Nelson's crowning victory at Trafalgar—that victory which ended once and for all Napoleon's dream of invading England ?

Looking back on the year that has gone, we have no need to remind ourselves of the hard knocks which we have taken ; they have been many and heavy. But let us not forget that we have given many and heavy hard knocks in return.

One Night of Triumph

Let us recapture for a moment the feelings with which we hailed the news of that day-long chase of Hitler's " pocket-battleship " through the waters of the South Atlantic ; let us hear again the thunder of the guns of " Ajax," " Achilles," and " Exeter " as they drove the " Graf Spee " before them ; let us remember how we listened-in to the sounds that came from Montevideo on that night of amazing tragedy and extraordinary triumph, how we were thrilled when the message came through that the " Graf Spee " had sailed—we thought to meet the British cruisers waiting with grim expectancy in the mouth of the Plate, but in reality to blow herself up on a mudbank in the river.

Let us remember, too, how not only the more unregenerate amongst us were stirred by that incident which recalled the exploits of Drake in those hard-hitting, hard-living Elizabethan days ; we were with the men in the " Altmark's " holds, and our hearts like theirs leaped with joy when we heard the words, " The Navy is here."

Then with what feelings of deep anxiety we heard of those hundreds of thousands of British soldiers and their French allies struggling to the coast after fighting for days against an enemy superior in numbers and vastly superior in equipment, of their spending days and nights on the bare beaches of Dunkirk exposed to the fire of the enemy and with no protection against the raining bombs save broken breakwaters and holes burrowed in the sand. Churchill prepared us for the worst ; we knew, even if we did not admit it in so many words, that the flower of the British army was in imminent danger—if not of destruction, at least of surrender. Yet that tightest of all tight corners was passed. The men whom it seemed nothing could save were brought off from those stricken beaches by a fleet of ships great and small ; and what was undoubtedly a military disaster could yet be claimed at the same time as a miracle of deliverance.

That miracle was wrought by British sea power ; but that other and greater miracle, the defeat of Hitler's aerial onslaught on Britain, and on London in particular, has been the work of those knights of the air, the pilots and gunners of the R.A.F. When the history of our age comes to be written, three great days will stand out in the record—August 15, September 15, and September 27 —days which, to quote Mr. Churchill, " proved to all the world that here at home in our own island we have the mastery of the air." On that day in mid-August, the day chosen by Hitler for his triumphal entry into London where he would dictate the terms of his victory, the Germans hurled hundreds of bombers and fighters against objectives in all parts of the country. All day there was tremendous air fighting over

Such little ships as those above, photographed in convoy in the Channel from an escorting destroyer, have done their full share with the bigger ships in ensuring that the 45,000,000 souls of these isles do not go hungry. Left, Mr. Churchill, during his tour of the Scottish defences at the end of October, looks out over the North Sea knowing that, thanks to the Navy, it is " all clear."
     Photos, P.N.A. and " Daily Mirror "

We Have had Bright Days—and Brighter Are to Come

The Royal Air Force has been Britain's first line of defence against the invaders, the Royal Navy the second, while for any ships or barges that might sneak across the Channel there are waiting on every mile of the sea coast and on the shores of every estuary such doughty defenders as these with their Tommy guns, ready to mow down every man who struggles through the surf.
Photo, Fox

the Channel, and shortly after midnight it was announced that in the course of the day's fighting the R.A.F. had "clawed down" from the air 180 of the German raiders. September 15—that was the eve of the day which, if reports speak truly, Hitler had chosen for his invasion day; it was the day on which, again to quote Mr. Churchill, "The R.A.F., aided by squadrons of their Czech and Polish comrades, cut to rags and tatters three separate waves of murderous assault upon the civilian population of their native land, inflicting a certain loss of 125 bombers and 53 fighters." Mr. Churchill was too moderate, for the official figure was given later as 185. Then on September 27 Goering tried again for the third time; hundreds of 'planes crossed the Kent coast in wave after wave, but of those hundreds only a score or two reached London. The whole of south-eastern England was littered with the refuse of broken Nazis; and when the day closed the careful statisticians at the Air Ministry added another 135 Germans to their score.

The battle is still joined. German raiders still keep us awake o'nights, but the "star-spangled thug," as Mr. Priestley has dubbed Field-Marshal Hermann, knows better now than to send over his massed squadrons during the hours of daylight. On the seas the Royal Navy has to counter not only the Nazi raiders and U-boats but the speedy ships of Mussolini's fleet; occasionally those ships' speed fails to save them, and if the Duce, seated in his great room at the Palazzo Venezia, calls on Monday mornings for the list of his fleet, he must run his pencil through the names of "Bartolomeo Colleoni," "Artigliere," of ten destroyers

and twenty-one submarines. If he wants them he will find them at the bottom of the Mediterranean, where we may be sure they will soon be joined by others.

On land here in Britain we have the greatest army that Britain has ever seen, waiting for the onslaught of the invader; in Egypt we have another army, nothing like so big but still filled with picked troops—Britons and Australians, New Zealanders, Tasmanians, who are waiting to cross swords with Graziani's columns when they have struggled along the desert road. Hundreds of thousands more are in Palestine, the Sudan and Kenya, in South Africa, in Canada, and the Indies, in Australia and New Zealand. They are the fighting men of the Empire; and if you want to know how they will fight when the moment comes, then there is no need to see what the history books tell of Crecy and Agincourt, of Blenheim and Fontenoy, of Albuera and Waterloo and Balaclava. There are plenty of men left alive who bear record to what was done on the bullet-strewn slopes of Gallipoli, the shell-torn wastes of the Somme.

Still there is another victory to record, the greatest of all. Even in peacetime there is surely no greater miracle than the existence in this tiny island of 45,000,000 people maintaining themselves at a high standard of life and culture. Think of the nice adjustment of means to ends, of the multitudinous variety of needs and their satisfaction; think of the intricate machinery of production and distribution, of buying and selling, of all the work involved in filling 45,000,000 hungry bellies, in clothing 45,000,000 backs, in

providing house room for 45,000,000 people of every social class and economic circumstance. This is a great achievement in peacetime, but how much greater in time of war, when Britain, so the Nazis boast, is a beleaguered island! Yet despite all that the U-boats and the mines, the surface raiders and the bombing 'planes, have been able to do, 45,000,000 British folk have lived, continue to live, and will live, within the shores of the island that is their home.

During the last war we faced starvation more than once; in this war we have not yet been near it, though maybe we shall have to face it before peace comes. We are spending ten millions a day; we are shouldering a burden which the economists of only yesterday would have held to be impossible; the standard of living of the great mass of our people is hardly, if at all, lower than it was before the war—indeed, in many cases it is higher, and rightly so.

So far from being a beleaguered island, we are an armed fortress, strong in our own strength and drawing reinforcements from every corner of the globe. In the last twelve months we have been baffled often, beaten sometimes, but despairing never. Through the streets, at the height of the Battle of London, drive the wedding cars with their bits of white ribbon, dodging the bomb holes and heaps of rubbish, and the book on which the young people plight their troth is damp with the water of the firemen's hose. No, we are not beaten yet—and " naught shall make us rue . . ."—but we all know that line of Shakespeare, if no other.

The Bully of Rome Strikes At Little Greece

On the 18th anniversary of Mussolini's so-called march on Rome, Fascist Italy delivered
an altogether unprovoked attack on Greece. So the war came to the Balkans—in part,
at least, because the Axis Powers had been unable to bring the Battle of Britain to a
successful conclusion—and the left arm of the pincers (see page 422) is extended to
keep pace with the right in Egypt.

A T 3 a.m. on October 28 the Italian
Minister in Athens, Signor Grazzi,
handed to General Metaxas, the
Dictator-Premier of Greece, an ultimatum
in which the Italian Government accused the
Greek Government of having allowed its
territorial waters and its coasts and ports to
be used by the British Fleet during war
operations, of having favoured the supplies
to the " alien British forces," and having
allowed the British Secret Service to organize
a service of military information in the Greek
Archipelago. It also referred to the " ter-
rorist policy " that had been adopted towards
the population of Ciamuria (the region in
northern Greece which was annexed from
Albania in 1913) and of the continued
attempts to create disorder in the Albanian
frontier zone. " All these provocations
cannot possibly be tolerated any longer by
Italy. Hence the Italian Government has
reached the decision to require the Greek
Government as a guarantee of its neutrality
and of Italian security to allow the Italian
forces to occupy for the duration of the
present conflict with Great Britain certain
strategic points on Greek territory." The
Greek Government was further asked not
to oppose this occupation, but if the Italian
troops did encounter resistance, then this,
it was stated, would be met by force of arms.
General Metaxas was swift with his reply.

He asked "What points ? " and when Grazzi
said he did not know, the Greek Premier
rejoined that he regarded the ultimatum as
a declaration of war by Italy against Greece.
The Italian Minister rejoined with a statement that the Italian troops would begin to
march at 6 o'clock.

In fact, the Italian military forces began
their invasion of Greece at about that time,
when the frontier from Albania was crossed
in several places. The army of invasion was
drawn from Italy's army of 200,000 men in
Albania, and the main thrusts were aimed
eastwards across the mountains towards
Florina and south in the direction of Janina.
The Greeks fought desperately in the
mountain passes to bar their passage, and
at one point they actually invaded Albania.
At the same time Italian troops were
reported to have landed on some of the
Greek islands in the Aegean Sea, and their
warplanes bombed the harbour of Athens,
the Corinth Canal, and other military
objectives.

Soon after King George of Greece and
General Metaxas had signed orders for a
general mobilization, they issued messages
to the Greek people. " At this great
moment," said King George, " I am sure
that every Greek man and woman will do
their duty to the end and will show themselves
worthy of the glorious history of Greece,"

**King George of the Hellenes is here seen with
General Metaxas, President of the Greek
Council. The King's grandfather was a
brother of our Queen Alexandra.**
Photo, Wide World

while General Metaxas urged the nation to
stand up and fight for Fatherland, wives and
children, and sacred traditions—to show
" whether we are truly worthy of our
ancestors and of the freedom won for us

King George VI to King George of Greece :
A message sent on October 28.

In this hour of Greece's need I wish to say to
the heroic Greek nation and to my cousin
George, King of the Hellenes, this :

We are with you in this struggle ; your cause
is our cause ; we shall be fighting against a
common foe.

There are doubtless hard trials to be borne,
but we shall both meet them in the firm faith
that ultimate victory is assured by the ever-
increasing strength of the free peoples

We may hope, indeed, that we are already
near the turn of the tide, when the power of
the aggressor will begin to ebb and our own
growing might to prevail.

Long live Greece and her leaders ; long live
the King of the Hellenes.

**Mr. Churchill to the President of the Greek
Council, General Metaxas :**

Italy has found threats and intimidation of no
avail against your calm courage. She has
therefore resorted to unprovoked aggression
against your coutrny, seeking justification for a
wanton attack in baseless accusations.

The way in which the Greek people, under
your trusted leadership, have faced the dangers
and provocations of recent months has gained
for Greece the admiration of the British people ;
the same qualities will uphold them in their
present hour of trial.

We will give you all the help in our power.

We fight a common foe and we will share a
united victory.

**This contour map of Greece, Albania, Bulgaria, and Turkey suggests the mountainous nature of
the country in which the fighting must take place. Italy is anxious to obtain bases from which
naval operations against the British Navy could be conducted in the Eastern Mediterranean, and
in particular her desire is to occupy Corfu and some of the islands between Greece and Crete
and off the coast of Turkey.**
Courtesy of the " Evening Standard"

by our forefathers." He concluded with the
words used by the Greeks on the eve of the
battle of Salamis in B.C. 480 : " Now above
all the battle."

Early in the day the Greek Government
sent an appeal to Britain to honour the
guarantee given on April 13, 1939. Speaking

Over the Balkans Break the Clouds of War

Greece has six Infantry divisions ; a typical infantryman is seen left at the " present." As for its air arm, the Greek air force comprises approximately 150 to 200 first-line but not all modern aircraft. A biplane bomber is seen above at the Tatoi aerodrome, near Athens.

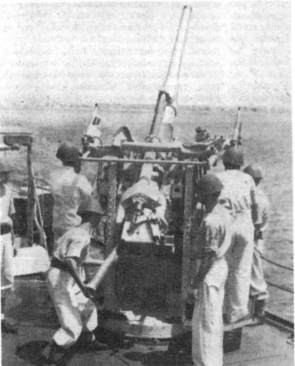

On the left is seen an anti-aircraft gun crew on board the coastal defence ship " Giorgios Averoff." This ship is an armoured cruiser of 9,300 tons and was refitted in France in 1927. Above, Greek troops with a machine-gun.

Two Greek destroyers belonging to the " Hydra " class are viewed from the deck of the " Averoff." These ships have a displacement of 1,350 tons with a complement of 156. They carry six 21-in. torpedo tubes and forty mines. For some years past a series of British naval missions have been in charge of Greek naval training and organization.

Photos, Wide World, Keystone, Planet News

With the Navy Britain Honours Her Pledge

An extensive view of Salonika, famous seaport of Greece. In 1915 when Greece asked Great Britain and France to reinforce her army with 150,000 troops, the Allies landed forces at Salonika during the campaign against the Bulgarians, and the town was held as a base for subsequent operations.

in the House of Commons on that day, Mr. Neville Chamberlain, then Prime Minister, had said that, " His Majesty's Government attach the greatest importance to the avoidance of disturbance by force or threats of force, of the status quo in the Mediterranean and the Balkan Peninsula. Consequently they have come to the conclusion that in the event of any action being taken which clearly threatened the independence of Greece or Rumania, and which the Greek or Rumanian Government respectively considered it vital to resist with their national forces, H.M. Government would feel themselves bound at once to lend the Greek or Rumanian Government, as the case might be, all the support in their power." Rumania succumbed to Axis pressure in September, 1940, but when it came to Greece's turn she chose the path of resistance largely, no doubt, because as a nation with a large seaboard and with many maritime connexions, she realized the immense weight that could be developed by Britain's sea power. So it was that on October 28 she asked for assistance, chiefly air and naval, and within a few hours this was being rendered.

Without that assistance Greece's position might be fairly considered to be far from happy. Her army is not, perhaps, much inferior in numbers to the Italian, but it cannot be called first class, lacking as it does modern equipment ; but if it is not mechanized to any extent, it must be remembered that Greece is a mountainous country with few roads where mechanized forces would possess no great advantage, while the Greek soldier enjoys the reputation of being the best marcher in Europe. The army is organized in four Army Corps with their headquarters at Athens, Larissa, Salonika, and Cavalla, and comprises thirteen infantry divisions and one cavalry division ; in peacetime its effective strength was some 70,000, but in wartime it is capable of being so expanded that 2,000,000 men may be called to the colours. But the Greek Air Force consists of only 150 to 200 'planes of all classes and is not to be compared, therefore, with Italy's more than 2,000 aircraft in the first line.

The disparity is even more marked in the matter of fleets. Italy is usually classed fifth among the great naval powers, but against the four battleships and 19 cruisers which she had in 1939, Greece can oppose only one large ship, the 30-year-old armoured cruiser " Georgios Averoff." She had two, but the converted mine-laying cruiser "Helle" was torpedoed by a submarine—no doubt an Italian—on August 15 last when lying at anchor off the island of Tinos. She possesses, however, a flotilla of smaller ships—10 destroyers, 11 torpedo boats, 4 motor torpedo boats, and 6 submarines, which should prove useful. But here, again, Italy possessed a year ago 82 destroyers and torpedo boats and 80 submarines, and both classes have recently been considerably increased. As regards personnel, the Greeks are a seafaring race and the quality of their seamanship is high.

Corfu, above, the little island belonging to Greece which the Italians covet as a naval base. It is forty miles in length. Left, standing on the lofty Acropolis, we see Athens spreading away in picturesque confusion to the Lycabetes Hill.
Photos, Fox and Ronesi

The Old and the Bold—the Young and the Brave

Left, Jack Potter, 55-year-old father of seven children, is twice armed, with hoe and rifle ; he was one of the first to enlist in the Home Guard. Above, Girl Guides, from 12 to 16, act as messengers for the Home Guard.

Mounted men of the Home Guard patrol wide stretches of country. Here one of them, his horse well used to the crack of the rifle, pots an imaginary parachutist.

The ramparts (circle) were once part of the Roman defences of Britain ; now, 1,600 years later, Home Guards find a new use for them. A special course of training on an estate in the Home Counties has helped to make the Home Guard an efficient military force ; commanders and section leaders are given a course in static defence and guerilla warfare in order to train their own units. Here they are seen practising throwing dummy grenades ; centre, right, they are attending a lecture on the art of bomb-throwing.

Photos, " The Times " and " Daily Mirror "

The Fight For France's Soul Goes On

While in Britain the air war went on, while in America Roosevelt and Willkie duelled
for the Presidency, while in the Balkans Italy launched her divisions against Greece
in France a fight went on between the defeatists and intriguers of the Laval clique and
those who believed in spite of all that France would rise again.

OF all the unhappy peoples of Europe
the French are perhaps the most
unhappy. After centuries of military
greatness, after fighting innumerable wars in
which, though sometimes defeated, they have
more often than not been victorious, Frenchmen today find themselves not only defeated
on the field of battle, but so crushed that
their Government seems to make a virtue of
national sacrifice, to wallow in humiliation.

After being defeated in one of the shortest
campaigns in modern history—if we reckon
from May 10, the date of the launching of
the German offensive, to June 17 when Pétain
asked for an Armistice, it lasted but thirty-
nine days—France is left helpless before the
traditional enemy from beyond the Rhine.
She is defenceless ; she is the helpless prey
of the victor. Things have come to such a
pass, indeed, that the possibility of France
declaring war on Britain—her old ally, her
co-victor in the Great War, her partner in
the *Entente cordiale*—is not to be ruled out.
It is seriously suggested that at Hitler's
command Frenchmen will fight side by side
with the men whom their fathers called the
" dirty Boches," against the soldiers and
sailors of a country which, as likely as not,
would not have been at war today if it had
not been for the disastrously mistaken and
short-sighted policies followed by the French
governments since the Armistice of 1918.

But on this side of the Channel we find it
difficult to believe that the soul of France can

Even in unoccupied France, the Pétain government has decreed that French children shall no
longer be educated in the old ideals of France. Here in a village school near Vichy the teacher
has written on the blackboard the words " Fatherland, Family, and Labour," which are now to
replace the former French watchword, " Liberty, Equality, Fraternity."   *Photo, " New York Times "*

Eighty-four-year-old Marshal Pétain is here walking with Admiral
Darlan, who was appointed to command the French Fleet at the outbreak of war and won high honour for his capacity in the evacuation
of Dunkirk. Following Oran, however, he was said to favour handing
over the French fleet to the Nazis.   *Photo, Planet News*

be so moribund, so well-nigh dead ; and it was in the hope of
reawakening the dormant spirit of France that Mr. Churchill
broadcast on October 21 to the French people.

" *C'est moi, Churchill, qui parle,*" was his dramatic opening ; " Frenchmen, for more than thirty years in peace and war I have marched with
you, and I am marching still along the same road. Tonight I speak to
you at your firesides wherever you may be or whatever your fortunes are.
I repeat that prayer round the Louis d'Or, ' God protect France.'

" Here at home in England," continued the Premier, " under the fire of
the Boche, we do not forget the ties and links that unite us to France,"
and he went on to say how important it was that " when good people get
into trouble because they are attacked and heavily smitten by the vile and
wicked they must be very careful not to get at loggerheads with one another."
He spoke of the common enemy who is always trying to bring this about ;
he reminded his listeners, too, that here in Britain we are still waiting for
the long-promised invasion and—a grim touch this—" so are the fishes."

He spoke of Hitler who, with his tanks and other mechanized weapons
and Fifth Column intrigues with traitors, has managed to subjugate for
the time being most of the finest races in Europe, while his " little Italian
accomplice trots along hopefully and hungrily, but rather wearily and very
timidly, at his side."

" They both wish to carve up France and her Empire as if it was a fowl.
To one a leg, to another a wing or, again, a portion of the breast. Not only
the French Empire will be devoured by these two ugly customers, but
Alsace Lorraine will go once again under the German yoke, and Nice,
Savoy, and Corsica—Napoleon's Corsica—will be torn from the fair realm
of France. But Herr Hitler is not thinking only of stealing other people's
territory or flinging gobbets of them to his little dog. I tell you truly, what
you must believe ; this evil man, this monstrous abortion of hatred and
deceit, is resolved on nothing less than the complete wiping out of the
French nation and the disintegration of its whole life and future."

" Excuse my speaking frankly," he said, " but this is not a time to
mince words. It is not defeat that France will be made to suffer at German
hands, but the doom of complete obliteration. Frenchmen," he called,
" re-arm your spirits before it is too late ! Never will I believe that the
soul of France is dead or that her place among the greatest nations of the
world has been lost for ever." Then came a last encouraging word. " Good-
night, then. Sleep and gather strength for the morning—for the morning
will come. Vive la France ! Long live also the forward march of the
common people in all the lands towards their just and true inheritance,
towards the better time."

So spoke France's old ally, not in siren tones of blandishment,
but forthright, resolute and brave. France's enemy also made his
appeal. We do not know what he said, but we know something
of what he did. We know that for weeks past he has been intrigu-
ing with that sinister figure, Pierre Laval. We know that the two

'Collaboration' Cloaks the Shame of Surrender

Drawing by Illingworth, by permission of "The Daily Mail."

met on October 22 and that following the meeting it was announced that France was definitely out of the war and was willing to collaborate with Germany in post-war reconstruction. After his meeting near Paris with Laval, the Fuehrer went on to Hendaye, facing the Spanish frontier in the Pyrenees, and in his special railway carriage had two conferences with General Franco, head (*Caudillo*) of the Spanish state. The conversations, it was announced, were conducted in the " cordial spirit of comradely friendship that unites the two nations."

On his way home Hitler met Pétain somewhere in occupied France and, said Vichy, " the interview took place in an atmosphere of great courtesy. The Marshal was received with the honours due to his rank." The two chiefs made a general examination of the situation, and agreement was reached on their collaboration in the reconstruction of Europe. What was agreed upon was left to be surmised, but from many quarters there came reports of the terms which, it was stated, had been presented to Pétain, and which he had or had not accepted. These terms were said to be as follows : Alsace and Lorraine to be ceded to Germany, and Nice to Italy. Tunis to be divided between France and Italy, and a portion of Morocco to go to Spain. France to cede Indo-China to Japan, and the French Colonies to be placed under a triple mandate exercised by France, Germany and Italy. French prisoners-of-war, numbering 1,800,000, to be liberated, and certain industrial and economic concessions made to France to enable her to return to normal conditions. Then one report had it that the French forces in North Africa and Syria should be used to " protect the Italian flank," while another stated that France would be required to place her Mediterranean fleet and air force stationed in North Africa at the disposal of the Axis for use against Britain.

This, then, constituted Hitler's bid for France's soul—and body. While Pétain was still hesitating, King George sent a personal

message to him. He declared that the British people were in good heart and were determined to fight until victory had been won, and that in the benefits of that victory France should share. Any other outcome of the battle would mean France's eclipse. Meanwhile, the British people looked with sympathy on the ordeal through which the French were passing, and trusted that these difficult days would not be made more difficult by any act on the part of the French Government.

President Roosevelt also made his contribution, but in his case it was more of a warning than an appeal. In a Note which Mr. Cordell Hull handed to the French Ambassador in Washington it was stated in frank but friendly language that the military " collaboration " of France with the Axis Powers might precipitate the occupation of Martinique and French Guiana by the

American Republics, in accordance with the decisions come to at the Havana Conference in July, 1940.

Then a communiqué was issued in London on behalf of General de Gaulle and his movement of Free Frenchmen. " We cannot believe," it ran, " that Hitler will find a single Frenchman who will willingly consent to the mutilation and subjugation of his native country," and it concluded by saying that " more than ever the Free French Forces proclaim their resolution to continue our fight at the side of the Allies in order to save the honour and the integrity of the country, together with that civilization for which France has been, and must remain, the torch-bearer." There, surely, spoke the true France.

A street in Vichy seen through a pastrycook's window. This shop was once well-known for its apple tarts, but today it exhibits a tray of sweetened toast.

Comfortably seated in a hotel bar at Vichy, Laval, Vice-Premier and Foreign Minister, is holding forth on the future of France, while Flandin, who was Prime Minister in 1934, listens dejectedly. Marquet, Minister for the Interior, is on the right.   *Photos, E.N.A.*

Bombed Out! Blasted Out! But Not Bowled Out!

THE photographs in this page are but a few examples of the typical British humour that has been in this war, as it was in the last, a factor of incalculable value in keeping up the morale of the people. Owners of shops, boarding houses, cinemas, and many other premises only just able to do business, have met tragedy with a smile and have invited continued patronage with an ingenious humour that will surely have its reward.

Photos, Central Press, Fox, B.I.F., Photopress, L.N.A., "News Chronicle"

Victory in the Air Battle of Britain is Assured

Not only, as Capt. Harold Balfour, M.P., declared, can we weld together determination and confidence to hold our present air position, but we also have, as the Premier said on October 21, the assurance that before many months are passed we shall have command of the air. Meantime the battle of London and Britain continues.

STATEMENTS by two members of the Government during the third week of October confirmed the British people in their confidence of ultimate victory in the war in the air. First came the assurance from the Premier, in his broadcast to the French people on the evening of October 21, that " in 1941 we shall have command of the air." Two days after the Under-Secretary for Air (Capt. Harold Balfour, M.P.) said in a speech that, looking at the air battle of Britain, we could weld our hard—nay, fierce—determination with resolute confidence at the position we held today.

Finally, in a broadcast on October 24, Air Marshal Sir Philip Joubert spoke of new developments in hand to improve the performance of our Hurricanes and Spitfires, which would be faster, climb higher, and be more heavily armed than those we had been using up to date. Moreover, we had on the stocks several types of newer and better fighters which should be as much an improvement on present types as these latter were upon their predecessors.

Dealing with our attack upon Germany, Sir Philip said that the most satisfactory feature was the increase in our bombing effort. We could hope from now steadily to increase our pressure on Germany and on her ally, and by next spring, when the flow of American aircraft, already very considerable, became a flood, we should return to Germany with sevenfold interest the bombing that we had had to endure.

As a result of the enemy's raids on Tuesday, October 22, he lost three aircraft; we lost six and two of our pilots were saved. This is a measure of the drastic change in the

GERMAN & BRITISH AIRCRAFT LOSSES
German to April 30, 1940

Total announced and estimated—West Front, North Sea, Britain, Scandinavia 350

	German	British
May	1,990	258
June	276	177
July	245	115
Aug.	1,110	310
Sept.	1,114	311
Oct. 1-28	199	107
Totals, May to Oct. 28 ...	**4,934**	**1,278**

Daily Results

Oct.	German Losses	British Losses	British Pilots Saved	Oct.	German Losses	British Losses	British Pilots Saved
1	5	3	—	16	6	—	—
2	13	1	—	17	4	3	—
3	1	—	—	18	—	1	—
4	3	1	—	19	2	—	—
5	23	9	4	20	7	3	3
6	2	—	—	21	5	—	—
7	28	16	10	22	3	6	2
8	0	2	—	23	1	—	—
9	4	1	1	24	2	—	—
10	5	5	2	25	17	10	7
11	8	9	6	26	6	2	—
12	12	10	6	27	10	8	4
13	2	2	2	28	2	—	—
14	—	—	—				
15	18	15	9	**Totals**	**199**	**107**	**56**

None of the figures includes aircraft bombed on the ground or so damaged as to be unlikely to reach home.

From the beginning of the war up to Oct. 28, 2,722 enemy aircraft have been destroyed during raids on Britain. R.A.F. losses were 776, but the pilots of 382 British machines were saved.

Civilian Casualties. Intensive air attacks on Britain began on Aug. 8. Casualties during August, 1,075 killed, 1,261 seriously injured. During September : 6,954 killed ; 10,615 seriously injured.

Mass Raid Casualties in London. Sept. 7 : 305 killed ; 1,337 injured. Sept. 8 : 286 killed ; about 1,400 injured. Sept. 9 : about 400 killed, 1,400 injured.

Nazi policy, referred to in a previous article. The scale of the enemy attacks was considerably reduced and, risking fewer of his machines, he lost less. Single aircraft made a few raids on Tuesday morning and afternoon ; in the evening a larger force—though small compared with those used on many previous occasions—flew inland a little way, but was then chased out of the sky by our fighters, and two raiders crashed. Combats took place very high in the air and the enemy was obliged to go ever to a higher altitude to find safety. On the other hand, individual raiders sneaked down lower when they saw a chance. That same evening a fighter-bomber swooped down on to a bus climbing a steep Kentish hill. His machine-gun bullets fell near but did no harm. In London the night alert was over by midnight.

On Wednesday again the enemy raids did little damage either in London or elsewhere. After dusk a number of raiders glided in over the London area and dropped bombs, but because of the bad weather over the Channel and the accurate fire of our A.A. guns they found it almost impossible to reach their objectives. In the Home Counties and the London area houses were wrecked and people killed and injured by this aimless night bombing. The west of Scotland had what was perhaps the worst raid of the war, and there were attacks on places in Southern Scotland and on Merseyside. Among miraculous escapes was that of a baby found alive on top of the wreckage of a cottage in which its parents and three other persons had been killed.

In daylight raids on Thursday the Germans lost two Dornier-17 bombers—one shot down in the sea off the Kent coast and the other crashing at Eaton Socon, near St. Neots. Single raiders flew over the London district

All the six firemen in the photograph (left) sustained minor injuries in a raid on the night of October 25, but they kept smiling. The drivers and conductors of the London omnibuses and tramcars have carried on with commendable courage during raids, though the noise of their vehicles makes it wellnigh impossible for them to know when enemy 'planes are overhead. Now spotters are stationed at certain points, who tell the drivers whether it is safe to proceed. Right, one of them is giving directions.

Photos, Planet News, Central Press

Women Tore Up their Clothing for Tramcar Victims

During a daylight raid on London streets early on October 25, Nazi raiders, aiming maybe at a railway bridge, found a target in these tramcars crowded with city workers, which were halted at traffic lights.
Photo, Fox

The freakish effect of high explosive bombs is well shown in the photograph below. The front of the building has been completely cut off, but in each flat the kitchen range and gas stove are left standing intact.
Photo, Sport & General

and over places in Kent, Hampshire and Somerset, but the attacks were still on a small scale. At night larger numbers took part, but the raids, though widespread, were light. Wards were wrecked at a London children's hospital, but the children had been removed and there was only a skeleton staff in attendance. No one was seriously hurt. Fires were caused in a Midland town, and some damage to buildings at other places. The number of casualties throughout the country was " exceedingly small " said the official communiqué.

At dawn on Friday, October 25, an enemy machine dive-bombed a place on the outskirts of London. Six bombs fell and houses were wrecked. A little later came an Alert in the London district, when a large enemy force attacked several suburbs. A line of tramcars checked at traffic signals during the rush hours was bombed ; two were hit. Buses alongside them also felt the effect of blast and splinters. Women tore up clothing to provide first aid dressings for injured travellers. London Transport workers got the route clear again in a few hours. Elsewhere in the Metropolis a church was damaged by a bomb that fell near. The raiders flew very high in their approach, and our defences forced them to climb higher still as they made off, unloading their missiles with little attempt at aiming. The Nazi aircraft were said to have numbered about 400, attacking in formations of twenty to 100.

Night raids by single enemy aircraft began early on Friday; many fire bombs being dropped on the outskirts of London and in the Home Counties. An unscreened light is said to have attracted one raider. A famous London square was one of the places attacked. A Scottish train was machine-gunned, but kept on its way and there were

no casualties. A German communiqué announced in the usual pompous style that Italian airmen had been over Britain, and a Rome report said that 200 had taken part.

Beginning at dawn on Saturday, Oct. 26, raids by small Nazi formations of fighters and fighter-bombers continued throughout the day. A bomb which fell in a crowded London shopping centre killed six persons ; shops and flats above were demolished. Places in S.E. England and in the Midlands also were bombed. On Saturday night more London hospitals and churches were bombed. A stoker was killed in the boiler house of one hospital. A direct hit on a public house buried a number of people, and others in a car outside were killed. At an orphanage of which the chapel was damaged by a bomb there were no casualties among babies in a dormitory or older children at supper, but one of the sisters was injured. A heavy attack was made on a Midland town, and places in South-eastern England suffered also.

In a rather " breezy " bulletin describing Sunday's daylight raids the Air Ministry said that the German air force " continued to fidget about over the South of England " ; some of the Messerschmitts were " almost playful in their behaviour." Twenty of them, " milling about 20,000 feet above Surrey," formed into two sections and made dummy dive-attacks on each other. Then two broke off and dived steeply down in front of the Hurricanes as a further decoy. Bombs were dropped in the London area and at places in South-east England. Casualties were few.

The Air Ministry described Sunday night's raids as widespread but less severe, and spoke of a very quiet night in London. Many flares were dropped by the Nazis. There were raids on Merseyside, the Midlands and East Anglia.

Little Orphans the Nazis Nearly Killed

Photo, Fox

When towards the end of October a German bomb struck a Roman Catholic orphanage in London forty babies, sleeping in a dormitory less than fifteen yards from where the bomb exploded, and a number of boys who were having supper, were unhurt. The bomb crashed on the orphanage chapel, where the Sister Superior and three other sisters were saying prayers. The children had been put to bed just before the bomb hit the building. Here are some of them playing happily against a background of wreckage.

As They Were and As They Are: Holland House a

Holland House, Lord Ilchester's Jacobean mansion in Kensington and the last of London's great country houses, was bombed by Nazi airmen in October, so that all but the east wing is an empty shell. Above, as it was ; on the right, as it is today.

The Temple, one of the loveliest parts of old London, has been bombed several times of recent weeks, so that the quiet courts which Lamb and Dickens knew so well and loved are now littered with broken masonry. Even the old brick faces of the surviving houses are covered with bomb-raised dust.

O NE by one the great landmarks are being damaged or destroyed by the bombs showered upon the Metropolis by Hitler's airmen. In this page we illustrate two of the more recent victims—Holland House, one of England's greatest literary shrines, and for generations associated with men and women imbued with the liberal spirit, and the Temple, home of the legal fraternity and a peaceful relic of the olden time set between the bustle of Fleet Street and the Embankment with its clanging trams. After the war many of the fallen buildings will be reconstructed or rebuilt, but nothing can restore the grace and charm of the houses and churches, halls and streets, which were hallowed by so many associations and bore on their faces the patina of so many centuries.

Generally considered to be the finest of the ancient buildings in the Tem so that the magnificent carved minstrels' gallery, a gem of Tudor woodw 1576—and the other made from the timbers of Dr

Temple Bombed by Hitler's Huns

Up this fine staircase walked generations of great writers and talkers—Addison and Samuel Rogers, Charles James Fox and Macaulay. Now, alas! it has been damaged beyond repair by Nazi bombs.

nple Hall has now been largely wrecked. As a comparison of the two photographs on the right will show, a huge hole has been made in one end of the Hall, letely destroyed. Fortunately, the vaulted roof still stands and the two famous tables one given by Queen Elizabeth—it was she who opened the Hall in 1" were untouched. It was in the Middle Temple Hall that the first performance of Shakespeare's "Twelfth Night" was given in 1602.

ktus, H. N. King, "*The Times.*" *Keystone, W. F. Taylor and Wide World*

Bombs On Berlin—And Berliners Do Care!

London is much more in the front line than Berlin—at present, at least—but it is good
to know that the German capital is being visited to an ever-increasing extent by the
young men of the R.A.F. Here are some details of the raids of recent nights.

"Bombs on Berlin ? Never ! " That, up to only a few weeks ago, would have been the instant reaction of the German man in the street to the suggestion that the R.A.F. might drop bombs on Berlin just as the Luftwaffe was dropping bombs on London.

" That is quite out of the question," the German might have added. " Our Goering has given us the most definite assurances that Berlin cannot be and will not be bombed." In the last war Berlin was never raided from the air, nor did the British and French stage a victory march down the Unter den Linden ; so far from expecting their capital to be bombed, the Berliners, up to the beginning of last September, hardly gave a thought to the possibility of being raided. What they did expect was to see Herr Hitler emerge

we have six times as much chance of encountering bad weather. We may have dropped fewer bombs on Berlin, but they are better aimed."

Now that the nights are lengthening fast the R.A.F. is able to spend longer over Berlin's roof-tops, and very soon the Berliners may have to become reconciled to spending the whole of the night in the basements and cellars beneath the great apartment buildings. (Even so they will be quite as comfortable as on the stone floor of a London tube.) Already by 9 p.m. Berlin's streets are emptied as the crowds hurry to their shelters or make for buses and trains. By ten o'clock the city is dead, almost the only people out being the policemen.

One of the longest raids to date was made on the night of Sunday, October 20. A

Germans ; many of them even had their cockpit lights on."

" I was 200 yards away while the bombardment of this district was going on," he proceeded. " Many incendiary bombs and two bombs of the heaviest calibre fell in this district, the two H.E. missiles hitting a building and a street. Afterwards, I found a scene of great destruction. Men, women, and children were carrying their possessions away while rescue workers were recovering bodies from the debris. About 20 people were killed or wounded."

The All-Clear went ·at 4 o'clock on that Monday morning. Then for a few nights, owing to the foul weather, the Berliners were able to sleep in peace. But on Thursday, October 24, they had their longest warning. The All-Clear signal was not given until 7 a.m., and as they emerged from their retreats they saw flames lighting a great sector on the horizon. Of course, on this occasion as on every other, the Nazi propagandist bureau maintained that the British attack had been altogether ineffective ; the raiders had hit residential districts, workers' housing estates and bungalows. But the pilots' story was different. Their orders were to attack military objectives—the great railway stations, the goods yards, the gas works and electricity stations, the munition factories, and so on. There are plenty of these targets in the compact Berlin area—but there are now not quite so many as there used to be.

The Nazi authorities did their best to make the bitter pill of an admission that Berlin is not a safe area a little less unpalatable to the people by evacuating children (above), to the accompaniment of brass bands and the waving of swastika flags. Those who remained behind, however, saw many such proofs of the activities of the R.A.F., as the crater in a Berlin street seen on the right.
Photos, Associated Press

from the Chancellery on his way to the Tempelhof Aerodrome, there to take his victorious flight to London.

But if we could buttonhole a Berliner now he would have a very different story to tell. He might be angry, but more likely he would be disgusted, miserable, and fed up. He has had a taste of the medicine which he thought so appropriate for the Poles and the Belgians, the Dutch and the French, and, most of all, of course, for the wicked Englanders.

A high official of the R.A.F. in London stated that " We have now visited Berlin on fourteen separate nights since the beginning of September, with a total of 225 sorties by individual machines. In all we have already dropped over 200 tons of bombs on Berlin.

" Our difficulties are greater than those of the enemy," went on the R.A.F. spokesman. " London is only 100 miles from the nearest German bomber aerodrome and Berlin is 600 miles away from ours. That means that

graphic account of it was sent from Berlin by the correspondent of the Swedish paper, the " Stockholm Aftonbladet." " The attack was terrific," he said ; " I saw a principal street in a district inhabited chiefly by doctors, lawyers, and civil servants suddenly turned into a burning inferno. Bombs, shrapnel, glass, and stones came raining down. Houses were cut in half as though with a huge knife. As usual, the R.A.F. displayed great courage in face of the thick and fast anti-aircraft fire of the

How Our Airmen Fly in Attack and Defence

Interval

Vee Flight

Distance

Flight Line astern

Close up

Flight Line abreast

Open — I repeat, Open — Go

Flight Line abreast — Right up.

Flight Star

Flight Line astern — Up

Though every airman must fight and fly as an individual, the closest coordination is necessary when Flights and Squadrons go into action. Pilots are taught to take off, fly, manoeuvre and fight as a single unit, and the strictest orders are given and obeyed regarding the intervals and distances separating the aircraft when operating as Flights and Squadrons. This spacing of machines is planned so that the maximum protection is secured for each member of the unit. A closely packed, well-led flight can ward off onslaughts made by enemy machines from any direction and counter-attack with devastating effect. By unified action a fighter formation can break up an enemy bomber formation.

Top centre a fighter-flight in " V " formation ; in centre of page Fairey Battles in **Flight Line Abreast**. Below them, four Hurricanes in **Flight Star**. Fighters in formation have interval between wing tips about half-span of 'planes. With bomber formations this is one span (sketch, top left). Top right, with fighters this distance, from the rudder of one machine to nose of following, equals half a length ; with bombers it is one length. Centre, right, a method is shown which gives the signal to " **Close Up**."
Upper centre, fighters operating in " V ".formation spread out just prior to attacking. Left centre, Blenheims in **Flight Line Astern**. At bottom of page, Fairey Battles in **Flight Line Astern Up**.

In the Indies Holland Stands Fast

Amongst the allies of Britain is the Kingdom of the Netherlands, which brings to the war against Germany the immense resources of its territories in the East and West Indies. Below we give some account of Queen Wilhelmina's colonial empire.

HOLLAND was overrun by the Nazis in the course of a five-day campaign last May, but the Kingdom of the Netherlands is still at war with Germany. This is because the Kingdom is not a state in Europe possessed of a number of colonies or dependencies overseas, but one state, one political entity, with territories in Europe, Asia, and America. The one connecting link is the person of the sovereign, Queen Wilhelmina, who, with her responsible ministers, constitutes the central and supreme government and executive organ of the State.

It was for this reason that Queen Wilhelmina and the other members of the Dutch Royal Family sought safety in Britain when it became clear that the Nazis were bent on capturing them by their parachutists, or,

Netherlands West Indies need not detain us long. It comprises the colony of Surinam, or Dutch Guiana, on the mainland of South America, and the colony of Curaçao, two groups of islands off the coast of Venezuela. Surinam has an area of about 54,000 square miles with a population of 165,000 ; its capital is Paramaribo. The islands of Curaçao amount in all to only some 400 square miles, with a population of about 100,000 ; the capital is Willemstad. Surinam exports much tropical produce ; Curaçao's chief industry is oil-refining. Both colonies are ruled by a Governor assisted by a council, whose members are nominated by Queen Wilhelmina ; but in Surinam there is also a representative body—the States—an elective body. Perhaps we may add that the

The Governor-General of the Dutch East Indies, Jonkheer A. W. L. Tjarda van Starkenborgh Stachouwer, is seen at an official function.
Photo, Black Star

Netherlands' forces in Surinam consist of a civic guard and an infantry force of seven officers and 177 n.c.o.s and men ; while Curaçao is defended by one officer and 65 men, with the support of a man-of-war.

Very different is " Netherlands India," which comprises a number of islands in the East Indies between Asia and Australia—Java and Madura, Sumatra, Banka and Billiton, most of Borneo, Celebes, Bali and Lombok, Timor, and western New Guinea, to mention the most important. It has a total area of 730,000 square miles, and a population estimated at about 60,000,000, for the most part brown-skinned peoples of the Malay or Indonesian races, although there is a considerable admixture of other Orientals, chiefly Chinese. The natives include some of the most colourful peoples of the Orient, ranging from the shapely beauties of Java and the world-famous temple dancers of Bali to the fuzzy-haired savages of largely unexplored New Guinea. The white element

The Dutch East Indies form a large group of islands roughly extending from Dutch New Guinea in the east to Sumatra in the west.

failing capture, assassinating them by bombs. If the Queen, Princess Juliana, and the Cabinet had been taken or slain, then the Kingdom of the Netherlands would almost certainly have been disrupted. But with the Queen in England the Dutch Empire is assured of its legally constituted authority, and its constitutional organs continue to function. Though Holland be occupied by the Nazis, in the Dutch East Indies and the Dutch West Indies the Government of the Netherlands goes on.

She Rules 60 Millions Overseas

In Holland, Queen Wilhelmina rules perhaps for the time being we should say ruled—over nearly 9,000,000 Hollanders, but in Asia and America her subjects number rather more than 60,000,000. Indeed, the Dutch colonial empire is one of the great empires of the world, great in extent, vast in its riches, filled with exotic appeal. It is divided between the two Indies, the East and the West.

Batavia, which has been called the " Venice of the East," is the capital of the Dutch East Indies ; it has a population of 231,463. Many of the streets are built on either side of canals. Here is a typical scene along one of the city's waterways. The numerous rafts drawn up to the water's edge are constructed of bamboo.
Photo, Dorien Leigh

Vast and Rich is Queen Wilhelmina's Domain

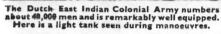

The Dutch East Indian Colonial Army numbers about 40,000 men and is remarkably well equipped. Here is a light tank seen during manoeuvres.

Most of the small but efficient Dutch fleet is usually stationed in East Indian waters. Among the ships is this minelayer, which is also equipped for minesweeping; its row of mines is waiting to be dropped overboard at the stern.

Rice is one of the most important products of the Dutch East Indies, and great quantities are exported; besides providing a living for the majority of the inhabitants, it is a staple diet for many of the native population. Whole families work in the paddy fields, and in this photo the young rice is being planted out.
Photos, Black Star

comprises some 200,000 Dutch nationals—officials, merchants, and traders.

The headquarters of the Dutch administration are in Java, where at Batavia the Governor-General, Jonkheer Stachouwer, a very great official with a position analogous to the Viceroy of India, has his seat. As in British India, some of the lands are under direct government, while others are subject native states. Supreme authority under the Crown is exercised by the Governor-General, but he is assisted by a council of four to six members; and there is a Volksraad, some of whose members are appointed by the Government and some elected by local councils. Since 1925 the Volksraad has been permitted to play a considerable part in local government.

Hollanders at Home in the Indies

Unlike most British officials in the East, the Dutch officials tend to regard the East Indies as their permanent home; they get long leave only once every ten years, and when they retire from the service they do not as a rule return to Holland; rather they buy a house in Java and spend the rest of their days in the comfortable surroundings to which they have become accustomed. Another striking difference is that there is no social ostracism for those who marry Javanese women; a Javanese woman marrying a European immediately ranks as a European.

The Dutch Indies are immensely rich in natural resources. In 1938 their share in the world production of rubber was 33 per cent, pepper 85 per cent, cinchona bark (quinine) 90 per cent, kapok 64 per cent, coconut products 29 per cent, tea 17 per cent, sugar 5 per cent, palm oil products 24 per cent, and coffee 4 per cent. In addition, in 1938 the Netherlands Indies produced 7,398,000 tons of crude petroleum, thus entitling it to rank fifth amongst the chief oil-producing countries of the world; and 27,700 tons of tin, giving it fourth place amongst the tin-producing countries. Much of this vast produce was dispatched to the home country in

exchange for manufactured goods; and the occupation of Holland by the Nazis gave rise to a very difficult situation. As regards sugar, it was eased when Britain purchased 100,000 tons from Java, and it may not be difficult to find fresh markets for the goods which in past years have been exported to Holland. Nor should it be difficult to find fresh sources of supply of those goods which were formerly exported to the Indies from Holland. Both Britain and America are already in the field, and Japan is falling over herself, as it were, to increase her share of the trade with the great Dutch islands. In this fact lies danger, for it is well known that Japan is interested not only economically but politically in the Indies; and during the last few months there have been several occasions when it seemed possible that Japan might aim a lightning blow at the islands, or at least attempt to secure bases such as have been granted by the French in Indo-China.

But the Dutch will not be caught napping, and in the Netherlands Indies there are main-

tained both an army and navy of considerable strength. The Royal Netherlands Indies Army consists of some 40,000 men; the battalions are mixed, composed of companies either of Europeans or of natives, but nearly all the officers and most of the n.c.o.s are Dutch. Several of the native princes, also, maintain bodies of armed troops. Then the Royal Navy in the Netherlands Indies consists of the coast defence ship "Soerabaja," three cruisers, "Tromp," "de Ruyter," and "Java," eight destroyers, fifteen submarines, and most of the other smaller vessels of the Dutch Navy. The main naval base is Surabaya on the North coast of Java. Next year's budget provides for an expenditure of nearly £55,000,000, half of which will be spent on strengthening the defences. More than 200 'planes are on order from America, and the strength of the Indies Army in Java is to be increased to 100,000 men. But the main defence of the Dutch East Indies, now as for generations past, is the British Navy.

Malta is Ready for Mussolini—If He Comes!

The first bomb to be dropped by an Italian raider on the island fell near this fine stone gateway in Valletta, Malta's capital, on June 11.

Circle, members of the Signal Station at a Field Telephone Exchange installed at Battalion H.Q. Right, troops grouped behind a powerful 6-inch howitzer and its limber which is being towed by a lorry during Army exercises.   *Photos, P.N.A. and Topical*

WHEN the Mediterranean Fleet was reinforced in September the ships called on their way to Alexandria at Malta. One of the first to enter the harbour was one of the Fleet's most modern battleships. A fierce air raid was in progress and all the islanders were in their shelters, but in accordance with traditional routine as his ship passed the breakwater at Valletta the Captain had his Marines paraded on the quarter-deck while the band played the ship's march and "There'll always be an England." Hearing the music and the cheers of the gunners at Fort Ricasoli, the Maltese rushed from their shelters and poured out in their thousands to the terraces and quays cheering wildly in their enthusiasm. As the battleship's band played the Admiral's salute the people answered by "Roll Out the Barrel" and "Rolling Home," singing them over and over again.

Camouflaged Italian 'planes run the gauntlet of furious A.A. fire as they circle above Malta's coastline. Accurate and deadly gunfire kept these raiders at a distance of five miles as they attempted to fly inland and forced them up to five thousand feet.

Photo, Keystone

They Served in That War and Serve Again in This

Air-Marshal A. W. Bishop, V.C., D.S.O. (circle) began his career as a fighting pilot in March, 1917, and headed the list of British aces, having brought down 72 German 'planes. He is now a director of Canada's Air Force training scheme, and in September he arrived in England at the invitation of the Air Ministry. The photograph on the right shows "Billy" Bishop in 1917 with his Nieuport Scout, a French single-seater with which he achieved spectacular success.

Photos, Planet News and Imperial War Museum

General Sir Hubert Gough, G.C.B., K.C.B., commanded the Fifth Army in the Battle of the Somme in 1916 and in the third Battle of Ypres in the following year. Heavily outnumbered and with few reserves, his Army was overwhelmed by the Germans in their attack of March, 1918. He was held responsible, as many have thought unjustly, and superseded. Shortly after the outbreak of the present war he took over the control of an A.R.P. depot in Chelsea, and played a leading part in the evacuation of London children. Below, he is seen at the A.R.P. depot with Mr. Lewis Casson, husband of Dame Sybil Thorndike; left, at the front during the last war.

Photos, Imperial War Museum, Keystone, and Elliott & Fry

Maj.-Gen. Sir Hugh Elles, K.C.B., D.S.O. (circle) commanded the Tank Corps during the last war; he is seen above with King George V at Suatrecourt in 1918. He is now Regional Commissioner for South-West England.

The Police Are in London's Front Line

London would not be London without its policemen, and in these days of war in particular it is difficult, if not impossible, to imagine a London in which they were not playing their part. How vital, how splendid a part is made clear in this article by Mr. Richard Capell, reprinted from the " Daily Telegraph."

ONE source only there is for self-satisfaction in these times—a conviction that one is pulling one's weight for all one is worth. On the strength of this the London police are justified in looking self-satisfied and feeling content with their lot.

It is a harder lot than in the idyllic times of " The Pirates of Penzance." Not, of course, that a murmur on that score is to be heard. The police are in the London battle with the firemen, the wardens, the busmen and all the others who are acting on the motto " It's dogged as does it ! "

All the same, there is no reason for not saying that the London police are today doing such a job of work as has fallen to no other police force in history.

To talk of anyone being exactly happy in the circumstances may seem to be stretching a point. On my own responsibility I should not venture so far. But when a hard-boiled police officer uses the phrase about his men it is worth quoting.

A divisional superintendent said to me : " The young men are happy to be in action. They felt out of it when fellows of their age went off to France and were fighting Germans, but in the last month or so they have had their share of what you may call the front line."

It is three years since the Metropolitan Commissioner, Sir Philip Game, started preparing for just such conditions as London is experiencing today, and the enemy can do much worse and still not upset the London police organization.

True, the oddities of the administration of London are a bit of a handicap to the police in wartime. Boroughs and police divisions are so far from coinciding that there may be three or even four different local authorities in one divisional area. Then there is the independent City Police, whose territory is represented on the Scotland Yard maps as a small white autonomous island in the middle of the 700 variously coloured square miles served by the Metropolitan Police, whose radius goes out 15 miles from Charing Cross.

How, in what may be called the domestic aspect, the preparation made by the police for emergencies works in practice was shown the other week when a sub-divisional station as near as nothing got a direct hit. Half the station was blown inside out, and there were casualties. But within an hour and a quarter the staff was efficiently at work in the emergency quarters long before allotted to it.

The strength of the Metropolitan Police is that of an army corps, or approaching 35,000 men, but they are none too many for the work to be done, which includes all the things you would expect and some others.

The sounding of the sirens—on R.A.F. instructions, of course—is one of the jobs of

The " alert " had been sounded when the young policeman, top centre, went on calmly regulating the traffic, but in a few moments he may be called upon to deal with such a casualty as the L.P.T.B. bus, left. The policeman, above, has to examine the identity cards of those desirous of entering bombed areas.

Photos, Sport & General, Wide World, and Fox

the police. There are 450 sirens in the Metropolitan area ; and since an unlucky bomb may put one or another out of action a large fleet of cars is ready equipped with sirens to go out and spread warnings.

Another job, as difficult as any, is the spotting of unexploded bombs. There are now inspectors who are being put through a special bomb course and are by way of becoming experts in discriminating between these tiresome engines

Friends and Helpers in Danger and Distress

A fireman and a policeman (above) who have been engaged in clearing the debris from a damaged building while a raid was still in progress, lie prone on the ground as another high explosive bomb whistles through the air.
Photos, Planet News

Practically every form of A.R.P. work comes within the province of the police, of whom now more than ever it is true, as Mr. Winston Churchill said some years ago, "that everyone, except the criminals, looks upon them as the friends and servants of the public." Right, police are rescuing an injured man from a wrecked building after a raid on October 21, 1940.

All night the stations receive reports from the public about unexploded bombs, and each has to be investigated, though generally there has been an explosion—far away. A distant bomb is taken by many people to be nearer than it is and assumed not to have gone off.

Then there are many reports received from the public of mysterious lights and suspected tappings—messages to the enemy, or so supposed—and these cannot be pooh-poohed out of hand, however fanciful. Incendiary bombs very often are first spotted by constables on their beats. "And it is wonderful," said a chief inspector who knows everything that has happened to a certain afflicted quarter of London in the last six weeks, "how many they have put out."

Strictly speaking, the work of rescuing persons caught in the collapse of houses does not belong to the police, but the occasions have been many when police officers have rushed in to aid the rescue squads or to begin the work before they were on the scene. After a bad night there is a stream of people calling at the station to inquire about relations and friends.

The compiling of casualty lists is part of the work of Scotland Yard. The lists are printed by the Yard's own press and are circulated to all stations. In these lists has appeared no insignificant number of Metropolitan policemen, for 54 have lost their lives and 372 have been injured.

A remarkable proportion of injuries received by Londoners in these weeks has been caused by glass: and, mentioning this, a police officer of authority made a remark worth quoting: "There is," he said, "far too much glass in London—unbroken glass. I am astonished that there should still be such expanses of it—all unprotected and a possible danger any day. Nine-tenths of it or more should be bricked up. Glasshouses should be turned into fortresses!"

He went on to marvel at the continued display of valuable goods in shop windows—jewelry in particular—often a few doors only from wrecked shops. This led to the question of looting.

While there has been a good deal of pilfering in damaged streets in some districts, looting—in the serious sense in which the police use the word—has been uncommon. That is to say that far too many Londoners have been indelicate enough to pocket an object or two that has caught their eye among wreckage; but the ruffians who set out to make a business of robbing disaster-stricken shopkeepers and householders are a tiny minority. Of concerted banditry there has been none at all.

Turning over sheet after sheet of detailed police reports, which descend on headquarters thick as October's drifting leaves in our neglected gardens, I see again and again the entry, "Morale good."

Were the actual labours of the London police all told in full it would still not be the whole tale.

Almost every Londoner, I imagine, must feel in some degree the heartening influence of the sight, amid the fantastic things we all see in these days, of the imperturbable policeman, stalwart and homely—the symbol of sane, established order. If you happen to have had a bad five minutes and the world still seems rocking, the sight of him helps to steady it. That is a service he has certainly rendered, though all unknowingly, to a number of citizens in these weeks.

Talking of the worst days in the East End, one who has seen much there said to me: "The East-Enders lean upon the police!" That surely is a tribute which any police force in the world would be proud of but one such as few can ever have evoked.

The London policeman, I have lately found, is in some ways different from the conventional idea we have of him. But there remains the traditional stolidity; and I only wish it were possible to convey the superbly placid tone with which this remark was made to me at one station where they knew as much as anyone about the new-style war: "We have settled down to the job; it is such a regular nightly occurrence, and we know what to expect."

OUR SEARCHLIGHT ON THE WAR

Humane Airmen

BY their ceaseless day and night vigil our airmen indirectly save thousands of lives. On many occasions, however, they do so by direct means, and, such is the British character, those rescued from death may well be the enemy. After the sinking by H.M.S. "Ajax" of three Italian destroyers on October 12, a Sunderland flying-boat of the R.A.F. was on patrol over the Mediterranean when the pilot sighted a ship in the distance. Having satisfied himself that she was the Italian ship "Aquileja," he resumed his patrol. A few miles farther on he found a vast patch of oil in which could be seen not only masses of wreckage but two boats and half a dozen Carley floats. The flying-boat turned back to the hospital ship and signalled a message, afterwards circling round the wreckage and diving several times to attract attention. The Italian ship altered course and steered towards the point indicated, and soon the Sunderland's pilot saw her lower a white motor dinghy and make for the floats. He himself searched a little time for survivors but, locating none, carried on with his patrol. Another Sunderland flying-boat, with an all-Australian crew, recently descended on the Atlantic and took aboard 21 survivors of a torpedoed merchantman who had been adrift in a lifeboat for $3\frac{1}{2}$ days. Twenty-four survivors of another British vessel were saved, through the good offices of three Blenheims of the Coastal Command, two of which remained flying round their raft and floats, while the third went off to get help and presently guided motor launches to the rescue.

Provincial 'Visitors' in London

OMNIBUSES of many hues and from divers provincial centres are being lent to the London Passenger Transport Board to help with the capital's traffic problem, and the first of the 2,000 promised are already to be seen on the streets. The impression their presence gives of solidarity, of practical sympathy in time of trouble, is very heartening to workers who are now in the front line of battle. So, too, are their varied colour schemes, which provide a gay contrast to the monotonous, if cheerful, red of London's own buses. The Halifax bus is orange and green with cream trimmings. That of Leeds is blue. Northampton's brown and Coventry's chocolate and yellow are perhaps a shade

London has "borrowed" 2,000 buses from the provinces. Here is a Manchester bus whose indicator is being changed for service in the metropolis.
Photo, Fox

more sober, and although Manchester's splendid scarlet vies with the city's own hue, Sheffield's cream and blue contribute another touch of friendly unfamiliarity to London's thoroughfares.

They Will Tell America

ON October 22 Mr. Joseph Kennedy, U.S. Ambassador to London, left for home, and in some quarters it is thought that he may not return, or, at any rate, not as representative of the United States. Even if he remains over there his influence will be only for Britain's good. His frankly expressed sympathies for this country, indeed, have earned for him the open detestation of Germany. In a last-minute talk to a "Daily Express" staff reporter he said : "You people are great. I'm going to tell them all about it at home." His views of the damage done by bombs—"It looks much worse on paper than it does when you see it yourself"—coincide with those of another American observer, Mr. Ralph Ingersoll, owner of a New York evening paper, who said that in 100 miles he had seen railways, stations, factories, airports, harbours where shipping went on normally, and not a single scar on any of them. But in London, said Mr. Ingersoll, he found more damage to non-military objectives than he had expected. "I am bewildered by the calmness and courage of the people. I shall go back to America with a message of good cheer and admiration for the British people."

' 47,000,000 Churchills '

GERMANY is puzzled by Britain's resistance to the Nazi air war, according to the Berlin correspondent of the Italian newspaper "Telegrafo." In his message on October 22 he said : "After the daily reading of German official communiqués, these questions are always asked : 'How is England able to resist? For how long? At the cost of what sacrifices will England be able to hold her ground? Can England—we ask ourselves—prolong her resistance? Is it really true that 47,000,000 Englishmen are 47,000,000 Churchills all determined to die under the ruined British Empire rather than give in?'" This comment is interesting coming as it does not long after the first suggestion of any doubt of ultimate victory which appeared in the Berlin newspaper "D.A.Z.": "Even in the hypothetical case of the Axis being unable to end the war successfully, Great Britain will on no account be able to annihilate Germany and Italy."

Nazis Fear We May Invade Them

BERLIN radio relayed on October 24 a talk by the commanding officer of a battery facing the Channel, in which he announced that Germany is fortifying the French and German coasts against possible invasion by Britain. Experts and labourers have been sent from the Rhineland, and, helped by troops already in the district, the work is being hurried along by day and night shifts. The officer stated that his section of the fortifications had been built in three and a

half weeks, and was the first to be completed. He concluded his talk with two test shots fired from his biggest gun, which had been installed "as the German High Command are anxious to do everything possible to secure the German-occupied coast from any possible landing and attack by the British."

Coastal Command's 'Private Blitzes'

PILOTS of a certain squadron of the Coastal Command, whose job it is to patrol the North Sea, are not satisfied with their allotted task of reconnaissance, and frequently ask and sometimes receive permission from

Mr. Joseph P. Kennedy, American Ambassador to Great Britain, waving a smiling farewell from the steps of the U.S. Embassy, as he left London for the United States on October 22. He was appointed in January, 1938.
Photo, Wide World

their commanding officer to spend their off-time seeking and attacking military targets. These jaunts, which are seldom fruitless, are known to the pilots and their crews as "private blitzes." The C.O.'s term for them is a little more dignified, as was shown recently when the board in the operations room, after noting details of the duties and expected time of return of two aircraft, bore the additional remark : "May be up to two hours late owing to private hostilities." On this occasion the elated pilots reported on their landing that they had registered direct hits on a minesweeper and a supply ship and a near-miss on a destroyer.

Propaganda Through Ridicule

THE broadcasts in French sent out by the B.B.C. are, it seems, immensely popular in unoccupied France. According to one letter received, an "entire village meets every night in the five or six houses which have sufficiently powerful wireless sets to get London on the short wave." The feature these listeners seem to appreciate most is the guying of the Germans through skits on the once familiar advertising slogans sent out by private wireless stations. One of the most popular is sung to a tune that was used to boost a well-known apéritif. The present words are :

    Radio-Paris ment ;
    Radio-Paris ment ;
    Radio-Paris est allemand.

This has caught on irresistibly among the young people of the French villages. Marshal Pétain's slogan, "Famille, travail, patrie," has been elaborated (by the B.B.C.) into "Famille dispersée, travail introuvable patrie humiliée," a true if biting comment on the present plight of the French nation.

I WAS THERE!

I Lived Under Nazi Rule in Jersey

We have already published an eye-witness account of the seizure of Jersey by the Germans (see page 51, Vol. 3). Mr. George Turner, a Jersey tomato-grower, remained on the island for more than three months before escaping to England, where he told the following story of the life of the islanders under Nazi rule.

ABOUT 300 Germans were the first to arrive in Jersey. I went on with my work until two of them came and wanted to know whether my house was my property. They went in, opened drawers and took £63, saying I would get a receipt

Mr. George Turner, the Jersey tomato-grower, who prefers the chance of being bombed in London to life in the Channel Islands under the rule of the Nazis.
Photo, "News Chronicle"

and would be given full marks to that value. When I went to an office in the town I got nothing.

The Germans were quite nice and courteous and did not lay a finger on me, but the next morning three more arrived, picked all my fruit and tomatoes and took them away.

I asked them about the money and they said "That will be all right." I never received anything.

I cannot say that they looted. It was all done by the officials in a very courteous way. They took all the flour in the island and commandeered the hotels, billeted themselves there and emptied the cellars.

They went straight to the town hall and interviewed Mr. John Pinel, the police magistrate. They appointed about 40 town guards, who patrolled the streets in couples, usurping the police force.

Although they are what might be termed tolerant they let you know that they are the bosses. If anyone carries a case he is stopped and made to show what is inside. If the Germans see anyone hanging about they put them to work on the fields.

There is nothing Prussian about their manner, but they said to us, "You will all be Prussians from now on and the Channel Islands belong to Germany for ever. The boats will come here now from Hamburg instead of from England, and if you want to go away you will go to Germany because you are German subjects now. Germany is a very good place, and England does not know how to govern." They also told us that Ribbentrop would be the boss for Germany in England.

They took the food from the boarding houses, went into the largest grocers' warehouse and packed great crates and sent them away. From the large drapers they sent all the women's lingerie away, and helped themselves from the jewellers.

Wireless is not allowed, and there is a curfew at 10 p.m. The banks are closed, and there are no cinemas.

The bread we had was dark brown. We had no sweetstuffs, no sugar, no butter, but a bit of margarine. When the German soldiers came they were ravenous, and the first thing they did was to have a good feed. Strangely, they never took the tobacco.

Describing his escape, Mr. Turner said:

One day four of us met in a hotel, and one man said, "I am going to make a bolt for it. There is a boat in the harbour."

This boat was captained by an Irishman, and he had been there for a long time. He was not allowed to move, but he had coal in his bunkers. He said he would take us to England for £3 5s. a head. Eventually nine of us, including a girl, made our way to the boat at 9 o'clock one night.

We all went to the quay by different routes, and I hid a small suitcase under my coat whenever I passed German soldiers.

About 4 a.m. the ship glided around the headland and we were away. In three days we reached England.—"*News Chronicle*"

Our Bomber Was Struck By Lightning

In an account of a raid over Germany (see page 249, vol. 3) a bomber pilot described the effects of bad weather conditions. Here "Tail-end Charlie"—the nickname for an air gunner, whose post is in the turret at the tail of a heavy bomber—tells what happened to him when his 'plane flew into a storm over the French coast.

"A SLICE of cake," said my pilot. I knew what he meant. This time we were not off to Berlin or Milan, or any of those far-flung places, sections of which have been flung even farther. We were to make a quick, sudden smash at Hitler's invasion bases, and be back in bed by three.

No trouble at all, so long as—it being full moon—old "Tail-End Charlie" kept a good look-out behind. Only the watchful tail-gunner, alone and alert in his little glazed house far out on the great bomber's tail, can see and deal with trouble when it comes streaking out of the sky in the shape of a Heinkel or a Messerschmitt.

The night was so bright, with a huge golden moon climbing up, that I turned my turret from side to side, looking for some of our squadron. It is astonishing how empty the sky may look when it is in fact full of aircraft, which have taken off from the same place at regular intervals and are circling around the same target. From beginning to end perhaps one hardly catches a glimpse of another.

We had not covered more than two-thirds of the way when we sailed slap into cloud.

At first it was only dim haze and wisps of pale vapour, with cumulus standing like snow-ruffed mountains about us. Then suddenly (remember "Tail-End Charlie" travels backwards, like a prawn, so that most of the things he sees are stale news to the rest of the crew) we plunged into absolute darkness. The clouds had engulfed us and rain beat down on the turret. Then our troubles began.

"We'll take her up out of this," I heard the pilot say through the intercommunicating

A bomber engaged in such work as is described in this page depends on its gunner for protection from fighter planes. Above is this important member of the crew of one of the Hampden bombers that are now armed with two Vickers K guns and a movable gun firing through the nose.
Photo, L.N.A.

502   *The War Illustrated*   *November 8th, 1940*

||||||||||||||||||||||||||||||||||||||||||||||||||||||||||||||||||| **I WAS THERE!** |||||||||||||||||||||||||||||||||||||||||||||||||||||||||||||||||||

telephone. Up we climbed through thrashing rain which suddenly turned into hail. Then I heard " whack ! whack ! whack ! " I knew what that was—ice flying off the airscrew and rattling down on the fuselage.

On the wings' leading edges the de-icers were working—expanding, deflating, like slow-breathing lungs, dispersing the ice.

Something flickered close to us. Were we over the target, with " Flak " coming up already ? It flickered again and again. " I don't like that lightning " I heard someone say in front. Then a strange thing happened. From the barrels of my four guns little sparks began to shoot backwards with a thin, dry crackling noise. Lightning shimmered in front and behind us and thunder bellowed all round.

Our flying became very " bumpy." We suddenly rose or fell at incredible speeds. I lurched about my turret, holding on tightly, wondering if the next bump would knock me out on the roof. All the time those little flickering sparks shot out of my guns.

The rain, flicking off from the tail-planes, carried blue flames away with it, little blue flames of electricity, " flick ! flick ! " blowing behind us. There came one enormous bump when we must have dropped 500 feet, then a pause. Then a purple flash filled the whole of my turret and there was a deafening report. I found myself completely blind. The aircraft rocked crazily. Not a sound came from those in front.

" Hello, captain ! Hello, captain ! " I called. Nobody answered

After a bit, light filtered back to my eyes. I was not blind after all. What was more, we were out of the clouds, and my guns had stopped firing off sparks. I could see that their several thousand cartridges had not gone off in my face as I had suspected.

" Hello, captain ! "

At last his voice came back to me, bringing me but little comfort.

" The 'plane has been struck by lightning," he said. " Have your parachute ready."

I took one glance at the cold sea, gleaming below, opened the turret doors, and reached for my parachute——

Well, we got back all right, and without having to jump. The lightning blast had done no harm to our " kite " ; but if ever " Met " (meteorological) matters go wrong with me again, I only hope I have as steady a captain and as stout an aircraft to bear me.

It was " cake " we had, all right—ice cake, with lightning to follow !

Among survivors from the " Empress of Britain " were Sergeant Speaston and his wife and their eight-year-old daughter Elizabeth. Taken on board different lifeboats, the family was reunited on reaching the shore.
Photo, Associated Press

We Were Bombed on " Empress of Britain "

Left a blazing wreck after she had been bombed and machine-gunned by enemy aircraft on October 26, the famous liner " Empress of Britain " blew up and sank while attempts were being made to salvage her. Below we give some eye-witness stories of survivors.

THE attack on the " Empress of Britain " began when enemy bombers dived out of the morning sky and raked the gun crew with machine-gun fire. Having put the liner's gun out of action, the pilots swept over the ship and dropped high-explosive bombs, one of which made a direct hit.

Incendiary bombs were dropped during a further onslaught, and the ship was ablaze amidships while passengers and crew took to the lifeboats or congregated in unaffected parts of the liner.

A member of the crew, J. P. Donovan, of Southampton, gave a vivid description of the scene on the forecastle. He said :

When the bombs began to drop about 40 or 50 of us lay down on the deck. Then the lights went out in the forward part and we made our way towards the forecastle by

torchlight. The stench left by the bombs was terrible.

Finally about 300 people were gathered in the forecastle, including a number of women and children. About half an hour after the attack some of the boats lowered from the starboard side came up forward and we got all the women and children into them.

When these boats were full we still had about 140 on the forecastle. In case there should not be enough boats for us we began to make rafts from all the wood we could find —cabin doors, between decks and awning spars.

Owing to the fire spreading a number of the boats had to be got away with only four men in them, the idea being to get them safely afloat and then get the people into them.

The trouble was that four men could not

row those heavy boats, and then the motorboat which could have towed them to where they were needed got a knock when it was being lowered and the engine would not start.

An assistant bo'sun named McKinnon and an R.A.F. officer did a good bit of work between them in getting the engine going. After that it was easy. The motor-boat towed the empty life-boats up to the ship, and it was not long after till we were all away. It was then the middle of the afternoon, between five and six hours after the attack.

All these hours the flames had been spreading forward, and when we got away the ship was burning within 10 feet of the bows. In a few minutes we would have had to take to the rafts.

Just before we got into the boats a flying boat came along and signalled that rescue ships were on the way. The rescue ships came up about three-quarters of an hour after, and we got into the boats. The Navy men were grand.

Another member of the crew said that a number of people were killed and injured by the explosion of the bombs and the aircraft's machine-guns. He went on :

She machine-gunned the bridge heavily, and a machine-gunner who was stationed there fought back very bravely. I heard Captain Sapsworth commending him highly. The skipper himself was very cool. He stayed on the bridge until it was burning under his feet, and he was on the fore part till the very end.

Mrs. A. Speaston, who was returning home to Glasgow with her eight-years-old daughter Elizabeth and her soldier husband, said :

I was on the promenade deck when the airraid warning sounded. I heard machineguns, and bullets thudded against the decks.

I was starting to run to the deck below when a great explosion hurled me down the stairs. I scrambled to my feet. My first thought was, of course, to find my little girl. But I was half dazed, and they took me to the boat deck. I found her there.

The youngest passenger was 11-months-old Neville Hart. He was saved by being lashed in a blanket to the back of a sailor, who slid down a 60 ft. rope into a lifeboat. Beryl Hart, his 19-year-old sister, said :

I was in a cabin next to mother's when the first bomb struck the liner. There was a great noise and her cabin was wrecked.

I heard mother calling and scrambled to her through the wreckage. We could hear fire crackling near us, but there was no panic and Neville was as good as gold.

The Hart family, including 11-months-old Neville, youngest survivor of the " Empress of Britain." When the ship was bombed they, with the other passengers, obeyed instructions and stayed below until the order to go on deck was given.   *Photo, Daily Mail*

Down On the Farm in the Front Line

ON the South-east coast, right in the " front line," Miss Mary Sinclair courageously runs her farm. She is surrounded by all the noise and confusion of war, aerial battles rage furiously over the farmhouse ; she has become accustomed to bombs, shells and machine-guns, and carries on her job in spite of everything. Her day begins at 6 a.m. and finishes at 9 p.m., all the work of the farm being done by herself. These photographs show Miss Sinclair at her round of tasks, and finally resting after the long day.

Photos by " News Chronicle" Staff Photographer R. Girling, Exclusive to THE WAR ILLUSTRATED.

OUR DIARY OF THE WAR

TUESDAY, OCT. 22, 1940   *416th day*

On the Sea—Admiralty announced that patrol vessels O.6 and O.7, formerly French, had been sunk by enemy light craft.

In the Air—R.A.F. bomber secured direct hit on enemy cargo ship off Hook of Holland. Owing to adverse weather conditions R.A.F. carried out no night bombing operations.

War against Italy—R.A.F. attacked enemy working parties and transport between Buqbuq and Sollum. Raids made on Dessie aerodrome, Assab, Bahar-Dar, Danghela, Gura and Asmara. South African Air Force attacked Birikau for fifth time.

Italian aircraft attacked island of Perim, in Straits of Bab el Mandeb. Bombs were dropped near Alexandria, but caused only slight damage.

Home Front—British fighters intercepted large formation of aircraft after crossing Kent coast. Fierce battle ensued and enemy was driven back. Sporadic raids on S.E. coast towns.

Less activity at night, but some raiders reached London. Houses damaged; large store wrecked; church struck. Nazi aircraft also reported over Midlands, where in one town considerable damage was done, and elsewhere.

Three German 'planes destroyed. Britain lost six fighters but pilots of two safe.

British and German long-range guns exchanged several shots across Straits of Dover.

General—M. Pierlot, Belgian Premier, and M. Spaak, Foreign Minister, arrived in London.

Hitler received M. Laval, Deputy Premier, during a visit to France.

WEDNESDAY, OCT. 23   *417th day*

On the Sea—Admiralty announced that H.M. minesweeper " Dundalk " had been sunk by enemy mine.

In the Air—R.A.F. attacked targets in Berlin area, including power stations and railway yards. Other forces bombed railways, wharves and warehouses at port of Emden, oil plants at Magdeburg and Hanover, goods yards, industrial targets and railway junctions in various places, docks at Hook of Holland and many aerodromes.

Two enemy supply ships in convoy off Frisian Islands torpedoed by Coastal Command Beaufort aircraft. Another vessel heavily machine-gunned.

War against Italy—Series of night raids made by R.A.F. on Gura. Other aircraft raided Asmara aerodrome, Gondar, Tessenie and Kassala. In Western Desert British aircraft raided Sidi Barrani.

Home Front—Enemy day activity confined to isolated attacks by single aircraft over S.E. and Midland areas.

During night bombers made gliding raids on London. Church severely damaged; houses and shops demolished. West of Scotland had severe raid over wide area, but only house property suffered.

Enemy lost one aircraft, Britain none.

General—Hitler met Franco on French-Spanish frontier.

M. Laval reported to Marshal Petain at Vichy on his meeting with Hitler.

THURSDAY, OCTOBER 24   *418th day*

On the Sea—Admiralty announced loss through enemy mines of H.M. trawlers " Velia " and " Lord Stamp."

In the Air—R.A.F. attacked ports of Ostend and Gravelines, a factory and goods yard near Calais and a convoy off Zeebrugge.

During night many objectives in Berlin were bombed, as well as oil plants at Hamburg, Hanover and Gelsenkirchen; docks and shipping at Hamburg, Cuxhaven, Bremerhaven, Wilhelmshaven, Rotterdam, Le Havre and Lorient; goods yards and railway com-

munications, several Channel ports and many aerodromes.

War against Italy—British bombers continued attacks on Italian lines in East Africa and Libya. Asmara, Gura and other centres bombed. Series of raids on Benghazi and Berka.

Home Front—Few enemy aircraft, operating singly, crossed coast. Bombs fell in London area, Kent, Hants and country district in Somerset. House and industrial buildings hit. Private school shattered and nurses' home partly wrecked in Hants.

Comparatively little activity during night. Areas attacked included Scotland and one Midland town, where fires were started which damaged commercial property and public buildings. German High Command stated Italian bombers took part for first time.

Enemy lost two aircraft. Britain none.

General—Hitler interviewed Marshal Pétain in French territory.

The Empress of Britain, 42,348-ton luxury liner, flagship of the Canadian Pacific fleet, brought the King and Queen back to England after their tour in Canada and the United States in 1939. She was sunk on October 26.
Photo, Topical

FRIDAY, OCTOBER 25   *419th day*

On the Sea—Admiralty announced that H.M. submarine " Swordfish " had sunk a German torpedo-boat off French coast, and H.M. submarine " Regent " destroyed Italian supply ship in Mediterranean.

Violent engagement involving heavy guns on both sides of Channel and British and German bombers centred round British convoy approaching Straits of Dover at dusk. Ships in convoy also opened fire. None received direct hits.

H.M. destroyer " Venetia " reported sunk by enemy mine.

In the Air—R.A.F. attacked docks and shipping at Kiel, Bremen, Cuxhaven, Amsterdam, Den Helder and Ostend; oil targets in Northern and Central Germany, power station at Hamburg, aerodromes, Channel gun positions and invasion ports.

Home Front—During day successive formations of enemy aircraft, mostly fighters, crossed S.E. coast at great height. Most were split up and dispersed, but some got through. Bombs fell on five crowded tramcars in London and casualties were heavy.

Night raiders, flying high, dropped bombs in various parts of London. Noted square hit by incendiaries. Number of destructive

fires started in Midland town. Several small coastal towns in Scotland suffered. Searchlights were machine-gunned.

Seventeen enemy aircraft destroyed. Ten British fighters lost, but pilots of seven safe.

SATURDAY, OCT. 26   *420th day*

On the Sea—British liner " Empress of Britain " was set on fire by enemy bomber and sank, following explosion, while on tow. Coastal Command Beaufort aircraft carried out torpedo attack on shipping off Norwegian coast. One supply ship sunk.

In the Air—Despite unfavourable weather R.A.F. heavily bombed many targets in Berlin, oil plants at Stettin, Leuna and Cologne, docks at Hamburg, Cuxhaven and Bremen, railway communications, 14 aerodromes and ports of Flushing and Antwerp.

Coastal Command aircraft successfully attacked power station at Brest.

Home Front—Day raiders over London dropped bombs among crowds in shopping centre, causing many casualties. S.E. coastal town bombed and machine-gunned. Castle in south England damaged.

Wide area attacked during night, but main force directed on London and Midlands.

Enemy lost six aircraft, Britain two.

General—Vichy announced that Marshal Pétain and Hitler had agreed on principle of collaboration. Free French Forces issued statement repudiating Hitler's proposals.

Italian press alleged " incidents " on Greek-Albanian frontier.

SUNDAY, OCT. 27   *421st day*

In the Air—R.A.F. successfully attacked Skoda works at Pilsen. Targets bombed in Germany included oil plants at Hamburg, Ostermoor, Hanover, Gelsenkirchen and Magdeburg; docks at Wilhelmshaven and Hamburg, goods yards at Krefeld, Hamm and Mannheim, Channel ports of Antwerp, Flushing, Ostend and Lorient, and 14 aerodromes.

Home Front—Intermittent raids by fighters and fighter-bombers. Bombs fell in London area, places in S.E. England and in Hants. London block of tenement flats hit.

Less activity during night than of late. Main attacks made on N.W. and Midlands.

Ten enemy aircraft destroyed. Eight British fighters lost but pilots of four safe.

General—Stated that Free French troops under Gen. de Larminat were advancing from Congo Valley and had nearly surrounded village and fortress of Lambarene in French Equatorial Africa.

MONDAY, OCT. 28   *422nd day*

On the Sea—Coastal Command aircraft made daylight attacks on shipping and convoys off Dutch and French coasts.

In the Air—R.A.F. heavily bombed shipping at Kiel, Wilhelmshaven, Bremen, Hamburg, Emden and Cuxhaven, and shipping in Boulogne harbour; oil plants at Homburg, Cologne and Hamburg; railway centres at Krefeld, Cologne, Coblenz and Mannheim; 19 aerodromes, and many A.A. batteries.

Home Front—Bombs fell during day over scattered points in E. Anglia and S.E. England.

During night enemy 'planes were reported over South-East, Merseyside, N.E. England and over Midlands, where in one town incendiaries caused many fires. Two bombs fell through London church into crypt, used as a shelter.

Enemy lost four aircraft, Britain none.

Greece—Greek Govt. rejected ultimatum from Rome demanding free passage of Italian troops to certain unspecified strategic points in Greece. Before expiry of ultimatum Italians launched attacks, which were strongly resisted, across Albanian border, and their aircraft raided Patras and other places.

General—Hitler and Mussolini met in Florence.

HAPPY LITTLE LONDONERS DOWN IN DEVON

All too many children are still to be found in the war-torn and war-threatened streets of London. Indeed, it is estimated that these children still number 290,000, even after the evacuations of late weeks. The best place for a child today is in the country, and fortunately many hundreds of thousands of little Londoners are benefiting from a change of scene. The fried-fish shop and the ice-cream tricycle are unknown in their new homes, but there is plenty of plain, wholesome fare. Here, in the Devon village of Lower Netherton, one of their new "Mothers" is handing out a morning ration of soup to evacuee children.

Photo, L.N.A.

Byron Would Have Been Proud of Greece Today

Byron, who went to Greece to help in her fight for independence from Turkish rule and died there at Missolonghi in 1824, would have hailed with delight the stand against Italian aggression made by the Greeks in these latter days. Below we describe the opening moves in the campaign.

AFTER a week the campaign in Greece showed no signs of a speedy conclusion. The Greeks, who had stood up marvellously well to Mussolini's bullying and who had refused to be rattled even when an "unknown" submarine sank their only cruiser, not only showed fight when the Italians invaded their country, but did fight to excellent purpose. In fact, the Italians soon realized that their attempt to rush the Greek defences and capture Salonika in a few hours or two or three days at most was doomed to failure.

The first Italian columns crossed the frontier from Albania in the early morning of Monday, October 28. From their movements it seemed that they were heading for Florina, in the north-west of Greece on the road to Salonika, and Janina (Yanina), the largest town (pop. 25,000) of the department of the same name in the province of Epirus. Another body of invaders moved along the coast southwards from Konispolis, probably with a view to preventing reinforcements from being sent to the Greek island of Corfu, which for years has been viewed by Mussolini with covetous eyes.

The war's first week went by, and the invaders appeared to have made little progress. In the Janina sector they claimed to have reached the little river Kalamas,

representing a gain of perhaps 10 miles. In the Florina sector, however, not only had their advance been halted, but the Greeks had delivered a strong counter-offensive. On November 1 the invader became the invaded, as considerable detachments of Greeks crossed the frontier into Albania, in a drive towards the town of Koritza (Korcha)—a small place of some 22,000 people, situated astride the road which runs southwards parallel to the frontier on the Albanian side and which must be used by the Italians on their way to Janina. If Koritza, which is also an Italian supply base, were captured, then their communications would be threatened.

That the Greeks fully appreciated the strategical importance of the place was obvious from their determined attack. In spite of a heavy bombardment those crack troops of the Greek Army, the kilted Evzones, sprang from their trenches and carried the heights dominating

King George of the Hellenes spent the years from 1923, when he abdicated, to 1935, when he was recalled to the throne of Greece, chiefly in London at Brown's Hotel. It was on a return visit to London that this photograph was taken.
Photo, Hay Wrightson

Koritza at the point of the bayonet. By evening the enemy resistance had been smashed, and the Greeks were left in occupation of the positions they had captured, five kilometres (three miles) within Albanian territory. Having won the heights, the Greeks brought up their artillery and consolidated their position, and at the same time extended their hold on the surrounding mountain region. In these operations they claimed to have taken over a thousand prisoners.

But if the Italians were slow in demonstrating their superiority in the fighting on land—and that superiority, let it be remembered, is entirely a matter of equipment, for the Greek islander, a peasant armed with a gun, is quite a match for the Italian drawn from the cities of the plain—in the air they proceeded to assert their predominance over the Greeks, who, indeed, have an almost insignificant air force. On the first day of the war the port of Patras was bombed and a number of people were killed and wounded; the number of casualties was all the greater because the Italian 'planes that came over were disguised with Greek markings and the streets were filled with spectators. On November 1 Salonika was raided; 40 people were killed and 80 wounded, all civilians, and 22 fires were caused in the harbour and amongst the shipping. In one of the first raids on the great Greek port Count Ciano's "Disperata," or "Suicide Squadron," was engaged, and the Italian Foreign Minister's activity in this unusual sphere was immediately recognized by his promotion to Lieut.-Col. of Aviation. The honours of the day—such as they were—were also shared by Mussolini's two sons, Vittorio and Bruno (that Bruno who has spoken so ecstatically of the joyous feeling he experienced when

When the Italians invaded Greece on October 28 they found themselves in a land of high and rugged mountains, of narrow passes and swift-flowing streams—a land far from ideal for the manoeuvring of their tanks and motorized columns. The field of initial operations is shown in this map of most of Greece and the adjoining areas of Albania and Yugoslavia.

Scenes in the New War Zone

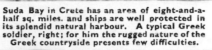

Suda Bay in Crete has an area of eight-and-a-half sq. miles. and ships are well protected in its splendid natural harbour. A typical Greek soldier, right; for him the rugged nature of the Greek countryside presents few difficulties.

The Corinth Canal, left, vital waterway in the coastal defence of Greece, connects the Gulfs of Corinth and Aegina. It is four miles in length and seventy feet wide. The canal was cut through solid rock and was completed in 1893. Stadium Street, a busy thoroughfare of Athens, is seen above with its cafés and shops.

On October 28, Patras was bombed by the Italians, and of its population of 52,000, one hundred and ten people were killed and three hundred wounded. The town was immediately evacuated, and later Italian raids caused far fewer casualties. Patras is one of the chief seaports of Greece, and is built on the slope of a hill overlooking the Gulf of Patras. The town's exports include currants, wine, oil and lemons. Here is a view of the place from the sea.

Photos, Fox, Keystone, E.N.A., and Central Press

No 'Walk-Over' for Mussolini's Legions

dropping bombs on the unarmed and completely defenceless natives of Abyssinia). Corfu, too, was bombed, and many casualties were caused in the little town's market-place. Many other towns and villages and the Greek lines of communication were similarly visited by the Italian airmen.

But by now the Greeks were not fighting alone. Following the appeal for aid addressed to the British Government by King George of the Hellenes and his Prime Minister, General Metaxas, it was decided to give instant assistance. The first announcement that British troops had landed on Greek territory was given by Mr. A. V. Alexander, First Lord of the Admiralty, in a broadcast in the Empire

and air advisers, arrived in Athens during the week-end.

Most important, however, was the intervention of the British air arm. Salonika was avenged when British and Greek 'planes made three heavy attacks on Koritza, doing heavy damage to the aerodrome and causing many casualties. Then there was the raid on Naples mentioned by Mr. Alexander. "Last night," reported the Air Ministry on November 1, "a small force of aircraft of Bomber Command made a successful attack on oil tanks and other objectives at Naples." Weather conditions were by no means ideal, but Rome admitted that "limited material damage was done in various parts of the town."

Left is General A. Papagos, who was appointed to be Commander-in-Chief of the Greek Army on October 29, 1940; he had previously been Chief of the General Staff. General Econmacolos, right, is in command of the Greek Air Force.   *Photos, Planet News*

On every hand there were expressions of surprise at Mussolini's blunder—to give the British an opportunity of establishing bases not only on the Greek mainland but in Crete and the Greek islands. Perhaps he believed that the Greeks would surrender as soon as his troops appeared over the frontier, and that King George would be deposed and Metaxas overthrown. If so, he was soon deceived, and another blow must have been the attitude of Turkey. "At a time when Britain is carrying on under difficult conditions the heroic struggle for its very existence," said President Inonu on Nov. 1, "it is my duty to proclaim that the bonds of alliance which unite us to her are solid and unbreakable."

programme on November 3. The announcement came almost at the end of the First Lord's speech, so that it had the appearance of an afterthought, but it was received with delight in Britain, intense gratification in Athens, and with apprehension in Rome. "We shall honour our pledge to the Greeks," said Mr. Alexander; "the Navy is there, air support is being given, military objectives in Naples have been bombed, and British troops landed in Greek territory. What we can do we will do." There were regrets that the Greek nation, in its determination to maintain its attitude of neutrality, had not permitted earlier anything in the nature of staff talks, but as soon as hostilities began the British forces in the Eastern Mediterranean moved to Greece's assistance. British troops were reported to have landed on the great island of Crete—third largest island in the Mediterranean ; British warships were sighted by the Italians at Leukas on the Greek coast opposite southern Italy ; and a British mission, led by Major-General Gambier-Parry, including naval, military

The bridge in the top photograph spans the River Sarantoporos that forms part of the boundary between Greece and Albania. On the left of it is the Albanian frontier post of Perati, and on the right the Greek frontier post of Mertzani ; in the lower photograph is a close-up view of the Greek post. The inscription above it is : "The ever-watchful guard."   *Photos, Wide World*

Who Are These Americans, Our Friends?

Written a few days before the citizens of the United States of America went to the polls
and chose Franklin Roosevelt for the third time as their President, this article tells something of the American people and of the vast country which is their home.

How often do we talk of America—of what America is saying, what America is doing ! The word rolls so easily off our tongues that there is never time for us to remember that the United States of America is not a country like England or Spain, and that there is more difference between the Americans who live in New York, say, and those who live in New Orleans, than there is between a man who was born within sound of Bow Bells and one whose birthplace was a homestead on an Australian ranch.

The U.S.A. is as big as a continent ; the forty-eight states in the Union which lie between the Atlantic and the Pacific have an area of 3,026,000 square miles, which may be compared with Europe's 3,800,000 square miles. It is farther from New York to San Francisco than it is from Liverpool to New York, and to cover the journey one must spend four or five days in the train, or if one prefers to go by road, drive for seven days, covering nearly 500 miles a day. But while Europe's population is about 550,000,000, the U.S.A. has only—*only*—some 130 millions living in its continental states ; 25,000,000 more have their homes in the Philippines, Alaska, and the other American possessions overseas. From these figures it will be clear that the U.S.A. is far less densely populated than Europe ; New York's population is rather more than 7,000,000, but Texas, the largest of the States and larger than Germany, Austria, and Czechoslovakia added together, has under six millions, for much of its area is practically unexplored tangle of forest and jungle. In Montana, which is considerably larger than Italy, there is a population of about half a million, as compared with Italy's 45,000,000. Wyoming is twice the size of Greece, but whereas the Greeks number nearly 7,000,000, Wyoming has only 225,000—2.3 people per square mile ; much of its area is still primeval wilderness in which the surviving Red Indians have their hunting ground.

Among America's 130,000,000 are to be found representatives of all the peoples of the world. Not for nothing has America been called the melting-pot, and it is not the least of her achievements that after a generation or two the immigrant who may hail from a country not only far distant but very different in culture, is absorbed and transformed into a good American.

Perhaps the most mistaken of the many mistaken beliefs which we on this side of the " Herring Pond " hold about the Americans is that the great majority of them are of our own stock, " speak the tongue that Shakespeare spake ; the faith and morals hold which Milton held." True, the English (Scottish, Welsh, and Irish) influence is still very marked, and, judging from the number of their alleged descendents, the Pilgrim Fathers who went to America in the " Mayflower " 300 years ago were exceedingly prolific. The most common name in the United States is Smith (though in many cases it may originally have been Schmidt), and Johnson, Brown, Williams, Miller, Jones, and Davies come next. But for many years

past the bulk of the men and women who have passed beneath the Statue of Liberty on their way to make a new home in the New World have come from the countries of continental Europe.

The last census, taken in 1930, revealed that more than 38,000,000 Americans were of " foreign white stock," i.e. they had either been born outside the U.S.A. or were the children of foreign-born parents. Of these 38,000,000, only some 4,300,000 were English, Scots, Welsh, and Ulstermen, and 3,000,000 more were Irish ; 6,800,000 were Germans, 4,500,000 Italians, 3,300,000 Poles and the same number Canadians ; 3,100,000 were Scandinavians and 2,600,000 Russians. There were also Czechs, Austrians, Hungarians, Dutchmen, and Frenchmen, Swiss, and Finns—indeed, men and women of all the European peoples, not to mention Mexicans, Cubans, and Filipinos, Japanese and Chinese, Armenians, Turks, and Syrians.

In course of time all these newcomers learn to speak English—or shall we say American ?—but a very large number of them continue to cherish their own languages. We are told that in the U.S.A. there are published every day 111 newspapers in foreign languages, ranging from thirteen in German to one each in Arabic, Cretan, and Portuguese. New York may claim to be the most cosmopolitan city in the world, for out of its 7,000,000 citizens there are 5,000,000 of " foreign white stock."

Then in addition to these " foreigners " there are some 12,000,000 negroes, descendants of the slaves we read about in " Uncle Tom's Cabin " and " Gone with

One of President Roosevelt's achievements against which no voice was raised during the pre-sidential election was the agreement for the joint defence [of the United States and Canada. Above, the President is seen, left, just after the conference on August 18, 1940. Next to him is the Canadian Prime Minister, Mr. Mackenzie King, and right, Mr. Stimson, U.S. Secretary for War.
Photo; Fox

the Wind." Slavery was abolished by President Lincoln's proclamation in 1862, but there are still negroes alive who were born slaves. Theoretically, the negro is on a level of equality with the white man, but in the South most of the states have laws which insist that there must be separate accommodation on railways, buses, and street cars for whites and negroes, and every obstacle is put in the way of negroes desiring to exercise the franchise. In the North, where there are now many millions of negroes, the tendency is for them to live apart in their own quarters in the towns, such as Harlem in New York, although there is no such ban as in the Southern States.

Yet in spite of this immense " foreign " element in the American population, it is probably true to say that the British element is still the most influential. The Americans are not British, and they have never forgotten that their ancestors beat ours at Bunker's Hill and Saratoga. Nevertheless, as Robert Waithman puts it in his book " Report on America," although they sometimes distrust, they seldom dislike the British people. " Perhaps it could be put in this way," he says : " the English are convinced that God is an Englishman, because they feel that with a Russian, German, or Japanese mind God would be too difficult to reach. The Americans think of God as an American. But if, on entering heaven, an American were to find that God was in fact an Englishman, the probability is that he would not be very alarmed."

But the most important fact about America is that in a world in which democracy has

130 Millions Under the Star-Spangled Banner

taken the count in so many countries, the U.S.A. still prides itself upon being the world's greatest democracy. It was in America that modern democracy had its birth when at Philadelphia on July 4, 1776, in the Declaration of Independence adopted by the Continental Congress, it was declared that " we hold these truths to be self-evident, that all men are created equal, that they are endowed by their Creator with certain un-alienable Rights, that among these are Life, Liberty, and the pursuit of Happiness. That, to secure these rights, Governments are instituted among Men, deriving their just

So vast is the territory of the U.S.A., so huge its population, that in common speech we refer to it and them as America and the Americans. Not surprisingly, it is a land of many contrasts; for example, the photograph on the right was taken in the Chinese quarter of San Francisco on the Pacific coast, while the other (below) shows the negro quarter of Harlem in New York, 3,000 miles away on the Atlantic.

wanted a man to trust in, a man to follow, and she found him in this liberal-minded son of one of New York's greatest and wealthiest families. Supposing, it has been often asked since then, that Roosevelt II had been a Hitler? Such was her mood, she might well have plunged forthwith along the totalitarian road. But he was no Hitler—fortunately for America—and fortunately for us.

powers from the consent of the governed . . ." and 90 years later, Abraham Lincoln, dedicating the National Cemetery at Gettysburg in which were interred soldiers slain in the Civil War, closed with the never-to-be-forgotten words: " We here highly resolve that these dead shall not have died in vain— that this nation under God shall have a new birth of freedom—and that government of the people, by the people, for the people, shall not perish from the earth."

Yet there was a time—only a few years ago, in fact—when it seemed that the political fabric of the United States was threatened with collapse, together with the whole economic and social structure. The blackest day in American history was Saturday, March 4, 1933, when after the boom America touched the bottom of the slump. There were perhaps 14 millions unemployed; the banks were closed, many of them never to open again; the stock market had crashed into ruin; on every hand there were the signs of poverty, distress, and intensest depression. On that day Franklin Delano Roosevelt assumed the Presidency, and hardly had he begun his inaugural address when the millions listening-in took from him fresh heart. " The only thing we have to fear is fear itself," he said, " a nameless, unreasonable, and unjustifiable terror," and he proceeded to outline a vast programme of reform. America breathed again; she

Looking through the steel lattice work of Brooklyn Bridge, we see that city of cloud-capped towers, New York, second only to London in size and population. In the foreground are the quays that line the shores of Manhattan, facing East River; the three most prominent sky-scrapers in the centre of the view are those of City Bank Farmers' Trust, Cities' Service, and Bank of Manhattan.

Photos, Topical, Dorien Leigh and Wide World

London By Night Through American Eyes

How does London at the height of the battle look to one who, though he is in it, is not actually of it ? Here is the answer in the shape of an account of his impressions of London by Mr. Ralph Ingersoll, proprietor of " P.M.," the New York evening newspaper, broadcast to America on October 29, and a few words spoken by Quentin Reynolds, London Correspondent of another famous American paper, " Collier's Weekly."

I HAVE been here nine days now (said Mr. Ingersoll). By day I have been talking to members of the Government. By night I have been visiting underground shelters, and over the week-end I made a two-day round of the military airports defending London

The city of London lives two lives, one by day and one by night. By day, life in the city is almost normal ; there is the cheerful noise of the traffic in the street, people come and go from offices and shops, restaurants are crowded at lunch time. Now and then there is the siren to startle the newcomer, but Londoners pay little attention to daytime raids. There is no rush for shelters, but if the sky is clear people look up to see if they can see the raider.

I shall have to wait till I get back to America to tell my bomb stories. Hereabouts the man who makes anecdotes of his narrow escapes is called a bomb bore, and people sidle away to talk of other things.

To the visitor who has not been here since the war the most startling change is the sudden end of the day at black-out time.

The papers publish the exact minute at which the black-out begins as our papers publish the weather—in one corner of a prominent page. In the half-hour preceding, the entire city of 8,000,000 people shut, curtain, board up and black out every window in their dwellings, offices, hotels, private homes—everywhere people live or work. The streets empty suddenly. The only lights that come on are hooded or masked, lights giving directions to shelters, first-aid posts, or showing obstructions in the highways.

The City Ready for the Germans

The only noises on the streets are the gears of the buses which run on through the night, the clap of boots on the pavements—usually the service boots of the police, the A.R.P. wardens and the Home Guardsmen, who challenge you in the dark when you cross their beat.

All but a few of the taxis have disappeared. Within a few minutes after the black-out the city is ready. It is a little after half-past six. Within a few minutes it comes : the evening siren. The Germans are methodical and punctual fellows.

They come droning through the black, and some nights the searchlights spout into the air to meet them round the edge of the city. Sometimes the tall fountains of light disappear up into the mist. Sometimes they break against low clouds in a white glow. Sometimes there are no searchlights and you can trace the approach of the 'planes by the sounds and flashes of the anti-aircraft guns. They thud far off over the horizon. Then those near the city bark with a hollow sound ; then all of a sudden you jump out of your boots when one goes off a few hundred yards away.

When they are close you can wait and count to 10 or 11 and then see the little flicks of exploding shells in the sky, and a minute later you can hear the thud, thud, thud, thud of the explosions themselves coming down from miles in the sky. It is a fine, heartening feeling to think that one of those shells may be knocking the tail off the man who is trying to drop nitro-glycerine on your head.

When the guns are quiet you can hear the droning buzz, quite distinct from the noise of transport 'planes flying back and forth from the La Guardia Field at home—for their motors are kept out of synchroniza-

Mr. Ralph A. Ingersoll, the American newspaper proprietor who broadcast to America on October 29 his impressions of wartime London. *Photo, Keystone*

tion to make it more difficult for the sound detectors to pick them up. Often they fly round and round trying to orient themselves.

That is life on the streets at night ; under the streets there is a whole other life, the life in the shelters. There is no precise pattern to the London shelter, they are improvised and of all sizes. The only generalization is that each is in the charge of an A.R.P. warden or a staff of wardens, and the people bring their own bedding. Most are crowded, and people sleep there in rows, shoulder to shoulder—all kinds of people, children and grown-ups, men and women.

In one of the big underground shelters in which I spent most of one night 8,000 people slept. There one could see the whole evolution of shelter life under one roof. Deep in one cavernous room people slept shoulder to shoulder, till they were so crowded, with no more room on the floor, that they slept propped against walls, curled up on metal stairs in unbelievable congestion. Cold and draughty at one end, it was thick and uncomfortable at another.

Yet a few hundred yards away a beginning had been made on bringing order out of this chaos. Hundreds of sturdy, triple-tier bunks had been installed, like camp beds one upon another, but made with heavy burlap instead of canvas. Each was numbered, and the occupant came back to the same bed every night.

The big shelters in the deep Tubes, 60 ft. underground, are at once the safest and the most depressing. In one you can walk a full half-mile, stepping over the feet of an absolutely solid carpet of sleeping humanity. In the middle of the tunnel you feel as if you could take a handful of air and press it between your hands and make a snowball of it. The night I was there there were 4,500 people jammed together.

The wardens and the nurses in the first-aid shelters were to me the most inspiring people I have met in London—calm, courageous, tireless volunteers, interested only in the people they look after. When rules are too few or too complicated they make their own with great good sense. They will one day erect monuments in this city to the unknown shelter warden.

I have said this before and I should like to say it again—not until you have been here and seen what it is like to live in an aerial

siege can you get any idea of the size of the problem of the magnificence with which the people of London are rising to meet it. Everywhere there is the calm and casual courage that takes your breath away in admiration.

The bombing of civilians is a brutal and ugly thing, but the heroism with which it is met and endured here restores one's confidence in humanity. Nowhere in nine days of walking and talking did I see the slightest evidence of indecision or faltering. Here Fascism has stubbed its toe on the character of a people who can " take it," and who obviously propose to take it until the last German raider has gone down in smoke or hot-footed it for home with two Spitfires on his tail.

A ND here is part of the commentary to the film " London Can Take It," spoken by Mr. Quentin Reynolds.

I am a neutral reporter. I have watched the people of London live and die ever since death in its most ghastly garb began to come here as a nightly visitor. I have watched them stand by their homes. I have seen them made homeless. I have seen them move to new homes. And I can assure you that there is no panic, no fear, no despair in London town ; there is nothing but determination, confidence and high courage among the people of Churchill's Island.

It is true that the Nazis will be over again tomorrow night and the night after that and every night. They will drop thousands of bombs and they'll destroy hundreds of buildings and they'll kill thousands of people. But a bomb has its limitations. It can only destroy buildings and kill people. It cannot kill the unconquerable spirit and courage of the People of London.

London can take it !

Mr. D. A. Deasy, a Battalion Chief of the New York City Fire Department who came to London to study our fire fighting methods, talking to a driver at London Fire Brigade Headquarters. *Photo, Associated Press*

They Keep the King's Peace in Palestine

The men of the Palestine Police of British birth share with their Arab comrades the traditional love for their horses of those who ride the deserts.

After a hard day's riding beneath the desert sun the first thought of the police is to water their horses. Top right, men of a mechanized section searching for a smugglers' lair in the mountains.

THE task of keeping the King's Peace in the wild and arid district of the Jordan Valley in Palestine falls to the Palestine Police. This fine body of men numbers about 170 officers and nearly 3,000 other ranks, of whom about 20 per cent, including all the officers, are British and 80 per cent of the other ranks Arabs. The British members of the force come from all parts of the United Kingdom. There are a mounted section and a mechanized section, and most of their work lies in the trackless and waterless wastes which lie around the Jordan.

Circle, is a constable of the Palestine Police well mounted and clothed in a uniform which, while smart, is admirably suited for the conditions under which his duties are performed. Above, a troop of the police are fording the river in the Jordan valley. One of the duties of the police is to guard the Jordan fords against drug smugglers, and this is trying work, for the precipitous cliffs on either side of the river make it almost intolerably hot.

Photos, British Official : Crown Copyright (special to THE WAR ILLUSTRATED)

Fighter Pilots See Their Fighters Building

The construction of the wings of fighters is being explained by experts to the visiting pilots. The pilot officer on the left has lessened the Nazi air strength by 11 'planes.

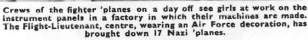

Crews of the fighter 'planes on a day off see girls at work on the instrument panels in a factory in which their machines are made. The Flight-Lieutenant, centre, wearing an Air Force decoration, has brought down 17 Nazi 'planes.

One day in October, 1940, when the pilots of a famous fighter squadron were not engaged in bringing down or driving off Nazi 'planes, they visited an aircraft factory, following upon a visit of the workers to their squadron. As a souvenir of the visit a miniature model of a fighter was presented to the Commanding Officer of the Squadron (circle). The visitors had destroyed at least 30 enemy machines between them. The one, left, in the photograph above, chatting to workers in the factory, was ship-wrecked and afloat on a raft for three days before he was rescued. At the end of their visit the pilots watched the finishing touches being given to a 'plane, left, and saw instances of the care and skill which enable them to have perfect confidence in the workmanship of their machines when they take them aloft.

Photos, British Official : Crown Copyright

New Turkey Is Like a Strong Man Armed

Following Italy's attack on Greece, Turkey's position became, if more difficult, at the same time more commanding. Now, as for centuries past, she is the guardian of the Straits, and she stands in the way of the Dictators' march on the oilfields of Irak and Iran.

In our fathers' days Turkey was the " sick man of Europe." She had been dying for centuries, and during the long reign of Abdul Hamid II (1876-1909)—that villainous old fellow who earned so well the title of " Abdul the Damned "—it seemed

in the Balkan War of 1912 Turkey was so soundly beaten by the Serbs, Greeks and Bulgars that she was almost driven out of Europe. True, in the next year when the victors fell out she recovered Adrianople with Bulgaria's aid, but the issue of the Great

itself was occupied, and nothing was left to the Turks save a tiny corner in Europe and Asia Minor—and even that was threatened with Italian and Greek domination.

In 1918 Turkey was down and out ; the sick man seemed to be really dead. Yet before long there were many signs of a national awakening, due almost entirely to that extraordinary man, one of the real makers of the modern world, Mustapha Kemal Pasha—Ataturk, as later he came to be styled. In 1922 Kemal chased the Greek invaders into the sea and bade successful defiance to the Allies in Constantinople. The last of the sultans, Mohammed VI, took refuge in the British cruiser " Malaya " and escaped to Malta. Turkey was proclaimed a republic with Kemal as its first President, while Ismet Pasha—now President Inonu—formed a cabinet.

Thus began a sweeping reformation. In the course of a few years Islam was disestablished as the state religion, and the new law code removed religion from public affairs altogether, and made it a matter of purely private choice ; the fez was abolished, and also the Arabic alphabet in favour of the Latin we use ourselves ; polygamy was frowned upon, women were unveiled and given the vote ; and in every sphere, legal and social, economic and political, the sexes were put on terms of equality.

So sweeping were the reforms, so rapid the pace with which they were effected, that it is not surprising that there were some of the older generation who protested, but the protests were soon silenced ; some of the discontented were given the opportunity to change their opinions in gaol, while the more hardened and hopeless cases were strung up by the hangman. Kemal knew his own mind and was in a hurry.

Yet, in spite of all, the nationalist revolution in Turkey shows every sign of being permanent. For the first time in history Turkey is now a homogeneous country ; perhaps it was from Kemal that Hitler learnt to " bring home " his Germans, for years ago Turkey arranged for an exchange of populations with Greece, so that now there is hardly a Turk

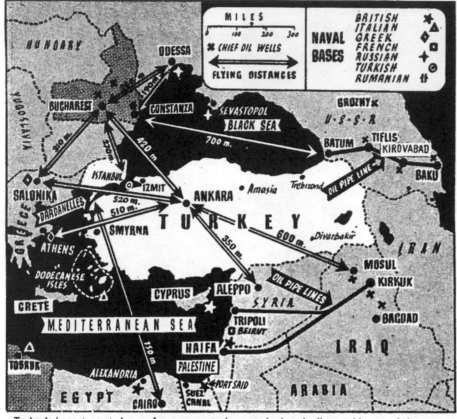

Turkey's importance today, as for many centuries past, is that she lies astride one of the most important of the world's waterways—the straits which connect the Black Sea with the Mediterranean. Even up to a generation or two ago she possessed vast territories in the Balkans and the Near East, but in the course of a succession of wars these were shorn away until now she stands out as a compact and racially homogeneous nation state.

that nothing could save her from dissolution. Province after province was lost to the " unspeakable Turk "—Carlyle's phrase—and after the old sultan died the process was quickened. In 1911 Italy seized Tripoli, and

War was even more disastrous. Despite her defeat of the British and French in the Dardanelles, by 1918 Turkey was completely crushed, and the conquerors deprived her of Syria, Palestine, and Arabia. Constantinople

The Commander-in-Chief of the Turkish Army and Air Force is Marshal Fevzi Chakmak, seen here reviewing a number of young Turkish air pilots. He served through the wars with Italy and in the Balkans and was one of the first members of Kemal's staff. Chief of the Navy is Vice-Admiral Sukor Okan (left).

Photos, Fox and Wide World

Astride the Straits Between Europe and Asia

At Ankara is the military academy where Turkish officers receive their military education. Above are some of the cadets mounted on motor-cycles and side-cars, three to each vehicle and all dressed in full war kit, starting off on a day's manoeuvres.

The soldiers of modern Turkey show every likelihood of living up to their fathers' reputation. These photographs show Turkish machine-gunners during manoeuvres, and another machine-gunner—this time in the Air Force—getting the feel of his guns before taking off on a practice flight from Eskisehir Air College, where men of the Turkish Air Force are trained.

Turkey's Navy, though not large, may at least be described as respectable. It comprises one battle cruiser, two light cruisers, four destroyers, and six submarines. Above we see one of the submarines, the "Dumlupinar," built in Italy in 1931 ; she has a surface displacement of 920 tons and an armament of one 4-inch gun, one machine-gun, and six torpedo tubes. Left centre, Turkish marines on parade in Ankara.

Photos, Keystone, Planet News, and René Zubar

Two Million Bayonets Bar the Aggressors' Path

Known today as Istanbul, yesterday as Constantinople, and before that as Byzantium, the great Turkish city is built on both shores of the Golden Horn, where the Sea of Marmora joins the Bosporus. In this photograph (left) the most prominent feature is the Mosque of Solyman the Great. The photograph on the right, showing a march past of Turkish peasants, was taken in Ankara.

Here are some more Turkish peasants photographed in Ankara on the occasion of a national festival. Their distinctive costume is rapidly becoming a thing of the past.

act of aggression leading to war in the Mediterranean area in which France and the United Kingdom are involved, and also to help France and the United Kingdom if, in fulfilling their guarantees to Greece and Rumania, they are involved in hostilities. It should be added that a protocol to the Ankara Treaty states that the obligations undertaken by Turkey cannot compel her to take action having as its effect, or involving as its consequence, entry into armed conflict with the U.S.S.R.

But though she has followed the paths of peace and asks nothing more than to be left alone, Turkey knows that her present position was secured by the sword and may have to be maintained by the sword. Hence no pains or money have been spared to build up the Turkish Army into a most formidable fighting force. Its strength in peacetime is 20,000 officers and 175,000 men; military service is compulsory from the age of twenty, and the annual contingent of recruits called to the colours is about 90,000. On a war footing an army of well over 2,000,000 men could take the field.

The Turkish Navy has been in the throes of reorganization for some time past. The principal vessel is the battle-cruiser "Yavuz," which won fame in the last war under the German flag as the "Goeben"; there are two cruisers and a handful of destroyers and submarines, and a number of smaller vessels.

The Turkish Air Force has been recently reorganized, and it is now equipped with fairly modern aircraft of British, American, Polish, and German makes, but its first-line strength is only 550 aeroplanes.

left in Greece and hardly a Greek left in Turkey.

Because of its compactness of territory, its uniformity of racial composition, present-day Turkey is far stronger than the Turkey of the Sultans. As we have seen, it is the creation of two soldiers, Kemal and his lieutenant, Inonu (who succeeded as President on Kemal's death in 1938), yet since the Greeks were driven out in 1922 Turkey has pursued a policy of "peace, retrenchment, and reform." Though Communism has been strictly suppressed in Turkey, the relations between Soviet Russia and Turkey have been of the best since 1920; and since 1930 another old enemy, Greece, has been accepted as a friend. Turkey joined Greece, Yugoslavia, and Rumania in the Balkan Entente concluded in 1934, and in 1937 she was a partner with Iran, Irak and Afghanistan in the Saadabad Pact of non-aggression.

Much more important, however, is her adhesion to the Anglo-Franco-Turkish Pact signed at Ankara on October 19, 1939 (see Vol. I, pp. 264 & 274); under this treaty Turkey promised to come to the aid of Britain and France if a European power commits an

Very different is Ankara, the capital of modern Turkey, from Istanbul, the other city which was for centuries the seat of the Ottoman Porte. Ankara, situated in the heart of the Anatolian highlands, is a new city built very largely on ground which only a few years ago was waste. Some idea of its character may be had from this photograph.

Photos, René Zuber

Italian 'Planes in Battle for Greece

(Six other types of the Regia Aeronautica are illustrated in page 289)

MARINE aircraft such as those shown here will doubtless play a large part in the struggle for bases in the islands of the Aegean, while the fighter, bomber and ground assault aeroplanes also shown are striving to subdue the Greek land forces.

1.—CANT Z 501
A four-seater flying-boat used for bombing and reconnaissance. Has a range of 800 miles, with a maximum speed of 170 m.p.h. The single engine is an Isotta-Fraschini Asso (XI RC 15). Armed with four 12·7 mm. machine-guns. Wing span, 73 ft. 10 in.

3.—BREDA 88
One of Italy's most modern aircraft, built for ground attack and fighting, and also used for light bombing and reconnaissance. Has a maximum speed of 330 m.p.h., with a range of 1,120 miles. Two Piaggio PXI engines (RC 40). Wing span, 50 ft. 10 in. The armament is three 12·7 mm. machine-guns and two 7·7 mm. guns. Ceiling, 27,850 ft.

4.—CR 32
An oldish type of biplane fighter. Fitted with a Fiat engine (A 30 RA), and has a range of 520 miles. Armed with two 12·7 mm. machine-guns. Wing span, 36 ft. 2 in. Maximum speed is 240 m.p.h. Ceiling, 26,200 ft.

2.—CANT Z 506 B
A three-engined float seaplane for bombing, torpedo dropping and reconnaissance. Armed with three 12·7 mm. guns. The top speed is about 229 m.p.h. Fitted with three Alfa Romeo engines (126 RC 34). Wing span 86 ft. 11 in. Range, 1,200 miles.

TYPES of aircraft used by Italy's Regia Aeronautica (Royal Italian Air Force) were illustrated in page 289, Vol. 3. Here are some further examples. The possession of a long sea coast has affected considerably the type of aircraft designed by Italy for war purposes, and seaplanes and flying-boats of the kind shown here are numerous in consequence. The Cant Z 501 flying-boat is extremely well armed, with two guns in a cockpit placed behind the engine nacelle, plus one in the front cockpit and another on the hull. The Z 506 B seaplane is designed primarily for torpedo work in addition to bombing and reconnaissance.

Italy has concentrated strongly on machines whose chief function is ground attack. Two are here illustrated. The Breda 88 is one of the most modern, attaining a speed of 330 m.p.h. and a ceiling of 27,850 feet. In eleven minutes this aircraft can climb to 16,400 feet. The Breda 65 has a shorter range and is considerably slower. Both these 'planes can be employed for light bombing and as fighters.

By contrast we show, in the CR 32, an almost obsolete biplane fighter that is still retained in service.

The Fiat BR 20 is typical of many of Italy's bombing and reconnaissance machines. Some were stated unofficially to have attempted an attack on Britain at the end of October, 1940. Two 18-cylinder radial engines are fitted, giving 1,000 h.p. at a height of 13,500 feet. This machine can climb to 16,400 feet in eighteen minutes.

Drawings taken by permission from "Chart of Italian Aircraft," issued by "Flight" Publishing Co. Ltd., Dorset House, Stamford Street, London, S.E.

5.—BREDA 65
Single-seater designed mainly for ground attack, but can be used as a two-seater and employed for reconnaissance or light bombing. Approximate range of 720 miles. Fitted with a Fiat engine (A 80 RC 41), and has a top speed of 265 m.p.h. Armament is two 12·7 mm. guns and two 7·7 mm. guns. Wing span, 39 ft. 8 in. Ceiling, 27,000 ft.

6.—FIAT BR 20
(Below, right and left.) A two-engined monoplane for bombing and reconnaissance, fitted with two Fiat engines (A 80 RC 41); maximum speed 263 m.p.h. Wing span of 70 ft. 6 in. The armament is four 12·7 mm. guns (two in a retractable turret on top of the fuselage). Approximate range 1,100 miles.

Like the Greeks of Old Who Triumphed at M

on and Salamis Theirs Is a Fight for Freedom

ALTHOUGH the peacetime strength of Greece's Army was only some 70,000, in time of war she can put a million and more men into the field. Man for man, the Greek soldier should prove more than a match for the Italian, and even the Greek equipment is apparently better than has been generally believed. "The Greek divisions," an Italian war correspondent has testified, "are well equipped and have good artillery and machine-guns and plenty of them." In these pages we have a number of illustrations of the Greek Army in training. 1. A sergeant explains how an automatic rifle works. 2. Infantrymen at drill. 3. More infantrymen, carrying a Bren gun and rifles, advancing; the men in the rear are practising throwing hand grenades. 4. Practising the art of firing grenades—one admirably suited to Greece's mountain terrain. 5. Like every other modern army the Greeks are equipped with gas masks; two of the patterns are illustrated here.

Photos, Keystone

'Old Sweats' Have a Job of Work in London

Men of the Auxiliary Military Pioneer Corps are actively engaged in the clearance of debris in the London area.　Above they are seen refreshing themselves on the edge of a bomb crater.　A crane driver gives "thumb-up" sign (top right).

Left, men of the Pioneer Corps engaged on salvage work are carrying the bronze horses and aspidistras out of a wrecked home.　Right, some of the Pioneers who are engaged in clearing away debris are arriving in a bombed area with two lorries loaded with wheelbarrows. Circle, Sir Warren Fisher, Commissioner for the London area, inspects salvage.

Photos, Planet News, " News Chronicle," Sport & General

Nazi Defeat in the Air Battle Now Made Clear

During the seven days, October 28 to November 4, the air offensive over Britain progressively decreased, and the publication by the Air Ministry of a review of the air Battle for Britain made it clear that in the twelve preceding weeks the R.A.F. and the A.A. defences had broken the Nazi air offensive.

IN twelve weeks of the Battle for Britain three Nazi aircraft and fourteen airmen were lost to every one of ours. Since August 8 the Luftwaffe has lost in all 2,433 bombers and fighters—in almost equal proportions. Over 6,000 German airmen were killed or taken prisoner as compared with 353 pilots lost by our own Fighter Command. An analysis of the enemy attacks reveals a constant change of tactics—and also a gradual weakening of the German effort. Dive-bombers were sent over to attack shipping convoys and harbours, but on August 8 24 Junkers 87s and 36 Messerschmitts were destroyed. On August 15, with a thousand bombers and fighters, the enemy made the biggest air attack on record, directed mainly against aerodromes and harbours. This cost him 180 aircraft, and in a single week 472

the raiders lost 133 machines, of which 91 were fighters. By the end of the month there were few bombers employed in day raids, which henceforth were made by Messerschmitts. But the R.A.F. continued to destroy them in number—for example, 28 on October 7 and 30 on October 29.

After the middle of October the raids diminished in intensity both by day and night. On November 3, for the first time in 57 nights, London had no Alert. There was a slow but constant increase in the number of night bombers destroyed during the month.

Enemy air attacks on Monday, October 28, were not on a big scale. Formations which crossed the South-east coast were broken up and dispersed, some being chased back to France by our fighters. Other groups dropped bombs at a few points in East Anglia.

GERMAN & BRITISH AIRCRAFT LOSSES

German to April 30, 1940

Total announced and estimated—West Front, North Sea, Britain, Scandinavia 350

	German	British
May	1,990	258
June	276	177
July	245	115
Aug.	1,110	310
Sept.	1,114	311
Oct.	241	119
Nov. 1-3	29	8
Totals, May to Nov. 3 ...	**5,005**	**1,298**

Daily Results

Oct.	German Losses	British Losses	British Pilots Saved	Oct.	German Losses	British Losses	British Pilots Saved
1	5	3	—	20	7	3	3
2	13	1	—	21	5	—	—
3	1	—	—	22	3	6	2
4	3	1	—	23	1	—	—
5	23	9	4	24	2	—	—
6	2	—	—	25	17	10	7
7	28	16	10	26	6	2	—
8	8	2	—	27	10	8	4
9	4	1	1	28	7	—	—
10	5	5	2	29	30	7	5
11	8	9	6	30	9	5	1
12	12	10	6	31	—	—	—
13	2	2	2		241	119	62
14							
15	18	15	9	Nov.			
16	6	—	—	1	18	7	2
17	4	3	—	2	10	—	—
18	—	1	—	3	1	1	—
19	2	—	—	Totals	29	8	2

None of the figures includes aircraft bombed on the ground or so damaged as to be unlikely to reach home.

From the beginning of the war up to Nov. 3, 2,793 enemy aircraft have been destroyed during raids on Britain. R.A.F. losses were 788, but the pilots of 384 British machines were saved.

Civilian Casualties. Intensive air attacks on Britain began on Aug. 8. Casualties during August, 1,075 killed, 1,261 seriously injured. During September: 6,954 killed; 10,615 seriously injured.

Mr. Churchill on Nov. 5 gave weekly average of killed and seriously wounded for September as 4,500; for October, 3,500. In first week of intense bombardment in September, 6,000 casualties; in the last week of October, only 2,000 casualties.

In times of peace Leicester Square was the hub of the London entertainment world. The Nazi bombers made direct hits upon it a few weeks ago, and here is the south side the day after. On the left of the street, opposite a collapsed restaurant, is the Leicester Square Cinema. A wrecked taxi, one of five, is seen, right, outside Thurston's Billiard Hall.

Photos, Planet News and Wide World

of his bombers and fighters were destroyed.

Dive-bombers were discredited, and even the introduction of a newer type—the Junkers 88—did not restore the balance. From the middle of August the numbers used fell off. But in daylight raids the Luftwaffe still kept to the big bombers for a time. In the fierce attack of September 7 the Germans lost 103; in an even more determined attempt made a week later the toll was 185 (later semi-officially increased to 232). More fighters were sent over as escorts, but even with a four-to-one ratio (September 27)

With matchless courage, crippled children sang songs while they were being carried to safety from an institution in South-eastern England on Monday night. Three bombs fell on the building, and debris was showered on the little ones, but their injuries were nothing worse than cuts and bruises. Though high explosive bombs exploded a few yards from the wards of a London hospital the surgeons went on with urgent operations

Here is Proof that 'London Can Take It'

The tenant of this bombed house was asleep when the Nazi bomber demolished part of his home. Although the window and the outside wall of his bedroom had disappeared, he finished dressing calmly under somewhat draughty conditions. Here he is seen at the washstand, indifferent to the damage.
Photo, Photopress

This little fruiterer's shop in London suffered badly from the effects of blast when a bomb exploded near by. The proprietor, himself an auxiliary fireman, is seen picking up fragments of his shattered shop-window which have been scattered over the display of piled-up fruit.
Photo, Associated Press

throughout the night. A boy of 15 was trapped for six hours when the concrete roof of a shelter fell and crushed his foot, but he held out bravely until the work of rescue could be completed. Bombs pierced the roof of a London church and penetrated to the crypt, where many people were sheltering. Several were killed by the explosions.

Four daylight attacks were attempted on London during Tuesday, October 29. In the morning about fifty fighters and fighter-bombers took part, and though a few slipped past our defences and dropped bombs, the majority were turned back. Later in the day an even larger party flew up the Thames Estuary, but again most were frustrated by our fighters and the guns. Thirty enemy aircraft were destroyed—a remarkable achievement considering that in this case they were high-performance fighter-bombers. Two fierce attacks were made on the Portsmouth area ; in the second one the raiders dropped bombs on shops and houses.

Besides the London area, night raiders

A trailer car that supplies warm clothes and hot food to those rendered homeless has been presented to the Westminster City Council. Here clothes and blankets are being packed into it ready for the next call.
Photo, Planet News

attacked Liverpool and places in Wales, N.E. and S.E. England and the South-east of Scotland. But along the S.E. coast of England the raiders encountered a new barrage. Many turned back, dropping their bombs over the open country and abandoning the attack on the capital. Some bombers by flying very high managed to get to London, but the raid petered out at an early hour.

On Wednesday, October 30, the Luftwaffe scaled down their daylight attacks on the S.E. area and on London. They took advantage of low cloud to fly in over the Kentish coast, but were nevertheless intercepted and driven off and scattered before they got far inland. Nine were shot down by the R.A.F. There was dive-bombing by ME 109s at a S.E. town, and one raider came down low and gunned motorists.

Throughout the Country the Same Brave Spirit

A "south-wester" blowing over the Straits may have accounted for the comparatively quiet night enjoyed by Londoners on Wednesday. The raid ceased at an early hour and was on a small scale again. A few bombs were dropped in the Midlands, and on an East Anglian town. A Junkers 88 came down near Ely ; two of the crew had baled out and two others surrendered to a woman.

A sky with low clouds on Thursday gave the raiders another chance of hit-and-run tactics, and they attacked several towns in this fashion. Only a few aircraft took part. There was an early Alert in the evening, but the Raiders Passed sounded before the night was far advanced. Some hours later there was another warning.

London had three daytime Alerts on Friday, and bombs were dropped on the outskirts. Italian aircraft were reported among the raiders which came in over the S.E. coast. The night attacks were bigger than of late,

A remarkable photograph of a parachute flare dropped by German night raiders over London. The tracer bullets that shot the flare down reveal themselves by their paths.
Photo, Fox

and were made from a number of directions. A heavy barrage was maintained for several hours, being especially fierce over the Thames Estuary.

On Saturday morning an attack by fighters and fighter-bombers was foiled and the raiders were turned back ; in a later attempt, by about a hundred aircraft, bombs were dropped in Kent and Essex and a few of the enemy flew high over London. The night raids ended before midnight and were on a small scale. A few bombs fell in the London area and others in the Home Counties, in Eastern and in S.E. England.

Diving out of low cloud, several lone raiders dropped bombs in London districts on Sunday morning, and turned their guns on to people in the streets. In East Anglia and in the Midlands the same tactics were used, but few bombs in all were dropped and little damage was done. After an Alert in the afternoon, followed before dusk by the Raiders Passed signal, London spent a night without a raid warning.

Five hundred people in Kent have made their homes in disused chalk-pits, 90 ft. below the ground. These shelters form a series of tunnels which connect the pits, and one tunnel, 300 ft. in length, provides accommodation for 240 "cave dwellers." Here we see a family at dinner. Table, chairs, and household utensils give a realistic atmosphere of the home above ground.

A fleet of 260 motor ambulances has been provided by the American colony in London to assist air-raid victims. The ambulances are driven by women in the M.T.C. and W.T.S. Here are four members of the service—who are all fully qualified in first aid—rescuing a victim.
Photo, Central Press

Nazi Threat of Shipping Blockade Fails Again

Despite heavy and increased submarine attacks on Britain's merchant shipping in
September accompanying the pseudo-solemn declaration of a "complete blockade"
the situation was satisfactory. By contrast, U-boat losses were severe.

ON August 17, 1940, Germany made a solemn declaration of "a complete blockade of the British Isles." By that time the world was in no doubt that both Germany and Italy were doing everything in their power, regardless of international law or the neutrality of nations, to sink all shipping then trading to this country or likely to do so. The declaration was made with the intention of frightening the shipowners of the few remaining neutral maritime countries in Europe who continued to employ their ships in the lucrative trade with Britain. In particular, the threat was aimed at the tramp shipping of Greece, pressure being brought to bear in that country to persuade the shipping companies to break the chartering contracts they had made with the British Ministry of Shipping ; as a bribe, alternative employment was offered in the non-existent overseas "import trade of Germany and Italy."

Whatever the real purpose of this declaration, the world was supposed to believe that a new campaign was opening at sea, many times more destructive than before. What happened ? The average weekly rate of sinkings of British, Allied and neutral shipping rose slightly from about 80,000 tons gross to 87,000 tons up to the beginning of October. This increase was mainly due to the high losses of one week, that ending on September 22. The total losses for this week amounted to 172,467 tons, of which British ships accounted for 145,036 tons—then the highest figure for any week since the beginning of the war, even including the losses in the combined operations during the evacuation of the B.E.F.

The middle of September thus represented a peak of the enemies' submarine activity, for the majority of the sinkings were undoubtedly due to the U-boats rather than to aircraft, mines, surface raiders or the coastal batteries. It was in conformity with the experience of the war of 1914-18 that there should be a falling off in losses during subsequent weeks ; a fortnight later the tonnage of British ships lost was the lowest recorded since the beginning of May. The success of our enemies was not attained without some sacrifice on their part. The Admiralty departed from its usual policy of silence in regard to anti-submarine activity to announce the sinking during the previous few weeks of seven German U-boats ; in addition, more than 20 Italian submarines had been sunk up to the end of September.

It was a satisfactory feature of the month that, although the merchant shipping losses were high, no armed merchant cruisers or transports were lost, as the accompanying table shows. Naval losses also were comparatively slight, in spite of considerable naval activity in the Mediterranean and off the "invasion ports."

Foremost among the losses of merchant ships during September was that of the Ellerman liner "City of Benares." She was torpedoed without warning on the night of September 17, about 600 miles out in the Atlantic, while conveying 90 children to Canada. The weather was tempestuous and many boats were swamped. The death roll was tragically high. Only thirteen of the children, together with six more travelling privately,

Merchant Shipping War Losses for September 1940			
	Sept. 3, 1939 Sept. 1, 1940 Tons gross	Sept. 1 Sept. 29 Tons gross	Sept. 3, 1939 Sep. 29, 1940 Tons gross
BRITISH :			
Liners, cargo vessels	1,522,102	290,710	1,812,812
Lost in naval operations	73,220	—	73,220
Naval auxiliaries ...	151,033	—	151,033
Naval trawlers	17,105	604	17,709
Totals ...	1,763,460	291,314	2,054,774
ALLIED ...	462,921	56,199	519,120
Totals ...	2,226,381	347,513	2,573,894
NEUTRAL ...	769,213	42,870	812,083
Totals ...	2,995,594	390,383	3,385,977

Enemy Losses to September 29, 1940			
	Sunk	Captured	Total
GERMAN ...	808,000	259,000	1,067,000
ITALIAN ...	140,000	151,000	291,000
Totals ...	948,000	410,000	1,358,000

In addition, about 33,000 tons of neutral shipping under enemy control have been sunk. The figures cover four weeks.

were rescued, and out of a total ship's company of 406, 248 were drowned. Forty-six of the survivors, including six children, were eight days in an open boat before a Sunderland flying-boat guided a warship to their rescue. In an attempt to excuse their action, the Germans first claimed that the liner had struck a mine and later that she was an armed merchant cruiser.

A week or two after the disaster it was announced that no more children would be sent abroad during the winter under the Government's scheme. It was revealed at the time that a liner with 320 evacuees on board had been torpedoed in August in the Atlantic ; the ship stayed afloat and all the children were taken off.

The "City of Benares" was the flagship of the Ellerman Line, being the largest ship of the fleet. Of 11,081 tons gross, she was built on the Clyde as recently as 1936.

The list of captured German merchant ships was added to during the month by the exploits of a converted Canadian coastal passenger ship. The Norddeutscher Lloyd cargo liner "Weser," 9,179 tons gross, left the port of Manzanillo, Mexico, on September 25, with a cargo of oil in barrels—reported to number 19,000—intended possibly for re-fuelling enemy warships. The same evening she was captured by the "Prince Robert," a Canadian vessel of 6,892 tons serving as an armed merchant cruiser. "The Weser" was one of the fastest and best equipped German ships of the cargo liner type.

There was further news of the activities of the German surface raiders. Early in September a raider sank the British tanker "Cymbeline," 6,317 tons gross, 600 miles from the Azores after a brief exchange of shots. The tanker was on her way from Gibraltar to Trinidad.

Among the neutral merchant ships sunk in September were three Spanish vessels, each of them torpedoed by Italian submarines. They were the "Cabo Tortosa" (3,302 tons), the trawler "Almirante Jose de Carranza" and the "Monte Moncayo" (4,291 tons). The enemies' warfare at sea respects neither law, humanity nor friendship.

In her efforts to break the stranglehold of the British blockade, Germany has relied upon her U-boats. All the evidence goes to prove that in the relentless R.A.F. raids on docks and ship-building yards German submarine construction has suffered severely. Here are two U-boats in the course of being built. In September seven were sunk by the Navy. *Photo, Wide World*

How Destroyers Bring the Food Ships Home

THE NAVY'S TASK

Mr. A. V. Alexander, First Lord of the Admiralty, speaking in London on October 29 :

Large numbers of enemy submarines have been destroyed, destroyers and cruisers sunk . . .

The Navy was today not only defending the British lifeline, but it stood between the dictators and the free peoples in the Western hemisphere.

I feel that so long as we can continue to resist successfully, as we are doing, with the courage and fortitude of our people and the gallantry of our pilots in the air attack on these islands, sea power will eventually encompass the destruction of the enemy.

I hope the Navy may look for even greater cooperation in this decisive sphere of fight for victory and freedom. At this moment 2,500 British and Allied ships are on the seas on mercantile voyages, and we are receiving raw materials and weapons of war in enormous volume. When this traffic is compared with the limited movement open to mercantile marine of the enemy, it can be appreciated how great the daily gratitude to the Navy should be.

No doubt new and ever more threatening and dangerous methods of attack must be expected, but I am confident that the technical skill and courage of the Navy, backed by the resources of the scientists, will see us through.

A most important though not spectacular part is played in sea warfare by the destroyers that convoy the merchant ships through home waters and are called on to meet attacks on their charges from under the sea, from aircraft and from the big guns on the coast of France. In the top photograph machine-gunners with pom-poms that send a hail of bullets into the air are ready for dive-bombers. In the lower photograph, a destroyer sends out from her funnel a smoke screen to hide a convoy from the shore guns.

Photos, " Daily Mirror " and Central Press

The Animals in the Zoo Don't Mind the Raids

The Zoo in Regent's Park is not only one of the favourite resorts of Londoners but a national institution. Hence this account, reprinted by permission from "The Times," of how it is faring during the weeks of bombing will be of interest even to many who have not—as yet—passed through its gates.

THE Zoo has not escaped its share of bombs any more than the rest of London; and, like the rest of London, it is carrying on. It has suffered material damage, but no casualties to its inhabitants beyond the death of Boxer, the young giraffe born at Whipsnade, who panicked when bombs fell in a paddock near the giraffe house and died from overstrained heart, and the escape of three humming birds through a hole in the birdhouse roof. Some serious damage to glass has been caused by the detonation of unexploded bombs—that task so gallantly performed by the bomb-disposal section of the R.E.s; but after representations were made in the right quarter, detonating is now done at a greater distance and with fuller precautions, so that it is no longer a source of trouble.

Looking after a Zoo in wartime involves its own peculiar responsibilities. For instance, if a bomb falls in it the inhabitants cannot be evacuated; yet they must continue to be fed and looked after. Luckily the two possible time bombs that fell in the Gardens without exploding were both small and not unduly near a populous district, and the animals' routine could continue until the R.E.s got round to digging the bombs up. Then, of course, there is the obvious danger of savage animals escaping after their cages have been damaged by a bomb. Luckily, the great majority of Zoo animals are not savage and could be easily dealt with by the Zoo's special A.R.P. staff.

The humming birds which escaped are doubtless gone for ever, but do not constitute a danger to the population of London. A demoiselle crane escaped into Regent's Park when its enclosure was damaged by a high-explosive bomb, but was recaptured by the offer of food after a few days; and a zebra which was liberated by a direct hit on the zebra house was rounded up without much

These penguins at the London Zoo follow A.R.P. instructions. They are waiting to be admitted to the shelter as the "Alert" sounds.

difficulty and shepherded into a shed in the stores yard to await the morning.

Experienced keepers can manage to recapture most animals; but if a brown bear, say, or a chimpanzee, or a large antelope were to be liberated and to prove difficult, there are rifles and scatter-guns which could be brought into play as a last resort.

The zebra house (bottom left) was bombed, but this zebra, inside at the time of the explosion, escaped unhurt.
Photos, Exclusive to THE WAR ILLUSTRATED

There remain the really dangerous animals. Of these, the poisonous snakes and spiders were all destroyed within a few hours of the declaration of war, since it was felt that, if released, they might elude capture. The only others in this category are the larger cats and Polar bears. All the dangerous larger cats have been placed in the lion house, and every night are shut up in the inner sleeping dens. These are so situated that it would take two bombs to release an inmate—one to break open the den and a second to break the bars of either the outdoor or the indoor cage. The odds against such a double event are so great that its possibility can be safely disregarded. The Polar bears (whom the keepers almost unanimously regard as the most alarming inmates of the Zoo) are each night shut in the underground tunnel behind their terrace, from which escape would appear to be impossible.

Bombs near the Zebras

The Zoo authorities feel that no apprehension need be entertained of danger from lions or tigers being added to danger from bombs. Meanwhile, they have kept the Gardens open as one of the few places of open-air entertainment in war-stricken London, and numbers of visitors have testified to the feeling of escape into a saner and more agreeable world that accompanies an afternoon's visit to the Zoo.

The animals themselves have been singularly little incommoded by the air raids. A bomb which fell just beside the old rodent

house made it unsafe, and all its inmates have had to be transferred to the north mammal house and the adjacent isolation ward; but none of them shows any trace of ill-effects. A hasty inspection of the zebra house in the middle of the night when the bomb fell on it gave the impression that at least half a dozen beasts must have been killed, yet none was even injured, apart from scratches. A roof beam came down between two zebras in a stall, but without touching them.

The stall with the female wild ass and her foal was smashed to bits; the mother escaped into the paddock, while the foal, slightly scratched, found a way out at the back over the ruins of the clerk of the works' office, and

There's No Danger of Bombs Opening the Cages

George, the camel, displays initiative after the raid ; he is hauling away some of the debris caused by bombs while the keepers help to clear the wreckage. George, top right, is seen taking cover.

was found in the morning sheltering, as one lady put it, " under the hippo "—in sober fact, in the stokehole beneath the hippopotamus house.

Monkey Hill received a direct hit, which freakishly blew half-a-ton or so of the concrete of the hill over the parapet without damaging the latter at all. The monkeys escaped because, like good citizens, they had

The Giraffe House is one of the most popular places in the Zoo ; fortunately, the bomb which caused this crater fell outside it and little damage was done, although the giraffe Boxer later died.

taken shelter. They were all in the inner fastnesses of the hill, and none was injured. Next morning, far from showing any sign of shock, they were enjoying the new opportunities for gymnastic play afforded by the crater and the tumbled blocks of concrete around it.

For a time the Zoo was largely without running water owing to a direct hit on a main ; but all needs were supplied by peripatetic water carts. Visitors had to be sent away unfed, as the top storey of the restaurant was

badly damaged by fire ; but now the catering service is re-established. The Zoo in fact is a microcosm of London. Hitler's bombs cause a certain amount of damage to it, and a considerable amount of inconvenience ; but they have not destroyed the morale or the routine of its inhabitants, animal or human, and it continues to function with a very respectable degree of efficiency.

This 14-ft. python (circle) is put into a strong box by its keeper and conveyed to a place of safety. Results of a bomb are seen above in the Monkey Hill enclosure. Three chimpanzees, right (with gas mask and tin hat !), wait and watch anxiously outside their shelter door.

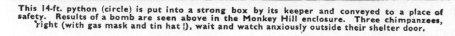

OUR SEARCHLIGHT ON THE WAR

Britain's Sympathy With Czechs

A MILITARY agreement between the British Government and the Provisional Czechoslovak Government was signed on October 25 by Lord Halifax and M. Jan Masaryk. It defines the principles on which the Czechoslovak armed forces will be organized, under their own Commander-in-Chief, for cooperation with the Allied Forces. The personnel of the Air Force, which has so distinguished itself, will be formed into Czechoslovak units attached to the R.A.F. The members will wear the normal R.A.F. uniform with distinctive badges. The land forces, which will be commanded by their own countrymen, will be organized out of troops now in Great Britain and the Middle East, and will be completed by mobilizing Czechoslovak citizens living in this country and by drafting volunteers from other countries. Czechoslovak regimental colours and badges will be retained. Dr. Benes, in a telegram to King George, said : '' This further act of Allied cooperation will meet with glad satisfaction in my sorely afflicted country, whose people it will encourage to redouble their opposition to German tyranny. The Czechoslovak soldiers and airmen will be proud to be, as the result of this agreement, more closely associated with their British brothers-in-arms.''

Eagle-Eyed Polish Airmen

F IGHTER squadrons composed of Polish airmen form a strong contingent of our Air Force. After their own country was overrun, about 200 officers and 2,000 airmen came to England and entered the R.A.F. Volunteer Reserve. When France capitulated these were reinforced by about 6,000 more who had been fighting with the Allies over there. Their success in accounting for the enemy has been striking, and one factor contributing to this is stated to be their exceptionally good eyesight. Two explanations have been given for this visual

On the side of a Hurricane of a Polish Squadron an amateur artist has been busy with a piece of chalk. The score justifies the claim, made by the inverted commas that it is "the" Polish Squadron.

Photo, British Official : Crown Copyright

superiority. First, because radio-telephony in Poland was poor compared with British standards, the Polish pilot had to rely entirely upon his eyes. Secondly, owing to the clarity of their country's atmosphere, the Poles are accustomed to focusing their eyes on points anything between 10 and 20 miles away, and are thus able to spot an aircraft before their more normally endowed British colleagues can see it. However this may be, one recently formed squadron shot

down 109 enemy machines during the month of September alone, and its total tally, as noted in the photograph below, is now 126.

First O.M. to the R.A.F.

T HE King conferred the Order of Merit on Marshal of the Royal Air Force Sir Cyril Newall when he received him at Buckingham Palace on October 29, on his appointment as Governor-General of New Zealand. The statutes of the Order were altered in 1935 to allow the honour to be awarded to officers of the R.A.F. as well as to those of the other Services ; but Sir Cyril is, nevertheless, the first airman to be admitted to this very exclusive Order. The other Service members are Field-Marshal Sir Philip W. Chetwode, Lt.-Gen. Lord Baden-Powell and Admiral of the Fleet Lord Chatfield.

Nazis Hide Our Raid Damage

I N the R.A.F. communiqués Duisburg is often included among the German towns in which military targets, such as the power station, receive our bombers' attention. A neutral business man who has just left Germany was granted a permit to make a two days' visit to the town, on condition that he first reported at the police-station there. Complying with this request, he was told that one day would be sufficient to transact business with the two firms he wished to see. Moreover, the police telephoned the managers to confirm that he was expected, and instructed both to conclude the interviews that day. This done, a policeman accompanied him to the appointments, and the route taken in each case was a roundabout one, although the surprised business man, who was well acquainted with the town, protested that they were going out of their way. Not once was the visitor left to his own devices, and he was firmly seen off by a prescribed train before nightfall. All of which tends to show how important it was felt to hide from neutral eyes the extent of the damage inflicted by the R.A.F. on just one town in Rhineland.

More Support for De Gaulle

L ONDON headquarters of the Free French Forces issued a communiqué on October 29 stating that General Legentilhomme had arrived in London and had placed himself at the disposal of General de Gaulle. General Legentilhomme, until the Franco-German Armistice, was in command of the Allied forces in French and British Somaliland at Jibuti under Sir Archibald Wavell, Commander-in-Chief of the Allied Forces in the Middle East. When the Armistice was declared he did his best to convince official and business people in Somaliland that it would pay them to back England. But Vichy got wind of this and dismissed him. He thereupon left Jibuti and went to Egypt. He is one of the survivors of the "Empress of Britain," having been rescued after many hours in an open boat.

Norway is Confident

H OW firm is the belief of the Norwegians that the Allies will win, and that the German interlopers will be banished from their country, is shown by a story going the rounds in Stockholm. A Norwegian went to one of the largest restaurants in Oslo and requested that a table should be reserved for him and his party for the day of King Haakon's return. The manager regretted, with unmixed satisfaction, that this was impossible, as every table had already been reserved not only for the first day but for the second and third as well. He offered one for the fourth day of celebration, and the applicant secured it with alacrity.

Bombs—and Bombs

M R. HOWE, Canadian Minister of Munitions, has gone to Washington to take part in conferences designed to speed up American production of war supplies. Before leaving Ottawa he announced that a huge new plant somewhere in Quebec was nearing completion, and by

Marshal of the Royal Air Force Sir Cyril Newall is the first airman to receive the Order of Merit. The Order was founded by King Edward VII in 1902 and is limited to 24 members who are distinguished by the letters O.M. after their names.

Photo, Keystone

February, 1941, would be turning out 500-lb. aerial bombs, with the eventual prospect of an output of 100,000 bombs a year.

Meanwhile, Germany is reported to have gone in for another form of '' ersatz.'' According to a radio statement from Moscow, the Nazis have started using bombs with concrete casings. '' The vast expenditure of metal in air bombing has induced Germany to look for substitutes, and concrete has been found suitable,'' said the speaker. '' The concrete bomb is said to have sufficient penetrating power to pierce two or three floors of an ordinary dwelling-house.'' This specification is of interest in view of the Nazi contention that military objectives only are sought by their airmen.

Homes Fit for Heroines

A FTER the Great Fire of 1666 which reduced most of London to ruins, Sir Christopher Wren submitted a comprehensive scheme for rebuilding the entire city. The plan, which is preserved at All Souls College, was approved by King Charles, but was shelved owing to expense and the sacrifice of many interests which would have been involved. The present destruction wrought by German bombers may eventually prove an indirect blessing, for one of the duties of Lord Reith, head of the new Ministry of Works and Buildings, is to report to the Cabinet on measures for the reconstruction of town and country after the war. The Government is alive to this immense opportunity for abolishing the slums and for so reorganizing the housing problem that those who have suffered the enemy's raids with such stoical endurance shall later enjoy better and brighter homes than they might ever have known.

I WAS THERE!

Eye Witness Stories of Episodes
and Adventures in the
Second Great War

Over Berlin I Shouted 'Let Them Go!'

During the R.A.F.'s four-hour raid on Berlin on the night of October 20-21, one heavy bomber scored a hit at 2,000 feet in the very heart of the city under a heavy barrage. The following story of this exploit was told by the sergeant-pilot on his return.

THE Irish sergeant-pilot of the 'plane which made the dive-bombing attack had with him as members of the crew another Irishman, a Scotsman and an Englishman. He said :

It was shortly before midnight when we got going. There was so much mist that I could only see the first of the two flares on the flare-path as we taxied out to take off. Straight away we flew into " muck," and it was not until we had climbed to 2,000 ft. that I saw the moon for the first time. I decided to continue flying at that height until we got to the coast, so as to make a landfall there, but it was hopeless. We could not see the ground at all. I then decided to climb to our operational height.

The first time that we saw the ground was when we struck the Dutch coast, but even then we could only just make out where the water met the land—nothing else.

Though this was my first trip to Berlin, it was the fifth time that my navigator had been over it. There was thick cloud right along the route until we got to within 100 miles of the German capital. That meant dead-reckoning navigation practically the whole way.

Then the cloud broke up a bit. We pinpointed ourselves here and there to make sure we were on course. When our estimated time of arrival was up we were south of Berlin, so swung north and went straight in, on to the south-east corner of the city.

Altogether we were 45 minutes over Berlin wangling our way in and then definitely pin-pointing the target. Twenty-five minutes of that time was spent over the centre of the city. Actually we were doing turns to get the full benefit of the moon. You could see lots of buildings and roadways if you got the angle right.

The ground defences were firing heavily from one corner of the city. Then from another corner they started peppering us heavily and the searchlights got on to us. But we had a couple of good landmarks to guide us to the target, and after a time the navigator picked them up.

He said, " I am sure that's it." I said, " All right ; down we go." I put the nose down. It is useless going down if you are not sure of your target, but the navigator was right.

During the last 50 miles to Berlin we had talked about making a dive attack, and I had said that if there was any chance at all I intended to go straight in. I got our target in the gun sights and held it there until we were quite near the ground. We were diving down at a good speed, and the target was getting bigger and bigger all the time.

Then I shouted, " Let them go !" and the bomb aimer pressed the button. After we had bombed, the defences really did let

us have it. The sky seemed alive with Flak (A.A. gun-fire). I put the aircraft into a vertical bank turn to get away, and out we went. I was swinging all over the place to get away.

Some of the German guns were high-angle guns, and we could see the flashes right back across the city. The rear gunner saw our bombs bursting in the target area ; then fires broke out. He said there seemed to be a line of fire and a great red glow with flames belching from it. While we were getting out I was doing stall turns, steep turns, and climbing and diving alternately.

Then suddenly I saw a balloon go up in flames. Fire from the guns on the ground must have hit it. There was a flash and the whole thing was ablaze.

At first I thought it was another aeroplane ; then I saw the cable quite clearly. Some of the blazing fabric came sliding down the cable. One of the chaps said it reminded him of the Indian rope trick.

It fell in our direction, and it seemed to be following us. That put the wind up us for a bit. It was several seconds before we got clear. Just after that I asked the navigator to give me a course for home.

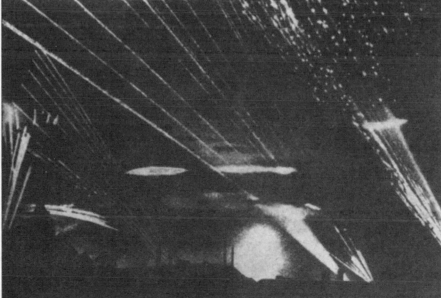

Just such a barrage of bursting shells as this was what the sergeant-pilot who here tells of the bombing of Berlin saw when he dived towards his objective. Above, crews ready and equipped for a recent raid over Berlin. The pilot with his arms stretched out is indicating the size of the " souvenir " he intends to drop on Berlin.   Photos, Associated Press, Keystone

IIIIIIIIIIIIIIIIIIIIIIIIIIIIIIIIIIIIIIIIIIIIIIIIIIIIIIIIIIIIIIIIIIIII **I WAS THERE!** IIIIIIIIIIIIIIIIIIIIIIIIIIIIIIIIIIIIIIIIIIIIIIIIIIIIIIIIIIIIIIIIIIIIIIIIII

Our Skipper Proved 'As Cool as Ice'

The heroism of some of the seamen in the convoys was recognized on October 29, when decorations were awarded to them. The story that led to the granting of the M.B.E. to Captain W. H. Dawson, whose ship came into port with everything breakable aboard her smashed to splinters, is told here by two of his crew.

CAPTAIN DAWSON's chief engineer, Harold George Travis, and his gunner, Robert Daniel Thomas, who were commended and rewarded for their bravery, told how their ship was brought into port after being attacked by E-boats and dive-bombers.

Gunner Thomas said :

It started at night. We were sailing in convoy down the Channel. Suddenly we

Captain W. H. Dawson, who was awarded the M.B.E. for his exploit against E-boats and dive-bombers, is here seen with his megaphone on the bridge of his ship.
Photo, " News Chronicle "

heard gunfire, then flares shot over our craft. We were being attacked by German E-boats. I was on watch and manned my gun.

Then I saw my first E-boat and I let her have it. She disappeared as suddenly as she came. Next came the roar of enemy 'planes and bombs fell around us. But that was a picnic compared with the events of the day.

Shortly after midday we saw spouts of water towards the head of the convoy—bombs were bursting. Another E-boat in the distance opened fire and was driven off—but she had given our position to 60 enemy dive-bombers.

We waited for them. They roared out of the sky, falling down on us—it seemed from a terrific height. I held my fire.

Skipper Dawson, was on the bridge. He was zigzagging the ship right and left as the bombers came down.

The first salvo left the first 'plane and we watched them all the way as they screamed down towards us.

Then the skipper said quietly, " Let them have it," and I did. The bombs fell on the port side and our boat shot out of the water. Great spouts swept over the bridge and washed the skipper across it. I was washed from my gun, but got back in time to let fly at the next German. Two 'planes came down, but who got them I don't know.

Eight salvos fell very close to us. Splinters were flying. I heard the crash of breaking wood and glass. My gun jammed and I took it to bits. Bombs were still falling.

I mended the gun and started firing again.

The skipper seemed as cool as ice—he's a cool stick, you know—and kept his ship swerving all the time.

Then the engineer—he had the worst time, I think—reported our auxiliary motors were broken. We were losing way, but the engine-room people went to work and repaired the damage.

Chief Engineer Travis declared :

It was rather unpleasant, you know. All the time we were being bombed the ship was jumping out of the water like a cork. In the engine-room we didn't know what was happening. The row was so great we couldn't hear the engines.

Water poured in through the skylights and began flooding the engine-room. Then we sprang a leak and more water came in. Our auxiliary motors broke down and we had trouble with the main engines.

We stuck the broken parts together and—well, here we are.—" *News Chronicle.*"

We Were Bombed on a London Tram

During an early morning air raid on London, on October 25, trams and buses in a busy street were severely damaged by a bomb, and several casualties occurred among the passengers on their way to work. Here are some eye-witness accounts of the scene by people who had fortunate escapes.

A PASSENGER in one of the trams was Mrs. M. Sell, who works in the offices of " The War Illustrated." She said :

I was on a tram which was going southwards from the City while an air raid warning was in progress. The top of our tram was empty, as far as I know, but there were a number of women inside. When we heard an explosion a little way off, one or two of them jumped up in dismay, but the conductor joked and made light of it and we went on.

Then we were held up by traffic lights—there were five trams in a row and one or two buses. Suddenly there was a second explosion right on top of us, and we all ducked instinctively on to the floor. Our tram was filled with thick smoke and dust and we could not see one another, but there was no panic and no one even screamed. As the dust cleared and we picked ourselves up, we found our hands were filled with fragments of glass from the windows. Still in silence, we emptied our hands and dusted ourselves down. I was dazed and could only think of searching for my hat which had been blown off.

When we got out of the tram we found that the one in front of us had been hit by a bomb, and passers-by who had been thrown to the ground were lying on the pavement. Women tore up their clothes to bandage the injured, and soldiers working near by took the wounded and people suffering from shock to a shop where they were given first aid before being taken to hospital. In the first shock I had hardly realized that I was hurt, but I had to go to hospital to have glass splinters removed from my face.

Miss Elsie Mackeson said :

The bomb scored a direct hit on the end of the tram behind the one in which I was a passenger.

People were flung all over the place, several of them being buried when the upper floor collapsed on the lower.

At first I thought the top of my head had been lifted off. I tried to help some of the others out, but the police and wardens were there in no time so I left it to them.

A bus passenger said :

We were travelling north when there were three terrific explosions. The bus windows were shattered into small pieces and the bus was filled with black fumes.

When the air cleared I saw that the conductor was injured on the head by glass, so I took him to a first aid post. Glass was strewn all over the road outside, and men and women were lying about on the pavement receiving first aid. Others were dead.

Trams and buses were sandwiched, and one tram was flattened. Ambulances arrived very quickly.

Here are two of the trams which were badly damaged when they were bombed as described by eye-witnesses in this page. During the rush hours the vehicles on this street are crowded with city workers.
Photo, Fox

Pigeons Have Their Place in Britain's Army

Above, a carrier pigeon is being prepared for a flight. The message, written on thin paper rolled up and placed in a quill, is attached to one of the bird's legs. Right, the pigeon carrying the message is released to speed on its way home.

The pigeon has got home to its base, and the message is being carefully detached. Between the two men is one of the wicker cages in which the birds are returned to the dispatching point.

SINCE the siege of Paris in 1870-71 carrier pigeons have been used by the French army to carry messages, and in 1916, during the last war, the British Army adopted this means of communication. The Royal Corps of Signals has now many hundreds of pigeons in training, all handled by men who are experts. They are particularly valuable when telephonic communication has broken down, and as some of them fly over a mile a minute and can travel over 100 miles a day, they are both a speedy and safe means of communication.

Above, the corporal in charge of the pigeons hands the message to a motor dispatch-rider, who will carry it on the last stage to headquarters. Right is the mobile pigeon loft to which the pigeons fly home. Pigeons used by the fighting services have a special food—"National pigeon mixture"—which is now supplied to their breeders.

Photos, Topical, Sport & General

OUR DIARY OF THE WAR

TUESDAY, OCT. 29, 1940   *423rd day*

In the Air—Despite snowstorms R.A.F. raided Berlin, oil plants at Homburg, Sterkrade and Magdeburg, shipyards and docks at Bremen, Wilhelmshaven, Den Helder, Ymuiden, Flushing and Ostend. Other aircraft attacked railway communications, 29 aerodromes, searchlight batteries, and A.A. gun positions.

War against Italy—Admiralty announced that British naval aircraft had attacked Maltezana, capital of Stampalia, Dodecanese.

R.A.F. made numerous raids and reconnaissances in Libya ; objectives included Bomba, Tobruk, Menastir and Sollum.

Cairo reported Italians had been routed near Blue Nile by Sudanese frontier force.

Home Front—Day raiders attempted four attacks on London, but few reached the capital. Three raids on Portsmouth area, damaging houses and shops. Scottish auxiliary squadron shot down 8 Messerschmitts over Kent. Italian bombers, protected by German fighters, took part.

Intermittent night attacks. Hotel, block of flats and R.C. church struck in London. Merseyside and Midlands raided.

Enemy lost 30 aircraft. Seven British fighters missing, but pilots of five safe.

Greek War—Athens communiqué stated that Greek troops held their positions against enemy attacks. Rome reported break in Greek line at S.E. tip of Albania. Italian forces reported to have landed at Corfu.

WEDNESDAY, OCT. 30   *424th day*

On the Sea—Admiralty announced that H.M. trawlers "Wave Flower" and "Joseph Burton" had been mined.

In the Air—Cherbourg attacked by R.A.F. in daylight. Night bombing operations included raids on docks at Antwerp and Flushing and naval bases at Emden. Coastal Command aircraft bombed Ostend Harbour.

War against Italy—Italians unsuccessfully attempted with a special device to torpedo ships in harbour at Gibraltar.

R.A.F. made reconnaissance flights over Greek and Italian coastal waters. Other formations raided Bardia and Tobruk, Massawa, Teclezan and Keren.

Home Front—Small formations of aircraft made daylight raids over S.E. coast, but damage was slight.

Night raids confined mainly to London and south and east England, though some bombs fell in Midlands. Church and rectory damaged in E. Anglia.

Nine enemy aircraft destroyed. Britain lost five fighters, but pilot of one safe.

Greek War—Athens reported that Greek resistance to Italian advance continued. Patras bombed five times.

THURSDAY, OCT. 31   *425th day*

In the Air—Coastal Command aircraft scored direct hit on enemy supply ship off Norway. No night bombing operations by R.A.F. owing to bad weather.

War against Italy—R.A.F. bombers made first raid on S. Italy and successfully attacked oil tanks and other targets at Naples.

Air battle over Mersa Matruh, when large force of Italian bombers and fighters attacked the town. Eight destroyed by R.A.F.

Home Front—Reduced daylight air activity over Britain. Bombs fell on towns in S.E. districts and S. Wales and Midlands.

Short night raid on London met by extensive barrage. Bombs fell in inner and outer suburb, and also in E. Anglia and a Midlands town. No aircraft shot down.

Greek War—Slight Italian advance southwards down west coast stubbornly contested by Greeks. Greek naval forces bombarded enemy right flank.

FRIDAY, NOV. 1   *426th day*

On the Sea—British convoy off Thames estuary reported attacked by enemy aircraft, but squadron of Spitfires counter-attacked and raiders were driven off with loss of eight.

German long-range guns heavily but unsuccessfully shelled British vessels in Straits of Dover.

British merchant ship "Eurymedon" and steamers "Matheran" and "Sulairia" reported sunk by U-boats.

In the Air—R.A.F. heavily bombed railway targets in Berlin, synthetic oil plants at Magdeburg, Krupps' works at Essen, railway junction at Osnabruck, 15 aerodromes and gun positions on French coast.

Home Front—Several formations of enemy aircraft and also isolated machines crossed British coasts and made for Portsmouth and London areas. Raiders were soon dispersed, but some bombs fell in London, Lincs., E. and S.E. counties. Naval A.A. guns shot down two raiders during dive-bombing attack on shipping in Thames estuary.

During night bombs fell in a few London areas, two Midland towns, few districts in Merseyside, and one in E. Scotland.

Enemy lost 18 aircraft. Seven British fighters lost, but pilots of two safe.

First award of Military Medal to women, three members of the W.A.A.F.

Greek War—Italians reported to have launched big attack from Koritza in direction of Florina. Athens reported violent artillery duel on Epirus front. In Florina sector Greeks advanced 3½ miles into Albanian territory and captured 9 Italian officers and 153 men.

Italian aircraft raided the Piraeus and Salonika. Athens raided for first time, but ineffectually. Corfu and Larissa also attacked.

General—Announced that General Smuts was visiting E. Africa, and on Oct. 27 met Mr. Anthony Eden in course of latter's inspection of Middle East Command.

SATURDAY, NOV. 2   *427th day*

In the Air—Owing to bad weather R.A.F. carried out no bombing operations.

Home Front—Two strong enemy formations attempted to reach London, but most were driven back. Few bombs fell in Kent and Essex. Night raids were on small scale and ended before midnight.

Nazis lost 10 aircraft, Britain none.

Greek War—Athens reported violent artillery duels in Epirus and W. Macedonian fronts. Positions occupied by Greek troops in Florina sector retained, and a new line of heights within Albanian territory occupied.

Italians reported to be marching on Janina after crossing Kalamas river in pontoons.

Greek fighters and A.A. guns prevented raiders from reaching Corinth Canal. Two waves of bombers raided Salonika, where 200 civilians were killed. Corfu, Patras and Janina were also attacked.

SUNDAY, NOV. 3   *428th day*

On the Sea—Admiralty announced that H.M. trawlers "Hickory" and "Lord Inchcape" had been sunk by enemy mines.

In the Air—Despite adverse weather conditions, R.A.F. carried out successful attacks on naval dockyards at Kiel and oil tanks and railway targets at Naples.

War against Italy—Cairo reported that two enemy 'planes had been shot down in raid on Malta, and two others damaged. S. African Air Force destroyed two Italian bombers in Kenya.

Home Front—Little daylight air activity. Few bombs fell in southern half of country. Diving aircraft delivered short bursts of machine-gun fire. No night raids on London. Enemy reported from N.E. England and E. Scotland, where tenement houses were demolished.

One enemy bomber destroyed. Britain lost one fighter.

Air Chief Marshal Sir Wilfrid Freeman appointed Vice-Chief of Air Staff.

Greek War—Announced that British troops had landed in Greek territory, that Navy was there, and that air support was being given.

Greek troops reported to have encircled Koritza after battle in which they made 1,200 prisoners and destroyed 30 tanks. Attacks in Florina sector repelled. Enemy made 15 bombing raids, mostly against positions captured from them. Salonika again raided.

MONDAY, NOV. 4   *429th day*

On the Sea—Admiralty announced that two more Italian submarines had been destroyed by our light forces. Two others had taken refuge at Tangier.

Armed merchant cruisers "Laurentic" and "Patroclus" reported sunk by U-boat, and H.M. trawler "Tilburyness" lost through enemy air action.

In the Air—Adverse weather hampered R.A.F. operations, but raids were made on Channel ports.

War against Italy—R.A.F. bombed Italian embarkation ports on east coast, including Bari and Brindisi, and Santo Quaranti, principal port for Epirus and Macedonian fronts.

Home Front—Small daylight raids when bombs fell in London area and at widespread points in Midlands and E. Anglia.

Night raids were resumed and enemy appeared over London and many parts of England and Scotland. S.E. coast town attacked by three bombers. Workers leaving factory in London area machine-gunned.

Greek War—Reported that town and valley of Koritza were being bombarded by Greeks, and that guerilla leader, Varda, and his band had cut off Italian force, numbering 30,000, near Janina. Stated that heavy naval engagement was in progress off Corfu, and that Italian warship had been sunk. British troops landed in Crete.

General—Tangier taken over by Spain.

H.M.S. "Laurentic," which has been sunk by U-boat. Before being taken over by the Navy and commissioned as an armed merchant cruiser, she belonged to the Cunard-White Star Line. She was built in 1927 and displaced 18,724 tons.
Photo, Fox

'AJAX' OF RIVER PLATE FAME HITS HARD AGAIN

This great column of smoke marks the end of the " Artigliere," an Italian destroyer sunk in the Mediterranean by H.M.S. " Ajax " on October 12, 1940. The British ship engaged three enemy destroyers, including the " Artigliere," which, after being disabled, was taken in tow by a consort; the latter cut the painter and left the damaged ship to her fate on sighting other British forces. The British ships threw rafts overboard to help the survivors and signalled their position. H.M.S. " York," from which this photograph was taken, sank the " Artigliere " with a shot that struck the magazine.

Photo, G.P.U.

Mussolini's Men Checked in the Mountain Battle

After a fortnight of war the Italians had made an inglorious showing in their invasion of Greek territory. The outstanding event was the defeat of the Alpini, described below, while the occupation of Crete made Italy's position even more vulnerable than heretofore. But the main Italian effort is yet to come.

SHORTLY before he launched his attack on Greece Mussolini is stated to have expressed his confidence that the Italian troops would be in Athens within 12 days. A fortnight after the offensive opened, however, the Italians had still a long way to go ; so far from having reached Athens, they had not yet sighted the rooftops of Janina. Moreover, in one section of the front the invaders had been driven back, and Koritza—one of the chief Italian supply bases in Albania—was threatened by Greek detachments which had succeeded in carrying at the point of the bayonet the heights which dominate the town. Then on November 11 came the news of another reverse to the Italian arms, one even more spectacular and unexpected.

" Between October 28 and November 10," ran an official bulletin issued in Athens on the latter date, " operations proceeded on a large scale in the mountainous and thickly wooded region of Smolika and Grammos in the north of the Pindus range, which resulted in the complete defeat and breaking-up of an Alpini division, one of the crack enemy divisions, supported by cavalry, Bersaglieri and a Fascist militia formation."

The Alpini division—it was the Third, from Venice—was mobilized long ago, and had seen service in Albania before the war began. No doubt it was selected by the Italian Command as being the one most capable of dealing a quick, decisive blow at the Greek forces in Epirus. When it made its attack it was supported by strong forces of artillery and tanks, with which it was confidently hoped the Greek communications would soon be threatened and severed.

The Alpini attempted a dash across the mountains with a view to reaching Metsovo, some 20 miles to the north-east of Janina, whence it might debouch on to the plains of Thessaly and Epirus and cut the Salonika-Athens railway at Larissa. The Alpini made some progress down the Sarantaporo and Aeos valleys, and as the enemy advanced the Greek light covering forces withdrew before them. Indeed, they did their best to draw the Italians ever deeper into the mountainous gorges, and for a week the northern entrance to the Aeos valley was deliberately left open so that more and more of the enemy might be enticed into the trap.

While the Italians were making their way along the rough mountain tracks—roads is hardly the word to use—the Greeks were being steadily reinforced, and night after night little bodies of Greek soldiers clambered into position on the lofty peaks which dominated the gorges along whose bottoms, several thousands of feet below, the Italians were making their painful way.

Then, at the opportune moment, the Greeks launched their counter-attack. For days they fought with characteristic stubbornness over most difficult country in cold and rain, often going hungry because of the difficulty of obtaining their viands ; such supplies and stores as reached them in their eyries were brought up with the aid of women from the neighbouring villages. At length the fierce fighting came to an end ; the enemy forces were completely overthrown and, in their haste to avoid being surrounded they retreated in disorder, hotly pursued by the Greeks. In their mad rush down the gorges they carried away with them Italian reinforcements which had been landed at Valona, and which were being rushed in motor-lorries to the aid of their comrades.

Whole platoons of the enemy flung away their arms and plunged into the mountain torrents, already considerably swollen by the autumn rains. Scores were swept away by the rushing stream before they could make the opposite bank, and were drowned. Hundreds more sought safety in flight across the mountains, and days afterwards the Greeks, patrolling the wooded heights, came upon heaps of enemy corpses already showing signs of having been mauled and half-devoured by mountain bears and wolves. Large numbers of prisoners were taken, and a great quantity of all sorts of war material fell into the hands of the victors. By November 10 the fighting was over ; the Alpini division had been destroyed.

Italy Sends a New General

That the seriousness of the defeat was realized in Italy was demonstrated by the appointment to the command of the Italian troops operating in Greece of General Soddu, who was formerly Italian Under-Secretary for War, and who was now recalled from Egypt, where he had been acting as Graziani's Vice-Chief of Staff. Generals Vercellino and Geloso were also dispatched to Albania to take over the command of the 9th and 11th Army Corps. These appointments presaged a determined effort to wipe out the shame of the Alpinis' defeat.

Elsewhere in Greece, almost the only signs of military activity were in Crete, which was occupied by British troops early in November. As the little British Expeditionary Force came ashore in Suda Bay they received a vociferous welcome from the Greek shepherds, shopkeepers and fishermen, who poured down to the waterfront and cheered wildly as the soldiers, in full war kit, were landed from British warships. Gifts of fruit and nuts, fresh milk and wine, were showered upon them, and in a very short time the newcomers had made themselves comfortable in a land whose hills and fields made a pleasant and welcome contrast with the sandy deserts of Egypt. Though the weather was calm and the landing was made in daylight, the Italians did nothing to hinder it. But a day or two later Italian bombers flew over Rhodes and dropped bombs in the neighbourhood of Candia and Canea and on, or rather near, the warships assembled in Suda Bay. They were soon driven off, however, by the ships' anti-aircraft guns.

By the occupation of Crete, Britain not only established herself across the lines of

In the mountainous country on the frontier between Albania and Greece, Greek pack artillery (light guns carried on mule-back) has proved a valuable arm. Here a train of these guns is marching towards the Albanian frontier, where they can traverse such rough mountain tracks as that seen in page 536, impassable even by the lightest mechanized vehicle. *Photo, Wide World*

Italian Objectives—But the Greeks Barred the Way

At the very opening of their offensive in Epirus the Italians claimed to have thrown pontoon bridges across the river Kalamas, but even ten days later they apparently had not succeeded in crossing it in any strength. Rising in the mountain masses of Michekeli, the Kalamas, as this photograph shows, flows along a rocky bed; in wintertime it is liable to flooding and must then present an even more formidable obstacle in the invader's path. It discharges into the Gulf of Goumenitsa, opposite the island of Corfu.
Photos, Catherine Harrison

In discussing the strategy of the war in Greece, mention is frequently made of the roads, railways in the mountain regions being non-existent. It should be stated that even the so-called roads are, in many cases, but tracks or bridle paths, such as the one shown in the photograph on the left, above; it follows the little river Acheron, which runs into the Ionian Sea at Speanza. Right, within the citadel at Janina. With its barracks, hotels, shops, banks, cinemas, and modern houses, Janina has spread far beyond the old town, where the Turkish pashas used to hold court.

Greece's Fortifications are the Gift of Nature

Picturesque in the extreme is the little Greek port of Parga, on the coast of Epirus. Today it is an objective of the Italian invaders ; in bygone days it was held at times by Turks, Venetians, French, and even English.

may well be proud. " There is one small, heroic country," declared Mr. Winston Churchill in the peroration of his speech at the Lord Mayor's luncheon at the Mansion House on November 9, " to whom our thoughts today go out in new sympathy and admiration. To the valiant Greek people and their armies, now defending their native soil from the latest Italian outrage—to them we send from the heart of old London our faithful promise that amid all our burdens and anxieties we will do our best to aid them in their struggle, and that we will never cease to strike at the foul aggressor in ever-increasing strength from this time forth until the crimes and treacheries which hang around the neck of Mussolini and disgrace the Italian name have been brought to con-dign and exemplary justice."

communication which linked Italy with Rhodes and the islands of the Dodecanese, but secured bases for her ships and aircraft which should soon prove to be of inestimable value in the war against Italy. Already, then, Mussolini must be regretting his move of October 28. If Greece had bowed before the blast, had given way to his menaces as Rumania gave way before Hitler, then, as he confidently expected, he would indeed have been in Athens in ten days. But the Greeks, strong in the strength of British sea power, called the Duce's bluff.

History may have to record that the invasion of Greece was the beginning of the end of Mussolini's dominion. Certain it is that we have secured an ally of whom we

Along the track, in the snow-topped Balkan mountains, passes a little caravan of mules (centre) ; for them it is passable, but not so, of a surety, for Mussolini's tanks and motor-lorries. Above is Koritza, one of Italy's principal bases in Albania, and the headquarters of the column operating against the Greeks in Epirus. A few days after the outbreak of the war the invader became the invaded, and the Greeks, crossing the frontier into Albania, carried the heights above Koritza by assault.

Photos, Catherine Harrison and Wide World

Don't We Really Know What We're Fighting For?

While the controversy over war aims continues, while men argue whether or not these war aims should be clearly stated by Mr. Churchill on behalf of the British Government, here is an article by E. Royston Pike which, it is hoped, may do something to clear the ground for future discussion.

THERE are some people about who profess that they are not quite clear in their own minds what we are fighting for. They admit that we are fighting for our self-preservation, but apparently to them self-preservation—like patriotism to Nurse Cavell—is not enough. Perhaps self-preservation—or saving our own skins—is too negative an idea ; these people want something more positive, something glowing with hope and pride, with the colours painted by expectation—something that will cheer them on their road through the fogs and storms, the clinging darkness, of this coming wartime winter.

Other peoples seem to experience no difficulty of this sort. Some of them find their inspiration in, revenge, that revenge which, as old Homer said, " is sweeter far than flowing honey." Revenge is a wonderful sharpener of swords, an unsurpassed hardener of resolution. Thus the Polish airmen, when they down a Dornier or send a Messerschmitt flaming into the sea, have the happy feeling that they have hit back at the men who invaded their country, bombarded their capital, burnt their homes, sacked their towns and villages. Probably there is not a man among them who has not some murdered friend to avenge, who does not grieve over someone carried away into Nazi slavery, some woman he has known widowed or treated with ruffianly violence. The Czechs, too, have their wrongs to avenge ; always before their eyes is the spectacle of their martyred state, their closed universities, their suppressed newspapers, the students and other patriots bludgeoned and imprisoned, driven into exile or shot. Then the French—such of them as have any fight left in them after the disasters and the disillusionments of late months—dream of restoring France to her once great place amongst the nations ; and

the Belgians and the Dutch, those of them who have escaped into the freedom of the outside world and those who have been condemned to remain at home under the rule of the swaggering Nazis—they, too, brood over the joy of restoration, of repaying old scores, of wiping out recent ignominies with the sponge of glorious revenge.

And we ? For most of us, probably, self-preservation is a sufficient urge for us to go on fighting, as it was for us to take up the sword. We know something at least of what Hitler's victory would mean for us, even though sometimes in unbelieving mood we say, "it couldn't happen here." Cradled as we have been in the ideals of a liberty which has grown and grown through more than a thousand years, speaking the speech of free men, and with ears attuned to the message of Milton and Cromwell, Pitt and Burke and Gladstone, it requires a really serious effort of concentration, a prolonged exercise of imagination, to think of England as it would be if the Nazis came and ruled.

If the Nazis Came to England

The King and Queen imprisoned in their rooms at Windsor Castle with German guards marching' up and down the pavement without ; a Gauleiter holding court in Buckingham Palace ; Mr. Churchill driven from office and taken into preventive custody —if not hanged from Nelson's Column in Trafalgar Square ; our M.P.s thrust out of Westminster and carted away in lorries to the concentration camp ; every newspaper worthy of the name suppressed, or if it continued to be printed, with men of the Gestapo sitting at the side of every sub-editor ; every preacher who dared to proclaim a gospel uncontaminated by Nazi myths hounded from his pulpit ; every

writer, every journalist of independent mind, every business leader who refused to be dragooned, every judge and magistrate who refused to pervert justice, every Trade Union official who refused to betray his men, every Socialist, every Liberal who refused to " abjure his errors " and lick the Nazis' boots—thrown into a concentration camp without a trial and without any hope of getting one. Surely, we say to ourselves, we shall never live to see the day when old Jews, just because they are old Jews, are cuffed and kicked, paraded through the streets, labelled opprobriously, and made to perform the filthiest tasks in the most humiliating way. Surely, we say, we shall never see a Nazi trooper cut an English girl's hair off because she has been too friendly with a Jew ; surely the bonfires of prohibited books will not be lit again at St. Paul's Cross, nor in place of our stolid, friendly "coppers," will men in black uniforms with pistols at their side harry and harass us, doing their best to make us a nation of spies and spied upon. Such things, we say, cannot happen here. But perhaps the Poles and Czechs, the French and the Belgians, the Dutch, and the Norwegians—perhaps they used that phrase, too ; indeed, no doubt many of them did. All the same, those things could happen there, because they did. And they might happen here.

In fact, there is every reason to believe that by now, after a year and more of war, they would already have happened here if it had not been for a few thousand young men diving through the air in their Hurricanes and Spitfires, but for the guns of the " Nelson," " Rodney," and Britain's other big ships ; and most of all, perhaps, but for that slender streak of water which Hitler's tanks and Hitler's men cannot cross.

Like the other countries that have fallen under Hitler's heel, Belgium is paying the heavy price of defeat. Many of her soldiers, taken prisoner during the campaign of last May, have been marched off from the prisoner-of-war camps to Germany, there to be employed as agricultural serfs to provide food for their conquerors. Often the means of transport in Germany are so bad that they have been forced to march the whole distance. Their sole hope of release from bondage lies in a British victory.

Photo, E.N.A.

Who Is This Man Franklin Roosevelt?

President Roosevelt's unprecedented triumph in the Presidential election on November 5 was hailed with delight by the lovers of Democracy and Liberty everywhere, and with corresponding gloom and rage by the partisans of the Axis. Here we tell something of Roosevelt the Man, and supplement the biographical details with a suggestion of what his victory may mean for our Country and our Cause.

WHAT sort of a man is this Roosevelt, who, defying what has always been regarded as one of the most rigid and unalterable, even though unwritten, laws of the American constitution, has just been re-elected for a third term as President of the United States of America ?

Both Roosevelt II, as the President is sometimes called, and his fifth cousin Roosevelt I —Theodore Roosevelt, who was President of the U.S.A. from 1901 to 1909—had a common ancestor in a Dutchman, one Van Rosenfelt, who emigrated to America about 1649 and made his home in New Amsterdam, later renamed New York ; Roosevelt I was

descended from one of his sons, and Roosevelt II springs from another. Both branches of the family settled in the State of New York, and it was in a pleasant, rambling old house at Hyde Park that Franklin Delano Roosevelt was born on January 30, 1882. As befitted the son of a wealthy country gentleman, Franklin went to the best schools, travelled with his tutor in Europe, and in due course went to Harvard. As a youth there was some idea of his entering the Navy, but ultimately he studied law at Columbia University, and was admitted to the New York Bar in 1907, and practised in the city for the next three years. By now he had married, in 1905, his sixth cousin, Anna Eleanor Roosevelt, a descendant of the other branch of the Roosevelt family and the niece of Roosevelt I.

Franklin Roosevelt's political life began with his election to the New York Senate in 1910—not as a Republican, the party of which Theodore Roosevelt was the head, but as a Democrat.

In 1912, when Theodore Roosevelt stood for the Presidency against Woodrow Wilson and Taft, Franklin Roosevelt was an active and ardent supporter of the Democrat, Wilson. Wilson won the election, and in the new Cabinet Franklin was given the appointment of Assistant Secretary to the Navy, a position which he held throughout the Great War until 1920. Then, as the Democratic candidate for the Vice-Presidency, he went down with Wilson in the hopeless fight against the Republican isolationists, and it seemed that his political career was at an end.

Then in 1921 fate dealt him a still harder blow. One day, when he was on a fishing and swimming trip in a friend's yacht, he was struck down by an attack of infantile paralysis. "What he suffered," writes Robert Waithman in his book "Report on America," "in the years when, a helpless cripple who first could not move his legs at all and then, painfully and slowly, learned to use crutches, what he learned to endure and how his spirit remained alive, is an untold story. The President could tell it, and Mrs. Roosevelt could, but neither of them is ever likely to do so. It is not a subject anyone talks about. But outsiders have said that when Roosevelt ' came back ' after this illness, he was afraid of nothing."

In 1924 he stood up on his crutches at the Democratic Convention and nominated Al Smith as the presidential candidate ; four years later he nominated Smith again ; Smith ran and was defeated by Hoover. Now it was Roosevelt's turn ; he stood for the Governorship of New York. He won ; it was the first step on the road to the White House. In 1932 he received the nomination as Democratic candidate for the Presidency, and at the election in November he carried 42 States out of the 48, and received a popular vote of 22,821,857 against Hoover's 15,761,841. But in accordance with the custom which then prevailed, he did not take office until the following March, and the actual date of his inauguration, March 4, 1933, was the blackest day in the history of modern America (see page 510) ; the Slump was at its worst, and millions of Americans were in despair. Hardly had Roosevelt begun to speak when, listening-in by their radio sets, the people took fresh heart. He spoke as a man inspired ; as a man who knew what ought to be done and was determined to do it.

Then the New Deal was born, and in a few weeks from the lobbies in Washington to the little parlours in the town's back o' beyond everyone was discussing N.R.A. (National Industrial Recovery Act, June 13, 1933) and A.A.A. (Agricultural Adjustment Act of May 12, 1933), P.W.A. (Public Works Administration) and W.P.A. (Works Progress Administration, instituted on May 6, 1935), C.C.C. (Civilian Conservation Corps) and T.V.A. (Tennessee Valley Authority). Thousands of millions of dollars were spent on a vast series of economic measures and social reforms ; a tremendous programme of public works was embarked upon, credit was cheapened, and everything was done to increase the purchasing power of the people. Old Age Pensions were introduced for the first time in the United States ; unemployment insurance was enlarged

From 1913 to 1920 Franklin Roosevelt was Assistant Secretary to the United States Navy, and as such he appears in these two photographs. In the upper one he is on board U.S.S. "Wyoming," with Rear-Admiral C. J. Badger. Even more interesting is the lower photograph, taken in 1919, where Mr. Roosevelt is on the extreme left, while on the right are Mr. Daniels, then U.S. Secretary of War, and the Prince of Wales (now the Duke of Windsor).

Photos, Topical

America's President Is Britain's Friend

and social insurance was introduced by the Social Security Act. Child labour in the factories was abolished ; trade unionism amongst the workers was encouraged by the Government ; house building was stimulated ; and the power of Wall Street was curbed, if not actually broken. The New Deal policy did not end unemployment, but it reduced the number of workless by seven, or perhaps as many as ten, millions, and in a hundred ways America caught up with the social legislation of the most advanced European countries—in some ways went beyond it.

Big business raged ; the great majority of the newspapers were ranged against the President ; the moneyed interests and most, but not all, of the upper classes took their stand against him. Yet all their rage and fury, their boundless opposition, was broken on the rock of the President's personality. In 1936, when he asked the electors to send him back to the White House for a second term, he won the most startling victory in American history. When the poll closed it was found that he had captured 46 States out of the 48, and polled 27,476,673 votes against Landon's 16,679,583.

Another four years went by—four years of unexampled activity in home affairs and of ever-increasing tension abroad. By now the President was a world figure, and when the election of 1940 came to be fought, both Democrats and Republicans were united on the main issues of his foreign policy. Though criticizing much of his home programme, they were at one with him in his resolve that everything possible should be done to help Britain defeat the

President Roosevelt with Mrs. Roosevelt in one of the President's scanty hours of leisure. They have four sons and one daughter.

aggressors. At the election on November 5 Roosevelt won 40 States and polled 26,000,000 votes against about 22,000,000 votes given to Wendell Willkie. On paper it was not so great a victory as that of four years before, yet in fact it was far greater, for the President had dared to do what only Theodore Roosevelt had dared to do before him—ask for a third term as President. Roosevelt I dared, but lost. ; Roosevelt II dared and triumphed.

More than ever today Franklin Roosevelt is a world figure ; perhaps more important for us is the fact that in America he holds a position of unchallenged supremacy, one even more dominating than was held by Lincoln or Washington himself. Pledged as he is to aid us to the utmost limit, we may expect in the immediate future many further expressions of American assistance—perhaps the famous bomb-sight, "flying fortresses," financial credits, more naval craft and a tremendous increase in the number of warplanes. Roosevelt knows, and the American people know, that if they want to keep out of war, then they must do their utmost to help Britain to hold the fighting line.

(From the Cartoon by Illingworth, by permission of "The Daily Mail.")

This photograph (transmitted across the Atlantic by wireless, hence its rough appearance) shows Mr. Roosevelt, after his return for a third term as President, waving thanks to his cheering supporters at his home at Hyde Park, New York State. On his left is Franklin Roosevelt, Junr., the third son, and his wife (formerly Ethel du Pont) ; next to them are John Roosevelt, fourth son, and his wife (formerly Anne Lindsay Clark) ; next again is Mrs. Sara Delano Roosevelt, the President's 84-year-old mother, and, extreme right, the President's wife.

Photos, Topical and Keystone

Back in Port the Letters Come Aboard

It is a great moment in the ships of the Royal Navy when the post arrives. Left, a picket boat of a warship discharges its load of mail bags; they are carried to the ship's post office, above, where the preliminary sorting takes place.

When the three Marines who act as sorters have finished their task of sorting out the letters and parcels for the men of each mess, one man from the mess comes to the hatch of the post office to collect those directed to his mates (circle). Then for a time there is silence on the lower deck (right), while at the mess tables every line from home is read and re-read.

Photos, British Official ; Crown Copyright

Our Heavy Tanks Make Light of Heavy Going

When tanks are on manoeuvres they do not look for easy ways or smooth going, but seek out every obstacle likely to make their course a hard one. Here heavy Infantry Tanks Mark 2, weighing 25 tons apiece, seen during exercises in the Northern Command. Their powers of progression over rough ground are being fully tested as they plough across the stony, waterlogged floor of a disused quarry.

Photo, G.P.U.

The Hawker Hurricane—A Perfect Fighter

Sectional Diagram Showing the Construction and Arming of a Well-Tried Machine Designed Seven Years Ago

THE Hawker Hurricane, which, in the estimation of both the British public and Goering's Luftwaffe, ranks only second to the Spitfire as a superlative fighter, is a clear proof of the foresight and preparedness of British air designers and the Air Command. Few realize that its design goes back nearly seven years, when the R.A.F. had nothing but biplane fighters in service. Designed by Mr. Sydney Camm, it made its first test flight in 1935, and was at once put into production with a then maximum speed of 325 m.p.h. It is believed that this was increased to approach 400 m.p.h. With a Rolls-Royce Merlin III 12-cylinder engine of 1,030 b.h.p. and a three-blade variable pitch airscrew it has a range of about 700 miles at a cruising speed of 230 m.p.h. at 25,000 feet. The pilot is protected by armour behind his seat and a bullet-proof windscreen in front.

The retracting under-carriage has off-centre hinges moving it sideways to clear the front spar when retracted. Hydraulic rams are used with hand and gravity controls in addition.

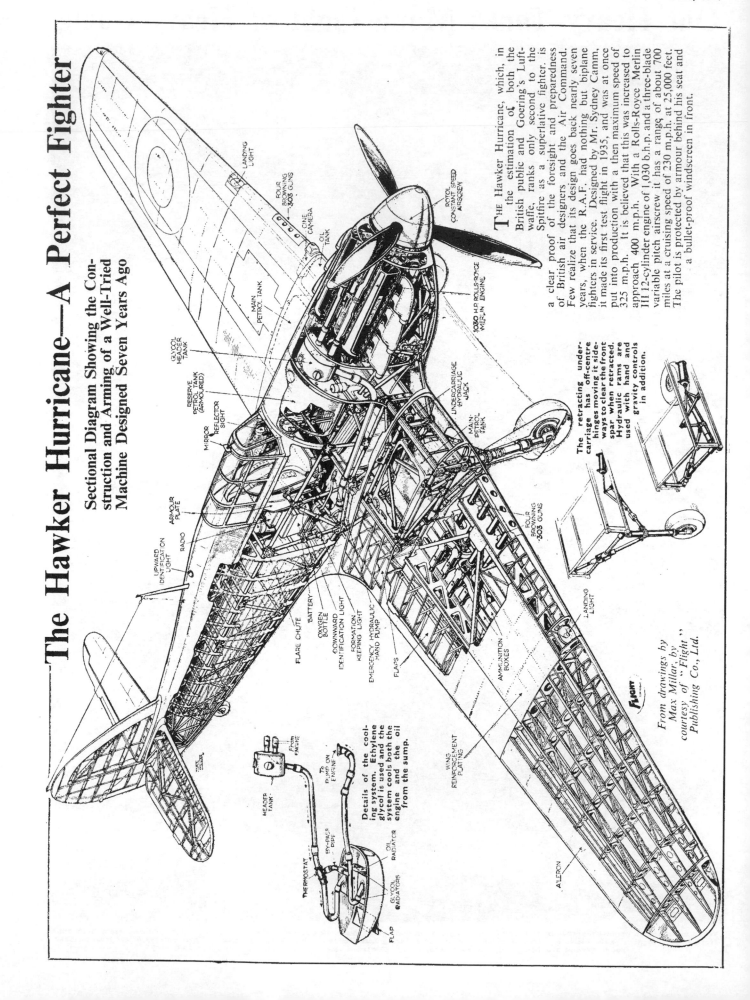

Details of the cooling system. Ethylene glycol is used and the system cools both the engine and the oil from the sump.

From drawings by Max Millar, by courtesy of "Flight," Publishing Co., Ltd.

Labels: LANDING LIGHT · FOUR BROWNING ·303 GUNS · CINE CAMERA · OIL TANK · ROTOL CONSTANT SPEED AIRSCREW · MAIN PETROL TANK · 1030 H.P. ROLLS-ROYCE MERLIN ENGINE · GLYCOL HEADER TANK · RESERVE PETROL TANK (ARMOURED) · MIRROR · REFLECTOR SIGHT · UNDERCARRIAGE HYDRAULIC JACK · MAIN PETROL TANK · ARMOUR PLATE · RADIO · UPWARD IDENTIFICATION LIGHT · BATTERY · FLARE CHUTE · OXYGEN BOTTLE · DOWNWARD IDENTIFICATION LIGHT · FORMATION KEEPING LIGHT · EMERGENCY HYDRAULIC HAND PUMP · FLAPS · FOUR BROWNING ·303 GUNS · AMMUNITION BOXES · LANDING LIGHT · WING REINFORCEMENT PLATING · AILERON · HEADER TANK · BY-PASS PIPE · FROM ENGINE · TO PUMP ON ENGINE · THERMOSTAT · OIL RADIATOR · GLYCOL RADIATORS · FLAP

This is the Hurricane Hawkers Build

WITH its clean, graceful lines, characteristic wing shape and distinctive engine note, the Hawker Hurricane is an aeroplane which is recognized by thousands of British people as it flies day after day over England to grapple with the marauding Luftwaffe. To many the sight of the Hurricanes is a welcome one, and the roar of their engines a most heartening sound, for, with the Spitfires, through long weeks of almost ceaseless warfare they have defended cities, towns and hamlets against the brutal, ruthless onslaughts of the enemy.

Few aeroplanes have earned fame so quickly, nor deserved it so well. In France Hurricane pilots early showed their mettle. In Norway Hurricanes fought and destroyed many German aircraft, and in the Mediterranean this 40-foot-span single-seater fighter has been in many combats with the Italian air force. How many of the enemy have been sent crashing out of the sky by Hurricanes of our many Home Defence squadrons only the Air Ministry knows.

The well-armed Messerschmitt 110 and the Heinkel 113 are no less swift than the Hurricanes, yet against this wonderful British aircraft, no longer new in design, these Nazi 'planes are constantly outfought.

Mr. Sydney Camm, who as chief designer at Hawker Aircraft Ltd., was responsible for the technical features of the Hawker Hurricane. The basic design of this fighter was entirely new.
Photo, "Flight"

Skilful pilotage and a great superiority in powers of manoeuvre the reasons. For its type the Hurricane is astonishingly nimble, and in spite of its high speed and comparatively large dimensions it can be turned and twisted about as can no enemy fighter. From pilots who fly it by day and by night it receives unstinted praise.

These incredibly beautiful clouds range from a height of about four thousand to ten thousand feet. A formation of 12 Hurricanes seen patrolling the vast expanse of sky above the lower cloud ranges.
Photo, P.N.A.

The Hurricane's armament is eight Browning 0·303 machine-guns (circle). These are mounted, four on each side, inside the wings. Ammunition boxes, feeds and the four Browning guns constitute the armament of one wing of the machine.
Photo, "Flight"

A formation of nine Hurricane machines (left) in search of enemy aircraft. These fighters can fly at an altitude of more than six miles. The clouds against which the 'planes are seen sometimes reach a height of 25,000 feet.
Photo, P.N.A.

Our A.A. Guns Shot Down 357 Raiders

Consistently splendid work has been done by our A.A. gunners since the Air Battle for Britain began. Some details are given below. A significant feature of the past week's air operations was the rout of an Italian force of bombers and fighters, thirteen of whom were destroyed near London without loss on Monday, November 11.

IN the House of Commons on Tuesday, November 5, the Premier spoke of the dwindling scale of the Nazi air attack. He hinted that other factors besides bad weather had accounted for this slowing down of the enemy offensive, and there is no doubt that new measures for the interception and destruction of night raiders are being taken.

An example of the freak results of blast from bombs is seen above. The tractor drawing a furniture van, and a part of the van itself, have been lifted bodily on to the top of another van.
Photo, Fox

Nothing spectacular need be looked for, but rather a gradual increase in the proportion of night bombers destroyed, as the cumulative effect begins to be felt of certain methods now being tried out.

On November 10 the Air Ministry News Service stated that 357 enemy aircraft had been shot down by anti-aircraft guns in thirteen weeks, and 400 since the beginning of the war—one-seventh of the total number destroyed. Since August 8, 112 fighters, 109 bombers and 49 doubtful types of enemy aircraft have been shot down. Many others just managed to limp home, badly mauled.

Monday's daylight raids were made on the London area, East Anglia and the Midlands. Casualties were few and the damage slight. The number of aircraft employed was small. Workers were machine-gunned when leaving a London factory early in the evening. Widespread night attacks of a heavy nature came after dusk, and continued for a long time.

Two lightning attacks on London were attempted on Tuesday, November 5, by raiders flying at about 25,000 feet. The first lot—forty in number—were turned back on the outer fringe of the capital ; the second, composed of about 20 aircraft, got only to within 40 miles of London before they were forced to flee. Night attacks began early, but the enemy aircraft were few in number. A London suburb was bombed some minutes

before the Alert was sounded. There was a good deal of material damage in outlying districts, but the casualties were not heavy.

Bombs were dropped in the Southampton area on Wednesday afternoon, when students were trapped in a school shelter and some killed and wounded. Houses and public buildings were damaged. Another heavy attack was made on London and the Home Counties at night. Two churches were hit, and in one case a bomb fell at the entrance to the crypt, where some hundreds of people had taken refuge. There were no casualties, and community singing was continued after a short pause.

The story of Thursday's daylight raids is like that of many other attempts : one formation came up the Thames Estuary and was driven back before reaching London ; a single raider approaching from East Anglia flew very high over London and was shot down after a hot chase. Two other formations made an abortive attack on Portsmouth. The machine shot down was a Messerschmitt fighter-bomber ; two Hurricanes sighted it when they were flying at 10,000 feet and it was some four miles higher in the sky. Climbing all the time, they chased it to London, and at Chiswick got within range. The enemy went still higher, but was closed with and engaged at 200 yards. The Hurricane pilots claimed to have " damaged " the Nazi, but on landing learned that, in fact, they had destroyed the raider.

At night the Nazis resumed their heavy attacks, using flares freely to light up their objectives. Central London was bombed, and the outskirts also were attacked.

Enemy dive-bombers which attempted to attack shipping on the East and South-east coasts of England on Friday, November 8, were signally defeated, despite their strong fighter escorts. **In a battle lasting only a few minutes fifteen of the Nazis were shot down by one squadron of our fighters.** Six more of the Junkers were probably destroyed at the same time, and a further two were known to have been damaged, and it seems that only two out of the twenty-five went scathless.

At night there was a resumption of the intensive raids on London. Liverpool was twice attacked, with incendiary bombs.

There was comparatively little daylight activity on Saturday, November 9. A raider which dropped bombs in the London area was later shot down by our fighters off the coast of Sussex. Three other raiders were

AIRCRAFT LOSSES OVER BRITAIN			
German to April 30, 1940			
Total announced and estimated—West Front, North Sea, Britain. Scandinavia 350			
	German	Italian	British
May	1,990	—	258
June	276	—	177
July	245	—	115
Aug.	1,110	—	310
Sept.	1,114	—	311
Oct.	241	—	119
Nov. 1-11	92	13	30
Totals, May to Nov. 11	5,068	13	1,320

Daily Results

Nov.	German Losses	Italian Losses	British Losses	British Pilots Saved
1 ...	18	—	7	2
2 ...	10	—	—	—
3 ...	1	—	1	—
4 ...	—	—	—	—
5 ...	7	—	5	2
6 ...	6	—	4	1
7 ...	8	—	5	5
8 ...	22	—	6	3
9 ...	7	—	—	—
10 ...	—	—	—	—
11 ...	13	13	2	—
Totals	92	13	30	13

None of the figures includes aircraft bombed on the ground or so damaged as to be unlikely to reach home.

From the beginning of the war up to Nov. 11, 2,846 enemy aircraft have been destroyed during raids on Britain. R.A.F. losses were 813, but the pilots of 405 British machines were saved.

Mr. Churchill on Nov. 5 gave weekly average of killed and seriously wounded for September as 4,500 ; for October, 3,500. In first week of intense bombardment in September 6,000 casualties ; in the last week of October, only 2,000 casualties. Totals announced for October : killed, men 2,791 ; women 2,900 ; children 643. Wounded and detained in hospital, men 4,228 · women 3,750 ; children 717.

destroyed during the night, one crashing on houses in a street at Bromley, Kent. Another was shot down off the Kentish coast, and the third met its doom over Lostwithiel.

Sunday's daylight raids were aimed in the morning at towns on the Kent and Sussex coasts and in the Scilly Isles. Though 24 bombs fell on one town in the south-east, and widespread damage was done, there was only one casualty.

Sunday night's air attacks were over soon after midnight, but while they lasted they were somewhat heavy. During one period raiders flew across London at the rate of one every minute. There were some poignant tragedies, as when six people in one family were killed while celebrating the christening of a baby ; the child was among the victims.

Thirteen Italian bombers and fighters, and twelve German aircraft were destroyed on Monday by two squadrons of Hurricanes. A Dornier bomber was also brought down by rifle fire by a Home Guard unit. Only two R.A.F. aircraft were lost in these engagements.

One of the greatest difficulties in restoring traffic on main streets in which a bomb has dropped is the repairing of cables and gas and water mains damaged by the explosions. In one crowded street a temporary bridge is being built over the crater which will allow one-way traffic to continue while repairs go on beneath it.
Photo, Sport & General.

GALLERY OF WAR PICTURES BY THE OFFICIAL ARTISTS

"George Anderson, Able Seaman, awarded M.B.E., and Lawrence Smith Halcrow, Steward, Commended, both of the S.S. ' Highlander.' " Sir Muirhead Bone. (*Right*) " Minesweeper." Hubert Freeth.

THE War of 1914 was a source of inspiration to many notable artists, and the pictures of Eric Kennington, Paul and John Nash, C. R. W. Nevinson, Sir John Lavery and Sir William Orpen—to mention a few at random—formed a contribution to the contemporary history of the War which was highly characteristic, and as an interpretation of the period still possesses great importance. So far the Second World War cannot be said to have inspired the artists of today to greater achievement, but the selection of subjects which we here reproduce from the exhibition of paintings by the Official War Artists recently brought together at the National Gallery, is at least typical of modern art.

" Lieut.-Gen. Sir A. F. Brooke, K.C.B."
R. G. Eves, R.A.

" An Air Gunner in a Turret—Sergeant
G. Holmes, D.F.M." J. Mansbridge.

" Able Seaman Povey, of H.M.S. ' Hardy.' "
Eric Kennington.

"Coldstream, Irish and Welsh Guards in Gymnasium." Anthony Gross. (*Above*)

"A Street in Louvain (just before the bridge was blown up in front of the German advance, May 1940)." Edward Ardizzone. (*Top right*)

"Bombing practice." W. Conor (*Left*)

"A North-East Coast Aerodrome." Keith Henderson.

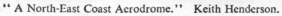

" The Withdrawal from Dunkirk." Charles Cundall.

" Norway, 1940."   Eric Ravilious.

" Manufacture of Battle Dress."   A. R. Thomson.

Abyssinia May Soon Flame into Revolt

Abyssinian chiefs are seen affirming their loyalty to their Emperor, Haile Selassie, at the latter's headquarters in the Sudan. The Emperor is completing plans for regaining his throne.

GALLABAT, on the borders of the Anglo-Egyptian Sudan and Abyssinia, lies at the foot of a slope on a small river, and has a population of about 3,000. On November 6 a British column, supported by units of the R.A.F., surprised and recaptured the place, the whole action occupying only three-quarters of an hour. Aircraft, tanks, armoured cars and artillery were employed, and the enemy suffered heavy casualties. The Italians counter-attacked, and though they claimed that they had recaptured the town, Cairo announced on Nov. 11 that the place was still held by the British. In the Kassala area British mobile forces have continued to maintain pressure on the Italian detachments. During these successful operations the Emperor Haile Selassie was reported to be "somewhere in the Sudan." He is in constant touch with Abyssinian chieftains and has done much to further the Allied cause against Italian aggression.

Gallabat is 85 miles north-west of Lake Tana, and has strategic importance since it passes the road to the lake. Three roads branch from it into the Sudan.

Addis Ababa, the Abyssinian capital, has been repeatedly bombed by the R.A.F., and military objectives have been extensively damaged. Italian air bases in the Western Desert have likewise suffered during the British raids. Hangars at Addis Ababa are seen on the left after direct hits have been scored.

Photos, British Official: Crown Copyright; Paramount Newsreel

Our Bombers Will Yet Destroy the Nazi Tyranny

In heartening words the Secretary of State for Air spoke on Nov. 6 of Britain's plan to strike with ever-increasing weight at German factories, shipyards and oil refineries and give the Germans "a strong taste of their own medicine." Below, in text and table, the doughty work of the Bomber Command during October is summarized.

DURING October the Bomber Command of the Royal Air Force carried out at least 484 raids on the two hundred "targets" listed in the table below—including 47 aerodromes and seaplane bases ; 39 railway junctions, sidings, stations or goods yards ; 37 dockyards, ports or naval bases ; 27 munition works, engine factories and chemical works ; 18 oil refineries, depots, or hydrogenation works ; and 11 power stations. A dozen or more times some of these key-points have been bombed; the effect on the transport system alone can be gauged by an extract from a letter quoted in " The Times " of Nov. 7 :

" A Swiss friend of ours lately returned to Bale from Hamburg, and had to change trains 52 times owing to the activities of the R.A.F."

Another index of the quickening tempo of the R.A.F. raids is given by a comparison of the number of our bombers lost in such operations during October (37 in all) with the total number (67) lost in similar operations during the thirteen months of war ending September 30, 1940. (This last figure also includes aircraft of the Coastal Command.) There is little doubt that under its new chief, Sir Charles Portal, the Bomber Command will strike ever harder during the months to come —and by day as well as by night.

A hint of this development is given by some of the Air Ministry's communiqués during October. Thus on October 3, "taking full advantage of the cover provided by low-lying clouds, bombers of the R.A.F. carried out a series of raids directed chiefly against coastal objectives from Rotterdam to Dunkirk. A large ironworks between Wesel and Halkern was also attacked during the afternoon by a bomber which flew across Holland and penetrated into Western Germany." Two days later, " a railway line outside Cherbourg, used by the Germans for bringing up supplies, was wrecked by Blenheims of the Coastal Command in a daylight raid." Again, next day, in a series of raids which began soon after dawn and lasted until the late afternoon, R.A.F. bombers attacked coastal objectives and shipping over an area extending from Harlingen in the north to Boulogne in the south-west. One of our

These 500-lb. bombs, being hauled out in pairs at an R.A.F. ammunition store, are destined for the bomb-racks of a long-range squadron about to make another of the long series of raids on Germany.   *Photo, Central Press*

pilots making for Calais was attacked by 12 Messerschmitts ; he shot down one and evaded the rest. Direct hits were scored on dockside warehouses at Calais, on a quay and on some twenty barges.

Another series of daylight raids was made a couple of days after, on targets in Germany and Holland. Railway sidings at Warendorf (50 miles east of Munster) were bombed.

Berlin was raided on October 26 for the twenty-sixth time. Soon after 9 p.m. our small heavy bombers opened an attack on objectives in the centre of the enemy capital. For the last 100 miles of the approach to Berlin our pilots had been hampered by

Sir Archibald Sinclair, Secretary for Air, in a Speech at Sheffield, Nov. 6.

It would be a great mistake to think that we are only concerned to defend ourselves against German attacks. . . . We are doing much more than that. We're attacking with our bomber squadrons the very roots of Nazi power and giving the Germans in Berlin and other German cities a strong taste of their own medicine. The weight of our bombing attack has increased, is increasing and will continue to increase. It is directed according to a carefully thought out plan. There in those factories where the Nazis refine their oil and make their guns and ships and aircraft and so forge the chains with which to bind the oppressed peoples of Europe, we shall seek them out and so, science and truth marching hand in hand, will break the power of tyranny and barbarism.

snowstorms, and driving snow made it difficult to locate the target. One British machine became iced up and went into a flat spin. Bombs were dropped to lighten the aircraft, but the spin continued, and the crew were warned to be ready to bale out. It was only after the bomber's trailing aerial had been wrenched off by contact with the ground that the pilot regained control.

Despite thick cloud down to 2,000 feet, on another occasion our bombers attacked Berlin for ninety minutes ; heavy bombs were dropped on the Moabit Power Station in a series of attacks at varying heights.

Bombing Raids by the R.A.F. on Germany and Enemy-Occupied Territory During October
(Compiled from Official Air Ministry Communiqués)

Numbers following place-names denote the days of the month on which raids were made

Aerodromes
Berlin, 7
Bleville, near Le Havre, 4
Bremen, 7
Brussels, 25, 26, 28
Bussum, 5
Cologne, 12
Cuxhaven, 25
De Kooy, 2, 9, 10, 11, 14
Diepholz, 6, 24
Diest, 7
Duisburg, 9
Eelde, 23
Eindhoven, 10
Flensburg, 2
Flushing, 9
Glisy, 27
Haamstede, 1, 9, 25
Halle, 12
Kloppenburg, 10
Krefeld, 9
Magdeburg, 14, 27
Merseburg, 10
Mulheim, 9
München-Gladbach, 10
Munster, 7, 12
Norderney, 10, 11, 13
Nordhausen, 14
Oldenburg, 2, 5
Oosvoorne, 10
Osthein, 10
Poix, 28
Querqueville, 27
Rheine, 29
Rotterdam, 12
Schipdel, 5
Schipol, 2, 7, 25, 27
Stade, 18
Sylt, 11, 14
Texel, 2, 5, 7, 9, 11, 13
Tondern, 10
Vught, 12
Wangerooge, 11
Wesel, 2, 13
Wesermunde, 14
Woensdrecht, 13
Ypenburg, 2, 26
Zwischenahn, 2

Aircraft Factories, Aircraft Stores, etc.
Amsterdam, 1, 7, 8, 10, 12
Berlin, 26, 27
Bremen, 23
Pilsen, 27
Wismar, 23

Gun Positions
Borkum, 13
Cap Gris Nez, 1, 7, 12, 15, 25
Terschelling, 13

Chemical Works, Munition Works, Metal Works, etc.
Berlin, 1, 7, 24
Bitterfeld, 12
Bottrop, 24
Brunsbüttel, 23
Cassel, 25
Cologne, 9, 15
Dortmund, 18
Duisburg, 13
Düsseldorf, 15
Essen, 2, 5, 8, 9, 12, 13, 29
Grevenbroich, 9, 15
Hamburg, 11
Hamm, 12
Hanau, 8
Herring, 12
Herringen, 12
Homburg, 28
Leipzig, 16
Leuna, 16
Lünen (nr. Dortmund), 15, 18
Neuhaldensleben, 14, 15
Oberhausen, 10
Osnabruck, 25
Schönebeck, 15
Torgau, 12
Wesel, 3
Wittenberg, 14

Canals, River Bridges, etc.
Anna Paulowna (south of Helder, Holland), 9
Dortmund-Ems, 12
Hanover, 12
Stralsund, 29

Oil Refineries, Hydrogenation Works, Oil Stores and Depots
Bohlen, 14
Bottrop, 2, 10
Cherbourg, 2
Cologne, 1, 9, 10, 12, 26, 27, 28
Duisburg, 13
Gelsenkirchen, 1, 8, 10, 13, 15, 24, 29
Hamburg, 2, 8, 10, 24, 25, 27, 28
Hanover, 10, 12, 14, 23, 24, 25, 27
Homburg, 9, 28, 29
Kiel, 15
Leuna, 10, 16, 26, 27, 29
Magdeburg, 10, 14, 15, 23, 27, 28, 29
Meisburg, 14
Ostermoor, 27
Reisholz, 10, 25
Saltzbergen, 15
Sterkrade, 1, 29
Stettin, 2, 14, 26, 27

Power Stations
Amsterdam, 12
Berlin, 7, 12, 23, 26, 27, 29
Brest, 26
Cologne, 1
Gelsenkirchen, 8
Hamburg, 24, 25
Kiel, 8, 25
Leuna, 16
Lorient, 12, 15
Reisholz, 9
Waldeck, 11

Railway Stations, Marshalling Yards, Supply Depots
Antwerp, 15
Berlin, 7, 12, 23, 24, 26, 27
Bottrop, 24
Bremen, 24, 26
Brussels, 9, 26
Celle, 26
Cherbourg, 3, 4
Coblenz, 1, 23, 28
Cologne, 1, 2, 5, 9, 12, 27, 28, 29
Dorsten, 27
Dortmund, 18, 26
Duisburg, 1
Duisburg-Ruhrort, 27
Düsseldorf, 9, 15
Ehrang, 7
Emmerich, 24
Frankfurt-am-Oder, 23
Gelseakirchen, 10
Göttingen, 14
Gremberg, 1, 2, 7, 8, 9
Halle, 15
Hamburg, 9
Hamm, 1, 5, 7, 10, 12, 13, 15, 23, 24, 27
Hanover, 14, 29
Homburg, 9
Koblenz, 9
Königshofen, 9
Krefeld, 15, 27, 28, 29
Lingen, 14
Mannheim, 7, 8, 27, 28
Munster, 25, 29
Nordhausen, 15, 29
Osnabruck, 5, 7, 18, 24, 27, 29
Schwerte, 13, 15, 18
Siedenburg, 24
Soest, 1, 7, 10, 15
Sterkrade Holten, 1
Warendorf, 9
Wesel, 9, 24

Road Bridges
Bremen, 12
Schwerte, 13

Barge Concentrations
Den Helder, 6
Dordrecht, 6
Enkhuizen, 6
Gravelines, 5
Harlingen, 6
Heusden, 3
Stavoren, 6

Naval Bases, Docks, Harbours, etc.
Amsterdam, 2, 5, 7, 9, 10, 25
Antwerp, 2, 11, 25, 26, 27, 30
Boulogne, 1, 6, 7, 8, 9, 10, 11, 12, 15, 28
Bremen, 8, 11, 16, 25, 26, 28, 29
Bremerhaven, 11
Brest, 5, 9, 10, 17
Calais, 1, 6, 7, 8, 9, 10, 11, 12, 13, 15, 26
Cherbourg, 2, 7, 10, 11, 30
Cuxhaven, 16, 24, 25, 26, 28
Den Helder, 10, 11, 14, 15, 25, 29
Dieppe, 7
Duisburg, 15, 18, 24
Dunkirk, 1, 3, 7, 12, 13, 24
Emden, 14, 18, 23, 28, 30
Enkhuizen, 6
Flushing, 1, 2, 5, 9, 10, 13, 15, 23, 24, 26, 27, 29, 30
Gravelines, 7
Hamburg, 2, 11, 13, 14, 15, 16, 18, 24, 25, 26, 27, 28, 29
Harlingen, 6
Hook of Holland, 24
Kiel, 8, 10, 11, 13, 16, 18, 25, 28
Le Havre, 7, 8, 9, 10, 12, 13, 14, 15
Le Treport, 11
Lorient, 7, 8, 15, 27
Lübeck, 18
Ostend, 2, 6, 7, 11, 12, 13, 15, 24, 25, 27, 29, 30
Rotterdam, 1, 2, 3, 5, 7, 9, 23, 24, 27
Stavoren, 6
Terneuzen, 15
Ushant, 2
Veere, 1
Wesermunde, 11
Wilhelmshaven, 2, 7, 8, 10, 11, 13, 24, 27, 28, 29
Wismar, 14
Ymuiden, 2, 29
Zeebrugge, 7, 8, 13, 15

Total No. Raids Oct. 1-31 484

'They Are Coming Just When Most Needed'

The First Lord on the American Destroyers, Empire Broadcast Nov. 3, 1940

THE enemy's mercantile marine has, to all intents and purposes, disappeared from almost every sea except the Baltic, soon to be frozen over, while food, munitions and materials arrive here in a continuous flow and reinforcements flow out to our armies and garrisons overseas. True, shipping losses have been heavy of late, for the tax upon our Naval forces has been great. I have no wish to deny it, and I make no promises and no prophecies. I merely say that the Admiralty has been overhauling every aspect of the problem of grappling with the enemy attacks by sea and air.

In this war against our mercantile marine I think often of Nelson's incessant cry for "more frigates." How often in the past months have I heard my professional advisers cry "more destroyers," and how welcome have been the fifty destroyers which America has sent us and for which, as head of the Navy, I tender the Navy's sincere and grateful thanks! I shall be equally thankful for any more that can be spared.

I have just read with deep interest a report of the handing over of some of these destroyers, of the American ensign being hauled down, of British crews marching on board as bands of the Royal Canadian Navy played "Hearts of Oak," an outward and visible sign of the sympathy and unity of purpose which unite two great democracies.

The White Ensign will fly at their ensign staffs in future, but many of us will in our mind's eye see the Stars and Stripes still fluttering there as well. After all, these ships and all their consorts in the Royal Navy today stand between the Western democracy and the ruthless aggression of the Nazi dictator.

The Prime Minister in Parliament, Nov. 5

WE have been in the last month at the lowest point of our flotilla strength. The threat of invasion has always been met. The great forces we are maintaining in the Mediterranean, in addition to the aircraft necessary for the protection of our innumerable convoys, have imposed upon the Royal Navy a gigantic task.

However, this period of stringency is perhaps passing. The fifty American destroyers are rapidly coming into service just when they are most needed, and the main flow of new construction started at the outbreak of the war is now coming along.

A drinking-water fountain is for British sailors a novel but much appreciated part of the equipment of the U.S destroyers ; a button is pressed and a stream of refreshing ice-cold water bubbles up.

A bicycle was among other gear taken over on one of the U.S. destroyers, and it is now used by the ship's "postman" to take the mail ashore. Here he is taking a trial run on deck with his new mount.

On board the American destroyers crossing the Atlantic a sharp watch was kept for U-boats The officer on the bridge (left) is well protected against Atlantic weather. British sailors (centre) on one of the American destroyers that they have recently taken over are at practice with one of the 4-in. guns that form part of the ship's main armament. Right, the British Commander of one of the destroyers takes a sight in mid-Atlantic.

Photos, British Official ; Crown Copyright

Now War Has Come to the Isles of Greece

Following the Italian invasion of Greece, the war was extended not only to the Balkan mainland but to the Greek islands which lie like stepping-stones between Europe and Asia. Some facts about these islands are given below, together with a suggestion of their strategical possibilities.

"THE Isles of Greece, the Isles of Greece ! Where Burning Sappho loved and sung. Where grew the arts of war and peace——" Byron loved Greece and loved still more the Greek islands, although it was in a squalid little port on the mainland that he breathed his last on that Easter Monday 116 years ago. There they lie, in the Aegean Sea, hundreds of them, great and small, relics of a land mass blown to pieces by the volcanic eruptions of ages ago. So many are they that the word archipelago, once applied to them alone, has now been extended to all other groups of islands which, like them, thickly stud the sea.

Most of the islands, which on the map and in reality appear as stepping-stones from Europe to Asia, belong to Greece, although two—Imbros and Tenedos, close to the entrance to the Dardanelles—are included in Turkey's territory. Imbros was occupied by the Greeks during the Great War and served as a base for the Allied operations against the Turks, but it was returned with Tenedos to Turkey by the Treaty of Lausanne of 1923. Then the Dodecanese Islands belong to Italy ; of them, more later.

The Greek islands are usually divided into three groups : the Aegean Islands, the Sporades (from the Greek "sporadikos," meaning "scattered"), and the Cyclades (derived from another Greek word, "kyklas," meaning " circular " : the Cyclades *encircled* the sacred island of Delos, while the Sporades were *scattered* near by).

The largest of the Aegean Islands is Mitylene (Mytilene) or Lesbos. It lies within sight of the coast of Asia Minor, and most of its surface is rugged and bare, though the valleys are very fertile, producing grapes, olives and grain. For centuries, like most of the other islands in the Aegean, it formed

part of the Sultan's dominions, but it was annexed in 1912 by Greece following her successes in the Balkan War. It has a population of some 160,000, practically all Greeks. Lemnos, too, is mountainous with fertile valleys affording rich pasture for sheep, but it is inhabited by only some 4,000 people. Mudros, on the island's south coast, lies at the head of a very fine land-locked bay, whose possibilities as a naval base were fully exploited during the Great War by the Allied fleets operating against the Turks in the Dardanelles. Then to the north lie Samothrace and Thasos.

Islands Fertile and Flourishing

In Chios, a little island to the south of Mitylene, about some 30 miles long and from eight to 15 miles broad, oranges and olives grow, and the vineyards form the basis of a flourishing industry. To the south-east, separated from Turkey by a strait only about a mile in width, is the little island of Samos, 27 miles by 14 ; like its neighbours, it is mountainous and fertile. Small as it is, it has a population of 80,000, engaged in producing oil and raisins, cotton, and tobacco for the cigarettes in whose making many of the women and girls of the island find employment.

The Sporades lie off the east coast of Greece. Some geographers speak of the Northern Sporades and the Southern, but the latter are more usually known nowadays as the Dodecanese Islands. The Sporades include Skiathos, Skopelos, Ikos, and Skyros ; both Skyros and Skiathos have fine harbours.

The Cyclades encircle the island of Delos, the smallest but the most famous of the group because of its having been a great centre of the religious, political and economic life of the ancient Greeks. Largest and

most fertile of the group is Naxos ; but all its fellows, Syros (Syra) and Tinos (where the Greek cruiser "Helle" was sunk by an Italian submarine on August 15 last), Andros, Melos (where the famous Venus de Milo was unearthed in 1820), and the rest, are gifted with a rich soil, and many are possessed of a considerable mineral wealth which, so far, has been hardly touched.

Between the Cyclades and Turkey lies the group of islands which, as mentioned above, is sometimes called the Lesser Sporades, but more usually the Dodecanese (Greek, " twelve islands "). The twelve islands are Stampalia (Astropalia), Scarpanto (Karpathos), Caso (Kasos), Piscopi (Tilos), Nisiro, Callimno (Kalymnos), Leros, Patmos, Cos, Symi, Calchi (Karchi) and Lipso. The islands were first occupied by Italy in 1912, during the Tripoli War, and they were finally ceded by Turkey to Italy in 1924.

Close to the Dodecanese, so close that it is sometimes counted as one of the group, is Rhodes, very much larger than any of the others, with its 545 square miles and a population of over 60,000, most of whom are Greeks and few of whom are inclined to look upon the Italians as anything more than unwelcome intruders. Rhodes has a history stretching far back into prehistoric times, and through all the centuries it has been famed for its delightful climate and the fertility of its soil. Its surface is traversed by a mountain range of considerable height, from which may be seen the rocky coast of Asia Minor, the cluster of islands to the north-west, and to the south-west the cloud-capped summit of Mount Ida in Crete. The only town is the capital, Rhodes, which still retains the walls and towers erected by the Knights of St. John before they evacuated the island in 1522. Not only Rhodes but

Here is a map of all the Greek islands in the Aegean sea, and a smaller one of the Dodecanese group and Rhodes, which is usually included among them. Crete is in many ways the most important of the isles of Greece, for it will afford a valuable base from which the R.A.F. can attack Albania and southern Italy. Right is the harbour of Candia, the chief port of Crete.

Photo, René Zuber

Welcome Bases for Britain at Italy's Back Door

Picturesque scenery characterizes most of the Isles of Greece, and typical of their beauty is this great valley seen through a line of cypress trees from the monastery of Aghia Moni, in Chios.

the Great War period was M. Venizelos, who was a native of Crete.

Crete has been described as one of the loveliest and most pleasant lands on earth, combining the beauty of continental Greece with the opulent charms of Italy. Its hilly slopes are terraced with vines, and in the valleys are wide-spreading olive groves and fruit orchards. Then, too, some of the grandest and most awe-inspiring mountain scenery in Europe is found in Crete, and seldom is the crest of Mount Ida, towering 8,000 feet above the sea, without its mantle of snow. The largest town is Candia (pop. 35,000), also known as Heraklion, but the capital is Canea (pop. 27,000). Inland and along the coast are many little villages, in which the spirit of the Middle Ages lingers yet. Even today roads are few and far between, most of the places being linked by mere bridle-paths, suitable only for donkeys or mules. Railways there are none, but Suda Bay was used by the British Navy during the Great War and more recently by the flying-boats of Imperial Airways.

Considering these things, then—considering the potentialities of the Greek islands in the Aegean and, still more, of Crete, as bases for the British Navy and Air Force, it seems all the more strange that Mussolini should have plunged into the invasion of Greece. For, in consequence of that invasion, Britain and Greece are now firm allies, and in the islands Britain is even now mustering her strength.

Relics of previous occupations are to be found in the Islands, and left is the ancient fortress of Mitylene, capital of Lesbos. Below is St. Catherine's Gate, a picturesque relic on Rhodes, once the stronghold of the Knights of St. John.　　　*Photos, Fox and Dorien Leigh*

several of the Dodecanese Islands—e.g. Stampalia and Leros (called the Italian Gibraltar)—have been recently bombed or bombarded by British ships and 'planes.

Eighty miles to the east of Rhodes and almost within a stone's throw of Turkey is the tiny island of Castelrosso, on whose four square miles more than 2,000 people have their homes. During the Great War the British occupied Castelrosso as a base for carrying on their air war against Turkey, and after they had been driven out it was reoccupied by the French. Yet, in spite of its proved value in time of war, the Allies in 1922 allowed the Italians not only to include it with the Dodecanese as part of their gains from Turkey, but gave their consent to its being fortified—just as later they permitted the fortifying of the little island of Pantelleria, between Sicily and Tunis.

Right in the entrance to the Aegean Sea lies the great Greek island of Crete, 3,200 square miles with a population of nearly 400,000—Greeks, and the best type of Greeks at that. For thousands of years Crete has been civilized, and of all the archaeological discoveries of recent years there have been few to rival the uncovering of the great Minoan civilization which had its centre at Knossos. Arabs and Crusaders, Venetians and Turks, have owned Crete in turn until, in 1913, she was formally united with the kingdom of Greece. The most dominating personality in Greek politics of

OUR SEARCHLIGHT ON THE WAR

Smuts Policy Strengthened

General Smuts recently paid a three days' visit to the South African troops now serving in East Africa, in the course of which he inspected all branches of the Service and had personal meetings with scores of officers and men of all ranks. "You are not only going to protect South Africa," he told them, "but you will lay the foundations here for something much bigger. You are going to kindle a light which will shine far beyond the boundaries of South Africa." On October 27 he conferred with Mr. Anthony Eden, who has been making a tour of inspection of areas under the Middle East Command. On November 3 General Smuts returned to the Union by air, and three days later the cause he upholds was further strengthened by a complete split in the opposition Nationalist Party. After a stormy session on November 6, General Hertzog resigned the leadership of the Party, and most of his supporters followed him, leaving Dr. Malan in possession. So has come to an end an uneasy partnership between branches of the Party which only last year decided to combine against General Smuts' war policy. The result is a severe blow to the Nationalist cause in the Union.

Enemy Torpedo Device Fails

British Naval authorities at Gibraltar announced on October 30 that an abortive attempt had been made by the enemy to torpedo ships in the harbour by means of a special device. One torpedo had exploded harmlessly at the harbour entrance, and another ran ashore without exploding at La Linea, the Spanish frontier town near Gibraltar, and was removed by the local authorities to Algeciras on a motor lorry. The next day a light torpedo-carrying motor-boat of unknown nationality grounded on the beach at La Linea and was also seized by the Spanish authorities. It carried no crew and was described as "a self-manoeuvred torpedo with a seat, and something which looked like a steering-wheel."

German Troops Invade England !

September 16 is thought to have been the day planned by Hitler for invading these shores in a fleet of specially prepared barges. The full story, so far as it is known, is told in page 456. But Hitler sees events, or the wishful anticipation of them, through his own magnifying and distorting spectacles, and the picture reproduced below appeared in a Government-controlled Berlin weekly paper with a wide circulation in order to gull the population into belief in a successful Nazi invasion of England. If such a photograph is authentic, the men in the so-called storm boat are training in their own waters.

No Walk-Over to 'Gib'

French radio stations stated on November 7 that Gibraltar had been transformed into an island by the cutting of a canal across the isthmus connecting the Rock with Spain. This neck of land, which is about 1½ miles long and ⅔ mile wide at its narrowest point,

La Linea

PRESUMED POSITION OF CANAL

Europa Point

Whether Spain wants Gibraltar or not, it may now be impossible to reach the Rock by land, for it has been announced that the British garrison has cut a canal through the sandy isthmus connecting it with the mainland.

Photo, courtesy of the "Daily Telegraph"

averages only about 10 feet above sea level. The northern end of the Rock rises from it almost perpendicularly. Between the British Lines and the Spanish Lines is a tract of neutral uninhabited ground. Behind the British Lines we had characteristically constructed a racecourse ; behind the Spanish Lines are fortifications and the town of La Linea. Gibraltar, which has been held by Britain for 236 years, has always been regarded as impregnable from the sea. She is

also now prepared for attack from the air. Women and children were evacuated in June, and those workers who remain spend the night in complete safety in the enormous electrically lighted shelters which were cut out of the rock through the foresight of General Ironside during his Governorship, 1938-39. There are vast stores of supplies, all underground, including 140,000,000 gallons of water, obtained by catchments. If the report concerning a canal on the north is true, Britain may view with complete equanimity the possibility of another siege of Gibraltar.

Italians are so Imaginative !

Here is the official Italian version, issued in Rome and repeated in the "Völkischer Beobachter" for October 30, of an encounter between one of Italy's submarines and a British ship. "An Italian submarine commander has a very smart action to record, in that he has sunk the English auxiliary cruiser 'Baron Erskine,' of 10,000 tons, by gunfire. The submarine had sighted two vessels, but owing to the extraordinarily rough sea was unable to use its torpedoes. In spite of enemy superiority the commander decided to exchange shots with his adversary and opened fire. He succeeded in sinking the 'Baron Erskine' within 18 minutes, and in extricating himself from the counter-attack made by the other ship. In recognition of this splendid action the commander and crew have been awarded a silver medal, two bronze medals, and nine military crosses."

This makes an impressive story, but, apart from the award of medals and crosses, it is almost entirely inaccurate. The steamship "Baron Erskine" is an ordinary merchantman of 3,657 tons, and is armed with one small gun for self-defence. She was alone when attacked by the submarine, and replied at once with her gun. The action, which was short, broke off when the submarine, having fired five shots without hitting, dived and was not seen again. The "Baron Erskine" thereupon resumed her voyage and in due course reached port. The number of honours (twelve) awarded for "sinking" a ship (doubled) of such tonnage (trebled) is lavish even for Mussolini.

A copy of the German photograph referred to in this page is reproduced above. It arrived in England by a circuitous route through Switzerland and Turkey, but it could only have propaganda value among the many millions of Germans whose total lack of knowledge of the sea might make the possibility of invasion by such fragile craft appear credible.

Eye Witness Stories of Episodes
and Adventures in the
Second Great War

Flames Drove Us Off the 'Empress'

The "Empress of Britain" was speedily avenged, for on November 5 the Admiralty announced that the U-boat which torpedoed and finally sank her had been destroyed. Below we give some further eye-witness stories of the fire, following the attack on the liner by German aircraft with high-explosive and incendiary bombs.

A MEMBER of the crew of the " Empress of Britain " said :

I cannot describe how quickly the fire spread. The ship caught fire within a few minutes as the result of hits by incendiary bombs. If it had not been for the fires we would never have had to leave the ship.

We managed to collect some of the injured and carry them aft, where some other men and I stayed with the ship's doctor helping to attend them until we were taken off.

A man who was among the last party to leave the forecastle said :

By the time we left the foremast was red-hot and the paint was falling off like strips of canvas.

An engine-room officer said :

We kept the engines running for about three-quarters of an hour after the attack, but the smoke and fumes were so bad below that we had to wear our gas masks as we went about our jobs. The lights were on, but we needed electric torches as well to see what we were doing. When the time came to abandon ship we had a bit of a struggle to get on deck.

George Larkin, a fireman, of Liverpool, said:

The first I heard was machine-gun fire. A moment later a bomb struck the ship. We were trapped, and we had to go right forward again through black choking smoke and fumes. Two men collapsed from suffocation before we reached safety by climbing to the upper deck.

James Cameron, a steward, whose home is in London, was greeted by his wife when he arrived at a hotel in the district where the survivors were landed. He had sent her and his child away some time ago to a town near the port where he was landed. Cameron came ashore wearing an artilleryman's overcoat, a trawlerman's jacket, and his own trousers. His hands were heavily bandaged.

Describing how he got his injuries, Cameron said :

I went down the rope to get into the boat, but when I got to the water the boat had disappeared. I hung on for a time and it was then that my hands were hurt. I then found an empty lifebelt box floating about. I was wearing my lifebelt, but I can swim only a few strokes. I managed to get to the box, and then it overturned and I was trapped inside it below the water. How I managed to free myself I do not know. . . . I have a vague memory of a pal of mine appearing from somewhere with a boathook, but I don't remember being pulled into the lifeboat.

One of the stewards said :

The women were very brave. One of them, a Mrs. Stratter, found herself on a raft. Not far away was a lifeboat, but as it had only four men in it it appeared that it could not reach the raft, so Mrs. Stratter and a steward swam to the boat.

With smoke pouring from her hull and two tugs attempting vainly to tow her to safety the crack Canadian Pacific liner "Empress of Britain" passes to her doom. The ship was attacked by enemy 'planes, first with machine-guns and then with incendiary bombs which set her afire amidships, before she was finally sunk by a U-boat. Her commander, Captain Sapsworth, remained on board until the decks were awash.

Photo, Associated Press; exclusive to THE WAR ILLUSTRATED

I WAS THERE!

We Serve Jam Puffs Down East at 5 a.m.!

Jam puffs at 5 a.m. may not sound very appetizing or appropriate, but—as Lorna Lewis tells in this sketch from "Time and Tide"— they are just the thing when served from a mobile canteen to the people emerging from their shelters after a night of bombing.

4 A.M. . . . Not perhaps one's favourite hour for rising, especially when the All Clear hasn't gone. But here we are, scrambling out of impromptu beds, loading up the mobile canteens with tea urns, milk jugs, cakes, sausage rolls, etc. Cramming stores into the vans, tea and snacks into ourselves, tin hats on to our heads. Pushing and blundering about sleepily with heavily-shaded torches, hoping to goodness that bombs and barrage won't break over us.

Then we're off for the East End shelters which the Ministry of Health has asked us to serve. Groping our way in the blackness, we pause for each unfamiliar red light on the road. Maybe it's a road diversion due to a newly-fallen unexploded bomb ; or rubble and glass on the road from bombed houses ; or a fresh crater. Anyhow, better treat all red lamps with respect.

My particular goal is down in one of dockland's poorest and most battered quarters. This shelter holds anything from 1,000 to 1,200 people and is under a big warehouse. Outside its entrance we open the side of the van, let down the counter, get out mugs from the drawers, by the light of a very small electric lamp. Then out of the darkness appear pale faces, the faces of men, women and children looking up at us. The sound of distant gunfire is drowned by coughing and a clamour of voices : " Tea, miss. . . Three teas, mate, and three nice cakes. . . Tea, ma. . . Five cups of you-an'-me, please. . . Two very speshul teas for this lady, my dear, and a sponge cake and bar of milk chocolate and a large Woodbine."

In this neighbourhood there's been no gas now for weeks. It is on the emergency efforts of our and other units that many thousands of London citizens go off to their work and the dangers of the day. From our van alone my colleague and I serve in under three hours about four hundred cups of tea. Soon the counter and the cash box are a mass of crumbs and stickiness, the floor is a flood of tea drips. Washing up is done in a small bucket and is on primitive lines ; we can only hope that what the customer's eye doesn't see the heart doesn't grieve over.

Sometimes there's a lull and we can have a little conversation with our clients.

" Well, what sort of a night did you have ? " " Might have been worse, miss. We had three more houses down at the end of the road and they chipped the bridge over at the back, but we didn't do so badly." " Couldn't say, mate, I slept right through." " A better night, thank Gawd, and I'll take a meat pie and a doughnut, please, miss. How was it up your end, miss ? "

Two good-tempered, robust-looking wardens bring out a collection of mugs left behind yesterday morning. The man had his home destroyed the first night of the blitzkrieg. I tell him I lost mine on the third, so he's beaten me by two days, and we all go into roars of hearty laughter. The woman warden says these bleeding bombs are a mistake and won't do Hitler any good. She also emphasizes what is already under discussion : that greatly though these breakfasts are needed and appreciated, yet as the weather gets worse and epidemics threaten, the whole question of solid hot meals for thousands of homeless people has got to be tackled by higher authorities, and tackled quickly.

The demand for cakes at this early hour is surprising to the inexperienced. Cakes, though, are sweet and sugar is scarce for most of us. Sugar gives energy and warmth, and is easy and quick to digest. Our friends eating jam puffs at 5.30 a.m. are unconsciously being more sensible than I at first supposed.

So darkness turns to light. . . The All Clear has sounded. People go off to work, which begins here anywhere between 6 and 8.30 a.m. Mothers and children and old people, armed with strange bundles of night wraps, trail home. Home . . . yes, but will it still be there ? How many have come out of that shelter of rest or restlessness to find that their house is a heap of ruins ? Maybe it hardly seemed worth keeping ; but poor and dilapidated as it was, it was home, and it was all they had.

I go into the shelter to collect cups, and am led to wonder what the catacombs of ancient Rome looked like. This shelter is divided by half-partitions into three compartments. Part is dark, part is light. Here are the very old and the very, and often wailing, young. Here are family parties lying on benches, sprawling on heaped bedding on the floor, huddling into corners, surrounded with babies, baskets, teacups, fruit-skins, toys, all the impedimenta of poorly equipped, ill-nourished people gallantly trying to make themselves comfortable in the most difficult circumstances. The atmosphere is not of the purest ; the sanitation still leaves much to be desired. But there's company and warmth, much cheerfulness, comparatively a feeling of safety ; and the promise by the authorities of better things to come.

It is, I admit, a relief to come into the open again and breathe the morning air. And now dawn has turned into daylight, the sun is rising, the sky is streaked with its friendly glow. What were dim, bulky shadows turn out to be ships and warehouses. Already a new day's work has begun for many. Cats and dogs chase each other merrily in the street, children shrilly hover round and ask what's in them tins, miss. We pack up the canteen, handing out final cups to night workers hurrying home, and wish each other good-morning. Another night has passed ; and we're all here.

" How d'you think we're doing ? " I ask a young sailor, a factory girl, and a stout woman in a shawl who are poring over today's picture paper.

" Oh, *we're* doing all right," is the reply ; and a homeless warehouseman joins in : " You know, miss ; I reckon 'e didn't know what 'e was up against."

A fleet of mobile canteens supply hot food and drinks to London's air-raid victims. In this page a vivid description is given of how these motorized kitchens supply the needs of men and women rendered homeless by, or sheltering from, Nazi bombs. Here is a group of people obtaining welcome refreshment from one of the canteens.   Photo, Fox

To the Rescue of Our Friends the Animals

Many pets have been rescued from bombed areas by workers of the People's Dispensary for Sick Animals. An Airedale, above, is being taken from a wrecked home in London's East End. Rescued cats, right, seen among debris; circle, a dog being handed to a P.D.S.A. official.

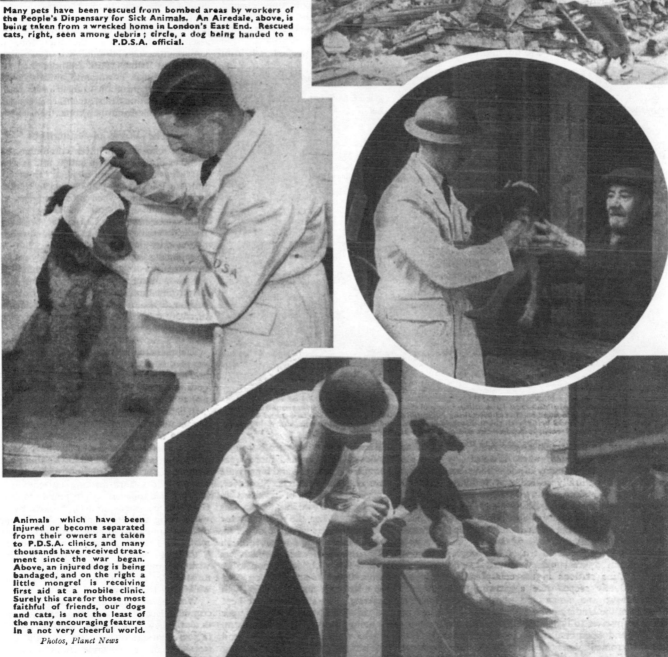

Animals which have been injured or become separated from their owners are taken to P.D.S.A. clinics, and many thousands have received treatment since the war began. Above, an injured dog is being bandaged, and on the right a little mongrel is receiving first aid at a mobile clinic. Surely this care for those most faithful of friends, our dogs and cats, is not the least of the many encouraging features in a not very cheerful world.

Photos, Planet News

Democracy Finds Itself in London's Tube Shelters

Since the air war was developed against London many hundreds of thousands of the people of the inner ring have found a reasonably safe, if neither comfortable nor pleasant refuge at night in the Tube stations. And there, deep underground, the democratic spirit has once again manifested itself.

AMONG the things that have happened, some foreseen and some not foreseen, since the aerial war opened against London, the use made by the public, on its own initiative, of London's magnificent underground railway system for shelter has become one of the biggest problems and one of the most impressive human spectacles of the war.

Whether the Government were right or wrong in refusing to countenance the provision of deep shelters, when they had an unexpected twelve months' grace to prepare for what could be foreseen, when the air war reached London it was too late in any case to get such work done for several months. Unfortunately, it was soon evident how inadequate was the shelter accommodation in poor and crowded areas.

The London Passenger Transport Board had informed the public since the war began that Tube stations were not and might

carrying blankets, pillows, food and drink, to stay all night at the pitch they had staked somewhere on a platform or in a corridor, or on stairs and escalators.

The first stations to be very overcrowded as the black-out hour approached were junctions or otherwise convenient centres. From Liverpool Street the tide moved on westward, filling up Holborn, Tottenham Court Road and Oxford Circus. From the south-east it came into the south London lines, and then pushed on south and south-west, where new hordes of people came pouring in from Victoria, Kennington, and Balham. The same happened in the north and north-west. Everywhere the river of humanity flowed into the only capacious underground shelters of the metropolis, and reached out all along the lines, to Ealing and Edgware and Tooting.

By the end of September the first rush from

The problem is not actually solved, but certain interesting developments can be traced, as the people of this valiant democracy have started to muddle through.

First, the officials at each station had to exclude the refugees until the traffic rush of people going home from work had eased somewhat. Many of the would-be shelterers, however, carrying suitcases or a discreet bundle wrapped with a blanket, took tickets and got out at another station, and waited patiently against the wall until there would be room to lie down on their staked claim to a night's repose. Crowds of other families, too poor to do this, waited in patient queues for hours outside the stations until they could be admitted. Now that bad weather is setting in this in itself has become another difficult problem, for many of these people begin to assemble at 2 or 3 in the afternoon, and cannot enter their station till five or six o'clock.

First at Tufnell Park Station, then soon after at Kentish Town and Camden Town, a necessary organization to keep order and to assist the station staffs in clearing up every morning came from the people themselves.

The Work of Volunteers

They chose a volunteer committee, each member of which wore a badge, and assumed authority in the general interest. These committees are rarely challenged by difficult individuals, and when this happens, the popular vote quells any disturbance. The committees have also assisted in organizing medical service, and in advising and helping overworked heads of families. But this spontaneous evolution of democracy remains unrecognized officially, and depends upon the cooperation of the Underground staffs. Meanwhile, officially-sponsored efforts to safeguard health and simplify the difficulties of cheap catering are being organized. Even entertainers, mostly from amateur theatres, now give shows in the stations at night.

The real credit for so far avoiding anything worse than some inconvenience to travellers, and for discovering an alternative to panic, goes to the masses of ordinary Londoners and not to their Councils or to the Government.

It is astonishing how the people in the overheated Underground stations contrive to sleep and resume work next day. In the still hours, after the last trains have ceased, while guns and bombs and lorries thunder on London's surface—in these artificial caverns and corridors hard-working citizens lie or lean huddled together. Multi-toned snores are the most persistent sounds, broken by the whimpering and crying of infants and small children, and the soothing or rebuke of tired mothers. Often the women are anxious that "the old man"—the breadwinner, there with his family—shall not be disturbed, for he must go straight off to work from the station, while they trek homeward with the children.

Wonders of pluck and endurance are the commonplace of these London workers, particularly the young women—waitresses, clerks, factory workers—who after a night on a staircase or a concrete floor, squeezed between others, turn up next morning at work, smiling, smart, and freshly made-up.

Here is the scene in Holland Park Tube Station, one of the first of 80 London Underground Stations at which food was provided so that those taking refuge in them should not have to depend on such " snacks " as they could bring with them. Electric urns are provided for hot drinks, and waitresses, interested in welfare work, look after the wants of those taking refuge.   *Photo, Fox*

not be used as shelters in an air raid ; but suddenly the stations were invaded by thousands of people, many of them homeless, all of them naturally scared and suffering from lack of sleep, who travelled every evening from the east and south-east areas which caught the first fury of the air bombardment. They came from areas densely crowded with small houses and with shelter accommodation for not one in ten of the people. They began a great trek westward to the nearest Tube stations in the central areas, and gradually seeped like a growing tide farther west and north and south. The officials of the Underground system could not bring themselves to turn the pathetic refugees adrift ; and when challenged for a decision, the Government wisely decided not to prohibit this invasion of the great transport system by thousands of families who came

the East End and the south-eastern boroughs had slowed down, as more and more basements, of commercial premises and big private houses, were opened for shelterers. Moreover, rapidly increasing numbers of residents in other districts began to crowd into the stations in their own areas. When the rush-hour for office and factory workers going home set in, it was often almost impossible to get through the crush of sweltering humanity. Mothers with babies, and sleepy children, soon to be joined by men and youths and working girls, thronged the platforms and corridors with makeshift bedding. The staircases were kept clear only so far as the station officials were able to keep going to order people off them. By tea-time the smell of the packed and motley crowds was pungent, and, remembering the entirely inadequate sanitary arrangements, there were grave fears of epidemic disease.

They Have Won Honour In Freedom's Cause

2nd Lieut. A. D. E. Curtis, Royal Engineers, M.C., for conspicuous gallantry and devotion to duty on active service.

Col. (temp. Brig.) A. C. L. Stanley - Clarke, C.B.E., for courage and distinguished services in the field.

Maj. R. L. Willott, Royal Engineers, D.S.O., for courage and conspicuous gallantry on active service.

Maj. C. H. C. Byrne, R.A.M.C., O.B.E., for bravery and outstanding courage during evacuation of hospital.

Lt.-Col. J. B. Gartside, Lancs. Fus., D.S.O., for conspicuous gallantry and courage while on active service.

Pilot Officer W. L. McKnight, D.F.C., for outstanding courage and conspicuous gallantry in the air.

Flt. Lieut. J. A. Kent, D.F.C., for gallantry in the air, Flight Cdr. in a Polish Squadron serving with R.A.F.

Aircraftman Gordon N. Patterson, bar to D.F.M., for displaying great bravery and courage in Belgium.

Flying Officer H. A. C. Bird-Wilson, D.F.C, for displaying conspicuous bravery. Shot down six aircraft.

Act. Flt. Lt. G. E. Ball, D.F.C., for destroying five enemy 'planes. He pursued one for 50 miles.

Sgt. Joan E. Mortimer, M.M., for displaying bravery when R.A.F. station to which she was attached was bombed.

Sgt. Helen E. Turner, M.M., for remaining at her telephone switchboard under severe aerial bombardment during attack on R.A.F. station.

Act. Asst. Sec. Officer E. Candlish-Henderson, M.M., for outstanding courage and devotion to duty during air raid.

These women of the W.A.A.F. are the first to win a military decoration

Lt. T. D. Wilson, Royal Armoured Corps (Hussars), M.C., for distinguished services and gallantry in the field.

Act. Squad. Leader A. V. R. Johnstone, D.F.C., for destroying four enemy 'planes, one at night.

Squad. Leader E.A. McNab, D.F.C., for leading his squadron with great success and destroying four aircraft.

Wing Cdr. F. V. Beamish, D.F.C., for displaying gallantry and conspicuous courage during operations in the air.

Lt. D. C. Mirrieless, Black Watch, M.C., for distinguished services and displaying gallantry in the field.

Patrol Officer M. C. Sadler, Bristol A.F.S., O.B.E., for working long under bombing and machine-gun attacks.

Sgt. E. Smith, G.M., for displaying gallantry and courage in helping to extinguish a serious fire.

Fireman A. V. Thomas, Bristol Fire Brigade, G.M., for courage, gallantry and devotion to duty during fire.

Sgt. W. V. Philpott, Bristol A.F.S., G.M., for conspicuous courage and devotion to duty under bombing attack.

Sgt. W. Bryant, Bristol A.F.S., G.M., for great courage in working under bombing and machine-gun attacks.

OUR DIARY OF THE WAR

TUESDAY, NOV. 5, 1940   *430th day*

On the Sea—Admiralty announced that two U-boats had been destroyed, one of which sank " Empress of Britain."

Reported that large British convoy in Atlantic, including liner " Rangitiki," was being attacked by German pocket battleship.

In the Air—R.A.F. carried out bombing attacks on oil sheds at Emden ; shipyards at Bremerhaven and Bremen ; power station at Hamburg ; ports of Boulogne, Dunkirk, Antwerp and Flushing ; many aerodromes.

War against Italy—R.A.F. reported to have made extensive reconnaissance flights in Greek and Italian coastal waters. Brindisi and Bari were attacked. During night of Nov. 4-5 targets at Naples were raided.

Other forces attacked objectives in Libya, and Metemma and Keren (Abyssinia).

Home Front—Three daylight attacks attempted on London and another in Dorset. Few bombs dropped in E. Kent, including Ramsgate. During night raiders bombed London, towns in E. Anglia, E. Scotland, Wales and Midlands.

Seven enemy aircraft destroyed. Five fighters lost, but pilots of two safe.

Greek War—Athens reported that Greeks had occupied new heights in Albania and were about to launch attacks on Koritza. Enemy aircraft bombed towns of the Piraeus, Patras and Volo.

Yugoslavia—Aircraft, said to be Italian, dropped bombs on Monastir.

WEDNESDAY, NOV. 6   *431st day*

On the Sea—Admiralty announced that H.M. submarine " Taku " had sunk large enemy tanker on Nov. 2.

In the Air—R.A.F. bombed oil refineries at Salzbergen, Hamstede aerodrome, Cuxhaven harbour and convoy off Den Helder.

Night operations included bombing of works at Spandau, suburb of Berlin, and railway junction west of city. Many other parts of Germany were heavily attacked.

War against Italy—Frontier post of Gallabat, on Sudan-Abyssinia frontier, captured by Italians in July, retaken by British.

Home Front—Southampton suffered daylight raid, resulting in casualties and damage to houses and public buildings. During night raids on London populous district was damaged. Two churches and block of flats hit. In crypt of one church nearly 600 people were sheltering, but all escaped. South coast town had its 175th raid.

Six enemy aircraft destroyed. Four British fighters lost, but pilot of one safe.

Greek War—Important new Greek advances reported. Positions gained have cut northern route for provisioning Koritza. On Epirus front Greeks made slight withdrawal from R. Kalamas.

Greek aircraft successfully bombed aerodromes of Koritza and Argyrokastro. R.A.F. attacked air base at Valona, Albania.

Africa—Lambarene, town in Gabon, surrendered to Free French Forces.

General Hertzog and his followers resigned from Nationalist Party.

General—Mr. Roosevelt re-elected to Presidency of U.S.A.

THURSDAY, NOV. 7   *432nd day*

In the Air—Aircraft of Bomber Command made heavy attacks on Krupps works at Essen ; synthetic oil plant at Cologne ; blast furnaces at Düsseldorf and Oberhausen ; docks on Dortmund-Ems Canal ; inland port of Duisburg ; shipping in Dunkirk harbour ; Lorient submarine base ; many aerodromes.

War against Italy—Fierce air fights over Gallabat which Italians tried to recapture.

Home Front—Three formations of enemy aircraft approached Britain, one entering Thames Estuary, the other two making for Portsmouth. All were dispersed. H.M.S. " Egret " destroyed one Junkers dive bomber and hit another.

Intensive night raids on London and Home Counties. Children's hospital suffered two direct hits. Bombs also fell in Midlands and in S.W. England.

Seven Nazi aircraft shot down. Britain lost five, but all pilots safe.

Greek War—Athens reported that fresh enemy attacks on Epirus front were repelled. In same sector 9 tanks were destroyed.

R.A.F. again bombed Valona aerodrome. Reconnaissances carried out over Greek and Italian coasts. Brindisi heavily raided.

FRIDAY, NOV. 8   *433rd day*

On the Sea—British steamer " Empire Dorado " reported to be sinking off Ireland after attack by Nazi sea raider.

In the Air—Strong force of R.A.F. bombers attacked railway stations and goods yards at Munich, and also hit famous beer cellar.

THE POETS & THE WAR
XXXVII
TO THE WORKERS OF LONDON
By M. D. Anderson

You should be proud, the humdrum and
  the weak,
Not versed in war nor schooled to high
  performance,
Who bear no shield but your own mute
  endurance,
Carry no sword but keen-edged Cockney
  laughter.
You should be proud indeed, for when
  men speak
Of this or that great hour of Time, here-
  after :
" London once saved Man's liberty,"
  they'll say,
" And those who fought their unheroic
  way
Through nameless dangers to mere drud-
  gery,
Helped thus to hold a new Thermopylae."
Are you not proud, the humdrum and the
  weak ?

—The Observer

Many other important targets in Germany and enemy-occupied territory were hit, including oil refineries, goods yards and 18 aerodromes.

Coastal Command aircraft made intense attack on submarine base at Lorient.

War against Italy—R.A.F. renewed attacks on aircraft factory at Turin and Pirelli magneto works at Milan.

Raids made on Tobruk and Derna (Libya) and on military centres in Abyssinia.

Home Front—Enemy dive bombers, escorted by fighters, attacked shipping off E. and S.E. coasts and were heavily engaged by R.A.F., fifteen being shot down by one squadron. Two more destroyed by guns of H.M.S. " Winchester," and three others hit. " Winchester " sustained slight damage. One merchant ship sunk and another damaged but reached port.

Intense A.A. barrage reduced number of night raiders over London. A.R.P. centre received direct hit.

Twenty enemy aircraft destroyed. Six British fighters lost, but three pilots safe.

Greek War—Italians claimed to have reinforced their bridgeheads across R. Kalamas. Greeks announced they had taken 150 more prisoners.

Yugoslavia—Italians bombed Monastir.

General—Roosevelt stated that half U.S. war output would go to Britain.

SATURDAY, NOV. 9   *434th day*

On the Sea—Admiralty announced that H.M. submarine " Sturgeon " had destroyed two enemy supply ships.

Announced that a British merchantman and the American steamer " City of Rayville " had been sunk off Australia by enemy mines. Latter was first U.S. loss of war.

In the Air—Aircraft of Bomber and Coastal Commands attacked submarine base at Lorient, docks at Boulogne and Calais, and many aerodromes.

War against Italy—Cairo stated that operations in Gallabat area were continuing.

R.A.F. raided Assab, Keren, and Agordat.

Home Front—Enemy daylight activity limited to few flights by single aircraft. Bombs fell in London area, Home Counties, Eastern England, Midlands, Liverpool and North-West. During night raiders flew over widespread areas of England and Wales.

Germany lost 7 aircraft, Britain none.

Greek War—Athens reported that Venezia Division of Alpini, on centre front in Pindus area, had been cut off, together with two regiments sent to relieve them.

General—Death of Mr. Chamberlain.

SUNDAY, NOV. 10   *435th day*

On the Sea—Admiralty announced that H.M. submarine H 49 was considered lost.

In the Air—Daylight attacks by R.A.F. on shipping at Boulogne and Calais. Targets bombed at night included oil plants, factories, docks, shipping, railway junctions, 14 aerodromes. Danzig bombed for first time.

War against Italy—Admiralty announced that Fleet Air Arm aircraft of H.M.S. " Ark Royal " carried out bombing attack on harbour and aerodrome at Cagliari, Sardinia.

R.A.F. raided Italian supply bases in Albania, including Sarande, Konispol and Valona. During night of Nov. 9-10 Naples was again raided.

Another attack made on Assab. Enemy twice raided Malta, but without material effect. Gallabat still in British hands.

Home Front—Enemy made raids on towns on Kent and Sussex coasts, and machine-gun attack on Scilly Isles. Strong force crossed Dorset coast but was dispersed.

At night bombs fell in many districts of London. A South coast town was heavily bombed. Damage and casualties occurred in areas of Thames Estuary.

Greek War—Italians attacked across R. Kalamas but were driven back and lost their bridgeheads. Greeks captured further strategic points dominating Koritza road at Berat, and made other advances.

Africa—Libreville, capital of Gabon, surrendered to Free French Forces.

MONDAY, NOV. 11   *436th day*

On the Sea—C.P.R. liner " Empress of Japan " reached port safely despite German claim of having left her sinking.

Three enemy aircraft destroyed by naval escort and others damaged when they attacked British convoy in North Sea.

In the Air—Daylight attacks made by R.A.F. on Lorient and several aerodromes. Weather precluded night operations.

War against Italy—R.A.F. raided Albanian port of Durazzo. Enemy naval base at Taranto also bombed.

Home Front—Strong formation of Italian aircraft routed when they attempted to attack shipping in Thames Estuary ; eight bombers and five fighters shot down by Hurricanes.

Several formations of German aircraft tried to reach London but few machines succeeded. Others attempted to attack convoy off Kent coast but were driven off.

Thirteen German and 13 Italian aircraft destroyed, one of former by Home Guard. Britain lost two fighters.

Greek War—Italians everywhere taking up defensive positions. Greeks captured many prisoners and much war material.

STRAIGHT AT THE TARGET THE TORPEDO-PLANE LAUNCHES ITS DEADLY MISSILE

In the brilliantly directed and highly successful attack on the Italian fleet in Taranto harbour, made on the night of November 11-12, the torpedo-carrying 'planes of the Fleet Air Arm covered themselves with glory. Torpedo-carrying aircraft were only just being developed at the end of the last war, but the technique of aerial torpedo attack has now been brought to a high state of perfection in the Air Arm of the Royal Navy.

Photo, Central Press

TARANTO: ITALY'S NAVAL STRONGHOLD

Where the Fleet Air Arm Triumphed

EVER since Italy entered the war, the Italian Navy has showed a marked preference for safe and sheltered havens rather than for the open seas, and no doubt it firmly believed that it had found one in the heavily-fortified harbour of Taranto, almost completely, land-locked and entered only through a channel 240 feet wide crossed by the swing bridge, seen left. Through the channel the largest warships can pass, though today there is some doubt about their emerging again. To the left of the bridge part of the ancient castle can be seen. In times of peace Taranto was a great fishing centre, and right are some of the fishing boats in the commercial harbour. Above is the Mare Piccolo, the main naval harbour. The white vessel is the Royal Yacht "Savoia," while alongside the quays are some of the older destroyers of the Italian Navy. On November 13, only a few hours after the devastating raid by the Fleet Air Arm, the port was bombed by the R.A.F.

Photos, Fox and Dorien Leigh

Taranto Was Indeed a 'Glorious Episode'

"If they won't come out of Taranto," Admiral Cunningham is reported to have declared,
"we shall blast them out." That, indeed, is what the Royal Navy did on November 11,
when the 'planes of the Fleet Air Arm bombed Italy's warships in Taranto harbour and
in a few minutes put three battleships out of action.

WHEN Mr. Churchill rose from his seat in the House of Commons on the afternoon of November 13 everyone could see that he was bubbling over with excitement. When he began to read his speech—carefully prepared as always—he read so fast that he left the reporters in the Press Gallery gasping. But very soon he was halted by the storm of cheering. "I have some news for the House," he announced. "It is good news. The Royal Navy has struck a crippling blow on the Italian Fleet."

When the cheering had died down, the Premier proceeded to tell of a truly "glorious

This sketch map shows the harbour of Taranto, scene of the Fleet Air Arm's great exploit on November 11, 1940. The smaller map shows the position of Taranto in relation to other points in Southern Italy bombed by the R.A.F. *Courtesy of the " Daily Telegraph "*

episode." He began by reminding the House that the Italians had possessed a battle fleet of six battleships—two of the Littorio class which had been put into service only lately and were, of course, among the most powerful vessels in the world, and four of the recently-reconstructed Cavour class. This fleet was considerably more powerful, on paper, than our Mediterranean Fleet, but it had consistently refused to accept battle. Then, with beaming face, Mr. Churchill announced that "on the night of November 11-12, when the main units of the Italian Fleet were lying behind their shore defences in their naval base at Taranto, our aircraft of the Fleet Air Arm attacked them in their stronghold.

"The reports of our airmen," he went on, "have been confirmed by photographic reconnaissance. It is now established that one battleship of the Littorio class is so badly down by the bows that her forecastle is under water, and she has a heavy list to starboard. One battleship of the Cavour class has been beached, and her stern, up to and including the after turret, is under water. This ship is also heavily listed to starboard. It has not yet been possible to establish the fact with certainty, but it appears probable that a second battleship of the Cavour class has also been severely damaged and beached. In the inner harbour of Taranto two Italian cruisers are listed to starboard and are surrounded by oil fuel,

and two Fleet auxiliaries are lying with their sterns under water."

Continuing his statement, the Premier recalled that the Italian communiqué of November 12, while admitting that one warship had been severely damaged, claimed that six of the attacking aircraft had been destroyed and probably three more shot down. In fact, however, only two British aircraft were missing, and even of these some of the crew had apparently been taken prisoner.

"As a result of a determined and highly successful attack," he concluded, "which reflects the greatest honour on the Fleet Air Arm, only three of the Italian battleships remain effective. This result, while it affects decisively the balance of naval power in the Mediterranean, also carries with it reactions upon the naval situation in other quarters of the globe."

Further details of the gallant and extraordinarily successful action were given later in the evening by the First Lord of the Admiralty, Mr. A. V. Alexander, in the course of a postscript to the nine o'clock news. He began with the reminder that when broadcasting on November 2 he had said that the Italian Admiralty regarded their capital ships as a capital investment and appeared determined to emerge from the war with their capital intact. "Today, I may be permitted to say we have imposed a severe capital levy on the Italian Navy."

Until the action at Taranto, the First Lord went on, our battle fleet in the Mediterranean was smaller in number than Italy's, but for reasons best known to themselves the Italians did not seek to exploit their superiority. They carefully avoided the action which Admiral Cunningham, Commander-in-Chief of the British Fleet in the Mediterranean, has always sought, and remained immobile behind the defences of their harbour. But in the event even these have failed to protect them. Within their inglorious shelter the Italian Fleet suffered on that November night a defeat which could have been redeemed in the public mind only had it shown itself willing to accept battle at sea. Now their numerical superiority has been reduced to inferiority in an action in which the dispositions of their admirals only allowed them to offer passive defence."

When the attack at Taranto was launched it was bright moonlight, and the 'planes of the Fleet Air Arm had to face strong anti-aircraft defences, supplemented by a balloon barrage.

There should have been 21 'planes—eleven carrying torpedoes and ten loaded with bombs and flares—but one bomber was delayed and another developed tank trouble and had to return. As soon as they appeared above their targets, the first wave of bombers dropped flares to illumine the path of the torpedo-carriers. With their engines roaring at full blast and with the wind screaming

Above is Admiral Sir Andrew Cunningham, Commander-in-Chief in the Mediterranean since 1939, who, after Taranto, was described by the First Lord of the Admiralty as "a gallant and skilful C.-in-C."
Photo, British Official: Crown Copyright

through their wires, these flew from 8,000 feet down to 5,000 feet, and then in a silent glide to 50 or even 20 feet above the water, when they fired their torpedoes. Nine torpedoes are known to have reached their marks; the other two may have done so, but the 'planes which carried them failed to return. After the torpedo-carriers had risen again into the air bomber No. 9 made its appearance—late, but not too late, for though all the fire of the ground defences and the ships' guns

In his broadcast account of Taranto on November 13 Mr. A. V. Alexander referred to the inspiring leadership of Rear-Admiral A. L. St. G. Lyster, right, backed by the captains of the two aircraft carriers. Left is Captain Bridge, commanding H.M.S. "Eagle."
Photos, Universal Pictorial Press and Elliott & Fry

A 'Crippling Blow' Struck at Italy's Fleet

At the outbreak of the last war H.M.S. "Eagle," one of the two aircraft carriers which made the attack on Taranto, was being built as a battleship for the Chilean Navy, but in 1917 she was bought by the British Government and completed as an aircraft carrier. She has a displacement of 22,600 tons, and a speed of 24 knots, while she carries normally 21 aircraft and a complement of 778.
Photo, Charles E. Brown

ITALIAN NAVAL LOSSES
June 11—Nov. 11, 1940

AT TARANTO

TWO BATTLESHIPS (I Cavour and I Littorio class) made ineffective.
ONE BATTLESHIP (Cavour class) severely damaged.
TWO CRUISERS heavily damaged and out of action ; two Fleet auxiliaries damaged.

EARLIER LOSSES

"**BARTOLOMEO COLLEONI**," cruiser, 5,000 tons, sunk by H.M.A.S. "Sydney" on July 19.
"**SAN GIORGIO**," an old cruiser of 9,232 tons, heavily damaged and beached in a Fleet Air Arm attack on Tobruk on June 11. Probably a total loss.
Nine destroyers and several sea-going torpedo boats and motor torpedo boats have been sunk.
At least 24 submarines have been sunk.
Submarine "**GALILEO GALILEI**" captured by H.M. trawler "Moonstone."

was concentrated upon it, it attacked the cruisers lying in the inner harbour with excellent effect.

Probably the attack lasted only a few minutes, but those few minutes were sufficient to wipe out Italy's superiority in capital ships, and to make it more than ever impossible for Mussolini to substantiate his frequent boast that the Mediterranean is Italy's sea.

The action at Taranto, declared Mr. Alexander, would help not only Britain's declared friends but free people everywhere. "It is a blow struck in full support of our gallant Greek ally, whose successful attacks on their treacherous enemy have thrilled us all. It will hearten them in proportion as it must depress the boastful and opportunist Mussolini, who, having waited to enter the war until he thought he was sure of the spoils of victory without fighting, now must see the writing on the wall and know that he is going to be beaten."

Concluding his broadcast, the First Lord paid tribute to the courage and skill of the Fleet Air Arm pilots, and of the Fleet Air Arm as a whole—that Arm which, off the Norwegian coast, in the British Channel and the Mediterranean, have destroyed at least 55 enemy aircraft, severely damaged at least an equal number, and sunk or damaged numbers of enemy warships and auxiliaries. "They are, indeed, worthy comrades of the pilots of the R.A.F." Then he proceeded to mention, in particular, the gallant and skilful Commander-in-Chief, Admiral Sir

Andrew Cunningham, and Rear-Admiral Lyster, whose inspiring leadership of the Fleet Air Arm has been backed by Captain Bridge and Captain Boyd of the aircraft carriers, "Eagle" and "Illustrious." (This mention of the "Illustrious," by the way, was the first public intimation of the completion of this newest of the Navy's aircraft carriers ; the "Eagle" is one of the oldest, and it seems most peculiarly appropriate that these two ships should have collaborated in one

of the most successful operations of the war to date.)

Not only at Taranto did the Navy strike at Mussolini. On the same night a squadron of our light forces operating on the main line of Italian communications with Albania, across the Straits of Otranto, intercepted off the Albanian port of Valona an enemy convoy consisting of four supply ships escorted by two destroyers. "Of the enemy supply ships," stated the Admiralty communiqué issued on November 13, "one was sunk outright, two were set seriously on fire, and almost certainly sank. The fourth was damaged, but succeeded in escaping under cover of a smoke screen. Both the escorting destroyers escaped at high speed under cover of smoke, but one of them was hit and damaged. No damage or casualties were sustained by our forces."

Still we have not finished the tale of victory. On that same Armistice Day 13 Italian aeroplanes paid for their temerity in raiding Britain, the majority of them being shot down before they managed to cross the coast. All in all, then, it was a black week for the Italians—the week which saw their defeat at Gallabat, the destruction of some of their crack troops in Greece, the bombing of their bases in Albania and Italy, and, as its climax, Taranto. These, said Mr. Alexander, are "blows inflicted upon each and every arm of the Italian forces."

Among the several types of 'planes used by the Fleet Air Arm is the Fairey Albacore biplane, one of which is seen above. It is designed for torpedo-carrying, spotting and reconnaissance, and machines of this type might have been employed in the attack on Taranto. It is powered with a Bristol Taurus sleeve-valve engine of over 1,000 h.p., and has an exceptional performance, but details of its speed and range and of its armament have not yet been disclosed.
Photo, Fox

Mussolini's Battleships Were Not Safe in Taranto

In the Fleet Air Arm's attack on Taranto on November 11, 1940 a ship of the Littorio class was left with her forecastle under water and a heavy list. Above is the "Littorio," one of four capital ships laid down between 1934 and 1938, the others of the same class being the "Vittorio Veneto," the "Impero," and the "Roma." They are of 35,000 tons with a main armament of nine 15-in. guns, besides twelve 6-in. guns and twelve 3·5-in. A.A. guns, and carry a complement of about 1,600. Their speed is 30 knots.

Another of the ships that the Fleet Air Arm put out of action for many months at least is one of the Conte di Cavour class. Italy possessed three ships of this class besides the "Cavour"—the "Giulio Cesare," the "Caio Duilio" and the "Andrea Doria." All four were completed between 1913 and 1916, but all have been reconstructed. They now carry ten 12·6 in. guns, twelve 4·7 in. guns and eight 3·9-in. A.A. guns, and have a tonnage of 23,622 and a speed of 27 knots. The reconstruction has made them practically new ships.   *Photos, Keystone*

More Than Fresh Laurels for the Fleet Air Arm

The aeroplanes of the Fleet Air Arm are specially designed for use with aircraft carriers, and the latest type to come into service is the Fairey Fulmar above. These 'planes, closely related to the famous Fairey Battle used by the R.A.F., are considerably faster than any hitherto employed by the Fleet Air Arm.   *Photo, Keystone*

Landing on the deck of an aircraft carrier is a ticklish business. An officer with two disks gives the pilot an indication as to the approach, and he is here making the signal to land.   *Photo, L.N.A.*

The new laurels which the Fleet Air Arm gathered at Taranto on November 11, 1940, are soon likely to be added to, for it is gaining strength apace. The first of six great new aircraft carriers has just been completed ; she is a ship of 23,000 tons, and on right is an impressive view of the stern, from which the 'planes take off. The photograph above, taken while Divine Service was being held, shows the great clear sweep of her deck. The first disclosure of this addition to the Navy's strength was made on November 13, when in a broadcast the First Lord of the Admiralty mentioned the completion of H.M.S. " Illustrious."

Photos, British Newsreel Association

'Jervis Bay's' Forlorn, Heroic Action

Many soul-stirring stories of the sea have been told of recent months, but surely the epic of the " Jervis Bay " will remain unsurpassed. Here we tell of the noble act of self-sacrifice and supreme bravery by which, though she, her captain and many of her crew were lost, the convoy entrusted to their charge sailed on.

SOMEWHERE in mid-Atlantic the big convoy of 38 merchantmen was proceeding steadily on its way on the afternoon of November 5. Suddenly, at 4.50 p.m., when the sun was still shining brightly in the sky, an enemy ship was reported on the port side. Almost as soon as she was sighted the raider opened fire from a distance of seven or eight miles on the largest ship in the convoy, the P. & O. liner " Rangitiki," which may have been taken for the escort vessel. There the German was mistaken, however. The escort ship was the auxiliary cruiser H.M.S. " Jervis Bay," formerly a liner of the Aberdeen and Commonwealth fleet, and as soon as the first shells screamed across the sea, Captain Fegen steered for the enemy without a moment's hesitation. He knew, none better, that his ship, armed only with 6-in. guns, had not a ghost of a chance against the raider, who was firing salvoes from apparently 11-in. guns (thus she may have been the " Deutschland," now renamed the " Luetzow," or the other pocket battleship, the " Admiral Scheer ").

Although completely outranged by the much heavier armament of the enemy, H.M.S. " Jervis Bay " continued to steer towards the raider, drawing the enemy fire away from her charges while at the same time she threw out a smoke screen with a view to cloaking their escape.

Very early in the action the " Jervis Bay " was heavily hit, and her steering-gear damaged. " Although partly out of control and seriously on fire," read the Admiralty statement issued on November 13, "she continued to hold the enemy fire while ships of the convoy were making their escape. The 'Jervis Bay' was continually hit by the enemy gunfire for nearly an hour, during which time she was engaged hotly in an attempt to divert the enemy gunfire from the convoy. She subsequently sank about three hours after the enemy was first sighted."

Survivors from the ship said that they realized fully what they were in for when they went out to tackle the Nazi battleship. But, to quote one of them, " I think everybody aboard was proud as our ship turned towards the enemy." Even when she had been holed below the waterline, when she was ablaze, developed a list and began to sink, her gun crews continued to pour shells at the distant enemy. When the flag was shot away a new ensign was nailed to the mast, and there it remained until the "Jervis Bay " took her last plunge. Early in the engagement Captain Fegen had his right arm badly shattered by a shell splinter ; but he staggered from the main bridge to the aft bridge in an attempt to control the ship from there, and then re-

turned to his original post. " Nobody saw him after that," said one of his officers ; and a member of the crew added : " I can see him standing on the bridge now. He was there when I last saw him after we abandoned ship."

" It was a cosy little scrap while it lasted," said one of the survivors when he got ashore at a Canadian port ; " our fellows were splendid. We sure gave Jerry everything we had until we could fight no longer. But," he went on, " it was an unequal fight. I guess we never had a chance ; but the ' Jervis Bay ' flayed right into the raider."

As the ship sank by the stern she was abandoned ; but the gunners, most of whom were formerly members of the Merchant Service who had never been in battle before, kept firing until the decks were awash. All but one of the boats had been destroyed, but the survivors plunged into the sea and made for the rafts. And there they were mercilessly raked by the fire of the enemy.

' They Did So Well For Us '

Meanwhile, the convoy was making good its escape. The " Jervis Bay " made the final sacrifice, but 33 out of the 38 ships which had been committed to her charge arrived safely in port. One of the ships, a Swedish freighter, remained near the scene of the action. " They did so well for us," said Captain Olander, " that I didn't like to leave. There she rode like a hero. She was right into the guns of the battleship. She didn't have a chance and we all knew it ; but there she stayed to the last to give us in the merchant ships a chance to run for it." When night had fallen he mustered his crew on deck and, putting the matter before them, decided to return to see if he could pick up any survivors of the " Jervis Bay." In spite of a rising sea, Captain Olander managed to reach the spot where the survivors were. He found three men dead in the only lifeboat which had been launched and four rafts on which a number of sur-

Capt. E. S. Fogarty Fegen, R.N., who went down with his ship, the " Jervis Bay." For his heroic conduct he was awarded on Nov. 16 a posthumous V.C.   *Photo, Vandyk*

vivors were still clinging, and he had the satisfaction of picking up 65 of them.

" It was glorious," said Captain Olander, when he got to Canada. " Never shall I forget the gallantry of the British captain, sailing forward to meet the enemy." And Captain Olander (see page 583), he too deserves a tribute. " He is a great man," said one of the men he rescued ; " he didn't have to risk himself and his ship to help us, but here he was right on the spot when we needed help badly. All our fellows are— well, we just can't put it into words. But we have the highest admiration for the Swedish captain and his men."

The Germans claimed at first that their surface naval forces operating against merchant shipping in the Atlantic Ocean had completely destroyed a British convoy, the total shipping sunk amounting to 86,000 tons ; and in London, too, it was feared that the losses would be very heavy. Greater far, indeed, would they have been, but for the sublime self-sacrifice of the " Jervis Bay " and her captain, that man cast in heroic mould.

The " Jervis Bay," an auxiliary cruiser of 14,164 tons, was on escort duty on November 5, 1940, in mid-Atlantic, when she was attacked by a Nazi raider. The result was a foregone conclusion, but, as Mr. Churchill said in the House of Commons on November 13, the spirit of the Royal Navy was exemplified in " the forlorn, heroic action fought by the captain, officers and ship's company of H.M.S. ' Jervis Bay ' in the Atlantic in giving battle against overwhelming odds to protect a merchant convoy which they were escorting, and thus securing the escape of by far the greater part of that convoy."
    Photo, Central Press

On to Koritza Pushed the Victorious Greeks

Following the defeat of Mussolini's crack division of Alpinis, the Greeks continued their successful resistance, coupled with a vigorous counter-offensive against the Italian invader. So successful, indeed, were they, that their achievements far exceeded what even their most sanguine well-wishers expected of them.

THREE weeks after the Italians began their attack on Greece, it was reported in Athens that there was not an Italian left on Greek soil, save prisoners, the wounded, and the dead. Moreover, along practically the whole of the front the Greeks had turned the tables on the aggressor and were themselves on Albanian soil.

For days the Greek highlanders, men who knew every inch of the ground and who were thoroughly acclimatized to the bitter weather encountered on these windswept and barren

One of the R.A.F. pilots who attacked the Italian troops on the move in the neighbourhood of Koritza had a thrilling story to tell on his return to his base. "We dived on them from about 20,000 feet," he said, "and released our bombs dead over the column, which was pretty tightly packed. I saw one bomb burst right in the centre of a big lorry. The Italians were running like hares. Then we hit a bridge (the one referred to here) fair and square, completely wrecking it, and the Italian reinforcements, which

had been using it, suffered heavily. Altogether," he concluded, "it was a most successful day."

In their move against Koritza the Greeks captured 3,500 prisoners and made a huge haul of war material, including 24 cannon, 38 trench mortars, nearly 300 machine-guns, 367 lorries, nearly 1,000 mules and horses, and the flags of two regiments. The prisoners, after a long march along the mountains, were taken by train to Athens, where, as the trains disgorged them on to the platform, they made a sorry enough showing, covered in mud, their uniforms torn, and the plumes in their hats bedraggled and broken. There was little in their appearance to suggest that these were men of some of Mussolini's finest regiments. So hungry-looking were they that some of the onlookers called out jestingly to the guards, "Look out, you fellows, or they will eat you!"

One of the Italian officers who was included among the prisoners said that on the evening of October 27 his regiment was ordered to take up its position on the frontier and on the following day move into Greece. "Our Colonel told us," he said, "what we now know to be all lies, that General Metaxas had assured Count Ciano that the Italian Army had been given permission to cross Greece and Yugoslavia, and that Greece would never oppose our might. With flags flying we marched at six o'clock in the morning. A terrible fire met us. The Greeks had trained their guns on the pass. We were unprepared and retreated in confusion. Next day we were surrounded by Greeks. I shall never forget those devils charging in skirts and yelling. I was captured in an unsuccessful counter-attack,

This map includes the Albanian-Greek frontier, where the Greeks turned the tables on the Italian invaders and penetrated some distance into enemy territory.

Map by courtesy of "The Times"

heights, worked steadily on across the mountain mass of Morova until they carried the heights above Koritza and thus had the Italians' advanced supply base at their mercy. With their mountain artillery and with four heavy guns which they had captured from the Italians, they dominated the enemy positions and the barracks and supply depots. Soon the Italians were seen to be evacuating the town, and fires from the burning houses and dumps illuminated the mountain sides. In this operation the Greeks received invaluable assistance from the 'planes of the R.A.F., which successfully bombed and machine-gunned the Italian motor transport columns, a farmhouse which was being used as Italian Army headquarters, and an important bridge—that which carries the road from Koritza to Elbasan, across the little river Devoli, along which enemy reinforcements were passing and along which, too, the retreating Italians might hope to move. This road, and also its continuation south from Koritza to Ersek, was completely dominated by the Greek guns; Ersek, indeed, was reported to have been captured, and also Leskoviku, still farther to the south-east.

This photograph, recently received in England, shows the swearing-in of some Greek conscripts, who were among the first to be enrolled after the Italian attack on their country. Compulsory military service in Greece begins at 21, and conscripts serve two years, followed by 19 years in the first reserve of the Army and eight years in the second reserve. Man for man, the Greeks have proved themselves quite the equal of their Italian foes.

Photo, Topical

Fiasco of Mussolini's First Invasion Attempt

The Italians have found that in the mountain passes between Albania and Greece cavalry is more useful than mechanized units. Here men of an Italian mounted division are advancing along a difficult road on the frontier.
Photo, Associated Press

General Soddu, left, was appointed Commander-in-Chief of the Italian Army, attempting to advance into Greece, when it was made plain that Italy's " blitzkrieg " was not going according to plan.   *Photo, E.N.A.*

Disembarking at an Albanian port, these Italian troops are to be rushed across country to reinforce their hard - pressed comrades on the Greek frontier.

mountains of Epirus and their muddy valleys do not lend themselves to lightning warfare," yet :" we will break the back of Greece."

" Today, the twenty-third day of the war," M. Nikoloudis, Under-Secretary for the Press, said on Nov. 19, " our heroic armies have purged the last corner of Greek soil which had been profaned by Italian Fascism. But we fight against an enemy six times our size numerically speaking, who has plenty of war material and means of every kind, and, above all, has a powerful air force. Greece has but little material and almost no aircraft. She has only the heroism of her soldiers and her airmen . . . Our appeal consists of one word : Aircraft ! "

which was ordered by our commander to cover the retreat. The Albanians on our left panicked. Our own tanks shelled them in an attempt to stop the panic which, however, spread along the whole line and caused it to fall back."

Another Italian officer had a similar story to tell. He spoke of moving forward into the mountains along deep defiles, where the trails were so narrow that even the mules lost their footing, so that many of them slipped and crashed down over the edge. " That was the end of them and their packs, too." When his column was halfway up a ravine on the Greek side of the frontier, the Greeks opened fire with rifles and machine-guns. " Taking what cover we could," he said, " we tried to reply, but the Greeks had chosen their positions too well. They had left us no targets that we could see. More machine-guns opened up. Even mounted guns were brought into action against us. It was impossible for us to try to advance farther ; it was quite as impossible to retreat. Suffering heavy casualties, we defended ourselves as best we could, from nine in the

morning to sundown. It was hopeless. So, in the end, we surrendered."

Swiftly the Italian retreat became a rout as the Greek centre, pushing on ever more strongly, threatened the whole Italian front with collapse. Bitter, indeed, must have been Mussolini's reflections when he heard the news that his army, which long ago should have been at Athens, was now in full retreat, and it was an infuriated man who screamed out on November 18 that though " the

Troops of an Italian unit mounted on motorcycles have made their way through a mountain pass in Albania into Greek territory. They wear on their helmets the cocks' plumes of the Bersaglieri.   *Photos, Associated Press*

In Syria the French are Still in Possession

Syria is one of the French territories that Mussolini hopes to secure by reason of his "victory," but as yet there seems to be small likelihood of his doing so. Not only is the British Navy in the way, but the French garrison—not to mention the Syrians themselves—are in no hurry to accept Italian domination.

BEFORE the Great War Syria was subject to the Sultan at Constantinople. In 1920, however, it was mandated to France by the League of Nations, and the mandate still holds, since the Franco-Syrian Treaty of 1936, providing for the abolition of the mandate and the recognition of Syria as a sovereign independent state, has not been ratified by the French parliament or by the League.

Shaped like a giant wedge between Turkey on the one hand and Palestine, Transjordan and Iraq on the other, Syria has an area of not quite 60,000 square miles. Fronting the

seeds yield a valuable oil. Fruits of all kinds are also grown, and olive groves, vineyards and fig gardens are many. Cotton production is on the increase, and Latakia tobacco is famous ; millions of sheep are pastured on the mountain slopes, and in the desert areas the camel is the beast-of-all-work of the tribesmen. In the Lebanon mountains iron has been worked from time immemorial, and there are traces of petroleum deposits.

Politically, Syria is divided into four territories : the Syrian Republic, the Lebanese Republic, the Government of Latakia, and the Government of Jebel Druze. Far the

the Lebanon mountains and the sea, is much smaller (3,800 square miles, and a population of 850,000). Its chief town is Beirut, which has long ranked as one of the most important ports in the Levant. To the north is Latakia (2,800 square miles ; inhabited by some 300,000 Alaouites), with the town of Latakia as its capital.

The fourth territory, Jebel Druze (2,400 sq. m.), lies in the extreme south of Syria, adjoining Transjordan ; its government has its seat at Es Suweideh. Its inhabitants, the Druses, are fanatical Moslem tribesmen, formidable fighters who not so long ago—in 1925 to be precise—rose in open rebellion against the French, who had recently come into their country. Fierce fighting extended even to the streets of Damascus, and for two days in October the ancient city was bombarded by the French guns. By the middle of 1926 the rebellion was over, but to this day the Druses have remained as an unreconciled element in the Syrian population.

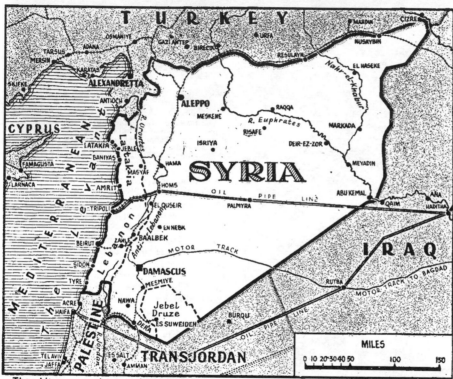

The white area on the map above shows Syria, the mandated French territory which is a key position in the Middle East. Alexandretta, or the Hatay, is an autonomous state under Turkish protection.
Courtesy of "News Chronicle"

Mediterranean and overlooking the fertile strip of coastal territory are the parallel mountain ranges of Lebanon and Anti-Lebanon ; beyond these, the table-land gradually merges into desert, crossed only by caravan roads and one or two motor tracks, and by the oil pipe-line, completed in 1934, which runs from Haditha on the Euphrates, through Palmyra and Homs, to the port of Tripoli on the Mediterranean.

Varied as are its surface features, Syria's population is even more diverse. Of its rather more than three and a half millions, the majority are Arabic-speaking Moslems, but there are also innumerable Turks, Turkomans, Kurds and Circassians, Armenians, Persians and Jews, Bedouins in the desert, and a few Europeans. About half a million are Christians belonging to different churches ; indeed, in Syria there is an almost bewildering variety of patriarchs, archbishops and bishops. Most of the people are farmers on a small scale, growing wheat and barley, maize and sesame, whose

largest of these is the first or Syria proper, whose 49,000 square miles take up practically the whole of the country with the exception of the coastal belt. Its capital is Damascus, historically the oldest of all living cities and one which still retains a predominant oriental atmosphere. Its bazaars are famous throughout the East ; and through its streets move caravans with tobacco from Baghdad and silk carpets from Persia, dark-hued Arabs in their camel-hair tarbooshes, pilgrims on the road to Mecca, and bearded Syrian merchants in coats of lamb's wool. As one of the greatest cities of the world of Islam Damascus may boast of its 250 mosques, but there are large Jewish and Christian quarters, and its most famous street is the one called Straight, down which tottered the newly-blinded Paul 1,900 years ago. Damascus' population may number some 230,000, but Aleppo, a great commercial centre in the northern part of the republic, is considerably larger, with perhaps 300,000 people.

The Lebanese Republic, which lies between

Repercussions of Surrender

The French administration has its headquarters at Beirut, and the present High Commissioner is M. Gabriel Puaux, who took office at the beginning of 1939. Before France collapsed she maintained an army consisting of five divisions of rather more than 100,000 men in Syria, but General Mittelhauser's fine force was quick to be affected by the disillusionment and conflicting loyalties that ensued. At first General Mittelhauser, the French Commander-in-Chief in the Near East, declared that whatever happened in Metropolitan France he would go on fighting, but when General Weygand, his predecessor as C.-in-C., brought pressure to bear upon him, Mittelhauser submitted to Vichy.

This submission was welcomed by many of the 35,000 or 40,000 conscripts and reservists who were concerned only with returning home at the earliest possible date, but it was bitterly resented by the resident Syrian garrison force, of about 10,000 French regulars, and their resentment was shared by the great majority of the native troops—numbering, perhaps, 50,000 men—who took not the slightest interest in the French political quarrel but were prepared, good soldiers that they were, to follow their officers wherever they might lead. The disaffection was intensified by the arrival of the Italian Mission, dispatched to supervise the demobilization and disarmament decreed by the terms of the armistice. We do not know what the Italians required, but it is safe to assume that they wanted to lay their hands on the great stores of military supplies, the tanks and guns, lorries and aeroplanes, and also to be permitted to occupy the principal aerodromes. Whatever they asked, they seem to have gone away disappointed ; M. Puaux and General Fougère, who replaced Mittelhauser as C.-in-C. last July, received the Italian generals with typical Gallic courtesy and expressed their willingness to cooperate with them in every way consistent with their loyalty to Marshal Pétain's government at Vichy. But it is significant that as the weeks pass more

Italy's Generals Were Sent Empty Away

Here is a view of Beirut, the principal seaport of Syria, and the home and the headquarters of the French Administration. It is situated on the Mediterranean about 60 miles from Damascus, and has had a long and chequered history, having belonged in turn to the Greeks, the Romans, the Crusaders and Moslems, while it was occupied by the British in October, 1918. The population is about 135,000.   *Photo, Dorien Leigh*

and more of the French dissentients cross the border into Palestine and Transjordan, to continue the fight side by side with their old allies.

If the Italians did indeed succeed in securing control of Syria, then the position of Britain in the Near East would be made infinitely more difficult, for a block of enemy or at least enemy-controlled territory would be interposed between Palestine and Turkey, Britain's ally. Moreover, the Italians would be able to replenish their dwindling oil supplies by way of the pipe-line from Iraq, which, as we have seen, reaches the Mediterranean at Tripoli ; since the war began the

flow of oil has ceased, much to the chagrin of Mussolini and to the disadvantage of his war effort, for it was from Iraq that Italy used to receive a considerable proportion of her oil supplies.

Britain's occupation of Crete and the Greek islands makes the Italian threat to Syria much less formidable ; and in any case the British island of Cyprus lies conveniently close—in fact, its mountains may be seen from the heights of Lebanon on a clear day. But there seems to be little likelihood at present of Mussolini securing a foothold in the great French dependency. Even if the French were inclined to submit, the Syrians them-

selves might be expected to put up a stern resistance against Italian domination. A large proportion of them were opposed to the French mandate, and if the French withdrew, Syria would almost certainly proclaim her independence ; after all, in so doing she would be carrying out the intention of the Treaty of 1936.

On the other hand, we might see the rise of a great Pan-Arabic realm, which would include not only the four territories of Syria, but Iraq and possibly Transjordan. But as yet the French are in possession, and, failing an attack by Italy or Germany, they are likely to remain so.

With Mr. Eden on His Tour of Empire

Men of an Indian division in an armoured car are on the look-out for enemy 'planes during operations in the Western Desert. They are fully equipped with anti-aircraft guns.
Photo, British Official: Crown copyright

On one occasion when Mr. Eden visited the military establishments in the Near (or Middle) East he and his party were conveyed in West-land Lysanders, two-seater monoplanes of extreme manoeuvrability which are highly favoured for reconnaissance and army coop-eration work. In this photograph we see the War Secretary entering his 'plane.
Photo, British Official: Crown Copyright

FOR some weeks in October and November, 1940, Mr. Anthony Eden, Secretary of State for War, toured the Near East, visiting numerous military establishments in Palestine, Egypt and the Sudan. Accompanied by General Sir Archibald Wavell, Commander-in-Chief in the Middle East, he inspected units of the Palestine garrison in Jerusalem, subsequently visiting Amman, the capital of Transjordania, where he was received by the Emir Abdullah of Transjordan, and inspected a desert patrol of the Arab Legion and a unit of the Transjordan Frontier Force. In Egypt Mr. Eden paid a surprise visit to the Fleet Club at Alexandria and was given an ovation by 5,000 officers and men of the Mediterranean Fleet and members of the R.A.F. He also inspected anti-aircraft defences at Alexandria. After a short stay at Suez, Mr. Eden spent some days with the field army in the Western Desert. At Khartum, on October 27, he met General Smuts, Prime Minister of the Union of South Africa. Broadcasting to the Forces in the Middle East on his return, Mr. Eden said that his journey had been a most vivid and encouraging experience. "Yours is the quality that commands success."

Here Mr. Eden is greeting a unit of the Transjordan Frontier Force during his visit to the Near East. This force polices the Jordan Valley and numbers 170 officers and nearly 3,000 other ranks. Other photographs of the Force appear in page 512.
Photo, British Official: Crown Copyright

How the Fleet Air Arm Attacked at Taranto

NAVAL and air history was made on the night of November 11-12, when torpedo- and bomb-carrying 'planes of the Fleet Air Arm delivered a devastating onslaught on the big ships of Mussolini's Navy lying so snugly at anchor in the harbour of Taranto. The story of the attack is given in page 563, but here, in this diagrammatic drawing, we have illustrated some of the 'planes with which the Fleet Air Arm is equipped and what we may suppose was the method of their attack on the great Italian naval base.

First we see the aircraft—Fairey Fulmars, Blackburn Skuas and Fairey Swordfish—taking off in waves from the deck of a monster aircraft carrier. The first flight is composed of the Fulmars—fast, heavily armed monoplane

fighters whose job it is to protect the bombers from attack by hostile 'planes. Close behind them—or rather, enclosed by them—come the Blackburn Skuas—dive-bombing monoplanes each of which may carry one 1,000 lb. bomb. Diving down at terrific speed on their targets, the Skuas release their bombs, then, flattening out, roar up again into the sky where for the nonce they join the protecting escort of fighters, while the third wave, composed of Fairey Swordfish torpedo-carrying 'planes, launch their torpedoes on the Italian battleships lying only a few feet below. Each Swordfish carries one torpedo—"Mouldies," as they are called in the Navy—but that torpedo is a miniature battleship weighing up to a ton and containing perhaps 500 lb. of T.N.T.

Specially Drawn for THE WAR ILLUSTRATED *by War Artists & Illustrators Ltd.*

Ferociously Mauled by the Bestial Nazi

For hours on
bert Morrison,
scarred Coven
his intense syr
dramatic photo
the intrepid fir

FROM dusk
town of
fame and prosperity as th
rayon and aircraft, was
Some 500 tons of hig
dropped, and the ca

In the savage onslaught on Coventry, the famous Cathedral, a gem of 14th-century architec
the tower standing (left and above). Among the other "targets" were two hospitals, a libr
large stores and shops, office buildings, a school, police station, and post office. Altogether
destroyed, and the damage in the heart of the city was particularly extensive. New

Photos, L.N.A. exclusive to THE WAR ILLUSTRATED; *and Fox, Associa*

ventry's Head Was Bloody but Unbowed

ng, accompanied by Mr. Her-
curity, walked through bomb-
rds and by his very presence
's stricken people (left). The
ventry street was taken when
gaged in combating the flames.

mber 14-15 Coventry, ancient
n in recent days has won fresh
motor-cars, sewing-machines,
fter wave of German 'planes.
and 30,000 incendiaries were
ed to be over a thousand.

Quaint reminder of the Lady Godiva story, the effigy of Peeping Tom was
carried to a place of safety (left). The two photographs given below
provide a grim contrast. They show Broadgate, in the centre of Coventry,
before the Nazi terror raid (bottom), and as it was on November 16, the
day when the King visited the still burning ruins.

ass of rubble with nothing but the outside walls and
hotels, clubs, cinemas, public baths, public shelters,
one kind and another were reported to have been
y's people told the King : "We carry on."
ror," and "The Times"

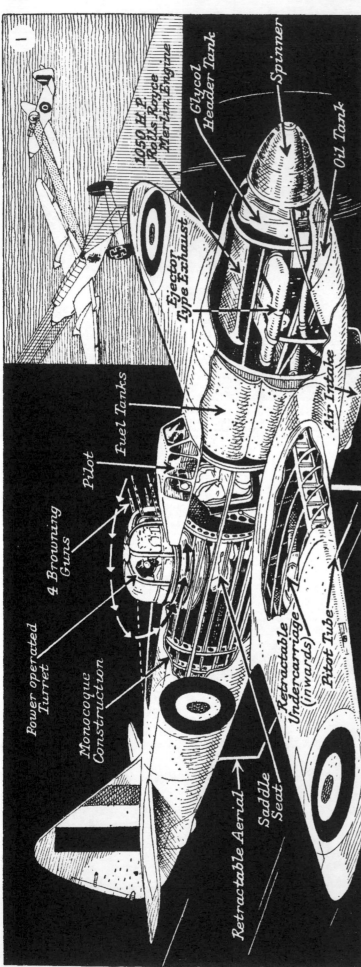

1

Power operated Turret

4 Browning Guns

Monocoque Construction

Pilot

Fuel Tanks

Retractable Aerial

Saddle Seat

Retractable Undercarriage (inwards)

Pilot Tube

Air Intake

Oil Tank

Spinner

Glycol Header Tank

1,050 H.P. Rolls-Royce Merlin Engine

Ejector Type Exhaust

4

3

2

BOULTON PAUL DEFIANT. With a performance which equals that of many single-seater fighters, this two-seater fighter is one of the most formidable aircraft in the service of the Royal Air Force. In addition to its fixed forward-firing machine-guns it has a four-gun turret behind the pilot's cockpit, and this combination endows the Defiant with a tremendous fire power. It is fitted with a 1,050 h.p. Rolls-Royce engine, and the span is 39 feet, 6 inches. Fine manoeuvrability, and splendid visibility for both pilot and gunner make it admirably suitable for defensive night flying. How its great field of fire can be used is shown in diagrams 1 to 4.

1. Attacking ME 110
A starboard attack on an ME 110. The German gunner's field of fire (shown by the patched section) is hopelessly restricted so that he is powerless to return the fire from the Defiant. Dotted beam shows Defiant's zone of fire.

2. Beam Attack on HE 111 K
A beam attack on an HE 111 K bomber. Again, the Nazi cannot protect himself because of the limited traverse (shown by the arrows) of his movable guns, above and below his fuselage.

3. Attacking DO 17 on Blind Spot
A Defiant comes close to pour bullets from its turret guns into a Dornier DO 17 caught in his blind spot. His movable guns installed above and below fuselage, shown by arrows, cover only a small field to the rear.

4. ME 109s in Defensive Circle
ME 109s fly in a defensive circle to ward off attacks. But a Defiant dives, and with his four guns the gunner fires a burst (shown dotted) on one of the enemy from a blind spot below.

Specially prepared for The War Illustrated *by War Artists and Illustrators Ltd.*

'A Good Week for Us—A Bad One for the Enemy'

One of the most active weeks in the air war is that whose principal happenings are reviewed in the chapter that follows. Italian attacks on Britain, and British on Italy; heavy raids on Hamburg and the wanton brutality of Coventry—these are some of the many incidents of an eventful period.

THE disastrous result of the first encounter between Italian raiders and our fighters over Britain, on Armistice Day, seems to have dissuaded the Regia Aeronautica for the present from pitting themselves against the R.A.F. Fifteen to twenty Italian bombers (Caproni 135) were accompanied by about three times as many fighters (CR 42, a type

Sergeant E. F. Sly, right, who has been awarded the Air Force Medal, was flying at a height of 900 feet when a pupil in another aircraft struck a wing of his 'plane and severed it from just beyond the engine. Though his machine was breaking up Sergeant Sly managed to land (below).

illustrated in page 289); eight bombers and five fighters were shot down by the R.A.F. in a few minutes, without loss. Mussolini could have found useful work for his aircraft much nearer home, for it was on the night of November 11-12 that machines of our Fleet Air Arm carried out a dashing attack on Italian warships at Taranto, as described in page 563, badly damaging three battleships, two cruisers and two Fleet auxiliaries. Two British aircraft were lost. On the night of November 13-14 a large force of bombers of the R.A.F. made a further attack on the docks and harbour at Taranto, and all our aircraft returned safely.

In a period of ten nights the R.A.F. had bombed Naples three times—October 31-November 1, November 4-5, and November 9-10. During this same period the port of Brindisi was bombed twice. On Armistice Day aircraft of the Fleet Air Arm from H.M.S. "Ark Royal" bombed the harbour and aerodrome at Cagliari, in Sardinia—without loss. Two shadowing enemy aircraft were destroyed by our fighters. So November 11 turned out to be a very unlucky day for Il Duce. Even the 900 miles of land and sea which separate his territory from Britain have not availed to protect his arms and engine factories from the R.A.F.; and on November 9, for example, our bombers flew 1,800 miles non-stop in order to batter the Fiat motor and aircraft works at Turin, and the Pirelli electrical accessories factories at Sesto San Giovanni, a few miles north of Milan. The Pirelli works had received a heavy attack some three weeks earlier, on October 20.

The Fleet Air Arm also struck heavy blows at the Italian air force. A Cant 501 aircraft was damaged on November 8, and on the same day our Fulmars intercepted a formation of S 79s and destroyed one. Next day they shot down a Cant 506, and on the 10th destroyed another of this type. A formation of nine S 79s was intercepted and one damaged.

Besides indirect help afforded by the British Naval and Air Force operations mentioned,

our forces have been assisting the Greeks with ever-increasing vigour in their resistance to the Italian invaders. Ports in Albania and on the Italian mainland have been bombed;

FIRST FIGHTER PILOT V.C.

ON November 14, 1940, it was announced that Flight Lieutenant James Brindley Nicolson, aged 23, of No. 249 Squadron, had been awarded the V.C. The official account stated that: "During an engagement near Southampton on August 16, Flight Lieutenant Nicolson's aircraft was hit by four cannon shells, two of which wounded him, while another set fire to the gravity tank. When about to abandon his aircraft owing to flames in the cockpit he sighted an enemy fighter, which he attacked and shot down, although, as a result of staying in his burning aircraft, he sustained serious burns to his hands, face, neck, and legs. Fl. Lt. Nicolson has always displayed great enthusiasm for air fighting, and this incident shows that he possesses courage and determination of high order. By continuing to engage the enemy after he had been wounded and his aircraft set on fire, he displayed exceptional gallantry and disregard for the safety of his own life."

Photos, British Official: Crown Copyright

AIRCRAFT LOSSES OVER BRITAIN			
German to April 30, 1940			
Total announced and estimated—West Front, North Sea, Britain, Scandinavia			350
	German	Italian	British
May	1,990	—	258
June	276	—	177
July	245	—	115
Aug.	1,110	—	310
Sept.	1,114	...	311
Oct.	241	—	119
Nov. 1-18	175	13	39
Totals, May to Nov. 18	5,151	13	1,329

Daily Results				
Nov.	German Losses	Italian Losses	British Losses	British Pilots Saved
1 ...	18	—	7	2
2 ...	10	—	—	—
3 ...	1	—	1	—
4 ...	—	—	—	—
5 ...	7	—	5	2
6 ...	6	—	4	5
7 ...	8	—	5	5
8 ...	22	—	6	3
9 ...	7	—	—	—
10 ...	—	—	—	—
11 ...	31	13	2	—
12 ...	1	—	—	—
13 ...	6	—	—	—
14 ...	19	—	2	2
15 ...	20	—	2	1
16 ...	5	—	—	—
17 ...	14	—	5	4
18 ...	—	—	—	—
Totals	175	13	39	20

None of the figures includes aircraft bombed on the ground or so damaged as to be unlikely to reach home.

From the beginning of the war up to Nov. 11, 2,846 enemy aircraft have been destroyed during raids on Britain. R.A.F. losses were 813, but the pilots of 405 British machines were saved.

Mr. Churchill on Nov. 5 gave weekly average of killed and seriously wounded for September as 4,500; for October, 3,500. In first week of intense bombardment in September 6,000 casualties; in the last week of October, only 2,000 casualties. Totals announced for October: killed, men 2,791; women 2,900; children 643. Wounded and detained in hospital, men 4,228; women 3,750; children 717.

supply ships en route to the scene of war have been destroyed; the Italian forces have been harried; roads and bridges over which supplies and reinforcements were being rushed have been persistently attacked by the R.A.F.

An outstanding feature of the German attacks on Britain during the week was the change of tactics seen in Thursday night's raid on Coventry. The Nazis claimed that this was the biggest raid in the history of air warfare. The raiders flew too high to discriminate, and in fact the damage was almost entirely confined to churches (including the Cathedral), cinemas, large hotels, stores, business premises and dwelling houses generally. Over 250 persons were killed and about 800 wounded. (Photographs of Coventry after the raid are printed in pages 574-575.)

The Germans stated that this savage attack on civilians was " in return for the abortive British raid on the party celebrations in Munich " on the previous Friday night. But they might just as well have intended it for a reprisal for our routine raid on Berlin during the night of November 13-14, when Molotov, the Russian Premier and Foreign Commissar, happened to be attending a farewell banquet at the Soviet Embassy.

While the Nazis were bombing Coventry and other British towns our R.A.F. bombers delivered a further heavy attack on Berlin; six terminal stations and goods yards were bombed. Other R.A.F. formations attacked

Italians Followed the Nazis to Disaster

28 enemy-occupied aerodromes, besides ports, harbours and shipping along the coasts from Norway to Brittany.

Germany's daylight raids on Britain, resumed in greater force, went ill for the Luftwaffe, which lost 19 aircraft on Thursday and 20 on Friday ; our own losses were two aircraft on each day. A large-scale attack was made on London on Friday night, when the German bombers came over in rapid succession and very heavy missiles were dropped. Five Nazi bombers were shot down. On the other side of the account is to be set the intensive and prolonged attack made on Hamburg by our bombers. Beginning at dusk on Friday, it continued until half-past five on Saturday morning, and on this occasion the R.A.F. selected targets in the city itself— but only military objectives. The R.A.F. also raided Kiel dockyards, and dropped bombs on Ostend and Calais among other places.

On Saturday night our bombers attacked Hamburg again—in even greater numbers : factories, oil works, goods yards, the enormous Blohm and Voss shipyards were battered. Earlier on Saturday, in daylight, the R.A.F. had raided the Dortmund-Ems canal and oil refineries at Bremen and Cologne. At dusk bombers of the Coastal Command had made dive-bombing attacks on aerodromes in Northern France.

On November 12 a force of eighty Italian 'planes that sought to raid England was routed over the Thames Estuary, and thirteen of them were shot down. Here is an Italian raider that was brought down during the raid.

Photo, Fox

A remarkable photograph showing a Dornier swooping from the clouds. As anti-aircraft shells burst round the machine three bombs are released on a London area.

Photo, Associated Press

On Saturday, November 16, the first air attack was made on the Hebrides, when a Nazi bomber flew over in daylight and gunned a lighthouse. Enemy attacks during the day were light, but in the night raids a South-coast town suffered severely, and elsewhere bombs were dropped in London and places in the Home Counties. A German bomber was shot down off the Kent coast.

Fourteen enemy aircraft were shot down during Sunday's daylight raids—one by H.M. paddle minesweeper " Southsea," which used to ply between the Isle of Wight and Portsmouth, and one by A.A. gunfire. Five of our fighters were lost, but four of the pilots are safe.

Mr. Arthur Greenwood, Minister without Portfolio, in a speech on Sunday said that " the past week has been a good one for us and a bad one for the enemy. Serious though the attacks have been on this country, the punishment we have suffered is nothing to that we have administered to the enemy. Germany has suffered fifty times as much industrial damage from bombing as Britain has." He said also that recent events had opened a new chapter in the war.

'Biddy' Treads the Path to Safety

Involved in the noise and flaming fury of the air raids, many a London horse has been killed when its stable has been shattered by Nazi bombs. " Biddy," whom we see in this photograph being led to safety, was more fortunate. For over nine hours she was imprisoned in her stall and remained quite imperturbable while rescuers were clearing away the wreckage so that she could be released. Three horses were killed beside her when the bomb fell, but eight others were saved.

Photo, Planet News

One More Italian Submarine Takes the Count

Late in October 1940 a British destroyer tracked down an Italian submarine and eventually forced it to the surface with depth charges. Here the submarine is seen surfacing.

Just as the submarine reached the surface the British flying-boat that had joined with the destroyer in the pursuit dropped a bomb which missed its mark by only a few yards. The photographs in this page were taken from the same flying-boat that dropped the bomb.

When the Italian submarine had been forced to the surface and the crew knew that the game was up, they swam for the destroyer. Helping hands were ready for them, life-lines were lowered and, as the empty davits of the destroyer, left, show, boats were lowered to rescue other survivors. Right, the submarine's bow rises as she takes her last plunge. Up to November 11 Italy had lost some 24 submarines

Photos, British Official: Crown Copyright

For 24 Years Arabs Have Been Our Friends

IN 1928 an independent Government of Transjordania was recognized by the British Government. This territory is governed by a local Arab administration under the Emir Abdullah Ibn Hussein, and its population is about 300,000, of whom 260,000 are Arab Moslems and 30,000 Arab Christians. The remaining 10,000 are mainly Circassians.

On the occasion of the 24th anniversary of the Arab world joining arms with Britain, celebrations took place in August in all Arab states. Men of the Transjordan desert patrol are seen left, during the parade at Amman, the Transjordanian capital. Above, the Emir Abdullah, ruler of Transjordania, addresses his people in Amman.

Here is an impressive array of armoured cars of the desert patrol, parading in the Square at Amman, where they were reviewed by Emir Abdullah.

Photos, British Official: Crown Copyright

NEVILLE CHAMBERLAIN: AN APPRECIATION
by LORD CAMROSE

THE ceremony at Westminster Abbey on November 14 saw the final passing from our midst of one of the most honest, self-sacrificing statesmen who ever achieved the glory of being First Minister of the Crown in this country.

Perhaps history will say that Neville Chamberlain was one of the most mis-understood statesmen of this country. After Munich many thousands of people made it definitely their opinion that Chamberlain was a political weakling; that he feared Hitler and his power, that he thought our only course was to conciliate the monster in any and every way.

Nothing could have been more untrue. Munich undoubtedly crystallized his view of Hitler and his works, but fear was never the motive which actuated his policy towards Hitler or, indeed, towards anything else. He was not built that way. Neville Chamberlain was the type of the solid, slow but sure-reasoning Englishman who has made the British Empire what it is today. There was nothing sham about him in any shape or form. Shy, unassuming, diffident of his own abilities, he was strong as steel when his mind was made up, and as determined, dogged and true as any statesman England has ever possessed.

*   *   *

What the Prime Minister said of his con-duct on May 8, when the House of Commons had registered its vote against him in partial but convincing form, characterized with exactitude the man Chamberlain was. Those who were present in the House that night will never forget the scene. The debate had travelled far from the real subject. He and his Government had been blamed for crimes which were not theirs at all. Mr. Lloyd George stung him to the remark—persistently miscon-strued by subsequent speakers— "Even I have my friends in the House, and we shall see what they think when the vote comes." Sir Samuel Hoare had delivered a speech which left the House freezingly cold and unsympathetic, and Mr. Churchill, who was to wind up the debate, was left with a difficult enough task. He vigorously de-fended the Government policy, for the rights and wrongs of which he took his full share of responsibility; but the vote revealed a sensational fall in the Government majority.

There were loud cheers and counter-cheers. Chamberlain rose from his seat on the Front Bench and walked slowly out of the House. As he went his followers, including men who had given an adverse vote, rose and cheered him, waving their order papers in the air. It was an expres-sion of respect and esteem such as the House has seldom seen. It was as though those who had voted against him wished him to know how much they regretted having to do so, and the conversation in a crowded and excited Lobby afterwards showed that the vote was against the Government and not the Leader.

It was Chamberlain's firm inten-tion right from the early days of 1939 that, if war came, he would offer Winston Churchill a seat in the War

Mr. Chamberlain, who was Britain's Prime Minister on the fateful September 3, 1939, and for the war's first eight months, died on November 9, 1940. The words of ap-preciation that follow are reproduced here by courtesy of the "Daily Telegraph."

Cabinet. Indeed, I can go farther, and say from personal knowledge that it was his original intention when he came into power to make the offer as soon as he had felt his feet as leader. He had always the greatest admiration for Churchill, but a fear of his restless genius in a peacetime Cabinet. When war came he acted on his preconceived plan. Winston was first of all to be a Minister without portfolio; but when it was decided that all the Service Ministers must be in the War Cabinet he became the First Lord instead.

*   *   *

Almost from the very first the two men achieved the kind of association that one would have thought impossible taking into account the relations between them for the last few years. They worked together in absolute accord; each seemed to find in the other the complement of himself. Chamber-lain immediately saw in Winston the forceful, imaginative genius which no other member of his Government possessed, and which has become so manifest since he became First Minister of the Crown. On the other hand, Winston learned to respect the slower, more precise and steady qualities traditional in the Chamberlain family.

They worked together for eight months with a loyalty and understanding of the most perfect character and, after the first months, passed almost unconsciously to terms of

intimacy and friendship. When the change came, and the chief became the assistant for the brief time fate permitted, the same loyalty and unity existed between them.

In the early days of the war Churchill quickly stood out as the leading figure in the Government. In the short space of time given to him after the advent to power of the man who had become a close and warm friend, Chamberlain was perhaps the most valuable member of Churchill's Government. He supplied ability of a kind that every Government needs, and the new Prime Minis-ter recognized the fact in no uncertain manner.

The combination of the two men was a wonderful thing for the country, and the Prime Minister made no secret of the trust he reposed in his former chief's sagacity and sure-mindedness. The letters which passed between the two men when the state of Chamberlain's health compelled his resignation were not the ordinary letters that are usually penned on such occasions; they were sincere expressions of mutual esteem and loyalty, every word of which came from the hearts of the writers.

*   *   *

Of Neville Chamberlain it has been said that he was cold, harsh and pitiless. Nothing could have been more wrong. Naturally of a modest and diffident nature, he possessed none of that joy of the clash of private debate and discussion so beloved of the ordinary politician, and his powers of putting his real personality across to his followers and to the public were limited thereby. In him capacity for self-assertion did not exist. When he did enter the discussion, clearness of mind and powers of logical reasoning quickly made him recognized; but he had none of the exhilaration in convivial discus-sion which has been so marked a habit in English political life and in which so many of our statesmen have excelled.

He was fond of good music, and his knowledge of natural history was unusually great. But he was never, and never could have been what is called a good "mixer." Few of the Members of the House of Commons really knew what was behind the seemingly cold façade which he presented in his public life. Those who did never ceased to regret that it was not possible to exhibit the kind and tolerant nature which was really his.

*   *   *

Munich will be discussed and de-bated for many years to come. It is already one of the landmarks in our history, a cross-roads in the terrible sequence which has led to the gigantic struggle on which we are engaged today. Chamberlain may have done the only thing possible in the circum-stances or he may have been totally mistaken in his whole policy; the argument on that will never cease. But nothing could be more true than the Prime Minister's statement: "Whatever else history may or may not say about these tremendous, terrible years, Neville Chamberlain acted in perfect sincerity according to his lights."

No statesman could earn a better epitaph than that.

MR. CHAMBERLAIN: THE LAST PORTRAIT
Photo, G.P.U.

I WAS THERE !

Eye Witness Stories of Episodes
and Adventures in the
Second Great War

All Aboard Were Proud of the 'Jervis Bay'

The "forlorn, heroic action of H.M.S. 'Jervis Bay,'" as Mr. Churchill
described it, is the subject of a separate article (see page 567), but
here several eye-witnesses of this heroic fight in mid-Atlantic tell
their stories.

A N officer of the "Jervis Bay" who was
picked up by the Swedish freighter
which Capt. Olander, with conspicuous bravery, took back to the scene of
the action, said :

It was a sunny evening when we picked
up the battleship on the port side at 4.50 on
November 5. She opened fire first and closed
to get into range.

We closed, too, leaving the convoy. I
think everybody aboard was proud as our
ship turned towards the enemy.

Our captain knew just what we were going
to get, but it did not matter.

We got between the enemy ship and the
convoy and dropped smoke floats to screen
the merchant ships from the raider. The
enemy was firing salvos.

Soon the "Jervis Bay" was hit. Her
steering gear was put out of action, though
her guns continued to fire, and she kept
fighting it out.

Holed below the waterline and ablaze,
the "Jervis Bay" began to list and sink. But
all the time the gun crews continued to pour
shells at the distant enemy.

The flag was shot away. A man ran up
the rigging with a new ensign, which remained
waving until the merchant cruiser took her
last plunge.

Struck several times, and with the steering
gear damaged, the "Jervis Bay" could
steam only in a straight line.

She could not get her guns to bear on the
German ship because she was heading for
her and the forward guns were out of action.

As the ship went down by the stern she was
abandoned. The Germans mercilessly fired
at the seamen as they took to the boats.

The officer went on :

One man on the forecastle did not hear
my order to leave. He stood there alone
with earphones over his head calmly continuing his duties while shells fell all around.
When someone brought the order to his
attention he laid the earphones down carefully and made his way to the boats without
a trace of haste.

All the lifeboats but one were burned
when we abandoned ship, but we threw four
rafts over. The raider ceased firing at the
"Jervis Bay" five minutes after we left,
concentrating on the convoy. She fired on
the other ships until well into the night,
throwing up star shells for illumination.

The officer said that the "Jervis Bay's"
crew fought like veterans. He remarked :

It was astonishing. Two-thirds of them
were formerly mem-
bers of the Merchant
Service who had
never been in battle
before.

Captain Fogarty
Fegen died a hero's
death and went down
with his blazing ship.
One of his arms was
almost shot away,
but he remained in
command until the
end.

The three survivors of
the crew of the immor-
tal fight of the "Jervis
Bay," below, were
wounded in the action
and are here seen in a
Canadian hospital.
They are, left to right,
J. Eggleston of Hull,
Dan Bain of Wick, and
Sam Patience of In-
verness.

Sub-Lieutenant J. G. Sergeant, another
survivor of the "Jervis Bay," summed up
the action in the words :

It was the Navy's job, and it was done.

Sub-Lieutenant Sergeant, who went to the
fire control station immediately "action
stations" was sounded, said :

We challenged the ship with a Verey
light signal, and she answered by firing. We
fired simultaneously with the raider.

Captain Fegen gave "full steam ahead,"
turning to port to bring us between the enemy
and the convoy. Then we laid a smoke screen.

The enemy opened fire at extreme
range. Captain Fegen had previously
promised that if he ever sighted the enemy
he would get as close as possible. He headed
for the enemy and tried to reduce the range.

The raider fired two salvos, missing us.
A third salvo hit us forward and carried away
one gun.

At the same time I went below, but I was
told that the bridge was blown away. Then
the ship was handled from the aft control.

Captain Olander, above left, of the Swedish
freighter which rescued sixty-five members of
the crew of the "Jervis Bay." Right is his
chief officer.   *Photos, Wide World*

When we first sighted the enemy it was
about 5 p.m. I should say that within 15
minutes we were disabled, unable to bring
our guns to bear. For the next half hour we
were being hit. The engine-room was hit,
then the enemy concentrated on the controls.

One of the skippers of the convoy on
landing in Britain said :

The raider was first sighted on the port
beam, and almost immediately began firing.

Her attention was evidently focused on
the big liner "Rangitiki," the largest ship in
the convoy. The German must have mistaken
the "Rangitiki" for an escort vessel, and was
obviously attempting to get rid of her first of
all. The gunfire was accurate and very heavy.

I WAS THERE!

At times we got as many as five shells in one burst.

The raider was about seven or eight miles distant, and my impression is that some of the salvos were from 11-in. guns. That makes me think she was of the Deutschland or Admiral Scheer class.

Everything was in favour of the attacking warship. The sea was calm and there was a clear atmosphere. The only handicap that the warship suffered from was that dusk was gathering.

We made our escape as quickly as we could, but we owe that escape mainly to the gallantry of our escort ship, the " Jervis Bay."

She went right out to meet the German challenge, although everyone knew what her fate would be. Her crew were facing almost certain death, but despite that they maintained the highest tradition of British seamen.

The " Jervis Bay," offering a perfect target, immediately came under fire of the German raider. The encounter was of short duration. A few sharp salvos caught the " Jervis Bay " and she went on fire. All the time she kept replying with her guns, but these were no match for the powerfully armed battleship.

Soon all was over. The " Jervis Bay " was ablaze and her guns ceased firing.

We do not know what happened to her crew or what the ultimate fate of the vessel was, but when we last saw her blazing we could only form one opinion.

Here are some of the R.A.F. men seen at their base on their return from Munich, listening to a fellow pilot relating some of his experiences. They have all taken part in the memorable raid on the German city, of which an account is given in this page. *Photo, Associated Press*

The " Jervis Bay's " action, however, gave us a chance to scurry to safety, and we did not need a second telling. As we steamed away in the gathering darkness we could still see the flash of guns on the far horizon.

Obviously after disposing of the " Jervis Bay " the raider turned her attention to the convoy. It was not until we were near port that we sighted other ships of the convoy like us, lucky to have escaped."—*Associated Press, British United Press, the " Daily Telegraph."*

We Flew Low Over Munich's Streets

" The bomb-aimer's dream of the perfect night " was how R.A.F. men regarded their surprise visit to Munich on November 8, when they bombed the hall where Hitler had been celebrating the anniversary of his 1923 Putsch. A Flight Lieutenant from New Zealand gave the following broadcast account of his part in the raid.

DESCRIBING the raid on the Munich railway yards, the Flight Lieutenant said :

This was our first trip to Munich. Our target was the railway locomotive and marshalling yards, almost in the centre of the city and only a short distance away from the famous Brown House of the Nazi Party.

Just before we took off the Senior Intelligence Officer came rushing over and said he thought that we might be interested to know that Hitler and some of the Nazi " Old Guard " were to be in Munich that night to celebrate the anniversary of the Beer Hall Putsch of 1923.

Everybody was flat out to get there. They had included in my bomb load one of the heaviest calibre bombs that we have so far carried. I talked things over with the observer, and we decided before we left that, as the Station Commander had been kind enough to entrust us with the delivery of this heavy-calibre bomb, we should go in as low as possible to make sure of getting the target.

It was a beautiful starlight night and there was almost a half-moon. We were checking up our course by the stars as we went out. Round Munich itself there was not a cloud in the sky.

We passed an enemy aerodrome—all lit up for night flying—but on the way out we weren't wasting any bombs on that. We saw one of our fellows flying about five miles in front of us, getting a packet of stuff thrown up at him over Mannheim. He flew straight through it, but we turned away to the left and avoided the town.

These R.A.F. pilots were determined to disturb Hitler's celebrations in the Munich Beer House, which marked the anniversary of the Nazi Putsch of 1923. Railway stations, electric installations, and goods yards were bombed throughout the favourite city of Hitler's " Old Guard." The Nazis will long remember this surprise British raid on November 8, for the broadcast of the Fuehrer's speech was postponed, and Marshal Goering, no doubt, had to seek fresh excuses for the presence of the R.A.F. bombers in order to reassure the German people. *Photo, Keystone*

I WAS THERE!

After Mannheim, Munich wasn't very far away and everybody was sitting up and taking notice. We were about twenty minutes flying time away when we first saw the Flak and the searchlights coming up around the city. The navigator got a bit worried because we were ten minutes in front of our estimated time of arrival, and he thought for a minute that we might have got off our course. Then we picked up a landmark—a goodish-sized lake—to the south of Munich and set course from there. Some of the other fellows had gone on ahead to light up the target and we could see their incendiaries bursting.

Flares were dropping all round as we went in. The guns on the ground were shooting quite well. I saw three flares shot down almost as soon as they had been dropped. We flew over to have a preliminary look at things and found we were about a mile south of the marshalling yards.

We were low enough, and it was so light that we could see houses and streets quite clearly. It was the bomb-aimer's dream of the perfect night. Altogether we stooged round for about twenty minutes, checking up on our target.

A 'plane of the Fleet Air Arm is seen taking off from one of our aircraft carriers in the Mediterranean. Bombers and torpedo-carriers of the Fleet Air Arm carried out the victorious attack on the Italian battleships at Taranto, a vivid account of which is given in page 563.   *Photo, Central Press*

We saw somebody else drop his stick of bombs slap on the target. The explosions lit up the locomotive sheds. We came down lower and they were shooting at us hard.

In the light of one of our own flares I saw a stationary engine in the yard. I could make out the glow from its fires and I noticed, incidentally, that it had steam up. We had to turn round and come back over the yards, making our run from south-east to north-west. Then we went whistling down.

Tracer seemed to be coming up right under the wings, and the bomb-aimer said that he could see it coming up towards him as he lay in the nose of the aircraft looking down through his tunnel. All the way down in the dive I could see the big black locomotive sheds in front of me.

The front gunner was shooting out searchlights, which I thought was a pretty good effort, and the rear gunner was having a try at the same game, but it was more difficult for him. I'd told them they could let loose with their guns and they didn't want telling twice. The bomb-aimer got the target right in his sight. He said, " I can see it ; I can see it absolutely perfectly." Then he called out, " Bombs gone—I've got it." As a matter of fact I don't see how he could have missed at that height.

Both he and the rear gunner saw the bombs burst. The rear gunner said that the heavy one made a dickens of an explosion. In the excitement I'd more or less forgotten that we had got this big bomb on board, and the force of the explosion gave the aircraft a tremendous wallop. If we'd come

down any lower we should have been blown up. As it was, we all thought we'd been hit. The effect was just as if a heavy shell had burst right under the rear turret.

There was a stunned silence for a few seconds ; then another babble of conversation as everybody decided we were all right. We were still low down Searchlights kept popping up. The front gunner put out

two and the rear gunner put out four. It was a remarkable sight to see the coloured tracer going down the beams of the light.

After that it was a race back, because we'd been told that the weather would close down over our base and that after two o'clock we'd be very lucky if we got in there, so we beetled back pretty rapidly. Altogether it was a perfect trip.

I Saw Them Swoop On Taranto

For more than 24 hours before the Fleet Air Arm attacked Taranto on November 11, Admiral Cunningham's fleet steamed between the Greek islands and the heel of Italy in an attempt to draw the Italian ships out to give battle. The following story is by a Press correspondent on board a British cruiser.

I WAS on board a heavy cruiser which, with a great array of other vessels ranging from heavy battleships to heavy and light cruisers and destroyers, steamed into Italian waters, challenging the Italians to come out and fight.

The warships afforded a screen while the Fleet Air Arm aircraft, in relays of bombers and torpedo-carriers, won their brilliant victory at Taranto.

Despite Nazi boasts that the Canadian Pacific liner " Empress of Japan " was left in a sinking condition when she was attacked by enemy aircraft in the Atlantic, the famous ship was safely docked at a British port on November 11. Her decks were raked by machine-gun fire, and one bomb caused slight damage. Capt. John Thomas, above, of Vancouver, handled the vessel so skilfully that he avoided a direct hit and zigzagged his ship out of danger. The greatest praise has been given to the Chinese quartermaster, Hoakin (right), for his endurance. He was on the bridge with Capt. Thomas, and each time the Nazi pilot tried to bomb the ship the quartermaster crouched at the wheel and steered the " Empress of Japan " out of reach.   *Photos, Associated Press*

I saw our 'planes disappear over the Italian coastline They dropped about eleven torpedoes among the Italian battleships.

The role of our raiders was not only to attack the ships in Taranto, but to seek to drive some of them out to sea, where they would have to give battle to our warships.

We steamed as part of Admiral Cunningham's great fleet between the Greek islands and the heel of Italy for more than 24 hours, until it became evident that the Italians did not dare risk fighting.

When there was no sign of the Italians, it was decided that the only chance to come to grips with them would be to strike hard at Taranto, where it was known that the main body of the Italian fleet was resting.

All the ships were at action stations. Standing silently at their posts were gunners wearing duffel lamb's-wool coats.

In the distance the thunder of heavy guns could be heard as the force which had gone ahead into the Taranto Straits got down to the work of destroying a convoy to Albania. At the same time the air was full of radio S O S messages from sinking Italian ships.

Towards dawn the fleet began another sweep which lasted well into the afternoon, but not even an enemy 'plane was sighted, although there were more than two score ships in these hostile seas offering possible targets for skilful and courageous pilots.

Air spotters from the " Illustrious " went to Taranto in daylight and saw the smashed and derelict warships resting on the sea bottom, with waves lapping at the decks and funnels.—" *British United Press.*"

Raids or No Raids Britain's Girls Carry On

The smooth running and easy stopping and starting of trolley-buses are a great improvement over the old-pattern trams, but swinging over the arm is no easy job for the new girl conductors.

The petrol-pump girls will be harder worked now that free rides and extra petrol bring more cars on to the roads. Left: this woman police sergeant does not feel at all embarrassed when playing the part of nurse.

The milk girls soon become familiar with their rounds, and, as seen above, quickly made friends with the ponies who draw their carts, but they cannot in these times reward them with a piece of sugar. The two girls, left, are engaged upon some of the most valuable work done by the A.T.S.; close up to the big anti-aircraft guns, they manipulate delicate instruments to make shell-burst recordings which provide much valuable data for aerial defence.

Photos, Fox, Keystone, and Planet News

OUR SEARCHLIGHT ON THE WAR

U.S.A. Cheers Taranto

ON the day following the great achievement of the Fleet Air Arm at Taranto, American newspapers were loud in their admiration of Britain's victory in the Mediterranean. Here is what the "New York Times" said about it: "The crippling of Italy's battle fleet at Taranto is a blow that will be heard round the world. The spirit of Nelson and Drake has taken wings. It must be galling for Mussolini to see his proudest battleships disabled, his crack regiments in Greece decimated, his troops in Egypt and Sudan checked, and his supply ships and transports sunk on his very doorstep. As he looks back on his miscalculation of last June, he may already see the folly of plunging his long suffering people into war." The "Herald-Tribune" also paid an emphatic tribute: "The effects of Taranto may well be tremendous. This smashing demonstration of British energy, resource and hitting power will immensely raise British prestige in Turkey and the Balkans."

Death Penalty For Aiding British

ANYONE in Norway harbouring or otherwise assisting British subjects is liable to be shot. Terboven, the German Commissioner, issued this order after discovering that some fishermen had connived, by keeping silence, at the escape from Leka, near Mamsos, of two British airmen. The latter, after baling out, persuaded the men to keep silent about their landing, and, having obtained a boat, put out to sea. The secret leaked out, however, the Germans gave chase and claimed to have caught them. Although it is now incumbent upon our former Allies to apprise the German authorities of the presence of an Englishman, it is doubtful, knowing the spirit of the Norwegians, whether they will do so.

German People Tired of 'Victories'

SIXTEEN Swedish journalists recently returned from a conducted tour of Germany and parts of France and Belgium, and their impressions have been recorded in various organs of the Swedish press. The Stockholm correspondent of "The Times" quotes from one of the best accounts, that of H. Nils Horney in the "Social Democraten." He did not see very much bomb damage, but as he was taken by road and not by train, and as none of the party were allowed to visit Hamburg, Bremen, or any other bombed coastal area, this is not surprising. But people in Berlin showed strong irritation at the bombing and quite openly criticized the A.A. defences, also daring to wonder how it was that the mighty Luftwaffe permitted the R.A.F. to cross the North Sea and half Germany without effective interference. The man in the street was apathetic about the possibility of an early end to the war, and nervy at the prospect of facing another winter of darkness and comparative privation. But H. Horney saw no signs of any revolutionary movement. As one German told him: "We will fight on in the German cause, but we are tired of victories."

American Arms for Home Guard

THE first shipment of rifles, revolvers and ammunition collected from homes in U.S.A. has arrived in this country and been distributed among members of the Home Guard who are on duty at a certain aircraft factory.

Hundreds of thousands more are on the way, dispatched by "The American Committee for the Defence of British Homes." These arms are the personal and spontaneous gift of game hunters and others, and constitute a unique and sympathetic tribute from private citizens of one country to those of another. Some are old frontier buffalo guns; others were made in 1873 and were used in the civil war in Louisiana; still others are the most modern type of revolver. But all are in perfect working order, and each weapon is accompanied by twenty rounds of ammunition, this being one of the conditions of collection in America. Many had little messages attached to them, of which the following rhyme is typical:

"Good friend, for Heaven's sake forbear
To let a German come too near;
Blest be the man whose aim is straight,
But woe to him who draws too late."

Creation of Far East C.-in-C.

FOR the first time Great Britain is to have a Commander-in-Chief, Far East, and the choice has fallen upon Air Chief Marshal Sir Robert Brooke-Popham. He is the sole survivor of the 1912 air battalion of the Royal Engineers, from which was evolved the Royal Flying Corps, and later the Royal Air Force. In announcing the new appointment the Downing Street communiqué stated that the holder will have under his command the General Officers Commanding Malaya, Burma, Hong-kong and the Air Officer Commanding, Far East. "The new Commander-in-Chief will consult and co-operate with the Naval Commanders-in-Chief, China and East Indies, and with the Commander-in-Chief, India, and it will also be his duty to maintain close touch with the Governors of Burma and the Colonies concerned and communicate with his Majesty's Governments in the Commonwealth of Australia and in New Zealand on all matters of interest to them." Sir Robert's headquarters will be Singapore, and since this great naval base is of supreme importance it will be one of his duties to coordinate the operations of all the British and Dominions land, sea, and air forces available.

'Biggest Swindle of All Time'

THESE words have been used, by one of the instigators, to describe the arrangement by which German workers were induced to pay in instalments for the "people's car," to be delivered at some unspecified date. The scheme was started in 1938, to meet the demand by Brinkmann, under-secretary to Dr. Funk at the Ministry of Economics, for 30,000,000 marks a week from the working people. Dr. Ley, the Labour leader, brought into conference, suggested selling them motor-cars, and in May of that year an enormous factory for cheap cars was started at Fallersleben. On August 1 German workers were informed that the "volkswagen" would cost 990 marks, plus 200 marks for two years' insurance after leaving the factory, that the Fuehrer desired that every workman should possess his own car, and that everyone earning more than 200 marks a week would be expected to take part. This immediately furnished 6,000,000 subscribers who started paying 5 marks a week. They have been doing this ever since, although the manufacture of the car has been postponed until after the war, and the factory has switched over to munitions. This means that the Nazi war chest benefits to the tune of 1,500 million marks a year for 4½ years.

The Rape of Tangier

COLONEL YUSTE, officer commanding the Spanish troops in Tangier, proclaimed himself Governor of the port on November 4, having apparently deposed the French administrator, and dissolved the Committee of Control, the Assembly, and the Mixed Bureau of Information, international institutions by which this neutral zone had been administered since 1928. Great Britain, like the majority of the Governments concerned, protested against this high-handed unilateral

Taking the Axe from the Axis
Drawn by Zec, reproduced by permission of the "Daily Mirror"

act, but was merely met by the assurance that absolute neutrality in the zone would be maintained. France is the principal loser by the Spanish coup, for not only did she control the harbour and railways, but a good deal of French money had been invested in the international zone during the last ten years. Washington also is concerned about the Spanish assumption of control, and on November 15 it was announced that representations had been made to the Spanish Government on the ground that "certain treaty rights" were involved. As it is said that America has been approached for a loan of 100 million dollars to buy food and to help in the revival of Spanish trade, it will be interesting to see what sort of a case will be made for the virtual annexation of international territory.

Foxes and Dogs as Food

FROM November 8 a new regulation, issued by the German Reich Minister of the Interior, requires that bodies of dogs, foxes and badgers should be subjected to official inspection, and certified as free from trichina, before delivery for human consumption. It is pointed out in Berlin that these animals are eaten not because there is any scarcity of meat, but because Germans formerly liked dog very much, and that even in 1912 they ate 10 tons of it.

OUR DIARY OF THE WAR

TUESDAY, NOV. 12, 1940   *437th day*
On the Sea—Admiralty announced that 24 ships of convoy of 38 attacked by Nazi raider on Nov. 5 in mid-Atlantic had reached port. Although hit and burning, H.M.S. " Jervis Bay," escort vessel, continued fighting, until final explosion sank her.

British freighter " Balmore " reported sinking after enemy air attack.

In the Air—R.A.F. bombers attacked oil plants at Gelsenkirchen and Cologne, inland port of Duisburg-Ruhrort, and railway centres and factories in Ruhr and near Cologne. Submarine base at Lorient heavily bombed, as well as docks at Flushing and Dunkirk and many aerodromes.

War against Italy—R.A.F. again bombed Durazzo, destroying power house. Bahardar, Italian East Africa, raided by our bombers.

Home Front—Small number of single aircraft made daylight raids on Britain. Fairly strong night attack on London. Cinema hit ; working-class district bombed ; two American Ambulance stations struck. Raids also took place on Merseyside and Midlands.

One enemy aircraft shot down.

Greek War—Local skirmishing reported from Kalamas area. Greeks continued to bring in material and prisoners from Pindus area, including entire Albanian company.

General—Molotov arrived in Berlin for talks with Hitler and Ribbentrop.

Africa—Port Gentil, second port of Gabon, surrendered to Gen. de Gaulle.

WEDNESDAY, NOV. 13   *438th day*
On the Sea—Premier announced that on night of Nov. 12-13 Fleet Air Arm had attacked main Italian naval forces at Taranto, by which enemy lost three battleships, two cruisers and two Fleet auxiliaries.

During same night British light naval squadron heavily damaged convoy of supply ships bound for Albania ; one was sunk, two set on fire, fourth damaged. Enemy destroyer also damaged.

Six more ships of convoy attacked on Nov. 5 reached port. British freighter " Empire Wind " reported sunk.

In the Air—British bombers attacked Berlin, damaging railway station, goods yard and other objectives. Other places bombed were power station at Cologne, docks at Duisburg-Ruhrort, industrial targets at Dortmund and Düsseldorf, battery of coke ovens at Lintfort, oil plants at Gelsenkirchen, Hanover and Leuna, aerodromes at Haamstede, Kreuzbruck and Lübeck, seaplane base at Norderney, docks at Wilhelmshaven.

War against Italy—R.A.F. bombed docks and harbour at Taranto.

Home Front—Scattered daylight raids attempted, most in S.E. England. Damage and casualties in two Kent coast towns and one Midland. During night bombs fell in London area and in E. and S.E. England, but little damage and few casualties occurred.

Six enemy aircraft shot down.

British long-range guns fired salvos across Straits of Dover.

Greek War—Greek aircraft bombed Koritza aerodrome. After successful attack in Pindus region Greek troops captured new line of heights in Albanian territory. Enemy reported to have retreated on Epirus front.

General—Sir R. Brooke-Popham appointed to newly-created post of Commander-in-Chief Far East.

THURSDAY, NOV. 14   *439th day*
In the Air—Heavy R.A.F. attack on Berlin ; bombed targets included railway stations, goods yards and two power stations. Hamburg and Bremen also raided. Attacks made on 26 aerodromes and on ports from Stavanger to Lorient.

Home Front—Strong formations of enemy aircraft approached S.E. coast, but were

intercepted, 15 dive-bombers and 2 fighters being destroyed. Few bombs fell in Kent and in one South-coast town.

During night raids on London a hospital, nursing home and ambulance station were hit.

Coventry suffered heavy night attack. Cathedral wrecked ; library, baths, four churches, five cinemas, two hotels, two clubs, seven stores and twelve public houses were among other buildings demolished.

Bombs also fell in other Midland towns and in widespread districts of England and North Wales.

Enemy lost 19 aircraft ; Britain two, but both pilots safe.

British long-range guns shelled French coast.

Greek War—Series of Greek counter-attacks, resulting in a general advance, reported from all three sectors.

General—Molotov left Berlin for Moscow.

FRIDAY, NOV. 15   *440th day*
On the Sea—Thirty-two out of 38 convoy ships attacked on Nov. 5 now stated to have reached port.

Admiralty announced loss of H.M. minesweepers " Rinovia," " Sevra," " William Wesney," " Girl Helen," and " Stella Orion."

Free French patrol boat " Le Poulmic " reported sunk by enemy action.

In the Air—R.A.F. carried out large-scale operations against railway communications, shipyards, docks and public utility services in Hamburg. Other aircraft raided Kiel dockyard and ports of Ostend and Calais. Coastal Command aircraft bombed targets ranging from Norway to France. Military stores at Rennes successfully attacked, also several aerodromes.

War against Italy—R.A.F. again bombed Valona, destroying landing jetty.

Home Front—Enemy made daylight raids over Kent, Thames Estuary and outskirts of London, but were routed by our fighters.

London subjected to heaviest night attack of the war. Buildings damaged included three hotels, two clubs, several hospitals, churches and chapels, a rest centre for the homeless, shops, houses and flats.

Twenty Nazi aircraft shot down. Britain lost two fighters, but one pilot safe.

Artillery duel fought across Straits of Dover.

Greek War—Major battle developing along entire length of front. Greek air force and R.A.F. bombed aerodromes at Koritza and Argyrokastro.

SATURDAY, NOV. 16   *441st day*
In the Air—Another heavy and successful attack by R.A.F. on Hamburg. Antwerp docks bombed. Daylight raids carried out on Cologne and Bremen, and on Dortmund-Ems Canal.

Coastal Command aircraft attacked Dunkirk and many aerodromes in N. France.

War against Italy—Cairo reported that Metemma had been pounded by British artillery.

Home Front—Daylight raids on London negligible. Hebrides attacked for first time when bomber machine-gunned a lighthouse. During night heavy attack made on South Coast town ; five streets seriously damaged and many houses in a wider area. Casualties were heavy. Two S.E. towns also attacked, and one in East Anglia. London hospital damaged.

Five enemy aircraft shot down.

Greek War—Italians reported to be evacuating Koritza after setting fire to the town. Greek cavalry pursuing retreating Italian forces in Pindus sector. On Epirus front enemy continued withdrawal from banks of R. Kalamas.

General—V.C. awarded posthumously to Captain Fegen of H.M.S. " Jervis Bay."

New R.A.F. Army Cooperation Command created, first holder being Air Marshal Sir A. S. Barratt. Other new appointments made.

SUNDAY, NOV. 17   *442nd day*
On the Sea—Admiralty announced that British light forces had carried out naval bombardment of Mogadishu, main port of Italian Somaliland.

In the Air—R.A.F. made large-scale attack on German invasion ports.

Night attacks concentrated on oil refineries at Gelsenkirchen. Other aircraft bombed industrial targets in the Ruhr, rail and river communications, naval base at Lorient, and many aerodromes.

War against Italy—Cairo announced another raid by R.A.F. on Brindisi. In Albania military supplies at Elbasan were attacked. In Libya Benghazi and Tobruk were bombed, and farther east Gura, Zula, Adagalla and Massawa were raided.

Home Front—Formation of enemy aircraft crossed Kent coast making for London, and another flew into Thames Estuary. Both were intercepted and scattered. Bombs fell during day at three places on Sussex coast, and in East Anglia. During night raids bombs damaged houses near South coast. In London a hospital, child welfare clinic and many houses were hit.

Enemy lost 14 aircraft. Five British fighters lost, but pilots of four safe.

Violent long-range gun duel across Straits of Dover.

Greek War—Greek forces thrusting forward into Albania and now said to be dominating Koritza.

General—King Boris of Bulgaria visited Hitler, who also received Suñer, Spanish Foreign Minister.

MONDAY, NOV. 18   *443rd day*
On the Sea—Admiralty announced that British light forces bombarded Dante, Italian Somaliland.

H.M.S. " Lowestoft," escorting convoy in North Sea, shot down Heinkel seaplane which attacked it.

In the Air—R.A.F. bombers attacked synthetic oil works at Leuna. Coastal Command aircraft shot down Dornier flying-boat and Heinkel seaplane.

War against Italy—Nairobi reported that S. African armoured cars inflicted heavy casualties on Italian forces near Somaliland frontier.

Home Front—During minor day attacks bombs fell on East coast and coasts of Sussex and Kent, and at few points in London area. West Country town subjected to series of raids. Night raiders reported near a Welsh town ; in Liverpool region ; over N.E. town ; and in Midlands.

Greek War—Fresh Italian troops still holding Koritza, and strong air reinforcements machine-gunned Greek troops. Violent fighting around the town. Italians driven back across River Kalamas.

TARANTO : THE EVIDENCE OF THE CAMERA

Only a few hours after the Fleet Air Arm's brilliantly successful attack on Taranto, R.A.F. pilots on November 12 and 14 carried out daring flights over the scene, in order to secure photographic evidence of the damage done to Mussolini's warships. Despite the intense anti-aircraft barrage, they flew over the port at between 6,000 and 8,000 feet, and so as to secure the most satisfactory results they made many runs over their objective. Four of their photographs are reproduced in this and the two following pages. The one above shows a 23,622-ton battleship of the Cavour class beached on the east shore of the outer harbour. Her original position is marked 2A on the map in page 590, and that in which she now lies, 2B.

Photo, British Official : Crown Copyright

After the Fleet Air Arm Had Done Its Work

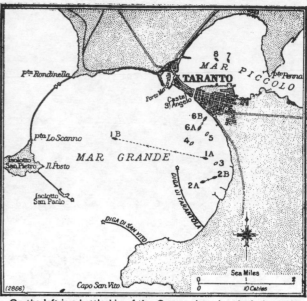

On the left is a battleship of the Cavour class, beached about 300 yards from the shore. A number of small craft cluster about her bow, which points towards the harbour. To protect her from torpedo attack, nets have been suspended round the ship. The diagram of Taranto, above, shows the position of the Italian battleships when the attack was made, marked A, while B marks the positions to which damaged ships were towed. 3, 4 and 5 show undamaged battleships.

Two 10,000-ton cruisers of the Trento class, marked 7 and 8 on the map, lying in the inner harbour, show evidence of damage to their hulls and oil is oozing from them. Nearer in shore is another 10,000-ton cruiser, and alongside the quays are light cruisers of the Condottieri type and some destroyers.

Photos, British Official : Crown Copyright

The R.A.F. Recorded It for the World to See

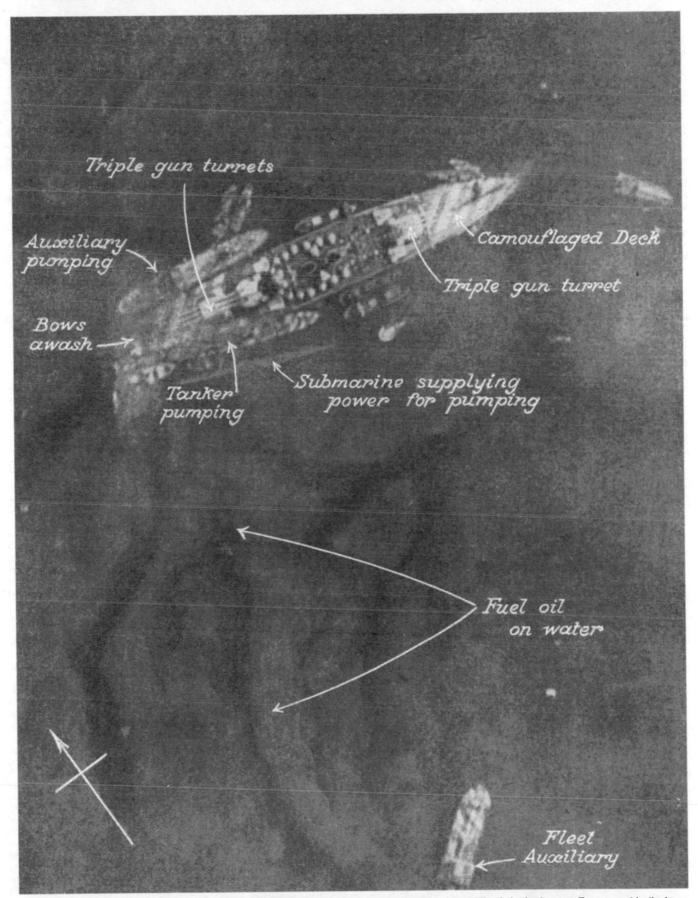

Triple gun turrets

Auxiliary pumping

Bows awash

Tanker pumping

Submarine supplying power for pumping

Camouflaged Deck

Triple gun turret

Fuel oil on water

Fleet Auxiliary

This photograph shows the 35,000-ton battleship of the Littorio class (see page 565) lying in the middle of the harbour at Taranto and badly down by the bows. The tankers alongside are probably pumping out oil fuel to lighten the ship, for dark streams of oil can be seen to the left of the ship. In securing these remarkable photographs, only ordinary Service type cameras were used.

Koritza Falls: Long Live Greece!

Having been practically surrounded for several days, Koritza fell to the Greek arms on November 22. The story of its capture is told below, together with some fresh details of the campaign and the striking help afforded to the Greeks by the 'planes of our R.A.F.

BEFORE daybreak on November 22 the first Greek detachments entered Koritza, and at nine o'clock the main body made its triumphal entry into the place, with bands playing and flags flying. The population received them with tears of joy, while from many a window fluttered a Greek flag, hidden for years in anticipation of just this day of deliverance. Shortly afterwards the capture of the town was announced in Athens by General Metaxas, and at once there broke out demonstrations of patriotic enthusiasm. The great square in front of the King's palace was a sea of waving flags, in which the blue and white of Greece was mixed with the red, white and blue of the Union Jack ; military bands marched through the streets, and the British soldiers in the capital were carried shoulder-high.

In Rome the news was announced only a few days after Mussolini's threat that " we will break Greece's back." The Italian communiqué quoted by Rome radio said that : " After 11 days of fighting two divisions, deployed on the defensive along the Greco-Albanian frontier and Koritza, have been withdrawn west of the city. Through this period fierce fighting has taken place. Our losses are considerable. Equally serious, perhaps more so, are the enemy's. Italian reinforcements are concentrating on the new line."

For several days Koritza had been threatened, and at the last there was fierce hand-to-hand fighting, in which the Italians were driven out of their shallow trenches by Greeks armed with bayonets and trench knives. Once they had abandoned the town the Italians fled along the roads to the west. Soon the retreat became a rout, and as they fled the Italians left behind them hundreds of lorries, numbers of heavy guns, complete with tractors and ammunition, many anti-tank and anti-aircraft guns, complete with shells, vast stores of food, and many big dumps of petrol.

As the invaders quitted Greek soil they committed a number of barbarities which were indignantly reported by the Greek authorities. " The Italians are looting and plundering the villages they are leaving," said a communiqué issued in Athens on November 23. " The village of Sayiades and other freed villages present horrible scenes where the Italians are leaving traces of savagery and barbarity. In the village of Bassibikon women and girls have been raped and killed, while many women and children have been carried off as hostages. Their fate is still unknown." As the retreat continued more burning villages and destroyed homesteads marked the Italians' path.

Hard on their heels followed the Greeks, although at times the pace was too hot for them to keep in touch. West of Koritza the invaders were pursued by a number of their own tanks, manned by Greeks who had

Air Commodore J. H. D'Albiac, who was stated on Nov. 18 to be in command of the British Forces in Greece—R.A.F. squadrons and auxiliary units. He was born in 1894 and commissioned in the R.A.F. in 1918.
Photo, Vandyk

taken them in a skirmish. So swift was the pursuit that the Greek H.Q. lost contact with their advanced units and supplies had to be dropped from 'planes of the R.A.F. to the most advanced. " It's like manna coming down from Heaven," said one Greek warrior as he watched the bundles of food and ammunition being dropped from the skies.

Along the whole front of a hundred miles the Greeks advanced, pushing the Italians steadily before them, until the national soil was completely cleared of their presence. At not one point but several the Greek columns invaded Albania, where they were hailed as deliverers by the native population. On the day following the fall of Koritza, it was reported in Athens that Argyrokastro, the Italian base in southern Albania, had also been captured, together with Konispol, not far from the coast, opposite Corfu ; in the Koritza sector the Greek advanced units were reported to be at Pogradets, 25 miles to the north-west of Koritza, on the shores of Lake Ochrida. They were said to be heading for Elbasan, which lies only some 20 miles south of Tirana, the Albanian capital. If this place, too, were carried, then the Italian situation in the heart of Albania would indeed become desperate, and they might be compelled to withdraw to the coast.

But even on the coast their position was far from happy, for there they were bombed time and again by the British R.A.F. Within 36 hours, indeed, of the beginning of the war in Greece, the R.A.F. was in action against targets in Albania ; and without belittling in the least the magnificent achievements of the Greek army and tiny air force, it may be asserted that the victory could hardly have been won without the powerful support of the British war 'planes. At Valona the landing jetty was completely destroyed and Durazzo was also heavily damaged, while British bombers created havoc in Brindisi and Bari, the ports of embarkation of Italian reinforcements and supplies. These attacks, delivered

March on Albania—1940.   *Cartoon by Illingworth, reproduced by courtesy of the " Daily Mail"*

Soon the Italian Defeat Became a Rout

A general view of Koritza, the fall of which on November 22 signalized the first great victory of the Greeks over the Italians. Mountains which overlook the town gave the Greeks a dominating position above it.
Photo, Planet News

in the opening hours of the war, gave the Greeks time to mobilize, with the result that, when the Italians pressed across the frontier they found the Greeks in large numbers standing across their path. Held up on the Kalamas River the Italians flung their dive bombers at the Greeks, and the result might have been serious had not they been able to call upon the R.A.F. The British fighters soon turned the tide of battle, and for some days there was hardly an Italian 'plane to be seen. Meanwhile, far behind the front, our bombers were maintaining their offensive—on Valona and Durazzo, on Tirana and the Italian base ports.

This British aid was generously acknowledged by the Greeks. In a broadcast message

This photograph was the first received in London of Italian soldiers captured by the Greeks during their advance into Albania. Owing to their headlong retreat they were very hungry. The photograph was radioed from Athens to New York and thence to London.
Photo, Associated Press

to the Greek people and army, after the fall of Koritza, General Metaxas, after declaring the nation's "profound gratitude to the valiant Greek Army, to the heroic Air Force, and to our indomitable Navy, for the glorious pages which they have added to our history of 3,000 years," went on to express "the grateful acknowledgement of the Hellenic nation to our valiant British allies, for the whole-hearted aid they have rendered to our struggle, and for all the exploits scored by their inconquerable Navy and brilliant Air Force."

And Britain, too, was proud of her ally. "We are all inspired by this feat of Greek valour against an enemy so superior in numbers and equipment," telegraphed Mr. Churchill to General Metaxas. This recalls the classic age. Ζήτω ἡ Ελλάς (Zeeto hee Hellas. Long Live Greece!)

The shaded portion of this map to the right of the dotted frontier line shows the area of Greece occupied in whole or in part by the Italians in their first attack. That to the left of the frontier line shows the Greek advance into Albania up to November 24.

The first Englishman to give his life in support of Greece's fight for freedom was Sergeant John Merifield, of West Hartlepool, aged 20, who was an observer-gunner in a 'plane over Albania. A symbolic bust of him is being made by the Greek sculptor, M. Phalerias, from the same stone with which the Parthenon is built.
Photo, "Daily Mirror"

Egypt Sticks to Her Treaty with Britain

On his assumption of office Egypt's new Premier made on Nov. 21 a fresh declaration
of that country's determination to abide in the most complete manner by the terms
of the Anglo-Egyptian alliance. Below we tell of that alliance, and of the war that,
in spite of Egypt's non-belligerency, is being waged in her Western Desert.

"EGYPT has a treaty with Britain, and she will stick to it. Tell that to the whole world, and leave nobody any illusions about it." It was Hussein Sirry Pasha speaking, Egypt's new Prime Minister, called to the helm by King Farouk following the sudden death of Hassan Pasha Sabry, who collapsed in the Chamber of Deputies at Cairo on November 14. The Premier followed this forthright declaration of policy by a reference to Britain's triumph at Taranto and powerful aid to Greece. "Nothing succeeds like success," he said, "and deeds speak more strongly than words, especially in the East."

Britain's treaty with Egypt was concluded in 1936, but since 1883, when Britain established a virtual protectorate over the country, the relations between Britain and Egypt have been peculiarly close. From 1883 to 1907 the real ruler of Egypt was Lord Cromer, though his nominal position was merely that of British Agent and Consul-General. Cromer's brilliant administration produced order out of chaos, and in particular he re-established the finances, developed agriculture, improved irrigation, and raised the standard of living of the peasants, who now, as always, make up the majority of the population. Up to 1914 Egypt was still, at least in name, a part of the Turkish dominions, but on Turkey's entry into the war a British protectorate was declared in December of that year. The Khedive was deposed and succeeded by a nominee of the British as Sultan. Following the war a strong Nationalist movement developed, and in 1922 Sultan Fuad was acknowledged as King. Then on August 26, 1936, Egypt and Britain signed a treaty of mutual alliance, and Egyptian independence was fully recognized.

By the terms of this treaty Britain withdrew the British troops from Cairo and Egypt as a whole, with the exception of the Suez Canal zone. She was also permitted to use Alexandria and Port Said as naval bases for the time being, while the Egyptian Government undertook to construct a number of roads, bridges and railways, so as to afford easy communication between the Canal zone, Cairo, Alexandria, and Mersa Matruh, on the edge of the Western Desert. The Sudan was recognized as an Anglo-Egyptian condominium (joint control of one state by two other states). Britain further undertook the defence of Egypt, while Egypt, for her part, gave an undertaking to give Britain all the help in her power in the case of war.

That help, particularly in the way of providing bases for Britain's military, naval and air effort against Italy, has been readily afforded, and on the outbreak of war Egypt at once severed diplomatic relations with Germany, and, in due course, with Italy. As yet, however, Egypt is not at war with the Axis Powers, although since September 13 an Italian army of invasion has been operating on Egyptian soil in the extreme west.

Between the Italians and their objectives—Alexandria, Cairo, the Delta, and the Suez Canal—is a large and ever-growing Imperial army, under the command of Lieut.-Gen. Henry M. Wilson. "Some months ago," Mr. Churchill told the House of Commons on November 21, "the defence of Egypt and the Canal against greatly superior numbers of the enemy looked a rather difficult and rather doubtful affair, but at the present time it gives us a measure of confidence that we should be able to give a good account of ourselves

when the invading forces fall upon us—when they do fall upon us."

Marshal Graziani, however, does not seem to be in any hurry to cross swords with the army which stands across his path. In ten weeks the Italian line was only slightly advanced from the point reached in September, and that advance was the result not of large-scale operations but of what may be described as infiltration tactics in which little units of two or three guns and a tank, supported by a few lorry loads of infantry, have been principally engaged. Even so, the farthest Italian outpost is still only Maktila, 15 miles along the coast to the east of Sidi Barrani. Some 12 miles to the south there is another group of camps, making, with Sidi Barrani and Maktila, a fortified triangle. Then separated by a gap of 18 or 20 miles is another Italian outpost grouped around Bir Sofafi.

Meanwhile, as Graziani has not yet ventured his main attack, the British in Egypt are doing all they can to defeat the Italians in Greece. "We are sending every 'plane, gun and bullet we can spare," declared British G.H.Q. at Cairo on November 21; it is fully realized that time is short, and it may not be long before the Axis tide sets in against the Greeks, although they have staggered military opinion already with their successes.

But, all the same, a close watch is being kept on Graziani and his army in the Western Desert, for it is on Egyptian soil that Greece's fate, and probably the British Empire's, too, will ultimately be decided.

Hussein Sirry Pasha, Egypt's new Prime Minister, left, succeeded Hassan Sabry, whose death occurred on November 14. In referring to relations between his country and Great Britain, the new Prime Minister said, "Our cooperation is most close and cordial."
Photo, Universal Picture Press

Egypt has an efficient if not very large modern army. Here we see an armoured car of a motorized unit being ferried across a river during exercises. Before the war the strength of the army was some 25,000 men.
Photo, Keystone

Free France Has Its Standard in Egypt

The first French unit to fight for a Free France in the Middle East has been formed from a contingent of the French Colonial Infantry who, at the time of the collapse of their country, decided to join General de Gaulle's forces. This nucleus has been greatly increased by members of other units. The flag of Free France, the Tricolour, is seen beside the Union Jack at a ceremony at Ismailia when the French flag was presented to standard-bearers of the Free French Orient Legion.

Photo, Keystone

Enemies but Companions in Misfortune

Above, Italian soldiers captured by the British in the Middle East in October 1940 are being marched through the streets of Cairo. Circle, one of the Italian airmen brought down in England on November 11, 1940. The British prisoners below are awaiting an escort after being captured in Flanders last summer; the photograph has only just reached England from Germany by way of a neutral country.   *Photos, Keystone, Topical and E.N.A.*

'San Demetrio' was Worthy of the 'Jervis Bay'

One of the 33 ships in the convoy that was attacked in mid-Atlantic on November 5 by a German surface raider and which owed their preservation to the sacrifice of their escort, H.M.S. "Jervis Bay" (see page 567), was the tanker, "San Demetrio." Below we give the story of her escape—in itself a thrilling deed of daring on the high seas.

SOON after they sighted a German raider, about 4.30 on the afternoon of November 5, the "San Demetrio" and the 37 other ships forming the convoy received the signal to scatter from their escort. When the men of the "San Demetrio" saw the "Jervis Bay" for the last time she was "standing up to the enemy like a hen standing up to a great tom-cat, while her brood of chickens made off." They saw the gallant ship turn first to port and then to starboard, so as to bring her broadsides to bear on her gigantic adversary. They saw her steering straight for the raider and holding her fire, while the merchantmen in her charge slipped away under cover of smoke in the gathering dusk.

The "San Demetrio" sheered off, but blazed away with her guns at the German warship until shells started to fall around her and she was badly hit. She caught fire, and the order was given to abandon ship. Having taken to the boats, her crew dropped astern, and ten minutes later they saw her start to blaze. As the shells whined over the boats the men pulled away.

That night they saw four burning ships—one of them the "Jervis Bay"—and a great flare in the sky which they took to be a magazine exploding. Every now and again star shells burst as the raider continued its hunt for other of the convoy's ships.

In one of the boats were 16 officers and men, among them an American seaman and a seaman from the Shetland Islands. The weather had been fine, but by midnight a full gale was blowing. They lay to a sea anchor, keeping the boat's head up to it with the oars. The Shetland Islander sat at the tiller; the Second Officer said "he knew all about small boats." By dawn great seas were running. They sighted a "Swede," which may have been the ship that so gallantly turned back and picked up survivors of the "Jervis Bay" (see page 583), but they could not reach her, nor did she see the boat—at one moment buried in the trough of the sea, and at the next running on its crest.

At midday they sighted a tanker to leeward, and at 5 p.m. they got alongside. It was their own ship—the "San Demetrio"! She was still burning and gasolene lay on the water all round her, so they decided not to board that night, and pulled ahead, hoping to drift with her through the night.

What was their disgust when, at daybreak, she was not in sight! But the weather had moderated, and it was now possible to get a sail up. Then, by one of those extraordinary chances of the sea, they fell in with the "San Demetrio" again. Though she was still blazing, the men decided that it was better to board her than to freeze to death in the lifeboats, so they got aboard.

She was white-hot amidships, her bridge and accommodation were gutted. There was a fierce fire still burning aft, and she was down by the bows. Down below the engineers set about getting steam on the pumps in an engine-room flooded to the floor plates, while on deck the remaining hands fought the fire with buckets and fire extinguishers, chipping off the burning cork insulation. There was gasolene washing over the decks, and every time she pitched more gasolene gushed up through the shell splinter holes.

By 5.30 p.m. the Chief Engineer had 80 lb. steam pressure and the hoses could be used instead of buckets. By daybreak next day all the fires were out and most of the rents in the decks and upper works were plugged.

Practically all the food had been destroyed, but they found a joint of beef and four cases of eggs already cooked by the flames—both quite good when the outside was chipped off. The Chief Engineer cooked potatoes and onions by steam, and there was plenty of tinned butter.

The main difficulty, when once the engines had been got going and she had been brought to an even keel, was the compass, which had been shot from the binnacle and, though replaced, behaved in a peculiar manner. The bridge, indeed, was gone; there were no charts but only a 6d. atlas, and only four spokes were left on the steering-wheel. That night, when steering north by compass, they found the Pole Star dead astern, so after that they gave the compass up and sailed by a mixture of stars and weather. The American sailor cheered everyone up by saying, "we are bound to hit something sometime between Narvik and Gibraltar."

Eight days after the raider's attack the "San Demetrio" made a landfall. She had no signalling flags; they had all been burnt. The only flag she had left was her Red Ensign, and that had been flying throughout her voyage—a symbol of the Merchant Navy's courage and determination.

Then to the intense satisfaction of her Chief Engineer she was able to discharge her cargo through her own pipes with her own pumps, and, furthermore, it was 11,000 tons out of the 11,200 with which she sailed.

The "San Demetrio," 8,073 tons, is a sister ship of the "San Alberto," torpedoed in December, 1939 (see Vol. I, page 603). The helmsman of the "San Demetrio" (top left), who, despite the wheel being broken, steered the ship to safety. Second Officer Hawkins (below left) brought the tanker—"by guess and by God," as he phrased it—through her hazardous course to a British West Coast port. The ship's bridge is seen below. *Photos, J. Hall and "Daily Express"*

'Wrens' on Duty with the Fleet Air Arm

Standing on the wing of a 'plane, a Wren messenger of the Women's Royal Naval Service (right) is seen carefully delivering a last order to the pilot just as he is about to take off.

These two Wrens (below) are watching with evident interest, from the signalling tower at a western Fleet Air Arm Depot a naval patrol making its way out to sea.

There are few jobs that these women are not capable of tackling. A Wren is seen, above, cleaning the barrel of a machine-gun. Below, a group is being instructed by an Air Arm man in the correct method of packing a parachute.

Photos, Central Press, Keystone

THE Women's Royal Naval Service, known popularly as the Wrens, is one of the branches of the women's war activity that was originally organized during the last war, in 1917. Its purpose was, and is, to release from routine and clerical duties men who could be better employed in duties for which their naval training and technical knowledge made them most suitable. The Wrens do general work as messengers, cooks, waitresses and cleaners, while some of them are in charge of stores, equipment and accounts. In this war many Wrens have also been employed with the Fleet Air Arm, and some have been trained to pack parachutes. They have proved themselves apt in learning the exact way in which the work should be done, and in performing it with perfect accuracy.

American 'Planes for Britain's Air Force

Here we have an account by Mr. Grenville Manton of some of the latest types of bombers and fighters which are being produced in the U.S.A. to the order of the British Government, and soon to be added to the ever-mounting strength of the R.A.F.

Here is an inspector checking over the ammunition belt of one of the machine-guns in the wing of a Curtiss P.-40 multi-gun fighter.

AFTER months of unremitting combat the R.A.F. is stronger, more formidable, and better equipped than ever before. While the Luftwaffe has been losing thousands of machines and men, Britain has been making good her own losses, and today is building up a gigantic air power which, as time passes, will far exceed anything the enemy possesses or has possessed.

In the immense task of amassing a great fleet of fighters and bombers she is securing vital aid from the United States. American aircraft are being shipped to England in ever-growing numbers. Piloted by British airmen, some have been flown across the Atlantic on non-stop delivery flights. In the coming months the flow will widen and expand, as President Roosevelt's fifty-fifty plan by which we are to receive half the output of American aircraft factories is geared up.

For years the aircraft industry in the United States has shown itself to be one of the most progressive in the world. Research, experiment and development in that great country have given the world of aviation new mechanical features and devices. The metal variable-pitch propeller was first evolved and brought to practical form in the U.S.A. So was the retractable undercarriage. The automatic pilot is an American invention, and much of the progress made in radio equipment and blind-flying instruments in recent years is due to the ingenuity and patience of engineers, pilots and scientists associated with aviation on the other side of the Atlantic.

For a long time American commercial aircraft—giant flying boats and big high-speed air-liners—have been in the front rank. All these things show clearly that in the United States aeroplane manufacturers thoroughly understand their work. Their machines have been employed all over the world, and since the beginning of the war American aircraft have been used against the enemy.

One American type with which people in England have been long familiar is the Lockheed Hudson. This fine reconnaissance-bomber machine has been used in large numbers by the Coastal Command, mainly on work over the North Sea, and it has been in many combats with the Luftwaffe. It is powered with two Wright Cyclone radial engines which give together a total of 1,700 h.p. at 6,000 feet. The Hudson was not designed in the first place as a military aircraft.

The Lockheed Company, famous as the makers of some of America's finest aircraft, is working at top speed to produce a great number of bombers for the R.A.F. Top is a scene in one of the Lockheed assembly-shops with fuselages undergoing completion. Scenes such as the one shown in the lower photo, taken at Mitchel Field, New York, are an everyday occurrence, when batches of new aeroplanes destined for the R.A.F. stand ready for delivery.

Photos, Fox, Wide World and Planet News

Many Models of Magnificent Performance

This American Grumman single-seater is now being used by the R.A.F., as well as the U.S. Navy. It is a mid-wing monoplane powered with a 1,050 h.p. Pratt and Whitney Twin Wasp radial engine, and, in addition to machine-guns mounted in the wings, it has others fitted on top of the fuselage and firing through the arc of the airscrew.

One of the most interesting fighters produced in the United States is the Bell Airacobra shown above. Its most striking feature is the position of the engine behind the pilot. Numbers of these interceptors are to be used by R.A.F. fighter squadrons.

A magnificent twin-motored bomber is the Douglas Boston (known as the DB-7 in the United States), and it is already in the service of the R.A.F. With a crew of three it can touch 330 m.p.h., and has a long range. Germany will feel the power of these machines in the very near future.

Typically American is the design of this pugnacious-looking fighter, the Brewster Buffalo. It is being inspected by H.R.H. the Duke of Kent in this photograph. Its performance is a close secret.

Photos, Wide World ; British Official: Crown Copyright

It is a development of the Lockheed 14 "Super Electra" air liner, and the fact that it performs so well under the arduous conditions of air warfare shows how well its conversion from commercial to military requirements has been made. For more than a year this ex-transport 'plane has shown its mettle, flying in all weathers, bombing Nazi bases, spotting U-boats, and often fighting its way homewards against tremendous odds.

But soon the Hudson, after valiant service, is to be replaced by other American machines of higher speed and better all-round performance. One of these is the Douglas DB-7, known in the R.A.F. as the Boston. This is a monoplane with a span of 61 feet and two Pratt and Whitney Twin Wasp engines which develop 1,200 h.p. each. An unusual feature of this aircraft, which is equipped for dive-bombing as well as precision bombing, is the tricycle undercarriage. It has exceptionally clean lines and is capable of a maximum speed of 320 m.p.h., a cruising speed of 280 m.p.h., and a range of about 1,200 miles. Armament consists of four fixed machine-guns mounted in the nose of the fuselage, and there is another gun on a movable mounting in a position behind the wing.

The U.S. Army Air Corps has been equipped for some years with ultra-large bombers to meet the specific requirements of America, and this has resulted in various types of four-engined long-range machines reaching a high state of development. The biggest of these is the Consolidated B-24. It has four 1,200 h.p. Pratt and Whitney Twin Wasp engines, and is credited with a top speed of well over 300 m.p.h. A hundred and twenty B-24s have been ordered by the British Government for the R.A.F. The Boeing "Flying Fortress" is another four-engined bomber which will probably be in the service of the R.A.F. in the near future.

There has been some controversy concerning the wisdom of using such large aircraft in this war, the argument on the one hand being that machines of this size would be too vulnerable when opposed by fighters or anti-aircraft fire. But there is another view, and that is that the big bomber with its huge load-carrying capacity, its great range and ability to fly in the sub-stratosphere where it would be difficult to locate and attack, would be a very powerful and efficient military machine. We shall have to wait until they have been in action before this or the other theory is proved.

There is another American bomber which must be mentioned : the Martin 167-A3. It was originally ordered by the French, and some of them saw service in France in the early days of the conflict. Powered with two Twin Wasp engines, it can carry 1,250 lb. of bombs, and has a maximum range of 2,470 miles. Its top speed is 316 m.p.h. and it cruises at 248 m.p.h. The Martin was not designed solely as a bomber, but is intended as a multi-seat fighter, as a reconnaissance machine, and also for low-flying attacks on ground forces. It is fairly well armed, and in spite of its size—its span is 61 feet—it has good powers of manoeuvre. But its most suitable role is that of bomber.

Several months ago much publicity was given to the fact that 90 dive-bombers in the service of the U.S. Navy were being transferred to Britain. These machines are

They Will Help to Put the R.A.F. on Top

Curtiss 77 SBC-4 Helldivers. They are powered with Wright Cyclone 1,200 h.p. engines and are single-bay wire-braced biplanes. They are regarded in America as obsolete, but they have no mean performance and will be useful in reinforcing still further the R.A.F.

In the fighter class great efforts are being made by U.S. manufacturers to evolve machines of the very highest performance. Hitherto they have favoured the comparatively small monoplane powered with a big air-cooled radial engine, and some very fine machines of this style have been produced. The Curtiss Hawk 75-A, which was supplied to l'Armée de l'Air and which has also been used in England to some extent, is a good example. It has a 900 h.p. Wasp engine, is very manoeuvrable, and has a speed in the region of 320 m.p.h. Another radial-engined fighter which is being supplied to our air arm is the Brewster Buffalo (800 h.p. Wright Cyclone). In appearance the Buffalo is very unusual, with its heavily-cowled engine and tubby, round fuselage.

One other American fighter, which is being supplied to the Fleet Air Arm for service with aircraft carriers, is the Grumman G-36 four-gun machine. It has a 1,050 h.p. motor, which gives it a speed of 330 m.p.h.

Well in advance of these radial-engined fighters in all-round performance is the Curtiss P-40, a 37-foot-span low-wing monoplane which in general appearance closely resembles the redoubtable Hawker Hurricane. It is powered with an Allison 1,250 h.p. liquid-cooled engine, the only aero motor of this type at present manufactured in the U.S.A. Performance figures of this fine aeroplane, which is being turned out at the rate of three every day for the R.A.F., cannot yet be divulged. But it can be taken for granted that in maximum speed and rate of climb it is as good as any fighter which has so far been on active service.

Two more types of fighters, which are produced by leading aircraft constructors in the U.S.A., will form the equipment of some of our squadrons before long. Each is of revolutionary design. One is the Bell Airacobra, an Allison-engined, 34-feet cantilever monoplane in which the outstanding feature is the location of the power unit in the fuselage behind the pilot. A shaft of special design drives the tractor airscrew. A tricycle undercarriage which is retractable is another unusual feature of this aircraft, for which a top speed of over 400 m.p.h. is claimed. Details as to its armament have not been released, but it is reputed to have four ·303 machine-guns and also a 37 mm. cannon. The other new fighter which will ultimately be delivered to England in large numbers is the Lockheed P-38. It has two Allison engines, a tricycle undercarriage, and is heavily armed. It can attain a speed of 404 m.p.h., and is one of the most advanced machines so far produced.

As in England, the call for more and more aircraft is being answered in America by a stupendous effort, and the joint demands of both countries are resulting in a close co-operation between the American and British aeroplane industries. Each will help the other in the drive forward in output, technical development and other factors which are vital in Democracy's fight for freedom.

Looking very like our wonderful Hawker Hurricanes, these Curtiss P-40 fighters are amongst the latest machines which are now being built in the U.S.A. in quantities. With British aeroplanes these fine American fighters will soon play their part in grappling with the Luftwaffe.

Photo, Fox

No Glittering Lamps of Piccadilly but the

While Londoners sleep or try to sleep in the Tubes or Andersons or under the dining-room table, the gunners manning the anti-aircraft defences are ever on the alert, and from time to time the silence of the night is blasted by the deep roar, the rumble, the crash of the guns. Few there are who are permitted to see an anti-aircraft battery in action, but here, in this photograph, we are permitted to view the dramatic scene. Raiders have

e of Guns Are the Lights o' London Now

been reported overhead, and the inky blackness is shattered by the bursts of flame belched forth as the shells go shrieking overhead. Not the least strange feature of the scene is the Y.M.C.A. mobile canteen, through whose open window a girl worker serves out hot drinks. Ordinarily, the canteen would be blacked-out the brilliant lighting is due to the photographer's flashlight, which was set off the moment the guns flashed.

Chiefs of the Air Commands in Britain

Air Marshal Sir Arthur Barratt

Air Marshal Sir Arthur Barratt takes up a new post in charge of the Army Cooperation Command. His experience of Army co-operation dates from 1914, when he went to France with No. 3 Squadron, and throughout the war was engaged in flying duties closely connected with the Army. At the outbreak of the present war he was C.-in-C. of the British Air Forces in France.

Photo, Lafayette

Air Marshal Sir Richard Peirse

The new Chief of the Bomber Command, Air Marshal Sir Richard Peirse (above), had been Deputy Chief of the Air Staff, Air Ministry, since 1937. He has attained to his present post at the early age of forty-eight. He served throughout the last war, when he won the D.S.O., and he was made a K.C.B. in the Birthday Honours list of 1940. He has also the Air Force Cross. From 1930 to 1933 he was Deputy Director of Operations and Intelligence at the Air Ministry, and from 1933 to 1936 he was Air Officer Commanding the Forces in Palestine and Transjordan.

Photo, P.N.A.

Air Marshal Sir Charles Portal

Sir Charles Portal (above) succeeds Sir Cyril Newall as Chief of the Air Staff. He joined the Army as a dispatch rider and at the age of 25 was promoted Colonel. He was awarded the D.S.O. and bar and the M.C. He won distinction as a fearless airman, and after the war joined the R.A.F. with a permanent commission. He commanded the British Forces at Aden from 1934 to 1935, and in 1936 was appointed instructor at the Imperial Defence College. He was Director of Air Organization, Air Ministry, in 1937-8. In March 1940 he was appointed C.-in-C. of the Bomber Command.

Photo, Planet News

Air Marshal Sir Frederick Bowhill

Sir Frederick Bowhill (left centre), who retains his post as C.-in-C. the Coastal Command, began his career in the Merchant Service, but in 1913 entered the Navy. In the last war he served with the R.F.C. (Naval Wing), the R.N.A.S., and the R.A.F., being awarded the C.M.G. and D.S.O. He has held several important staff appointments, the last before his present post being Air Member for Personnel on the Air Council.

Photo, Topical

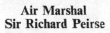

Air Marshal W. Sholto Douglas

At the outbreak of the last war Air Vice-Marshal Douglas, now Air Officer C.-in-C. Fighter Command and temporary Air Marshal, was a 2nd Lieut. in the R.F.A., but in January 1915 he joined the R.F.C. in France and between 1917 and 1918 commanded Nos. 43 and 84 Fighter Squadrons, being awarded the M.C. and D.F.C.

Photo, British Official : Crown Copyright

Air Vice-Marshal E. L. Gossage

Air Vice-Marshal E.L. Gossage (right centre), who succeeds Air Vice-Marshal Boyd in the Balloon Command, was commissioned in the R.F.A. in 1912 and was seconded for service with the R.F.C. in 1915, and after the war was granted a permanent commission in the R.A.F. He was Air Attaché at the British Embassy, Berlin, 1930-31 and Senior Air Staff Officer Air Defence of Great Britain 1931-34. His previous appointment was that of Air Officer Commanding No. 11 Group.

Photo, Wide World

'Coventrated' Is What the Nazis Called It

Gloating over the death and destruction wrought at Coventry by their aimless bombing, the Nazis invented a word for this perversion of aerial warfare. Historians of the future will point to the contrast presented by the work of the R.A.F. Bomber Command, here referred to, whose precise and effective attacks on military objectives are the marvel of military experts.

ON Tuesday night (Nov. 19-20) the Nazis made a very heavy bombing attack on a Midland town, which they said was Birmingham. For hours it was subjected to a hail of bombs of all sorts, and firemen were gunned at their work by low-flying raiders. The German communiqué said that 450 tons of bombs had been dropped. Five of the raiders were shot down. Next night there came another devastating attack on a town in the East Midlands, lasting nine hours. In these raids, as in the one made on Coventry the week before, working-class districts seemed to have been deliberately selected for destruction.

From 7 p.m. on Friday until near six next morning a town in the West Midlands felt the force of another of the intensive Nazi raids. An art gallery, municipal buildings, churches, schools and shops were damaged. Elsewhere attacks were made on Merseyside, and bombs were dropped also in the London area.

In describing Tuesday's attack the Nazis used a word—" coventrated "—which they said they had coined to denote mass air attacks such as the one of Nov. 14 on Coventry. On Nov. 20 there took place at Coventry the mass burial, in four long trench graves, of 172 victims of the raid. An American observer described the line of dry-eyed, grim-faced mourners which filed past; he said that Coventry now knew the meaning of " totalkrieg " and " blitzkrieg," and had taken a tacit vow to crush those who coined these words. Not only Coventry but the whole Empire will remember, too, the perverted and inhuman act of the enemy who, from the symbol of

Coventry's suffering, manufactured a term to describe his foul murder of civilians.

On account of the apparent impunity with which the Nazi night bombers were able to operate over places in the Midlands or elsewhere, there were a good many criticisms of our defence measures, and people wanted to know why more of the enemy aircraft were not destroyed, since they flew low and remained for a long while over the area. A group of Midland M.P.s decided to make the strongest possible recommendations to Mr. Churchill that the defences of Birmingham and other big industrial towns should be the immediate and urgent concern of the Government. Partly to blame for the prevalent discontent was the over-optimism of recent official statements about night-defence methods said to be under trial. It is clear that the enemy has not yet solved this problem for himself, or the R.A.F.—despite its courage, skill, and enterprise—would not be able to carry out so scathelessly the remarkable counter-bombing attacks that are made night after night upon German objectives.

An outstanding example was the bombing, on the night of Nov. 19-20, of the gigantic Skoda works at Pilsen, in Bohemia. This trip—1,400 miles there and back—was made in very bad weather, though over the objective itself there was a moonlit and cloudless sky. The inland port of Duisburg-Ruhrort has figured again and again in Air Ministry communiques. It is the largest river port in the world, linking the Rhine with the Ruhr, and has four railway stations. Here comes the coal from the Ruhr, and here

AIRCRAFT LOSSES OVER BRITAIN

German to April 30, 1940
Total announced and estimated—West Front, North Sea, Britain, Scandinavia ... 950

	German	Italian	British
May	1,990	—	258
June	276	—	177
July	245	—	115
Aug.	1,110	—	310
Sept.	1,114	—	311
Oct.	241	—	119
Nov. 1-25	197	20	40
Totals, May to Nov. 25	**5,173**	**20**	**1,330**

Daily Results for November (1-25)

Day	German Losses	Italian Losses	British Losses	British Pilots Saved
1	18	—	1	2
2	10	—	—	—
3	1	—	1	—
4	—	—	—	—
5	7	—	5	2
6	6	—	4	1
7	8	—	5	5
8	22	—	6	3
9	7	—	—	—
10	—	—	—	—
11	31	13	2	—
12	1	—	—	—
13	6	—	—	—
14	19	—	2	2
15	20	—	2	1
16	5	—	—	—
17	14	—	5	4
18	3	—	—	—
19	5	—	—	—
20	—	—	—	—
21	1	—	1	—
22	2	—	—	—
23	4	7	—	—
24	3	—	—	—
25	4	—	—	—
Totals	**197**	**20**	**40**	**20**

None of the figures includes aircraft bombed on the ground or so damaged as to be unlikely to reach home.

From the beginning of the war up to Nov. 25, 2,961 enemy aircraft have been destroyed during raids on Britain. R.A.F. losses were 825, but the pilots of 413 British machines were saved.

Mr. Churchill on Nov. 5 gave weekly average of killed and seriously wounded civilians for September as 4,500 ; for October, 3,590. In first week of intense bombardment in September, 6,000 casualties ; in the last week of October, 2,000 casualties.

Four long rows of trenches received 172 coffins of the Coventry victims—persons who were killed by Nazi bombs on November 15. As far as possible each coffin bore the name of the deceased. A memorial will eventually be erected over the grave.
Photo, Planet News

Night Bombers Still Manage To Get Through

hundreds of barges unload oil, grain and iron. On Wednesday night (Nov. 20-21) Duisburg-Ruhrort was selected by the Bomber Command for a large-scale attack. Our medium bombers were over the target soon after 11 p.m. and kept up the attack for many hours. Soon after midnight the R.A.F. heavy bombers came along, and pilots reported 34 bursts on the objective, besides fires too numerous to count. Not until 5 a.m. on Thursday did the attacks cease.

By shooting down seven out of twenty Italian C R 42s off Dover on Saturday afternoon a Spitfire squadron brought its bag of enemy aircraft to well over a hundred. Though by flying high the Italians tried to elude our fighters, the Spitfires attacked them from above and beneath and routed them in

fighters and harassed by gunfire from the ground, the raiders dropped bombs promiscuously and demolished shops and houses.

The main enemy attack on Saturday night was directed against a South-coast town where, besides the usual bombing of churches, cinemas, schools and large stores, much damage was done to working-class dwellings.

Three German aircraft were destroyed during Sunday—a Dornier 215 brought down in the Channel, in swift punishment for gunning a West of England aerodrome; a Junkers 88 near Cheltenham; and a Messerschmitt 109 off the South-east coast. On Sunday night a hundred bombers attacked a West of England town, which the Germans claimed was Bristol.

In the Graeco-Italian theatre of war the aid given by our R.A.F. is beginning

The Diocesan flag, top right, flutters challengingly before the shattered porch of this church in south-east England. A curiously Oriental effect was obtained as a result of the bombing of a shopping arcade, above, in a Midland town.   *Photos, James Topham and Associated Press*

a short time. Four German Me 109s were also destroyed on this day. Nazi fighter-bombers made three attempts to penetrate inland, and in one attack a fierce combat took place over a London park. Pursued by

Jack and Jill, the famous ravens at the London Zoo, have been bombed out of their home. Jill has not yet been traced, and here is Jack looking very disconsolate.   *Photo, Planet News*

to tell, and the brave defenders are no longer obliged to remain immobile under the dive-bombing attacks of the Italian assault 'planes. A fighter unit of the R.A.F. which arrived on Nov. 18 moved to its operational base next morning, and in the afternoon destroyed eight Italian biplanes and one monoplane fighter; two others were shot down, but our pilots were unable to confirm destruction. We suffered no losses. The Italians were escorting a score of bombers carrying out low-level attacks when our men came upon them. In one combat the enemy went spinning down as if out of control, then straightened out and attacked a British fighter whose previous encounter had taken him down to 200 feet; the Britisher dived to 50 feet, and fired a burst that caused the enemy to crash in flames.

In an air battle over Eastern Libya on Nov. 20 15 of our fighters tackled sixty Italian C R 42s; seven of the Italians were destroyed and three more were shot down, the pursuit in some cases being taken down to within 200 feet of the ground.

British airmen invariably carry a "memento" in the form of a brick when they bomb Germany. The tail gunner of a Whitley Bomber Squadron displays his missile before setting out over enemy territory.   *Photo, Fox*

Strange Things Happen When Bombs Fall!

Sometimes the seemingly impossible happens when bombs fall, and here in this page we illustrate strange examples of the effects of H.E. and blast. A motor-car is given a lift; crockery and a top floor have an astounding escape; while the figure at the base of the Lord Clyde statue in Waterloo Place, London, has only a broken nose.

Photos, "Daily Mirror"

India's Contribution to Our War Effort

In a debate in the House of Commons on Nov. 20, Mr. Leopold Amery, Secretary of State for India, gave an impressive picture of India's war effort. Some of the facts and figures he quoted are given below, followed by some account of the political conditions which prevent that effort from being even more powerful.

IN the war of 1914-1918 India put something like 1,500,000 trained men into the field ; she could do so again if so many men were needed and steps were taken to equip them.

In peacetime the army in India consisted of some 160,000 men of the Indian Army and some 50,000 troops of the British Army. Since the war began the Indian Army has been rapidly expanded until today it numbers some 500,000 men of all arms, trained, equipped and mechanized on a modern scale. There is no scarcity of willing recruits, for in India there is an abundance of splendid military material—for instance, the Gurkha fighting men of Nepal, and the forces of the ruling princes of India, with their great martial traditions and long record of loyalty to the Imperial Crown. Some thirty of these "private armies" are now serving with His Majesty's forces in British India, and one, the Bikaner Camel Corps, is on active service in the Middle East. Soon after war began expeditionary forces of British and Indian troops were sent, at the request of the British Government, to reinforce garrisons in Egypt, Aden, and Singapore ; and at the same time units of the

Rt. Hon. Leopold Stennett Amery, M.P., Secretary of State for India. He has travelled extensively in the Near East and in all the British Dominions. *Photo, Lafayette*

R.A.F. were transferred from their stations in India to reinforce the Imperial garrisons in the Middle East and Malaya.

An Indian Air Force Volunteer Reserve is being created, with flights at Karachi, Delhi, Bombay, Calcutta, and Madras. All its personnel will not only be found in India, but trained and commissioned there. Young Indians, indeed with their quick minds and sensitive hands, take naturally to flying, and there is great enthusiasm for air service in India. Quite a number of Indian pilots are already serving in the R.A.F.,

The Royal Indian Navy has been more than trebled since the outbreak of war, and it is being steadily increased as new vessels are constructed in India, Australia, and the United Kingdom. Indefatigably occupied with the task of escorting convoys and keeping India's ports and coasts clear of enemy mines and submarines, the R.I.N. is worthily maintaining the high traditions of its past.

In material, as in man power, India today is far more advanced than she was in 1914. It has been stated that of the 40,000 items needed to equip a modern army, more than 20,000 were being produced in India before the end of the first year of war. Since then,

Marquess of Linlithgow, Viceroy and Governor-General of India. He is the thirty-third of the line, which began with the appointment of Warren Hastings as Governor-General of Fort William (Calcutta) in 1774. *Photo, Central Press*

India has become still more a vast arsenal, and very shortly, in something like 90 per cent of military supplies, she will be self-sufficient. Broadly speaking, India is aiming, in cooperation with the Dominions and Colonies east and south of Suez at meeting in very large measure all the needs of our armies in the Middle and Far East. With this end in view the Eastern Group Supply Conference, attended by representatives of the Governments of Australia, New Zealand, the Union of South Africa, Rhodesia, the East African Colonies, Palestine, Burma, and Malaya, sat at Delhi from October 25 to Nov. 25 ; and a special mission under the leadership of Sir Alexander Roger, appointed by Mr. Herbert Morrison while he was Minister of Supply, is also at work in India, seeking to devise means of expanding still farther the production of munitions and supplies.

Yet, great as is India's war effort, it would be greater far but for the political differences and deep suspicions which distract the country. India, it should be remembered, is as big as all Europe with the exception of Russia ; its 375 millions comprise people of many different races, speaking more than 200 different languages, and living at every stage of culture, from the lowest barbarism to the highest degree of civilization. Politically, India consists of British India and a large number of native states whose rulers are allied by treaty with the King-Emperor. The central government at Delhi is headed by the Viceroy and Governor-General, and consists of an Executive Council of British and Indian ministers appointed by the Crown ; there is also a Federal Legislature, composed of the Legislative Assembly and the Council of State, whose members are partly elected and partly nominated. At Delhi is also the

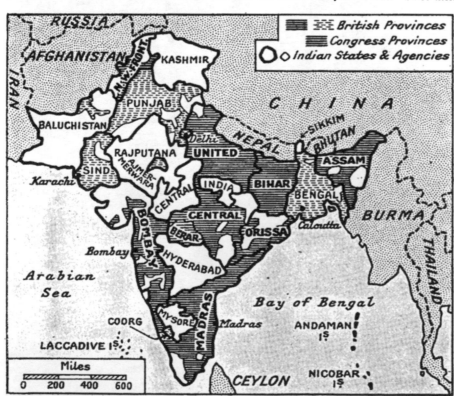

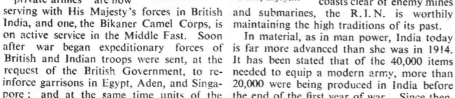

India, with a total area of 1,808,679 sq. miles and a population of some 375 millions, is a continent rather than a country. This map shows the principal territorial divisions, those of the Governors' Provinces which have "Congress" majorities being specially marked, while the dominions of the Princes are left white. Burma was separated from India on April 1, 1937.

They Are Proud to Serve the King-Emperor

A soldier of the Indian Army, left, carrying one of the new "V.B." Mark 3 machine-guns, while his companion holds ammunition equipment. This gun is remarkable for its absence of recoil, its accuracy and mobility. The medals of the Indian captain, above, are eloquent of long and gallant service.

These Indian recruits from an ex-Service Association at Fort William are being inspected by Brigadier C. M. Maltby. They are then being sent on to be trained for work in the Indian Coastal Defence. The strength of the Indian war effort has been increased by 100,000 men, and every effort has been made to secure the maximum number of Indians to officer the powerfully-equipped Army. India has sent large contingents of soldiers overseas, in addition to strengthening her vital home defences.

Photos, Lubinski, Keystone, Topical Press

All Races and Creeds United Against Nazism

Considerable additions are being made to the Royal Indian Navy, and here we see a new member of the fleet gliding down the slipway. Right is a typical Indian pilot of the Royal Air Force in India, undergoing training at a British station.

Photos, British Official: Crown Copyright; G.P.U.

sympathy with Germany, and certainly they have not the slightest wish to see Nazism supplant the British Raj. Mr. Gandhi has expressed most clearly his sympathy with Britain in her fight against Nazism, though his belief in non-violence makes him oppose anything savouring of war-mindedness in India. But the Viceroy's declaration of India's belligerency without consulting the Indian parties or people has been widely criticized.

The Indian attitude towards the war has been summarized by Sir Firozkhan Noon, High Commissioner for India. The Indian states, comprising one-third of the country; the Moslems, numbering 90 millions; the Sikh community, with its martial traditions; the Liberals; the Hindu Mahasabha, a strong and independent organization—all these were behind the war effort; and even the Congress, while it advanced technical reasons for standing aside, had before the war strongly condemned what it regarded as British tardiness in repelling German aggression on Austria and Czechoslovakia.

On August 8 the Viceroy issued a statement which affirmed that the attainment by India of free and equal partnership in the British Commonwealth was the proclaimed and accepted goal of the Imperial Crown and of the British Parliament. At the same time, Lord Linlithgow invited the Indian political leaders to join his Executive Council and to establish a War Advisory Council. The invitation was rejected, but the offer was repeated by the Viceroy on November 20.

Chamber of Princes, in which the rulers of the allied states are represented.

British India is divided into 14 provinces, containing about four-fifths of the total population; and on eleven of these far-reaching powers of self-government were conferred by the Government of India Act of 1935. These ": Governors' Provinces," as they are called, have elected legislatures, although the franchise is extremely limited, as the immense majority of the people are quite illiterate and therefore politically dumb. In each province there is a ministry which, though chosen by the Governor, is responsible to the legislature. In eight of the eleven provincial legislatures (Bombay, Madras, United Provinces, Bihar, Orissa, Central Provinces, Assam, and N.W. Frontier Province) there is a " Congress " majority, i.e. one drawn from the Indian National Congress, whose aim is Indian independence or, at least, Dominion Home Rule, and whose strength is derived in the main from the Hindu population. Its leader is Mahatma Gandhi, though his authority has been frequently challenged by the left wing, whose most prominent spokesman is Jawaharlal Nehru, a Socialist but, unlike Gandhi, no pacifist. On November 5, 1940 Nehru was sentenced to four years' imprisonment for making speeches calculated to hamper the country's war effort.

Besides the Congress, the only organized political party in India is the Moslem League, led by Mr. Jinnah, which opposes the Congress Party largely because it fears that in a Congress-dominated India the rights of the Moslem minority would be adversely affected. Both the Congress and Moslem League, however, are at one in their demand for independence in greater or lesser measure. It was because they were dissatisfied with the slow progress made towards the long pro-

mised Dominion status that the Congress governments in the eight provinces resigned last August, whereupon the provinces reverted to autocratic rule. In Punjab, Sind and Bengal coalition governments are in office. Neither the Congress Party nor the Moslem League have any

This unique photograph of a session of the Working Committee of the Indian Congress was taken by Pandit Jawaharlal Nehru. It shows Mahatma Gandhi addressing Congress workers of the United Provinces. On his left is Mrs. Vijayalakshmi Pandit, who as Minister for Public Health United Provinces, was India's first woman Minister, and on his right is ex-Premier Pant of the United Provinces.

Photo, Central Press

I Saw the Fight from 'Rangitiki's' Bridge

One of the main targets of the German raider which attacked the
"Jervis Bay" convoy (see pages 567 and 583) was the 17,000-ton
liner "Rangitiki," which, however, docked safely. Her commander
here tells the story of his ship's ordeal under shell-fire and of the
"Jervis Bay's" heroic fight which enabled her to escape.

WHEN his ship reached port, Capt.
Barnett of the "Rangitiki" said:
"It was at four o'clock in the
afternoon that an unidentified ship was
sighted hull down on the port beam and
steering gradually closer to us.

The look-out in the crow's nest passed
the message and the top masts of the enemy
must have been 20 miles away when we first
sighted her. By 4.45 we could see she was a
warship of heavy calibre.

The whole convoy was doing about nine
knots. About 5.15 the enemy suddenly
opened fire with her forward turret at a range
which I should estimate to be nearly 15,000
yards.

It was obvious that the target was the
"Jervis Bay" or the "Rangitiki," as we
were the largest ship and our 17,000 tons
and our two funnels must have made an
attractive target. At the same time the
convoy, acting swiftly to orders, turned to
starboard and dispersed.

It seemed lucky, although it really wasn't,
that no one ran into another ship. While
this operation was going on the enemy
had turned to a parallel course to the convoy
and began to concentrate its fire on the
"Jervis Bay," which had commenced to
steam towards the enemy.

She was firing all the time, but her salvos
appeared to fall short.

The raider's second salvo hit the "Jervis
Bay" amidships on the port side, evidently
putting her engines out of action, as she lost
way immediately. The third salvo struck her
just before the bridge and the fourth aft,
setting her afire.

Then the enemy concentrated its fire on
our ship, but she did not have so much luck.
Her first salvo fell on our starboard quarter
about 400 yards short. The second straddled

Here at sea is the "Rangitiki," the largest ship in the convoy under the escort of "Jervis Bay."
Top is her commander, Captain Henry Barnett; below left, her purser, Mr. A. Swift, with
Mrs. B. Lee, stewardess, on his left and Miss W. Taylor on his right, photographed on board the
"Rangitiki" after she had reached port.   *Photos, Planet News and Fox*

us amidships, but the third, instead of
finishing us, straddled us again just forward
of the bridge.

One shell went right over us less than 50
yards away, and it smothered the bridge
with spray and shell fragments, which struck
the ship forward but did no appreciable
damage. The enemy by this time was
apparently bringing its secondary armament
into play, as we have found since small pieces
of shell on the deck.

Meantime all the ships in the convoy were
using their smoke floats, and if it had not
been for a light wind from the south-east
which enabled the smoke to screen us, I
think we might not have escaped, and nor
would a lot of others.

The other skippers carried out a very
gallant action with their manoeuvres, and
fortunately as night fell with only a quarter-
moon we made good our escape.

Capt. Barnett paid a high tribute to all his
officers, engineers and crew. He also spoke
highly of the conduct of his passengers.
They were all magnificent. The passengers
on board included seven women. Although
the ship was at times enveloped by shell fragments and spray they were calm throughout.

MISS RUTH SHANNON, who was a passenger
returning from New Zealand to do war
work, told a graphic story. She said:

I was just getting up from afternoon rest
when I heard a terrific crash on the starboard
side, where my cabin was situated. In a
few minutes stewardesses told us to put on
our lifebelts and we were taken to the port
alleyway.

Later a sing-song was arranged by the
officers and we all joined in singing such
songs as "Roll out the Barrel." Everyone
was very cheerful and there was absolutely
no panic of any kind.

At dinnertime, some two hours later, we
were told that dinner would be served in the
ordinary way in the saloon, and we sat down
with our lifebelts on, although I am afraid

THOUSANDS of holiday-makers have crossed the Solent in the Southern Railway's paddle-steamer "Southsea," above right. She is now H.M. minesweeper "Southsea," commanded by Lieutenant C. C. M. Pawley, R.N.R., and has earned fame by bringing down an enemy aircraft. On November 17, 1940, she was attacked by a Dornier 17, and her 20-year-old gunner secured a direct hit with his first shot. His mate is 22 years of age. Left are the two gunners.
Photos, Wright & Logan and Topical

we did not make as good a dinner as we usually do. The only difference in the dining-room was that the lights were lowered, but the service was, as usual, excellent.

When the immediate danger was over and the passengers were able to resume their normal life on board there was a feeling of gratefulness to the captain and officers. On the last night before they reached the West-coast port the passengers insisted that the captain should come for a few minutes to the dining saloon.

Miss Shannon concluded :
The captain had been on the bridge for many hours. In fact, I was told he had not taken off his clothes for seven days. We had dinner, and then it was proposed that we should sing "Auld Lang Syne," and we joined hands, skipped around the tables and chairs, and sang.

I do not think I am giving away a secret when I say that all the women passengers went up to the captain and kissed him !
"*Daily Telegraph.*"

We Watched the Bomb Taken for a Ride!

The work of the bomb-disposal squads of the Royal Engineers has already been described (see page 338), but the reactions of the public to the removal of delayed-action bombs are amusingly depicted in the following dispatch by Helen Kirkpatrick.

AT first when the manager of a famous London hotel approached tables of lunchers with the news, everyone, from the Chief Whip, Capt. Margesson, to lowly correspondents, looked startled.

" What do you mean ?—the police have ordered everyone out of the hotel during the procession ? "

" That's the order," said the manager, spreading his hands in deprecating fashion. " Actually the police said that everyone must go thirty yards from the street for the procession, but I'd advise three thousand yards."

In good order the guests paid their bills and left by the back door, not, as might be thought, in fear of what first seemed the Gestapo-like activities of the British police, but in genuine respect for a procession which was to pass down a famous London thoroughfare on the stroke of three.

Peeping out behind a solid stone building a good 30 yards from the street, we watched the mysterious procession passing.

Slowly from unseen crowds equally well hidden behind buildings all along the street came cheers. Not from windows which had been left open and untenanted, but muffled by yards of stone between them and the majestic sight.

There on a large Army lorry, escorted by outriders, sat the biggest bomb we had ever seen that close, and, sitting beside it, seeming to stroke it into a brief quiescence, sat the calm figure of an Army engineer.

As it roared its way down the street towards—we hoped—some eager marshes, the police shed their Gestapo role and welcomed us back.
(*From the story by Helen Kirkpatrick, London Correspondent of the "Chicago Daily News," printed in the "Daily Telegraph".*)

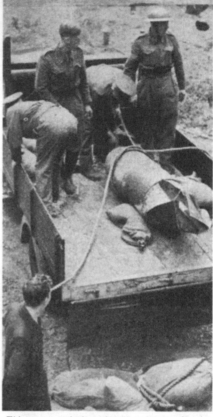

This apparently harmless bomb reposing in a lorry is actually a delayed-action bomb ready to pass in " procession " to some " eager marshes." *Photo, Fox*

Kipling Would Have Enjoyed My Journey

Among the unsung heroes of wartime England are the lorry-drivers who " deliver the goods " in fair weather and foul and are not deterred from driving through nightly air raids. Mr. Campbell Dixon, the " Daily Telegraph " reporter, who spent a night with north-bound drivers, wrote the following note of appreciation of their work.

KIPLING should have written this story. He loved machines, the traffic of high seas and highways, and men in greasy overalls doing a brave job of work.

Yes, Kipling should have ridden in my place the other night and seen how the lorry drivers of England are pounding nightly through blitz and fog and darkness, carrying food for the housewife, spare parts for the factory and raw materials to keep a million wheels turning.

The lorry I rode in was one of Tillings', said to control more lorries and vans than any other company in the world. It weighs seven tons and carries a 15-ton load from London to Manchester between darkness and dawn.

It was bright moonlight when we crossed the Thames, shimmering like a Whistler Nocturne, passed the blind houses of northern

suburbs, and roared through sleeping villages set in a fairyland of oak and grass, silver beneath the moon.

Soon came disenchantment. At one place a board at a junction said, " Air Raid." Sirens and even gunfire were drowned by the roaring Diesel engine, but there was no mistaking the import of the searchlights.

Often the lights followed a 'plane along our road. Then the driver would reach under the seat for a steel helmet. Nothing dropped and one by one the lights went out.

These night drivers know the roads of England as most of us know our street. Every now and then my driver would indicate a local landmark : " Sleepy hollow " ; " Our boys have supper there " ; " Café on the right is where I saw two girls fight with razors. Bit rough."

I WAS THERE!

At a half-way house at 2 a.m. with frost biting sharply, we met drivers from the North. Hot tea, sausage and mashed, and I was on another lorry, London bound.

Five more hours' pounding through moonlight and ground mist, with the barrage of London now glittering silently, and I was back in the West End, full of admiration for the unknown army that delivers England's goods.—*Daily Telegraph.*

We Were Rescued by an American Destroyer

The first job to fall to one of the American destroyers transferred to the British Navy was to rescue from the sea the crew of a Royal Air Force heavy bomber. On October 31 the captain of the aircraft broadcast the following story of the crew's 22 hours in the Atlantic in a rubber dinghy.

MANY people have said what a welcome addition the American destroyers would be to our fleet. I am sure that no one is likely to give them a more hearty and grateful welcome than my crew and myself did one afternoon a couple of weeks ago when, after drifting aimlessly about in a rubber dinghy off the coast of Ireland for a very long time, we suddenly saw on the crest of a wave the funnels of a destroyer.

It happened like this. We had been detailed to escort a convoy and had met it inward bound at about midday. Several hours later, while we were still on patrol, the rear gunner reported a trace of smoke from the starboard engine. I was not unduly worried, but I decided to return to base at once and the wireless operator reported to base that we were doing so. But almost immediately our trouble increased, the engine got very hot—and so did I.

I saw clouds of smoke pouring from the engine, the temperature shot right up, and I had to throttle the engine back to prevent it catching fire. We were only at about 500 feet at the time and the aircraft would not maintain height on the other engine. I told the crew to stand by for a landing on the sea. This we must have done with quite a crack, in spite of my efforts to hold off as long as possible and reduce speed, as the fuselage broke nearly in two just forward of the leading edge of the wings. The cockpit immediately began to fill with water, and I climbed out through the escape hatch in the roof and found the rest of the crew in the sea with the dinghy which was just opening. The wireless operator had hit himself jumping in and had swallowed a lot of salt water when he went under; he was very nearly unconscious. We got him in after quite a struggle, and the rest of the crew came aboard in turn. The aircraft had sunk by the time the last had got in.

This happened at about 4 o'clock in the afternoon; there were about three hours of daylight remaining, and, of course, we hoped very much that SOS we had sent out would have been received and that we should be picked up or at least sighted that afternoon. We were at the time within sight of land, but a strong south-westerly wind was carrying us away out to sea. Darkness fell without a sight of ships or aircraft, and we resigned ourselves to at least another fourteen hours afloat.

There were only three things to do all night—to keep awake, to keep warm and to try to keep the boat as dry as possible. We had all, except the rear gunner, swallowed some salt water and were seasick. We found three exercises which seemed the most practicable for keeping warm. First we would pat our hands briskly on our thighs; that warmed both hands and thighs and was our commonest exercise. Then we did the "cabman's swing," swinging our arms across our chests. Finally we smacked each other on the back. We did our best to keep cheerful, and as my watch was watertight and working I reported the time every half-hour and the number of hours to daylight.

At first we shipped water quite often as the tops of the waves broke over us. Later, though the seas were steadily rising with the wind increasing through the night, we became quite expert at riding the huge Atlantic rollers, and found that if we kept two of us facing into the wind and two with their backs to it we could watch the waves and by leaning away from the bad ones ease ourselves over the top of them without shipping water very often.

The night passed very slowly indeed. I had decided not to open the rations till morning, as I knew we should be much hungrier then. I am afraid I adopted rather a "Captain Bligh of the Bounty" line over the rations, as I wanted to make them last

One of the U.S.A. destroyers transferred to the Royal Navy is the "W. C. Wood," and here is a photograph of her new captain (who by a coincidence bears the same name)—Commander D. E. Wood, standing beside the bell of his ship.   *Photo, Associated Press*

for three days. Dawn crept upon us at about 6.30 after an apparently interminable night of back-slapping and wave-climbing. It was quite light by 7.30 and we were out of sight of land, but suddenly, to our joy, we saw a ship in the west. It got larger and was heading almost in our direction; then it altered course and came straight for us. We stood up in turn and waved and we all shouted, but she was to windward and neither saw nor heard us. We saw several aircraft during the morning, but even those fairly near did not spot us because the sea was a mass of "white horses."

Suddenly, about 2 p.m., we thought we saw some ships in the distance. All the morning, however, we had been seeing low islands and lighthouses, which proved to be merely the crests of waves breaking in the distance, so I didn't have much faith in any of these ships. Then we started looking again, and to our joy saw from the crest of a wave a flotilla of destroyers steaming towards us in line abreast. The second pilot recognized the four funnels and flush deck of the American destroyers, and we thought that they would pass on either side of us. Then, as they drew near, they altered course away from us so that we passed to port of the port ship of the line. We held the rear gunner up and he waved our green canvas paddle. Just as we had about given up hope again we saw people waving from the decks and she turned in a circle round us.

Soon after, she came alongside and threw us a line, at first shouting directions in German, as they had mistaken our uniforms. The ship was rolling heavily and when our navigator caught hold of the rope ladder he could not get a foothold, and as his hands were too cold to keep a grip he fell into the sea. A sailor at once jumped in, put a line round him and he was lifted out. The rest of the crew and myself were able to climb aboard. We were taken below and had our skins practically rubbed off us before we were wrapped in blankets and put in officers' cabins, with tea and rum and hot food, all extremely welcome.

As soon as I was warm I borrowed some clothes and went on the bridge to thank the captain. I learned that it was he who had first spotted us when he saw through his glass our yellow skull-caps and life-saving jackets, and dinghy, which he thought was some wreckage as we appeared and disappeared on the distant waves.

The lives of many airmen have been saved by rubber dinghies with which aircraft are equipped. As recounted in this page, the crew of a wrecked aircraft spent 22 hours in their dinghy before they were rescued by an American destroyer that had been transferred to the British Navy. *Photo, British Official: Crown Copyright*

OUR SEARCHLIGHT ON THE WAR

De Gaulle Scores Further Successes

VICHY is becoming increasingly perturbed about the Free French gains in Equatorial Africa. On Aug. 26 the Governor of Chad Territory announced that it refused to accept the French capitulation and would continue to fight on the side of Britain. This courageous lead was followed three days later by the announcement that French Congo and the Cameroons also repudiated the Pétain Government and had joined the Allies. The colony of Gabon at first put up resistance, and on October 27 it was reported that Free French Forces under the command of General de Larminat were advancing on the village and fortress of Lambarene. On November 6 they were captured. Four days later Libreville, the capital of Gabon, surrendered to General de Gaulle's adherents, and the warships "Savorgnan de Brazza" and "Commandant Domine" of the Free French Navy entered the harbour. On November 12 Port Gentil, the second port of Gabon, surrendered. General Weygand, who is in French North Africa, whither he was sent as a special commissioner of the Vichy Government to check the movement of the French colonies towards General de Gaulle, is said to be bitterly disappointed at this effect of France's capitulation, and in those circles in France which believed in the possibility of Franco-German cooperation there is a feeling of something like despair.

Small States Join the Axis

AT the Belvedere Palace in Vienna, on November 20, Count Czaky, Hungarian Foreign Minister, signed, with Ribbentrop, Ciano and Kurusu, Japanese Ambassador in Berlin, a Protocol binding his country to the Three-Power Military Pact of September 27. Hitler, who stood by and watched, had hoped that similar Protocols would have been signed at the same time by King Boris of Bulgaria and Suñer, Spanish Foreign Minister, whom he had recently summoned to Berchtesgaden for conferences. But Ribbentrop ended a speech of welcome to Hungary with the words, "Other States will follow." By the Protocol she undertakes to assist the other signatories "with all political, economic and military means" if any of them is attacked by a Power not yet involved in the war. The ceremony at the Belvedere Palace is merely a formal confirmation of what was already an accomplished fact, for Hungary has for some time had to submit to the use of her territory and her resources by Germany. Making the best of a bad business, Hungarian officials at Budapest maintained that "Hungary's position is now similar to that of Japan, namely, the closest collaboration in the common aim of the signatories of the tripartite pact, but without belligerency." On November 23 General Antonescu, Rumanian dictator, signed a similiar Protocol on behalf of his country, and he was followed by Dr. Tuka, Slovak Prime Minister. But Hitler's plan of compelling Bulgaria to join the Axis has either been postponed—or rejected by King Boris himself.

Enemy Activities in Syria

BARON von Oppenheim, a German archaeologist of note, arrived some weeks ago on the Syrian frontier with a party numbering over thirty, his ostensible object being the study of the architecture of the Omayyad castles. The French Commissioner, M. Puaux, having a well-founded distrust of "missions," at first refused him entry, but Berlin put a little pressure on Vichy, and M. Puaux had to give in. Von Oppenheim, who speaks Arabic fluently, is now said to be in the Syrian desert, visiting the Ruwalla tribe. But in addition to his genuine archaeological achievements, the Baron has won success in diplomacy, and was for some years attached to the German embassy in Turkey, and it is not without significance that the territory of the Ruwalla tribe lies near the Iraq Petroleum Company's pipeline, which runs across the desert from Kirkuk to Haifa, and furnishes a principal source of supply for H.M. Fleet in the Mediterranean.

The other member of the Axis is definitely not persona grata in Syria. It was reported on November 20 that half of Mussolini's Armistice Commission had gone home, and the rest were soon leaving. Their aims—to ingratiate themselves with the civil population, and to secure military, naval and air

GEORGE CROSS AND MEDAL

KING GEORGE has chosen the design for the George Cross and the George Medal, the honours which he created on September 23 "for men and women in all walks of civilian life." (There is also a small military division.) Both are in silver. The Cross was designed and modelled by Mr. Percy Metcalfe, C.V.O., R.D.I., the artist responsible for the King's Coronation Medal. It has four equal limbs and in the centre is a circular medallion bearing the design of St. George and the Dragon, taken from the reverse of the gold coinage, surrounded by the inscription "For Gallantry." In the angle of each limb are the letters G VI. The reverse of the Cross is plain, and on it will be inscribed the name of the recipient and date of award. The ribbon is dark blue, threaded through a bar adorned with laurel leaves.

The Medal is 1·42 in. diam. The obverse shows the crowned effigy of the King, surrounded by the inscription GEORGIUS VI D.G. BR. OMN. REX ET INDIAE IMP., and is identical with that of service medals in general. The reverse depicts St. George slaying the Dragon, a design adapted by Mr. George Kruger Gray, C.B.E., A.R.C.A., F.S.A., after the bookplate designed by Mr. Stephen Gooden, A.R.A., for the Royal Library at Windsor Castle. The ribbon is red with five narrow vertical stripes of blue.

bases for operations in the Middle East—have met with complete failure. This set-back, coming on top of Taranto, reverses in Greece, and Italian air losses in Britain, has, it would seem, infuriated the Duce.

Press Censors in Norway

BERLIN controls even the headlines in the Norwegian newspapers. According to a writer in the "Manchester Guardian," a young Norwegian, one of the many refugees who are still arriving by boat from that unhappy country, produced a "Direction to Newspapers," issued by the German Reichskommissar after an attack on Bergen by the R.A.F. This instruction to editors of the morning papers was as follows:

The reports should have one of the following headlines, among which the editor is free to choose for himself:

1. The King dispatches his help from England; Bergen bombed.
2. Royal greetings from Bergen.
3. Cordial thanks, King Haakon, for your bombing of Bergen.
4. Was King Haakon aware that his British friends were attacking Bergen?
5. As soon as the King is established in London, Norwegian citizens are killed by bombs.
6. King Haakon carries on with the war; Bergen his first victims.

All the headline writers in the morning papers chose No. 4 as being the least offensive. But the Reichskommissar evidently felt that he had been stupidly lenient, for within an hour of two the editors of the evening papers were circularized to the effect that they might report the bombardment of Bergen, but that headline No. 4 was cancelled.

Messerschmitts' Weak Point

THE Air Ministry News Service has been collecting extracts from the reports of pilots who have destroyed Messerschmitt 109 fighters carrying single bombs. It seems that these machines can fly very high and very fast, thus escaping more easily, but their construction is such that they cannot stand up to attack. "I gave it about a seven-second burst," said a Spitfire pilot. "No other action was necessary, as it disintegrated and fell from the sky in hundreds of pieces." "The Me. disintegrated," said another. "The tail was struck first, then the rudder. The petrol tank was alight and the panels were falling off." A Hurricane pilot, describing his encounter, said: "Everything poured out and bits flew off." And still another reported: "Pieces were flying off in all directions." How different is the resistance of our own fighters! The condition of one Hurricane, whose wounded pilot made a safe landing near Folkestone, has already been described in page 278, but we may here repeat the awed comment of one expert after examining the battered machine: "It's not flying, it's a miracle!"

Nazi Winter Invasion Plans

ACCORDING to reports from neutral sources, the German troops stationed along the French coast believe that the invasion of Britain may be attempted during foggy weather this coming winter. Rehearsals were still being carried out recently, to the disgust of the troops. They hate the sea, and hope that their units may not form part of the million or so men whom the German Command, it is said, proposes to send across the Channel to widely separated places, reckoning that the British defence forces will be so dispersed that at least one contingent could effect a landing and hold it until vast German reinforcements converged upon it. The plan looks well on paper, but it appears to disregard the existence of our coastal patrols, both naval and air.

Perhaps It Is Not So Bad to Be an Evacuee!

The best sport these youngsters from the East End of London have hitherto enjoyed has been fishing for " tiddlers " in a London park. Now they are guests at one of the Duke of Bedford's houses, Sarratt Mill in Hertfordshire, and though the catches may not be big, novel conditions lend zest to their sport.

First-hand stories of adventures on the sea add a new joy to life for boys and a small girl evacuated from London to a fishing village in Devon. No doubt, too, the old salt loves to tell them!

At Blackpool, this grandmother from the East End of London (left) enjoys a paddle perhaps even more than her charges. Lady Brooke Popham sees that the little Londoners to whom she has given a home have a good time ; above, a bunch of them enjoy a ride in the gardeners' truck while Lady Brooke Popham consoles one of them who, being a Londoner, perhaps feels safer on a tram.

Photos, Topical, Fox and " Daily Mirror "

OUR DIARY OF THE WAR

TUESDAY, NOV. 19, 1940   *444th day*

On the Sea—British light naval forces sank German E-boat in North Sea.

Admiralty announced that H.M. submarine "Rainbow" was overdue and must be considered lost.

In the Air—R.A.F. bombed Skoda works at Pilsen, Bohemia ; munition stores and other objectives in Berlin ; shipyards and docks at Kiel, Hamburg, and Bremerhaven ; synthetic oil plants at Gelsenkirchen and Hamburg ; power station at Hamborn ; railway yards and junctions at Bremen, Berlin and Aurich ; inland port of Duisburg-Ruhrort.

Coastal Command aircraft attacked naval base at Lorient and harbour at Barfleur.

German liner "Europa" reported to have been hit during recent R.A.F. raid on Bremen docks.

War against Italy—Night raids by R.A.F. on Tirana and Durazzo. Destructive attack made on Assab.

Five Italian tanks destroyed and others damaged at Hileiquat, 15 m. south of Sidi Barrani.

Cairo reported that enemy raids on Alexandria had been intensified.

Home Front—Very little enemy air activity during day. Heavy night raids, particularly in Midlands. Birmingham had its severest attack, lasting 9 hours. Extensive damage done and many casualties. London hotel again struck. Church, convent, hospital, and L.C.C. institution hit. Five enemy aircraft destroyed.

Greek War—Newly arrived R.A.F. fighters in Greece shot down nine Italian aircraft. Greeks reported capture of Erseka, 20 m. south of Koritza.

General—King Leopold reported to have visited Hitler at Berchtesgaden.

WEDNESDAY, NOV. 20   *445th day*

In the Air—R.A.F. made large-scale attack on Duisburg-Ruhrort. Other forces bombed ports of Lorient, Cherbourg, Dunkirk, and Ostend, and several aerodromes.

War against Italy—R.A.F. scored success in Eastern Libya, bringing down 10 Italian fighters. During night Benghazi, Berka, and Benina were raided, as were Gura, Massawa, and Asmara in Italian East Africa.

During night British naval unit, assisted by air cooperation, successfully bombarded Maktila camp, on Libyan coast.

Home Front—After day of slight activity enemy launched another, but minor, night attack on Midlands. Bombs also fell in London area, in South-coast town and in many other widespread districts. One town in S.W. England had its 202nd raid.

Greek War—Greeks reported to have launched new offensive on wide front. Attacks continued on Morova mountains overlooking Koritza.

General—Hungary joined Three-Power Pact between Germany, Italy and Japan.

THURSDAY, NOV. 21   *446th day*

In the Air—No night bombing operations by R.A.F. owing to unfavourable weather.

War against Italy—R.A.F. bombers raided Tepelini, Albania. In Libya, Derna, Bomba and Bardia were bombed.

Home Front—During day bombs fell in East Anglia and Home Counties and in a town in South England. At night Liverpool had two short raids. Bombs fell at several places in East Anglia and in widely separated places in southern half of England. One enemy aircraft destroyed ; Britain lost one fighter.

Greek War—Italians abandoned Koritza and retreated northwards to Elbasan and Pogradets. Greeks began to occupy the town. General Greek advance throughout Epirus front reported. Tanks, 200 motor vehicles, much war material and many prisoners captured. Argyrokastro aerodrome bombed.

General—Air Marshal O. T. Boyd, newly-appointed Deputy to A.O.C., Middle East Command, taken prisoner after forced landing over Sicily.

King George opened new session of Parliament.

FRIDAY, NOV. 22   *447th day*

In the Air—R.A.F. made intensive attack on Merignac aerodrome, near Bordeaux. Many successful raids also made over Germany. Coastal Command aircraft bombed Stavanger aerodrome.

War against Italy—During night R.A.F. made successful raid on Bari.

Home Front—Bombs fell during day in

THE POETS & THE WAR
XXXIX
TO THE FIGHTER PILOT
By Greta Briggs

He is so young and joyous, yet he bears
The fate of nations on his shoulders now.
His roaring Spitfire thunders up the sky ;
To him the drone of engines seems a song.
He rides the cloud-pavilioned lists that lie
Between earth's surface and the evening star;
His feats of arms are such as men have not
Dared heretofore. His brief reports can vie
With all the ballads of those knights and kings
Whose deeds were red-hot news in Camelot.

He has a threefold England in his charge :
The old-world England we have loved so long,
And then the splendid England of today,
And, finally, the England yet to be !
We pass him in the street—a knight who wears
Not golden spurs, perhaps, but shining wings.
                    —*Daily Telegraph*

Home Counties village and town on South coast. Concentrated 11-hours night attack on West Midland town ; much damage and many casualties occurred. Bombs also fell in London area, in N.E. town, South-coast town, and elsewhere. Two enemy aircraft destroyed.

Dover area shelled from French coast.

Greek War—Italian retreat continued. Large quantities of war material fell into Greek hands. Occupation of Koritza completed. R.A.F. bombed and destroyed communications of retreating Italians at Pogradets. On Epirus front Greeks advancing in direction of Premeti and Tepelini.

Italians bombed Cephalonia and Corfu, and Tygani in Samos. Four destroyers from Leros later bombarded Samos.

SATURDAY, NOV. 23   *448th day*

In the Air—Large force of bombers attacked objectives at Turin, including the Royal Arsenal and Fiat Works.

R.A.F. bombed goods yards and railway stations in Berlin and Leipzig ; inland port of Duisburg-Ruhrort ; canal wharves at Cologne ; railway sidings at Dortmund ; oil targets at Wanne Eickel and Dortmund ; Krupps works at Essen ; several aerodromes.

Coastal Command aircraft raided marine bases in northern and western France.

Spitfire squadron routed twenty Italian fighters in Straits of Dover, shooting down seven without loss to itself.

War against Italy—R.A.F. attacked group of Italian aerodromes in desert and on coast around Tobruk.

Home Front—Enemy aircraft made three daylight raids over S.E. England. One small formation penetrated to London and bombs fell in a southern suburb and in a town on Thames Estuary.

At night Southampton had its worst raid of the war ; many buildings demolished or damaged, and casualties heavy. Another South-coast town was also bombed.

Eleven enemy machines shot down, seven being Italian.

Greek War—Greek advance continued along whole front. Italians retreating towards Valona, abandoning vast quantities of equipment. R.A.F. bombed Elbasan, Albania.

General—Rumanian dictator, General Antonescu, and Dr. Tuka, Slovak Premier, signed protocols in Berlin by which their countries join the Axis.

SUNDAY, NOV. 24   *449th day*

On the Sea—Admiralty announced loss by mines of H.M. trawler "Kingston Alalite" and H.M. drifter "Reed."

British steamer "Port Hobart" wirelessed that she was being shelled by raider off West Indies.

In the Air—R.A.F. carried out extensive raids over invasion ports on French coast.

Bomber Command concentrated night attacks on shipyards and industrial plants at Hamburg. Other targets included Altona gas works, docks at Wilhelmshaven and Den Helder, aerodromes, seaplane bases, A.A. and searchlight positions.

Coastal Command aircraft bombed aerodrome at Christiansand. Other aircraft attacked harbour of Hook of Holland.

War against Italy—Heavy daylight raid by R.A.F. on Durazzo. Military stores and motor transport column successfully attacked in Tepelini area.

Cairo stated that Metemma, opposite Gallabat, had virtually been evacuated by Italians. R.A.F. attacked Red Sea port of Assab.

Home Front—Enemy daylight activity was slight. Few bombs fell in Kent. Big night attack on Bristol. Churches, chapels, schools, cinemas, shops and houses demolished ; casualties were considerable. Bombs also fell in London.

Three enemy aircraft shot down.

Greek War—Athens reported that Greek advanced units entered Pogradets and proceeded towards Elbasan. Mountain town of Moscopole fell to Greeks. Konispol, opposite Corfu, captured.

General—Death of Lord Craigavon, Prime Minister of Northern Ireland.

MONDAY, NOV. 25   *450th day*

On the Sea—Steamer "Patria" sank in Haifa harbour following explosion.

In the Air.—R.A.F. bombers attacked naval base and dockyards at Kiel and Wilhelmshaven. Other aircraft bombed docks at Hamburg and Willemsoord, seaplane base at De Mok, and several enemy aerodromes.

War against Italy.—R.A.F. carried out reconnaissance over Sicily, Taranto and Bari. Assab on Red Sea was again bombed.

Home Front—Bombs fell during day on coastal towns in S. and S.E. England, but damage was slight. No night raids as weather was unfavourable.

Four enemy aircraft shot down.

Greek War—Italian retreat fast becoming a rout. Greek advance continued along whole front. R.A.F. harassed retreating enemy and bombing his convoys and motor transports. Italians reported to be forming new line on Tomor mountains, east of Berat.

Empire—First contingent of airmen trained in Canada arrived in London.

TO THE RESCUE OF A FAITHFUL FRIEND IN DISTRESS

Terrified by the noise, dazed by the disaster which has come so suddenly upon their homes, many a dog and cat has dashed off, it knows not where. Sometimes the pathetic fugitives have been killed ; sometimes they have returned when the bombing was over and have been found shivering on deserted doorsteps ; many of them have been picked up by the rescue workers of the animal welfare societies who, even durin the worst of the bombing, periodically patrol the streets. This little wire-haired terrier fell into a bomb crater and injured his leg, but is now in the good hands of the People's Dispensary for Sick Animals Mobile Rescue Squad.

Photo, Kosmos

Still the Greeks Drove On in Triumph

After a month of war the Italians in the Balkans had lost terrain, men and materials ;
they were in full retreat to the coast. The story of the fall of Pogradets and the
fighting about Argyrokastro is told below.

AFTER five days of hard fighting Pogradets, the Albanian town 20 miles north-west of Koritza on the shores of Lake Okrida, fell on the afternoon of December 1, when Greek patrols entered the place, hard on the heels of the retreating enemy. The Italian resistance was particularly strong towards the end of the struggle, but throughout the night in heavy snow the Greeks fought their way, foot by foot, up the heights which dominated the town from either side. Once they had been carried the fall of the town was inevitable. When the Greeks entered they found that most of the houses were in ruins and all the inhabitants had fled. Considerable quantities of munitions were seized, however, together with a number of tanks and lorries which the Italians abandoned as they sped along the road to Elbasan.

Elbasan, only 20 miles south of Tirana, the Albanian capital, now became the Greeks' objective, and the Italians were reported to be making desperate efforts to hold it. For if Elbasan, too, fell, then their hold on the centre of Albania would be precarious. Without giving the Italians time to consolidate, the Greeks pushed on westwards along the road to Elbasan, while the trail was blazed before them by the 'planes of the R.A.F. and the Greek Air Force.

Meanwhile, heavy fighting was proceeding to the south in the Argyrokastro sector. This town was used by the Italians as their principal supply base on the Epirus front, and for days its fate lay in the balance. Several times, indeed, its fall was rumoured, but the Italians put up a determined resistance, throwing a number of reinforcements into the fight. Among these was the Modena division, which was dispatched from Rome

ALBANIA is a land of quite high mountain ranges, mostly parallel with the coast, and valleys watered by small streams. On this map the Greek thrusts from the east and south are shown by black arrows.

only a few days before it went into action against the Greeks in front of Argyrokastro ; but fresh as they were, the Italians were unable to withstand the Greek onslaught. One regiment in particular, the 42nd, was badly cut up when the Greeks carried their hilltop position by assault shortly before daybreak.

"The Italians maintained a very strong position on the hill for three days," the Greek captain who led his men in the charge which put the Italians to flight told Mr. Leland Stowe, Special Correspondent of the "Daily Telegraph" with the Greek Army. "If they had had real morale they could have held it. Our artillery barrage was laid down in the middle of the night. Then we charged into darkness with bayonets and grenades. It was the hottest hand-to-hand fighting I have yet seen on this front. The Fascists broke under it. Many of their officers were killed in trying to make their men fight."

The Greek officer in charge of the operations was reported to have stated that " it was the hardest position we have tackled yet. Several trees and bushes seemed to be covering the next with a machine-gun. Mortars and hand grenades met our Evzones. During the day we could not move a foot, so deadly was the fire of the Italian snipers. During the night our mountain-guns fired, setting the pine trees ablaze and lighting up the plateau. The Greeks then attacked under cover of darkness, and after less serious fighting the position was taken, though the losses on both sides were heavy."

On the other hand, in fairness to the enemy it must be said that on many occasions they fought with as much courage and endurance as the Greeks. One party of Black-

ARGYROKASTRO (left), principal base of the Italian Army in south-west Albania, which the Greeks vigorously attacked at the end of November. Italians were forced back into the narrow streets as they defended the town.

Above, left to right: General A. Papagos, C.-in-C. of the Greek Forces ; General Metaxas, Prime Minister ; and Major - General Gambier Parry, leader of the British military mission to Greece, photographed together in Athens.

Photos, Sport & General, E.N.A.

shirts, in particular, may be singled out for honourable mention ; after the troops to which they had been attached surrendered, they continued to fight on until all had been killed. Generally speaking, the bad morale, which became so apparent following the collapse of the Italian first line, was confined to the troops of the regular army, whose heart was most obviously not in the struggle : the Blackshirts, on the other hand, for their

Brothers-in-Arms in the Balkan War

BRITISH SOLDIERS are as good " mixers " as they are fighters and never allow difficulties of language to interfere with friendship. Right, British and Greek troops have found a bond in mugs of tea. The Greeks can be distinguished by their mushroom-shaped helmets.
Photo, British Official: Crown Copyright

The Greek soldiers in the photograph below are among those who took part in the heroic stand against the Italian invaders. They are holding a sandbagged position on the frontier. Against a fresh Italian advance the Greeks would have a much more favourable line to hold.
Photo, Keystone

THE ITALIAN FAILURE to overrun Greece in a few days, was minimized by releasing photographs for publication showing the immense difficulties of the advance; one of these photos of transport sunk in mud, is reproduced above. The Italian propaganda, however, declared that, all the same, the advance was "proceeding according to schedule."
Photo, Associated Press

Besides airmen and aircraft, British aid to Greece has included anti-aircraft guns and their crews who have already had practice in the Middle East. Left, one of the guns is in action and Greek soldiers stand by to watch the excellent marksmanship of the gunners.
Photo, British Official: Crown Copyright

Britain Helps to Hit the Italians Hard

BRITISH TROOPS IN GREECE received a splendid welcome when they arrived in that country at the beginning of November 1940. All Greece was jubilant at Britain's prompt fulfilment of her guarantee of aid. Here is a British mechanized unit passing through a Greek town, watched by enthusiastic sightseers.   *Photos, British Official : Crown Copyright*

part were sustained by political fervour. Most of the Italians taken prisoner made a very poor showing compared with the Greeks. They cringed and crawled before their captors as if expecting some particularly harsh treatment, and it was with almost ludicrous alacrity that they saluted every Greek they saw, whether officer or private. Man for man the Greeks were obviously far superior, and if it were not for the comparative poorness of Greek equipment, their victory might have been presaged from the outset. The Greeks were particularly weak in mechanized transport, and Arthur Merton, Special Correspondent of the " Daily Telegraph " with the Greek forces in the field, spoke of seeing the Greeks' guns drawn by farm tractors, of bullock carts laden with supplies and of bakers' carts drawn by old horses crawling along behind the marching columns. A high Greek officer told him that if only they had 100 more modern army vehicles, they would have been able to follow up the retreating Italians much more closely and to inflict even greater losses upon them instead of losing contact with them be-

cause of the speed with which they made off.

Gradually, however, the Greek deficiencies in material were remedied, as large quantities of Italian war material fell into their hands. Soon, scores of Italian trucks were employed in transporting captured war material to the Greek dumps, and it was quite common to see donkeys trudging along the mountain paths, heavily laden with Italian rifles or boxes of cartridges. Sometimes the donkeys were in tow by Greek soldiers riding Italian bicycles.

That far greater and more vital deficiency, the lack of aircraft, was remedied by the R.A.F., which gave the Greeks invaluable assistance. It was not long before Valona and Durazzo were both practically untenable as bases, and the Italians were reported to be using the anchorage—it is no more—of San Giovanni di Medua, in the extreme north of Albania. Then of the air combats, we may take as typical that of November 28, when a small patrol of British fighter aircraft encountered 20 fighter CR 42s. Our aircraft at once attacked, and in less than a minute seven Italian aircraft were shot down !

Here is an Evzone (kilted Greek soldier) in his picturesque uniform, talking to a genial, bearded Italian prisoner.

Britain's Railwaymen Are Fighting Through

In their bombing attacks on London and the provinces the Nazis hope so to block and hamper the lines of communication that there will be a complete breakdown in the people's life. That breakdown has not occurred, and will not occur, thanks in large measure to the splendidly brave work of the railwaymen, some of whose deeds are recorded here.

BRITAIN's railwaymen are fighting through. Drivers and firemen, motormen and guards, signalmen, shunters, and permanent-way men, are going on duty by day and by night, and nothing that the raiders can do has been able to stop them. They have been driving trains which have been machine-gunned and bombed; they have worked the signal levers whilst bombs were actually falling and their signal boxes were on fire; they have placed trains of coal-wagons as screens and volunteered to work trains past unexploded bombs; they have fought fires in wagons of ammunition and explosives in the most imminent danger. They have inspected the tracks during night air attacks and have searched for unexploded bombs so that the train services may be rapidly restored. These are just a few of the ways in which British railwaymen have shown, and are showing, their mettle.

In numerous cases incendiary bombs have been attacked and extinguished by railwaymen, and in one instance as many as ten of these bombs were dealt with by one man. In another case hundreds of incendiary bombs, with some high explosive bombs, were dropped on a railway siding; wagons were set on fire in all directions, but the staff, with a total disregard for their personal safety, worked for several hours putting out the fires and moving the wagons from the danger area. A wagon of ammunition fuses on fire was unloaded and saved by a checker and his gang; a train of ammunition and petrol was promptly moved away from a blazing building by a yard inspector; and a wagon of high-explosive bombs on fire was tackled by a shunter who with other men removed a sheet and the topmost layer of bombs, which by that time were quite hot.

Following an attack at a large goods centre the foreman, assisted by members of the staff, successfully evacuated some 50 horses and assisted in putting out fires which had broken out; action was taken at the same time to remove blazing wagons to prevent the fires spreading. At another goods station more than 80 horses were removed after incendiary bombs had dropped.

An engine-driver and fireman who were sheltering under the wheels of the tender of their engine when it was struck by a bomb, climbed back on to the footplate, flooded the boiler to reduce steam pressure, and extinguished the fire by means of the injector hose pipe and ballast thrown into the firebox, thus preventing the explosion of the boiler. All the time further bombs were dropping.

Signal and telegraph men working near a works which was heavily attacked were without shelter, and although they were badly shaken by the explosions, and extensive damage had been caused to the permanent way and signal wires, they recommenced work immediately the danger was past, and temporarily restored main line telegraph circuits.

Nor are these acts confined to the men on the trains and on the tracks; the captains of railway steamers who brought their ships crowded with refugees safely to port under fire, and men like the ship's officer who picked up a large bomb which fell on the deck and threw it overboard just in time—it exploded immediately on reaching the water—typify the fine courage shown in the railway marine departments.

Railwaymen at the docks continue to work in spite of enemy action, so that essential war supplies and foodstuffs are landed and transported. A coal-shipping foreman put out nine incendiary bombs which fell in the neighbourhood of an unexploded bomb; piermasters, dockgatemen and members of the docks staff put out fires with a trailer pump whilst bombs were dropping; and when a bomb fell into the hold of a ship, two dock-checkers, with the help of a crane driver who stuck to his post, lowered stretchers through the fumes into the hold, with the result that the whole of the casualties were removed within twenty minutes.

Railway clerks are also showing commendable calmness in carrying on their duties and in quickly adapting themselves to meet emergencies. On a recent occasion a goods clerk when off duty was awakened at 2.50 a.m. by the pilot of a British aircraft which had fallen across the railway lines. The clerk opened up the station office, made contact with the

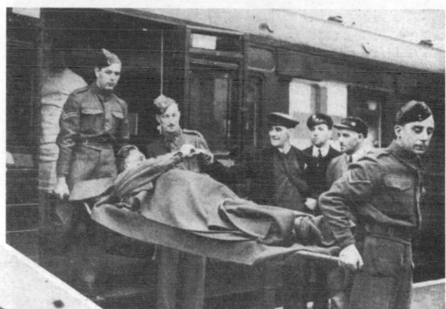

RAILWAYS have made ample provision for dealing with casualties, for on all of them there are well-equipped ambulance trains. The wounded are looked after on the train by Red Cross nurses and R.A.M.C. orderlies, but the train crews show their sympathy with a cheery word and a "fag."

EVACUEE CHILDREN are interested in the engine-driver and fireman of the train that are to take them from sorely-tried London to the safety of the countryside. Many of the children, girls as well as boys, like to have a look at the locomotive that is taking them to safety.

Photos, Keystone

Magnificent Work in Keeping the Lines Open

ROOF SPOTTING on the railways is an arduous task. On the vigilance and timely warning of those employed at the great London railway stations the safety of many hundreds of people may depend. High up above the metals of an L.M.S station a roof-spotter scans the sky with his binoculars; he puts safety first, but the smooth working of traffic is an ever-present concern.

THE SOUTHERN RAILWAY before the war employed a weed-killer train that sprayed the permanent way and kept it as neat as a garden path. Now the train has been converted into a fire-engine to deal with embankment fires that might mark the track at night. Manned by six fully-trained fire fighters, it can spray a fire for two-and-a-half hours without refilling.
Photos, Keystone and Planet News

railway control office, the aerodrome and the police, and took his station-master to the site, so enabling the line to be cleared quickly. Another clerk at a suburban station was thrown across the booking-hall when three bombs dropped beside the station at 5.50 p.m.; although bruised and suffering from shock he remained on duty until after midnight helping to clear up tickets and books, and was again on duty at 9.0 a.m. the following day. Yet another clerk, who was on duty in the early hours of the morning when bombs fell and fires started, carried current books and records to safety, and gave assistance in putting out the fires although the station was a target for further bombs. A high sense of duty was also displayed during a period of intense activity by a restaurant-car attendant whose calm courage whilst a train was passing through a danger-zone allayed the alarm of passengers and enabled tea to be served without a hitch.

But perhaps most deserving of a " special mention " are the railway engineering staffs, who are always on the alert for instant action night and day carrying out the work of repairing damage caused to the railways by air attacks.

Splendid Work of Engineers

They have effected some remarkably speedy repairs, as the following examples show :

During the course of an air raid a large calibre bomb fell on a viaduct carrying eight railway lines. It passed through the crown of an arch and exploded underneath. The force of the explosion formed a crater about 50 ft. by 30 ft. and seriously shattered and displaced the remainder of the arch. The two adjoining arches with the supporting piers were also damaged badly. After a test two lines were opened for urgent traffic. Timber-work was constructed by gangs working day and night to support the damaged masonry and the space beneath the arches was filled with well-packed quarry refuse and stone clippings, watered and tamped to ensure consolidation. Concrete and brickwork retaining walls were built to keep in the filling, and thus a length of viaduct was converted into a solid embankment. Eighteen days afterwards two further tracks were opened and six days later two additional lines were brought into use, the remaining tracks being again available soon afterwards.

On one occasion bombs had destroyed 100 yards of track in the West of England. In spite of continued air raids, a staff of 60 relayers got busy on the job. Materials were rushed to the site by 7.30 p.m. By 8.45 p.m. the up line was repaired and reopened, and by 11.15 p.m. the down line was restored by men who had been on duty 17 hours. Meanwhile, a trainload of passengers had been transferred to an emergency road service and had resumed their journeys with a delay of 2½ hours. At the conclusion of this race against time to restore the tracks—one of many such—one of the men said, " That's one for Hitler, anyway ! "

In another instance a crater 50 ft. by 20 ft. blocked all lines leading to a vital area. Within eight hours tons of debris were removed, damaged rails, sleepers, fishplates, and screws were replaced, and three tracks

Things to Remember when the Train is Late

were reopened again. Elsewhere, a bomb dropped on a carriage-shed where a fire-fighting train was stationed. Within half an hour a clear passage was made for the train by permanent-way engineers and plate-layers, after which other damage was speedily put right.

Early one morning a bridge carrying four railway tracks was damaged by a bomb, putting one section of the track out of service. Reserve buses maintained the connexions whilst railway engineers decided upon a plan of action. High-tension cables were moved and entrenched, a new crossover 200 ft. long was built, and the automatic signalling over two miles of track was reversed, with the result that the train services were restored by 6 p.m. the next day.

During another raid a signal box was destroyed by fire. A new box was necessary, and a temporary structure 31 ft. long, 8 ft. wide, and 7 ft. high was built complete with a new stairway—the floor involved threading the joists through the signal levers—and all the steelwork in the supporting girders was stripped, red-leaded, and repaired within 17½ hours. In yet another instance a direct hit by a bomb on the negative rail of an electric line, as a result of which several lengths of rail were buckled, the conductor rail displaced, and sleepers were smashed, was restored within 6 hours.

Bombs dropped on a railway line and damaged the platforms and tracks at a station. All lines were affected, but the station reopened for traffic in 12 hours.

A bomb fell on a main line making a crater 50 ft. in diameter under the running lines. A brick retaining wall supporting the line was blown into a cutting, blocking one line. Certain lines were cleared in 5 hours, others by the end of the day, and the whole of the tracks were opened inside three days.

Night and Day They Are Ready

Charts, maps and drawings dealing with every detail of the railways, including bridges, tunnels, lines, signals, telephones, lighting and drainage, are consulted night and day by the engineering staffs, who follow up every report received even when bombs and fragments of anti-aircraft shells may be falling. They are showing unexampled coolness and courage in dealing with any and every emergency from bomb craters or fallen debris to unexploded bombs; and the immediate repairs which are effected enable the train services to be got going again, as nearly as possible normally.

The examples quoted go to show that the railways are well justified in their claim that they are doing their utmost to maintain the train services. Both management and men show a fine spirit of devotion to duty, and it is obvious—indeed, it is stressed on both sides—that their achievements are made possible only through the close cooperation which exists between the companies and the Railway Trade Unions in the maintenance of the railway transport services. Let us remember these things when next we experience some inconvenience when going to or from work; and let us remember, too, that if the information concerning emergency travelling facilities is on the meagre side, the publication of details of these services might give the enemy the very news that they would like to have in planning further raids.

THE PERMANENT WAY of the railways even in peacetime is constantly patrolled to see that it is in order. In the days of air raids a more careful watch must be kept. Above, a ganger is doing his daily round on a northern line; at any moment he may be called upon to take his gang for a rush job at some point that has suffered damage.

Raid or no raid the work of the parcel-sorters at the big railway stations goes on. Each parcel must be weighed, sorted, and dispatched to its proper train. The parcel-offices are generally above ground, so that all the protection that those who work in them can have is steel helmets, though the roof spotter will warn them of imminent danger.

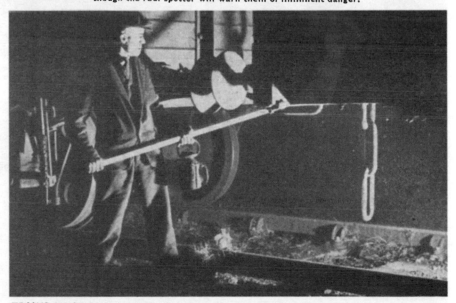

TRAINS MUST RUN has been the slogan of the railway workers, but nowhere has it been more difficult to carry out than in the marshalling-yards of the great goods depots. Even in peacetime, when the yards were brilliantly lighted, it was dangerous work. It is doubly so now that the shunters have to do their work by the light of lanterns. *Photos, "News Chronicle" and Fox*

Chelsea Pensioners in the Wars Again

CHELSEA ROYAL HOSPITAL, home of the famous Chelsea Pensioners, suffered damage as the result of one of the intensive night raids on London by the enemy. The Royal Hospital, which was founded during the reign of Charles II, was designed by Sir Christopher Wren and opened in 1694. This well-known institution was one of the first of its kind for old and disabled soldiers left alone in the world. The Hospital accommodates about 550 " in-pensioners " as distinguished from " out-pensioners." There is also accommodation for six officers, who are known as Captains of Invalids.

CHELSEA PENSIONER, H. A. Rattray, circle, aged one hundred, was in the Hospital when it was bombed, but the Nazis could not subdue his spirits. Result of bomb damage is seen above. A hole was torn in the wall of one of the buildings, causing damage to all five floors.

SIR CHRISTOPHER WREN'S GREAT HALL has not been used since the 17th century for dining, the purpose for which the great architect intended it. Since the Hospital was bombed, however, pensioners now take their meals in this handsome Hall, looked down upon by the portraits of many famous soldiers. Some of the pensioners are seen above waiting for their meals to be served.

Photos, G.P.U., Planet News, " News Chronicle "

Despite Nazi Attacks Britain's Air Strength Grows

By fierce and desperate attacks on our production centres the Luftwaffe tried to stem the rising tide of Britain's aerial expansion, but without serious check to that steady growth which they fear. Then they turned again on London, still carrying on its manifold activities undaunted by three months of indiscriminate bombing.

THOUGH the Nazis claimed that their heavy bombing of Coventry and other Midland towns was in reprisal for British attacks on Munich and other German centres, the true motive was not by any means so naive and simple. Alarmed by the steady and rapid increase in Britain's aerial strength, which by now was approaching parity with their own, the Nazis switched over the air assault from London—where months of continued bombing had left civilian morale virtually untouched and had done insignificant military damage—to certain centres of aircraft production in the Midlands, the South and the West. Here, though, of course, production was hindered to some extent, nothing was done to check in any serious degree the flow of aircraft and munitions to our Air Force. Bombs were merely unloaded on to any large or prominent target, and in the process of hitting some few real military objectives a whole host of much less important buildings were destroyed—less important, that is, to war effort.

Some of the wildness of the Luftwaffe's aim can be attributed to mere wantonness. It seems probable that the Germans were not well prepared for precision bombing by the approach method, which with some types at least of their bomb-sights would be extremely difficult. Probably the Nazis expected to be able to smash our Air Force and ground defences, and then to bomb our cities unhindered at low levels. For important targets which needed precise aim they would rely on their dive-bombers. These schemes went agley, thanks to the indomitable courage and brilliant skill of our fighter pilots, and so mass attacks with bombers by daylight were abandoned as fruitless, and the scale of daylight raids was reduced. But on Saturday, Nov. 30, the Nazis returned to their earlier tactics and made strong attempts to reach London in daylight with numbers of their fighter-bombers. Three of the enemy were shot down. and although two of our machines were lost the pilots were saved. As usual, most of the raiders were dispersed soon after crossing the coast and only a small number got through to the capital.

By night also the attack on London was intensified again towards the end of the month, and on Friday, Nov. 29, from an early hour of the evening until about midnight, there were widespread and continuous raids on the Metropolitan and Home Counties areas. Many incendiary bombs were dropped besides high explosives, and a German news agency stated that 36,000 of the former and 400 tons of H.E. bombs had been used " by several hundred 'planes."

In the earlier part of the week the enemy raids varied a good deal. Four day raiders were destroyed on Tuesday : two bombers and two fighter-bombers. On the previous afternoon two other enemy aircraft had been shot down in the Channel—one a patrolling seaplane which the Germans used to rescue their airmen who baled out from damaged aircraft. It was escorted by eight Messerschmitts, which did nothing to protect it but made off for France at great speed.

Eleven raiders, flying at a height of between three and four miles, were destroyed on Wednesday over Kent. One Spitfire squadron

BRISTOL has been one of the towns to suffer heavily in the new Nazi policy of bombing the industrial centres at random. Several churches, the University, a museum, and an art school were bombed. One church in the suburbs was practically destroyed, as can be seen.
Photos, " Daily Mirror " and " News Chronicle "

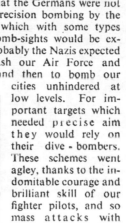

SOUTHAMPTON was one of the towns selected by the Luftwaffe on which to wreak their savage spite, for it had been attacked before the big raid of November 30, 1940. Most of the damage was once more done in residential districts, and many householders were forced to leave their homes and pile their furniture on the pavement.

Our Bombers and Fighters Harass the Italians

H.M.S. LONDONDERRY, a British escort ship of 990 tons, did some successful shooting while she was on convoy duty in November. Enemy 'planes attacked the convoy and a Junkers bomber was brought down ; the gun crew received the congratulations of the captain of their ship, Commander J. S. Dalison, R.N.

Photo, British Official : Crown Copyright

was responsible for seven of the enemy, and within a quarter of an hour all the Germans had turned back. On Thursday six enemy aircraft were shot down and the R.A.F. lost seven, the pilot of one of our machines being saved. Major Helmuth Wieck, leader of the Richthofen squadron, was among the pilots shot down by the R.A.F. on Thursday. The German report claimed that Wieck had shot down " his 56th enemy aircraft." He is stated to have baled out but came down in the Channel. In Friday's fighting five Nazi machines were destroyed—four single bombers shot down in the Channel and one Messerschmitt off Dungeness. Two of our machines were lost, but not their pilots.

On Saturday night Southampton had its worst raid, which lasted seven hours. First the attack was made with fire bombs and then high explosives were dropped to widen the area of destruction. The centre of the town was deliberately bombed on this occasion, and churches, theatres, cinemas and hotels, with many other large buildings, were set on fire. So intense was the glare from the many fires that a newspaper could be read out of doors. On Sunday night again Southampton bore the full brunt of the Nazi terror. Flares were dropped and then incendiaries, followed later by high explosive bombs. One district was attacked with machine-guns.

As a result of these two nights of terror, thousands were rendered homeless and wide areas were laid waste. Considering all things, the casualties (about 370) were light.

Five enemy aircraft were brought down on Saturday and eight destroyed in Sunday's daylight operations.

London had a peaceful night on Monday, Dec 2, for the Nazi bombers were busy raiding Bristol. Beginning soon after dusk the attack was carried on until nearly midnight. Indiscriminately the enemy bombed large buildings and the dwellings of the workers. A children's hospital was set on fire. Another town in the S.W. was raided for the seventh successive night, but the A.A. guns made such good shooting that no bombs were dropped in the area.

Throughout the week the R.A.F. in Greece collaborated with the land forces in pursuing the retreating Italians, bombing supply columns and checking the flow of reinforcements. Ten enemy aircraft were shot down during Wednesday and Thursday by R.A.F. fighters. Raids were made on Valona, Santi Quaranta, Durazzo and Elbasan. The harbour of Valona on the Straits of Otranto is specially important to Italy, for across the fifty-mile-wide channel come the transports and food ships to maintain her forces in Albania. Dominance of the port by our aircraft would paralyse those forces ; capture of Valona by the Greek and British arms might lead to combined operations in which our Mediterranean Fleet could take a hand.

An R.A.F. bomber, after being badly holed by A.A. shells, managed to land on the 20-feet-wide shore of a small Greek island. Here the crew were bombed eight times in a single day, but got across to the mainland and eventually by walking and travelling by car and train made their way back to their base—where they had been reported " missing, believed killed."

During this same active period our naval aircraft bombed Port Laki in the Dodecanese island of Leros, and also Tripoli in Libya. In each case damage was done to enemy ships. On Thursday night Brindisi in Italy was heavily attacked by R.A.F. aircraft and much damage done to fuel tanks, the arsenal, railway station and quays.

Caught in the barrage during the British pursuit of the Italian fleet, according to a report from Vichy, M. Chiappe (former Paris Prefect of Police) was killed on Wednesday when the aeroplane taking him to his new post as High Commissioner in Syria was shot down south of Sardinia, an accident that may have unfortunate results for the Pétain government's hold on Syria.

Another facet of the many-sided work of the Royal Air Force is shown by an incident in the Channel when H.M. destroyer " Javelin " was slowly making her way home after a brush with the enemy's light forces on Friday, in which she had been disabled by a torpedo. Repeated attacks by Nazi aircraft were frustrated by patrolling R.A.F. machines ; a Dornier 17, a Junkers 88, and another Dornier were shot down by our Spitfires, and later another Junkers 88 was badly mauled and sent limping away. " Javelin " got safely to port.

The GREEK AIR FORCE, though small in numbers and with but few 'planes of modern design, has shown the same indomitable pluck as the Greek Army and held its own against superior enemy air forces until it was reinforced by the R.A.F. Here formidable missiles are being loaded on a twin-engine bomber to harass the retreating Italians.

Photo, Sport and General

The Royal Air Force Now Plays its Part in Greece

HELP FOR GREECE in fulfilment of the Prime Minister's promise of " all possible aid " materialized when men and machines of the R.A.F. arrived to take part in the good work of bombing the Italians. The ground staff arrived by sea, and in the top photograph a contingent has just disembarked at a Greek port from a British warship. Below, officers of the R.A.F. who have flown to a Greek aerodrome are unloading their kit. These photographs are among the first showing the R.A.F. in Greece (R.A.F.G.) to arrive in this country.

Photos, British Official : Crown Copyright

Cagliari Was a Resounding British Victory

Another smashing blow was delivered at Italy's Navy on November 27, when Vice-Admiral
Somerville intercepted a large force of enemy ships off Sardinia. But more important
than the damage inflicted on the vessels themselves was the effect of the enforced withdrawal from Taranto on the Italian communications with Albania and Libya.

FOLLOWING the smashing attack made by the dive-bombers of the Fleet Air Arm on Italian warships in Taranto Harbour on the night of November 11-12, the Italian Naval Command—which is probably only another name for Mussolini—seems to have decided that Taranto was too hot for them. So most of the ships which had escaped damage put out to sea, sailed round the toe of the Italian boot, and headed towards the Tyrrhenian Sea.

But they were soon stopped. The British Fleet was also at sea, and soon after 10 o'clock on the morning of Wednesday, November 27, our forces, operating westwards of Sardinia, received reports from their reconnaissance aircraft that enemy forces, consisting of two battleships and a large number of cruisers and destroyers, were at sea about 75 miles to the north-eastwards.

At once the British ships increased to full speed, and altered course in the hope of bringing the enemy to action. A few minutes after noon, four enemy cruisers were sighted, hull down, over the horizon, and at 12.21 p.m. our advanced light units opened fire. The enemy cruisers replied, but hardly had they discharged their first salvo when they turned away and retired to the north-eastward at high speed, throwing out a smoke screen as they ran.

Half an hour later two enemy battleships—one, the "Vittorio Veneto," one of the newest and most powerful in the world, and one of the Cavour class—accompanied by cruisers, were sighted, and they opened fire on the British cruisers. These were forced by the much heavier metal of the enemy to make a slight turn away, but within a few minutes the enemy battleships themselves turned away, and our cruisers at once resumed their pursuit of the Italian cruisers.

The British slower units rapidly fell astern, but now the twenty-three-year-old battle-cruiser "Renown" (Captain C. E. B. Simeon, R.N.), flying the flag of Vice-Admiral Sir James Somerville, rushed ahead, doing her utmost to bring the enemy's heavy ships to action. Such was the speed at which the enemy retired, however, that by 1.10 p.m. the chase, having been carried to within a few miles of the enemy's coast, was abandoned. By this time the enemy had scattered, but they were followed up by our reconnaissance 'planes, and it was revealed that one cruiser, believed to be of the eight-inch gun type, was seriously on fire aft; one destroyer of the Grecale class seemed to be down by the stern, listing heavily and stopping; and another enemy destroyer was listing slightly and losing way.

Repeatedly, during the pursuit and afterwards, aircraft of the Fleet Air Arm launched from H.M.S. "Ark Royal" (Captain C. S. Holland, R.N.) attacked. One force of the Swordfish aircraft delivered a torpedo attack on enemy battleships, and one torpedo was

bombed a formation of three six-inch gun cruisers of the Condottieri class, one of which was damaged in the boiler room.

Our aircraft returned safely from these operations, and the only ship hit of the British units engaged was H.M.S. "Berwick" (Captain G. L. Warren, R.N.), which received two hits. One officer and six ratings were killed and nine ratings wounded, but the damage done to the ship itself was slight.

At 2.35 p.m. the British forces were attacked by ten enemy bombers, escorted by fighters, but the attack was frustrated by the fighters of the Fleet Air Arm. At 4.40 p.m. enemy aircraft came over again—15 bombers in three waves—and though the fighters of the Fleet Air Arm beat off most of the raiders, some of the enemy aircraft succeeded in attacking H.M.S. "Ark Royal," which disappeared from sight between splashes from about 30 bombs falling close to her. The great ship emerged from the spray, however, with all her guns firing

VICE - ADMIRAL SIR JAMES SOMERVILLE (below) commanded the squadron which put the Italian Navy to flight off Sardinia on November 27. He it was who prevented the French warships at Oran from escaping on July 3, 1940. Right, the anchor chain of his flagship, H.M.S. "Renown," is being brought in board.

furiously, having sustained neither damage nor casualties. After the action Admiral Somerville sent a special message to Captain Holland. "I wish to congratulate you and your ship's company," he said, "on the magnificent and resolute way in which you carried out your reconnaissance duties. As for the bombing, it was an inspiring sight to see the 'Ark Royal' emerge from a complete curtain of water, with every gun blazing efficiently. I am proud of you."

One British fighter did not return from intercepting the enemy bombers, but two Italian planes were disposed of—one Cant Z 506 three-engined float 'plane, and one RO 43 float 'plane.

Once again, then, the Italian Fleet had more than met its match in the Mediterranean. Now it was reported to be in the harbour of Cagliari, in southern Sardinia—a port which can hardly appear to be a safer sanctuary than Taranto. But much more important is the fact that in withdrawing his ships from Taranto and Southern Italy, Mussolini has not only uncovered the Adriatic, for only some light units are maintained at Brindisi and Bari, but laid open his communications with Libya.

observed to hit the "Vittorio Veneto." Another Swordfish force attacked three eight-inch gun cruisers; the rear ship, a 10,000-ton ship of the Bolzano class, was almost certainly hit by a torpedo, and the leading ship of the formation was observed to have reduced speed immediately after this attack. Then a force of Skuas dive-

H.M.S. "BERWICK" was the only ship of the British force in action off Sardinia to sustain damage. She received two hits, but no vital part was struck and she was not rendered unfit for service. The "Berwick" is a 10,000-ton cruiser of the Kent class, completed in 1926, but with the others of her type she was reconstructed in 1935-38.

Photos, Wide World, Lafayette and Topical

New Machines Will Add to Fleet Air Arm Glories

Each Pilot makes away in his own particular fashion after firing Torpedo

Plane taking evasive action before the Attack

Navigator-Observer releasing Torpedo

Torpedo must strike Water dead in line with Target

Act of releasing Torpedo starts Internal Mechanism working. Course & Depth have been set already.

Taking aim

HAWORTH

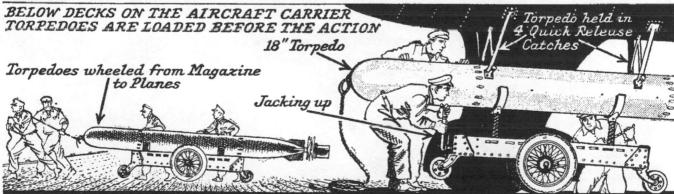

BELOW DECKS ON THE AIRCRAFT CARRIER TORPEDOES ARE LOADED BEFORE THE ACTION

Torpedo held in 4 Quick Release Catches

18" Torpedo

Torpedoes wheeled from Magazine to Planes

Jacking up

THE FLEET AIR ARM, after months of fine but unadvertised work, won fame and glory at Taranto on Nov. 11 and in the action off Sardinia on Nov. 27, 1940. In those two actions the torpedoing was carried out chiefly by Fairey Swordfish aircraft, but lately a new and improved type of torpedo-carrying 'plane, the Fairey Albacore (see page 564), which has been put into service, adds considerably to the striking power of aircraft carriers. This diagram indicates the method of attack and of the carrying and launching of the torpedo. It strikes the water with the tremendous impetus, some 300 miles an hour, given it by the speed of the machine. The Fairey Albacore can be used also as a dive-bomber or for general reconnaissance. To carry the 500-lb. weight of an 18-in. torpedo the 'plane is quite big —50 ft. in length and sturdily built, being all

metal except for the fabric covering of the wings. The Bristol-Taurus sleeve-valve engine gives 1,050 h.p. Its small size allows the pilot a clear view.

The Machine in Action

The 'planes are stored below decks with wings folded backwards. There the torpedoes are wheeled from the magazines on trolleys and jacked up to the fastening gear on the 'planes. The machine-guns are loaded and the 'planes raised to the flight deck in huge lifts. The crews climb aboard. On expeditions such as those of Taranto and the Sardinian Sea, there is usually only one observer, who navigates for all—the rest of the 'planes, to save weight, carry only pilot and rear gunner (who releases the torpedo). When the 'planes are taking off the huge aircraft carrier forges ahead into the wind to give them some help. Once away from the ship the navigator must find his own way without

using wireless, which would disclose the position of the ship. This needs high skill, for the flight may take four or five hours—he does it by dead reckoning.

The Aerial Torpedo Attack

The planes usually take evasive action to confuse the enemy gunners ; sometimes smoke screens are laid first. To drop the torpedo the 'plane comes down to 150 ft. or less, in order to prevent the mechanism which keeps the torpedo at a given distance beneath the surface being damaged as the torpedo strikes the water. As the 'plane swoops low over the water at about 1,000 yards from, and in line with, its target the rear gunner releases the torpedo, which speeds towards its mark, and the pilot must then extricate himself as best he can.

Specially drawn for THE WAR ILLUSTRATED *by Haworth*

To the Rescue of Our Animal Friends C

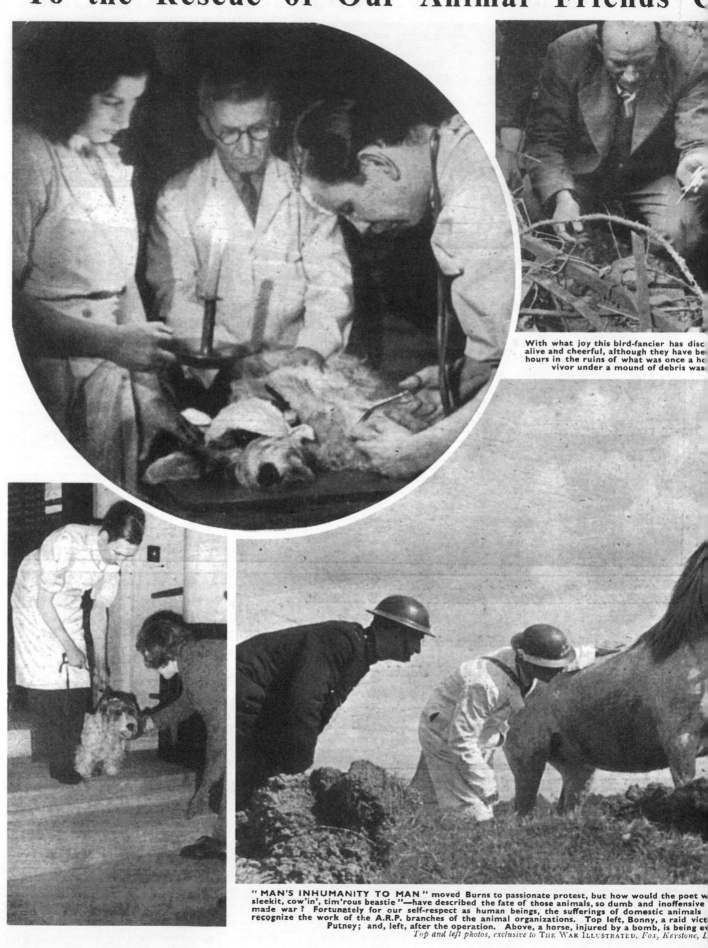

With what joy this bird-fancier has disc
alive and cheerful, although they have be
hours in the ruins of what was once a h
vivor under a mound of debris was

" MAN'S INHUMANITY TO MAN " moved Burns to passionate protest, but how would the poet w
sleekit, cow'in', tim'rous beastie "—have described the fate of those animals, so dumb and inoffensive
made war ? Fortunately for our self-respect as human beings, the sufferings of domestic animals
recognize the work of the A.R.P. branches of the animal organizations. Top left, Bonny, a raid vict
Putney; and, left, after the operation. Above, a horse, injured by a bomb, is being ev

Top and left photos, exclusive to THE WAR ILLUSTRATED. *Fox, Keystone, L*

in the Flaming Fury of Man-made War

rs still
an ten
ge sur-

tifully of a field-mouse—" Wee,
in all the flaming fury of man-
oticed, and we must gratefully
n table of a R.S.P.C.A. clinic at
d for treatment.

More than 7,000 animals have been rescued by the mobile sur-
geries of the Peoples' Dispensary for Sick Animals; above, a terrier
retrieved from a wrecked house. The Rev. J. N. Sykes (left), a
Stepney vicar, has built a shelter for bombed-out cats; here
they are kept safe until they can be collected by the **Dumb
Friends' League.**

Under the Nazis 'Poland Has Forgotten Laughter'

More than a year has passed since the fighting in Poland, but war is still proceeding
within what were once its bounds—between the Nazi overlords and the people who,
if the conquerors have their way, are doomed to be slaves in the land of their fathers.

CHOPIN's works, his preludes and nocturnes, his mazurkas and polonaises, must no longer be performed in Poland. Zeromski's novels and Henryk Sienkiewicz's, in particular those which tell of the dramatic conflict between Slav and Teuton, have been removed from the public libraries and booksellers are forbidden to show them. The gramme of radium which was given by American women to Mme. Curie, who in turn gave it to the Radium Institute in Warsaw, has been taken away to Germany. For Chopin, Zeromski, Sienkiewicz and Mme. Curie were all Poles; and nothing must be left in Poland which might serve to remind its unhappy people that their race has produced men and women of whom the whole world might well be, and is, proud, and that only a short time ago they, a free and happy people, were enjoying the fruits of an age-old culture and were living in peace in their own land.

From the very first day of their invasion the Germans have aimed at the complete destruction of the Polish nation, and now for a year and more they have been engaged in carrying it out with systematic cruelty and deadly efficiency. The campaign in which they overran the country was ruthless in the extreme, but the methods they have employed since the end of hostilities are no less ruthless and even more barbarous. Without the slightest appearance of legality they have imprisoned and killed thousands of men and women; they have expropriated and evicted from their homes and lands hundreds of thousands of innocent folk; and they are now engaged in deliberately starving out millions of people.

Provinces which are overwhelmingly Polish in their character have been incorporated in the Reich. The language of their inhabitants is Polish, the place-names are Polish, the architecture of the churches and houses, the national memorials, the title-deeds of property—all testify to their Polish character. Yet these provinces are now being subjected to rigid and complete Germanization. Place-names are being changed into German: thus Gdynia, that supreme achievement of Polish post-war town planning, is to be known henceforth as Gotenhafen. National and local records are being destroyed; public and private libraries and art collections are being transferred to the Reich; national monuments of one kind or another have been destroyed. Even the Reststaat, that portion of central Poland about Warsaw which was given a kind of fictitious autonomy under a Governor-General, has now been incorporated in the Reich.

"The Fuehrer has decided," Governor Frank announced on August 15, "that the Reststaat is not to be regarded as occupied territory, but is to form an integral part of the area under the rule of Greater Germany. In this area the German National Socialist party is building up its bastion for all time. The Polish nation is again just as it was 700 years ago, under the protective rule of the German nation. Henceforth, the Vistula will remain an East German river."

'Never Again a Polish State'

"Polish schools may continue," went on Frank; "we shall also permit the printing of Polish newspapers and we shall treat loyally those Polish officials who are loyal. But I warn you against any attempt at opposition. . . I demand from the Poles that they perform labour service for the community, and in exchange I offer them the security of their lives and property, and cultural development. There will never be a Polish state again."

Under the rule of Germany, it is all too clear, Poland is destined to become a nation of slaves—one which will not be allowed to develop its own civilization, its own religion, science and art, because such activities, intellectual and spiritual, increase moral strength. Slaves must be kept in ignorance; and so not only have the universities and high schools been closed, or at least thoroughly Germanized, but listening-in to the wireless has been forbidden, the theatres are shut, and the cinemas show only German propaganda films. Even the publication of Polish books has been prohibited, and Polish newspapers, in spite of Frank's promise, remain suppressed.

Yet Frank is reported to have informed neutral newspapermen that Poland under the German administration is highly prosperous, and that the majority of the Polish people are cheerfully cooperating with the German administration, being more than pleased at having been delivered by the German government from "playing the part of England's flunkey . . ."

"Listening to these cynical lies"—we are now quoting from a statement made by Polish women in a document which was smuggled out of Poland and published in America by the Committee of Polish-American Women on November 27—"we tremble lest the world might believe them. This hell is all around us. It is smothering us and we are its hopeless victims. History fails to record a Calvary such as that which we women of Poland are living through now. We are suffering as Catholics and as Poles, as mothers, as wives, as sisters and as daughters.

"We are living in hell," the document goes on. "Our husbands, brothers, and fathers have perished in mass murders which have wiped out tens of thousands. They die slowly in dungeons or perish from starvation and cold in war prisoners'' camps. Our sons—the future and pride of the nation—have either perished like their fathers—boys of 12 and 14 were by no means lacking among those who were shot—or are registered and taken away to alleged labour camps in Germany, whence there is no return. Our daughters—our little girls, dearest joy of our lives—are being apprehended on the streets or abducted from their homes under cover of night, imprisoned in company with prostitutes, and deported to German brothels. Crime, ruin and misery have ploughed through the length and breadth of the land. Poland has forgotten laughter.

"We endeavour not to abandon ourselves to despair," the statement concludes. "We believe in Divine justice. We have faith in the victory of the Allies and we wait the day of their triumph. Should this day be slow in arriving Poland may be free, but there will be no Poles."

THE CELEBRATION AT CRACOW on the first anniversary of German rule in Poland, on October 26, 1940, was attended by a number of the Nazi chiefs. Seated, left to right are: Otto Meissner, Franz Seldte, Adolf Hühnlein, Victor Lütze, Dr. Frank, Governor-General of Poland, Wilhelm Frick, Walter Daluege, and Herr Stuckhart.

Photo, Associated Press

They Celebrate a Year's Tyranny in Poland

A GREAT DISPLAY OF NAZI POWER was made in Cracow during the anniversary celebrations on October 26, 1940, one feature being a march past of the military police, whose duty has been the terrorization of the Polish people. The Governor-General, Dr. Frank, accompanied by the guests of honour, seen in the opposite page, is here watching the parade. The goose-step is absent, but the Prussian eagle is much in evidence.

Photo, Associated Press

Aden: Britain's Other—and Lesser—Gibraltar

Always a vitally important link in the chain of Imperial communications, Aden possesses an added importance today from the fact that it is the nearest British stronghold to the Italian possessions in East Africa. In this article something is said of the colony's present state, and of its remarkable development to one of the great ports and fortresses of the world.

ONE of the hottest and driest places on the face of the globe—and one of the strongest. That is Aden, Britain's colony at the entrance to the Red Sea, which is sometimes compared to Gibraltar.

There is some natural resemblance between the two, for Aden, like Gibraltar, consists of little more than a big rock, joined by a narrow isthmus of sand to the mainland. Like Gibraltar, too, it is practically barren, and for its water it has to depend on cisterns and imported supplies. Then, too, it is a fortress; but, despite the improvements made in recent years, it can hardly rival in this

failed to carry out the bargain, and so, on January 16, 1839, naval and military forces under Capt. James Haines captured the town and annexed it to the dominions of Queen Victoria: it was the first of the innumerable additions to British territory which her reign was to see. Soon afterwards the Red Sea route to India was developed, and Aden began to enjoy an altogether new prosperity. It was made a coaling station for the new steamships of the P. & O. Line, and when the Suez Canal was opened in 1869 its growth was still more rapid. In due course, too, a flourishing trade was developed with the Arab principalities and tribes of the interior and along the coast.

But its commercial importance is overshadowed in these days by its strategical. It is one of the key bases of Britain's naval power—one of the chain which begins at Dover, runs through Gibraltar, Malta and Alexandria on the one hand, and to Singapore and

One of the 'planes at an aerodrome in Aden, first established as an R.A.F. Command in 1928, and now a base for attacks on Italian East Africa, is ready to take off at any moment.

Hongkong on the other. For many years it was an outlying territory of the Indian Empire, governed from Bombay, but since April 1, 1937, it has been a Crown Colony—Britain's youngest colony, although, as we have seen, it has been British for rather more than a century. It is under the control of a Governor and Commander-in-Chief, who is responsible to the Colonial Office. The present Governor is Mr. Hathorn Hall, who succeeded Sir Bernard Reilly last October.

The area of the Colony is only 75 square miles, but the Aden Protectorate, stretching to west and east for some 700 miles along the southern coast of Arabia and up-country to a depth of about 100 miles, covers about 112,000 sq. miles and comprises the territories and dependencies of a number of Arab chiefs, who have treaties of alliance with H.M. Government. The eastern part of the Protectorate is known as the Hadramaut, and consists of rich and fertile valleys ruled over by various sultans and emirs. Then the island of Sokotra, 70 miles by 20, which lies 150 miles from Cape Guardafui on the African coast, and 220 from the southern coast of Arabia, is also included within the Protectorate. Sokotra is peopled by a mixture of negroes, Arabs and Indians, fisherfolk and pastoralists for the most part, living on their catches and the produce of their sheep, cows and goats, and was formally annexed by Britain in 1886.

Another little island included in the Aden Protectorate is Perim, 97 miles west of Aden in the Strait of Bab-el-Mandeb; it is at the very entrance of the Red Sea, one-and-a-half miles from the Arabian shore and nine from the African. Tiny as it is—its area is only 5 square miles—it has a deep and spacious

respect the great stronghold at the farther side of Europe. On the other hand, the danger of an attack from the land, at least, is far smaller than in the case of Gibraltar, for behind Aden is a vast and dreary waste of desert, inhabited by wandering tribes of Arabs—most of whom find it convenient, not to say profitable, to keep on good terms with the British.

Little more than a century has passed since the British first came to Aden. It was in 1837 that a ship under British colours was wrecked close to what was then a squalid little village, and the crew and passengers who struggled ashore were maltreated by the Arabs in the vicinity. The Bombay government complained to the Sultan of Sana on whose territory the outrages had been committed, whereupon the Sultan promised to make compensation for the plunder of the vessel and, moreover, to sell his town and port to the British. But the Sultan's son

In the hinterland of Aden armoured-cars and aeroplanes are of paramount importance. 'Planes have made communication easy with places previously inaccessible except by long journeys on camelback, while armoured-cars, such as the one seen above being prepared for a day's work on patrol, form an important part in the defence of this Empire outpost. *Photos, Keystone, exclusive*

Guardian of the Great Route to the East

ADEN, lying at the entrance to the Red Sea, on one of the world's principal traffic routes, has been in British occupation for rather more than a hundred years. The top photograph shows the outer harbour, facing the town and protected by the island of Sirah. Steamer Point, below, Aden's inner harbour, is on the west side of the peninsula. It is the official, residential, and commercial centre of the colony.

Photos exclusive to THE WAR ILLUSTRATED

Where Britons and Indians Keep Watch Together

harbour, and until recently was an important coaling station on the East Indian route.

Aden itself—that is, the town and its neighbourhood—has a population of some 50,000. The town is built on the eastern shore of the peninsula, in the crater of an extinct volcano, and the scenery of barren, cinder-like rocks is depressing in the extreme. As for the climate, it may be described as that of a perpetual Turkish bath. Judged by the standards of the Tropics it is by no means unhealthy, for malaria is unknown, and recently a fresh water supply has been discovered in the village of Sheikh Othmar.

For the most part, its inhabitants are Arabs and African Somalis, all speaking Arabic dialects, but there are also, of course, large numbers of military, naval and air personnel.

Aden produces little save cigarettes and salt; but it imports vast quantities of oil and petrol, cotton goods, grain, coal and foodstuffs, while amongst its exports are salt, coffee, gums, hides and skins and tobacco. But, as previously indicated, its importance is military and naval rather than commercial; certainly with its gunboats, submarines and 'planes it is an ever-present thorn in the side of Mussolini's African realm.

A bugler of an Indian regiment now at Aden sounds the réveillé. He typifies India's magnificent response to the call to arms.

ONE "AIRMAN" = 10 "GUNNERS"
INVINCIBLE
ARTILLERY
FIRST ON THE FIELD
LAST TO RETIRE

N° 2 BOMBPROOF

ADEN'S DEFENCE is shared between British and Indian troops and the R.A.F. In the top photograph a heavy machine-gun detachment of the Indian Army is at exercises in the open ground behind the town. The lower photograph shows one of the old forts, still bombproof, on the walls of which the R.A. and the R.A.F. have exchanged pleasantries, the R.A. in black paint and the R.A.F. in white.
Photos, exclusive to THE WAR ILLUSTRATED

Ninety-Nine—then it Was a Hundred!

WHEN No. 609 (West Riding) Squadron took off in their Spitfires from a southern aerodrome the score on the "bag pad" had stood at 99 for several days.

They were off to patrol at 15,000 ft., along a strip of coastline nearly 60 miles from their base. And all hoped that the Nazi fighter-bombers would come in that way, so that the squadron's score could be raised to 100—or more.

"Not a Jerry did we see," explained a flight-lieutenant later, "and we'd decided to return to our aerodrome when I heard by radio that a bomber was machine-gunning some troops 100 miles to the north.

"Detaching ourselves from the rest, I and a pilot officer who had recently joined us and had never before seen a Jerry, flew off to intercept.

SPITFIRE PILOTS of the No. 609 (West Riding) Squadron happily surveying the swastika which, as its inscription tells, was taken from their squadron's hundredth victim. Left, returning from patrol are the two Spitfires which put the Junkers 88 down.

"I looked at my map and decided that the bomber would take a certain course home and almost certainly fly low instead of wasting time gaining height.

"Down we went to about 200 ft., and presently my companion shouted over the radio in an astonished voice that a bomber had just passed beneath him.

"We swung round and gave chase. As we got near, hedge-hopping and skimming hilltops, the Nazis fired off some recognition signals to confuse us into believing they were in a British bomber, but we were close enough to see it was a Junkers 88.

"We both gave it a few bursts at short range and saw it crash near a wood and burst into flames."

The squadron's score now is 103, but their proudest possession (until the 200 mark is reached !) is a swastika from that Junkers 88, suitably inscribed to commemorate their 100th victim.

Yorkshire will be specially proud of 609's achievements (which have earned them a D.S.O. and seven D.F.C.s) because it was founded and was originally manned by Auxiliary Air Force personnel from Leeds, Halifax and other big West Riding cities.

I find that today the pilots are not all Yorkshiremen because promotions, postings and casualties have brought about many changes. The ground staff, however, are still mostly from Yorkshire.

The pilots who have contributed to the 100 bag include a journalist, a law student, a solicitor, a wool merchant, dye manufacturer, and an American who was a professional parachute jumper in private life. Several Poles have now joined the squadron.

"We reckon we've worked out the best fighting tactics of any squadron," said one of the pilots. "The trouble nowadays is that the Messerschmitt pilots will not stay to fight. And gosh ! Don't we hope we meet some of those Wops !"

Story by Geoffrey Edwards and photos by "News Chronicle" Staff Photographer Ross-White: exclusive to THE WAR ILLUSTRATED.

Two more glimpses of the famous 609 Squadron are given below. In one, a hand of cards helps to pass the time ; while, right, pilots stand at the door of the mess waiting to take off—and so have an opportunity of contributing something to their second century.

OUR SEARCHLIGHT ON THE WAR

Britain's First Air Minister

NORTHCLIFFE the journalist and Rothermere the financier—the two brothers Harmsworth between them revolutionized the Press of this country. Alfred's fame will endure as long as the " Daily Mail " continues to appear, but Harold, who died on November 26, eighteen years after

VISCOUNT ROTHERMERE, whose death occurred in Bermuda on November 26, left England last May to carry out a special mission in U.S.A. Lord Rothermere was seventy-two.
Photo, Keystone

his more famous elder brother, will be remembered not so much for his creation of the " Sunday Pictorial," but as being, in Mr. Churchill's words, " one of the first Englishmen to realize the vital, or perhaps mortal, significance of two great new facts which broke brutally upon the post-war world at the beginning of 1933 : the power of the air and the arrival of Hitler." Lord Rothermere was Britain's first Air Minister, holding that office in the Lloyd George government from 1917 to 1918, and since the aeroplane became something more than a toy, his newspapers gave their powerful encouragement to aerial development.

Landslide Sabotage in Norway

SCANDINAVIANS are adept at making use of the natural phenomena of their countries, and it is said that a number of recent rockslides, which have broken the Oslo-Bergen railway in ten places and damaged important highways, cannot be attributed to recent rains. This original means of sabotage is thought to be the work of a new organization of patriotic Norwegians whose object is to hamper the troops in occupation. A number of arrests have been made, and meanwhile German repair squads are labouring to restore normal traffic along roads and railway. A state of siege has been declared in the region, and angry Nazi soldiers and policemen have taken charge of the damaged ways and are closely interrogating travellers.

America's New Bases

RAPID progress has been made in settling upon sites in British North Atlantic colonies to be leased to U.S.A. for air and naval bases. Each Colony has been visited in turn by a Board of Inspection under Rear-Admiral J. W. Greenslade, of the U.S. Navy, and discussions have been held with the Governors and consultations with the British C.-in-C. of the America and West Indies Station. Seven sites have been chosen—in Bermuda, Bahamas, Jamaica, Antigua, St. Lucia, British Guiana and Trinidad—and the work of surveying them is proceeding rapidly. Building has already started at another site, Placentia Bay, Newfoundland. President Roosevelt has allotted £12,500,000 for the immediate development of this chain of defence bases.

Nazi Financial Swindles

GERMAN Army Orders have brought to light a widespread swindle that had evidently received official countenance and been practised in the occupied territories. It consisted in tendering to shopkeepers, in exchange for their goods, worthless German banknotes of high denomination which had been preserved from the period of inflation after the last war. As the German currency had been stabilized in 1923 at the rate of 1,000,000,000,000 old marks to the new mark, these notes have no value whatsoever except as curios. The way this barefaced fraud has been discovered is particularly interesting. German Army Orders were issued condemning the practice and forbidding it *in the West*, where the Nazis are anxious to pose as the friends of France, but no prohibition on this point has been issued to the troops in Poland and in the Balkans, and the swindle is presumably continuing unabated. This is in addition to the officially sponsored habit of fixing arbitrary rates of exchange for the mark, a method by which the helpless conquered countries have been considerably despoiled.

France Might Have Fought Against Us

A RECENT dispatch sent by a special correspondent of the Free French news agency discloses that one of the German peace terms brought back from Paris by M. Laval, after his meeting there with Hitler on October 22, provided for the use of all ports in France and the French Empire for the harbouring and provisioning of German ships. General Huntziger, War Minister, strenuously opposed this Article, telling the Cabinet that it was a trap set by the Nazis to bring about war between England and France. " When German ships come into French ports for supplies," he told them, " Britain will be obliged to bombard them. We shall not be able to reply to these attacks, and this will inevitably lead to hostile acts, more and more accentuated, with regard to Britain, and finally we shall be drawn into war." General Huntziger won the support of the majority of the Cabinet against M. Laval and Admiral Darlan.

Tragedy Overtakes New Commissioner

VICHY, submitting meekly to the demands of Berlin, recently dismissed M. Gabriel Puaux from his appointment of High Commissioner for France in Syria and the Lebanon on the grounds that he had " handled the mandatory affairs in a manner incompatible with the spirit of Vichy." In his place they appointed M. Jean Chiappe, a Corsican, who, as Chief of Police in Paris from 1926 to 1934, became notorious for his ruthless methods. He was concerned in the latter year with the Paris demonstrations over the Stavisky scandal and was dismissed by M. Daladier, then in power. The dismissal was followed by demonstrations in his favour by Royalist and Fascist groups. Later he became president of the Paris municipal council, and when the Nazis entered Paris he cooperated with them. On November 27 the aircraft carrying M. Chiappe to Syria to take up his new appointment was lost over the Northern Mediterranean. It was stated that while British and Italian ships were engaged off Sardinia his slow-moving Air France 'plane got involved in the air action simultaneously taking place and was shot down by a fighter, alleged to be British.

Empire Airmen Arrive in England

THE first batch of airmen trained in Canada under the Empire Air Training Scheme have arrived in London. All are observers and have had six months' training from R.A.F. instructors. The atmospheric conditions obtaining in Canada have enabled them to put in a larger number of flying hours than are usually possible to men in this country in the same period. Some entered the Service straight from school ; others had been engaged in civil occupations of various kinds before joining up. The average age is 24, and all are fighting fit, full of enthusiasm, and give the impression of being a remarkably efficient body of young men. This contingent is the forerunner of many others, pilots, gunners and observers, who will be arriving at frequent intervals from all parts of the British Commonwealth to help the mother country in her great fight for the freedom of the world.

FIRST CONTINGENT OF AIRMEN TRAINED IN CANADA under the Empire Air Training Scheme arrived in London on October 25. They are taking up their duties with the R.A.F., and they were trained by R.A.F. instructors. Flying conditions in Canada enabled them to record a larger number of flying hours than is usual in Britain. *Photo, Wide World*

I WAS THERE !

Eye Witness Stories of Episodes
and Adventure in the
Second Great War

We Got the 'Sussex' Home to Port

The gallantry of the crew of the New Zealand cargo-ship "Sussex" was described in a broadcast on November 26 by Mr. Ronald Cross, Minister of Shipping. How the ship's company fought the fire caused by German bombs is here told by Captain Clarke, who brought his badly-damaged ship safe to port.

CAPTAIN PETER BOOTH CLARKE, D.S.C., sailed in Q ships in the last war and took part in the Zeebrugge raid. Telling the story of the "Sussex," he said :

We were "inward bound" with a cargo of food and a large quantity of explosive packed in steel cylinders.

Suddenly a German bomber flew at a great altitude over our starboard bow. The anti-aircraft crew raced to their stations and we waited. Suddenly the bomber altered course and dived. As it came down it loosed a volley of machine-gun fire and fired from its cannon.

Our gunners opened fire. I think they hit the machine, but not seriously. When it was at a low altitude the 'plane dropped two heavy high explosive bombs. Both made direct hits. The first blew the funnel away and damaged the decks, the other fell aft of No. 2 hold, tore its way through the timber and started a fire.

The 'plane circled around us to see what damage had been done and to finish us off if necessary. When it came down low we opened fire on it again from our gun and with rifles fired from the bridge. We drove the 'plane off, but not before one lad named Croxford had been badly wounded by bullets. He was a member of the gun crew and refused to leave his gun.

The 'plane hovered around us for nearly three-quarters of an hour and then came down lower and signalled us to stop. It was then within range and we opened fire again from our gun. That was the answer they got.

All our navigational instruments had been destroyed by the bombs and the ship was circling round. The wireless had been damaged and it was impossible to send out any signals of distress.

The fire started by the second bomb had by this time spread to the cargo.

A young assistant steward, F. Trundley, of London, perched himself on top of a number of cylinders and with a hosepipe played water around to keep the flames from reaching the spot. As he squatted on top of the cylinders he laughed and joked with other members of the crew and urged them on to greater efforts. It was a great display of courage.

The 'plane must have thought we were completely finished, for it made off.

It was not until afternoon that we managed to get the fire under control. We then tried to steer by a boat compass, but the efficiency of this had been impaired by the explosions and so we had to use the sun.

To add to our difficulties we ran into a thick blanket of fog and we didn't know where we were. Once we collided with a trawler from which we got our position. Soon afterwards a warship came along and escorted us to port.

The British cargo-ship "Sussex" of 11,066 tons, which was brought safely into port through the gallantry of her crew.
Photo, P. A. Vicary

We are sorry we did not shoot down the enemy and hope we shall meet him again and have better luck.—"*News Chronicle.*"

How We Chased the Italians to Their Lair

Following the British aerial attack on the Italian Navy at Taranto came the naval engagement off Sardinia on November 27. Throughout this action, Reuter's Special Correspondent with the Navy was on board a British cruiser, and below we give his graphic story of the battle.

IT was ten in the morning when the electrifying news came from the "Ark Royal's" aircraft that a large force of Italian ships had been sighted steaming south-east twenty miles off the south coast of Sardinia and seventy miles away from our position.

At this time our main fighting force consisted of cruisers and the battle-cruiser "Renown." At full speed ahead we steamed eastward to contact the remainder of our forces, which included a battleship and destroyers. "Hoist Battle Pennants" came the signal from the flagship, the "Renown," and a few seconds later the silken ensigns floated proudly from the masts right down our battle lines as we smashed ahead to engage the enemy force.

It was a perfect day with a brilliant sun and a sky speckled with faint wisps of white cloud, and I found it difficult to realize we were about to plunge into the hell of a naval action.

The eyes of every man above decks were straining eagerly for the first glimpse of the enemy.

Ploughing along astern of us came the capital ships, while the destroyers were ahead. Smoke fouling the sun-lit horizon told us we were nearing the Italian ships, who had apparently turned on their original course, and were steaming back towards Cagliari, Sardinia.

We pushed forward at high speed in an endeavour to cut them off. I could feel the tremendous wave of excitement which flowed through the ship as, just after noon, the masts of the enemy ships came within vision of the naked eye ahead and slightly to starboard.

Breathless seconds passed and then other ominous shapes loomed up, the sun reflecting dully on their hulls. They were fifteen miles away.

Puffs of black smoke appeared in the sky above them as their anti-aircraft fire peppered the torpedo bombers who had taken off from the aircraft carrier to make a preliminary attack. Rapidly the distance narrowed.

I glanced astern and saw the battle cruiser well up with us, but the pace was too hot for

MEN OF THE SUSSEX. One member of the gun crew Croxford (left), although badly wounded by bullets, refused to leave his gun. Centre, Capt. P. B. Clarke, the skipper, who navigated his ship to port with a boat's compass. Frederick Trundley (right), eighteen-year-old assistant steward, stood on cases of explosives and fought flames with a hose.
Photos. G.P.U., Keystone

TWO AIRCRAFT CARRIERS that have covered themselves with glory in the Mediterranean are H.M.S. " Ark Royal " and H.M.S. " Illustrious," here seen in consort. The " Ark Royal " (right), was engaged in Admiral Somerville's action off Sardinia, and though at one time she was hidden by spray thrown up by bombs she emerged with all her guns firing.   *Photo, Topical*

the battleship in spite of miracles worked in her engine-room.

Although making her best speed, she was too far away to take an effective part in the subsequent engagement, thus giving the enemy a marked superiority.

The enemy opened fire first. From my perch on the after bridge I saw at 12.22 an evil spurt of flame come from amid the faint shapes of the enemy craft, and long seconds afterwards water spouts spumed into the air well short of the cruisers in the centre of the line. Dull booms penetrated through the cotton-wool stuffed in my ears two minutes later, and I saw clouds of orangy smoke billowing from the turrets of two of our cruisers.

Suddenly the iron deck beneath my feet seemed to jump, and the whole ship shuddered as the guns of the fore turrets, with a deafening colossal roar, sent shells screeching over the 20,000 yards of water.

The whole cruiser squadron was now in action, and writhing coils of smoke, which almost hid the ships, were diamonded eerily with red flame as their guns sent salvos roaring over towards the enemy.

Gun flashes stabbed out from the Italian squadrons, which were now steaming on the port side on a parallel course to us. Shells plunged into the sea around the cruisers, kicking up vicious columns of water.

Barely 30 ft. away below the after-bridge the muzzles of six guns were elevated to their extreme range to pound the Italians. As they belched out their high velocity shells I was stunned and dazed by the fearful noise, and it felt as though my face and chest were being buffeted by heavy bolsters.

We were concentrating our fire on an enemy cruiser. When it was reported that the cruiser was on fire we concentrated our salvos on another cruiser for the remainder of the action.

They were obviously drawing away behind the smoke screen. When for blessed seconds the inferno of our fire ceased, I heard the dull boom of the battle-cruiser's guns, and could see the vivid flashes of her 15-in. broadsides.

In our own tower everyone with me on the bridge ducked as two enemy shells screamed horribly overhead and smashed into the sea away on the starboard side. Again we ducked as another salvo landed close on the port quarter and shell fragments whistled above us. The Italian battleships appeared to be firing at the cruiser " Berwick."

I noticed no shells falling round the battle-cruiser astern, although her guns were still firing. By this time the Italian Fleet had nearly disappeared over the horizon, running for the shelter of the shore batteries.

Our ships were then within a few miles of the enemy coast, and were forced to abandon the pursuit as the superior speed of the enemy ships had taken them out of range.

I Flew with the Bombers to Bari

The R.A.F.'s activities over the Italian port of Bari increased after the invasion of Greece. Here is an account, by a special correspondent of the " News Chronicle," of a typical bombing raid which wreaked destruction on oil refineries and storage plants.

WE took off during the night from somewhere in the Middle East in perfect moonlight and headed towards our objective through a rhapsody in blue—under a blue sky, over blue waters and blue islands.

Inside the 'plane all was dark, save where the moonlight leaked through the gunports and through the glass dome in the top of the fuselage. The uniform roar of the motors was broken only by occasional orders which came through over headphones.

Everybody else on board had something to do, every minute watching or working in some way. I curled up, my head on my parachute, my feet on yards and yards of a machine-gun belt, my middle suspended over a case of incendiary bombs—and slept.

Suddenly I was roused by a member of the crew who shoved me up under the glass dome, which was like an inverted goldfish bowl, and from which I could see far away on the port bow a red light which seemed like a rising and falling flame.

At first I thought we were witnessing a giant conflagration, but as we neared I could see the light was the product of scores of tracer bullets.

But that was not Bari, it was only a foretaste of what we saw when we had gone a few minutes farther up the coast.

As we neared Bari the anti-aircraft guns joined in, their shell bursts winking silently —because of the noise of the motors—like malignant sparks. We must have come down a bit, for the anti-aircraft shells, instead of bursting beneath us, began bursting alongside and then above us. The fire increased in intensity until we could hear shells bursting above the noise of the engines.

Afterwards I asked the 'plane's crew, veterans of raids on Germany, how Italian A.A. fire compared with that of the Germans. They agreed the Italian fire lacked nothing in vigour compared with the German, yet it was incomparably worse aimed. But it seemed incredible that nothing was hit.

Time after time we flew over the target. Each time something interfered with perfect marksmanship until finally we had been trailing our coat tails because of the Italian " flak " for nearly an hour. In the middle of this a voice from the headphones said,

" Don't look now, but I think someone is shooting at us."

Visibility was decreased considerably by cloud, but it was still possible to make out the outlines of Bari's port and town.

I watched, fascinated. The last time I had seen Bari was in April, 1939, when from there and from Brindisi I had witnessed the sailing of Mussolini's armada to the conquest of Albania.

Eventually aiming conditions were perfect. Down went our bombs. We turned and I caught a glimpse of a very promising fire, blazing with so much fierce vigour that it seemed almost certain that oil tanks were hit. As we sped away from Bari, three times the sky flashed with big explosions.

The homeward course took us above the clouds over Taranto, presumably, since we had no bombs left just to give the already sorely harassed A.A. gunners at that port something to worry about.

Once again there was a brilliant fireworks display of searchlights, shells and tracer bullets. Once again the uppermost reaction was to wonder that all that produced no result.

The way back was far too cold for sleep. After a long dull haul a vivid red band of light on the rim between earth and sky showed us dawn and home.

The sand of the desert is one of the difficulties that the Royal Air Force has to contend with in the East. Bombs must be cleared of every vestige of it before the fuses can be put in.

Home Front Personalities of the War

Major - General T. R. Eastwood, who succeeded Lieut.-Gen. Sir H. R. Pownall as Inspector-General of the Home Guard in September, 1940. Major-Gen. Eastwood has been Commandant of the Royal Military College, Sandhurst, since 1938. He was born in 1890, and before the last war became A.D.C. to the Earl of Liverpool, Governor-General of New Zealand. He served with distinction in Gallipoli and France, 1914-18.

Commander Lord Teynham, R.N., Naval Control Service Officer for the Port of London. Lord Teynham, who was born in 1896, was educated at Osborne and Dartmouth Colleges, and served in the Second Cruiser Squadron, Grand Fleet, during the last war. He has charge of all operational merchant shipping in the Port of London and their preparation for convoy.

Army Reform Committee. This is a Standing Committee which examines how the military organization of Britain may be simplified and " ensures that there shall be no dislocation or interruption of the war effort "; its chairman is Sir James Grigg, Permanent Under-Secretary for War. Its membership includes, left to right above : Sir Percy Bates, chairman of Cunard White Star Line ; Lieut.-Gen. H. C. B. Wemyss, Adjutant-General to the Forces ; Lieut.-Gen. Sir Robert Haining, Vice-Chief, Imperial General Staff ; Mr. G. W. Dunkley, whose services have been placed at the War Office's disposal by the Iraq Petroleum Co. ; and General Sir W. Venning, Quarter-Master-General to the Forces. Mr. R. J. Sinclair is also a member of the Committee.

Photos, Lafayette, L.N.A., Fox, Elliott & Fry, Associated Press

Mr. W. B. Chrimes, C.B.E., Director of Communal Feeding to the Ministry of Food, was born in 1883. The Ministry of Food want every industrial worker and poor person in the country to have square meals at reasonable prices. A survey has been made of the catering facilities available throughout Great Britain, and, in cooperation with the Ministry of Labour, canteens are being installed for factory workers. Mr. Chrimes is managing director of a large grocery firm in Liverpool. He is also Chairman of the Liverpool Child Welfare Association.

Captain Oliver Lyttelton, M.P., President of the Board of Trade, was born in 1893. During the last war he was continuously on active service, received the D.S.O., and M.C., and was three times mentioned in dispatches. He became President of the Board of Trade when that office was vacated by Sir Andrew Duncan. At that time he had no seat in Parliament, but when the Aldershot constituency fell vacant owing to the elevation of Lord Wolmer to the peerage, Capt. Lyttelton was returned unopposed as Conservative M.P. on Nov. 26, 1940.

Saved From War's Perils on the High Seas

The solitary figure on a capsized boat is Captain Whitehead of Leeds, who was the sole survivor of a ship torpedoed and sunk in the Atlantic. He clung to a piece of wreckage for eight hours before climbing on the boat, and four hours later was seen by an Anson flying-boat that brought a warship to his rescue.

The Germans, left, were saved from a U-boat that surfaced when it was threatened with destruction; they are entraining at a northern port on their way to a prison camp. The British seamen above, rescued from a torpedoed merchant-ship by another, are being transferred to a warship.

Photos, British Official: Crown Copyright; J. H. Hall and Associated Press

Life-Saving Speed-boats of the R.A.F.

THE Royal Air Force now has its own lifeboat service. It consists of a number of launches, which might be described as speed-boats, for they are among the fastest small craft afloat. They are fitted with radio so that they can keep in touch with 'planes and ships, while they carry life-saving apparatus and a first-aid equipment so complete as to make them almost miniature hospital ships. The launches are plying not only in home waters but in the Mediterranean as well, and they have been instrumental in saving many lives from aircraft shot down or forced down in the sea. Not only British airmen owe their lives to these craft, but, in accordance with the humane traditions of all three British fighting services, the crews of enemy aircraft as well. At the same time the Nazis do all they can to rescue their own men who become casualties and fall in the sea. They, too, employ speed-boats, dashing out from the Channel ports ; and " floating sick-bays " have been sighted at various points off the the French coast.

Above is one of the high-speed launches of the R.A.F. going all out. The design of the hull raises the bow when she is going at full speed so that she skims over the water making hardly any bow wave. Left, one of the launches on service in the Near East is leaving her moorings.

Photos, British Official : Crown Copyright

Perched on the front of the cabin is the look-out man, above, who communicates with the officer at the controls with a speaking-tube. His perch, with his legs dangling, is none too secure.

OUR DIARY OF THE WAR

TUESDAY, NOV. 26, 1940   *451st day*
In the Air—R.A.F. made large-scale attack on armament factories and other targets at Cologne. Other forces bombed railways in Berlin, arsenal at Turin, shipping and docks at Rotterdam, Flushing, Antwerp, Calais, and Boulogne.

Coastal Command aircraft attacked naval base at Lorient, oil targets at Ghent, shipping off Dutch coast, and many aerodromes.

War against Italy—Bombers of R.A.F. raided Valona harbour, Albania, registering direct hits on a big ship, on quays and docks and on aerodrome buildings.

Home Front—During day few enemy aircraft crossed coast, most of which were shot down. Bombs fell in Sussex coastal town. Bristol raided again both by daylight and at night. London was also bombed.

Four enemy 'planes shot down.

Greek War—Greek troops continued to press forward on Albanian territory. Among other war material six aircraft abandoned by enemy were captured near Koritza.

WEDNESDAY, NOV. 27   *452nd day*
On the Sea—Admiralty announced that British naval forces in Mediterranean made contact with Italian fleet, and that enemy retired at high speed towards his base. One enemy cruiser set on fire by gunfire and two destroyers badly hit. Aircraft of Fleet Air Arm torpedoed a battleship of Littorio class. Enemy bombers scored two hits which slightly damaged H.M.S. "Berwick."

Coastal Command aircraft torpedoed two German tankers near Frisian Islands.

In the Air—R.A.F. again directed main offensive against Cologne. Other aircraft bombed invasion ports of Antwerp, Le Havre and Boulogne, and several aerodromes.

Home Front—Heavy night raid on Plymouth, 'planes coming over in continued relays. Bombs fell intermittently in London.

Enemy lost 11 aircraft. Two British fighters lost but both pilots safe.

Greek War—Greeks continuing their action on Albanian territory. Air Force successfully bombed enemy concentrations, columns and batteries.

Italian 'planes active on front ; they also bombed villages in Epirus, Corfu, Cephalonia, Crete and port of Patras.

Rumania—Iron Guard executed 64 political prisoners in Bucharest.

General—Sir Robert Kindersley announced that in one year's effort £475,532,981 had been raised by war savings.

General Catroux appointed High Commissioner of Free France and Gen. de Gaulle's representative in Near East.

THURSDAY, NOV. 28   *453rd day*
On the Sea—Admiralty announced loss of H.M. trawlers "Dungeness" and "Fontenoy" as result of air attack.

In the Air—R.A.F. attacked principally Dusseldorf and Mannheim areas, where goods yards, naval armament factories and gas works were hit. Other forces bombed synthetic oil plant at Politz ; naval shipbuilding yards at Stettin ; docks at Cuxhaven ; railway communications, military storehouses and aerodromes.

Attacks were also made on ports at Antwerp, Boulogne and Le Havre.

War against Italy—R.A.F. bombers carried out raids at Santi Quaranta, causing withdrawal of enemy destroyers bombing Corfu ; attacks also made on Durazzo and Elbasan. Brindisi was heavily bombed.

Successful raid by British bombers on Sidi Barrani, Bomba and Tmimi.

Home Front—About 40 Nazi aircraft crossed Kent coast during morning, but were dispersed by our fighters. Night raiders were reported over East Anglia, Wales, Midlands, N.E., S.W., and N.W. England ; Merseyside had its heaviest raid of the war.

Six enemy aircraft shot down. Britain lost seven fighters ; pilot of one safe.

Greek War—Greeks occupied number of heights overlooking Argyrokastro. Italian resistance reported to be stiffening and their air force increasingly active. R.A.F. shot down 10 Italian aircraft on Nov. 27 and 28.

FRIDAY, NOV. 29   *454th day*
On the Sea—British light naval forces made contact with those of enemy in English Channel and pursued them to Brest, inflicting damage. H.M.S. "Javelin" hit by torpedo but reached port. R.A.F. fought off series of air attacks on "Javelin."

Admiralty announced naval bombardment of targets at Ras Alula, near Cape Gardafui, Italian Somaliland.

In the Air—R.A.F. made concentrated raids on naval yards at Bremen and riverside wharves and docks at Cologne.

Coastal Command aircraft bombed ports at Hamburg, Cologne, Boulogne and Le Havre. Enemy supply ship sunk off Holland.

War against Italy—C.-in-C. Mediterranean Fleet reported successful attacks by Fleet Air Arm on Port Laki (Leros), in the Dodecanese, and on Tripoli (Libya).

Home Front—Small forces of enemy aircraft crossed coast during day. Bombs fell mostly in South London. Night attack on London, Home Counties and N.W. England.

Five enemy aircraft shot down. Britain lost two fighters.

Greek War—Greek advance continued despite Italian reinforcements from Northern Albania. Italians transferred supply bases from Valona and Durazzo to northern anchorage of San Giovanni di Medua.

SATURDAY, NOV. 30   *455th day*
In the Air—Coastal Command aircraft made dawn attack on Lorient.

Owing to adverse weather R.A.F. night bombing operations were cancelled.

War against Italy—Italians stated that French battleship "Lorraine" was partly destroyed by their bombers during raid on Alexandria.

Home Front—Big Nazi daylight raid attempted but most 'planes were dispersed by British fighters. Some bombs fell in London. Air activity also reported over S.E. and W. coasts of England and East Anglia.

Heavy night raid on Southampton, centre of city being deliberately attacked. Every type of building in main streets suffered severely ; many churches destroyed.

Five enemy aircraft shot down. Britain lost two fighters, but both pilots safe.

Greek War—Pogradets captured by Greek assault units. Fierce fighting continued along whole front, Italian resistance having stiffened. Greeks closing in on Argyrokastro.

Rumania—Serious disorders reported following execution of political prisoners by Iron Guard. Enormous crowds attended re-burial of Codreanu, former Iron Guard leader shot in 1938, and representatives of Hitler, Mussolini and Franco were present.

SUNDAY, DEC. 1   *456th day*
On the Sea—British patrol of motor torpedo-boats damaged German supply ship "Santos" off mouth of Scheldt.

Admiralty announced that H.M. submarine "Triad" was overdue and presumed lost.

In the Air—Coastal Command made daylight attack on naval base at Lorient. Other aircraft bombed military camp at Kristiansand, and gasworks at Esbjerg, Denmark.

R.A.F. made night bombing attack on naval shipbuilding yards at Wilhelmshaven.

Home Front—Enemy activity over S.E. England during day, but no aircraft penetrated deeper than outskirts of London.

During night Southampton was again heavily raided. Bombs also fell in London and Home Counties and elsewhere.

Eight enemy aircraft destroyed. Britain lost five fighters, but all pilots safe.

Greek War—Athens reported considerable advance on all fronts. More than 150 prisoners captured in region of Premeti, as well as much war material. Fierce artillery duel in progress near Argyrokastro.

R.A.F. damaged important bridge on Italian supply road in S.W. Albania. Military buildings in Tepelini were bombed.

MONDAY, DEC. 2   *457th day*
On the Sea—Five British ships in North Atlantic reported by radio that they had been torpedoed.

In the Air—Coastal Command aircraft attacked shipping off Norwegian coast. Bombers raided submarine base at Lorient.

War against Italy—R.A.F. bombed military targets at Naples. Aerodromes of Catania and Augusta in Sicily attacked with incendiaries. Reported that R.A.F. had made heavy attack on Benina aerodrome, Western Desert. Enemy troops and motor transport on Metemma-Gondar road, Italian East Africa, were bombed and machine-gunned, and successful raid carried out on large camp at Gubba.

Home Front—Enemy air activity over Britain was slight except for another heavy night raid on Bristol.

Two enemy fighters shot down.

Greek War—Greek forces continued to advance from Lake Ochrida to Adriatic seaboard, in spite of stubborn rearguard actions. Reported that 5,000 Italians surrendered on northern front. Heights commanding Santi Quaranta captured. R.A.F. bombed military objectives at Valona.

General—Britain signed financial agreement with Spain by which further supplies and imports to Spain will be facilitated.

H.M. DESTROYER JAVELIN (Commander A. F. Pugsley, R.N.) was damaged by a torpedo fired from an enemy destroyer during a naval engagement in the Channel on November 29. She is one of the new " J " class destroyers and was completed in June, 1939. She has a displacement of 1,695 tons and carries six 4·7-in. guns and ten torpedo tubes.
Photo, Wright & Logan

POLES MAKE SURE WHAT SCOTLAND STANDS WHERE IT DID

Through the fortunes of war Poles are unable to fight the enemy in their own country, but tens of thousands of this supremely gallant nation have found their way to Britain, where they are playing a most useful part in the war against the common foe. Here we see some Polish troops who have taken over the defence of a sector of the Scottish coast in the Coastal Defence Scheme. This is one of the few photographs of coastal defence works of which publication has been permitted.

Photo. British Official : Crown Copyright

Black Days for Italy in Albania

The second month of the Greco-Italian war began with a further series of Italian reverses as encouraging to the Allies as humiliating to the bullies of the Axis. As is told below, the Italians were in full retreat along the whole front, and their plight was emphasized by a host of changes in the High Command.

DECEMBER opened blackly enough for the Italians in Albania. All along the line they were in full retreat, but particularly in the south. Never for a moment did the Greeks relax their pressure, though it would be difficult to conceive of conditions making for harder campaigning, what with the rugged and barren ground and the bitter weather. Nothing, it seemed,

MARSHAL PIETRO BADOGLIO, Duke of Addis Ababa, was relieved on Dec. 6, " at his own request," of the position of Chief of the Italian General Staff which he had held since 1925.   *Photo, Keystone*

kastro sector. Operating along the coast road and across the hills from the east, the Greeks bombarded the Italians in front of the town, while at the same time their warships were reported to be in action against the harbour forts. An Italian destroyer in the harbour was hit by R.A.F. bombers, and was amongst the spoils of victory.

While the Italians were suffering these reverses in the south, their retreat continued in the north. Their withdrawal from Pogradets was reported to be skilful, but all along the way to Elbasan they were harried by the 'planes of the R.A.F., while the roads and mountain tracks they had to follow were knee-deep in mud and snow. Then they were also exposed to attacks by bands of Albanian guerillas, organized and led by local chiefs who had been amongst the supporters of King Zog.

Meanwhile, the Italian Air Arm continued its terroristic raids against the Greek civilian population. During the first month of the war, it was officially announced by Athens radio, 604 people were killed and 1,070 wounded in Italian air raids on undefended towns and villages in Greece. Corfu was the

chief sufferer. " This beautiful old place," the announcer said, " has been severely damaged for no other reason than that here Fascist vandalism can be carried out in comparative safety as the island is barely an hour's flight from Sicily. As for the famous fortifications in Corfu, about which we hear so much from the Italians, these were installed 500 years ago, and now serve only to give protection to hundreds of homeless people, huddled in their vaults."

So the war went on, and every day that passed saw the Italians being driven ever nearer to the sea. The Greek Army did, indeed, make a magnificent showing. " Surely this Greek Army today," said Mr. Leland Stowe, the " Daily Telegraph's " Special Correspondent with the Greek Army, " is just about the highest-spirited army in the world. Regardless of mud, rain and snow, regardless of hundreds of gorges, precipices and snow-covered peaks which must be conquered, day after day they march on." Their appearance, he discovered, was

The black arrows on this map show the steady Greek drive into Albania; shaded portions indicate territory occupied by the Greek forces up to the beginning of December. At that time the Italian fortified line roughly stretched from Elbasan to Tepeleni, while in the Pogradets sector the Greeks held a strong mountain line west of the town.
By courtesy of the " Daily Telegraph "

could stop that gallant little army which the Italians had been taught to despise.

Town after town was evacuated by the Italians. First they abandoned Argyrokastro, their principal supply base in the south. The town had been under fire for some days before the Greek patrols entered it on December 4.

When this latest triumph was announced Athens went wild with joy. British soldiers, sailors and airmen danced a Highland fling on the stage at a theatre; the church bells crashed out and the sirens from ships in the Piraeus joined in the joyous tumult; and King George and General Metaxas, together with British officers, appeared on the balcony of the palace.

The Greeks wasted no time in occupying Argyrokastro, but pushed on along the road towards Tepeleni, methodically clearing the Italians from the positions which they had taken up in the hills on either side. As they retreated, the Italians were bombed along the road by the Greek Air Force and the R.A.F., and Tepeleni itself was heavily " plastered."

About the same time the Italians were driven out of Premeti, some 20 miles across the mountains from Argyrokastro, and on December 5 they suffered a far worse blow when the Greeks entered in triumph the port of Santi Quaranta—which the Italians had renamed Port Edda, in honour of Mussolini's daughter, Count Ciano's spouse. Santi Quaranta ranks after Valona and Durazzo in importance, but since the war began it had been used extensively as a base for the troops operating in the Argyro-

SANTI QUARANTA, the most southerly port in Albania, was evacuated by the Italians during the first week in December. This photograph of the little port was taken in April, 1939, when, after the Italian occupation of Albania, troops were embarked from Santi Quaranta to be sent farther south to threaten the Greek frontier.
Photo, Wide World

The Greeks Have a Word for 'Thumbs Up!'

A BRITISH MECHANIZED UNIT in a Greek town on its way to the front has pulled up by the roadside to get the latest news from a Greek soldier in his traditional uniform. The self-consciousness that a British tourist feels in trying to speak a foreign language does not affect the British soldier. Judging by the smiles the answer is " thumbs up ! "

Photo, British Official: Crown Copyright

Comrades-in-Arms on the Field of Glory

GREECE'S CHEERY SOLDIERS are never happier than when they line up to receive the mugs of tea from their British comrades before joining such a tea party as that seen in the photograph in page 619. They have appreciated British additions to their rations almost as much as British military aid. The improvised stone fireplaces, on which their British comrades-in-arms make a strong brew, are the work of the Army cooks.

entirely deceptive, for they are little fellows, not averaging much more than 5 ft. 5 in. in height, and most of them look as if their uniforms are one or two sizes too big for them. To hear their animated chatter one might suspect them almost incapable of a well-organized effort. Yet, in fact, these " iron-muscled, warm-hearted men, these humble, unassuming sons of Greece," are extraordinarily efficient. " After a night of forced marches," continued the famous American journalist, " over killing mountain roads, it is a common thing for Greek

soldiers to shout and cheer as you pass them. Plugging slowly along through rain on mule-back, Greeks will yell ' macaronis,' and gesticulate eloquently to indicate what they will do to the Italians when they catch up with them. Their gestures are masterpieces of mimicry, and are always accompanied by diabolical but good-natured grins."

Only a few weeks before, Greece had been despised by her powerful enemy across the Adriatic ; now she was feared, and that fear had its repercussions in the Italian High Command. Marshal Badoglio was the first to

go—retired " at his own request " on December 6 ; he was followed within a day or two by General de Vecchi, Governor and C.-in-C. of the Dodecanese Islands, who apparently despaired of holding out in an impossible situation. Then, on December 8 it was reported from Rome that Admiral Cavagnari, Chief of Naval Staff, Vice-Admiral Somigli, the Deputy Chief, and Vice-Admiral Bacci, C.-in-C. of the Fleet, had all been superseded. Finally, there were reports in Cairo that Graziani, too, had asked to be relieved of his command.

GENERAL SIR ARCHIBALD WAVELL, the British Commander-in-Chief in the Middle East, was responsible for the prompt aid sent to the Greeks when they appealed for help against the Italian invaders. Towards the end of November he arrived in Greece, and is here seen, centre, soon after landing from the flying-boat in which he made the journey, inspecting emplacements for anti-aircraft guns.   *Photos, British Official : Crown Copyright*

Captains of a Greece Reborn to Greatness

King George, Premier Metaxas and General Papagos are Greece's leaders in her fight
with Italy—that fight which began with an altogether unprovoked invasion of Greece,
but soon developed into a struggle for the possession of Albania. Here we give biographies-
in-little of the Greek " Big Three."

TWICE has King George II ascended the throne of Greece. The first time was in 1922, when he succeeded his father Constantine ; the second was in 1935, when he returned after twelve years of exile, during which Greece had been a republic.

King George of the Hellenes (to give him his proper style) is a man of fifty. He has no queen, for his wife Elizabeth, elder daughter of the late King Ferdinand and Queen Marie of Rumania, obtained a divorce some months before his re-accession to the throne. The Crown Prince, or Diadoch, as the Greeks style him, is the King's brother, Prince Paul. Their sister, Princess Helen, is the former wife of King Carol, who abdicated the Rumanian throne last September. The Duchess of Kent is their first cousin.

During his enforced absence from Greece King George spent much time in England ; his headquarters in London was Brown's Hotel in Dover Street. He came to know England well, and to like English people and English things and ways of life—so much so, indeed, that they gave point to Mussolini's gibe that Greece's sovereign is in effect an Englishman. But first and foremost he is a lover of his own country, and throughout his reign he has devoted himself wholeheartedly to the reconstruction of the national finances and economic system, which were so sorely tried by the many wars in which Greece has been engaged since 1912.

' Only One Metaxas in Greece '

Greece's Prime Minister is General John Metaxas, who was born in 1871 in the island of Ithaca. After serving as a lieutenant on the General Staff during the war with Turkey of 1897, he spent several years at the War Academy in Berlin, where he created an excellent impression. The story runs that he was offered a position in the German

Army, but he refused it. " There are many Metaxas in Germany," he is reported to have said, " but there is only one in Greece." In 1913 he became Chief of the Greek General Staff, but early in the Great War he resigned when his plan for the forcing of the Dardanelles by the Greeks was rejected by the British High Command. In 1916 he fell foul of the Allies, and was forced to leave Greece. On his return a few years later he was placed on the retired list, and then embarked on what was to prove a stormy career as a politician. Once he was banished, several times he was a minister ; then, as the head of the Union Royalist Party, he favoured the restoration of the monarchy, and after George's return became Minister of War, and in April 1936 Prime Minister. From January 1938 he has been practically dictator, ruling

GENERAL JOHN METAXAS—soldier first, then politician—in appearance rather suggests the latter, but his military abilities found plentiful scope in framing the plans for the defence of his country against Italy.
Photo, Mondiale

unscrupulous politicians are capable, are in a fit position to judge the achievements of Metaxas' regime.

In the light of Greece's amazing stand against the Italian aggressor, there can be little doubt that the Greek people have profited largely by the stern disciplining to which they have been subjected by their little, but plump and sturdy, dictator.

Papagos the C.-in-C.

While Metaxas rules the home front, and perhaps frames the strategy which is proving so successful in the mountains of the Balkans, the Greek Army in the field is commanded by Lt.-Gen. Alexander Papagos. Born in 1886, Papagos went to the Ecole de Guerre in Paris to finish his military education, and he may have profited from Foch's lectures there. In the Balkan Wars he served in the cavalry, and rose to the command of a brigade.

When the Greeks invaded Asia Minor in 1921 he was well to the front, but, unlike King Constantine, he knew when to stop. His advice was overruled and in the end the Turks chased the Greeks into the sea. Through the years of the Republic Papagos remained a royalist, and it was he who, in 1935, came to London to invite Prince George to return to his distracted country. Under Metaxas he devoted himself to the rebuilding of the Greek Army, and he was responsible for the supervision of the fortifications in the north to which the name of the Metaxas Line is generally given.

When the present war broke out Papagos was given the appointment of Commander-in-Chief of the Greek Forces, and his first Order of the Day breathes the very spirit of confidence. " We will write new and glorious pages in our history," he said. " We will fight to the last breath."

When King George II of the Hellenes returned to Athens in 1935 to re-ascend the throne, he declared that he would restore to Greece " happiness and glory." He is seen here with Admiral Sakellariou on board a Greek man-o'-war.
Photo, Sport & General

with what some people would call a firm hand, and others, who have suffered from it, a rod of iron. All political parties have been abolished, and most of the leaders of the Opposition have been banished or imprisoned. All this has appeared rather shocking to those worthy democrats who believe that every country would do well to copy the Parliamentary institutions of Britain, forgetting that in this country the soil has been prepared by many centuries of gradually-increasing popular participation in the government. Greece is a poor country, economically backward and politically immature ; and only those who have lived in Athens and have seen for themselves the excesses of which an unbridled press and

GENERAL PAPAGOS, now Commander-in Chief of the Greek Army, is seen above on his arrival in London on November 9, 1935 to invite King George to return to Greece. He was at that time War Minister.
Photo Wide World

Albania: Land of the Men of the Eagle

One of the most picturesque countries of Europe—if also one of the most remote from
the main stream of modern life—Albania is now the battlefield on which Greek and
Italian are struggling for the mastery. Here is an account of the little country and of its
people, who ere long may once again enjoy their independence.

WE call it Albania ; the Albanians call it
Shquiperia. It is a small country,
only some ten thousand square miles
in area—not very much bigger than Wales—
and it holds a population of only a million or
so, not so many as live in Birmingham. It
is not surprising that it is so sparsely peopled,
for nearly the whole of the little land is
covered by outlying ranges of the Balkan
mountain mass. For the most part its surface is bleak and barren, and its soil, save in a
few favoured regions, is infertile.

Like country, like people. The Albanians
(Shquipetars, they call themselves—" Sons of
the Eagle ") are of pure Aryan stock, and
for many centuries they have been renowned
as warlike mountaineers, possessors of an
untamed and untamable spirit. In the
remote villages local chieftains have held and
still hold sway, and the blood feud, or
vendetta, is still approved by public opinion
and, is still much too often carried into
practice. The Albanians have all the barbaric virtues ; their word is their bond, and
they would rather die than violate the duties

King Zog of Albania is here seen at his desk
after he was driven into exile by the Italian
invasion of his country in April, 1939. As
Ahmed Beg Zogu he became President of the
Albanian Republic in 1925 and was proclaimed
King on September 1, 1928. *Photo, Associated Press*

of hospitality. Yet they are inclined to look
on theft as a very minor peccadillo, and even
murder is countenanced and not considered a
crime if it be committed in revenge or in
satisfaction for some slight which can be
wiped out only in blood.

Of the million Albanians, about seven in
every ten are Moslems, while three are
Christians—two members of the Orthodox
Church, and one a Roman Catholic. The
differences of creed, however, are hardly
reflected in everyday life, and in actual
practice there is very little to distinguish the
Moslem from his Christian brother. The

Moslems go to their mosques and the
Christians to their churches, but the Moslems,
like the Christians, have as a rule only one
wife apiece, and not all the Moslem women go
veiled. The people as a whole are divided
into Ghegs in the north and Tosks in the
south, the dividing line being the River
Shkumbi, on which Elbasan stands. It may
be added that there are tens of thousands of
Albanians outside Albania ; there are many
in Macedonia and in Greek Epirus, and
just as the finest soldiers of the Turkish
Sultan were Albanians, so today the Greek
Evzones, corresponding to our Brigade of
Guards, are largely Albanian in their racial
origin.

Albania is primarily an agricultural and
pastoral country, but its farming is carried on
in the most primitive fashion. The farmers
merely scratch the surface with their hoes or
with wooden ploughs drawn by oxen, and
the shepherds find it advisable to carry a gun
to keep off the robbers. There are vast tracks
of forest land, and other extensive areas
which are altogether uncultivated ; in the
interior are the large estates of the Moslem
beys. Cattle-breeding is carried on, and
every little farmer has his pigs—at least,
every Christian farmer, for to the Moslem
swine are taboo. In some places there are
vineyards, and in many more there are primitive distilleries for the production of brandy
from various fruits. Like most peasants, the
Albanian loves to indulge in a good drinking
bout now and again.

The villages are generally isolated, and as
often as not the only man who can read or
write is the priest. Village is linked to village
by tracks which are seldom deserving of the
name of roads. There are no railways in
Albania, and the only motor road is that

The market-place in a small
town in Albania presents an
animated scene when the
peasants come in to sell their
produce. More than half of
the people of Albania are
Mahomedans ; in the Moslem
areas the men still wear the
fez and until a few years ago
the women were veiled.

Photo, Dorien Leigh

TIRANA, the capital of
Albania, is a town of small
population and, like the other
towns of the country, it is
primitive in comparison with
most European cities. Right
is the Main Square with the
mosque in the background.
Tirana has been the capital
only since 1921, Durazzo
having formerly been the
seat of Government.

Photo, Topical

The 'Conquest' Italy Is Now Fast Losing

ALBANIA for the most part is a country of steep mountains—a continuation of the Alpine range of Dalmatia. In the south there is fertile country in the river valleys, with grazing land on the slopes. The coast is marked by rocky headlands, swamps and lagoons. This mountain valley, with maize growing in the foreground, well illustrates the sort of landscape against which the Greeks are scoring their successes.   *Photo, Dorien Leigh*

which runs from Durazzo to Elbasan and the Italians have extended to Koritza, and perhaps the Turkish military highway running from Santi Quaranta to Argyrokastro and then across the frontier to Janina in Greece.

On the coast and in the valleys where the hills broaden out to form little basins are a number of small towns. The capital is Tirana, set well inland in an arm of the coastal plain and so comparatively immune from attack from the sea. It is in the centre of a Moslem district, and its rather ramshackle architecture has a suggestion of the East. Its population has been put as high as thirty thousand, but it is sometimes claimed that both Scutari, in the far north (almost in Yugoslavia), and Koritza, reputed to be the finest town in the country, which was captured by the Greeks on November 22, 1940, are more populous. The principal ports are Valona (10,000) and Durazzo (9,000), both of which have been severely hammered by 'planes of the R.A.F. since the war began. Two other places whose names are frequently mentioned nowadays are Elbasan (14,000) and Argyrokastro, or Gjinokaster as the Albanians call it (11,000).

One of the most backward countries in Europe, Albania is believed to possess considerable mineral wealth. There are salt pits at Valona, and bitumen and asphalt are also extracted near by. Coal and iron have been located, and there is a small oilfield in the Devoli valley; the concession is owned by an Italian company, the Azienda Italiana Petroli Albania (A.I.P.A.). This, it may be remarked, is Mussolini's only oilfield.

Mussolini's—for since 1939 Albania has been part of the dominions of the Italian King-Emperor. For many hundreds of years Albania

belonged to Turkey, but on November 28, 1912 her independence was proclaimed at Valona. For a few months in 1914 she had a ruler, Prince William of Wied, but on the outbreak of the Great War the Prince went back to Germany, and shortly afterwards most of Albania was overrun by the Austrians. Her independence was proclaimed afresh in 1917, and by 1920 it had been recognized by the Great Powers. In 1925 a Republic was set up with Ahmed Beg

DURAZZO, chief port of Albania, has been repeatedly subjected to intensive attack by the R.A.F. The town stands on the Adriatic, and was known to the Romans of old as Dyrrachium. This street scene in Durazzo shows primitive houses and an equally primitive electric-light standard.   *Photo, Will Roness*

Zogu, a Moslem and hereditary chief of the Mati clan, as president, and three years later the president was proclaimed king as Zog I.

Zog made vigorous but not altogether successful efforts to modernize his country in the space of a few years, but at least he maintained some degree of public order and did much to curb the violence of the vendetta custom which had brought sorrow and misery to so many. He also introduced a measure of land reform, aimed at improving the condition of the poor peasants and at breaking up the estates of the bigger landowners. Something was done for education, too, and the Albanians, who under the Turks had been forbidden to use their own language, might now go to Albanian schools, several of which were for girls as well as for boys. Colleges and technical schools were established in the principal towns. Then another factor making for progress was the establishment of a really reliable force of gendarmes, with British officers under General Percy.

But these steps along the road of progress aroused much opposition among the more conservative elements in the country. There were several attempts at rebellion and assassination, and plots and arrests were the order of the day. Reforms cost money, too, and unfortunately the only country willing and eager to lend to struggling little Albania was Italy, so dangerously close. Mussolini cast his covetous eyes on the mineral wealth of the little country, but he was even more interested in its possibilities as a base for his future military operations in the Balkans. So on Good Friday, 1939, he sent his troops into Albania; Zog was driven out with little difficulty, and the country was formally incorporated into the Italian Empire.

Australia Is Beating Her Own Fine Record

An Australian motor auxiliary cruiser of the Sydney Harbour Patrol is seen with " patients " aboard. These were " victims " of an imaginary air raid which was carried out on the great city. The ship is taking the " victims " from one side of the immense harbour to the other.

AUSTRALIA is preparing for any eventuality, and plans to increase the Army to 300,000 by the end of March 1941. The Home Defence Force will number 210,000 and the A.I.F. will be increased to 90,000. The Prime Minister, Mr. Menzies, stated in September that 50 patrol craft were under construction in Australian shipyards, and an extensive programme of naval construction has been carried out during the past year.

These men are shown during their intensive military course of instruction at Ingleburn, near Sydney, Australia. They are learning to operate batteries of howitzers.

AUSTRALIAN INFANTRYMEN are seen above embarking at a port " down-under " for service overseas. The factories of New South Wales are working 24 hours a day in a magnificent effort to speed up Australian wartime production ; right, punching holes in steel helmets.

Photos, British Official: Crown Copyright ; Keystone and Wide World

The Long Arm of the R.A.F. Strikes Over the Desert

ITALY'S AIR FORCE lost eight 'planes in the battle of Mersa Matruh on the Egyptian coast on October 31, 1940, while another, an S 79, right, was brought down in the desert. Its crew were buried where they fell, and below a British airman places a cross made from the remains of the 'plane on the grave.

HURRICANES IN THE MIDDLE EAST have given an unpleasant surprise to Mussolini's Aeronautica Regia, which is even less able to meet them on equal terms than Hitler's Luftwaffe. Above, on an aerodrome in the Western desert pilots are making ready to take off on a patrol. In the middle photograph the patrol has received a report that enemy aircraft are approaching over the desert and has broken formation to attack them.

Photos, British Official: Crown Copyright

When the Netherlands Navy Came to Britain

Quite a number of Allied forces are now assembled or taking shape in the British Isles.
Here is an account by Henry Baerlein of one of them—the Navy and Air Force which
are proud to owe allegiance to Queen Wilhelmina.

WHEN the Nazis invaded and overran Holland most of the ships comprising the Dutch Navy in home waters —cruisers, destroyers, torpedo boats, mine-layers and submarines—managed to escape, and are now doing valuable work from certain British ports. Passenger vessels, cargo ships, pilot vessels and trawlers came over with them. Some of the trawlers have been turned into minesweepers (others continue their fishing career), while useful work is being done by all the vessels. Thus a fine Dutch liner is now not only the depot ship of her station, but houses a number of young Dutchmen who are being trained for the sea. Some of

torpedo boat suffered a very near miss from a bomb which so severely damaged the star-board engine that five months were required in a British dockyard before it was made satisfactory ; nevertheless, that engine carried on during the passage to England and collapsed only while entering the harbour.

One of the cargo ships was bringing over some 1,500 German prisoners when a Nazi 'plane began to bomb it. The officer in charge caused the hatches to be thrown open so that the captives should have a sight of their friends above ; he refused prisoners' requests to hoist a German flag, and disposed various machine-guns in case any funny business

Academy of Den Helder, and if they display the necessary qualities of character and leadership, there is nothing to prevent them from rising to any higher post.

The Dutch Navy consists of volunteers—who in peacetime are in the majority—and of conscripts ; the former, after a training period of eighteen months, may remain with the colours until they retire on a pension (at the age of 45 for the men, 50 for warrant-officers, and 55 for officers). About a thousand conscripts are normally called up every year, as a rule men who in civilian life have to do with the sea as fishermen or who have been engaged in Holland's vast fleet of barges. After eighteen months of service they join the reserve. In the present war the men of fifteen years were called upon. Most of them are in Britain, where they go about their business as efficiently as a certain naval detachment which got to Ostend from the south of Holland. There a French officer provided them with a boat which had been the victim of sabotage : there was sand in the lubricating oil ! For twenty-four hours these industrious Dutch worked away, with a large rusty file and a pocket-knife, the only available implements. They cleaned the engine and crossed the sea without mishap.

Bombs Were an Odd Experience!

We are accustomed to regard the Dutch as an imperturbable people, and there have been many instances of their bravery and nonchalance in the face of danger. An example was the case of a militiaman at one of their ports when the Nazis were bombing it. This man, who in civilian life was a lampshade-maker, had become an officer's servant. He was on his way back from market with two baskets of food suspended from the handle-bars of his bicycle. When the bombs fell round him he said it was an odd experience and one he was not used to, but he could not let his officer wait for lunch. And such imperturbability is not the only fine attribute of the Dutch sailors who now put to sea from various British ports.

Some account of the activities of Dutch airmen in Britain has been given in page 371. Various modifications have since been made, and British bombers have been allotted to them in place of their own seaplanes, on account of the question of spare parts. Netherlands pilots have been accustomed to flying three-engine 'planes under all conditions, both in Europe and the East Indies, so that they adapted themselves without the least difficulty to their present twin-engine machines, of which they speak with a glow of affection. These airmen, who will shortly be reinforced by others from the East Indies, are doing admirable work in reconnaissance, in assisting the convoys and in spotting U-boats. Now and then some amusing experiences have lightened the stern realities of war, as when a Dutch pilot made a safe landing in the dark on a stretch of sand which the Army had made dangerous for an invader. Up to this day he does not know how he managed it : for one thing, he was lucky—as fortunate as a comrade whose propeller cut away a barrage balloon—and it must also be admitted that the Army's protective work had not been quite completed.

HOLLAND'S NAVY, many of the ships of which are now in British waters, has impressed all observers with the smartness not only of the men but of the ships. This seaman of a Dutch destroyer has soon got to work with paint-pot and brush on one of the guns during a short spell in port.
Photo, British Official : Crown Copyright

them, having been born in England, have now had to learn the language of their ancestors.

Among both officers and men there is the greatest enthusiasm for their present work; it has been so successful—many details cannot be given, of course—that they have received from time to time the congratulations of the British authorities. These Dutch sailors have much in common with their British comrades, and it was a great relief to them that they managed to escape from the clutches of the Nazis. Most of the vessels were so crowded, what with seamen and the personnel of the shore establishments, that if they had been sunk on the way it would indeed have been a disaster, but they all arrived safely.

The Dutch are an ingenious race, and their engines behaved well. A heavily laden

should be attempted. One of the sailors behind the guns was a Jew, and for the entire thirty-six hours this man declined to budge. Nothing, he said, would induce him to miss such a chance. However, his only contact with the Nazis was to assist in feeding them, and as he handed down each plate he said : " This is from a Jew."

In the Dutch Navy a man is judged not by his race or colour, but by his capacity. On the passenger ship where the writer spent a few interesting days, a number of the men were of mixed Dutch and Indian descent. (The larger part of the Dutch Navy, by the way, has always been centred in the splendid Netherlands East Indies.) Like their European colleagues, most of these young men remain ordinary seamen, but if they have gone through the high school and the Naval

Training to Fight for Holland's Liberation

At the Dutch Naval College in England a cadet, left, is learning knotting and splicing, a necessary part of every sailor's training. Besides a few clothes the Dutch cadets brought nothing away from Den Helder except one cherished possession, the standard presented to the College by Queen Wilhelmina, proudly displayed above. Right, the Dutch Minister of Defence, Lieut.-Colonel Dyxhoorn, is taking the salute during an inspection of Dutch warships in British waters.

DUTCH CADETS of the Royal Netherlands Navy who escaped from the Naval College at Den Helder when the Germans overran Holland, are now in training, some at a country house in England, and others at a new establishment at Sourabaya in the Dutch East Indies. Soon after the cadets were installed in their new home in the East Indies there was a ceremonial parade (above) in which a number of cadets took part.

Photos, Fox, Central Press, Topical and Netherlands Press Service

Many a Good Deed Done by the Scouts

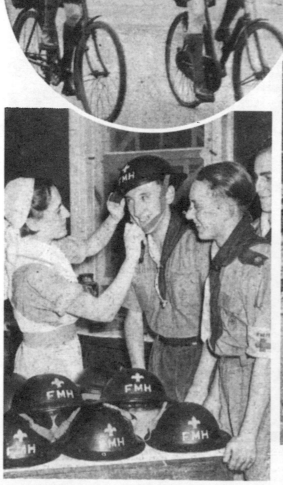

BOY SCOUTS find abundant opportunities for service in a world at war. Top left, a messenger receiving necessary instructions from an A.R.P. official at an East London post. The 18th Rochdale Troop have turned poultry farmers (right). Chester has formed a squad of A.R.P. messengers, and local Scouts have provided a large proportion of its strength ; two of these are seen, circle, wearing gas-masks.

FIRST AID is another Scout "speciality." Left, are some Scouts who help at the Finchley Memorial Hospital. In the North of England Scouts give a hand in forestry work; these boys are chopping down a tree so as to give a clear path to the tractor.
Photos, Claude Fisher, Fox, Keystone

Courageous Coventry Goes into Action

COVENTRY was so savagely bombed by the Nazis on the night of November 14 that they gloatingly coined a word—"coventrated"—to describe it. Yet the people of the ancient Midland city, with a courage which, as the King said, is an example to the whole world, immediately set about the work of clearance and reconstruction. While the smoke was still rising from the shattered buildings, squads of Civil Defence workers, ably supported by the military, went into action with splendid effect. The photographs in this page, of street clearance, salvage of household and office effects, and demolition of a dangerous wall, were all taken when the Nazi raid was still a very recent memory.

Photos, Keystone

The King in Southampton, One of the Places W

SOUTHAMPTON WAS BOMBED BY THE NAZIS, not for the first time, but far more ferociously than ever before, on the night of Saturday, November 30, and again the following night. The centre of the city was deliberately attacked, with the double object of terrorizing the people and of hampering to the greatest possible extent Britain's war effort. Some 370 people were killed or seriously wounded, thousands lost their homes, and hundreds more were thrown out of employment. On December 5 the King, as we see here, accompanied by Mr. Herbert Morrison, the

rdinary Men and Women Have Died for Freedom

Regional Commissioner, Sir Harry Butlar, and the Mayor, Councillor W. Lewis, toured the city so as to satisfy himself that all that could be done was being done for the stricken town. He found Southampton undaunted. "The Germans," as the "New York Times" put it, "can no more destroy the spirit of this seaport city than King Canute could push back the waves. It will be rebuilt. The deep ship sirens will echo through the streets again. New armies of Americans will visit it with a new reverence as one of the places where ordinary men and women died for freedom."

MAKING MUNITIONS and shipbuilding are the two most important war industries, and an adequate supply of workers has been one of the chief concerns of the Minister of Labour. On May 29, 1940, the Government announced a scheme for training additional workers, and this busy scene, recently photographed, is in a workshop of a Government Centre where 17,000 men are now being trained as mechanics. Among them are men of varied occupations, including barristers, solicitors, artists, journalists and day labourers. The centres are open alike to unemployed and employed men, provided the latter are not in reserved occupations. They must undertake to work on completion of their training in any part of the country to which they may be sent.

Photo, exclusive to THE WAR ILLUSTRATED

R.A.F. Reply to Nazi Boast of New Air War Chapter

According to the Nazis their recent heavy and indiscriminate bombing of our provincial towns began what they called " industrial warfare " and opened up a new chapter in the air war. The R.A.F., striking the enemy at his bases in France and the Low Countries, is heavily bombing aerodromes whence the raiders set out for Britain.

ACCORDING to the Nazi newspapers, total war against England has only just begun—with the " stupendous bombardment of destruction " waged against Coventry, Southampton, Bristol and London. The " Nachtausgabe " says that England's southern port (Southampton) was destroyed, but it is significant that the Luftwaffe attacked the town itself rather than the port. In this connexion the views of an American official observer—Major-General J. E. Chaney, of the U.S. Army Air Corps—are significant. The General, speaking of the ten-day Nazi onslaught of last August, pointed out that docks seemed then to have been spared from attack and suggested that this was because the Germans expected to be able to use them for landing troops and material during the projected invasion. Perhaps the same reason operates today, when there are ideas in the air that the Nazis are tuning up for another invasion attempt.

The indiscriminate bombing of provincial towns has been coupled with an intensified U-boat attack on British shipping by submarines operating from bases on the Atlantic seaboard of France. This time the Nazis did not boast in advance about the coming onslaught, though they are now in full chorus about what they call " industrial warfare " and " retaliatory attacks," with which they declare that a new chapter of the war has begun. These terms may cloak but will not conceal the true purpose of the air attacks— mass murder and widespread destruction, by which Britain's morale is intended to be broken. No longer is there any pretence that the Nazi bombers attack only military objectives ; in fact, the German communiqué describing the London raid of Dec. 9 said that " sticks of incendiaries were dropped on certain districts and whole blocks of houses were set on fire." With the realization of this ruthless and brutal motive there is beginning to be heard—not only in Britain but in the Dominions—a demand that the morale of the German civilian population shall be put to a like ordeal.

Major-Gen. Chaney, in his review of the Battle of Britain, compared the ratio of German to British losses in the three earlier phases of the conflict : Aug. 8-15, 6 to 1 ; Sept. 5-15, 4 to 1 ; Sept. 27 onwards, 1·9 to 1. The reason for the smaller number of German casualties in the third phase is that the Nazis used fighter-bombers instead of big bombers, and that they then resorted to night attacks, besides flying at much greater altitudes. One other reason is that the Nazis latterly have provided more armour protection for their pilots and the vitals of their aircraft. As a counter to this, our fighters are now being armed with a shell gun as well as powerful machine-guns.

The new weapon, a Hispano-Suiza 20-mm. gun, fires through the airscrew hub and was a standard armament for some types of French fighter 'plane. It works on the same principle as the Swiss Oerlikon shell-gun, which fires 470 rounds per minute with a muzzle velocity of 2,700 feet per second ; with armour-piercing ammunition, a hardened steel plate one inch thick can be penetrated at a range of 2,000 feet. The armour above and behind the pilot's seat on a Me. 109 shot down in Britain was 8 mm. thick (about 5-16 inch) : at a range of 3,280 feet armour nearly twice as thick (15 mm. or about 7-12 inch) would be pierced.

Fourteen Nazi aircraft were shot down by the R.A.F. on Thursday, with the loss of two of our fighters, one of our pilots being saved. Eight Me. 109s were destroyed by a single R.A.F. squadron. On the previous night Düsseldorf had been bombed for twelve hours, armament works and gas plants being fiercely attacked. That same night other of our bombers visited Turin and bombed munition works. During Thursday night the Germans made a heavy attack on a South-coast town, and despite an intense A.A. barrage were able to cause much material damage and many casualties. On Friday a town in the South-west (Bristol) was heavily raided.

There was little enemy activity over Britain on Saturday—partly, perhaps, because the R.A.F. during Friday night had carried out one of their most intensive raids on airfields in Holland, Belgium and France. Weather conditions were also responsible for the grounding of the Nazi bombers. Over a region extending from the Plain of Orleans to Holland our bomber squadrons attacked the Nazi bases from which raiders set out for Britain. Coming down to 500 feet, our men dropped fire and explosive bombs, and gunned the aerodromes. About one in ten of the enemy's temporary aerodromes in the areas mentioned were attacked.

Düsseldorf was again severely raided on Saturday night, when some 4,000 incendiaries, besides numbers of H.E. bombs, were dropped on places of military importance. Other

BRISTOL'S AIR RAID DAMAGE has been heavy and some notable buildings have been damaged. Among them is the Dutch House, a remarkably picturesque structure dated 1676, which is said to have been brought from Holland. It stands at the corner of Wine Street and High Street in the oldest part of the city.
Photo, " Daily Mirror "

Over Berlin & All Germany Our Bombers Roam

R.A.F. RAIDS ON GERMANY AND ENEMY-OCCUPIED TERRITORY DURING NOVEMBER
Compiled from Official Air Ministry Communiqués
Numbers following place-names denote the days of the month on which raids were made

Aerodromes

Abbeville, 7, 16
Amiens, 10, 27
Arras, 16, 20
Buer, 1, 17
Cambrai, 15, 16
Christiansand, 24
DenMok, 5, 25
Doullens, 8, 15
Haamstede, 6, 13
Merignac, 19, 22
St. Malo, 11, 15
Schipol, 1, 19, 27
Soesterberg, 3
Stavanger, 14, 15, 22
Vannes-Meucon, 14, 20

Amiens-Glisy, Bomlitz, Berlin, Brest, Coblenz, Dunkirk, Eindhoven, Emden, Knocke, Lannian, Leeuwarden, Le Touquet, Lille, Lubeck, Magdeburg, Montivilliers, Norderney, Oostvoorne, Rennes, Rheine, Rosendael, Rouen, St. Brieuc, St. Leger, St. Omer, Tournai, Tubingen, Ursei—raided once.

Aircraft Factories, etc.

Amsterdam, 8, 10
Bremen, 14
Hamburg, 16
Nurnberg, 8

Gun Positions, etc.

Cap Gris Nez, 1, 6, 15
Kloppenubrg, 5
Magdeburg, 5
Oldenburg, 5

Chemical Works, Munition Works, etc.

Berlin, 6, 19
Cologne, 6, 13, 26, 27
Düsseldorf, 6, 7, 13, 27
Essen, 1, 7, 10, 13, 23, 29
Gelsenkirken, 1, 29
Hamburg, 15, 16, 24
Mannheim, 10, 28
Pilsen, 19, 27

Berhausen, Boulogne, Castrop-Rauxel, Dortmund, Dresden, Geldern, Homburg, Leipzig, Lintfort, Nurnberg, Oberhausen, Salzbergen, Solingen, Uberlingen, Ulm, Weimar—raided once.

Oil Refineries, Oil Stores and Depots

Cologne, 12, 13, 16, 28
Gelsenkirchen, 1, 7, 8, 10, 12, 13, 17, 19, 27, 29
Hamburg, 14, 15, 16, 19, 24, 27, 28
Homburg, 6, 28, 29
Leuna, 6, 13, 18, 19, 29
Magdeburg 1, 27, 29
Wanne Eickel, 19, 22, 23

Emden, Frankfort, Ghent, Lutzendorf, Ostermoor, Salzbergen, Sterkrade, Stettin, Vlaardingen, Wesserling—raided once.

Bremen, Dortmund, Hanover, Ruhland—raided twice.

Railway Stations, Marshalling Yards, etc.

Berlin, 1, 6, 13, 14, 19, 23
Cologne, 6, 8, 26, 27, 28, 29
Dortmund, 19, 22, 23
Duisberg-Ruhrort, 8, 19
Düsseldorf, 13, 28
Gelsenkirchen, 17, 22
Hamburg, 15, 16, 29
Hamm, 6, 8, 27
Krefeld, 28, 29
Leipzig, 19, 23
Mainz, 6, 9
Mannheim, 8, 10, 27, 28
Munster, 10, 29
Osnabruck, 1, 8, 19, 27, 29

Aurich, Bremen, Coblenz, Danzig, Dessau, Dorsten, Dresden, Halle, Hildesheim, Hook of Holland, Le Havre, Ludwigshaven, Mors, Munich, Neuff, Nordhausen, Pretzsch, Rheine, Saarbrucken, Soest, Stuttgart—raided once.

Naval Bases, Docks, Harbours, Canals, etc.

Antwerp, 5, 10, 16, 27, 28
Boulogne, 4, 5, 9, 10, 15, 23, 24, 27, 28, 29
Bremen, 5, 28, 29
Bremerhaven 5, 13, 19
Calais, 5, 9, 10, 13, 15
Cherbourg, 10, 20, 30
Cologne, 23, 26, 29
Den Helder, 6, 24, 25, 29
Dortmund-Ems Canal, 7, 13, 16
Duisberg-Ruhrort, 1, 6, 7, 8, 10, 12, 13, 17, 19, 20, 22, 23, 27
Dunkirk, 5, 6, 7, 10, 12, 15, 16, 20
Flushing, 3, 5, 8, 10, 12, 19, 27, 29
Hamburg, 15, 16, 19, 24, 25, 27, 28, 29
Kiel, 3, 10, 15, 19, 25, 28
Le Havre, 4, 7, 8, 10, 14, 19, 27, 28, 29
Lorient, 7, 8, 9, 10, 11, 12, 14, 17, 19, 20, 23, 26 to 29
Ostend, 4, 14, 15, 19, 20, 27, 29
Wilhelmshaven, 13, 24, 25, 28, 29

Amsterdam, Barfleur, Borkum, Emden, Heligoland, Hook of Holland, Ludwigshaven, Mannheim, Norderney, Stettin, Vegesack, Willemsoord—raided once.
Cuxhaven, Rotterdam, Ymuiden—raided twice.

Power Stations

Berlin, 2, 20
Cologne, 13, 26, 27
Hamburg, 5, 15, 16, 19, 24
Brest, Dresden, Düsseldorf, Hamborn, Kiel, Magdeburg—raided once

Total Raids Nov. 1-30 380

AT A FIGHTER AERODROME in the South of England, a " kitty " was subscribed to go to the squadron that first brought down 600 enemy 'planes. It was won by Flt.-Lieut. J. C. Mungo Park, D.F.C., right, and Pilot Officer H. M. Stephens, D.F.C., left.

Photo, British Official : Crown Copyright

BERLIN has been forced by the R.A.F. to "take it" despite the promises of the Nazi leaders that no enemy aircraft could ever reach the city. Civilians have been employed in clearing up the debris after bombs had fallen, and in the photograph they are filling in a crater in a street close to a military objective.
Photo, Planet News

squadrons visited Antwerp, Dunkirk, Calais and Boulogne, and bombed a long list of aerodromes in France and the Low Countries. Brest and Lorient, whence submarines sally forth, were attacked also ; Lorient had been raided fifteen times during November, and is given no respite.

On Sunday night, after two days and one night without an Alert, London had an early warning which ushered in what proved to be the worst air attack for three weeks past and was met by the heaviest barrage for some time. First flares were dropped, followed by incendiaries and H.Es, and damage was done both in the central area and the outskirts. Other raiders attacked places along the Thames Estuary and in the South-east of England. In the London area nine hospitals, four churches and a convent were hit.

Over Greece and Albania the R.A.F. had

destroyed 37 Italian aircraft up to Dec. 6, with the loss of only two of our fighters. In all, since she entered the war, Italy has lost 290 'planes, against 53 lost by the R.A.F. Italian aircraft are said to be poor in quality and the personnel to be inadequately trained ; there are signs also that the pilots have little enthusiasm for their task. Diving down into narrow valleys, our own aircraft bombed road junctions, attacked troop concentrations and harassed the Italian columns retreating before the Greeks. Two hits were scored on an Italian destroyer in the harbour at Santi Quaranta, before this place was abandoned by the enemy. Later, the vessel fell into the hands of the Greeks. The port of Valona has been repeatedly bombed, and also Italian shipping off the Albanian coast. In Libya our bombers made a devastating attack on Castel Benito, near the town of Tripoli, on Saturday night.

AIRCRAFT LOSSES OVER BRITAIN

				German	Italian	British
May	...	...	...	1,990	—	258
June	...	...	...	276	—	177
July	...	...	...	245	—	115
Aug.	...	...	...	1,110	—	310
Sept.	...	...	...	1,114	—	311
Oct.	...	...	...	241	—	119
Nov.	...	...	...	201	20	53
Dec. 1-8	...	...	...	28	—	7
Totals, May to Dec. 8				**5,205**	**20**	**1,350**

Daily Results

Dec.	Ger. Losses	Br. Losses	Br. Pilots Saved	Dec.	Ger. Losses	Br. Losses	Br. Pilots Saved
1	... 8	5	5	6	... —	—	—
2	... 2	—	—	7	... 2	—	—
3	... —	—	—	8	... 11	—	—
4	... 1	—	—	Totals	28	7	6
5	... 14	2	1				

From the beginning of the war up to **Dec. 8, 3,023 enemy aircraft** destroyed during raids on Britain. R.A.F. losses **846**, but **428** pilots saved.

British bombers lost in operations in November against German or enemy-occupied territory were **48** ; German aircraft destroyed over these regions numbered **8**. In the East and in the Mediterranean **Britain lost 18** aircraft, against **59 Italian destroyed**. Unofficial estimate for the whole war period gave an **Italian loss of at least 290** 'planes.

Mr. Churchill on Nov. 5 gave weekly average of killed and seriously wounded civilians for September as **4,500** ; for October, **3,500**.

In Britain We Fight the Murder Raids

MONKS are now to be seen as firemen at Buckfast Abbey, Buckfastleigh, Devon, the great stone church which has been rebuilt entirely by the monks, who began their work in 1908. Now their fear is that bombs may undo the work of many years, and here they are wheeling their fire-pump out for daily practice.

LIVERPOOL, it has now been revealed, is the north-western city that has been mentioned many times as one of the Nazi objectives since the blitzkrieg in the air was carried to provincial cities. Here the Lord Mayor, seen left with an air-raid warden, is watching a civilian rescue squad at work in a demolished building. In the ruins that fill the huge crater people were still trapped when the photograph was taken.

Photos, "Daily Mirror"

Nazis Had a Brief Success in the Shipping War

One week in October was a black week in the war against our Mercantile Navy. The losses were the heaviest since war began, but the weekly average for the month was lower than that for September, so the Nazi success was brief. This, with stories of seamen's gallantry and a table of losses for the five weeks, is described here by Mr. D. E. Maxwell.

THE British public, inevitably concerned with the progress of the war overhead, was reminded of its debt to the British seamen when the Ministry of Shipping issued its first merchant shipping casualty list on October 17. The fact that the list was long overdue—it covered approximately the first six months of the war—possibly emphasized that, unlike conditions on land or in the air, the war at sea had been waged with all the strength Germany could command and cared to risk from the first day, when the passenger liner "Athenia" was torpedoed without warning, and sixteen seamen, three stewardesses and 193 passengers were killed or drowned. For the seamen of many countries, but Britain in particular, there had been no respite from attacks by torpedo, from the menace of mines sown indiscriminately, or from the danger of the lurking raider. But for the courage, endurance and sacrifice of her seamen, Britain's war effort would have long since been paralysed for want of food and raw materials.

The first casualty list contained the names of 917 members of the Merchant Navy and fishing fleets; it was made up of 45 masters and skippers, 192 deck and engine-room officers, 19 radio officers and 661 men. The First Lord of the Admiralty later announced that in the first year of the war the number, crews and passengers, lost and saved was approximately : 3,327 lost, 15,635 saved, and 1,100 taken prisoner or interned.

In regard to shipping losses, the uncomfortably steady rate of sinkings during the previous four months was maintained in October. The position was regarded as serious, particularly since the British losses of one week were the heaviest since the outbreak of war.

That the Government was alive to the menace represented by the intensified attack on Britain's vital trade routes was demonstrated later in Parliament—as it had not been demonstrated before. "This is a

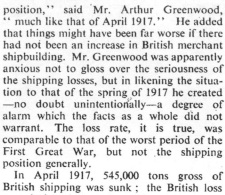

Merchant Shipping War Losses For October 1940

	Sept. 3, 1939 Sept. 29, 1940	Sept. 30 Nov. 3	Sept. 3, 1939 Nov. 3, 1940
	Tons gross	Tons gross	Tons gross
BRITISH :			
Liners, cargo vessels	1,852,937	313,428	2,166,415
Lost in naval operations	73,220	—	73,220
Naval auxiliaries ...	151,033	—	151,033
Naval trawlers ...	17,709	3,751	21,460
Totals ...	2,094,949	317,179	2,412,128
ALLIED :	544,977	60,242	605,219
Totals ...	2,639,926	377,421	3,017,347
NEUTRAL :	825,127	46,630	871,757
Totals ...	3,465,053	424,051	3,889,104

The figures above cover five weeks

Enemy Losses to October 31, 1940

	Sunk	Captured	Total
GERMAN :	873,478	259,161	1,132,639
ITALIAN :	214,899	150,762	365,661
Totals ...	1,088,377	409,923	1,498,300

In addition about 44,190 tons under enemy control or useful to the enemy have been sunk.

position," said Mr. Arthur Greenwood, " much like that of April 1917." He added that things might have been far worse if there had not been an increase in British merchant shipbuilding. Mr. Greenwood was apparently anxious not to gloss over the seriousness of the shipping losses, but in likening the situation to that of the spring of 1917 he created —no doubt unintentionally—a degree of alarm which the facts as a whole did not warrant. The loss rate, it is true, was comparable to that of the worst period of the First Great War, but not the shipping position generally.

In April 1917, 545,000 tons gross of British shipping was sunk ; the British loss rate during the worst month so far of the Second Great War, September, was less than this by nearly 40 per cent, though it was higher than the average for the whole of 1917. Further, in 1917 there was a marked shortage of Allied shipping such as did not exist in October 1940. On the former occasion, the crisis arose largely owing to the Government's concentration on warship building at the expense of the construction of merchant ships. As Mr. Greenwood indicated, no such vital error had been committed in 1940—or, if the building programme had at one time been slightly unbalanced in favour of men-of-war, a safer equilibrium had been established by the end of October.

However, in relation to the actual supply of tonnage at that time, of far greater importance than the British shipbuilding programme was the vast amount of shipping controlled by countries now allied to the British cause, including the Norwegian and Dutch fleets. While, as the Minister of Shipping revealed, the tonnage under the British flag was slightly less than at the outbreak of war, that flying the flags of our Allies amounted to about 8,000,000 tons gross—equivalent to nearly two years' losses at the current high rate of sinkings. The problem in the autumn of 1940 was not that

DESTROYER ESCORTS are still the best means of dealing with the menace to convoys from U-boats, and above a destroyer is dropping depth charges over her stern round the spot where an enemy submarine has been located. When more destroyers come from U.S.A. still more damage will be done to the U-boat forces. The top photograph shows fifteen-year-old Desmond Lock, bellboy of the "Highland Patriot" a U-boat victim, arriving early in October at a West Coast port in naval rig-out after being rescued by a British warship.   *Photos, British Official : Crown Copyright ; and Keystone*

The Fight Against the U-Boat Menace Goes On

BRITISH SHIPYARDS work at full pressure to make good the losses caused by Hitler's intensive U-boat campaign against our convoys. Riveters are here seen at work on the deck of a new ship at a British shipyard. Beside it the framework of another vessel is shown, while in the background a third ship has been completed and launched. On December 5 it was announced that the U.S.A. was placing 150 merchant ships at Britain's disposal.   *Photo, Central Press*

a shortage of ships existed but that means had eventually to be found to replace the losses that might possibly occur in 1941 and 1942 and to strengthen our escorting forces.

The black week of October was that which ended the 20th, when 47 British, Allied and neutral ships were sunk, totalling 205,781 tons gross. This figure had only been exceeded in one week, but on that occasion many of the ships were lost in the combined naval operations off the Channel ports. The British losses in the week 13-20, 154,279 tons, were slightly higher (by 5,600 tons) than those of the previously worst week of the war (September 15-22), while the Allied losses were the highest since the evacuation of the B.E.F. from France

Lowest Week's Losses Since May

This record was, of course, to be deplored, but the figures for the following week served as a reminder that monthly or average totals were of more importance than weekly figures. By contrast, the total for the week ended on October 27—16,860 tons, including 9,986 tons of British ships—was the lowest since the beginning of May. The result of these violent fluctuations was that the average weekly loss of British and Allied tonnage for October was noticeably less than in September—75,000 tons against 90,000 tons—though it was still slightly above the average for August—71,000 tons.

In the week ended on October 20 the majority of the British losses occurred in the Atlantic and were evidently due to a concentration of U-boats, based on ports all along the Norwegian and Continental coastline as far south as the Pyrenees. The exceptional effort soon petered out. The Germans may have been assisted by such Italian submarines as had been able to slip past Gibraltar. Also one or two fruitful attacks on convoys may have been made by more than a single submarine. For what it is worth—usually very little indeed—a German communiqué issued on October 19 claimed that of 31 ships sunk by U-boats "during the past few days," 26 were in "strongly protected" convoys. The brief success was undoubtedly accompanied by losses of enemy submarines, and their highly-skilled officers and crews.

The weekly average loss for October would have been less than that for August,

as well as September, if the total had not included one of the finest and most beautiful passenger liners flying the British flag. The "Empress of Britain," of 42,348 tons gross, flagship of the Canadian Pacific fleet, was sunk at 2.5 a.m. on the night of October 27-28 (see pages 502, 504 and 555). The liner had been attacked by a German bomber in the early morning two days previously about 150 miles from the Irish coast.

The "Empress of Britain," though belonging to the C.P.R., whose head office is in Canada, was, like all the fleet of Canadian Pacific Steamships, Ltd., registered in Great Britain. She was one of the fastest and most luxurious ships in Empire services, and the most notable merchant ship in the world to have been sunk during the war so far.

Another regrettable loss was that of the Royal Mail liner "Highland Patriot," a fine ship of 14,172 tons gross. She was torpedoed without warning homeward bound from South America. Fortunately, only three

of the crew of 139 lost their lives and all the 33 passengers were rescued, although the liner was not in convoy.

A typical incident demonstrating the resourcefulness and daring of the merchant seamen who are aiding in the war against totalitarianism as the allies of Britain, was the escape from Dakar during the month of two Polish coastal ships, the "Rozewie" of 766 tons and the "Kroman" of 1,864 tons. The French authorities planned to seize six Polish ships which had been berthed at Dakar. Steel cables with electric alarms were placed at the mouth of the harbour. The masters decided to make a dash for safety, braving the powerful French artillery units. The "Rozewie" slipped under the nose of a French battleship at the dead of night, started the alarm, broke the cable and managed to reach open sea. The "Kroman" escaped later, without navigation papers or certain parts of her machinery.

While, as already pointed out, the merchant shipping losses continued at a rate which could be regarded with anything but complacency, the Allied shipping position was still so satisfactory at the end of October that a fair tonnage of the Norwegian and Dutch fleets was left unchartered to the Ministry of Shipping, free to engage in trades remote from the theatre of war. A further safeguard against a shipping crisis was provided when Italy wantonly attacked her small but tenacious neighbour Greece on October 28. A considerable proportion of the Greek merchant fleet—which included about 1,600,000 tons gross of ocean-going tramp ships, the largest tramp fleet in the world next to that of Great Britain—was already chartered to the Ministry of Shipping. But the addition to the countries ranged against the dictators of another sea power, in the commercial sense, provided a welcome assurance for the future.

Imports of between 4,000,000 and 5,000,000 tons continued to arrive at British ports.

THIS U-BOAT is seen from a Messerschmitt 'plane. Members of the crew on the conning-tower are clearly visible. R.A.F. attacks against the important U-boat base of Lorient in German-occupied France have been repeatedly pressed home, for with the acquisition of Atlantic seaports the U-boats seek to paralyse British shipping.   *Photo, Planet News*

OUR SEARCHLIGHT ON THE WAR

Nazis Try to Wreck Oil Plant

FROM New York comes a curious tale of an attempt by a Nazi raiding party to destroy the oil refineries on the island of Curaçao, in the Dutch West Indies. These works were taken under Allied protection on May 11 last to prevent them from falling into enemy hands. According to an eye-witness story, the attempt was made on the night of July 28, when two British tankers were tied up at the dock taking on supplies of aviation petrol. The landing party from a Nazi raider crept ashore on the opposite side of the island, intending to steal over to the refineries unseen, but they were detected and a fight ensued. Details are lacking, but it would appear that the tankers left the port and manoeuvred so as to be able to train their guns on the shore. The raiders started using machine-guns and hand grenades, the tankers replied with gunfire. It was a short and sharp encounter. Whether the British defenders suffered any losses was not stated, but next day it was declared that 35 members of the raiding party were either killed or wounded.

American Flash Bomb for R.A.F.

THE United States Army Air Corps has released to the R.A.F. a secret flash bomb on which their experts have been experimenting for some years. It is a device for securing detailed photographs from a high altitude by night, and will be of great value in reconnaissance flights over enemy

country. The flash from the bomb, which is similar to that produced by a photographic flash bulb, acts upon a photo-electric cell in the aeroplane which actuates the shuttle of the camera, and photographing becomes automatic. Dangerous daylight flights for the purpose of obtaining information about damage done to enemy objectives, or to ascertain the disposition of forces, will soon be unnecessary.

Attempt to Assassinate Quisling

GREAT tension has resulted in Norway from the unsuccessful attempt on December 1 to assassinate the leader of the Norwegian Nazi party, Quisling. After addressing a none too friendly gathering at Fredrikstad, he was walking at the head of a Nazi youth procession through the streets of the town when a bomb was thrown which exploded immediately ahead. Several people were badly hurt, but Quisling himself escaped, although the police had to intervene to save him from molestation by the excited crowd.

The same evening he started to address a meeting at Sarpsburg, but so threatening was the attitude of the audience that again he had to be rescued, while a free fight broke out, followed by arrests and the removal of more injured persons to hospital. Hatred and hostility towards the Nazis have intensified during recent weeks, and a dangerous spirit is rising in the country which is feared by some to presage civil war.

Finland's Independence Day

HELSINKI celebrated Finnish Independence Day on December 6 with a military parade and many large patriotic meetings. At least half of those taking part in the parade were engaged a year ago in the great

FLASH BOMB lighting was used to take the aerial photograph above from a height of 5,000 feet. Its clarity is remarkable, for it has not been in any way retouched. Left, Major George W. Gordon, a U.S. observer, who conducted the first experiments with the bombs, is examining one of them. With him is the pilot who flew the 'plane from which experimental photographs were taken.   *Photos, Associated Press*

struggle with Russia. Field-Marshal Mannerheim inspected disabled men who attended in wheeled chairs, and M. Ryti, Premier and acting President, delivered an oration in which he said : " We must make ready for any eventuality, and maintain and strengthen our capacity and will for defence." Hitler, who had withheld any message of encouragement when Finland was fighting for her life last winter, cabled his good wishes.

Journalists Inspect Italian Warships

WITH the object of disproving British claims of damage inflicted on Italian warships during the naval battle of November 27, Mussolini invited fifteen neutral journalists to make a tour of inspection of ships said to have taken part in the engagement. The privileged correspondents were shown over five warships and reported that the only scars to be seen on the battleships " Vittorio Veneto " and " Giulio Cesare " were a few bare patches due, they were told, to the paint being peeled off the gun turrets by the firing of their own 15-in. batteries. No damage of any kind was found on the three cruisers " Fiume," " Pola " and " Gorizia." Two comments can be made about this report. The first is that the only damage observed by British aircraft on the battleships was a torpedo hit on one of them, and this would not be apparent to a visitor shown only the upper deck. The second is that out of seven 10,000-ton cruisers taking part in the action three only were seen. There is nothing to prove that the other four are intact.

Rumania in the German Grip

WHEN General Antonescu, Rumanian premier, was in Berlin to sign the Axis pact on November 23, he also arranged a 10-year economic pact between the two countries. Under this agreement, Germany allows Rumania long-term credits for the development of her industry and agriculture, German technical aid is made available, and private investment of German capital in Rumania will be encouraged. In exchange for these privileges Rumania is to develop and extend her communications with Germany, including railways, roads, and oil pipe-lines. The first of the new decrees empowers General Antonescu to expropriate all oil-pipes, lines, pumping stations and reservoirs, as well as the property on which they stand. The second decree provides for the seizure of all Danube barges, tugs, tankers and sea-going ships owned or used by companies with Jewish shareholders.

Rules for the Inhabitants of Brest

COMPLYING with instructions issued by the Kreiskommandantur (German District Command), the unhappy mayor of Brest has had to appeal to his fellow townsmen to observe regulations which were set out in " La Dépêche de Brest et de l'Ouest." They ran as follows :

1. *National Emblem.* By order of the head of the military administration in France, the French population is forbidden to wear the tricolour emblem in public, in whatever form. No object displayed to the public must be decorated with the French national colours.

2. *Insult to Italians.* The inhabitants are strictly forbidden to insult the Italians and in particular the Italian Vice-Consul at Brest, M. Vittorio Job. If the Vice-Consul is insulted afresh the city of Brest will be fined 50,000 francs on each occasion.

3. *Throwing of Stones or Sundry Debris at German Soldiers.* Acts of this sort will be repressed with extreme severity. If the culprits are not discovered, the city risks being subjected to a considerable fine.

The mayor counts on the spirit of understanding of the population for the avoidance of incidents the consequences of which may be serious for the whole community

I WAS THERE!

Eye Witness Stories of Episodes and Adventures in the Second Great War

'Are Youse Guys English?' They Asked Us

Reported "missing, feared killed," the crew of an R.A.F. bomber—pilot, observer and air gunner—arrived safely at their base in Greece after a two-days' journey which, as the squadron leader describes below, developed into a triumphal progress through the Greek countryside.

AN R.A.F. squadron raided one of the Albanian ports, and because of cloud its bombs had to be released at a very low altitude. A big ship was hit and damage to docks caused. Two of the aircraft were hit by anti-aircraft shells. One, badly damaged, had great difficulty in making its way back to base. He reported that his companion had also been hit, one engine being seen to stop, and that it was likely the aircraft had crashed into the sea.

Nothing more was heard for two days and the crew and aircraft were officially posted as missing. The squadron leader eventually told the following story of the adventures of this aircraft.

Just as we had released our bombs we received direct hits from anti-aircraft shells. One tore a large hole in the port engine cowling, but it continued to function in spite of the fact that oil was pouring out. The other engine was hit and stopped almost immediately.

The aircraft was holed in many places and there was one enormous rent right through one wing, but the aircraft would still fly, though the force of the explosion had thrown it on its back.

Not one of us was injured, though the notebook in our air gunner's pocket was torn in half by a piece of shrapnel. We flew on slowly, unable to make height on our one engine. The cockpit was full of petrol fumes, and I feared we should pass out. We were a sitting bird, all right, but no one came after us.

We flew for nearly two hours and then spotted a tiny island. We found only one place to attempt a landing—a strip of beach about 20 yards wide. I gave the chance of jumping to the crew, but they preferred to stand by me. Well, we put the aircraft down safely, although the wheels would not come down and we made a belly landing.

There were more difficulties with which to contend. The observer went forward to some peasants, who immediately rushed away screaming. We put our hands up and yelled: "Inglese; Inglese." A look of wonderment spread over one man's face, and he replied with a definite American accent: "Are youse guys English?"

Locals came to the number of about a thousand and looked extremely dangerous, only being kept back by our Americanized friend.

At last we persuaded the villagers of this tiny island that we were friendly, and they found us their only car. It did not last long. It was destroyed soon after by a bomb, one of many that fell that day on this entirely defenceless island. We were bombed eight times in a single day, the only casualties occurring among the civilian population.

Later we persuaded the owner of a fishing boat to take us to the mainland. We set off at night, going to sleep on the deck, but cold and hungry. Rough waves continually swept the deck. After 20 hours at sea the weather was so rough that the skipper was forced to put into a port near by, fortunately on the mainland.

Here we had a grand reception. All of us were carried shoulder high round the village, being kissed by men, women, and children alike. Bouquets showered on us; we were given bottles of local wine, and finally led by the mayor and corporation to the town hall.

I had to make a speech, but as it was in English I do not imagine much of it got over. The most popular part was when I said "Mussolini" in grim tones and made a sign. That fairly brought the house down. A car was found for us, and amid wild cheers and enthusiasm and loaded with gifts we set off across the mountain trail. After a long journey we came to another town, where we were again treated like conquering heroes.

Eventually, after walking, travelling by car and by train, we got back to our base. My crew and I are agreed we would not have missed this grand tour of Greece for anything. It has made us feel that war in this part of the world is really worth while, and we are instilled with renewed enthusiasm.

I Was in a Channel Destroyer Battle

On Friday, November 29, a naval action took place in the English Channel between British and German destroyers. The following eye-witness account of the engagement is by the "Daily Mirror" Naval Correspondent, who was on board one of the British destroyers.

WE had been at "action stations" about eleven hours when at about 5 a.m. suddenly we turned about and from the leader, H.M.S. "Javelin" (see illustration in page 644), there flashed a message.

The lean grey ships leapt forward in unison and raced full steam ahead. On we sped. Each ship's 4,000 h.p. engines were humming at their highest pitch.

Suddenly a star-shell burst, hung in the sky and flooded the scene with a white light.

On our starboard bow, little more than two miles away, I saw two German destroyers. There were three, I learned afterwards. But in the split second before hell's lid was lifted I picked out two dark shapes from the tumbling waves.

Then the enemy's guns crashed and our guns and the guns of our sister ships spoke. The air was filled with the roar of guns and bursting shells, flying metal and the reek of cordite.

More star shells. "Javelin," our leader, three hundred yards away on our starboard bow, took a torpedo in her nose. We swung towards her the better to bring our guns and torpedoes to bear on the enemy.

The roar of guns and the whang of the enemy's five-inch shells, that sounded like the crack of a giant whip, persisted.

Torpedoes were the enemy's parting shot. As they launched them and the British destroyers closed in with their guns blazing and registering hits, they swung their noses southwards, put up a smoke screen, piled on steam and fled.

"Pursue!" We pursued.

But behind their smoke screen in the pre-dawn darkness they slipped us. We raked the Channel till dawn, but there was no sign of the marauding destroyers.

"Lost 'em, eh?" said a Cockney gunner

AT A GREEK AIRFIELD, R.A.F. officers are seen inspecting bombs intended to be released on an Italian port in Albania. The fine work of the R.A.F., which operates from Greek bases against the enemy positions in Albania, is the background to the adventure described above.
Photo, British Official: Crown Copyright

as I passed him. "Blimey, I wish I'd brought my —— bike."

Just before dawn it was reported that "Javelin," whom we had thought lost, was afloat. And our leader was unhurt. At daybreak we found her. She had gaping wounds, but the white ensign still flew from her mast. We gave her three rousing cheers as we passed. They cheered back.

Another destroyer took the wounded on board and raced back to port. "Javelin" was the only British ship to sustain casualties or damage.

Tugs came out and took "Javelin" in tow. Slowly all day they have been towing her back to port.

Enemy 'planes have attacked us several times. It is now 8 p.m. With me are officers with grimy, unshaven faces, eyes bloodshot and heavy.

Later.—We are in port. All except "Javelin" are loading ammunition. Then a spot of sleep. "For tomorrow, by the living God, they'll try the game again."

That is, if the Germans dare to come out and fight.

'Proud of the Crew of My Flaming Bomber'

A story of outstanding courage and endurance lies behind the award on December 4 of the D.S.O. to Pilot Officer Geoffrey Cheshire and the D.F.M. to Sergeant Henry Davidson of the R.A.F. How the bombing of Cologne goods yards was carried out by a severely damaged 'plane and injured crew is told here by Pilot Officer Cheshire himself.

ARRIVING back at his base, Pilot Officer Cheshire made his report, which began in correct service fashion, "I have the honour to report that on the night of November 11-12th the . . . aircraft was damaged. . . ." In a less formal account he said :

We were off just before midnight, and set course for the oil refinery at Wesseling, Cologne. We went straight to the target, but unluckily the clouds were there before us. We could not see the ground at all. We circled for fifty minutes hoping that it would clear ; then we decided to attack the railway goods yard at Cologne before that was

cleared a little, and to my amazement I saw that, not only were the engines still there, but that they were both running. Then the bomb-aimer came up through the well, his face streaming with what looked like blood. He was holding his head, and could not stand upright. I could not possibly help him, since it was all I could do to regain control of the aircraft. Suddenly he shouted "fire" and staggered towards the tail.

A little later I looked round and saw the wireless operator coming through the door with flames licking his flying suit. He was on fire himself. The bomb-aimer dashed up to him and beat the flames out with his hands.

come to, thinking that the turret had been blown completely off and that it was falling through the sky. It turned out that it was he who had said "I've been hit," and the next thing he remembers is helping to throw out the incendiary bombs and being told to go back for his parachute in case the other end of the aeroplane should fall off.

During this time the wireless operator and I were alone in the cabin. He had collapsed on the floor and said, "I'm going blind, sir." His face was burned completely black, and it looked as though blood was streaming from his eyes. When the crew returned I sent the second pilot back for the first-aid outfit and told the others to look after the wireless operator who at first refused to be helped. He got to his feet and said, "I must get to the wireless." As soon as his burns had been attended to, he clambered to his wireless and started to send out messages saying that we were on our way back to base. But first he had to explain the setting of the dials to the rear gunner, and when everything was ready he had his hand guided to the key. For forty minutes he stood like that, tapping out his message, but the aerial had been shot away, and nothing got through. Half an hour after the explosion we had got clear of the anti-aircraft fire.

Then we took stock. We found the front turret holed, both doors gone, and the ten-foot hole in the fuselage itself. The fuselage had been twisted, and that accounted for the wallowing motion of the aircraft, but we were able to maintain height, and by running the engines carefully could make a decent speed. It took us five hours to get home—there was an eighty-mile wind against us.

All those hours the wireless operator made no moan or complaint, although he was suffering from the intense cold as well as from his burns. When we told him we would land at the nearest aerodrome, he begged that we should go the extra 100 miles, so that we could all get back to our friends and let them see that we were safe. It was a crew to be proud of, not one of them showed even the slightest trace of fear or doubt as to our ability to get through.

That the aircraft was able to cover the distance is the finest tribute possible to the designers, manufacturers, and workmen. The whole of the skin and ribs had been blown off one side of the fuselage, and on the other side all the rivets were missing. There was very little left to hold the tail plane on, but we bombed the goods yard, and in spite of all they could do to us, we safely made the journey home.

WHILE OVER GERMANY this heavy bomber was hit by an A.A. shell ; although a large part of the fuselage was blown out by the explosion, the magnificent cooperation on the part of the crew, described by Pilot Officer Cheshire in this page, brought the machine safely home.
Photo, British Official : Crown Copyright

obscured, too. We could see the yard clearly enough. The anti-aircraft gunfire, which had been very severe and accurate for the last hour, slowed down, and it seemed as though we could not miss our new target. The bomb doors were open, the wireless operator was standing by to drop the great flare and the bomb-aimer had started giving the usual alterations of course.

Then anti-aircraft fire opened up intensely again, and one shell burst very close. It was what is technically known as a near miss, but it was near enough for fragments to hit us. There was a blinding explosion from the front, the perspex of the front turret was blown away, and there was another terrific explosion in the fuselage. The shell had touched off the flare.

The explosions had hurled the control column out of my hands, and the cabin filled with dense black smoke. I remember asking the bomb-aimer if he had dropped his bombs, but the only answer I got was, "I've been hit." Very soon the smoke

Then he disappeared down the fuselage again. He seemed to have recovered completely, and it turned out that what I had taken to be blood was only oil.

Then the cabin cleared of smoke, and things seemed to be fairly all right, except that the aircraft was flying in an erratic sort of way. Back in the body of the machine the crew were working frantically to get rid of the incendiaries and anything that might explode. We carried on and dropped our bombs. We hadn't made the journey for fun, and the job had to be done as best we could do it.

Then the second pilot came forward and reported that the fire seemed to be under control. On seeing fire break out he had gone for the fire extinguisher. But by the time he had got back again the wireless operator had pushed the blazing flare down the "chute" and the bomb-aimer was stamping the flames out. So the second pilot went back to the tail gunner, cooped up in his little glass turret, who had been knocked out by the explosion. He had

December 20th, 1940   The War Illustrated   669

IIIIIIIIIIIIIIIIIIIIIIIIIIIIIIIIIIIIIIIIIIIIIIIIIIIIIIIIIIIIIIIIIIIIIIIIIIIIIIII I WAS THERE! IIIIIIIIIIIIIIIIIIIIIIIIIIIIIIIIIIIIIIIIIIIIIIIIIIIIIIIIIIIIIIIIIIIIIIIIIIIIIIIIIIII

Our Jackie Mumbled : 'Only Did Me Best'

When eight people were trapped in the cellar of a bombed house at Birmingham, six were rescued by Jack Reynolds, an eighteen-year-old A.R.P. messenger who, as recounted in this letter to the "Daily Mirror," wormed his way into the wreckage and helped them out.

Jack Reynolds, young and brave, the story of whose fine rescue work in Birmingham is told in this page, is seen reading a letter of praise and congratulation from the Earl of Dudley, Midlands Regional Commissioner.

Photo, " Daily Mirror "

DESCRIBING the " incident " in which young Jack Reynolds displayed conspicuous bravery, a Birmingham group warden said :

One night two houses were hit by a high explosive bomb. The incident was reported at the post by a warden two minutes later.

Eight people were trapped in the cellar of one house. We heard them calling to us through a hole on a level with the garden.

The big bay window frame, which had been blown out by the explosion, lay across it.

I shone my torch into the cellar and counted six people and two dogs.

The ceiling had collapsed at the far end, and at our end was held up only by a loose beam which looked like slipping at any moment.

Young Jackie Reynolds was by my side. He said : " Shall I go down ? I can slip in quite easily." I told him he would be risking his life, but all he said was : " I'll do me best. Just tell me what to do."

He slithered down feet first and got busy in the light of several torches. He helped up the three people nearest to us, a man and two women.

We heaved them up, but the remaining three (two women and a man) and the two dogs were not going to be so easy.

The man was lying back in his invalid chair unconscious. His wife, a heavy woman, was face down on his lap, also unconscious, her feet hidden in the debris.

First we passed some water down to Jackie for the woman. It revived her a lot. Jackie talked away to her.

Now came his most delicate and difficult task. The woman was not so difficult, because she could at least walk, and he helped her up to us, but the man and wife were heavy.

I asked him if he could manage to roll one at a time on to a sheet of corrugated iron if we let it down. He gave us the usual reply : " I'll do me best."

He passed the dog up first. Then we slid down the corrugated iron sheet, which he wedged firmly. Then I dropped the end of a rope down to him and told him to tie it firmly round the man's chest.

Jackie is not a strong lad. But again he said : " I'll do me best." After a hard struggle he managed to tie the rope and roll the man only a little on to the metal sheet.

While Jackie guided, we pulled the man from under his wife and so up to the opening. Jackie could not turn the woman over on her back, but he managed to get her head and chest on to the sheet.

The woman was the sixth person Jackie had rescued, and it had taxed his strength severely.

But before he allowed himself to be helped up, he borrowed my torch to see if he could find the other two women. They were invisible under the debris, and, as the rescue squad were working from behind the house to reach them, we left it to them and helped Jackie up.

He mumbled something about " Only did me best " and vanished.

I Was Boarded by the Fishermen's Patrol

Among the vessels flying the White Ensign which keep watch over coastal traffic round our shores are the trawlers of the " Fishermen's Patrol." A master mariner who was challenged and inspected by one of them describes their vigilance and efficiency in the following story.

STEALTHILY the little old coaster nosed her way among the shoals off the East Coast on her homeward journey to the Port of London.

I say " stealthily " because at the best of times this coast is no place for a careless seaman, and now we must take care to avoid, with the assistance of our naval instructions, " certain obstructions " which are intended for the benefit of someone else.

And for the enlightenment of any landsman who thinks, or might have thought, that a waterborne invading force could pounce upon these shores of ours, I can say from personal experience that coastal navigation is an anxious enough job for us who know, from years of experience, the narrow channels, the shoals, the set of the tides and how they are affected by various directions of wind, apart from the above-mentioned " certain obstructions."

Heaven knows how any square-headed stranger from over the water would get on ! And on top of all such difficulties he would have to contend with the Fishermen's Patrol.

No smart naval force, this, although the White Ensign flutters over their seaworthy counters ; but a rough, ruthless set of men whose families have for centuries wrested a living from off the stormy coast of Britain. If you have any business near the British coast you had better be sharp about answering their questions, or you might get hurt.

We had seen these patrol trawlers off and on all day—they seemed to be everywhere, rolling and pitching to and fro with as masterful a majesty as any battleship. As darkness came on, we were, by wartime regulations, compelled to anchor. But as it was not possible for us to get into a port or sheltered anchorage, we had to let go some miles out to sea, with a half-tide sandbank to give us a lee till the morning.

Right up to the time our anchor chain rattled out through the hawser pipe a little

Yarmouth drifter shadowed us a mile off our starboard quarter, and when we were brought up he steamed close alongside and hailed us.

Crossing from one side of the wheelhouse to the other to answer, I found myself looking down the business end of a gun, manned by a tough-looking bunch in cloth caps and blue guernseys, who, I am sure, would have been delighted had I replied in German, or even said a word out of place. They would have blown us sky-high at the slightest provocation.

They train the gun on you first and hail you afterwards ; and the gun crew stand by all ready while you answer. So great care was necessary on my part in giving their skipper, briefly and clearly, the information he required. The trawler sheered off into the night. I went below, had supper, and turned in.

I was wakened just before daylight by the sound of a boat alongside and heavy footsteps on the deck. Jumping out of my bunk to investigate, I started up the companion steps only to find my way balked by a huge fisherman in sea-boots. Somewhat surprised at this intrusion, I stepped back into the cabin and he followed me.

" Are you the master of this vessel ? " I told him that I was. " Your papers, please."

There was no dilly-dallying. In a few seconds he satisfied himself about the essential items concerning the ship. In the meantime another of his men was conducting a rapid but efficient examination of the crew and their quarters forward. A third and fourth had already taken a hatch off and looked down the hold. In two or three minutes they had examined every section of the ship and every member of the crew. They were gruff, unyielding, and thorough, but they missed nothing.

And once they decided that all was well they bluntly apologized for troubling us— " We have to do this, you know "—and pulled away to the drifter. They had been watching us all night.—" *Daily Mail.*"

The guns of trawlers and drifters now acting as minesweepers receive periodical overhauls by gunners of the Royal Navy. A gunnery officer at an East Coast port is watching the changing of a Lewis gun ammunition drum.

Photo, Planet News

They Are Ready for Any Invaders in the Shetlands

SHETLAND Islanders have resolved that no Nazis shall ever set foot on their islands, and they are prepared for everything. The Shetlands—situated as they are on a possible air and sea route from Nazi-occupied Norway to the Faroes, Iceland and Greenland—are of much strategic importance, and though naval officers have to some extent supervised the defensive preparations, the islanders, men, women and children, have worked with a will and have marshalled their own resources most effectively.

One thing that the Shetlanders have discovered is that whale oil drums filled with sand make obstacles on the roads that an invader would find extremely awkward. In the top photograph, amidst the barren and treeless country, one of these ingenious devices is being inspected by naval and military officers. In the lower photograph women and children are at work filling the sandbags with which the drums are packed.

Photo, British Official : Crown Copyright

Sniper of the Modern Army Sees but Is Unseen

From a few yards away the netting, above, is indistinguishable from the bed of nettles in which it is placed, but inside it is a sniper, right, who can see without being seen.

The strange formation in the branching tree trunk is worn by a sniper. It is a camouflage visor, designed by a famous artist, and is practically indistinguishable from the trunk.

SNIPERS today are not picked out from the troops in the firing line simply because they are good shots. They are still that, but they are also highly trained specialists who have undergone a course of training at the Army School of Sniping in the Aldershot Command. Everything that can possibly be of value is added to the natural gifts of hands and sight which have already made the men good marksmen, and famous shots from all over the Empire coach them in the finer points of marksmanship.

A most important part of the course is that concerned with camouflage and taking cover, and so a famous big-game hunter teaches them how to see without being seen. Many of the sharpshooters are recruited from the ghillies and stalkers of the grouse moors and deer forests of Scotland, who in the course of their work have learned much that will be of use to them as snipers. They have developed a far keener sight than the average man.

The camouflage cloak worn by this sniper is painted to harmonize exactly with the surrounding vegetation, and it makes him as nearly as possible an invisible man.

Photos, Topical

OUR DIARY OF THE WAR

TUESDAY, DEC. 3, 1940   *458th day*

In the Air—R.A.F. made daylight attacks on aerodromes in Northern France. Bad weather restricted night operations, but attacks were made on goods yards at Ludwigshaven and railway junction at Mannheim, blast furnace plant at Essen and port of Dunkirk.

War against Italy—Violent R.A.F. attack on Kassala.

Home Front—Single enemy aircraft made few daylight flights over East Anglia, S.E. and S.W. England. Bombs fell in London outskirts and at other widespread places.

Night raiders dropped incendiaries over London, starting fires. Heavy attack on Midlands towns, particularly Birmingham, where extensive damage was done. Bombs also fell in scattered areas in the Home Counties.

Greek War—Athens claimed that Greek Army was within 1½ miles of Santi Quaranta, and that two heights dominating Argyrokastro had been captured. Fresh heights occupied north-west of Pogradets.

WEDNESDAY, DEC. 4   *459th day*

In the Air—R.A.F. made sustained attack on targets in Düsseldorf area. Other objectives included ports of Antwerp and Calais, several aerodromes and A.A. gun positions.

Enemy bomber shot down over Dutch coast.

War against Italy—R.A.F. bombers heavily damaged Italian destroyer off Santi Quaranta. Greek Navy later captured it.

Other forces bombed selected targets at Turin, including the Royal Arsenal.

Home Front—Bombs dropped during day over Dover. Two raids on East Anglian town. Midlands were again attacked at night, bombs being dropped in a number of districts. London and Home Counties were also raided.

Greek War—Greek patrols entered outskirts of Santi Quaranta. Italians evacuating Argyrokastro and Premeti.

R.A.F. shot down eight enemy aircraft and severely damaged seven others. Italian troops retreating in Tepelini-Klisura area were successfully attacked by British bombers and fighters.

General—First Free French Cross of Liberation awarded posthumously to Colonial civil servant in French West Africa.

THURSDAY, DEC. 5   *460th day*

On the Sea—Armed merchant cruiser H.M.S. " Carnarvon Castle " was in action at long range with heavily armed German raider in South Atlantic. " Carnarvon Castle " was slightly damaged and put into Montevideo for repairs.

Admiralty announced loss while minesweeping of H.M. trawlers " Ethel Taylor," " Amethyst," " Elk," " Calverton," and H.M. drifter " Christmas Rose."

In the Air—Coastal Command aircraft attacked chemical factory at Eindhoven, Rotterdam airport, Haamstede aerodrome, and submarine base at Lorient. Night bombing operations were cancelled owing to bad weather.

Home Front—Successive formations of enemy fighters and fighter-bombers which flew over East Kent were scattered by our fighters. Bombs were dropped, causing damage and casualties.

During night South Coast town was heavily bombed. Large fires caused in nurses' home attached to hospital. Extensive damage to houses, shops, and a cinema. London was also raided for short time.

Fourteen enemy aircraft shot down. Two British fighters lost, but pilot of one safe.

Long-range artillery duel across Straits of Dover. R.A.F. bombers flew to attack enemy positions.

Greek War—Greeks occupied Premeti, enemy suffering heavy losses. Greek aircraft heavily bombed enemy colums at Elbasan and in valley of R. Skumbi. To south of Argyrokastro Greeks occupied Libohovo. Italians evacuated Delvino.

FRIDAY, DEC. 6   *461st day*

In the Air—R.A.F. heavily bombed aerodromes in France and Low Countries. Channel ports of Dunkirk, Calais and Boulogne were also attacked.

THE POETS & THE WAR

XL

THE ALLY

By Lord Dunsany

I saw a gaunt shape walking in the snow
    When winter came. He lifted up his
        hand
And said in accents of a king's command,
Heil Hitler ! Thousands round him bent
        them low,
And did not rise again. Some uttered slow
    The same words, then were silent.
        Through that land
I saw him stride, and his tall figure
        stand
Gazing upon Berlin spread out below.
Then in the streets the voices died away
    That called on Hitler, and deep stillness
        came,
    And in the stillness, like a little flame
A new voice rose and gathered strength
        to say,
Feeble at first, then fierce and still more
        wild,
Heil Famine !   And the gazing monster
        smiled.

—*Sunday Times*

Home Front—Very little daylight activity. During night a south-western town was heavily attacked, damage being done to a hospital, numerous buildings and roads. Enemy 'planes were also over London, Midlands and Wales.

Greek War—Greeks occupied Santi Quaranta and entered outskirts of Argyrokastro. Further Greek advance made west of Premeti towards Klisura. In north Greek forces said to be advancing along river valleys to Elbasan and Berat.

Another R.A.F. bombing attack made on Valona.

General—Resignation of Marshal Badoglio announced. He was succeeded by General Ugo Cavallero.

SATURDAY, DEC. 7   *462nd day*

On the Sea—Disclosed that H.M.S. " Kelly," flotilla leader, was torpedoed in May off German North Sea coast by an E-boat, but is now back in service.

In the Air—R.A.F. bombers carried out sustained attack on targets in Düsseldorf area. Other objectives bombed included Antwerp, Dunkirk, Calais, Boulogne, several aerodromes, and naval shipyards and docks at Lorient and Brest.

War against Italy—Attack made on shipping off southern Albanian coast by R.A.F. bombers. Durazzo and Valona were heavily bombed.

R.A.F. bombers made successful raid on Castel Benito, near Tripoli.

Home Front—Enemy air activity was on reduced scale. No raids were made at night. Two enemy bombers shot down.

Greek War—Italians retreating along coast north of Santi Quaranta. Beyond Premeti Greeks pushing Italians on towards Klisura and Tepelini. On northern front Greeks continued advance towards key towns of Elbasan and Berat.

General—Announced that President Roosevelt had pledged American aid for Greece.

General Cesare de Vecchi, Governor of Dodecanese Islands, dismissed and succeeded by General Ettore Bastico.

SUNDAY, DEC. 8   *463rd day*

On the Sea—Reported from Buenos Aires that H.M. cruiser " Enterprise " was engaging Nazi raider in S. Atlantic.

British cruiser captured German supply ship " Idarwald " off Cuba.

In the Air—R.A.F. renewed attacks on targets in Düsseldorf area. Other forces bombed submarine base at Lorient; shipping and harbour installations at Bordeaux and Brest; ports of Flushing, Dunkirk and Gravelines; and several aerodromes.

War against Italy—In Western Desert R.A.F. bombers made night attack on Benina aerodrome. In the Sudan British patrols continued extensive activities in Gallabat area.

Home Front—After quiet day London suffered heavy night attack, wave after wave of raiders coming over. Considerable damage resulted from high explosive and incendiary bombs. Seven hospitals, four churches, a convent, three vicarages, two hotels, private houses, A.R.P. posts and shelters were hit, and a number of people killed or seriously injured. Bombs also fell in many districts between London and the south and east coasts, as well as in a few localities in southern England.

Three enemy aircraft shot down.

Greek War—Greeks occupied Argyrokastro and Delvino. Much material seized and many prisoners taken.

Italians reported to be continuously retreating towards Himara, on the coast, from area of Santi Quaranta and that of Argyrokastro.

AUXILIARY CRUISER 'CARNARVON CASTLE,' a vessel of 21,222 tons, was in action on December 5 with a heavily-armed raider in the South Atlantic, north-east of the River Plate estuary. The fight, which lasted 90 minutes, ended with the damaged raider steaming away at high speed. The British ship also sustained damage and put into Montevideo for repairs.

Photo, Topical Press

ONE OF THE GUNS THAT BLEW THE ITALIANS OUT OF EGYPT'S SKY

Anti-aircraft guns forming part of the western defences of Egypt have often been in action since Italy entered the war, and they helped to keep the sky clear of Italian raiders during Wavell's great offensive. One of the big guns is here seen on the coastline with its crew ready for action. The huge tires of the mounting help to prevent it from sinking into the sand. Such guns are very effective in desert warfare, for visibility beneath the glaring sun is usually good, and " cloud-dodging " is possible for attacking 'planes only on comparatively few days of the year.

Photo, British Official: Crown Copyright

Wavell's Army of the Nile Routs Graziani's

After months of waiting for a further move on Graziani's part, the British in Egypt delivered
a sudden blow at the Italian invaders in the Western Desert of Egypt. Below we describe
the opening phase of what was indeed a magnificent victory.

GENERAL SIR ARCHIBALD WAVELL, Commander-in-Chief of the British Forces in the Middle East, leant crosslegged against his desk in his headquarters at Cairo. About him were grouped a number of British, American and Turkish correspondents, and to them he made this dramatic declaration: " Gentlemen," he said, " I have asked you here to tell you that our forces began to carry out an engagement against the Italian armies in the Western Desert at dawn this morning [Dec. 9]." Then he went on to describe how the British troops had begun their advance, and concluded by saying that already he had received word that one of the Italian camps had been taken.

The British offensive against Graziani had been most carefully planned and prepared, and it would have taken place earlier if, as Mr. Churchill pointed out in the House of Commons on December 10, the Italian invasion of Greece had not made it necessary for a considerable part of the Royal Air Force in Egypt to be dispatched to aid the Greek Army in their heroic defence of their native land. " The serious temporary diminution of our Air Force in Egypt," said Mr. Churchill, " made it necessary somewhat to delay the execution of the offensive plans which had been matured, and it was not until the beginning of this month that the Air Force in Egypt was once again in a position to afford the necessary support to a forward movement."

But the delay was employed to good advantage. Although the opposing patrols were in more or less daily contact, the main bodies of the British and Italian armies were separated by some 75 miles of desert, and the crossing of this barren and shelterless waste unobserved by the enemy presented a pretty problem. Most of the work was done at night. First, dumps of ammunition, petrol, food and military supplies of all kinds were brought up from the base and buried in the sands far ahead of the British lines. Again at night the British troops were marched ever nearer to the Italian positions,

while during the hours of daylight they rested motionless, their khaki uniforms and camouflaged equipment fading imperceptibly into the dull brown of the desert. Even if the Italian 'planes had attempted a reconnaissance they might still have failed to spot the troops spread out below them, but in fact the skies were kept clear by the fighters of the R.A.F.

Then on the night of Sunday, December 8, the final stage began. By forced marches

LT.-GEN. SIR HENRY MAITLAND WILSON is here seen (centre) watching the arrival of further military equipment in Egypt. He has been Commander-in-Chief in Egypt since 1939, and it was he who, at the head of troops drawn from his Army of the Nile, delivered the onslaught in the Western Desert which in the space of a few hours drove the Italians out of their carefully-prepared positions at Sidi Barrani and its protective screen of forts.   *Photo, British Official: Crown Copyright*

the British armoured columns, drawn from General Sir Maitland Wilson's Army of the Nile, were brought right up against the Italian outposts. They moved without lights with the utmost stealth and as quietly as might be, following the faint tracks scored in the sand, keeping their course by compass and helped on their way by the stars that glittered overhead. Long before dawn the guns and tanks and armoured cars were all in the positions allotted to them, and far away to the rear the signallers and engineers had completed the lines which linked them with their bases in Egypt.

Some time before dawn on December 9 waves of British bombers went over on their way to plaster the Italian aerodromes. Dawn brought zero hour, and with a rush and a roar the British and Imperial troops, supported by a contingent of the Free French

forces, went into action. Their first objectives were the forts or fortified camps, built of rock and concrete and defended by anti-tank and anti-aircraft guns as well as field artillery, which the Italians had established in the desert east and south of Sidi Barrani, that cluster of whitewashed mud hovels which was made the Italian advanced headquarters in September. The first of these forts to fall was Nibeiwa, 15 miles south of Sidi Barrani; here 500 prisoners and much

war material fell into the hands of the British, while the Italian General was killed and his second-in-command captured. Later in the day another stronger and more important position nearer to the coast was attacked; again 500 prisoners and much material fell to the victors. At the same time other British forces reached the coast to the west of Sidi Barrani, thus threatening, indeed cutting, Graziani's communications with Buqbuq and Sollum.

In all these operations the British Mediterranean Fleet and the Royal Air Force cooperated closely with the army. British warships bombarded the Italian positions on the coast, in particular Sidi Barrani and Maktila, the little village some 15 miles to the east which marked the farthest point of Graziani's advance into Egypt.

Several communiqués told of the aid rendered by the R.A.F. On the night of Saturday, December 7, the Italian aerodrome at Castel Benito—named in honour of Mussolini, and the principal Italian Air Force depot in Libya—was heavily bombed, much damage being done to hangars, offices, ammunition and petrol dumps. Then on the two following days R.A.F. bombers attacked all the Italian aerodromes from Derna to Sidi Barrani, while the fighters— Hurricanes in the main—machine-gunned enemy troop concentrations and columns of

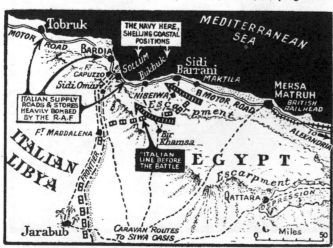

SIDI BARRANI, Graziani's advanced post in Egypt which was captured by the British on the afternoon of December 11, is situated on the Mediterranean coast, rather less than half-way between the Libyan-Egyptian frontier and Mersa Matruh. On this map arrows mark the direction of the British thrusts on December 9.
By courtesy of the " Daily Telegraph "

Where Our 'Victory of the First Order' Was Won

SOMEWHERE IN EGYPT Indian infantrymen, forming a part of the British Army in the Western Desert, take cover behind rocks when an Italian aeroplane drops bombs in their vicinity. Graziani's air arm was far superior in numbers to Air Chief Marshal Sir Arthur M. Longmore's, but never for a moment did it assert its superiority—not even when numbers of R.A.F. 'planes were sent from Egypt to aid the Greeks. By the beginning of December the opportunity was lost, and henceforth it was the R.A.F. which did the bombing. Every Italian aerodrome, from Derna to Sidi Barrani, has been plastered time and again.

ITALIAN TROOPS are here seen taking cover at Sollum soon after they invaded Egypt on September 13. Three days later they reached Sidi Barrani, but from there they extended their hold only as far as Maktila, 15 miles to the east, and for two months Graziani devoted all his efforts to improving the coast road along which the advance had been made and laying down a water supply. Then, on December 9, the British struck, and in two days the Italians were driven out of positions which they had spent two months in consolidating.

Photos, Keystone

Egypt Freed from the Threat of Invasion

transport wherever they were to be spotted. Particular attention was paid to the road along the coast, so that in a very short time it deserved still more its reputation of one of the world's worst; yet along this road, which Graziani made strenuous efforts to improve, all the Italian supplies and reinforcements had to move. Large fires were reported west of Buqbuq, and in many places enemy motor transport was seen to be burning on the road, adding to the dislocation of their troop movements. Twenty-two enemy aircraft were reported shot down or destroyed in the first day's fighting. Pausing only to refuel, the British aircraft attacked far and wide.

In a communiqué issued on December 10 G.H.Q. Cairo briefly reported that "operations in the Western Desert are successfully continuing. Prisoners so far captured are reported to exceed 4,000, also a number of medium tanks." Within 36 hours of the opening of the British offensive the British had driven a wedge between the Italian force at Sidi Barrani—report had it that it consisted of two divisions, principally of Libyan troops—and the main Italian army which was strung out along the road running through Buqbuq and Sollum into Libya. A number of the camps with which the Italians had dotted the desert had been stormed and the process of cleaning up enemy pockets was proceeding satisfactorily.

When Mr. Churchill addressed the House of Commons on December 10 he said that it was too soon to forecast either the scope or the result of the considerable operations which were in progress, but at least "the preliminary phase had been successful." He spoke with statesmanlike caution, but within a few hours the news flashed from Cairo emphasized his understatement.

A special communiqué issued from British G.H.Q. in Cairo on the night of December 11 stated: "This afternoon Sidi Barrani was captured, with a large number of prisoners, including three generals. Advance elements of our mechanized forces are now operating westwards, and considerable additional captures have been made." A little later a naval communiqué from Alexandria announced that: "During last night and today naval forces have been harassing the enemy retreating along the coast and bombarding enemy columns on the roads

round Sollum." The number of prisoners taken mounted apace. The first figure was 1,000; then it was 4,000, then 6,000; then it jumped to 20,000 and over 30,000 with thousands more still pouring in, together with vast quantities of tanks, guns, and military equipment and supplies of every kind.

So that when Mr. Churchill again addressed the House on December 13 he was able to announce that the operations constituted a "victory of the first order"—one which removed all our anxieties for the defence of Egypt, so acute only three or four months ago. He spoke of the capture of Sidi Barrani and of the whole coastal region, with the exception of one or two points. "We do not yet know," he said, "how many Italians were caught in the encirclement, but it would not be surprising if at least the best part of three Italian divisions, including numerous Blackshirt formations, have been either destroyed or captured." Then he went on: "In the meanwhile the pursuit to the westward continues with the greatest vigour. The Air Force are bombing and the Navy are shelling the principal road open to the retreating enemy, and considerable additional captures have already been reported besides those which fell within the original encirclement." Thus, he concluded, "the British guarantee and pledge that Egypt would be effectively defended against all comers has been in every way made good."

So far from being a mere foray, as had been first suggested, the British attack was now revealed as an offensive on a large scale. Over the desert and along the coastal road the British swept on, driving the Italians before them. Only here and there were the enemy able to make a stand; at Sidi Barrani itself, for example, where Blackshirt detachments offered a tough but altogether unavailing resistance. From Buqbuq, taken on December 10, the British armoured columns continued their progress to the west. On the night of December 12 there came a report over the Turkish radio at Ankara that Sollum, too, had been taken.

This report was regarded as premature, but there was no doubt that Graziani's situation was critical. One after the other his ring of forts in the desert had been over-run, and the retreating Italians were forced to converge on the coast road which was under continual fire both from the sea and the air. At Sollum the coastal plain abruptly rises into the Libyan Plateau, and only two narrow passes connect the coast road of Libya with that which runs along the Egyptian shore. These passes were now

DESERT DUST is one of the adverse conditions that faced the British troops during their advance against the Italians. Above, the leaders of pack donkeys are ankle deep in it, while, left, a car makes its own smoke screen of sand.
Photos, British Official: Crown Copyright

packed with an indescribable medley of Italian troops; moving westwards was a great mass of wounded and fugitives, while in the opposite direction the motorized units which Graziani ordered up from Benghazi to reinforce his reeling front, endeavoured to push their way. The traffic jam was terrific, and while some of the Italians struggled to go forward and others strove to go back, all alike were exposed to a wellnigh continuous attack from the air, as the R.A.F. bombers came over and discharged their death-dealing loads. For in the air, as on the ground, the British were now indisputable masters.

Laying the Foundations of Victory in Libya

IN THE SANDS of the Western Desert deep-dug gun emplacements are almost an impossibility, and camouflage becomes of the greatest importance. Left is an example of cover that would hide the gun from the air. Above, Indian troops are learning to use "Molotov Cocktails," the mixture in bottles which hurled at a passing tank puts it out of action.

TROOPS OF THE INDIAN ARMY played a great part in holding the line against the Italians in North Africa. These riflemen of an Indian regiment are occupying a sandbagged position in the British first line.

THE R.A.F. is harassing the Italians not only from the air but on land as well, for it has an armoured car section now operating in the Middle East. Some of the formidable array of cars, above, have here been drawn up on the desert ready to start out on patrol.

THE INDIAN TROOPS had thorough training in the changed conditions of modern warfare before they went to the front. One of the things that they learned was how to deal with tanks. Left, men of a famous Indian regiment are advancing armed with light anti-tank guns.

Photos, British Official: Crown Copyright

In Albania the Italians Retreated Still

While the British drove the Italians out of the positions they had so carefully consolidated in Egypt, their gallant allies, the Greeks, continued their victorious offensive in Albania. Below we review the developments following upon the capture of Argyrokastro.

WHEN in the first week of December the Italians were driven out of Argyrokastro, their principal supply base in southern Albania, they retreated across the mountains towards Tepelini, an important road junction on the way to Valona. At the same time the Italians who had been occupying Santi Quaranta on the sea coast withdrew northwards in the direction of Fort Palermo and Chimarà. But the first fell on Dec. 13, and Chimarà, too, was outflanked.

The Greeks kept in close touch with the Italian rearguard, although their advance was marked by a laudable caution. They knew, none better, that the enemy was strong in tanks and armoured cars, and they were careful to avoid giving him any opportunity of using them to any effect. In front of their marching detachments they flung a screen of cavalry, and they also made full use of their experience in mountain warfare, using precipitous paths which were quite inaccessible to the Italian mechanized transport.

Inland, too, the Greeks gradually but inexorably drove the Italians before them until they were within range of Tepelini, whence it is only a matter of some 30 miles to Valona. Dispite the desperate efforts of the Italian Alpine troops, a number of villages were occupied by the Greeks, who by now had developed to a fine art their tactits of the offensive which proved as successful as economical in man-power. Usually they refrained from making a frontal assault, but gradually worked round on either side of the villages or towns which were their objectives until they occupied the heights, and so compelled the Italians down below in the valleys to choose between extermination or evacuation. Again and again these tactics proved their worth, and from place after place the Italians streamed away north or west, leaving behind them quantities of war material which they had not time to destroy.

The Greek communiqués were masterpieces of concise statement. "Fighting

The objectives of the Greek advance into Albania from the south and the south-east are shown on this map by black arrows. On the coast the main objective is Chimarà (Himara).   *By courtesy of the "Daily Express"*

continued successfully today," read the one issued on December 9; "we have advanced farther." Next day it was stated that "our offensive action continued with success along the whole of the front. Some strong positions were taken with the bayonet. The enemy suffered heavy losses. Three 100-mm. guns fell into our hands." Another 24 hours went by and the Greek G.H.Q. announced that: "Our advance continues in various directions of the front, despite violent enemy reaction. Much booty and many prisoners have fallen into our hands."

Klisura, a strongly fortified key-point in central Albania, was evacuated by the Italians on December 10, when the general advance of the Greeks was stated to have been greatly accelerated. The enemy were now not merely retiring but were literally in flight, and if more prisoners were not taken it was entirely due to the mountainous character of the region in which the battle was being fought. Then, on December 9, the day on which the British opened their offensive against the Italians in Egypt, a strong Italian column was annihilated in Northern Albania while defending strong positions on the mountain massif. The Greek mountain artillery got range and blasted the Italians from their positions. When the Greek infantry went forward to occupy the ground

they discovered several ravines full of Italian dead, and vast quantities of war material which had been left behind as the enemy fled.

By now the weather conditions had taken another turn for the worse. The cold was extreme; dense mist hampered the use of aircraft, and deep snow made it next to impossible to drag the heavy guns across the mountains. So severe was the weather that it was reported that the wolves had been driven from the heights to seek the comparative shelter of the valleys, where they were often encountered on the roads. In such conditions the highly mechanized Italian Army was at a serious disadvantage compared with the Greeks, whose transport was still almost entirely drawn by horse and mule. All the same, the Greeks were severely tried by the bitter conditions and they strove to penetrate into the valleys of the Devoli and Skumbi, where it was hoped milder conditions would be encountered. But this effort

POGRADETS (above), with the capture of which the whole area south-east of Lake Okrida was in Greek hands; this street scene in the little town is typical of Albania. The top photograph shows a frontier station on the boundary between Greece and Yugoslavia, across which Hitler may perhaps come to Mussolini's aid if his situation becomes desperate.   *Photos, G. Bull*

From Triumph to Triumph the Greeks Press On

ARGYROKASTRO. This picturesque town, clambering up a hillside, was finally occupied by the Greeks on December 8. It was the main Italian forward base in South Albania. The enemy was vigorously shelled by the Greek forces from the mountains, seen in the background.
Photo, P. Luck

brought them up against the main line of defence running through Tirana, Elbasan, Berat and Valona, which the Italians were feverishly fortifying and would obviously do their utmost to hold. For if that line were penetrated, even at one point, then the Italians would be compelled to abandon practically the whole of Albania and be driven to find a last line of resistance on the coast itself.

In spite of the unfavourable weather conditions, the Anglo-Hellenic Air Arm continued their attacks whenever possible. It was not long before Italy's last remaining aerodromes in Albania, those at Durazzo and Tirana, had been so bombed—not to mention several days of torrential rain—that they were reported to be no longer capable of being used. Valona, too, was raided time and again, munition dumps, buildings, and ships in the harbour receiving direct hits. So severe was the damage at this, Italy's chief " invasion port," that to an increasing extent the Italians were driven to make use of the roadstead of San Giovanni di Medua in the extreme north of Albania.

As the struggle developed there were reports of growing confusion behind the Italian lines. Prisoners spoke of disputes between the commanders of the various units, who endeavoured to shift on to one another the blame of the successive defeats. Changes in the High Command, too, had added to the difficulty of the situation. Not once but several times did Mussolini " swop horses in crossing the stream " ; first General Prasca gave place to General Soddu ; then Badoglio was said to be in charge, and he in turn was sup-

planted by General Cavallero. But one of the most important factors in the situation was the striking comparison between the individual quality of the troops engaged. The Italians were fighting for a cause for which they had no heart ; they had been told by their officers to expect a triumphal parade, and instead they found themselves bogged in icy swamps, staggering through blizzards across mountain heights, bombed and machine-gunned from

the air, and exposed to the attacks of an enemy who could not only shoot with a sniper's accuracy but wield a bayonet with devilish skill. The Greeks, on the other hand, were inured to the climate and had vast experience of mountain war ; they were fighting, if not in their own country, at least in one with which they were closely associated. Their hearts were in the struggle, and they had the proud consciousness of knowing that theirs was the honour of being the first to defeat the much-vaunted troops of the Totalitarian despot.

ALBANIA'S COUNTRYSIDE admittedly makes hard going, and the Italian propagandists have gladly seized on the fact as an excuse for the dismal failure of their troops. This photograph, recently released by the Italian Censor, shows some of General Soddu's troops on a rough road, but, significantly, it is not stated whether they are going forward or back. *Photo, Associated Press*

German High Seas Raider

A Disguised Merchant Ship Preying on Ocean Traffic

Specially drawn by Haworth for
THE WAR ILLUSTRATED

THESE RAIDERS are usually merchant or passenger ships strengthened and heavily armed, but still retaining the superficial appearance of harmless vessels. Such ships are continually trying to slip out of Germany in order to take toll of our shipping and, if possible, to divert some of our warships to search for the raiders.

1. As the Victim Sees Her

The raider as she might appear to a merchant ship's captain through his binoculars. Naturally she would not fly the Swastika, but the ensign of a neutral country, changed from day to day.

2. The Raider Approaches

The torpedo tubes of a raider are hidden behind high bulwarks, and the torpedo gunners, A, lie down beside them until the moment for action. The crew of the 5.9-inch gun—concealed in the dummy after deckhouse, B—stand by.

3. Disguise is Dropped

When the victim is near enough the heavy metal false plating, C, is dropped to expose, at port or starboard, a pair of 5-inch guns, D. The torpedo tubes fore and aft would be used only in an emergency. The A.A. gun, E (concealed as a deckhouse), and several batteries of machineguns, F, complete the armament. Searchlights, G, are mounted beneath the captain's bridge. The aircraft would be stored partly dismantled in the hold. Some 300 mines, stored below, are brought up in a small lift, H, and run along a set of lines on the deck ready for laying.

Martinique : Vichy's Outpost in America

Here is a brief account of that French island in the West Indies which appears in the
news from time to time, not because of its own importance, but on account of the
French warships and American warplanes which for months past have been immobilized
at Fort de France, its capital.

IF France had not collapsed we should probably not be hearing very much about Martinique, for as one of the many islands in the West Indies it lies well away from the main scene of the war. But when the Nazis overran France and there was some question of the all-too-subservient men of Vichy granting them rights over the French Navy and colonies, Martinique came into prominence with a rush.

At once the Americans made it plain that there could be no question of the Nazis securing a territorial foothold on the American continent. The situation was made still more difficult when it became known that Admiral Robert, in command of the French warships at Martinique, had declared that he felt it his bounden duty to obey the orders received from Vichy and make for French ports, which he could not do without coming into conflict with the British warships which maintained a strict blockade of the island in anticipation of just such a dash. For obviously the British could not allow Admiral Robert's ships—which included the aircraft carrier "Béarn," the cruiser "Emile Bertin," and the training cruiser "Jeanne d'Arc"—to go to France, where they would at once come under the control of the Nazis ; still less could they run any risk of the 110 American dive-bombers and pursuit 'planes, taken on board the "Béarn" before France collapsed, to be brought within reach of the Nazis.

As the U.S.A. wanted neither to see the Nazis in Martinique nor a repetition in American waters of the Oran episode, President Roosevelt sent Admiral Greenslade to Martinique last August, and after a few days it was understood that a reasonable compromise had been effected. The ships were to be virtually decommissioned and laid up in the harbours of the island, while their

crews should be demobilized. The problem of the ownership of the American 'planes remained unsettled ; the British claimed that they should be handed over to them since they had been ordered when France was fighting as Britain's ally, and Britain had now assumed the liability for all orders delivered by the Anglo-French Purchasing Commission. An alternative suggestion was that they should be sent to French Indo-China.

But the 'planes are still there, although they have been unloaded on to the quayside ; and there, too, are the ships and the men. So far from having been completely im-

mobilized, there is at least a suspicion that the French naval forces in Martinique are being used to reinforce the garrison. There have been reports that the French colonial troops were practising repelling landing-parties, that ammunition was being transported from the ships to the land batteries, and that pilots and crews for the warplanes were ready in the Colombian port of Barranquilla, waiting for an opportunity of slipping

MARTINIQUE'S CAPITAL, Fort de France, rises in tiers of picturesque houses from the seashore towards the mountainous country of the interior. It is the chief port of the island, and through it most of the considerable trade is carried. The population of Fort de France is about 50,000.
Photo, Wide World

through the patrol maintained by the British squadron and the American Navy.

And what sort of a place is this Martinique? It is an island of tropical beauty and riches, lying between the British islands of Dominica and St. Lucia in the chain of the Lesser Antilles. Its area is about 380 square miles, and it is about 40 miles long by 20 miles wide. It was first colonized by the French in 1635, and as the aborigines, the cannibal Caribs, were gradually dispossessed and finally exterminated, the French settlers,

the "habitants," grew rich in producing cotton and tobacco, sugar and coffee. The labour for the plantations was supplied by thousands of black slaves imported from Africa ; slavery, indeed, was not abolished until 1860. Several times the island has been British, but in 1814 it was finally returned to France. Since then the only events which have broken the monotony of everyday life have been hurricanes and earthquakes, and,

in particular, that vast eruption of Mt. Pelée in 1902, when 40,000 people were wiped out in a few hours.

Of Martinique's 250,000 people only a few thousand are whites—officials and their families for the most part. The rest are of every colour from dull copper to pure black, for in their veins is mingled the blood of Caribs and negroes and Chinese (imported to add to the island's labour supply), with, of course, a dash of pure French. For the most part they are an indolent crowd living on a low level of culture in a land where life on so low a level is easy and pleasant. They work on the plantations, producing sugar and cocoa, pineapples, bananas and coffee, or on their small holdings. Rum is one of the chief productions of the colony, and the islanders see that not all of it is exported. They display a pronounced aversion from hard work, and so the island is still largely undeveloped. Like so many of the French overseas possessions, in a word, Martinique has been for years in a neglected backwater.

'PLANES BUILT FOR FRANCE in the United States had arrived at Martinique on their way across the Atlantic on board the 22,000-ton French aircraft-carrier Béarn, seen in the lower photograph, when France collapsed. At Martinique they were unloaded, and in the top photograph we see French sailors busy keeping them in good condition.   *Photos, Associated Press, Central Press*

H.M.S. "KELLY," FLOTILLA LEADER, the story of whose salving by a remarkable feat of seamanship is told in the opposite page, is seen here after she had been torpedoed off the German coast in May 1940. In the lower photograph the crew are mustered on deck, while in the top photograph she is waiting to be taken in tow; H.M.S. "Bulldog" is standing by. H.M.S. "Kelly" is one of the K class of destroyers which, with the J class, were at the outbreak of war the newest and best armed destroyers in the British Navy. The German destroyers which, since the collapse of France, have been slipping out into the Channel from ports on the French north and west coasts, are of similar quality.

Photos, Central Press and Fox

Torpedoed, Bombed, 'Kelly' Lived Through It All

One of the finest sea stories of the war is that which tells of the magnificent fight put up by H.M. destroyer " Kelly " against German torpedo and bomb attacks last May. For months details were not permitted to be published, but now we are able to describe the way in which " Kelly " outfought the Nazis. She is now back with the Fleet.

ONE day last May the Germans published an official communiqué in which they claimed that in operations off the German coast one of their motor torpedo-boats had torpedoed and sunk a British destroyer. But in actual fact the ship in question—the flotilla leader " Kelly "—though she was torpedoed and badly damaged, was not sunk. By dint of tremendous efforts she was towed across the North Sea to England, there to be repaired and in due course go into service again.

It was a Thursday evening in May, and " Kelly " was leading a destroyer flotilla operating against a German minelaying force off the enemy coast. An escorting aircraft having reported a submarine ahead, " Kelly " and a sister destroyer, " Kandahar," proceeded to hunt her. A further report from the aircraft of having sighted the enemy minelaying force presently decided the captain of " Kelly," Lord Louis Mountbatten, to abandon the hunt and rejoin his flotilla, by then passing out of sight over the horizon. While overtaking them another destroyer, the " Bulldog," joined " Kelly " and " Kandahar."

It was now 10.30 p.m., twilight and windless, with banks of mist forming on the calm surface of the sea. A quarter of an hour later a blurred object was sighted in the mist from the bridge of the " Kelly " some 600 yards away on the port beam, and simultaneously the track of a torpedo was seen advancing swiftly towards them. It passed under the bridge, and then came the explosion. A sheet of flame rose above the level of the bridge. The " Kelly " lifted bodily with the force of the detonation, which blew a large hole in her side, extending downwards to the keel. The foremost boiler room was blown open to the sea. The entire ship was enveloped in steam, which escaped with a deafening roar, and in black smoke and fumes from the explosion. Everybody in the foremost boiler room was killed instantly. The men in the after boiler room and engine room remained quietly at their posts until ordered on deck.

" Bulldog," who had been some distance astern, presently reappeared, and, the smoke having cleared somewhat, sighted " Kelly " lying like a log on the water, down by the bows and with a heavy list to starboard. By this time the fog had become very thick, but " Bulldog," with assured seamanship, took " Kelly " in tow and was heading for home in an incredibly short time.

In the meantime, torpedoes, depth charges and all movable top-weight were thrown overboard, and wounded men were being extricated from the tangle of twisted metal and wreckage amidships. They were transferred to the after superstructure, as the sick bay had been completely demolished, and, working in the darkness by the light of a few hand-torches, the surgeon laboured just as in days past they worked in the cockpit of the " Victory." One man he mentioned specially—a stoker, terribly wounded and bleeding, who lay for hours without uttering a groan or a complaint. An 18-year-old telegraphist forced his way through a small hole into the main wireless office where five men were trapped and gave injections of morphia to the wounded, knowing that if the ship foundered he could not escape.

Early next morning " Kandahar " rejoined, and the wounded were transferred to her. Her Volunteer Reserve surgeon did marvels for the seriously hurt. During this operation, while the two ships were lying alongside each other, the first German bombers appeared. They were beaten off by gunfire, and by an air escort of three Hudsons which had just arrived. Later, two more destroyers joined as escort, and in the afternoon two cruisers as well. Repeated bombing attacks were made by the enemy and were beaten off. During the afternoon those of the dead who had been recovered from the wreckage were buried at sea, volleys being fired as each shotted hammock slid overboard.

At Any Moment She Might Sink

Saturday wore on, the wind and sea rising steadily. The " Kelly " was labouring with a heavy list, and yawing from side to side almost unmanageably. As her list had increased and it seemed as if she might sink at any moment, the captain decided to send everybody out of the ship not required to fight the guns. The other destroyers had stopped when the enemy made another—their heaviest—bombing attack. No hits were scored. Eighteen officers and men, volunteers selected from a whole ship's company that volunteered to remain on board, were left in " Kelly." The two had repeatedly parted, and further attempts at towing were abandoned until the weather moderated. " Kelly " was then lying water-logged and stationary, when aircraft reported two enemy submarines in her direct path, and her captain, realizing he was merely a sitting target, decided to transfer his volunteer party temporarily to " Bulldog."

So all through the hours of darkness the " Kelly " lay abandoned, with the seas churning through her boiler rooms. And all through the night the escorting destroyers steamed in an endless chain patrol round their stricken leader. In the dawn two tugs arrived, and the volunteer party returned to " Kelly " and got her in tow. The wind and sea, which had dropped in the night, rose again, and waves swept her from end to end. At noon further bombing attacks were carried out by the enemy, who this time nearly succeeded in hitting, but still did no damage. The whole electrical system of the ship being out of action, the guns were worked by hand, the crews scrambling over the wreckage from one gun to another as each came to bear on the attacking aircraft. The able seaman who had volunteered to act as cook kept rushing from his stew pots to his gun and back again in the lulls to his cooking. He persisted in wearing a large white apron and steel helmet throughout these activities.

The spirit of this ship's company was dauntless throughout. Even when darkness fell for the fourth night and every moment increased the risk of capsizing or foundering, the little band of volunteers remained cheerful and enthusiastic.

On the Monday afternoon, having been 91 hours in tow or hove-to, " Kelly " and her escort arrived at a repair yard through miles of cheering spectators.

Captain Lord Louis Mountbatten (inset), who was on the bridge of H.M.S. " Kelly " when she was torpedoed in May 1940, was the commander of H.M.S. " Javelin," leader of the British destroyer flotilla in the Channel action of Nov. 29. Lord Louis Mountbatten is a cousin of the King. In the lower photograph " Kelly " is seen as she arrived in port with her starboard deck awash.

Photos, British Official : Crown Copyright ; and Baron

Our 'Knights of the Air' Learn Their Job

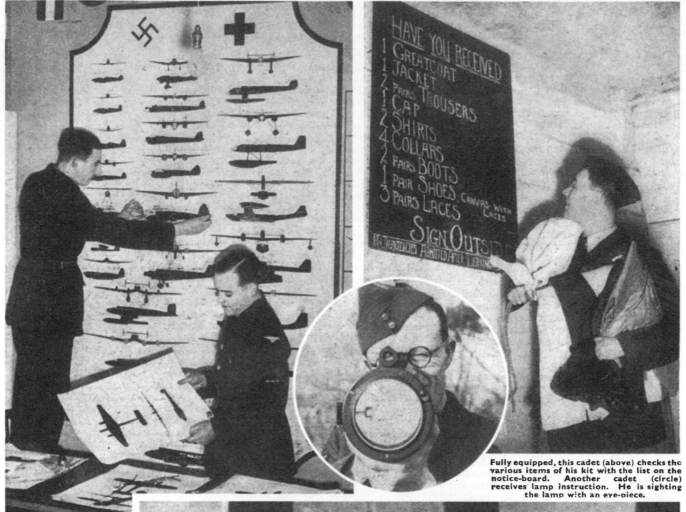

Fully equipped, this cadet (above) checks the various items of his kit with the list on the notice-board. Another cadet (circle) receives lamp instruction. He is sighting the lamp with an eye-piece.

R.A.F. CADETS are seen above at work on a wall of the "Aircraft Recognition" room at their training centre. These realistic silhouettes and drawings are intended to familiarize the cadet with various types of machines. On the left-hand side of the wall-panel are depicted German 'planes, while those shown on the right are Italian.

THE NAVIGATION SCHOOL is one of the most important sections of the training centre, for it is here that navigation officers, observers, and pilots learn their job. The whole crew of a 'plane must have a knowledge of this subject in case the navigator is disabled. Before the war instruction in navigation was given at the School of Air Navigation where pilots went through various courses, including the special "N" course. Now such schools are widely distributed throughout the Empire.

Photos, Planet News

Demolition Spells Danger for the Pioneers

MEN OF THE PIONEER CORPS (as the Auxiliary Military Pioneer Corps is now more simply styled) take their lives in their hands when they undertake the task of clearing up after bombs have fallen. While such work is going on a first aid squad stands by, ready to treat any minor injury. *Photos, Planet News*

Amid Egypt's Desert Sands the Army of the I

Trained for Its Swift Victory Over the Italians

BRITAIN'S ARMY OF THE NILE— to use the fine title bestowed upon it by Mr. Churchill—is a truly Imperial force in which British and Indians, Rhodesians, Australians and New Zealanders are proud to serve as comrades-in-arms. When Italy declared war in the summer of 1940 this Army was charged with the defence of Egypt against a foe far superior in numbers. Yet it was the first to assume the initiative, for its desert patrols cut the Italian wire on the Libyan-Egyptian frontier within an hour or two of the declaration of war, and during the ensuing months maintained a brilliant offensive. Then, on December 9, Maitland Wilson's men struck at Graziani, and in a few hours the Italians were in flight. This photograph, taken last autumn, is of a number of newly-arrived reinforcements drilling and marching in the desert sand, exposed to the pitiless blaze of the Egyptian sun. In the background is seen a portion of the escarpment which, stretching for some two hundred miles from the Nile to the borders of Libya, is an important feature of the Western Egyptian landscape.

Photo, British Official: Crown Copyright

At Home and in Egypt the R.A.F. is On Top

Signs of Britain's growing strength in the air are to be seen in the vigorous offensive carried out by the R.A.F. and the R.A.A.F. in the Battle of Egypt, despite the dispatch of many bomber and fighter squadrons to Greece. Another heartening sign is the successful cooperation with land forces which is so manifest in both theatres of war. In the Battle of Britain we are holding our own.

AFTER the heavy attack of Sunday, December 8, on London, there was no evening Alert in the Metropolitan area until Wednesday, soon after dusk. An intense barrage came into operation for a time and then there was a lull. The attack flared up again some time later, to be followed by another quiet period, after which raiders converged upon the London area from several directions to drop bombs. A somewhat heavy raid was made also on Birmingham ; other enemy aircraft raided an East Anglian town, doing little damage, and also visited places in the north-west, south-west, and Wales. Aircraft, believed to be German, were heard over Liverpool during the night. In Birmingham six churches, eleven schools and two cinemas were damaged, besides

in good order and were conducted to shelters. Midland towns were attacked again, and other bombers went on to the Liverpool area and various other places. Fire bombs were dropped on a London suburb, but little damage was done. During the afternoon two enemy formations made a fruitless attempt to attack London, but were dispersed and turned back over the Thames Estuary.

In a statement on Thursday the Air Ministry referred to the new shell-guns with which our fighters have recently been armed. A formation of four of our aircraft attacked ten to fifteen Messerschmitt 109s, and over the Channel a young British pilot tackled two of the enemy. Missing one, he turned to the other and fired deliberately from dead astern. The Nazi machine exploded like a bursting shell.

Until Sunday night there was little further activity ; two bombs were dropped on a Thames Estuary town on Saturday night. Next evening, raiders visited many parts of Britain.

In the Battle of Egypt, which opened at dawn on Dec. 9 with a British attack on the Italians in Libya, the Royal Air Force played a most important part. It is clear now that the heavy bombing of Castel Benito (near Tripoli) and Benina (near Benghazi) on the previous nights was a preparation for the

AIRCRAFT LOSSES OVER BRITAIN			
	German	Italian	British
May	1,990	—	258
June	276	—	177
July	245	—	115
Aug.	1,110	—	310
Sept.	1,114	—	311
Oct.	241	—	119
Nov.	201	20	53
Dec. 1-15	36	—	7
Totals, May to Dec. 15	**5,213**	**20**	**1,350**

Daily Results

Dec.	Ger. Losses	Br. Losses	Br. Pilots Saved	Dec.	Ger. Losses	Br. Losses	Br. Pilots Saved
1 ...	8	5	5	9 ...	1	—	—
2 ...	2	—	—	10 ...	1	—	—
3 ...	—	—	—	11 ...	2	—	—
4 ...	1	—	—	12 ...	4	—	—
5 ...	14	2	1	13 ...	—	—	—
6 ...	—	—	—	14 ...	—	—	—
7 ...	2	—	—	15 ...	—	—	—
8 ...	1	—	—	**Totals**	**36**	**7**	**6**

From the beginning of the war up to **Dec. 15**, 3,032 enemy aircraft destroyed during raids on Britain. R.A.F. losses 846, but 426 pilots saved.

British bombers lost in operations in November against German or enemy-occupied territory were **48** ; German aircraft destroyed over these regions numbered 8. In the East and in the Mediterranean **Britain lost 18 aircraft, against 59 Italian destroyed.** Unofficial estimate for the whole war period gave an **Italian loss of at least 290 'planes.**

Mr. Churchill on Nov. 5 gave weekly average of killed and seriously wounded civilians for September as 4,500 ; for October, 3,500.

five hangars were hit, and dumps of petrol and bombs were destroyed. Office buildings and barracks were set on fire, and eight aircraft destroyed on the ground. Our pilots came down as low as 250 feet so as to use their machine-guns more effectively. These successful operations did much to paralyse the resistance of the Italian air force during the days that followed.

A feature of the lightning offensive of December 9 was the close cooperation between the R.A.F. and the ground forces. Throughout the day our aircraft harassed the

NAZI PRISONER AIRMEN, above, who have come down in Britain, are in a destroyer on their way to a remote internment camp. For the damage they and others have done the R.A.F. makes such reprisals as are seen, right, an aerial photograph of Stettin, the great German port 30 miles from the Baltic. It was taken at the beginning of an R.A.F. raid and shows : (1) the flash of a bursting bomb ; (2) a bomb exploding close to the viaduct that carries the Berliner Strasse over the railway ; (3) a fire caused by an incendiary bomb.
Photos, Associated Press and British Official : Crown Copyright

many houses. Three high explosive bombs fell on a hospital. An enemy bomber was destroyed in the air during Wednesday night by a direct hit from A.A. guns.

Many Nazi 'planes (estimated at over a hundred) took part in a heavy raid on Sheffield on the night of Thursday, Dec. 12. Bombs fell on a store next door to a theatre, where a large audience was listening to a dance band. The people left the building

advance of Dec. 9. Castel Benito is the chief Italian administrative centre in Libya, and here are assembled the big stocks of petrol needed by the Regia Aeronautica. By low-altitude attacks

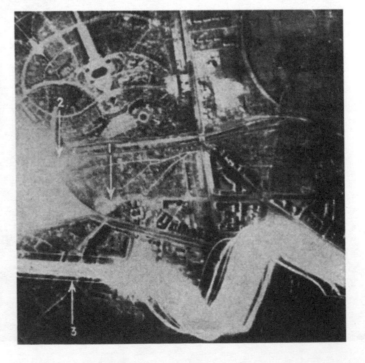

Sport and Science Suffer from the Casual Bomb

THIS BOMB exploded in open parkland after being jettisoned from a German bomber fleeing before British fighters. This remarkable photograph was taken by a Press photographer from his car while he was driving in a South-eastern district. *Photo, Fox*

One Nazi bomb, early in December, struck a sports outfitter's shop in London. All that survived was a pile of bicycles, some of which, however, will be fit to take the road when peace comes. *Photo, Topical*

GREENWICH OBSERVATORY has not escaped bombs, and the worst damage was done to the dome which houses the big altazimuth, an instrument for ascertaining the exact position of stars. Though the structure was damaged the lenses were not, and the instrument can be repaired and reassembled. *Photo, Sport & General*

enemy in the Western Desert, continually bombing and gunning troops and transport columns. In front of the advancing British columns our fighters carried out offensive patrols and shot down Italian 'planes. Farther afield, Italian aerodromes were bombed, and at night even more extensive attacks were made on airfields whence support might have come to the forward areas.

On Tuesday and afterwards the R.A.F. continued its attacks on all enemy aerodromes in the Desert. Other squadrons bombed camps, dumps, and transport concentrations; as the enemy retreated along the coast he was bombed by aircraft and came also under the fire of Royal Naval units off the shore. In the operations which resulted in the capture of Sidi Barrani on Wednesday and in cutting off large Italian forces, the R.A.F. and the R.A.A.F. again rendered yeoman service. One R.A.A.F. squardon shot down seven of the enemy during covering operations.

Aircraft of the Fleet Air Arm bombed Tripoli in the night of Dec. 13-14; other Naval aircraft cooperated with the R.A.F. in attacks in the coastal region. On Friday our 'planes bombed and gunned troops retreating along the Tobruk-Bardia road, and

attacked most of the enemy's aerodromes in the battle area. During the week-end the R.A.F. bombed Bardia, Derna and Sollum; at the last key-point the barracks were severely damaged and other military objectives attacked. In patrol work one of our fighter squadrons shot down 14 S79s and

4 CR42s; other R.A.F. squadrons accounted for three more of each type. In one week the Italians lost 103 'planes.

Our air forces in the Western Desert attack are under the command of Air Commodore Collishaw, an ace of the war of 1914-18, who accounted then for 68 enemy machines.

The Tragedy of the Temple: a Personal Story

Of all London's air battle wounds few have called forth louder lamentations than those inflicted by the flying " knights of the New Order " in Europe upon the ancient home of the champions of Christendom. Here is the story of its futile devastation by Mr. George Godwin, who lived there when the landmine fell and still resides amidst the ruins.

FOR the Templars themselves, both Inner and Middle, the unmerited disaster inflicted upon the Temple is a personal matter ; and for those whose homes are— or were—in this pleasant place the loss is an intimate affair about which it is not easy to write. The Temple is very old. It possesses overhanging houses that were not so very new when Queen Elizabeth came down the narrow lane to Middle Temple Hall to witness Master Will's first production of " Twelfth Night."

The sister Societies of the Inner and Middle Temple possess still (as yet un-destroyed) a Round Church that dates from 1185. By this ancient monument, lovingly restored a century since at a cost of £70,000, we know the antiquity of the place.

The Temple's story thrusts back to the days when the Knights Templars, some of whose bones rest yet in its Church, left the pleasant lands of France and England to defend the faithful from the Saracens. Baldwin II gave them quarters in his palace in Jerusalem. It was said to stand where once the Temple of Solomon stood ; hence the name Templar. At the time of the transfer of legal practice from the monks to the lay profession it happened that the Templars had become rich, arrogant and corrupt. Their wealthy and powerful society was disbanded by Papal decree ; their London home passed to the legal profession.

The Temple has only two outstanding examples of architectural masterpieces : its Round Church and the Hall of the Middle Temple, said to be the most perfect Eliza-bethan Hall in London, whose equal or near-equal is to be found only at Cambridge. Yet, despite many buildings of little or no merit, the Inns form a pattern, taken as a whole, which achieves beauty in a way that escapes even many who love it well. Some of its ancient courts see little of the sun, though others are made almost rustic by ancient plane trees and the music of a fountain whose splashings jewel the backs of the fattest pigeons in the world. It is from these ancient courts that the faultless lawns issue and flow gently down to the Victoria Embankment. Under the shade of their great trees one can drowse through a summer afternoon in perfect peace ; and at night, if it so happens that your chambers overlook the lawn, you may hear, as the writer has done, the strangely haunting hoot of a tawny owl.

Here, surrounded by its walls and pro-tected by its great gates, the Temple lives a life of its own. It has two communities : those who practise law from chambers and those who live in them. Some years ago, when the writer was a student, there was a popular book called " Still Life In The Middle Temple." It was a charming book de-picting the days and ways of the Temple folk. Today, it is fairly safe to say—if such things are done—that the author has turned more than once in his grave since last September.

It was in that month that the trouble began. It began in a more or less gentlemanly sort of way. One made oneself comfortable in a deck-chair, and then the siren sounded and one retired behind brick walls.

The Inner Temple Hall Devastated

Then it became rougher and the first bomb came down.

That evening was one of those when London takes on a peculiar colour magic of her own. From my windows overlooking the shaven lawn the Pegasus that tipped off the top of the Inner Temple Library Clock Tower seemed to swim in a sea of mother-of-pearl. I often sat there of an evening held by nothing but the quiet loveliness of the scene.

That night there was one particularly terrible detonation. When I opened my window shutters next morning I learned the meaning of it. The Clock Tower had been hit. Two of its four sides were torn away (see page 346). The winding staircase was visible, and outside the door that gives on to the Library I could see the Librarian's notices fluttering in the wind.

Shortly after that a bomb passed right through the Inner Temple Hall. It devastated the interior and blew the stained-glass windows far and wide. It was followed shortly after by another, almost geometrically in line with the two first, a stone's throw from where Charles Lamb was born. A gas main blew up, and a tall, stout house was split like an apple.

Little by little the Temple, always so beautifully groomed, began to take on a dilapidated air. Here and there a stricken building poured its disrupted fabric across the road ; everywhere windows framed splintered glass.

Even so, we who have long been about the place took heart of grace. At least our incomparable Church was undamaged still, and our flawless Elizabethan Hall.

Then, on the night of October 16, while we slept or lay and listened to the most

PUMP COURT, one of the most beautiful parts of the Temple, has suffered heavy damage from Nazi raiders. The beautiful red brick houses that line it were built after it had been destroyed by fire in 1679. More of the damage is shown in the photograph in page 490.
Photo, Fox

Lawless Crime Lays Waste the Lawyers' Home

we gazed at what had been so little time before a thing perfect in every way.

All was wrecked. Gone the beautiful carved screen and minstrels' gallery which tradition tells us was made from the timbers of the defeated Armada. Gone the stately perfection of the Hall's furniture : only heaped-up debris and dirt incredible (see pages 490 491). But, even worse, the great gap at the eastern end through which the dawn looked upon the wreck and three numbed men. . .

The Temple, as I have said, is very old. In its eight centuries it has known danger, but never before has it suffered harm. When Wat Tyler led his hundred thousand to Temple Bar and there burnt that City gate, the lawyers rested secure behind their great gates. When the Great Fire razed old London, the last of its flames licked at, but never leapt, the Temple's eastern walls.

Now, after a period many times the total length of Germany's existence as a Power, what was beautiful has been marred ; where there was quiet there is perpetual noise ; where all was orderliness the heaped-up debris impedes the wayfarer and does very much worse to the hearts of those who feel that this London haunt of ancient peace is, in some very personal way, their own.

terrific din then yet experienced, there descended slowly upon us, swaying below its monstrous canopy, a great landmine. It floated down until its detonator touched the roof of a house where Crown Office Row meets Harcourt Buildings at right-angles, by an archway that gives on to Middle Temple Lane.

It was about three o'clock in the morning that I was awakened by some sudden instinctive awareness. My bedroom is upon the ground floor, its window overlooking the lawn. The landmine had detonated two houses away.

In times when nearly all of us who live in London can tell a tale of bomb or mine, it is unnecessary to say that it is not a pleasant thing to have one's windows, together with heavy wooden shutters and their iron fitments, shot at high velocity across the room in a shower of glass ; to feel the ceiling descend, with a black cloud of filth and soot, upon one's head.

At five, shaken but intact, I went with the porter and a warden round the Inns. We were the first to enter the Middle Temple Hall. Here, thirty years ago, I had come shyly in my sleeveless gown to eat my first dinner. Here, a callow youth, I had learned the ceremonial of the mess, one descended from those same old Templars who trounced the Saracens. Here I was called to the Bar.

We had come, three shaken men, into the Hall by an entrance near the high table, and

THE HALLS of both the Inner and Middle Temple have suffered severely from bombs. Top is the Inner Temple Hall, built in 1862, with effigies of a Crusader and a Knight Templar blown from their pedestals standing among the ruins. The lower photo shows the end of Middle Temple Hall, struck on October 16, with the gap seen in a photograph of the interior in page 491.

Photos, Sport & General, Fox

Our Men Are Now at Home in Iceland

During these winter months a considerable force of British and Canadian troops are in Iceland, preventing its use by U-boats or Nazi flyers. Some description of the island—so wintry in name but, as will be seen, not altogether so in features and character.

BRITISH troops landed in Iceland on May 10, just a month after the invasion of Denmark—the island's sister State—by the Nazis; and soon after they were joined by a contingent of Canadians. By now they have made many friends amongst the islanders and have come to know the country—but not, perhaps, to love it, for Iceland's scenery is as different from that of the English countryside as are the almost boundless prairies of Canada.

How gaunt and grim is Iceland's landscape will be apparent from this photograph of one of the island's few roads winding its way across a rocky terrain to the snow-capped hills. Judged by Western engineering standards these roads are not of a very high order, but all the same they reflect very great credit on the men who have made them.

Photo, Dorien Leigh

Iceland is an Arctic land—in the winter the seas to the north are sometimes completely frozen over—and there are icefields in many parts of the country. On the north and east great cliffs of basalt rise almost perpendicularly from the sea, while both here and on the west the coast is riven by many picturesque fjords. Yet in this land of ice in name and character there are plentiful traces of volcanic activity, and in the north are several sand deserts. There are swift-flowing rivers, splendid waterfalls cascading over the rocks, and, of course, the famous geysers in the hot spring regions. Geyser, indeed, is derived from the Icelandic word meaning " to gush."

All this is suggestive of a grim landscape, and indeed Iceland has none of the soft beauty of woods and fields. There are a few trees and those few are small ; seldom can

grain be got to ripen, and the chief agricultural crops are hay, cabbages, potatoes, and rhubarb. As for livestock, cattle and sheep are bred extensively ; and ponies, surefooted little beasts, are still the principal means of transport, although now that the roads have been much improved nearly 2,000 motor vehicles have been licensed. There are no railways in the island.

Of Iceland's total area, some six-sevenths is unproductive bogland or rocky, moss-covered waste, and although a considerable proportion of the population manage to make a living out of the fisheries, cod and herring, it is not surprising that the population of 2·7 persons per square mile is the lowest in Europe. Of the 120,000 Icelanders, about 40,000 have their homes in the capital, Reykjavik, on the west coast, which is also the country's principal port.

It need hardly be said that there was no resistance to the British and Canadian troops, since they came as friends ; but there would have been no resistance if it had been the Nazis who came ashore, since Iceland has not even the smallest army or navy, but is a completely defenceless island community. Yet since 1918 she has been acknowledged by the world as a sovereign State, and her only political link with Denmark is through the

common Sovereign, in very much the same way, for instance, as Canada's only political link with Britain is King George. King Christian of Denmark, now a prisoner in the hands of the Nazis, is also King of Iceland. Since the German occupation of Denmark, however, the Althing, as Iceland's Parliament is called, has proclaimed a state of autonomy, and there is now a British minister in Iceland, Mr. Howard Smith. The Althing consists of two houses, an upper and lower, and there is a responsible ministry of five politicians—familiarly known as the Icelandic Quintuplets. They form a National Government based on a coalition of the Progressive Party, the Social Democratic Party, and the Independence Party, and the present Prime Minister is Hermann Jonasson.

The existence of the Independence Party is a reminder that there are many in Iceland who long before the war had been agitating for the severance of the last slender link which connects Iceland and Denmark. By the Act of Union of 1918 Iceland and Denmark, as two free and independent sovereign States, were united by a personal bond of union under the common king, and it was stipulated that if after December 31, 1940, within three years a new treaty of union were not negotiated, then the alliance should be abrogated. Today the Independence Party is the largest political group, and it may well be that by 1943 Iceland may have made a formal declaration of complete independence.

Nazi Efforts to Win the Young

Most of the Icelanders are pro-British in sentiment, but there is a very considerable minority who have been infected by Nazi ideas. For some years before the war Germans were ostentatious in their patronage of Icelandic culture, literature, and institutions ; most of the doctors and scientists in the island have been trained in Germany, and Icelandic scholars have always received a most friendly welcome from the German universities. Then the Nazis did everything in their power to win the sympathies of young Icelanders of both sexes by sending them teachers of skiing and rock-climbing, inviting Icelandic football and athletic teams to Germany, supporting the Icelandic Flying Club by loaning gliders and gliding instructors, and so on.

There is even a Nazi Party in Iceland, organized on the lines of the parent Party in Germany, and this party still exists, although most of its former leaders have found it advisable to leave the island for Germany.

There have been stories of attacks on British soldiers in cafés and in the streets of Reykjavik by young Nazis who had had more than was good for them, but generally speaking the mass of the Icelandic people are most friendly towards Britain and sympathize strongly with the democratic ideals of which she is the champion. As is the way of the British soldier wherever the path of duty may lead him, he has become not only a familiar but a highly popular figure with the Icelanders, particularly the youngsters. Even the babies, we are told, have now learned to call out " Hello, what is your name ? " and " Goo'bye," when they see a man in khaki passing along the street.

Midway on the Air Route Across the Atlantic

Though Iceland lies at the back of beyond geographically and politically speaking, it is on what might well become the direct air route from Europe to North America. From Iceland to the Shetlands is a matter of 500 miles, and about the same to Greenland. This fact in itself is sufficient to explain that occupation of the island by British troops which as likely as not forestalled Hitler in his designs on the American continent. The photograph, left, shows a British "Walrus" seaplane at a port on the Icelandic coast.

British troops landed in Iceland on May 10, 1940, and the island is now held by a joint British and Canadian force. It did not take very long for our soldiers to become on the best of terms with the islanders—particularly with the youngsters, some of whom, as the photograph below shows, have the makings of good footballers.

Hot springs of volcanic origin are one of the amenities with which Nature does something to console the Icelanders for the rigours of their climate. Above is a view of washing-day in this generally bleak and barren land. Another of Nature's gifts to Iceland is the Midnight Sun, which during the summer months shines in perpetual splendour. On the right is a British camp with the sun shining brightly at midnight.

Photos, British Official: Crown Copyright; Dorien Leigh

OUR SEARCHLIGHT ON THE WAR

Present from the R.A.F.

DURING the precipitate flight of the Italians from Santi Quaranta a destroyer escorting two cargo boats left the port with the Italian headquarters staff aboard. Bombers of the R.A.F., engaged in harrying the retreating enemy and patrolling the Albanian coast, attacked the destroyer, two direct hits being scored and several near misses. While the cargo boats fled, the warship had to stop and was listing heavily when the British aircraft left. Later the half-submerged ship was captured by units of the Greek Navy, and she is being recommissioned for service with their Fleet. A plaque has been fixed on the bridge bearing the inscription : " Presented to the Greek Navy by the Royal Air Force."

Tank Veteran's New Command

ON December 9 the War Office announced that two important appointments had been made. The first is that of Lieut.-Gen. H. R. L. G. Alexander, who succeeds Gen. Auchinleck, now C.-in-C. India, as C.-in-C. Southern Command. Gen. Alexander, who has an outstanding record, was in command of the B.E.F. during the last days of the evacuation from Dunkirk.

The other appointment is a new one : Maj.-Gen. G. le Q. Martel is to be commander

Major-General Martel's new command, the Royal Armoured Corps, came into being in 1939, when all the cavalry regiments except the Household Cavalry, the Scots Greys, and the Royal Dragoons, had been mechanized.
Photo, Associated Press

of the Royal Armoured Corps, into which the Royal Tank Corps, later the Royal Tank Regiment, was merged. General Martel, who is 51, served on the staff of the Tank Corps in France for 18 months in 1917-18, was assistant Director of Mechanization at the War Office from October 1936 to December 1937, and thereafter deputy director of the same branch until February 1939. For some time after the Great War he was at the Staff College, Camberley. Here, in a garage-workshop attached to his house, he set about building a one-man tank, using parts of cheap motor-cars. This later developed into a two-man tank, and General Martel has worked with tanks ever since, except for the interval after February, 1939, when, by reason of the automatic system of Army promotion, he took command of the 50th division. With the

creation of this new post an expert specialist officer will be responsible for the development of the armoured forces of the Army.

Two Enemy Spies Hanged

TWO spies, Jose Waldberg and Karl Meier, were hanged in Pentonville Prison on December 10, the first spy execution to be announced in Britain during this war. The one was a German, the other a Dutch subject of German extraction, and both had been sentenced on November 22 after a secret trial at the Old Bailey. These two enemy agents were arrested soon after their surreptitious arrival in this country. They were posing as refugees from enemy-occupied territory, and their instructions were to move about among the people, listening in trains and buses, in cafés, and in the streets, to careless talkers, picking up in this and other ways as much military information as possible, particularly with regard to aero-dromes, troop concentrations, gun emplacements, and ammunition dumps. They had a wireless transmitting set, and at dusk they were to erect the aerial in a country field and communicate directly to the German secret service what they had learnt during the day. They would then carefully conceal the set, pass the night hiding in woods or an empty building, and emerge in the morning to resume their search for information. The radio set, which was of German manufacture, was contained in a small leather bag, about 8 in. square. Another case contained three 90-volt and two 45-volt batteries. There were two aerials, the main one being coiled ready for use. The men had been told that they would soon be relieved by German invading forces.

One Against Seventy-Five

RECENTLY a 20-year-old Spitfire pilot, making a lone patrol over the Channel at 10,000 feet, was gratified by the appearance below him of a tight formation of 75 German machines—35 bombers protected by 40 fighters. Making a steep dive into the middle of the posse, he selected a machine, attacked it savagely at close range, sent it flaming into the sea, and disabled another one. He then made off at speed before the Nazis could manoeuvre sufficiently to open fire without danger of bringing down one of their own aircraft. When later he examined his own Spitfire, there were only two bullet holes in it.

Refugee Industry in London

THE first factory to be created specifically for wartime refugees has been opened in London. It is the conception of Mr. Ernest Bevin, and will now constitute an international centre for the diamond-polishing industry, which, until the German invasion, was largely concentrated in Antwerp. The workpeople come chiefly from Belgium and Holland, and are all expert in the skilled processes of cleaving, sawing, and polishing. When their countries were overrun about

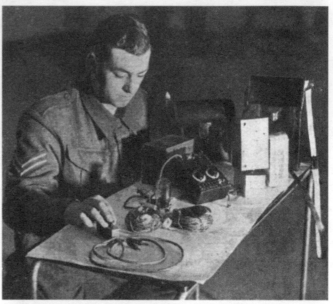

THE WIRELESS SET carried by the two Nazi spies executed at Pentonville prison on December 10, 1940, is being examined by an expert. It was not always carried about by the men, but hidden at some convenient spot from which it might be brought out for use at night. *Photo, L.N.A.*

8,000 of these highly trained craftsmen, largely Jews, fled to France, and only about half that number eventually reached England. But as the price of cut diamonds has trebled since the war, it is hoped that, even starting with small numbers, this new British industry will flourish. The only other country with a diamond-polishing industry is the United States, and it is also here that the principal markets for cut diamonds are found.

Deputy Air Chief, Middle East

AIR MARSHAL ARTHUR WILLIAM TEDDER has been appointed Deputy to the Air Officer C.-in-C., R.A.F., Middle East, and has arrived at Cairo. This is the second appointment to the post to be made within a month, for on November 21 Air Marshal O. T. Boyd, the newly-appointed Deputy, who was flying over the Mediterranean to take up his duties, had to make a forced landing in Sicily and was taken prisoner by the Italians. Air Marshal Tedder began his flying career in the R.F.C. in 1916, and since 1938 has been Director-General of Research and Development, Air Ministry. He had two years' experience, 1936-38, as Air Officer C.-in-C., Far East.

Communist Push in Bulgaria

IT was reported from Sofia by a " Times " correspondent on December 10 that during the previous ten days thousands of leaflets had been circulated in Bulgaria announcing that Soviet Russia is proposing a " pact of mutual assistance " by which Bulgaria would receive " the Adrianople district west of the Enos-Media Line from Turkey, and the whole of the Aegean coast from Greece." What is termed the Enos-Media Line constituted the old frontier between Bulgaria and Turkey before the second Balkan War. So great has been the effect of this campaign that 100,000 signatures have already been obtained in the provinces urging the Government to accept the Russian proposals. The Germans, feeling that the leaflet was both anti-Turkish and anti-Greek, decided to produce and distribute it themselves. But pro-Russian feeling among the population is now so great that if Bulgaria were to join the Axis there is a danger of severe internal difficulties.

I WAS THERE !

Eye Witness Stories of Episodes and Adventures in the Second Great War

We Hit the German Raider Fair Amidships

The German sea raider which sank the "Haxby" (see page 471, Vol. 3) encountered the armed merchant cruiser "Carnarvon Castle" in the South Atlantic on December 5, and after some damage had been inflicted on both sides the raider made off. The following short eye-witness account is by a member of the ex-liner's crew.

ONE of the "Carnarvon Castle's" gunners, describing the action, said: Early on Thursday (December 5) the "Carnarvon Castle" picked up a German ship and fired a shot across her bow. As a precaution, in view of several unpleasant surprises we have had in recent weeks, the captain ordered the crew to battle stations. At 8.5 a.m., without warning, the German opened fire and the battle was on.

The captain immediately ordered the gunners to straddle the enemy, seeking the

and forced her to tack to port to bring her remaining guns to bear on us. Altogether she hit us 22 times, but not seriously.

One shell burst close to a gun crew. One little fellow, whose arm was smashed by a piece of steel at his gun, turned to his comrades and said: "I haven't let you down, mates, have I ? " He was taken to the infirmary, but he died, and he was buried with honours, with others, after the battle.

Before the German got away she fired two torpedoes. They missed. As she disappeared in her smokescreen we saw her settling down by the stern.

We were short of ammunition, so we decided to go to Montevideo, and turned southward. First we saw the "Queen of Bermuda," which took off our 22 Germans from the "Itape" (a Brazilian steamer, which was stopped for the purpose off the Brazilian coast). A number of ratings from the "Queen of Bermuda" were transferred to us.

A few hours later we picked up the "Enterprise," who signalled asking if we needed any assistance. We said "No," and she made northward at full speed. That German's bound for Davy Jones's locker.

CAPT. HARDY, of the "Carnarvon Castle," whose ship, as recounted in this page, was hit 22 times by a German raider, but in the end forced the enemy to retire. *Photo, Vandyk*

range. The German did likewise, and with good effect. Captain Hardy kept the ship on a straight course till the Germans found the range, and were ready for a direct hit. Then, at the last moment, he changed the course.

It was evident from the first that the German had the heavier guns—at least two 8-inchers—and she did her utmost to bring them to bear. Besides, the German was long and low, with very little freeboard, making her very hard to hit.

In spite of that we hit her fair amidships, put out of commission the guns on that side

I Drove Along Greece's Most-Bombed Road

A vivid picture both of the difficulties to be surmounted by the Greek soldiers and of the spirit which animates them is given in the following dispatch by a Special Correspondent of British United Press, who drove along a bomb-scarred mountain road in an army supply lorry.

THE most terrifying drive of my life taught me how supplies for the Greek Army get through in spite of the Italian bombers. I drove along the most-bombed road in Greece in an ancient two-ton Ford lorry carrying several hundred-gallon drums of petrol and ten soldiers.

The tough Army driver, George Cuovo, had not made the trip before and did not know the distance between his starting point and his destination. Italian bombers had scored fourteen direct hits along the road, which hangs on the edge of a mountain as though placed there as an after-thought. On one side is a bottomless precipice. On the other is a mountain-side without the slightest cover, topped with cloud-capped peaks. The driver had been told to get the petrol through, and he did.

George, myself, and the interpreter packed the driver's cabin, while the soldiers, who were rejoining their units, squeezed in behind among the drums of petrol. We lurched and swayed round hairpin bends without knowing what might be round the corner.

Twice we came at breakneck speed upon bomb craters which seemed to cut the road completely. One of them drew a warning yell from the stoic soldiers, who stood swaying on the back of the lorry—the only expression of fright they had given as the driver swung the lorry round the innumerable bends, only feebly lit by his dimmed head-lamps.

Each time we squeezed through on a narrow strip of mud between the crater and the edge of the precipice, though pebbles and loosened earth rattled away down into the abyss.

There were fourteen of these craters. And as if this, plus the hazards of hairpin bends, darkness, and lack of headlights, were not enough, George insisted on smoking. Steering with one hand, he fished in

his deep pockets for matches. Finding none, he opened the door of his cabin and yelled up to the soldiers, one of whom handed him a box. Then a match was extracted after several tries, and George's cigarette was lit.

ALBANIA'S PRECIPITOUS ROADS, such as the one above, provide a vivid background for the experiences of the driver of a supply lorry, described in this page. *Photo, Percy Luck*

During the eternity that these operations appeared to last the unwieldy lorry lurched under his one hand and repeatedly made a bee-line for the precipice, but always came back to the road just in time. I died a thousand deaths on that journey, but my sympathies were with those soldiers who stood among the shifting petrol drums. I was too limp at the end of it to ask them how they felt.

When I think what that ride would be like with only three Italian bombers at work I just thank my lucky stars that I am not a lorry driver in the Greek Army.

'The —— Swine' Said the Nurse

Here is a plain account of what happened to a children's hospital on the outskirts of London when on a night in last November it was bombed by a Nazi raider. Written by an eye-witness, Nelson Davies, it is reprinted here by arrangement with the "Star."

THERE is a children's hospital on the outskirts of London which is one of the best of its kind in England. Many of the children there have never been able to walk ; some of them, tiny victims of paralysis, may never know what it is to leave their beds ; others have permanent troubles which bar them from all the ordinary joys of childhood.

The other night all the little ones had been finally tucked up, some of them hugging their favourite toys, and the lights in the wards had been dimmed. Sleep had descended on the hospital.

Then, in a flash, the peacefulness of the wards was torn to shreds. Coming down almost as one, ten bombs fell on the buildings and their grounds, and the explosions which followed merged into one undulating roar.

It was difficult for those of us who ran from the First Aid Post attached to the hospital to measure the extent of the damage at first. But we had the cries of the children for our guide.

They were not yells or screams, but rather half-choked calls, like " Sister, please, *please*, come and hold my hand," and " Sister, I'm frightened ; please, can we have a light ? "

We went through broken glass and other debris into the first ward of the blocks, fearing what we should find inside.

The moon, shining through the torn windows, gave us our light, and we saw rows of white faces in their cots. On the floor was a figure. It was a probationer nurse, hit by a bomb splinter in the leg.

We thought we had been quick on the spot, but she had already received attention from the Sister, who, on our entry, was walking round the cots, soothing and assuring the children.

The cries had almost ceased by now. There were a few whimpers from some of the younger ones, but the Sister had done her work well. " How many of the children are hurt ? " someone asked urgently. " I think they are all safe ! " replied the Sister.

And so it was. Glass and dirt had crashed down all over the ward, and great pieces of paper-covered glass hung by tiny shreds over the heads of some of the cots ; but not a child was injured.

The nurse was carried out. As I followed I felt a tug at my coat. One of the elder children had reached out from his cot. I leaned down to him.

" D'yer think Nurse is hurt very badly ? " he asked, his voice full of concern. I was able to assure him that she would be soon back among them.

The next ward had received a direct hit, but we learned that it was used as a day nursery and that there was no one—but wait, there was someone there. One little girl had been put to bed in the room.

One of our party was somehow inside the wreckage the next moment, and soon came out carrying a tiny form. It was the baby, two years old or so—and miraculously alive. And not only alive, as we discovered when we reached the Aid Post, but not too badly injured. Her leg was in plaster, following a recent operation. Her little face was white, except where the blood flowed from her two wounds. She cried a little as the doctor attended to her, but only a little.

Then it was that one of the nurses, who had probably never used such a word before, expressed what was in the minds of all of us. " The —— swine ! " she said.

'We See Lorient Clearly When We Attack It'

A squadron of the R.A.F. which dates back to the last war is now taking its share in the vast work of the Coastal Command. Some account of its operations over the German-occupied ports of France, and a description of a very successful bombing attack on Lorient, broadcast in November by a Flight Lieutenant, is given below in his own words.

LATELY our squadron has been doing its bit in making the ports on the other side of the Channel uncomfortable for their temporary tenants. Cherbourg, Brest and Lorient have been most frequently on our daily lists.

Our attacks on Lorient are now regular news. Lorient, on the Brittany coast, about 90 miles south of Brest, has become a U-boat base and maintenance depot. It isn't giving away any secrets to say that our targets there are power stations, naval yards, slipways, torpedo workshops, and so on. Some of us have been so often to Lorient lately that we must know the way into and around it better than its temporary German inhabitants. Now we know every yard of the country and its landmarks. We always see Lorient clearly when we attack it—at dusk or dawn, or in light provided by the moon or by our flares. And the enemy always gives us a hot reception. All sorts of stuff come up at us—light and heavy shells, flaming red things which we call " onions," and what-not.

The other night the armourers of our squadron were given their first operational flight. Their job is on the ground—to fit and load our bombs. The idea in taking them with us was that they could study what happens when their bombs burst.

" How did you get on ? " one of them was asked afterwards.

" Coo—great stuff," was the reply. " All the colours of the rainbow. Lovely it was from the gallery seat." I don't think I would choose the word " lovely " myself !

I wonder if I can give you a sort of mental picture of how we set about things on one of these raids. An hour before the take-off we assemble in the Operations Room to be told all about the job in hand. Then off everyone goes to attend to his own particular end of things. The observer gets the weather report ; a gunner, who is also the wireless operator, makes certain that the guns are O.K. Then he checks up the recognition signals and the wireless frequencies and sees that the pigeons are in wicker basket—we always take homing pigeons with us. And the pilot gets into his head all he can about the trip and the targets.

Before we leave the ground I test the microphone which enables me to talk to the gunner in the rear turret and to the rest of the crew.

" Hello, gunner—are you all right behind ? "

And then to the observer : " Hello, observer ; course to steer, please."

As we approach Lorient the observer shouts, " I see the target—yes, I've got it ! " " O.K." I say. " Master switch and fusing switch on ! " These are the switches which control the fusing and the release of the bombs. Round just once more to make quite certain. The docks and the outlines of the naval buildings show up a little more clearly. Then I throttle the engines back.

" Running on now," I tell the observer. " O.K.," he says. " Left, left—that's it— steady—a shade right—hold it—*now !* "

He presses the electric button which releases the bombs. The aircraft gives a slight shudder as they go through the doors.

" Bombs gone ! " cries the observer. Down they go, hundredweight after hundredweight of high explosive. My observer is watching for the results. Have we scored hits or just got near misses ? I see many bright flashes. Then big flames flicker skywards like the fiery tongues of monster serpents. Showers and towers of ruddy sparks burst from the ground.

My observer nearly jumps from his seat, waving his hands in excitement. " We've hit it—we've hit it ! " he yells. " We've damned well hit it ! " Then home we go, our umpteenth visit to Lorient on the Brittany coast has ended.

In this page is the story of a children's hospital which was bombed by a Nazi raider. All too often hospitals have been hit, and this photo shows but one of many of these homes of mercy that have been so brutally served.

War Personalities—Premiers of Empire

Rt. Hon. J. M. Andrews

When Lord Craigavon died on November 24, his place as Prime Minister of Northern Ireland was taken by Mr. James Miller Andrews, who had been Minister of Finance in the Craigavon cabinet since 1937. The new Premier was born in 1871, and has been one of Co. Down's representatives in the Parliament of Northern Ireland since 1921. From 1921 to 1937 he was Minister of Labour. Like his late chief, he is an advocate of the closest cooperation between the Government of Northern Ireland and the British Government.

Rt. Hon. R. G. Menzies

On April 20, 1939, Mr. Robert Gordon Menzies, of the United Australian Party, became Prime Minister of the Commonwealth of Australia. His rise to that high office was rapid, for he first entered the Victorian Parliament in 1926 and the Commonwealth Parliament in 1934; before, in Mr. Lyons's government, he had been Attorney-General and Minister for Labour. He is 46 years of age. After the general election of September 1940 he reconstructed his Cabinet with the support of the Country Party.

General the Rt. Hon. J. C. Smuts

Since South Africa has been a Dominion General Smuts has done yeoman service to the Empire. In the last war he commanded for a time the British troops in East Africa, and afterwards was Minister Without Portfolio in the war cabinet. His counsel was of great service throughout the struggle, while he played a prominent part in the Versailles Peace Conference. After General Hertzog's government was defeated on a motion that South Africa should keep out of the war, General Smuts formed a new Ministry and ensured South Africa's full cooperation.

Rt. Hon. W. L. Mackenzie King

Now 66 years of age, Mr. William Lyon Mackenzie King first entered on a political career as M.P. for Waterloo, North Ontario, in 1908. He has held many high offices and has three times represented Canada at Imperial Conferences. He was Prime Minister, except for a three months' interval, from 1921 to 1930, and has now held that office since 1935. On the evening of Sunday, September 3, 1939, Mr. Mackenzie King said during a broadcast, "Canada has already answered the call," and under his leadership the Dominion's wonderful war effort has grown rapidly.

Rt. Hon. G. M. Huggins

A surgeon by profession, Mr. Godfrey Martin Huggins, Prime Minister of Southern Rhodesia, spent two and a half years holding post-graduate appointments at St. Thomas's Hospital and afterwards was House Physician and then Medical Superintendent of the Hospital for Sick Children, Great Ormonde Street. In 1911 he went to Southern Rhodesia as a general practitioner, and is still a consulting surgeon. He became a member of the Legislative Council in 1923 and Prime Minister in 1934. He was born in 1883.

Rt. Hon. P. Fraser

The Prime Minister of New Zealand, Mr. Peter Fraser, was born in Scotland in 1884, but in 1910 emigrated to New Zealand, where he worked for a time on a farm. In due course he joined the New Zealand Labour Movement and became President of the Party. He was first elected to the New Zealand Parliament in 1918, and in December 1935 became Minister for Education, Health and Marine in Mr. Savage's Government. He succeeded Mr. Savage as Prime Minister of the Dominion in April 1940.

Photos, Photo Press, Lafayette, Hay Wrightson, Barratt's

Men of 'Free French' Navy Stand Ready

Captain Foch, top left, grandson of Marshal Foch, is now in the French Naval Air Force, and was one of General de Gaulle's envoys at Dakar.

Admiral Muselier, top right, who was appointed by General de Gaulle to command the 'Free French" Navy, leaving a ship after an inspection

Right, an officer of the French sloop "Commandant Duboc," one of the units of the Free French Navy, is seen at the rangefinder when the crew are at gun practice stations.

The "Commandant Duboc," below, a sloop of 630 tons, played a prominent part in General de Gaulle's expedition to Dakar in Sept., 1940.

Photos, British Official : Crown Copyright; Topical Press and Associated Press

On Convent as on Home the Bombs Descend

When a convent in the south-west outskirts of London was bombed during the "blitz" the refectory, above, was one of the parts destroyed by fire.

The nuns unperturbed girt up their robes and helped in salvage work. Here, with the aid of a fireman, they remove the damaged effigy of a saint.

Incendiary bombs from a "Molotov breadbasket" fell on the main building of the convent and the fire got a hold before the firemen arrived. Left, the next morning nuns are sweeping out the water that flooded the floor of the chapel. Right is the beautiful staircase covered with debris, but the mural paintings escaped injury. The firemen (circle) who had fought all night to save the building received in the morning a most welcome token of gratitude from the nuns—cups of tea.

Photos, Keystone and Planet

OUR DIARY OF THE WAR

MONDAY, DEC. 9, 1940   *464th day*

On the Sea⁓Reported that a Dutch submarine had been lost in war operations.

In the Air⁓R.A.F. bombed aircraft factory at Bremen, naval base at Lorient and docks at Boulogne.

War against Italy⁓British advanced forces in Western Desert made contact at dawn with Italian forces on a broad front south of Sidi Barrani. More than 1,000 prisoners were taken.

R.A.F. cooperated with Army and harassed enemy troops in Western Desert and raided Italian aerodromes. Twenty-two enemy aircraft reported shot down.

During night of Dec. 8-9 naval units bombarded Maktila Camp and Sidi Barrani in support of operations.

In Italian East Africa a Rhodesian squadron bombed defended positions north-east of Kassala and other aircraft raided troops and motor concentrations at Khor Aftit, on Chown Gondar road.

Home Front⁓No enemy raids either by day or night. German bomber shot down in North Sea by R.A.F. fighters.

Greek War⁓Greeks advancing towards Himara, threatening flank of Italian forces withdrawing north from Santi Quaranta. Number of important mountain positions occupied.

R.A.F. carried out offensive reconnaissances near Valona.

General⁓War Office announced appointment of Gen. G. Le Q. Martel to newly created Command of Royal Armoured Corps.

TUESDAY, DEC. 10   *465th day*

On the Sea⁓Canadian destroyer "Saguenay" reported damaged by torpedo in Eastern Atlantic but reached port safely.

In the Air⁓Bombers of the R.A.F. attacked number of targets in Western Germany and enemy-occupied territory and docks at Channel invasion ports.

War against Italy⁓British advance in Western Desert continued. Over 4,000 prisoners and a number of tanks captured. Two Italian divisions at Sidi Barrani reported cut off by British troops reaching coast at point between there and Buqbuq. Some Free French units operating with British.

During night of Dec. 10-11 British naval forces harassed enemy retreating along coast and bombarded Italian columns on roads round Sollum.

R.A.F. continued bombing of all Italian aerodromes in Libyan Desert, as well as camps, troop concentrations and motor transport. Aircraft of Fleet Air Arm attacked barracks at Bardia.

Reported that Addis Ababa railway had been severely damaged by R.A.F. bombers on Dec. 8.

Home Front⁓Number of single enemy aircraft penetrated into East Kent and Essex and a few bombs were dropped.

One enemy fighter shot down.

Long-range artillery duel across Straits of Dover.

Greek War⁓Greek offensive continued successfully throughout whole front. Severe battles in Pogradets sector. North-west of Pogradets important heights were captured. R.A.F. again successfully raided Valona.

WEDNESDAY, DEC. 11   *466th day*

In the Air⁓R.A.F. bombed invasion ports and a number of aerodromes. Targets in Western Germany included power stations, inland docks and railway yards.

War against Italy⁓British forces captured Sidi Barrani and large number of prisoners, including three generals. Advanced elements of mechanized forces now operating westwards and additional captures made.

Home Front⁓During day small numbers of enemy aircraft were active over Channel and S.E. coast and bombs fell in one town.

At night raiders made heavy attack on Birmingham. Six churches, 11 schools, two cinemas and very many houses were damaged. A West of England town was also raided and considerable damage done. Bombs also fell in other areas, in West Midland region, in London and East Anglia.

Enemy fighter shot down over Kent. One night bomber destroyed over London by A.A. fire.

Greek War⁓Greek advance continuing along 80-mile front. All Italian counter-attacks repulsed. Greek left wing advancing towards Himara.

General⁓Air-Marshal A. W. Tedder appointed Deputy to Air Officer C.-in-C., Middle East.

THURSDAY, DEC. 12   *467th day*

On the Sea⁓Admiralty announced that German merchant ship "Rhein" had been captured by Dutch sloop "Van Kinsbergen."

H.M. drifter, "Evening Primrose," attacked by bomber in North Sea, brought raider down in flames.

War against Italy⁓More than 20,000 prisoners, with tanks and guns, taken in Western Desert. Enemy retreat continuing. Royal Navy cooperated by bombarding focal points of enemy's retreat. R.A.F. continued ceaseless bombing of aerodromes and troops.

British naval units carried out bombardment of Kismayu, Italian Somaliland, damaging Italian supplies.

Home Front⁓Small formations of enemy aircraft crossed Kent coast, but were intercepted by our fighters. Few bombs fell on outskirts of London and at places in S.E.

During night raiders attacked Sheffield. Incendiaries started many fires. Streets blocked by wrecked tramcars and debris of buildings. Many churches hit or damaged by blast. London was also raided, as well as Liverpool and towns in East Anglia, N.E. and N.W. England.

Three enemy aircraft shot down over S.E. England, and one bomber off S.W. coast.

Greek War⁓Greeks advancing along coast and nearing Himara. Two more command-

ing heights captured in Premeti sector. Tepelini now threatened. More positions captured in Pogradets sector.

General⁓Lord Lothian, British Ambassador to U.S.A., died.

Announced that Gen. Hertzog had resigned his seat in S. African Parliament.

FRIDAY, DEC. 13   *468th day*

On the Sea⁓Admiralty announced that armed merchant cruiser, H.M.S. "Forfar" had been torpedoed and sunk.

Announced that H.M. submarine "Sunfish" had torpedoed and sunk German supply ship off Norwegian coast, and damaged an oil tanker.

In the Air⁓R.A.F. bombed shipbuilding yards at Kiel, factories and other targets at Bremen, docks and aerodromes in Holland. Coastal Command aircraft attacked submarine base at Bordeaux.

War against Italy⁓Remnants of beaten Italian army continued withdrawal from Egypt closely pursued by British troops. Several thousand more prisoners captured, including two generals.

R.A.F. maintained incessant attacks on enemy aerodromes and troop and motor concentrations in Libya. During night Derna was heavily raided. Bardia again attacked. Fifteen Italian 'planes brought down.

Home Front⁓No bombs dropped in any area by daylight. At night raiders did some damage at few points on East Coast.

Greek War⁓Greeks continued relentless drive towards Valona and reached coast north of Chimara, where they captured fortified positions. Fierce battle for Tepelini in progress.

SATURDAY, DEC. 14   *469th day*

On the Sea⁓British liner "Western Prince" torpedoed in Atlantic; most passengers saved.

Italian submarine "Naiade" sunk off N. African coast by British destroyers.

In the Air⁓Coastal Command aircraft attacked ports of Brest and Lorient.

War against Italy⁓In Western Desert British advanced forces continued to press back enemy over Libyan frontier. Estimated that 26,000 prisoners have been taken, with guns, tanks and much equipment. Eight Italian divisions said to have been cut up.

British naval forces continued operations along coast between Sidi Barrani and Bardia.

R.A.F. continued to support Army by attacking aerodromes, fuel dumps, and motor transport and troops. Fleet Air Arm attacked Tripoli during night of Dec. 13-14. In Sudan harassing activities continued unabated.

Home Front⁓Enemy air activity slight during day. At night Thames Estuary town was attacked and many houses destroyed.

Greek War⁓Operations continued successfully. Important heights, many prisoners and much equipment captured. Fierce battle raging in Tepelini area. R.A.F. twice raided Valona.

General⁓Marshal Pétain announced that M. Laval had left Government and his post as Foreign Minister was taken by M. Flandin.

SUNDAY, DEC. 15   *470th day*

War against Italy⁓Operations proceeding on Libyan frontier where British troops have now penetrated into Italian territory. R.A.F. maintained raids on Italian landing grounds and aerodromes; Bardia suffered particularly heavy attack.

Considerable air activity reported from Italian East Africa; Asmara, Gura, Zula and Danghilla among places raided.

Home Front⁓No bombs dropped over Britain during day. At night there was widespread activity. Many incendiaries and high explosives fell in a N.E. town. Towns in Midlands also attacked. London had short raid. E. Anglian town attacked.

LORD LOTHIAN, remembered perhaps better as Philip Kerr, was one of Lord Milner's "kindergarten" in South Africa. In 1916 Mr. Lloyd George, then Premier, made him his private secretary, and he was Under-Secretary for India, 1931-32. In April 1939 he was appointed Ambassador to U.S.A., where he died on December 12. *Photo, Barratt's*

SHELLS FOR THE GUNS THAT BATTERED GRAZIANI

Through a truly tropical scene these gunners of a British field artillery unit are man-handling shells for their guns emplaced somewhere in the Western Desert. In large measure General Wavell's smashing victory over the Italian invaders was due to the accurate and long-sustained shooting of the artillery arm of the Imperial Army of the Nile.

Photo, British Official : Crown Copyright

This Is How They Stormed Sidi Barrani

Most important of the actions which opened General Wavell's great offensive against the Italians in the Western Desert of Egypt was the capture of Sidi Barrani, Graziani's advanced supply base. Some account of the battle has been given in an earlier page (see page 674), but we are now in a position to provide a much more detailed and comprehensive narrative.

A T dawn on Monday, December 9, the Italians holding the desert fort of Nibeiwa, some 15 miles to the south of Sidi Barrani, heard some shots which were returned by their patrols. The firing soon died down and the garrison went on with the preparations for breakfast. But while they were consuming their coffee and rolls they heard again the crackle of rifle-fire and, much more ominous, a heavy rumbling. Rushing to the walls, they were amazed to see advancing towards them across the desert numbers of British and Indian troops, supported by tanks. At the same time the British artillery opened up, and while a barrage of 60 lb. shells was dropping on the Italian fortifications facing the east, tanks, field guns, and lorries filled with infantry swept up from the west, where no attack had been expected. In confusion the Italians turned some of their guns round and fired furiously at the attackers. But the British tanks were already charging up the embankment, their guns spouting death, while a hail of shells fell on the fort from the guns established way back in the desert. Then the infantry were unloaded from their lorries, fixed bayonets, and prepared to charge. The Italian tanks were never got into action because their crews, caught in their tents by the cannonade, were unable to penetrate the curtain of fire. Then the horses and mules were so terrified by the noise that they stampeded, adding to the confusion that prevailed within the compound. Still the British tanks came on : they breached the walls and drove here and there amongst the medley of men and animals. Behind them rushed the British and Indian infantry, shooting, thrusting, stabbing with their bayonets.

BATTLE OF SIDI BARRANI. Based on the details of the fighting which have come to hand, this map shows the approximate course of the three days' operations which ended on December 11 with the capture of Sidi Barrani by the Imperial Army of the Nile.

Once the attackers were inside the fort the Italians had no protection beyond their tents and a few dug-outs and trenches which had been constructed against air raids. "Many jumped into refuge trenches," said an Italian surgeon afterwards. "They did not know it, but they were jumping into their own graves because the shells came pouring into the trench after them. Shrapnel hit a medicine chest, and when a barrel of creosote burst the men thought it was poison gas."

Another Italian officer described the attack as being "the nearest thing to hell ever seen on this earth;" Colonel Giusfreda, Chief of Staff to General Maletti, Commander of an Italian armoured column, who was amongst the slain, told the British officer

who took him prisoner that "the action was brilliantly conceived and even more brilliantly executed. We were taken completely by surprise." By 8 o'clock all resistance had ceased, and Nibeiwa was in British hands (see page 723).

As soon as Nibeiwa had been captured the British forces re-formed behind the shattered walls and moved to attack the Tummar group of forts, which lay to the north between Nibeiwa and Sidi Barrani. These, too, fell in the course of that first day of battle. Meanwhile, a British armoured column hurried across the desert, and in the space of a few hours reached Buqbuq on the coast, thus cutting the road between Sidi Barrani and Sollum. Their advance was furthered by a tremendous bombardment from ships of the British Mediterranean Fleet, which moved up and down the coast shelling the Italian positions and columns of motor transport.

On board the ships the course of the battle was followed over the wireless, and one who was there said it was like listening to an intensely exciting B.B.C. sports commentary. One of the messages overheard came from the commander of a British tank who said, "I am stopped in the middle of 200 men—no, 500 men—with their hands up. For heaven's sake send up the blankety blank infantry." Another ran, "I am two miles south of the first Buq in Buqbuq." This place, known to every British soldier as Bugbug, was captured on December 10 by the Armoured Brigade, which took 14,000 prisoners—so many that they sent out an S O S for the infantry, saying that they were anxious to continue their advance without having to bother about acting as

ANTI-TANK GUNS mounted in the Western Desert in readiness for the assault by Graziani's tanks. In the event, however, the Italian tank arm was handled very ineffectively, and scores of tanks were amongst the huge booty captured by the Army of the Nile.
Photo, British Official: Crown Copyright

Dry and Barren Was the Field of Combat

Photos. British Official : Crown Copyright

WATER is a major problem both for Wavell and for Graziani. Wells are few and far between in the Western Desert, and the precious fluid has to be brought by lorry and stored in tanks sunk deep in the sand.

GUNS OF THE ROYAL ARTILLERY preparing the way for the British advance against the Italian forts on the Libyan frontier are covered with thin rope netting, which, seen from an angle, blends perfectly with the sand. In the desert camouflage is all the more necessary as natural cover is so slight. Inset, a British soldier is using a bomb crater as protection while he explodes a land-mine left by the retreating enemy.

Photos, British Official : Crown Copyright

Australians On the Way to Meet the Italians

AUSTRALIANS, just detrained at the railhead at Mersa Matruh, are setting off to "footslog" through a fog of penetrating and choking dust. It was with boundless pride that the news was received " down under " of the part played by the " Aussies " in their first major action.

Photo, Australian Official

division which had just stormed the Tummar camps, assisted by an armoured brigade which was operating eastwards from Buqbuq. On the night of December 10 they bivouacked in the desert, then at dawn the long columns of lorries continued their march across the plain. Soon the enemy positions came in sight, and at a distance of about 3,000 yards the British came under a heavy fire. The lorries were taken up a little farther, however, before the infantry " debused." Then the men went into the attack—on the left wing a famous South Country regiment, Highland troops in the centre, and a Midland regiment on the right. The Italians were holding a strongly-entrenched position, protected by many well-sited machine-guns. Throughout the battle a sandstorm was raging—" hellish " is the word used by a major to describe it. " The Blackshirts," he went on, " stuck to their guns surprisingly well. It was extremely hard to see them in their trenches among the sand dunes, and there were plenty of them." As the infantry were held up by a withering fire the call went forth for artillery and tanks.

Charge of the Highlanders

So there came rumbling into action a squadron of the most modern British battle-tanks. They smashed their way through on the left flank, enabling the South Country regiment to carry the positions opposite them by storm. The artillery cleared the way for the Midlanders on the right flank, so that they, too, were able to make some progress. But the centre was still held up, and at last the Brigadier, hearing of the successes on either flank, gave the order to advance. With fixed bayonets the Highlanders then charged across the desert through a hail of bullets, and in a few minutes were amongst the Black-shirts with their bayonets. By 2 o'clock the Scots had gained a foothold on a low ridge looking down on Sidi Barrani with the Mediterranean and British ships beyond.

Meanwhile, the tanks on the British left wing had nosed their way along the shore, and British forces were drawing near from Maktila, driving a host of fugitives before them. About 3 o'clock in the afternoon the Highlanders holding the ridge attacked again. Racing down over the scrubby slopes, they charged into the ruins of Sidi Barrani. For a short time there was fierce hand-to-hand fighting ; then group after group of the defenders held up their hands, waving handkerchiefs and shirts and crying " Ci rendiamo "—we surrender. Some of the Blackshirts tried to escape along the road to the west, but when they came up against the British armoured brigade they, too, surrendered. The number of prisoners taken was stated to be in the neighbourhood of 15,000, but they were pouring in so rapidly that it was impossible to keep an accurate check ; nor was it possible to make an inventory of the quantities of war supplies of every kind which fell to the conquerors.

On the day following the battle General Gallina, who was taken prisoner together with several of his divisional generals, asked and was granted permission to address his troops ; he thanked them for having fought like good Fascists. The British, too, were loud in their praises of the enemy. " The Italians fought bravely," said one British major, " you can take my word for that."

warders. Soon a battalion of Indian infantry took charge of the prisoners, and the Armoured Brigade continued its pursuit of the Italians along the road to Sollum, at the same time cutting off those columns of Italian troops who were painfully making their way to the coast from their positions in the desert.

Meanwhile, the British columns had been drawing near to Sidi Barrani, as one by one the forts surrounding it were overrun. Nibeiwa, as we have seen, was the first to fall on the morning of December 9 ; shortly afterwards Maktila, 15 miles to the east along the coast, was also carried. Here it was that the Libyan troops were so terrified by the noise of the 15-inch guns used by the Fleet in their bombardment of the place that they deserted their Italian officers and fled along the road to Sidi Barrani. Many of them were intercepted by the British tanks and wiped out, but the remainder staggered into Sidi Barrani, where they were flung into the firing-line alongside a crack division of Blackshirts.

By nightfall on that same Monday Tummar East and Tummar West, two camps just north of Nibeiwa, were both in British hands, and on Wednesday, December 11, Habsa or

Point 90 also capitulated. On the same day the Italian commander at Sofafa, where a division was holding an exceedingly strong group of four forts, was tricked into disaster. For three days the British forces had been detailed to stand by, not attacking but simply keeping a watchful eye on his movements. News of the reverse which his colleagues had suffered was allowed to trickle through, with the result that by the Wednesday morning the Italian had taken the decision to evacuate. At breakfast-time hundreds of lorries and large numbers of men, including part of the 63rd Metropolitan Division and some Blackshirts, set out from the encampment and started to creep westwards along the desert. This was the moment the R.A.F. had been waiting for. They dive-bombed and machine-gunned the marchers, and when the column was last seen it was marching straight into a British tank unit which had been detailed to intercept it.

Now the way was clear to the final assault on Sidi Barrani, which already had been heavily bombed and bombarded from land, sea and air. It was held by Blackshirt regiments under General Gallina, in command of the 23rd Corps, and it was now attacked by a British brigade of the Indian

At Battalion H.Q. They Waited for Zero Hour

IN THE WESTERN DESERT the Battalion Headquarters of one of the regiments with the Army of the Nile were established in an old Roman tomb, a relic of the days when Egypt was a province of the Roman Empire. Telephones and typewriters were installed, while the niches where the coffins of the Roman dead once lay served as bunks for the officers. To give a last touch of modernity to the scene these were named after the dwarfs who divide their fame with "Snow White."

Photo, British Official: Crown Copyright

The Invader Invaded: the War in Libya

General Wavell opened his offensive in Egypt on December 9. Sidi Barrani fell on December 11, and before the week was out the Italians had been driven out of Egypt and the Imperial Army of the Nile had followed the defeated, dispirited and, in part at least, demoralized enemy over the frontier into Libya.

WHILE one part of Wavell's Army of the Nile surrounded Sidi Barrani and after storming its ring of forts captured the place—or what was left of it—on December 11, other large detachments raced westwards in pursuit of the fleeing enemy. One armoured brigade made for Buqbuq, main centre for the distribution of food and water to Graziani's advance troops. For a day they were held up south-east of the village ; then on the afternoon of December 10 they carried it by assault. Many thousands of prisoners were taken, but a considerable number of Italian troops escaped and made for Sollum, some 30 miles to the west. They were closely followed by the British as they hurried along the coastal road, and on their way they were harried, too, by bombers of the R.A.F. and by ships of the Mediterranean Fleet lying off the shore.

With a view to heading off the fugitives, one of the British armoured columns swept around west of Buqbuq and flung itself astride the road to Sollum. Hardly had they done so when they saw coming towards them a whole division of Italian regulars— the 64th (Catanzaro) division under General Amico. The Italians were taken completely by surprise when they marched into the ambush of British tanks and armoured cars. So surprised, indeed, were they that they showed little fight, and practically all of the 14,000 men composing the division were captured, together with vast quantities of war material which they left strewn along both sides of the road. An infantry brigade having come up took charge of the prisoners and marched them away down " Victory Avenue," as the Italians had named the road between Sollum and Sidi Barrani. But theirs was no victory march—just two long columns of dusty and tired conscripts, every

ON THE EVE OF THE BATTLE
General Wavell's Order of the Day to the Troops in the Western Desert

THE result of the fighting in the Western Desert will be one of the decisive events of the war.

The crushing defeat of the Italian forces will have an incalculable effect not only upon the whole position in the Middle East, not only upon the military situation everywhere, but on the future of freedom and civilization throughout the world. It may shorten the war by very many months.

It must be the firm determination of every man to do everything that in him lies, without thought of self, to win this decisive victory.

In everything but numbers we are superior to the enemy. We are more highly trained, we shoot straighter, we have better equipment. Above all, we have stouter hearts, greater traditions, and we are fighting for a worthier cause.

The Italians entered the war treacherously, without a reason, because they expected a cheap and easy victory. Let us show them their mistake by inflicting on them a stern and costly defeat.

Mr. Winston Churchill has sent us every wish for good fortune in this fighting, and his assurance that all the acts, decisions, valour, and violence against the enemy will, whatever their upshot, receive the resolute support of his Majesty's Government.

We have waited long in the Middle East ; when our chance comes let us strike hard. The harder the blows we strike against these servants of tyranny and selfish lust for power, the sooner we shall bring peace and freedom back into the world and be able to return to our own free, peaceful homes.

200 or 300 being guarded by a single cheerfully grinning Cockney private.

Through storms of dust and rain the British tanks and armoured cars poured across the desert towards Sollum, and the weather had cleared somewhat when on the morning of December 16 the attack was launched on this, Mussolini's last stronghold in Egypt. The walls having been breached by artillery fire, the tanks charged into the village, closely followed by the infantry. Some of the defenders slipped away along the road to the west, but the great majority— so many that it was difficult to count them— fell into the hands of the conquerors, as well as huge masses of war material and 15

Italian 'planes which had already been rendered unserviceable by British air attacks earlier in the week. Those Italians who had escaped retreated up Halfiya Pass—Hell Fire Pass, the British called it. From machine-gun positions skilfully sited in the side of the escarpment the Italians poured a withering fire on to our mechanized units as they forced their way up. But nothing could stop the advance. The Italians fled in disorder, and soon the British tanks were crunching through the wire which marked the boundary between Egypt and Libya.

First news of the British invasion of Libya was contained in an Italian communiqué issued on Dec. 15 which referred to " bloody encounters in the desert zone of Fort Capuzzo, Sollum and Bardia." Fort Capuzzo was stormed the next day ; then came the news that three forts to the south, Musaid, Sidi Omar and Shefferzen, had also been carried by another of the British armoured columns. This was on Tuesday, December 17. Still farther to the south Australian cavalry charged, sword in hand, the Italians holding the oasis of Jarabub and carried the place by assault.

Fresh from these victories the Imperial Army—British and Indians, Australians and New Zealanders, with their Free French and Polish allies—continued their march into Libya, the tanks and armoured cars closely followed by battalions of infantry conveyed in lorries. Some of the invaders moved straight on Bardia, Mussolini's big base and port 12 miles inside Libyan territory, and soon it was cut off. Others drove across the desert and reached the coast 20 miles beyond Bardia and some 30 miles inside Libya.

Bardia itself was now a blazing inferno, as it was shelled from the land, bombed from the air and bombarded from the sea. The night sky was lit up with the pin-points of bursting

MAJ.-GEN. R. N. O'CONNOR, who is in direct command of the Imperial Army in the Western Desert, served with distinction in the last war. Besides the D.S.O. with bar and the M.C. he was awarded the Italian Silver Medal for Valour.

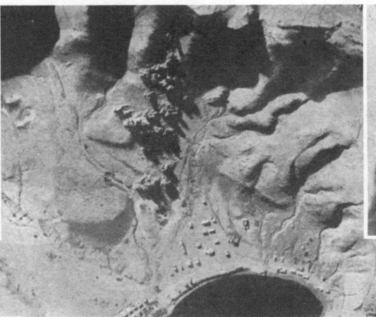

SOLLUM, seen from the air in this unique photograph, was retaken by the British on December 16, 1940, after being in Italian hands since the beginning of the previous September. In the meantime it had been heavily fortified by Graziani, and on the foreshore and in the gully leading to it military buildings can be discerned.   *Photos, Central Press, " Daily Mirror " and E.N.A.*

MAJOR-GENERAL M. O'MOORE CREAGH, who was in command of the Armoured Division that dashed along the coast into Libya, began his career in the Army as a cavalryman, but soon applied cavalry tactics to mechanized units.

Sollum and Fort Capuzzo Fall to the British

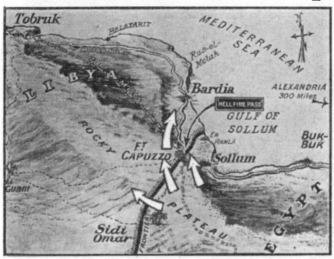

FORT CAPUZZO AND SOLLUM fell on December 16, and at once the British forces moved on against Bardia, twelve miles into Libya. The white arrows in the map above show the general direction of the British advance. On the right is the port of Bardia, so mercilessly hammered by the R.A.F.   *Photo, E.N.A., map by courtesy of the "Daily Telegraph"*

A.A. shells and great strings of "flaming-onions"; flares floodlit the landscape, and huge columns of smoke floated upwards and blotted out the stars. The place was strongly held, for within its walls were bottled up the whole of the 62nd division under General Berti, together with what was left of the 63rd division and some of the Blackshirts who had managed to escape from Sidi Barrani. They put up a strong resistance but, surrounded on every side, their surrender was deemed to be merely a matter of time.

By now even the Italians at home were allowed to know something—but only something—of the disaster which had befallen their arms in Africa. Writing his weekly screed, Gayda, Mussolini's mouthpiece, declared that the British had concentrated 300,000 men in Egypt and that 800 tanks and armoured cars supported their advance; and an announcer over the Rome radio declared that the British were using a tank of a new model, much more powerful and better protected than the earlier types.

In the House of Commons on December 19 Mr. Churchill reviewed this "memorable battle," as he well styled it, "spread over this vast expanse of desert with swiftly-moving mechanized columns circling in and out of the mass and posts of the enemy, and with fighting taking place over an area as large as Yorkshire." The figure of 30,000 prisoners taken was, he said, a considerable understatement, and to them should be added a hundred serviceable guns and 50 tanks, together with a great quantity of invaluable stores. Yet the Army of the Nile, after continuous fighting throughout the week, had lost less than a thousand killed and wounded of all ranks, British, Indian and Imperial troops.

MARSHAL GRAZIANI, C.-in-C. of the Italian armies in North Africa, partaking of a meal in the desert. He is a hard-bitten old warrior, with an unenviable reputation for harshness towards the natives.   *Photo, G.P.U.*

BLENHEIM BOMBERS of the R.A.F. Middle East Command are seen above breaking formation to land at their desert aerodrome on their return from a successful raid. Air Commodore Collishaw (inset), who is directing the R.A.F. cooperation with the Army in the Western Desert.   *Photos, British Official: Crown Copyright; Planet News*

Poles and Free French Share in the Triumph

POLISH TROOPS cooperated with the British forces in the Western Desert, and a motorized Polish column is seen above. General Sir Archibald Wavell (circle), C.-in-C. of the Army of the Nile, talks to men of a Yorkshire regiment.

While Bardia was still holding out, Marshal Graziani sent a message to Mussolini, explaining the disaster which had befallen him. He reminded the Duce of the great difficulties which hampered his march into Egypt—the inadequate communications and the almost entire lack of water. By December preparations for a further advance were almost complete, but since early in October aerial reconnaissances revealed a British concentration east of Mersa Matruh, and so there was, Graziani declared, no surprise. The attack was launched on December 9. "Against the positions occupied by our troops in the flat desert territory the enemy poured masses of armoured cars, tanks, light and heavy arms, supported by mobile batteries and aerial forces. As soon as the terrific aerial bombardment ceased, armoured units advanced from all directions against our troops . . .

"Against the armoured mass operating concentrically over a wide front the opposition of our anti-tank guns and artillery, forced to disperse their fire on a number of very mobile objectives, was ineffectual. It is in the crushing superiority of the armoured units employed *en masse* that the reason for the enemy's initial success is to be found."

FREE FRENCH FORCES gave invaluable support to the British troops during the final assault upon Sollum on December 16. A motorized detachment of a French unit is seen "debussing" from Army lorries upon the desert.   *Photos, British Official : Crown Copyright*

'Mid Snow and Rain the Greeks Still Advanced

Though the weather conditions were appalling, the war between Greek and Italian in the Albanian mountains continued on its bloody way. Below we give a picture of the battle-front after fifty days of war, when the Italians were being relentlessly driven back on Valona.

AFTER fifty days of fighting the front formed by the opposing armies of Italians and Greeks ran in a jagged line across the mountains of south-central Albania. It was not a continuous line, for the character of the country, so rugged and barren, so precipitous in places, so reft by narrow gorges carved out of the rock by the rushing mountain streams, forbade anything in the nature of a connected system of strong points and trenches; but wherever the Greeks could secure a foothold they continued their advance against the Italians, who, for their part, were obliged to keep to the roads, for only along roads could their motorized transport move.

By the middle of December, then, the "line" ran from the shores of Lake Ochrida to the west of Pogradets, and thence across the mountains in a south-westerly direction to just south of Klisura, which already was under Greek fire and on the point of being

December 18 was the scene of the rout of the Italian Fourth Grenadiers, the King of Italy's personal bodyguard, by the Greeks, who charged them with the bayonet. A little to the north is Himara (Chimarà), which was also being bombarded. Indeed, it was rumoured that the Italians had abandoned it, though another report stated that they were dragging their heavy artillery up the mountains in a last desperate effort to save the place. For if Chimara, Tepelini and Klisura fell, then Valona itself could hardly be held; and Valona's harbour might provide a splendid base for the British Navy. Not without reason, then, did Mussolini order that big naval guns should be put into position on the little island of Saseno—the "Gibraltar of the Adriatic," as the Italians have called it—which lies at the entrance of the Bay of Valona.

Throughout these operations the weather was appalling. Mr. Arthur Merton, Special

Correspondent of the "Daily Telegraph," telegraphed that thick clouds were overhanging the whole country, creating a most depressing atmosphere, and torrential rains were sweeping over the land, converting the roads into morasses of rising mud. Sleet and hail alternated with the rain, and the mountains were covered with thick snow. Water was pouring down the mountain-sides, converting streams into roaring torrents which swept away bridges in their onrush.

Yet nothing seemed to be able to deter the Greeks. On his way across the mountains Mr. Merton passed endless convoys carrying supplies to the front line. "Their covered wagons or open carts on which the drivers huddled under pieces of canvas, trying to protect themselves from the driving rain and wind, were drawn by sturdy little horses or mules. Cheerfulness was the characteristic of all these wayfarers. There were always greetings for us. Through thick, slippery

WAR COUNCIL IN ATHENS. Left to right: Major-General M. D. Gambier-Parry, Chief British Liaison Officer with the Greek Army; General Metaxas, Prime Minister of Greece; King George; Air Vice-Marshal J. H. D'Albiac, commanding the British forces in Greece; and General Papagos, Greek C.-in-C.

abandoned by the Italians. Then, after dipping in the valley of the Viosa and up the opposite slope, it faced Tepelini, an Italian supply centre, which also was reported to have been abandoned. Between Tepelini and the coast the line ran across Mt. Skiovika. Here on the ridge the Italians had established themselves in strong positions, but on Dec. 16 the Greeks, fighting in a furious snowstorm, swept through the Italian defences and stormed one after the other the gun emplacements and machine-gun nests. The Italians made five attempts to recapture the hill, but the Greeks mowed them down until the slopes were a shambles. At last the Italians —men of the Alpini division—had had enough of this useless slaughter, and retired northwards in disorder. The Modena division, which counter-attacked in the west of the river Drinos, was also repulsed.

The "line" reached the sea in the neighbourhood of Porto Palermo, which on

ALBANIA'S HILLS glimpsed from an R.A.F. 'plane. The photograph gives some idea of the nature of the country through which the Italians were forced to retreat. In narrow defiles beneath the precipitous mountain-side they had little chance of escaping the bombs that rained on them from the air.
Photos, British Official; Crown Copyright; and Fox

Athens Was a City of Victory Smiles

ENTHUSIASM IN ATHENS grew steadily as the news of the Allied victories began to come through. Top, British sailors in the Greek capital are being received with hearty handclaps. In the lower photograph young Greek recruits crowd on to a tram to make a triumphant tour of Athens before joining their units.

THE GREEK AIR FORCE was small, but proved its worth against the Italians time and again. Young Greeks are keen to join it, and training is in full swing. Here recruits are learning to use the various types of guns mounted on the aircraft in which they will fly.

Photos, British Paramount Newsreel and Sport & General

mire which hindered every step, they ploughed their way." On a summit of some 6,000 feet, where conditions were truly Arctic, old men and women and even little children were picking up stone and slate from the hill-side and carrying it to the road to make it passable for wheeled transport. " Equally pathetic, but inspiring, was the sight of those thousands of horses and mules, drenched and shivering with cold, but struggling to bear the loads which are their contribution to their masters' success in the battle."

Very different was the spirit of the Italians, few of whom had any real interest in the struggle. In some places, it is true, they put up a fierce resistance, but in others they acted as if they were completely demoralized. Thus we are told of one village, Vassilikon in the Pindus sector, which was evacuated by the Italians without a shot being fired as soon as they heard that the Greeks were approaching. When the Greeks entered the place they found that the fires were still burning in the bakeries and bread ovens ; in the houses and encampment water was still hot in the basins. Half-eaten meals lay on the tables, and in one officer's tent his clothes were laid out neatly on his camp bed ; in another the soap was still wet on a shaving-brush. Some 1,500 bicycles were found in or about the village ; apparently they had been brought up in readiness for the victory parade which the Italians had planned so confidently to hold in Janina.

Terrible Conditions at the Front

But, all the same, the Italians were still holding strong positions and were not only better equipped than the Greeks but probably more numerous. The Greeks profited by the enormous captures of Italian war material, and were as quick to use the Italian lorries as they were to turn round the Italian guns and tanks. But in the terrible weather conditions that prevailed on the mountain battlefield their plight was pitiable. Numbers of the men were without even a single blanket, as 200,000 blankets had been destroyed by a fire in Athens on the eve of the war ; many more had to share a blanket with a comrade. Their boots, too, were in a shocking state after weeks of marching and clambering about the rocks. As one Greek corps commander put it, " If my men are able to do so much with so little essential clothing, how much more could be done if they were more adequately provided ! "

Meanwhile, in spite of the opening of the offensive in Egypt, the R.A.F. and the Royal Navy continued their aid to our Greek allies. Air Vice-Marshal D'Albiac stated on December 21 that the strength of the R.A.F. in Greece was expected to be increased as soon as the weather improved, when large scale operations would begin. Since the beginning of the war, he added, 39 Italian 'planes had definitely been destroyed in the Balkans, while 12 others had probably been destroyed, as against only nine British 'planes lost. Valona had been raided 18 times and Durazzo eight times.

As for the Royal Navy, on December 18 ships of the Mediterranean Fleet swept the Adriatic Sea as far north as Bari and Durazzo, while a force of battleships, under the command of the C.-in-C., heavily bombarded Valona. No opposition was encountered from the enemy.

The Italians Were Also Driven Out of Gallabat

GALLABAT fell to the British on November 6, 1940, after an action lasting only about three-quarters of an hour ; right, two British soldiers are seen inspecting the ruins of the fort just after the Italians had been forced to abandon it.

Artillery had shelled the fort heavily before the attack was made. Circle, is one of the guns in action during the bombardment. Aircraft, tanks, and armoured cars gave efficacious support to the British and Indian troops.

Photos, British Official ; Crown Copyright

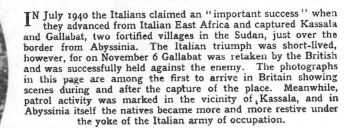

IN July 1940 the Italians claimed an "important success" when they advanced from Italian East Africa and captured Kassala and Gallabat, two fortified villages in the Sudan, just over the border from Abyssinia. The Italian triumph was short-lived, however, for on November 6 Gallabat was retaken by the British and was successfully held against the enemy. The photographs in this page are among the first to arrive in Britain showing scenes during and after the capture of the place. Meanwhile, patrol activity was marked in the vicinity of Kassala, and in Abyssinia itself the natives became more and more restive under the yoke of the Italian army of occupation.

ITALIAN PRISONERS taken when Gallabat was captured being marched away to internment (left) ; among them were 17 deserters, an early indication of the Italian lack of morale. Above, British troops in possession of the fort are watching for any sign of a counter-attack by the enemy. One was made, but was successfully repulsed.

Sudan's Defence Force Fights for the Empire

SUDANESE INFANTRYMEN at bayonet practice. They take readily to this form of fighting. Right is one of their sergeants.

SUDAN DEFENCE FORCE is the designation of the fine body of soldiers raised among the natives of the Anglo-Egyptian Sudan. Since the declaration of war it has rapidly expanded and has already proved its capacity for attack as well as defence in actions against the Italians in Eritrea. Above, a member of the camel patrol of the Force, attached to an Indian infantry brigade, is on the qui vive on the frontier. The Southern Sudan is a tsetse fly area, and as animals are particularly susceptible to this pest all the patrols of the Sudan Defence Force operating there are mechanized. Right, a patrol is leaving a lorry that has brought the men to their post. All the mechanized units in this area are provided with water and petrol to last 15 days.

Photos, British Official: Crown Copyright

South Africans in Action on the Kenya Front

TROOPS OF THE UNION now operating with other Imperial troops on the Kenya front occupy some very lonely posts. The mortar detachment, left, is holding a sand-bagged emplacement in a commanding position in the Turkana area, immediately south of the Anglo-Egyptian Sudan, but lest there is any doubt that they keep their spirits up their dug-out is named the "Merry Mortars."

Below is Lieut.-General D. P. Dickinson, G.O.C. the East African Forces in Kenya, with Colonel Dan Pienaar, a South African brigade commander, on his right.

SOUTH AFRICANS were quick to cross swords with the Italians. On June 11, 1940, the day after Italy entered the war, bombers of the South African Air Force attacked objectives in Abyssinia, and on July 29 South African troops, the first volunteers for service outside the Union, arrived in Kenya, to be followed later by a much larger contingent. They were in action on December 16 when South African and East African troops, with Gold Coast Askaris and supported by armoured cars, artillery, and South African Air Force 'planes, raided the Italian post at El Wak, on the frontier of Italian Somaliland. Some 50 of the enemy were killed, and 20 Italians and a hundred natives were taken prisoner. Just before the attack was opened the Italian commander fled into the interior in a mule cart !

SKY-WATCHERS with the South African forces in Kenya have built a crow's-nest in a leafless tree to be used as a look-out for Italian air raiders approaching from Eritrea.

Photos, G.P.U., and Sport & General

On the Mediterranean Shore They Made Re

WAVELL'S OFFENSIVE, which in the course of one short week drove the Italians out of their strongly fortified positions in the Western Desert of Egypt and sent them reeling back across the frontier into Libya, was the result of most careful planning and preparation. Once the operation had been conceived by the master-brain, its execution was confided to a band of most able assistants, who in many cases had had years of experience of desert

Phot

or ' One of the Decisive Events of the War '

al :

warfare and in particular were intimately acquainted with the Egyptian terrain. For weeks and months the preparations went on with never a hitch. This photograph shows men of the Royal Engineers laying a concrete foundation for one of the big guns, which in due course pummelled the Italian defences into dust. Beyond the toilers is a native village of mud-walled and flat-roofed huts, clustered beneath the grateful shade of the palms.

HAPPY NEW YEAR?—GLANCES BACK & FORWARD

By the Editor

WISHFUL thinking has just been at its zenith. But remember Hamlet : " Nothing is either good or bad, but thinking makes it so." When wishing our friends a Happy New Year for 1941 most of us must have had a mental reservation in trying to equate our wishing with our thinking.

With the approach of Christmas I had the thought to turn over some old leaves of " The War Illustrated " in the intervals of preparing new ones for my readers to turn in in 1941. The result, if not too joyous, is not too depressing . . . we have not hesitated to " keep our Christmas merry still." Optimist though I be I am heavily conscious that however happily we may have celebrated the swift-footed hours of the festive season we cannot quite have been blind to the veiled spectre of 1941 when we broadcast our wishes for a Happy New Year.

We are assuredly at the threshold of the Testing Year, and if thinking could really make it so we should all give a special vehemence to the " Happy." But what did the bells that rang out the old year tell us ? I found an answer of sorts in those year-old pages of " The War Illustrated " which I looked over again in contemplative mood. Too often where I looked for souvenirs of victory and progress, I found records of disaster, dismay, disillusionment . . . bad stuff on which to build up hope and confidence. Yet out of things evil good has often issued.

The hopes that were springing in the breasts of all lovers of liberty and freedom when the first New Year of this monstrous War was ushered in were doomed to disappointment and the need to think intensively on good rather than on evil if we thus could " make it so " had become clamant in one of the loveliest summers that have ever smiled on this dear island of ours.

' Neutrality ' a Broken Reed

BY odd chance the hopes of liberty-loving peoples everywhere were resting at the start of 1940 on a small heroic nation that had dared to stand up to a gigantic tyranny, just as the same eyes of admiration are today bent upon little valiant Greece standing up to the still more loathsome onslaught of Mussolini's Imperial Italy. Not that we can compare Finland with Greece save in the spirit of the two peoples. The geographical difficulty presented to Britain and her ally France in carrying the necessary aid to the Finns in their immortal stand against Russian aggression might, and could have been overcome had Norway and Sweden been ready to make a stand for freedom at the side of the democracies to which they naturally belong, instead of clinging to a futile " neutrality " which they were both powerless to maintain.

All that followed of disaster can in large measure be traced to this. Norway, too late in accepting Allied aid, merely led to her complete Nazi domination when the Allies had to withdraw from Trondheim on May 2. Sweden saved herself from material harm at the cost of accepting a Nazi domination that may be less apparent than real, betraying in the act everything that democracy implies. The end of Finland's heroic stand could have been no otherwise in the circumstances. The whole course of the War might well have been changed if the then free nations of Scandinavia had invited the cooperation of the Allies instead of opposing it while Finland was upright—even France, in full action with Britain, might well have found herself before the political rot in her body politic had time to eat its way down to her very vitals. A new health might have come to her.

It would be foolish to deny how high the star of Nazidom was mounting then ; how much these events were to affect the vastly greater events of later months . . . and of tomorrow.

" WE shan't win the War by Wishful Thinking " was one of our headlines in the issue of January 15. " Britain's Shipwrights Are Outpacing the Nazis," was another headline of the week before, and the pictures showed shipping losses from U-boat action were speedily being made good by the energy of our shipbuilders . . . more than good. No such headline is likely to appear in any early number of 1941. " Where Will the Blow Fall in the West ? " we were asking at the end of January, when the shameful French debacle at Sedan, must have seemed as remote as a collision in stellar space if any one had had the prevision to foretell it. The War was still " phoney " then. " Allies and Neutrals Present a Firm Front " (the world still accepted the false gospel of Maginot) : Belgium would stand firm on the Albert Canal and Holland would hold back the Hun by flooding her defensive areas if he ever attempted to invade these two stalwart die-hard neutrals !

The Editor's New Year Wish

OUR surest Hope of Survival through 1941 and of Progress on the Way to Final Victory over the Forces of Evil is based upon Our having withstood and overcome the horrors and misfortunes of 1940 and achieving Our First Major Victory by Land, Sea and Air in the Near East. May 1941 prove the Year of Great Things for the British Empire and All Nations of Free Men !

A SERIES of articles "On the Fringes of the War" dealt with Denmark, Belgium, Holland, Rumania, Hungary, which had all been woven into the unpatterned warp and woof of Nazi Europe along with once mighty France months before the approach of the second wartime Christmas. In April so little did the peoples of France and Britain know of the alarming rot that was feverishly eating out the body and soul of France (thanks to the most brutal and corrupting censorship at Paris) that picturesque ceremonies (complete with military bands) could take place when the French handed over sectors of their ill-conceived and inadequately fortified Maginot extension line to the British and we could headline the picture-record " From Strength to Strength on the Western Front " . . . just seven weeks before the B.E.F. and " the little boats of England " at Dunkirk were providing History with the raw material for one of the greatest epics of heroism and human endurance its pages are ever likely to enshrine . . . a vast disaster made glorious by British valour.

" Happy New Year " wishes for 1940 had foreseen none of these world-shaking events.

But, little though we knew in January 1940 that we were so soon to face Britain's blackest hour—we hoped, trusted, and believed we should see a turn of the tide in 1940, nor have we been disappointed.

Even when the blitzkrieg on London was at its worst, even when the Nazis vowed to continue to "Coventrate" all our great cities one by one, even when the intensified submarine campaign was taking toll of British and Allied shipping at a formidable and indeed alarming rate, the tide was turning.

On the day that the unspeakable Mussolini announced his entry into the War Mr. Duff Cooper, in his broadcast, prophecied that Italy " which has never won a war, will prove more of a liability than an asset." A safe prophecy, which the Fascist fiascos in Albania and on the Egyptian frontier have speedily confirmed. Indeed, Italy's entry has proved the real bright spot of 1940. But somehow the liability she has thrown upon the

Axis, by Mussolini in his conceit and folly trying to secure, on the cheap, a little military gilt for the embellishing of his gingerbread Empire, will have to be met. And how ?

Nazi policy may not have fully provided for the new situation before it developed. If it had, then the Nazis are the most far-seeing of strategists. The thrust to the East was always an essential feature of their policy, the absorbing of Rumania and Hungary were preliminaries, but of which the "Drang nach Osten " has received a jolt for which Hitler has his " great friend Benito Mussolini " solely to thank. He may thank him in several ways. One that is not unlikely is to let Benito sizzle in his own Balkan stewpot rather than weaken the Nazi preparations for the one supreme task that remains to the mechanized conqueror of Europe—the Invasion of Britain. So long as Britain stands inviolate in her island stronghold—let her head be bloody but unbowed—the Nazi plan of world dominion has failed and will eventually crumble.

This implies a supreme effort to reduce Great Britain in 1941. With Italy shaping so badly under the hammering of our Army of the Nile and the Greeks gaining new strength from their victories, so considerably aided by British naval and air support, Hitler's alternative to a supreme effort against the British Isles would be speedily to occupy all France, take possession of the considerable elements of the French Fleet which the anti-British Darlan commands, secure a foothold in French North Africa, if not its complete domination, and force Italy, with her Fleet, to do his bidding not as a partner but as a cringing servant. Spain and Portugal would also have to be forced in.

The Year of Decision Has Dawned

BRITAIN would have much to say and more to do if Nazi policy took that direction, but not more than she could do. So that the likelier turn of events in 1941 is a genuine and desperate effort to invade this country, with intensified air attacks, U-boat torpedoing and long-distance bombing of our convoys, in order to force an issue. That, at least, is what we must be prepared to meet. General Wavell's brilliant defence of Egypt and rout of the Italians in Libya is a glorious achievement, indeed, a major battle of the War, and synchronising so accurately with the Greek triumph, it might well be the turning-point of the War in the East, but the true turning-point of the War will not be reached until the ever-present menace of the Invasion of Britain has been boldly met and defeated.

We may reasonably hope that the vast and urgently-needed supplies of war materials from America will soon be transformed from the astronomical figures of the dollars they are to cost and the overwhelming numerals of 'planes, tanks, ships and boats and other war supplies which have filled millions of columns in the American press for a year or more, into things of hard reality landed here in Britain. Our good American friends are lively talkers about what they are going to do : the best wish we can send them in this first week of the New Year is that, for our sake and their own, they will take our Mr. Morrison's advice and " Go to it ! "

And so in ending this page of random reflections one may say that, bearing in mind the terrible trials from which we have just emerged unbowed in 1940, and looking with eager eye and no trembling of the lip as the Fates are fingering the curtain that occludes the coming events of 1941, there is much to justify our wishfully thinking that before the third Christmas of the War comes round the tide will indeed have turned for all the world to see and will be running strong for the nations that are fighting for freedom . . . even though interludes of trial and tribulation are still ahead of us.

The Spahis Were Amongst the Conquerors

SPAHIS, the native cavalry of France's African Empire, are represented amongst General Wavell's Army now engaged in Egypt and Libya. After the collapse of France many of them took the southward road from Syria and joined the Free French Forces. As these two photographs show, they are fine soldiers obviously well used to desert warfare.   *Photos, British Official : Crown Copyright*

Anti-Aircraft Battery

How the Guns Are Trained on the Nazi Raiders

Specially drawn for THE WAR ILLUSTRATED *by War Artists & Illustrators Ltd.*

Mobile A.A. Gun (3-inch)

(A), barrel; (B), recuperator; (C), breech; (D), shell; (E), loader; (F), elevating quadrant; (G), loading tray; (H), road wheels; (J), davits for raising wheels; (K), legs; (L), transversor; (M), elevator.

Predictor

Operators (B) keep the aircraft in view: (A) feeds in the figures for height, delivered to him from the height-and-range finder. In following the raider with their telescopes, operators (B) set in motion calculating machinery, and the wheel turned by (A) also plays its part. Operators (C) balance " the figures resulting from (A) and (B). As a result, the proper figures for the fuse setting appear on dial (D) and are given to the gunners.

Height-and-Range Finder. A simplified diagram of the range-finding portion. At eyepiece (B) the observer sees half-images from both apertures, coming from the pentagonal prisms (F) and (K) by way of the objective lenses (J) and (E); by manipulating the two deflecting prisms (G) and (H), the two half-images are made to coincide; simultaneously an index is moved over the range scale and the figure is read off at (A). (C) is the eyepiece prism; (D), halving glass; (L), frame tube; (M), outer tube; (N), (O), beams from object.

These picture diagrams show how an A.A. battery is linked up with its predictor, height-and-range finder and sound locator. A pictorial layout is given immediately above, and at the top are details of the gun and the instruments that direct its fire. The sound locator is used to find the aircraft when visual methods (by the predictor) are not practicable : its giant ears are turned until the sound of the approaching raider is loudest, and the information thus gathered is passed on to the gunners. The predictor forecasts the likely position of the aircraft (from course, bearing, speed, etc.) and enables the gunners to aim and fuse their shells to meet the raider in its flight. The height-and-range finder supplies certain essential particulars for the predictor calculations.

Uneasy Interlude in the War by Night

Whatever might have been its causes or motives, the slackening of the Luftwaffe's attack on Britain led to no such diminuendo in our own assault. Some of the chief targets of our bombers are listed below. The need for increased vigilance and for the increasing effort of all was stressed by the Premier in his review of the war situation on Dec. 19.

SHEFFIELD was the main objective of enemy bombers on Sunday night, December 15-16. This was the town's second heavy raid in four days, and again the Nazis began by dropping incendiaries; these were soon put out by the A.R.P. personnel. At another industrial town in the North many incendiaries were dropped during a raid lasting some hours. So prompt was the fire-fighting service that no conflagrations developed, and it might have been on this account that the raiders dropped no high-explosive bombs. Two bombs were dropped in an East Midlands area.

The R.A.F. on Sunday night carried out raids on railways, factories, and public utility services in the Berlin area. The city's underground railway was damaged and traffic was dislocated. Elsewhere our bombers attacked Frankfort-on-Main, the Kiel shipyards, and the port of Bremen.

There were Nazi raids on a small scale and of short duration on Monday night. The heaviest attack was that made on a West Midland town, where a bomb demolished a social club, beneath which was a wardens' post. Two wardens and three children were killed. One raider over the London area dropped three bombs, but there were no casualties. Five bombs fell in a town on the Thames Estuary and damaged houses.

R.A.F. bombers attacked Mannheim and Ludwigshaven on Monday night, and some of the fires they caused are shown in the remarkable air photo printed in this page. Up to Wednesday night Mannheim (chief industrial centre of the Upper Rhine) had been raided 31 times and Ludwigshaven 13 times. Early on Tuesday morning Coastal Command aircraft attacked the enemy submarine base at Bordeaux; a column of flame 300 feet high was seen to spring up.

No bombs were dropped on Britain during Tuesday, December 17; one enemy bomber was shot down in the afternoon by our fighters. Next afternoon another would-be raider was brought down by the R.A.F. Neither on Tuesday nor Wednesday night were Nazi aircraft observed over Britain, but our own bomber squadrons were very active on both nights. Mannheim—its many fires still raging—was again bombed on these dates, and on Wednesday night our pilots made the long trip to Italy to carry out the eleventh attack on vital factories in the Milan area; docks at Genoa and an aerodrome in Northern Italy were bombed also.

On Thursday evening London had its first Alert since Monday night; raiders attacked places in the Home Counties, and in the outskirts of the Metropolitan area. A bomber was shot down during daylight off the South-west coast. Liverpool and the Merseyside area were heavily attacked on the nights of Dec. 20, 21 and 22.

The recent slowing down of the Nazi aerial offensive caused some speculation, but no remission of our vigil or slackening of our effort. In Parliament on December 19 the Premier said that we were not afraid of any blow which might be struck against us, but we must make increasing preparations. The attacks in the air had slackened somewhat because of the weather, he went on, but they might easily have slackened in preparation for some other form of activity. Of the problem of the night raider Mr. Churchill said that every method of dealing with air fighting by night was being studied with passion and zeal by able and brilliant scientists and officers. So far we had been no more successful in stopping the German night raider than the Germans had been successful in stopping our aeroplanes that had ranged freely over Germany. We had struck very heavy blows, he added, and he instanced the raids on Mannheim.

ENEMY AND BRITISH AIRCRAFT LOSSES

	German	Italian	British
May ...	1,990	—	258
June ...	276	—	177
July ...	245	—	115
Aug. ...	1,110	—	310
Sept. ...	1,114	—	311
Oct. ...	241	—	119
Nov. ...	201	20	53
Dec. 1-19	39	—	7
Totals, May to Dec. 19	**3,716**	**20**	**1,350**

Daily Results

Dec.	Ger. Losses	Br. Losses	Br. Pilots Saved	Dec.	Ger. Losses	Br. Losses	Br. Pilots Saved
1 ...	8	5	5	12 ...	4		
2 ...	—	—	—	13 ...			
3 ...	—	—	—	14 ...			
4 ...	1	—	—	15 ...			
5 ...	14	2	1	16 ...	—		
6 ...	—	—	—	17 ...	1		
7 ...	2	—	—	18 ...	1		
8 ...	1	—	—	19 ...	1		
9 ...	1	—	—				
10 ...	1	—	—	Totals	39	7	6
11 ...	2						

From the beginning of the war up to Dec. 19, 3,035 enemy aircraft destroyed during raids on Britain. R.A.F. losses 846, but 426 pilots saved.

British bombers lost in November over German or occupied territory, 48. In the East and in the Mediterranean **Britain lost 18 aircraft, against 59 Italian destroyed.** In **Western Desert** offensive, Dec. 7-19, 85 Italian aircraft destroyed in the air, and 56 destroyed on the ground or captured. British losses were 13 aircraft (five pilots saved).

Mr. Churchill on Nov. 5 gave weekly average of killed and seriously wounded civilians for September as 4,500; for October, 3,500. **Official figures for November:** Killed, 2,289 men; 1,806 women; 493 children under age 16. Wounded, 3,493 men; 2,251 women; 458 children

R.A.F. RAIDS UP TO DECEMBER 18, 1940

Outstanding objectives: figures denote number of raids carried out.

Antwerp, 28	Hamburg, 58
Berlin, 33	Hamm, 85
Boulogne, 66	Hanover, 26
Bremen, 52	Havre, Le, 29
Brest, 20	Kiel, 32
Calais, 50	Krefeld, 19
Cape Gris Nez, 23	Lorient, 33
Cherbourg, 22	Magdeburg, 20
Cologne, 51	Mannheim, 31
Dortmund, 35	Osnabruck, 35
Duisburg-Ruhrort, 33	Ostend, 49
Dunkirk, 41	Rotterdam, 25
Düsseldorf, 19	Schipol, 35
Emden, 37	Stavanger, 23
Essen, 32	Texel, 26
Flushing, 49	Waalhaven, 19
Gelsenkirchen, 37	Wilhelmshaven, 33

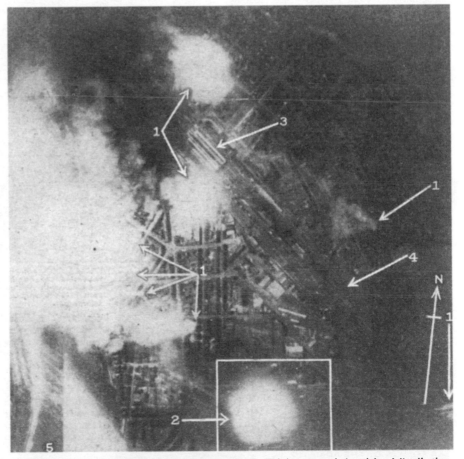

MANNHEIM, after the R.A.F. raid of December 16-17. This important industrial and distributing centre is built on a tongue of land between the rivers Rhine and Neckar. Opposite, on the other bank of the Rhine, is Ludwigshaven, also a much-visited target of our bombers. (1) north: fires burning fiercely N. and S. of (3) the Central Station; south: fires in the Lindenhof district; east: fires near the great marshalling yard (4), which is one of the main objectives. (2) the Heinrich Lanz armament works ablaze. (5) the Rhine. *British Official: Air Ministry Photo: Crown Copyright*

Not Even in the Adriatic Is Italy Safe

As the war in Albania proceeds and the Greeks continue to maintain their amazing offensive against the Italians, the Adriatic Sea becomes an ever more likely scene of armed conflict. Indeed, on Dec. 18, Britain's Mediterranean Fleet made a comprehensive sweep of its lower portion.

In places the Adriatic is more than 100 miles in width, but at its narrowest—the Straits of Otranto which divide the heel of Italy from Albania—it is less than fifty. And there it is that danger lurks for Italy. All Mussolini's transports have to cross that narrow channel, and every day that passes makes it. more and more problematical whether the Italians will be able much longer to keep the channel open. For the Greeks are pressing northwards along the mountain paths that lead to Valona, an important port in Albania and the one which lies nearest to Italy. If Valona falls, then the British Navy will be able to make it a base for ships and 'planes operating against the Italian fleet and Italian towns and harbours. Valona has served Mussolini well; the time may come, and very soon, when it will serve Britain better. For Britain is not only a great sea power; she has captains who know how to use that power—something that Mussolini has never learnt.

As seas go, the Adriatic is small enough— its length is only some 470 miles—but it possesses a most decided strategical importance, for it separates Italy from the Balkans, always a storm-centre of European politics. Its Italian shore is for the most part low and uninteresting; and in the north, particularly around Venice, are marshy swamps and lagoons. The opposite shore, however, is steep and rocky with many inlets and innumerable islands. On this side there are a number of good harbours and roadsteads, whereas the Italian coast is very deficient in this respect.

Because of this deficiency Italy has long coveted the Dalmatian coast line, and to some extent her territorial ambitions in that quarter were satisfied following the Great War. By the Secret Treaty of London, signed on April 26, 1915, Italy was promised, in return for her

forthcoming participation in the struggle on the side of the Allies, most of the province of Dalmatia, together with the islands which fringed its shore; Valona, too, was made part of the bargain, together with the little island of Saseno and the coast to the south as far as Chimara.

But when the terms of peace came to be determined by the treaty-makers in 1919, President Wilson would have nothing to do with the secret treaty and set his face sternly against the satisfaction of Italy's ambitions at the expense of the new kingdom of Yugoslavia; he had excellent grounds for doing so, inasmuch as the Italian population of Dalmatia was less than 4 per cent. The Treaty of St. Germain in 1919 gave Italy most of Istria, in the Adriatic's north-east, together with the great port of Trieste, but the Treaty of Rapallo, made between Italy and Yugoslavia in 1920, added to Italy's gains the port of Zara—which, at least, was predominantly Italian in its population—and the island of

that the Adriatic was " our sea "; but of the two countries Italy was in the better position, because, with both Brindisi and Saseno in her hands, she could close at will the Straits of Otranto.

Mussolini was not satisfied, however. For years it was part of his accepted policy to secure in one way or another the whole of the Dalmatian coast, and to some extent this ambition was realized when in 1939 Italian troops seized Albania—that conquest in the Balkan region of the new Italian Empire which they are now so rapidly losing to the Greeks.

Why the Duce should want Dalmatia is not altogether clear, unless it be that he regards it as a jumping-off board for aggression in the Balkans. Possibly, too, he is desirous of securing more and better harbours for the Italian fleet, though here again the need for them is not altogether obvious if the Adriatic Sea be, indeed, already an Italian lake, as has so frequently been claimed. On the Italian

DURAZZO is the chief port of Albania, and on May 8, 1939, its people witnessed the humiliating spectacle of Italian troops landing to rob the country of its independence. Though a town of only 9,000 inhabitants, it is the only one of the four Albanian ports that has up-to-date equipment.   *Photos, British Official: Crown Copyright; and Fox*

Lagosta. The little island of Saseno was retained by the Italians when they withdrew their troops from Albania; and in 1924 Fiume, which for some years had possessed a more or less independent status, was added to the Italian crown. Yugoslavia was left with a very large Adriatic coastline, so that, equally with Italy, she could claim

side the principal ports are Brindisi, Bari, Ancona, Venice, Trieste, Pola and Fiume. All are places of considerable size, and Venice and Pola rank as naval bases. Brindisi is the Brundisium of the ancient Romans, whose principal naval station it was on the Adriatic Sea. For more than 2,000 years it has been the starting-point for the East, and its importance was enhanced when it was made the land terminus of the overland route to India, made possible by the opening of the Suez Canal; before the war passenger liners left there frequently for Greece, Egypt, Turkey and India.

Bari lies seventy miles to the north-west, and has some importance as a railway centre and manufacturing town. Ancona has one

SEA ROUTES OF THE ADRIATIC between Italian and Albanian ports and between the Italian ports are shown in this map, together with the distances that separate them. Bari and Brindisi are the ports on which the Italian troops in Albania depend for their supplies.

Ports on What Italians Claimed as 'Our Lake'

DUBROVNIK (Ragusa), situated in Yugoslavia on the Dalmatian coast, has been for centuries one of the principal ports of the Adriatic, though today its population is only about 14,000. The harbour is partly closed by sand, so large ships use Gravosa, four miles distant.

of the best harbours in Italy, where are established naval construction yards. Trieste was formerly the principal port of the Austria-Hungarian Empire, and it is still the chief channel of trade between Central Europe and the countries on the Adriatic and in south-east Europe ; shipbuilding has been for long one of its chief industries. Pola was Austria-Hungary's chief naval station, and, as already mentioned, it is a base of the Italian fleet in the Adriatic. Fiume was the port through which, before the Great War, practically all the shipping trade of Hungary passed, but in recent years it has suffered through its allotment to Italy.

Rivals for Italy's Harbours

Of the Yugoslavian ports the most important is Split (Spalato in Italian)—indeed, its harbour is sometimes said to be the finest on the Adriatic coast. The town, with a population of some 35,000, is the capital of the province of Dalmatia ; and with its good communications by road, railway and steamer it has long been of considerable commercial importance. After a stormy history it passed

VALONA (oval), the Albanian port which is one of the main objectives of the Greeks ; the photo shows the Palace of the Prefecture. Above, is a view of Trieste (250,000), the great port, which is a principal outlet of Central Europe.

from the Venetians to the Austrians, who ceded it to the newly-created kingdom of the Serbs, Croats and Slovenes in 1919.

Then there is Ragusa, or Dubrovnik as it is now called ; this lies towards the southern end of the Dalmatian coast, and of late years it has regained some of the importance it enjoyed in medieval times. Many a relic of its ancient greatness has survived to gladden the eyes of the tourists who have stepped ashore for a few hours from their cruising liner. To the south is the Albanian port of Durazzo, which still dreams of the days when it was the port opposite Brundisium, on the main highway from Rome across the Balkans to Byzantium, the Constantinople of later days and the Istanbul of today.

So we come to the last of the Adriatic ports, Valona, which is situated on an excellent harbour. During the Great War it was occupied by the Italians, who made it a naval and military base in their operations against the Austrians in the Balkans. When peace came they evacuated the place, but, as mentioned above, retained in their possession the little island of Saseno lying at the entrance to the bay. They seized it again on Good Friday of 1939—but for how long ?

BARI is the port from which most of the Italian troops embark for Albania. Its harbour has been frequently raided by British airmen and much damage has been done. The place has a population of approximately 200,000.　　*Photos, Dorien Leigh, Wide World and E.N.A.*

OUR SEARCHLIGHT ON THE WAR

Flandin Steps Into Laval's Shoes

MARSHAL PÉTAIN, in a message broadcast on December 14 by Lyons Radio, made a dramatic announcement: "Frenchmen! I have just taken a decision which I trust is in the interests of the country. M. Pierre Laval is no longer a member of the Government. M. Pierre Etienne Flandin has taken the portfolio of Foreign Affairs. Constitutional Act No. 4, which nominated my successor (Laval), is cancelled. It is for high reasons of internal policy that I have taken this decision. It has no repercussions at all on our relations with Germany. I remain at the helm—National Revolution continues." M. Flandin, who thus becomes Foreign Minister for the second time—the first was January-June, 1936—has held many posts in the French Cabinet, including that of Prime Minister, November 1934-June 1935. He has twice served under the premiership of M. Laval, first as Minister of Finance, 1931-32, and then as Minister without Portfolio, 1935-36. After the Munich crisis M. Flandin sent a congratulatory message to Hitler; before war broke out he worked for a rapprochement between France and Germany and was in favour of sacrificing the alliance with Britain. Since the Armistice he has kept in the background, except for some recent speeches in which he stressed the need for "wholehearted and loyal collaboration with Germany in the construction of the New Europe." M. Flandin has always been closely connected with Germany, while M. Laval has been a man of Italy rather than Germany. The new Foreign Minister, who is 6 ft. 4 in. in height and looks a typical big-business man, speaks English fluently. He had an English tailor, used to join English house parties for grouse and pheasant shooting, and described himself as "an old and faithful friend of Britain."

'La Libre Belgique'

DESPITE the Gestapo, Belgian patriots are producing a secret newspaper in occupied Belgium. Like its forerunner in the Great War, it is called "La Libre Belgique," and a few copies of an August issue have reached free territory. Among other things it contains an account of an incident that had already leaked through—the deliberate bombing of Brussels by German 'planes and their attempt to lay this act of treachery at Britain's door. "In the night of August 17-18 an aeroplane dropped bombs on the centre of Brussels, causing deaths and injuries. What was the nationality of the guilty machine? The Germans went to great trouble not to prove (we are still awaiting their proofs) but to make believe that it was a British aeroplane. The people of Brussels were not deceived for a moment . . . Whereas almost every night Brussels is awakened by furious anti-aircraft fire, nothing was heard of it on the night in question. If this was a British aeroplane, why did not the Germans fire at it?"

Underground Food Trains

LONDON's night life underground is becoming highly organized. The provision of bunks and facilities for heating and cooking is adding enormously to the comfort of the stoical shelterers, and recently those availing themselves of the Tube stations gave a rousing welcome to a new form of train that drew up at their dormitory platforms. It was a food train, carrying hot drinks, meat pies, sausage rolls, sandwiches, and so on, and it had received a ceremonial send-off from Bank Station in the presence of the Lord Mayor, the Minister of Food, and the Chairman of the London Passenger Transport Board. There are now six of these "Tube Refreshments Specials." They leave six London Transport depots every afternoon laden with seven tons of food. Statistics show that in one night Tube shelterers consume 30,000 buns, more than 21,000 slabs of cake and 13,000 gallons of cocoa. These items, as well as soup, sausages and pies, are supplied from 134 canteens serving 80 stations, and 1,000 women are employed in the service.

R.A.F. Fighters' Cannon

IT has been known for some time that British fighters are being equipped with cannon, and that these have accounted for many raiders recently shot down. It was not until December 12, however, that the Air Ministry News Service released a specific instance of their successful use. This victory was gained over the Channel by a 21-year-old R.A.F. pilot who has already won the D.F.C. and bar. According to his account, the Messerschmitt, when struck by the shell, just exploded into little bits in the air. The chief advantages of the cannon over the machine-gun are its longer range and greater damaging power. The shell easily pierces the armour plating encasing German aircraft, whereas with the machine-gun penetration was difficult.

Badge For Bomb Disposal Units

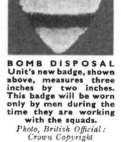

BOMB DISPOSAL Unit's new badge, shown above, measures three inches by two inches. This badge will be worn only by men during the time they are working with the squads.
Photo, British Official : Crown Copyright

A SPECIAL badge which will be worn by personnel of bomb disposal units is being introduced by the War Office. The design is a bomb embroidered in gold on a red background, and the badge will be sewn on the left sleeve between the elbow and the wrist. Only the men of the Royal Engineers actually engaged in this dangerous work will be entitled to wear the badge; it will be withdrawn from personnel when their turn of duty expires.

Italy Foots Another Bill

BLOW after blow is being struck at Italy—in the Mediterranean, in Albania, in the Western Desert—and now comes the news that she is having to pay in hard cash for the privilege of bombing Egypt. The Egyptian Government has instructed the Official Trustee to make a valuation of Italian property in Egypt which may be devoted to paying compensation to raid sufferers. It is expected that a total sum of £15,000,000 will be assessed in this way. Alexandria's raid victims have already had £15,000 allocated for their relief. Indignation against the Italians increases daily, and a suggestion has been made in the Egyptian Parliament to make reprisals against those not yet interned, who are given a small daily subsistence allowance by the Official Trustee.

Red Cross Parcel Ship

FORTY-ONE THOUSAND parcels a week are being made up in this country for prisoners of war in Germany, and 10,000 a week will shortly be sent from Canada. The difficulties of transport are, however, so colossal that more than 150,000 parcels have been delayed between the Spanish frontier and Geneva, owing to insufficiency of Spanish rolling stock and disorganization of the rail transport. Through occupied France the obstructions have been legion. Now a new route has been arranged, and a ship chartered by the British Red Cross has taken aboard at Lisbon 200 tons of food parcels and 160 tons of clothing, and will convey these to Marseilles. Once the cargo leaves Lisbon the organization of the journey will be undertaken by the International Red Cross, who also will be responsible for the subsequent rail journey from Marseilles to Geneva, and for the handing over of the parcels to the German authorities for transmission to the camps

TUBE REFRESHMENTS SPECIAL is the name given to the special train which carries food for distribution to the various stations on the London Transport system used by shelterers from air raids. Here we see the provisions being checked by officials before they are loaded on board the train.
Photo, Fox

I WAS THERE!

Eye Witness Stories of Episodes
and Adventures in the
Second Great War

This is What I Saw in Nibeiwa Camp

As British troops made their triumphant advance in the Western Desert of Egypt they were scavenging the stores and equipment of an entire Italian army. The fantastic scene is dramatically pictured in the following dispatch from a Special Correspondent of the "Daily Telegraph," who visited Nibeiwa Camp shortly after its capture.

FOLLOWING the British army's advance in Egypt, a press correspondent drove across a landscape strewn with millions of pounds' worth of war material. He said:

It was a staggering sight. There were places where lorries were dotted across the desert as far as I could see in every direction.

For mile after mile dumps of ammunition, camouflaged with scrub, were neatly displayed alongside the tracks. Big barrels of diesel oil were tumbled about in huge heaps everywhere.

The most fantastic thing I found was Nibeiwa Camp. It was more of a military township housing thousands of men than a camp, and it was full to bursting with stores.

Men must have spent days collecting stones from the face of the desert to build these mile-long walls, complete with ramparts, bastions, machine-gun nests, tank traps, land mines, and artillery emplacements. Tents and dugouts, counter-sunk well below the level of the earth, must have meant hours of arduous digging in tough, stony ground.

Dispersed at regular intervals over a couple of square miles were vehicles ranging from 6 h.p. Fiat runabouts to 10-ton trucks. A score of medium tanks had already been removed by the British salvage corps and grouped outside the walls. Bicycles, motorcycles, and mules were scattered everywhere.

Cookhouses and the quartermasters' stores were bulging with tinned goods. Case after case was filled with yard-long packets of macaroni. I found British troops varying their rations with strange diets of quince jelly, tomato extract, tunny fish and spaghetti in sauce. Wooden casks and canvas bottles brimmed with excellent Chianti. There were liqueurs and mineral water in almost every tent. Tins of olive oil were stacked six feet high.

British and Indian Tommies were gazing spellbound at this evidence of luxury. Some officers' messes had elegant silverware. There was plenty of perfumery. Gorgeous pieces of dress uniform in gilt, satin and velvet looked doubly incongruous amid desert dust.

Then I wandered on, noting new surprises at every step. The dead Gen. Maletti's tunic with four flamboyant rows of decorations, a tent full of beautiful wireless equipment, a handsome young Italian with a grenade in one hand and a rifle in the other lying dead on the roof of a tent.

As I progressed to the front line I met big Fiat and Lancia lorries, brimful of dusty, dishevelled captives. Generals and colonels had been removed from their special camp to make room for new arrivals. And still prisoners were being taken. . . .

They Showed Me How to Fly a Spitfire

The first batch of Canadian-trained airmen arrived in England during the week-end of November 23, 1940. The training of a fighter pilot under the Empire scheme is described below by the "Daily Mail" correspondent Walter Farr, who spent a day as a pupil at a flying-school in Ottawa.

STANDING waiting for me on the flying ground was a man who has spent years training fighter pilots at a famous flying school in England.

Now, with other R.A.F. officers, he has come to Canada to take charge of the training of fighters here.

The instructor eyed me carefully.

"Ever piloted a 'plane?" he asked.

"No," I said.

"The important part of a fighter pilot's training is aerobatics," he said. "It teaches you to be nippy in the air."

I said the questions everybody was asking were, How do the fighter pilots get hardened to flinging themselves about? What is the secret of their brilliance?

"You will understand after the flight we are going to make," the instructor told me.

He handed me a Service parachute—it is extremely heavy, and I found getting into it rather like getting into a strait-jacket—a leather helmet with headphones fitted inside, and a speaking-tube gadget. He pointed to a little metal ring on the left side of the parachute and said, "Only in case of trouble pull that when you jump out."

We clambered into a two-seater American-made Harvard trainer. He sat in front, I in the back seat with a complete set of duplicate controls in front of me—joystick, rudder controls, everything. One thing he had which I had not was a mirror fixed above his right eye so that he could watch me.

"Strap him in tight," he ordered the mechanics.

Four straps were fixed over my shoulders and held by a pin on the chest. "In case of emergency just pull out the pin," I was told.

Above the roar of the machine I could hear the instructor's voice perfectly in the headphones.

At least a hundred other Harvard trainers, each carrying pupil and instructor, were whizzing about the 'drome, taking off, landing, practising formation flying. At two nearby reserve 'dromes there was the same intensive activity.

We had to queue up to take off. We shot up high above the aerodrome.

"Feel all right?" asked the instructor. "O.K. We will now do a loop."

The 'plane somersaulted at terrific speed, and I saw a bit of Ottawa blot out the pale blue Canadian sky and a bit of wing mixed up in the picture. I felt myself hanging by straps. Then we flattened out again. The instructor glanced at me through the mirror.

"Feel all right?" he repeated. "O.K. We will now fly on our backs."

We spun over and went along upside down for a few hundred yards. "Now, if you feel O.K., we will do a roll off the top."

We looped again, then, instead of flattening out at once, began spiralling down at terrific speed. I felt a terrific dragging at my cheeks, my head throbbed and I got a sort of hang-over feeling in the stomach.

We flattened out again. My head felt hot as if all the blood had rushed to it.

"I expect you'd like a little air," said the instructor, opening a window in the transparent celluloid cover over the cockpit. Air never tasted better.

He saw me in the mirror mopping my brow

ITALIAN MOTOR VEHICLES were captured by the hundred during the British advance in the Western Desert. Many of them were still fit for service, but scattered about the sands were such wrecks as these, caught by British fire—tangled masses of metal left behind in the trail of a defeated army.
Photo, British Paramount News

724   *The War Illustrated*   *January 3rd, 1941*

IIIIIIIIIIIIIIIIIIIIIIIIIIIIIIIIIIIIIIIIIIIIIIIIIIIIIIIIIIIIIIII **I WAS THERE !** IIIIIIIIIIIIIIIIIIIIIIIIIIIIIIIIIIIIIIIIIIIIIIIIIIIIIIIIII

and said, " Perhaps we'd better fly along and take a look at the scenery for a while.

" One of the big objects of this aerobatics stuff is that it tests whether a man would be capable of handling controls in emergencies," continued the instructor.

We did some more stunts, steep turns, banking, flying in and out of clouds. I was beginning to get used to it. I began to release my grip on the cockpit sides, sit back and relax.

Then came a voice in the 'phone.

" Of course, Spitfires and Hurricanes move much faster than this."

We finished up the lesson with a bombing dive, and flew over a nearby lake.

" See that white buoy floating down there ? " asked the instructor. " That's the bombing target."

We shot up higher, poised like a hawk, then plunged from five thousand feet straight down, reaching a speed of three hundred miles an hour. There was again that pulling feeling on the cheeks and head throbs.

" The 'plane is now said to be ' mushing,' " said the instructor. " In other words it is falling faster than the engine could move it."

One thousand feet—two thousand feet— we roared down. " At this second I would have dropped my bomb," said the instructor.

The machine by now was skimming upwards again. " That is how 'planes bomb Berlin," explained the instructor.

We landed and, to my astonishment, I was able to have luncheon. Long before I had finished the instructor excused himself and went off to make a flight with more pupils. He does this day and night.

CANADIAN AIRMEN having completed their training under R.A.F. instructors in Canada are seen with a British sergeant. The latter points out 'planes in flight. A vivid description of a day spent by Walter Farr as a pupil at an Ottawa flying-school is given in the preceding page.
Photo, " News Chronicle "

Two of My Torpedoes Hit a Nazi Ship

In the middle of December 1940, H.M. submarine " Sunfish " (see page 462, Vol. II) returned to port after an underwater patrol off the Norwegian coast, where she sank a German supply ship and badly damaged a tanker. Her commander, Lieutenant George Colvin, here tells of the " Sunfish's " achievements.

ON his return to port Lieut. Colvin said that he had done several patrols without having the luck to see anything. He continued :

On this one we were sent to do part of the North Sea. One day about teatime we saw, close inshore, a merchant ship of about 4,000 tons, deeply laden. She was in an un- favourable position for attacking, but we saw that in a few minutes it would be too late to attack her. So we closed at high speed and I fired torpedoes from long range.

There was a long wait while they ran towards their target. I was watching with the periscope kept low in case it should be seen. I could see only the upper works of the ship.

After some minutes there were two heavy explosions, and I saw two great humps of water. The ship had been hit by two of my torpedoes.

Within a minute I raised the periscope to its full extent, and by that time there was no trace left of the ship. She had a heavy cargo, probably iron ore, and she must have broken up and sunk like a stone.

If the " Sunfish " had surfaced for survivors we might have been attacked by 'planes, so we turned and went away. Next day we operated at another part of the coastline. We were submerged all the time. Just after sunset I saw a steamer close astern. It was getting dark, and difficult to see, so we turned quickly to attack.

I fired. The torpedoes were running true, but suddenly the ship turned and they missed.

Next day, the last of the patrol, we sighted a tanker of about 4,000 tons creeping along close to shore. I fired torpedoes and heard them explode, but I was unable to see whether they had hit.

But I came up to periscope depth and saw that the tanker had stopped and was blowing off steam from her funnels after turning a complete circle. A small Diesel coaster of about 200 tons came alongside her.

Half an hour later the tanker got under way and went off slowly, with the coaster in attendance. She was crippled. That was the last hour of our patrol, and we turned and left for our base.—" *Daily Express.*"

H.M. SUBMARINE "SUNFISH," whose commander, Lieut. Colvin (arrow), recounts in this page the memorable feat performed by his ship off the Norwegian coast in December 1940. In April the "Sunfish" accounted for four Nazi ships amounting to a tonnage of over 16,000. This photograph shows the submarine at her base with her crew lined up on deck.
Photo, G.P.U.

Thanks to Them You Got Your Xmas Greetings

(1) In some sorting offices enemy action had resulted in the failure of the electric light, yet sorting went on by the light of guttering candles.   (2) Steel helmets protected the postmen from shrapnel and falling masonry.   (3) The Post Office engineers have been busy repairing damaged telephone cables; hundreds of telephone wires must be joined up correctly.   (4) Working on the top floor of a London telephone exchange, these girls are wearing their steel helmets and have their gas-masks handy.

Photos, Fox, Keystone, L.N.A., and "News Chronicle"

WORDS OF HOPE AND WARNING FOR 1941

The Address to America with which Lord Lothian Closed his Career of Service

The Grim Picture That Has Been Dispelled

WHEN I last made a public speech in the United States we had just experienced a terrific shock—the overthrow of France. If you recall those dismal days you will remember there was something like despair among many diplomatic and business circles in Washington, New York, and other cities of the United States. Hitler had announced that he would dictate peace in London in August, or, at the latest, in the middle of September. And hadn't he always been right over his military dates ? Those June and July dates were indeed gloomy days for us and for you. But that grim picture has been dispelled, at any rate for the present, by the action of the people of a small island in the North Sea, nobly and valiantly aided by the young nations of the British family across the seas.

First there was the retreat from Dunkirk. . . . Then came Mr. Winston Churchill, with almost the whole of the rest of the world on the run, standing undaunted in the breach, defying in matchless oratory the apparently irresistible power and prestige of Hitler and National Socialism. Then came reports from your own air attachés that the R.A.F. had taken the measure of the German air force despite its superiority in numbers and was on the high road to establishing its supremacy over the British Isles. Then followed the great air battles of August and September in which the Germans lost nearly 200 machines in a day and five or six to one in pilots. Then came the brutal bombing of London, and especially East London, by night. But there was no flinching before Hitler's attempted intimidation no crying for peace, no suggestion that, though we were almost alone, we had had enough.

And, finally, has come the gradual petering out of the much-heralded invasion of Britain.

Thus, if Hitler won the first round of the great battle which began in Norway in April, we have won the second, for without the conquest of Britain Hitler cannot win the war. But do not think that Hitler's Nazidom is going to be easily overthrown. Hitler is certainly going to make another attempt next year—and earlier rather than later—to beat down our resistance by new methods of still greater violence and to open the way to world war and domination by the Nazis.

The True Nature of National Socialism

I DO not think even now we realize the true nature of National Socialism. Modern National Socialism is the reassertion of the strongest tradition in German and Prussian history—belief in an all-powerful military State creating order and discipline at home by ruthless Gestapo methods and expanding its wealth and power by ruthless conquest abroad.

Under Hitler the free nations of Europe are never going to reappear. They are going to be reduced permanently to political, economic and military impotence so that they can act as suppliers of serfs to the ruling German race.

Hitlerism cannot stop and become peaceful. Nazi Germany is organized for war and totalitarian economics and for nothing else. Its economic system, like everything else, is built on fraud. War and preparation for war is its only real remedy for unemployment.

This war, therefore, is not a war between nations like the last war. It is more of a revolution than a war—a revolutionary war, waged by Hitler and his military totalitarian machine, against all other nations and the free world in which we have lived, so as to make them military, political and economic satellites in a totalitarian world empire. Then Hitler will have given the world peace—the peace of death; and employment—employment of the slave.

Our Navy is Strung Out Terribly Thin

HITLER has lost the second round of the war. But we think he is certainly going to renew the attack on Britain with all his might this winter and spring. This time he is going to concentrate on the sea . . . [and] our Navy, with the tremendous tasks which rest on it, none of which it has shirked or evaded, is strung out terribly thin.

We think this is a situation which concerns you almost as much as it concerns us. It has long been clear that your security, no less than ours, depends upon our holding the Atlantic impregnable and you the Pacific. So long as this is so the way of life to which we are attached can continue, and our free economic system can resist totalitarian attack. But if one of these two navies fails and the unity of the British Commonwealth begins to disappear, the control of trade routes begins to pass to Axis powers, and those controlling bastions of sea-power which now keep war away from America become the jumping-off points from which it can be menaced.

We have both, therefore, a vital interest in decisively defeating the now rapidly maturing naval attack on British communications. It is the best way of preventing a spread of the war, and an essential step towards that victory which will eventually follow the failure of Hitler to destroy Great Britain, both in the air and on the sea, is the uninterrupted flow of American munitions to the British Isles.

With America's Help We Are Sure of Victory

WE have no illusions, therefore, about 1941. It is going to be a hard, dangerous year . . . But we aren't in the least dismayed. With help from you we are confident that we can win, and win decisively, by 1942, if not before.

We are confident, first of all, for spiritual reasons. The core of Hitlerism is moral rottenness and the belief that the use of utter brutality, ruthless power and the prosecution of domination is the road to greatness both in individuals and in nations. Hitlerism is a tragedy in Germany. Its doctrine is not true. All history proves it wrong.

The core of the Allied creed, for all our mistakes of omission and commission, is liberty, justice and truth, and that, we believe, will infallibly prevail if we have resolution and the courage to resist to the end.

But on the side of armaments also we have great growing assets. The curve of our munition and aeroplane production is steadily rising—despite bombing. The number of our divisions, of our aeroplanes and our pilots is also steadily going up. What is more, the important young nations of the Commonwealth, Canada, Australia, South Africa and New Zealand, are fast getting into their stride.

Indian troops and Indian munitions are now coming into the battle fronts, and ever-increasing resources are coming from colonies and territories loyal to a man and proud of their membership of the Commonwealth.

The whole of this growing aggregation of power is now being mobilized. Its first task is to defend that great ring of defensive positions which lie around you—Britain itself, Gibraltar, Cape Town, Egypt, the Suez Canal, Singapore. As long as we can hold these positions we and the democratic world beyond them are safe.

Our second task is to enable us to deliver increasingly formidable blows at Germany itself and at her allies, one of whom is already beginning to crack, and to bring assistance to the subjugated peoples who are now once more beginning to show signs of resistance to Hitler's will. But that result is not yet secure. It will be put to the test in 1941. If we can stave off the attack on Britain ; if we can outlast next year still holding all the positions I have mentioned, Hitlerism in the end must go down.

By ourselves we cannot be sure of this result —though we will try our best . . . but with your help in aeroplanes, munitions and ships, and on the sea and in the field of finance now being discussed between your Treasury and ours, we are sure of victory.

Britain Was Never More Truly Democratic

THE last thing I want to say concerns the future. There were two things which I found the ordinary citizens of Britain thinking about. The first was that all his and her suffering and sacrifice should, if possible, end not all wars, for human nature is not probably yet ready for that, but the kind of total war Hitler is waging, with its hideous mutilation and destruction from the air, its brutal persecution of conquered peoples. The second was that after this war no one who had done his duty should be thrown on the scrap-heap of unemployment, with nothing but bonus or dole. Somehow or other employment must be found for everybody.

Some people are spreading a legend that democracy is disappearing from Britain and that she will come out at the end of the war a Fascist or Communist State. Nothing could be further from the truth. I have never known Britain more truly democratic. The British are not going to change their essential character. It has shown itself in this war. They will move forward, of course, with the times, but without revolutionary violence.

But the more people think about the future the more they are drawn to the conclusion that all real hope depends on some form of cooperation between the United States and the British Commonwealth of Nations . . . The only nucleus round which a stable, peaceful, democratic world can be built after this war is if the United States and Great Britain possess between them more aeroplanes, ships of war and key positions of world power such as I have described than any possible totalitarian rival. Then only will political and industrial freedom be secure.

I HAVE done. I have endeavoured to give you some idea of our present position and dangers, the problems of 1941 and our hopes for the future. It is for you to decide whether you share our hopes and what support you will give us in realizing them.

We are, I believe, doing all we can. Since May there is no challenge we have evaded, challenge we have refused. If you back us you won't be backing a quitter.

The issue now depends largely on what you decide to do. Nobody can share that responsibility with you. It is the great strength of democracy that it brings responsibility down squarely on every citizen and every nation. And before the Judgement Seat of God each must answer for his own actions.—*From the Address which Lord Lothian, British Ambassador to Washington, penned just before his sudden passing on Dec. 12,* 1940.

Thanks to Them Britain Is Not Hungry

" ACTION STATIONS ! " is the order, and the men who guard Britain's food convoys leap to their gun to beat off an enemy attack.　Day in, day out, in blazing sun and freezing cold, these ever-vigilant guardians of our vital ocean life-lines are instantly prepared for the Nazi U-boat or bomber seeking to destroy their precious charges.　In the last war the convoy system triumphed over the submarine menace in the end.　But today the air weapon has greatly strengthened the Germans' striking power, and the problem of safeguarding merchant shipping is proving much harder to solve.

Photo, Planet News

OUR DIARY OF THE WAR

SUNDAY, DEC. 15, 1940   *470th day*

In the Air—R.A.F. bombed important targets in Berlin area, including railways, factories and utility services. Other aircraft attacked inland port of Frankfort-on-Main, Kiel shipyards and port of Bremen.

War against Italy—Operations proceeding on Libyan frontier where British troops have now penetrated into Italian territory. R.A.F. bombed Appolonia, Bomba, Derna and Benina.

During night of December 14-15 and 15-16 R.A.F. attacked Bardia, Tmimi, Gazala, Tobruk, El Gubbi and El Adem. Bardia suffered particularly heavy raid. Our fighters shot down 12 enemy aircraft.

Long-range bombers carried out heavy raid on Naples during night of December 14-15. Five direct hits on concentration of cruisers and destroyers. Aerodrome, railway station and junctions also attacked.

Considerable air activity reported from Italian East Africa; Assab, Gura, Zula, Bahadar and Gondar among places raided.

Home Front—No bombs dropped over Britain during day. Widespread activity at night. Sheffield area heavily attacked. Another north of England industrial town also raided, and an urban district in East Midlands.

Five enemy machines brought down.

Greek War—Athens reported successful local combats in which fresh heights, numerous prisoners and machine-guns had been captured. Enemy aircraft resumed intensive action.

MONDAY, DEC. 16   *471st day*

In the Air—R.A.F. made sustained attack on targets at Mannheim and suburbs. Other aircraft dropped heavy bombs on submarine base at Bordeaux. Several aerodromes were also attacked, and six merchant vessels off French coast.

War against Italy—British troops occupied Sollum and Fort Capuzzo, and captured frontier forts of Musaid, Sidi Omar and Shefferzen.

Bari raided by R.A.F. during night of December 16-17.

During night of December 15-16 Gura and Asmara, East Africa, were raided by R.A.F. bombers.

Frontier post of El Wak, Italian Somaliland, successfully raided by S. African and E. African troops.

Home Front—Enemy day activity slight. Few bombs fell in E. Anglia and S.E. England. At night bombs were dropped in London area, a Thames Estuary town, Liverpool area and the Midlands.

Greek War—Greeks continued to advance north of Premeti and westwards from Ersek. Italians retired with losses towards Klisura. Enemy said to have evacuated Chimarà and neighbouring villages. Heavy night attack made by R.A.F. on Durazzo.

TUESDAY, DEC. 17   *472nd day*

In the Air—R.A.F. bombers again attacked industrial targets at Mannheim. Other aircraft bombed ports and aerodromes on Channel coasts.

War against Italy—New British forces reached Bardia sector, where severe fighting was reported. Prisoners now number 40,000. Reconnaissance flights showed enemy retreating towards Derna. R.A.F. fighters machine-gunned retiring troops between Bardia and Tobruk. Derna raided during night. Heavy night raid on Benina aerodrome, 18 aircraft being destroyed.

Assab bombed both by night and day.

Reported that offensive patrolling had recommenced on considerable scale in northern frontier district of Kenya.

Enemy raided Port Sudan, causing some damage.

Home Front—During daylight enemy air activity was very slight. No night raids. One enemy bomber shot down by our fighters.

Greek War—Klisura defile being bombarded from all sides. Fires seen at Klisura caused by blowing up of ammunition dumps. Advance made north of Premeti. In coastal sector Greeks continue to force enemy to abandon positions.

General—By request of German Ambassador Abetz, Laval was released from confinement to which he was sent after dismissal.

WEDNESDAY, DEC. 18   *473rd day*

On the Sea—British motor torpedo-boats carrying out offensive patrol off Belgian coast made successful attack on large armed enemy supply ship; it was seen to break up

---

and sink. Enemy escort ship engaged by machine-gun fire and hit.

In the Air—Another heavy bombing attack made on Mannheim and four new fires started. Other aircraft bombed submarine base at Lorient.

War against Italy—Operations in Bardia area continued. Town was shelled by Navy and bombed day and night by R.A.F.

R.A.F. bombed Pirelli works at Milan, docks at Genoa and an aerodrome in Northern Italy.

Home Front—No air activity over Britain either by day or night. German bomber shot down over Dover.

Greek War—Successful local operations carried out at various points on the front. Further prisoners and material captured.

R.A.F. bombed Valona seaplane base, docks and warehouses.

THURSDAY, DEC. 19   *474th day*

In the Air—Coastal Command aircraft bombed aerodrome at Le Touquet.

Despite bad weather R.A.F. attacked targets in the Ruhr and Western Germany, including synthetic oil plants, power stations and a railway junction.

Aircraft of Coastal Command successfully bombed Bergen-Oslo railway.

War against Italy—Bardia encircled by British; two enemy divisions believed trapped.

During night of Dec. 18-19 R.A.F. heavily raided Bardia and Derna, doing great damage.

On Sudan front patrols were again active in Kassala and Gallabat areas.

Brindisi was heavily bombed during night.

Home Front—Very little hostile air activity during day. At night bombs were dropped in the Home Counties.

Enemy bomber shot down off S.W. coast.

Greek War—New positions occupied after successful engagements. More prisoners and war material captured. Very heavy fighting reported from coast north of Chimarà, where Italians were counter-attacking.

FRIDAY, DEC. 20   *475th day*

On the Sea—Admiralty announced that H.M. submarine "Truant" had sunk Italian supply ship in convoy off Cape Spartivento during night of Dec. 13-14, and large tanker off Calabrian coast on Dec. 15-16.

In the Air—R.A.F. bombed Berlin, causing many fires and explosions in target area. Attacks made on Channel invasion ports. Docks at Amsterdam also bombed. Many aerodromes raided. Gun positions near Cap Gris Nez attacked. Supply ship hit.

War against Italy—Italian rearguard at Bardia putting up strong defence. During night R.A.F. carried out highly successful raid on Castel Benito aerodrome. Nineteen enemy aircraft destroyed. Benghazi and Berka also bombed.

Home Front—Slight activity by single enemy aircraft during day. Few bombs fell in London area. At night raiders were over most parts of Britain. Merseyside had very heavy attack. Countless incendiaries dropped over Liverpool. Tannery and storage yard fired. Prolonged raid on inland N.W. town.

Greek War—Tepelini and Klisura under bombardment by Greek artillery. Farther north Greek advance maintained and fresh heights won.

SATURDAY, DEC. 21   *476th day*

In the Air—R.A.F. bombed oil plants in the Ruhr and Rhineland. Other targets included factories, inland docks, railways and aerodromes. Other forces attacked docks and harbour works at Rotterdam, Flushing, Antwerp, Ostend and Calais.

War against Italy—Enemy troops holding Bardia defences being harassed by artillery fire. British forces clearing areas to northwest and west. Nine hundred more prisoners captured.

R.A.F. bombed oil refinery at Porto Marghera, near Venice.

Home Front—Slight enemy activity during day. At night raiders again attacked Liverpool and Merseyside, and there was much damage and many casualties. Bombs also fell in widely separated places in Britain.

Three enemy aircraft destroyed.

German long-range guns shelled Dover.

Greek War—Severe battles continued in all sectors. Greeks reported to have advanced beyond Chimarà. Big battle still in progress in Tepelini-Klisura area.